Fodor's 16th Edition

P9-APT-352

Japan

Fodor's Travel Publications • New York, Toronto, London, Sydney, Auckland
www.fodors.com

CONTENTS

MAPS

Circled letters in text correspond to letters on the photographs. For more information on the sights pictured, turn to the indicated page number Ⓐ＞ on each photograph.

DESTINATION JAPAN

Delicate cherry blossoms stir in the wind, snowcapped mountains shelter valley towns, sacred structures whisper of history and lore: you've entered Japan, a land of exquisite and ancient beauty. Temples that date to the 6th century, castles that cascade in tiers down to earth, and venerated shrines transport you across a grand sweep of time into a colorful, rich, and turbulent past. Bullet trains, meanwhile, shuttle you between these sights, and world-class restaurants, shopping, urban sprawl, and crackling human energy remind you that Japan is a postindustrial giant, a critical player on the global stage. You may find little in Japan that reminds you of home, but you will find much to explain why the Japanese love their country as they do.

TŌKYŌ

Ⓐ J 43

Some 30 million people live in Tōkyō or within commuting distance, and the flow of dynamic humanity charges the city's atmosphere. Immense, crowded, and endlessly fascinating though Japan's capital may be, it isn't lovely. Some blocks are eyesores. But amid plain backdrops you'll find great beauty, as at a Kabuki performance at the Ⓑ**Kabuki-za,** graceful Ni-jū-bashi (Two-Tiered Bridge), or the Sensō-ji temple complex. Likewise, for all its massed humanity, Tōkyō is one of the safest cities in the world. Don't be flustered by its sprawl. Virtually any place you'll want to see is within a five-minute walk of a train station, and all station signs are marked in

English. Like most big cities, Tōkyō stitches together several colorful neighborhoods—Asakusa, Ginza, Tsukiji, Shinjuku, and dozens more—each with its own texture. In Shinjuku, the two towers of the ©**Tōkyō Tochō** complex soar above the sky-line, providing sweeping views from observation platforms. Down at street level here, impeccably mannered Tōkyō reaches the height of urban edginess. For a break from the crush, duck into splendid Shinjuku Gyo-en National Garden. Or join thousands of passionate baseball fans for a home game at the Bunkyo area's Ⓐ**Tōkyō Dome.** The Ⓓ**Shimbashi** district, once geisha central, still houses geisha discreetly amid neon blare, while in Ⓔ**Kappa-bashi,** the crafting of plastic food rises to the level of pop art. In hip Hara-juku, where you can view the (often imported) fashion of the moment, the young cut loose from grown-up norms. Fresh or hokey, fleeting trends rest on the bedrock of traditional Japan in this exciting, exasperating, mov-able feast of a city.

Ⓓ 75

Ⓔ 74

7

Ⓐ 185

SIDE TRIPS FROM TŌKYŌ

Ⓑ 204

If Tōkyō were rows of Quonset huts, it would still be worth staying in for the side trips nearby. Start with lunch in Yokohama's Ⓑ**Chinatown,** where more than 150 restaurants serve every major regional Chinese cuisine. Here, silks, spices, herbal medicines, and all things Chinese beckon from a warren of shops in narrow lanes. Far removed from such urban bustle lie Nikkō and the Ⓒ**Tōshō-gū** shrine complex, stirring in its sheer scale alone. Some call it sublime, some excessive, but no one finds it dull. At a nearby national park, Chūzenji-ko (Lake Chūzenji) and waterfalls

Ⓒ 181

Ⓓ❯219

like Ⓐ**Kegon-no-taki** nourish the spirit. The national park and resort area of Hakone puts you close to majestic Ⓓ**Fuji-san,** which you can climb in summer without special gear. In Hase, the 37-foot Ⓔ**Daibutsu**—the Great

Buddha—has sat for seven centuries, serenely gazing inward. The temples and shrines of nearby Kamakura, 13th-century capital of Japan, remind you that this was an important religious as well as political center. Break away from the tourists and enjoy a moment of peace: the clamor of Tōkyō falls silent here in the ancient heart of Japan.

Ⓔ❯196

NAGOYA, ISE-SHIMA, AND KII PENINSULA

Ⓑ 234

Sacred sites, traditional crafts, and untamed natural beauty head the list of reasons to visit this region west of Tōkyō. At Ise-Shima National Park the highly venerated Ise Jingū (Grand Shrines of Ise) sit amid groves of ancient trees and, in accordance with Shintō tradition, are rebuilt with new wood every 20 years. A loop around the Kii Peninsula takes you past magnificent coastal scenery, fishing villages, and Yoshino-san, with perhaps the finest springtime display of cherry blossoms in Japan. Inland, the mountain monastery of Ⓓ**Kōya-san,** founded in 816, looms almost as large as myth with its 120 temples. To truly appreciate Kōya-san, stay overnight in one of the temples. Old Japan resonates in Ⓑ©**Gifu,** famous for its oiled-paper umbrellas, paper

lanterns, and for U-kai, the ancient practice of fishing with cormorants. Farther north, in Inuyama, sweeping views of the river and hills from the upper floors make the local castle a gem. And though not especially handsome, Japan's fourth-largest city, Nagoya, with its easygoing residents,

© 234

D 244

can grow on you. It has some sightseeing moments, notably at Ⓐ**Nagoya-jō** and the Ⓔ**Tokugawa Bijutsukan,** whose many priceless objects include a National Treasure: 12th-century illustrated hand scrolls of *The Tale of Genji,* widely considered the world's first novel.

Ⓔ 230

JAPAN ALPS AND THE NORTH CHŪBU COAST

Ⓐ 259

Soaring mountains, slices of old Japan, and superb hiking, skiing, and hot-springs soaking make this region enticing. So does the gorgeous natural color, from the flowering trees of spring to the rich hues of autumn. To the west, along the Sea of Japan, the Chūbu region's coastal scenery contrasts nicely with the mountain experience. After the 1998 Winter Olympics in Nagano, new roads and a bullet train line have made the region more accessible, and Nagano is a good base if taking the waters is high on your list. Yudanaka Onsen's thermal springs are popular with people bent on relaxing, and

Ⓑ 255

with snow monkeys, who gather for warmth. Nearby at the renowned hot springs at Ⓐ**Kusatsu,** a bracing pinch of arsenic (far from toxic levels) spikes the mineral waters. Just viewing the waters can be fulfilling at Ⓑ**Shiraito-no-taki** and Ryugaeshi-no-taki, reachable from tony Karuizawa, the St. Moritz of the Ⓓ**Japan Alps.** Hiking there, whether on torii-crowned Ⓕ**Tate-yama** or on the trails around Kamikōchi, tones both body and soul. Urban pleasures, including

Ⓒ 270

first-rate nightlife, flourish in sophisticated yet friendly Kanazawa, gracefully sharing space with the venerable examples of Japanese art and architecture. The city's ©**Kenrokuen** ranks as one of the three finest gardens in the country. The less crowded, tranquil garden at Gyokusenen lends itself to meditation. Fine

museums, shrines, traditional crafts, and Naga-Machi (Samurai District) round out the spell of the enchanting town. Traditional Japan also remains alive in ©**Takayama,** where, in April and October, drummers set the pulse for raucous ancient festivals. Along the coast, a trip around Noto-hantō (Noto Peninsula) rewards you with dreamlike seascapes and charming villages such as Wajima, renowned for its lacquerware. On Sado-ga-shima (Sado Island) the pace of life recalls centuries past. Japan changes slowly in these mountains and along these shores. Savor it.

E⟩ 264

F⟩ 253

KYŌTO

Ⓐ 311

Twelve centuries of history and tradition echo in gracious Kyōto, in gardens, castles, and museums, and nearly 2,000 temples and shrines. For 10 of those centuries, Kyōto was the imperial capital, and over that millennium the city gave birth to classical Japanese customs, aesthetics, and arts. Glorious sights abound, with gold-leafed Ⓐ**Kinkaku-ji** topping nearly any list of favorites. At Ⓒ**Kiyomizu-dera,** built on a steep hillside, views of the temple match views from it, while Kōryū-ji serves as both a place of worship and a trove of National Treasures. One of the

Ⓑ 312

Ⓒ 303

Ⓓ ▷ 301

Ⓔ ▷ 319

most beloved is the sublime Ⓑ**Miroku Bosatsu** statue of the Buddha, created nearer to his time than to our own. Also beloved, 10,000 torii guard the paths that lead, uphill and heavenward, from the shrine of Ⓔ**Fushimi-Inari Taisha.** Secular, but no less devoted to ceremony, are the geisha of the Ⓓ**Gion** district. Secular, too, but with a religious following, are the gastronomic shrines serving *kaiseki ryōri*, an elegant meal that engages all senses. Like the food, the crafts here approach perfection: dolls, fans, ceramics, and creations by masters of the Kyō-yuzen silk-dyeing technique. Pick up your mementos here; you won't find better. And you may not find a better time in all Japan.

NARA

While ancient Nara may not match Kyōto for sheer volume of sacred sites, its shrines and parks count among Japan's finest, and its crafts and cuisine are superb. Head straight for Ⓑ**Nara Kōen,** a splendid park where tame deer see handouts as a birthright. Get crackers at a stall, buy off Bambi, and enjoy the park's temples, Ⓒ**Kasuga Taisha** among them. Its main shrines are National Treasures. Other must-sees near the park are the resplendent Tōdai-ji and the Daibutsu-den, which houses a 53-foot bronze Buddha. From here, it's a train or bus ride to the temples of western Nara. The finest is Ⓐ**Hōryū-ji,** with its Great Treasure Hall and 7th-century wooden buildings. You can visit Nara in a day, but you may find yourself wanting to linger.

Ⓐ⟩ 364   Ⓑ⟩362

Ⓒ⟩ 361

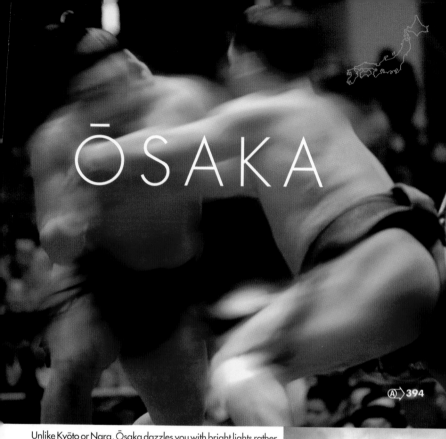

ŌSAKA

Ⓐ➲ 394

Unlike Kyōto or Nara, Ōsaka dazzles you with bright lights rather than tradition, but it does possess Ⓒ**Ōsaka-jō,** a match for any castle in the country, and sumō wrestling at the Ⓐ**Ōsaka Furitsu Taiikukaikan.** Japan is passionate about sumō, whose origins are tied to ancient Shintō rites, and Osakans are among its biggest fans. Despite the bulk of the wrestlers, their quickness is amazing; some years ago in an exhibition, novice sumō wrestlers tossed beefy NFL linemen around like schoolboys. The Americans never asked for a rematch. Bunraku puppet masters ply a gentler art at the National Bunraku Theater. Ōsaka is famous for the perfection of this dramatic form. For neon and nightlife, hop on a subway to Ⓑ**Dōtombori-dōri.** Unwind and dine among the locals, who have a reputation as food-lovers. Be sure to sample delicacies like *okonomiyaki,* grilled pancakes with vegetables and meat. You won't spend a week in Ōsaka, but a day or two has its rewards.

Ⓑ➲ 382

Ⓒ➲ 379

For a break from traditional Japan, try Kōbe—typified more by its harbor skyline, with the ©**Hotel Okura Kōbe** rising above the water, than by sights like Ⓐ**Ikuta Jinja,** a Shintō shrine. European and Japanese influences have long mingled in this city on Ōsaka Bay. One result is Kitano-chō, worth a visit for its old Western-style homes, including delightful Choueke Yashiki. Shopping is one of Kōbe's strong points, and at the Ⓑ**Tasaki Shinju** company, you'll learn how pearls get from mollusk to necklace. International accents lace the culinary scene, where pride of place goes to pricey, world-famous Kōbe beef. Yes, it's marbled, but don't worry: you'll be eating fish again soon.

KŌBE

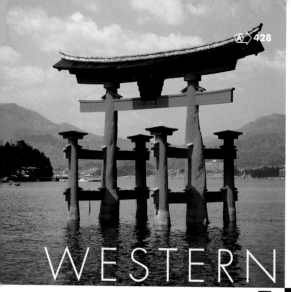

Ⓐ 428

WESTERN HONSHŪ

Ⓑ 418

Mountains divide this region into an urban south and a rural north. Today Hiroshima stands tall and modern in the south, while the charred ©**Gembaku Dōmu,** a sobering icon of the atomic age, testifies to darker times. Offshore at Miyajima, the famous Ⓐ**O-torii** appears to float on the water. Also in the south is Himeji-jō, one of Japan's most beloved castles. In nearby Ⓑ**Bizen,** masters craft the famous local pottery, while Kurashiki, with its buildings and willow-shaded canals, envelops you in an older time. On the northern coast, don't miss history-rich Hagi and the gems called Tsuwano and Matsue, two towns special even in this lovely corner of Japan.

© 423

Ⓐ▷458

Thanks to its isolation—now ended by bridges to Honshū—the island of Shikoku has held on to its traditions, and staved off the industry that blights parts of Japan. Your rewards for leav-

SHIKOKU

Ⓑ▷457

ing the beaten path to come here include great hiking with dramatic scenery, some of the freshest seafood in the country, and a chance to make a fool of yourself (that's the idea) at the rollicking Ⓐ**Awa Odori** festival in Ⓑ**Tokushima.** Tokushima is also a good place to try your hand at traditional crafts, such as papermaking, or to watch masters at work. Visit the mellow city of Ⓒ**Kōchi,** rugged Shōdo-shima island, and the superb Takamatsu gardens. Take the waters at Dogo Onsen Hon-kan and at the beach. This is a Japan you've never dreamed of.

Ⓒ▷460

KYŪSHŪ

Ⓐ 497

Lush Kyūshū, southernmost of Japan's main islands, has everything from an active and accessible volcano, at Aso-san National Park, to the quiet hills of charming Nagasaki, a harbor town often called the San Francisco of Japan. The city's ©**Kōshibyō** (Chinese Mansion) reflects one thread of foreign influence. The wooden houses at Oranda-zaka (Holland Slope) testify to another. Not far from the artsy spa of Ⓐ**Yufuin,** volcanic grandeur accents pastoral views, and at the Ⓑ**Beppu** hot springs, kitsch, neon, and tour groups prevail. Beppu's people-watching can be riveting, and the spa's inelegance is as fascinating as anything else on this enchanting isle.

Ⓑ 495

© 483

TŌHOKU

If you overlook Tōhoku—Honshū's six northern prefectures— you'll be among millions of travelers, Japanese and foreign, who do. That's their loss and, potentially, yours. The main island's urban metabolism slows down here; friendliness rises and natural beauty abounds. Ⓐ**Zaō-san** draws skiing enthusiasts, and even nonskiers come for the *juhyō*, snow-covered fir trees that resemble fairy-tale monsters. With its caldera lake and great hiking, the mountain also merits a visit in summer. A short hop east lies modern Sendai, Tōhoku's largest city and a

Ⓐ 517

Ⓑ 506

Ⓒ 514

good base for trips to Zaō-san and ©**Matsu-shima,** a bay studded with 250 pine-clad islands that is one of Japan's three official scenic wonders. In southern Tōhoku, the five lakes of different hues, known as ®**Go-shiki-numa,** and ©**Inawashiro-ko,** Japan's third-largest lake, are neighbors. In nearby Kitakata, mud-wall storehouses will eat up your film, and in Aizu-Waka-matsu you'll see how a wealthy Samurai lived (in 38 rooms,

Ⓓ⟩ 533

Ⓔ⟩ 506

for starters). Northern Tōhoku is even more rugged—from rocky cliffs to volcanic peaks—and the autumn foliage in its national parks puts on one of the planet's great shows. Let your hair down at celebrations up north, such as the lively ©**Nebuta Festival** in Aomori and the Ⓓ**Kantō Festival** in Akita. Make time for traditional Kakunodate, a kind of Kyōto in miniature, and nearby alpine Tazawa-ko, Japan's deepest lake. Top it off with a day trip to windblown Tappi-Zaki. Honshū ends here; across the chilly water lies Hokkaidō. You've come far from Tōkyō, in every imaginable way.

Ⓕ⟩ 529

HOKKAIDŌ

Ⓐ 575

Barely tamed and beautiful, Japan's northernmost island is also its last frontier—a world away from Honshū's urban hives. You won't find shrines or castles here; the Japanese started settling Hokkaidō in earnest in the 19th century. What you will find are glorious landscapes, abundant hiking and skiing opportunities, and a good, modern base in the island's capital, Sapporo. In February the ©**Sapporo Snow Festival** dazzles with huge ice sculptures, and the city's nightlife

©⟩549

Ⓓ⟩563

zone, Susukino, glitters with neon year-round. To the south lie famous hot springs at Ⓑ**Noboribetsu Onsen** and, next door, Jigokudani (Valley of Hell), a volcanic crater that belches boiling water and sulfurous vapors. West of Sapporo, strange rock formations accent the dramatic coast of Ⓓ**Shakotan-hantō.** Try to fit Nakayama Tōge (a mountain pass) and three lakes—Tōya-ko, Shikotsu-ko, and Ⓐ**Mashū-ko**—into your plans as well. To the east is the town of Nibutani, a last toehold of the indigenous Ainu people, muscled aside as Japanese from the south moved to Hokkaidō. Northeast lie three great national parks: wild Shiretoko by the sea, lake-filled Akan, and mountainous Daisetsu-zan, with its dramatic Ⓔ**Sōun-kyō** ravine. You can walk the northern tip of Japan at Sōya-misaki and hike the rugged islands of Rebun-tō and Rishiri-tō nearby. Feel the peace. And if you're returning to any big Japanese city, brace yourself for the shock.

Ⓔ⟩579

GREAT ITINERARIES

Highlights of Japan
14 to 16 days

Many people don't see much more of Japan than Tōkyō, Kyōto, and the blur of the suburbs through the windows of a bullet train. If you want to explore the country at a slower pace, reduce the journey from a 170-mph whiz to a slow meander among temples, shrines, hot springs, mountains, and major cities. Begin with three days in Tōkyō. So few days in a megalopolis of millions may seem brief, but once you get caught up in the buzz of the city you'll soon be dashing from Shinjuku's skyscrapers to Ginza's boutiques. Be sure to take advantage of your jet lag and start your first day off with the early morning tuna auction at the Chūō Oroshiuri Ichiba, the Tsukiji fish market. If you have an extra day to spare, consider using it for a day trip to nearby Kamakura, the 13th-century capital of Japan, or to Fuji-san.

NIKKŌ
1 to 2 days. If you're still in big-city mode you may wish to approach Nikkō as a day trip, but a longer stay will allow you to soak up the atmosphere of the ancient temples and shrines in a gorgeous moun-tain setting. Tōshō-gū ranks as one of Japan's best shrines, and nearby Ⓐ Chūzenji-ko (Lake Chūzenji) and the Kegon-no-taki (Kegon Falls) are impressive.
☞ *Nikkō* in Chapter 2

ISE
1 day. Ise Jingū (Grand Shrines of Ise), with their harmonious architecture and cypress-forest setting, provide one of Japan's most spiritual experiences. The nearby city of Toba is an introduction to Japan's pearl-diving traditions.
☞ *Ise-Shima National Park and the Kii Peninsula* in Chapter 3

NARA
1 day. During the 8th century Nara served as the capital of Japan, and many cultural relics of that period, including some of the world's oldest wooden structures, still stand among forested hills and parkland. You can cover most major sights on foot in a day. Be sure to visit Nara's 53-ft-high *Daibutsu* (Great Buddha) and to make friends with the affable deer of Nara Kōen.
☞ *Chapter 6*

KYŌTO
3 days. For many visitors Kyōto *is* Japan, and few leave disappointed. Wander in and out of temple precincts like Ginkaku-ji, spot geisha strolling about Gion, and dine on *kaiseki ryōri*, an elegant culinary event that engages all the senses. Outside the city center, day-trip to hillside Arashiyama,

the gardens of the Katsura Rikyū, and the temple of Enryaku-ji atop Hiei-zan.
☞ *Chapter 5*

KURASHIKI
1 day. This rustic town, an important trading port in centuries past, retains its picturesque 17th-century buildings. The 1930s classi-cal-style Ōhara Bijutsukan houses a fine collection of European art. The Kurashiki Mingeikan displays crafts from around the world, including pottery from nearby Bizen.
☞ *The San-yō Region* in Chapter 9

HIROSHIMA
2 days. A quick glance at the busy, attractive city of Hi-roshima gives no clue to the

events of August 6, 1945. Only the city's Heiwa Kinen Kōen (Peace Memorial Park)—with its memorial museum and its Gembaku Dōmu, a twisted, half-shat-tered structural ruin—serves as a reminder of the horror of the day the world first saw the destructive potential of atomic weapons. From Hiroshima, make a quick trip to the island of Miyajima to see the famous floating torii of the Itsukushima Jinja, a shrine built on stilts above a tidal flat.
☞ *The San-yō Region* in Chapter 9

BEPPU OR YUFUIN
2 days. You don't need to be shaken by an earthquake to realize that Japan is very

seismically active. One of locals' favorite pastimes is relaxing in an *onsen* (hot spring), and Beppu, on the southernmost island of Kyūshū, has been a hot-springs resort for centuries. You can soak in mineral water or bubbling mud or bury yourself in therapeutic sand. With entertainment complexes, neon signs, and souvenir shops, Beppu can be a bit much. A quiet alternative is nearby Yufuin, with crafts galleries and thermal baths. ☞ *Beppu and Yufuin in Chapter 11*

By Public Transportation The train ride from Tōkyō's Asakusa Station to Nikkō takes less than two hours. Return to Tōkyō to catch either the Hikari or Kodama Shinkansen (bullet train) from Tōkyō Station to Nagoya. The private Kintetsu Railway can take you from Nagoya south

Traditional and Contemporary
9 days

Yes, Japan is a modern country with its skyscrapers, lightning-fast train service, and splendid neon lights. But it's also rich in history, culture, and tradition. Japan is perhaps most fascinating when you see these two faces at once: a 17th-century shrine sitting defiantly by a tower of steel and glass and a geisha chatting on a cell phone. A trip to Japan's major cities and holiest mountains combines the best of both worlds.

ŌSAKA
1 day. Ōsaka's amazing airport serves as an impres-

B⟩ 379

A⟩ 184

sive gateway to Japan. But the high-tech, undulating terminal is usually all that visitors see of this city before catching the express to nearby Kyōto. Although by no means picturesque, Ōsaka does provide a taste of urban Japan outside the capital, along with a few traditional sights. The handsome castle ⑧Ōsaka-jo nestles among skyscrapers, and the neon of

Dōtombori flashes around the local Kabuki theater. Osakans are passionate about food, and you're bound to find some of the finest in the country here. ☞ *Chapter 7*

KŌYA-SAN
1 day. More than 100 temples belonging to the Shingon sect of Buddhism stand on one of Japan's holiest mountains, 30 mi south of Ōsaka. An exploration of the atmospheric cemetery of Okuno-in takes you past interesting examples of headstone art and 300-year-old cedar trees. ☞ *Kōya-san and Yoshino-san in Chapter 3*

to Ise in 80 minutes. This railway can also take you from Ise to Kyōto, with connections to Nara. Less than two hours away from Kyōto by the San-yō Shinkansen is Kurashiki; you may need to change trains at Okayama. This same line will connect you to Hiroshima and Fukuoka, where you can catch the JR Nichirin Line to Beppu. Regular bus service connects Beppu and Yufuin.

© 301

KYŌTO

3 days. With nearly 2,000 temples and shrines, exquisite crafts, and serene gardens, Kyōto embodies traditional Japan. But the city is a bustling metropolis in its own right, with high-tech industries and contemporary architecture. A splendid modern-art gallery, Kindai Bijutsukan, cozies up to the buildings of the ©Heian Jingū (Heian Shrine). I. M. Pei designed the main structure of the Miho Bijutsukan, a museum built into a hillside to the north of Kyōto, which displays traditional Japanese art and Asian and Western antiquities. And Kyōto Eki, Hiroshi Hara's modern, once-controversial, marble-and-glass train station, is as significant as any of Kyōto's ancient treasures.
☞ Chapter 5

HIMEJI

1 day. The city's most famous sight, Himeji-jō, also known as the White Egret Castle (Shirasag-jō), dominates the city and its skyline. The castle takes only an afternoon to see, but museums near the train station are also worth a visit if you have an interest in Japan's modern architecture.

Kenzō Tange designed the informative Hyōgo Ken Shiryōkan (Hyōgo Prefectural Museum of History), and boxer-turned-architect Tadao Andō is responsible for the Himeji Bungaku Kan (Museum of Literature), which is celebrated more for its unique minimalist exterior than for the exhibits inside.
☞ The San-yō Region in Chapter 9

TŌKYŌ

3 days. ⒹJapan's capital, it seems, has much in common with everyone's vision of the future. The neon of Kabuki-chō, the city's wildest nightlife venue, is said to have inspired the cityscapes in *Blade Runner*, and Andrei Tarkovsky used images of the Tōkyō Metropolitan Expressway in his futuristic film masterpiece *Solaris*. Shibuya's bottle-blonde schoolgirls and the chic twentysomethings of Aoyama beat the nation's fashion drum, and buildings such as Philippe Starck's imaginative Asahi Beer headquarters tower over traditional structures like Asakusa's Sensō-ji. Sumō wrestlers observe centuries-old rituals before grappling in an ultramodern stadium. The venue sits next door to a space-age museum, the Edo-Tōkyō Hakubutsukan, that houses the treasures of Old Edo, a stimulating contrast typical of Tōkyō.
☞ Chapter 1

By Public Transportation
From Ōsaka's Nankai Namba Station you can reach Kōya-san in 90 minutes by the private Nankai Line and a cable car. You'll have to pass through Ōsaka again to get to Kyōto; frequent daily Hikari and Kodama Shinkansen make the 15-minute trip from Ōsaka to Kyōto. From Kyōto the Shinkansen will whisk you to Himeji in 45 minutes. Head back to Kyōto to catch the Shinkansen to Tōkyō.

770 km (477 mi)

Haguro-San

Niigata

410 km (254 mi)

Nikko

Nagano

Fukui

Himeji
120 km (74 mi)
Kyōto

Fuji Go-ko

Tōkyō
125 km (78 mi)

Ōsaka
80 km (50 mi)

Fuji-San

Nara

480 km (298 mi)

Kōya-san

Shingu

Ⓓ 34

Lakes and Mountains
8 days

With 80% of Japan's surface covered by mountains, you're bound to meet up with one sooner or later. Fuji-san, Japan's tallest peak, is one of the country's most enduring images, but several other mountains also provide a focus for a wonderful visit. Most of the country's lakes are small and shallow, but usually clear and scenic.

SAPPORO

2 days. This pleasant and accessible city serves as a good base for exploring the dramatic landscape of Hokkaidō. Mountains encircle Sapporo, the venue for the 1972 Olympic Games, and draw Japanese skiers in winter. Take day trips out to Tōya-ko or Shikotsu-ko, picturesque caldera lakes where you can boat or fish, and Noboribetsu Onsen, where you can soak in hot springs set against striking mountain scenery.
☞ *Sapporo and Otaru and the Shakotan-hantō in Chapter 13*

DAISETSU-ZAN NATIONAL PARK

2 days. One of Japan's most popular spots for hiking and skiing reflects the essence of Hokkaidō: soaring mountain peaks, hidden gorges, cascading waterfalls, forests, and hot springs. Sheer cliff walls and stone spires make for a stunning drive through the Sōun-kyō ravine. Take a cable car up to the top of Hokkaidō's tallest mountain, Asahi-dake; hike or ski for a couple of hours; and then unwind at a hot spring below.
☞ *Central Hokkaidō and the Northern Cape in Chapter 13*

HAGURO-SAN

2 days. This mountain, the most accessible of the Dewa-san range, a trio of sacred mountains in Tōhoku, is worth the trip not only for the lovely climb past cedars, waterfalls, and shrines but also for the thatched shrine at the top. You may even happen upon one of the many festivals and celebrations that take place at the shrine throughout the year. The rigorous climb itself, up 2,446 stone steps to the summit, is the main draw; however, it's possible to take a bus up or down the mountain.
☞ *Tōhoku West Coast in Chapter 12*

FUJI-SAN AND FUJI GO-KO

2 days. Climbing ⒺMount Fuji requires an early start, ideally you should reach the summit before dawn in order to greet the sunrise. The climb takes five hours but is not arduous. The trip up is safe only in July and August, but the views of the mountain are rewarding any time of year. The nearby resort area at Fuji Go-ko (Fuji Five Lakes) is one place to take in some of those views, and it's the best place to set up base camp for your climb. You can skate and fish here in the winter, boat and hike in the summer.
☞ *Fuji-Hakone-Izu National Park in Chapter 2*

Transportation

Many countryside areas are difficult to reach by public transportation, so you may want to rent a car for parts of this trip, and combine it with trains, buses, and even flights. Note that flights, in addition to being quicker, are often equal in price to if not cheaper than trains. Although Sapporo has some direct flights from Europe and the United States, if you're bound for Hokkaidō you usually have to transfer in Tōkyō. If you do choose to use the train to Daisetsu-zan National Park, it'll take two hours from Sapporo to Kamikawa, the nearest station. Heading to Haguro-san by rail is possible, but it's easier to take the hour-long flight out of Sapporo to tiny Shōnai Airport in Sakata, only 30 minutes away by bus or car from Haguro-san. You can hop on a plane from Shōnai Airport for the hour-long trip to Tōkyō, or use the Shinkansen, which takes more than four hours to reach Tōkyō and may require you to change trains. From Tōkyō a bus or train will take you to Fuji-san.

Ⓔ ⟩ 219

FODOR'S
CHOICE

Even with so many special places in Japan, Fodor's writers and editors have their favorites. Here are a few that stand out.

DINING

Kanawa Restaurant, Hiroshima. This Western Honshū city prides itself on its oysters; savor them on this barge with river views. *$$$$* ☞ p. 425

Kitayama, Yufuin, Kyūshū. After soaking in hot springs, try high-grade sake in this 120-year-old former *minka* (village house). *$$$–$$$$* ☞ p.498

Heichinrou, Tōkyō. Dine on first-rate Cantonese food while taking in a spectacular view of the Imperial Palace. *$$–$$$$* ☞ p. 126

Yagembori, Kyōto. A teahouse in the geisha district serves the city's best traditional kaiseki cuisine, artistically presented on beautiful handmade ceramics. *$$–$$$* ☞ p. 329

Ⓐ **Sagano, Kyōto.** Tofu simmered in savory broth is subtle and delicate at this gorgeous Arashiyama-district retreat. *$$* ☞ p. 332

Sasa-no-yuki, Tōkyō. An eight-course banquet showcases this restaurant's delectable take on traditional Buddhist vegetarian cuisine—and they've been serving it for 300 years. *$$* ☞ p. 126

Farm Grill, Tōkyō. Tōkyō yuppies meets California-style cuisine in this vast, minimally decorated space. *$* ☞ p. 118

LODGING

Ⓔ **Four Seasons Hotel, Tōkyō.** Every polished inch is evidence of the million dollars or so that it cost to complete each guest room here. *$$$$* ☞ p. 136

Ⓙ **Hiiragiya, Kyōto.** This 1818 inn skillfully combines ancient and modern: where else can you find cedar baths with chrome taps? *$$$$* ☞ p. 338

Palace Hotel, Tōkyō. Rooms are low-key and tasteful at this deluxe retreat, and the staff is particularly helpful. *$$$$* ☞ p. 133

Yamakyu, Takayama. This affordable Japanese inn set in old wooden buildings in an enchanting Japan Alps town provides tatami-mat rooms, large public baths, and meals. *$$* ☞ p. 268

Sakaeya, Beppu, Kyūshū. Meals prepared in a hot spring–heated backyard oven are included in the reasonable rates at this beautiful wooden inn. *$* ☞ p. 497

Sawanoya Ryokan, Tōkyō. The owners of this popular budget inn make guests feel welcome and at home. *$* ☞ p. 138

PARKS AND GARDENS

Ginkaku-ji, Kyōto. One of the two gardens at this tranquil temple provides changing perspectives as you stroll through it; the other is a dry garden with two dazzling sand shapes for quiet contemplation. ☞ p. 300

Katsura Rikyū, Kyōto. The loveliness of this vast estate's numerous gardens and rustic teahouses makes it worth your while to plan in advance to visit—as you must. ☞ p. 314

Kenrokuen, Kanazawa. The Japanese have designated this remarkable attraction on the North Chūbu Coast one of the country's three most beautiful gardens. ☞ p. 270

Ⓕ **Nara Kōen, Nara.** This sprawling park is home to tame deer and many famed temples and shrines. ☞ p. 362

Sankei-en, Yokohama. The many varieties of trees and flowers here ensure that something is blooming—or changing color—any time of year. Several traditional buildings add to the natural beauty. ☞ p. 204

Ⓒ **Shinjuku Gyo-en, Tōkyō.** Renowned for cherry blossoms in April and chrysanthemums in October, this park is an oasis of quiet in one of the city's most frenetic areas. ☞ p. 104

SIGHTS AND SCENES

Ⓖ **Chūō Oroshiuri Ichiba.** Getting up early to watch 90% of the fish consumed in Tōkyō being auctioned off is truly memorable. ☞ p. 79

Daibutsu-den, Tōdai-ji, Nara. The world's largest wooden structure houses a colossal 8th century bronze Buddha. ☞ p. 360

Fuji-san. One sighting of the elegant profile of the country's highest mountain, near Tōkyō, repays many times over the effort of traveling to Japan. ☞ p. 219

Ⓑ **Geisha, Gion, Kyōto.** These traditional female entertainers in richly brocaded kimono hurry down alleys to appointments in this Kyōto neighborhood. ☞ p. 301

Ⓗ **Gembaku Dōmu, Hiroshima.** Only this building was left unreconstructed after an atomic bomb leveled this Western Honshū city. ☞ p. 423

TEMPLES AND SHRINES

Byōdō-in, Uji, Kyōto. The Phoenix Hall of this temple is one of Japan's finest religious buildings. ☞ p. 319

Ⓘ **Hase-dera, Kamakura.** The haunting sight of hundreds of statues of Jizō—the bodhisattva associated with the souls of lost children—will stay with you after seeing this temple. ☞ p. 196

Hōryū-ji, Nara. Japan's oldest temple compound houses a fine collection of Buddhist art. ☞ p. 364

Ise Jingū, Ise-Shima. The austere beauty of the Grand Shrines of Ise is especially intriguing when you consider that the structures are completely rebuilt every 20 years. ☞ p. 239

Ⓓ **Itsukushima Jinja, Miyajima.** Itsukushima's striking vermilion torii stands in Hiroshima Bay, near the tiny island of Miyajima. ☞ p. 428

Kiyomizu-dera, Kyōto. You get a splendid panorama of the city from the cliff-side main hall of this spacious temple complex. ☞ p. 303

Sensō-ji, Tōkyō. A walk through the grounds of this Edo-period temple complex in the traditional Asakusa district is like a journey back in time. ☞ p. 72

1 TŌKYŌ

A state-of-the-art financial marketplace, a metropolis of exquisite politeness, a city that is monstrously large yet has astonishing beauty in its details—these are a few of the myriad ways to describe Tōkyō, and all contain more than a grain of truth. Ultimately, with its ultramodern speed and its smattering of old-Japanese haunts, Tōkyō is the sum of its districts and neighborhoods—among them Ueno, Asakusa, Ginza, Tsukiji, Shibuya, and Shinjuku.

By Jared
Lubarsky

TŌKYŌ: Of all major cities in the world, it is perhaps the hardest to understand or to see in any single perspective. To begin with, consider the sheer, outrageous size of it. Tōkyō incorporates 23 wards, 26 smaller cities, seven towns, and eight villages—altogether sprawling 88 km (55 mi) from east to west and 24 km (15 mi) from north to south. The wards alone enclose an area of 590 square km (228 square mi), which in turn house some 12 million people. More than 3 million of these residents pass through Shinjuku Eki, one of the major hubs in the transportation network, every day.

Space, that most precious of commodities, is so scarce that pedestrians have to weave in and around utility poles as they walk along the narrow sidewalks—yet mile after mile, houses rise only one or two stories, their low uniformity broken here and there by the sore thumb of an apartment building. Begin with that observation, and you discover that the very fabric of life in this city is woven of countless, unfathomable contradictions.

Tōkyō is a state-of-the-art financial marketplace, where billions of dollars are whisked electronically around the globe every day in the blink of an eye—and where automatic teller machines shut down at 9 PM. (There's no service after 5 PM on weekends and holidays, and the machines levy a service charge of ¥105 for withdrawals on Sunday.) A city of astonishing beauty in its small details, Tōkyō also has some of the ugliest buildings on the planet and generates more than 20,000 tons of garbage a day. It installed its first electric light in 1877 yet still has hundreds of thousands of households without a bathtub.

Life was simpler here in the 12th century, when Tōkyō was a little fishing village called Edo (pronounced "eh-doh"), near the mouth of the Sumida-gawa on the Kantō Plain. The Kantō was a strategic granary, large and fertile; over the next 400 years it was governed by a succession of warlords and other rulers. One of them, Dōkan Ōta, built the first castle in Edo in 1457. That act is still officially regarded as the founding of the city, but the honor really belongs to Ieyasu ("ee-eh-ya-su"), the first Tokugawa shōgun, who arrived in 1590. A key figure in the civil wars of the 16th century, he had been awarded the eight provinces of Kantō in eastern Japan in exchange for three provinces closer to Kyōto, the imperial capital. Ieyasu was a farsighted soldier; the swap was fine with him. On the site of Ōta's stronghold, he built a mighty fortress of his own—from which, 10 years later, he was ruling the whole country.

By 1680 there were more than a million people here, and a great city had grown up out of the reeds in the marshy lowlands of Edo Bay. Tōkyō can only really be understood as a jō-ka-machi—a castle town. Ieyasu had fought his way to the shogunate, and he had a warrior's concern for the geography of his capital. Edo-jō (Edo Castle) had the high ground, but that wasn't enough; all around it, at strategic points, he gave large estates to allies and trusted retainers. These lesser lords' villas would also be garrisons, outposts on a perimeter of defense.

Farther out, he kept the barons he trusted least of all—whom he controlled by bleeding their treasuries. He required them to keep large, expensive establishments in Edo; to contribute generously to the temples he endowed; to come and go in alternate years in great pomp and ceremony; and, when they returned to their estates, to leave their families—in effect, hostages—behind.

All this, the Edo of feudal estates, of villas and gardens and temples, lay south and west of Edo-jō. It was called Yamanote—the Bluff, the uptown. Here, all was order, discipline, and ceremony; every man had his rank and duties (very few women were within the garrisons). Almost from the beginning, those duties were less military than bureaucratic. Ieyasu's precautions worked like a charm, and the Tokugawa dynasty enjoyed some 250 years of unbroken peace, during which nothing very interesting ever happened uptown.

But Yamanote was only the demand side of the economy: somebody had to bring in the fish, weed the gardens, weave the mats, and entertain the bureaucrats during their free time. To serve the noble houses, common people flowed into Edo from all over Japan. Their allotted quarters of the city were jumbles of narrow streets, alleys, and cul-de-sacs in the low-lying estuarine lands to the north and east. Often enough, the land assigned to them wasn't even there; they had to *make* it by draining and filling the marshes (the first reclamation project in Edo dates to 1457). The result was Shitamachi—literally "downtown," the part below the castle, which sat on a hill. Bustling, brawling Shitamachi was the supply side: it had the lumberyards, markets, and workshops; the wood-block printers, kimono makers, and moneylenders. The people here gossiped over the back fence in the earthy, colorful Edo dialect. They went to Yoshiwara—a walled and moated area on the outskirts of Edo where prostitution was under official control. (Yoshiwara was for a time the biggest licensed brothel area in the world.) They supported the bathhouses and Kabuki theaters and reveled in their spectacular summer fireworks festivals. The city and spirit of the *Edokko*—the people of Shitamachi—have survived, while the great estates uptown are now mostly parks and hotels.

The shogunate was overthrown in 1867. The following year, Emperor Meiji moved his court from Kyōto to Edo and renamed it Tōkyō: the Eastern Capital. By now the city was home to nearly 2 million people, and the geography was vastly more complex. As it grew, it became not one but many smaller cities, with different centers of commerce, government, entertainment, and transportation. In Yamanote rose the commercial emporia, office buildings, and public halls that made up the architecture of an emerging modern state. The workshops of Shitamachi multiplied, some of them to become small jobbers and family-run factories. Still, there was no planning, no grid. The neighborhoods and subcenters were worlds unto themselves, and a traveler from one was soon hopelessly lost in another.

The firebombings of 1945 left Tōkyō, for the most part, in rubble and ashes. That utter destruction could have been an opportunity to rebuild on the rational order of cities like Kyōto, Barcelona, or Washington. No such plan was ever made. Tōkyō reverted to type: it became once again an aggregation of small towns and villages. One village was much like any other; the nucleus was always the *shōten-gai,* the shopping arcade. Each arcade had at least one fishmonger, grocer, rice dealer, mat maker, barber, florist, and a bookstore. You could live your whole life in the neighborhood of the shōten-gai. It was sufficient to your needs.

People seldom moved out of these villages. The vast waves of new residents who arrived after World War II—about three-quarters of the people in the Tōkyō metropolitan area today were born elsewhere—just created more villages. People who lived in the villages knew their way around, so there was no particular need to name the streets. Houses were numbered not in sequence but in the order in which they were built. No. 3 might well share a mailbox with No. 12. And people still take their local geography for granted—the closer you get to the place you're looking for, the harder it is to get coherent directions. Away from main streets and landmarks, even a taxi driver can get hopelessly lost.

Tōkyō Overview (Boxes Refer to Detail Maps)

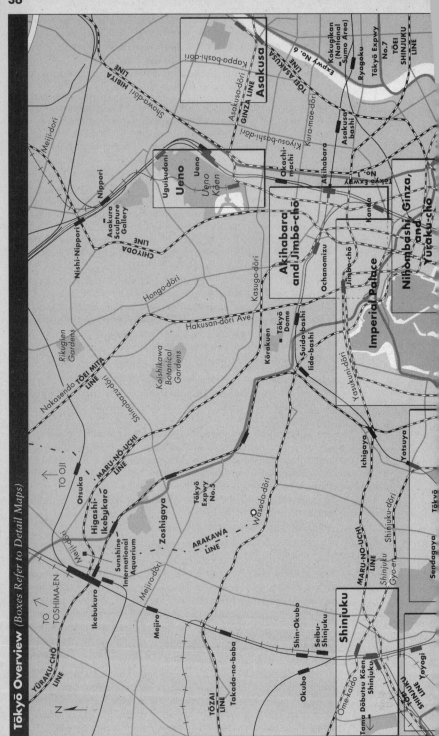

Asakusa

Ueno

Akihabara and Jimbō-chō

Nihombashi, Ginza, and Yūraku-chō

Imperial Palace

Shinjuku

TŌEI ASAKUSA LINE

Expwy No. 6

Kokugikan (National Sumo Area)

Ryōgoku

Tōkyō Expwy No. 7

TŌEI SHINJUKU LINE

Kappa-bashi-dōri

Asakusa-bashi

Kura-mae-dōri

Kiyosu-bashi-dōri

GINZA LINE

Akihabara

Kanda

HIBIYA LINE

Showa-dōri

Meiji-dōri

Asakusa-dōri

Okachi-machi

Tōkyō Expwy No. 1

Uguisudani

Ueno Kōen

CHIYODA LINE

Nippori

Nishi-Nippori

Asakura Sculpture Gallery

Ochanomizu

Jimbō-chō

Suido-bashi

Iida-bashi

Yasukuni-dōri

Hongo-dōri

Kasuga-dōri

Hakusan-dōri Ave

Tōkyō Dome

Kōrakuen

Rikugien Gardens

Koishikawa Botanical Gardens

TŌEI MITA LINE

Nakasendo

Shinobazu-dōri

MARU-NO-UCHI LINE

Ōtsuka

TO OJI

TO TOSHIMA-EN

Higashi-Ikebukuro

Zōshigaya

Tōkyō Expwy No.5

Waseda-dōri

Ichigaya

Yotsuya

Sunshine International Aquarium

ARAKAWA LINE

Meijiro-dōri

MARU-NO-UCHI LINE

Shinjuku Gyo-en

Shinjuku-dōri

Sendagaya

Tōkyō

Ikebukuro

Mejiro

Takada-no-baba

Ōkubo

Shin-Ōkubo

Seibu-Shinjuku

Shinjuku

Ome-Kaidō

Tama Dōbutsu Kōen Shinjuku

TŌZAI LINE

YŪRAKU-CHŌ LINE

Meiji-dōri

SHINJUKU LINE

TŌEI Yoyogi

N

KEY

JR Trains
Shinkansen (Bullet Train)
Subway
Private rail line
Street car

TO TŌKYŌ DISNEYLAND, KASAI SEASIDE PARK AND TŌKYŌ SEALIFE PARK

TO TŌKYŌ

Eitai-dōri

TŌZAI LINE

YŪRAKU-CHŌ LINE

Sumidagawa

Tsukuda-Jima

Kiyosumi-dōri

Nihombashi

Tōkyō

Chūō-dōri

Shōwa-dōri

Shin Ōhashi-dōri

Tsukiji

Shōwa-chō

Yūraku-chō

Tsukiji and Shimbashi

Hama Rikyū Tei-en

PORT OF TŌKYŌ

Uchibori-dōri

Hibiya Park

Shimbashi

TOEI ASAKUSA LINE

Shiba Rikyū Tei-en

Hibiya-dōri

Hamamatsu-chō

TOEI MITA LINE

Sakurada-dōri

Tōkyō Tower

Sotobori-dōri

Sakurada-dōri

Ta-machi

Dai-ichi Keihin

Tōkyō Expwy No.1

TO DAIBA

Tōkyō Kaigan-dōri

Akasaka-mitsuke

Akasaka Palace

Aoyama-dōri

Gaien-Higashi-dōri

Roppongi

Sengaku-ji

TO SHINAGAWA

TOEI ASAKUSA LINE

Shinagawa

Tōkyō Expwy No.3

Tōkyō Expwy No.4

Sendagaya

Shina-no-machi

Aoyama-it-chōme

Aoyama Outer Garden

Meiji Jingū Outer Garden

Omotesandō

Tōkyō Expwy No.2

National Park for Nature Study

Meguro-dōri

Sakurada-dōri

TO SHINAGAWA SUIZOKUKAU

Gotanda

Meguro

HIBIYA LINE

Meiji-dōri

CHIYODA LINE

GINZA LINE

HANZŌMON LINE

Meiji Jingū-mae

Harajuku

Ebisu

MEGURO

Meiji Jingū Inner Garden

Yoyogi Kōen

Shibuya and Harajuku

Shibuya

Daikanyama

Nakameguro

1 mile

1 km

0

0

Tōkyō Subway

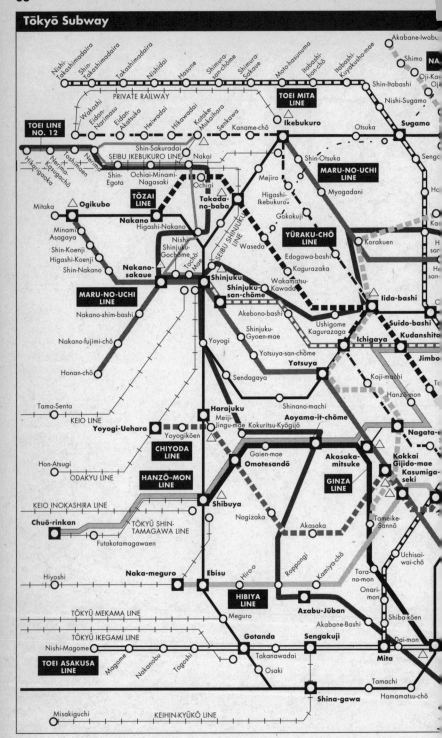

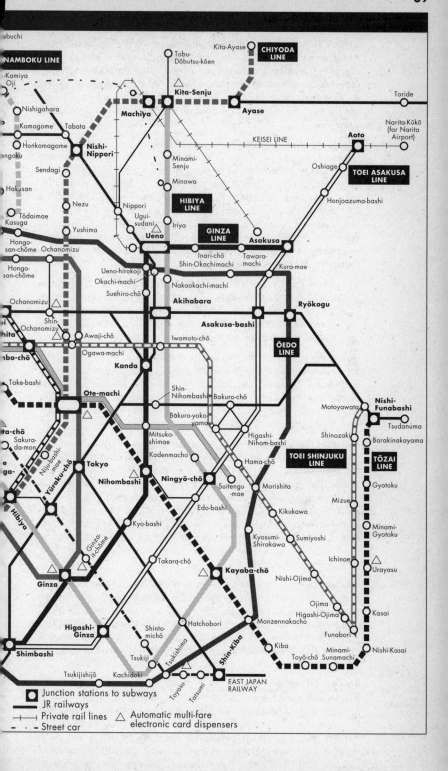

abuchi

NAMBOKU LINE

-Kamiya
Oji

Nishigahara

Komagome · Tabata

Honkomagome

ngoku

**Nishi-
Nippori**

Sendagi

Hakusan

Nezu

Tōdaimae
Kasuga

Hongo-
san-chōme · Ochanomizu

Hongo-
san-chōme

Ochanomizu

Shin-
Ochanomizu

hita

Awaji-chō

nbo-chō

Ogawa-machi

Take-bashi

Kanda

Ote-machi

a-chō

Sakura-
da-mon

Niju-bashi-
mae

ga-

Tokyo

Yūraku-chō

Nihombashi

Ginza-
it-chōme

Hibiya

Kyo-bashi

Ginza

Takara-chō

**Higashi-
Ginza**

Shimbashi

Shinto-
michō

Tsukijishijō · Kachidoki

Tsukiji

Tsukishima

Yushima

Nippori

Ugui-
sudani

Ueno

Tobu-
Dōbutsu-kōen

Kita-Senju

Machiya

Minami-
Senju

Minowa

Iriya

**HIBIYA
LINE**

**GINZA
LINE**

Inari-chō
Shin-Okachimachi

Ueno-hirokoji

Okachi-machi

Suehiro-chō

Nakaokachi-machi

Akihabara

Iwamoto-chō

Shin-
Nihombashi · Bakuro-chō

Bakuro-yoko-
yama

Mitsuko-
shimae

Kodenmacho

Ningyō-chō

Suitengu
-mae

Edo-bashi

Kayaba-chō

Nishi-Ojima

Hatchobori

Shinto-
michō

Kita-Ayase

**CHIYODA
LINE**

Toride

Ayase

KEISEI LINE

Oshiage

Aoto

**TOEI ASAKUSA
LINE**

Narita-Kūkō
(for Narita
Airport)

Honjoazuma-bashi

Asakusa

Tawara-
machi

Kura-mae

Ryōkogu

Asakusa-bashi

**ŌEDO
LINE**

Motoyawata

**Nishi-
Funabashi**

Shinozaki

Tsudanuma

Barakinakayama

Higashi-
Nihom-bashi

Hama-chō

**TOEI SHINJUKU
LINE**

**TŌZAI
LINE**

Morishita

Gyotoku

Kikukawa

Mizue

Minami-
Gyotoku

Kyosumi-
Shirakawa · Sumiyoshi

Ichinoe

Urayasu

Ojima

Higashi-Ojima

Kasai

Monzennakacho

Funabori

Kiba

Minami-
Sunamachi

Nishi-Kasai

Toyō-chō

Shin-Kiba

**EAST JAPAN
RAILWAY**

Toyosu · Tatsumi

Junction stations to subways
JR railways
Private rail lines
Street car
**Automatic multi-fare
electronic card dispensers**

Fortunately, there are the *kōban:* small police boxes, or substations, usually with two or three officers assigned to each of them full time, to look after the affairs of the neighborhood. You can't go far in any direction without finding a kōban. The officer on duty knows where everything is and is glad to point the way. (The substation system, incidentally, is one important reason for the legendary safety of Tōkyō: on foot or on white bicycles, the police are a visible presence, covering the beat. Burglaries are not unknown, of course, but street crime is very rare.)

Outsiders, however, rarely venture very far into the labyrinths of residential Tōkyō. Especially for travelers, the city defines itself by its commercial, cultural, and entertainment centers: Ueno, Asakusa, Ginza, Roppongi, Shibuya, Harajuku, and Shinjuku. Megaprojects to develop the waterfront and the Ebisu area in the 1980s and 1990s added yet others to the list. The attention of Tōkyō shifts constantly, seeking new patches of astronomically expensive land on which to realize its enormous commercial energy. Even with the collapse of the speculative bubble in 1992, you can't buy a square yard anywhere in the city's central wards for much less than $1,000.

Tōkyō is still really two areas, Shitamachi and Yamanote. The heart of Shitamachi, proud and stubborn in its Edo ways, is Asakusa; the dividing line is Ginza, west of which lie the boutiques and depāto, the banks and engines of government, the pleasure domes and cafés. Today there are 13 subway lines in full operation that weave the two areas together.

Tōkyō has no remarkable skyline, no prevailing style of architecture, no real context into which a new building can fit. Every new project is an environment unto itself. Architects revel in this anarchy, and so do the designers of neon signs, show windows, and interior spaces. The kind of creative energy you find in Tōkyō could flower only in an atmosphere where there are virtually no rules to break.

Not all of this is for the best. Many of the buildings in Tōkyō are merely grotesque, and most of them are supremely ugly. In the large scale, Tōkyō is not an attractive city—neither is it gracious, and it is certainly not serene. The pace of life is wedded to the one stupefying fact of population: within a 36-km (22-mi) radius of the Imperial Palace live almost 30 million souls, all of them in a hurry and all of them ferocious consumers—not merely of things but of culture and leisure. Still uncertain about who they are and where they are going, they consume to identify themselves—by what they wear, where they eat, and how they use their spare time.

Sooner or later everything shows up here: Van Gogh's *Sunflowers,* the Berlin Philharmonic, Chinese pandas, Mexican food. Even the Coney Island carousel is here—lovingly restored down to the last gilded curlicue on the last prancing unicorn, back in action at an amusement park called Toshima-en. Tōkyō is a magnet, and now the magnet is drawing you. What follows here is an attempt to chart a few paths for you through this exciting, exasperating, movable feast of a city.

Tōkyō Glossary

Key Japanese words and suffixes in this chapter include *-bashi* (bridge), *bijutsukan* (art museum), *-chō* (street or block), *-chōme* (street), *chūō* (central), *depāto* ("deh-*pah*-to," department store), *dōri* (avenue), *eki* (train station), *gaijin* (foreigner), *-gawa* (river), *-gū* (Shintō shrine), *guchi* (exit), *hakubutsukan* (museum), *higashi* (east), *-in* (Buddhist temple), *izakaya* (pub), *-ji* (Buddhist temple), *-jima* (island), *jingū* or *jinja* (Shintō shrine), *-jō* (castle), *kita* (north), *kōen* (park), *-ku* (section or ward), *kūkō* (airport), *machi* (town), *matsuri* (festival), *minami* (south), *-mon* (gate), *nishi* (west), *Shinkansen* (bullet train, literally "new trunk line"), *shita* (lower, downward), *torii* ("*to*-ree-ee," gate), *-ya* (shop, as in hon-ya, bookshop), *yama* (mountain), *yamanote* (the hilly part of town).

Pleasures and Pastimes

Depending on your point of view, Tōkyō has more than 400 years of history—or barely 50. What survives here of the old—temple architecture, performing arts, traditions of craft and design—may not compare to what you find in Kyōto, but the rewards of Tōkyō's museums and theaters are rich indeed. What's new is relentlessly so: Tōkyō is an affluent mass market for the latest products and designs, services, and amusements—an unbeatable place to shop and party.

Dining

The Japanese are more cautious than they were a decade ago about expense-account entertaining, but wining and dining still play a role in cementing the all-important personal contacts that make the wheels of business, and government, turn. It's still standard practice for Tōkyō's white-collar legions to work late, unwind with their colleagues in a favorite restaurant, and catch the last train home. Social critics point to an alarming rise in the percentage of young singles out in the working world who still live with their parents—but these are the bearers of most of the city's discretionary income, and they flock to whatever new restaurants the magazines have declared in fashion. The range of options is astonishing: It's hard to think of a national cuisine of any prominence that goes unrepresented.

Some of those choices can be hideously expensive. For every budget-buster, however, there are any number of bargains—good cooking of all sorts, at prices ordinary travelers can afford. The options, in fact, go all the way down to street food and *yakitori* (Japanese-style chicken kebabs) joints under railroad trestles, where many Japanese go when they have to spend their own money. Food and drink, incidentally, are safe wherever you go. For more details on Japanese cuisine, *see* Chapter 14, *and* Dining *in* Smart Travel Tips A to Z.

Lodging

Hotels throughout the city are clean and safe, with excellent service. Tōkyō has a wide range of lodging possibilities, from luxurious suites to functional business-hotel rooms to claustrophobic capsule-hotel cubicles. For a short course on accommodations in Japan, *see* Lodging *in* Smart Travel Tips A to Z.

Performing Arts

Japan is justly proud of its music, dance, and theater traditions, which are quite unique: unless you happen to catch one of the infrequent (and expensive) performances of a company on tour abroad, you'll never really see the like of Kabuki, Nō, or Bunraku anywhere else.

Kabuki has been pleasing Japanese audiences from all walks of life for more than 300 years. It's the kind of theater—a combination of music, dance, and drama, with spectacular costumes and acrobatics, duels, and quick changes and special effects thrown in—that you can enjoy without understanding a word the actors say. Nō, on the other hand, is an acquired taste. A ritual masked drama that has remained virtually unchanged since the 14th century, Nō moves at a stately—nay, glacial—pace to music and recitation utterly different from anything Western. Bunraku is Japan's puppet theater, like Kabuki a popular form of entertainment, but with roots in the western part of the country. The puppets themselves are so expressive and intricate in their movements that each requires three people to move it around on stage.

Three theaters in Tōkyō present Kabuki, including the landmark Kabuki-za, first built exclusively for that purpose in 1925. Four traditional schools, each with its own performance space, specialize in Nō; there's also the National Nō Theater, and—on rare occasions—night performances by torchlight in the courtyards of temples. Bunraku is not found as often in Tōkyō as it is in Ōsaka, but if there's a performance anywhere in town during your stay, it's decidedly worth seeing.

Shopping

In the late 1990s upscale consumer goods in Tōkyō—designer clothing, cultured pearls, home electronics—spiraled down from the insanely expensive to the merely costly. Fashions by internationally known designers like Issey Miyake, Rei Kawakubo, Hanae Mori, Yōji Yamamoto, Hiroko Koshino, and Kansai Yamamoto are priced more reasonably in Tōkyō's boutiques and depāto than they are abroad. Among things more traditionally Japanese, good buys include pottery, fabrics, folk-craft objects in wood and bamboo, cutlery, lacquerware, and handmade paper. You can find regional specialties from all over Japan, amounting to an enormous range of goods from which to choose. The selections in conveniently located arcades and the crafts sections of major depāto make one-stop shopping easy.

EXPLORING TŌKYŌ

The distinctions of Shitamachi (literally "downtown," to the north and east) and Yamanote (literally "uptown," to the south and west) have shaped the character of Tōkyō since the 17th century and will guide you as you explore the city. At the risk of an easy generalization, it might be said that downtown has more to *see,* uptown more to *do.* Another way of putting it is that Tōkyō north and east of the Imperial Palace embodies more of the city's history and traditional way of life; the glitzy, ritzy side of contemporary, international Tōkyō generally lies south and west.

The city has been divided into 10 exploring sections in this chapter, 6 in Shitamachi—starting in central Tōkyō with the Imperial Palace District—and 4 uptown in Yamanote. It can be exhausting to walk from one part of Tōkyō to another—you'll look in vain for places outdoors just to sit and rest en route—and bus travel can be particularly tricky. Fortunately, no point on any of these itineraries is very far from a subway station, and you can use the city's efficient subway system to hop from one area to another, to cut a tour short, or to return to a tour the next day. The area divisions in this book are not always contiguous—Tōkyō is too spread out for that—but they generally border each other to a useful degree. As you plan your approach to the city, by all means skip parts of an area that don't appeal or combine parts of one tour with those of another in order to get the best of all worlds.

The listings in this chapter include subway and JR train lines and stops as well as station exit names and numbers in cases where they're most helpful—which is quite often, as several stations have multiple (sometimes more than 15) exits.

Great Itineraries

You need three days just to take in the highlights of Tōkyō and still have time for some shopping and nightlife. With four or five days you can explore the city in greater depth, wander off the beaten path, and appreciate Tōkyō's museums at leisure. Eight days would allow for day trips to the scenic and historical sights nearby.

IF YOU HAVE 3 DAYS

Start *very* early (why waste your jet lag?) with a visit to the Tōkyō Chūō Oroshiuri Ichiba (Tōkyō Central Wholesale Market) while it's still in high gear; then use the rest of the day for a tour of the Imperial Palace and environs. Spend the next morning at Buddhist Sensō-ji in Asakusa, and from there head to Ueno Kōen for an afternoon with its many museums, vistas, and historic sites. Start your last day with a morning stroll through Ginza to explore its fabled shops and depāto. In the afternoon, see the Shintō Meiji Jingū and take a leisurely walk through the nearby Harajuku and Omotesandō fashion districts to the Nezu Institute of Fine Arts—a perfect oasis for your last impressions of the city.

IF YOU HAVE 4 OR 5 DAYS

Follow the itinerary above and add to it (or punctuate it with) a morning of browsing in Akihabara, Tōkyō's electronics discount quarter, visiting the nearby Shintō Kanda Myōjin as well. Spend the afternoon on the west side of Shinjuku, Tōkyō's 21st-century model city; savor the view from the observation deck of architect Kenzō Tange's monumental Tōkyō Tochō complex; and cap off the day with a walk through the greenery of Shinjuku Gyo-en National Garden. The luxury of a fifth day would allow you to fill in the missing pieces that belong to no particular major tour: the Buddhist Sengaku-ji in Shinagawa, the remarkable Edo-Tōkyō Hakubutsukan in Ryōgoku, a tea ceremony, or any of the shops that haven't yet managed to stake a claim on your dwindling resources. See a sumō tournament, if there's one in town; failing that, you could still visit the Kokugikan, National Sumō Arena, in the Ryōgoku district, and some of the sumō stables in the neighborhood.

IF YOU HAVE 8 DAYS

With a week or more, you can make Tōkyō your home base for a series of side trips (☞ Chapter 2). After getting your fill of Tōkyō, take a train out to Yokohama, with its scenic port and Chinatown. A bit farther afield but still easily accessible by train is Kamakura, the 12th-century military capital of Japan. The Daibutsu (Great Buddha) of the Kōtoku-in is but one of the National Treasures of art and architecture here that draw millions of visitors a year. For both Yokohama and Kamakura, an early morning start will allow you to see most of the important sights in a full day and make it back to Tōkyō by late evening. As Kamakura is the most popular of excursions from Tōkyō, avoid the worst of the crowds by making the trip on a weekday. Still farther off, but again an easy train trip, is Nikkō, where the founder of the Tokugawa shogunal dynasty is enshrined. Tōshō-gū is a monument unlike any other in Japan, and the picturesque Lake Chūzen-ji is in a forest above the shrine. Two full days, with an overnight stay, would allow you an ideal, leisurely exploration of both. Yet another option would be a trip to Hakone and a climb to the summit of Mt. Fuji.

When to Tour Tōkyō

The best of all possible times to be in Tōkyō are from early to mid-April, in cherry-blossom season—though two or three days of chill and rain will sometimes come and dampen the enjoyment—and during the second half of May. The next best times are late September and October. Avoid the rainy season, from late June through mid-July, if you can, and only come in August if you must visit in the summer, knowing that you'll get blasted with heat and high humidity. Because mid-August is also one of the few periods when the Japanese themselves can take vacations—the others are the two or three days before and after New Year's and the first week of May—reservations are at a premium for planes, trains, and hotels.

Imperial Palace District

Kōkyo, the Imperial Palace, occupies what were once the grounds of Edo-jō. When Ieyasu Tokugawa chose the site for his castle in 1590, he had two goals in mind. First, it would have to be impregnable; second, it would have to reflect the power and glory of his position. He was lord of the Kantō, the richest fief in Japan, and would soon be shōgun, the military head of state. The fortifications he devised called for a triple system of moats and canals, incorporating the bay and the Sumida-gawa into a huge network of waterways that enclosed both the castle keep (the stronghold, or tower) and the palaces and villas of his court—in all, an area of about 450 acres. The castle had 99 gates (36 in the outer wall), 21 watchtowers (of which 3 are still standing), and 28 armories. The outer defenses stretched from present-day Shimbashi Eki to Kanda. Completed in 1640 and later expanded, it was at the time the largest castle in the world.

The walls of Edo-jō and its moats were made of stone from the Izu Peninsula, about 96 km (60 mi) to the southwest. The great slabs were brought by barge—each of the largest was a cargo in itself—to the port of Edo (then much closer to the castle than the present port of Tōkyō is now) and hauled through the streets on sledges by teams of 100 or more men. Thousands of stonemasons were brought from all over the country to finish the work. Under the gates and castle buildings, the blocks of stone are said to have been shaped and fitted so precisely that a knife blade could not be slipped between them.

The inner walls divided the castle into four main areas, called *maru*. The *hon-maru*, the principle area, contained the shōgun's audience halls, his private residence, and, for want of a better word, his seraglio: the *ō-oku*, where he kept his wife and concubines, with their ladies-in-waiting, attendants, cooks, and servants. At any given time, as many as 1,000 women might be living in the ō-oku. Intrigue, more than sex, was its principal concern, and tales of the seraglio provided a rich source of material for the Japanese literary imagination. Below the hon-maru was the *ni-no-maru*, where the shōgun lived when he transferred his power to an heir and retired. Behind it was the *kita-no-maru*, the northern area, now a public park; south and west was the *nishi-no-maru*, a subsidiary fortress.

Not much of the Tokugawa glory remains. The shogunate was abolished in 1868, and in Emperor Meiji's move from Kyōto to Edo, which he renamed Tōkyō, Edo-jō was chosen as the site of the Imperial Palace. Many of its buildings had been destroyed in the turmoil of the restoration of the emperor, others fell in the fires of 1872, and still others were simply torn down. Of the 28 original *tamon* (armories), only 2 have survived. The present-day Imperial Palace, which dates to 1968, is open to the public only twice a year: on January 2 and December 23 (The Emperor's Birthday), when many thousands of people assemble under the balcony to offer their good wishes to the imperial family. In 1968, to mark the completion of the current palace, the area that once encompassed the hon-maru and ni-no-maru was opened to the public as the Imperial Palace East Garden. There are three entrance gates—Ōte-mon, Hirakawa-mon, and Kita-hane-bashi-mon. You can easily get to any of the three from the Ōte-machi or Takebashi subway station.

Numbers in the text correspond to numbers in the margin and on the Imperial Palace map.

A Good Walk

A good place to start is **Tōkyō Eki** ①. The Ōte-machi subway stop (on the Chiyoda, Marunouchi, Tōzai, Hanzō-mon, and Toei Mita lines) is a closer and handier connection, but the old redbrick Tōkyō Eki building is a more compelling choice. (The Tōkyō Station Hotel, incidentally, which wanders along the west side of Tōkyō Eki on the second and third floors, serves a fairly decent breakfast for ¥1,700.) Leave the station by the Marunouchi Central Exit, cross the street in front at the taxi stand, and walk up the broad divided avenue that leads to the Imperial Palace grounds. To your left is Marunouchi, to your right Ōtemachi: you're in the heart of Japan, Incorporated—the home of its major banks and investment houses, its insurance and trading companies. Take the second right, at the corner of the New Marunouchi Building; walk two blocks, past the gleaming brown-marble fortress of the Industrial Bank of Japan, and turn left. Ahead of you, across Uchibori-dōri (Inner Moat Avenue) from the Palace Hotel, is **Ōte-mon,** one of three entrances to the **Imperial Palace East Garden** ②.

Turn right as you leave the East Garden through Ōte-mon. Where the wall makes a right angle, you will see the Tatsumi, or Ni-jū Yagura (Double-Tiered Watchtower), one of three surviving watchtowers on the original fortifications. Here the sidewalk opens out to a parking lot for tour buses and the beginning of a broad promenade. In the far corner to your right, where the angle of the wall turns again, is the Kikyō-mon, a gate used primarily for deliveries to the palace. At the far end of the parking lot is Sakashita-mon, the gate used by the officials of the Imperial Household Agency itself.

From here to Hibiya Kōen, along both sides of Uchibori-dōri, stretches the concourse of the **Imperial Palace Outer Garden** ③. This whole area once lay along the edge of Tōkyō Bay. Later, the shōgun had his most trusted retainers build their estates here. These in turn gave way to the office buildings of the Meiji government. In 1899 the buildings were relocated, and the promenade was planted with the wonderful stands of pine trees you see today.

Walk along the broad gravel path to **Ni-jū-bashi** ④ (Two-Tiered Bridge) and the Sei-mon (Main Gate). Ni-jū-bashi makes its graceful arch over the moat here from the area inside the gate. The building in the background, completing the picture, is the Fushimi Yagura, built in the 17th century. It is the last of the three surviving original watchtowers.

Continue on the gravel walk past the Sei-mon, turn right, and pass through the **Sakurada-mon** ⑤. Before you do, turn and look back down the concourse: you will not see another expanse of open space like this anywhere else in Tōkyō.

Look south across the street as you pass through the gate; the broad avenue that begins on the opposite side is Sakurada-dōri. World-renowned architect Kenzō Tange's Metropolitan Police Department building is on the west corner. The stately brick building on the east corner is the old Ministry of Justice. Sakurada-dōri runs through the heart of official Japan; between here and Kasumigaseki are the ministries—from Foreign Affairs and Education to International Trade and Industry—that compose the central government. Turn right at Sakurada-mon and follow the Sakurada Moat uphill along Uchibori-dōri.

A five-minute walk will bring you to where Roppongi-dōri branches in from the left; look in that direction and you will see the approach to the squat pyramid of the **Kokkai-Gijidō** ⑥, which houses the Japanese parliament. You might want to walk in for a closer look. If not, bear right as you continue to follow the moat along Uchibori-dōri to the next intersection, at Miya-zaka. Across the street are the gray-stone slabs of Japan's Supreme Court, the **Saikō Saibansho** ⑦. This and the **Kokuritsu Gekijō** ⑧ (National Theater), next door, are worth a short detour.

46

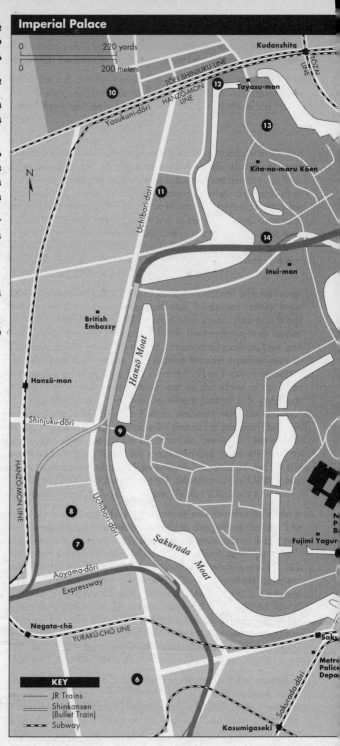

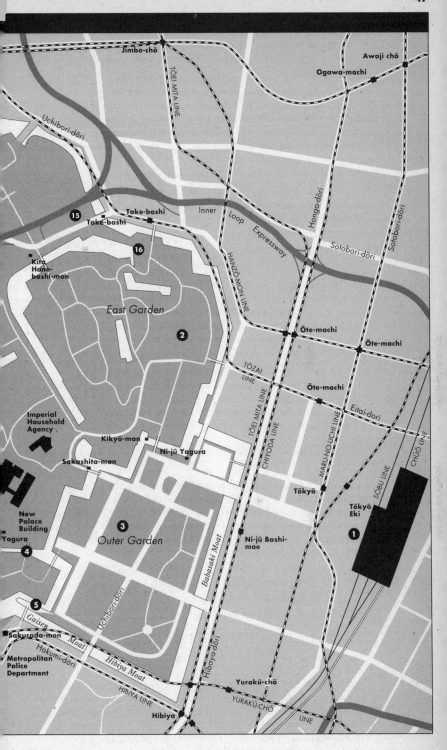

Jimbo-chō

Awaji chō

Ogawa-machi

Uchibori-dōri

TŌEI MITA LINE

Take-bashi

15 Take-bashi

Inner Loop Expressway

Hongo-dōri

Sotobori-dōri

Sotobori-dōri

16

Kita Hane-bashi-mon

HANZŌ-MON LINE

East Garden

2

Ōte-machi

Ōte-machi

TŌZAI LINE

Ōte-machi

Eitai-dori

Imperial Household Agency

TŌEI MITA LINE

CHIYODA LINE

MARU-NO-UCHI LINE

SŌBU LINE

CHŪŌ LINE

Kikyō-mon

Ni-jū Yagura

Sakashita-mon

Tōkyō

Tōkyō Eki

1

New Palace Building

3

Outer Garden

Babasaki Moat

Ni-jū Bashi-mae

Yagura

4

5

Gaisen Moat

Sakurada-mon

Hakumi-dōri

Hibiya Moat

Hibiya-dōri

Uchibori-dōri

Metropolitan Police Department

HIBIYA LINE

Yurakū-chō

YURAKŪ-CHŌ LINE

Hibiya

Cross back to the palace side of the street and continue north on Uchibori-dōri. At the top of the hill, on your right, a police contingent guards the road to the **Hanzō-mon** ⑨—the western gate to the new Imperial Palace. Here, where the road turns north again, begins the Hanzō Moat.

North along the Hanzō Moat is a narrow strip of park; facing it, across the street, is the British Embassy. Along this western edge of his fortress, the shōgun kept his personal retainers, called *hatamoto*, divided by *ban-chō* (district) into six regiments. Today these six ban-chō are among the most sought-after residential areas in Tōkyō, where high-rise apartments commonly fetch ¥100 million or more.

At the next intersection, review your priorities again. You can turn right and complete your circuit of the palace grounds by way of the Inui-mon, or you can continue straight north to the end of Uchibori-dōri to **Yasukuni Jinja** ⑩, the Shrine of Peace for the Nation.

If you do go to Yasukuni Jinja, make time for a short visit on the way to the **Yamatane Bijutsukan** ⑪, a few minutes' walk past the intersection on the east side of Samban-chō.

Leave Yasukuni Jinja the way you came in, cross the street, turn left, and walk down the hill. The entrance to **Chidori-ga-fuchi Kōen** ⑫ is about 50 yards from the intersection, on the right. The green strip of promenade is high on the edge of the moat, lined with cherry trees. Halfway along, it widens, and opposite the Fairmount Hotel a path leads down to the Chidori-ga-fuchi Boathouse. Beyond the boathouse, the promenade leads back in the direction of the Imperial Palace.

If you have the time and stamina for a longer tour, retrace your steps from the boathouse, leave the park the way you came in, turn right, and continue down the hill to the entrance to Kita-no-maru Kōen, through Tayasu-mon, one of the largest and finest of the surviving *masu* (box) gates to the castle. Inside, you come first to the octagonal **Nippon Budōkan** ⑬, site of major rock concerts and martial arts contests.

Opposite the main entrance to the Budōkan, past the parking lot, a pathway leads off through the park back in the direction of the palace. Cross the bridge at the other end of the path, turn right, and then right again before you leave the park on the driveway that leads to the **Kōgeikan** ⑭, a museum devoted to works of traditional craftsmanship by the great modern masters.

Return to the park exit and cross the street to the palace side. Ahead of you is the Inui-mon. This gate is used primarily by members of the imperial family and by the fortunate few with special invitations to visit the palace itself. A driveway here leads to the Imperial Household Agency and the palace. A bit farther down the hill is the Kita-Hane-bashi-mon, one of the entrances to the Imperial Palace East Garden.

At the foot of the hill is Take-bashi—although the name means Bamboo Bridge, the original construction has, of course, long since given way to reinforced concrete. Here, depending on your reserves of time and energy, you might want to cross the street to see the collection of modern Japanese and Western work in the **Tōkyō Kokuritsu Kindai Bijutsukan** ⑮. On the palace side of Take-bashi sits the finely reconstructed **Hirakawa-mon** ⑯, the East Garden's third entrance, which will complete the loop on this walk. From here follow the moat as it turns south again around the garden. In a few minutes you'll find yourself back at Ōte-mon, tired, perhaps, but triumphant.

TIMING

The Imperial Palace area covers a lot of ground—uphill and down—and even in its shorter versions the walk includes plenty to see. Allow at least an hour for the East Garden and Outer Garden of the palace itself. Plan to visit Yasukuni Jinja after lunch and spend at least an hour there. The Yūshūkan (at Yasukuni Jinja) and Kōgeikan museums are both small and should engage you for no more than half an hour each, but the modern art museum will repay a more leisurely visit—particularly if there's a special exhibit. Set your own pace, but assume that this walk will take you the better part of a full day.

Avoid Monday, when the East Garden and museums are closed; the East Garden is also closed on Friday. In July and August heat will make the palace walk grueling—bring hats, parasols, and bottled water.

Sights to See

⑫ **Chidori-ga-fuchi Kōen.** High on the edge (*fuchi* means "edge") of the Imperial Palace moat, this park is pleasantly arrayed with cherry trees. Long before Edo-jō was built, there was a lovely little lake here, which Ieyasu Tokugawa incorporated into his system of defenses. Now you can rent a rowboat at **Chidori-ga-fuchi Boathouse,** roughly in the middle of the park, and explore it at your leisure. The park entrance is near Yasukuni Jinja, west and downhill from the corner of Yasukuni-dōri and Uchibori-dōri. ☎ 03/3234–1948. ⌦ *Boat rentals ¥300 for 30 mins.* ⊙ *Park daily sunrise–sunset; boathouse Apr.–Sept., Tues.–Sun. 9:30–4:30; Oct.–Mar., Tues.–Sun. 9:30–5. Subway: Hanzō-mon and Toei Shinjuku lines, Kudanshita Eki (Exit 2).*

⑨ **Hanzō-mon.** The house of the legendary Hattori Hanzō once sat at the foot of this small wooden gate. Hanzō was the leader of the shōgun's private corps of spies and infiltrators—and assassins, if need be. They were the menacing, black-clad *ninja,* perennial material for historical adventure films and television dramas. The gate is a minute's walk east from the subway. *Subway: Hanzō-mon Line, Hanzō-mon Eki (Exit 3).*

⑯ **Hirakawa-mon.** The approach to this gate crosses the only wooden bridge that spans the Imperial Palace moat. The gate and bridge are reconstructions, but Hirakawa-mon is especially beautiful, looking much as it must have when the shōgun's ladies used it on their rare excursions from the seraglio. Hirakawa-mon is the north gate to the East Garden, southeast of Take-bashi. *Subway: Tōzai Line, Take-bashi Eki (Exit 1A).*

② **Imperial Palace East Garden.** The entrance to the East Garden, Kōkyo Higashi Gyo-en, is the ☞ Ōte-mon, once the main gate of Ieyasu Tokugawa's castle. In lieu of an admission ticket, collect a plastic token at the office on the other side of the gate. As you walk up the driveway you pass, on the left, the National Police Agency *dōjō* (martial arts hall). The hall was built in the Taishō period (1912–25) and is still used for *kendō* (Japanese fencing) practice. On the right is the Ōte Rest House, where for ¥100 you can buy a simple map of the garden.

There was another gate at the top of the driveway, where feudal lords summoned to the palace would descend from their palanquins and proceed on foot. The gate itself is gone, but two 19th-century guardhouses survive, one outside the massive stone supports on the right and a longer one inside on the left. The latter, known as the **Hundred-Man Guardhouse,** was defended by four shifts of 100 soldiers each. Past it, to the right, is the entrance to what was once the *ni-no-maru,* the "second circle" of the fortress. It's now a grove and garden, its pathways defined by rows of perfect rhododendrons, with a pond and a waterfall in the northwest corner. At the far end of the ni-no-maru is the **Suwa**

Tea Pavilion, an early 19th-century building relocated here from another part of the castle grounds.

The steep stone walls of the **hon-maru** (the "inner circle"), with the Moat of Swans below (the swans actually swim in the outer waterways), dominate the west side of the garden. Halfway along, a steep path leads to an entrance in the wall to the upper fortress. This is **Shio-mi-zaka**, which translates roughly as "Briny View Hill," so named because in the Edo period the ocean could be seen from here.

Nothing remains on the broad expanse of the hon-maru's lawn to recall the scores of buildings that once stood here, connected by a network of corridors. But you can see the stone foundations of the castle keep at the far end of the grounds. As you enter, turn left and explore the wooded paths that skirt the perimeter. Here you'll find shade, quiet, and benches where you can sit, rest your weary feet, and listen to birdsong. In the southwest corner, through the trees, you can see the back of the **Fujimi Yagura,** the only surviving watchtower of the hon-maru; farther along the path, on the west side, is the **Fujimi Tamon,** one of the two remaining armories.

The foundations of the keep make a platform with a fine view of **Kita-no-maru Kōen** and the city to the north. The view must have been even finer from the keep itself. Built and rebuilt three times, it soared more than 250 ft over Edo. The other castle buildings were all plastered white; the keep was black, unadorned but for a golden roof. In 1657 a fire destroyed most of the city. Strong winds carried the flames across the moat, where it consumed the keep in a heat so fierce that it melted the gold in the vaults underneath. The keep was never rebuilt.

To the left of the keep foundations there is an exit from the hon-maru that leads northwest to the Kita-Hane-bashi-mon. To the right, another road leads past the **Toka Music Hall**—an octagonal tower faced in mosaic tile, built in honor of the empress in 1966—down to the ni-no-maru and out of the gardens by way of the northern **Hirakawa-mon.** If you decide to leave the hon-maru the way you came in, through the Ōte-mon, stop for a moment at the rest house on the west side of the park before you surrender your token, and look at the photo collection. The pairs of before-and-after photographs of the castle, taken about 100 years apart, are fascinating. ✉ *Free.* ☉ *Weekends and Tues.–Thurs. 9–3. Subway: Tōzai, Marunouchi, or Chiyoda line; Ōte-machi Eki (Exit C10).*

❸ **Imperial Palace Outer Garden.** When the office buildings of the Meiji government were moved from this area in 1899, the whole expanse along the east side of the palace was turned into a public promenade and planted with stands of pine. The Outer Garden affords the best view of the castle walls and their Tokugawa-period fortifications: Ni-jū-bashi and the Sei-mon, the 17th-century Fujimi Yagura watchtower, and the Sakurada-mon. *Subway: Chiyoda Line, Ni-jū-bashi-mae Eki (Exit 2).*

⑭ **Kōgeikan** (Crafts Gallery of the National Museum of Modern Art). Built in 1910, the Kōgeikan was once the headquarters of the Imperial Guard. It is a rambling redbrick building, Gothic Revival in style, with exhibition halls on the second floor. The exhibits are all too few, but many of the craftspeople represented here—masters in the traditions of lacquerware, textiles, pottery, and metalwork—have been designated by the government as Living National Treasures. The most direct access to the gallery is from the Take-bashi subway station on the Tōzai Line. Walk west and uphill about 10 minutes, on the avenue between Kita-no-maru Kōen and the Imperial Palace grounds; the entrance will be on the right. ✉ *1–1 Kita-no-maru Kōen, Chiyoda-ku,* ☎ *03/3211–7781.* ✉ *¥420 (includes admission to National Museum of Modern*

Art); additional fee for special exhibits. ☉ *Tues.–Sun. 10–4:30. Subway: Hanzō-mon and Toei Shinjuku lines, Kudanshita Eki (Exit 2); Tōzai Line, Takebashi Eki (Exit 1b).*

⑥ Kokkai-Gijidō (National Diet Building). This chunky pyramid houses the Japanese parliament. Completed in 1936 after 17 years of work, it is a building best contemplated from a distance. On a gloomy day it seems as if it might well have sprung from the screen of a German Expressionist movie. ✉ *1–7–1 Nagata-chō, Chiyoda-ku. Subway: Marunouchi Line, Kokkai-Gijidō-mae Eki (Exit 2).*

⑧ Kokuritsu Gekijō (National Theater). Architect Hiroyuki Iwamoto's winning entry in the design competition for the Kokuritsu Gekijō building (1966) is a rendition in concrete of the ancient *azekura* (storehouse) style, invoking the 8th-century Shōsōin Imperial Repository in Nara. The large hall seats 1,746 and presents primarily Kabuki theater, ancient court music, and dance. The small hall seats 630 and is used mainly for Bunraku puppet theater and traditional music. ✉ *4–1 Hayabusa-chō, Chiyoda-ku,* ☏ *03/3265–7411.* ☉ *Varies depending on performance. Subway: Hanzō-mon Line, Hanzō-mon Eki (Exit 1).*

★ **④ Ni-jū-bashi** (Two-Tiered Bridge). This is surely the most photogenic spot on the grounds of the former Edo-jō, which you can approach no closer than the head of the short stone bridge called the **Sei-mon Sekkyō**. Cordoned off on the other side is the **Sei-mon**, through which ordinary mortals may pass only on January 2 and December 23. The guards in front of their small, octagonal, copper-roof sentry boxes change every hour on the hour—alas, with nothing like the pomp and ceremony of Buckingham Palace. Ni-jū-bashi arcs over the moat from the area inside Sei-mon. In the background the **Fushimi Yagura** watchtower makes for a picturesque backdrop. The bridge is a minute's walk north of the subway; follow the Imperial Palace moat to the courtyard in front of the gate. *Subway: Chiyoda Line, Ni-jū-bashi-mae Eki (Exit 2).*

⑬ Nippon Budōkan. With its eight-sided plan based on the Hall of Dreams of Hōryū-ji in Nara, the Budōkan was built as a martial arts arena for the Tōkyō Olympics of 1964. It still hosts tournaments and exhibitions of jūdō, karate, and kendō, as well as concerts. Tōkyō promoters are fortunate in their audiences, who don't seem to mind the exorbitant ticket prices and poor acoustics. From the Kudanshita subway stop walk west uphill toward Yasukuni Jinja; the entrance to Kitano Maru Kōen and the Budōkan is a few minutes' walk from the station, on the left. ✉ *2–3 Kitano Maru Kōen, Chiyoda-ku,* ☏ *03/3216–5100. Subway: Tōzai, Hanzō-mon, and Toei Shinjuku lines; Kudanshita Eki (Exit 2).*

Ōte-mon. This gate is the main entrance to the Imperial Palace East Garden. In former days it was the principal gate of Ieyasu Tokugawa's castle. The masu style was typical of virtually all the approaches to the shōgun's impregnable fortress: the first portal leads to a narrow enclosure, with a second and larger gate beyond, offering the defenders inside a devastating field of fire upon any would-be intruders. Most of the Ōte-mon was destroyed in 1945 but was rebuilt in 1967 on the original plans. The outer part of the gate, however, survived. *Subway: Tōzai, Marunouchi, and Chiyoda lines; Ōte-machi Eki (Exit C10).*

⑦ Saikō Saibansho (Supreme Court). Designed by Shinichi Okada, the Supreme Court building was the last in a series of open architectural competitions sponsored by the various government agencies charged with the reconstruction of Tōkyō after World War II. Its fortresslike planes and angles speak volumes for the role of the law in Japanese society—here is the very bastion of the established order. Okada's winning design was one of 217 submitted. Before the building was finished, in 1968, the open competition had generated so much controversy that the government did not hold another one for almost 20 years. Guided tours are available, but under restrictive conditions: you must be 16 years old or above to take part; tours musts be reserved two weeks in advance; and there is no interpretation in English. Tours are conducted weekdays (except July 20–August 31 and national holidays); they begin at 3 and take about an hour. ⊠ *4–2 Hayabusa-chō, Chiyoda-ku,* ☎ *03/ 3264–8111 for public relations office (Kōhōka) for permission to visit inside. Subway: Hanzō-mon Line, Hanzō-mon Eki (Exit 1).*

❺ Sakurada-mon (Gate of the Field of Cherry Trees). By hallowed use and custom, the small courtyard between the portals of this masu gate is where joggers warm up for their 5-km (3-mi) run around the palace. *Subway: Yūraku-chō Line, Sakurada-mon Eki (Exit 3).*

❶ Tōkyō Eki. The work of Kingo Tatsuno, one of Japan's first modern architects, Tōkyō Eki was completed in 1914. Tatsuno modeled his creation on the railway station of Amsterdam. The building lost its original top story in the air raids of 1945, but it was promptly repaired. More recent plans to tear it down entirely were scotched by a protest movement. Inside, it seems to be in a constant state of redesign and renovation, but the lovely old facade remains untouched. The best thing about the place is the **Tōkyō Station Hotel,** on the west side on the second and third floors. ⊠ *1–9–1 Marunouchi, Chiyoda-ku,* ☎ *03/ 3231–2511.*

⓯ Tōkyō Kokuritsu Kindai Bijutsukan (National Museum of Modern Art, Tōkyō). Founded in 1952 and moved to its present site in 1969, this was Japan's first national art museum. It mounts a number of major exhibitions of 20th-century Japanese and Western art throughout the year but tends to be rather stodgy about how it organizes and presents these exhibitions and is seldom on the cutting edge. The second through fourth floors house the permanent collection, which includes the painting, prints, and sculpture of Rousseau, Picasso, Tsuguji Fujita, Ryūzaburo Umehara, and Taikan Yokoyama. ⊠ *3 Kita-no-maru Kōen, Chiyoda-ku,* ☎ *03/3561–1400 or 03/3272–8600,* Ⓦ*www.momat.go.jp. Subway: Tōzai Line, Take-bashi Eki (Exit 1b); Hanzō-mon and Tōei Shinjuku lines, Kudanshita Eki (Exit 2).*

⓫ Yamatane Bijutsukan. The museum, which specializes in *nihon-ga*— traditional Japanese painting—from the Meiji period and later, has a private collection of masterpieces by such painters as Taikan Yokoyama, Gyoshū Hayami, Kokei Kobayashi, and Gyokudō Kawai. The exhibitions, which sometimes include works borrowed from other collections, change every two months. The decor and display at the Yamatane make it an oasis of quiet and elegance in the surrounding world of high finance, and the chance to buy the lavish catalog of the collection is well worth the visit. An interior garden was designed by architect Yoshio Taniguchi, who also did the Museum of Modern Art. ⊠ *2 Samban-chō, Chiyoda-ku,* ☎ *03/3239–5911,* 𝐅𝐀𝐗 *03/3239–5913.* 💲 *¥500.* 🕙 *Tues.–Sun. 10–4:30. Subway: Tōzai and Tōei Shinjuku lines, Kudanshita Eki (Exit 2).*

❿ Yasukuni Jinja (Shrine of Peace for the Nation). Founded in 1869, Yasukuni Jinja is dedicated to the approximately 2.5 million Japanese who have died since then in war or military service. Since 1945 Yasukuni has been the periodic focus of passionate political debate, given that the Japanese constitution expressly renounces both militarism and state sponsorship of religion. Even so, hundreds of thousands of Japanese come here every year, simply to pray for the repose of friends and relatives they have lost.

The shrine is not one structure but a complex of buildings that includes the **Main Hall** and the **Hall of Worship**—both built in the simple, un-adorned style of the ancient Shintō shrines at Ise—and the **Yūshūkan,** a museum of documents and war memorabilia. Also here are a **Nō the-ater** and, in the far western corner, a sumō-wrestling ring. Both Nō and sumō have their origins in religious ritual, as performances offered to please and divert the gods. Sumō matches are held at Yasukuni in April, during the first of its three annual festivals.

Pick up a pamphlet and simplified map of the shrine in English just in-side the grounds. Just ahead of you, in a circle on the main avenue, is a statue of Masujiro Omura, commander of the imperial forces that subdued the Tokugawa loyalist resistance to the new Meiji government. From here, as you look down the avenue to your right, you see the enor-mous steel outer *torii* of the main entrance to the shrine at Kudanshita; to the left is a bronze inner torii, erected in 1887. (These Shintō shrine arches are normally made of wood and painted red.) Beyond the inner torii is the gate to the shrine itself, with its 12 pillars and chrysanthe-mums—the imperial crest—embossed on the doors.

Though some of the displays in the Yūshūkan have English labels and notes, the English is not very helpful; fortunately, most objects speak clearly enough for themselves. Rooms on the second floor house an especially fine collection of medieval swords and armor. Perhaps the most bizarre exhibit is the *kaiten* (human torpedo) on the first floor. The kaiten was a black cylinder about 50 ft long and 3 ft in diameter, with 3,400 pounds of high explosives in the nose. The operator, squeezed into a seat with a periscope in the center of the tube, worked the directional vanes with his feet. The kaiten was carried into battle on the deck of a ship and launched, like a kamikaze plane, on its one-way journey.

If time permits, turn right as you leave the Yūshūkan and walk past the other implements of war—cannons, ancient and modern, and a tank, incongruously bright and gay in its green-and-yellow camouflage paint—arrayed in front of the pond at the rear of the shrine. There is, unfortunately, no general admittance to the teahouses on the far side, but the pond is among the most serene and beautiful in Tōkyō, espe-cially in spring, when the irises bloom. ⊠ *3–1–1 Kudankita, Chiyo-daku,* ☏ *03/3261–8326.* ☑ *¥300.* ☉ *Grounds daily, usually 9–9. Museum Mar.–Oct., daily 9–5; Nov.–Feb., daily 9–4:30. Subway: Hanzō-mon and Toei Shinjuku lines, Kudanshita Eki (Exit 2).*

NEED A BREAK?   The specialty at the moderately priced **Tony Roma's,** as it is in this chain's umpteen locations, is charcoal-broiled spareribs. It is on the west side of Uchibori-dōri north of the British Embassy, at the intersec-tion straight west of Inui-mon. ⊠ *1 Samban-chō, Chiyoda-ku,* ☏ *03/ 3222–3440.*

Akihabara and Jimbō-chō

This is it: the greatest sound-and-light show on earth. Akihabara is a merchandise mart for anything—and everything—that runs on elec-tricity, from microprocessors and washing machines to television sets and gadgets that beep when your bathwater is hot. Wherever you go in the world, if people know nothing else about Japan, they recognize the country as a cornucopia of electronics equipment and household appliances. About 10% of what Japan's electronics industry makes for the domestic market passes through Akihabara.

Just after World War II there was a black market here, around the railroad station, where the Yamanote Line and the crosstown Sōbu Line intersect. In time, most of the stalls were doing a legitimate business in radio parts, and in 1951 they were all relocated in one dense clump under the tracks. Retail and wholesale suppliers then spread out into the adjacent blocks and made the area famous for cut-rate prices.

Few visitors to Tōkyō neglect this district; the mistake is to come here merely for shopping. Akihabara may be consumer heaven, but it is also the first stop on a walking tour through the general area known as Kanda—where the true Edokko, the born-and-bred Tōkyōites of the old town, claim their roots—to the bookstalls of Jimbō-chō. In a sense this tour is a journey through time: it's a morning's walk from satellite broadcast antennas to the hallowed precincts of the printed word.

Numbers in the text correspond to numbers in the margin and on the Akihabara and Jimbō-chō map.

A Good Walk

Start at the west exit of JR Akihabara Eki. (There's also a stop, Nakaokachi-machi, nearby on the Hibiya subway line, but the JR provides much easier access.) Come out to the left after you pass through the wicket, head into the station square, turn right, and walk to the main thoroughfare. Ahead of you on the other side of the street you'll see the **LAOX** ⑰ building, one of the district's major discount stores.

Before you get to the corner, on the right is a little warren of stalls and tiny shops that cannot have changed an iota since the days of the black market—except for their merchandise. Wander through the narrow passageways and see an astonishing array of switches, transformers, resistors, semiconductors, printed circuit cards, plugs, wires, connectors, and tools. The labyrinth is especially popular with domestic and foreign techno mavens, the people who know—or want to know—what the latest in Japanese electronic technology looks like from the inside.

If you turn left at the corner and cross the small bridge over the Kanda-gawa, you'll soon come to the **Kōtsū Hakubutsukan** ⑱—a detour you might want to make if you have children in tow. If not, turn right at the corner and walk north on Chūō-dōri. Music blares at you from hundreds of storefronts as you walk along; this is the heart of the district. Most larger stores on the main drag have one floor—or even an entire annex—of products for the foreign market, staffed by clerks who speak everything from English to Mandarin to Portuguese. Prices are duty free (don't forget to bring your passport). By far the biggest selections are to be found at rival stores **Yamagiwa** and **Minami** ⑲. Yamagiwa is just past the second intersection, on the right, and Minami is at the far end of the block.

At Minami, cross the street, continue north to the Soto Kanda 5-chōme intersection (there's an entrance to the Suehiro-chō subway station on the corner), and turn left onto Kuramae-bashi-dōri. Walk about five minutes—you'll cross one more intersection with a traffic light—and in the middle of the next block you'll see a flight of steps on the left, between two brick buildings. Red, green, and blue pennants flutter from the handrails. This is the back entrance to **Kanda Myōjin** ⑳.

Leave the shrine by the main gate. The seated figures in the alcoves on either side are its guardian gods; carved in camphor wood, they are depicted in Heian costume, holding long bows. From the gate down to the copper-clad torii on Hongo-dōri is a walk of a few yards. On either side are shops that sell the specialties famous in this neighborhood: pickles, miso, and sweet sake laced with ground ginger. On the

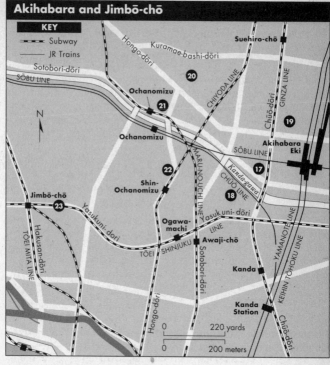

other side of the avenue are the wall and wooded grounds of the
Yūshima Seidō ㉑ Confucian shrine.

Cross Hongo-dōri and turn left, following the wall downhill. Turn right
at the first narrow side street, and right again at the bottom; the entrance to Yūshima Seidō is a few steps from the corner. As you walk
up the path, you'll see a statue of Confucius on your right; where the
path ends, a flight of stone steps leads up to the main hall of the
shrine—six times destroyed by fire, each time rebuilt. The last repairs
date to 1954. The hall could almost be in China: painted black, weathered and somber, it looks like nothing else you're likely to see in Japan.

Retrace your steps, turn right as you leave the shrine, and walk along
the continuation of the wall on the side street leading up to Hijiri-bashi
(Bridge of Sages), which spans the Kanda-gawa at Ochanomizu Eki
on the JR Sōbu Line. Cross the bridge—you're now back on Hongo-
dōri—and ahead of you, just beyond the station on the right, you'll
see the dome of the Russian Orthodox **Nikolai Cathedral** ㉒.

Continue south to the intersection of Hongo-dōri and Yasukuni-dōri.
Surugadai, the area to your right as you walk down the hill, is a kind of
fountainhead of Japanese higher education: two of the city's major private universities—Meiji and Nihon—occupy a good part of the hill. Not
far from these are a score of elite high schools, public and private. In the
1880s several other universities were founded in this area. They have
since moved away, but the student population here is still enormous.

Turn right on Yasukuni-dōri. Between you and your objective—the **bookstores of Jimbō-chō** ㉓—are three blocks of stores devoted almost exclusively to electric guitars, records, travel bags, skis, and skiwear. The
bookstores begin at the intersection called Surugadai-shita and continue along Yasukuni-dōri for about ½ km (¼ mi), most of them on the

south (left) side of the street. This area is to print what Akihabara is to electronics.

What about that computer or CD player you didn't buy at the beginning of your walk because you didn't want to carry it all this way? No problem. There's a subway station (Toei Mita Line) at the Jimbō-chō main intersection; go one stop north to Suidō-bashi, transfer to the JR Sōbu Line, and five minutes later you're back in Akihabara.

TIMING

Unless you do a lot of shopping, this walk should take you no more than a morning. Cultural landmarks are few, and you can explore them thoroughly in half an hour each. Getting from place to place will take up much of your time. Keep in mind that most stores in Akihabara do not open until 10 AM. Weekends draw hordes of shoppers, especially on Sunday, when the four central blocks of Chūō-dōri are closed to traffic and become a pedestrian mall.

Sights to See

㉓ Bookstores of Jimbō-chō. For the ultimate browse through art books, catalogs, scholarly monographs, secondhand paperbacks, and dictionaries in most known languages, the hon-ya (bookstores) of Jimbō-chō are the place. A number of the antiquarian booksellers here carry not only rare typeset editions but also wood-block-printed books of the Edo period and individual prints. At shops like **Isseido** (⊠ 1–7 Kanda Jimbō-chō, Chiyoda-ku, ☎ 03/3292–0071), open Monday–Saturday 10–6:30, and **Ohya Shōbō** (⊠ 1–1 Kanda Jimbō-chō, Chiyoda-ku, ☎ 03/3291–0062), open Monday–Saturday 10–6, it's still possible to find a genuine Hiroshige or Toyokuni print—if not in the best condition—at an affordable price. Wholesalers, distributors, and many of Japan's most prestigious publishing houses make their home in this area as well. The bookstores run for ½ km (¼ mi) on Yasukuni-dōri beginning at the Surugadai-shita intersection. *Subway: Toei Shinjuku and Toei Mita lines, Jimbō-chō Eki (Exit A7).*

⓴ Kanda Myōjin. This shrine is said to have been founded in 730 in a village called Shibasaki, where the Ōte-machi financial district stands today. In 1616 it was relocated, a victim of Ieyasu Tokugawa's ever-expanding system of fortifications. The present site was chosen, in accordance with Chinese geomancy, to afford the best view from Edo-jō and to protect the shrine from evil influences. The shrine itself was destroyed in the Great Kantō Earthquake of 1923, and the present buildings reproduce in concrete the style of 1616. Ieyasu preferred the jazzier decorative effects of Chinese Buddhism to the simple lines of traditional Shintō architecture. This is especially evident in the curved, copper-tile roof of the main shrine and in the two-story front gate.

Three principle deities are enshrined here: Ōkuninushi-no-Mikoto and Sukunohikona-no-Mikoto, both of whom appear in the early Japanese creation myths, and Taira-no-Masakado. The last was a 10th-century warrior whose contentious spirit earned him a place in the Shintō pantheon: he led a revolt against the Imperial Court in Kyōto, seized control of the eastern provinces, declared himself emperor—and in 940 was beheaded for his rebellious ways. The townspeople of Kanda, contentious souls in their own right, made Taira-no-Masakado a kind of patron saint, and even today—oblivious somehow to the fact that he lost—they appeal to him for victory when they face a tough encounter.

Some of the smaller buildings you see as you come up the steps and walk around the main hall contain the *mikoshi*—the portable shrines that are featured in one of Tōkyō's three great blowouts, the **Kanda Festival.** (The other two are the Sannō Festival of Hie Jinja in Nagata-chō and the Sanja Festival of Asakusa Jinja.) The essential shrine festival is a procession in which the gods, housed for the occasion in their mikoshi, pass through the streets and get a breath of fresh air. The Kanda Festival began in the early Edo period. Heading the procession then were 36 magnificent floats, most of which were destroyed in the fires that raged through the city after the earthquake of 1923. The floats that lead the procession today move in stately measure on wheeled carts, attended by the priests and officials of the shrine dressed in Heian-period (794–1185) costume. The mikoshi, some 70 of them, follow behind, bobbing and weaving, carried on the shoulders of the townspeople. Shrine festivals like Kanda's are a peculiarly competitive form of worship: piety is a matter of who can shout the loudest, drink the most beer, and have the best time. The festival takes place in August in odd-numbered years. Kanda Myōjin is on Kuramae-bashi-dōri, about a five-minute walk west from the Suehiro-chō stop (Exit 3) on the Ginza Line. ✉ *2–16–2 Soto Kanda, Chiyoda-ku,* ☎ *03/3254–0753.*

🐾 ⑱ **Kōtsū Hakubutsukan** (Transportation Museum). This is a fun place to take children. Displays explain the early development of the railway system and include a miniature layout of the rail services, as well as Japan's first airplane, which lifted off in 1903. To get here from JR Akihabara Eki, take the Denki-gai Exit, cross the bridge on Chūō-dōri over the Kanda-gawa, and turn right at the next corner. ✉ *1–25 Kanda Sudachō, Chiyoda-ku,* ☎ *03/3251–8481.* 🎫 *¥310.* ◎ *Tues.–Sun. 9:30–5.*

⑰ **LAOX.** Of all the discount stores in Akihabara, LAOX has the largest and most comprehensive selection, with four buildings in this area—one exclusively for musical instruments, another for duty-free appliances—and outlets in Yokohama and Narita. This is a good place to find cameras, watches, and pearls. ✉ *1–2–9 Soto Kanda, Chiyoda-ku,* ☎ *03/3255–9041.* ◎ *Mon.–Sat. 10–8, Sun. 10–7:30. JR Akihabara Eki (Nishi-guchi/West Exit).*

㉒ **Nikolai Cathedral.** Formally, this is the Holy Resurrection Cathedral. The more familiar name derives from its founder, St. Nikolai Kassatkin (1836–1912), a Russian missionary who came to Japan in 1861 and spent the rest of his life here propagating the Russian Orthodox faith. The building, planned by a Russian engineer and executed by a British architect, was completed in 1891. Heavily damaged in the earthquake of 1923, the cathedral was restored with a dome much more modest than the original. Even so, it endows this otherwise featureless part of the city with the charm of the unexpected. ✉ *4–1 Surugadai, Kanda, Chiyoda-ku,* ☎ *03/3295–6879.* 🎫 *Free.* ◎ *Tues.–Fri. 1–4. Subway: Chiyoda Line, Shin-Ochanomizu Eki (Exit B1).*

⑲ **Yamagiwa and Minami.** These rival giants have whole floors devoted to computer hardware, software, fax machines, and copiers. Yamagiwa has a particularly good selection of lighting fixtures, most of them—alas—for 220 volts. Both stores, however, have annexes with English-speaking staff for export models of the most popular appliances and devices. You should be able to bargain prices down a bit—especially if you are buying more than one big-ticket item. *Yamagiwa:* ✉ *4–1–1 Soto Kanda, Chiyoda-ku,* ☎ *03/3253–2111.* ◎ *Weekdays 10:30–7:30, weekends 10–7:30. Minami:* ✉ *4–3–3 Soto Kanda, Chiyoda-ku,* ☎ *03/3255–3730.* ◎ *Weekdays 10:30–7, weekends 10–7. JR Akihabara Eki (Nishi-guchi/West Exit).*

㉑ **Yūshima Seidō.** The origins of this shrine date to a hall, founded in 1632, for the study of the Chinese Confucian classics. The original building was in Ueno, and its headmaster was Hayashi Razan, the official Confucian scholar to the Tokugawa government. The shogunal dynasty found these Chinese teachings—with their emphasis on obedience and hierarchy—attractive enough to make Confucianism a kind of state ideology. Moved to its present site in 1691, the hall became an academy for the ruling elite. In a sense, nothing has changed: In 1872 the new Meiji government established the country's first teacher-training institute here, and that, in turn, evolved into Tōkyō University—the graduates of which still make up much of the ruling elite. ⊠ *1–4–25 Yūshima, Bunkyō-ku,* ☎ *03/3251–4606.* ▣ *Free.* ☉ *Apr.–Sept., Fri.–Wed. 10– 5; Oct.–Mar., Fri.–Wed. 10–4. Subway: Marunouchi Line, Ochano-mizu Eki (Exit B2).*

Ueno

JR Ueno Eki is Tōkyō's version of the Gare du Nord: the gateway to and from Japan's northeast provinces. Since 1883, when the station was completed, it has served as a terminus in the great migration to the city by villagers in pursuit of a better life.

Ueno was a place of prominence long before the coming of the railroad. When Ieyasu Tokugawa established his capital here in 1603, it was merely a wooded promontory, called Shinobu-ga-oka (Hill of Endurance), overlooking the bay. Ieyasu gave a large tract of land on the hill to one of his most important vassals, Takatora Toda, who designed and built Edo-jō. Ieyasu's heir, Hidetada, later commanded the founding of a temple on the hill. Shinobu-ga-oka was in the northeast corner of the capital. In Chinese geomancy, the northeast approach required a particularly strong defense against evil influences.

That defense was entrusted to Tenkai (1536–1643), a priest of the Tendai sect of Buddhism and an adviser of great influence to the first three Tokugawa shōguns. The temple he built on Shinobu-ga-oka was called Kanei-ji, and he became the first abbot. The patronage of the Tokugawas and their vassal barons made Kanei-ji a seat of power and glory. By the end of the 17th century it occupied most of the hill. To the magnificent Main Hall were added scores of other buildings—including a pagoda and a shrine to Ieyasu—and 36 subsidiary temples. The city of Edo itself expanded to the foot of the hill, where Kanei-ji's main gate once stood. And most of what is now Ueno was called *Mon-zen-machi*: "the town in front of the gate."

The power and glory of Kanei-ji came to an end in just one day: April 11, 1868. An army of clan forces from the western part of Japan, bearing a mandate from Emperor Meiji, arrived in Edo and demanded the surrender of the castle. The shogunate was by then a tottering regime; it capitulated, and with it went everything that had depended on the favor of the Tokugawas. The Meiji Restoration began with a bloodless coup.

A band of some 2,000 Tokugawa loyalists assembled on Ueno Hill, however, and defied the new government. On May 15 the imperial army attacked. The *Shōgitai* (loyalists), outnumbered and surrounded, soon discovered that right was on the side of modern artillery. A few survivors fled; the rest committed ritual suicide—and took Kanei-ji with them—torching the temple and most of its outbuildings.

The new Meiji government turned Ueno Hill into one of the nation's first public parks. The intention was not merely to provide a bit of greenery but to make the park an instrument of civic improvement and to show off the achievements of an emerging modern state. It would serve as the site of trade and industrial expositions; it would have a national museum, a library, a university of fine arts, and a zoo. The modernization of Ueno still continues, but the park is more than the sum of its museums. The Shōgitai failed to take everything with them:

some of the most important buildings in the temple complex survived or were restored and should not be missed.

Numbers in the text correspond to numbers in the margin and on the Ueno map.

A Good Walk

The best way to begin is to come to JR Ueno Eki on the JR Yamanote Line and leave the station by the *Kōen-guchi* (Park Exit), upstairs. Directly across from the exit is the Tōkyō Bunka Kaikan, one of the city's major venues for classical music.

Follow the path to the right of the Bunka Kaikan to the information booth, where you can pick up a useful detailed map of the park in English; northwest of the booth (turn left, away from Ueno Eki) is the **Kokuritsu Seiyō Bijutsukan** 24. The Rodins in the courtyard—*The Gate of Hell, The Thinker,* and the magnificent *Burghers of Calais*—are authentic castings from Rodin's original molds.

Turn right at the far corner of the Seiyō and walk along a stretch of wooded park; you come next to the museum of science, the **Kokuritsu Kagaku Hakubutsukan** 25; at the next corner is the main street that cuts through the park. Turn left on this street, and cross at the traffic signal some 50 yards west to the main entrance of the **Tōkyō Kokuritsu Hakubutsukan** 26, which has one one of the world's greatest collections of East Asian art and archaeology.

Turn right as you leave the museum complex, walk west, and turn right at the first corner; this road dead-ends in about five minutes in the far northwest corner of the park, opposite the gate to **Kanei-ji** 27. (The gate is usually locked; use the side entrance to the left.) The only remarkable remaining structure here is the ornately carved vermilion gate to what was the mausoleum of Tsunayoshi, the fifth shōgun. Tsunayoshi is famous in the annals of Tokugawa history for his disastrous fiscal mismanagement and his *Shōrui Awaremi no Rei* (Edicts on Compassion for Living Things), which, among other things, made it a capital offense for a human being to kill a dog. Stretching away to the right is the cemetery of Kanei-ji, where several Tokugawa shōguns had their mausoleums. These were destroyed in the air raids of 1945, but the gate that led to the tomb of the fourth shōgun, Ietsuna, remains.

Retrace your steps to the main gate of the Tōkyō Kokuritsu Hakubutsukan, and cross the street to the long esplanade, with its fountain and reflecting pool. Keep to the right as you walk south. The first path to the right brings you to the **Tōkyō-to Bijutsukan** 28 and its small but impressive permanent collection of modern Japanese painting.

At the south end of the esplanade is the central plaza of the park. (Look to your left for the police substation, a small steel-gray building of futuristic design.) To the right is the entrance to the **Ueno Zoo** 29. Opened in 1882, the zoo gradually expanded to its present 35 acres, and the original section here on the hill was connected to the one below, along the edge of **Shinobazu Pond** 30, by a bridge and a monorail. The process of the zoo's expansion somehow left within its confines the 120-ft, five-story Kanei-ji Pagoda, built in 1631 and rebuilt after a fire in 1639.

A few steps farther south, on the continuation of the esplanade, is the path that leads to **Tōshō-gū** 31—the shrine to the first Tokugawa shōgun, Ieyasu. The entrance to the shrine is marked by a stone torii built in 1633.

From Tōshō-gū, return to the avenue, turn right, and continue walking south. Shortly you'll see a kind of tunnel of red-lacquered torii, with

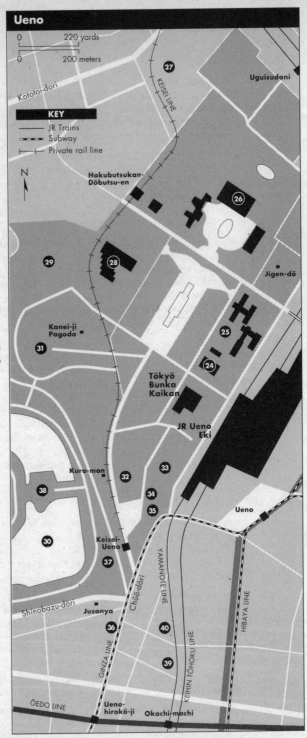

Ueno

a long flight of stone steps leading down to the shrine to Inari, a Shintō deity of harvests and family prosperity. Shrines of this kind are found all over the downtown part of Tōkyō, tucked away in alleys and odd corners, always with their guardian statues of foxes—the mischievous creatures with which the god is associated. Just below the Inari shrine is a shrine to Sugawara Michizane (854–903), a Heian-period nobleman and poet worshiped as the Shintō deity Tenjin. Because he is associated with scholarship and literary achievement, Japanese students visit his various shrines by the hundreds of thousands in February and March to pray for success on their college entrance exams.

Return to the avenue and continue south. On the left side is a flight of stone steps to **Kiyomizu Kannon-dō** ㉜, one of the important temple structures that survived the Meiji-Tokugawa battle of 1868.

Leave Kiyomizu by the front gate, on the south side. As you look to your left, you will see a two-story brick administration building, on the other side of which is the **Ueno-no-Mori Bijutsukan** ㉝. After a stop in the museum, continue south, and you soon come to where the park narrows to a point. Two flights of steps lead down to the main entrance on Chūō-dōri. Before you reach the steps, you'll see the **Shōgitai Memorial** ㉞ on the left, and a few steps away, with its back to the gravestone, the **statue of Takamori Saigō** ㉟.

Leave the park and walk south, keeping to the west side of Chūō-dōri until you get to the corner where Shinobazu-dōri comes in on the right. About a block beyond this corner, you'll see a building hung with banners; this is **Suzumoto** ㊱, a theater specializing in a traditional narrative comedy called *rakugo*.

Turn right at the Shinobazu-dōri intersection and walk west. A few doors from the corner is Jusan-ya, a nearly three-century-old family-run shop that sells handmade boxwood combs. Directly across the avenue is an entrance to the grounds of Shinobazu Pond; just inside, on the right, is the small black-and-white building that houses the **Shitamachi Hakubutsukan** ㊲. Japanese society in the days of the Tokugawa shōguns was rigidly stratified. In Tōkyō—then called Edo—the common people lived "below the castle," most of them in long, single-story tenements called *nagaya,* one jammed up against the next along the narrow alleys and unplanned streets of Ueno and the areas nearby. They developed a unique culture and way of life, which this museum celebrates.

From in front of the museum, a path follows the eastern shore of Shinobazu Pond. On the island in the middle of the pond is **Benzaiten** ㊳, a shrine to the patron goddess of the arts. You can walk up the east side of the embankment to the causeway and cross to the shrine. Then cross to the other side of the pond, turn left in front of the boathouse, and follow the embankment back to Shinobazu-dōri. Off to your right as you walk, a few blocks away and out of sight, begin the precincts of Tōkyō University, the nation's most prestigious seat of higher learning, alma mater to generations of bureaucrats. Turn left as you leave the park and walk back in the direction of the Shitamachi Hakubutsukan.

When you reach the intersection, cross Chūō-dōri and turn right; walk past the ABAB clothing store and turn left at the second corner. At the end of this street is **Tokudai-ji** ㊴, a temple over a supermarket, and the bustling heart of **Ame-ya Yoko-chō Market** ㊵. There are more than 500 little shops and stalls in this market, which stretches from the beginning of Shōwa-dōri at the north end to Ōkachi-machi at the south end. Ōkachi-machi means "Ōkachi Town"; the *ōkachi*—the "honorable infantry," the samurai of lowest rank in the shōgun's service—lived in the area.

From here follow the JR tracks as you wander north. In a few minutes you'll find yourself back in front of Ueno Eki.

TIMING

Exploring Ueno can be one excursion or two: an afternoon of cultural browsing or a full day of discoveries in one of the great centers of the city. Avoid Monday, when most of the museums are closed. Ueno out of doors is no fun at all in February or the rainy season of late June to mid-July; mid-August can be brutally hot and muggy. In April, the cherry blossoms of Ueno Kōen are glorious.

Sights to See

40 **Ame-ya Yoko-chō Market.** The history of Ame-ya Yoko-chō (often shortened to Ameyoko) begins in the desperate days immediately after World War II. Ueno Eki had survived the bombings—virtually everything around it was rubble—and anyone who could make it here from the countryside with rice and other small supplies of food could sell them at exorbitant black-market prices. Sugar was a commodity that couldn't be found at any price in postwar Tōkyō. Before long, there were hundreds of stalls in the black market selling various kinds of *ame* (confections), most of them made from sweet potatoes. These stalls gave the market its name: Ame-ya Yoko-chō means "Confectioners' Alley."

Shortly before the Korean War, the market was legalized, and soon the stalls were carrying a full array of watches, chocolate, ballpoint pens, blue jeans, and T-shirts that had somehow been "liberated" from American PXs. In years to come the merchants of Ameyoko diversified still further—to fine Swiss timepieces and French designer luggage of dubious authenticity, cosmetics, jewelry, fresh fruit, and fish. The market became especially famous for the traditional prepared foods of the New Year, and during the last few days of December, as many as half a million people crowd into the narrow alleys under the railroad tracks to stock up for the holiday. ✉ *Ueno 4-chōme, Taitō-ku.* ☉ *Most shops and stalls daily 10–7. JR Ueno Eki (Hirokō-ji Exit).*

38 **Benzaiten.** Perched in the middle of Shinobazu Pond, this shrine is for the goddess Benten. She is one of the Seven Gods of Good Luck, a pantheon that emerged some time in the medieval period from a jumble of Indian, Chinese, and Japanese mythology. As matron goddess of the arts, she is depicted holding a lutelike musical instrument called a *biwa*. The shrine, with its distinctive octagonal roof, was destroyed in the bombings of 1945. The present version is a faithful copy. You can rent rowboats and pedal boats at a nearby boathouse. ☎ *03/3828–9502 for boathouse.* ☉ *Boathouse daily 9:30–5.* ✍ *Rowboats ¥600 for 1 hr, pedal boats ¥600 for 30 mins. JR Ueno Eki; Keisei private rail line, Keisei-Ueno Eki (Ikenohata Exit).*

27 **Kanei-ji.** In 1638 the second Tokugawa shōgun, Hidetada, commissioned the priest Tenkai to build a temple on Shinobu-ga-oka Hill in Ueno to defend his city from evil spirits. Tenkai turned for his model to the great temple complex of Enryaku-ji in Kyōto, established centuries earlier on Mt. Hiei to protect the imperial capital. The main hall of Tenkai's temple, called Kanei-ji, was moved to Ueno from the town of Kawagoe, about 40 km (25 mi) away, where he had once been a priest; it was moved again, to its present site, in 1879, and looks a bit weary of its travels. ✉ *1–14–11 Ueno Sakuragi, Taitō-ku,* ☎ *03/3821–1259.* ✍ *Free, contributions welcome.* ☉ *Daily 9–5. JR Ueno Eki (Kōen-guchi/Park Exit).*

32 **Kiyomizu Kannon-dō** (Kannon Hall). This National Treasure was a part of Abbot Tenkai's grand attempt to echo in Ueno the grandeur of Kyōto, but the echo is a little weak. The model for it was Kyōto's magnificent

Kiyomizu-dera, but where the original rests on enormous wood pillars over a gorge, the Ueno version merely perches on the lip of a little hill. And the hall would have a grand view of Shinobazu Pond—which itself was landscaped to recall Biwa-ko (Lake Biwa), near Kyōto—if the trees in front of the terrace were not too high and too full most of the year to afford any view at all. The principal Buddhist image of worship here is the Senjū Kannon (Thousand-Armed Goddess of Mercy). Another figure, however, receives greater homage. This is the Koso-date Kannon, who is believed to answer the prayers of women having difficulty conceiving children. If their prayers are answered, they return to Kiyomizu and leave a doll, as both an offering of thanks and a prayer for the child's health. In a ceremony held every September 25, the dolls that have accumulated during the year are burned in a bonfire. ✉ *1–29 Ueno Kōen, Taitō-ku,* ☎ *03/3821–4749.* 🎫 *Free.* ☉ *Daily 7–5. JR Ueno Eki (Kōen-guchi/Park Exit).*

🐾 **㉕ Kokuritsu Kagaku Hakubutsukan** (National Science Museum). This conventional natural history museum displays everything from dinosaurs to moon rocks, but it provides relatively little in the way of hands-on learning experiences. Kids seem to like it anyway—but otherwise this is not a place to linger if your time is short. ✉ *7–20 Ueno Kōen, Taitō-ku,* ☎ *03/3822–0111.* 🎫 *¥420; additional fees for special exhibits.* ☉ *Tues.–Sun. 9–4:30. JR Ueno Eki (Kōen-guchi/Park Exit).*

㉔ Kokuritsu Seiyō Bijutsukan (National Museum of Western Art). Along with castings from the original molds of Rodin's *Gate of Hell, The Burghers of Calais,* and *The Thinker,* the wealthy businessman Matsukata Kojiro acquired some 850 paintings, sketches, and prints by such masters as Renoir, Monet, and Cézanne. He kept the collection in Europe. The French government sent it to Japan after World War II—Matsukata left it to the country in his will—and it opened to the public in 1959 in a building designed by Swiss-born architect Le Corbusier. Since then, the museum has diversified a bit and ushered in the new millennium with a luxurious special exhibition hall; more recent acquisitions include works by Reubens, Tintoretto, El Greco, Max Ernst, and Jackson Pollock. The Seiyō is one of the best-organized, most pleasant museums to visit in Tōkyō. ✉ *7-7 Ueno Kōen, Taitō-ku,* ☎ *03/3828–5131.* 🎫 *¥420; additional fee for special exhibits.* ☉ *Tues.–Thurs. and weekends 9:30–4:30, Fri. 9:30–7:30. JR Ueno Eki (Kōen-guchi/Park Exit).*

㉚ Shinobazu Pond. Shinobazu was once an inlet of Tōkyō Bay. When the area was reclaimed, it became a freshwater pond. The abbot Tenkai, founder of Kanei-ji on the hill above the pond, had an island made in the middle of it, on which he built ☞ **Benzaiten** for the goddess of the arts. Later improvements included a causeway to the island, embankments, and even a racecourse (1884–93). Today the pond is in three sections. The first, with its famous lotus plants, is a sanctuary for about 15 species of birds, including pintail ducks, cormorants, great egrets, and grebes. Some 5,000 wild ducks migrate here from as far away as Siberia, sticking around from September to April. The second section, to the north, belongs to Ueno Zoo; the third, to the west, is a small lake for boating.

During the first week of June, the path is lined on both sides with the stalls of the annual All-Japan Azalea Fair, a spectacular display of flowering bonsai shrubs and trees. Nurserymen in *happi* (workmen's) coats sell a variety of plants, seedlings, bonsai vessels, and ornamental stones. ✉ *Shinobazu-dōri, Ueno, Taitō-ku.* 🎫 *Free.* ☉ *Daily sunrise–sunset. Keisei private rail line, Keisei-Ueno Eki (Higashi-guchi/East Exit); JR Ueno Eki (Kōen-guchi/Park Exit).*

★ **③⑦ Shitamachi Hakubutsukan.** Shitamachi (literally, the "Lower Town") lay originally between Ieyasu's fortifications, on the west, and the Sumida-gawa, on the east. As it expanded, it came to include what today constitutes the Chūō, Taitō, Sumida, and Kōtō wards. During the Edo period some 80% of the city was allotted to the warrior class and to temples and shrines. In Shitamachi—the remaining 20% of the space— lived the common folk, who made up more than half the population. The people here were hardworking, short-tempered, free-spending, quick to help a neighbor in trouble—and remarkably stubborn about their way of life. The Shitamachi Museum preserves and exhibits what remained of that way of life as late as 1940.

The two main displays on the first floor are a merchant house and a tenement, intact with all their furnishings. This is a hands-on museum: you can take your shoes off and step up into the rooms. On the second floor are displays of toys, tools, and utensils donated, in most cases, by people who had grown up with them and used them all their lives. There are also photographs of Shitamachi and video documentaries of craftspeople at work. Occasionally various traditional skills are demonstrated, and you're welcome to take part. This don't-miss museum makes great use of its space, and there's even a passable brochure in English. ✉ *2–1 Ueno Kōen, Taitō-ku,* ☎ *03/3823–7451.* ⌲ *¥300.* ☉ *Tues.–Sun. 9:30–4:30. Keisei private rail line, Keisei-Ueno Eki (Higashi-guchi/East Exit); JR Ueno Eki (Kōen-guchi/Park Exit).*

③④ Shōgitai Memorial. Time seems to heal wounds very quickly in Japan. Only six years after they had destroyed most of Ueno Hill, the Meiji government permitted the Shōgitai to be honored with a gravestone, erected on the spot where their bodies had been cremated. *JR Ueno Eki (Kōen-guchi/Park Exit); Keisei private rail line, Keisei-Ueno Eki (Higashi-guchi/East Exit).*

③⑤ Statue of Takamori Saigō. As chief of staff of the Meiji imperial army, Takamori Saigō (1827–77) played a key role in forcing the surrender of Edo and the overthrow of the shogunate. Ironically, Saigō himself fell out with the other leaders of the new Meiji government and was killed in an unsuccessful rebellion of his own. The sculptor Takamura Kōun's bronze, made in 1893, sensibly avoids presenting him in uniform. *JR Ueno Eki (Kōen-guchi/Park Exit); Keisei private rail line, Keisei-Ueno Eki (Higashi-guchi/East Exit).*

③⑥ Suzumoto. Originally built around 1857 for Japanese comic monologue performances called *rakugo* and since rebuilt, Suzumoto is the oldest theater operation of its kind in Tōkyō. A rakugo comedian sits on a purple cushion, dressed in a kimono, and tells stories that have been handed down for centuries. Using only a few simple props—a fan, a pipe, a handkerchief—the storyteller becomes a whole cast of characters, with all their different voices and facial expressions. The audience may have heard his stories 20 times already and still laughs in all the right places. There is no English interpretation, and even for the Japanese themselves, the monologues are difficult to follow, filled with puns and expressions in dialect—but don't let that deter you. For a slice of traditional pop culture, rakugo at Suzumoto is worth seeing, even if you don't understand a word. The theater is on Chūō-dōri, a few blocks north of the Ginza Line's Ueno Hirokō-ji stop (Exit 3). ✉ *2-7-12 Ueno, Taitō-ku,* ☎ *03/3834–5906.* ⌲ *¥2,500.* ☉ *Continual performances daily 12:20–4:30 and 5:20–9.*

③⑨ Tokudai-ji. This is a curiosity in a neighborhood of curiosities: a temple on the second floor of a supermarket. Two deities are worshiped here. One is the bodhisattva Jizō, and the act of washing this statue is

HOW TO
USE THIS GUIDE

Great trips begin with great planning, and this guide
makes planning easy. It's packed with everything you
need—insider advice on hotels and restaurants, cool
tools, practical tips, essential maps, and much more.

COOL TOOLS

Fodor's Choice Top picks are marked throughout with a star.

Great Itineraries These tours, planned by Fodor's experts,
give you the skinny on what you can see and do in the time
you have.

Smart Travel Tips A to Z This special section is packed with
important contacts and advice on everything from how to get
around to what to pack.

Good Walks You won't miss a thing if you follow the numbered bullets on our maps.

Need a Break? Looking for a quick bite to eat or a spot to
rest? These sure bets are along the way.

Off the Beaten Path Some lesser-known sights are worth a
detour. We've marked those you should make time for.

POST-IT® FLAGS

Dog-ear no more!

"Post-it" is a registered trademark of 3M.

Favorite restaurants • Essential maps •
Frequently used numbers • Walking tours
• Can't-miss sights • Smart Travel
Tips • Web sites • Top shops • Hot
nightclubs • Addresses • Smart contacts
• Events • Off-the-beaten-path spots •
Favorite restaurants • Essential maps •
Frequently used numbers • Walking
tours • Can't-miss sights • Smart
Travel Tips • Web sites • Top shops • Hot
nightclubs • Addresses • Smart contacts •
Events • Off-the-beaten-path spots • Favorite
restaurants • Essential maps • Frequently
used numbers • Walking tours •

ICONS AND SYMBOLS

Watch for these symbols throughout:

★	Our special recommendations
✕	Restaurant
🏠	Lodging establishment
✕🏠	Lodging establishment whose restaurant warrants a special trip
☙	Good for kids
☞	Sends you to another section of the guide for more information
✉	Address
☏	Telephone number
FAX	Fax number
WEB	Web site
💳	Admission price
☺	Opening hours
$-$$$$	Lodging and dining price categories, keyed to strategically sited price charts. Check the index for locations.
①❶	Numbers in white and black circles on the maps, in the margins, and within tours correspond to one another.

ON THE WEB

Continue your planning with these useful tools found at **www.fodors.com**, the Web's best source for travel information.

"Rich with resources." —*New York Times*

"Navigation is a cinch." —*Forbes* "Best of the Web" list

"Put together by people bursting with know-how."
                                        —*Sunday Times* (London)

Create a Miniguide Pinpoint hotels, restaurants, and attractions that have what you want at the price you want to pay.

Rants and Raves Find out what readers say about Fodor's picks—or write your own reviews of hotels and restaurants you've just visited.

Travel Talk Post your questions and get answers from fellow travelers, or share your own experiences.

On-Line Booking Find the best prices on airline tickets, rental cars, cruises, or vacations, and book them on the spot.

About our Books Learn about other Fodor's guides to your destination and many others.

Expert Advice and Trip Ideas From what to tip to how to take great photos, from the national parks to Nepal, Fodors.com has suggestions that'll make your trip a breeze. Log on and get informed and inspired.

Smart Resources Check the weather in your destination or convert your currency. Learn the local language or link to the latest event listings. Or consult hundreds of detailed maps—all in one place.

believed to help safeguard your health. The other, principal image is of the Indian goddess Marishi, a daughter of Brahma, usually depicted with three faces and four arms. She is believed to help worshipers overcome various sorts of difficulties and to help them prosper in business. ✉ *4–6–2 Ueno, Taitō-ku. JR Yamanote and Keihin-tōhoku lines, Ōkachi-machi Eki (Higashi-guchi/East Exit) or Ueno Eki (Hirokō-ji Exit).*

★ **㉖** **Tōkyō Kokuritsu Hakubutsukan** (Tōkyō National Museum). This complex of four buildings grouped around a courtyard is one of the world's great repositories of East Asian art and archaeology. The Western-style building on the left, with its bronze cupolas, is the **Hyōkeikan.** Built in 1909, it was devoted to archaeological exhibits; it was closed in 1999 and the greater part of the collection transferred to the new, larger **Heiseikan,** behind it. Look especially for the flamelike sculpted rims and elaborate markings of Middle Jōmon–period pottery (circa 3500 BC– 2000 BC), so different from anything produced in Japan before or since. Also look for the terra-cotta figures called *haniwa,* unearthed at burial sites dating from the 4th to the 7th century. The figures are deceptively simple in shape and mysterious and comical at the same time in effect.

In the far left corner of the museum complex is the **Hōryū-ji Hōmotsukan** (Gallery of Hōryū–ji Treasures). In 1878 the 7th-century Hōryū-ji in Nara presented 319 works of art in its possession—sculpture, scrolls, masks, and other objects—to the Imperial Household. These were transferred to the National Museum in 2000 and now reside in this gallery designed by Yoshio Taniguchi. There is a useful guide to the collection in English, and the exhibits are well explained. Don't miss the hall of carved wooden *gigaku* (Buddhist processional) masks.

The central building in the complex, the **Honkan,** was built in 1937 and houses Japanese art exclusively: paintings, calligraphy, sculpture, textiles, ceramics, swords, and armor. The more attractive **Tōyōkan,** on the right, completed in 1968, is devoted to the art of other Asian cultures. Altogether, the museum has some 87,000 objects in its permanent collection, with several thousand more on loan from shrines, temples, and private owners. Among these are 84 objects designated by the government as National Treasures. The Honkan rotates the works on display several times during the year; it also hosts two special exhibitions a year, April–May or June and October–November, which feature important collections from both Japanese and foreign museums. These, unfortunately, can be an ordeal: the lighting in the Honkan is not particularly good, the explanations in English are sketchy at best, and the hordes of visitors make it impossible to linger over a work you especially want to study. ✉ *13–9 Ueno Kōen, Taitō-ku,* ☎ *03/3822– 1111,* ⓦ *www.tnm.go.jp.* 🎫 *¥420.* ☉ *Tues.–Sun. 9:30–4:30. JR Ueno Eki (Kōen-guchi/Park Exit).*

㉘ **Tōkyō-to Bijutsukan** (Tōkyō Metropolitan Art Museum). The museum displays its own collection of modern Japanese art on the lower level and rents out the remaining two floors to various art institutes and organizations. At any given time, there will be at least five exhibits in the building: work by promising young painters, for example, or new forms and materials in sculpture or modern calligraphy. Completed in 1975, the museum was designed by Maekawa Kunio, who also did the nearby Metropolitan Festival Hall. ✉ *8–36 Ueno Kōen, Taitō-ku,* ☎ *03/3823– 6921,* ⓦ *www.tef.or.jp/tmm/eng/index.html.* 🎫 *Permanent collection free, fees vary for other exhibits (usually ¥300–¥800).* ☉ *Daily (except 3rd Mon. of month) 9–4:30. JR Ueno Eki (Kōen-guchi/Park Exit).*

★ **㉛** **Tōshō-gū.** Ieyasu, the first Tokugawa shōgun, died in 1616 and the following year was given the posthumous name Tōshō-Daigongen (The

Great Incarnation Who Illuminates the East). The Imperial Court declared him a divinity of the first rank, thenceforth to be worshiped at Nikkō, in the mountains north of his city, at a shrine he had commissioned before his death. That shrine is the first and foremost Tōshō-gū. The one here, built in the ornate style called *gongen-zukuri,* dates from 1627. Miraculously, it survived the disasters that destroyed most of the other original buildings on the hill—the fires, the 1868 revolt, the 1923 earthquake, the 1945 bombings—making it one of the few early Edo-period buildings in Tōkyō. The shrine and most of its art are designated National Treasures.

Two hundred *ishidoro* (stone lanterns) line the path from the stone entry arch to the shrine itself. One of them, just outside the arch to the left, is more than 18 ft high—one of the three largest in Japan. This particular lantern is called *obaketoro* (ghost lantern) because of a story connected with it: it seems that one night a samurai on guard duty slashed at the ghost—*obake*—that was believed to haunt the lantern. His sword was so good it left a nick in the stone, which can still be seen. Beyond these lanterns is a double row of 50 copper lanterns, presented by the feudal lords of the 17th century as expressions of their piety and loyalty to the regime.

The first room inside is the **Hall of Worship**; the four paintings in gold on wooden panels are by Tan'yū, one of the famous Kano family of artists who enjoyed the patronage of emperors and shōguns from the late 15th century to the end of the Edo period. Tan'yū was appointed *goyō eshi* (official court painter) in 1617. His commissions included the Tokugawa castles at Edo and Nagoya as well as the Nikkō Tōshō-gū. The framed tablet between the walls, with the name of the shrine in gold, is in the calligraphy of Emperor Go-Mizuno-o (1596–1680). Other works of calligraphy are by the abbots of Kanei-ji. Behind the Hall of Worship, connected by a passage called the *haiden,* is the sanctuary, where the spirit of Ieyasu is said to be enshrined.

The real glories of Tōshō-gū are its so-called **Chinese Gate,** which you reach at the end of your tour of the building, and the fence on either side. Like its counterpart at Nikkō, the fence is a kind of natural history lesson, with carvings of birds, animals, fish, and shells of every description; unlike the one at Nikkō, this fence was left unpainted. The two long panels of the gate, with their dragons carved in relief, are attributed to Hidari Jingoro—a brilliant sculptor of the early Edo period whose real name is unknown (*hidari* means "left"; Jingoro was reportedly left-handed). The lifelike appearance of his dragons has inspired a legend. Every morning they were found mysteriously dripping with water. Finally it was discovered that they were sneaking out at night to drink from the nearby Shinobazu Pond, and wire cages were put up around them to curtail this disquieting habit. ⊠ *9–88 Ueno Kōen, Taitō-ku,* ☎ *03/ 3822–3455.* ▨ *¥200.* ⊙ *Daily 9–5. JR Ueno Eki (Kōen-guchi/Park Exit).*

㉝ **Ueno-no-Mori Bijutsukan.** Although the museum has no permanent collection of its own, it makes its galleries available to various groups, primarily for exhibitions of modern painting and calligraphy. ⊠ *1–2 Ueno Kōen, Taitō-ku,* ☎ *03/3833–4191.* ▨ *Prices vary depending on exhibition, but usually ¥400–¥500.* ⊙ *Sun.–Wed. 10–5:30, Thurs.–Sat. 10–7:30. JR Ueno Eki (Kōen-guchi/Park Exit).*

🖐 **㉙** **Ueno Zoo.** The zoo houses some 900 different species, most of which look less than enthusiastic about being here. First built in 1882 and several times expanded without really modernizing, Ueno is not among the most attractive zoos in the world. But it does have a giant panda (quartered near the main entrance), and you might decide the zoo is worth a visit on that score alone. On a pleasant Sunday afternoon, however, upwards of 20,000 Japanese are likely to share your opinion; don't expect to have a leisurely view. ⊠ *9–83 Ueno Kōen, Taitō-ku,* ☎ *03/ 3828–5171.* 🔄 *¥600; free on Mar. 20, Apr. 29, and Oct. 1.* ⊙ *Tues.– Sun. 9:30–4. JR Ueno Eki (Kōen-guchi/Park Exit); Keisei private rail line, Ueno Eki (Dōbutsu-en Exit).*

Asakusa

In the year 628, so the legend goes, two brothers named Hamanari and Takenari Hikonuma were fishing on the lower reaches of the Sumida-gawa when they dragged up a small, gilded statue of Kannon—an aspect of the Buddha worshiped as the goddess of mercy. They took the statue to their master, Naji-no-Nakamoto, who enshrined it in his house. Later, a temple was built for it in nearby Asakusa. Called Sensō-ji, the temple was rebuilt and enlarged several times over the next 10 centuries—but Asakusa itself remained just a village on a river crossing a few hours' walk from Edo.

Then Ieyasu Tokugawa made Edo his capital and Asakusa blossomed. Suddenly, it was the party that never ended, the place where the free-spending townspeople of the new capital came to empty their pockets. For the next 300 years it was the wellspring of almost everything we associate with Japanese popular culture.

The first step in that transformation came in 1657, when Yoshiwara—the licensed brothel quarter not far from Nihombashi—was moved to the countryside farther north: Asakusa found itself square in the road, more or less halfway between the city and its only nightlife. The village became a suburb and a pleasure quarter in its own right. In the narrow streets and alleys around Sensō-ji, there were stalls selling toys, souvenirs, and sweets; acrobats, jugglers, and strolling musicians; sake shops and teahouses—where the waitresses often provided more than tea. (The Japanese have never worried much about the impropriety of such things; the approach to a temple is still a venue for very secular enterprises of all sorts.) Then, in 1841, the Kabuki theaters—which the government looked upon as a source of dissipation second only to Yoshiwara—moved to Asakusa.

Highborn and lowborn, the people of Edo flocked to Kabuki. They loved its extravagant spectacle, its bravado, and its brilliant language. They cheered its heroes and hissed its villains. They bought wood-block prints, called *ukiyo-e,* of their favorite actors. (*Ukiyo* means "the floating world" of everyday life; *e* means "picture." The genre flourished in the 18th and 19th centuries.) Asakusa was home to the Kabuki theaters for only a short time, but that was enough to establish it as *the* entertainment quarter of the city—a reputation it held unchallenged until World War II.

When Japan ended its long, self-imposed isolation in 1868, where else would the novelties and amusements of the outside world first take root but in Asakusa? The country's first photography studios appeared here in 1875. Japan's first skyscraper, a 12-story mart called the Jū-ni-kai, was built in Asakusa in 1890 and filled with shops selling imported goods. The area around Sensō-ji had by this time been designated a public park and was divided into seven sections; the sixth section, called Rok-ku, was Tōkyō's equivalent of 42nd Street and Times Square. The nation's first movie theater opened here in 1903—to be joined by dozens more, and these in turn were followed by music halls, cabarets, and revues. The first drinking establishment in Japan to call itself a "bar" was started in Asakusa in 1880; it still exists.

Most of this area was destroyed in 1945. As an entertainment district, it never really recovered, but Sensō-ji was rebuilt almost immediately. The people here would never dream of living without it—just as they would never dream of living anywhere else. This is the heart and soul of Shitamachi, where you can still hear the rich, breezy downtown Tōkyō accent of the 17th and 18th centuries. Where, if you sneeze in the middle of the night, your neighbor will demand to know the next morning why you aren't taking better care of yourself. Where a carpenter will refuse a well-paid job if he doesn't think the client has the mother wit to appreciate good work when he sees it. Where you can still go out for a good meal and not have to pay through the nose for a lot of uptown pretensions. Even today the temple precinct embraces an area of narrow streets, arcades, restaurants, shops, stalls, playgrounds, and gardens. It is home to a population of artisans and small entrepreneurs, neighborhood children and their grandmothers, and hipsters and hucksters and mendicant priests. In short, if you have any time at all to spend in Tōkyō, you really have to devote at least a day of it to Asakusa.

Numbers in the text correspond to numbers in the margin and on the Asakusa map.

A Good Walk

For more information on depāto and individual shops mentioned in this walk, *see* Shopping, *below.*

Start at Asakusa Eki, at the end of the Ginza Line. This was in fact Tōkyō's first subway, opened from Asakusa to Ueno in 1927; it became known as the Ginza Line when it was later extended through Ginza to Shimbashi and Shibuya. When you exit the station, take a minute to check out the Asahi Beer headquarters, complete with a golden flame atop the building, across the Sumda-gawa; Philippe Starck designed the unique structure. Follow the signs, clearly marked in English, to Exit 1. When you come up to the street level, turn right and walk west along Kaminari-mon-dōri. In a few steps you will come to a gate, on your right, with two huge red lanterns hanging from it: this is **Kaminari-mon** ㊶, the main entrance to the grounds of Sensō-ji.

Another way to get to Kaminari-mon is via the "river bus" ferry from Hinode Pier (☞ Boat & Ferry Travel, *below*), which stops in Asakusa at the southwest corner of the park, called Sumida Kōen. Walk out to the three-way intersection, cross two sides of the triangle, and turn right. Kaminari-mon is in the middle of the second block.

Take note of the Asakusa Bunka Kankō Center (Asakusa Tourist Information Center; 03/3842–5566), across the street from Kaminari-mon. A volunteer staff with some English is on duty here daily 10–5 and will happily load you down with maps and brochures.

From Kaminari-mon, Nakamise-dōri—a long, narrow avenue lined on both sides with small shops—leads to the courtyard of Sensō-ji. One shop worth stopping at is Ichiban-ya, about 100 yards down on the right, for its handmade, toasted *sembei* (rice crackers) and its seven-pepper spices in gourd-shape bottles of zelkova wood. At the end of Nakamise-dōri, on the right, is Sukeroku, which specializes in traditional handmade dolls and models clothed in the costumes of the Edo period. Just beyond Sukeroku is a two-story gate called Hozō-mon.

At this point, take an important detour. Look to your left as you pass through the gate. Tucked away in the far corner is a vermilion-color building in the traditional temple style (just to the left of the pagoda, behind an iron railing) that houses the Sensō-ji administrative offices: walk in, go down the corridor on the right to the third door on the

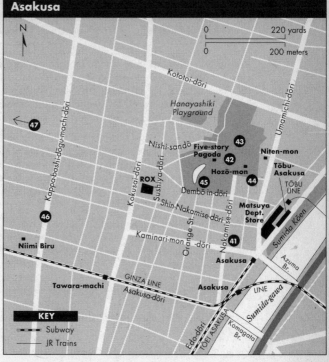

Asakusa

left, and ask for permission to see the Garden of Dembō-in. There is no charge. You simply enter your name and address in a register and receive a ticket. Hold on to the ticket: you'll need it later.

Return to Hozō-mon and walk across the courtyard to **Sensō-ji Main Hall** ㊷. To the left of the Main Hall is the Five-Story Pagoda. To the right is **Asakusa Jinja** ㊸—a shrine to the Hikonuma brothers and their master, Naji-no-Nakatomo. Near the entrance to the shrine is the east gate to the temple grounds, Niten-mon.

From Niten-mon, walk back in the direction of Kaminari-mon to the southeast corner of the grounds. On a small plot of ground here stands the shrine to Kume-no-Heinai, a 17th-century outlaw who repented and became a priest of one of the subsidiary temples of Sensō-ji. Late in life he carved a stone statue of himself and buried it where many people would walk over it. In his will, he expressed the hope that his image would be trampled upon forever. Somehow, Heinai came to be worshiped as the patron god of lovers—as mystifying an apotheosis as you will ever find in Japanese religion.

Walk south again from Heinai's shrine along the narrow street that runs back to Kaminari-mon-dōri, parallel to Nakamise-dōri. On the left you pass a tiny hillock called Benten-yama and the **Toki-no-kane Shōrō** ㊹, a 17th-century belfry. Opposite Benten-yama is a shop called Naka-ya, which sells all manner of regalia for Sensō-ji's annual Sanja Festival.

Next door is Kuremutsu, a tiny ramshackle *nomiya* (Japanese pub) dating back nearly 100 years and open only in the evening. Just up the street from Kuremutsu is Hyaku-suke, the last place in Tōkyō to carry government-approved skin cleanser made from powdered nightingale droppings. Ladies of the Edo period—especially the geisha—swore by the cleanser. The wonderful variety of handcrafted combs and cosmetic brushes, intended for actors and dancers in traditional Japanese theater, makes for interesting gifts and souvenirs. The shop is closed on Tuesday.

Three doors up, on the same side of the street, is Fuji-ya, a shop that deals exclusively in *tenugui*—printed cotton hand towels. Owner Keiji Kawakami designs and dyes all of the tenugui himself. They unfold to about 3 ft, and many people buy them for framing. When Kawakami feels he has made enough of one pattern, he destroys the stencil.

Turn right at the corner past Fuji-ya and walk west on Dembō-in-dōri until you cross Nakamise-dōri. On the other side of the intersection, on the left, is Yono-ya, purveyor of pricey handmade boxwood combs for traditional Japanese coiffures and wigs. Some combs are carved with auspicious motifs, like peonies, hollyhocks, or cranes, and all are engraved with the family benchmark.

Now it's time to cash in the ticket you've been carrying around. Walk west another 70 yards or so, and on the right you will see an old dark wooden gate; this is the side entrance to **Dembō-in** ㊺, the living quarters of the abbot of Sensō-ji. The only part of the grounds you can visit is the garden: go through the small door in the gate, across the courtyard and through the door on the opposite side, and present your ticket to the caretaker in the house at the end of the alley. The entrance to the garden is down a short flight of stone steps to the left.

Turn right as you leave Dembō-in and continue walking west on Dembō-in-dōri. You'll pass a small Shintō shrine with a number of small statues of the bodhisattva Jizō; this is a shrine for prayers for the repose of the souls of *mizuko*—literally "water children"—those who were aborted or miscarried.

Farther on, in the row of knockdown clothing stalls along the right side of the street, is the booth of calligrapher Kōji Matsumaru, who makes *hyōsatsu*, the Japanese equivalent of doorplates. A hyōsatsu is a block of wood, preferably cypress, hung on a gatepost or an entranceway, with the family name on it in India ink. The hyōsatsu is the first thing people will learn about a home, and the characters on it must be felicitous and well formed—so one comes to Matsumaru. Famous in Asakusa for his fine hand, he will also render Western names in the *katakana* syllabic alphabet reserved for foreign words, should you decide to take home a hyōsatsu of your own.

Opposite the row of clothing stalls, on the corner of Orange-dōri, is the redbrick Asakusa Public Hall; performances of Kabuki and traditional dance are sometimes held here, as well as exhibitions of life in Asakusa before World War II. Across the street is Nakase, one of the best of Asakusa's many fine tempura restaurants.

Now review your options. If you have the time and energy, you might want to explore the streets and covered arcades on the south and west sides of Dembō-in. Where Dembō-in-dōri meets Sushiya-dōri, the main avenue of the Rok-ku entertainment district, there is a small flea market. Turn right here, and you are in what remains of the old movie-theater district. Nishi-Sandō—an arcade where you can find kimonos and yukata (cotton kimono) fabrics, traditional accessories, fans, and festival costumes at very reasonable prices—runs east of the movie theaters, between Rok-ku and Sensō-ji. If you turn to the left at the flea market, you soon come to the ROX Building, a misplaced attempt to endow Asakusa with a glitzy vertical mall. Just beyond it, you can turn left again and stroll along Shin-Nakamise-dōri (New Street of Inside

Shops). This arcade and the streets that cross it north–south are lined with stores selling clothing and accessories; purveyors of crackers, seaweed, and tea; and restaurants and coffee shops. This is Asakusa's answer to the suburban shopping center.

Turn south, away from Dembō-in on any of these side streets; return to Kaminari-mon-dōri; turn right, and walk to the end of the avenue. Cross Kokusai-dōri, turn left, and then right at the next major intersection onto Asakusa-dōri; on the corner is the entrance to Tawara-machi Eki on the Ginza subway line. Head west on Asakusa-dōri; at the second traffic light, you'll see the Niimi Biru building across the street, on the right. Atop the Niimi Biru is the guardian god of Kappa-bashi: an enormous chef's head in plastic, 30 ft high, beaming, mustached, and crowned, as every chef in Japan is crowned, with a tall white hat. Turn right onto Kappa-bashi-dōgu-machi-dōri to explore the shops of **Kappa-bashi** ㊻, Tōkyō's wholesale restaurant supply district.

At the second intersection, on the right, is the main showroom of the Maizuru Company, virtuosos in the art of counterfeit cuisine: the plastic models of food you see in the front windows of most popularly priced Japanese restaurants. In 1960 models by Maizuru were included in the Japan Style Exhibition at London's Victoria and Albert Museum. Here you can buy individual pieces of plastic sushi or splurge on a whole Pacific lobster, perfect in coloration and detail down to the tiniest spines on its legs. A few doors down is Biken Kōgei, a good place to look for the folding red-paper lanterns that grace the front of inexpensive bars and restaurants.

Across the street from Maizuru is Nishimura, a shop specializing in *noren*—the short divided curtains that hang from bamboo rods over the doors of shops or restaurants to announce that they are open for business. Nishimura also carries ready-made noren with motifs of all sorts, from white-on-blue landscapes to geisha and sumō wrestlers in polychromatic splendor. They make wonderful wall hangings and dividers.

In the next block, on the right (east) side of the street, is Kondo Shōten, which sells all sorts of bamboo trays, baskets, scoops, and containers. A block farther, look for Iida Shōten, which stocks a good selection of embossed cast-iron kettles and casseroles, called *nambu* ware.

On the far corner is Union Company, which sells everything you need to run a coffee shop (or the make-believe one in your own kitchen): roasters, grinders, beans, flasks, and filters of every description.

The intersection here is about in the middle of Kappa-bashi. Turn left and walk about 100 yards to the next traffic light; just past the light, on the right, is **Sōgen-ji** ㊼—better known as the Kappa Temple, with its shrine to the imaginary creature that gives this district its name.

From Sōgen-ji retrace your steps to the intersection. There is more of Kappa-bashi to the north, but you can safely ignore it; continue east, straight past Union Company down the narrow side street. In the next block, on the left, look for Tsubaya Hōchōten. Tsubaya sells cutlery for professionals—knives of every length and weight and balance for every imaginable use, from slicing sashimi to turning a cucumber into a paper-thin sheet to making decorative cuts in fruit.

Continue on this street east to Kokusai-dōri and then turn right (south). As you walk, you'll see several shops selling *butsudan,* Buddhist household altars. The most elaborate of these, hand-carved in ebony and covered with gold leaf, are made in Toyama Prefecture and can cost as much as ¥1 million. No proper Japanese household is without at least a modest butsudan; it's the spiritual center of the family, where reverence for ancestors and continuity of the family traditions are expressed. In a few moments, you will be back at Tawara-machi Eki—the end of the Asakusa walk.

TIMING

Unlike most of the other areas to explore on foot in Tōkyō, Sensō-ji is admirably compact. You can easily see the temple and environs in a morning. The garden at Dembō-in is worth half an hour. If you decide to include Kappa-bashi, allow yourself an hour more. Some of the shopping arcades in this area are covered, but Asakusa is essentially an outdoor experience. Be prepared for rain in June, heat and humidity in July and August.

Sights to See

THE SENSŌ-JI COMPLEX

★ Dedicated to the goddess Kannon, **Sensō-ji** is the heart and soul of Asakusa. Come for its local and historical importance, its garden, its 17th-century Shintō shrine, and the wild Sanja Matsuri in May. ⊠ *2–3–1 Asakusa, Taitō-ku,* ☎ *03/3842–0181.* ☎ *Free.* ☉ *Temple grounds daily 6–sundown. Subway: Ginza Line, Asakusa Eki (Exit 1/Kaminari-mon Exit).*

㊸ Asakusa Jinja. Several structures in the temple complex survived the bombings of 1945. The largest, to the right of the Main Hall, is a Shintō shrine to the putative founders of Sensō-ji. In Japan, Buddhism and Shintoism have enjoyed a comfortable coexistence since the former arrived from China in the 6th century. It's the rule, rather than the exception, to find a Shintō shrine on the same grounds as a Buddhist temple. The shrine, built in 1649, is also known as Sanja Sanma (Shrine of the Three Guardians). The Sanja Festival, held every year on the third weekend in May, is the biggest, loudest, wildest party in Tōkyō. Each of the neighborhoods under Sanja Sanma's protection has its own mikoshi, and on the second day of the festival, these palanquins are paraded through the streets of Asakusa to the shrine, bouncing and swaying on the shoulders of the participants all the way. Many of the "parishioners" take part naked to the waist, or with the sleeves of their tunics rolled up, to expose fantastic red-and-black tattoo patterns that sometimes cover their entire backs and shoulders. These are the tribal markings of the Japanese underworld.

Near the entrance to Asakusa Jinja is another survivor of World War II: the east gate to the temple grounds, **Niten-mon,** built in 1618 for a shrine to Ieyasu Tokugawa (the shrine itself no longer exists) and designated by the government as an Important Cultural Property.

★ ㊺ **Dembō-in.** Believed to have been made in the 17th century by Kōbori Enshū, the genius of Zen landscape design, the garden of Dembō-in, part of the living quarters of the abbot of Sensō-ji, is the best-kept secret in Asakusa. Anyone can see the front entrance to Dembō-in from Nakamise-dōri—behind an iron fence in the last block of shops—but the thousands of Japanese visitors passing by seem to have no idea what it is. (And if they do, it somehow never occurs to them to visit it themselves.) The garden of Dembō-in is usually empty and always utterly serene, an island of privacy in a sea of pilgrims. Spring, when the wisteria blooms, is the ideal time to be here. As you walk along the path that circles the pond, a different vista presents itself at every turn. The only sounds are the cries of birds and the splashing of carp.

A sign in English on Dembō-in-dōri, about 150 yards west of the intersection with Naka-mise-dōri, indicates the entrance, through the side door of a large wooden gate. For permission to see the abbot's garden, apply at the temple administration building, between Hozō-mon and the Five-Story Pagoda, in the far corner. ☎ *03/3842–0181 for reservations.* ☑ *Free.* ☉ *Daily 9–4; may be closed if abbot has guests.*

NEED A BREAK? | The tatami-mat rooms in **Nakase,** a fine tempura restaurant, look out on a perfect little interior garden—hung, in May, with great fragrant bunches of white wisteria. Carp and goldfish swim in the pond; you can almost lean out from your room and trail your fingers in the water as you listen to the fountain. Nakase is expensive: lunch (11–3) at the tables inside starts at ¥3,000; more elaborate meals by the garden start at ¥7,000. It's across Orange Street from the redbrick Asakusa Public Hall. ✉ *1–39–13 Asakusa, Taitō-ku,* ☎ *03/3841–4015. No credit cards. Closed Tues.*

④ **Kaminari-mon** (Thunder God Gate). This is the proper Sensō-ji entrance, with its huge red-paper lantern hanging in the center. The original gate was destroyed by fire in 1865. The replica that stands here now was built after World War II. Traditionally, two fearsome guardian gods are installed in the alcoves of Buddhist temple gates to ward off evil spirits. The Thunder God (Kaminari-no-Kami) of the Sensō-ji main gate is on the left. He shares his duties with the Wind God (Kaze-no-Kami) on the right. Few Japanese visitors neglect to stop at **Tokiwa-dō,** the shop on the west side of the gate, to buy some of Tōkyō's most famous souvenirs: *kaminari okoshi* (thunder crackers), made of rice, millet, sugar, and beans.

Kaminari-mon also marks the southern extent of **Nakamise-dōri,** the Street of Inside Shops. The area from Kaminari-mon to the inner gate of the temple was once composed of stalls leased to the townspeople who cleaned and swept the temple grounds. The rows of redbrick buildings now technically belong to the municipal government, but the leases are, in effect, hereditary: some of the shops have been in the same families since the Edo period.

④ **Sensō-ji Main Hall.** The **Five-Story Pagoda** and the **Main Hall** of Sensō-ji are both faithful copies in concrete of originals that burned down in 1945. It took 13 years, when most of the people of Asakusa were still rebuilding their own bombed-out lives, to raise money for the restoration of their beloved Sensō-ji. To them—and especially to those involved in the world of entertainment—it is far more than a tourist attraction: Kabuki actors still come here before a new season of performances; sumō wrestlers come before a tournament to pay their respects; the large lanterns in the Main Hall were donated by the geisha associations of Asakusa and nearby Yanagi-bashi. Most Japanese stop at the huge bronze incense burner, in front of the Main Hall, to bathe their hands and faces in the smoke—it's a charm to ward off illnesses—before climbing the stairs to offer their prayers.

The Main Hall, about 115 ft long and 108 ft wide, is not an especially impressive piece of architecture. Unlike in many other temples, however, part of the inside has a concrete floor, so you can come and go without removing your shoes. In this area hang the Sensō-ji's chief claims to artistic importance: a collection of votive paintings on wood, from the 18th and 19th centuries. Plaques of this kind, called *ema*, are still offered to the gods at shrines and temples, but they are commonly simpler and smaller. The worshiper buys a little tablet of wood with the picture already painted on one side and inscribes a prayer on the other. The temple owns more than 50 of these works, which were removed to safety in 1945 and so escaped the air raids. Only eight of them, depicting scenes from Japanese history and mythology, are on display. A catalog of the collection is on sale in the hall, but the text is in Japanese only.

Lighting is poor in the Main Hall, and the actual works are difficult to see. This is also true of the ceiling, done by two contemporary masters of Nihon-ga (traditional Japanese-style painting); the dragon is by Ryūshi Kawabata, and the motif of angels and lotus blossoms is by Inshō Dōmoto. One thing that visitors cannot see at all is the holy image of Kannon itself, which supposedly lies buried somewhere deep under the temple. Not even the priests of Sensō-ji have ever seen it, and there is in fact no conclusive evidence that it actually exists.

Hozō-mon, the gate to the temple courtyard, serves as a repository for sutras (Buddhist texts) and other treasures of Sensō-ji. This gate, too, has its guardian gods; should either of them decide to leave his post for a stroll, he can use the enormous pair of sandals hanging on the back wall—the gift of a Yamagata Prefecture village famous for its straw weaving.

㊹ Toki-no-kane Shōrō (belfry). The tiny hillock Benten-yama, with its shrine to the goddess of good fortune, is the site for this 17th-century belfry. The bell here used to toll the hours for the people of the district, and it was said that you could hear it anywhere within a radius of some 6 km (4 mi). The bell still sounds at 6 AM every day, when the temple grounds open. It also rings on New Year's Eve—108 strokes in all, beginning just before midnight, to "ring out" the 108 sins and frailties of humankind and make a clean start for the coming year. Benten-yama and the belfry are at the beginning of the narrow street that parallels Nakamise-dōri.

NEED A BREAK? **Kuremutsu,** formerly a tiny old teahouse, has been turned into a fairly expensive *nomiya*—literally, a "drinking place," the drink of choice in this case being sake. It's open evenings, Friday–Wednesday. ✉ 2–2–13 Asakusa, Taitō-ku, ☎ 03/3842–0906.

ELSEWHERE IN ASAKUSA

★ ㊼ Kappa-bashi. The more than 200 wholesale dealers in this area sell everything the city's restaurant and bar trade could possibly need to do business, from paper supplies to steam tables, from signs to soup tureens. In their wildest dreams the Japanese themselves would never have cast Kappa-bashi as a tourist attraction, but indeed it is.

For one thing, it is *the* place to buy plastic food. From the humblest noodle shop or sushi bar to neighborhood restaurants of middling price and pretension, it's customary in Japan to stock a window with models of what can be eaten inside. The custom began, according to one version of the story, in the early days of the Meiji Restoration, when anatomical models made of wax first came to Japan as teaching aids in the new schools of Western medicine. A businessman from Nara decided that wax models would also make good point-of-purchase advertising for restaurants. He was right: the industry grew in a modest way at first, making models mostly of Japanese food, but in the boom years after 1960, restaurants began to serve all sorts of cookery ordinary people had never seen before, and the models offered much-needed reassurance: "So *that's* a cheeseburger. It doesn't look as bad as it sounds. Let's go in and try one." By the mid-1970s, the makers of plastic food were turning out creations of astonishing virtuosity and realism, and foreigners had discovered in them a form of pop art. ✉ *Nishi-Asakusa 1-chōme and 2-chōme, Taitō-ku.* ☉ *Most shops daily 9–6. Subway: Ginza Line, Tawara-machi Eki (Exit 1).*

㊼ Sōgen-ji. In the 19th century, so the story goes, there was a river in the present-day Kappa-bashi district and a bridge. The surrounding area was poorly drained and was often flooded. A local shopkeeper began a project to improve the drainage, investing all his own money, but met with little success until a troupe of *kappa*—mischievous green water sprites—emerged from the river to help him. The local people still come to the shrine at Sōgen-ji to leave offerings of cucumber and sake—the kappa's favorite food and drink.

A more prosaic explanation for the name of the district points out that the lower-ranking retainers of the local lord used to earn extra money by making straw raincoats, also called kappa, that they spread to dry on the bridge. To get here, walk north on Kappa-bashi-dōgu-machi-dōri from the Niimi Biru to the fifth intersection and turn left. ⊠ *3–7–2 Matsugaya, Taitō-ku,* ☎ *03/3841–2035.* ☎ *Free.* ☉ *Temple grounds sunrise–sunset. Subway: Ginza Line, Tawara-machi Eki (Exit 1).*

Tsukiji and Shimbashi

Tsukiji is a reminder of the awesome disaster of the great fire of 1657. In the space of two days, it leveled almost 70% of Ieyasu Tokugawa's new capital and killed more than 100,000 people. Ieyasu was not a man to be discouraged by mere catastrophe, however; he took it as an opportunity to plan an even bigger and better city, one that would incorporate the marshes east of his castle. Tsukiji, in fact, means "reclaimed land," and a substantial block of land it was, laboriously drained and filled, from present-day Ginza to the bay.

The common people of the tenements and alleys, who had suffered most in the great fire, benefited not at all from this project; land was first allotted to feudal lords and to temples. After 1853, when Japan opened its doors to the outside world, Tsukiji became Tōkyō's first foreign settlement—the site of the American legation and an elegant two-story brick hotel, and home to missionaries, teachers, and doctors. Today this area is best known for the largest fish market in Asia.

Almost nothing remains in Shimbashi to recall its golden age—the period after the Meiji Restoration, when this was one of the most famous geisha districts of the new capital. Its reputation as a pleasure quarter is even older. In the Edo period, when there was a network of canals and waterways here, it was the height of luxury to charter a covered boat (called a *yakata-bune*) from one of the Shimbashi boathouses for a cruise on the river; a local restaurant would cater the excursion, and a local geisha house would provide the companionship. A dwindling number of geisha still work in Shimbashi. They entertain at some 30 or so *ryōtei* (traditional restaurants) tucked away on the backstreets of the district, but you're unlikely to encounter any while exploring the area.

Numbers in the text correspond to numbers in the margin and on the Tsukiji and Shimbashi map.

A Good Walk

TSUKIJI

Take the Tōei Ōedo Line subway to Tsukiji-shijō Eki, leave the station by Exit A1 onto Shin-Ōhashi-dōri, and turn right. After walking about 30 paces, you will come to the back gate of the fish market, which extends from here southeast toward the bay. Alternatively, take the Hibiya Line subway to Tsukiji Eki (signs in English to the FISH MARKET are posted in the station), come up on Shin-Ōhashi-dōri (Exit 1), and turn southeast. Cross Harumi-dōri, walk along the covered sidewalk for about 110 yards to the traffic light, and turn left. Walk to the end of the street (you'll will see the stone torii of a small shrine), and turn

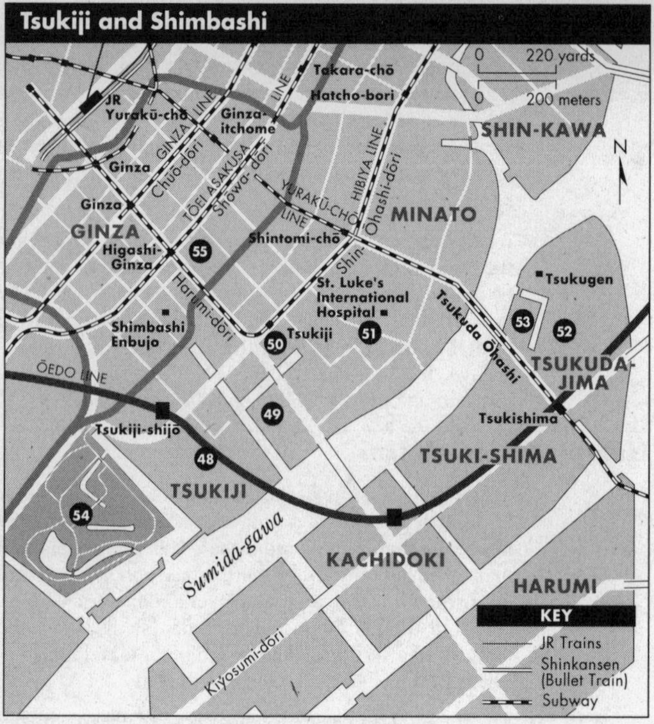

right. If you reach this point at precisely 5 AM, you'll hear a signal for the start of Tōkyō's greatest ongoing open-air spectacle: the fish auction at the **Tōkyō Chūō Oroshiuri Ichiba** ㊽, the Central Wholesale Market.

By 9 AM the business of the Central Market is largely finished for the day, but there is still plenty to do and see. You'll have missed the auctions, but you can still explore the maze of alleys between the market and Harumi-dōri, where you'll come across the **Backstreet Shops of Tsukiji** ㊾. You'll find all kinds of eateries, as well as food and cookware stores. For a close-up shot of Japanese daily life, this is one of the best places in Tōkyō to visit.

From the Central Market, go back to Shin-Ōhashi-dōri; turn right; and walk to the next block, past Harumi-dōri. On the right, as you approach the Hibiya subway line's Tsukiji Eki, are the grounds of **Tsukiji Hongan-ji** ㊿. Looking much like a transplant from India, this temple is the main branch in Tōkyō of Kyōto's Nishi Hongan-ji. Continue northeast on Shin-Ōhashi-dōri, and turn right at the next corner. When you come to a small park, turn left and follow the path through it. At the end of the path, turn right, keeping St. Luke's International Hospital on your immediate left. About 30 yards down this street, in a traffic island on the right, are two unassuming stone **Tsukiji memorials** (51) that mark the true importance of the area in the modern history of Japan.

St. Luke's International Hospital, across the street, was founded in 1900 by Dr. Rudolf Teusler, an American medical missionary. The chapel on the second floor of the charming brick-and-granite old wing of the hospital is quite lovely. Covering the several square blocks north of the hospital was the foreign settlement created after the signing of the U.S.-Japan Treaty of Commerce in 1858. Among the residents here in the latter part of the 19th century was a Scottish surgeon and missionary named Henry Faulds. Intrigued by the Japanese custom of putting their thumbprints on documents for authentication, he began the research that established for the first time that no two people's fingerprints are alike. In 1880 he wrote a paper for *Nature* magazine suggesting that this fact might be of some use in criminal investigation.

After you've seen the hospital, review your priorities. From here you can retrace your steps to the Hibiya Line station on Shin-Ōhashi-dōri and take the subway to Higashi-Ginza and Shimbashi. Or you can take a longish but rewarding detour to **Tsukuda-jima** ⑫. If you choose the latter, walk north from the hospital, parallel to the Sumida-gawa and one block west of it, for two blocks. Cross the main intersection here and turn right. The street rises to become the Tsukuda Ōhashi (Tsukuda Bridge). Just before it crosses the water, you'll find a flight of steps up to the pedestrian walkway that brings you to the island.

Tsukugen, a shop on the first street along the breakwater as you leave the bridge, is famous for its delicious *tsukudani*—whitebait boiled in soy sauce and salt—the island's most famous product. At the end of the breakwater, turn right. From here it's a short walk to the gate of the **Sumiyoshi Jinja** ⑬, a shrine established by fishermen from Ōsaka when they first settled on the island in the 17th century.

If you've opted not to visit Tsukuda-jima, retrace your steps from St. Luke's to the Tsukiji subway station and walk southwest again on Shin-Ōhashi-dōri. Pass the turnoff to the Central Market on your left and the Asahi Newspapers Building on your right. The avenue curves and brings you to an elevated walkway. The entrance to the gardens of **Hama Rikyū Tei-en** ⑭ is on the left. (The path to the left as you enter the garden leads to the "river bus" ferry landing, from which you can leave this excursion and begin another: up the Sumida to Asakusa.)

On your way to Hama Rikyū Tei-en, as you walk west on Shin-Ōhashi-dōri, keep on the right side of the street. After you cross Harumi-dōri, take the first narrow street on the right; just past the next corner, on the left, is Edo-Gin, a venerable sushi bar that serves sizable portions of market-fresh sushi. Lunchtime set menus are bargains.

SHIMBASHI

North of the entrance to Hama Rikyū Tei-en is a major intersection, where Shin-Ōhashi-dōri crosses Shōwa-dōri. If you turned left on Shōwa-dōri you'd pass an O marker commemorating the starting point of Japan's first railway service, between Shimbashi and Yokohama, in 1872. Turn right instead onto Shōwa-dōri. At the next major intersection turn right again and then left at the third corner. Walk northeast in the direction of Higashi-Ginza Eki. In the second block, on your right, is the Shimbashi Enbujo, which hosts Kabuki performances and other traditional theater. On the left is the Nissan Motor Company headquarters.

A brisk minute's walk will bring you to the intersection of Harumi-dōri. Turn left, and on the next block, on the right, you'll see the **Kabuki-za** ⑮, built especially for Kabuki performances.

Just in front of the Kabuki-za is the Hibiya subway's Higashi-Ginza stop, where you can make your way back from whence you came.

TIMING

The Tsukiji walk offers few places to spend time *in*; backtracking and getting from point to point, however, can consume most of a morning—especially if you decide to devote an hour or so to Tsukuda-jima. The backstreet shops will probably require no more than half an hour. Allow yourself an hour or more to explore the Central Market and the nearby shops; if fish in all its diversity holds a special fascination for you, take two or three hours. Remember that in order to see the fish auction in action, you'll need to get to the Central Market before 6:30 AM; by 9 AM the business of the market is largely finished for the day.

This part of the city can be brutally hot and muggy in August; during the O-bon holiday, in the middle of the month, Tsukiji is comparatively lifeless. Mid-April and early October are best for strolls in the Hama Rikyū Garden.

Sights to See

★ ㊾ **Backstreet Shops of Tsukiji.** Because of the area's proximity to the fish market, there are scores of fishmongers here—but also sushi bars, restaurants, and stores for pickles, tea, crackers, kitchen knives, baskets, and crockery. Markets like these provide a vital counterpoint to the museums and monuments of conventional sightseeing; they bring you up close to the way people really live in the city. If you have time on your itinerary for just one market, this is the one to see. The area that these shops occupy is between the Tōkyō fish market and Harumi-dōri. ✉ *5–2–1 Tsukiji, Chūō-ku. Subway: Tōei Ōedo Line, Tsukiji-shijō Eki (Exit A1); Hibiya Line, Tsukiji Eki (Exit 1).*

(54) **Hama Rikyū Tei-en** (Detached Palace Garden). The land here was originally owned by the Owari branch of the Tokugawa family from Nagoya, and it extended to part of what is now the fish market. When one of the family became shōgun in 1709, his residence was turned into a shogunal palace—with pavilions, ornamental gardens, pine and cherry groves, and duck ponds. The garden became a public park in 1945, although a good portion of it is fenced off as a nature preserve. None of the original buildings survive, but on the island in the large pond is a reproduction of the pavilion where former U.S. president Ulysses S. Grant and Mrs. Grant had an audience with the emperor Meiji in 1879. The building can now be rented for parties. The path to the left as you enter the garden leads to the "river bus" ferry landing, from which you can leave this excursion and begin another: up the Sumida to Asakusa. ✉ *1–1 Hamarikyū–Teien, Chūō–ku,* ☎ *03/3541–0200.* 🎫 *¥300.* ⏲ *Daily 9–4:30. Subway: Tōei Ōedo Line, Tsukiji-shijō Eki (Exit A1); Hibiya Line, Tsukiji Eki (Exit 1).*

★ (55) **Kabuki-za.** Soon after the Meiji Restoration and its enforced exile in Asakusa, Kabuki began to reestablish itself in this part of the city. The first Kabuki-za was built in 1889, with a European facade. Here, two of the hereditary theater families, Ichikawa and Onoe, developed a brilliant new repertoire that brought Kabuki into the modern era. In 1912 the Kabuki-za was taken over by the Shochiku theatrical management company, which replaced the old theater building in 1925. Designed by architect Shin'ichirō Okada, it was damaged during World War II but was restored soon after. For information on performances *see* Nightlife and the Arts, *below.* ✉ *4–12–15 Ginza, Chūō-ku,* ☎ *03/3541–3131,* WEB *www.shochiku.co.jp/play/kabukiza/theater. Subway: Hibiya Line, Higashi-Ginza Eki (Exit 3).*

(53) **Sumiyoshi Jinja.** A few steps from the breakwater at the north end of Tsukuda-jima, this shrine dates from the island's earliest period, when Ōsaka fishermen settled here. The god enshrined here is the protector of those who make their livelihood from the sea. Once every three years (2002, 2005, 2008), on the first weekend in August, the god is brought out for his procession in an eight-sided palanquin, preceded by huge, golden lion heads carried high in the air, their mouths snapping in mock ferocity to drive any evil influences out of the path. As the palanquin passes, the people of the island douse it with water, recalling the cus-

tom, before the breakwater was built, of carrying it to the river for a high-spirited dunking. ✉ *1–1 Tsukuda, Chūō-ku,* ☎ *03/3531–6525.* 🎫 *Free.* ☉ *Daily dawn–sunset. Subway: Yūraku-chō and Tōei Ōedo lines, Tsukishima Eki (Exit 6).*

★ ㊽ **Tōkyō Chūō Oroshiuri Ichiba** (Tōkyō Central Wholesale Market). The city's fish market used to be farther uptown, in Nihombashi. It was moved to Tsukiji after the Great Kantō Earthquake of 1923, and it occupies the site of what was once Japan's first naval training academy. Today the market sprawls over some 54 acres of reclaimed land. Its warren of buildings houses about 1,200 wholesale shops, supplying 90% of the fish consumed in Tōkyō every day and employing some 15,000 people. Most of the seafood sold in Tsukiji comes in by truck, arriving through the night from fishing ports all over the country.

What makes Tsukiji a great show is the auction system. The catch—more than 100 varieties of fish in all, including whole frozen tuna, Styrofoam cases of shrimp and squid, and crates of crabs—is laid out in the long covered area between the river and the main building. Then the bidding begins. Only members of the wholesalers' association can take part. Wearing license numbers fastened to the front of their caps, they register their bids in a kind of sign language, shouting to draw the attention of the auctioneer and making furious combinations in the air with their fingers. The auctioneer keeps the action moving in a hoarse croak that sounds like no known language, and spot quotations change too fast for ordinary mortals to follow.

Different fish are auctioned off at different times and locations, and by 6:30 AM or so, this part of the day's business is over, and the wholesalers fetch their purchases back into the market in barrows. Restaurant owners and retailers arrive about 7, making the rounds of favorite suppliers for their requirements. Chaos seems to reign, but everybody here knows everybody else, and they all have it down to a system.

A word to the wise: the 52,000 or so buyers, wholesalers, and shippers who work at the Central Market may be a lot more receptive to casual visitors than they were in the past, but they are not running a tourist attraction. They're in the fish business, moving some 636,000 tons of it a year to retailers and restaurants all over the city, and this is their busiest time of day. The cheerful banter they use with each other can turn snappish if you get in their way. Also bear in mind that you are not allowed to take photographs while the auctions are under way (flashes are a distraction). The market is kept spotlessly clean, which means the water hoses are running all the time. Boots are helpful, but if you don't want to carry them, bring a pair of heavy-duty trash bags to slip over your shoes and secure them above your ankles with rubber bands. ✉ *5–2–1 Tsukiji, Chūō-ku,* ☎ *03/3542–1111.* 🎫 *Free.* ☉ *Business hrs Mon.–Sat. (except 2nd and 4th Wed. of month) 5–4. Subway: Tōei Ōedo Line, Tsukiji-shijō Eki (Exit A1); Hibiya Line, Tsukiji Eki (Exit 1).*

㊿ **Tsukiji Hongan-ji.** Disaster seemed to follow this temple since it was first located here in 1657: it was destroyed at least five times thereafter, and reconstruction in wood was finally abandoned after the Great Kantō Earthquake of 1923. The present stone building dates from 1935. It was designed by Chūta Ito, a pupil of Tatsuno Kingo, who built Tōkyō Eki. Ito's other credits include the Meiji Jingū in Harajuku; he also lobbied for Japan's first law for the preservation of historic buildings. Ito traveled extensively in Asia; the evocations of classical Hindu architecture in the temple's domes and ornaments were his homage to India as the cradle of Buddhism. ✉ *3–15–1 Tsuk-*

iji, Chūō-ku, ☎ *03/3541–1131.* ☎ *Free.* ☉ *Daily 6–4. Subway: Hibiya Line, Tsukiji Eki (Exit 1).*

Edo-Gin, one of the area's older sushi bars, founded in 1924, is legendary for its portions—slices of raw fish that almost hide the balls of rice on which they sit. Dinner is pricey, but the set menu at lunch is a certifiable *bāgen* (bargain) at ¥1,000. Walk southwest on Shin-Ōhashi-dōri from its intersection with Harumi-dōri. Take the first right and look for Edo-Gin just past the next corner, on the left. ☒ *4–5–1 Tsukiji, Chūō-ku,* ☎ *03/3543–4401. AE, MC, V. Closed Sun. Subway: Hibiya Line, Tsukiji Eki (Exit 1).*

51 **Tsukiji memorials.** The taller of the two unassuming stone memorials pays tribute to Ryōtaku Maeno and Gempaku Sugita. With a group of colleagues, these two men translated the first work of European science into Japanese. Maeno and his collaborators were samurai and physicians. Maeno himself was in the service of the Lord Okudaira, whose mansion was one of the most prominent in Tsukiji. In 1770 Maeno acquired a Dutch book on human anatomy in Nagasaki. It took his group four years to produce its translation. At this time Japan was still officially closed to the outside world, and the trickle of scientific knowledge accessible through the Dutch trading post at Nagasaki—the only authorized foreign settlement—was enormously frustrating to the eager young scholars who wanted to modernize their country. Maeno and his colleagues began with barely a few hundred words of Dutch among them and had no reference works or other resources on which to base their translation, except the diagrams in the book. It must have been an agonizing task, but the publication in 1774 of *Kaitai Shinsho* (New Book of Anatomy) had a tremendous influence. From this time on, Japan would turn away from classical Chinese scholarship and begin to take its lessons in science and technology from the West.

The other stone memorial commemorates the founding of Keiō University by Yūkichi Fukuzawa (1835–1901), the most influential educator and social thinker of the Meiji period. The son of a low-ranking samurai, Fukuzawa was ordered by his lord to start a school of Western learning, which he opened in Tsukiji in 1858. Later the school was moved west to Mita, where the university is today. Engraved on the stone is Fukuzawa's famous statement: HEAVEN CREATED NO MAN ABOVE ANOTHER, NOR BELOW. Uttered when the feudal Tokugawa regime was still in power, this was an enormously daring thought. It took Japan almost a century to catch up with Fukuzawa's liberal and egalitarian vision.

52 **Tsukuda-jima.** In 1613 the shogunate ordered a group of fishermen from the village of Tsukuda, now part of Ōsaka, to relocate here, on an island reclaimed from mudflats at the mouth of the Sumida-gawa. Officially, they were brought here to provide the castle with whitebait; unofficially, their role was to keep watch and report on any suspicious maritime traffic in the bay. Over the years more and more land has been reclaimed from the bay, more than doubling the size of the island and adding other areas to the south and west. The part to explore is the original section: a few square blocks just west and north of the Tsukuda Ōhashi. This neighborhood—with its maze of narrow alleys, its profusion of potted plants and bonsai, its old houses with tile roofs—could almost have come straight out of the Edo period. ☒ *1–1 Tsukuda, Chūō-ku. Subway: Yūraku-chō and Ōedo lines, Tsukishima Eki (Exit 6).*

Nihombashi, Ginza, and Yūraku-chō

Tōkyō is a city of many centers. The municipal administrative center is in Shinjuku. The national government center is in Kasumigaseki. For almost 350 years Japan was ruled from Edo Castle, and the great stone ramparts still define—for travelers, at least—the heart of the city. History, entertainment, fashion, traditional culture: every tail you could want to pin on the donkey goes in a different spot. Geographically speaking, however, there is one and only one center of Tōkyō: a tall, black iron pole on the north side of Nihombashi—and if the tail you were holding represented high finance, you would have to pin that one right here as well.

When Ieyasu Tokugawa had the first bridge constructed at Nihombashi, he designated it the starting point for the five great roads leading out of his city, the point from which all distances were to be measured. His decree is still in force: the black pole on the present bridge, erected in 1911, is the Zero Kilometer marker for all the national highways.

In the early days of the Tokugawa Shogunate, Edo had no port; almost everything the city needed was shipped here. The bay shore was marshy and full of tidal flats, so heavily laden ships would come only as far as Shinagawa, a few miles down the coast, and unload to smaller vessels. These in turn would take the cargo into the city through a network of canals to wharves and warehouses at Nihombashi. The bridge and the area south and east became a wholesale distribution center, not only for manufactured goods but also for foodstuffs. The city's first fish market, in fact, was established at Nihombashi in 1628 and remained here until the Great Earthquake of 1923.

All through the Edo period, this was part of Shitamachi. Except for a few blocks between Nihombashi and Kyō-bashi, where the city's deputy magistrates had their villas, it belonged to the common people—not all of whom lived elbow to elbow in poverty. There were fortunes to be made in the markets, and the early millionaires of Edo built their homes in the Nihombashi area. Some, like the legendary timber magnate Bunzaemon Kinokuniya, spent everything they made in the pleasure quarters of Yoshiwara and died penniless. Others founded the great trading houses of today—Mitsui, Mitsubishi, Sumitomo—which still have warehouses nearby.

It was appropriate, then, that when Japan's first corporations were created and the Meiji government developed a modern system of capital formation, the Tōkyō Stock Exchange (Shōken Torihikijo) would go up on the west bank of the Nihombashi-gawa. A stone's throw from the exchange now are the home offices of most of the country's major securities companies, which in the hyperinflated bubble economy of the 1980s and early '90s were moving billions of yen around the world electronically—a far cry from the early years of high finance, when the length of a trading day was determined by a section of rope burning on the floor of the exchange. Trading finished when the rope had smoldered down to the end.

A little farther west, money—the problems of making it and of moving it around—shaped the area in a somewhat different way. In the Edo period there were three types of currency in circulation: gold, silver, and copper, each with its various denominations. Determined to unify the system, Ieyasu Tokugawa started minting his own silver coins in 1598 in his home province of Suruga, even before he became shōgun. In 1601 he established a gold mint; the building was only a few hundred yards from Nihombashi, on the site of what is now the Bank of Japan. In 1612 he relocated the Suruga plant to a patch of reclaimed land west of his castle. The area soon came to be known informally as Ginza (Silver Mint).

The value of these various currencies fluctuated. There were profits to be made in the changing of money, and this business eventually came under the control of a few large merchant houses. One of the most successful of these merchants was a man named Takatoshi Mitsui, who had a dry-goods shop in Kyōto and opened a branch in Edo in 1673. The shop, called Echigo-ya, was just north of Nihombashi. By the end of the 17th century it was the base of a commercial empire—in retailing, banking, and trading—known today as the Mitsui Group. Not far from the site of Echigo-ya stands its direct descendant: Mitsukoshi depāto.

Rui wa tomo wo yobu goes the Japanese expression: "Like calls to like." From Nihombashi through Ginza to Shimbashi is the domain of all the noble houses that trace their ancestry back to the dry-goods and kimono shops of the Edo period: Mitsukoshi, Takashimaya, Matsuzakaya, Matsuya. All are intensely proud of being at the top of the retail business, as purveyors of an astonishing range of goods and services.

The district called Yūraku-chō lies west of Ginza's Sukiya-bashi, stretching from Sotobori-dōri to Hibiya Kōen and the Outer Garden of the Imperial Palace. The name derives from one Urakusai Oda, younger brother of the warlord who had once been Ieyasu Tokugawa's commander. Urakusai, a Tea Master of some note—he was a student of Sen no Rikyū, who developed the tea ceremony—had a town house here, beneath the castle ramparts, on land reclaimed from the tidal flats of the bay. He soon left Edo for the more refined comforts of Kyōto, but his name stayed behind, becoming Yūraku-chō—the Pleasure (*yūraku*) Quarter (*chō*)—in the process. Sukiya-bashi was the name of the long-gone bridge near Urakusai's villa that led over the moat to the Silver Mint.

The "pleasures" associated with this district in the early postwar period stemmed from the fact that a number of the buildings here survived the air raids of 1945 and were requisitioned by the Allied forces. Yūraku-chō quickly became the haunt of the so-called *pan-pan* women, who provided the GIs with female company. Because it was so close to the military post exchange in Ginza, the area under the railroad tracks became one of the city's largest black markets. Later, the black market gave way to clusters of cheap restaurants, most of them little more than counters and a few stools, serving yakitori and beer. Office workers on meager budgets and journalists from the nearby *Mainichi, Asahi,* and *Yomiuri* newspaper headquarters would gather here at night. Yūraku-chō-under-the-tracks was smoky, loud, and friendly—a kind of open-air substitute for the local taproom. The area has long since become upscale, and no more than a handful of the yakitori stalls remains.

Numbers in the text correspond to numbers in the margin and on the Nihombashi, Ginza, and Yūraku-chō map.

A Good Walk

For more information on depāto and individual shops mentioned in this walk, *see* Shopping, *below.*

NIHOMBASHI

Begin at Tōkyō Eki. Take the Yaesu Central Exit on the east side of the building, cross the broad avenue in front of you (Sotobori-dōri), and turn left. Walk north until you cross a bridge under the Shuto Expressway and turn right at the second corner, at the **Nihon Ginkō** ㊝. From here walk east two blocks to the main intersection at Chūō-dōri. On your left is the Mitsui Bank, on your right **Mitsukoshi** ㊝ depāto. The small area around the store, formerly called Suruga-chō, is the birthplace of the Mitsui conglomerate.

Turn right on Chūō-dōri. As you walk south, you'll see on the left a shop founded in 1849, called Yamamoto Noriten, which specializes in *nori,* the ubiquitous dried seaweed used to wrap *maki* (sushi rolls) and *onigiri* (rice balls); nori was once the most famous product of Tōkyō Bay.

Nihombashi, Ginza, and Yūraku-chō

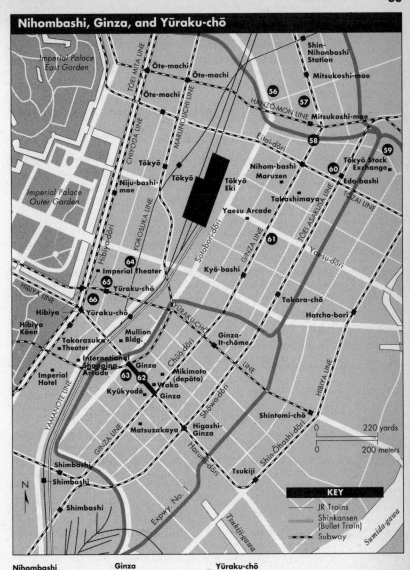

At the end of the next block is the **Nihombashi** ⑤⑧ (this is name of the bridge itself, as well as the neighborhood), shaken but not stirred by the incessant rumbling of the expressway overhead. Before you cross the bridge, notice on your left the small statue of a sea princess seated by a pine tree: a monument to the fish market that stood here before the 1923 quake. To the right is the Zero Kilometer marker, from which all highway distances are measured. On the other side, also to the right, is a plaque depicting the old wooden bridge. In the Edo period the south end of the bridge was set aside for posting public announcements— and for displaying the heads of criminals.

Turn left as soon as you cross the bridge and walk past the Nomura Securities Building to where the expressway loops overhead and turns south. This area is called Kabuto-chō, after the small **Kabuto Jinja** ⑤⑨ here on the left, under the loop. Just across the street from the shrine is the Tōkyō Stock Exchange.

At the main entrance to the Stock Exchange, turn right. Walk south two blocks to the intersection at Eitai-dōri and turn right again. Walk west on Eitai-dōri, turn right onto Shōwa-dōri, and then left on the first small street behind the Bank of Hiroshima. Just off the next corner is a restaurant called Taimeiken. On the fifth floor of this building is the delightful little private **Kite Museum** ⑥⓪—well worth the detour for visitors of all ages.

Retrace your steps to Eitai-dōri, continue west, and turn left onto Chūō-dōri. One block south, on the left, is the Takashimaya depāto; on the right is Maruzen, one of Japan's largest booksellers.

Look right at the next intersection; you'll see that you've come back almost to Tōkyō Eki. Below the avenue from here to the station runs the Yaesu Underground Arcade, with hundreds of shops and restaurants. The whole area here, west of Chūō-dōri, was named after Jan Joosten, a Dutch sailor who was shipwrecked on the coast of Kyūshū with William Adams—hero of James Michener's novel *Shōgun*—in 1600. Like Adams, Joosten became an adviser to Ieyasu Tokugawa, took a Japanese wife, and was given a villa near the castle. "Yaesu" (originally Yayosu) was as close as the Japanese could come to the pronunciation of his name. Adams, an Englishman, lived out his life in Japan; Joosten drowned off the coast of Indonesia while attempting to return home.

On the southeast corner of the intersection is the **Burijisuton Bijutsukan** ⑥①, one of Japan's best private collections of early modern painting and sculpture, both Western and Japanese.

GINZA

Consider your feet. By now they may be telling you that you'd really rather not walk to the next point on this excursion. If so, get on the Ginza Line—there's a subway entrance right in front of the Burijisuton Bijutsukan—and ride one stop to **Ginza** ⑥②. Take any exit directing you to the 4-chōme intersection (yon-*chō*-me *kō*-sa-ten). When you come up to the street level, orient yourself by the Ginza branch of the Mitsukoshi depāto, on the northeast corner, and the round Sanai Building on the southwest.

From Ginza 4-chōme, walk west on Harumi-dōri in the direction of the Imperial Palace. From Chūō-dōri to the intersection called **Sukiya-bashi** ⑥③, named for a bridge that once stood here, your exploration should be free-form: the side streets and parallels north–south are ideal for wandering, particularly if you are interested in art galleries— of which there are 300 or more in this part of Ginza.

YŪRAKU-CHŌ

From the Sukiya-bashi intersection, walk northwest on the right side of Harumi-dōri. Pass the curved facade of the Mullion Building depāto complex and cross the intersection. You'll go through a tunnel under the JR Yamanote Line tracks, and then turn right. Walk two long blocks east, parallel to the tracks, until you come to the gleaming white expanse of the **Tōkyō International Forum** (64).

The plaza of the Tōkyō International Forum is that rarest of Tōkyō rarities—civilized open space: a long, tree-shaded central courtyard with comfortable benches to sit on and things to see. Freestanding sculpture, triumphant architecture, and people strolling—actually *strolling*—past in both directions are all here. Need a refreshment? Café Wien, next to the Plaza Information Center, serves pastry and coffee.

From the southwest corner of the Forum, turn left and walk halfway down the block to the main entrance of the International Building. On the ninth floor you'll find the **Idemitsu Bijutsukan** (65). After a stop inside, continue west along the side of the International Building toward the Imperial Palace to Hibiya-dōri.

Turn left, and less than a minute's walk along Hibiya-dōri will bring you to the **Dai-ichi Mutual Life Insurance Company Building** (66). Across the avenue is Hibiya Kōen, Japan's first Western-style public park, which dates to 1903. Its lawns and fountains make a pretty place for office workers from nearby buildings to have lunch on a warm spring afternoon, but it doesn't provide compelling reasons for you to make a detour. Press on, past the Hibiya police station, across the Harumi-dōri intersection, and at the second corner, just before you come to the Imperial Hotel, turn left.

At the end of the block, on the corner, is the Takarazuka Theater, where all-female casts take the art of musical review to the highest levels of camp. Continue southeast, and in the next block, on both sides of the street (just under the railroad bridge), are entrances to the International Shopping Arcade (☞ Shopping, *below*), the last point of interest on this walk. Stores here sell kimonos and happi coats, pearls and cloisonné, prints, cameras, and consumer electronics: one-stop shopping for presents and souvenirs.

Turn left down the narrow side street that runs along the side of the arcade to the Hankyū depāto—the horned monstrosity in the pocket park on the corner is by sculptor Taro Okamoto—and you will find yourself back on Harumi-dōri, just a few steps from the Sukiya-bashi crossing. From here you can return to your hotel by subway, or a minute's walk will bring you to JR Yūraku-chō Eki.

TIMING

There's something about this part of Tōkyō—the traffic, the numbers of people, the way it exhorts you to keep moving—that can make you feel you've covered a lot more ground than you really have. Take this walk in the morning; when you're done, you can better assess the energy you have left for the rest of the day. None of the stops along the way, with the possible exception of the Bridgestone and Idemitsu museums, should take you more than 45 minutes. The time you spend shopping, of course, is up to you. In summer make a point of starting early, even though many stores and attractions do not open until 10 or 11: by midday the heat and humidity can be brutal. On weekend afternoons (October–March, Saturday 3–6 and Sunday 12–5; April–September, Saturday 3–7 and Sunday 3–6), Chūō-dōri is closed to traffic from Shimbashi all the way to Kyō-bashi and becomes a pedestrian mall with tables and chairs set out along the street. That's great if you plan only to shop, but keep in mind that some of the museums and other sights in the area close on Sundays.

Sights to See

61 **Burijisuton Bijutsukan** (Bridgestone Museum of Art). This is one of Japan's best private collections of French Impressionist art and sculpture and of post-Meiji Japanese painting in Western styles by such artists as Shigeru Aoki and Tsuguji Fujita. The collection, assembled by Bridgestone Tire Company founder Shōjiro Ishibashi, includes work by Rembrandt, Picasso, Utrillo, and Modigliani as well. The Bridgestone also puts on major exhibits from private collections and museums abroad. ⊠ *1–10–1 Kyō-bashi, Chūō-ku,* ☎ *03/3563–0241.* ☞ *¥700.* ☼ *Tues.–Sun. 10–5:30. Subway: Ginza Line, Kyō-bashi Eki (Meijiya Exit), Nihombashi Eki (Takashimaya Exit).*

66 **Dai-ichi Mutual Life Insurance Company Building.** Built like a fortress, the edifice survived World War II virtually intact and was taken over by the Supreme Command of the Allied powers. From his office here, General Douglas MacArthur directed the affairs of Japan from 1945 to 1951. The room is kept exactly as it was then. It can be visited by individuals and small groups without appointment; you need only to sign in at the reception desk in the lobby. ⊠ *1–13–1 Yūraku-chō, Chiyoda-ku,* ☎ *03/3216–1211.* ☞ *Free.* ☼ *Weekdays 10–4:30. Subway: Hibiya Line, Hibiya Eki (Exit B1).*

62 **Ginza.** Ieyasu's Silver Mint moved out of this area in 1800. The name *Ginza* remained, but only much later did it begin to acquire any cachet for wealth and style. The turning point was 1872, when a fire destroyed most of the old houses here, and the main street of Ginza, together with a grid of parallel and cross streets, was rebuilt as a Western quarter. It had two-story brick houses with balconies, the nation's first sidewalks and horse-drawn streetcars, gaslights, and, later, telephone poles. Before the turn of the 20th century, Ginza was already home to the great mercantile establishments that still define its character. The **Wako** depāto, for example, on the northwest corner of the 4-chōme intersection, established itself here as Hattori, purveyors of clocks and watches. The clock on the present building was first installed in the Hattori clock tower, a Ginza landmark, in 1894.

Many of the nearby shops have lineages almost as old, or older, than Wako's. A few steps north of the intersection, on Chūō-dōri, **Mikimoto** (⊠ *4–5–5 Ginza*) sells the famous cultured pearls first developed by Kokichi Mikimoto in 1883. His first shop in Tōkyō dates to 1899. South of the intersection, next door to the Sanai Building, **Kyūkyodō** (⊠ *5–7–4 Ginza*) carries a variety of handmade Japanese papers and related goods. Kyūkyodō has been in business since 1663 and on Ginza since 1880. Across the street and one block south is **Matsuzakaya** depāto, which began as a kimono shop in Nagoya in 1611. Exploring this area—there's even a name for browsing: Gin-bura, or "Ginza wandering"—is best on Sunday from noon to 5 or 6 (depending on the season), when Chūō-dōri is closed to traffic between Shimbashi and Kyō-bashi. *Subway: Ginza and Hibiya lines, Ginza Eki.*

65 **Idemitsu Bijutsukan.** With its four spacious rooms, the Idemitsu is one of the largest and best designed private museums in Tōkyō. The strength of the collection lies in its Tang and Song dynasty Chinese porcelain and in Japanese ceramics—including works by Ninsei Nonomura and Kenzan Ōgata, and masterpieces of Old Seto, Oribe, Old Kutani, Karatsu, and Kakiemon ware. The museum also houses an outstanding examples of Zen painting and calligraphy, wood-block prints, and genre paintings of the Edo period. Of special interest to scholars is the resource collection of shards from virtually every pottery-making culture of the ancient world. ⊠ *3–1–1 Marunouchi, Chiyoda-ku,* ☎ *03/ 3213–9402.* ⊡ *¥800.* ⊙ *Tues.–Sun. 10–4:30. Subway: Yūraku-chō Line, Yūraku-chō Eki (Exit A1).*

⑤⑨ Kabuto Jinja. This shrine, like the Nihombashi itself, is another bit of history lurking in the shadows of the expressway. Legend has it that a noble warrior of the 11th century, sent by the Imperial Court in Kyōto to subdue the barbarians of the north, stopped here and prayed for assistance. His expedition was successful, and on the way back he buried a *kabuto,* a golden helmet, on this spot as an offering of thanks. Few Japanese are aware of this legend, and the monument of choice in Kabuto-chō today is the nearby Tōkyō Stock Exchange. ⊠ *1–8 Kabuto-chō, Nihombashi, Chūō-ku. Subway: Tōzai Line, Kayaba-chō Eki (Exit 10).*

⑥⓪ Kite Museum. Kite flying is an old tradition in Japan. The Motegi collection includes examples of every shape and variety from all over the country, hand-painted in brilliant colors with figures of birds, geometric patterns, and motifs from Chinese and Japanese mythology. Call ahead, and the museum will arrange a kite-making workshop (in Japanese) for groups of children. ⊠ *1–12–10 Nihombashi, Chūō-ku,* ☎ *03/3271– 2465,* WEB *www.tako.gr.jp.* ⊡ *¥200.* ⊙ *Mon.–Sat. (except national holidays) 11–5. Subway: Tōzai Line, Nihombashi Eki (Exit C5).*

⑤⑦ Mitsukoshi. Takatoshi Mitsui made his fortune by revolutionizing the retail system for kimono fabrics. The drapers of his day usually did business on account, taking payments semiannually. In his store (then called Echigo-ya), Mitsui started the practice of unit pricing, and his customers paid cash on the spot. As time went on, the store was always ready to adapt to changing needs and merchandising styles: garments made to order, home delivery, imported goods, and even—as the 20th century opened and Echigo-ya changed its name to Mitsukoshi— the hiring of women to the sales force. The emergence of Mitsukoshi as Tōkyō's first depāto, also called *hyakkaten* (hundred-kinds-of-goods emporium), actually dates to 1908, with a three-story Western building modeled on Harrods of London. This was replaced in 1914 by a five-story structure with Japan's first escalator. The present flagship store is vintage 1935. ⊠ *1–4–1 Nihombashi Muro-machi, Chūō-ku,* ☎ *03/3241–3311.* ⊙ *Daily 10–7. Subway: Ginza and Hanzō-mon lines, Mitsukoshi-mae Eki.*

⑤⑧ Nihombashi (Bridge of Japan). Why, back in 1962, the expressway *had* to be routed directly over this lovely old landmark is one of the mysteries of Tōkyō and its city planning—or lack thereof. There were protests and petitions, but they had no effect—planners argued the high cost of alternative locations. At that time Tōkyō had only two years left to prepare for the Olympics, and the traffic congestion was already out of hand. So the bridge, with its graceful double arch and ornate lamps, its bronze Chinese lions and unicorns, was doomed to bear the perpetual rumble of trucks overhead—its claims overruled by concrete ramps and pillars. *Subway: Tōzai and Ginza lines, Nihombashi Eki (Exits B5 and B6); Ginza and Hanzō-mon lines, Mitsukoshi-mae Eki (Exits B5 and B6).*

⑤⑥ Nihon Ginkō (Bank of Japan). The older part of the Bank of Japan is the work of Tatsuno Kingo, who also designed Tōkyō Eki. Completed in 1896, the bank is one of the very few surviving Meiji-era Western buildings in the city. ⊠ *2–2–1 Nihombashi Hongoku-chō, Chūō-ku,* ☎ *03/3279–1111,* WEB *www.boj.or.jp. Subway: Ginza (Exit A5) and Hanzō-mon (Exit B1) lines, Mitsukoshi-mae Eki.*

63 Sukiya-bashi. The side streets of the Sukiya-bashi area are full of art galleries, several hundred in fact. The galleries operate a bit differently here than they do in most of the world's art markets: A few, like the venerable **Nichidō** (⊠ 5–3–16 Ginza), **Gekkōso** (⊠ 7–2–8 Ginza), **Yoseidō** (⊠ 5–5–15 Ginza), **Yayoi** (⊠ 7–6–16 Ginza), and **Kabuto-ya** (⊠ 8–8–7 Ginza), actually function as dealers, representing particular artists, as well as acquiring and selling art. The majority, however, are rental spaces. Artists or groups pay for the gallery by the week, publicize their shows themselves, and in some cases even hang their own work. It's not unreasonable to suspect that a lot of these shows, even in so prestigious a venue as Ginza, are vanity exhibitions by amateurs with money to spare—but that's not always the case. The rental spaces are also the only way for serious professionals, independent of the various art organizations that might otherwise sponsor their work, to get any critical attention; if they're lucky, they can at least recoup their expenses with an occasional sale. *Subway: Ginza, Hibiya, and Marunouchi lines, Ginza Eki (Exit C4).*

64 Tōkyō International Forum. This postmodern masterpiece, the work of Uruguay-born American architect Raphael Viñoly, is the first major convention and art center of its kind in Tōkyō. Viñoly's design was selected in a 1989 competition that drew nearly 400 entries from 50 countries. Opened in January 1997, the forum is really two buildings. On the east side of the plaza is Glass Hall, the main exhibition space—an atrium with an 180-ft ceiling, a magnificent curved wooden wall, and 34 upper-floor conference rooms. The west building has six halls for international conferences, exhibitions, receptions, and concert performances—the largest with seating for 5,012.

The **Cultural Information Lobby** (☎ 03/5221–9084), in the west building, has the latest schedules of conventions and events in the forum itself; it also has an English-speaking staff and an excellent audiovisual library on tourist attractions, festivals, and events all over Japan—making this a worthwhile first stop when you come to town. Another useful resource is the information office of the **JNTO** (Japan National Tourist Organization; ☎ 03/3201–3331), at the north end of the lower concourse. ⊠ *3–5–1 Marunouchi, Chiyoda-ku,* ☎ *03/5221–9000,* WEB *www.tif.or.jp.* ☉ *Cultural Information Lobby daily 10–6:30; JNTO weekdays 9–5, Sat. 9–noon. Subway: Yūraku-chō Line, Yūraku-chō Eki (Exit A-4B).*

NEED A BREAK?   Amid all of Tōkyō's bustle and crush, you actually can catch your breath in the open space of the plaza of the Tōkyō International Forum. If you also feel like having coffee and a bite of pastry, stop in at **Café Wien,** next to the Plaza Information Center. ⊠ *3–5–1 Marunouchi, Chiyoda-ku,* ☎ *03/3211–3111.* ☉ *Daily 9 AM–10 PM. Subway: Yūraku-chō Line, Yūraku-chō Eki (Exit A-4B).*

Akasaka

Modern-day Akasaka is just a 15-minute taxi ride west of the Imperial Palace, but little more than 100 years ago, the gentle slopes of this area were still covered with tea bushes and *akane*—a plant that produces a red dye, and thus gave Akasaka (*aka* means red; *saka,* hill) its name. In 1936, with the construction of the granite ziggurat that houses the National Diet, the seat of the Japanese government moved to Nagata-chō, on the heights just to the north, and Akasaka blossomed in a different fashion. It became the favored haunt of politicians and their wealthy industrial backers: a quarter of discretely walled-off geisha houses and ryōtei, where deals were cut that shaped the country's future.

After World War II, a number of countries—most importantly, the United States—established embassies in the area. Deluxe hotels like the Okura and the Hilton (the latter now removed to Shinjuku) put even more of an international spin on Akasaka's upscale image. When TBS Television established its broadcast facilities and corporate headquarters here in 1960, the area grew downright glittery. None of this deterred the ryōtei clientele. Akasaka remained the venue of choice for quiet backroom discussions of politics and high finance. Today the few surviving ryōtei define the character of the area in one way, just as the new TBS Building—a postmodern confection of 1994, all flash and no fire—defines it in another. There's more to Akasaka than meets the eye—and less.

Numbers in the text correspond to numbers in the margin and on the Akasaka map.

A Good Walk

To begin this walk, take the Chiyoda subway line to Kokkai Gijidō-mae Eki and follow signs to Exit 5 and the Capitol Tōkyū Hotel exit. The rear entrance to the hotel will be directly across the street. (You can also take the Namboku Line to Tameike-Sannō Eki and use the hotel exit.) To save yourself a climb up the hill and around the hotel, enter the building through this rear entrance and take the elevator to the main lobby. You may want to stop here for breakfast; the dining room in the lobby overlooks an especially fine traditional Japanese pond and garden. Leave the hotel by the main entrance, and the torii of the **Hie Jinja** ⑥⑦ will be straight ahead of you.

Leave Hie Jinja by its east gate and walk down the hill to Akasaka's main street, Sotobori-dōri. On the opposite side, two smaller avenues run parallel to Sotobori-dōri: Ta-machi-dōri and Hitotsugi-dōri. On these two streets, and the narrow alleys between them, are the majority of Akasaka's small bars, restaurants, and cafés. The few remaining ryōtei and geisha houses are at the southern end of this area.

Turn right on Sotobori-dōri and walk toward the Akasaka-mitsuke subway station. The five-way intersection at Aoyama-dōri is just beyond it. The Suntory Building and the **Suntory Bijutsukan** ⑥⑧ stand across the intersection on the left, on the other side of the overpass.

Cross the street and the bridge over the moat on the far side of the Suntory Building and walk to the Hotel New Otani Tōkyō and Towers, on the left. The New Otani complex—1,600 guest rooms, banquet halls, upscale shopping arcades, acres of bars and restaurants, tennis courts, and office towers—is perhaps better described as a minicity than a hotel. The lounge in the main lobby, looking out on a lovely Japanese garden, is a particularly good place to stop for a drink.

Retrace your steps to the Suntory Building, turn right (west) and walk uphill along Aoyama-dōri, which goes all the way through the area to Shibuya. Five minutes at a brisk pace will bring you to the walls of the **Geihinkan** ⑥⑨, also known as Akasaka Detached Palace, on your right. A few minutes farther along, across the avenue on the left, just before you reach the Canadian Embassy, you'll see the glass facade of the **Sōgetsu Kaikan** ⑦⑩, headquarters of one of the more important modern schools of *ikebana*, flower arranging. Two blocks farther west, you come to the Aoyama Twin Tower Building and the Aoyama-1-chōme station on the Ginza and Hanzō-mon subway lines. From here you can ride one stop to Gaien-mae to get to the start of the next walk in Aoyama and Harajuku.

TIMING

Akasaka makes for a fairly easy walk. Even with a break and a stroll through the garden of the New Otani Hotel, it should take you no more

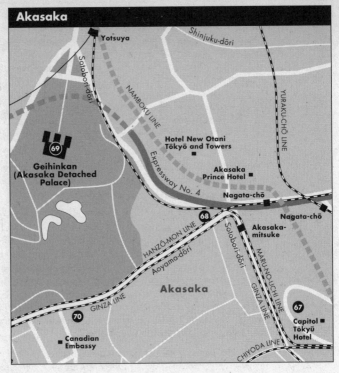

than two hours. Weekdays are best, especially if you plan to have a lesson in flower arrangement at the Sōgetsu Kaikan—for which you should budget an hour more.

Sights to See

⑥⑨ Geihinkan (Akasaka Detached Palace). Built in 1909, this was the home of the crown prince, who later became the Taishō emperor; the Geihinkan has served since 1974 as an official state guest house for visiting foreign dignitaries. Inspired by the Louvre and the Palace of Versailles, the architecture and the grounds and gardens bear witness to the fierce determination of the Meiji government to imitate the achievements of the West. The Geihinkan is a seven-minute walk west on Aoyama-dōri from the Akasaka-mitsuke intersection. ⊠ *2–1–1 Moto-Akasaka, Minato-ku,* ☎ *03/3478–1111. Subway: Yūraku-chō and Marunouchi lines, Akasaka-mitsuke Eki (Exit 8).*

⑥⑦ Hie Jinja. This shrine dates to the late 15th century and is dedicated principally to the Shintō deity Oyamakuni-no-kami. During the Edo period, the shrine became a favorite of the Tokugawa shogunate, which believed that Oyamakuni-no-kami took the city under his special protection. Several festivals take place here. By far the most important, held in alternate years, is the Sannō Matsuri (June 15), with processions of palanquins and attendants in historical costume that evoke the Tokugawa era—when the event was known as the Festival Without Equal. For the rest of the year, the shrine holds a special appeal for those seeking protection against miscarriages; in the main courtyard note the statue of the female monkey holding her offspring. Worshipers also visit the shrine to protect themselves against traffic accidents; it's not unusual to see a Shintō priest blessing a new car. Hie Jinja has been destroyed several times in fires. The present building dates to 1959, the torii to 1962. ⊠ *2–10–5 Nagata-chō, Chiyoda-ku.* ☒ *Free.* ☉ *Daily* *sunrise–sunset. Subway: Ginza and Marunouchi lines, Akasaka-mitsuke Eki (Exit 8).*

70 **Sōgetsu Kaikan.** The schools of ikebana, like those of other traditional arts, from music and dance to calligraphy and tea ceremony, are highly stratified organizations. Students rise through levels of proficiency, paying handsomely for lessons and certifications as they go, until they can become teachers themselves. At the top of the hierarchy is the *iemoto*, the head of the school, a title usually held within a family for generations. The Sōgetsu School of flower arrangement is a relative newcomer to all this. It was founded by Sōfū Teshigahara in 1927, and, compared to the older schools, it espouses a style flamboyant, free-form, and even radical. Detractors call it overblown, but it draws students and admirers from the world over, and it has made itself wealthy in the process. The main hall of the Sōgetsu Kaikan, created by the late Isamu Noguchi, one of the masters of modern sculpture, is well worth a visit. Noguchi's moving composition of carved stone slabs, cantilevered walkways, and flowing water are typical of his later career and reflect the influence of Zen aesthetics and his lifelong interest in the design of gardens and public spaces. Lessons in flower arrangement are given in English on Monday from 10 to noon. Sōgetsu Kaikan is a 10-minute walk west on Aoyama-dōri from the Akasaka-mitsuke intersection or east from the Aoyama-itchōme subway stop. ⊠ *7–2–21 Akasaka, Minato-ku,* ☎ *03/3408–1209.* ✍ *¥4,850 for 1st lesson, ¥3,800 thereafter. Reservations must be made a day in advance. Subway: Ginza and Marunouchi lines, Akasaka-mitsuke Eki; Ginza and Hanzō-mon lines, Aoyama-itchōme Eki (Exit 4).*

68 **Suntory Bijutsukan.** On the 11th floor of the Suntory Building, this museum houses a fine small collection of traditional paintings, prints, lacquerware, glassware, and costumes. It also holds special loan exhibits throughout the year. For the size of the museum, the admission price is high (and can be higher still for special exhibits), but its displays are carefully selected and well displayed. ⊠ *1–2–3 Moto-Akasaka, Minato-ku,* ☎ *03/3470–1073,* WEB *www.suntory.co.jp.* ✍ *¥1,000.* ☉ *Tues.– Thurs. and weekends 10–5, Fri. 10–7. Subway: Ginza and Marunouchi lines, Akasaka-mitsuke Eki (Exit B).*

NEED A
BREAK?

The Garden Lounge, in the main lobby of the Hotel New Otani Tōkyō and Towers, looks out on an immaculately sculpted 400-year-old Japanese garden, with red-lacquered bridges over ponds and waterfalls and winding paths: a perfect, if pricey, spot to unwind and have something to drink. At ¥2,800, the lunch buffet (11:30–2), with Continental and Chinese dishes, is a pretty good deal. ⊠ *4–1 Kioi-chō, Chiyoda-ku,* ☎ *03/5226–0246. Subway: Ginza and Marunouchi lines, Akasaka-mitsuke Eki (Exit 8).*

Aoyama, Harajuku, and Shibuya

Who would have known? As late as 1960, this was as unlikely a candidate as any area in Tōkyō to develop into anything remotely chic. True, there was the Meiji Jingū, which gave the neighborhood a certain solemnity and drew the occasional festival crowd. Between the Shrine and the Aoyama Cemetery to the east, however, the area was so unpromising that the municipal government designated a substantial chunk of it for low-cost public housing. Another chunk, called Washington Heights, was being used by U.S. occupation forces—who spent their money elsewhere. The few young Japanese people in Harajuku and Aoyama were either hanging around Washington Heights to practice their English or attending the Methodist-founded Aoyama Gakuin (Aoyama University)—and seeking their leisure farther south in Shibuya.

Then Tōkyō won its bid to host the 1964 Olympics, and Washington Heights was turned over to the city for the construction of the Olympic Village. Aoyama-dōri, the avenue through the center of the area, was improved; under it ran the extension of the Ginza Line subway, and later the Hanzō-mon Line. Public transportation is the chief ingredient in Tōkyō's commercial alchemy; suddenly, people could get to Aoyama and Harajuku easily, and they did—in larger and larger numbers, drawn by the Western-style fashion houses, boutiques, and design studios that decided this was the place to be. By the 1980s the area was positively *smart*. Two decades have passed since then, and parts of the area have gone a bit downhill, but it should still be high on your list of places to explore in Tōkyō.

On weekends the heart of Harajuku belongs to high school and junior high school shoppers, who flock here with hoarded sums of pocket money and for whom last week was ancient history. Harajuku is where the market researchers come, pick 20 teenagers off the street at random, give them ¥2,000, and ask them to buy a tote bag. Whole industries convulse themselves to keep pace with those adolescent decisions. Stroll through Harajuku—with its outdoor cafés, its designer ice cream and Belgian waffle stands, its ever-changing profusion of mascots and logos—and you may find it impossible to believe that Japan is in fact the most rapidly aging society in the industrial world.

Shibuya is south and west of Harajuku and Aoyama. Two subway lines, three private railways, the JR Yamanote Line, and two bus terminals move about a million people a day through Shibuya. The hub's commercial character is shaped by the fierce battle for supremacy between the Seibu and Tōkyū depāto. As fast as one of them builds a new branch, vertical mall, or specialty store, its rival counters with another. Shops, restaurants, and amusements in this area target a population of university students, young office workers, and consumers younger still.

Numbers in the text correspond to numbers in the margin and on the Aoyama, Harajuku, and Shibuya map.

A Good Walk

For more information on depāto and individual shops mentioned in this walk, *see* Shopping, *below*.

AOYAMA

Begin outside of the Gaien-mae subway station on Aoyama-dōri. This is also the stop for the Jingū Baseball Stadium, home field of the Yakult Swallows. You'll see it across the street from the Chichibu-no-miya Rugby and Football Ground. The stadium is actually within the **Meiji Jingū Gai-en** ⑦ (Outer Garden). The National Stadium—Japan's largest stadium, with room for 75,000 people, and the seat from which the city hosted the 1964 Summer Olympics—sits on the other side of this park.

From Gaien-mae, continue west some five blocks toward Shibuya, and turn left at the intersection where you see the Omotesandō subway station on the right-hand side of the avenue. Hold tight to your credit cards here: This is the east end of Omotesandō, Tōkyō's premier fashion boulevard, lined on both sides with the boutiques of couturiers like Issey Miyake, Missoni, Calvin Klein, and Comme des Garçons. At the far end of the street (a 15-minute walk at a brisk pace), across the intersection to the right, you'll see the walls of the **Nezu Institute of Fine Arts** ⑫.

From the Nezu Institute of Fine Arts, retrace your steps to Aoyama-dōri. If you turned left here, you would come in due course (it's a longish walk) to Shibuya, by way of the Aoyama Gakuin University campus on the left. **Aoyama Kodomo-no-Shiro** ⑦, for the child with you (or in you), is also to the left on Aoyama-dōri. To make your way to Harajuku, continue straight across Aoyama-dōri northwest on Omotesandō.

HARAJUKU

On the north side of Aoyama-dōri, Omotesandō becomes a broad divided boulevard lined with ginko trees, sloping gently downhill—and down-market—to the intersection of Meiji-dōri. True, a few conservative fashion houses dot the west boulevard, like Mori Hanae and Ralph Lauren. But the pulse of Harajuku beats at the rate of the adolescents who—with less to spend, perhaps, than a couturier's clientele—still take their apprenticeship as consumers very seriously indeed.

On the left side of the boulevard as you approach the Meiji-dōri intersection is the Oriental Bazaar, a store especially popular with foreign visitors for its extensive stock of Japanese, Korean, and Chinese souvenirs at reasonable prices; browse here for scroll paintings and screens, kimono fabrics, antiques, ceramics, and lacquerware. A few doors down is Kiddyland, one of the city's largest toy stores. On the northwest corner of the intersection itself is La Foret. With some 110 boutiques on five floors, this was one of the earliest of Tōkyō's characteristic vertical malls.

Here you might want to make a brief detour, to the right on Meiji-dōri and left at the corner of the third narrow side street, called Takeshita-dōri, which rises to JR Harajuku Eki at the other end. This is where the youngest of Harajuku's consumers gather, from all over Tōkyō and the nearby prefectures, packing the street from side to side and end to end, filling the coffers of stores with names like Rap City and Octopus Army. If Japanese parents ever pause to wonder where their offspring might be on a Saturday afternoon, Takeshita-dōri is the likely answer.

Retrace your steps to La Foret, turn right, and walk uphill on the right side of Omotesandō to the first corner. Turn right again, and a few steps from the corner on this small street you'll find the **Ōta Kinen Bijutsukan** ⑦—an unlikely setting for an important collection of traditional wood-block prints. Return to Omotesandō and walk up to the intersection at the top. Across the street to your right look for JR Harajuku Eki; straight ahead is the entrance to the Meiji Jingū Inner Garden and the **Meiji Jingū** ⑦ itself.

When you have finished exploring the grounds of the shrine, you have two options. You can leave the Inner Garden on the northwest side and walk west about five minutes from Sangū-bashi Eki on the private Odakyū railway line to the **Tōken Hakubutsukan** ⑦ to see its collection of swords. From there you can return to Sangū-bashi Eki and take the train two stops north to Shinjuku, the next major exploring section. The other possibility is to return to Harajuku Eki and take the JR Yamanote Line one stop south to Shibuya.

SHIBUYA

Begin your exploration of this area at JR Shibuya Eki.; use the **Statue of Hachiko** ⑦, in the plaza on the north side of the station, as a starting point. Cross the intersection and walk southwest on Dōgen-zaka. In a minute the street will fork at a vertical mall called the 109 Fashion Community; bear right on Bunka-mura-dōri and walk about four blocks to where the street suddenly narrows. Ahead of you will be the main branch of the Tōkyū depāto chain. Cross to the entrance and turn left to the **Bunka-mura** ⑦ complex of theaters, exhibition halls, shops, and restaurants on the next corner. Les Deux Magots, in the sunken courtyard of the complex is a good place for a light meal.

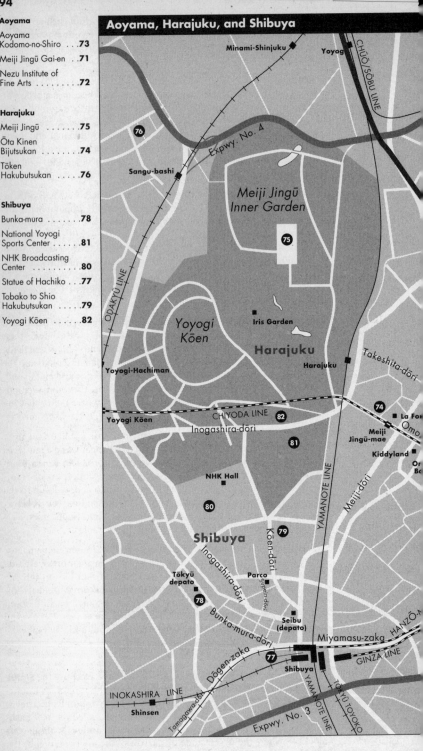

Aoyama, Harajuku, and Shibuya

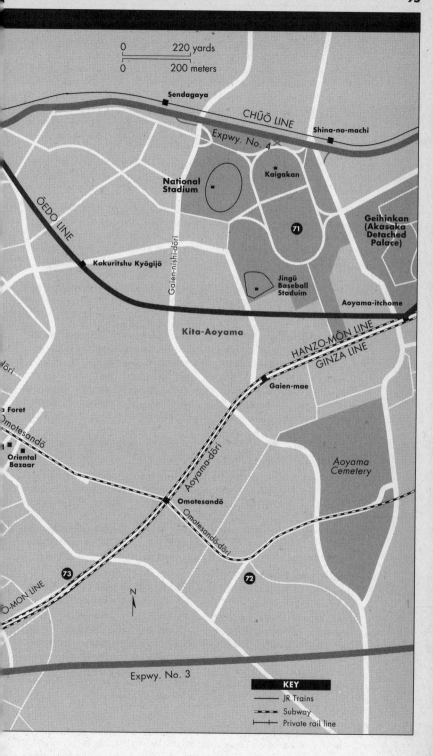

0 220 yards
0 200 meters

Sendagaya

CHŪO LINE

Expwy. No. 4

Shina-no-machi

Kaigakan

National
Stadium

ŌEDO LINE

71

Geihinkan
(Akasaka
Detached
Palace)

Kokuritshu Kyōgijō

Jingū
Baseball
Staduim

Aoyama-itchome

Kita-Aoyama

HANZO-MÔN LINE

GINZA LINE

Gaien-nishi-dōri

Gaien-mae

Foret

Omotesandō

Oriental
Bazaar

Aoyama-dōri

Aoyama
Cemetery

Omotesandō

Omotesandō-dōri

73

72

N

Ō-MON LINE

Expwy. No. 3

KEY

JR Trains
Subway
Private rail line

Return to Bunka-mura-dōri and walk back toward Shibuya station on the left side of the street to the second corner. Turn left at the first traffic light and walk north, crossing Sentā-gai, a street lined with fast-food shops, down-market clothing stores, and game centers, to Inogashira-dōri. Ahead of you, across the street, will be the entrance to Supein-dōri, the heart of Shibuya's appeal to young consumers: a narrow brick-paved passageway, climbing to a flight of steps at the other end, supposedly inspired by the Spanish Steps in Rome. Spain-dōri leads to Kōen-dōri, the smartest street in the neighborhood, by way of Parco (on the left), a vertical mall developed by the Seibu depāto conglomerate. The Parco Theater, on the top floor, has an interesting calendar of plays and art films. Farther up Kōen-dōri, on the right, is the **Tobako to Shio Hakubutsukan** ㉙, an interesting paean of sorts to the uses of tobacco and salt.

Turn left at the top of Kōen-dōri, and you'll see the **NHK Broadcasting Center** ㉚ across the street on your right. The building next to it, at the far north corner, is the 4,000-seat NHK Hall, the pride of which is a 7,640-pipe organ, the foremost of its kind in the world. West of the NHK Hall, across the street, is the **National Yoyogi Sports Center** ㉛. From here you can finish off Shibuya in either of two ways: Retrace your steps to JR Shibuya Eki, or walk through **Yoyogi Kōen** ㉜ along the extension of Omotesandō to Harajuku and the JR station there.

TIMING

Aoyama and Harajuku together make a long walk, with considerable distances between the sights. Ideally, you should devote an entire day to it, giving yourself plenty of time to browse in shops. You can see Meiji Jingū in less than an hour; the Nezu Institute warrants a leisurely two-hour visit. Don't be afraid to come on weekends; there are more people on the streets, of course, but people-watching is a large part of the experience of Harajuku. Spring is the best time of year for the Meiji Inner Garden; as with any other walk in Tōkyō, the June rainy season is horrendous, and the humid heat of midsummer can quickly drain your energy and add hours to the time you need for a comfortable walk.

Shibuya is fairly compact; you can easily cover it in about two hours. Unless you switch into shopping mode, no particular stop along the way should occupy you for more than half an hour; allow a full hour for the NHK Broadcasting Center, however, if you decide to take the guided tour. Spring is the best time of year for Yoyogi Kōen, and Sunday the best day. The area will be crowded, of course, but Sunday affords the best opportunity to observe Japan's younger generation on display.

Sights to See

㉓ **Aoyama Kodomo-no-Shiro** (National Children's Castle). This complex includes a swimming pool, a gym, and an audiovisual library. The 1,200-seat theater presents a range of concerts, plays, and other performances regularly throughout the year, especially for kids. At the Omotesandō subway station on the Ginza, Hanzō-mon, and Chiyoda lines, take the exit for Aoyama Gakuin and walk southwest on Aoyama-dōri about five minutes. Aoyama Kodomo-no-Shiro is on the right side of the avenue. ✉ 5–53–1 Jingū-mae, Shibuya-ku, ☎ 03/3797–5666. ☑ ¥500. ☉ Tues.–Fri. 12:30–5, weekends 10–5. Subway: Omotesandō Eki (Exit B2).

㉘ **Bunka-mura.** This six-story theater and gallery complex is a venture of the next-door Tōkyū depāto and one of the liveliest venues in Tōkyō for music and art, hosting everything from science-fiction film festivals to opera, from ballet to big bands. The design of the building would be impressive if there were any vantage point from which to see it whole. The museum on the lower-level Garden Floor often has well-planned, interesting exhibits on loan from major European museums. ✉ *2–2–4–1 Dōgen-zaka, Shibuya-ku, ☎ 03/3477–9111; 03/3477–9999 for ticket center.* ✉ *Theater admission and exhibit prices vary with events.* ☉ *Ticket counter in lobby open daily 10–7. Subway, JR, and private rail lines: Shibuya Eki (Kita-guchi/North Exit for JR Yamanote Line, Ginza subway line, and private rail lines; Exits 5 and 8 for Hanzō-mon subway line).*

<table>
<tr><td>

NEED A
BREAK?

</td><td>

Les Deux Magots, sister of the famed Paris café, in the Bunka-mura complex, serves a good selection of beers and wines, sandwiches, salads, quiches, tarts, and coffee. There's a fine art bookstore next door, and the tables in the courtyard are perfect for people-watching. ✉ *Bunka-mura, lower courtyard, 2–24–1 Dōgen-zaka, Shibuya-ku, ☎ 03/3477–9124. Subway, JR, and private rail lines: Shibuya (Kita-guchi/North Exit for JR Yamanote Line, Ginza subway line, and private rail lines; Exits 5 and 8 for Hanzō-mon subway line).*

</td></tr>
</table>

75 **Meiji Jingū.** The Meiji shrine honors the spirits of the emperor Meiji, who died in 1912, and the empress Shōken. It was established by a resolution of the Imperial Diet the year after the emperor's death to commemorate his role in ending the long isolation of Japan under the Tokugawa Shogunate and setting the country on the road to modernization. Completed in 1920 and virtually destroyed in an air raid in 1945, it was rebuilt in 1958 with funds raised in a nationwide public subscription.

The two torii at the entrance to the grounds of the jingū, made from 1,700-year-old cypress trees from Mt. Ari in Taiwan, tower 40 ft high; the crosspieces are 56 ft long. Torii are meant to symbolize the separation of the everyday secular world from the spiritual world of the Shintō shrine. The buildings in the shrine complex, with their curving green copper roofs, are also made of cypress wood. The surrounding gardens have some 100,000 flowering shrubs and trees, many of which were donated by private citizens.

The annual festival at Meiji Jingū takes place on November 3, the emperor's birthday, which is a national holiday. On the festival day and at New Year's, as many as a million people come to offer prayers and pay their respects. A variety of other festivals and ceremonial events are held at Meiji Jingū throughout the year; check by phone or on the shrine Web site to see what's scheduled during your visit. Even on a normal weekend the shrine draws thousands of visitors, but this seldom disturbs its mood of quiet gravitas: the faster and more unpredictable the pace of modern life, the more respectable the Japanese seem to find the certainties of the Meiji era.

The **Jingū Nai-en** (Inner Garden), where the irises are in full bloom in the latter half of June, is on the left as you walk in from the main gates, before you reach the shrine. Beyond the shrine is the **Treasure House,** a repository for the personal effects and clothes of Emperor and Empress Meiji—perhaps of less interest to gaijin than to the Japanese. ✉ *1–1 Kamizono-chō, Yoyogi, Shibuya-ku, ☎ 03/3379–5511,* WEB *www.meijijingu.or.jp.* ✉ *Shrine free, Treasure House ¥500, Inner Garden ¥500.* ☉ *Shrine daily sunrise–sunset. Inner Garden Mar.–Oct., daily 9–4:30; Nov.–Feb., daily 9–4. Treasure House daily 10–4 (closed 3rd Fri. of month). Subway: Chiyoda Line, Meiji-jingū-mae Eki; JR Yamanote Line, Harajuku Eki (Exit 2).*

71 **Meiji Jingū Gai-en** (Meiji Outer Garden). This park is little more than the sum of its parts. The Yakult Swallows play at **Jingū Baseball Stadium** (✉ *13 Kasumigaoka, Shinjuku-ku, ☎ 03/3404–8999*); the Japanese baseball season runs between April and October. The **National**

Stadium (✉ 10 Kasumigaoka, Shinjuku-ku, ☎ 03/3403–1151) was the main venue of the 1964 Summer Olympics and now hosts soccer matches. Some World Cup matches will be played here when Japan cohosts the event with Korea in autumn 2002. and East across the street from the National Stadium is the **Kaigakan** (Meiji Memorial Picture Gallery; ✉ 9 Kasumigaoka, Shinjuku-ku, ☎ 03/3401–5179), open daily 9–4:30 (¥500), which you needn't plan to see unless you are a particular fan of the emperor Meiji and don't want to miss some 80 otherwise undistinguished paintings depicting events in his life. *Subway: Ginza and Hanzō-mon lines, Gai-en-mae Eki (Exit 2); JR Chūō Line, Shina-no-machi Eki.*

㉛ National Yoyogi Sports Center. The center consists of two paired structures created by Kenzō Tange for the 1964 Olympics. Tange's design, of flowing ferroconcrete shell structures and cable-and-steel suspension roofing, successfully fuses traditional and modern Japanese aesthetics. The stadium, which can accommodate 15,000 spectators for swimming and diving events, and the annex, which houses a basketball court with a seating capacity of 4,000, are open to visitors when there are no competitions. ✉ 2–1–1 *Jinnan, Shibuya-ku,* ☎ 03/3468–1171. *Pool* ¥550. ☉ *Daily noon–4. JR Yamanote Line, Harajuku Eki (Exit 2).*

★ **㉒ Nezu Institute of Fine Arts.** This museum houses the private art collection of Meiji-period railroad magnate and politician Kaichirō Nezu. The permanent display in the main building (1955) and the annex (1990) includes superb examples of Japanese painting, calligraphy, and ceramics—some of which are registered as National Treasures—and Chinese bronzes, sculpture, and lacquerware. The institute also has one of Tōkyō's finest gardens, with more than 5 acres of shade trees and flowering shrubs, ponds, and waterfalls, and seven tea pavilions. Walk southeast on Omotesandō-dōri from the intersection of Aoyama-dōri about 10 minutes, where the street curves away to the left. The Nezu Institute is opposite the intersection, on the right, behind a low sandstone-gray wall. ✉ 6–5–1 *Minami-Aoyama, Minato-ku,* ☎ 03/3400–2536, WEB *www.nezu-muse.or.jp/indexže.html.* ¥1,000. ☉ *Tues.–Sun. 9–4. Subway: Ginza and Hanzō-mon lines, Omotesandō Eki (Exit A5).*

NEED A
BREAK?

How can you resist a café with a name like **Yoku Moku**? As you approach, you'll probably notice a steady stream of very smartly dressed young people on their way in and out. Tables alfresco in the tree-shaded courtyard continue to make Yoku Moku, which established itself as Japan's primo confectionery just after World War II, an Aoyama favorite. Its blue-tile front is on Omotesandō-dōri near the Nezu Institute. The café is open daily 10:30–6. ✉ 5–3–3 *Minami-Aoyama, Shibuya-ku,* ☎ 03/5485–3340. *Subway: Ginza, Chiyoda, and Hanzō-mon lines, Omotesandō Eki (Exit A4).*

㉚ NHK Broadcasting Center. The 23-story Japanese National Public Television facility was built as the Olympic Information Center in 1964. NHK (Nippon Hōsō Kyōkai) runs a "Studio Park" tour, in Japanese only, in the main building, during which you can see the latest developments in broadcast technology. The center is a 15-minute walk on Kōen-dōri from JR Shibuya Eki. ✉ 2–2–1 *Jinnan, Shibuya-ku,* ☎ 03/3465–1111. ¥200. ☉ *Daily 10–5. Closed 3rd Mon. of month, except Aug.*

★ **㉔ Ōta Kinen Bijutsukan** (Ōta Memorial Museum of Art). The gift of former Tōhō Mutual Life Insurance chairman Seizō Ōta, this is probably the city's finest private collection of ukiyo-e, traditional Edo-period wood-block prints. The works on display are selected and changed periodically from the 12,000 prints in the collection, which includes some extremely rare work by artists such as Hiroshige, Sharaku, and Utamaro. From JR Harajuku Eki, walk southwest downhill on Omote-sandō-dōri and turn left on the narrow street before the intersection of Meiji-dōri. The museum is less than a minute's walk from the corner, on the left. ✉ *1–10–10 Jingū-mae, Shibuya-ku,* ☎ *03/3403–0880.* 🎫 *¥500, special exhibitions ¥800.* ☉ *Tues.–Sun. 10:30–5. Closed from 1st to 4th of each month for new installations.*

⑦ Statue of Hachiko. The subject of at least one three-hanky motion picture, Hachiko is Japan's version of the archetypal faithful dog. Hachiko's master, a professor at the University of Tōkyō, would take the dog with him every morning as far as Shibuya Eki on his way to work, and Hachiko would go back to the station every evening to greet him on his return. One day in 1925 the professor failed to appear; he had died that day of a stroke. Every evening for the next seven years, Hachiko would go to Shibuya and wait there hopefully until the last train had pulled out of the station. Then the dog died, too, and his story made the newspapers. A handsome bronze statute of Hachiko was installed in front of the station, funded by thousands of small donations from readers all over the country. The present version is a replica; the original was melted down for its metal in World War II—but it remains a familiar landmark where younger people, especially, arrange to meet. ✉ *JR Shibuya Eki, West Plaza.*

⑦ Tobako to Shio Hakubutsukan (Tobacco and Salt Museum). A museum that displays examples of every conceivable artifact associated with tobacco and salt since the days of the Maya might not seem, at first, to serve a compelling social need, but the existence of the T&S reflects one of the more interesting facts of Japanese political life. Tobacco and salt were both made government monopolies at the beginning of the 20th century. Sales and distribution were eventually liberalized, but production remained under exclusive state control, through the Japan Tobacco and Salt Public Corporation, until 1985. The corporation was then privatized. Renamed Nihon Tabako Sangyō (Japan Tobacco, Inc.), it continues to provide comfortable, well-paying second careers—called *amakudari* (literally, "descent from Heaven")—for retired public officials. It remains Japan's exclusive producer of cigarettes, still holds a monopoly on the sale of salt, and dabbles in real estate, gardening supplies, and pharmaceuticals—ringing up sales of some $17 billion a year. Japan Tobacco, Inc., in short, has more money than it knows what to do with: so why not put up a museum? What makes this museum noteworthy is the special exhibit on the fourth floor of ukiyo-e on the themes of smoking and traditional salt production. T&S is a 10-minute walk on Kōen-dōri from Shibuya Eki. ✉ *1–16–8 Jinnan, Shibuya-ku,* ☎ *03/3476–2041,* 🌐 *www.jtnet.ad.jp.* 🎫 *¥100.* ☉ *Tues.–Sun. 10–5:30. Subway, JR, and private rail lines: Shibuya Eki (Kita-guchi/North Exit).*

⑦ Tōken Hakubutsukan (Japanese Sword Museum). It's said that in the late 16th century, before Japan closed its doors to the West, the Spanish tried to establish a trade here in weapons of their famous Toledo steel. The Japanese were politely uninterested; they had already been making blades of incomparably better quality for more than 600 years. Early Japanese sword smiths learned the art of refining steel from a pure iron sand called *tamahagane,* carefully controlling the carbon content by adding straw to the fire in the forge. The block of steel was repeatedly folded, hammered, and cross-welded to an extraordinary strength, then "wrapped" around a core of softer steel for flexibility. At one time there were some 200 schools of sword making in Japan; swords were prized not only for their effectiveness in battle but for the beauty of the blades and fittings and as symbols of the higher spirituality of the warrior caste. There are few inheritors of this art today. The Japanese Sword Museum offers a unique opportunity to see the works of noted sword smiths, ancient and modern—but don't expect any detailed explanations of them in English. ⊠ *4–25–10, Yoyogi, Shibuya-ku,* ☎ *03/3379–1386.* 🔒 *¥525.* ☉ *Tues.–Sun. 9–4. Odakyū private rail line, Sangū-bashi Eki.*

㉜ Yoyogi Kōen. Once a parade ground for the Imperial Japanese Army, this area was known in the immediate postwar period—when it was appropriated by the occupying forces for military housing—as Washington Heights. During the Tōkyō Games of 1964, it served as the site of the Olympic Village, and in 1967 it became a public park. On Sunday and holidays, a flea market takes place in the park, along the main thoroughfare that runs through it, opposite the National Yoyogi Sports Center. ⊠ *Jinnan 2-chōme. Subway: Chiyoda Line, Meiji Jingū-mae Eki (Exit 2); JR Yamanote Line, Harajuku Eki (Omotesandō exit).*

Shinjuku

If you have a certain sort of love for big cities, you're bound to love Shinjuku. Come here, and for the first time Tōkyō begins to seem *real*. Shinjuku is where all the celebrated virtues of Japanese society—its safety and order, its grace and beauty, its cleanliness and civility—fray at the edges.

To be fair about all this, the area has been at the fringes of respectability for centuries. When Ieyasu, the first Tokugawa shōgun, made Edo his capital, Shinjuku was at the junction of two important arteries leading into the city from the west. It became a thriving post station, where travelers would rest and refresh themselves for the last leg of their journey; the appeal of this suburban pit stop was its "teahouses," where the waitresses dispensed a good bit more than sympathy with the tea.

When the Tokugawa dynasty collapsed in 1868, the 16-year-old emperor Meiji moved his capital to Edo, renaming it Tōkyō, and modern Shinjuku became the railhead connecting it to Japan's western provinces. As the haunt of artists, writers, and students, it remained on the fringes of respectability; in the 1930s Shinjuku was Tōkyō's bohemian quarter. The area was virtually leveled during the firebombings of 1945—a blank slate on which developers could write, as Tōkyō surged west after the war. By the 1970s property values in Shinjuku were the nation's highest, outstripping even those of Ginza. Three subways and seven railway lines converge here. Every day more than 3 million commuters pass through Shinjuku Eki, making this the city's busiest and most heavily populated commercial center. The hub at Shinjuku—a vast, interconnected complex of tracks and terminals, depāto and shops—divides that property into two distinctly different subcities, Nishi-Shinjuku (West Shinjuku) and Higashi-Shinjuku (East Shinjuku).

After the Great Kantō Earthquake of 1923, Nishi-Shinjuku was virtually the only part of Tōkyō left standing; the whims of nature had given this one small area a gift of better bedrock. That priceless geological stability remained largely unexploited until the late 1960s, when technological advances in engineering gave architects the freedom to soar. Some 20 skyscrapers have been built here since then, including the Tōkyō Tochō complex, and Nishi-Shinjuku has become Tōkyō's 21st-century administrative center.

By day the quarter east of Shinjuku Eki is an astonishing concentration of retail stores, vertical malls, and discounters of every stripe and description. By night it is an equally astonishing collection of bars and clubs, strip joints, hole-in-the-wall restaurants, pinball parlors, and peep shows—just about anything that amuses, arouses, alters, or intoxicates is for sale in Higashi-Shinjuku, if you know where to look. Drunken fistfights are hardly unusual here; petty theft is not unknown. Not surprisingly, Higashi-Shinjuku has the city's largest—and busiest—police substation.

Numbers in the text correspond to numbers in the margin and on the Shinjuku map.

A Good Walk

For more information on depāto and individual shops mentioned in this walk, *see* Shopping, *below.*

NISHI-SHINJUKU

JR trains and subways will drop you off belowground at Shinjuku Eki; head for the west exit. You'll need to get up to the street level, in front of the Odakyū depāto, with the Keiō depāto on your left, to avoid the passageway under the plaza. Walk across the plaza, through the bus terminal, or take the pedestrian bridge on the north side. Traffic in front of the station is rather confusing—what you're looking for is the wide divided avenue on the other side, called Chūō-dōri (YON-GŌ GAIRO on some street markers) between the Fuji Bank on the left and the Dai-ichi Kangyō Bank on the right. Walk west on Chūō-dōri one block to the Shinjuku Center Building, cross at the traffic light, and turn right. In the next block is the tapering shape of the Yasuda Fire and Marine Insurance Building; the **Seiji Tōgō Museum** ⑧ is on the 42nd floor.

Retrace your steps to Chūō-dōri, turn right, and walk west to where the avenue dead-ends at Kyū-gō Gairo, also called Higashi-dōri. You'll see the 52-story Shinjuku Sumitomo Building, ahead of you to the right, and to the left the unmistakable shape of the Tōkyō Tochō complex—but you'll need to make a slight detour to reach it. Cross Kyū-gō Gairo, turn left, and walk south past the front of the Keiō Plaza Inter-Continental, the first of the high-rise hotels to be built in the area, to the next corner.

Across the street you'll see the blue phallic shape of the sculpture in front of the Shinjuku Monolith Building. Turn right and walk down-hill on Fureai-dōri. In the middle of this next block, on the left, is the Shinjuku NS Building. Opposite the NS Building, to the right, are the steps to the Citizens' Plaza of the adored and reviled **Tōkyō Tochō** ⑧.

From here you have two options. You can turn east and walk back along any of the streets parallel to Chūō-dōri that return you to Shinjuku Eki. You may want to stop (especially if you haven't included Akihabara on your Tōkyō itinerary) at one of the giant discount electronics stores in the area—Yodobashi and Doi are a block from the station—to get an eye- or bagful of the latest gadgets that Japan is churning out.

Or if you have energy to spare, leave the Tōkyō Tochō complex the way you came in, turn right, and walk west to Kōen-dōri, which runs along the east side of Shinjuku Chūō Kōen. Cross Kōen-dōri, turn left, and walk south about five minutes, past the end of the park (avoiding the expressway on-ramp), to the **Shinjuku Park Tower Building** ⑧, at the corner of the Kōshū Kaidō (Kōshū Highway). The Park Hyatt, on the topmost floors of this building, is a good place to stop for lunch or high tea.

From the intersection turn right and walk about five minutes south-west on the Kōshū Kaidō to the **Tōkyō Opera City** ⑧. There's an entrance to the Hatsudai subway station on the west side of the courtyard. Stop in at the Tower Building and see the architecture of the performance spaces of the Shin Kokuritsu Gekijō complex, and then ride the Keiō Shin-sen Line one stop back to Shinjuku Eki.

Shinjuku

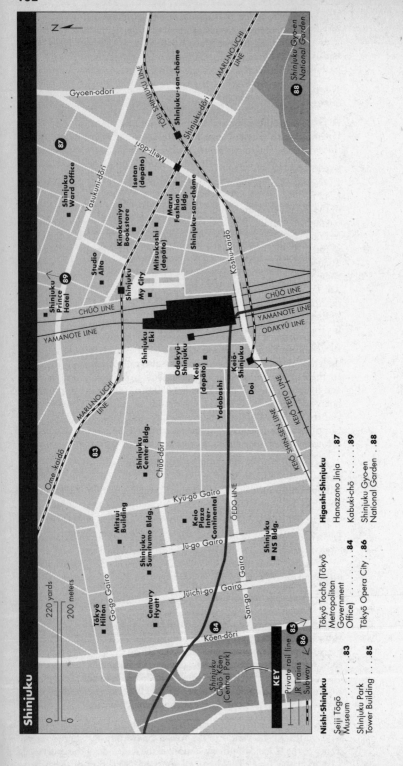

Nishi-Shinjuku

Seiji Tōgō
Museum **83**
Shinjuku Park
Tower Building **85**

Tōkyō Tochō (Tōkyō
Metropolitan
Government
Office) **84**
Tōkyō Opera City . . **86**

Higashi-Shinjuku

Hanazono Jinja . . . **87**
Kabuki-chō **89**

Shinjuku Gyo-en
National Garden . . **88**

KEY

————— Private rail line
———— JR Trains
- - - - - Subway

HIGASHI-SHINJUKU

From the east exit of Shinjuku Eki, you can't miss the huge video screen on the facade of Studio Alta. Under this building begins Subnade—the most extensive underground arcade in Tōkyō, full of shops and restaurants. Studio Alta is at the northwest end of Shinjuku-dōri, which on Sunday, when the area is closed to traffic, becomes a sea of shoppers. Turn right, and as you walk southeast, Kinokuniya Bookstore looms up on your left; the sixth floor is devoted to foreign-language books, including some 40,000 titles in English. On the next block, on the same side of the street, is Isetan depāto, with a foreign customer-service counter on the fifth floor. Mitsukoshi depāto and the Marui Fashion Building are on the opposite side of Shinjuk-dōri.

At the Isetan corner, turn left onto Meiji-dōri and walk north. Cross Yasukuni-dōri, and another minute will bring you to **Hanazono Jinja** ㊿. From here you can take two different directions—indeed, to two different worlds. You can retrace your steps to Isetan depāto and the Shinjuku-san-chōme subway station, and take the Marunouchi Line one stop east to Shinjuku-Gyo-en-mae, a few steps from the north end of **Shinjuku Gyo-en National Garden** ㊿. Visit the gardens and take the subway back to Shinjuku Eki. Another option is to walk back from Hanazono Jinja as far as Yasukuni-dōri and take a right. Two blocks farther on is the south end of rough-and-tumble **Kabuki-chō** ㊾, and from here you can easily return to Shinjuku Eki on foot.

If you'd like to finish the day with a kaiseki or bentō box meal, head for Yaozen, on the 14th floor of Takashimaya Times Square.

TIMING

Plan at least a full day for Shinjuku, if you want to see both the east and west sides. Subway rides can save you time and energy on the longer versions of these walks, but walking distances are still considerable. The Shinjuku Gyo-en National Garden is worth at least an hour, especially if you come in early April, in *sakura* (cherry blossom) time. The Tōkyō Tochō complex can take longer than you'd expect; lines for the elevators to the observation decks are often excruciatingly long. Sunday, when shopping streets are closed to traffic, makes the best day to tramp around Higashi-Shinjuku; the rainy season in late June and the sweltering heat of August are best avoided.

Sights to See

㊿ **Hanazono Jinja.** Constructed in the early Edo period, Hanazono is not among Tōkyō's most imposing shrines, but it does have one of the longest histories. Chief among the deities enshrined here is Yamatotakeru-no-Mikoto, a legendary hero, supposedly a 4th-century imperial prince, whose exploits are recounted in the earliest Japanese mythologies. His fame rests on the conquest of aboriginal tribes, which he did at the bidding of the Yamato Court. When he died, legends say, his soul took the form of a swan and flew away. Prayers offered here are believed to bring prosperity in business. The shrine is a five-minute walk north on Meiji-dōri from the Shinjuku-san-chōme subway station. ⊠ *5–17–3 Shinjuku, Shinjuku-ku,* ☎ *03/3200–3093.* ☜ *Free.* ☽ *Daily sunrise–sunset. Subway: Marunouchi Line, Shinjuku-san-chōme Eki (Exits B2 and B3).*

㊾ **Kabuki-chō.** In 1872 the Tokugawa-period formalities governing geisha entertainment were dissolved, and Kabuki-chō became Japan's largest center of prostitution. Later, when vice laws got stricter, prostitution just went a bit further underground, where it remains—deeply deplored and widely tolerated.

In an attempt to change the area's image after World War II, plans were made to replace Ginza's fire-gutted Kabuki-za with a new one in Shinjuku. The plans never came to fruition—the old theater was rebuilt. But the project gave the area its present name. Kabuki-chō's own multipurpose theater is the 2,000-seat **Koma Gekijō** (⊠ 1–19–1 Kabuki-chō, Shinjuku-ku). The building, which also houses several discos and bars, serves as a central landmark for the quarter.

Kabuki-chō means unrefined nightlife at its best and raunchy seediness at its worst. Neon signs flash; shills proclaim the pleasures of the places you particularly want to shun. Even when a place looks respectable, ask prices first—drinks can cost ¥5,000 or more in hostess clubs—and avoid the cheap *nomiya* (bars) under the railway tracks. All that said, you needn't be intimidated by the area: it *can* be fun, and it remains one of the least expensive areas of Tōkyō for nightlife. *JR Shinjuku Eki (Higashi-guchi/East Exit for JR lines; Exit B10, B11, B12, or B13 for Marunouchi Line).*

㉝ Seiji Tōgō Museum. The painter Seiji Tōgō (1897–1978) was a master of putting on canvas the grace and charm of young maidens. More than 100 of his works from the museum collection are on display here at any given time. This is also the museum that bought Van Gogh's *Sunflowers*. Yasuda CEO Yasuo Gotō acquired the painting in 1987 for ¥5.3 billion—at the time the highest price ever paid at auction for a work of art. He later created considerable stir in the media with the ill-considered remark that he'd like the painting cremated with him when he died. The gallery has an especially good view of the old part of Shinjuku. ⊠ *Yasuda Fire and Marine Insurance Bldg., 42nd floor, 1–26–1 Nishi-Shinjuku, Shinjuku-ku,* ☎ *03/3349–3081,* ⓦⓔⓑ *www.yasuda.co.jp/museum/museumžtitleže.html.* ⊡ *Varies depending on exhibit.* ◷ *Tues.–Thurs. and weekends 9:30–4:30, Fri. 9:30–6:30. Marunouchi and Toei Shinjuku subway lines (Exit A18), JR, Keiō Shin-sen and Teitō private rail lines: Shinjuku Eki (Nishi-guchi/West Exit or Exit N4 from the underground passageway).*

★ ㊳ Shinjuku Gyo-en National Garden. This lovely 150-acre park was once the estate of the powerful Naitō family of feudal lords, who were among the most trusted retainers of the Tokugawa shōguns. In 1871, after the Meiji Restoration, the family gave the grounds to the government, which—not quite ready yet to put such gems at the disposal of ordinary people—made it an imperial property. After World War II, the grounds were finally opened to the public. It's a perfect place for leisurely walks: paths wind their way through more than 3,000 kinds of plants, shrubs, and trees; artificial hills; ponds and bridges; and thoughtfully placed stone lanterns. There are different gardens in Japanese, French, and English styles as well as a greenhouse (the nation's first, built in 1885) filled with tropical plants. The best times to visit are April, when 75 different species of cherry trees—some 1,500 trees in all—are in bloom, and the first two weeks of October, during the chrysanthemum exhibition. ⊠ *11 Naitō-chō, Shinjuku-ku,* ☎ *03/3350–0151.* ⊡ *¥200.* ◷ *Tues.–Sun. 9–4; also open Mon. 9–4 in Apr. cherry-blossom season. Subway: Marunouchi Line, Shinjuku Gyo-en-mae Eki (Exit 1).*

㉟ Shinjuku Park Tower Building. The Shinjuku Park Tower has in some ways the most arrogant, hard-edged design of any of the skyscrapers in Nishi-Shinjuku, but it does provide any number of opportunities to rest and take on fuel. You might have picked a day, for example, when there's a free chamber-music concert in the atrium. Or you might have come for lunch at **Kushinobo** (☎ 03/5322–6400), on the lower level, for delicately deep-fried bamboo skewers of fish and vegetables. You might want simply to have an evening drink at the **Cafe Excelsior** (☎ 03/5322–6174). Or if you're here in the afternoon, indulge yourself and ride up to the skylighted bamboo garden of the Peak Lounge on the 41st floor of the **Park Hyatt Hotel** (☎ 03/5322–1234) for high tea and a spectacular view of the city. ⊠ *3–7–1 Nishi-Shinjuku, Shinjuku-ku. JR Shinjuku Eki (Nishi-guchi/West Exit).*

★ ⑧④ **Tōkyō Tochō** (Tōkyō Metropolitan Government Office). Work on architect Kenzō Tange's grandiose city hall complex, which now dominates the western Shinjuku skyline, began in 1988 and was completed in 1991. Built at a cost of ¥157 billion, it was clearly meant to remind observers that Tōkyō's annual budget is bigger than that of the average developing country. The complex consists of a main office building, an annex, the Metropolitan Assembly building, and a huge central courtyard, often the venue of open-air concerts and exhibitions. The design has inspired a passionate controversy: Tōkyōites either love it or hate it. It's been called everything from a "fitting tribute" to a "forbidding castle." The main building soars 48 stories, splitting on the 33rd floor into two towers. On a clear day, from the observation decks on the 45th floors of both towers, you can see all the way to Mt. Fuji and to the Bōsō Peninsula in Chiba Prefecture. Several other skyscrapers in the area have free observation floors—among them the Shinjuku Center Building, the Shinjuku Nomura Building, and the Shinjuku Sumitomo Building—but city hall is the best of the lot. The Metropolitan Government Web site, incidentally, is an excellent source of information on sightseeing and current events in Tōkyō. ⊠ *2–8–1 Nishi-Shinjuku, Shinjuku-ku,* ☎ *03/5321–1111,* WEB *www.metro.tokyo.jp.* 🎫 *Free.* ☉ *North and south decks both open daily 9:30–9:30. Marunouchi and Toei Shinjuku subway lines; JR; Keiō Shin-sen and Teitō private rail lines: Shinjuku Eki (Nishi-guchi/West Exit).*

⑧⑥ **Tōkyō Opera City.** Completed in 1997, this is certain to be the last major cultural project in Tōkyō for the foreseeable future. The west side of the complex is the Shin Kokuritsu Gekijō (New National Theater), consisting of the 1,810-seat Opera House, the 1,038-seat Playhouse, and an intimate performance space called the Pit, with seating for 468. Architect Helmut Jacoby's design for this building, with its reflecting pools and galleries and granite planes of wall, deserves real plaudits: the Shin Kokuritsu Gekijō is monumental and approachable at the same time.

The east side of the complex consists of a 55-story office tower—an uninspired atrium-style slab, forgettable in almost every respect—flanked by a sunken garden and art museum on one side and a concert hall on the other. The concert hall is astonishing: The sheer cost of the wood alone, polished panels of it rising tier upon tier, is staggering to consider. The amount of research involved to perfect the acoustics in its daring vertical design is even harder to imagine. ⊠ *3–20–2 Nishi-Shinjuku, Shinjuku-ku,* ☎ *03/5353–0700 for concert hall; 03/ 5351–3011 for National Theater,* WEB *www.tokyooperacity-cf.or.jp. Keiō Shin-sen private rail line: Hatsudai Eki (Higashi-guchi/East Exit).*

AROUND TŌKYŌ

The sheer size of the city and the diversity of its institutions make it impossible to fit all of Tōkyō's interesting sights into neighborhoods and walking tours. Plenty of worthy places—from Tōkyō Disneyland to sumō stables to the old Ōji district—fall outside the city's neighborhood repertoire. Yet no guide to Tōkyō would be complete without them. The sights below are marked on the Tōkyō Overview map at the beginning of this chapter.

Amusement Centers

🄲 **Kasai Seaside Park.** With two artificial beaches, a bird sanctuary, and the ☞ **Tōkyō Sea Life Park** aquarium spread over a stretch of landfill between the Arakawa and the Kyū-Edogawa rivers, Kasai Seaside Park is one of the major landmarks in the vast effort to transform Tōkyō Bay into Fun City. The **Daia to Hana no Dai-kanransha** (Great Ferris Wheel of Diamonds and Flowers), the tallest Ferris wheel in Japan, takes passengers on a 17-minute ride to the apex, 384 ft above the ground, for a spectacular view of the city. On a clear day you can see all the way to Mt. Fuji; at night, if you're lucky, you reach the top just in time for a bird's-eye view of the fireworks over the Magic Kingdom, across the river. To get here, take the JR Keiyō Line local train from Tōkyō Eki to Kasai Rinkai Kōen Eki; the park is a five-minute walk from the south exit. ⊠ *Rinkai-chō, Edogawa-ku,* ☎ *03/5696-4741.* ⊡ *Free, Ferris wheel ¥700.* ⊙ *Ferris wheel Sept.–July, Tues.–Fri. 10–8, weekends 10–9; Aug., weekdays 10–8, weekends 10–9.*

☾ **Kōrakuen.** The Kōrakuen stop on the Marunouchi subway line, about 10 minutes from Tōkyō Eki, lets you out in front of the **Tōkyō Dome,** Japan's first air-supported indoor stadium, built in 1988 and home to the Tōkyō Giants baseball team. Across the Tōkyō Expressway from the stadium is the **Kōrakuen Amusement Park**—chiefly noted for its stomach-churning giant roller coaster. ⊠ *1–3–61 Kōraku, Bunkyō-ku,* ☎ *03/3817-6098.* ⊡ *Full day to all rides ¥2,800, ¥800 5–closing.* ⊙ *Weekdays 10–6, weekends 9:30–6.*

☾ **Tōkyō Disneyland.** Since the amusement park opened in 1983, some 10 million people have been coming here every year. And at Tōkyō Disneyland, Mickey-san and his coterie of Disney characters entertain just the way they do in the California and Florida Disney parks, though the park is smaller than the parks in the United States.

There are several types of admission tickets. If you plan to see most of the attractions, the Tōkyō Disneyland Passport, at ¥5,500, is the most economical buy; also available are a weekday after–6 PM passport, at ¥2,900, and a weekend (and national holiday) after–5 PM passport, at ¥4,500. You can buy tickets in advance in Tōkyō Eki, near the Yaesu North Exit—look for red-jacketed attendants standing outside the booth—or from any travel agent, such as the Japan Travel Bureau.

The simplest way to get to Disneyland is by JR Keiyo Line from Tōkyō Eki to Maihama; the park is just a few steps from the station exit. From Nihombashi you can also take the Tōzai Line subway to Urayasu and walk over to the Tōkyō Disneyland Bus Terminal for the 15-minute ride, which costs ¥230. ⊠ *1–1 Maihama, Urayasu-shi,* ☎ *045/683–3333,* WEB *www.tokyodisneyland.co.jp.* ⊙ *Daily 9–8 (closing time may vary, so check before you go). Closed 6 days in Dec., 6 days in Jan., and 3 days in Feb.*

☾ **Toshima-en.** This large, well-equipped amusement park in the northwestern part of Tōkyō has four roller coasters, a haunted house, and seven swimming pools. What makes it special is the authentic Coney Island carousel—left to rot in a New York warehouse, discovered and rescued by a Japanese entrepreneur, and lovingly restored down to the last gilded curlicue on the last prancing unicorn. From Shinjuku, the new Tōei Ōedo Line subway goes directly to the park. ⊠ *3–25–1 Koyama, Nerima-ku,* ☎ *03/3990–3131.* ⊡ *All-day pass ¥3,800.* ⊙ *Thurs.–Mon. 10–6.*

Tōkyō Tower. In 1958, Tōkyō's fledgling TV networks needed a tall antenna array to transmit signals. Just emerging from the devastation of World War II, the nation's capital was also hungry for a landmark—a symbol for the aspirations of a city still without a skyline. The result was Tōkyō Tower: an unabashed knockoff of Paris's Eiffel Tower, but at 333 m (1,093 ft) even higher. The Grand Observation Platform, at 150 m (492 ft), and the Special Observation Platform, at 250 m (820 ft), quickly became major tourist attractions; they still draw some 3 million visitors a year, the vast majority of them Japanese youngsters on their first trip to the big city. A modest aquarium and a wax museum round out the tower's appeal as an amusement complex. The tower does provide a spectacular view of the city, and it gives Godzilla something to demolish periodically. This is a good diversion for kids, but get here soon: the antennas were originally built for analog broadcasting, and with Japan set to convert entirely to digital communications by 2010, a real demolition is already on the planning board. By 2003, a new 700-m (2,297-ft) tower will rise to take its place. ⊠ *4–2–8 Shiba-Kōen, Minato-ku,* ☎ *03/3433–5111.* ⊠ *¥820 to Grand Observation Platform, ¥600 additional to Special Observation Platform; aquarium ¥1,000; wax museum ¥870.* ☉ *Mar. 16–July 24 and Sept.–Nov. 15, daily 9–8; Jul. 25–Aug., daily 9–9; Nov. 16–Mar. 15, Mon.–Thurs. 9–7, Fri.–Sun. 9–8. Subway: Hibiya Line, Kamiyachō Eki (Exit 2).*

Zoo and Aquariums

🔄 **Shinagawa Suizokukan.** The fun part of this aquarium in southwestern Tōkyō is walking through an underwater glass tunnel while some 450 species of fish swim around and above you. There are, however, no pamphlets or explanation panels in English. Avoid Sundays, when the dolphin and sea lion shows draw crowds in impossible numbers. Take the local Keihin-Kyūkō private rail line from Shinagawa to Ōmori-kaigan Eki. Turn left as you exit the station and follow the ceramic fish on the sidewalk to the first traffic light; then turn right. You can also take the JR Tōkaidō Line to Oimachi Eki; when you arrive here, board a free shuttle to the aquarium from the No. 6 platform at the bus terminal. ⊠ *3–2–1 Katsushima, Shinagawa-ku,* ☎ *03/3762–3431.* ⊠ *¥900.* ☉ *Wed.–Mon. 10–4:30, dolphin shows 3 times daily, on varying schedule.*

🔄 **Sunshine International Aquarium.** The Sunshine International Aquarium has some 750 kinds of sea creatures on display and sea lion performances four times a day (except when it rains). An English-language pamphlet is available, and most of the exhibits have some English explanation. Take the JR Yamanote Line to Ikebukuro Eki (Exit 35) and walk about eight minutes west to the Sunshine City complex. You can also take the Yūraku-chō Line subway to Higashi-Ikebukuro Eki (Exit 2); Sunshine City and the aquarium are about a three-minute walk north. ⊠ *3–1–3 Higashi-Ikebukuro, Toshima-ku,* ☎ *03/3989–3466.* ⊠ *¥1,600.* ☉ *Sept. 3–July 19, Mon.–Sat. 10–6, Sun. 10–6:30; July 20–Sept. 2, daily 10–8:30.*

🔄 **Tama Dōbutsu Kōen.** More a wildlife park than a zoo, this facility in western Tōkyō gives animals room to roam; moats typically separate them from us. You can ride through the Lions Park in a minibus. To get here, take a Keiō Line train toward Takao from Shinjuku Eki and transfer at Takahata-Fudō Eki for the one-stop branch line that serves the park. ⊠ *7–1–1 Hodokubo, Hino-shi,* ☎ *0425/91–1611.* ⊠ *¥600.* ☉ *Thurs.–Tues. 9:30–4.*

🔄 **Tōkyō Sea Life Park.** The three-story cylindrical complex of this aquarium houses more than 540 species of fish and other sea creatures within three different areas: "Voyagers of the Sea" ("Maguro no Kaiyū"), with migratory species; "Seas of the World" ("Sekai no Umi"), with species from foreign waters; and the "Sea of Tōkyō" ("Tōkyō no Umi"), devoted to the creatures of the bay and nearby waters. To get here, take the JR Keiyō Line local train from Tōkyō Eki to Kasai Rinkai Kōen Eki; the aquarium is a 10-minute walk or so from the south exit. ⊠ *6–2–3 Rinkai-chō, Edogawa-ku,* ☎ *03/3869–5152.* ⊠ *¥700.* ☉ *Thurs.–Tues. 9:30–5.*

Off the Beaten Path

Asakura Sculpture Gallery. Outsiders have long since discovered the Nezu and Yanaka areas of Shitamachi—much to the dismay of the handful of foreigners who have lived for years in this charming, inexpensive section of the city. Part of the areas' appeal lies in the fact that some of the giants of modern Japanese culture lived and died here, including novelists Ōgai Mori, Sōseki Natsume, and Ryūnosuke Akutagawa; scholar Tenshin Okakura, who founded the Japan Art Institute; painter Taikan Yokoyama; and sculptors Kōun Takamura and Fumio Asakura. If there's one single attraction here, it's probably Asakura's home and studio, which was converted into a gallery after his death in 1964 and now houses many of his most famous pieces. The tearoom on the opposite side of the courtyard is a haven of quietude from which to contemplate his garden.

From the north wicket (Nishi-guchi/West Exit) of JR Nippori Eki, walk west—Tennō-ji temple will be on the left side of the street—until you reach a police box. Turn right, then right again at the end of the street; the museum is a three-story black building on the right, a few hundred yards from the corner. ✉ *7–18–10 Yanaka, Taitō-ku,* ☏ *03/ 3821–4549.* 🎟 *¥400.* ⊙ *Tues.–Thurs. and weekends 9:30–3:30.*

Odaiba. Tōkyō's latest leisure and commercial-development complex rises on more than 1,000 acres of landfill, connected to the city by the Yurikamome monorail from Shimbashi. Visitors come for the arcades, shopping malls, and museums, as well as the city's longest stretch (albeit artificial) of sand beach, along the boat harbor. There's also a Ferris wheel—a neon phantasmagoric beacon for anyone driving into the city across the Rainbow Bridge. With hotels and apartment buildings as well, this is arguably the most successful of the megaprojects on Tōkyō Bay.

From Shimbashi Eki (JR Karasumori Exit; Toei Asakusa subway line, Exit A2; Ginza subway line, Exit 4) follow the blue seagull signs to the monorail. You can pick up a map of Odaiba in English at the entrance. The Yurikamome Line makes 10 stops between Shimbashi and the terminus at Ariake; fares range from ¥310 to ¥370, but the best strategy is to buy a ¥1,000 prepaid card that allows you to make multiple stops at different points in Odaiba. The monorail runs every three to five minutes from 6 AM to 12:13 AM.

The first monorail stop on the island is **Odaiba Kaihin Kōen,** the closest point to the beach and the site of two massive shopping complexes. Aqua City has four floors of boutiques, movie theaters, cafés, and eateries—including a Starbucks and Hanashibe, an excellent sake-brewery restaurant on the third level. Overlooking the harbor is Decks Tōkyō Beach, a five-story complex of shops, restaurants, and boardwalks in two connected malls. Daiba Little Hong Kong, on the sixth and seventh floors of the Island Mall, has a collection of Cantonese restaurants and dim sum jōints on neon-lighted "streets" designed to evoke the real Hong Kong. At the Seaside Mall, a table by the window in any of the restaurants affords a delightful view of the harbor—especially at sunset, when the *yakata-bune,* the traditional covered boats designed for floating geisha parties, drift down the Sumida-gawa from Yanagibashi and Ryōgoku, their red paper lanterns twinkling in the half-light while the passengers wine and dine.

Architecture buffs should make time for **Daiba,** the second stop on the monorail, if only to contemplate the futuristic **Fuji Television Nippon Broadcasting Building** (✉ 2–4–8 Daiba, Minato-ku, ☏ 0180/993–188). From its fifth-floor Studio Promenade, you can watch programs being produced. The observation deck on the 25th floor affords a spectacular view of the bay and the graceful curve of the Rainbow Bridge. Admission is ¥500, and it's open Tuesday–Sunday 10–8.

Get off the monorail at the third stop, Fune no Kagakukan, for a visit to the **Fune-no-Kagakukan** (Museum of Maritime Science; ✉ 3–1 Higashi-Yashio, Shinagawa-ku, ☎ 03/5500–1111), which houses an impressive collection of models and displays on the history of Japanese shipbuilding and navigation. Built in the shape of an ocean liner, the museum is huge; if you're interested in ships, plan at least an hour here to do it justice. There are no English-language explanations at the museum. Anchored alongside the museum are the ferry *Yōtei-maru,* which for some 30 years plied the narrow straits between Aomori and Hokkaidō, and the icebreaker *Sōya-maru,* the first Japanese ship to cross the Arctic Circle. The museum is open daily 10–5; admission is ¥1,000.

The fun part of the **Nihon Gagaku Miraikan** (National Museum of Emerging Science and Innovation; ✉ 2–41 Aomi, Kōtō-ku, ☎ 03/3570–9151) is on the third floor, where you can watch robots in action, write with light pens, and play with various things that move. The rest of the museum is what the Japanese call *ō-majime* (deeply sincere)—five floors of thematic displays on environment-friendly technologies, life sciences, and the like with high seriousness and not much fun. The director of this facility, Dr. Mamoru Mohri, was Japan's first astronaut, who in 1992 logged some 460 hours in space aboard the NASA Spacelab-J Endeavor. Some of the exhibits have English-language explanations. It's a short walk here from the Museum of Maritime Science. Admission is ¥500, and it's open Sunday–Thursday 10–5, Friday–Saturday 10–7.

The fifth stop on the Yurikamome circuit of Odaiba is Aomi, gateway to the **Palette Town** complex of malls and amusements at the east end of the island. The uncontested landmark here is the Ferris wheel, modeled after the London Eye, the biggest in the world. It reaches 377 ft high and has 64 gondolas that carry six people each on a 16-minute circuit; the Ferris wheel is open daily 10–10 and costs ¥900. Adjacent to the Ferris wheel is Mega Web, ostensibly a complex of rides and multimedia amusements but in fact a showcase for the Toyota Motor Corporation. You can ride a car (hands off—the ride is electronically controlled) over a 1-km (½-mi) course configured like a roller coaster but moving at a stately pace. You can have any car you want, of course, as long as it's a Toyota. The **Venus Fort** shopping mall (✉ Palette Town 1-chōme, Aomi, Kōtō-ku, ☎ 03/3599–0700) at Aomi consists of galleries designed to suggest an Italian Renaissance palazzo, with arches and cupolas, marble fountains and statuary, and painted vault ceilings. The mall is chock-full of boutiques by the likes of Jean Paul Gaultier, Calvin Klein, Ralph Lauren, and all the other usual suspects.

★ **Ryōgoku.** Two things make this working-class shitamachi neighborhood worth a special trip: this is the center of the world of sumō wrestling as well as the site of the extraordinary Edo-Tōkyō Hakubutsukan. Just five minutes from Akihabara on the JR Sōbu Line, Ryōgoku is easy to get to, and if you've budgeted a leisurely stay in the city, it's well worth a morning's expedition.

The **Edo-Tōkyō Hakubutsukan** (✉ 1–4–1 Yokoami, Sumida-ku, ☎ 03/3626–9974, ᴡᴇʙ www.edo-tokyo-museum.or.jp) opened in 1993, more or less coinciding with the collapse of the economic bubble that had made the project possible. Money was no object in those days; much of the 30,000 square meters of the museum site is open plaza—an unthinkably lavish use of space. From the plaza the museum rises on massive pillars to the permanent exhibit areas on the fifth and sixth floors.

The escalator takes you directly to the sixth floor—and back in time 300 years. You cross a replica of the Edo-period Nihombashi Bridge into a truly remarkable collection of dioramas, scale models, cutaway rooms, and even whole buildings: an intimate and convincing experience of everyday life in the capital of the Tokugawa shōguns. Equally elaborate are the fifth-floor re-creations of early modern Tōkyō, the "Enlightenment" of Japan's headlong embrace of the West, and the twin devastations of the Great Kantō Earthquake and World War II. If you only visit one nonart museum in Tōkyō, make this it.

To get to the Edo-Tōkyō Hakubutsukan, leave Ryōgoku Eki by the west exit, immediately turn right, and follow the signs. The moving sidewalk and the stairs bring you to the plaza on the third level; to request an English-speaking volunteer guide, use the entrance to the left of the stairs instead, and ask at the General Information counter in front of the first-floor Special Exhibition Gallery. The fee for the museum is ¥600; special exhibits cost extra. The museum is open Tuesday–Wednesday and weekends 10–6, Thursday–Friday 10–8 (closed December 28–January 4 and on Tuesdays when Monday is a national holiday).

Walk straight out to the main street in front of the west exit of Ryōgoku Eki, turn right, and you come almost at once to the **Kokugikan** (National Sumō Arena), with its distinctive copper-green roof. If you can't attend one of the Tōkyō sumō tournaments, you may want to at least pay a short visit to the **Sumō Hakubutsukan** (⊠ 1–3–28 Yokoami, Sumida-ku, ☎ 03/3622–0366), in the south wing of the arena. There are no explanations in English, but the museum's collection of sumō-related wood-block prints, paintings, and illustrated scrolls includes some outstanding examples of traditional Japanese fine art. Admission is free and it's open weekdays 10–4:30.

Sumō wrestlers are not free agents; they must belong to one or another of the stables officially recognized by the Sumō Association. Although the tournaments and exhibition matches take place in different parts of the country at different times, all the stables—now some 30 in number—are in Tōkyō, most of them concentrated on both sides of the Sumida-gawa near the Kokugikan. Wander this area when the wrestlers are in town (January, May, and September are your best bets) and you're more than likely to see some of them on the streets, in their wood clogs and kimonos. Come 7 AM–11 AM, and you can peer through the doors and windows of the stables to watch them in practice sessions. One of the easiest to find is the **Tatsunami Stable** (⊠ 3–26–2 Ryōgoku), only a few steps from the west end of Ryōgoku Eki (turn left when you go through the turnstile and left again as you come out on the street; then walk along the station building to the second street on the right). Another, a few blocks farther south, where the Shuto Expressway passes overhead, is the **Izutsu Stable** (⊠ 2–2–7 Ryōgoku).

Sengaku-ji. One day in the year 1701, a young provincial baron named Asano Takumi-no-Kami, serving an official term of duty at the shōgun's court, attacked and seriously wounded a courtier named Yoshinaka Kira. Kira had demanded the usual tokens of esteem that someone in his high position would expect for his goodwill; Asano refused, and Kira humiliated him in public to the point that he could no longer contain his rage.

Kira survived the attack. Asano, for daring to draw his sword in the confines of Edo Castle, was ordered to commit suicide. His family line was abolished and his fief confiscated. Headed by Kuranosuke Ōishi, the clan steward, 47 of Asano's loyal retainers vowed revenge. Kira was rich and well protected; Asano's retainers were *rōnin*—masterless samurai. It took them almost two years of planning, subterfuge, and hardship, but on the night of December 14, 1702, they stormed Kira's villa in Edo, cut off his head, and brought it in triumph to Asano's tomb at Sengaku-ji, the family temple. Ōishi and his followers were sentenced to commit suicide—which they accepted as the reward, not the price, of their honorable vendetta—and were buried in the temple graveyard with their lord.

The event captured the imagination of the Japanese like nothing else in their history. Through the centuries it has become the national epic, the last word on the subject of loyalty and sacrifice, celebrated in every medium from Kabuki to film. The temple still stands, and the graveyard is wreathed in smoke from the bundles of incense that visitors still lay reverently on the tombstones.

The story gets even better. There's a small museum on the temple grounds with a collection of weapons and other memorabilia of the event. One of these items dispels forever the myth of Japanese vagueness and indirection in the matter of contracts and formal documents. Kira's family, naturally, wanted to give him a proper burial, but the law insisted this could not be done without his head. They asked for it back, and Ōishi—mirror of chivalry that he was—agreed. He entrusted it to the temple, and the priests wrote him a receipt, which survives even now in the corner of a dusty glass case. "Item," it begins, "One head."

Take the Toei Asakusa subway line to Sengaku-ji Eki (Exit A2), turn right when you come to street level, and walk up the hill. The temple is past the first traffic light, on the left. ⊠ *2–11–1 Takanawa, Minato-ku,* ☎ *03/3441–5560,* WEB *www.cssi.co.jp.* ⌧ *Temple and grounds free, museum ¥200.* ⊘ *Daily 7–6, museum daily 9–4.*

Toden Arakawa Line. Want to take a trip back in time? Take the JR Yamanote Line to Ōtsuka, cross the street in front of the station, and change to the Toden Arakawa Line—Tōkyō's last surviving trolley. Heading east, the trolley takes you through the back gardens of old neighborhoods on its way to Ōji—once the site of Japan's first Western-style paper mill, built in 1875 by Ōji Paper Company, Ltd., the nation's oldest joint-stock company. The mill is long gone, but the memory lingers on at the **Akuka-yama Ōji Paper Museum.** Some exhibits here show the process of milling paper from pulp. Others illustrate the astonishing variety of products that can be made from paper. The museum is a minute's walk from the trolley stop at Asuka-yama Kōen: you can also get here from the JR Ōji Eki (Minami-guchi/South Exit) on the Keihin–Tōhoku Line, or the Nishigahara Eki (Asuka-yama Exit) on the Namboku Line subway. ⊠ *1–1–3 Ōji, Kita-ku,* ☎ *03/3916–2320.* ⌧ *¥300.* ⊘ *Tues.–Sun. 10–4:30.*

DINING

At last count, there were more than 190,000 bars and restaurants in Tōkyō. In the bubble economy of the late 1980s, when money seemed to be no meaningful obstacle to anything, dining out became grotesquely expensive: it was possible to spend $1,000 on a steak dinner. The feeding frenzy is over now; wining and dining are still a major component of the Japanese way of life, but a far more sober mood prevails, and that is reflected in the range and cost of restaurants. The high end of the market, of course, has not disappeared, but Tōkyō's myriad choices also include a fair number of bargains—good cooking of all sorts that you can enjoy even on a modest budget. Food and drink, even at street stalls, are safe wherever you go.

For an international city, Tōkyō is still stubbornly provincial in many ways. Whatever the rest of the world has pronounced good, however, eventually makes its way here: French, Italian, Chinese, Indian, Middle Eastern, Latin American. It's hard to think of a cuisine of any prominence that goes unrepresented, as Japanese chefs by the thousand go abroad, hone their craft, and bring it home to this city.

Restaurants in Japan naturally expect most of their clients to be Japanese, and the Japanese are the world's champion modifiers. Only the most serious restaurateurs refrain from editing some of the authenticity out of foreign cuisines; in areas like Shibuya, Harajuku, and Shinjuku, all too many of the foreign restaurants cater to students and young office workers, who come mainly for the *fun'iki* (atmosphere). Choose a French bistro or Italian trattoria in these areas carefully, and expect to pay dearly for the real thing. That said, you can count on the fact that the city's best foreign cuisine is world-class.

A number of France's two- and three-star restaurants, for example, have established branches and joint ventures in Tōkyō, and they regularly send their chefs over to supervise. The style almost everywhere is still nouvelle cuisine: small portions, with picture-perfect garnishes and light sauces. More and more, you find interesting fusions of French and Japanese culinary traditions. Meals are served in poetically beautiful presentations, in bowls and dishes of different shapes and patterns. Recipes make imaginative use of fresh Japanese ingredients, like *shimeji* mushrooms and local wild vegetables.

In recent years Tōkyōites have also had more and more opportunities to experience the range and virtuosity of Italian cuisine; chances are good that a trattoria here will measure up to even Tuscan standards. Indian food here is also consistently good—and relatively inexpensive. Local versions of California-style American cooking are often admirable. Chinese food is the most consistently modified; it can be quite appetizing, but for repertoire and richness of taste, it pales in comparison to Hong Kong fare. Significantly, Tōkyō has no Chinatown.

The quintessential Japanese restaurant is the *ryōtei,* something like a villa, most often walled off from the bustle of the outside world and divided into a number of small, private dining rooms. These rooms are traditional in style, with tatami-mat floors, low tables, and a hanging scroll or a flower arrangement in the alcove. One or more of the staff is assigned to each room to serve the many dishes that compose the meal, pour your sake, and provide light conversation. Think of a ryōtei as an adventure, an encounter with foods you've likely never seen before and with a centuries-old graceful, almost ritualized style of service unique to Japan. Many parts of the city are proverbial for their ryōtei; the top houses tend to be in Akasaka, Tsukiji, Asakusa, and nearby Yanagi-bashi, and Shimbashi.

A few pointers are in order on the geography of food and drink. The farther "downtown" you go—into Shitamachi—the less likely you are to find the real thing in foreign cuisine. There is superb Japanese food all over the city, but aficionados of sushi swear (with excellent reason) by Tsukiji, where the central fish market supplies the neighborhood's restaurants with the freshest ingredients; the restaurants in turn serve the biggest portions and charge the most reasonable prices. Asakusa takes pride in its tempura restaurants, but tempura is reliable almost everywhere, especially at branches of the well-established, citywide chains. Every depāto and skyscraper office building in Tōkyō devotes at least one floor to restaurants; none of them stand out, but all are inexpensive and quite passable places to lunch. When in doubt for dinner, note that Tōkyō's top-rated international hotels also have some of the city's best places to eat and drink.

Dining out in Tōkyō does not ordinarily demand a great deal in the way of formal attire. If it's a business meal, of course, and your hosts or guests are Japanese, dress conservatively: for men, a suit and tie; for women, a dress or suit in a basic color, stockings, and a minimum of jewelry. On your own, you'll find that only a very few upscale Western venues (mainly the French and Continental restaurants in hotels) will even insist on ties for men; follow the unspoken dress codes you'd observe at home and you're unlikely to go wrong. For Japanese-style dining on tatami floors, keep two things in mind: wear shoes that slip on and off easily and presentable socks, and choose clothing you'll be comfortable in for a few hours with your legs gathered under you.

Price-category estimates for the restaurants below are based on the cost of a main Western-style course at dinner or a typical Japanese-style meal per person, excluding drinks, taxes, and service charges; a restaurant listed as $$ can easily slide up a category to $$$ when it comes time to pay the bill.

CATEGORY	COST*
$$$$	over ¥9,000
$$$	¥6,000–¥9,000
$$	¥2,500–¥6,000
$	under ¥2,500

per person for a main course at dinner

Akasaka

Indian

$–$$ ✕ **Moti.** Vegetarian dishes at Moti, especially the lentils and eggplant, are very good; so is the chicken *masala*, cooked in butter and spices. Moti has the inevitable Indian friezes, copper bowls, and white elephants, but the owners have not gone overboard on decor. The appeal here is food, as it should be. Cooks here are recruited from India by a family member who runs a restaurant in Delhi. There are other branches of Moti in Tōkyō, but the Akasaka branch, right by the Chiyoda Line subway station, is the easiest to get into and the most comfortable. ✉ *Kimpa Bldg., 3rd floor, 2–14–31 Akasaka, Minato-ku,* ☎ *03/3584–6640. AE, DC, MC, V. Subway: Chiyoda Line, Akasaka stop (Exit 2).*

Italian

$$–$$$ ✕ **La Granata.** On the basement level of the Tōkyō Broadcasting Systems building, La Granata and its companion restaurant, Granata Moderna, are both very popular with the media crowd upstairs—deservedly so: the chefs prepare some of the most accomplished, professional Italian food in town. La Granata is decked out trattoria style, with brickwork arches and red checkered tablecloths; Granata Moderna has the same menu but reaches for elegance with a polished rosewood bar, art-deco mirrors, and stained glass. Specialties worth trying include spaghetti with garlic and red pepper and the batter-fried zucchini flowers filled with mozzarella and asparagus. ✉ *TBS Kaikan, basement, 5–3–3 Akasaka, Minato-ku,* ☎ *03/3582–5891. AE, MC, V. Subway: Chiyoda Line, Akasaka Eki (Exit 1A).*

Japanese

$$–$$$ ✕ **Kisoji.** The specialty here is *shabu-shabu* (thin slices of beef cooked in boiling water at your table and dipped in sauce). Normally, this is an informal—if pricey—sort of meal; after all, you do get to play with your food a bit. Kisoji, however, adds a dimension of posh to the experience: private dining rooms with tatami seating, elegant little rock gardens, and alcoves with flower arrangements—all the tasteful appointments of a traditional ryōtei. ✉ *3–10 Akasaka, Minato-ku,* ☎

03/3588–0071. AE, MC, V. Subway: Ginza and Marunouchi lines, Akasaka-mitsuke Eki (Belle Vie Akasaka Exit).

Akasaka-mitsuke

American

$$$ ✕ **Tōkyō Joe's.** The very first foreign branch of famed Miami Joe's opened in Ōsaka, a city where volume-for-value really counts in the reputation of a restaurant. The Tōkyō branch upholds its reputation the same way—by serving enormous quantities of stone crab, with melted butter and mustard-mayonnaise. The turnover here is fierce; waiters in long red aprons scurry to keep up with it, but service is remarkably smooth. The crabs are flown in fresh from the Florida Keys, their one and only habitat. There are other choices on the menu, but it's madness to order anything else. Top it all off—if you have room—with key lime pie. ✉ *Akasaka Eight-One Bldg. B1, 2–13–5 Nagata-chō, Chiyoda-ku,* ☎ *03/3508–0325. AE, DC, MC, V. Subway: Ginza and Marunouchi lines, Akasaka-mitsuke Eki (Belle Vie Akasaka Exit).*

Japanese

$ ✕ **Sawanoi.** The homemade *udon* noodles served at Sawanoi make for a perfect light meal or a midnight snack. The menu, available in English, lists a range of noodle dishes, hot and cold, served in combination with seafood, vegetables, or meat. Try the *inaka* (country-style) udon, which has bonito, seaweed flakes, radish shavings, and a raw egg dropped in to cook in the hot broth. For a heartier meal, chose the *tenkama* set, which consists of hot udon and tempura that you dip in a delicate soy-based sauce. Sawanoi is one of the last remaining neighborhood shops in this stylish business district, and its decor is a bit on the grungy side. Excellent food and friendly service more than make up for it. ✉ *Shimno Bldg., 1st floor, 3–7–13 Akasaka, Minato-ku,* ☎ *03/3582–2080. No credit cards. Closed Sun. Subway: Ginza and Marunouchi lines, Akasaka-mitsuke Eki (Belle Vie Akasaka Exit).*

Aoyama

Japanese

$$–$$$$ ✕ **Maisen.** You're likely to spend some time soaking in a Japanese bath-
★ house; eating in one is a different story. Maisen was converted from a former *sentō* (public bathhouse) in 1983, and you'll find the old high ceiling, characteristic of bathing rooms built during the first quarter of the 20th century, as well as the original signs instructing bathers where to change, intact. Large bouquets of seasonal flowers help transform the large, airy space into a pleasant dining room. *Tonkatsu* (deep-fried pork cutlets) is Maisen's chef d'oeuvre. Though it's more expensive than the regular tonkatsu roast, consider trying *kuroi buta no hire* (fillet of Chinese black pork), which is very juicy and tender. Spoon a generous serving of sauce—sweet, spicy, or extra thick for black pork—over the cutlets and the shredded cabbage that comes with the sets. Miso soup and rice are also included. Or consider salmon dishes, of which the most elegant is the *oyako* set: bite-size pieces of salmon with salmon roe. There are no-smoking rooms upstairs. ✉ *4–8–5 Jingū-mae, Shibuya-ku,* ☎ *03/3470–0071. No credit cards. Ginza, Chiyoda, and Hanzō-mon lines, Omotesandō Eki (Exit A2).*

$–$$ ✕ **Higo-no-ya.** This restaurant specializes in a style called *kushi-yaki,* which refers simply to a variety of ingredients—meat, fish, vegetables— cut into bits and grilled on bamboo skewers. There's nothing ceremonious or elegant about kushi-yaki; it resembles the more familiar yakitori, except that there is more variety to it. At Higo-no-ya you can feast on such dishes as shiitake mushrooms stuffed with minced chicken; scallops wrapped in bacon; and bonito, shrimp, and eggplant with ginger. The decor here is a postmodern-traditional cross, with wood beams painted black, paper lanterns, and sliding paper screens. There's tatami, table, and counter seating. Also, a helpful English menu is available. ⊠ *AG Bldg. B1, 3–18–17 Minami-Aoyama, Minato-ku,* ☎ *03/3423–4462. AE, V. No lunch. Subway: Ginza, Chiyoda, and Hanzō-mon lines, Omotesandō Eki (Exit A4).*

Asakusa

Japanese

$$ ✕ **Tatsumiya.** This is a ryōtei with at least two delightfully untraditional features: it is neither inaccessible nor outrageously expensive. Most ryōtei tend to oppress the first-time visitor a little with the weight of their antiquity and the ceremonious formality of their service. Tatsumiya, which opened in 1980, takes a different attitude to the past: the rooms are almost cluttered with antique chests, braziers, clocks, lanterns, bowls, utensils, and craft work (some of which are for sale). The cuisine itself follows the kaiseki repertoire, derived from the tradition of the tea-ceremony meal. Seven courses are offered, including something raw, something boiled, something vinegared, something grilled. You must arrive before 8:30 for dinner. ⊠ *1–33–5 Asakusa, Taitō-ku,* ☎ *03/3842–7373. Jacket and tie. No credit cards. Closed Mon. and 3rd Sun. of month. No lunch. Subway: Ginza and Toei Asakusa lines, Asakusa Eki (Exit 1 or 3).*

$–$$ ✕ **Aoi-Marushin.** If not the most elegant, this is surely the largest tempura restaurant in Tōkyō, with six floors of table and tatami seating. Aoi-Marushin is used to—nay, enjoys—having foreign customers and makes a visit easy with English menus. This is essentially a family restaurant; don't expect much in the way of decor—just lots of food at very reasonable prices. Asakusa is a must on any itinerary, and tempura *teishoku* (an assortment of delicately batter-fried fish, seafood, and fresh vegetables) is the specialty of the district. Aoi-Marushin's location, just a few minutes' walk from the entrance to Sensō-ji, makes it an obvious choice after a visit to the temple. ⊠ *1–4–4 Asakusa, Taitō-ku,* ☎ *03/3841–0110. AE, MC, V. Subway: Ginza and Toei Asakusa lines, Asakusa Eki (Exit 1).*

Azabu-jūban

Korean

$$ ✕ **Sankō-en.** With the embassy of the Republic of Korea a few blocks away, Sankō-en is in a neighborhood thick with barbecue joints; from the outside, not much seems to distinguish one from another. From the beginning, however, Sankō-en drew customers in droves, not just from the neighborhood but from trendy nearby Roppongi as well. It opened one branch, then another, and moved the main operation to new quarters—and customers are still lining up at all hours to get in. Korean barbecue is a smoky affair; you cook your own dinner—thin slices of beef and brisket and vegetables—on a gas grill at your table. Sankō-en also makes a great salad to go with its brisket. ⊠ *1–8–7 Azabu-jūban, Minato-ku,* ☎ *03/3585–6306. Reservations not accepted. AE, V. Closed Wed. Subway: Namboku and Toei Ōedo Lines, Azabu-jūban Eki (Exit 7).*

Daikanyama

Contemporary

$$–$$$ ✕ **Tableaux.** The mural in the bar depicts the fall of Pompeii, the ban★ quettes in the restaurant are upholstered in red leather, and the walls are papered in antique gold. So with pony-tailed waiters gliding hither and yon, you suspect that somebody here really *believes* in Los Angeles. Tableaux may lay on more glitz than it really needs, but the service is cordial and professional, and the food is superb. Try *bruschetta* (toasted bread with tomato, basil, and olive oil), fettuccine with smoked salmon and sun-dried tomatoes, or grilled pork chop stuffed with chutney, onion, and garlic. Tableaux's bar is open until 1:30 AM. ⊠ *Sunroser Daikanyama Bldg., basement, 11–6 Sarugaku-chō, Shibuya-ku,* ☎ *03/5489–2201. AE, DC, MC, V. No lunch. Tōkyū Toyoko private rail line, Daikanyama Eki (Kita-guchi/North Exit).*

Pan-Asian

$–$$ ✕ **Monsoon Cafe.** Thanks to places like this, the demand for "ethnic" food—which by local definition means spicy and primarily Southeast Asian—continues apace in Tōkyō. The Monsoon Cafe complements its eclectic menu with an aggressively "ethnic" decor: rattan furniture, brass tableware from Thailand, colorful papier-mâché parrots on gilded stands, Balinese carvings, and ceiling fans. The best seats in the house are on the balcony that runs around the four sides of a huge atrium-style central floor space. Try the Vietnamese steamed spring rolls, the Indonesian grilled chicken with peanut sauce, or the Chinese-style beef with oyster sauce. The place stays open until 5 AM daily. ⊠ *15–4 Hachiyama-chō, Shibuya-ku,* ☎ *03/5489–3789. AE, DC, MC, V. Tōkyū Toyoko private rail line, Daikanyama Eki (Kita-guchi/North Exit).*

Ebisu

Eclectic

$–$$ ✕ **Ninnikuya.** In Japanese, *ninniku* means "garlic"—an ingredient conspicuously absent from the traditional local cuisine and one that the Japanese were once supposed to dislike. Not so nowadays, if you can believe the crowds that cheerfully line up for hours to eat at this cluttered little place in the Ebisu section. Owner-chef Eiyuki Endo discovered his own passion for the savory bulb in Italy in 1976. Since then he has traveled the world for interesting garlic dishes. Endo's family owns the building, so he can give free rein to his artistry without charging a lot. There is no decor to speak of, and you may well have to share a table, but it's all good fun. Try the littleneck clams Italian style with garlic rice, or the Peruvian garlic chicken. Ninnikuya is a little hard to find, but anybody you ask in the neighborhood can point the way. ⊠ *1–26–12 Ebisu, Shibuya-ku,* ☎ *03/3446–5887. Reservations not accepted. No credit cards. Closed Mon. No lunch. JR and Hibiya Line, Ebisu Eki (Higashi-guchi/East Exit).*

Ginza

American

$ ✕ **Farm Grill.** Tōkyō could use a few more restaurants like the Farm
★ Grill, which specializes in innovative California-style cuisine in generous portions at truly reasonable prices. Generous also is the space, vast by any standard: there's seating at the Farm Grill for 260, at wood-block pedestal tables with rattan chairs. The focus here is on hearty salads and sandwiches, pasta and rotisserie entrées, and rich desserts—the carrot cake is pretty good, the linzertorte to die for. Try the Caesar salad, pasta Malibu (penne with chicken, mushrooms, bacon, mozzarella, and fresh herbs), or the house chili. There are more than 90 entries on the wine list, a good percentage of them at ¥1,500 or less. The all-you-can-eat dinner buffet at the Farm Grill is ¥1,900 for women, ¥2,900 for men. Can this be politically correct? Add ¥1,000 for all you can drink, and the question will probably trouble you less. ⊠ *Ginza Nine 3 Gokan, 2nd floor, 8–5 Ginza, Chūō-ku,* ☎ *03/5568–*

6156. *AE, DC, MC, V. No lunch. JR Yamanote Line and Ginza and Toei Asakusa subway lines: Shimbashi Eki (Exit 5).*

Indian

$$-$$$ ✕ **Ashoka.** The owners of the Ashoka set out to take the high ground—to provide decor commensurate with a fashionable address. The room is hushed and spacious, incense perfumes the air, the lighting is recessed, the carpets are thick, and the waiters have spiffy uniforms. Floor-to-ceiling windows overlook Chūō-dōri, the main street in Ginza. *Thali*, a selection of curries and other specialties of the house, is served up on a figured brass tray. *Khandari nan*, a flat bread with nuts and raisins, is excellent. So is chicken *tikka*, boneless chunks marinated and cooked in the tandoor. All in all, this is a good show for the raj. ✉ *Pearl Bldg., 2nd floor, 7–9–18 Ginza, Chūō-ku,* ☎ *03/3572–2377. AE, DC, MC, V. Subway: Marunouchi and Ginza Lines, Ginza Eki (Exit A4).*

Japanese

$$$-$$$$ ✕ **Rangetsu.** The increase in Japan's consumption of beef over the past century has much to do with the popular appeal of shabu-shabu and sukiyaki, the house specialties here. Inside, tables for four or more people in semiprivate rooms are equipped with a tabletop stove. Only one dish can be cooked at your table, but this shouldn't stop you from trying both shabu-shabu and sukiyaki. Rangetsu is one block from the Ginza 4-chōme crossing, on the side closest to the Wako clock. ✉ *3–5–8 Ginza, Chūō-ku,* ☎ *03/3567–1021. AE, DC, MC, V. Subway: Marunouchi and Ginza lines, Ginza Eki (Exit A9 or A10).*

$$-$$$$ ✕ **Ōshima.** One reason Tōkyō is such a great city for food is that it easily supports a great variety of restaurants serving the regional cuisines from all over the country. Ōshima is devoted to the cooking of Kanazawa, the city on the Sea of Japan that during the Edo period earned the nickname "Little Kyōto" for the richness of its craft traditions. Kanazawa cuisine is noted for its seafood; the grilled fresh yellowtail at Ōshima is a delight. But the specialty of the house is a stew of duck and potatoes called *jibuni*. The waitresses dress in kimonos of Kanazawa's famous Yuzen dyed silk. The exquisite table settings make use of Kutani porcelain and Wajima lacquer bowls. ✉ *Ginza Core Bldg. 9F, 5–8–20 Ginza, Chūō-ku,* ☎ *03/3574–8080. AE, MC, V. Subway: Ginza, Hibiya, and Marunouchi lines, Ginza Eki (Exit A5).*

Ichiyaga

Italian

$$ ✕ **Restorante Carmine.** Everybody pitched in, so the story goes, when Carmine Cozzolino opened this unpretentious little neighborhood restaurant in 1987: friends designed the logo and the interior, painted the walls (black and white), and hung the graphics, swapping their labor for meals. And they're good meals, too. For a real Italian five-course dinner, this could be the best deal in town. Specialties of the house include pasta twists with tomato and caper sauce, and veal scallopini à la marsala. The tiramisu is a serious dessert. Carmine's is not easy to find, but it's well worth the effort. When you exit the station, ask for help finding the street Ushigome-chūō-dōri. Follow the street uphill for about 10 minutes; the sign for the restaurant will be on the left. ✉ *1–19 Saiku-machi, Shinjuku-ku,* ☎ *03/3260–5066. No credit cards. Subway: Namboku and Yūraku-chō lines, Ichigaya Eki (Exit 5).*

Japanese

$$ ✕ **Healthy Kan.** Beloved by its regular Japanese and gaijin clientele,
★ Healthy Kan serves an array of traditional vegetarian and fish dishes. The daily menu, listed on a white board, offers a complete Japanese meal that includes *haigo* (brown rice) or soba served either hot or cold

depending on the season. For something different, try the tempeh set. A classic Indonesian dish, Kan's tempeh—seasoned with either soy or miso—is dressed up to look Japanese. *Komatsuna* (mustard spinach), or a comparable leafy green vegetable such as spinach or chrysanthemum leaves, in addition to tasty *hijiki* (edible algae) and pickles, is served on the side. Healthy Kan is a casual place; it's easy to linger over a glass of home-pureed vegetable juice or a piece of homemade cake (desserts run out early, so call ahead to reserve something). The menu is written in English. ✉ *Asahi Roku-ban-chō Mansion, 2nd floor, 6–4 Chiyoda-ku,* ☎ *03/3263–4023. No credit cards. Closed Sun. Subway: Yūraku-chō Line, Ichigaya Eki (Exit 3).*

Ikebukuro

Japanese

$$ ✗ **Sasashū.** This traditional-style pub is noteworthy for stocking
★ only the finest and rarest, the Latours and Mouton-Rothschilds, of sake: these are wines that take gold medals in the annual sake competition year after year. It also serves some of the best izakaya food in town—and the Japanese wouldn't dream of drinking well without eating well. Sasashū is a rambling two-story building in traditional style, with thick beams and step-up tatami floors. The specialty of the house is salmon steak, brushed with sake and soy sauce and broiled over a charcoal hibachi. ✉ *2–2–6 Ikebukuro, Toshima-ku,* ☎ *03/3971–6796. AE, DC, MC, V. Closed Sun. No lunch. JR Yamanote Line; Yūraku-chō, Marunouchi and Ōedo subway lines: Ikebukuro Eki (Exit 19).*

Kyō-bashi

French

$$$$ ✗ **Chez Inno.** Chef Noboru Inoue studied his craft at Maxim's in Paris and Les Frères Troisgros in Roanne; the result is brilliant, innovative French food. Try fresh lamb in wine sauce with truffles and finely chopped herbs, or lobster with caviar. The main dining room, with seating for 28, has velvet banquettes, white-stucco walls, and stained-glass windows. A smaller room can accommodate private parties. Across the street is the elegant Seiyō Hotel—making this block the locus of the very utmost in Tōkyō upscale. ✉ *3–2–11 Kyō-bashi,* ☎ *03/3274–2020. Reservations essential. Jacket and tie. AE, DC, V. Closed Sun. Subway: Ginza Line, Kyō-bashi Eki (Exit 2); Yūraku-chō Line, Ginza-Itchōme Eki (Exit 7).*

Italian

$$–$$$$ ✗ **Attore.** The Italian restaurant of the elegant Hotel Seiyō Ginza, Attore is divided into two sections. The "casual" side, with seating for 60, has a bar counter, banquettes, and a see-through glass wall to the kitchen; its comfortable decor is achieved with track lighting, potted plants, marble floors, and Indian-looking print tablecloths. The "formal" side, with seating for 40, has mauve wall panels and carpets, armchairs, and soft recessed lighting. On either side of the room, you get some of the best Italian cuisine in Tōkyō. Chef Katsuyuki Muroi trained for six years in Tuscany and northern Italy and acquired a wonderful repertoire. Try pâté of pheasant and porcini mushrooms with white-truffle cheese sauce or the walnut-smoked lamb chops with sun-dried tomatoes. The menu is simpler, and the dishes are less expensive on the casual side of the restaurant. ✉ *1–11–2 Ginza, Chūō-ku,* ☎ *03/3535–1111. Reservations essential for formal dining room. Jacket and tie. AE, DC, MC, V. Subway: Ginza Line, Kyō-bashi Eki (Exit 2); Yūraku-chō Line, Ginza-Itchōme Eki (Exit 7).*

Meguro

Japanese

$ ★ ✕ **Tonki.** Meguro, a neighborhood distinguished for almost nothing else culinary, has the *ichiban-no* (number one) *tonkatsu ryōri* (deep-fried pork cutlet cookery) in Tōkyō. It's a family joint, with Formica-top tables and a fellow who comes around to take your order while you're waiting the requisite 10 minutes in line. And people do wait in line, every night until the place closes at 10:30. Tonki is one of those successful places that never went conglomerate; it kept getting more popular and never got around to putting frills on what it does best: pork cutlets, soup, raw cabbage salad, rice, pickles, and tea. That's the standard course, and almost everybody orders it, with good reason. ⊠ *1–1–2 Shimo-Meguro, Meguro-ku,* ☎ *03/3491–9928. DC, V. Closed Tues. and 3rd Mon. of month. JR Yamanote Line, Meguro Eki (Nishi-guchi/West Exit).*

Thai

$–$$$ ✕ **Keawjai.** Blink and you miss this little Thai restaurant, just a minute's walk or so from the east exit of Meguro Eki on Meguro-dōri. (The sign is faded, and the steps leading downstairs are barely noticeable.) But Keawjai is worth looking for: it's one of the few places in Tōkyō offering the subtle complexities of Royal Thai cuisines, and despite its size—only eight tables and four banquettes—the restaurant serves a remarkable range of dishes in different regional styles. The spicy beef salad is excellent (and *really* spicy), as are the baked rice with crabmeat served in a whole pineapple, and the red curry in coconut milk with chicken and cashews. The decor evokes Thailand with carved panels, paintings, and brass ornaments but manages to avoid clutter. The staff is all Thai, and the service is friendly and unhurried. ⊠ *Meguro Kōwa Bldg. B1, 2–14–9 Kami Ōsaki, Meguro-ku,* ☎ *03/5420–7727. MC, V. Closed 2nd and 3rd Mon. of month. JR and Namboku subway line, Meguro Eki (Higashi-guchi/East Exit).*

Niban-chō

Indian

$$–$$$ ✕ **Adjanta.** About 45 years ago the owner of Adjanta came to Tōkyō to study electrical engineering and ended up opening a small coffee shop near the Indian Embassy. He started out cooking a little for his friends; now the coffee shop is one of the oldest and best Indian restaurants in town. There's no decor to speak of. The emphasis instead is on the variety and intricacy of Indian cooking—and none of its dressier rivals can match Adjanta's menu for sheer depth. The curries are hot to begin with, but you can order them even hotter. There's a small boutique in one corner, where saris and imported Indian foodstuffs are for sale. Adjanta is open 24 hours. ⊠ *3–11 Niban-chō, Chiyoda-ku,* ☎ *03/3264–6955. AE, DC, MC, V. Subway: Yūraku-chō Line, Kōji-machi Eki (Exit 5).*

Nihombashi

Japanese

$ ✕ **Sasashin.** No culinary tour of Japan would be complete without a visit to an izakaya, where the food is hearty, close to home cooking, and is meant—to most of the local clientele, at least—mainly as ballast for the earnest consumption of beer and sake. Arguably one of the two or three best izakaya in Tōkyō, Sasashin spurns the notion of decor: there is a counter laden with platters of the evening's fare, a clutter of rough wooden tables, and not much else. It's noisy, smoky, crowded—and absolutely authentic. Try the sashimi, the grilled fish, or the fried tofu; you really can't go wrong by just pointing your finger to anything on the counter that takes your fancy. Sasashin is open evenings only, 5–10:30. ✉ 2–20–3 Nihombashi- Ningyōchō, Chūō-ku, ☎ 03/3668–2456. *Reservations not accepted. No credit cards. Closed Sun. and 3rd Sat. of month. No lunch. Subway: Hanzō-mon Line, Suitengū-mae Eki (Exit 7); Hibiya and Toei Asakusa lines, Ningyōchō Eki (Exits A1, A3).*

Omotesandō

French

$$$–$$$$ ✕ **Le Papillon de Paris.** This very fashion-minded restaurant is a joint venture of L'Orangerie in Paris and Madame Mori's formidable empire in couture. Muted elegance marks the decor, with cream walls, deep brown carpets, and a few good paintings. Mirrors add depth to a room that actually seats only 40. The menu, an ambitious one to begin with, changes every two weeks; the recurring salad of sautéed sweetbreads is excellent. The lunch and dinner menus are nouvelle and very pricey. This is a particularly good place to be on a late Sunday morning, for the buffet brunch (¥3,500), when you can graze through to what's arguably the best dessert tray in town. Le Papillon is on the fifth floor of the Hanae Mori Building, just a minute's walk from the Omotesandō subway station on Aoyama-dōri. ✉ *Hanae Mori Bldg., 5th floor, 3–6–1 Kita–Aoyama, Minato-ku,* ☎ *03/3407–7461. Reservations essential. AE, DC, MC, V. No dinner Sun. Subway: Ginza and Hanzō-mon lines, Omotesandō Eki (Exit A1).*

Roppongi

American

$$–$$$ ✕ **Spago.** This was the first venture overseas by trendsetting Spago of Los Angeles, and owner-chef-celebrity Wolfgang Puck still comes periodically to Tōkyō to oversee the authenticity of his California cuisine. Will duck sausage pizza with Boursin cheese and pearl onions ever be as American as apple pie? Maybe. Meanwhile, Spago is a clean, well-lighted place, painted pink and white and adorned with potted palms. Service is smooth, and tables on the glassed-in veranda attract a fair sample of Tōkyō's gilded youth. ✉ *5–7–8 Roppongi, Minato-ku,* ☎ *03/3423–4025. AE, DC, MC, V. Subway: Hibiya Line, Roppongi Eki (Exit 3).*

Contemporary

$–$$ ✕ **Roti.** Billing itself as a "modern Brasserie," Roti is basically inspired by the culinary aesthetic that emerged in the late 1960s in the United States: a creative use of simple, fresh ingredients that still lets the food speak for itself, and a fusing of Eastern and Western elements. Appetizers at Roti are more interesting than main dishes. Try the Vietnamese sea-bass carpaccio with crisp noodles and roasted garlic, or the calamari batter-fried in ale with red chili tartar sauce. Don't neglect dessert: the espresso chocolate tart is to die for. Roti stocks a fine cellar of some 60 Californian wines and has microbrewed ales from the famed Rogue brewery in Oregon as well as a selection of Cuban cigars. The best seats in the house are in fact outside, at one of the dozen tables around the big glass pyramid on the terrace. ✉ *Piramide Bldg. 1F, 6–6–9 Roppongi, Minato-ku,* ☎ *03/5785–3671. AE, MC, V. Subway: Hibiya Line, Roppongi Eki (Exit 1).*

Indonesian

$$ ✕ **Bengawan Solo.** The Japanese, whose native aesthetic demands a separate dish and vessel for everything they eat, have to overcome a certain resistance to the idea of *rijsttafel*—a kind of Indonesian smorgasbord of curries, salad, and grilled tidbits that tends to get mixed up on a serving platter. Nevertheless, Bengawan Solo has maintained its popularity with Tōkyō residents for about 40 years. The eight-course

rijsttafel is spicy hot and ample. If it doesn't quite stretch for two, order an extra *gado-gado* salad with peanut sauce. An amiable clutter of batik pictures, shadow puppets, carvings, and pennants makes up the decor. The parent organization, in Jakarta, supplies periodic infusions of new staff as needed and does a thriving import business in Indonesian foodstuffs. ⊠ *7–18–13 Roppongi, Minato-ku,* ☎ *03/3408–5698. AE, DC, MC, V. Subway: Hibiya Line, Roppongi Eki (Exit 2).*

Japanese

$$$$ ✕ **Inakaya.** The style here is *robatayaki,* the ambience pure theater. The centerpiece is a large U-shape counter. Inside, two cooks in traditional garb sit on cushions behind the grill, with a wonderful cornucopia of food spread out in front of them: fresh vegetables, seafood, skewers of beef and chicken. Point to what you want, or tell your waiter—each speaks some English. The cook will bring it up out of the pit, prepare it, and hand it across on an 8-ft wooden paddle. Expect a half-hour wait any evening after 7. Inakaya is open from 5 PM to 5:30 AM. ⊠ *Reine Bldg., 1st floor, 5–3–4 Roppongi, Minato-ku,* ☎ *03/3408–5040. Reservations not accepted. AE, DC, MC, V. No lunch. Subway: Hibiya Line, Roppongi Eki (Exit 3).*

$$$–$$$$ ✕ **Sushi Toshi.** This contemporary and colorful sushi shop in Roppongi caters to an eclectic clientele, all of whom can easily be seen thanks to the restaurant's U-shape counter. As in most sushi bars, a single order consists of two pieces from the superb array of the day's catch. In addition to *maguro* and *chūtoro* (both tuna, the latter coming from the middle section of the fish), *kompachi* (a close relative of *hamachi,* yellow tail) and *tai* (sea bream) are spectacular, and the scallops still smack of sea salt. Or if you don't see anything appealing in the glass case in front of you, ask one of the chefs to pull something from the tank. The usual pink pickled ginger, as well as *kamaboko* (white fish cakes) served on a *haran* (lily-flower) leaf, clears the palate between each "course." ⊠ *5–8–3 Nakano Bldg., 1st floor, Roppongi, Minato-ku,* ☎ *03/3423–0333. AE, DC, MC, V. Closed Sun. No lunch. Subway: Hibiya Line, Roppongi Eki (Exit 3).*

$–$$ ✕ **Ganchan.** Although the Japanese prefer their sushi bars to be immaculately clean and light, they expect yakitori joints to be smoky, noisy, and cluttered—like Ganchan. There's counter seating only, for about 15, and you have to squeeze to get to the chairs in back by the kitchen. Festival masks, paper kites and lanterns, gimcracks of all sorts, handwritten menus, and greeting cards from celebrity patrons adorn the walls. Behind the counter, the cooks yell at each other, fan the grill, and serve up enormous schooners of beer. Try the *tsukune* (balls of minced chicken) and the fresh asparagus wrapped in bacon. Ganchan is open from 5:30 PM to 1 AM Monday–Saturday and until 11 PM on Sunday and holidays. ⊠ *6–8–23 Roppongi, Minato-ku,* ☎ *03/3478–0092. V. No lunch. Subway: Hibiya Line, Roppongi Eki (Exit 1A).*

Shibuya

Japanese

$$–$$$$ ✕ **Tenmatsu.** The best seats in the house at Tenmatsu, as in any tempura-ya, are at the immaculate wooden counter, where your tidbits of choice are taken straight from the oil and served up immediately. You also get to watch the chef in action. Tenmatsu's brand of good-natured professional hospitality adds to the enjoyment of the meal. Here you can rely on a set menu or order à la carte delicacies like lotus root, shrimp, *unagi* (eel), and *kisu* (a small white freshwater fish). Call ahead to reserve a seat at the counter. ⊠ *1–6–1 Dōgen-zaka, Shibuya-ku,* ☎ *03/ 3462–2815. DC, MC, V. Subway/JR: Shibuya Eki (Minami-guchi/South Exit for JR lines, Exit 3A for Ginza and Hanzō-mon subway lines).*

Shinjuku

Japanese

$$$–$$$$ ✕ **Yaozen.** On the 14th floor of Takashimaya Times Square, Yaozen has a magnificent view of the city and serves elegant kaiseki banquets for parties of three or more between the normal lunch and dinner hours (reserve in advance). Standard fare, served by kimono-clad waitresses, is a prix-fixe meal in a bentō lunch box or on elegantly lacquered trays: try the two-tiered *okusama-gozen bentō*, which includes sashimi, simmered vegetables, and grilled fish. Small desserts with *hōjicha* (parched twig tea) are popular during tea time, but with a full-course meal, it's easy to skip, since so many of the foods—in traditional Japanese style—are prepared with *mirin* (sweet rice wine) and sugar. ⊠ *Takashimaya Times Square, 5–24–2 Sendagaya, Shibuya-ku,* ☎ *03/ 5361–1872. AE, DC, MC, V. JR/subway: Shinjuku Eki (Minami-guchi/South Exit for JR, Exit 2 for Toei Shinjuku Line).*

Shirokanedai

Seafood

$–$$ ✕ **Blue Point.** The name is a bit misleading: neither the restaurant nor the bar at this chic little establishment serves oysters. What they do serve are generous portions of good seafood, at reasonable prices, in an informal trattoria-style setting—and they stay open until 3 AM on weekdays, 4 AM on weekends. Blue Point cuts corners here and there (there are processed bacon bits in the Caesar salad), but the clientele doesn't come for haute cuisine; the chief appeal, weather permitting, is to dine by candlelight at one of the 10 sidewalk tables, with their blue-and-white checkered oilcloths and the tall French windows behind them. Try the seafood risotto with saffron or the bouillabaisse. Tōkyō's well-heeled clubbers love this place. ⊠ *4–19–19 Shirokanedai, Minato-ku,* ☎ *03/3440–3928. MC, V. Subway: Toei Mita and Namboku lines, Shirokanedai Eki (Exit 1).*

Spanish

$$ ✕ **Sabado Sabadete.** Catalonia-born jewelry designer Mañuel Benito loves to cook. For a while he indulged this passion by renting out a bar in Aoyama on Saturday nights and making an enormous paella for his friends; to keep them happy while they were waiting, he added a few tapas. Word got around: soon, by 8 it was standing room only, and by 9 there wasn't room in the bar to lift a fork. Inspired by this success, Benito found a trendy location and opened his Sabado Sabadete full-time in 1991. The highlight of every evening is still the moment when the chef, in his bright red Catalan cap, shouts out "Gohan desu yo!"—the Japanese equivalent of "Soup's on!" and dishes out his bubbling-hot paella. Don't miss the empanadas or the *escalivada* (a Spanish ratatouille with red peppers, onions, and eggplant). ⊠ *Genteel Shirokanedai Bldg., 2nd floor, 5–3–2 Shirokanedai, Minato-ku,* ☎ *03/ 3445–9353. No credit cards. Closed Sun. Subway: Toei Mita and Namboku lines, Shirokanedai Eki (Exit 1).*

Shōtō

French

$$$$ ✕ **Chez Matsuo.** Shōtō is the kind of area you don't expect Tōkyō to have—at least not so close to Shibuya Eki. It's a neighborhood of stately homes with walls half a block long, a sort of sedate Beverly Hills. Chez Matsuo opened here in 1980, in a lovely old two-story Western-style house. The two dining rooms on the first floor, and the private "Imperial Room" on the second, overlook the garden, where you can dine by candlelight on spring and autumn evenings. Owner-chef Matsuo stud-

ied as a sommelier in London and perfected his culinary finesse in Paris. His food is nouvelle; the specialty of the house is *suprême* (breast and wing) of duck. ✉ *1–23–15 Shōtō, Shibuya-ku,* ☎ *03/3465–0610. Reservations essential. AE, DC, MC, V. Subway/JR: Shibuya Eki (Kita-guchi/North Exit for JR Yamanote Line, Ginza subway line, and private rail lines; Exit 5 or 8 for Hanzō-mon subway line).*

Tora-no-mon

Chinese

$$$–$$$$ ✕ **Toh-Ka-Lin.** Year after year the Hotel Okura is rated by business travelers as one of the three best hotels in the world. That judgment has relatively little to do with its architecture, which is rather understated. It has to do instead with its polish, its impeccable standards of service—and, to judge by Toh-Ka-Lin, the quality of its restaurants. The style of the cuisine here is eclectic; two stellar examples are the Peking duck and the sautéed quail wrapped in lettuce leaf. The restaurant also has a not-too-expensive midafternoon meal ($$) of assorted dim sum and other delicacies—and one of the most extensive wine lists in town. ✉ *Hotel Okura, 2–10–4 Tora-no-mon, Minato-ku,* ☎ *03/3505–6068. AE, DC, MC, V. Subway: Hibiya Line, Kamiya-chō Eki (Exit 4B); Ginza Line, Tora-no-mon Eki (Exit 3).*

Tsukiji

Japanese

$$–$$$$ ✕ **Edo-Gin.** In an area that teems with sushi bars, this one maintains its reputation as one of the best. Edo-Gin serves up generous slabs of fish that drape over the vinegared rice rather than perch demurely on top. The centerpiece of the main room is a huge tank, in which the day's ingredients swim about until they are required; it doesn't get any fresher than that! ✉ *4–5–1 Tsukiji, Chūō-ku,* ☎ *03/3543–4401. Reservations not accepted. AE, DC, MC, V. Closed Sun. Subway: Hibiya Line, Tsukiji Eki (Exit 1); Toei Ōedo Line, Tsukiji-shijō Eki (Exit A1).*

$$ ✕ **Takeno.** Just a stone's throw from the Tōkyō central fish market, Takeno is a rough-cut neighborhood restaurant that tends to fill up at noon with the market's wholesalers and auctioneers and office personnel from the nearby Dentsu ad agency and Asahi *Shimbun* (newspaper) company. There's nothing here but the freshest and the best—big portions of it, at very reasonable prices. Sushi, sashimi, and tempura are the staple fare; prices are not posted because they vary with the costs that morning in the market. ✉ *6–21–2 Tsukiji, Chūō-ku,* ☎ *03/3541–8697. Reservations not accepted. No credit cards. Closed Sun. Subway: Hibiya Line, Tsukiji Eki (Exit 1); Toei Ōedo Line, Tsukiji-shijō Eki (Exit A1).*

Tsukishima

Japanese

$ ✕ **Nishiki.** Toss out the window any notions you might have about the delicacy and artistic presentation of Japanese food when you come to Nishiki, one of the dozens of *monjya-yaki* restaurants that line the streets of Tsukishima, a five-minute subway ride from Yūraku-chō. A close relative of the western Japanese meal-in-a-pancake innovation *okonomi-yaki*, monjya-yaki, Tōkyō residents swear, is a cuisine that's genuinely Shitamachi—old Tōkyō downtown. Unlike okonomi-yaki, however, monjya-yaki uses no eggs and less flour; this makes frying the pancakes somewhat of a challenge, but that's half the fun. The menu lists more than 20 eclectic combinations, of which the most popular are sliced potatoes and mayonnaise, *tara-ko* (cod roe), and *mochi* (rice cakes), as well as the standard mix of beef, pork, shrimp, and squid seasoned in soy sauce. ⊠ *3–11–10 Tsukishima, Chūō-ku,* ☎ *03/3534–8697. No credit cards. Closed Tues. No lunch weekdays. Subway: Yūraku-chō and Ōedo lines, Tsukishima Eki (Exit 7).*

Uchisaiwai-chō

Chinese

\$\$–\$\$\$\$ ✕ **Heichinrou.** This branch of one of the oldest and best restaurants in
★   Yokohama's Chinatown is on the top floor of a prestigious office building about five minutes' walk from the Imperial Hotel, and it commands a spectacular view of Hibiya Kōen and the Imperial Palace grounds. Be sure to call ahead to reserve a table by the window. The cuisine is Cantonese; pride of place goes to the *kaisen ryōri,* an elaborate multicourse meal of steamed sea bass, lobster, shrimp, scallops, abalone, and other seafood dishes. The decor is rich but subdued, lighting is soft, and table linens are impeccable. Much of the clientele comes from the law offices, securities firms, and foreign banks on the floors below. Heichinrou has a banquet room that can seat 100 and a VIP Room with separate telephone service for power lunches. ⊠ *Fukoku Seimei Bldg., 28th floor, 2–2–2 Uchisaiwai-chō, Chiyoda-ku,* ☎ *03/ 3508–0555. Jacket and tie. AE, DC, MC, V. Closed Sun. Subway: Toei Mita Line, Uchisaiwai-chō Eki (Exit A6).*

Ueno

Japanese

\$\$ ✕ **Sasa-no-yuki.** With its cross between the traditional *shōjin ryōri* (Bud-
★   dhist vegetarian cuisine) and formal kaiseki dining, Sasa-no-yuki has been serving homemade silky, soft, and sensuous tofu in an array of styles for the past 300 years. The seating is on tatami, the garden has a waterfall, and the presentation of the food is truly artistic. In addition to a few nontofu à la carte items, there are three all-tofu sets, the most basic of which is a three-course meal including *ankake* tofu (bean curd in a sweet soy sauce), *kake shōyu* tofu (simmered with chicken and shiitake mushrooms), and *unsui* (a creamy tofu crepe filled with tiny morsels of sea scallops, shrimp, and minced red pepper). For the best sampling, choose the eight-course banquet, which includes *yuba-kōya* tofu, a delicious crepe soaked in soy milk. ⊠ *2–15–10 Negishi, Taitō-ku,* ☎ *03/3873–1145. AE, DC, MC, V.* ۞ *Tues.–Sun. 11–9. Closed Mon. JR Uguisudani Eki (Kita-guchi/North Exit).*

Yūraku-chō

Japanese

\$\$–\$\$\$ ✕ **Robata.** You might find this place a little daunting at first: it's old and funky, impossibly cramped, and always packed. But chef-owner Takao Inoue, who holds forth here with an inspired version of Japanese home cooking, is also a connoisseur of pottery; he serves his own work on pieces acquired at famous kilns all over the country. There's no menu; the best thing you can do is tell Inoue-san (who speaks some English) how hungry you are and how much you want to spend, and leave the rest to him. A meal at Robata—like the pottery—is simple to the eye but subtle and satisfying. Typical dishes include steamed fish with vegetables, stews of beef or pork, and seafood salad. ⊠ *1–3–8 Yūraku-chō, Chiyoda-ku,* ☎ *03/3591–1905. No credit cards. Closed 3rd Mon. of month. No lunch. Subway: Hibiya, Chiyoda, and Toei Mita lines, Hibiya Eki (Exit A4).*

LODGING

There are three things you can virtually take for granted when you look for a hotel in Tōkyō: cleanliness, safety, and service—impeccable almost anywhere you finally set down your bags. The factors that will probably determine your choice, then, are cost and location.

The relation between the two is not always what you'd expect. Real estate in Tōkyō is horrendously expensive; normally, the closer you get to the center of town, the more you ought to be paying for space. That's true enough for business property, but when it comes to hotels at the upper end of the market, the logic doesn't seem to apply: a night's lodging is not likely to cost you much less in Roppongi, Shinjuku, Ikebukuro, Meguro, or Asakusa than it would for a view of the Imperial Palace.

The reasons aren't complicated. A substantial number of Tōkyō's present hotels were built in the outlying subcenters during the "bubble" of the 1980s and early 1990s, when real estate speculation made prices outrageous everywhere. The bubble encouraged a "spare-no-expense" approach to hotel design: atriums, oceans of marble, interior decorators fetched in from London and New York. The cost of construction per square foot did not vary much from place to place, and that remains reflected in what you can anticipate paying for your room. Business travelers might have good reason to choose one location over another, but if you're in Tōkyō on vacation, that factor may be only marginally important. Nor should transportation be a concern: wherever you're staying, Tōkyō's subway and train system—comfortable (except in rush hours), efficient, inexpensive, and safe—will get you back and forth.

Down-market hotels, of course, provide less in the way of services and decor, but this affects the cost of accommodations—per square foot—less than you might imagine. Deluxe hotels make a substantial part of their profits from their banquet and dining facilities; they charge you more, but they can also give you more space. Farther down the scale, you pay somewhat less, but the rooms are disproportionately smaller. Nay, they can be positively tiny.

Tōkyō accommodations can be roughly divided into five categories: international (full-service) hotels, business hotels, *ryokan,* "capsule" hotels, and hostels.

International (full-service) hotels are exactly what you would expect; most also tend to be priced in the $$$ and $$$$ categories. Virtually all have a range of Western and Japanese restaurants, room service, direct-dial telephones, minibars, *yukata* (cotton bedroom kimonos), concierge services, and porters. Most have business and fitness centers. A few also have swimming pools. At least 90% of the guest rooms are Western style; the few Japanese rooms available (with tatami mats and futons) are more expensive.

Business hotels are meant primarily for travelers who need no more than a place to leave luggage, sleep, and change. Rooms are small; an individual guest will often take a double rather than suffer the claustrophobia of a single. Each room has a telephone, a small writing desk, a television (sometimes the pay-as-you-watch variety), slippers, a yukata, and a prefabricated plastic bathroom unit with tub, shower, and washbasin; the bathrooms are scrupulously clean, but if you're basketball-player size, you might have trouble coming to your full height inside. The hotel facilities are limited usually to one restaurant and a 24-hour receptionist, with no room service or porters. Business hotels are not listed below in a separate category, but entries in the $$ price category can be assumed to be of this type.

There are two kinds of ryokan. One is an expensive traditional inn, with impeccable personal service, where you are served dinner and breakfast in your room. The other is an inexpensive hostelry that offers rooms with tatami mats on the floors and futon beds; meals might be served in rooms, but more often they aren't. Tōkyō ryokan fall in the latter category. They are often family-run lodgings, where service is less a matter of professionalism than of good will. Many offer the choice of rooms with or without baths. Because they have few rooms and the owners are usually on hand to answer their guests' questions, these small, relatively inexpensive ryokan are very hospitable places to stay and especially popular with younger travelers.

Capsule hotels are literally plastic cubicles stacked one on top of another. They are used by very junior business travelers or commuters who have missed their last train home. (Very rarely, a capsule hotel will have a separate floor for women; otherwise, women are not admitted.) The capsule—marginally bigger than a coffin or a CAT scanner—has a bed, an intercom, and (in the luxury models) a TV in the ceiling. Washing and toilet facilities are shared. One such place is **Green Plaza Shinjuku** (⊠ 1–29–2 Kabuki-chō, Shinjuku-ku, ☎ 03/3207–4923), two minutes from Shinjuku Eki (Higashi-guchi/East Exit for JR lines; Exit B10, B11, B12, or B13 for Marunouchi Line). It is the largest of its kind, with 660 sleeping slots. Check-in starts at 3 PM; checkout in the morning is pandemonium. A night's stay in a capsule is ¥4,200.

Separate categories are provided in this section for (1) hotels near Narita Airport and (2) youth hostels and dormitory accommodations. All rooms at the hotels listed below are Western style and have private baths, unless otherwise specified.

CATEGORY	COST*
$$$$	over ¥30,000
$$$	¥21,000–¥30,000
$$	¥10,000–¥21,000
$	under ¥10,000

All prices are for a double room, excluding service and tax.

Akasaka-mitsuke

$$$$ 🏨 **Akasaka Prince Hotel.** Rooms from the 20th to the 30th floor of this ultramodern, 40-story, Kenzō Tange–designed hotel afford the best views of the city, especially at night. The room decor of white and pale grays accentuates the light from the wide windows that run the length of the room. The result is a feeling of spaciousness, though the rooms are no larger in size than those in other deluxe hotels. A welcome feature is the dressing mirror and sink in an alcove before the bathroom. The marble and off-white reception areas on the ground floor are pristine—maybe even a bit sterile. The hotel does a lot of wedding and convention business; the Grand Ballroom can accommodate up to 2,500 guests. ⊠ *1–2 Kioi-chō, Chiyoda-ku, Tōkyō-to 102-0094,* ☎ *03/3234–1111,* FAX *03/3205–5163,* WEB *www2.princehotels.co.jp. 693 rooms, 68 suites. 8 restaurants, 3 bars, 2 coffee shops, no-smoking room, massage, shops, business services, travel services. AE, DC, MC, V. Subway: Ginza and Marunouchi lines, Akasaka-mitsuke Eki (Exit 7).*

$$$$ 🏨 **Hotel New Otani Tōkyō and Towers.** The New Otani is virtually a town unto itself. When all rooms are occupied and all banquet facilities are in use, the traffic flow in and out of the restaurants, lounges, and shopping arcades seems like rush hour at a busy railway station.

The hotel's redeeming feature is its peaceful, 10-acre manicured garden; rooms that overlook it are the best in the house. Among the many restaurants and bars are La Tour d'Argent, Japan's first Trader Vic's, and the revolving Sky Lounge. ⊠ *4–1 Kioi-chō, Chiyoda-ku, Tōkyō-to 102-0094,* ☎ *03/3265–1111; 0120/112–211 toll free,* 𝔽𝔸𝕏 *03/3221–2619,* 𝕎𝔼𝔹 *www.newotani.co.jp. 1,549 rooms (30 on 21st floor for women only), 51 suites. 33 restaurants and bars, coffee shop, no-smoking rooms, pool, spa, driving range, 2 tennis courts, shops, baby-sitting, chapel, business services, travel services. AE, DC, MC, V. Subway: Ginza and Marunouchi lines, Akasaka-mitsuke Eki (Exit 7).*

Asakusa

$$$–$$$$ 🏨 **Asakusa View Hotel.** If you want an elegant place to stay in the heart of Tōkyō's old Asakusa area—which was actually resurrected after the World War II fire bombings—then this hotel is the only choice. Off the smart marble lobby a harpist plays in the tea lounge, and expensive boutiques line the second floor. The standard pastel guest rooms are similar to what you find in all modern Tōkyō hotels, but you also have access to communal *hinoki* (Japanese cypress) bathtubs that overlook a sixth-floor Japanese garden. Ask for rooms on the 22nd and 23rd floors, which afford a view of the Senjō-ji grounds. There are Chinese, French, Italian, and Japanese restaurants and a bar that will keep your personal bottle. ⊠ *3–17–1 Nishi-Asakusa, Taitō-ku, Tōkyō-to 111-0035,* ☎ *03/3847–1111,* 𝔽𝔸𝕏 *03/3842–2117,* 𝕎𝔼𝔹 *www.viewhotels.co.jp/asakusa/index-english.html. 333 room, 9 suites. 4 restaurants, 2 bars, coffee shop, no-smoking rooms, pool, health club, concierge floor. AE, DC, MC, V. Subway: Ginza Line, Tawara-machi Eki (Exit 3).*

$$ 🏨 **Ryokan Shigetsu.** Just off Nakamise-dōri and inside the Sensō-ji grounds, this small inn could not be better located for a visit to the temple. Half the rooms are Japanese-style (futon bedding, tatami floors) and half are Western, plainly but comfortably furnished. All rooms have private baths, and there's also a public bath on the sixth floor with a view of the Sensō-ji pagoda. ⊠ *1–31–11 Asakusa, Taitō-ku, Tōkyō-to 111-0032,* ☎ *03/3483–2345,* 𝔽𝔸𝕏 *03/3483–2348,* 𝕎𝔼𝔹 *www.roy.hi-ho.ne.jp/shigetsu. 11 Western-style rooms, 12 Japanese-style rooms. Restaurant, Japanese baths. AE, MC, V. Subway: Ginza Line, Asakusa Eki (Exit 1/Kaminari-mon exit).*

Ebisu

$$$$ 🏨 **Westin Tōkyō.** In Yebisu Garden Place, one of the last grand, pharaonic development projects to go up in Tōkyō before the real estate bubble burst in 1994, the Westin provides easy access to Mitsukoshi depāto, the Tōkyō Metropolitan Museum of Photography, an elegant concert hall, and the Taillevent-Robuchon restaurant, this last housed in a full-scale reproduction of a Louis XV château. The decor of the hotel itself is updated art nouveau, with an excess of marble and bronze. Rooms are spacious, and suites are huge by Japanese standards. ⊠ *1–4 Mita 1-chōme, Meguro-ku, Tōkyō-to 153-0062,* ☎ *03/5423–7000,* 𝔽𝔸𝕏 *03/5423–7600,* 𝕎𝔼𝔹 *www.starwood.com/westin. 445 rooms, 20 suites. 5 restaurants, 2 bars, coffee shop, no-smoking rooms, health club, shops, concierge floor, business services, travel services. AE, DC, MC, V. Subway (Hibiya Line)/JR station: Ebisu Eki (Higashi-guchi/East Exit).*

Hakozaki

$$$$ 🏨 **Royal Park Hotel.** This hotel would recommend itself if only for the connecting passageway to the Tōkyō City Air Terminal, where you can complete all your check-in procedures before you climb on the bus for

Tōkyō Lodging

ASAKUSA

TO NARITA AIRPORT

Kappa-bashi-dōri

Asakusa

Kaminarimon-dōri

Inari-chō

Tawara-machi

Showa-dōri

Uguisudani

Ueno

UENO

Ueno Kōen

Ueno

Okachi-machi

Kiyosu-bashi-dōri

Kasuga-dōri

Asakusa-bashi

HAMA-CHŌ

NIHOMBASHI

EITAI

Sumidagawa

Eit-ai-dōri

AKIHABARA

Akihabara

Nihombashi

TUSHIMA

Hongo-san-chōme

Ochanomizu

Kasuga-dori

JIMBO-CHŌ

Kanda

Tōkyō

Chuo-dōri

Showa-dōri

YURAKU-CHŌ

Yūraku-chō

Ginza

GINZA

Hongo-dōri

Hakusan-dōri

Suido-bashi

Jimbo-chō

Imperial Palace

Uchibori-dōri

Hibiya

Hibiya Kōen

Koishikawa Botanical Gardens

Korakuen

Korakuen Garden

Iida-bashi

Yoshukuni-dōri

Ichigaya

ICHIBAN-CHŌ

Akasaka-mitsuke

Akasaka

Myogadani

Edogawa-bashi

Kagurazaka

Waseda-dōri

Yotsuya

Akasaka Palace

AKASAKA

Sotobori-dōri

Aoyama-dōri

Gaien

Gokokuji

Waseda

ŌEDO LINE

Akebo-no-bashi

Shinjuku-dōri

Shina-no-machi

Meiji Jingū Outer Garden

Aoyama-it-chōme

Meijiro-dōri

Meijiro

Shin-Okubo

Seibu-Shinjuku

SHINJUKU

Shinjuku Gyo-en

Sendagaya

Meiji-dōri

HARAJUKU

Meiji-Jingū-mae

Takada-no-baba

Okubo

Omekaido

Shinjuku

Yoyogi

Meiji Jingū Inner Garden

Harajuku

Yoyogi Kōen

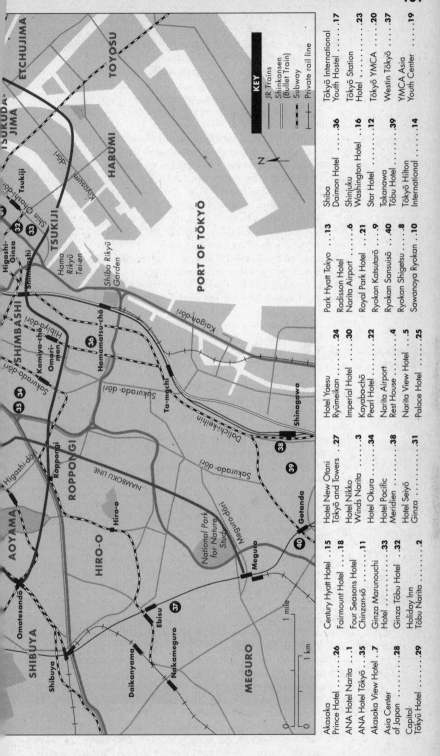

Narita Airport. At the end of an intensive trip, there's no luxury like being able to pack, ring for the bellhop, and not have to touch your baggage again until it comes off the conveyor belt back home. Built in 1989, the 20-story Royal Park is well designed: the large, open lobby has perhaps a bit more marble than it needs, and the inevitable space-age chandelier, but this is offset by wood-paneled columns, brass trim, and lots of comfortable lounge space. Guest rooms, done in coordinated neutral grays and browns, are well proportioned; deluxe twins have handsome writing tables instead of built-in desktops. Ask for a room on one of the executive floors (16–18) with a northeast view of the Sumida-gawa. Another good option would be a room lower down (sixth–eighth floors) on the opposite side, overlooking the hotel's delightful fifth-floor Japanese garden. ⊠ *2–1–1 Nihombashi, Kakigara-chō, Chūō-ku, Tōkyō-to 103-0014,* ☎ *03/3667–1111,* FAX *03/3667–1115,* WEB *www.royalparkhotels.co.jp. 450 rooms, 9 suites. 7 restaurants, 3 bars, coffee shop, no-smoking room, shops, concierge floor, business services, travel services. AE, DC, MC, V. Subway: Hanzō-mon Line, Suitengū-mae Eki (Exit 4).*

$$ 🛏 **Kayaba-chō Pearl Hotel.** Rooms here are strictly utilitarian, but the price is low, unless you sleep late: there's a charge of 30%–50% of your room rate for late checkout (after 10 AM). The hotel is just across the bridge from Tōkyō City Air Terminal, a five-minute walk from Exit 3 or 4B of Kayaba-chō Eki on the Hibiya or Tōzai Line. ⊠ *1–2–5 Shinkawa, Chūō-ku, Tōkyō-to 104-0033,* ☎ *03/3553–2211,* FAX *03/3555–1849. 262 rooms. Restaurant. AE, DC, MC, V. Subway: Kayaba-chō Eki.*

Hibiya

$$$$ 🛏 **Imperial Hotel.** The location of these prestigious quarters could not be better: in the heart of central Tōkyō, between the Imperial Palace and Ginza. The finest rooms, high up on the 30th floor in the New Tower, afford views of the palace grounds. The Old Imperial Bar incorporates elements from the 1922 version of the hotel, which Frank Lloyd Wright designed. The Imperial opened its doors in 1891, and from the outset the hotel has been justly proud of its Western-style facilities and Japanese service. Now, with its tower addition, the hotel is a vast complex, but it still retains its personalized service. Rooms range from standard twin size to suites that are larger than many homes. ⊠ *1–1–1 Uchisai-wai-chō, Chiyoda-ku, Tōkyō-to 100-0011,* ☎ *03/3504–1111,* FAX *03/3581–9146,* WEB *www.imperialhotel.co.jp. 1,005 rooms, 54 suites. 13 restaurants, 4 bars, no-smoking room, indoor pool, massage, health club, shops, concierge floor, business services, travel services. AE, DC, MC, V. Subway: Hibiya Line, Hibiya Eki (Exit 5).*

Higashi-Ginza

$$$–$$$$ 🛏 **Ginza Tōbu Hotel.** This hotel's relatively reasonable prices, friendly service, and comfortable rooms make it something of a bargain for the Ginza area. Standard rooms have blond-wood furniture and quilted bedspreads in pastel prints. The more expensive concierge floors have much larger rooms, with extras such as terry bathrobes and hair dryers; breakfast, afternoon tea, and complimentary cocktails in the lounge are part of the package. There are also French and Japanese restaurants (the excellent Muraki among the latter), as well as a 24-hour coffee shop. ⊠ *6–13–10 Ginza, Chūō-ku Tōkyō-to 104-0061,* ☎ *03/3546–0111,* FAX *03/3546–8990,* WEB *www.tobu.co.jp. 190 rooms, 16 suites. 2 restaurants, 2 bars, coffee shop, concierge floor, business services, travel services. AE, DC, MC, V. Subway: Hibiya and Toei Asakusa lines, Higashi-Ginza Eki (Exit A1).*

Higashi-Gotanda

$ 🏨 **Ryokan Sansuisō.** If you're traveling on a tight budget and want to immerse yourself in Japanese culture, consider this basic ryokan near the Toei Asakusa Line's Gotanda stop. The proprietor will greet you with a warm smile and a bow and escort you to a small tatami room with a pay TV and a rather noisy heater/air-conditioner mounted in the wall. Some rooms are stuffy (you can't open a window), and only two have private baths, but the Sansuisō is clean, easy to find, and only 20 minutes on the subway from Tōkyō Eki and Ginza. The midnight curfew poses a problem for night owls. This hotel is a member of the Japanese Inn Group; the Japan National Tourist Organization (☎ 03/3201–3331) can help make reservations. ⊠ *2–9–5 Higashi-Gotanda, Shinagawa-ku, Tōkyō-to 141-0022,* ☎ *03/3441–7475,* 𝔽𝔸𝕏 *03/3449–1944. 9 rooms, 2 with bath. AE, MC, V. Subway/JR: Gotanda Eki (Exit A3 for Toei Asakusa Line, Higashi-guchi/East Exit for JR Yamanote Line).*

Kudan-Minami

$$–$$$ 🏨 **Fairmount Hotel.** Nostalgia buffs love the Fairmount; here's a place
★   in relentlessly high-tech Tōkyō with pull-chain ventilators, real tile in the bathrooms, and furniture (a little chipped) that Sears & Roebuck must have phased out of its catalog in 1955. The hotel has all that and exposed water pipes—left that way even after a major renovation, neatly wrapped and painted, of course, but exposed just the same. The hotel isn't seedy, mind you, just old (it was built in 1951) and a bit set in its ways. The best thing about the seven-story Fairmount is its frontage on the park that runs along the east side of the Imperial Palace grounds; rooms facing the park afford a wonderful view of the moat and Chidorigafuchi Pond, where Tōkyō couples take rented rowboats out on summer Sunday afternoons. ⊠ *2–1–17 Kudan-Minami, Chiyoda-ku, Tōkyō-to 102-0074,* ☎ *03/3262–1151,* 𝔽𝔸𝕏 *03/3264–2476. 207 rooms, 2 suites. Restaurant, bar. AE, DC, MC, V. Subway: Hanzō-mon and Tōzai lines, Kudanshita Eki (Exit 2).*

Kyō-bashi

$$$$ 🏨 **Hotel Seiyō Ginza.** The muted pastels and grays of the decor, the thick pile of the carpets, and the profusion of cut flowers all combine to create an atmosphere more like an elegant private club than a hotel. Location and personalized service are the two reasons to choose the exclusive Seiyō, where double rooms start at ¥45,000. In hailing distance of Ginza, it caters to celebrities and those who require a direct line in their rooms to a personal secretary who takes care of their every need. A staff of some 220 outnumbers the guests by a considerable margin. Rooms and suites, it must be noted, are smaller than what most Westerners might expect for the price. There are four restaurants, including the Attore for Italian food and the Pastorale for French-Continental. ⊠ *1–11–2 Ginza, Chūō-ku, Tōkyō-to 104-0061,* ☎ *03/3535–1111,* 𝔽𝔸𝕏 *03/3535–1110. 51 rooms, 28 suites. 3 restaurants, bar, lounge, patisserie, health club, concierge, business services, travel services. AE, DC, MC, V. Subway: Ginza Line, Kyō-bashi Eki (Exit 2); Yūraku-chō Line, Ginza-Itchōme Eki (Exit 7).*

Marunouchi

$$$$ 🏨 **Palace Hotel.** The service here is extremely helpful and professional;
★   much of the staff has been with the hotel for more than 10 years. The location is ideal: only a moat separates the hotel from the outer gardens of the Imperial Palace; Ginza and the financial districts of Marunouchi are both a short taxi or subway ride away. The lobby spaces

are rectangular and uninspiring; an air of calm conservatism bespeaks the Palace's half century as an accommodation for the well-to-do and well connected. The tasteful, low-key guest rooms are spacious; try for one on the upper floors facing the Imperial Palace. ⊠ *1–1–1 Marunouchi, Chiyoda-ku, Tōkyō-to 100-0005,* ☎ *03/3211–5211,* FAX *03/3211–6987,* WEB *www.palacehotel.co.jp. 384 rooms, 6 suites. 7 restaurants, 2 bars, coffee shop, no-smoking rooms, shops, business services, travel services. AE, DC, MC, V. Subway: Chiyoda, Marunouchi, Hanzō-mon, Tōzai, and Mita lines; Ōte-machi Eki (Exit C-13B).*

$$$ 🏨 **Tōkyō Station Hotel.** Kingo Tatsuno, one of Japan's first modern architects, modeled the Tōkyō Eki building on the railway station of Amsterdam. Completed in 1914, it was saved in 1990 from the wrecker's ball by a determined historical preservation movement—one of the few times, in this part of the city, that cultural values triumphed over commerce. The original charming facade remains—so far—untouched. The hotel is on the west side of the station building, on the second and third floors; the windows along the corridor look out over the station rotunda. The hotel's frosted glass and flocked wallpaper, its heavy red drapes, and its varnished wooden staircases have seen better days, but many travelers appreciate the wide corridors and high ceilings. If you're moving on from Tōkyō by train to another part of the country, the location is ideal. ⊠ *1–9–1 Marunouchi, Chiyoda-ku, Tōkyō-to 100-0005,* ☎ *03/3231–2511,* FAX *03/3231–3513,* WEB *www.tshl.co.jp. 58 rooms. AE, DC, MC, V. Subway/JR: Tōkyō Eki (Marunouchi Central Exit).*

$$ 🏨 **Ginza Marunouchi Hotel.** Since it opened in 1976, the Ginza Marunouchi has been a popular choice for tour groups, both foreign and Japanese, for one reason: given its location—a subway stop from Ginza—the cost of accommodations here is very reasonable. Guest rooms are compact and clean, but there's nothing particularly remarkable about the decor or the service. ⊠ *4–1–12 Tsukiji, Chūō-ku, Tōkyō-to 104-0045,* ☎ *03/3543–5431,* FAX *03/3543–6006. 114 rooms. Restaurant. AE, DC, MC, V. Subway: Hibiya and Toei Asakusa lines, Higashi-Ginza Eki (Exit 6).*

Nagata-chō

$$$$ 🏨 **Capitol Tōkyū Hotel.** The Tōkyū Hotel chain's flagship operation, the Capitol was built in 1963, but it feels a bit like a grand hotel of a bygone era and commands a loyal repeat clientele among foreign business travelers. It's also relatively small, even by Tōkyō standards, but with two full-time staff members to every guest, service is excellent. Guest rooms are furnished in dark wood, but *shōji* (sliding paper screens) on the windows create a feeling of soft warmth and light. Ask for one of the rooms that overlook the adjacent Hie Jinja. Two of the hotel's dining rooms, the Origami breakfast café and the Tea Lounge, also have views of the shrine. To the left of the lobby is a small garden with a pond. ⊠ *2–10–3 Nagata-chō, Chiyoda-ku, Tōkyō-to 100-0014,* ☎ *03/3581–4511,* FAX *03/3581–5822,* WEB *www.capitoltokyu.com. 440 rooms, 19 suites. 5 restaurants, 2 bars, coffee shop, no-smoking rooms, pool, massage, steam room, shops, concierge floor, business services, travel services. AE, DC, MC, V. Subway: Chiyoda and Marunouchi lines, Kokkai Gijidō-mae Eki (Exit 5); Ginza and Namboku lines, Tameike-Sannō Eki (Exit 5).*

Nishi-Shinjuku

$$$$ 🏨 **Park Hyatt Tōkyō.** An elevator whisks you to the 41st floor, where the hotel begins with an atrium lounge enclosed on three sides by floor-to-ceiling plate-glass windows. The panorama of Shinjuku spreads out before you; the tops of neighboring skyscrapers add to the three-

dimensional spectacle. Service is so efficient and personal, the staff members seem to know your name before you introduce yourself. The mood of the hotel is contemporary and understated. Guest rooms, from the 42nd to the 50th floor, are large by any standard. King-size beds have Egyptian-cotton sheets and down-feather duvets; other appointments include pale olive-green carpets and black-lacquer cabinets. Even bathrooms have views, with tubs situated by windows. The Park Hyatt's restaurants include the Girandole (Continental cuisine), the Peak Lounge, and the very popular New York Grill, with an open kitchen that specializes in steaks and seafood. ⊠ 3–7–1–2 Nishi-Shinjuku, Shinjuku-ku, Tōkyō-to 163-1090, ☎ 03/5322–1234, FAX 03/5322–1288, WEB www.tokyo.hyatt.com. 155 rooms, 23 suites. 3 restaurants, 2 bars, coffee shop, no-smoking rooms, indoor pool, massage, sauna, steam room, aerobics, health club, library, business services. AE, MC, V. Subway/JR: Shinjuku Eki (Nishi-guchi/West Exit).

$$$$ ⊞ **Tōkyō Hilton International.** A short walk from the megalithic Tōkyō Metropolitan Government Office, the Hilton is a particular favorite of Western business travelers. When it opened in 1984, it was the largest Hilton in Asia but opted away from the prevailing atrium style in favor of more guest rooms and banquet facilities; as a result, the lobby is on a comfortable, human scale. A copper-clad spiral staircase reaching to the mezzanine floor above highlights the bar-lounge. Shōji screens instead of curtains bathe the guest rooms in soft, relaxing light. The Imari Room, with its displays of museum-quality traditional pottery, is one of Tōkyō's more elegant places to dine. ⊠ 6–6–2 Nishi-Shinjuku, Shinjuku-ku, Tōkyō-to 160-0023, ☎ 03/3344–5111; 0120/489–992 toll free, FAX 03/3342–6094, WEB www.hilton.com. 757 rooms, 50 suites. 5 restaurants, bar, no-smoking rooms, indoor and outdoor pool, sauna, 2 tennis courts, shops, cabaret, dance club, concierge floor, business services, travel services. AE, DC, MC, V. JR: Shinjuku Eki (Nishi-guchi/West Exit). Subway: Marunouchi Line, Nishi-Shinjuku Eki (Exit C8); Toei Ōedo Line, Tochō-mae Eki (all exits).

$$$–$$$$ ⊞ **Century Hyatt Hotel.** This Hyatt has the trademark atrium-style lobby: seven stories high, with open-glass elevators soaring upward and three huge chandeliers suspended from above. Single rooms tend to be small and lack good views from their windows; larger rooms are designed to create the impression of a separate sitting area. The Hyatt emphasizes its cuisine; at any given time, there is almost sure to be a special "gourmet fair" in progress, celebrating the food of one country or another and supervised by visiting celebrity chefs. ⊠ 2–7–2 Nishi-Shinjuku, Shinjuku-ku, Tōkyō-to 160-0023, ☎ 03/3349–0111, FAX 03/3344–5575, WEB www.centuryhyatt.co.jp. 750 rooms, 16 suites. 5 restaurants, 2 bars, coffee shop, no-smoking room, indoor pool, shops, concierge floor, business services, travel services. AE, DC, MC, V. Subway/JR: Shinjuku Eki (Nishi-guchi/West Exit).

$$–$$$ ⊞ **Shinjuku Washington Hotel.** This is truly a business hotel, where service is computerized as much as possible. The third-floor lobby has an automated check-in and checkout system; you are assigned a room and provided with a plastic card that opens the door and the minibar. The clerk at the counter will explain the process, but after that you're on your own. ⊠ 3–2–9 Nishi-Shinjuku, Shinjuku-ku, Tōkyō-to 160-0023, ☎ 03/3343–3111, FAX 03/3342–2575. 1,638 rooms. 5 restaurants, bar, coffee shop, no-smoking rooms. AE, DC, MC, V. Subway/JR: Shinjuku Eki (Minami-guchi/South Exit).

$$ ⊞ **Star Hotel.** Rates at this small, friendly hotel are more reasonable than
★ those at most other places in the area. The staff speaks only Japanese but is sympathetic to sign language. The rooms are clean but not spacious. A small, pleasant restaurant serves Japanese and Western food. Don't expect a doorman or a porter to help with your bags, but the size

of the Star at least allows the people at the front desk to remember your name without the help of a computer. ⌧ *7–10–5 Nishi-Shinjuku, Shinjuku-ku, Tōkyō-to 160-0023,* ☎ *03/3361–1111,* FAX *03/3369–4216. 214 rooms. 2 restaurants, bar, coffee shop, no-smoking rooms. AE, DC, MC, V. Subway/JR: Shinjuku Eki (Nishi-guchi/West Exit).*

Roppongi

$ ⊞ **Asia Center of Japan.** Established mainly for Asian students and other Asian visitors on limited budgets, these accommodations have become generally popular with foreign travelers for their easy access (a 15-minute walk) to the nightlife of Roppongi. You get good value for what you pay: rooms are small, minimally furnished, and not very well sound-proofed—but they are clean and comfortable. To get here, walk toward Roppongi on Gaien-higashi-dōri from the Akasaka post office on the corner of Aoyam-dōri, and take the first side street on the left. ⌧ *8–10–32 Akasaka, Minato-ku, Tōkyō-to 107-0052,* ☎ *03/3402–6111,* FAX *03/3402–0738. 220 rooms, 114 with bath. Bar, cafeteria. No credit cards. Subway: Ginza and Hanzō-mon lines, Aoyama-it-chōme Eki (Exit 4).*

Sekiguchi

$$$$ ⊞ **Four Seasons Hotel Chinzan-sō.** Where else will you have a chance
★ to sleep in a million-dollar room? That's about what it cost, on aver-age, to build and furnish each of the accommodations in this elegant hotel, which opened in 1992. Rooms are large by any standard; conservatory suites have their own private garden patios. Huge woolen area rugs woven in Ireland accent the Italian marble floor in the lobby. Built on what was once the estate of an imperial prince, Chinzan-sō rejoices in one of the most beautiful settings in Tōkyō; in summer the gardens are famous for their fireflies. The hotel's complimentary shuttle-bus service to the Waseda subway station (Tōzai Line) and limousine service to Tōkyō Eki make it easy to get downtown. ⌧ *2–10–8 Sekiguchi, Bunkyō-ku, Tōkyō-to 112-0014,* ☎ *03/3943–2222,* FAX *03/3943–2300,* WEB *www.fourseasons.com. 233 rooms, 50 suites. 4 restaurants, bar, coffee shop, lounge, no-smoking rooms, indoor pool, barbershop, hair salon, hot tub, Japanese baths, massage, gym, shops, chapel, concierge, business services, travel services. AE, DC, MC, V. Subway: Yūraku-chō Line, Edogawa-bashi Eki (Exit 1A).*

Shiba Kōen

$$ ⊞ **Shiba Daimon Hotel.** This moderately priced hotel a minute's walk from Zōjō-ji is popular with Japanese travelers. The staff is a bit ill at ease with guests who cannot speak Japanese but no less willing to help. The decor is unremarkable, but the rooms are reasonably spacious for the price. A good restaurant on the ground floor serves Japanese and Chinese breakfast and Chinese fare in the evening. ⌧ *2–3–6 Shiba-kōen, Minato-ku, Tōkyō-to 105-0011,* ☎ *03/3431–3716,* FAX *03/3434–5177. 96 rooms. Restaurant, no-smoking room. AE, DC, MC, V. JR: Hamamatsu-chō Eki (Kita-guchi/North Exit). Subway: Toei Asakusa Line, Daimon Eki (Exit A3).*

Shinagawa

$$$–$$$$ ⊞ **Hotel Pacific Meridien.** Just across the street from JR Shinagawa Eki, the Pacific Meridien sits on grounds that were once part of an imperial-family estate. The decor is pastel and lilac all the way to the Sky Lounge on the 30th floor, which overlooks Tōkyō Bay. The entire back wall of the coffee lounge on the ground floor is glass, the better to contemplate a tranquil Japanese garden, sculpted with rocks and waterfalls. The hotel markets itself to convention groups and business travelers. ✉ *3–13–3 Takanawa, Minato-ku, Tōkyō-to 108-0074,* ☎ *03/ 3445–6711,* FAX *03/3445–5137. 913 rooms, 41 suites. 6 restaurants, 3 bars, coffee shop, no-smoking rooms, pool, shops, concierge, business services, travel services. AE, DC, MC, V. JR Yamanote Line, Shinagawa Eki (Nishi-guchi/West Exit).*

$$$ 🏨 **Takanawa Tōbu Hotel.** The Takanawa Tōbu, a five-minute walk from Shinagawa Eki, provides good value for the price—particularly since the rate includes a buffet breakfast. Rooms are smallish and uninspired in decor, the bathrooms are the claustrophobic prefabricated plastic units beloved of business hotels, and there's no proper sitting area in the lobby, but the hotel atones for these shortcomings with a friendly staff (which speaks a bit of English) and a cozy bar. There's also a small Western restaurant, the Boulogne. ✉ *4–7–6 Takanawa, Minato-ku, Tōkyō-to 108-0074,* ☎ *03/3447–0111,* FAX *03/3447–0117. 190 rooms. Restaurant, bar. AE, DC, MC, V. JR Yamanote Line, Shinagawa Eki (Nishi-guchi/West Exit).*

Tora-no-mon

$$$$ 🏨 **ANA Hotel Tōkyō.** The ANA Hotel arrived on the Tōkyō scene in 1986, and it typifies the ziggurat-atrium style that seems to have been a requirement for hotel architecture at the time. The reception floor, with its two-story fountain, is clad in enough marble to have depleted an Italian quarry. Guest rooms are airy and spacious; those who stay on the concierge floor (35th floor) can use a separate breakfast room and a private cocktail lounge. In general, the interior designers have made skillful use of artwork and furnishings to take some of the chill off the ANA's relentless modernism. There are Chinese, French, and Japanese restaurants and three bars; the Astral Lounge on the top (37th) floor affords a superb view of the city. The hotel is a short walk from the U.S. Embassy. ✉ *1–12–33 Akasaka, Minato-ku, Tōkyō-to 107-0052,* ☎ *03/3505–1111; 0120/029–501 toll free,* FAX *03/3505–1155,* WEB *www.anahotels.com. 872 rooms, 29 suites. 8 restaurants, 4 bars, no-smoking rooms, pool, hair salon, sauna, gym, shops, concierge floor, business services, travel services. AE, DC, MC, V. Subway: Ginza and Namboku lines, Tameike-Sannō Eki (Exit 13); Namboku Line, Roppongi-itchō Eki (Exit 3).*

$$$$ 🏨 **Hotel Okura.** Year after year, a poll of business travelers ranks the
★   Okura, for its exemplary service, among the best two or three hotels in Asia. The hotel opened just before the 1964 Olympics, and, understated in its sophistication, human in its scale, it remains a favorite of diplomatic visitors. The spacious guest rooms are tastefully furnished; amenities include remote-control draperies, hair dryers, and terry bathrobes. The odd-number rooms, 871–889 inclusive, overlook a small Japanese landscaped garden. The Okura Art Museum, on the hotel grounds, displays a fine collection of antique porcelain, mother-of-pearl, and ceramics; tea ceremonies take place here Monday–Saturday 11– 4 (no charge for guests of the hotel). The main building is preferable to the south wing—which you reach by an underground shopping arcade—and the Japanese-style rooms are superb. ✉ *2–10–4 Tora-no-mon, Minato-ku, Tōkyō-to 105-0001,* ☎ *03/3582–0111; 0120/003– 751 toll free,* FAX *03/3582–3707,* WEB *www.okura.com. 798 rooms, 11 Japanese-style rooms, 48 suites. 8 restaurants, 3 bars, coffee shop, no-smoking rooms, indoor and outdoor pool, massage, steam room, gym, shops, chapel, concierge, business services, travel services. AE, DC, MC, V. Subway: Hibiya Line, Kamiya-chō Eki (Exit 3); Ginza Line, Tora-no-mon Eki (Exit 4B).*

Ueno

$ ◨ **Ryokan Katsutarō.** This small, simple, economical hotel is a five-minute walk from the entrance to Ueno Kōen and a 10-minute walk from the Tōkyō National Museum. The quietest rooms are in the back, away from the main street. A simple breakfast of toast, eggs, and coffee is served for only ¥500. To get here, leave the Nezu subway station by the Ike-no-hata Exit, cross the road, take the street running northeast, and turn right at the "T" intersection; Ryokan Katsutarō is 25 yards along Dōbut-suen-uramon-dōri, on the left-hand side. ⊠ *4–16–8 Ike-no-hata, Taitō-ku, Tōkyō-to 110-0008,* ☎ *03/3821–9808,* ᴘᴀX *03/3891–4789. 7 Japanese-style rooms, 4 with bath. Breakfast room, Japanese bath. AE, MC, V. Subway: Chiyoda Line, Nezu Eki (Exit 1/Ike-no-hata Exit).*

Yaesu

$$ ◨ **Hotel Yaesu Ryūmeikan.** It's hard to believe that a ryokan could still exist in the heart of the city's financial district, where the price of real estate is out of sight—but there is it, a three-minute walk from Tōkyō Eki. The Ryūmeikan hosts relatively few foreign guests in its mostly Japanese-style rooms, but a friendly, professional staff goes the extra mile to make them feel comfortable. Weekday evenings, a staff member who speaks English is usually available. Amenities are few—there are no nonsmoking rooms, for example, and a Japanese-style breakfast is served by reservation only—but for price and location this inn is hard to beat. ⊠ *1–3–22 Yaesu, Chūō-ku, Tōkyō-to 103-0028,* ☎ *03/3271–0971,* ᴘᴀX *03/3271–0977. 14 Japanese-style rooms, 7 Western-style rooms. Breakfast room, Japanese bath. AE, MC, V. JR and Marunouchi subway line, Tōkyō Eki (Yaesu North Exit); Tōzai subway line, Nihombashi Eki (Exit A3).*

Yanaka

$ ◨ **Sawanoya Ryokan.** The residential neighborhood, in a quiet area
★   northwest of Ueno Kōen, and the hospitality of the ryokan make you feel at home in this traditional part of Tōkyō. The family who operate this little inn truly welcome you; they'll help you plan trips and will arrange future accommodations. Two rooms have private baths, while the rest share Japanese-style common baths. No dinner is offered, but you can order a Continental (¥300) or Japanese (¥900) breakfast. Sawanoya is very popular with low-budget travelers; make a reservation by fax well before you arrive. To get here from the Nezu subway station, walk 300 yards north along Shinobazu-dōri and take the street on the right; Sawanoya is 180 yards on the right. ⊠ *2–3–11 Yanaka, Taitō-ku, Tōkyō-to 110-0001,* ☎ *03/3822–2251,* ᴘᴀX *03/3822–2252. 12 Japanese-style rooms. Breakfast room, Japanese baths. AE, MC, V. Subway: Chiyoda Line, Nezu Eki (Exit 1).*

Hostels and Dormitory Accommodations

$$ ◨ **Tōkyō YMCA.** The private rooms here come with and without bath. Both men and women can stay at the hostel, which is a three-minute walk from Awaji-chō Eki (Exit B-7) on the Marunouchi Line or seven minutes from Kanda Eki (Exit 4) on the Ginza Line. ⊠ *7 Kanda-mi-toshiro-chō, Chiyoda-ku, Tōkyō-to 101-0052,* ☎ *03/3293–1919,* ᴘᴀX *03/3293–1926. 40 rooms. No credit cards.*

$$ ◨ **YMCA Asia Youth Center.** Both men and women can stay here, and all rooms are private and have private baths. The hostel is an eight-minute walk from Suidō-bashi Eki, which is on the JR Mita Line. ⊠ *2–5–5 Saragaku, Chiyoda-ku, Tōkyō-to 101-0064,* ☎ *03/3233–0611,* ᴘᴀX *03/3233–0633. 55 rooms. No credit cards.*

$ ⊞ **Tōkyō International Youth Hostel.** In typical hostel style, you are re-
quired to be off the premises between 10 AM and 3 PM. Less typical is
the fact that for an additional ¥1,200 over the standard rate, you can
have breakfast and dinner in the hostel cafeteria. TIYH is a few minutes' walk from Iidabashi Eki on the JR, Tōzai, Namboku, and Yūraku-
chō lines. ⊠ *Central Plaza Bldg., 18th floor, 1–1 Kagura-kashi,
Shinjuku-ku, Tōkyō-to 162-0823,* ☎ *03/3235–1107,* FAX *03/3267–
4000. 138 bunk beds. No credit cards.*

Near Narita Airport

Transportation between Narita Airport and Tōkyō proper takes—at
best—about an hour. In heavy traffic, a limousine bus or taxi ride can
stretch to two hours or more. A sensible strategy for visitors with early
morning flights home would be to spend the night before at one of the
hotels near the airport, all of which have courtesy shuttles to the departure terminals; these hotels are also a boon to visitors en route elsewhere with layovers in Narita.

$$$ ⊞ **Radisson Hotel Narita Airport.** Set on 72 spacious acres of land, this
modern hotel feels somewhat like a resort—and has Narita's largest out-
door pool. A shuttle bus runs between the Radisson and the airport every
20 minutes or so (between 1 PM and 10 PM from Terminal 1, between
12:50 PM and 9:50 PM from Terminal 2); the trip takes about 20 min-
utes. ⊠ *650–35 Nanaei, Tomisato-machi, Inaba-gun, Chiba-ken 286-
0222,* ☎ *0476/93–1234,* FAX *0476/93–4834,* WEB *www.radisson.com. 496
rooms. Restaurant, no-smoking rooms, pool, 2 tennis courts, jogging,
shop. AE, DC, MC, V.*

$$–$$$ ⊞ **ANA Hotel Narita.** This 1990 hotel, like many others in the ANA
chain, aspires to architecture in the grand style; expect the cost of brass
and marble to show up on your bill. The amenities measure up, and
the proximity to the airport (about 15 minutes by shuttle bus) makes
this a good choice if you are in transit. ⊠ *68 Hori-no-uchi, Narita-
shi, Chiba-ken 286-0107,* ☎ *0476/33–1311; 0120/029–501 toll free,*
FAX *0476/33–0244,* WEB *www.anahotels.com. 422 rooms. 5 restaurants,
bar, coffee shop, no-smoking rooms, pool, shops. AE, DC, MC, V.*

$$–$$$ ⊞ **Holiday Inn Tōbu Narita.** The Western-style accommodations at this
hotel, a 10-minute ride by shuttle bus from the airport, provide the
standard—if unremarkable—range of amenities. You can also rent
one of its soundproof twin rooms for daytime-only use (11 AM–6 PM,
¥13,000). ⊠ *320–1 Tokkō, Narita-shi, Chiba-ken 286-0106,* ☎ *0476/
32–1234,* FAX *0476/32–0617,* WEB *www.basshotels.com. 500 rooms. 2
restaurants, coffee shop, bar, no-smoking rooms, pool, barbershop, hair
salon, massage, steam room, tennis court. AE, DC, MC, V.*

$$ ⊞ **Hotel Nikkō Winds Narita.** A regular shuttle bus (at Terminal 1, Bus
Stop 14; Terminal 2, Bus Stop 31) makes the 10-minute trip to this mod-
ern, efficient, all-purpose hotel with one restaurant serving Japanese,
French, and Chinese food. All rooms are soundproof. ⊠ *560 Tokkō,
Narita-shi, Chiba-ken 286-1016,* ☎ *0476/33–1111; 0120/582–586 toll
free,* FAX *0476/33–1108. 321 rooms. 5 restaurants, no-smoking rooms,
pool, sauna, 2 tennis courts, shops, meeting room. AE, DC, MC, V.*

$$ ⊞ **Narita View Hotel.** Boxy and uninspired, the Narita View offers no
view of anything in particular but can be reached by shuttle bus from
the airport in about 15 minutes. Short on charm, it tends to rely on
promotional discount "campaigns" to draw a clientele. You can also
rent rooms for daytime-only use from 11 to 6 for ¥6,500. ⊠ *700 Ko-
suge, Narita-shi, Chiba-ken 286-0127,* ☎ *0476/32–1111,* FAX *0476/32–
1078. 504 rooms. 4 restaurants, coffee shop, no-smoking rooms, hair
salon, massage. AE, DC, MC, V.*

$ ☒ **Narita Airport Rest House.** A basic business hotel without much in the way of frills, the Rest House offers the closest accommodations to the airport itself, less than five minutes away by shuttle bus. You can also rent one of its soundproof rooms for daytime-only use from 9 to 5 for about ¥5,000. ☒ *New Tōkyō International Airport, Narita-shi, Chiba-ken 286-0000,* ☎ *0476/32–1212,* FAX *0476/32–1209. 129 rooms. Restaurant, bar, coffee shop, no-smoking room. AE, DC, MC, V.*

NIGHTLIFE AND THE ARTS

The Arts

Few cities have as much to offer as Tōkyō does in the performing arts. It has Japan's own great stage traditions: Kabuki, Nō, Bunraku puppet drama, music, and dance. An astonishing variety of music, classical and popular, can be found here; Tōkyō is a proving ground for local talent and a magnet for orchestras and concert soloists from all over the world. Eric Clapton, Yo-Yo Ma, Winton Marsalis: whenever you visit, the headliners will be here. Tōkyō also has modern theater—in somewhat limited choices, to be sure, unless you can follow dialogue in Japanese, but Western repertory companies can always find receptive audiences here for plays in English. In recent years musicals have found enormous popularity here; it doesn't take long for a hit show in New York or London to open in Tōkyō.

Japan has yet to develop any real strength of its own in ballet and has only just begun to devote serious resources to opera, but for that reason touring companies like the Metropolitan, the Bolshoi, Sadler's Wells, and the Bayerische Staatsoper find Tōkyō a very compelling venue—as well they might, when even seats at ¥30,000 or more sell out far in advance.

Film presents a much broader range of possibilities than it did in the past. The major commercial distributors bring in the movies they expect will draw the biggest receipts—horror films and Oscar nominees—but there are now dozens of small theaters in Tōkyō catering to more sophisticated audiences.

Information and Tickets

One of the best comprehensive guides in English to performance schedules in Tōkyō is the "Cityscope" insert in the monthly *Tōkyō Journal* magazine. You can probably pick up the *Tōkyō Journal* at one of the newsstands at Narita Airport on your way into the city; if not, it's on sale in the bookstores at major international hotels. *Metropolis,* a free weekly magazine available at hotels, book and music stores, some restaurants and cafés, and other locations, lists up-to-date announcements of what's going on in the city. Another source, rather less complete, is the *Tour Companion,* a tabloid visitor guide published every two weeks that is available free of charge at hotels and at Japan National Tourist Organization offices.

If your hotel cannot help you with concert and performance bookings, call **Ticket Pia** (☎ 03/5237–9999) for assistance in English. Be warned: this is one of the city's major ticket agencies; the lines are always busy, and it can be maddeningly difficult to get through. When phone calls fail, try the **Playguide Agency,** which has outlets in most of the depāto and in other locations all over the city, for tickets to cultural events; you can stop in at the main office (☒ Playguide Bldg., 2–6–4 Ginza, Chūō-ku, ☎ 03/3561–8821, FAX 03/3567–0263; Yūraku-chō subway line, Ginza Itchōme Eki, Exit 4) and ask for the nearest counter. Note that agencies normally do not have tickets for same-day performances but only for advance booking.

Traditional Theater

BUNRAKU

The spiritual center of Bunraku today is Ōsaka, rather than Tōkyō, but there are a number of performances in the small hall of the Kokuritsu Gekijō. In recent years it has come into vogue with younger audiences, and Bunraku troupes will occasionally perform in trendier locations. Consult the "Cityscope" listings, or check with one of the English-speaking ticket agencies.

KABUKI

The best place to see Kabuki is at the **Kabuki-za,** built especially for this purpose, with its *hanamichi* (runway) passing diagonally through the audience to the revolving stage. Built originally in 1925, the Kabuki-za was destroyed in an air raid in 1945 and rebuilt in the identical style in 1951. Matinees usually begin at 11 and end at 4; evening performances, at 4:30, end around 9. Reserved seats are expensive and hard to come by on short notice; for a mere ¥800 to ¥1,000, however, you can buy an unreserved ticket that allows you to see one act of a play from the topmost gallery. The gallery is cleared after each act, but there's nothing to prevent you from buying another ticket. Bring binoculars—the gallery is very far from the stage. You might also want to rent an earphone set (¥650; deposit ¥1,000) to follow the play in English, but this is really more of an intrusion than a help—and you can't use the set in the topmost galleries. ⊠ *4–12–15 Ginza, Chūo-ku,* ☎ *03/5565–6000 or 03/3541–3131,* WEB *www.shochiku.co.jp/play/kabukiza/theater. Call by 6 PM the day preceding performance for reservations. Subway: Hibiya and Toei Asakusa lines, Higashi-Ginza Eki (Exit 3).*

The **Kokuritsu Gekijō** hosts Kabuki companies based elsewhere; it also has a training program for young people who may not have one of the hereditary family connections but want to break into this closely guarded profession. Debut performances, called *kao-mise*, are worth watching to catch the stars of the next generation. Reserved seats are usually ¥1,500–¥9,000. ⊠ *4–1 Hayabusa-chō, Chiyoda-ku,* ☎ *03/3230–3000. Subway: Hanzō-mon Line, Hanzō-mon Eki (Exit 1).*

The **Shimbashi Enbujō,** which dates to 1925, was built originally for the geisha of the Shimbashi quarter to present their spring and autumn performances of traditional music and dance. It's a bigger house than the Kabuki-za, and it presents a lot of traditional dance and conventional Japanese drama as well as Kabuki. Reserved seats commonly run ¥2,100–¥16,800, and there is no gallery. ⊠ *6–18–2 Ginza, Chūo-ku,* ☎ *03/5565–6000. Subway: Hibiya and Toei Asakusa lines, Higashi-Ginza Eki (Exit A6).*

NŌ

Somewhat like Kabuki, Nō is divided into a number of schools, the traditions of which developed as the exclusive property of hereditary families. The best way to see Nō is in the open air, at torchlight performances called Takigi Nō, held in the courtyards of temples. The setting and the aesthetics of the drama combine to produce an eerie theatrical experience. These performances are given at various times during the year. Consult the "Cityscope" or *Tour Companion* listings. Tickets sell out quickly and are normally available only through the temples.

Nō performances occasionally take place in public halls, like the **National Nō Theater,** but are primarily done in the theaters of the individual schools—which also teach their dance and recitation styles to amateurs. ⊠ *4–18–1 Sendagaya, Shibuya-ku,* ☎ *03/3423–1331. JR Chūo Line, Sendagaya Eki (Minami-guchi/South Exit); Ōedo subway line, Kokuritsu-Kyōgijō Eki (Exit A4).*

Among the most important of the Nō family schools in Tōkyō is the **Kanze Nō-gakudō,** founded in the 14th century. The current iemoto (head) of the school is the 26th in his line. ✉ 1–16–4 Shōtō, Shibuya-ku, ☎ 03/3469–5241. *Subway: Ginza and Hanzō-mon lines, Shibuya Eki (Exit 3A).*

Founded in the 14th century, the Hōshō School of Nō maintains a tradition of severe, stately—nay, glacially slow—movement that may strike audiences as more like religious ritual than theater. Performances take place at the **Hōshō Nō-gakudō.** ✉ 1–5–9 Hongo, Bunkyō-ku, ☎ 03/3811–4843. *Subway: Toei Mita Line, Suidō-bashi Eki (Exit A1).*

Johnny-come-lately in the world of Nō is the Umewaka School, founded in 1921. Classes and performances are held at the **Umewaka Nō-gakuin.** ✉ 2–6–14 Higashi-Nakano, Nakano-ku, ☎ 03/3363–7748. *JR Chūō Line, Higashi-Nakano Eki (Exit 2); Marunouchi and Ōedo subway lines, Nakano-saka-ue Eki (Exit A1).*

Modern Theater

The *Shingeki* (Modern Theater) movement began in Japan at about the turn of the 20th century, coping at first with the lack of native repertoire by performing translations of Western dramatists from Shakespeare to Shaw. It wasn't until around 1915 that Japanese playwrights began writing for the Shingeki stage, but modern drama did not really develop a voice of its own here until after World War II.

The watershed years came around 1965, when experimental theater companies, unable to find commercial space, began taking their work to young audiences in various unusual ways: street plays and "happenings"; dramatic readings in underground malls and rented lofts; tents put up on vacant lots for unannounced performances (miraculously filled to capacity by word of mouth) and taken down the next day. It was in this period that surrealist playwright Kōbō Abe found his stride and director Tadashi Suzuki developed the unique system of training that now draws aspiring actors from all over the world to his "theater community" in the mountains of Toyama Prefecture. Japanese drama today is a lively art indeed; theaters small and large, in unexpected pockets all over Tōkyō, attest to its vitality.

The great majority of these performances, however, are in Japanese, for Japanese audiences. You're unlikely to find one with program notes in English to help you follow it. Unless it's a play you already know well, and you're curious to see how it translates, you might do well to think of some other way to spend your evenings out.

Language poses no barrier to an enjoyment of the **Takarazuka**—Japan's own, wonderfully goofy all-female review. The troupe was founded in the Ōsaka suburb of Takarazuka in 1913 and has been going strong ever since; today it has not one but five companies, one of them with a permanent home in Tōkyō. Located for many years across the street from the Imperial Hotel, in Hibiya, the 2,069-seat **Tōkyō Takarazuka Theatre** was rebuilt in 2001, grander and goofier than ever. Tickets are ¥3,800–¥10,000 for regular performances, ¥2,000–¥5,000 for debut performances with the company's budding ingenues. Everybody sings; everybody dances; the sets are breathtaking; the costumes are swell. Where else but at the Takarazuka could you see *Gone With the Wind*, sung in Japanese, with a young woman in a mustache and a frock coat playing Rhett Butler? ✉ 1–1–3 Yūraku-chō, Chiyoda-ku, ☎ 03/5251–2001. *JR Yamanote Line, Yūraku-chō Eki (Hibiya-guchi Exit); Hibiya subway line, Hibiya Eki (Exit A5); Chiyoda and Toei Mita subway lines, Hibiya Eki (Exit A13).*

Music

Information in English about venues for traditional Japanese music (*koto*, *shamisen*, and so forth) can be a bit hard to find; check newspaper listings for concerts and school recitals. Western music poses no such problem: during the 1980s and early 1990s a considerable number of new concert halls and performance spaces sprang up all over the city, adding to what was already an excellent roster of public auditoriums. The following are a few of the most important.

Casals Hall, the last of the fine small auditoriums built for chamber music, before the Japanese bubble economy collapsed in the early '90s, was designed by architect Arata Isozaki—justly famous for the Museum of Contemporary Art in Los Angeles. In addition to chamber music, Casals draws piano, guitar, cello, and voice soloists. ⊠ *1–6 Kanda Surugadai, Chiyoda-ku,* ☎ *03/3294–1229. JR Chūō Line and Marunouchi subway line, Ochanomizu Eki (Exit 2).*

Iino Hall, built before Japan fell fatally in love with marble, maintains a reputation for comfort, intelligent programming, and excellent acoustics. Chamber music and Japanese concert soloists perform here. ⊠ *2–1–1 Uchisaiwai-chō, Chiyoda-ku,* ☎ *03/3506–3251. Subway: Chiyoda and Hibiya lines, Kasumigaseki Eki (Exit C4); Marunouchi Line, Kasumigaseki Eki (Exit B2); Ginza Line, Toranomon Eki (Exit 9); Toei Mita Line, Uchisaiwai-chō Eki (Exit A7).*

Ishi-bashi Memorial Hall's pride is its wonderful pipe organ. Alas, it seldom schedules organ concerts but is a favorite venue for piano and violin solo recitals, string quartets, and small chamber orchestras. ⊠ *4–24–12 Higashi Ueno, Taitō-ku,* ☎ *03/3843–3043. Subway: Ginza Line, Inari-chō Eki (Exit 3).*

Nakano Sun Plaza hosts everything from rock to Argentine tango. ⊠ *4–1–1 Nakano, Nakano-ku,* ☎ *03/3388–1151. JR and Tōzai subway line, Nakano Eki (Kita-guchi/North Exit).*

NHK Hall, home base for the Japan Broadcasting Corporation's NHK Symphony Orchestra, is probably the auditorium most familiar to Japanese lovers of classical music, as performances here are routinely re-broadcast on NHK-TV. ⊠ *2–2–1 Jinnan, Shibuya-ku,* ☎ *03/3465–1751. JR Yamanote Line, Shibuya Eki (Hachiko Exit); Ginza and Hanzō-mon subway lines, Shibuya Eki (Exits 6 and 7).*

New National Theatre and Tōkyō Opera City Concert Hall, with its 1,810-seat main auditorium, nourishes Japan's fledgling efforts to make a name for itself in the world of opera. ⊠ *3–20–2 Nishi-Shinjuku, Shinjuku-ku,* ☎ *03/5353–0788; 03/5353–9999 for tickets,* WEB *www. tokyooperacity-cf.or.jp. Subway: Keiō Shin-sen Line, Hatsudai Eki (Higashi-guchi/East Exit).*

Suntory Hall, in the Ark Hills complex, is among the most lavishly appointed of the concert auditoriums built in Japan in the past decade. It is also one of the best located for theatergoers who want to extend their evening out: there's an abundance of good restaurants and bars nearby. ⊠ *1–13–1 Akasaka, Minato-ku,* ☎ *03/3505–1001. Subway: Ginza and Namboku lines, Tameike-Sannō Eki (Exit 13).*

Tōkyō Bunka Kaikan (Tōkyō Metropolitan Festival Hall) was, in the 1960s and '70s, perhaps the city's premier showcase for orchestral music and visiting soloists and still gets major bookings. ⊠ *5–45 Ueno Kōen, Taitō-ku,* ☎ *03/3828–2111. JR Yamanote Line, Ueno Eki (Kōen-guchi/Park Exit).*

Tōkyō Dome, a 55,000-seat sports arena, hosts the biggest acts from abroad in rock and popular music. ⊠ *1–3–61 Kōraku, Bunkyō-ku,* ☎ *03/5800–9999. Subway: Marunouchi and Namboku lines, Kōraku-en Eki (Exit 2); Ōedo and Toei Mita lines, Kasuga Eki (Exit A2); JR Suidō-bashi Eki (Nishi-guchi/West Exit).*

Dance

Traditional Japanese dance, like flower arranging and the tea ceremony, is divided into dozens of styles, ancient of lineage and fiercely
proud of their differences from each other. In fact, only the aficionado
can really tell them apart. They survive not so much as performing arts
but as schools, offering dance as a cultured accomplishment to interested amateurs. At least once a year, teachers and their students in each
of these schools hold a recital, so that on any given evening there's very
likely to be one somewhere in Tōkyō. Truly professional performances
are given, as mentioned previously, at the Kokuritsu Gekijō and the Shimbashi Enbujō; the most important of the classical schools, however, developed as an aspect of Kabuki, and if you attend a play at the Kabuki-za,
you are almost guaranteed to see a representative example.

Ballet began to attract a Japanese following in 1920, when Anna
Pavlova danced *The Dying Swan* at the old Imperial Theater. The
well-known companies that come to Tōkyō from abroad perform to
full houses, usually at the Tōkyō Metropolitan Festival Hall in Ueno.
There are now about 15 professional Japanese ballet companies, several of which have toured abroad, but this has yet to become an art
form on which Japan has had much of an impact.

Modern dance is a different story—a story that begins with a visit in
1955 by the Martha Graham Dance Company. The decade that followed was one of great turmoil in Japan; it was a period of dissatis-
faction—political, intellectual, artistic—with old forms and conventions.
The work of pioneers like Graham inspired a great number of talented
dancers and choreographers to explore new avenues of self-expression.
One of the fruits of that exploration was Butō, a movement that was
at once uniquely Japanese and a major contribution to the world of
modern dance.

The father of Butō was the dancer Tatsumi Hijikata (1928–86). The
watershed work was his *Revolt of the Flesh,* which premiered in 1968.
Others soon followed: Kazuo Ono, Min Tanaka, Akaji Marō and the
Dai Rakuda Kan troupe, and Ushio Amagatsu and the Sankai Juku.
To most Japanese, their work was inexplicably grotesque. Dancers performed with shaved heads, dressed in rags or with naked bodies painted
completely white, their movements agonized and contorted. The images were dark and demonic, violent and explicitly sexual. Butō was
an exploration of the unconscious: its gods were the gods of the Japanese village and the gods of prehistory; its literary inspirations came
from Mishima, Genet, Artaud. Like many other modern Japanese
artists, the Butō dancers and choreographers were largely ignored by
the mainstream until they began to appear abroad—to thunderous critical acclaim. Now they are equally honored at home. Butō does not
lend itself to conventional spaces (a few years ago, for example, the
Dai Rakuda Kan premiered one of its new works in a limestone cave
in Gunma Prefecture), but if there's a performance in Tōkyō, "Cityscope"
will have the schedule. Don't miss it.

Film

One of the best things about foreign films in Japan is that the distributors invariably add Japanese subtitles rather than dub their offerings,
the way it's done so often elsewhere. The original sound track, of course,
may not be all that helpful to you if the film is Polish or Italian, but
the vast majority of first-run foreign films here are made in the United
States. Choices are limited, however, and films take so long to open in
Tōkyō that you've probably seen them all already at home. And tickets are expensive—around ¥1,800 for general admission and ¥2,500–
¥3,000 for a reserved seat, called a *shitei-seki*.

The native Japanese film industry has been in a slump for more than 20 years, though it has intermittent spasms of recovery. Now and again a Japanese entry—usually by an independent producer or director—will walk off with an unexpected prize at a European film festival and then get the recognition it deserves at home. Rarely, a Japanese film (like the 1997 *Shall We Dance?*) will be a box office success abroad. The major studios, however, are for the most part a lost cause, cranking out animations, low-budget gangster movies, and sentimental comedies to keep themselves afloat.

First-run theaters that have new releases, both Japanese and foreign, are clustered for the most part in three areas: Shinjuku, Shibuya, and Yūraku-chō-Hibiya-Ginza. At most of them, the last showing of the evening starts at around 7. This is not the case, however, with the best news on the Tōkyō film scene: the handful of small theaters that take a special interest in classics, revivals, and serious imports. Somewhere on the premises will also be a chrome-and-marble coffee shop, a fashionable little bar, or even a decent restaurant. Most of these small theaters have a midnight show—at least on the weekends. The **Bunka-mura** complex in Shibuya has two movie theaters, a concert auditorium (Orchard Hall), and a performance space (Theater Cocoon); it is the principal venue for many of Tōkyō's film festivals. ✉ *2–24–1 Dōgen-zaka,* ☎ *03/3477–9999. JR Yamanote Line, Shibuya Eki (Hachiko Exit).*

Chanter Cine, a three-screen cinema complex, tends to show British and American films by independent producers but also showcases fine work by filmmakers from Asia and the Middle East. ✉ *1–2–2 Yūraku-chō, Chiyoda-ku,* ☎ *03/3591–1511. Subway: Hibiya, Chiyoda, and Toei Mita lines; Hibiya Eki (Exit A5).*

Cine Saison Shibuya occasionally gets in recent releases by award-winning directors from such countries as Iran, China, and South Korea as well as popular releases. ✉ *Prime Bldg., 2–29–5 Dōgen-zaka, Shibuya-ku,* ☎ *03/3770–1721. JR Yamanote Line, Shibuya Eki (Hachiko Exit).*

Haiyū-za is primarily a repertory theater, but its **Haiyū-za Talkie Nights** screens notable foreign films. ✉ *4–9–2 Roppongi, Minato-ku,* ☎ *03/3401–4073. Subway: Hibiya Line, Roppongi Eki (Exit 4A).*

Nightlife

Tōkyō has more sheer diversity of nightlife than any other Japanese city. That diversity can be daunting—if not downright hazardous. Few bars and clubs have printed price lists; fewer still have lists in English. That drink you've just ordered could set you back a reasonable ¥1,000; you might, on the other hand, have wandered unknowingly into a place that charges you ¥15,000 up front for a whole bottle—and slaps a ¥20,000 cover charge on top. If the bar has hostesses, it is often unclear what the companionship of one will cost you, or whether she is there just for conversation. There is, of course, a certain amount of safe ground: hotel lounges, jazz clubs, bars, and cabarets where foreigners come out to play—and the unspoken rules of nightlife are pretty much the way they are anywhere else. But wandering off the beaten path in Tōkyō can be like shopping for a yacht: if you have to ask how much it costs, you probably can't afford it anyhow.

There are five major districts in Tōkyō that have an extensive nightlife and have places that make foreigners welcome. The *kinds* of entertainment will not vary much from one to another; the tone, style, and prices will.

Akasaka nightlife concentrates mainly on two streets, Ta-machi-dōri and Hitotsugi-dōri, and the small alleys connecting them. The area has several cabarets and nightclubs, and a wide range of wine bars, coffee shops, late-night restaurants, pubs, and "snacks"—counter bars that will serve (and charge you for) small portions of food with your drinks, whether you order them or not. Akasaka is sophisticated and upscale, not quite as expensive as Ginza and not as popular as Roppongi. Being fairly compact, it makes a convenient venue for testing the waters of Japanese nightlife.

Ginza is probably the city's most well-known entertainment district, and one of the most—if not *the* most—expensive in the world. It does have affordable restaurants and pubs, but its reputation rests on the exclusive hostess clubs where only the highest of high rollers on corporate expense accounts can take their clients. In recent years many corporations have been taking a harder look at those accounts, and Ginza as a nightlife destination has suffered in the process.

Roppongi draws a largely foreign crowd and is the part of Tōkyō where Westerners are most likely to feel at home, though the area's reputation as a haunt of the rich and beautiful has taken a battering recently as petty crime and general unpleasantness dog Roppongi's once-flourishing nightlife. With the cool kids getting their kicks in Aoyama and Azabu and even the stiletto-heel brigade migrating to Shibuya, Roppongi's club scene is in decay. It's best for barhopping.

Shibuya, less expensive than Roppongi and not as raunchy as Shinjuku, attracts mainly students and young professionals to its many *nomiya* (inexpensive bars). There's something a bit provincial about it, in that respect, and there are few places where you can count on communicating in English, but if you know a little Japanese, this is a pleasant and inexpensive area for an evening out.

Shinjuku's Kabuki-chō is the city's wildest nightlife venue. The options range from the marginally respectable down to the merely sleazy to where you can almost hear the viruses mutating. Bars (straight, gay, cross-dress, S&M), nightclubs, cabarets, discos, hole-in-the-wall pubs, love-by-the-hour hotels: Kabuki-chō has it all. Just stay clear of places with English-speaking touts out front, and you'll be fine. If you're a woman unescorted, however, you probably want to stay out of Kabuki-chō after 9 PM; by then there are bound to be a few men drunk enough to make nuisances of themselves.

Bars

Agave. Tucked away in a basement just off Roppongi's main drag, Roppongi-dōri, is the perfect place for anyone who craves mariachi and a margarita. With more than 400 types of tequila on offer at Agave, lovers of Mexican firewater won't be disappointed. You can line your stomach with a selection of nachos and other snacks before a slammer session. ⊠ *Clover Bldg. B1F, 7–15–10 Roppongi, Minato-ku,* ☎ *03/ 3497–0229. Drinks from ¥800.* ☉ *Mon.–Thurs. 6:30 PM–2 AM, Fri. 6:30 PM–4 AM, Sat. 6 PM–4 AM. Subway: Hibiya Line, Roppongi Eki.*

Charleston. For years this has been the schmoozing and hunting bar for Tōkyō's single foreign community, and the young Japanese who want to meet them. It's noisy and packed until the wee small hours. ⊠ *3–8–11 Roppongi, Minato-ku,* ☎ *03/3402–0372. Drinks from ¥800.* ☉ *Nightly 6 PM–5 AM. Subway: Hibiya Line, Roppongi Eki.*

Den. Launched by the mammoth beer and whiskey maker Suntory, Den is partly an exercise in corporate-image making. Meant to express the company's ecoconsciousness and its roots in traditional Japanese culture, the motif here is a confection of stones, trees, and articles of folkcraft. Den draws a fashionable crowd from the TV production, PR, and design companies in this part of town. ⊠ *DST Bldg., 1st floor, 4– 2–3 Akasaka, Minato-ku,* ☎ *03/3584–1899. Drinks from ¥800.* ☉ *Mon.–Thurs. 6 PM–2 AM, Fri. 6 PM–4 AM, Sat. 6 PM–11 PM.. Subway: Marunouchi Line, Akasaka-mitsuke Eki (Belle Vie Akasaka Exit).*

Ginza Inz 2. Inside this building and one floor up is a collection of small, popular-priced bars and restaurants where people who work in the area go after hours. One such bar is the **Americana** (☎ 03/3564–1971), where drinks start at ¥800. Farther along the hallway is the **Ginza Swing** (☎ 03/3563–3757), which hosts live bands playing swing jazz. The cover varies but is usually ¥2,800; drinks start at ¥700. Ginza Inz 2 is one building east of the Kōtsū Kaikan Building; you can recognize the latter by the circular sky lounge on the roof. ⊠ *2–2 Nishi-Ginza, Chūō-ku. Subway/JR: Yūraku-chō Eki (Central Exit).*

Highlander. The Highlander Bar in the Hotel Okura purports to stock 224 brands of Scotch whiskey, 48 of them single malts. This is a smart place to meet business acquaintances or to have a civilized drink. ⊠ *Hotel Okura, 2–10–4 Tora-no-mon, Minato-ku,* ☎ *03/3505–6077. Drinks from ¥1,100.* ◷ *Mon.–Sat. 11:30 AM–1 AM, Sun. 11:30 AM– midnight. Subway: Ginza Line, Tora-no-mon Eki (Exit 3).*

The Old Imperial Bar. Comfortable and sedate, this is the pride of the Imperial Hotel, decorated with elements saved from Frank Lloyd Wright's earlier version of the building—alas, long since torn down. ⊠ *Imperial Hotel, 1–1–1 Uchisaiwai-chō, Chiyoda-ku,* ☎ *03/3504– 1111. Drinks from ¥1,000.* ◷ *Daily 11:30 AM–midnight. Subway: Hibiya Eki (Exit A13).*

Wine Bar. Racks and casks and dimly lighted corners: the atmosphere at this European-style bistro appeals to Japanese and gaijin. This is a good place to take a date before moving on to the dance clubs. ⊠ *5– 6–12 Ginza, Chuo-ku,* ☎ *03/3569–7211. Drinks from ¥600.* ◷ *Daily 5 PM–11:30 PM. Subway: Ginza and Hibiya lines, Ginza Eki (Ginza exit).*

Beer Halls

Kirin City. There's somewhat less glass-thumping and mock-Oktober-fest good cheer here than at other brewery-sponsored beer halls, but the menu of grilled chicken, fried potatoes, onion rings, and other snacks to wash down with a brew is just as good. The clientele tends to be groups of white-collar youngsters from area offices, unwinding after work. ⊠ *Bunshōdo Bldg., 2nd floor, 3–4–12 Ginza, Chūō-ku,* ☎ *03/ 3562–2593. Beer ¥460.* ◷ *Daily 11:30–11. Subway: Ginza, Hibiya, and Marunouchi lines, Ginza Eki (Exit A13).*

Sapporo Lion. For a casual evening of beer and ballast—anything from yakitori to spaghetti—the Sapporo Lion is a popular and inexpensive choice. The entrance is off Chūō-dōri, near the Matsuzakaya depāto. ⊠ *6–10–12 Ginza, Chūō-ku,* ☎ *03/3571–2590. Beer from ¥590.* ◷ *Mon.–Sat. 11:30–11. Subway: Ginza, Hibiya, and Marunouchi lines, Ginza Eki (Exit A3).*

What the Dickens. Sixteenth-century English-style pubs have been the big trend in Tōkyō in the past few years, and this is the king of them all, particularly for the gaijin crowd. In a former Aum Shinri Kyō headquarters in Ebisu (the cult held responsible for the gas attack in the Tōkyō subway), it is nearly always packed. There are live stage acts and poetry readings (first Sunday of the month), and live music starts nightly at 8:30. ⊠ *1–13–3 Ebisu-Nishi, Shibuya-ku, Roob 6 Bldg., 4th floor,* ☎ *03/3780–2099.* ◷ *Sun. 5 PM–midnight, Tues.–Wed. 5 PM–1 AM, Thurs.–Sat. 5 PM–2 AM. Subway: Hibiya Line, Ebisu Eki (JR Ebisu Nishi-guchi/West Exit).*

Dance Clubs

The club scene is alive in Tōkyō but less well than it was before the uptown crowd started to feel the pinch in its discretionary income. Dance clubs have always been ephemeral ventures, anyhow. They disappear fairly regularly, to open again with new identities, stranger names, and newer gimmicks—although the money behind them is usually the same. Even those listed here come with no guarantee they'll be around when you arrive, but it can't hurt to investigate. Where else can you work out, survey the vinyl-miniskirt brigades, and get a drink at 3 AM?

Bul-let's. Billed as an "ambient space," this club is so laid-back there are even a couple of mattresses in the middle of the room for those too tired to cut a rug. DJs spin minimal and electronica to a young and groovy crowd—a haven for lounge lizards in the maelstrom of Roppongi. ⊠ *B1F 1–7–11 Nishi-Azabu, Minato-ku,* ☎ *03/3401–4844. ¥1,000–¥2,000 (varies by event).* ⊙ *Daily 10 PM–late (varies by event). Subway: Hibiya and Ōedo lines, Roppongi Eki.*

Geoid/Flower. Geoid's way-after-hours (it opens at 5 AM) techno beats keep after-Roppongi party clubbers going until it closes at 1 PM—the same day. It's on Telebi Asahi-dōri, halfway between Roppongi and Hiro-o. ⊠ *Togensha Visiting Bldg., basement, 3–5–5 Nishi-Azabu, Minato-ku,* ☎ *03/3479–8161.* ⊠ *¥2,500 (varies by event).* ⊙ *Sat. 5 AM– 1 PM. Subway: Hibiya and Ōedo lines, Roppongi Eki.*

Luners. At this two-story venue, barflies sit it out with a martini upstairs while hard-core dancers head for the packed dance floor in the basement. DJ offerings usually include house, trance, or a combination of the two, with monthly gay/mixed parties attracting Tōkyō's out-and-out clubbers. ⊠ *Fukao Bldg., 1st floor and basement, 1–4–5 Azabu-jūban, Minato-ku,* ☎ *03/3586–6383.* ⊠ *¥3,000–¥3,500 (varies by event).* ⊙ *Fri.–Sun. 10 PM–5 AM. Subway: Ōedo Line, Azabu-jūban Eki (Exit 7).*

Maniac Love. Known by Tōkyōites for its consistently excellent techno, garage, and ambient music, Maniac Love proves that Japanese DJs have technique to support their style. It helps that they tend to become experts in their genres by collecting even the most obscure tracks. The club also hosts regular Sunday-morning after-hours parties from 5 AM. The ¥1,000 after-hours entry fee includes free coffee. ⊠ *5–10–6 Minami-Aoyama, off Kottō-dōri,* ☎ *03/3406–1166.* ⊠ *¥2,500, ¥1,000 for after-hours party.* ⊙ *Sun.–Fri. until 5 AM (Sun. after-hours party usually ends by lunchtime); Sat. until 10 AM. Subway: Ginza and Hanzō-mon lines, Omotesandō Eki.*

Milk. In the basement beneath What the Dickens Pub, this place is a milk bar à la *Clockwork Orange.* With tables shaped like nude women and obscene inflatable goodies, this club caters to young Tōkyōites who yearn for digital sounds, techno, or even hard rock in an erotic atmosphere. Milk hosts hip live acts and avant-garde events. DJs and the types of music change daily. ⊠ *1–13–3 Ebisu-Nishi, Roob 6 Bldg., basement and 2nd-level basement, Shibuya-ku,* ☎ *03/5458–2826.* ⊠ *¥3,500, with 2 drinks.* ⊙ *Nightly 8 PM–4 AM. JR Yamanote and Hibiya subway line: Ebisu Eki (JR Ebisu Nishi-guchi/West Exit).*

Organ Bar. The eclectic selection at the Organ Bar, an avant-garde addition to Shibuya's nightspots, ranges from jazz to disco with a spot of poetry reading thrown in for good measure. There are no actual organs (musical or bodily) to speak of. ⊠ *Kuretake Bldg. 3F, 4–9 Udagawa-chō, Shibuya-ku,* ☎ *03/5489–5460.* ⊠ *Sun.–Thurs. ¥1,000, Fri. and Sat. special events ¥2,000.* ⊙ *Nightly 9 PM–4 AM. JR Yamanote and Ginza and Hanzō-mon subway lines: Shibuya Eki (Hachiko Exit).*

328 (San-ni-pa). A fixture on the club scene since the early '90s, 328 hosts all genres of music. Across the street from Hobson's Ice Cream and next to the police box at the Nishi-Azabu intersection, 328 is often crowded due to its reputation for providing a consistently good time. It's rumored that musician Ryuichi Sakamoto and famous fashion designers sometimes stop by. ⊠ *3–24–20 Nishi-Azabu, basement, Minato-ku,* ☎ *03/3401–4968.* ⊠ *¥2,500, with 2 drinks.* ⊙ *Nightly 8 PM– 5 AM. Subway: Hibiya and Ōedo lines, Roppongi Eki, then a 10-min walk; from Shibuya, take Roppongi-bound bus.*

Live Music
Body and Soul. Owner Kyoko Seki has been a jazz fan and an impresario for nearly 20 years. There's nothing fancy about this place—just good, serious jazz, some of it played by musicians who come in after hours, when they've finished gigs elsewhere, just to jam. ⊠ *Anise Minami-Aoyama Bldg., B1 floor, 6–13–9 Minami-Aoyama, Minato-ku,* ☎ *03/5466–3348.* ⊡ *Cover charge ¥3,500–¥4,000, drinks from ¥700.* ☉ *Mon.–Sat. 7 PM–12:30 AM. Subway: Hibiya Line, Roppongi Eki.*

Club Quattro. More a concert hall than a club, the Quattro hosts one show nightly, with a heavy accent on world music—especially Latin and African—by Japanese and foreign groups. Audiences tend to be young and enthusiastic. ⊠ *Parco IV Bldg., 32–13 Utagawa-chō, Shibuya-ku,* ☎ *03/3477–8750.* ⊡ *Cover charge ¥2,500–¥7,000.* ☉ *Shows usually start at 7 PM. Subway/JR: Shibuya Eki (Kita-guchi/North Exit for JR Yamanote Line and Ginza subway line; Exits 5 and 8 for Hanzō-mon subway line).*

Skyline Lounges
New York Bar. All the style you would expect of one of the city's top hotels combined with superior views of Shinjuku's skyscrapers and neon-lighted streets make the New York Bar one of Tōkyō's premier nighttime venues. The price of the drinks may encourage you to sip quite slowly as you enjoy the view. And while the cover charge may be steep, the quality of the jazz on offer equals that of the view. ⊠ *Park Hyatt Hotel 52F, 3–7–1–2 Nishi-Shinjuku, Shinjuku-ku,* ☎ *03/5322–1234. Cover charge ¥1,700 (from 8 PM Mon.–Sat., 7 PM Sun.). Drinks start at ¥800.* ☉ *Mon.–Sat. 5 PM–midnight, Sun. 4 PM–11 PM. Subway: Ōedo Line, Tochō-mae Eki.*

Top of Akasaka. On the 40th floor of the Akasaka Prince Hotel, you can enjoy some of the finest views of Tōkyō. If you can time your visit for dusk, the price of one drink gets you two views—the daylight sprawl of buildings and the twinkling lights of evening. ⊠ *Akasaka Prince, 1–2 Kioi-chō, Chiyoda-ku,* ☎ *03/3234–1111. Drinks start at ¥1,000. Table charge ¥800 per person.* ☉ *Weekdays noon–2 AM, weekends noon–midnight. Subway: Ginza and Marunouchi lines, Akasaka-mitsuke Eki (Exit D).*

OUTDOOR ACTIVITIES AND SPORTS

Participant Sports

Golf
Golfing can be a daunting prospect for the casual visitor to Tōkyō: The few public courses are far from the city, and booking a tee time on even a week's notice is almost impossible. What you can do, however, if the golf bug is in your blood, is groove your swing at one of the many practice ranges in Tōkyō itself. Most driving ranges are open from 11 AM to 7 or 8 at night and will rent you a club for around ¥200. At **Golf Range Pinflag** (⊠ 1–7–13 Tsukiji, Chūō-ku, ☎ 03/3542–2936; Hibiya subway line, Tsukiji Eki [Exit 4]), a bucket of 24 balls costs ¥350, and you can generally get a tee without waiting very long. At the **Meguro Gorufu-jō** (⊠ 5–6–22 Kami-Meguro, Meguro-ku, ☎ 03/3713–2805; Tōkyū Toyoko private railway line, Nakameguro Eki), you buy a prepaid card for ¥2,000, which allows you to hit up to 142 balls. The centrally located **Shiba Gofuru-jō** (⊠ 4–8–2 Shiba Kōen, Minato-ku, ☎ 03/5470–1111; Toei Mita subway line, Shiba Kōen Eki [Exit A4]) has three decks of practice tees. A bucket of only 20 balls costs ¥650 weekdays, ¥900 weekends.

Jogging

The venue of choice for runners who work in the central wards of Chūō-ku and Chiyoda-ku is the **Imperial Palace Outer garden.** Sakurada-mon, at the west end of the park, is the traditional starting point for the 5-km (3-mi) run around the palace—though you can join in anywhere along the route. Jogging around the palace is a ritual that begins as early as 6 AM and goes on throughout the day, no matter what the weather. Almost everybody runs the course counterclockwise. Now and then you may spot someone going the opposite way, but freethinking of this sort is frowned upon in Japan.

Swimming and Fitness

Pools and fitness centers abound in Tōkyō, but the vast majority of them are for members only. At the major international hotels, you would have guest privileges at these facilities, but if your accommodations are further downscale, places to swim or work out are harder to find. The fitness center at **Big Box Seibu Sports Plaza Athletic Club** (⊠ 1–35–3 Takadano-baba, Shinjuku-ku, ☎ 03/3208–7171) is open to non-members for ¥4,000; use of the pool, which is only available on Sunday 10–6, is an additional ¥1,500. The **Clark Hatch Fitness Center** (⊠ 2–1–3 Azabu-dai, Minato-ku, ☎ 03/3584–4092) has a full array of machines for mortification of the flesh and charges a guest fee of ¥2,600 for nonmembers. It does not have a pool. You don't have to be a resident to use one of the facilities operated by the various wards of Tōkyō; one of the best of these is the **Minato Ward Shiba Pool** (⊠ 2–7–2 Shiba Kōen, Minato-ku, ☎ 03/3431–4449), which is open Tuesday–Saturday 9:30–8 and Sunday–Monday 9:30–5. The pool charges only ¥300 for two hours of swimming.

Spectator Sports

Baseball

Since 2001, when superstar Ichirō Suzuki moved to the Seattle Mariners and made the All-Star team in his first major-league season, baseball frenzy has never been greater in Japan. The game, to be sure, has been a national obsession for more than a century—but don't imagine that it's played quite the same way here as it is elsewhere. The pace and style, the fans and their worldview, are uniquely Japanese. An afternoon in the bleachers, when a despised rival like the Hanshin Tigers are in town from Ōsaka, will give you insights into the temper of everyday life available nowhere else.

The Japanese baseball season runs between April and October. Same-day tickets are hard to come by; try the **Playguide** ticket agency (☎ 03/3561–8821). **Ticket Pia** (☎ 03/5237–9999) handles mainly music and theater but can also book and sell tickets to sporting events. Depending on the stadium, the date, and the seat location, expect to pay from ¥1,900 to ¥8,000 for an afternoon at the ballpark.

Baseball fans in Tōkyō are blessed with a choice of three home teams. The Yomiuri Giants and the Nippon Ham Fighters both play at the 55,000-seat **Tōkyō Dome.** ⊠ 1–3–61 Kōraku, Bunkyō-ku, ☎ 03/5800–9999. *Subway: Marunouchi and Namboku lines, Kōraku-en Eki (Exit 2); Ōedo and Toei Mita lines, Kasuga Eki (Exit A2); JR Suidō-bashi Eki (Nishi-guchi/West Exit).*

The home ground of the Yakult Swallows is **Jingū Baseball Stadium,** in the Outer Gardens of Meiji Jingū. ⊠ 13 Kasumigaoka, Shinjuku-ku, ☎ 03/3404–8999. *Subway: Ginza Line, Gaien-mae Eki (Exit 2).*

Soccer

Soccer is one of the marketing miracles of Japan. It was launched as a full-fledged professional sport only in 1993, and within three years—buoyed by a stunningly successful media hype—was drawing crowds of 6 million spectators a season. Much of that success was due to superstars like Gary Linaker and Dragan Stojkovic, who came to Japan to finish out their careers and train the inexperienced local teams. By 1990, the J. League had 26 teams in two divisions, and European and Latin American clubs were scouting for talented Japanese players. The popularity of soccer waned for a time but has revived again—thanks in part to Japan's successful bid to co-host the 2002 World Cup, and in part by the introduction in 2001 of legalized gambling on the results of the J. League's 13 weekly matches. (The biggest payoff in the "Toto" pools is ¥100 million.)

The original J. League marketing plan called for the fledgling soccer clubs to be sponsored by small cities in the provinces, many of them with moribund economies and declining populations; these cities would build modest stadiums for their clubs and ride the popularity of soccer back to prosperity. The plan worked, with one odd result: Tōkyō never acquired a home team. Now it has two, FC Tōkyō and Tōkyō Verde, both of which play at the 50,000-seat **Tōkyō Stadium** in Tama. The J. League season has two 15-week schedules, one beginning in mid-March and the other in mid-August; visitors to Tōkyō have a pretty fair window of opportunity to see a match. Tickets cost ¥1,000–¥6,000 and can be ordered through **Playguide** (☎ 03/3561–8821) or **Ticket Pia** (☎ 03/5237–9999). ✉ *376–3 Nishi-machi, Chōfu-shi,* ☎ *0424/ 40–0555. JR Keiō Line, Tobitakyū Eki.*

Sumō

Sumō wrestling dates back some 1,500 years. Originally it was not merely a sport but a religious rite, performed at shrines to entertain the gods that presided over the harvest. Ritual and ceremony are still important elements of sumō matches—contestants in unique regalia, referees in gorgeous costumes, elaborately choreographed openings and closings. To the casual spectator a match itself can look like a mostly naked free-for-all. Stripped down to silk loincloths, the two wrestlers square off in a dirt ring about 15 ft in diameter and charge straight at each other; the first one to step out of the ring or touch the ground with anything but the soles of his feet loses. Other than that, there are no rules—not even weight divisions: a runt of merely 250 pounds can find himself facing an opponent twice his size.

Of the six Grand Tournaments (called *basho*) that take place during the year, Tōkyō hosts three of them: in early January, mid-May, and mid-September. The tournaments take place in the **Kokugikan,** the National Sumō Arena, in the Ryōgoku district on the east side of the Sumida-gawa. Matches go from early afternoon, when the novices wrestle, to the titanic clashes of the upper ranks at around 6 PM. The price of admission buys you a whole day of sumō; the most expensive seats, closest to the ring, are tatami-floor loges for four people, called *sajiki.* The loges are terribly cramped, but the cost (¥9,200–¥11,300) includes all sorts of food and drink and souvenirs, brought around to you by Kokugikan attendants in traditional costume. The cheapest seats cost ¥3,600 for advanced sales, ¥2,100 for same-day box office sales. For same-day box office sales you should line up an hour in advance of the tournament. You can also reserve tickets through **Playguide** (☎ 03/3561–8821) or **Ticket Pia** (☎ 03/5237–9999). ✉ *1–3–28 Yokoami, Sumida-ku,* ☎ *03/3622–1100. JR Sōbu Line, Ryōgoku Eki (Nishiguchi/West Exit).*

SHOPPING

Horror stories abound about prices in Japan—and some of them are true. Yes, a cup of coffee can cost $10, if you pick the wrong coffee shop. A gift-wrapped melon from a department-store gourmet counter can cost $100. And a taxi ride from the airport to central Tōkyō does cost about $200. Take heart: the dollar has risen quite a bit against the yen over the past few years, and with a little ingenuity and effort you can find a wide range of gifts and souvenirs at bargain prices.

Some items are better bought at home: why go all the way to Tōkyō to buy European designer clothing? Concentrate on Japanese goods that are hard to get elsewhere, especially traditional handicrafts and fabrics. Such things can be found in areas easy to reach by public transportation. If time is limited, stick to hotel arcades and depāto, or focus on one particular shopping district.

In some smaller stores and markets, prices might be given in *kanji* (Japanese ideographs)—but the clerk can always write the price of an item for you in Arabic numbers, or display it on a calculator.

Salespeople are invariably helpful and polite. In the larger stores they greet you with a bow when you arrive—and many of them speak at least enough English to help you find what you're looking for. There is a saying in Japan: *o-kyaku-sama wa kami-sama,* "the customer is a god"—and since the competition for your business is fierce, people do take it to heart.

Japan has an across-the-board 5% value-added tax (VAT) imposed on luxury goods as well as on restaurant and hotel bills. This tax can be avoided at some duty-free shops in the city (don't forget to bring your passport). It is also waived in the duty-free shops at the international airports, but because these places tend to have higher profit margins, your tax savings there are likely to be offset by the higher markups.

Stores in Tōkyō generally open at 10 AM or 11 AM and close at 8 PM or 9 PM.

Shopping Districts

Akihabara and Jimbō-chō
For the ultimate one-stop display of photographic and electronic gadgetry, Akihabara is high-tech heaven; here, block after block of multistory buildings stock everything that beeps, buzzes, computes, or responds to digital suggestions. Portable tape and CD players appeared here long before they made it across the ocean. The best deals in Japan can be found in Akihabara, but prices are generally comparable to those in American discount stores. West of Akihabara, in Jimbō-chō, you'll find pretty much whatever you're looking for in dictionaries and art books, rare and out-of-print editions (Western and Japanese), and prints. *For Akihabara: JR Yamanote and Sōbu lines, Akihabara Eki (Denki-gai Exit); Hibiya Line, Akihabara Eki. For Jimbō-chō: Hanzō-on, Toei Shinjuku, and Toei Mita lines, Jimbō-chō Eki.*

Aoyama
Shopping in Aoyama can empty your wallet in no time: this is where many of the leading Japanese and Western designers have their cash-cow boutiques. European and American imports will be high, but Japanese designer clothes are usually 30%–40% lower than they are elsewhere. Aoyama tends to be a showcase, not merely of couture but of the latest concepts in commercial architecture and interior design. *Subway: Chiyoda, Ginza, and Hanzō-mon lines, Omotesandō Eki*

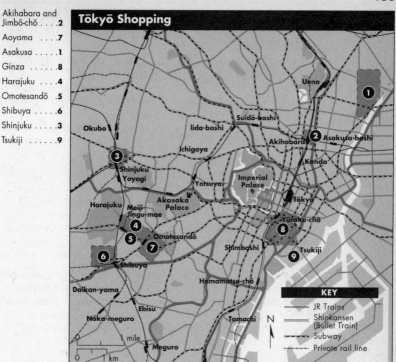

Tōkyō Shopping

(Exits A4, A5, B1, B2, and B3); Ginza, Hanzō-mon, and Toei Ōedo lines, Aoyama-itchōme Eki.

Asakusa

While sightseeing in this area, take time to stroll through its arcades. Many of the goods here are the kind of souvenirs you would expect to find in any tourist trap, but if you look a little harder, you'll find small backstreet shops that have been making beautiful wooden combs, delicate fans, and other items of fine traditional craftsmanship for generations. Also here are the cookware shops of Kappa-bashi-dōgu-machi-dōri, with everything from sushi knives to plastic lobsters. *Subway: Toei Asakusa Line, Asakusa Eki (Kaminarimon Exit); Ginza Line, Asakusa Eki (Exit 1) and Tawara-machi Eki (Exit 3).*

Ginza

Ginza was the first entertainment and shopping district in Tōkyō, dating to the Edo period (1603–1868), and once consisted of long, willow-lined avenues. The willows have long since gone, and the streets are now lined with depāto and boutiques. The exclusive stores in this area sell quality merchandise at higher prices. *Subway: Marunouchi, Ginza, and Hibiya lines, Ginza Eki (Exits A1–A10); Yūraku-chō Line, Ginza 1-chōme stop. JR Yamanote Line, Yūraku-chō Eki.*

Harajuku

The average shopper in Harajuku is under 20; a substantial percentage are under 16. This shopping and residential area extends southeast from Harajuku Eki along both sides of Omotesandō and Meiji-dōri; the shops that target the youngest consumers concentrate especially on the narrow street called Takeshita-dōri. Most stores focus on moderately priced clothing and accessories, with a lot of kitsch mixed in, but there are also several upscale fashion houses in the area such as Ralph

Lauren. *Subway: Chiyoda Line, Meiji Jingū-mae Eki (Exits 1–5); JR Yamanote Line, Harajuku Eki.*

Omotesandō

Known as the Champs-Elysées of Tōkyō, this long, wide avenue, which runs from Aoyama-dōri to Meiji Jingū, is lined with cafés and designer boutiques. There are also several antiques and print shops here, as well as one of the best toy shops in Tōkyō—Kiddyland. Omotesandō is perfect for browsing, window-shopping, and lingering over a café au lait before strolling to your next destination. *Subway: Chiyoda, Ginza, and Hanzō-mon lines, Omotesandō Eki (Exits A4, A5, B1, B2, and B3).*

Shibuya

This is primarily an entertainment district geared toward teenagers and young adults. The shopping in Shibuya also caters to these groups, with many reasonably priced smaller shops and a few depāto that are casual yet chic. *JR Yamanote Line; Tōkyū and Keiō Shinsen private rail lines; Ginza and Hanzō-mon subway lines: Shibuya Eki (Nishi-guchi/West Exit for JR, Exits 3–8 for subway lines).*

Shinjuku

Shinjuku is not without its honky-tonk and sleaze, but it also has some of the city's most fashionable depāto. Shinjuku's merchandise reflects the crowds—young, stylish, and hip. In the station area are several discount electronics and home-appliance outlets. *JR Yamanote Line; Odakyū private rail line; Marunouchi, Toei Shinjuku, and Toei Ōedo subway lines: Shinjuku Eki.*

Tsukiji

Best known for its daily fish-market auctions, Tsukiji also has a warren of streets that carry useful, everyday Japanese items that serve as a lens onto the lives of the Japanese. This is a fascinating area to poke around after seeing the fish auction and before stopping in the neighborhood for a fresh-as-can-be sushi lunch. *Toei Ōedo Line, Tsukiji-shijō Eki (Exit A1); Hibiya Line, Tsukiji Eki (Exit 1).*

Specialty Stores

Books

Bookstores of Jimbō-chō. If you love books, put the shops on the ½-km (¼-mi:) strip of Yasukuni-dōri high on your Tōkyō itinerary. The Japanese print aesthetic and concern with paper and production quality put Japanese books in a category of their own. If you don't read Japanese, then art books, coffee-table books, and old prints make a trip here worthwhile. *Subway: Toei Mita, Toei Shinjuku, and Hanzō-mon lines, Jimbō-chō Eki (Exit A5).*

ENGLISH-LANGUAGE BOOKSTORES

Most top hotels have a bookstore with a modest selection of English-language books. The stores below are all open daily. The best place in Tōkyō for foreign-language books and periodicals—for price if not for selection—is on the seventh floor of **Tower Records** in Shibuya (⊠ 1–22–14 Jinnan, Shibuya-ku, ☎ 03/3496–3661; Hanzō-mon and Ginza subway lines, Shibuya Eki [Exit6]). Unlike the "dedicated" booksellers, Tower sticks pretty much to popular titles, but it carries a wide range of newspapers from all over the world. **Jena Bookstore** (⊠ 5–7–1 Ginza, Chūō-ku, ☎ 03/3571–2980) carries a wide range of books and is near the Ginza and Marunouchi subway lines' exits in Ginza. For a wide selection of English and other non-Japanese-language books, try **Kinokuniya Bookstore** (⊠ 3–17–7 Shinjuku, Shinjuku-ku, ☎ 03/3354–0131; Marunouchi subway line, Shinkuju Eki [Exits B7, B8, B9]), which carries some 40,000 books and magazine titles. It's closed the third

Wednesday of each month, except in April, July, and December. Kinokuniya also has a branch store in the **Tōkyū Plaza Building** (✉ 1–2–2 Dōgen-zaka, Shibuya-ku, ☎ 03/3463–3241; JR Yamanote Line, Shibuya Eki [Minami-guchi/South Exit]), across from Shibuya Eki. **Maruzen** (✉ 2–3–10 Nihombashi, Chūō-ku, ☎ 03/3272–7211), one of Japan's largest booksellers, prospers in large part on its imports—which are sold at grossly inflated rates of exchange. On the second floor you can find books in Western languages on any subject from Romanesque art to embryology. There's an extensive collection here of books about Japan and also a small crafts center. The store is on Chūō-dōri south of the Tōzai and Ginza lines' Nihombashi stops. **Yaesu Book Center** (✉ 2–5–1 Yaesu, Chūō-ku, ☎ 03/3281–1811), near Tōkyō Eki and the Imperial Palace, has a small selection of English books that includes popular paperbacks, business titles, and Japanese culture and travel books.

Ceramics

It's true that pottery and fine ceramics can fill up and weigh down your luggage, but the shops will pack wares safely for travel—and they do make wonderful gifts. The Japanese have been crafting extraordinary pottery for more than 2,000 years, but this art really began to flourish in the 16th century, with the popularity and demand for tea-ceremony utensils. Feudal lords competed for possession of the finest pieces, and distinctive styles of pottery developed in regions all over the country. Some of the more prominent styles are those of Arita in Kyūshū, with painted patterns of flowers and birds; Mashiko, in Tochigi Prefecture, with its rough textures and simple, warm colors; rugged Hagi ware, from the eponymous Western Honshū city; and Kasama, in Ibaraki Prefecture, with glazes made from ash and ground rocks. Tōkyō's specialty shops and depāto carry fairly complete selections of these and other wares.

Kisso. This store carries an excellent variety of ceramics in modern design, made with traditional glazes, as well as a restaurant and a gift shop. ✉ *Axis Bldg., basement, 5–17–1 Roppongi, Minato-ku,* ☎ *03/3582–4191.* ☉ *Mon.–Sat. 11:30–2 and 5:30–10. Subway: Hibiya and Toei Ōedo lines, Roppongi Eki (Exit 3); Namboku Line, Roppongi-itchōme Eki (Exit 1).*

Tachikichi. Pottery from different localities around the country is sold here. ✉ *5–6–13 Ginza, Chūō-ku,* ☎ *03/3573–1986.* ☉ *Mon.–Sat. 11–7. Subway: Ginza, Hibiya, and Marunouchi lines, Ginza Eki (Exit B3).*

Dolls

Many types of traditional dolls are available in Japan, each with its own charm. Kokeshi dolls are long, cylindrical, painted, and made of wood, with no arms or legs. Fine examples of Japanese folk art, they date from the Edo period (1603–1868). Daruma, papier-mâché dolls with rounded bottoms and faces, are often painted with amusing expressions. They are constructed so that no matter how you push them, they roll and remain upright. Legend has it they are modeled after a Buddhist priest who remained seated in the lotus position for so long that his arms and legs atrophied. Hakata dolls, made in Kyūshū's Hakata City, are ceramic figurines in traditional costume, such as geisha, samurai, or festival dancers.

Kyūgetsu. In business for more than a century, Kyūgetsu sells every kind of doll imaginable. ✉ *1–20–4 Yanagibashi, Taitō-ku,* ☎ *03/3861–5511.* ☉ *Weekdays 9:15–6, weekends 9:15–5:15. Subway: Toei-Asakusa Line, Asakusa-bashi Eki (Exit A3).*

Sukeroku. Come to this shop for traditional handmade Edokko dolls and models, clothed in the costumes of the Edo period. ✉ *2–3–1 Asakusa, Taitō-ku,* ☎ *03/3844–0577.* ☉ *Daily 10–5. Subway: Ginza Line, Asakusa Eki (Exit 1).*

Electronics

The area around Akihabara Eki has more than 200 stores with discount prices on stereos, refrigerators, CD players, and anything else that plugs in or responds to digital commands. The larger of these stores have sections or floors (or even whole annexes) of goods made for export. These products come with instructions in most major languages, and if you have a tourist visa in your passport, you can purchase them duty free. The main store of **Yamagiwa** (✉ 4–1–1 Soto Kanda, Chiyoda-ku, ☏ 03/3253–2111), one of the area's largest discounters, is a few minutes' walk from the Denki-gai exit of JR Akihabara Eki. Over the years it has established branches and annexes in the neighboring blocks, specializing in computers, peripherals, office equipment, and export models of consumer electronics. This branch is open daily until 7:30. **Minami** (✉ 4–3–3 Soto Kanda, Chiyoda-ku, ☏ 03/3255–3730) lacks some of the variety of rival Yamagiwa but still manages to stock the major brands of every electronic gizmo you're likely to want to buy. Like most of the big discounters in the area, Minami is a few minutes' walk from the Denki-gai Exit of JR Akihabara Eki. It's open daily until 7 (7:30 on Friday and Saturday.)

Doi (✉ 1–18–15 Nishi-Shinjuku, Shinjuku-ku, ☏ 03/3348–2241) carries a complete line of consumer electronics. It's open daily until 9 and is located within a block of Shinjuku Eki (Exit 5 for Toei Shinjuku subway line, Minami-guchi/South Exit for JR lines).

The mammoth discount camera chain **Yodobashi** (✉ 1–11–1 Nishi-Shinjuku, Shinjuku-ku, ☏ 03/3346–1010) has its flagship store in Shinjuku. In addition to cameras, it sells a vast range of other products, from cellular phones and computers to DVD players and boom boxes. It's open daily until 9.

Folk Crafts

Japanese folk crafts, called *mingei*—among them bamboo vases and baskets, fabrics, paper boxes, dolls, and toys—achieve a unique beauty in their simple and sturdy designs. Be aware, however, that simple does not mean cheap. Long hours of loving hand labor go into these objects. And every year there are fewer and fewer craftspeople left, producing their work in smaller and smaller quantities. Include these items in your budget ahead of time: The best of it—worth every cent—can be fairly expensive.

Bingo-ya. A complete selection of crafts from all over Japan can be found here. ✉ 10–6 *Wakamatsu-chō, Shinjuku*, ☏ 03/3202–8778. ☉ *Tues.–Sun. 10–7. Subway: Tōzai Line, Waseda Eki (Babashita-chō Exit).*

Oriental Bazaar. Here are three floors of just about everything you might want in a traditional Japanese (or Chinese or Korean) handicraft souvenir, from painted screens to pottery to antique chests, at fairly reasonable prices. Kimonos are downstairs. ✉ 5–9–13 *Jingū-mae, Shibuya-ku*, ☏ 03/3400–3933. ☉ *Fri.–Wed. 10–7. Subway: Chiyoda Line, Meiji Jingū-mae Eki (Exit 4).*

Foodstuffs and Wares

This hybrid category includes everything from crackers and pickled foods to standard restaurant-supply items like cast-iron kettles, paper lanterns, and essential food-kitsch like plastic sushi sets. Unless otherwise noted, shops below are centered either on Asakusa's Kappa-bashi-dōgu-machi-dōri or on the Tsukiji fish market.

The Backstreet Shops of Tsukiji. In Tsukiji, between the Central Wholesale Market and Harumi-dōri, among the many fishmongers, you'll also find stores where you can buy pickles, tea, crackers, kitchen knives, baskets, and crockery. For a picture of real Japanese life, it is not to be missed. ✉ *5–2–1 Tsukiji, Chūō-ku. Subway: Toei Ōedo Line, Tsuk-iji-shijō Eki (Exit A1); Hibiya Line, Tsukiji Eki (Exit 1).*

Biken Kōgei. If you want to take home an *aka-chōchin* (folding red-paper lantern) like the ones that hang in inexpensive bar and restaurant fronts, look no farther. ✉ *1–5–16 Nishi-Asakusa, Taitō-ku,* ☎ *03/3842–1646.* ⊙ *Mon.–Sat. 9–6, Sun. 11–4 (but call in advance to confirm Sun. hrs). Subway: Ginza Line, Tawara-machi Eki (Exit 3).*

Iida Shōten. Solid, traditional *nambu* ware, such as embossed cast-iron kettles and casseroles, is Iida Shōten's specialty. ✉ *2–21–6 Nishi-Asakusa, Taitō-ku,* ☎ *03/3842–3757.* ⊙ *Mon.–Sat. 9:30–5:30, Sun. 10–5. Subway: Ginza Line, Tawara-machi Eki (Exit 3).*

Kondo Shōten. If you're of the mind that your kitchen won't be complete without a bamboo tray, basket, scoop, or container of some sort, stop in at Kondo Shōten. ✉ *3–1–13 Matsuya, Taitō-ku,* ☎ *03/ 3841–3372.* ⊙ *Weekdays 9:30–5:30, Sat. 9:30–4:30. Subway: Ginza Line, Tawara-machi Eki (Exit 3).*

Maizuru Company. Somebody actually has to *make* all that plastic food you see in restaurant windows in Japan, and real masters of the craft—the Rembrandts of counterfeit cuisine—tend to work for Maizuru. Their models are so good that the company was chosen some years back to take part in the "Japan Style" Exhibition at the Victoria and Albert Museum in London. Stop in here for some of the most unusual gifts and souvenirs you're likely to find anywhere in Tōkyō. ✉ *1–5–17 Nishi-Asakusa, Taitō-ku,* ☎ *03/3843–1686.* ⊙ *Daily 9–6. Subway: Ginza Line, Tawara-machi Eki (Exit 3).*

Nishimura. This shop specializes in *noren*—the curtains that shops and restaurants hang to announce they're open. A typical fabric is cotton, linen, or silk, most often dyed to order for individual shops. The store also sells premade noren of an entertaining variety for your decorating pleasure. ✉ *1–10–10 Matsuya, Taitō-ku,* ☎ *03/3844–9954.* ⊙ *Mon.–Sat. 9–5. Subway: Ginza Line, Tawara-machi Eki (Exit 3).*

Tokiwa-dō. Come here to buy some of Tōkyō's most famous souvenirs: *kaminari okoshi* (thunder crackers), made of rice, millet, sugar, and beans. The shop is on the west side of Asakusa's Thunder God Gate, the Kaminari-mon entrance to Sensō-ji. ✉ *1–3 Asakusa, Taitō-ku,* ☎ *03/3841–5656.* ⊙ *Daily 9–8:45. Subway: Ginza Line, Asakusa Eki (Exit 1).*

Tsubaya Hōchōten. Tsubaya sells high-quality cutlery for professionals. Its remarkable array of *hōchō* (knives) is designed for every imaginable use, as the art of food presentation in Japan requires a great variety of cutting implements. The best of these carry the Traditional Craft Association seal: hand-forged tools of tempered blue steel, set in handles banded with deer horn to keep the wood from splitting. ✉ *3–7–2 Nishi-Asakusa, Taitō-ku,* ☎ *03/3845–2005.* ⊙ *Daily 9–5:45. Subway: Ginza Line, Tawara-machi Eki (Exit 3).*

Union Company. Coffee paraphernaliacs, beware: roasters, grinders, beans, flasks, and filters of every shape and description will make your eyes bulge in anticipation of the caffeine ritual. Japanese *kōhi* (coffee) wares are ingenious and remarkable. ✉ *2–22–6 Nishi-Asakusa, Taitō-ku,* ☎ *03/3842–4041.* ⊙ *Mon.–Sat. 9–6, Sun. 10–5. Subway: Ginza Line, Tawara-machi Eki (Exit 3).*

Yamamoto Noriten. The Japanese are resourceful in their uses of products from the sea. *Nori*, the paper-thin dried seaweed used to wrap *maki* sushi and *onigiri* (rice balls), is the specialty here. Here's a tip if you plan to bring some home with you: buy unroasted nori and toast it yourself at home; the flavor will be far better than that of the preroasted sheets. ✉ *1–6–3 Nihombashi Muro-machi, Chūō-ku,* ☎ *03/3241–0261.* ⊙ *Daily 9–6:30. Subway: Hanzō-mon and Ginza lines, Mitsukoshi-mae Eki (Exit A1).*

Kimonos

Unless they work in traditional Japanese restaurants, Japanese women now wear kimonos mainly on special occasions, such as weddings or graduations, and like tuxedos in the United States, they are often rented instead of purchased. Kimonos are extremely expensive and difficult to maintain. A wedding kimono, for example, can cost as much as ¥1 million.

Most visitors, naturally unwilling to pay this much for a garment that they probably want to use as a bathrobe or a conversation piece, settle for a secondhand or antique silk kimono. These vary in price and quality. You can pay as little as ¥1,000 in a flea market, but to find one in decent condition, you should expect to pay about ¥10,000. However, cotton summer kimonos, called yukatas, in a wide variety of colorful and attractive designs, can be bought new, complete with sash and sandals, for ¥7,000–¥10,000.

Hayashi. This store specializes in ready-made kimonos, sashes, and dyed yukata. ⊠ *2–1–1 Yūraku-chō, Chiyoda-ku,* ☎ *03/3501–4012.* ◐ *Mon.–Sat. 10–7, Sun. 10–6. Subway: Ginza, Hibiya, and Marunouchi lines, Ginza Eki (Exit C1).*

Lacquerware

For its history, diversity, and fine workmanship, lacquerware rivals ceramics as the traditional Japanese craft nonpareil. One warning: lacquerware thrives on humidity. Cheaper pieces usually have plastic rather than wood underneath. Because these won't shrink and crack in dry climates, they make safer—and no less attractive—buys.

Inachu. Specializing in lacquerware from the town of Wajima, a famous crafts center on the Noto Peninsula, this is one of the most elegant (and expensive) crafts shops in Tōkyō. ⊠ *1–5–2 Akasaka, Minato-ku,* ☎ *03/3582–4451.* ◐ *Mon.–Sat. 10–6. Subway: Marunouchi and Namboku lines, Tameike-Sannō Eki (Exit 9).*

Miscellaneous

Handmade combs, towels, and cosmetics are other uniquely Japanese treasures to consider picking up while in Tōkyō.

Fuji-ya. Master textile creator Keiji Kawakami's cotton *tenugui* ("teh-*noo*-goo-ee") hand towels are collector's items, often as not framed instead of used as towels. Kawakama is also an expert on the history of this Edo-period craft. His *Tenugui Fuzoku Emaki* (roughly, *The Scroll Book of Hand Towel Customs and Usages*) is the definitive work on the hundreds of traditional towel motifs that have come down from the Edo period: geometric patterns, plants and animals, and scenes from Kabuki plays and festivals. The shop is near the corner of Dembō-in-dōri on Naka-mise-dōri. ⊠ *2–2–15 Asakusa, Taitō-ku,* ☎ *03/3841–2283.* ◐ *Fri.–Wed. 10–7 Subway: Ginza Line, Asakusa Eki (Exit 6).*

Hyaku-suke. Hyaku-suke is the last place in Tōkyō to carry government-approved skin cleanser made from powdered nightingale droppings. Ladies of the Edo period—especially the geisha—swore by the cleanser. They mixed the powder with water and patted it on gently as a boon to their complexion. These days this 100-year-old-plus cosmetics shop sells little of the nightingale powder, but its theatrical makeup for Kabuki actors, geisha, and traditional weddings—as well as interesting things to fetch home like seaweed shampoo, camellia oil, and handmade wool cosmetic brushes bound with cherrywood—makes it a worthy addition to your Asakusa shopping itinerary. ⊠ *2–2–14 Asakusa, Taitō-ku,* ☎ *03/3841–7058.* ◐ *Wed.–Mon. 11–5. Subway: Ginza Line, Asakusa Eki (Exit 6).*

Jusan-ya. A shop selling handmade boxwood combs, this business was started in 1736 by a samurai who couldn't support himself as a feudal retainer. It has been in the same family ever since. Jusan-ya is on Shinobazu-dōri, a few doors west of its intersection with Chūō-dōri in Ueno. ☒ *2–12–21 Ueno, Taitō-ku,* ☎ *03/3831–3238.* ☾ *Mon.–Sat. 10–7. Subway: Ginza Line, Ueno Hirokō-ji Eki (Exit 6); JR Ueno Eki (Shinobazu Exit).*

Naka-ya. If you want to equip yourself for Sensō-ji's annual Sanja Festival in May in Asakusa, this is the place to come. Best buys here are *sashiko hanten,* which are thick, woven firemen's jackets, and happi coats, cotton tunics printed in bright colors with Japanese characters—*ukiyo-e*—which are available in children's sizes. ☒ *2–2–12 Asakusa, Taitō-ku,* ☎ *03/3841–7877.* ☾ *Daily 10–7. Subway: Ginza Line, Asakusa Eki (Exit 6).*

Yono-ya. Traditional Japanese coiffures and wigs are very complicated, and they require a variety of tools to shape them properly. Tasumi Minekawa is the current master at Yono-ya—the family line goes back 300 years—who deftly crafts and decorates a stunning array of very fine boxwood combs. Some combs are carved with auspicious motifs, such as peonies, hollyhocks, or cranes, and all are engraved with the family benchmark. ☒ *1–37–10 Asakusa, Taitō-ku,* ☎ *03/3844–1755.* ☾ *Daily 10–7. Subway: Ginza Line, Asakusa Eki (Exit 1).*

Paper

What packs light and flat in your suitcase won't break, doesn't cost much, and makes a great gift? The answer is traditional handmade *washi* (paper), which the Japanese make in thousands of colors, textures, and designs and fashion into an astonishing array of useful and decorative objects.

Kami Hyakka. Operated by the 110-year-old Okura Sankō wholesale paper company, this showroom displays some 512 different types and colors of paper—made primarily for stationery, notes, and cards rather than as crafts material. ☒ *2–4–9 Ginza, Chūō-ku,* ☎ *03/3538–5025.* ☾ *Tues.–Sat. 10:30–7. Subway: Yūraku-chō Line, Ginza-Itchōme Eki (Exit 5).*

Kami-no-Takamura. Specialists in washi and other papers printed in traditional Japanese designs, this shop also carries brushes, inkstones, and other tools for calligraphy. ☒ *1–1–2 Higashi-Ikebukuro, Toshima-ku,* ☎ *03/3971–7111.* ☾ *Mon.–Sat. 11–6:30. JR: Ikebukuro Eki (Exit 35).*

Kyūkyodō. Kyūkyodō has been in business since 1663—in Ginza since 1880—selling its wonderful variety of handmade Japanese papers, paper products, incense, brushes, and other materials for calligraphy. ☒ *5–7–4 Ginza, Chūō-ku,* ☎ *03/3571–4429.* ☾ *Mon.–Sat. 10–7:30, Sun. 11–7. Subway: Ginza, Hibiya, and Marunouchi lines, Ginza Eki (Exit A2).*

Ōzu Washi. In business since the 17th century, this shop has one of the largest washi showrooms in the city and its own gallery of antique papers. ☒ *2–6–3 Nihombashi-Honchō, Chūō-ku,* ☎ *03/3663–8788.* ☾ *Mon.–Sat. 10–6. Subway: Ginza Line, Mitsukoshi-mae Eki (Exit A4).*

Yushima no Kobayashi. Here, in addition to shopping for paper goods, you can also tour a papermaking workshop and learn the art of origami. ☒ *1–7–14 Yushima, Bunkyō-ku,* ☎ *03/3811–4025.* ☾ *Mon.–Sat. 9–5. Subway: Chiyoda Line, Yushima Eki (Exit 5).*

Pearls

Japan remains one of the best places in the world to buy cultured pearls. They will not be inexpensive, but pearls of the same quality cost considerably more elsewhere. It's best to go to a reputable dealer, where you know that quality will be high and you will not be misled.

Mikimoto. Kokichi Mikimoto created his technique for cultured pearls in 1893. Since then the name *Mikimoto* has been associated with the best quality in the industry. Prices are high, but design and workmanship are uniformly first rate. ✉ *4–5–5 Ginza, Chūō-ku,* ☎ *03/3535–4611.* ◷ *Daily 10:30–6:30; closed 3rd Wed. of month. Subway: Ginza, Hibiya, and Marunouchi lines, Ginza Eki (Exit A9).*

Tasaki Pearl Gallery. Tasaki sells pearls at slightly lower prices than does Mikimoto. The store has several showrooms and hosts English tours that demonstrate the technique of culturing pearls and explain how to maintain and care for them. ✉ *1–3–3 Akasaka, Minato-ku,* ☎ *03/5561–8881.* ◷ *Daily 9–6. Subway: Ginza Line, Tameike-Sannō Eki (Exit 9).*

Toys

Hakuhinkan (Toy Park). This is reputedly the largest toy shop in Japan. It's on Chūō-dōri, the main axis of the Ginza shopping area. ✉ *8–8–11 Ginza, Chūō-ku,* ☎ *03/3571–8008.* ◷ *Daily 11–8. Subway: Ginza and Toei Asakusa lines, Shimbashi Eki (Exit 1).*

Arcades and Shopping Centers

If you don't have the time or energy to dash about Tōkyō in search of the perfect gifts, you may want to try some of the arcades and shopping centers, which carry a wide selection of merchandise. Most of these are used to dealing with gaijin.

Axis. On the first floor of this Gaien-higashi-dōri complex in Roppongi, **Living Motif** is a home-furnishings shop with high-tech foreign and Japanese goods of exquisite design. **Nuno,** in the basement, sells cutting-edge fabrics of its own design and manufacture, from natural fibers like hemp and linen to high-tech metal synthetics. Be sure to look at the restaurant-store **Kisso,** which sells, along with lacquered chopsticks and fine baskets, an extraordinary selection of unique, modern handmade ceramics in contemporary designs, shapes, and colors. ✉ *5–17–1 Roppongi, Minato-ku. Subway: Hibiya and Toei Ōedo lines, Roppongi Eki (Exit 3); Namboku Line, Roppongi Itchōme Eki (Exit 1).*

International Shopping Arcade. This collection of shops in Hibiya has a range of goods—including cameras, electronics, pearls, and kimonos—and a sales staff with excellent English. The arcade is conveniently located near the Imperial Hotel, and the shops are all duty free. ✉ *1–7–23 Uchisaiwai-chō, Chiyoda-ku. Subway: Chiyoda and Hibiya lines, Hibiya Eki (Exit A13).*

Nishi-Sandō. This Asakusa arcade sells kimono and yukata fabrics, traditional accessories, fans, and festival costumes at very reasonable prices. It runs east of the area's movie theaters, between Rok-ku and the Sensō-ji complex. ✉ *Asakusa 2-chōme, Taitō-ku. Subway: Ginza Line, Asakusa Eki (Exit 1).*

Boutiques

Japanese boutiques pay as much attention to interior design and lighting as they do to the clothing they sell; like anywhere else, it's the image that moves the merchandise. Although many Japanese designers are represented in the major upscale depāto, you may enjoy your shopping more in the elegant boutiques of Aoyama and Omotesandō—most of which are within walking distance of one another.

Comme Des Garçons. This is one of the earliest and still most popular "minimalist" design houses, where you can get almost any kind of ¥7000 tank top you want, as long as it's black. ✉ *5–2–1 Minami-Aoyama, Minato-ku,* ☎ *03/3406–3951.* ◷ *Daily 11–8. Subway: Ginza, Chiyoda, and Hanzō-mon lines, Omotesandō Eki (Exit A5).*

From 1st Building. This building houses the boutiques of several of Japan's leading designers, including Issey Miyake and Comme Ça du Mode, as well as several restaurants. "Produced" by Yasuhiro Hamano, whose atelier designs many of Tōkyō's trendiest commercial spaces, From 1st is one of the earliest and liveliest examples of the city's chic vertical malls. ⊠ *5–3–10 Minami-Aoyama, Minato-ku. Subway: Ginza, Chiyoda, and Hanzō-mon lines, Omotesandō Eki (Exit A5).*

Hanae Mori Building. This glass-mirrored structure, designed by Kenzō Tange, houses the designs of the doyenne of Japanese fashion, Mori Hanae, whose clothing has a classic look with a European influence. The café on the first floor is a good vantage point for people-watching, Harajuku's favorite sport. ⊠ *3–6–1 Kita-Aoyama, Minato-ku,* ☏ *03/3406–1021.* ◷ *Daily 10:30–7. Subway: Ginza, Chiyoda, and Hanzō-mon lines, Omotesandō Eki (Exit A1).*

Koshino Junko. Shop here for sophisticated clothing and accessories with a European accent. ⊠ *6–5–36 Minami-Aoyama, Minato-ku,* ☏ *03/3406–7370.* ◷ *Mon.–Sat. 10–8. Subway: Ginza, Chiyoda, and Hanzō-mon lines, Omotesandō Eki (Exit B1).*

Depāto

Most Japanese department stores are parts of conglomerates that include railways, real estate, and leisure industries. The stores themselves commonly have travel agencies, theaters, and art galleries on the premises, as well as reasonably priced restaurants on the upper or basement floors, with coffee shops strategically located in between.

Major depāto accept credit cards and provide shipping services. Some staff members speak English. If you're having communication difficulties, someone will eventually come to the rescue. On the first floor you'll invariably find a general information booth with useful maps of the store in English.

A visit to a Japanese depāto is not merely a shopping excursion—it's a lesson in Japanese culture. Plan to arrive just before it opens: promptly on the hour, two immaculately groomed young women face the customers from inside, bow ceremoniously, and unlock the doors. Walk through the store: the staff are all standing at attention, in postures of nearly reverent welcome. Notice the uniform angle of incline: many stores have training sessions to teach their new employees the precise and proper degree at which to bend from the waist.

Visit the food specialty departments on the lower levels—and be prepared for an overwhelming selection of Japanese and Western delicacies. No Japanese housewife in her right mind would shop here regularly for her groceries. A brief exploration, however, will give you a pretty good picture of what she might select for a special occasion—and the price she's prepared to pay for it. Many stalls have small samples out on the counter, and nobody will raise a fuss if you help yourself, even if you make no purchase.

Most major depāto close one or two days a month, different stores on different days of the week—but normally on Tuesday or Wednesday. These schedules vary considerably; in holiday gift-giving seasons, for example, they may be open every day. To be on the safe side, call ahead.

Ginza/Nihombashi

Matsuya. The slightly frazzled presentation here is a welcome change from the generally refined and immaculately ordered shopping in the Ginza/Nihombashi area. The merchandise at Matsuya is meant for a younger crowd, and shoppers with the patience to comb through the hordes of goods will be rewarded with many finds, particularly in women's clothing. ⊠ *3–6–1 Ginza, Chūō-ku,* ☎ *03/3567–1211.* ⊙ *Daily 10–8. Subway: Ginza, Marunouchi, and Hibiya lines, Ginza Eki (Exits A12 and A13).*

Matsuzakaya. The Matsuzakaya conglomerate was founded in Nagoya and still commands the loyalties of shoppers with origins in western Japan. Style-conscious Tōkyōites tend to find the sense of fashion here a bit countrified. ⊠ *6–10–1 Ginza, Chūō-ku,* ☎ *03/3572–1111.* ⊙ *Mon.–Thurs. 10:30–7:30, Fri.–Sat. 10:30–8, Sun. 10:30–7. Subway: Ginza, Marunouchi, and Hibiya lines, Ginza Eki (Exits A3 and A4).*

Mitsukoshi. Founded in 1673 as a dry-goods store, Mitsukoshi later played one of the leading roles in introducing Western merchandise to Japan. It has retained its image of quality and excellence, with a particularly strong representation of Western fashion designers, such as Chanel, Lanvin, and Givenchy. Mitsukoshi also stocks a fine selection of traditional Japanese goods. ⊠ *1–4–1 Nihombashi Muro-machi, Chūō-ku,* ☎ *03/3241–3311.* ⊙ *Daily 10–7. Subway: Ginza and Hanzō-mon lines, Mitsukoshi-mae Eki (Exits A3 and A5).* ⊠ *4–6–16 Ginza, Chūō-ku,* ☎ *03/3562–1111.* ⊙ *Mon.–Sat. 10–8, Sun 10–7:30. Subway: Ginza, Marunouchi, and Hibiya lines, Ginza Eki (Exits A6, A7, A8).*

Takashimaya. The kimono department here, one of the best in Tōkyō, draws its share of brides-to-be to shop for their weddings. In addition to a complete selection of traditional crafts, antiques, and curios, Takashimaya sells very fine Japanese and Western designer goods and so has a broad, sophisticated appeal. ⊠ *2–4–1 Nihombashi, Chūō-ku,* ☎ *03/3211–4111.* ⊙ *Daily 10–7. Subway: Ginza Line, Nihombashi Eki (Exits B1 and B2).*

Wako. Deftly avoiding the classification of a mere depāto by confining itself to a limited selections of goods at the top end of the market, Wako is particularly known for its glassware, jewelry, and accessories—and for some of the handsomest, most sophisticated window displays in town. ⊠ *4–5–11 Ginza, Chūō-ku,* ☎ *03/3562–2111.* ⊙ *Mon.–Sat. 10:30–6. Subway: Ginza, Marunouchi, and Hibiya lines, Ginza Eki (Exits A9 and A10).*

Shibuya

Parco. Owned by Seibu depāto, Parco is actually not one store but four, vertical malls filled with small retail stores and boutiques, all in hailing distance of one another in the commercial heart of Shibuya. Parco Part 1 and Part 4 (Quattro) cater to a younger crowd, stocking "generic" unbranded casual clothing, crafts fabrics, and accessories from foreign climes; Quattro even has a club that hosts live music. Part 2 is devoted mainly to upmarket designer fashions, and Part 3 sells a mixture of men's and women's fashions, tableware, and household furnishings. A major overhaul of all four buildings, scheduled for completion in 2002, was under way at press time; the company plans eventually to open a fifth outlet in the area. ⊠ *15–1 Udagawa-chō, Shibuya-ku,* ☎ *03/3464–5111.* ⊙ *Parts 1, 2, and 3 daily 10–8:30; Quattro daily 11–9. Subway: Ginza and Hanzō-mon lines, Shibuya Eki (Exits 6 and 7).*

Seibu. The mammoth main branch of this depāto—where even many Japanese customers get lost—is in Ikebukuro. The Shibuya branch, which still carries an impressive array of merchandise, is smaller and more manageable. Seibu is the flagship operation of a conglomerate that owns a railway line and a baseball team, the Seibu Lions. When the Lions win the pennant, prepare to go shopping: All the Seibu stores have major sales the following day (be prepared for even bigger crowds than usual). This store has an excellent selection of household goods, from furniture to china and lacquerware. ⊠ *21–1 Udagawa-chō, Shibuya-ku,* ☎ *03/3462–0111.* ⊙ *Mon.–Tues. and weekends 10–8, Thurs.–Fri.*

10–9. Subway/JR: Shibuya Eki (Hachiko exit for JR lines, Exits 6 and 7 for Ginza and Hanzō-mon lines).

Tōkyū. Tōkyū's marketing strategy is apparently to harvest the spin from its Bunka-mura cultural complex next door, but this hasn't been all that successful in drawing young consumers away from rival Seibu. The store carries a good selection of imported clothing, accessories, and home furnishings, but the ambience overall is a bit conservative. ✉ *2–24–1 Dōgen-zaka, Shibuya-ku,* ☎ *03/3477–3111.* ☉ *Wed.–Mon. 10–8. Subway/JR: Shibuya EKi (Hachiko exit for JR lines, Exit 3A for Ginza and Hanzō-mon lines).*

Tōkyū Hands. Known commonly just as "Hands," this do-it-yourself and hobby store stocks an excellent selection of carpentry tools, sewing accessories, kitchen goods, plants, and other related merchandise. The toy department is unbearably cute, and the stationery department has a comprehensive selection of Japanese papers. ✉ *12–18 Udagawa-chō, Shibuya-ku,* ☎ *03/5489–5111.* ☉ *Daily 10–8; closed 2nd and 3rd Mon. of month. Subway/JR: Shibuya Eki (Hachiko exit for JR lines, Exits 6 and 7 for Ginza and Hanzō-mon lines).*

Shinjuku

Isetan. Often called the Bloomingdale's of Japan—a description that doesn't quite do this store justice—Isetan has become a nearly universal favorite, with one of the most complete selections of Japanese designers in one place. If you're looking for distinctive looks without paying designer prices, this is the place for you: the store carries a wide range of knockoff brands. But expect to look long and hard for something that fits; these clothes are made specifically for the Japanese market. Ceramics, stationery, and furniture here are generally of high quality and interesting design; the folk-crafts department carries a small but good selection of fans, table mats, and other gifts. ✉ *3–14–1 Shinjuku, Shinjuku-ku,* ☎ *03/3352–1111.* ☉ *Mon.–Thurs. 10–7:30, Fri.–Sun. 10–8. Subway/JR: Shinjuku Eki (Higashi-guchi/East Exit for JR lines; Exits B2, B3, B4, and B5 for Marunouchi Line).*

Keiō. This no-nonsense depāto has a standard but complete selection of merchandise. A me-too operation, it seems somehow to have avoided creating an image uniquely its own. ✉ *1–1–4 Nishi-Shinjuku, Shinjuku-ku,* ☎ *03/3342–2111.* ☉ *Daily 10–8. Subway/JR: Shinjuku Eki (Nishi-guchi/West Exit for JR lines, Exit A10 for Marunouchi Line).*

Marui. Marui is not so much a depāto as a group of specialty stores that focus on young fashions and household effects. Wildly successful for its easy credit policies, Marui is where you go when you've just landed your first job, moved into your first apartment, and need to outfit yourself presentably on the cheap. Twice a year, in February and July, prices are slashed dramatically in major clearance sales. If you're in the neighborhood, you'll know exactly when the sales are taking place: The lines will extend into the street and around the block. (Let it not be said that Japanese men do not care about fashion: The most enthusiastic customers line up, from 6 AM, for the men's sales.) ✉ *3–30–16 Shinjuku, Shinjuku-ku,* ☎ *03/3354–0101.* ☉ *Thurs.–Tues. 11–8. Subway/JR: Shinjuku Eki (Nishi-guchi/West Exit for JR lines; Exits A1, A2, A3, and A4 for Marunouchi Line).*

Odakyu. Slightly snazzier than neighboring Keiō depāto, Odakyu is a very family-oriented store, particularly good for children's clothing. Across the street from the main building is Odakyu Halc, with a varied selection of home furnishings and interior goods on its upper floors. ✉ *1–1–3 Nishi-Shinjuku, Shinjuku-ku,* ☎ *03/3342–1111.* ☉ *Daily 10–8. Subway/JR: Shinjuku Eki (Nishi-guchi/West Exit for JR lines, Exit A10 for Marunouchi Line).*

TŌKYŌ A TO Z

To research prices, get advice from other travelers, and book travel arrangements, visit www.fodors.com.

AIR TRAVEL

The airlines of more than 50 different countries fly in and out of Tōkyō; among them, direct flights are available from hub cities in the United States, Canada, Great Britain, Australia, and New Zealand.

See Air Travel *in* Smart Travel Tips A to Z for more information on Tōkyō's airports and airlines that serve the area.

AIRPORTS AND TRANSFERS

Tōkyō has two airports, Narita and Haneda. Narita Kūkō is 80 km (50 mi) northeast of Tōkyō and serves all international flights, except those operated by (Taiwan's) China Airways, which uses Haneda Kūkō. Narita added a new terminal building in 1992, which has somewhat eased the burden on it, but it can still be bottlenecked. In both terminals there are money exchange counters just inside the customs inspection area and just outside, in the arrivals lobby. In the shopping-restaurant area between the two wings is the Japan National Tourist Organization's Tourist Information Center, where you can get free maps, brochures, and other information. Directly across from the customs area exits at both terminals are the ticket counters for Airport Limousine Buses to Tōkyō.

Haneda Kūkō, 16 km (10 mi) southwest of Tōkyō, serves all domestic flights. At Haneda, Japan Airlines (JAL), All Nippon Airways (ANA), and Japan Air System have extensive domestic flight networks.
➤ AIRPORT INFORMATION: **Haneda Kūkō** (☎ 03/5757–8111). **Narita Kūkō** (☎ 0476/34–5000).

AIRPORT TRANSFERS BETWEEN NARITA AIRPORT AND CENTER CITY
Two services, the Airport Limousine Bus, operated by Airport Transport Service Co., and the Airport Express Bus, operated by IAE Co., run from Narita to various major hotels in the $$$$ category (☞ Lodging, *above*) and to the JR Tōkyō and Shinjuku stations; the fare is ¥2,400–¥3,800, depending on your destination. Even if you're not staying at one of the route's drop-off points, you can take the bus as far as the one closest to your hotel and then use a taxi for the remaining distance. Keep in mind that these buses only run every hour, and they do not run after 11 PM. The trip is scheduled for 70–90 minutes but can take two hours in heavy traffic. Ticket counters are in the arrival lobbies, directly across from the customs-area exit. Buses leave from platforms just outside terminal exits, exactly on schedule; the departure time is on the ticket.

A bus to the Tōkyō City Air Terminal (TCAT) leaves approximately every 10–20 minutes from 6:45 AM to 11 PM; the fare is ¥2,900, and you can buy tickets at the hotel bus ticket counter. TCAT is in Nihombashi in north-central Tōkyō, a bit far from most destinations, but from here you can connect directly with Suitengū Eki on the Hanzō-mon subway line, then to anywhere in the subway network. A taxi from TCAT to most major hotels will cost about ¥3,000.

Taxis are rarely used between Narita Airport and central Tōkyō—at ¥20,000 or more, depending on traffic and where you're going, the cost is prohibitive. Station-wagon taxis do exist, and the meter rates are the same as for the standard sedans, but they are not always available. Limousines are also very expensive; from Narita Airport to the Imperial Hotel downtown, for example, will set you back about ¥35,000.

Trains run every 30–40 minutes between Narita Airport Train Station and Keisei-Ueno Eki on the privately owned Keisei Line. The Keisei Skyliner takes 57 minutes and costs ¥1,920. The first Skyliner leaves Narita for Ueno at 9:25 AM, the last at 9:58 PM; from Ueno to Narita, the first Skyliner is at 6:30 AM, the last at 5:25 PM. It only makes sense to take the Keisei, however, if your final destination is in the Ueno area; otherwise, you must change to the Tōkyō subway system or the Japan Railways loop line at Ueno (the station is adjacent to Keisei-Ueno Eki) or take a cab to your hotel.

Japan Railways trains stop at both terminals. The fastest and most comfortable is the Narita Limited Express (N'EX), which makes 23 runs a day in each direction. Trains from the airport go directly to the central Tōkyō Eki in just under an hour, then continue to Yokohama and Ōfuna. Daily departures begin at 7:43 AM; the last train is at 9:43 PM. The one-way fare is ¥2,940 (¥4,980 for the first-class "Green Car" and ¥5,380 per person for a private compartment that seats four). All seats are reserved, and you'll need to reserve one for yourself in advance, as this train fills quickly. The less elegant *kaisoku* (rapid train) on JR's Narita Line also runs from the airport to Tōkyō Eki, by way of Chiba; there are 16 departures daily, starting at 7 AM. The fare to Tōkyō is ¥1,280 (¥2,210 for the Green Car); the ride takes 1 hour and 27 minutes.

➤ CONTACTS: **Airport Transport Service Co.** (☎ 03/3665–7232 in Tōkyō; 0476/32–8080 for Terminal 1, New Tōkyō International Airport, Narita; 0476/34–6311 for Terminal 2). **IAE Co.** (☎ 0476/32–7954 for Terminal 1, New Tōkyō International Airport, Narita; 0476/34–6886 for Terminal 2). **Japan Railways** (☎ 03/3423–0111 for JR East InfoLine).

AIRPORT TRANSFERS BETWEEN HANEDA AIRPORT AND CENTER CITY

The monorail from Haneda Airport to Hamamatsu-chō Eki in Tōkyō is the fastest and cheapest way into town; the journey takes about 17 minutes, and trains run approximately every 5 minutes; the fare is ¥470. From Hamamatsu-chō Eki, change to a JR train or take a taxi to your destination.

A taxi to the center of Tōkyō takes about 40 minutes; the fare is approximately ¥8,000.

➤ CONTACT: **Tōkyō Monorail Co., Ltd.** (☎ 03/3434–3171).

BOAT AND FERRY TRAVEL

The best ride in Tōkyō, hands down, is the *suijō basu* (river bus), operated by the Tōkyō Cruise Ship Company from Hinode Pier, from the mouth of the Sumida-gawa upstream to Asakusa. The glassed-in double-decker boats depart roughly every 20–40 minutes, weekdays 9:50–6:15, weekends and holidays 9:50–6:55 (with extended service to 7:35 July 9–September 23). The trip takes 40 minutes and costs ¥660. The pier is a seven-minute walk from Hamamatsu-chō Eki on the JR Yamanote Line.

The Sumida-gawa was once Tōkyō's lifeline, a busy highway for travelers and freight alike. The ferry service dates to 1885. Some people still take it to work, but today most passengers are Japanese tourists. On its way to Asakusa, the boat passes Tsukiji's Central Wholesale Market, the largest wholesale fish and produce market in the world; the old lumberyards and warehouses upstream; and the Kokugikan, with its distinctive green roof, which houses the sumō wrestling arena, the Sumō Museum, and headquarters of the Japan Sumō Association.

Another place to catch the ferry is at the Hama Rikyū Tei-en (Detached Palace Garden: open daily 9–4:30), a 15-minute walk from Ginza. Once part of the imperial estates, the gardens are open to the public for a separate ¥300 entrance fee. The ferry landing is inside, a short walk to the left as you enter the main gate. Boats depart every 35–45 minutes every weekday 10:25–4:10; the fare between Asakusa and Hama Rikyū is ¥620.

In addition to the ferry to Asakusa, the Tōkyō Cruise Ship Company also operates four other lines from Hinode Pier. The Harbor Cruise Line stern-wheeler makes a 50-minute circuit under the Rainbow Bridge and around the inner harbor. Departures are at 10:30, 12:30, 1:30, and 3:30 (and 4:45 in August). The fare is ¥800. If you visit in August you should definitely opt for the evening cruise; the lights on the Rainbow Bridge and neighboring Odaiba are spectacular. Two lines connect Hinode to Odaiba itself, one at 20-minute intervals from 10:10 to 6:10 to Odaiba Seaside Park and the Museum of Maritime Science at Aomi Terminal (¥400–¥520), the other every 20 minutes from 9 to 5:40 to the shopping/amusement center at Palette Town and on to the Tōkyō Big Sight exhibition grounds at Ariake (¥350). The Kasai Sealife Park Line cruise leaves Hinode hourly from 10 to 4 and travels through the network of artificial islands in the harbor to the beach and aquarium at Kasai Rinkai Kōen in Chiba; the one-way fare is ¥800. The Canal Cruise Line connects Hinode with Shinagawa Suizokukan aquarium, south along the harborside. There are nine departures daily between 10:40 and 4:40; the one-way fare is ¥600.

➤ BOAT AND FERRY INFORMATION: **Tōkyō Cruise Ship Company** (✉ 2–7–104 Kaigan, Minato-ku, ☎ 03/3457–7830).

BUS TRAVEL

Because Tōkyō has no rational order bus routes are impossibly complicated. The Tōkyō Municipal Government operates some of the lines; private companies run the rest. There is no telephone number even a native Japanese can call for help. And buses all have tiny seats and low ceilings. Unless you are a true Tōkyō veteran, forget about taking buses.

CAR RENTAL

Congestion, lack of road signs in English, and the difficulty of parking make driving in Tōkyō impractical. That said, should you wish to rent a car, contact one of the following companies, with offices all around Tōkyō and Japan: Avis Rent-A-Car, Hertz Asia Pacific (Japan), Nippon Rent-A-Car Service, or Toyota Rent-A-Lease. The cost is approximately ¥15,000 per day. An international driver's license is required.

You can hire large and comfortable chauffeured cars (the Japanese call them *haiya*) for about ¥5,000 per hour for a midsize car, up to ¥18,000 per hour for a Cadillac limousine. Call Hinomaru. The Imperial, Okura, and Palace hotels also have limousine services.

➤ LOCAL AGENCIES: **Avis Rent-A-Car** (☎ 03/5550–1015). **Hertz Asia Pacific (Japan) Ltd.** (☎ 0120/489–882 toll free). **Hinomaru** (☎ 03/3505–0707). **Nippon Rent-A-Car** (☎ 03/3469–0919). **Toyota Rent-A-Lease** (☎ 03/3263–6324).

EMBASSIES AND CONSULATES

The following embassies and consulates are open weekdays, with one- to two-hour closings for lunch. Call for exact hours.

➤ AUSTRALIA: **Australian Embassy and Consulate** (✉ 2–1–14 Mita, Minato-ku, ☎ 03/5232–4111; subway: Toei Mita Line, Shiba-Kōen Eki [Exit A2]; Toei Ōedo and Namboku lines, Azabu-jūban Eki [Exits 2 and 4]).

➤ CANADA: **Canadian Embassy and Consulate** (✉ 7–3–38 Akasaka, Minato-ku, ☎ 03/5412–6200; subway: Hanzō-mon and Ginza lines, Aoyama-itchōme Eki [Exit 4]).

➤ New Zealand: **New Zealand Embassy** (✉ 20–40 Kamiyama-chō, Shibuya-ku, ☎ 03/3467–2270; subway: Chiyoda Line, Yoyogi-kōen Eki [Minami-guchi/South Exit]).

➤ United Kingdom: **British Embassy and Consulate** (✉ 1 Ichiban-chō, Chiyoda-ku, ☎ 03/3265–5511; subway: Hanzō-mon Line, Hanzō-mon Eki [Exit 4]).

➤ United States: **U.S. Embassy and Consulate** (✉ 1–10–5 Akasaka, Minato-ku, ☎ 03/3224–5000; subway: Namboku Line, Tameike-Sannō Eki [Exit 13]).

EMERGENCIES
➤ Contacts: **Ambulance and Fire** (☎ 119). **Police** (☎ 110).

DOCTORS AND DENTISTS
The International Catholic Hospital (Seibō Byōin) accepts emergencies and takes regular appointments Monday–Saturday 8 AM–11 AM; outpatient services are closed the third Saturday of the month. The International Clinic also accepts emergencies. Appointments there are taken weekdays 9–noon and 2:30–5 and on Saturday 9–noon. St. Luke's International Hospital is a member of the American Hospital Association and accepts emergencies. Appointments are taken weekdays 8:30 AM–11 AM. The Tōkyō Medical and Surgical Clinic takes appointments weekdays 9–5 and Saturday 9–noon.

The Yamauchi Dental Clinic, a member of the American Dental Association, is open weekdays 9–12:30 and 3–5:30, Saturday 9–noon.
➤ Contacts: **International Catholic Hospital** (Seibō Byōin; ✉ 2–5–1 Naka Ochiai, Shinjuku-ku, ☎ 03/3951–1111; subway: Seibu Shinjuku Line, Shimo-Ochiai Eki [Nishi-guchi/West Exit]). **International Clinic** (✉ 1–5–9 Azabu-dai, Roppongi, Minato-ku, ☎ 03/3582–2646 or 03/3583–7831; subway: Hibiya Line, Roppongi Eki [Exit 3]). **St. Luke's International Hospital** (✉ 9–1 Akashi-chō, Chūō-ku, ☎ 03/3541–5151; subway: Hibiya Line, Tsukiji Eki [Exit 3]; Yūraku-chō Line, Shintomichō Eki [Exit 6]). **Tōkyō Medical and Surgical Clinic** (✉ 32 Mori Bldg., 3–4–30 Shiba Kōen, Minato-ku, ☎ 03/3436–3028; subway: Toei Mita Line, Onarimon Eki [Exit A1]; Hibiya Line, Kamiyachō Eki [Exit 1]; Toei Ōedo Line, Akabane-bashi Eki). **Yamauchi Dental Clinic** (✉ Shirokanedai Gloria Heights, 1st floor, 3–16–10 Shirokanedai, Minato-ku, ☎ 03/3441–6377; JR Yamanote Line, Meguro Eki [Higashi-guchi/East Exit]; subway: Namboku and Toei Mita lines, Shirokanedai Eki [Exit 1]).

EMERGENCY SERVICES
Assistance in English is available 24 hours a day on the Japan Helpline. The Tōkyō English Life Line (TELL) is a telephone service available daily 9 AM–4 PM and 7 PM–11 PM for anyone in distress who cannot communicate in Japanese. The service will relay your emergency to the appropriate Japanese authorities and/or will serve as a counselor.
➤ Contacts: **Japan Helpline** (☎ 0120/461–997 toll free). **Tōkyō English Life Line** (TELL; ☎ 03/5774–0992).

LATE-NIGHT PHARMACIES
No drugstores in Tōkyō are open 24 hours a day. The American Pharmacy stocks American products. It's near the Tourist Information Center and is open Monday–Saturday 9:30–8:30 and Sunday 10–6:30. Note that grocery stores frequently carry such basics as aspirin.

Nagai Yakkyoku is open Wednesday–Monday 10–7 and will mix a Chinese and/or Japanese herbal medicine for you after a consultation. You can't have a doctor's prescription filled here, but you can find something for a headache or stomach pain. A little English is spoken.
➤ Contacts: **American Pharmacy** (✉ Hibiya Park Building, 1–8–1 Yūraku-chō, Chiyoda-ku, ☎ 03/3271–4034; Hibiya subway line, Hi-

biya Eki [Exit A3]). **Nagai Yakkyoku** (✉ 1–8–10 Azabu-jūban, Minato-ku, ☎ 03/3583–3889; Namboku and Toei Ōedo subway lines, Azabu-jūban Eki [Exit 7]).

LOST AND FOUND

The Central Lost and Found Office of the metropolitan police is open weekdays only, 8:30–5:15; someone should be able to speak English here. If you leave something on a JR train, report it to the lost-and-found office at any station. You can also call either of the two central JR Lost Property Offices, one at Tōkyō Eki (open daily 8:30–8), the other at Ueno Eki (open weekdays 10–6, Saturday 10–4). If you leave something on a subway car, contact the Teitō Rapid Transit Authority (TRTA) at its Ueno Lost Properties Office (open weekdays 9:30–7, Saturday 9:30–4). If you leave something in a taxi, contact the Tōkyō Taxi Kindaika Center. The center is open 24 hours, but only Japanese is spoken here.

➤ CONTACTS: **Central Lost and Found Office** (✉ 1-9-11, Kōraku, Bunkyō-ku, ☎ 03/3814–4151). **JR Lost Property Office** (✉ Tōkyō Eki, ☎ 03/3231–1880; ✉ Ueno Eki, ☎ 03/3841–8069). **Teitō Rapid Transit Authority** (☎ 03/3834–5577). **Tōkyō Taxi Kindaika Center** (✉ 7-3-3 Minami-Suna, Koto-ku, ☎ 03/3648–0300).

LODGING

The Japanese Inn Group is a nationwide association of small ryokan and family-owned tourist hotels. Because they tend to be slightly out of the way and provide few amenities, these accommodations are priced to attract budget-minded travelers. The association has the active support of the Japan National Tourist Organization. The best way to get information about the member inns in Tōkyō and throughout Japan—and arrange bookings on the spot—is to visit the JNTO Tourist Information Center (open weekdays 9–5, Saturday 9–noon) on the lower level of the Tōkyō International Forum.

➤ CONTACT: **JNTO Tourist Information Center** (✉ Tōkyō International Forum B1, 3–5–1 Marunouchi, Chiyoda-ku, ☎ 03/3201–3331; subway: Yūraku-chō Line, Yūraku-chō Eki [Exit A-4B]).

MAIL AND SHIPPING

Most hotels have stamps and will mail your letters and postcards; they will also give you directions to the nearest post office. The main International Post Office is on the Imperial Palace side of JR Tōkyō Eki. For cables, contact the KDD International Telegraph Office.

➤ MAJOR SERVICES: **International Post Office** (✉ 2–3–3 Ōte-machi, Chiyoda-ku, ☎ 03/3241–4891; Tōkyō Eki). **KDD International Telegraph Office** (✉ 2–3–2 Nishi-Shinjuku, Shinjuku-ku, ☎ 03/3344–5151; Tōei Ōedo subway line, Tochō-mae Eki [any exit]).

MONEY MATTERS

Most hotels will change both traveler's checks and notes into yen. However, their rates are always less favorable than at banks. Because Japan is largely free from street crime, you can safely consider changing even hefty sums into yen at any time; three places that may be familiar to you are American Express International and Citibank. The larger branches of most Japanese banks have foreign exchange counters where you can do this as well; the paperwork will be essentially the same. All major branch offices of the post office have ATM machines that accept Visa, MasterCard, American Express, Diners Club, and Cirrus cards. You can also use cards on the Cirrus network at Citibank ATMs. Banking hours are weekdays 9–3.

➤ CONTACTS: **American Express International** (✉ 4–30–16 Ogikubo, Suginami-ku, ☎ 03/3220–6100; JR Chuo Line, Ogikubo Eki [Higashi-guchi/East Exit]). **Citibank** (⊠ Ōte Center Bldg. 1F, 1–1–3 Ōte-machi, Chiyoda-ku, ☎ 0120/110–330 toll free for members; 03/3215–0051 for nonmembers; Chiyoda, Marunouchi, Hanzō-mon, Tōzai, and Mita subway lines; Ōte-machi Eki [Exit C-13B]).

SUBWAY TRAVEL

Thirteen subway lines serve Tōkyō; nine of them are operated by the Rapid Transportation Authority (Eidan) and four by the Tōkyō Municipal Authority (Toei). Maps of the system, bilingual signs at entrances, and even the trains are color-coded for easy identification. Japan Travel Phone can provide information in English on subway travel. Subway trains run roughly every five minutes from about 5 AM to midnight; except during rush hours, the intervals are slightly longer on the newer Toei lines.

The network of interconnections (subway to subway and train to subway) is particularly good. One transfer—two at most—will take you in less than an hour to any part of the city you're likely to visit. At some stations—such as Ōte-machi, Ginza, and Iidabashi—long underground passageways connect the various lines, and it does take time to get from one to another. Directions, however, are clearly marked. Less helpful is the system of signs that tell you which of the 15 or 20 exits (exits are often numbered and alphabetized) from a large station will take you aboveground closest to your destination; only a few stations have such signs in English. Exit names or numbers have been included in the text where they'll be most useful. You can also try asking the agent when you turn in your ticket; she or he may understand enough of your question to come back with the exit number and letter (such as A3 or B12), which is all you need.

Subway fares begin at ¥160. Toei trains are generally a bit more expensive than Eidan trains, but both are competitive with JR lines. From Ueno across town to Shibuya on the old Ginza Line (orange), for example, is ¥190; the ride on the JR Yamanote Line will cost you the same. The Eidan (but *not* the Toei) has inaugurated an electronic card of its own, called Metrocard. The denominations are ¥1,000, ¥3,000, and ¥5,000. Automatic card dispensers are installed at some subway stations. Remember to hold onto your ticket during your trip; you'll need it again to exit the station turnstile.
➤ CONTACT: **Japan Travel Phone** (☎ 03/3201–3331).

TAXIS

In spite of the introduction of ¥340 initial-fare cabs, Tōkyō taxi fares remain among the highest in the world. Most meters start running at ¥660 and after the first 2 km (1 mi) tick away at the rate of ¥80 every 274 meters (about ⅕ mi). Keep in mind that the ¥340 taxis (which are a very small percentage of those on the street) are only cheaper for trips of 2 km (1 mi) or less; after that the fare catches up with the ¥660 cabs. The ¥340 taxis have a sticker on the left-rear window.

There are also smaller cabs, called *kogata,* that charge ¥640 and then ¥80 per 290 meters (⅕ mi). If your cab is caught in traffic—hardly an uncommon event—the meter registers another ¥80 for every 1½ minutes of immobility. Between 11 PM and 5 AM, a 30% surcharge is added to the fare.

You do get very good value for the money, though. Taxis are invariably clean and comfortable. The doors open automatically for you when you get in and out. Drivers take you where you want to go by the shortest route they know and do not expect a tip. Tōkyō cabbies are not, in general, a sociable species (you wouldn't be either if you had to drive for 10–12 hours a day in Tōkyō traffic), but you can always count on a minimum standard of courtesy. And if you forget something in the cab—a camera, a purse—your chances of getting it back are almost 100% (☞ Lost and Found, *above*).

Hailing a taxi during the day is seldom a problem. You would have to be in a very remote part of town to wait more than five minutes for one to pass by. In Ginza, drivers are allowed to pick up passengers only in designated areas; look for short lines of cabs. Elsewhere, you need only step off the curb and raise your arm. If the cab already has a fare, there will be a green light on the dashboard, visible through the windshield; if not, the light will be red.

Night, when everyone's been out drinking and wants a ride home, changes the rules a bit. Don't be astonished if a cab with a red light doesn't stop for you: the driver may have had a radio call, or he may be heading for an area where a long, profitable fare to the suburbs is more likely. (Or the cab driver may simply not feel like coping with a passenger in a foreign language. Refusing a fare is against the law—but it's done all the time.) Between 11 PM and 2 AM on Friday and Saturday nights, you have to be very lucky to get a cab in any of the major entertainment districts; in Ginza it is almost impossible.

TELEPHONES

For directory information on Tōkyō telephone numbers, dial 104; for elsewhere in Japan, dial 105. These services are only in Japanese, but the NTT Information Customer Service Centre, open weekdays 9–5, has service representatives who speak English, French, Spanish, Portuguese, Korean, and Chinese.

➤ CONTACT: **NTT Information Customer Service Centre** (☎ 0120/364–463 toll-free).

TOURS

EXCURSIONS

Sunrise Tours, a division of the Japan Travel Bureau, runs a one-day bus tour to Nikkō on Monday, Tuesday, and Friday between April and October, at ¥13,500 (lunch included). Japan Amenity Travel and the Japan Gray Line conduct Mt. Fuji and Hakone tours, with return either by bus or train; one-day trips cost from ¥12,000 to ¥15,000 (lunch included), and two-day tours cost ¥26,500 (meals and accommodation included). Some of these tours include a quick visit to Kamakura. There are also excursions to Kyōto via Shinkansen that cost from ¥49,500 to ¥82,100; you can arrange these Shinkansen tours through Japan Amenity Travel or Japan Gray Line.

ORIENTATION TOUR

April–June and mid-September–November, Sunrise Tours conducts a Thursday-morning (8–12:30) "Experience Japanese Culture" bus-and-walking tour (¥7,000), which includes a calligraphy demonstration, a tea ceremony, and a visit to the Edo-Tōkyō Hakubutsukan. Both Sunrise Tours and the Japan Gray Line operate a number of other bus excursions around Tōkyō with English-speaking guides. The tours vary with the current demands of the market. Most include the Tōkyō Tower Observatory, the Imperial East Garden, a demonstration of flower arrangement at the Tasaki Pearl Gallery, and/or a Sumida-gawa cruise to Sensō-ji in Asakusa. These are for the most part four-hour morning or afternoon tours; a full-day tour (seven hours) combines most of what is covered in half-day excursions with a tea ceremony at Happō Garden and lunch at the traditional Chinzan-sō restaurant. Costs range from ¥4,000 to ¥12,900. Tours are conducted in large, air-conditioned buses that set out from Hamamatsu-chō Bus Terminal, and there is also free pickup and return from major hotels. (If you travel independently and use the subway, you could probably manage the same full-day itinerary for under ¥3,000, including lunch.)

PERSONAL GUIDES

The Japan Guide Association will introduce you to English-speaking guides. You'll need to negotiate your own itinerary and price with the guide. Assume that the fee will be ¥25,000–¥30,000 for a full eight-hour day. The Japan National Tourist Organization can also put you in touch with various local volunteer groups that conduct tours in English; you need only to pay for the guide's travel expenses, admission fees to cultural sites, and meals if you eat together.

SPECIAL-INTEREST TOURS

Sunrise Tours also offers a "Geisha Night" tour (4:30–7) of Tōkyō on Tuesday and Friday mid-March–November. Dinner is included. Other evening tours include Kabuki drama at the Kabuki-za, and sukiyaki dinner. Prices are ¥5,000–¥9,500, depending on which portions of the tour you select. Sunrise Tours has a free-schedule trip to Tōkyō Disneyland, but this operates only on Tuesday and Friday and works in only one direction: buses pick you up at major hotels but leave you to manage your own way back to Tōkyō at the end of the day. The cost for the trip is ¥9,500.

➤ TOUR CONTACTS: **Japan Amenity Travel** (✉ 5–13–12 Ginza, Chūō-ku, ☎ 03/3542–7200; Hibiya subway line, Higashi-Ginza Eki [Exit 4]). **Japan Gray Line** (✉ 3–3–3 Nishi Shimbashi, Minato-ku, ☎ 03/3433–5745; JR Yamanote Line, Shimbashi Eki [Nishi-guchi/West Exit]). **Japan Guide Association** (☎ 03/3213–2706). **Japan National Tourist Organization** (✉ Tōkyō International Forum B1, 3–5–1 Marunouchi, Chiyoda-ku, ☎ 03/3201–3331; subway: Yūraku-chō Line, Yūraku-chō Eki [Exit A-4B]). **Sunrise Tours Reservation Center, Japan Travel Bureau** (☎ 03/5620–9500).

TRAIN TRAVEL

The JR Shinkansen (bullet train) and JR express trains on the Tōkaidō Line (to Nagoya, Kyōto, Kōbe, Ōsaka, Hiroshima, and the island of Kyūshū) use Tōkyō Eki in central Tōkyō. The JR Shinkansen and express trains on the Tōhoku Line (to Sendai and Morioka) use Ueno Eki. JR Shinkansen and express trains on the Jōetsu Line (to Niigata) use both Tōkyō Eki and Ueno Eki. JR express trains to the Japan Alps (Matsumoto) use Shinjuku Eki. The *Hokuriku* Shinkansen travels from Tōkyō Eki to Nagano; it uses the Jōetsu Shinkansen tracks to Takasaki, where it branches off for Nagano.

If you buy a Japan Rail Pass for further travel throughout the country, you can use it on all JR trains except the *Nozomi* Shinkansen out of Tōkyō on the Tōkaidō Line. *See* Train Travel *in* Smart Travel Tips A to Z for information on Japanese rail networks and on obtaining JR Passes.

Japan Railways (JR) trains in Tōkyō are color-coded, making it easy to identify the different lines. The Yamanote Line (green or silver with green stripes) makes a 35-km (22-mi) loop around the central wards of the city in about an hour. The 29 stops include the major hub stations of Tōkyō, Yūraku-chō, Shimbashi, Shinagawa, Shibuya, Shinjuku, and Ueno.

The Chūō Line (orange) runs east to west through the loop from Tōkyō to the distant suburb of Takao. During the day, however, these are limited express trains that don't stop at most of the stations inside the loop. For local cross-town service, which also extends east to neighboring Chiba Prefecture, you have to take the Sōbu Line (yellow).

The Keihin Tōhoku Line (blue) goes north to Ōmiya in Saitama Prefecture and south to Ōfuna in Kanagawa, running parallel to the Yamanote Line between Tabata and Shinagawa. Where they share the loop, the two lines usually use the same platform—Yamanote trains on one side and Keihin Tōhoku trains, headed in the same direction, on the other. This requires a little care. Suppose, for example, you want to take the loop line from Yūraku-chō around to Shibuya, and you board a blue train instead of a green one; four stops later, where the lines branch, you'll find yourself on an unexpected trip to Yokohama.

JR Yamanote Line fares start at ¥130; you can get anywhere on the loop for ¥260 or less. Most stations have a chart in English somewhere above the row of ticket vending machines, so you can check the fare to your destination. If not, you can simply buy the cheapest ticket and pay the difference at the other end. In any case, hold on to your ticket: you'll have to turn it in at the exit. Tickets are valid only on the day you buy them, but if you plan to use the JR a lot, you can save time and trouble with an Orange Card, available at any station office. The card is electronically coded; at vending machines with orange panels, you insert the card, punch the cost of the ticket, and that amount is automatically deducted. Orange Cards come in ¥1,000 and ¥3,000 denominations.

Shinjuku, Harajuku, and Shibuya are notorious for the long lines that form at ticket dispensers. If you're using a card, make sure you've lined up at a machine with an orange panel; if you're paying cash and have no change, make sure you've lined up at a machine that will change a ¥1,000 note—not all of them do.

Yamanote and Sōbu Line trains begin running about 4:30 AM and stop around 1 AM. The last departures are indicated at each station—but only in Japanese. Bear in mind that 7 AM–9:30 AM and 5 PM–7 PM trains are packed to bursting with commuters; avoid the trains at these times, if possible. During these hours smoking is not allowed in JR stations or on platforms.

➤ CONTACT: **Japan Railways** (☎ 03/3423–0111).

TRANSPORTATION AROUND TŌKYŌ

Daunting in its sheer size, Tōkyō is, in fact, an extremely easy city to negotiate. If you have any anxieties about getting from place to place, remind yourself first that a transportation system obliged to cope with 4 or 5 million commuters a day simply *has* to be efficient, extensive, and reasonably easy to understand. Remind yourself also that virtually any place you're likely to go as a visitor is within a 15-minute walk of a train or subway station—and that station stops are always marked in English. Of course, exceptions to the rule exist—the system has its flaws. In the outline here you'll find a few things to avoid and also a few pointers that will save you time—and money—as you go.

Excellent maps of the subway system, with major JR lines included as well, are available at any station office free of charge. You'll find the same map in the monthly *Tour Companion* magazine. Hotel kiosks and English-language bookstores stock a wide variety of pocket maps, some of which have suggested walking tours that also mark the locations of JR and subway stations along the way. A bit bulkier to carry around, but by far the best and most detailed resource, is the *Tōkyō City Atlas: A Bilingual Guide* (Kodansha International, second edition; ¥2,100), which contains subway and rail-system guides and area maps. Because all notations are in both English and Japanese, you can always get help on the street, even from people who do not speak your language, just by pointing at your destination.

The standard postal system the Japanese themselves use to indicate addresses in Tōkyō begins with the ward—designated by the suffix *-ku* (as in Minato-ku)—followed by the name of the district within the ward, such as Roppongi or Nishi-Azabu. The district is usually divided into numbered subsections, sometimes designated by the suffix -*chōme*; the subsections can be further divided into units of one or more blocks, each with its own building numbers. Apartment blocks will often have a final set of digits on the address to specify an apartment number. Thus, *Taitō-ku 1–4–301 Asakusa 3-chōme* will be recognizable to the mail carrier as "Apartment No. 301 in Building 4 on the first block of Asakusa subsection No. 3 in Taitō Ward"—but don't count on the driver of a taxi you hail on the other side of the city having the faintest idea how to find it. And don't count on the blocks or the building numbers appearing in any rational geographic order, either. The whole system is impossibly complicated, even for the Japanese. People usually direct each other to some landmark or prominent building in a given neighborhood and muddle on from there. Bear in mind that addresses written in Japanese appear in reverse order, that is, with the postal code, prefecture, and ward first and the name of the person or establishment last; however, Japanese addresses written in English follow Western order, with the name first and the ward, prefecture, and postal code last. The system used throughout this guide follows the Western order: 1–4–301 Asakusa, 3-chōme, Taitō-ku.

Information on trains is available in English from the JR East InfoLine (weekdays 10–6). The Japan Travel Phone (daily 9–5) provides information in English on all domestic travel, buses, and trains.
➤ CONTACTS: **Japan Travel Phone** (☎ 03/3201–3331; 075/371–5649 for the Kyōto area). **JR East InfoLine** (☎ 03/3423–0111).

VISITOR INFORMATION

The Tourist Information Center (TIC) in the Tōkyō International Forum, at the north end of the lower concourse, is an extremely useful source of free maps and brochures. The center also advises on trip planning in Japan. Make a point of dropping by early in your stay in Tōkyō; it's open weekdays 9–5, Saturday 9–noon.

The Asakusa Tourist Information Center, opposite Kaminari-mon, has some English-speaking staff and plenty of maps and brochures; it's open daily 9:30–8.

A taped recording in English on festivals, performances, and other events in the Tōkyō area operates 24 hours a day and is updated weekly. Two free weekly magazines, the *Tour Companion* and *Metropolis*, available at hotels, book and music stores, some restaurants and cafés, and other locations, carry up-to-date announcements of what's going on in the city. The better of the two is *Metropolis*, which breaks its listings down in separate sections for Art & Exhibitions, Movies, TV, Music, and After Dark. *Tōkyō Journal* (¥600), available at newsstands in Narita Airport and at many bookstores that carry English-language books, is a monthly magazine with similar listings. The *Japan Times*, a daily English-language newspaper, is yet another resource for entertainment reviews and schedules.

NTT (Japanese Telephone Corporation) can help you find information (in English), such as telephone numbers, museum openings, and various other information available from its databases. It's open weekdays 9–5.
➤ TOURIST INFORMATION: **Asakusa Tourist Information Center** (✉ 2–18–9 Kaminari-mon, Taitō-ku, ☎ 03/3842–5566; subway: Ginza Line, Asakusa Eki [Exit 2]). **Metropolis** (☎ 03/3423–6931, WEB www.metropolis.co.jp). **NTT** (☎ 0120/36–4463 toll free). **Tourist Information Center** (TIC; ✉ Tōkyō International Forum, 3–5–1 Marunouchi, Chiyoda-ku, ☎ 03/3201–3331; subway: Yūraku-chō Line, Yūraku-chō Eki [Exit A-4B]).

2 SIDE TRIPS FROM TŌKYŌ

Most people are drawn to Nikkō first by Tōshō-gū, the astonishing shrine to the first Tokugawa shōgun Ieyasu. Kamakura, the 13th-century capital of Japan, has a great legacy of historical and cultural sights. And no matter how many pictures of Fuji-san you've seen, the genuine majesty of this dormant volcano will fill you with awe. Yokohama, which demographers now include in the greater Tōkyō conurbation, is a port city with an international character all its own.

By Jared
Lubarsky

NIKKŌ—which means "sunlight"—is the site not simply of the Tokugawa shrine but also of a national park, Nikkō Kokuritsu Kōen, on the heights above it. The centerpiece of the park is Chūzenji-ko, a deep lake some 21 km (13 mi) around, and the 318-ft Kegon-no-taki, Japan's most famous waterfall. "Think nothing splendid," asserts an old Japanese proverb, "until you have seen Nikkō." Whoever said it first might well have been thinking more of the park than of the shrine below.

One caveat: The term "national park" does not quite mean what it does elsewhere in the world. In Japan pristine grandeur is hard to come by; there is *nowhere* in this country where intrepid hikers can go to contemplate the beauty of nature for very long in solitude. If a thing's worth seeing, it's worth exploiting: this world view tends to fill the national parks with bus caravans, ropeways and gondolas, scenic overlooks with coin-fed telescopes, signs that tell you where you may and may not walk, fried noodle joints and vending machines, and shacks full of kitschy souvenirs. That's true of Nikkō, and it's true as well of Fuji-Hakone-Izu National Park, southwest of Tōkyō, another of Japan's most popular resort areas.

The park's chief attraction is, of course, Fuji-san—spellbinding in its perfect symmetry, immortalized by centuries of poets and artists. South of Fuji-san, the Izu Peninsula projects out into the Pacific, with Suruga Bay to the west and Sagami Bay to the east. The beaches and rugged shoreline of Izu, its forests and highland meadows, and its numerous hot-springs inns and resorts (*izu* means "spring") make the region a favorite destination for the Japanese, especially honeymooners.

Kamakura and Yokohama, both close enough to Tōkyō to provide ideal day trips, could not make for more contrasting experiences. Kamakura is an ancient city—the birthplace, one could argue, of the samurai way of life. Its place in Japanese history begins late in the 12th century, when Minamoto no Yoritomo became the country's first shōgun and chose this site, with its rugged hills and narrow passes, as the seat of his military government. The warrior elite of the Kamakura period took much of their ideology—and their aesthetics—from Zen Buddhism, endowing splendid temples that still exist today. A walking tour of Kamakura's Zen temples and Shintō shrines is a must for anyone with a day to spend out of Tōkyō. Yokohama, too, can lay claim to an important place in Japanese history: in 1869, after centuries of isolation, this city became the first important port for trade with the West and the site of the first major foreign settlement. Twice destroyed, the city retains very few remnants of that history, but it remains Japan's largest port and has an international character that rivals—if not surpasses—that of Tōkyō. Its waterfront park and its ambitious Minato Mirai bayside development project draw visitors from all over the world.

Side Trips Glossary

Key Japanese words and suffixes for this chapter include *bijutsukan* (art museum), *-chō* (street or block), *chūō* (central), *daimyō* (feudal lord), *-den* (hall), *-dō* (temple or hall), *dōri* (avenue), *eki* (train station), *gaijin* (foreigner), *-gawa* (river), *-gū* (Shintō shrine), *-gun* (district), *-hama* (beach), *-hara* (plain), *-in* (Buddhist temple), *-ji* (temple), *jingū* or *jinja* (Shintō shrine), *kita* (north), *-ko* (lake), *kōen* (park), *-ku* (section or ward), *machi* (town), *michi* (street), *-mon* (gate), *onsen* (hot springs), *-san* (mountain, as in Fuji-san, Mt. Fuji), *-shima* (island), *Shinkansen* (bullet train, literally "new trunk line"), *shōgun* (commander in chief), *torii* ("*to*-ree-ee," gate), and *yama* (mountain).

Pleasures and Pastimes

Dining

Nikkō has no shortage of popular restaurants catering to its tourist trade. It also has a small number of truly elegant upscale places to eat, in both Western and traditional Japanese style. Several in each category are listed below. The local specialty is a kind of bean curd called *yuba*; dozens of restaurants in Nikkō serve it in a variety of dishes you would not have believed possible for so prosaic an ingredient. Other local favorites are *soba* (buckwheat) and *udon* (wheat-flour) noodles—both inexpensive, filling, and tasty options for lunch.

Three things about Kamakura make it a fairly good place to look for a restaurant. It's on the ocean (properly speaking, on Sagami Bay), which means that seafood is good nearly everywhere. Kamakura is a major tourist stop, and it has long been a prestigious place to live, a favorite with Japan's worldly and well-to-do, and with its more successful writers, artists, and intellectuals. On a day trip from Tōkyō, you can feel confident picking a place for lunch almost at random.

Yokohama, as befits a city of more than 3 million people, lacks little in the way of food, from quick-fix lunch counters to elegant dining rooms, and has almost every imaginable cuisine. Your best bet is Chinatown—Japan's largest Chinese community—with more than 100 restaurants representing every regional style. If you fancy Greek food, or Italian, or Indian instead, this international port is still guaranteed to provide an eminently satisfying meal. For more on Japanese cuisine, *see* Chapter 14 *and* Dining *in* Smart Travel Tips A to Z.

CATEGORY	COST*
$$$$	over ¥7,000
$$$	¥3,000–¥7,000
$$	¥1,500–¥3,000
$	under ¥1,500

per person for a main course at dinner

Lodging

Yokohama and Kamakura are treated here as day trips, and as it's unlikely that you'll stay overnight in either city, no accommodations are listed for them. Nikkō is something of a toss-up: you can easily see Tōshō-gū and be back in Tōkyō by evening. But when the weather turns glorious in spring or autumn, why not spend some time in the national park, staying overnight at Chūzen-ji, and returning to the city the next day? Fuji-san and Hakone, on the other hand—and more especially the Izu Peninsula—are pure resort destinations. Staying overnight is an intrinsic part of the experience, and it makes little sense to go without hotel reservations confirmed in advance.

In both Nikkō and the Fuji-Hakone-Izu area are modern, Western-style hotels that operate in a fairly standard international style. More common, however, are the Japanese-style *kankō* (literally, "sightseeing") hotels and the traditional *ryokan* (inns). The undisputed pleasure of a ryokan is to return to it at the end of a hard day of sightseeing, luxuriate for an hour in a hot bath with your own garden view, put on the *nemaki* (sleeping gown) provided for you, and sit down to a catered private dinner party. There's little point to staying at a kankō hotel, on the other hand, beyond being able to say you've had the experience and survived with your good humor intact. Like everywhere else in Japan, these places do most of their business with big, boisterous tour groups. The turnover of guests is ruthless at kankō hotels, and the cost is way out of proportion to the service they provide.

The price categories listed below are for double occupancy, with private bath, but you'll find that most kankō and ryokan normally quote per-person rates, which include breakfast and dinner. Remember to stipulate whether you want a Japanese or Western breakfast. If you don't want dinner at your hotel, it's usually possible to renegotiate the price, but the management will not be happy about it; the two meals are a fixture of their business. The typical ryokan takes great pride in its cuisine—and very often with good reason: the evening meal is an elaborate affair of 10 or a dozen different dishes, based on the fresh produce and specialties of the region, served to you—nay, *orchestrated*—in your room on a wonderful variety of trays and tableware designed to celebrate the season.

Be aware that hotels may add a surcharge to the basic rate at various times—weekends, nights before local festivals, July–August, October, over the New Year—in other words, whenever you're likely to want a room. In peak season, July 15–August 31, prices can increase by 40%. Call ahead or check with your travel agent for the prevailing rate at the time. For a short course on accommodations in Japan, *see* Lodging *in* Smart Travel Tips A to Z.

CATEGORY	COST*
$$$$	over ¥25,000
$$$	¥17,000–¥25,000
$$	¥10,000–¥17,000
$	under ¥10,000

All prices are for a double room, excluding service and tax.

Onsen

Japan's biggest natural headache—the slip and slide of vast tectonic plates deep below the archipelago that spawn volcanoes and make earthquakes an everyday fact of life—provides one of Japan's greatest delights as well: thermal baths. Wherever there are volcanic mountains—Japan is mostly volcanic mountains—you can usually count on drilling or tapping into springs of hot water, rich in all sorts of restorative minerals. Any place where this happens is called, generically, an *onsen*; any place where lots of spas have tapped these sources, to cash in on the Japanese passion for total immersion, is an *onsen chiiki* (hot-springs resort area). The Izu Peninsula is particularly rich in onsen. It has, in fact, one-fifth of the 2,300-odd officially recognized hot springs in Japan.

The spas in famous areas like Shuzenji or Yugashima take many forms. The ne plus ultra is that small, secluded Japanese inn, up in the mountains, where you sleep on futons on tatami floors, in a setting of almost poetic traditional furnishings and design. Such an inn will have its own *rotemburo*, an open-air mineral-spring pool, in a screened-off nook with a panoramic view, for the exclusive use of its guests. For a room in one of these inns on a weekend, or in high season, you often have to book months in advance. (High season is late December to early January, late April to early May, the second and third weeks of August, and the second and third weeks of October.) More typical is the large resort hotel, geared mainly to groups, with one or more large indoor mineral baths of its own. Where whole towns and villages have developed to exploit a local supply of hot water, there will be several of these large hotels, an assortment of smaller inns, and probably a few modest public bathhouses, with no accommodations, where you just pay an entrance fee for a soak of whatever length you wish. For more on bathing in Japan *see* Chapter 14.

NIKKŌ

At Nikkō there is a monument to a warlord who was so splendid and powerful that he became a god. In 1600, Ieyasu Tokugawa (1543–1616) won a battle at a place called Seki-ga-hara, in the mountains of south-central Japan, that left him the undisputed ruler of the archipelago. He died in 1616, but the Tokugawa Shogunate would last another 252 years, holding in its sway a peaceful, prosperous, and united country.

A fitting resting place would have to be made for the founder of such a dynasty. Ieyasu ("ee-eh-*ya*-su") had provided for one in his will: a mausoleum at Nikkō, in a forest of tall cedars, where a religious center had been founded more than eight centuries earlier. The year after his death, in accordance with Buddhist custom, he was given a *kaimyō*—an honorific name to bear in the afterlife. Thenceforth, he was Tōshō-Daigongen: the Great Incarnation Who Illuminates the East. The imperial court at Kyōto declared him a god, and his remains were taken in a procession of great pomp and ceremony to be enshrined at Nikkō.

The dynasty he left behind was enormously rich. Ieyasu's personal fief, on the Kantō Plain, was worth 2.5 million *koku* of rice. One koku, in monetary terms, was equivalent to the cost of keeping one retainer in the necessities of life for a year. The shogunate itself, however, was still an uncertainty. It had only recently taken control after more than a century of civil war. The founder's tomb had a political purpose: to inspire awe and to make manifest the power of the Tokugawas. It was Ieyasu's legacy, a statement of his family's right to rule.

Tōshō-gū was built by his grandson, the third shōgun, Iemitsu (it was Iemitsu who established the policy of national isolation, which closed the doors of Japan to the outside world for more than 200 years). The mausoleum and shrine required the labor of 15,000 people for two years (1634–36). Craftsmen and artists of the first rank were assembled from all over the country. Every surface was carved and painted and lacquered in the most intricate detail imaginable. Tōshō-gū shimmers in the reflections from 2,489,000 sheets of gold leaf. Roof beams and rafter ends with dragon heads, lions, and elephants in bas-relief; friezes of phoenixes, wild ducks, and monkeys; inlaid pillars and red-lacquer corridors—Tōshō-gū is everything a 17th-century warlord would consider gorgeous, and the inspiration is very Chinese.

Foreign visitors have differed about the effect Iemitsu achieved. Victorian-era traveler Isabella Bird, who came to Nikkō in 1878, was unrestrained in her enthusiasm: "To pass from court to court," she writes in her *Unbeaten Tracks in Japan,* "is to pass from splendour to splendour; one is almost glad to feel that this is the last, and that the strain on one's capacity for admiration is nearly over." Fosco Mariani, a more recent visitor, felt somewhat different: "You are taken aback," he observes in his *Meeting with Japan* (1959). "You ask yourself whether it is a joke, or a nightmare, or a huge wedding cake, a masterpiece of sugar icing made for some extravagant prince with a perverse, rococo taste, who wished to alarm and entertain his guests." Clearly, it is impossible to feel indifferent about Tōshō-gū. Perhaps, in the end, that is all Ieyasu could ever really have expected.

Exploring Nikkō

Numbers in the margin correspond to points of interest on the Nikkō Area map.

Tōshō-gū Area

The town of Nikkō is essentially one long avenue—Sugi Namiki (Cryptomeria Avenue)—extending for about 2 km (1 mi) from the railway stations to Tōshō-gū. Tourist inns and shops line the street, and if you have time, you might want to make this a leisurely stroll. The antiques shops along the way may turn up interesting—but expensive—pieces like armor fittings, hibachi, pottery, and dolls, and the souvenir shops sell ample selections of local wood carvings.

The best way to see the Tōshō-gū precincts is to buy a multiple-entry ticket: ¥1,000 for Rinnō-ji, the Daiyū-in Mausoleum, and Futara-san Jinja; ¥1,300 for these sights as well as the Sleeping Cat and Ieyasu's tomb at Daiyū-in (separate fees are charged for admission to other sights). There are two places to purchase the multiple-entry ticket: one is at the entrance to Rinnō-ji, in the corner of the parking lot, at the top of the path called the Higashi-sandō (East Approach) that begins across the highway from Shinkyō; the other is at the entrance to Tōshō-gū, at the top of the broad Omote-sandō (Central Approach), which begins about 300 ft farther west.

❶ Built in 1636 for shōguns and imperial messengers on their visits to the shrine, the original **Shinkyō** (Sacred Bridge) was destroyed in a flood; the present red-lacquer wooden structure—under repair at press time but scheduled for completion "sometime" in 2002—dates to 1907. Buses leaving from either railway station at Nikkō go straight up the main street to the bridge, opposite the first of the main entrances to Tōshō-gū. The fare is ¥190. The Shinkyō is just to the left of a modern bridge, where the road curves and crosses the Daiya-gawa.

❷ A Nikkō landmark, the **Kanaya Hotel** has been in the same family for more than 100 years. The main building is a delightful, rambling Victorian structure that has hosted royalty and other important personages—as the guest book attests—from around the world. The long driveway that winds up to the hotel at the top of the hill is just below the Sacred Bridge, on the same side of the street.

The **Monument to Masatane Matsudaira**—opposite the Sacred Bridge, at the east entrance to the grounds of Tōshō-gū—pays tribute to one of the two feudal lords charged with the construction of Tōshō-gū. Matsudaira's great contribution was the planting of the wonderful cryptomeria trees (Japanese cedars) surrounding the shrine and along all the approaches to it. The project took more than 20 years, from 1628 to 1651; the result was some 36 km (22 mi) of cedar-lined avenues—planted with more than 15,000 trees in all. Fire and time have taken their toll, but thousands of these trees still stand in the shrine precincts, creating a setting of solemn majesty the buildings alone could never have achieved. Thousands more line Route 119 east of Nikkō on the way to Shimo-Imaichi.

★ ❸ Rinnō-ji belongs to the Tendai sect of Buddhism, the head temple of which is Enryaku-ji, on Mt. Hiei near Kyōto. The main hall of Rinnō-ji, called the **Sanbutsu-dō**, is the largest single building at Tōshō-gū; it enshrines an image of Amida Nyorai, the Buddha of the Western Paradise, flanked on the right by a Senju (Thousand-Armed) Kannon, the goddess of mercy, and on the left by a Bato-Kannon, regarded as the protector of animals. These three images are lacquered in gold and date from the early part of the 17th century. The original Sanbutsu-dō is said to have been built in 848 by the priest Ennin (794–864), also known as Jikaku-Daishi. The present building dates from 1648.

In the southwest corner of the Rinnō-ji compound, behind the abbot's residence, is an especially fine Japanese garden called the **Shōdō-en,**

Nikkō Area

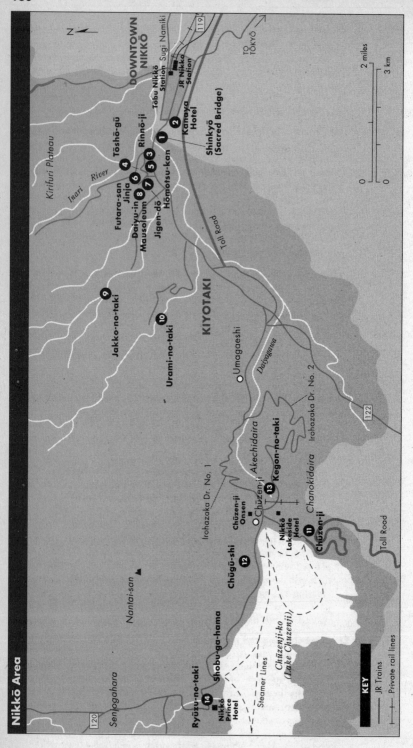

N

DOWNTOWN NIKKŌ

Sugi Namiki

119

TO TOKYO

Tōbu Nikkō Station

JR Nikkō Station

Kaneya Hotel

Shinkyō (Sacred Bridge)

Tōshō-gū

Rinnō-ji

2

1

Futara-san Jinja

Daiyu-in Mausoleum

Jigen-dō

Hōmotsu-kan

4

3

6

5

8

7

Kirifuri Plateau

Inari River

Toll Road

Jakko-no-taki

9

Urami-no-taki

10

KIYOTAKI

Umagaeshi

Daiyagawa

Irohazaka Dr. No. 2

122

Akechidaira

Irohazaka Dr. No. 1

Chūzen-ji Onsen

Chūzen-ji

Kegon-no-taki

13

Chanokidaira

Chūzen-ji

Nikkō Lakeside Hotel

11

Toll Road

Nantai-san

Chūgū-shi

12

Shobu-ga-hama

Senjogahara

Ryūzu-no-taki

14

Nikkō Prince Hotel

120

Chūzenji-ko (Lake Chuzenji)

Steamer Lines

KEY

JR Trains

Private rail lines

2 miles

3 km

0

0

created in 1815 and thoughtfully designed to afford the visitor a different perspective of its rocks, ponds, and flowering plants from every turn in the path. To the right of the entrance to the garden is the **Hōmotsu-den** (Treasure Hall) of Rinnō-ji, a museum with a collection of some 6,000 works of lacquerware, painting, and Buddhist sculpture. The museum is rather small, and only a few of the pieces in the collection—many of them designated National Treasures and Important Cultural Properties—are on display at any given time.

Gohōten-dō, in the northeast corner of Rinnō-ji, behind the Sanbutsu-dō, enshrines three of the Seven Gods of Good Fortune. These three Buddhist deities are derived from Chinese folk mythology: Daikoku and Bishamon, who bring wealth and good harvests, and Benten, patroness of music and the arts. ✉ *Rinnō-ji ¥1000 (multiple-entry ticket includes admission to the Daiyū-in Mausoleum and Futara-san Jinja), Shōdō-en and Treasure Hall ¥300. ☉ Apr.–Oct., daily 8–5 (last entry at 4); Nov.–Mar., daily 8–4 (last entry at 3).*

★ ❹ With its riot of colors and carvings, inlaid pillars, red-lacquer corridors, and extensive use of gold leaf, **Tōshō-gū**, the 17th-century shrine to Ieyasu Tokugawa, is magnificent, astonishing, and never for a moment dull.

The west gate of Rinnō-ji brings you out on the Omote-sandō, which leads uphill to the stone torii of the shrine. The **Five-Story Pagoda** of Tōshō-gū—a reconstruction dating from 1818—is on the left as you approach the shrine. The 12 signs of the zodiac decorate the first story. The black-lacquer doors above each sign bear the three hollyhock leaves of the Tokugawa family crest.

From the torii a flight of stone steps brings you to the front gate of the shrine—the Omote-mon, also called the Nio-mon (Gate of the Deva Kings), with its fearsome pair of red-painted guardian gods. From here the path turns to the left. In the first group of buildings you reach on the left is the **Shinkyū** (Sacred Stable). Housed here is the white horse—symbol of purity—that figures in many of the shrine's ceremonial events. Carvings of pine trees and monkeys adorn the panels over the stable. The second panel from the left is the famous group of three monkeys—"Hear no evil, see no evil, speak no evil"—that has become something of a trademark for Nikkō, reproduced endlessly on plaques, bags, and souvenirs of every sort. A few steps farther, where the path turns to the right, is a granite font where visitors purify themselves before entering the inner precincts of Tōshō-gū. The **Kyōzō** (Sutra Library), just beyond the font, is a repository for some 7,000 Buddhist scriptures, kept in a huge revolving bookcase nearly 20 ft high; it's not open to the public.

As you pass under the second (bronze) torii and up the steps, you'll see on the right a belfry and a tall bronze candelabrum; on the left is a drum tower and a bronze revolving lantern. The two works in bronze were presented to the shrine by the Dutch government in the mid-17th century. (Under the policy of national seclusion, only the Dutch retained trading privileges with Japan, and even they were confined to the tiny artificial island of Dejima, in the port of Nagasaki. They regularly sent tokens of their esteem to the shogunate to keep their precarious monopoly.) Behind the drum tower is the **Yakushi-dō**, which enshrines a manifestation of the Buddha as Yakushi Nyorai, the healer of illnesses. The original 17th-century building was famous for a huge India-ink painting on the ceiling of the nave, *The Roaring Dragon*, so named for the rumbling echoes it seemed to emit when visitors clapped their hands beneath it. The painting was by Yasunobu Kanō (1613–85), from a family of artists that dominated the profession for 400 years. The Kanō school was founded in the late 15th century and patronized by successive military governments until the fall of the Tokugawa Shogunate in 1868. The leadership was hereditary; the artists who trained in the Kanō ateliers specialized in Chinese-style ink paintings, landscapes, and decorative figures of birds and animals—typically for screens and the paneled sliding doors that stand as the interior "walls" of Japanese villas and temples. The Yakushi-dō was destroyed by fire in 1961, then rebuilt; the dragon on the ceiling now is by Nampu Katayama (1887–1980).

The centerpiece of Tōshō-gū is the **Yomei-mon** (Gate of Sunlight), at the top of the second flight of stone steps. A designated National Treasure, it's also called the Higurashi-mon (Twilight Gate)—implying that you could spend all day until sunset looking at its richness of detail. And rich it is indeed: dazzling white, 36 ft high, the gate has 12 columns, beams, and roof brackets carved with dragons, lions, clouds, peonies, Chinese sages, and demigods, painted in vivid hues of red, blue, green, and gold. On one of the central columns, there are two carved tigers; the natural grain of the wood is used to bring out the "fur." To the right and left of the Yomei-mon as you enter, there are galleries running east and west for some 700 ft, their paneled fences also carved and painted with a profusion of motifs from nature: pine and plum branches, pheasants, cranes, and wild ducks.

The portable shrines that appear in the annual Tōshō-gū Festival on May 17–18 are kept in the **Mikoshigura,** a storeroom to the left as you come through the Twilight Gate into the heart of the shrine. The paintings on the ceiling, of *tennin* (Buddhist angels) playing harps, are by Ryōkaku Kanō.

The "official" entrance to the Tōshō-gū inner shrine, through which mere mortals may not pass, is the **Kara-mon** (Chinese Gate). Like its counterpart, the Yomei-mon, on the opposite side of the courtyard, the Kara-mon is a National Treasure—and, like the Yomei-mon, carved and painted in elaborate detail with dragons and other auspicious figures. The Hon-den (Main Hall) of Tōshō-gū is enclosed by a wall of painted and carved panel screens; opposite the right-hand corner of the wall, facing the shrine, is the **Goma-do,** a hall where annual prayers were once offered for the peace of the nation—and where now, for a very modest fee, Japanese couples can be married in a traditional Shintō ceremony, with an ensemble of drums and reed flutes and shrine maidens to attend them.

The **Hon-den** (Main Hall) of Tōshō-gū is the ultimate purpose of the shrine. You approach it from the rows of lockers at the far end of the enclosure; here you remove and store your shoes, step up into the shrine, and follow a winding corridor to the Hai-den (Oratory)—the anteroom, resplendent in its lacquered pillars, carved friezes, and coffered ceilings bedecked with dragons. Over the lintels are paintings of the 36 great poets of the Heian period, by Mitsuoki Tosa (1617–91), with their poems in the calligraphy of Emperor Go-Mizuno-o. Deeper yet, at the back of the Oratory, is the Nai-jin (Inner Chamber)—repository of the Sacred Mirror that represents the spirit of the deity enshrined here. To the right is a room that was reserved for members of the three principal branches of the Tokugawa family; the room on the left was for the chief abbot of Rinnō-ji—who was always a prince of the imperial line.

Behind the Nai-jin is the Nai-Nai-jin, the Innermost Chamber. No visitors come this far. Here, in the very heart of Tōshō-gū, is the gold-lacquer shrine where the spirit of Ieyasu resides—along with two other deities, whom the Tokugawas later decided were fit companions. One was Hideyoshi Toyotomi, Ieyasu's mentor and liege lord in the long wars of unification at the end of the 16th century; the other was Minamoto no Yoritomo, brilliant military tactician and founder of the earlier (12th-century) Kamakura Shogunate (Ieyasu, born Takechiyo Matsudaira, son of a lesser baron in what is today Aichi Prefecture, claimed Yoritomo for an ancestor).

Recover your shoes and return to the courtyard. Between the Goma-do and the **Kagura-den** (a hall where ceremonial dances are performed to honor the gods) is a passage to the **Sakashita-mon** (Gate at the Foot of the Hill). Above the gateway is another famous symbol of Tōshō-gū, the Sleeping Cat—a small panel said to have been carved by Hidari Jingoro (Jingoro the Left-handed), a late-16th-century master carpenter and sculptor credited with important contributions to numerous Tokugawa-period temples, shrines, and palaces. A separate admission charge (¥520) is levied to go beyond the Sleeping Cat, up the flight of 200 stone steps through a forest of cryptomeria to **Ieyasu's tomb.** The climb is worth making, if only for the view of the Yomei-mon and Kara-mon from above—the tomb itself is unimpressive. ○ *Apr.–Oct., daily 8–5; Nov.–Mar., daily 8–4.*

An unhurried visit to the precincts of Tōshō-gū should definitely include the **Hōmotsu-kan** (Treasury House), which houses a collection of antiquities from its various shrines and temples. From the west gate of Rinnō-ji, turn left off the Omote-sandō, just below the pagoda, on to the cedar-lined avenue to Futarasan Jinja. A minute's walk will bring you to the museum, on the left. ▦ *¥500.* ○ *Apr.–Oct., daily 9–5; Nov.– Mar., daily 9–4.*

★ **6** The holy ground at Nikkō is far older than the Tokugawa dynasty, in whose honor it was improved upon. To the gods enshrined at **Futara-san Jinja,** Ieyasu Tokugawa must seem but a callow newcomer. Founded in the 8th century, Futara-san is sacred to the Shintō deities Okuni-nushi-no-Mikoto (god of the rice fields, bestower of prosperity), his consort Tagorihime-no-Mikoto, and their son Ajisukitaka-hikone-no-Mikoto. Futara-san actually has three locations: the Hon-sha (Main Shrine), at Tōshō-gū; the Chū-gushi (Middle Shrine), at Chūzenji-ko; and the Okumiya (Inner Shrine), on top of Mt. Nantai.

The bronze torii at the entrance to the shrine leads to the **Kara-mon** (Chinese Gate) and the **Hon-den** (Sanctum)—the present version of which dates from 1619. To the left, in the corner of the enclosure, is an antique bronze lantern, some 7 ft high, under a canopy. Legend has it that the lantern would assume the shape of a goblin at night; the deep nicks in the bronze were inflicted by swordsmen of the Edo period— on guard duty, perhaps, startled into action by a flickering shape in the dark. This proves, if not the existence of goblins, the incredible cutting power of the Japanese blade, a peerlessly forged weapon. To get to Futara-san, take the avenue to the left as you're standing before the stone torii at Tōshō-gū and follow it to the end. ▦ *¥200, ¥1,000 multiple-entry ticket includes admission to Rinnō-ji and Daiyū-in Mausoleum.* ○ *Apr.–Nov., daily 8–5; Dec.–Mar., daily 9–4.*

7 Tenkai (1536–1643), the first abbot of Rinnō-ji, has his own place of honor at Tōshō-gū: the **Jigen-dō.** To reach it, take the path opposite the south entrance to Futara-san Jinja that passes between the two sub-temples called Jōgyō-do and Hokke-dō. Connected by a corridor, these two buildings are otherwise known as the Futatsu-dō (Twin Halls) of Rinnō-ji and are designated a National Cultural Property. Founded in 848, the Jōgyō-do now holds many of Rinnō-ji's artistic treasures. The path between the Twin Halls leads roughly south and west to the Jigen-dō compound: the hall itself is at the north end of the compound, to the right. At the west end sits the Go-ōden, a shrine to Prince Kitashirakawa (1847–95), the last of the imperial princes to serve as abbot. Behind it are his tomb and the tombs of his 13 predecessors. 🔲 *Free.* ⊗ *Apr.–Nov., daily 8–5; Dec.–Mar., daily 9–4.*

★ ❽   The second of the grandiose Tokugawa monuments at Nikkō is the **Daiyū-in Mausoleum,** resting place of the third shōgun, Iemitsu (1604–51)—who imposed a policy of national isolation on Japan that was to last more than 200 years. Iemitsu, one suspects, had it in mind to upstage his illustrious grandfather; he marked the approach to his own tomb with no fewer than six different decorative gates. The first is another Nio-mon—a Gate of the Deva Kings—like the one at Tōshō-gū. The dragon painted on the ceiling is by Yasunobu Kanō (1613–85). A flight of stone steps leads from here to the second gate, the Niten-mon, a two-story structure protected front and back by carved and painted images of guardian gods. Beyond it, climb two more flights of steps to the middle courtyard. As you climb the last steps to Iemitsu's shrine, you'll pass a bell tower on the right and a drum tower on the left; directly ahead is the third gate, the remarkable **Yasha-mon,** so named for the figures of *yasha* (she-demons) in the four niches. This structure is also known as the Botan-mon (Peony Gate) for the carvings that decorate it.

On the other side of the courtyard is the **Kara-mon** (Chinese Gate), gilded and elaborately carved; beyond it is the **Hai-den,** the shrine's oratory. The Hai-den, too, is richly carved and decorated, with a dragon-covered ceiling. The Chinese lions on the panels at the rear are by two distinguished painters of the Kanō school. From the oratory of the Daiyū-in a connecting passage leads to the **Hon-den** (Sanctum). Designated a National Treasure, it houses a gilded and lacquered Buddhist altar some 9 ft high, decorated with paintings of animals, birds, and flowers, in which resides the object of all this veneration: a seated wooden figure of Iemitsu himself.

As you exit the shrine, on the west side, you come to the fifth gate: the **Koka-mon,** built in the style of the late Ming Dynasty of China. The gate is normally closed, but from here another flight of stone steps leads to the sixth and last gate—the cast copper **Inuki-mon,** inscribed with characters in Sanskrit—and Iemitsu's tomb. 🔲 *Included in ¥1,000 multiple-entry ticket to Tōshō-gū, ¥1,300 ticket also allows you to visit the Sleeping Cat and Ieyasu's tomb.* ⊗ *Apr.–Oct., daily 8–5; Nov.–Mar., daily 8–4.*

If you take the **Nishi-sandō** (West Approach) south from Futara-san Jinja, you'll soon come to an exit from the Tōshō-gū area on the main road. At this point you may have given Nikkō all the time you had to spare. If so, turn left, and a short walk will bring you back to the Shinkyō (Sacred Bridge). If not, turn right, and in a minute or so you will come to the Nishi-sandō bus stop, where you can take the local bus to Chūzenji-ko.

To Chūzenji-ko (Lake Chūzen-ji)

Falling water is one of the special charms of the Nikkō National Park area; visitors going by bus or car from Tōshō-gū to Chūzen-ji often

❾   stop off en route to see the **Jakko-no-taki** (Jakko-no Falls), which descend in a series of seven terraced stages, forming a sheet of water about 100 ft high. About 1 km (½ mi) from the shrine precincts, at the Tamozawa bus stop, a narrow road to the right leads to an uphill walk of some 3 km (2 mi) to the falls.

⑩ "The water," wrote the great 17th-century poet Bashō about the **Urami-no-taki** (Urami-no Falls), "seemed to take a flying leap and drop a hundred feet from the top of a cave into a green pool surrounded by a thousand rocks. One was supposed to inch one's way into the cave and enjoy the falls from behind." It's a steep climb to the cave, which begins at the Arasawa bus stop, with a turn to the right off the Chūzenji road; the falls and the gorge are striking—but you should make the climb only if you have good hiking shoes and are willing to get wet in the process.

The real climb to Chūzenji-ko begins at **Uma-gaeshi** (literally, "horse return"). Here, in the old days, the road became too rough for horse riding, so riders had to alight and proceed on foot. The lake is 4,165 ft above sea level. From Uma-gaeshi the bus climbs a one-way toll road up the pass; the old road has been widened and is used for the traffic coming down. The two roads are full of steep hairpin turns, and on a clear day the view up and down the valley is magnificent—especially from the halfway point at **Akechi-daira** (Akechi Plain), from which you can see the summit of **Nantai-san** (Mt. Nantai), reaching 8,149 ft. Hiking season lasts from May through mid-October; if you push it, you can make the ascent in about four hours. Uma-gaeshi is about 10 km (6 mi) from Tōbu Eki in Nikkō, or 8 km (5 mi) from Tōshō-gū. (Note: Wild monkeys make their homes in these mountains, and they've learned the convenience of mooching from visitors along the route. Be careful—they have a way of not taking no for an answer.)

The bus trip from Nikkō to the national park area ends at Chūzen-ji **⑪** village, which shares its name with the temple established here in 784. **Chūzen-ji** is a subtemple of Rinnō-ji, at Tōshō-gū. The principal object of worship at Chūzen-ji is the **Tachi-ki Kannon,** a 17-ft standing statue of the Buddhist goddess of mercy, said to have been carved more than 1,000 years ago by the priest Shōdō from the living trunk of a single Judas tree. You reach the temple grounds by turning left (south) as you leave the village of Chūzen-ji and walking about 1½ km (1 mi) along the eastern shore of the lake. ☎ ¥300. ☉ Apr.–Oct., daily 8–5; Mar. and Nov., daily 8–4; Dec.–Feb., daily 8–3:30.

⑫ **Chūgū-shi,** a subshrine of the Futara-san Jinja at Tōshō-gū, is the major religious center on the north side of Lake Chūzen-ji, about 1½ km (1 mi) west of the village. The **Hōmotsu-den** (Treasure House) houses an interesting historical collection, including swords, lacquerware, and medieval shrine palanquins. ☎ Shrine free, Treasure House ¥300. ☉ Apr.–Oct., daily 8–5; Nov.–Mar., daily 9–4.

Near the bus stop at Chūzen-ji village is a **gondola** (¥900 round-trip) to the Chanoki-daira (Chanoki plateau). About 1,000 ft above the lake, it commands a wonderful view of the surrounding area. A few minutes' walk from the gondola terminus is a small **botanical garden.**

What draws the crowds of Japanese visitors to Chūzen-ji, more than
★ ⑬ anything else, is **Kegon-no-taki,** the country's most famous waterfall. Fed by the eastward flow of the lake, the falls drop 318 ft into a rugged gorge; an elevator (¥530) takes you to an observation platform at the bottom. The volume of water over the falls is carefully regulated, but it's especially impressive after a summer rain or a typhoon. In the winter the falls do not freeze completely but form a beautiful cascade of icicles. The elevator is just a few minutes' walk east from the bus stop at Chūzen-ji village, downhill and off to the right at the far end of the parking lot.

If you've budgeted an extra day for Nikkō, you might want to consider a walk around the lake. A paved road along the north shore extends for about 8 km (5 mi), one-third of the whole distance, as far as the "beach" at Shobu-ga-hama. Here, where the road branches off to the north for Senjogahara, are the lovely cascades of **Ryūzu-no-taki** (Dragon's Head Falls). The falls are less dramatic than Kegon, perhaps, but they're blessed with a charming woodland setting and a rustic coffee shop, where you can sit and enjoy the play of the waters as they tumble into the lake. To the left is a steep footpath that continues around the lake to Senju-ga-hama and then to a campsite at Asegata. The path is well marked but can get rough in places. From Asegata it's less than an hour's walk back to Chūzen-ji village.

Dining

$$$-$$$$ ✕ **Fujimoto.** At what may be Nikkō's most formal Western-style restaurants, finer touches include plush carpets and art-deco fixtures, stained and frosted glass, a thoughtful wine list, and a maître d' in black tie. The menu blends elements of French and Japanese cooking styles and ingredients; the fillet of beef in mustard sauce is particularly excellent. Fujimoto closes at 7:30, so plan on eating early. ⊠ *2339–1 Sannai,* ☎ *0288/53–3751. AE, DC, MC, V. Closed Fri.*

$$$ ✕ **Gyōshintei.** This is the only restaurant in Nikkō devoted to *shōjin ryōri,* the Buddhist-temple vegetarian fare that evolved centuries ago into haute cuisine. Gyōshintei is done in the style of a *ryōtei* (traditional inn), with all-tatami seating. It differs from a ryōtei in that it has one large, open space where many guests are served at once, rather than a number of rooms for private dining. Gyōshintei serves until 7. ⊠ *2339–1 Sannai,* ☎ *0288/53–3751. AE, DC, MC, V. Closed Thurs.*

$$-$$$ ✕ **Masudaya.** Masudaya started out as a sake maker more than a century ago, but for four generations now, it has been the town's best-known restaurant. The specialty is *yuba* (bean curd)—which the chefs transform, with the help of local vegetables and fresh fish, into a sumptuous high cuisine. The building is traditional, with a lovely interior garden; the assembly line–style service, however, detracts from the ambience. Masudaya offers one set-menu nine-course kaiseki-style meal; the kitchen plans to feed 100–120 customers a day and simply stops serving when the food is gone. Reservations, therefore, are a must. It's on the main street of Nikkō, about halfway between the railway stations and Tōshō-gū. ⊠ *439–2 Ishiya-machi,* ☎ *0288/54–2151. No credit cards. Closed Thurs. No dinner.*

$$-$$$ ✕ **Meiji-no-Yakata.** Not far from the east entrance to Rinnō-ji, Meiji-no-Yakata is an elegant 19th-century Western-style stone house, originally built as a summer retreat for an American diplomat. The food, too, is Western style; specialties of the house include fresh rainbow trout from Chūzenji-ko, roast lamb with pepper sauce, and melt-in-your-mouth filet mignon made from local Tochigi beef. The ambience is informal, and high ceilings and hardwood floors help make this a very pleasant place to dine. The restaurant closes at 7:30. ⊠ *2339–1 Sannai,* ☎ *0288/ 53–3751. AE, DC, MC, V. Closed Wed.*

$$ ✕ **Sawamoto.** Charcoal-broiled *unagi* (eel) is an acquired taste, and there's no better place in Nikkō to acquire it than at Sawamoto. The place is small and unpretentious—with only five plain-wood tables—and service can be lukewarm, but Sawamoto is reliable for a light lunch or dinner of unagi on a bed of rice, served in an elegant lacquered box. Eel is considered a stamina builder: just right for the weary visitor on a hot summer day. Sawamoto closes at 7. ⊠ *Kami Hatsuishi-machi,* ☎ *0288/54–0163. No credit cards.*

Lodging

Nikkō

$$–$$$$
★ 🏨 **Nikkō Kanaya Hotel.** A little worn around the edges after a century of operation, the Kanaya still has the best location in town—just across the street from the Tōshō-gū precincts. The hotel is very touristy; daytime visitors, especially Westerners, come to browse through the old building and its gift shops. The helpful staff is better at giving information on the area than the city information office. Rooms vary a great deal, as do their prices—up to ¥33,000 per person on holiday weekends. The more expensive rooms are all spacious and comfortable, with wonderful high ceilings; in the annex you fall asleep to the sound of the Daiya-gawa murmuring below by the Sacred Bridge. Horseback riding and golf are available nearby. ⊠ *1300 Kami Hatsuishi-machi, Nikkō, Tochigi-ken 321-1401,* ☎ *0288/54–0001,* FAX *0288/53–2487,* WEB *www.kanayahotel.co.jp. 77 rooms, 62 with bath. 2 restaurants, bar, pool. AE, DC, MC, V.*

$ 🏨 **Turtle Inn Nikkō.** This member of the Japanese Inn Group provides friendly, modest, and cost-conscious accommodations with or without a private bath. Breakfasts and dinners, simple and inexpensive, are served in the dining room, but you needn't opt for these if you'd rather eat out. Keep in mind that rates go up about 10% in high season, from late July through August. To get to the Turtle Inn Nikkō, take the bus bound for Chūzen-ji from either railway station and get off at the Sōgō Kaikan-mae bus stop. The inn is two minutes from the bus stop and within walking distance of Tōshō-gū. ⊠ *2–16 Takumi-chō, Nikkō, Tochigi-ken 321-1433,* ☎ *0288/53–3168,* FAX *0288/53–3883. 7 Western-style rooms, 5 Japanese-style rooms. Restaurant. AE, MC, V.*

Chūzen-ji

$$$–$$$$
🏨 **Chūzen-ji Kanaya.** On the road from the village to Shobu-ga-hama, this branch of the Nikkō Kanaya has a boathouse and restaurant on the lake. The atmosphere is like that of a private club. The simple, tasteful rooms are decorated in pastel colors and have floor-to-ceiling windows overlooking the lake or grounds. ⊠ *2482 Chū-gūshi, Nikkō, Tochigi-ken 321-1661,* ☎ *0288/51–0001,* FAX *0288/51–0051,* WEB *www.kanayahotel.co.jp. 60 rooms. Restaurant, boating, fishing, waterskiing. AE, DC, MC, V. MAP.*

$$–$$$
🏨 **Nikkō Lakeside Hotel.** In the village of Chūzen-ji at the foot of the lake, the Nikkō Lakeside has no particular character, but the views are good and the transportation connections (to buses and excursion boats) are ideal. Prices vary considerably from weekday to weekend and season to season. Check ahead. ⊠ *2482 Chū-gūshi, Nikkō, Tochigi-ken 321-1661,* ☎ *0288/55–0321,* FAX *0288/55–0771. 100 rooms. Restaurant, tennis, boating, fishing, bicycles. AE, DC, MC, V. MAP.*

Shobu-ga-hama

$$–$$$
🏨 **Nikkō Prince Hotel.** This hotel is within walking distance of Ryūzu-no-taki (Ryū-no Falls). The Prince chain is one of Japan's largest and most successful leisure conglomerates, with hotels in most major cities and resorts. With many of its accommodations in two-story maisonettes and rustic detached cottages, the chain tends to market itself to families and small groups of younger excursionists. The architecture favors high ceilings and wooden beams, with lots of glass in the public areas to take advantage of the view. ⊠ *Shobu-ga-hama, Chū-gūshi, Nikkō, Tochigi-ken 321-1692,* ☎ *0288/55–1111,* FAX *0288/55–0669,* WEB *www.princehotels.co.jp. 60 rooms. Restaurant, pool, 2 tennis courts. AE, DC, MC, V. MAP.*

Nikkō A to Z

To research prices, get advice from other travelers, and book travel arrangements, visit www.fodors.com.

CAR TRAVEL

It's possible, but unwise, to go by car from Tōkyō to Nikkō. The trip will take at least three hours, and merely getting from central Tōkyō to the toll-road system can be a nightmare. Coming back, especially on a Saturday or Sunday evening, is even worse. If you absolutely *must* drive, take the Tōkyō Expressway 5 (Ikebukuro Line) north to the Tōkyō Gaikandō, go east on this ring road to the Kawaguchi interchange, and pick up the Tōhoku Expressway northbound. Take the Tōhoku to Utsunomiya and change again at Exit 10 (marked in English) for the Nikkō–Utsunomiya Toll Road, which brings you from there into Nikkō.

TOURS

From Tōkyō, Japan Amenity Travel and Sunrise Tours both operate one-day motor-coach tours to Nikkō, which include Tōshō-gū and Chūzenji-ko. The Japan Amenity tour (¥14,500, lunch included) operates daily March 19–November 30; the Sunrise tour (¥13,500, lunch included) operates Monday, Tuesday, and Friday, March 19–November 30.

➤ TOUR CONTACTS: **Japan Amenity Travel** (☎ 03/3542–7200, FAX 03/3542–7501, WEB www.jam-trip.co.jp). **Sunrise Tours** (☎ 03/5796–5454, FAX 03/5495–0680, WEB www.jtb.co.jp/sunrisetour).

TRAIN TRAVEL

Far easier and more comfortable than driving yourself are the Limited Express trains of the Tōbu Railway, with two direct connections every morning, starting at 7:30 AM (additional trains on weekends, holidays, and in high season) from Tōbu Asakusa Eki, a minute's walk from the last stop on the Ginza subway line in Tōkyō. The one-way fare is ¥2,740. All seats are reserved. Bookings are not accepted over the phone; consult your hotel or a travel agent. The trip from Asakusa to the Tōbu Nikkō Eki takes about two hours, which is quicker than the JR trains. If you're visiting Nikkō on a day trip, note that the last return trains are at 4:29 PM (direct express) and 7:42 PM (with a transfer at 7:52 at Shimo-Imaichi).

If you have a JR Pass, use JR service, which connects Tōkyō and Nikkō, from Ueno Eki. Take the Tōhoku–Honsen Line limited express to Utsunomiya (about 1½ hours) and transfer to the train for JR Nikkō Eki (45 minutes). The earliest departure from Ueno is at 5:10 AM; the last connection back leaves Nikkō at 8:03 PM and brings you into Ueno at 10:48 PM. More expensive but faster is the *Yamabiko* train on the north extension of the Shinkansen; the one-way fare, including the surcharge for the express, is ¥5,430. The first one leaves Tōkyō Eki at 6:04 AM (or Ueno at 6:18 AM) and takes about 50 minutes to Utsunomiya; change there to the train to Nikkō Eki. To return, take the 9:43 PM train from Nikkō to Utsunomiya and catch the last *Yamabiko* back at 10:40 PM, arriving in Ueno at 11:26 PM.

TRANSPORTATION AROUND NIKKO

In Nikkō itself, you won't need much in the way of transportation but your own two feet; nothing is terribly far from anything else. Local buses leave the Tōbu Nikkō Eki for Lake Chūzen-ji, stopping just above the entrance to Tōshō-gū, approximately every 30 minutes from 6:15 AM. The fare to Chūzen-ji is ¥1,100; the ride takes about 40 minutes. The last return bus from the lake leaves at 7:39 PM, arriving back at Tōbu Nikkō Eki at 9:17. Cabs are readily available; the one-way fare from the Tōbu Nikkō Eki to Chūzen-ji is about ¥6,000.

VISITOR INFORMATION

You can do a lot of preplanning for your visit to Nikkō with a stop at the Japan National Tourist Organization office in Tōkyō, where the helpful English-speaking staff will ply you with pamphlets and field your questions about things to see and do. Closer to the source is the Tourist Information and Hospitality Center in Nikkō itself, about halfway up the main street of town between the railway stations and Tōshō-gū, on the left; don't expect too much in the way of help in English, but the center does have a good array of guides to local restaurants and shops, registers of inns and hotels, and mapped-out walking tours.

➤ TOURIST INFORMATION: **Japan National Tourist Organization** (☎ 03/ 2301–3331, WEB www.jnto.go.jp). **Nikkō Tourist Information and Hospitality Center** (☎ 0288/54–2496).

KAMAKURA

Kamakura, about 40 km (25 mi) southwest of Tōkyō, is an object lesson in what happens when you set the fox to guard the hen house.

For the aristocrats of Heian-period (794–1185) Japan, life was defined by the imperial court in Kyōto. Who in his right mind would venture elsewhere? In Kyōto there was grace and beauty and poignant affairs of the heart; everything beyond was howling wilderness. Unfortunately, it was the howling wilderness that had all the estates: the large grants of land, called *shōen,* without which there would be no income to pay for all that grace and beauty. Somebody had to go *out there*, to govern the provinces and collect the rents, to keep the restive local families in line, and to subdue the barbarians at the fringes of the empire. Over time a number of the lesser noble families consigned to the provinces began to produce not only good poets and courtiers but good administrators. To the later dismay of their fellow aristocrats, some of them—with their various clan connections, vassals, and commanders in the field—also turned out to be extremely good fighters.

By the 12th century two clans—the Taira ("*ta*-ee-ra") and the Minamoto, themselves both offshoots of the imperial line—had come to dominate the affairs of the Heian court and were at each other's throats in a struggle for supremacy. In 1160 the Taira won a major battle that should have secured their absolute control over Japan but in the process made one serious mistake: having killed the Minamoto leader Yoshitomo, they spared his 13-year-old son, Yoritomo, and sent him into exile. Yoritomo bided his time, gathered support against the Taira, and planned his revenge. In 1180 he launched a rebellion and chose Kamakura—a superb natural fortress, surrounded on three sides by hills and guarded on the fourth by the sea—as his base of operations.

The rivalry between the two clans became an all-out war. By 1185 Yoritomo and his half-brother, Yoshitsune, had destroyed the Taira utterly, and the Minamoto were masters of all Japan. In 1192 Yoritomo forced the imperial court to name him shōgun; he was now de facto and de jure the military head of state. The emperor was left as a figurehead in Kyōto; the little fishing village of Kamakura became—and for 141 years remained—the seat of Japan's first shogunal government.

The Minamoto line came to an end when Yoritomo's two sons were assassinated; power passed to the Hōjō family, who remained in control, often as regents for figurehead shōguns, for the next 100 years. In 1274 and again in 1281 Japan was invaded by the Mongol armies of China's Yuan dynasty. On both occasions typhoons—the original kamikaze (literally, "divine wind")—destroyed the Mongol fleets, but the Hōjō family were still obliged to reward the various clans they had rallied to the defense of the realm. A number of these clans were unhappy with their portions—and with Hōjō rule in general. The end came suddenly, in 1333, when two vassals assigned to put down a revolt switched sides. The Hōjō regent committed suicide, and the center of power returned to Kyōto.

Kamakura reverted to being a sleepy backwater on the edge of the sea. It remained relatively isolated until the Yokosuka Railway line was built in 1889; and it wasn't until after World War II that the town began to develop as a residential area for the well-to-do. Nothing secular survives from the days of the Minamoto and Hōjō; there wasn't much there to begin with. The warriors of Kamakura had little use for courtiers, or their palaces and gardened villas; the shogunate's name for itself, in fact, was the *bakufu*—literally, the "tent government." As a religious center, however, the town presents an extraordinary legacy. The bakufu endowed shrines and temples by the score in Kamakura, especially temples of the Rinzai sect of Zen Buddhism. The austerity of Zen, its directness and self-discipline, had a powerful appeal for a warrior class that in some ways imagined itself on perpetual bivouac. Most of those temples and shrines are in settings of remarkable beauty; many are designated National Treasures. If you can afford the time for only one day trip from Tōkyō, you should probably spend it here.

Exploring Kamakura

Numbers in the margin correspond to points of interest on the Kamakura map.

There are three principal areas in Kamakura, and you can easily get from one to another by train. From Tōkyō come first to Kita-Kamakura for most of the important Zen temples, including Engaku-ji and Kenchō-ji. The second area is downtown Kamakura, with its shops and museums and the venerated shrine Tsuru-ga-oka Hachiman-gū. The third is Hase, to the southwest, a 10-minute train ride from Kamakura on the Enoden Line. Hase's main attractions are the great bronze figure of the Amida Buddha, at Kōtoku-in, and the Kannon Hall of Hase-dera. There is a lot here to see, and even to hit just the highlights will take you most of a busy day. You may need to edit your choices—especially if you want to leave yourself enough time for the Enoshima resort area, described at the end of this section.

If your time is limited, you may want to visit only Engaku-ji and Tōkei-ji in Kita-Kamakura before riding the train one stop to Kamakura. If not, follow the main road all the way to Tsuru-ga-oka Hachiman-gū and visit four additional temples en route.

Kita-Kamakura (North Kamakura)

Hierarchies were important to the Kamakura Shogunate. In the 14th century it established a ranking system called *Go-zan* (literally, "Five Mountains") for the Zen Buddhist monasteries under its official sponsorship. The largest of the Zen monasteries in Kamakura, **Engaku-ji**, founded in 1282, ranked second in the Five Mountains hierarchy. Here, prayers were to be offered regularly for the prosperity and well-being of the government; Engaku-ji's special role was to pray for the souls of those who died resisting the Mongol invasions in 1274 and 1281. The temple complex once contained as many as 50 buildings. Often damaged in fires and earthquakes, it has been completely restored.

Engaku-ji belongs to the Rinzai sect of Zen Buddhism. Introduced into Japan from China at the beginning of the Kamakura period (1192–1333), the ideas of Zen were quickly embraced by the emerging warrior class. The samurai especially admired the Rinzai sect, with its emphasis on the ascetic life as a path to self-transcendence, and the monks of Engaku-ji played an important role as advisers to the shogunate in matters spiritual, artistic, and political. The majestic old cedars of the temple complex bespeak an age when this was both a haven of quietude and a pillar of the state.

Among the National Treasures at Engaku-ji is the **Shari-den** (Hall of the Holy Relic of Buddha), with its remarkable Chinese-inspired thatched roof. Built in 1282, it was destroyed by fire in 1558 but rebuilt in its original form soon after, in 1563. The Shari-den is supposed to enshrine a tooth of the Gautama Buddha himself, but it's not on display. In fact, except for the first three days of the New Year, you won't be able to go any farther into the hall than the main gate. Such is the case, alas, with much of the Engaku-ji complex: this is still a functioning monastic center, and many of its most impressive buildings are not open to the public. The accessible National Treasure at Engaku-ji is the **Ōkane**, the Great Bell, on the hilltop on the southeast side of the complex. The bell—Kamakura's most famous—was cast in 1301 and stands 8 ft tall. It's rung only on special occasions, such as New Year's Eve.

The two buildings open to the public at Engaku-ji are the **Butsunichi-an**, which has a long ceremonial hall where you can enjoy the Japanese tea ceremony, and the **Obai-in**. The latter is the mausoleum of the last three regents of the Kamakura Shogunate: Hōjō Tokimune, who led the defense of Japan against the Mongol invasions; his son Sadatoki; and his grandson Takatoki. Off to the side of the mausoleum is a quiet garden with apricot trees, which bloom in February. When you leave Kita-Kamakura Eki, you'll see the stairway to Engaku-ji just in front of you. ☒ *409 Yama-no-uchi,* ☎ *0469/22–0478.* ☒ *¥200.* ☉ *Nov.–Mar., daily 8–4; Apr.–Oct., daily 8–5.*

★ ⑯ **Tōkei-ji,** a Zen temple of the Rinzai sect, holds special significance for the study of feminism in medieval Japan. More popularly known as the Enkiri-dera, or Divorce Temple, it was founded in 1285 by the widow of the Hōjō regent Tokimune as a refuge for the victims of unhappy marriages. Under the shogunate, a husband of the warrior class could obtain a divorce simply by sending his wife back to her family. Not so for the wife; no matter what cruel and unusual treatment her husband meted out, she was stuck with him. If she ran away, however, and managed to reach Tōkei-ji without being caught, she could receive sanctuary at the temple and remain there as a nun. After three years (later reduced to two), she was officially declared divorced. The temple survived as a convent through the Meiji Restoration of 1868. The last abbess died in 1902, and her headstone is in the cemetery behind the temple, beneath the plum trees that blossom in February. Tōkei-ji was later reestablished as a monastery.

The **Hōmotsu-kan** (Treasure House) of Tōkei-ji has a number of Kamakura-period wooden Buddhas, ink paintings, scrolls, and works of calligraphy on display, some of which have been designated by the government as Important Cultural Objects. The library, called the Matsuga-oka Bunko, was established in memory of the great Zen scholar D. T. Suzuki (1870–1966). Tōkei-ji is on the southwest side of the JR tracks (the side opposite Engaku-ji), less than a five-minute walk south from the station on the main road to Kamakura (Route 21–the Kamakura Kaidō), on the right. ☒ *1367 Yama-no-uchi,* ☎ *0467/22–1663.* ☒ *Tōkei-ji ¥100, Treasure House additional ¥300.* ☉ *Tōkei-ji Apr.–Oct., daily 8:30–5; Nov.–Mar., daily 8:30–4; Treasure House Tues.–Sun. 10–3.*

★ ⑰ In June, when the hydrangeas are in bloom, **Meigetsu-in** becomes one of the most popular places in Kamakura. The gardens transform into

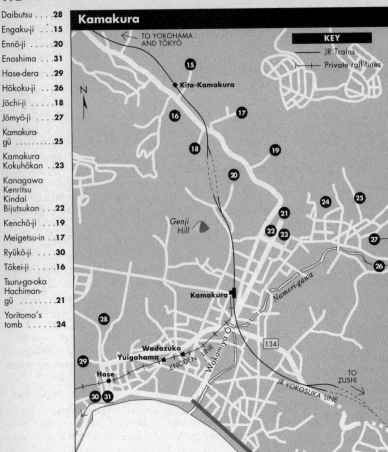

Kamakura

a sea of color—pink, white, and blue—and visitors can number in the thousands. A typical Kamakura light rain shouldn't deter you; it only showcases this incredible floral display to best advantage. From Tōkei-ji walk along Route 21 toward Kamakura for about 20 minutes until you cross the railway tracks; take the immediate left turn onto the narrow side street that doubles back along the tracks. This street bends to the right and follows the course of a little stream called the Megetsu-gawa to the temple gate. ⊠ *189 Yama-no-uchi,* ☎ *0467/24–3437.* ⌨ *¥300.* ⊙ *Apr.–May and July–Oct., daily 9–4:30; June, daily 8–5:30; Nov.–Mar., daily 9–4.*

In the Five Mountains hierarchy established by the Kamakura Shogunate, **Jōchi-ji** was ranked fourth. The buildings now in the temple complex are reconstructions; the Great Kantō Earthquake of 1923 destroyed the originals. The garden here is especially fine. Take note of the figures of the Seven Gods of Good Fortune in the northwest corner—a curious group of Indian, Chinese, and Japanese deities, believed to bring wealth and long life and widely revered from the 15th to 17th century.

Jōchi-ji is on the south side of the railway tracks, a few minutes' walk farther southwest of Tōkei-ji in the direction of Kamakura. Turn right off the main road (Route 21) and cross over a small bridge; a flight of moss-covered steps leads up to the temple. ✉ *1402 Yama-no-uchi,* ☎ *0467/22–3943.* 🎫 *¥150.* 🕐 *Daily 9–4:30.*

★ ⑲ Founded in 1250, **Kenchō-ji** was the foremost of Kamakura's five great Zen temples—and lays claim to being the oldest Zen temple in all of Japan. It was modeled on one of the great Chinese monasteries of the time and built for a distinguished Zen master who had just arrived in Japan from China. Over the centuries, fires and other disasters have taken their toll on Kenchō-ji, and although many buildings have been authentically reconstructed, the temple complex today is half its original size. Near the San-mon (Main Gate) is a **bronze bell** cast in 1255; it's the temple's most important treasure. The San-mon and the **Hattō** (Lecture Hall) are the only two structures to have survived the devastating Great Kantō Earthquake of 1923. Like Engaku-ji, Kenchō-ji is a functioning temple of the Rinzai sect, where novices train and lay people can come to take part in Zen meditation. The entrance to Kenchō-ji is about halfway along the main road from Kita-Kamakura Eki to Tsuru-ga-oka Hachiman-gū, on the right. ✉ *8 Yama-no-uchi,* ☎ *0467/22–0981.* 🎫 *¥300.* 🕐 *Daily 8:30–4:30.*

In the feudal period Japan acquired from China a belief in Enma, the lord of hell, who, with his court attendants, judges the souls of the departed and determines their destination in the afterlife. Kamakura's
★ ⑳ **Ennō-ji,** otherwise undistinguished, houses some remarkable statues of these judges—as grim and merciless a court as you're ever likely to confront. To see them is enough to put you on your best behavior, at least for the rest of your excursion. Ennō-ji is a minute's walk or so from Kenchō-ji, on the opposite (south) side of the main road to Kamakura. A few minutes' walk along the main road to the south will bring you to Tsuru-ga-oka Hachiman-gū. ✉ *1543 Yama-no-uchi,* ☎ *0467/25–1095.* 🎫 *¥200.* 🕐 *Mar.–Nov., daily 9–4; Dec.–Feb., daily 9–3:30.*

Kamakura

When the first Kamakura shōgun, Minamoto no Yoritomo, learned he was about to have an heir, he had the tutelary shrine of his family moved to Kamakura from nearby Yui-ga-hama and ordered a stately avenue to be built through the center of his capital from the shrine to the sea. Along this avenue would travel the procession that brought his son—if there were a son—to be presented to the gods. Yoritomo's consort did indeed bear him a son, Yoriie ("yo-*ree*-ee-eh"), in 1182; Yoriie was brought in great pomp to the shrine and then consecrated to his place in the shogunal succession. Alas, the blessing of the gods did Yoriie little good. He was barely 18 when Yoritomo died, and the regency established by his mother's family, the Hōjō, kept him virtually powerless until 1203, when he was banished and eventually assassinated. The Minamoto were never to hold power again, but Yoriie's memory lives on in the street—Wakamiya Oji, "the Avenue of the Young Prince"—that his father built for him.

A bus from Kamakura Eki (Sign 5) traces the following route, with stops at most access roads to the temples and shrines. However, you may want to walk out as far as Hōkoku-ji and take the bus back; it's easier to recognize the end of the line than any of the stops in between. You can also go by taxi to Hōkoku-ji—any cab driver knows the way—and walk the last leg in reverse. In any event, downtown Kamakura is a good place to stop for lunch and shop. Restaurants and shops selling local crafts objects, especially the carved and lacquered woodwork called *Kamakura-bori,* abound on Wakamiya Oji and the street parallel to it, Komachi-dōri.

★ ❷ The Minamoto shrine, **Tsuru-ga-oka Hachiman-gū,** is dedicated to the legendary emperor Ōjin, his wife, and his mother, from whom Minamoto no Yoritomo claimed descent. At the entrance, a small, steeply arched vermilion bridge—the **Taiko-bashi** (Drum Bridge)—crosses a stream between two lotus ponds. The ponds were made to Yoritomo's specifications. His wife, Masako, suggested placing islands in each. In the larger **Genji Pond,** to the right, filled with white lotus flowers, she placed three islands. Genji was another name for the Minamoto clan, and three is an auspicious number. In the smaller **Heike Pond,** to the left, she put four islands. Heike ("*heh*-ee-keh") was another name for the rival Taira clan, which the Minamoto had destroyed, and four—homophonous in Japanese with the word for "death"—is very unlucky indeed.

On the far side of the Drum Bridge is the **Mai-den.** This hall is the setting for a story of the Minamoto celebrated in Nō and Kabuki theater; it bears telling here. Though Yoritomo was the tactical genius behind the downfall of the Taira and the establishment of the Kamakura Shogunate, it was his dashing half-brother, Yoshitsune, who actually defeated the Taira in battle. In so doing, he won the admiration of many, and Yoritomo came to believe that he had ambitions of his own. Despite Yoshitsune's declaration of allegiance, Yoritomo had him exiled and sent assassins to have him killed. Yoshitsune spent his life fleeing from one place to another until, at the age of 30, he was betrayed in his last refuge and took his own life.

Earlier in his exile, Yoshitsune's lover, the dancer Shizuka Gozen, had been captured and brought to Kamakura. Yoritomo and his wife, Masako, commanded Shizuka to dance at the family shrine, as a kind of penance. Instead, she danced to the joy of her love for Yoshitsune and her concern for his fate. Yoritomo was furious, and only Masako's influence kept him from ordering her death. When he discovered, however, that Shizuka was carrying Yoshitsune's child, he ordered that if the child were a boy, he was to be killed. A boy was born. Some versions of the legend have it that the child was slain; others say he was placed in a cradle, like Moses, and cast adrift in the reeds. This heartrending drama is enacted once a year during the Spring Festival (early or mid-April, when the cherry trees bloom) on the stage at the Mai-den.

Beyond the Mai-den, a flight of steps leads to the shrine's Hon-dō (Main Hall). To the left of these steps is a gingko tree that—according to legend—was witness to a murder that ended the Minamoto line in 1219. From behind this tree, a priest named Kugyō leapt out and beheaded his uncle, the 26-year-old Sanetomo, Yoritomo's second son and the last Minamoto shōgun. The priest was quickly apprehended, but Sanetomo's head was never found. Like all other Shintō shrines, the Hon-gū is unadorned; the building itself, an 1828 reconstruction, is not particularly noteworthy.

To reach Tsuru-ga-oka Hachiman-gū from the east side of Kamakura Eki, cross the plaza, turn left, and walk north along Wakamiya Oji. Straight ahead is the first of three arches leading to the shrine, and the shrine itself is at the far end of the street. ⊠ *2–1–31 Yuki-no-shita,* ☎ *0467/22–0315.* ◨ *Free.* ◷ *Daily 9–4.*

❷ The **Kanagawa Kenritsu Kindai Bijutsukan** (Prefectural Museum of Modern Art), on the north side of the Heike Pond at Tsuru-ga-oka Hachiman-gū, has a collection of Japanese oil paintings and watercolors, woodblock prints, and sculpture. ⊠ *2–1–53 Yuki-no-shita,* ☎ *0467/22–5000.* ◨ *¥800–¥1,200, depending on exhibition.* ◷ *Tues.–Sun. 10–5.*

(23) The **Kamakura Kokuhōkan** (Treasure Museum) was built in 1928 as a repository for many of the most important objects belonging to the shrines and temples in the area. Many of these are designated Important Cultural Properties. The museum, located along the east side of the Tsuru-ga-oka Hachiman-gū shrine precincts, has an especially fine collection of devotional and portrait sculpture in wood from the Kamakura and Muromachi periods; the portrait pieces may be among the most expressive and interesting in all of classical Japanese art. ⊠ *2–1–1 Yuki-no-shita,* ☎ *0467/22–0753.* 🏛 *¥400.* ☉ *Tues.–Sun. 9–4.*

OTHER KAMAKURA SIGHTS

The man who put Kamakura on the map, so to speak, chose not to leave it when he died: it's only a short walk from Tsuru-ga-oka Hachiman-gū to the tomb of the man responsible for its construction, Minamoto no Yoritomo. If you've already been to Nikkō and seen how a later dynasty of shōguns sought to glorify their own memories, you (24) may be surprised at the simplicity of **Yoritomo's tomb,** but the route of your excursion takes you this way anyhow, and you may as well stop and pay your respects. Cross the Drum Bridge at Tsuru-ga-oka Hachiman-gū and turn left. Leave the grounds of the shrine and walk east along the main street (Route 204) that forms the T-intersection at the end of Wakamiya Oji. A 10-minute walk will bring you to a narrow street on the left—there's a bakery called Bergfeld on the corner—that leads to the tomb, about 300 ft off the street to the north and up a flight of stone steps. 🏛 *Free.* ☉ *Daily 9–4.*

(25) **Kamakura-gū** is a Shintō shrine built after the Meiji Restoration of 1868 and dedicated to Prince Morinaga (1308–36), third son of the emperor Go-Daigo. When Go-Daigo overthrew the Kamakura Shogunate and restored Japan to direct imperial rule, Morinaga—who had been in the priesthood—was appointed supreme commander of his father's forces. The prince lived in turbulent times and died young: when the Ashikaga clan in turn overthrew Go-Daigo's government, Morinaga was taken into exile, held prisoner in a cave behind the present site of Kamakura-gū, and eventually beheaded. The **Hōmotsu-kan** (Treasure House) on the grounds of Kamakura-gū is of interest mainly for its collection of paintings depicting the life of Prince Morinaga. To reach Kamakura-gū, walk from Yoritomo's tomb to Route 204, where you'll turn left; at the next traffic light, a narrow street on the left leads off at an angle to the shrine, about five minutes' walk west. The Treasure House is in the northwest corner of the grounds, next to the shrine's administrative office. ⊠ *154 Nikaidō,* ☎ *0467/22–0318.* 🏛 *Kamakura-gū free, Treasure House ¥300.* ☉ *Daily 9–4:30.*

(26) Visitors to Kamakura tend to overlook **Hōkoku-ji,** a lovely little Zen temple of the Rinzai sect that was built in 1334. Over the years it had fallen into disrepair and neglect, until an enterprising priest took over, cleaned up the gardens, and began promoting the temple for meditation sessions, calligraphy exhibitions, and tea ceremony. Behind the main hall are a thick grove of bamboo and a small tea pavilion—a restful oasis and a fine place to go for *matcha* (tea-ceremony green tea). The temple is about 2 km (1 mi) east on Route 204 from the main entrance to Tsuru-ga-oka Hachiman-gū; turn right at the traffic light by the Hōkoku-ji Iriguchi bus stop and walk about three minutes south to the gate. ⊠ *2–7–4 Jōmyō-ji,* ☎ *0467/22–0762.* 🏛 *Hōkoku-ji free, bamboo garden ¥200, tea ceremony ¥700.* ☉ *Daily 9–4.*

(27) **Jōmyō-ji,** founded in 1188, is the only one of the Five Mountains Zen monasteries in the eastern part of Kamakura. It lacks the grandeur and scale of Engaku-ji and Kenchō-ji—naturally enough, as it was ranked behind them, in fifth place—but it still merits the status of an Impor-

tant Cultural Property. To reach it from Hōkoku-ji, cross the main street (Route 204) that brought you the mile or so from Tsuru-ga-oka Hachiman-gū, and take the first narrow street north. Jōmyō-ji is about 300 ft from the corner. ⊠ *3–8–31 Jōmyō-ji,* ☎ *0467/22–2818.* 🖃 *Jōmyō-ji ¥100, tea ceremony ¥500.* 🕙 *Daily 9–4.*

Hase

The single biggest attraction in Hase ("*ha*-seh") is the Kōtoku-in's ★ ㉘ **Daibutsu** (Great Buddha)—sharing the honors with Fuji-san, perhaps, as the quintessential picture-postcard image of Japan. The statue of the compassionate Amida Buddha sits cross-legged in the temple courtyard, the drapery of his robes flowing in lines reminiscent of ancient Greece, his expression profoundly serene. The 37-ft bronze figure was cast in 1292, three centuries before Europeans reached Japan; the concept of the classical Greek lines in the Buddha's robe must have come over the Silk Route through China during the time of Alexander the Great. The casting was probably first conceived in 1180, by Minamoto no Yoritomo, who wanted a statue to rival the enormous Daibutsu in Nara. Until 1495 the Amida Buddha was housed in a wooden temple, which was washed away in a great tidal wave. Since then the loving Buddha has stood exposed, facing the cold winters and hot summers for the last five centuries.

It may seem sacrilegious to some actually to walk inside the Great Buddha, but for ¥20 you can enter the figure from a doorway in the right side and explore (until 4 PM) his stomach. To reach Kōtoku-in and the Daibutsu, take the Enoden Line train from the west side of JR Kamakura Eki three stops to Hase. From the east exit, turn right and walk north about 10 minutes on the main street (Route 32). ⊠ *4–2–28 Hase,* ☎ *0467/22–0703.* 🖃 *¥200.* 🕙 *Apr.–Sept., daily 7–6; Oct.–Mar., daily 7–5:30.*

★ ㉙ The only Kamakura temple facing the sea, **Hase-dera** is one of the most beautiful, and saddest, places of pilgrimage in the city. Flanking the steep flight of stone steps that lead to the temple grounds are hundreds of small stone images of Jizō, one of the bodhisattvas in the Buddhist pantheon who have deferred their own ascendance into Buddha-hood to guide the souls of others to salvation. Jizō is the savior of children— particularly the souls of the stillborn, aborted, and miscarried; the mothers of these children dress the statues of Jizō in bright red bibs and leave them small offerings of food, strangely touching acts of prayer.

The **Kannon-do** (Kannon Hall) at Hase-dera enshrines the largest carved-wood statue in Japan: the votive figure of Jūichimen Kannon, the 11-headed goddess of mercy. Standing 30 ft tall, the goddess bears a crown of 10 smaller heads, symbolizing her ability to search out in all directions for those in need of her compassion. No one knows for certain when the figure was carved. According to the temple records, a monk named Shōnin carved two images of the Jūichimen Kannon from a huge laurel tree in 721. One was consecrated to the Hase-dera in present-day Nara Prefecture; the other was thrown into the sea in order to go wherever the sea decided that there were souls in need, and that image washed up on shore near Kamakura. Much later, in 1342, Ashikaga Takauji—the first of the 15 Ashikaga shōguns who followed the Kamakura era—had the statue covered with gold leaf.

The **Amida Hall** of Hase-dera enshrines the image of a seated Amida Buddha, who presides over the Western Paradise of the Pure Land. Minamoto no Yoritomo ordered the creation of this statue when he reached the age of 42; popular Japanese belief, adopted from China, holds that your 42nd year is particularly unlucky. Yoritomo's act of piety earned him another 10 years—he was 52 when he was thrown by a horse and died of his injuries. The Buddha is popularly known as the *yakuyoke* (good-luck) Amida, and many visitors—especially students facing graduation and entrance exams—make a point of coming here to pray. To the left of the Amida Hall is a small restaurant where you can buy good-luck candy and admire the view of Kamakura Beach and Sagami Bay. To reach Hase-dera from Hase Eki, walk north about five minutes on the main street (Route 32) towards Kōtoku-in and the Daibutsu, and look for a signpost to the temple on a side street to the left. ✉ 3–11–2 Hase, ☎ 0467/22–6300. ✆ ¥300, including Treasure House. ☉ Mar.–Sept., daily 8–5; Oct.–Feb., daily 8–4:30.

Ryūkō-ji and Enoshima

The Kamakura story would not be complete without the tale of Nichiren (1222–82), the monk who founded the only native Japanese sect of Buddhism and who is honored at the temple **Ryūkō-ji.** Nichiren's rejection of both Zen and Jōdo (Pure Land) teachings brought him into conflict with the Kamakura Shogunate, and the Hōjō regents sent him into exile on the Izu Peninsula in 1621. Later allowed to return, he continued to preach his own interpretation of the Lotus Sutra—and to assert the "blasphemy" of other Buddhist sects, a stance that finally persuaded the Hōjō regency, in 1271, to condemn him to death. Execution was to take place on a hill to the south of Hase. As the executioner swung his sword, legend has it a lightning bolt struck the blade and snapped it in two. Taken aback, the executioner sat down to collect his wits, and a messenger was sent back to Kamakura to report the event. On his way he met another messenger, who was carrying a writ from the Hōjō regents commuting Nichiren's sentence to exile on the island of Sado-ga-shima.

Followers of Nichiren built Ryūkō-ji in 1337, on the hill where he was to be executed, marking his miraculous deliverance from the headsman. Although there are other Nichiren temples closer to Kamakura—Myōhon-ji and Ankokuron-ji, for example—Ryūkō-ji not only has the typical Nichiren-style main hall with gold tassels hanging from its roof but also a beautiful pagoda, built in 1904. To reach it, take the Enoden Line west from Hase to Enoshima—a short, scenic ride that cuts through the hills surrounding Kamakura to the shore. From Enoshima Eki walk about 300 ft east, keeping the train tracks on your right, and you'll come to the temple. ✉ 3–13–37 Katase, Fujisawa, ☎ 0466/25–7356. ✆ Free. ☉ Daily 10–4.

The Sagami Bay shore in this area has some of the closest beaches to Tōkyō, and in the hot, humid summer months it seems as though all of the city's teeming millions pour onto these beaches in search of a vacant patch of rather dirty gray sand. Pass up this mob scene and press on instead to **Enoshima.** The island is only 4 km (2½ mi) around, with a hill in the middle. Partway up the hill is a shrine where the local fishermen used to pray for a bountiful catch—before it became a tourist attraction. Once upon a time it was quite a hike up to the shrine; now there's a series of escalators, flanked by the inevitable array of stalls selling souvenirs and snacks. The island has a number of cafés and restaurants, and on clear days some of them have spectacular views of Fujisan and the Izu Peninsula. To reach the causeway from Enoshima Eki to the island, walk south from the station for about 3 km (2 mi), keeping the Katase-gawa on your right.

To return to Tōkyō from Enoshima, take a train to Shinjuku on the Odakyū Line. From the island walk back across the causeway and take the second bridge over the Katase-gawa. Within five minutes you'll come to Katase-Enoshima Eki. Or you can retrace your steps to Kamakura and take the JR Yokosuka Line to Tōkyō Eki.

Dining

$$$–$$$$ ✕ **Kaseiro.** In an old Japanese house on the main street from Hase Eki to the Daibutsu at Kōtoku-in, this establishment serves the best Chinese food in the city. The dining-room windows look onto a small, restful garden. Meals are served 11–7:30. ✉ *3–1–14 Hase, Kamakura,* ☎ *0467/22–0280. AE, DC, MC, V.*

$$–$$$$ ✕ **Hachinoki Kita-Kamakura-ten.** You can dine on traditional *shōjin ryōri* (the vegetarian cuisine of Zen monasteries) here in an old Japanese house on the Kamakura Kaidō (Route 21) near the entrance to Jōchi-ji. There's some table service, but most seating is in tatami rooms, with beautiful antique wood furnishings. Allow plenty of time; this is not a meal to be hurried through. Meals are served Tuesday–Friday 11–2, weekends 11–4. ✉ *350 Yama-no-uchi, Kamakura,* ☎ *0467/22–8719. DC, V. Closed Mon. No dinner.*

$–$$$ ✕ **Tori-ichi.** This elegant restaurant serves traditional Japanese *kaiseki.*
★   In an old country-style building, waitresses in kimonos bring out sumptuous multicourse meals, including one or more subtle-tasting soups, sushi, tempura, grilled fish, and other delicacies. Meals are served Wednesday–Monday noon–2 and 5–8. ✉ *7–13 Onari-machi, Kamakura,* ☎ *0467/22–1818. No credit cards. Closed Tues.*

Kamakura A to Z

To research prices, get advice from other travelers, and book travel arrangements, visit www.fodors.com.

TOURS

No bus company in Kamakura conducts guided tours in English. You can, however, take one of the Japanese tours, which depart from Kamakura Eki eight times daily, starting at 9 AM. Purchase tickets at the bus office to the right of the station. There are two itineraries, each lasting a little under three hours; tickets, depending on what the tour covers, are ¥2,250 and ¥3,390. The last tours leave at 1 PM. These tours are best if you have limited time and would like to hit the major attractions but don't want to linger anywhere or do a lot of walking. Take John Carroll's book *Trails of Two Cities: A Walker's Guide to Yokohama, Kamakura and Vicinity* (Kodansha International, 1994) with you, and you'll have more information at your fingertips than any of your fellow passengers.

On Saturday and Sunday the Kanagawa Student Guide Federation has a free guide service. Students show you the city in exchange for the chance to practice their English. Arrangements need to be made in advance through the Japan National Tourist Office in Tōkyō. Be at Kamakura Eki by 10 AM.

Tours from Tōkyō, through companies such as Japan Amenity Travel and Sunrise Tours, depart every day, often combined with trips to Hakone. You can book through, and arrange to be picked up at, any of the major hotels. Before you do, however, be certain that the tour covers everything in Kamakura that you want to see, as many include little more than a passing view of the Daibutsu (Great Buddha) in Hase. Given how easy it is to get around—most sights are within walking distance of each other, and others are short bus or train rides apart— you're better off seeing Kamakura on your own.

➤ TOUR CONTACTS: **Japan Amenity Travel** (☎ 03/3542–7200, FAX 03/3542–7501, WEB www.jam-trip.co.jp). **Japan National Tourist Office** in Tōkyō (☎ 03/3201–3331, WEB www.jnto.go.jp). **Kanagawa Student Guide Federation** (☎ 045/584–6412). **Sunrise Tours** (☎ 03/5796–5454, FAX 03/5495–0680, WEB www.jtb.co.jp/sunrisetour).

TRAIN TRAVEL

Traveling by train is by far the best way to get to Kamakura. Trains run from Tōkyō Eki (and Shimbashi Eki) every 10–15 minutes during the day. The trip takes 56 minutes to Kita-Kamakura and one hour to Kamakura. Take the JR Yokosuka Line from Track 1 downstairs in Tōkyō Eki (Track 1 upstairs is on a different line and does not go to Kamakura). The cost is ¥780 to Kita-Kamakura, ¥890 to Kamakura (or use your JR Pass).

To return to Tōkyō from Enoshima, take a train to Shinjuku on the Odakyū Line. There are 11 express trains daily from here on weekdays, between 8:38 AM and 8:45 PM; 9 trains daily on weekends and national holidays, between 8:39 AM and 8:46 PM; and even more in summer. The express takes about 70 minutes to make the trip and costs ¥1,220. Or you can retrace your steps to Kamakura and take the JR Yokosuka Line to Tōkyō Eki.

VISITOR INFORMATION

Kamakura and Enoshima each have their own Tourist Associations, although it can be problematic getting help in English over the phone. Your best bet is the Kamakura Station Tourist Information Center, which has a useful collection of brochures and maps. And since Kamakura is in Kanagawa Prefecture, visitors heading here from Yokohama can preplan their excursion at the Kanagawa Prefectural Tourist Association office in the Silk Center, on the Yamashita Park promenade.

➤ TOURIST INFORMATION: **Enoshima Tourist Association** (⊠ Kugenuma Kaigan 4–3–17, Fujisawa-shi, ☎ 0466/37–4141). **Kamakura Station Tourist Information Center** (⊠ Komachi 1–1–1, Kamakura-shi, ☎ 0467/22–3350). **Kamakura Tourist Association** (⊠ Onari-machi 1–12, Kamakura-shi, ☎ 0467/23–3050). **Kanagawa Prefectural Tourist Association** (⊠ Silk Center 1F, Yamashita-chō 1, Naka-ku, Yokohama-shi, ☎ 045/681–0007, ⓌⒺⒷ www.kanagawa-kankou.or.jp).

YOKOHAMA

In 1639 the Tokugawa Shogunate adopted a policy of national seclusion that closed Japan to virtually all contact with the outside world—a policy that remained in force for more than 200 years. Then, in 1853, a fleet of four American warships under Commodore Matthew Perry sailed into the bay of Tōkyō (then Edo) and presented the reluctant Japanese with the demands of the U.S. government for the opening of diplomatic and commercial relations. The following year Perry was back, setting foot first on Japanese soil at Yokohama—then a small fishing village on the mudflats of the bay, some 20 km (12½ mi) southwest of Tōkyō.

Two years later New York businessman Townsend Harris became America's first diplomatic representative to Japan. In 1858 he was finally able to negotiate a commercial treaty between the two countries; part of the deal designated four locations—one of them Yokohama—as treaty ports. With the agreement signed, Harris lost no time in setting up his residence in Hangaku-ji, in nearby Kanagawa, another of the designated ports. Kanagawa, however, was also one of the 53 relay stations on the Tōkaidō, the highway from Edo to the imperial court in Kyōto, and the presence of foreigners—perceived as unclean barbarians—offended the Japanese elite. Die-hard elements of the warrior class, moreover, wanted Japan to remain in isolation and were willing to give their lives to rid the country of intruders. Unable to protect foreigners in Kanagawa, in 1859 the shogunate created a special settlement in Yokohama for the growing community of merchants, traders, missionaries, and assorted other adventurers drawn to this exotic new land of opportunity.

The foreigners (predominantly Chinese and British, plus a few French, Americans, and Dutch) were confined here to a guarded compound about 5 square km (2 square mi)—placed, in effect, in isolation—but not for long. Within a few short years the shogunal government collapsed, and Japan began to modernize. Western ideas were welcomed, as were Western goods, and the little treaty port became Japan's principle gateway to the outside world. In 1872 Japan's first railway was built, linking Yokohama and Tōkyō. In 1889 Yokohama became a city; by then the population had grown to some 120,000. As the city prospered, so did the international community.

The English enjoyed a special cachet in the new Japan. Was not Britain, too, a small island nation? And did it not do great things in the wide world? These were people from whom they could learn and with whom they could trade, and the Japanese welcomed them in considerable numbers. (You can still watch the occasional game of cricket at the Yokohama Country and Athletic Club—once the exclusive bastion of British trading companies like Jardine Matheson.) The British, in turn, helped Japan recover its sovereignty over the original treaty ports, and by the early 1900s Yokohama was the busiest and most modern center of international trade in all of east Asia.

Then Yokohama came tumbling down. On September 1, 1923, the Great Kantō Earthquake devastated the city. The ensuing fires destroyed some 60,000 homes and took more than 40,000 lives. During the six years it took to rebuild the city, many foreign businesses took up quarters elsewhere, primarily in Kōbe and Ōsaka, and did not return.

Over the next 20 years Yokohama continued to grow, as an industrial center—until May 29, 1945, when in a span of four hours, some 500 American B-29 bombers leveled nearly half the city and left more than half a million people homeless. When the war ended, what remained became—in effect—the center of the Allied occupation. General Douglas MacArthur set up headquarters here, briefly, before moving to Tōkyō; the entire port facility and about a quarter of the city remained in the hands of the U.S. military throughout the 1950s.

By the 1970s Yokohama was once more rising from the debris; in 1978 it surpassed Ōsaka as the nation's second-largest city, and the population is now inching up to the 3.5 million mark. Boosted by Japan's postwar economic miracle, Yokohama has extended its urban sprawl north to Tōkyō and south to Kamakura—in the process creating a whole new subcenter around the Shinkansen station at Shin-Yokohama.

The development of air travel, and the competition from other ports, has changed the city's role in Japan's economy. The great liners that once docked at Yokohama's piers are now but a memory, kept alive by a museum ship and the occasional visit of a luxury vessel on a Pacific cruise. Modern Yokohama thrives instead in its industrial, commercial, and service sectors—and a large percentage of its people commute to work in Tōkyō. Is Yokohama worth a visit? Not, one could argue, at the expense of Nikkō or Kamakura, and not if you are looking for history in the physical fabric of the city: most of Yokohama's late-19th- and early 20th-century buildings are long gone. In some odd, undefinable way, however, Yokohama is a more *cosmopolitan* city than Tōkyō. The waterfront is fun, and city planners have made an exceptional success of their port redevelopment project. The museums are excellent. And if you spend time enough here, Yokohama can still invoke for you the days when, for intrepid Western travelers, Japan was a new frontier.

Exploring Yokohama

Numbers in the margin correspond to points of interest on the Yoko-hama map.

Large as Yokohama is, the central area is very negotiable. As with any other port city, much of what it has to offer centers on the waterfront—in this case, the Bund, on the west side of Tōkyō Bay. The downtown area is called Kannai (literally, "within the checkpoint"); this is where the international community was originally confined by the shogunate. Though the center of interest has expanded to include the waterfront and Ishikawa-chō, to the south, Kannai remains the heart of town.

Think of that heart as two adjacent areas. One is the old district of Kannai, bounded by Basha-michi on the northwest and Nippon-ōdori on the southeast, the Keihin Tōhoku Line tracks on the southwest, and the waterfront on the northeast. This area contains the business offices of modern Yokohama. The other area extends southeast from Nippon-ōdori to the Moto-machi shopping street and the International Cemetery, bordered by Yamashita Park and the waterfront to the northeast; in the center is Chinatown, with Ishikawa-chō Eki to the southwest. This is the most interesting part of town for tourists.

Whether you are coming from Tōkyō, Nagoya, or Kamakura, make Ishikawa-chō Eki your starting point. Take the south exit from the station and head in the direction of the waterfront. Within a block of Ishikawa-chō Eki is the beginning of **Moto-machi,** the street that follows the course of the Nakamura-gawa to the harbor. This is where the Japanese set up shop 100 years ago to serve the foreigners living in Kannai. The street is now lined with smart boutiques and jewelry stores that cater to fashionable young Japanese consumers.

The **International Cemetery,** better known locally as the Gaijin Bochi, is a Yokohama landmark and a reminder of the port city's heritage. It was established in 1854 with a grant of land from the shogunate; the first foreigners to be buried here were Russian sailors assassinated by xenophobes in the early days of the settlement. Most of the 4,500 graves on this hillside are English and American, and about 120 are of the Japanese wives of foreigners; the inscriptions on the crosses and headstones attest to some 40 different nationalities who lived and died in Yokohama. From Moto-machi Plaza, it's a short walk to the north end of the cemetery.

The **Yamate Shiryōkan** (Yamate Archive) holds a collection of materials from the city's 19th-century European enclave. The building, which is just south of the International Cemetery, is the oldest surviving wooden structure in Yokohama. ✉ *247 Yamate-chō, Naka-ku,* ☏ *045/622–1188.* 🎟 *¥200.* ⏱ *Daily 11–4.*

Once the barracks of the British forces in Yokohama, the **Minato-no-Mieru-Oka Kōen** (Harbor View Park) affords a spectacular nighttime view of the waterfront, the floodlighted gardens of Yamashita Park, and the Bay Bridge. The park, about 300 ft east of the Yamate Archive, is the major landmark in this part of the city—known, appropriately enough, as the Bluff (*yamate*). Foreigners were first allowed to build here in 1867, and it has been prime real estate ever since—an enclave of consulates and churches and international schools, private clubs and palatial Western-style homes.

Yamashita Kōen is perhaps the only positive legacy of the Great Kantō Earthquake of 1923. The debris of the warehouses and other buildings that once stood here was swept away, and the area was made into a 17-acre oasis of green along the waterfront. The fountain, representing

202

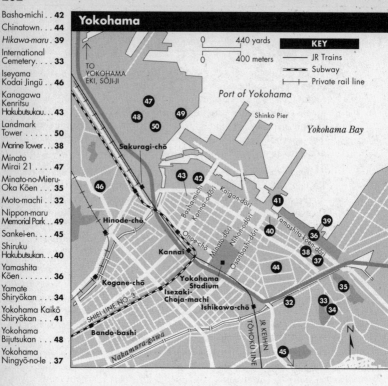

Yokohama

Port of Yokohama

Yokohama Bay

the Guardian of the Water, was presented to Yokohama by San Diego, California, one of its sister cities. To get here from the Bluff, walk northwest through Minato-no-Mieru-Oka Kōen and the neighboring French Hill Park and cross the walkway over Moto-machi. Turn right on the other side and walk one block down toward the bay to Yamashita-Kōen-dōri, the promenade along the park.

37 The **Yokohama Ningyō-no-Ie** (Yokohama Doll Museum) houses a collection of some 4,000 dolls from all over the world. In Japanese tradition, dolls are less to play with than to display—either in religious folk customs or as the embodiment of some spiritual quality. Japanese visitors to this museum never seem to outgrow their affection for the Western dolls on display here, to which they tend to assign the role of timeless "ambassadors of good will" from other cultures. The museum is worth a quick visit, with or without a child in tow. It's just across from the southeast end of Yamashita Park, on the left side of the promenade. ⊠ *18 Yamashita-chō, Naka-ku,* ☎ *045/671–9361.* ☜ *¥300; multiple-entry ticket to Doll Museum, Marine Tower, and Hikawa-maru, ¥1,550.* ☺ *Tues.–Sun. 10–5.*

38 For an older generation of Yokohama residents, the 348-ft decagonal **Marine Tower,** which opened in 1961, was the city's landmark structure; civic pride prevented them from admitting that it falls lamentably short of an architectural masterpiece. The tower has a navigational beacon at the 338-ft level and purports to be the tallest lighthouse in the world. At the 328-ft level, an observation gallery provides 360-degree views of the harbor and the city, and on clear days in autumn or winter, you can often see Fuji-san in the distance. Marine Tower is in the middle of the second block northwest from the end of Yamashita Park, on the left side of the promenade. ⊠ *15 Yamashita-chō, Naka-ku,* ☎ *045/641–7838.* ☜ *¥700; multiple-entry ticket to Marine Tower and*

Hikawa-maru ¥1,300; multiple-entry ticket to Marine Tower, Hikawa-maru, and Yokohama Doll Museum ¥1,550. ☉ *Dec.–Feb., daily 10–7; Mar.–July and Nov., daily 10–9; Aug., daily 10–10; Sept.–Oct., daily 10–9:30.*

③⑨ Moored on the waterfront, more or less in the middle of Yamashita Park, is the **Hikawa-maru,** which for 30 years shuttled passengers between Yokohama and Seattle, Washington, making a total of 238 trips. A tour of the ship evokes the time when Yokohama was a great port of call for the transpacific liners. The Hikawa-maru has a French restaurant, and in summer there's a beer garden on the upper deck. ☎ *045/641–4361.* 🎫 *¥800; multiple-entry ticket to Hikawa-maru and Marine Tower ¥1,300; multiple-entry ticket to Hikawa-maru, Marine Tower, and Yokohama Doll Museum ¥1,550.* ☉ *Daily 9:30–9.*

④⓪ The **Shiruku Hakubutsukan** (Silk Museum) pays tribute to the period at the turn of the 20th century when Japan's exports of silk were all shipped out of Yokohama. The museum has an extensive collection of silk fabrics and an informative exhibit on the silk-making process. People on staff are very happy to answer questions. In the same building, on the first floor, are the main offices of the Yokohama International Tourist Association and the Kanagawa Prefecture Tourist Information Service. The museum is at the northwestern end of the Yamashita Park promenade, on the second floor of the Silk Center Building. ✉ *1 Yamashita-chō, Naka-ku,* ☎ *045/641–0841.* 🎫 *¥300.* ☉ *Tues.–Sun. 9–4.*

④① The **Yokohama Kaikō Shiryōkan** (Yokohama Archives of History), housed in what was once the British Consulate, has some 140,000 items recording the history of Yokohama since the opening of the port to international trade. Across the street is the monument to the U.S.–Japanese Friendship Treaty. Walk west from the Silk Building, at the end of the Yamashita Park promenade, to the corner of Nihon-ōdori; the archives are on the left. ✉ *3 Nihon-ōdori, Naka-ku,* ☎ *045/201–2100.* 🎫 *¥200.* ☉ *Tues.–Sun. 9:30–4:30.*

④② From Shinko Pier, running southwest to Kannai, is **Basha-michi** (literally, "Horse-Carriage Street"). The street was so named in the 19th century, when it was widened to accommodate the horse-drawn carriages of the city's new European residents. This redbrick-paved thoroughfare and the streets parallel to it have been restored to evoke that past, with faux-antique telephone booths and imitation gas lamps. Here you'll find some of the most elegant coffee shops, patisseries, and boutiques in town. In the block northeast of the Kannai Eki, as you walk toward the waterfront, is **Kannai Hall** (look for the red-orange abstract sculpture in front), a handsome venue for chamber music, Nō, classical recitals, and the occasional visits of such groups as the Peking Opera. If you're planning to stay late in Yokohama, you might want to check out the listings.

④③ A few blocks north of Kannai Eki (use Exit 8), on Basha-michi, is the **Kanagawa Kenritsu Hakubutsukan** (Kanagawa Prefectural Museum), built in 1904—one of the few buildings in Yokohama to have survived both the Great Kantō Earthquake and World War II. Most exhibits here have no explanations in English, but the galleries on the third floor have some really remarkable medieval wooden sculptures (including one of the first Kamakura shōgun, Minamoto no Yoritomo), hanging scrolls, portraits, and armor. The exhibits of prehistory and of Yokohama in the early modern period are of much less interest. ✉ *5–60 Minami Naka-dōri, Naka-ku,* ☎ *045/201–0926.* 🎫 *¥300, special exhibitions ¥800.* ☉ *Tues.–Sun. 9–4:30 (closed last Tues. of month and day after a national holiday).*

★ ㊹ Yokohama's **Chinatown** (Chūka-gai) is the largest settlement of Chinese in Japan—and easily the city's single most popular tourist attraction, drawing more than 18 million visitors a year. Its narrow streets and alleys are lined with some 350 shops selling foodstuffs, herbal medicines, cookware, toys and ornaments, and clothing and accessories: if China exports it, you'll find it here. Wonderful exotic aromas waft from the spice shops. Even better aromas drift from the quarter's 160-odd restaurants, which serve every major style of Chinese cuisine: this is the best place for lunch in Yokohama. Chinatown is a 10-minute walk southeast of Kannai Eki. When you get to Yokohama Stadium, turn left and cut through the municipal park to the top of Nihon-ōdori. Then take a right, and you'll enter Chinatown through the Gembu-mon (North Gate), which leads to the dazzling red-and-gold, 50-ft-high Zenrin-mon (Good Neighbor Gate).

Around Yokohama

★ ㊺ **Sankei-en** was once the estate and gardens of Hara Tomitaro, one of Yokohama's wealthiest men, who made his money as a silk merchant before becoming a patron of the arts. On the extensive grounds of the estate he created is a kind of open-air museum of traditional Japanese architecture, some of which was brought here from Kamakura and the western part of the country. Especially noteworthy is Rinshunkaku, a villa built for the Tokugawa clan in 1649. There is also a tea pavilion, Chōshūkaku, built by the third Tokugawa shōgun, Iemitsu. Other buildings include a small temple transported from Kyōto's famed Daitoku-ji and a farmhouse from the Gifu district in the Japan Alps (around Takayama). The garden was opened to the public in 1906.

Walking through Sankei-en is especially delightful in spring, when the flowering trees are at their best: plum blossoms in February and cherry blossoms in early April. In June come the irises, followed by the water lilies. In autumn the trees come back into their own with tinted golden leaves. To reach Sankei-en, take the JR Keihin Tōhoku Line to Negishi Eki and a local bus from there for the 10-minute trip to the garden. ⊠ *58–1 Honmoku San-no-tani, Naka-ku,* ☎ *045/621–0635.* ☞ *Inner garden ¥300, outer garden ¥300, farmhouse ¥100.* ☼ *Inner garden daily 9–4, outer garden daily 9–4:30.*

㊻ **Iseyama Kodai Jingū,** a branch of the nation's revered Grand Shrines of Ise, is the most important Shintō shrine in Yokohama—but probably worth a visit only if you have seen most of everything else in town. The shrine is a 10-minute walk west of Sakuragi-chō Eki. ⊠ *64 Miyazaki-chō, Nishi-ku,* ☎ *045/241–1122.* ☞ *Free.* ☼ *Daily dawn-dusk.*

㊼ If you want to see Yokohama urban development at its most self-assertive, **Minato Mirai 21** is a must. The aim of this project, launched in the mid-1980s, was to turn some three-quarters of a square mile of waterfront property, lying east of the JR Negishi Line railroad tracks between the Yokohama and Sakuragi-chō stations, into a model "city of the future." As a hotel, business, international exhibition, and conference center, it's a smashing success.

㊽ Minato Mirai 21 is the site of the **Yokohama Bijutsukan** (Yokohama Museum of Art), designed by Kenzō Tange. The 5,000 works in the permanent collection include paintings by both Western and Japanese artists, including Cézanne, Picasso, Braque, Klee, Kandinsky, Kishida Ryūsei, and Yokoyama Taikan. ⊠ *3–4–1 Minato Mirai, Nishi-ku,* ☎ *045/221–0300.* ☞ *¥500.* ☼ *Mon.–Wed. and weekends 10–5:30, Fri. 10–7:30 (closed day after a national holiday). Subway: Sakuragi-chō.*

49 On the east side of ☞ **Minato Mirai 21,** where the Ō-oka-gawa (Ō-oka River) flows into the bay, is **Nippon-maru Memorial Park.** The centerpiece of the park is the *Nippon-maru,* a full-rigged three-masted ship popularly called the *Swan of the Pacific.* Built in 1930, now retired from service as a training vessel and an occasional participant in Tall Ships festivals, it is open for guided tours. Adjacent to the ship is the **Yokohama Maritime Museum,** a two-story collection of ship models, displays, and archival materials that celebrate the achievements of Yokohama Port from its earliest days to the present. ⊠ *2–1–1 Minato Mirai, Nishi-ku,* ☎ *045/221–0280.* ☜ *Ship and museum ¥600.* ⊘ *Mar.–June and Sept.–Oct., Tues.–Sun. 10–4:30; July–Aug., Tues.–Sun. 10–6; Nov.–Feb., Tues.–Sun. 10–4 (closed day after a national holiday). JR station: Sakuragi-chō.*

50 The 70-story **Landmark Tower,** in Yokohama's Minato Mirai, is Japan's tallest building. The observation deck on the 69th floor has a spectacular view of the city, especially at night; you reach it via a high-speed elevator (¥1,000) that carries you up at an ear-popping 45 kph (28 mph). The Yokohama Royal Park Hotel occupies the top 20 stories of the building. On the first level of the Landmark Tower is the Mitsubishi Heavy Industry Corporation's **Minato Mirai Industrial Museum,** with rocket engines, power plants, a submarine, various gadgets, and displays that simulate piloting helicopters—great fun for kids. ⊠ *3–3–1 Minato Mirai, Nishi-ku,* ☎ *045/224–9031.* ☜ *Museum ¥500.* ⊘ *Museum Tues.–Sun. 10–4:30.*

Part of the Landmark Tower complex is the **Dockyard Garden,** a restored dry dock with stepped sides of massive stone blocks, originally built in 1896. The long, narrow floor of the dock, with its water cascade at one end, makes a wonderful year-round venue for concerts and other events; in summer (July through mid-August), the beer garden installed here is a perfect refuge from the heat. ⊠ *Subway: Sakuragi-chō.*

Minato Mirai is a work in progress, adding to itself year by year with ever more ambitious commercial projects. The courtyard on the northeast side of the ☞ **Landmark Tower** connects to **Queen's Square,** a huge atrium-style vertical mall with dozens of shops (mainly for clothing and accessories) and restaurants. The complex also houses the Pan Pacific Hotel Yokohama and **Yokohama Minato Mirai Hall,** the city's major venue for classical music.

The **Yokohama Cosmo World** amusement park complex claims—among its 30 or so rides and attractions—the world's largest water-chute ride. It's west of Mirato Mirai and Queen's Square, on both sides of the river. ⊠ *11 Shin Minato-machi, Naka-ku,* ☎ *045/641–6591.* ☜ *Park free, rides ¥100–¥700 each.* ⊘ *Mid-Mar.–Nov., Tues.–Thurs. 11–9, Fri.–Sun. 11–10; Dec.–mid-Mar., Tues.–Sun. 11–8. Subway: Sakuragi-chō.*

OFF THE BEATEN PATH

Sōji-ji – One of the two major centers of the Sōtō sect of Zen Buddhism, Sōji-ji, in Yokohama's Tsurumi ward, was founded in 1321. The center was moved here from Ishikawa, on the Noto Peninsula (on the Sea of Japan, north of Kanazawa), after a fire in the 19th century. There's also a Sōji-ji monastic complex at Eihei-ji in Fukui Prefecture. The Yokohama Sōji-ji is one of the largest and busiest Buddhist institutions in Japan, with more than 200 monks and novices in residence. The 14th-century patron of Sōji-ji was the emperor Go-Daigo, who overthrew the Kamakura Shogunate; the emperor is buried here, although his mausoleum is off-limits to visitors. However, you can see the **Buddha Hall,** the **Main Hall,** and the **Treasure House.** To get to Sōji-ji, take the JR Keihin Tōhoku Line two stops from Sakuragi-chō to Tsurumi. From the station walk five minutes south (back toward Yokohama), passing Tsurumi University on your right. You'll soon reach the stone lanterns that mark the entrance to the temple complex. ⊠ 2–1–1 Tsurumi, Tsurumi-ku, ☎ 045/581–6021. ☒ ¥300. ⊙ Sōji-ji Center daily dawn–dusk, Treasure House Tues.–Sun. 10–4:30.

Dining

\$\$\$–\$\$\$\$ ✕ **Kaseiro.** A smart Chinese restaurant with red carpets and gold-tone walls, Kaseiro serves Beijing cuisine—including, of course, Peking Duck and shark-fin soup—and is the best of its kind in the city. ⊠ 164 Yamashita-chō, Naka-ku, ☎ 045/681–2918. Jacket and tie. AE, DC, V.

\$\$\$–\$\$\$\$ ✕ **Miroir.** One of the most elegant venues in town, Miroir is on the sec-
★   ond floor of a seven-story banquet facility called Excellent Coast, be-
tween the Moto-machi and Chinatown districts. The facade of the building evokes the Paris Opera House; the restaurant itself is a bit more casual and understated than its surroundings. The classic French food is excellent, and service is exceptional. Vegetarians, beware: the speciality of the house is *wagyū*—roasts and fillets of tender, marbled Japanese beef—in rich red wine sauces. For some unfathomable reason, Miroir is only open Tuesday–Friday for dinner, from 5:30 to 8. ⊠ 105 Yamashita-chō, Naka-ku, ☎ 045/211–2252. Jacket and tie. AE, DC, MC, V. Closed weekends and Mon. No lunch.

\$\$\$–\$\$\$\$ ✕ **Rinka-en.** If you visit Sankei-en, you might want to have lunch at this traditional country restaurant, which serves kaiseki-style cuisine. The owner, by the way, is the granddaughter of Hara Tomitaro, who donated the gardens to the city. Rinka-en stays open noon–5:30. ⊠ Honmoku San-no-tani, Naka-ku, ☎ 045/621–0318. Jacket and tie. No credit cards. Closed Wed. and Aug.

\$\$\$–\$\$\$\$ ✕ **Scandia.** Scandia, near the Silk Center and the business district, is known for its smorgasbord. It's popular for business lunches as well as for dinner and stays open until midnight, later than many other restaurants. ⊠ 1–1 Kaigan-dōri, Naka-ku, ☎ 045/201–2262. No credit cards. No lunch Sun.

\$\$\$–\$\$\$\$ ✕ **Seryna.** This establishment is famous for its *ishiyaki* steak, which is grilled on a hot stone, as well as for its *shabu-shabu*—thin slices of beef cooked in boiling water at your table and dipped in one of several sauces. (Shabu-shabu is onomatapoetic for the sound the beef makes as you swish it through the water with your chopsticks.) ⊠ Shin-Kannai Bldg. B1, 4–45–1 Sumiyoshi-chō, Naka-ku, ☎ 045/681–2727. AE, DC, MC, V.

\$\$\$ ✕ **Jukei Hanten.** Jukei Hanten is the city's best choice for Szechuan cooking. Food is what really matters here; don't expect much in the way of decor. ⊠ 164 Yamashita-chō, Naka-ku, ☎ 045/641–8288. AE, DC, MC, V.

\$\$–\$\$\$ ✕ **Aichiya.** One of the specialties at this seafood restaurant is *fugu* (blow-
★   fish)—a delicacy that must be treated with expert care, as chefs must remove organs that contain a deadly toxin before the fish can be consumed. Fugu is served only in winter. The crabs here are also a treat. Aichiya stays open 3–10. ⊠ 7–156 Isezaki-chō, Naka-ku, ☎ 045/251–4163. Jacket and tie. No credit cards. Closed Mon.

\$–\$\$\$ ✕ **Rome Station.** Rome Station is a popular venue for Italian food; the spaghetti *vongole* (with clam sauce) is particularly good. The restaurant is between Chinatown and Yamashita Park. ⊠ 26 Yamashita-chō, Naka-ku, ☎ 045/681–1818. No credit cards.

\$–\$\$ ✕ **Saronikos.** The Akebono-chō district of Yokohama, west and south of Kannai Eki, has long been home to a small cluster of Greek restaurants; sailors off the Greek ships in port still drift over this way to bring gifts of feta cheese, spices, and *sirtaki* music tapes to friends and relatives of the owners. Saronikos is among the best of these restaurants, not the least because it invests more effort in the food than in tarted-up reproductions of the Parthenon and other pretensions to decor. Try eggplant with garlic, the Greek salad—and, of course, moussaka. Saronikos stays open 6 PM–1 AM. ⊠ *3–30 Akebono-chō, Naka-ku,* ☎ *045/251– 8980. No credit cards. Closed 1st and 3rd Mon. of each month. No lunch.*

Yokohama A to Z

To research prices, get advice from other travelers, and book travel arrangements, visit www.fodors.com.

AIRPORTS AND AIRPORT TRANSFERS

From Narita Airport, a direct limousine-bus service departs once or twice an hour between 6:45 AM and 10:20 PM for Yokohama City Air Terminal (YCAT). The fare is ¥3,500. YCAT is a five-minute taxi ride from Yokohama Eki. JR Narita Express trains going on from Tōkyō to Yokohama leave the airport every hour from 8:13 AM to 1:13 PM and 2:43 to 9:43 PM. The fare is ¥4,180 (or ¥6,730 for the first-class Green Car coaches). Or you can take the limousine-bus service from Narita to Tōkyō Eki and continue on to Yokohama by train. Either way, the journey will take more than two hours—closer to three, if traffic is heavy.

The Airport Limousine Information Desk provides information in English daily 9–6; you can also get timetables on its Web site. For information in English on Narita Express trains, call the JR Higashi-Nihon Info Line, available daily 10–6.
➤ CONTACTS: **Airport Limousine Information Desk** (☎ 03/3665–7220, WEB www.limousinebus.co.jp). **JR Higashi-Nihon Info Line** (☎ 03/ 3423–0111).

BUS TRAVEL

Most of the things you'll want to see in Yokohama are within easy walking distance of a JR or subway station, but this city is so much more negotiable than Tōkyō that exploring by bus is a viable alternative. Buses, in fact, are the best way to get to Sankei-en. The city map available in the visitor centers in Yokohama and Shin-Yokohama stations has most major bus routes marked on it, and the important stops on the tourist routes are announced in English. The fixed fare is ¥210. One-day passes are also available for ¥600.

EMERGENCIES

The Yokohama Police station has a Foreign Assistance Department.
➤ CONTACTS: **Ambulance or Fire** (☎ 119). **Police** (☎ 110). **Washinzaka Hospital** (⊠ 169 Yamate-chō, Naka-ku, ☎ 045/623–7688). **Yokohama Police station** (☎ 045/623–0110).

ENGLISH-LANGUAGE MEDIA
BOOKS
Yurindo has a good selection of popular paperbacks and books on Japan in English. The Minato-Mirai branch is open daily 11–8; the store on Isezaki-chō opens an hour earlier.
➤ CONTACTS: **Yurindo** (⊠ Landmark Plaza 5F, 3–3–1 Minato-Mirai, Nishi-ku, ☎ 045/222–5500; ⊠ 1–4–1 Isezaki-chō, Naka-ku, ☎ 045/ 261–1231).

SUBWAY TRAVEL
One line connects Asamino, Shin-Yokohama, Yokohama, Totsuka, and Shōnandai. The basic fare is ¥200. One-day passes are also available, at ¥740. A second line, the Minatomirai Line, is scheduled to open between Motomachi and Yokohama Eki in 2003.

TAXIS

There are taxi stands at all the train stations, and you can always flag a cab on the street. Vacant taxis show a red light in the windshield. The basic fare is ¥660 for the first 2 km (1 mi), then ¥80 for every additional 350 meters (⅕ mi). Traffic is heavy in downtown Yokohama, however, and you will often find it faster to walk.

TOURS

Teiki Yuran Bus offers a full-day (9–3:45) sightseeing bus tour that covers the major sights and includes lunch at a Chinese restaurant in Chinatown. The tour is in Japanese only, though pamphlets written in English are available at most sightseeing stops. Buy tickets (¥6,360) at the bus offices at Yokohama Eki (east side) and at Kannai Eki; the tour departs daily at 9 AM from Bus Stop 14, on the east side of Yokohama Eki. A half-day tour is also available, with lunch (9:30–1, ¥3,850) or without (2–5:30, ¥3,000).

The sightseeing boat *Marine Shuttle* makes 40-, 60-, and 90-minute tours of the harbor and bay for ¥900, ¥1,400, and ¥2,000, respectively. Boarding is at the pier at Yamashita Park. Boats depart roughly every hour between 10:20 AM and 6:30 PM. Another boat, the *Marine Rouge*, runs 90-minute tours departing at 11, 1:30, and 4, and a special two-hour evening tour at 7 (¥2,500).

➤ TOUR CONTACT: Marine Shuttle (☎ 045/671–7719).

TRAIN TRAVEL

JR trains from Tōkyō Eki leave approximately every 10 minutes, depending on the time of day. Take the Yokosuka, the Tōkaidō, or Keihin Tōhoku Line to Yokohama Eki (the Yokosuka and Tōkaidō lines take 30 minutes, and the Keihin Tōhoku Line takes 40 minutes). From there the Keihin Tōhoku Line (Platform 3) goes on to Kannai and Ishikawa-chō, Yokohama's business and downtown areas. If you're going directly to downtown Yokohama from Tōkyō, the blue commuter trains of the Keihin Tōhoku Line are best. From Shibuya Eki in Tōkyō, the Tōkyū Toyoko Line, which is private, connects directly with Yokohama Eki and hence is an alternative if you leave from the western part of Tōkyō.

From Nagoya and Points South, the Hikari and Kodama Shinkansen stop at Shin-Yokohama Eki, 8 km (5 mi) from the city center. Take the local train from there for the seven-minute ride into town.

Yokohama Eki is the hub that links all the train lines and connects them with the city's subway and bus services. Kannai and Ishikawa-chō are the two downtown stations, both on the Keihin Tōhoku Line. Trains leave Yokohama Eki every two to five minutes from Platform 3. From Sakuragi-chō, Kannai, or Ishikawa-chō, most of Yokohama's points of interest are within easy walking distance; the one notable exception is Sankei-en.

VISITOR INFORMATION

The Yokohama International Tourist Association arranges visits to the homes of English-speaking Japanese families. These usually last a few hours and are designed to give gaijin a glimpse into the Japanese way of life. To arrange a visit or to find out more information, call the Yokohama International Tourist Association.

The Yokohama Tourist Office, in the central passageway of Yokohama Eki, is open daily 10–6 (closed December 28–January 3). A similar office with the same closing times is in Shin-Yokohama Eki. The head office of the Yokohama Convention & Visitors Bureau, open weekdays 9–5 (except national holidays and December 29–January 3), is in the Sangyō Bōeki Center Building, across from Yamashita Kōen.

➤ TOURIST INFORMATION: **Yokohama Convention & Visitors Bureau**
(✉ 2 Yamashita-chō, Naka-ku, ☎ 045/641–4759). **Yokohama International Tourist Association** (☎ 045/641–4759). **Yokohama Tourist Office** (✉ Yokohama Eki, ☎ 045/441–7300; ✉ Shin-Yokohama Eki, ☎ 045/473–2895).

FUJI-HAKONE-IZU NATIONAL PARK

Fuji-Hakone-Izu National Park, southwest of Tōkyō between Suruga and Sagami bays, is one of Japan's most popular resort areas. The region's main attraction, of course, is Fuji-san, a dormant volcano—it last erupted in 1707—rising to a height of 12,388 ft. The mountain is truly beautiful, utterly captivating in the ways it can change in different light and from different perspectives. Its symmetry and majesty have been immortalized by poets and artists for centuries. Keep in mind that during spring and summer, Fuji-san often hides behind a blanket of clouds, to the disappointment of the crowds of tourists who travel to Hakone or the Fuji Five Lakes to see it.

Apart from Fuji-san itself, each of the three areas of the park—the Izu Peninsula, Hakone and environs, and the Five Lakes—has its own special appeal. Izu has a dramatic rugged coastline, beaches, and onsen. Hakone has mountains, volcanic landscapes, and lake cruises. The Five Lakes form a recreational area with some of the best views of Fuji-san. And in each of these areas there are monuments to Japan's past.

Though it's possible to make a grand tour of all three areas at one time, most people make each of them a separate excursion from Tōkyō. Because these are tourist attractions where people are accustomed to foreign visitors, there's always someone to help out in English if you want to explore off the beaten path.

Izu Peninsula

Numbers in the margin correspond to points of interest on the Fuji-Hakone-Izu National Park map.

Atami

51 *48 mins southwest of Tōkyō by Kodama Shinkansen.*

The gateway to the Izu Peninsula is **Atami**. Most Japanese honeymooners make it no farther into the peninsula, so Atami itself has a fair number of hotels and traditional inns. When you arrive, collect a map from the **Atami Tourist Information Office** (☎ 0557/85–2222) at the train station.

★ The major sight in Atami is the **MOA Bijutsukan,** which houses the private collection of the messianic religious leader Okada Mokichi. Okada (1882–1955), who founded a movement called the Sekai Kyūsei Kyō (Religion for the Salvation of the World), also acquired more than 3,000 works of art, dating from the Asuka period (6th and 7th centuries) to the present day, including a number of particularly fine *ukiyo-e* (Edo-era wood-block prints) and ceramics. On a hill above the station and set in a garden full of old plum trees and azaleas, the museum also affords a sweeping view over Atami and the bay. ✉ 26–2 Momoyama, Atami, ☎ 0557/84–2511. 🎫 ¥1,600. ⏱ Fri.–Wed. 9:30–5.

Barely worth the 15-minute walk from Atami Eki is the **Oya Geyser,** which used to gush on schedule once every 24 hours but stopped after the Great Kantō Earthquake. Not happy with this, the local chamber of commerce rigged a pump to raise the geyser for four out of every five minutes and gives it top billing in its tourist brochures.

Fuji-Hakone-Izu National Park

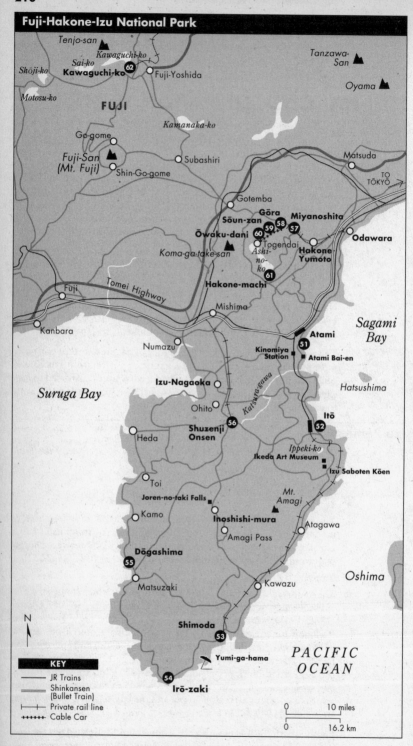

Tenjo-san

Tanzawa-San

Kawaguchi-ko

Sai-ko

Shōji-ko

Kawaguchi-ko

Fuji-Yoshida

Oyama

Motosu-ko

FUJI

Kamanaka-ko

Go-gome

Matsuda

**Fuji-San
(Mt. Fuji)**

Subashiri

TO
TOKYO

Shin-Go-gome

Gotemba

Gōra

Sōun-zan

58 **Miyanoshita**

59

Ōwaku-dani

60 57

Odawara

Koma-ga-take-san

Togendai

**Hakone
Yumoto**

_Ashi-
no-
ko_

61

Hakone-machi

Tomei Highway

Mishima

_Sagami
Bay_

Atami

Kanbara

51

Numazu

**Kinomiya
Station**

Atami Bai-en

Suruga Bay

Hatsushima

Izu-Nagaoka

Katsura-gawa

Ohito

Itō

56

52

**Shuzenji
Onsen**

Ippeki-ko

Heda

Ikeda Art Museum

Izu Saboten Kōen

Toi

Joren-no-taki Falls

_Mt.
Amagi_

Kamo

Inoshishi-mura

Atagawa

Amagi Pass

Dōgashima

55

Oshima

Matsuzaki

Kawazu

Shimoda

53

_PACIFIC
OCEAN_

Yumi-ga-hama

N

54

Irō-zaki

KEY

——	JR Trains
═══	Shinkansen (Bullet Train)
┼┼┼	Private rail line
┿┿┿	Cable Car

0   10 miles

0   16.2 km

The time to visit the **Atami Bai-en** (Plum Garden) is in late January or early February, when its 850 trees bloom. If you do visit, also stop by the small shrine in the shadow of an enormous old camphor tree: the tree has been designated a National Monument. Atami Bai-en is 15 minutes by bus from Atami or an eight-minute walk from Kinomiya Eki, the next stop south of Atami served by local trains.

If you have the time and the inclination for a beach picnic, it's worth taking the 25-minute high-speed ferry (round-trip ¥2,340) from the pier over to **Hatsu-shima.** There are nine departures daily between 7:30 and 5:20; call ☎ 0557/81–0541 for reservations. You can easily walk around the island, which is only 4 km (2½ mi) in circumference, in less than two hours. Use of the **Picnic Garden** (open daily 10–3) is free.

LODGING

$$$$ 🏨 **Taikansō.** A traditional Japanese inn with exquisite furnishings and
★ individualized service, this villa was once owned by the Japanese artist Yokoyama Taikan. Views of the sea must have been his inspiration. The prices (¥31,000–¥47,000) may seem astronomical—well, they *are* astronomical—but bear in mind that they include a multicourse dinner of great artistry, served in your room, and breakfast the next morning. The inn is a 10-minute walk from Atami Eki. ✉ *7–1 Hayashi-ga-oka-chō, Atami, Shizuoka-ken 413-0131,* ☎ *0557/81–8137,* 𝔽𝔸𝕏 *0557/83–5308. 44 Japanese-style rooms. AE, DC, MC, V. MAP.*

$$–$$$ 🏨 **New Fujiya Hotel.** A modern resort hotel and a useful base for sightseeing, the New Fujiya is inland (five minutes by taxi from Atami Eki). Only the top rooms have a view of the sea. Service is impersonal but professional, and a foreign visitor is no cause for consternation. ✉ *1–16 Ginza-chō, Atami, Shizuoka-ken 413-0013,* ☎ *0557/81–0111. 158 Western-style rooms, 158 Japanese-style rooms. 3 restaurants, bar, indoor pool, hot springs, sauna. AE, DC, MC, V.*

Itō

52 *25 mins south of Atami by JR local; 1 hr, 40 mins southwest of Tōkyō via Atami by Kodama Shinkansen, then JR local.*

The hot-springs resort of Itō, 16 km (10 mi) south of Atami, traces its history of associations with the West to 1604, when William Adams (1564–1620), the Englishman whose adventures served as the basis for James Clavell's novel *Shōgun,* came ashore.

Four years earlier Adams had beached his disabled Dutch vessel, *De Liefde,* on the shores of Kyūshū and became the first Englishman to set foot on Japan. The authorities, believing that he and his men were Portuguese pirates, put Adams in prison, but he was eventually befriended by the shōgun Ieyasu Tokugawa, who brought him to Edo (present-day Tōkyō) and granted him an estate. Ieyasu appointed Adams his adviser on foreign affairs. The English castaway taught mathematics, geography, gunnery, and navigation to shogunal officials and in 1604 was ordered to build an 80-ton Western-style ship. Pleased with this venture, Ieyasu ordered the construction of a larger oceangoing vessel. These two ships were built at Itō, and Adams lived there from 1605 to 1610.

This history was largely forgotten until British Commonwealth occupation forces began coming to Itō for rest and recuperation after World War II. Adams's memory was revived, and since then the Anjin Festival (the Japanese gave Adams the name *anjin*—which means "pilot") has been held in his honor every August. A monument to the Englishman stands at the mouth of the river.

One reason the British forces chose Itō is that there are some 800 thermal springs in the area. These springs—and the beautiful, rocky, indented coastline nearby—remain the resort's major attractions. Some 150 hotels and inns serve the area. In addition to the hot springs, the Itō area has a number of other attractions.

Izu Saboten Kōen (Izu Cactus Park) consists of a series of pyramidal greenhouses set up at the base of Komuro-san (Mt. Komuro) that contain 5,000 kinds of cacti from around the world. The park is 20 minutes south of Itō Eki by bus. ⊠ *1317–13 Futo,* ☎ *0557/51–1111.* ☞ *¥1,800, ¥800 after 5.* ☉ *Mid-Mar.–mid-Oct., daily 8:40–8:30; mid-Oct.–mid-Jan., daily 8:40–4.*

The **Ikeda 20-Seiki Bijutsukan** (Ikeda 20th-Century Art Museum), at Lake Ippeki, has a collection of works by Picasso, Dalí, Chagall, and Matisse and a number of wood-block prints. The museum is a 15-minute walk from Izu Saboten Kōen. ⊠ *614 Aza-Sekiba, Totari,* ☎ *0557/45–2211.* ☞ *¥800.* ☉ *Sept.–June, daily 10–4:30; July–Aug., daily 10–5:30.*

Komuro-san Kōen (Mt. Komuro Park) has, on its east side, 3,000 cherry trees of 35 varieties that bloom at various times throughout the year. A cable car takes you to the top of the mountain. The park is about 20 minutes south of Itō Eki by bus. ☞ *Free, round-trip to mountain top ¥400.* ☉ *Daily 9–4.*

Shimoda and Irō-zaki (Irō Point)
1 hr south of Itō by Izu Railways.

South of Itō, the coastal scenery is lovely—each sweep around a headland gives another picturesque sight of a rocky, indented shoreline. There are several spa towns en route to Shimoda. Higashi-Izu (East Izu) has a number of hot-springs resorts, of which **Atagawa** is the most fashionable. South of Atagawa is **Kawazu,** a place of relative quiet and solitude, with pools in the forested mountainside and waterfalls plunging through lush greenery. For history, however, none of these resort towns have the distinction of **Shimoda.**

❺❸

Shimoda's encounter with the West began when Commodore Matthew Perry, bearing a commission from the U.S. government to open—by force, if necessary—diplomatic relations with Japan, anchored his fleet of black ships off the coast here in 1854. To commemorate the event, the three-day Kurofune Matsuri (Black Ship Festival) is held every year in mid-May. Shimoda was also the site, in 1856, of the first American Consulate.

The first American consul to Japan was New York businessman Townsend Harris—who soon after his arrival in Shimoda asked the Japanese authorities to provide him with a female servant; they sent him a young girl named Saitō Kichi. The arrangement brought her only a new name—Tōjin (the Foreigner's) Okichi—and a tragic end. Harris soon sent her away, compounding poor Okichi's shame and ridicule. She tried and failed to rejoin a former lover, moved to Yokohama, and later returned to Shimoda in an unsuccessful attempt to run a restaurant. Okichi took to drink and drowned herself in 1890. **Hōfuku-ji** was Okichi's family temple. The museum-annex displays a life-size image of her, and just behind the temple is her grave—where incense is still kept burning in her memory. The grave of her lover, Tsurumatsu, is at Tōden-ji, a temple about midway between Hōfuku-ji and Shimoda Eki. ⊠ *18–26 1-chōme, Shimoda,* ☎ *0558/22–0960.* ☞ *¥300.* ☉ *Daily 8–5.*

The major sight on a Shimoda walk is **Ryosen-ji,** the temple where the negotiations took place that led to the United States–Japan Treaty of Amity and Commerce of 1858. The **Hōmotsu-den** (Treasure Hall) of Ryosen-ji contains some personal articles that belonged to Tōjin Okichi. ⊠ *3–12–12 Shimoda, Shimoda-shi,* ☎ *0558/22–2805.* ☞ *Treasure Hall ¥500.* ☉ *Daily 8:30–5.*

The **Shimoda tourist office** (☎ 0558/22–1531), in front of the station, has the easiest of the local English itineraries to follow. The 2½-km (1½-mi) tour covers most major sights, and all of those concerning Okichi. On request, the tourist office will also find local accommodations for you.

(54) The southernmost part of the Izu Peninsula is **Irō-zaki** (Irō Point), reached either by bus or sightseeing boat from Shimoda. If you visit in January, you're in for a special treat: a blanket of daffodils covers the cape. Your best plan, in any case, is to take the boat one way and the bus the other; both take about 40 minutes. The bus from Shimoda Eki stops at **Yumi-ga-hama,** one of the prettiest sandy beaches on the whole Izu Peninsula, then continues to Irō-zaki, the last stop on the route.

From the bus stop at the end of the line from Shimoda Eki, it's a short walk to the **Irō-zaki Jungle Park,** with its 3,000 varieties of colorful tropical plants. Beyond the park you can walk to a lighthouse at the edge of the cliff. ✉ *546–1 Irō-zaki, Minami-Izu,* ☎ *0558/65–0050.* 🎫 *¥900.* ⏲ *Daily 8–5.*

LODGING

$$$–$$$$ 🏨 **Shimoda Prince Hotel.** This modern V-shape resort hotel faces the Pacific, steps away from a white-sand beach. The decor is more functional than aesthetic, but the panoramic view of the Pacific from the picture windows in the dining room makes this one of the best hotels in town. The Prince is just outside Shimoda, 10 minutes by taxi from the station. Among numerous facilities, the Prince has a Continental-style main dining room, a Japanese restaurant, and a terrace lounge. ✉ *1547–1 Shira-hama, Shimoda, Shizuoka-ken 415-8525,* ☎ *0558/22–2111,* FAX *0558/22–7584. 70 Western-style rooms, 6 Japanese-style rooms. 2 restaurants, bar, pool, sauna, 3 tennis courts, shops, nightclub. AE, DC, MC, V.*

$$$–$$$$ 🏨 **Shimoda Tokyū Hotel.** Perched just above the bay, the Shimoda Tokyū has impressive views of the Pacific from one side (where rooms cost about 10% more) and mountains from the other. The lobby areas lack character and warmth, but that's typical of Japanese resort hotels. Prices run significantly higher in midsummer. ✉ *5–12–1 Shimoda, Shimoda, Shizuoka-ken 415-8510,* ☎ *0558/22–2411. 107 Western-style rooms, 10 Japanese-style rooms. 2 restaurants, bar, outdoor café, sushi bar, pool, hot springs, shops. AE, DC, MC, V.*

Dōgashima

(55) *1 hr northwest of Shimoda by bus.*

The sea has eroded the coastal rock formations into fantastic shapes near the little port town of Dōgashima. A sightseeing boat from Dōgashima Pier makes 20-minute runs to see the rocks (¥920). In the typical Japanese excess of kindness, a recorded loudspeaker—which you can safely ignore—recites the name of every rock you pass on the trip. To get to Dōgashima from Shimoda, you'll need to use bus service (¥1,360). Shimoda is the end of the line for travelers by train; to continue around the Izu Peninsula from Shimoda, or go north through the central mountains, you must use buses, which run frequently during the day. (Whatever your destination, always check the time of the last departure to make sure that you are not left stranded.) Going south, the bus from Shimoda rounds the point at Irō-zaki and continues on to Dōgashima.

The **Nishi-Izu Tourist Office** (☎ 0558/52–1268) is near the pier, in the small building behind the bus station.

LODGING

$$$$ 🏨 **Dōgashima New Ginsui.** Every guest room overlooks the sea at the New Ginsui, which sits atop cliffs above the water. This is the smartest

luxury resort on Izu's west coast. Service is first class, despite its popularity with tour groups. Room charges include a seafood kaiseki dinner, served in your room, and buffet breakfast. ⊠ 2977–1 Nishina, Nishi-Izu-chō, Dōgashima, Shizuoka-ken 410-3514, ☎ 0558/52–1211, ℻ 0558/52–1210. 90 Japanese-style rooms. Restaurant, pool, shops, nightclub. AE, DC, MC, V. MAP.

Shuzenji Onsen

56 2 hrs north of Shimoda by bus, 32 mins south of Mishima by Izu-Hakone Railways.

Shuzenji—a hot-springs resort in the center of the peninsula, along the valley of the Katsura-gawa—enjoys a certain historical notoriety as the place where the second Kamakura shōgun, Minamoto no Yoriie, was assassinated early in the 13th century. Don't judge the town by the area around the station; most hotels and hot springs are 2 km (1 mi) to the west.

If you've planned a longer visit to Izu, consider spending a night at **Inoshishi-mura,** en route by bus between Shimoda and Shuzenji. The scenery in this part of the peninsula is dramatic, and the specialty of the house at the local inns is roast mountain boar. In the morning, a pleasant 15-minute walk from Inoshishi-mura brings you to **Joren-no-taki,** where you can gaze at the waterfall before rejoining the bus.

LODGING

$$$$ 🏯 **Ryokan Sanyōsō.** The former villa of the Iwasaki family, founders
★ of the Mitsubishi conglomerate, the Sanyōsō is furnished with museum-quality antiques; this is as luxurious and beautiful a place to stay as you'll find on the Izu Peninsula. The best rooms—which are quite expensive at up to ¥70,000—have traditional baths made of fragrant cypress wood that look out on exquisite little private gardens. Breakfast and dinner, served in your room, are included in the rate. The Sanyōsō is a five-minute taxi ride from Izu-Nagaoka Eki. ⊠ 270 Mama-no-ue, Izu-Nagaoka-chō, Shizuoka-ken 410-2204, ☎ 0559/48–0123, ℻ 0559/47–0610. 21 Western and Japanese-style rooms. Restaurant. AE, DC, MC, V.

$$ 🏯 **Kyorai-An Matsushiro-kan.** Though this small family-owned inn, five minutes by bus or taxi from Izu-Nagaoka Eki, is nothing fancy, the owners make you feel like a guest in their home. Some English is spoken. Japanese meals are served in a common dining room. Room-only reservations (no meals) are accepted only on weekdays. ⊠ 55 Kona, Izu-Nagaoka, Shizuoka-ken 410-2201, ☎ 0559/48–0072, ℻ 0559/48–4030. 16 Japanese-style rooms. Restaurant. AE, DC, MC, V.

Hakone

The national park and resort area of Hakone is a popular day trip from Tōkyō and a good place for a close-up view of Fuji-san. A word of caution, though, before you dash off to see Fuji-san: the mountain is often swathed in clouds, especially in summer. And on summer weekends it often seems that all of Tōkyō has come out to Hakone with you. Expect long lines at cable cars and traffic jams everywhere.

You can cover the best of Hakone in a one-day trip out of Tōkyō, but if you want to try the curative powers of the thermal waters or do some hiking, then stay overnight. Two of the best areas are around the old hot-springs resort of Miyanoshita and the western side of Koma-ga-take-san (Mt. Koma-ga-take). The route may sound complex, but in fact this is one excursion from Tōkyō so well defined that you really can't get lost—no more so, at least, than any of the thousands of Japanese tourists ahead and behind you.

The first leg of the journey is from Odawara or Hakone-Yumoto by train and cable car through the mountains to Togendai, on the north shore of Ashi-no-ko (Lake Ashi). The scenery en route is spectacular, but if you have problems with vertigo you might be better off on the bus. The long way around, from Odawara to Togendai, takes about an hour—in heavy traffic, an hour and a half. The trip over the mountains will take about two hours.

Credit the difference to the Hakone Tōzan Tetsudō Line—possibly the slowest train you'll ever ride. It takes 54 minutes to travel the 16 km (10 mi) from Odawara to Gōra (38 minutes from Hakone-Yumoto), using three switchbacks to inch its way up the side of the mountain. The steeper it gets, the grander the view.

57 Trains do not stop at any station en route for any length of time, but they do run frequently enough to allow you to disembark, visit a sight, and catch another train. The first stop to make is **Miyanoshita,** a small but very pleasant and popular resort. Especially charming is the 19th-century Western-style **Fujiya Hotel.** Even if you're not staying there, drop in for a morning coffee on the first floor overlooking the garden and, on the way out, take a peek at the vintage collection of old books and magazines in the library.

★ Past Miyanoshita, by all means get off the train to visit the **Hakone Chōkoku-no-mori Bijutsukan** (Hakone Open-Air Museum). Established in 1969, the museum has an astonishing collection of 19th- and 20th-century Western and Japanese sculpture, most of it on display in a spacious, handsome garden. There are works here by Rodin, Moore, Arp, Calder, Giacometti, Takeshi Shimizu, and Kōtarō Takamura. One section of the garden is devoted to Emilio Greco. Inside are works by Picasso, Léger, and Manzo, among others. Chōkoku-no-mori is within a minute's walk of Miyanoshita Eki; directions are posted in English. ✉ *1121 Mi-no-taira,* ☎ *0460/2–1161.* 🎟 *¥1,600.* ⊙ *Mar.–mid-July and late Sept.–Oct., daily 9–4:30; mid-July–late Sept., daily 9–8:30; Nov.–Feb., daily 9–4.*

58 The final stop on the line is **Gōra,** a small town at the lower end of the Sōun-zan cable car and a jumping-off point for hiking and exploring. Ignore the little restaurants and souvenir stands here: get off the train as quickly as you can and make a dash for the cable car at the other end of the station. If you let the rest of the passengers get there before you, and perhaps a tour bus or two, you may stand 45 minutes in line.

59 The cable car up to **Sōun-zan** departs every 20 minutes and takes 10 minutes (¥410; free with the Hakone Free Pass [☞ Fuji-Hakone-Izu National Park A to Z, *below*]) to the top. There are four stops en route, and you can get off and reboard the cable car at any one of them if you've paid the full fare. At Kōen-kami, the second stop on the cable car from Gōra, is the **Hakone Bijutsukan,** sister institution to the MOA Museum of Art in Atami. The museum, which consists of two buildings set in a garden, houses a modest collection of porcelain and ceramics from China, Korea, and Japan. ✉ *1300 Gōra,* ☎ *0460/2–2623.* 🎟 *¥900.* ⊙ *Fri.–Wed. 9–4.*

★ **60** At Sōun-zan a gondola swings up over a ridge and crosses the valley called **Ōwaku-dani** on its way to Togendai. The landscape here is blasted and desolate, sulfurous billows of steam escaping through holes from some inferno deep in the earth. Why this fascinates the Japanese—who need no reminders that they live on a chain of volcanic islands—is anybody's guess. At the top of the ridge is one of the two stations where you can leave the gondola. From the station a ¼-km (½-mi) walking course wanders among the sulfur pits in the valley. Local entrepreneurs make a passable living boiling eggs in these holes and selling them to tourists at exorbitant prices. Just below the station is a restaurant, where the food is truly terrible—but on a clear day the view of Fuji-san is perfect. Next to the gondola station is the **Ōwaku-dani Shizen Kagakukan** (Ōwaku-dani Natural History Museum), an uninspired collection of exhibits on the ecosystems and volcanic history of the area, none of which have explanations in English. The museum is open daily 9–4:30; admission is ¥400. Remember, if you get off the gondola here, you—and others in the same situation—will have to wait for someone to make space on a later gondola before you can continue down to Togendai and Ashi-no-ko (but again, the gondolas come by every minute). ⊠ *Gondola in same building as cable car terminus at Sōun-zan.* 🎫 *¥1,330, free with Hakone Free Pass.* ⊙ *Gondolas depart every minute.*

From Ōwaku-dani the descent by gondola to Togendai on the shore of **Ashi-no-ko** takes 25 minutes. There is no reason to linger at Togendai; it is only a terminus for buses to Hakone-Yumoto and Odawara and to the resort villages in the northern part of Hakone. Head straight for the pier, a few minutes' walk down the hill, where boats set out on the lake for Hakone-machi. The ride is free with your Hakone Free Pass; otherwise, buy a ticket (¥970) at the office in the terminal. A few ships of conventional design ply the lake; the rest are astonishingly corny Disney knockoffs. One, for example, is rigged like a 17th-century warship. There are departures every 30 minutes, and the cruise to Hakone-machi takes about 30 minutes. With still water and good weather, you will get a breathtaking reflection of the mountains in the waters of the lake as you go.

61 The main attraction in **Hakone-machi** is the **Hakone Sekisho** (Hakone Barrier). In days gone by, the town of Hakone was on the Tōkaidō, the main highway between the imperial court in Kyōto and the shogunate in Edo (present-day Tōkyō). The road was the only feasible passage through this mountainous country. Travelers could scarcely avoid passing through Hakone—which made it an ideal place for a checkpoint to control traffic. The Tokugawa Shogunate built the barrier here in 1618; its most important function was to monitor the *daimyō* (feudal lords) passing through—to keep track, above all, of weapons coming into Edo, and womenfolk coming out.

When Ieyasu Tokugawa came to power, Japan had been through nearly 100 years of bloody struggle among rival coalitions of daimyō. Ieyasu emerged supreme from all this, mainly because some of his opponents had switched sides at the last moment, in the Battle of Sekigahara in 1600. The shōgun was justifiably paranoid about his "loyal" barons—especially those in the outlying domains, and he required the daimyō to live in Edo for periods of time every two years. It was an inspired policy. The rotation system turned the daimyō into absentee landlords, which undercut their bases of power. They had to travel both ways in processions of great pomp and ceremony and maintain homes in the capital befitting their rank—expenses that kept them perennially strapped for cash. When they did return to their own lands, they had to leave their wives behind in Edo, hostages to their good behavior. A noble lady coming through the Hakone Sekisho without an official pass, in short, was a prima facie case of treason.

The checkpoint served the Tokugawa dynasty well for 250 years. It was demolished only when the shogunate fell, in the Meiji Restoration of 1868. An exact replica, with an exhibition hall of period costumes and weapons, was built as a tourist attraction in 1965. The restored Hakone Sekisho is a few minutes' walk from the pier, along the lakeshore in the direction of Moto-Hakone. ⊠ *Ichiban-chō, Hakone-machi,* ☎ *0460/3–6635.* ☒ *¥300.* ⊙ *Mar.–Nov., daily 9–4:30; Dec.–Feb., daily 9–4.*

Lodging

LAKE ASHI

$$–$$$$ 🏨 **Hakone Prince Hotel.** The location of this resort complex at Hakone-
★ en is perfect, with the lake in front and the mountains of Koma-ga-
take behind. The Hakone Prince draws both tour groups and individual
travelers, and it's also a popular venue for business conferences. The
main building has both twin rooms and triples; the Japanese-style
Ryū-gū-den annex, which overlooks the lake and has its own thermal
bath, is absolutely superb. The rustic-style cottages in the complex sleep
three–four guests; these are only open from mid-April through Novem-
ber. ⊠ *144 Moto-Hakone, Hakone-machi, Ashigarashimo-gun, Kana-
gawa-ken 250-0522,* ☎ *0460/3–7111,* ℻ *0460/3–7616,* 🌐
*www.princehotels.co.jp. 96 rooms in main bldg., 12 in chalet, 77 in
lakeside lodge, 73 total in 2 annexes. 2 restaurants, bar, coffee shop,
dining room, lounge, 2 pools, Japanese baths, 7 tennis courts, shops.
AE, DC, MC, V. CP.*

MIYANOSHITA

$$–$$$$ 🏨 **Fujiya Hotel.** Built in 1878, this Western-style hotel with modern ad-
★ ditions is showing signs of age, but that somehow adds to its charm.
The library, with its stacks of old books, would make a character out
of Dickens feel positively at home. In the gardens behind the hotel is
an old imperial villa, which serves as a dining room. The Fujiya combines the best of traditional Western decor with the exceptional service
and hospitality of a fine Japanese inn. There are both Western and Japanese restaurants. ⊠ *359 Miyanoshita, Hakone-machi, Kanagawa-ken
250-0522,* ☎ *0460/2–2211,* ℻ *0460/2–2210,* 🌐 *www.fujiyahotel.co.jp.
149 Western-style rooms. 3 restaurants, 2 pools, hot springs, 18-hole
golf course. AE, DC, MC, V.*

SENGOKU

$$ 🏨 **Fuji-Hakone Guest House.** A small, family-run Japanese inn, this guest
house has simple tatami rooms with the bare essentials. The owners,
Mr. and Mrs. Takahashi, speak English and are a great help in plan-
ning trips off the beaten path. The inn is between Odawara Eki and
Togendai; take a bus from the station (Lane 4), get off at the Senkyōro-
mae stop, and walk one block. The family also operates the nearby
Moto-Hakone Guest House (⊠ *103 Moto-Hakone,* ☎ *0460/3–7880*),
which has five Japanese-style rooms that share a typical Japanese-
style bath. ⊠ *912 Sengoku-hara, Hakone, Kanagawa-ken 250-0631,*
☎ *0460/4–6577. 12 Japanese-style rooms. Hot springs. AE, MC, V.*

Fuji Go-ko (Fuji Five Lakes)

While Hakone is to the southeast of Fuji-san, Fuji Go-ko is to the north—
affording the best view of the mountain and the best base for a climb
to the summit. With its various outdoor activities, from skating and
fishing in winter to boating and hiking in summer, this is a popular re-
sort area for families and business conferences.

The five lakes are, from the east, Yamanaka-ko, Kawaguchi-ko, Sai-
ko, Shōji-ko, and Motosu-ko. Kawaguchi and Yamanaka are the
largest and most developed as resort areas, with Kawaguchi more or
less the centerpiece of the group. You can visit this area on a day trip
from Tōkyō, but unless you want to spend most of it on buses and trains,
plan on staying overnight.

From Kawaguchi-ko Eki, it's a 5- to 10-minute walk to the lakeshore.
62 Kawaguchi-ko is the most developed of the five lakes, ringed with weekend retreats and vacation lodges—many of them maintained by companies and universities for their employees. If you turn right and walk along the shore, another five minutes will bring you to the gondola for a quick ride up to **Tenjo-san** (Mt. Tenjo; 3,622 ft). At the top there is an observatory, from which the whole of Lake Kawaguchi is before you, and beyond the lake is a classic view of Fuji-san. Back down the gondola and across the road is the pier from which excursion boats leave on 30-minute tours of the lake. The promise, not always fulfilled, is to have two views of Fuji-san: one of the thing itself and the other inverted in its reflection on the water.

One of the little oddities at Lake Kawaguchi is the **Fuji Hakubutsukan.** Don't be diverted by the conventional exhibits on the first floor of local geology and history; head straight upstairs (you must be 18 or older) and browse in the museum's astonishing collection of—well, for want of a euphemism—phalluses. Mainly made from wood and stone and carved in every shape and size, these figures played a role in certain local fertility festivals. The museum is on the north shore of the lake, next to the Fuji Lake Hotel. ⊠ *3964 Funatsu, Mizuminako, Kawaguchi-ko-machi,* ☎ *0555/73–2266.* ☎ *Ground floor ¥200, ground and 2nd floors ¥500.* ☉ *Mar.–Oct., daily 9–4; Nov.–Feb., Sat.–Thurs. 9–4. Closed 3rd Tues. of month.*

The largest of the recreational facilities at Lake Kawaguchi is the
Fuji-kyū Highland. Not particularly worth a visit unless you have children in tow, it does have an impressive assortment of rides, roller coasters, and other amusements. The park stays open all year and in the winter has superb skating, with Fuji-san for a backdrop. Fuji-kyū Highland is about 15 minutes' walk east from Kawaguchi-ko Eki. ☎ *0555/23–2111.* ☎ *Full-day pass ¥4,300.* ☉ *Daily 9–5.*

Buses from Kawaguchi-ko Eki go to all the other lakes. The farthest west is **Motosu-ko,** the deepest and clearest of the Fuji Go-ko, which takes about 50 minutes. Many people consider **Shōji-ko,** the smallest of the lakes, to be the prettiest—not least because it still has relatively little vacation-house development. The **Shōji Trail** leads from the Shōji-ko to Fuji-san through Aoki-ga-hara (Sea of Trees), a forest with an underlying magnetic lava field that makes compasses go haywire. Any number of people go into Aoki-ga-hara every year and never come out, some of them on purpose—the forest seems to hold a morbid fascination for the Japanese as a place to commit suicide and disappear. If you're planning to climb Fuji-san from Motosu-ko, go with a guide.

Sai-ko, between Shōji-ko and Kawaguchi-ko, is the third-largest lake of the five, with only moderate development. From the western shore there is an especially good view of Fuji-san. Near Sai-ko there are two natural caves, an ice cave and a wind cave. You can either take a bus or walk to them. The largest of the five lakes is **Yamanaka-ko,** 35 minutes by bus to the southeast of Kawaguchi. Yamanaka-ko is the closest lake to the popular trail up Fuji-san that starts at Go-gōme, and many climbers use this resort area as a base.

Lodging

KAWAGUCHI-KO

$$$–$$$$ **Fuji View Hotel.** Conveniently located on Lake Kawaguchi, the Fuji View is a little threadbare but comfortable. The terrace lounge offers fine views of the lake and of Fuji-san beyond. The staff speaks English and is helpful in planning excursions. Many of the guests are on group excursions and take two meals—dinner and breakfast—in the hotel, but it's possible to opt for the room rate alone. Rates are significantly higher on weekends and in August. ⊠ *511 Katsuyama-mura, Minami Tsuru-gun, Yamanashi-ken 401-0310,* ☎ *0555/83–2211,* FAX *0555/ 83–2128. 40 Western-style rooms, 30 Japanese-style rooms. 2 restaurants, 9-hole golf course, 3 tennis courts, boating. AE, DC, MC, V. MAP.*

YAMANAKA-KO

$$ ⊞ **Hotel Mount Fuji.** The best resort hotel on Lake Yamanaka, the Mount Fuji offers all the facilities for a recreational holiday, and its guest rooms are larger than those at the other hotels on the lake. The lounges are spacious, and they have fine views of the lake and mountain. Rates are about 20% higher on weekends. ⊠ *1360-83 Yamanaka, Yamanaka-ko-mura, Yamanashi-ken 401-0501,* ☎ *0555/62–2111. 153 Western-style rooms, 4 Japanese-style rooms. 3 restaurants, pool, 2 tennis courts, ice-skating. AE, DC, MC, V.*

Fuji-san

★ There are six routes to the summit of **Fuji-san** (Mt. Fuji), but only two are recommended: from Go-gōme (fifth station), on the north side, and from Shin-Go-gōme (new fifth station), on the south. From Go-gōme you have a five-hour climb to the summit—the shortest way up—and a three-hour descent. From Shin-Go-gōme the ascent is slightly longer and stonier, but the way down, via the *sunabashiri,* a volcanic sand slide, is faster.

The Climb

The ultimate experience of climbing Fuji-san is to reach the summit just before dawn and to greet the extraordinary sunrise. *Go-raikō* (The Honorable Coming of the Light [here *go* means "honorable"]), as the sunrise is called, has a mystical quality because the reflection shimmers across the sky just before the sun itself appears over the horizon. Mind you, there is no guarantee of seeing it: Fuji-san is often cloudy, even in the early morning.

The climb is taxing but not as hard as you might think scaling Japan's highest mountain would be. That said, the air *is* thin, and it *is* humiliating to struggle for the oxygen to take another step while some 83-year-old Japanese grandmother blithely leaves you in her dust (it happens: Japanese grannies are made of sterner stuff than most). Have no fear of losing the trail on either of the two main routes. Just follow the crowd—some 196,000 people make the climb during the official season, July 1–August 26 (outside of this season the weather is highly unpredictable and potentially dangerous, and climbing is strongly discouraged). In all, there are 10 stations to the top; you start at the fifth. There are stalls selling food and drinks along the way, but at exorbitant prices, so bring your own.

Also along the route are huts where, dormitory style, you can catch some sleep. A popular one is at the Hachi-gōme (eighth station), from which it is about a 90-minute climb to the top. The mountain huts (about ¥7,000 with two meals, ¥5,000 without meals) are open only in July and August—and should be avoided at all costs. The food is vile. There is no fresh water. The bedding is used by so many people and so seldom properly aired, you'd feel better sleeping on fish skins. Sensible folk leave Go-gōme at midnight with good flashlights, climb through the night, and get to the summit just before dawn. Camping on the mountain is prohibited.

Be prepared for fickle weather around and atop the mountain. Summer days can be unbearably hot and muggy, and the nights can be a shocking contrast of freezing cold (bring numerous warm layers and be prepared to put them all on). Wear strong hiking shoes. The sun really burns at high altitudes, so wear protective clothing and a hat; gloves are a good idea, too. Use a backpack, as it keeps your hands free and serves a useful function on the way down: instead of returning to Go-gōme, descend to Shin-Go-gōme on the volcanic sand slide called the *sunabashiri*—sit down on your pack, push off, and away you go.

Fuji-Hakone-Izu National Park A to Z

To research prices, get advice from other travelers, and book travel arrangements, visit www.fodors.com.

BUS TRAVEL

Buses connect Tōkyō with the major gateway towns of this region, but except for the trip to Kawaguchi-ko or Mt. Fuji the price advantage doesn't really offset the comfort and convenience of the trains. If you're interested only in climbing Mt. Fuji, take one of the daily buses directly to Go-gōme from Tōkyō; they run July through August and leave Shinjuku Eki at 7:45 AM, 8:45 AM, and 7:30 PM. The last bus allows sufficient time for the tireless to make it to the summit before sunrise. The journey takes about 2 hours and 40 minutes from Shinjuku and costs ¥2,600. Reservations are required; book seats through the Fuji Kyūkō Highway Bus Reservation Center, the Keiō Highway Bus Reservation Center, the Japan Travel Bureau (which should have English-speaking staff), or any major travel agency.

To return from Mt. Fuji to Tōkyō, take an hour-long bus ride from Shin-Go-gōme to Gotemba (¥1,500). From Gotemba take the JR Tōkaidō and Gotemba lines to Tōkyō Eki (¥1,890), or take the JR Line from Gotemba to Matsuda (¥480) and change to the private Odakyū Line from Shin-Matsuda to Shinjuku (¥750).

Direct bus service runs daily from Shinjuku Eki in Tōkyō to Kawaguchi-ko every hour between 7:10 AM and 10:10 PM (¥1,700). Buses go from Kawaguchi-ko station to Go-gōme (the fifth station on the climb up Mt. Fuji) in about an hour; there are eight departures a day (9:30, 10:10, 10:55, 11:30, 12:45, 1:50, 3:30, and 5:30) until the climbing season (July–August) starts, when there are 15 departures or more, depending on demand. The cost is ¥1,700.

From Kawaguchi-ko, you can also take a bus to Gotemba, then change to another bus for Sengoku; from Sengoku there are frequent buses to Hakone-Yumoto, Togendai, and elsewhere in the Hakone region. On the return trip, three or four buses a day make the two-hour journey from Kawaguchi-ko to Mishima (¥2,130), skirting the western lakes and circling Fuji-san; at Mishima you can transfer to the JR Shinkansen Line for Tōkyō or Kyōto. A shorter bus ride (70 minutes, ¥1,470) goes from Kawaguchi-ko to Gotemba with a transfer to the JR local line.

From Kawaguchi-ko, you can also connect to the Izu Peninsula. Take the bus to Mishima and from there go by train either to Shuzenji or Atami.

The Tōkai Bus Company covers the west coast and central mountains of the Izu area well with local service; buses are not especially frequent, but they do provide the useful option of just hopping off and exploring if you happen to see something interesting from the window.

➤ BUS INFORMATION: **Fuji Kyūkō Highway Bus Reservation Center** (☎ 03/5376–2222). **Keiō Highway Bus Reservation Center** (☎ 03/5376–2222). **Japan Travel Bureau** (☎ 03/3284–7605). **Tōkai Bus Company** (☎ 0557/36–1112 for main office; 0557/22–2511 Shimoda Information Center).

CAR TRAVEL

Having your own car makes sense only for touring the Izu Peninsula, and only then if you're prepared to cope with less than ideal road conditions, lots of traffic (especially on holiday weekends), and the paucity of road markers in English. From Tōkyō take the Tōmei Expressway as far as Ōi-matsuda (about 84 km [52 mi]); then pick up Routes 255 and 135 to Atami (approximately 28 km [17 mi]). From Atami you'll drive another 55 km (34 mi) or so down the east coast of the Izu Peninsula to Shimoda. It takes some effort—but exploring the peninsula *is* a lot easier by car than by public transportation. The best solution is to call either the Nippon or Toyota rental agency in Tōkyō and book a car to be picked up at the Shimoda branch, and then you can go to Shimoda by train. From Shimoda you can drive back up the coast to Kawazu (35 minutes), on to Yūgashima (one hour), and then to Shuzenji (30 minutes).

➤ CONTACTS: **Nippon Interrent** (☎ 03/3469–0919). **Toyota Rent-a-Car** (☎ 03/3263–6321).

TOURS

Sunrise Tours, a division of the Japan Travel Bureau, operates a tour to Hakone, including a cruise across Lake Ashi and a trip on the gondola over Ōwaku-dani (¥15,000 includes lunch and return to Tōkyō by Shinkansen; ¥12,000 includes lunch and return to Tōkyō by bus). Sunrise tours depart daily from Tōkyō's Hamamatsu-chō Bus Terminal and some major hotels.

Once you are on the Izu Peninsula itself, sightseeing excursions by boat are available from a number of picturesque small ports. The Fujikyū Kōgyō company operates a daily ferry to Hatsushima from Atami (23 minutes, ¥1,170 round-trip) and another to the island from Itō (23 minutes, ¥1,150). Izukyū Marine offers a 40-minute tour (¥1,530) by boat from Shimoda to the coastal rock formations at Irō-zaki; from Dōgashima, you can take the Dōgashima Marine short (20 minutes, ¥720) or long (50 minutes, ¥1,020) tours of the rugged Izu west coast.

➤ TOUR CONTACTS: **Dōgashima Marine** (☎ 0558/52–0013). **Fujikyū Kōgyō** (☎ 0557/81–0541). **Izukyū Marine** (☎ 0558/22–1151). **Sunrise Tours** (☎ 03/5796–5454).

TRAIN TRAVEL

Trains are by far the easiest and fastest ways to get to the Fuji-Hakone-Izu National Park area. The gateway stations of Atami, Odawara, and Kawaguchi-ko are well served by comfortable express trains from Tōkyō, on both JR and private railway lines. These in turn connect to local trains and buses that can get you anywhere in the region you want to go. Call the JR Higashi-Nihon Info Line (10–6 daily, except December 31–January 3) for assistance in English.

The *Kodama* Shinkansen from Tōkyō to Atami costs ¥3,570 and takes 51 minutes; JR Passes are valid. The JR local from Atami to Itō takes 25 minutes and costs ¥320. Itō and Atami are also served by the JR *Odoriko* Super Express (not a Shinkansen train). The Tōkyō–Itō run takes 1¾ hours and costs ¥4,070; you can also use a JR Pass. The privately owned Izukyū Railways, on which JR Passes are not valid, makes the Itō–Shimoda run in one hour for ¥1,570.

The Izu-Hakone Railway Line runs from Tōkyō to Mishima (1 hour, 36 minutes, ¥4,090), with a change at Mishima for Shuzenji (31 minutes, ¥500); this is the cheapest option if you don't have a JR Pass. With a JR Pass, a Shinkansen–Izu Line combination will save about 35 minutes and will be the cheapest option. The Tōkyō–Mishima Shinkansen leg (62 minutes) costs ¥4,400; the Mishima–Shuzenji Izu Line leg (31 minutes) costs ¥500.

The transportation hub, as well as one of the major resort areas in the Fuji Five Lakes area, is Kawaguchi-ko. Getting there from Tōkyō requires a change of trains at Ōtsuki. The JR Chūō Line *Kaiji* and *Azusa* express trains leave Shinjuku Eki for Ōtsuki on the half hour from 7 AM to 8 PM (more frequently in the morning) and take approximately one hour. At Ōtsuki, change to the private Fuji-Kyūkō Line for Kawaguchi-ko, which takes another 50 minutes. The total traveling time is about two hours, and you can use your JR Pass as far as Ōtsuki; otherwise, the fare is ¥1,280. The Ōtsuki–Kawaguchi-ko leg costs ¥1,110. Also available are two direct service rapid trains for Kawaguchi-ko that leave Tōkyō in the morning at 6:08 and 7:10 on weekdays, 6:09 and 7:12 on weekends and national holidays.

One train on weekends and national holidays (the *Holiday Kaisoku Picnic-gō*) offers direct express service from Shinjuku, leaving at 8:10 and arriving at Kawaguchi-ko Eki at 10:37. From March through August, JR puts on additional weekend express trains for Kawaguchi-ko, but be aware that on some of them only the first three cars go all the way to the lake. Coming back, you have a choice of late-afternoon departures from Kawaguchi-ko that arrive at Shinjuku in the early evening. Check the express timetables before you go; you can also call either the JR Higashi-Nihon Info Line or Fuji-kyūukō Kawaguchi-ko Eki for train information.

➤ TRAIN INFORMATION: **Fuji-kyūukō Kawaguchi-ko Eki** (0555/72–0017). **Izukyū Corporation** (☎ 0557/53–1111 for main office; 0558/22–3202 Izukyū Shimoda Eki. **JR Higashi-Nihon Info Line** (☎ 03/3423–0111). **Odakyū Reservation Center** (☎ 03/3481–0130).

TRANSPORTATION AROUND
FUJI-HAKONE-IZU NATIONAL PARK

Trains will serve you well in getting from major point to point anywhere in the northern areas of the National Park region and down the eastern coast of the Izu Peninsula. For the Hakone area, the best way to get around is with a Hakone Free Pass, issued by the privately owned Odakyū Railways. This coupon ticket (¥5,500 from Shinjuku Eki in Tōkyō—from which trains leave every 12 minutes for Odawara) allows you to use any mode of transportation in the Hakone area, including the Hakone Tōzan Railway, the Hakone Tōzan bus, the Hakone Ropeway, the Hakone Cruise Boat, and the Sōun-zan cable car. There's a surcharge of ¥870 on the Hakone Free Pass for the upscale *Romance Car,* with comfortable seats and big observation windows, which goes one stop beyond Odawara to Hakone-Yumoto. Beyond Hakone-Yumoto, travel is either on the privately owned Hakone Tōzan Tetsudō Line or by bus.

Reservations are required for the *Romance Car*; buy tickets at any Odakyū Odakyū Travel Service counter or major travel agency, or call the Odakyū Reservation Center. If you have a JR Pass, it is cheaper to take a *Kodama* Shinkansen from Tōkyō Eki to Odawara (the faster *Hikari* does not stop at Odawara) and buy the Hakone Free Pass there (¥4,130) for travel within the Hakone region only. The coupon is valid for three days.

From Hakone-machi buses run every 15–30 minutes to Hakone-Yumoto Eki on the private Odakyū Line (40 minutes, ¥930), and Odawara Eki (one hour, ¥1,150), where you can take either the Odakyū *Romance Car* back to Shinjuku Eki or a JR Shinkansen to Tōkyō Eki. The buses are covered by the Hakone Free Pass.

For the west coast and central mountains of Izu, there are no train connections; unless you are intrepid enough to rent a car, the only way to get around is by bus (☞ Bus Travel, *above*).

From Shimoda, the end of the line on the private Izukyū Railway down the east coast of the peninsula, you travel by bus around the southern cape to Dōgashima. From there, another bus takes you up the west coast as far as Heda and then turns inland to Shuzenji. From Shimoda, you can also take a bus directly north to Shuzenji through the Amagi Mountains (one departure daily at 10:45 AM, ¥2,180). Leaving Shuzenji, take the private Izu-Hakone railway line through the mountains to Mishima. If this is the end of your trip, you can change at Mishima to a *Kodama* Shinkansen for Tōkyō or Kyōto. If you're heading north instead to Ashi-no-ko and Fuji-san, take one of the hourly buses (¥1,140) for the 50-minute trip from Mishima Eki to Hakone-machi.
➤ TRANSPORTATION CONTACTS: **Hakone–Tozan Railway** (☏ 0465/24–2115). **Izu–Hakone Railway** (☏ 0465/77–1200). **Izukyū Corporation** (☏ 0557/53–1111 main offices; 0558/22–3202 Izukyū Shimoda Eki). **Odakyū Reservation Center** (☏ 03/3481–0130).

VISITOR INFORMATION

Especially in summer and fall, the Fuji-Hakone-Izu National Park area is one of the most popular vacation destinations in the country, and most towns and resorts have local visitor information centers. Few of them have staff members who speak fluent English, but you can still pick up local maps and pamphlets, as well as information on low-cost inns, pensions, and guest houses.
➤ TOURIST INFORMATION: **Atami Tourist Association** (✉ 12–1 Ginza-chō, Atami-shi, ☏ 0557/85–2222). **Fuji-Kawaguchiko Tourist Association** (✉ 3631–5 Funatsu, Kawakuchiko-machi, Minami-Tsurugun, ☏ 0555/72–2460). **Hakone-machi Tourist Association** (✉ 698 Yūmoto, Hakone-machi, ☏ 0460/5–8911). **Nishi-Izu Tourist Office** (✉ Dogashima, Nishi-Izu-chō, Kamo-gu, ☏ 0558/52–1268). **Shimoda Tourist Association** (✉ 1–1 Soto-ga-oka, Shimoda-shi, ☏ 0558/22–1531).

3 NAGOYA, ISE-SHIMA, AND THE KII PENINSULA

Japan's fourth-largest city, Nagoya purrs along most contentedly, burdened neither by a second-city complex nor by hordes of tourists. To its southeast are Ise-Shima National Park and the revered Grand Shrines of Ise. Around the untamed Kii Peninsula, views of steep-walled gorges and thickly forested headlands nudging down into pristine bays abound. Fine sandy beaches await in Shirahama, and inland is Yoshino-san, justly famous for its unmatched display of cherry blossoms. For a spiritual retreat, there's Kōya-san, the complex of ancient Buddhist temples set among groves of towering Japanese cypress.

By John
Malloy Quinn

SOMETIMES GIVEN A BAD RAP or dismissed altogether as an unattractive, industry-bent sprawl of concrete, Nagoya in fact has the capacity to pleasantly surprise any visitor who can give it the time.

There is indeed a fair amount of history here, despite the fact that you first notice the bright white skyscrapers sprouting from the ultra-modern station—almost a city in itself. An extensive underground network of shopping malls stretches outward in all directions below the wide, clean streets. Prices are very reasonable, and the variety of goods is astounding.

Prosperous locals and comfortable foreign residents alike will tell you that although Nagoya is undeniably a big and hardworking city, it has a certain small-town feel to it. "Stay awhile, and you know *everyone*," they might say. The laid-back and cheerful attitude provides a refreshing contrast to the endless bustle and impersonality of most large cities.

Away from the city you'll find a wealth of religious architecture, including the famous shrines of Ise and the remarkable temple-mountain, Kōya-san. Add to these the scenic beauty of the Kii Peninsula and the traditional arts of Gifu and Seki, and you have more than enough reasons to visit this corner of Japan.

Nagoya, Ise-Shima, and the Kii Peninsula Glossary

Key Japanese words and suffixes for this chapter include the following: *-bashi* (bridge), *-chō* (street or block), *-chōme* (street), *-dōri* (street or avenue), *eki* (train station), *gaijin* (foreigner), *gawa* (river), *hama* (beach), *-in* (Buddhist temple), *-ji* (Buddhist temple), *jingū* (Shintō temple), *jinja* (Shintō shrine), *-jō* (castle), *-ken* (prefecture), *kōen* ("ko-en," park), *-ku* (section or ward), *kyō* (gorge), *-mon* (gate), *onsen* (hot springs), *sakura* (cherry blossoms), *-san* (mountain, as in Kōya-san, Mt. Kōya), *-shima* or *-jima* (island), *Shinkansen* (bullet train, literally "new trunk line"), *taisha* (shrine), *torii* ("to-ree-ee," gate), and *yama* (mountain).

Pleasures and Pastimes

Castles

Nagoya has a large castle, and although a replica, it's a rather beautiful one. North of Nagoya, in the town of Inuyama, you'll find the genuine ancient article, and its views out over the city and the Kiso-gawa delight those who climb its steep and narrow wooden staircases to the original interior.

Dining

Local Nagoya dishes include *kishimen,* white, flat noodles with a velvety smoothness; *misonikomi udon,* thick noodles cooked in an earthenware pot full of hearty red miso soup with chicken, egg, wood mushrooms, and green onions (you may want to try it with the chili pepper served on the side); *moriguchizuke,* a Japanese pickle made from a special radish, either with or without sweet sake; and *uiro,* a sweet cake made of rice powder and sugar, most often eaten during the tea ceremony. The most highly prized food product of the region is the *ko-chin,* a specially fattened and uniquely tender kind of chicken. Other than these items, Nagoya's cuisine is mostly Kyōto style, but you can also find every type of Japanese and international food in this cosmopolitan city.

Away from the city, on the Ise Peninsula, lobster is especially fine. On the Kii Peninsula, farmers raise cattle for Matsuzaka beef—the town of Matsuzaka is 90 minutes by train from Nagoya. However, the best beef is typically shipped to Tōkyō, Kyōto, and Ōsaka.

For more details on Japanese cuisine, *see* Chapter 14 *and* Dining *in* Smart Travel Tips A to Z.

CATEGORY	COST*
$$$$	over ¥4,500
$$$	¥2,500–¥4,500
$$	¥1,500–¥2,500
$	under ¥1,500

per person for a main course at dinner

Lodging

Nagoya has a range of lodging—from clean, efficient business hotels to large luxury hotels with additional amenities—in three major areas: the district around JR Nagoya Eki, downtown, and the Nagoya-jō area. Though *ryokan* (traditional Japanese inns) are listed below, international-style hotels are often more convenient if you want flexible dining hours.

Temples are another lodging option, especially if you are heading to Kōya-san. Furnishings are rather spartan, but sufficient, and you may be expected to attend morning prayer service. Futons, baths, and amenities are much the same as in ryokans, but the food in temples may be strictly vegetarian. You won't go hungry, nor be pressed into following the faith, and it's a fascinating experience.

For a short course on accommodations in Japan, *see* Lodging *in* Smart Travel Tips A to Z.

CATEGORY	COST*
$$$$	over ¥20,000
$$$	¥15,000–¥20,000
$$	¥10,000–¥15,000
$	under ¥10,000

All prices are for a double room, excluding service and tax.

Outdoor Activities and Sports

Beyond Nagoya many outdoor diversions await. In Gifu city and Inuyama, look for *u-kai*, fishing with cormorants. Gifu's season runs from mid-May to mid-October, and Inuyama's is from June through September. It's great fun if not a particularly active endeavor: the birds are on leashes and do all the work catching the fish. Inuyama also has riverboat rides down the Kiso-gawa. Placid rafting, through steep, green gorges filled with mineral-tinted water, can be done on the Kii Peninsula at Doro-kyō (Doro Gorge). The highest waterfall in Japan is near Nachi. Fine scenery and hiking are possibilities in Ōsugi-kyō, near Owase. For swimming, the most popular beach in the region is at Shirahama, but beautiful bays, lovely beaches, and rocky coves can be found on the Kii Peninsula's entire coast.

Shopping

Craftspeople in and around Nagoya produce several unique items, such as cloisonné, *paulownia* (wood chests), and tie-dyed fabrics. Nagoya is home to the world's largest producer of porcelain, Noritake. The nearby towns of Seto and Tajimi have famous ceramics traditions as well—and factory outlets. In Gifu you can buy paper lanterns and umbrellas. In Seki the traditional skill in forging samurai swords is still practiced. Toba, on the Shima-hantō (Shima Peninsula), is where, in 1893, Kokichi Mikimoto perfected the technique for harvesting pearl-bearing oysters in 1893. Don't expect too many bargains: because of the labor-intensive farming methods, pearls are expensive everywhere.

Temples and Shrines

There's no shortage of religious architecture on the Shima and Kii peninsulas, but two Buddhist temple complexes, Kōya-san and Yoshino-san, are exceptional. Kōya-san, founded in 816, is the more popular of the two. To get a real sense of the place, spend a night at one of its temples.

South of Nagoya are the Grand Shrines of Ise. The shrines, rebuilt every 20 years for the last 1,500 years, are among the most sacred in Japan. Nai-kū, the Inner Shrine, is the home of worship to Amaterasu, the sun goddess and highest Shintō deity.

Exploring Nagoya, Ise-Shima, and the Kii Peninsula

After you've seen the main sights of Nagoya, take a ride out of the city to see fishing with cormorants, pottery, and lantern and sword making. For a second (and longer) excursion, visit the Grand Shrines of Ise, the Shima Peninsula, and the Kii Peninsula, including Kōya-san and Yoshino-san. A logical place to finish the second trip is Nara, which is covered in Chapter 6.

Numbers in the text correspond to numbers in the margin and on the Nagoya and the South Gifu-ken, Ise-Shima, and the Kii Peninsula maps.

Great Itineraries

Nagoya's sights can be seen in a day, and its cosmopolitan atmosphere deserves at least a one-night stay. Tajimi, a major ceramics center, is a short jaunt from the city. The unique tradition of fishing with cormorants may be still observed at Gifu or Inuyama. Kōya-san's mystical temple complex exudes an almost supernatural spirituality, and a visit to nearby Yoshino-san in cherry-blossom season is highly recommended. Farther afield, there is the junglelike, green wilderness of Doro-kyō (Doro Gorge) and the fine beach at Shirahama.

IF YOU HAVE 3 DAYS

With such limited time, head straight from ⊞ **Nagoya** ①–⑧ to ⊞ **Inuyama** ⑩, perhaps stopping in **Tajimi** ⑪ on the way. In Tajimi you can visit the factory outlets, observe some kilns, and even make your own pottery. In Inuyama, see the castle and in the evening enjoy u-kai. If you don't return to Nagoya for a night's sleep, plan to get a very early start the next day for the most mystical place in the region, the 9th-century Buddhist complex of temples at Kōya-san. From there you could go on to Yoshino-san, or go straight to Nara.

IF YOU HAVE 7 DAYS

Start your trip with a full day and night in ⊞ **Nagoya** ①–⑧, covering the castle, the Tokugawa Bijutsukan, Atsuta Jingū, and Noritake China Factory to see the making of porcelain. On the next day go up to ⊞ **Gifu** ⑨ to visit the umbrella- and lantern-making shops. Include the Shangyo Shinko Center in Seki on your tour if sword-making demonstrations are occurring that day—usually the first Sunday of the month—or **Tajimi** ⑪ for some fun with ceramics. The next stop is ⊞ **Inuyama** ⑩ with its original castle and great strolls down by the Kisogawa. Enjoy a ceremonial tea at the Jo-an Teahouse. If you're here during u-kai, be sure to take in the spectacle. On the next day return to Nagoya to change trains for **Ise** ⑫ and a visit to venerated Ise Jingū, one of Japan's three most important Shintō shrines. For the fourth night continue out onto the peninsula to **Toba** ⑬, home of Mikimoto pearls, and the fishing town of ⊞ **Kashikojima** ⑭. On your fifth day backtrack north to Taki to pick up the train to ⛩ **Shingū** ⑰, where you can spend the night after taking a river trip through **Doro-kyo** ⑱. If you have time, the falls near **Nachi** ⑲ should not be missed. On day six take a four-hour bus ride north to ⛩ **Yoshino-san** ㉕ first thing in the morning. This is a particularly worthy inclusion at cherry-blossom time, if you can stand crowds or get up early enough the next day to beat them. On day seven take a train to Hashimoto and on to ⛩ **Kōya-san** ㉔ and plan to spend the night at a Buddhist temple. From Kōya-san it's easy to reach Kyōto, Nara, and Ōsaka.

IF YOU HAVE 9 DAYS

Keep to the seven-day itinerary as far as ⛩ **Kashikojima** ⑭. Then on the way down the peninsula, you could stop off at Misedani for a bus ride and hike up into the scenic ⛩ **Ōsugi-kyo** ⑯, coming back out and heading south by train again to stop for the night in the town of **Owase** ⑮, should ⛩ **Shingū** ⑰ prove too far. Or skip Ōsugi and spend the extra time taking in the spectacular sights and sounds of Nachi-no-taki (Nachi Falls), an easy bus ride from **Nachi** ⑲. Just south from there, you can stop off and enjoy one or more of the fine hot springs in the area, such as Katsuura or Yukawa. Continue along the coast of the Kii Peninsula to spend a night or two at the spa and beach resort of ⛩ **Shirahama** ㉒. From there, via Wakayama, go to ⛩ **Kōya-san** ㉔ for a full 24 hours in and around the monasteries. Then go to ⛩ **Yoshino-san** ㉕ for the next night before exiting the region by taking the train to Nara.

When to Tour Nagoya, Ise-Shima, and the Kii Peninsula

Springtime throughout Japan is the most popular season for travel, especially so when cherry trees bloom in early to mid-April. The weather can be sunny and warm but nowhere near as hot as it can get in late July and August. Autumn is another popular season, especially on the Kii Peninsula, where the Pacific Ocean stays warm and the trees turn their fall colors under bright blue skies. Winter can still be quite warm and sunny in coastal Wakayama-ken, and to a lesser extent, in Mie-ken, so don't be overly afraid of visiting at that time, either.

NAGOYA

By Shinkansen, 1½–2 hrs west of Tōkyō, 1 hr east of Ōsaka, 40 mins east of Kyōto.

During the Tokugawa period (1603–1868), Nagoya was already an important stop on the Tōkaidō post road between Kyōto and Edo (Tōkyō). In 1612 Ieyasu Tokugawa established Nagoya town by permitting his ninth son to build a castle. In the shadow of this magnificent fortress, industry and merchant houses sprang up, as did pleasure quarters for samurai. As a result, the town quickly grew in strategic importance. Supported by taxing the rich harvests of the vast surrounding Nobi plain, the Tokugawa family used the castle as its power center for the next 250 years. By the early 1800s Nagoya's population had grown to around 100,000. Although it was smaller than Edo, where the million-plus population surpassed even that of Paris, Nagoya had become as large as the more established cities of Kanazawa and Sendai.

With the Meiji Restoration in 1868, when Japan began trade with the West in earnest and embraced Western ideas and technology, Nagoya developed rapidly. In 1889, with a population of 157,000, it became a city. When the harbor opened to international shipping in 1907, Nagoya's industrial growth accelerated. By the 1930s it was supporting Japanese expansionism in China with munitions and aircraft. The choice of industry was Nagoya's downfall: very little of the city was left standing by the time the Japanese surrendered unconditionally, on August 14, 1945.

Less than two months after the war's end, ambitious and extensive reconstruction plans were laid, and Nagoya began its remarkable comeback as an industrial metropolis. Today the fourth-largest city in Japan, Nagoya bustles with 2.2 million people living in a 520-square-km (200-square-mi) area. Industry is still booming, with shipbuilding, food processing, and the manufacture of textiles, ceramics, machine tools, automobiles, railway rolling stock, even aircraft. Nagoya Port sees as much trade as ports in Yokohama and Kōbe.

When they rebuilt Nagoya after the war, urban planners laid down a grid system, with wide avenues intersecting at right angles. Hisaya-odōri, a broad avenue with a park in its 328-ft-wide median, bisects the city. At Nagoya's center, an imposing 590-ft-high television tower (useful for getting your bearings) stands as a symbol of modernity. Nagoya-jō is north of the tower, Atsuta Jingū is to the south, Kenchū-ji is to the east, and the JR station is to the west. The Sakae subway station serves as the center of the downtown commercial area, and a second commercial area is next to the JR station.

➊ **JR Nagoya Eki** is like a small city in itself, with a variety of shops in, under, and around the station complex. Look for the big red question-mark icon to find the **Tourist Information Center** (TIC; ☎ 052/541-4301) in the middle of JR Nagoya Eki's central corridor, open daily from 8:30 to 6:45.

➋ The **Nagoya International Center,** or Kokusai Senta (Government Center), as it's known locally, is a wise stop on any foreigner's Nagoya itinerary. Venture one stop from the JR station on the Sakura-dōri Line to the Kokusai Senta station (or take the seven-minute walk through the underground walkway that follows the line), and the center's friendly, multilingual staff will provide you with a wealth of info on Nagoya. You can also get your hands on brochures in several languages about wherever in Japan you might be heading next. ✉ *47–1 Sakura-dōri, Nagono 1-chōme, Nakamura-ku,* ☎ *052/581–0100.* ⊙ *Tues.–Sat. 9–8:30, Sun. 9–5.*

➌ Originally constructed by Tokugawa Ieyasu for one of his sons in 1612, **Nagoya-jō** was severely damaged in 1945 and in 1959 was rebuilt of reinforced concrete. The castle as it stands is notable for its impressive size and for the pair of gold-plated dolphins—one male, one female—mounted atop the *donjon* (principal keep). Inside the castle a museum houses collections of armor, paintings, and Tokugawa family treasures salvaged from the original structure. Instead of there being the usual narrow, steep wooden staircases, an elevator whisks you between floors. Inside the east gate of Nagoya-jō, **Ninomaru Tei-en** (Ninomaru Gardens) has a traditional teahouse built of *hinoki* (Japanese cypress), surrounded by peaceful gardens. A traditional tea ceremony costs ¥500.

To get here by bus from Nagoya Eki, take the Nishi-ku 2 bus and get off at Nagoya-jō Seimon-mae (Main Gate). By subway, go to the Shiyakusho (City Hall) station on the Meijo Line, which is on the Higashiyama and Sakura-dōri lines from the JR station. Nagoya-jō's east gate is one block north of the subway exit. ☎ *052/231–1700.* ✉ *¥500.* ⊙ *Daily 9:30–4:30.*

Delicate colors and intricate hand-painted designs characterize the china of Noritake, the world's largest manufacturer of porcelain. A free,
➍ informative tour of the **Noritake China Factory** is given at 10 and 1 by

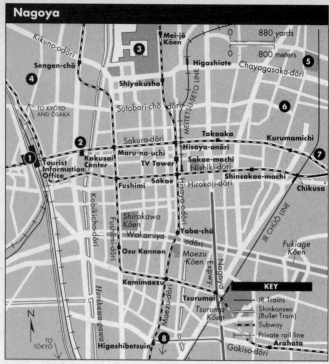

an English-speaking guide, and a short film about the porcelain is also shown. Make a reservation in advance and allow 1–1½ hours for the tour. At the company shop, in front of the north gate, you aren't likely to find any serious bargains, but you may discover pieces not available elsewhere. The factory is a 15-minute walk north of JR Nagoya Eki or five minutes from the Kamejima subway station (one stop north of the JR station on the Higashiyama Line) and is closed the second Sunday of each month. ⊠ 1–36 Mei-eki dōri 3-chōme (north of Kikui-dōri), Noritake-Shin-machi, Nishi-ku, ☎ 052/561–7114 factory; 052/572–5072 shop. ☉ Factory weekdays 10–4, shop Tues.–Sun. 9–5.

★ ❺ Because the pieces in the **Tokugawa Bijutsukan** (Tokugawa Art Museum) are so valuable, the museum displays only a portion of the more than 20,000 art objects, heirlooms, and furnishings at any one time. Most of the relics were handed down from the Tokugawa family to their descendants, the Owari clan, before becoming a part of the collection. The 12th-century hand scrolls illustrating *The Tale of Genji*, widely considered to be the world's first novel, have been designated a National Treasure. If you're visiting specifically to see the scrolls, telephone the museum to make sure they are on display. If not, look for the photos and a later incarnation of the scrolls in Room 6 of the museum.

From Sakae station, take the Meitetsu Seto Line; from Nagoya Eki, take either the Meijo Line or the JR Chūō Line to the Ōzone station, from which you can walk about 10 minutes south. Your other option is to catch a bus from the Green No. 7 stop at the Eki-mae bus station (or the Shiyakusho stop across from Nagoya-jō) to the Shindeki bus stop, then walk three minutes north. ☎ 052/935–6262. ⊡ ¥1,200. ☉ Tues.–Sun. 10–5 (last entry at 4:30).

One of few survivors of the World War II bombs that flattened Nagoya, **Kenchū-ji** is famous for its original 1651 two-story gate. From the JR station, take the Sakura-dōri subway line to the Kuruma-michi station, and then walk three blocks north and turn left and continue for about 1,200 ft; the temple will be on your right. ☎ *052/935–3845.* ✉ *Free.* ⊗ *Daily 9–4:30.*

❼ **Higashiyama Kōen,** a huge expanse of green, encompasses a zoo, botanical gardens, amusement park rides, and a sky tower, offering welcome respite (with a view) from city air, traffic, and noise. The food in the tower restaurant is unspectacular, but it's not a bad place to sit and refuel. Best of all, the park is only 16 minutes from Nagoya Eki. To get there, take the Higashiyama Line to the Higashiyama-kōen station. ☎ *052/782–2111 zoo and botanical gardens; 052/781–5586 sky tower.* ✉ *Zoo and botanical gardens ¥500, sky tower ¥500.* ⊗ *Zoo and botanical gardens Tues.–Sun. 9–4:30; sky tower Tues.–Sun. 9–9:30; tower restaurant Tues.–Sun. 9–9.*

❽ For 1,700 years a shrine has been at the site of **Atsuta Jingū.** After Ise, Atsuta Jingū is the second most important shrine in the country. The **Hōotsukan** (Treasure House) holds one of the emperor's three imperial regalia—the Kusanagi-no-Tsurugi (Grass-Mowing Sword). Nestled among trees more than 1,000 years old, the shrine is an oasis of tradition in the midst of bustling, modern industrialism. Sixty festivals and 10 religious events are held here each year—check with the tourist office to see what's on when you're coming. From Nagoya Eki take the Higashiyama Line east to Sakae Eki; then take the Meijo Line south to Jingū-nishi Eki. ☎ *052/671–4151.* ✉ *Shrine free, Treasure Museum ¥300.* ⊗ *Daily (except last Wed.–Thurs. of each month) 9–4:30.*

Around Nagoya

Nagoya Minato Suizoku-kan (Port of Nagoya Public Aquarium). This is not your average fish tank; practically everything that swims is present. One of the largest in Japan, the aquarium is known especially for its Antarctic Zone. To get here, take the Meijo Line south from Sakae to Nagoya-ko (Nagoya Port). ✉ *1–3 Minato-machi, Minato-ku,* ☎ *052/654–7080.* ✉ *¥1,500.* ⊗ *Apr.–mid-July and Sept.–Nov., Tues.–Sun. 9:30–5:30; mid-July–Aug., Tues.–Sun. 9:30–8; Dec.–Mar., Tues.–Sun. 9:30–5.*

Arimatsu Narumi Shibori Mura (Arimatsu Cloth Dyeing Village). This village once flourished as a *shibori* (tie-dyed cotton) production center, and more than 10 dye houses are still active. At Arimatsu Narumi Shibori Kaikan, you can learn about the history and techniques of the dyeing process and buy exquisite samples of the cloth, which often features striking, alive-looking bright white designs on the deepest indigo. Arimatsu Eki is 25 minutes south of Nagoya on the Meitetsu Nagoya Line. ✉ *60–1 Hashi Higashi-minami, Arimatsu-chō, Midori-ku,* ☎ *052/621–0111.* ✉ *Free.* ⊗ *Thurs.–Tues. 9–4.*

OFF THE
BEATEN PATH

TADO-SAN SUIGŌ TENBO COURSE – If you seek the refreshment and scenery of a hike—and have four to five hours to spare—consider this 14-km (9-mi) loop up to the green plateau of Tado Sanjo Park, then down through maple-lined Tado-kyō (Tado Gorge). The trail begins as a series of switchbacks to the northwest. From the top of the trail, continue west and downhill to meet and follow the river south and then back east, ending where you started. To get there from JR Nagoya Eki, take the Kintetsu or JR train southwest to Kuwana Eki, and then go north on the local line to Tado Eki. The train ride is 35 minutes. Then walk northwest of Tado Eki, cross the river, and head north toward Uga Shrine.

Dining and Lodging

$$$$ ✕ **Kisoji.** Come here for a reasonably priced (¥4,500) *shabu-shabu* dinner (thinly sliced beef and vegetables boiled in broth at your table) and sashimi courses from ¥5,000 to ¥7,000. Western decor prevails, but waitresses wear kimonos. Private tatami rooms are available if you make a reservation. ✉ *Nishiki 3-chōme, Naka-ku,* ☎ *052/951–3755. AE, MC, V.*

$$$$ ✕ **Okura Restaurant.** This is the place where Western businesspeople
★ often entertain their Japanese partners. Choose from Chinese, French, and Japanese cuisine—each on its own floor. Recommended dishes include sautéed abalone, roast duck, steak, and lobster. ✉ *Tōkyō Kaijo Bldg., 23rd–25th floors, 23-34 Sakae 1-chōme, Naka-ku,* ☎ *052/201–3201. Reservations essential. AE, DC, V.*

$–$$$ ✕ **Jin-maru Nishina.** Locals come here to eat and drink at reasonable prices. Whether you relax at the bar, tatami-seating, or tables, the atmosphere is lively and friendly. Everything from Korean-style kimchee dishes to Taiwan-style noodles is served, along with superb sashimi and draft beers—including Guinness! ✉ *Tōkyō Kaijo Bldg., 1st floor, 23-34 Sakae 1-chōme, Naka-ku,* ☎ *052/203–5885. No credit cards. Closed Sun. No lunch.*

$$ ✕ **Yamamotoya.** Nothing but *misonikomi-udon* (udon in a hearty broth with green onions and mushrooms) is served at this basic restaurant. A big, steaming bowl of this hearty, cold-chasing specialty can be had for just ¥1,500. ✉ *2–4–5 Sakae, Naka-ku,* ☎ *052/471–5547. No credit cards.*

$–$$ ✕ **Capricciosa.** This interesting, festive eatery serves unbeatably priced
★ Italian food. Bowls of pasta are massive—one order is more than enough to feed two. Try the *ika-sumi* (squid-ink) spaghetti or authentic thin-crust pizza. The place is three blocks west of Sakae Eki on the south side of Nishiki-dōri, on the second floor. ✉ *ARK Biru, 2nd floor, Nishiki 3–22–7, Naka-ku,* ☎ *052/953–1647. Reservations not accepted. No credit cards.*

$$$$ ⌂ **Nagoya Castle Hotel.** Next to Nagoya-jō, this hotel is a good choice for avid sightseers—its hourly shuttle from Nagoya Eki makes it doubly convenient. Dark-wood paneling and gold carpet grace the lobby filled with comfortable chairs. Guest rooms are spacious, pleasantly furnished, and hung with oil paintings. Ask for a room with a view of Nagoya-jō, which is a treat at night when spotlights illuminate the castle. ✉ *3–19 Hinokuchi-chō, Nishi-ku, Nagoya, Aichi-ken 451-8551,* ☎ *052/521–2121,* FAX *052/531–3313. 237 Western-style rooms, 1 Japanese-style suite, 5 suites. 3 restaurants, indoor pool, hair salon, health club, shops. AE, DC, MC, V.*

$$$$ ⌂ **Nagoya Hilton.** Soft live music, which accompanies the nightly dessert buffet, drifts into the cavernous lobby of the Hilton, giving it an intimate feel. Pink granite with gold accents and live trees help fill the space. Light pink, green, and gold decorate the large guest rooms as well, perfectly complementing the light-wood furnishings and translucent *shōji* (window screens). Views from the 28th-floor Sky Lounge are magnificent. The staff is friendly and multilingual, and the hotel is only five minutes by taxi from Nagoya Eki. ✉ *3–3 Sakae 1-chōme, Naka-ku, Nagoya, Aichi-ken 460-0008,* ☎ *052/212–1111,* FAX *052/212–1225. 422 rooms, 28 Western-style and Japanese-style suites. 3 restaurants, coffee shop, indoor pool, sauna, tennis court, health club, shops, concierge floor. AE, DC, MC, V.*

$$$$ ⌂ **Nagoya Kanko Hotel.** The Imperial Family, professional ballplay-
★ ers, and airline crews are among those regularly served by this, the oldest hotel in Nagoya. A lavish renovation put the well-located, first-class Nagoya Kanko at the top of the ranks with savvy international trav-

elers. Soft-toned carpets and upholstery contrast with dark-wood furnishings. In the lobby, white-brick walls are accented with rich wood paneling. Members of the friendly and attentive staff speak several languages. The breakfast buffet in the tearoom is a particularly good value, at only ¥1,000. If you run short of cash, head to the ATM in the lobby. ✉ *19–30 Nishiki 1-chōme, Naka-ku, Nagoya, Aichi-ken 460-8608,* ☎ *052/231–7711,* FAX *052/231–7719,* WEB *www.nagoyakankohotel.co.jp. 375 rooms, 7 suites. 5 restaurants, 2 bars, room service, shops, concierge, business services. AE, DC, MC, V.*

$$$–$$$$ 🏨 **Hotel Castle Plaza.** A top-notch, reasonably priced hotel, the Castle Plaza has more amenities than most in its price range. The few Japanese-style rooms available are larger than the Western-style rooms. Eleven on-site restaurants serve Japanese and various international cuisines. It's a five-minute walk from the main railway station. ✉ *4–3–25 Meieki, Nakamura-ku, Nagoya, Aichi-ken 450-0002,* ☎ *052/582–2121,* FAX *052/582–8666. 258 Western-style rooms, 4 Japanese-style rooms, 1 suite. 11 restaurants, indoor pool, sauna, gym. AE, MC, V.*

$$$ 🏨 **International Hotel Nagoya.** Close to shopping and dining in Sakae, the International Hotel is a favorite with business travelers. It's 35 years old but doesn't look half its age. Rooms are in bright tones and are fairly spacious. The gold-tone lobby is full of paintings and antique furnishings and has some shops. ✉ *3–23–3 Nishiki, Naka-ku, Nagoya, Aichi-ken 460-0003,* ☎ *052/961–3111,* FAX *052/962–5937. 265 Western-style rooms, 4 Japanese-style rooms, 11 suites. 4 restaurants, bar, shops. AE, DC, MC, V.*

Nightlife

Sakae-chō has a high concentration of restaurants and bars. During the day shoppers and strollers pack its streets, but late at night the area fills mostly with patrons of shady bars called "snacks," places where high fees are charged for women to pour drinks and provide companionship. Unless you've got a lot of cash to burn, avoid such places.

Expats hang out at **Shooter's Sports Bar and Grill** (✉ Pola Nagoya Bldg., 2nd floor, 9–26 Sakae 2-chōme, Naka-ku, ☎ 052/202–7774). Pool tables and the big-screen TV are the main draws, but special events such as All You Can Drink Night (¥1,500) on Monday and Ladies Night on Wednesday pack them in as well. It's open daily from 11:30 AM to 3 AM. Its location just south of Fushimi Subway Station Exit Number 5 is not hard to find.

A young crowd gathers at the wild, five-floor **iD Cafe** (✉ Mitsukoshi Bldg., 1–15 Sakae 3-chōme, Naka-ku, ☎ 052/251–0382). On Wednesday night, foreigners showing a valid gaijin card and passport can enter this dance club free, and drinks are only ¥300.

Getting Around

Four subway lines run under the city's main avenues; the Sakura-dōri and Higashiyama lines have stops under JR Nagoya Eki. The minimum subway fare is ¥200, the maximum is ¥320, and the system is easy to manage, as all subway signs are written in both Japanese and English.

Visitor Information

The city **tourist information office** (✉ 1–4 Meieki 1-chōme, Nakamura-ku, ☎ 052/541–4301) will give you city maps and make hotel reservations. There is another branch of the tourist office in the center of JR Nagoya Eki; both are open 9–5 daily.

SOUTH GIFU-KEN

Just north of Nagoya, among the foothills of the Hida Sanmyaku (Hida Mountains), old Japan resonates in the area's umbrella, lantern, pottery, and sword makers; in its fishing with cormorants; and in the ancient castle, Inuyama-jō.

Gifu

❾ *20 mins northwest of Nagoya on the JR Tōkaidō Line or Meitetsu Honsen Line.*

Gifu, known for its paper-lantern and umbrella making, as well as cormorant fishing, is also a center of clothing manufacture, and you'll see more than 2,000 wholesale shops within a couple of city blocks as you leave the station. *Kasa* (oiled-paper umbrellas) are made in small family-owned shops and can be bought in Gifu's downtown stores. *Chōchin* (paper lanterns) are made locally as well.

Brightly blooming trees and flowers everywhere attest to the locals' love of color—as do the trains, painted a bright magenta. On summer evenings you can witness u-kai, an organized opportunity to party while watching an ancient way of catching fish. Fishermen, dressed in traditional reed skirts, glide down the river in their boats. Suspended in front of each boat is a brazier full of burning pinewood that attracts *ayu* (river smelt) to the surface. *U* (cormorants), up to 12 per boat, are slipped overboard on leashes to snap up the fish. Because of a small ring around each of the birds' necks, the birds cannot swallow the fish whole. Instead, their long necks expand to hold as many as five wiggling fish. When a bird can't take in another ayu, the fisherman hauls it back to the boat, where it regurgitates its neckful. After many successful hauls, a bird is rewarded with a cut-up fish to swallow. Ayu, which eat only green algae from the rocks, are indeed delicious, and a bucketful of them smells like sliced watermelon.

If you're interested in the craft of kasa making, visit the **Sakaida Umbrella Company** (✉ 27 Kanō Nakahiroe-machi, ☎ 058/272–3865), an authentic studio and shop 10 minutes on foot southeast of the JR station. It's open weekdays 7–5 except at lunchtime.

To watch chōchin being crafted, head to the **Murase Gifu Lantern Company** (✉ 23 Imako-machi, ☎ 0582/62–0572), north of and next to the city hall. Take the Meitetsu bus (bound for Takatomi) from Shin-Gifu Eki-mae to Shiyakusho-mae. It's open daily from 10 to 5:30.

U-kai (☎ 0582/62–0104 Gifu City U-kai Office; 0582/62–4415 Tourist Information Office) can be viewed for free from the banks of the Nagara-gawa, just east of Nagara Bridge at around 7:30 PM. Your other option is to buy a ticket for one of approximately 130 boats that ply the waters, each carrying from 10 to 30 spectators. Allow two hours for a u-kai outing: an hour and a half to eat and drink and a half hour to watch the fishing. Boat trips (¥3,300) begin at about 6 PM nightly; reservations, made through Gifu City U-kai Office or Tourist Information Center, are essential. Though you can usually buy food on-board, you're better off bringing your own. There's no fishing on nights during a full moon.

An unusual statue of Buddha (45 ft tall), with a 6-ft-long ear as a symbol of omnipotent wisdom, is housed in **Shōhō-ji**. The statue, completed

South Gifu-ken, Ise-Shima, and the Kii Peninsula

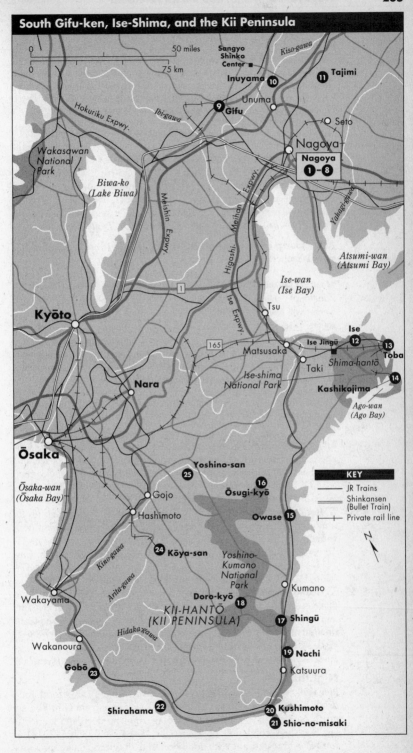

centuries ago, is one of the three largest Buddhas in Japan. It was constructed of pasted-together paper *sutra* (prayers), coated with clay and stucco and then lacquered and gilded; it took 38 years to complete. The orange-and-white temple is 15 minutes by bus from the Gifu JR station. Take Bus 11 (Nagara–Sagiyama) to Gifu Park, walk south along the main road two blocks, then turn right (west); the temple will be on your right. ⊠ 8 *Daibutsu-chō*, ☎ *058/264–2760*. ⊡ ¥150. ⏲ *Apr.–Nov., daily 8:30–5; Dec.–Mar., daily 9–4*.

A major Gifu landmark is **Gifu-jō.** The castle is relatively new (1951), having replaced a 16th-century structure destroyed by an 1891 earthquake. You can either walk—quite a workout—or take the cable car from Gifu Park (¥600 one-way, ¥1050 round-trip). The castle commands a fine view of the city and the surrounding mountains, and the cool breeze are refreshing, especially if you've climbed the hill. There's also a small historical museum in the surrounding park (¥300). ⊠ *Gifu-jō, Ōmiya-chō*, ☎ *058/263–4853*. ⊡ ¥200. ⏲ *Daily 9–5*.

A city **tourist information office** (☎ 058/262–4415) is at the train station. It's open daily from 10 to 7.

OFF THE
BEATEN PATH

SANGYO SHINKO CENTER (Sword Industry Promotion Center) – Seki is a traditional center of sword production. A trip to the Shangyo Shinko Center will help you appreciate the artistry and skill of Japanese swordsmiths. Free demonstrations are held on the first Sunday of the month from March to September and in November and, during the Seki Cutlery Festival, the second weekend in October. The festival is a good time to look for bargains on world-class cutlery. Seki is 30 minutes northeast of Gifu via the Meitetsu Honsen Line. Ask for directions at the station. ☎ *0575/22–3131*. ⊡ *Free*.

Lodging

$$$$ 🏨 **Ryokan Sugiyama.** Close to the Nagara River, and embodying a tasteful blend of traditional and modern, Sugiyama is Gifu City's best Japanese inn. The presence of the river adds to the mood of peace and quiet. Very good food, including ayu, is usually served in the rooms. ⊠ *73–1 Nagara, Gifu-shi, Gifu-ken 502-0071*, ☎ *058/231–0161*, 𝔽𝔸𝕏 *058/233–5250*. 49 rooms. AE. MAP.

$$$ 🏨 **Hotel 330 Grand Gifu.** This tall, modern hotel prides itself on its imported American art and furnishings. The place is an outstanding value, with comfortable Western-style rooms done in grays and lilacs. To get here, walk one block north and two blocks west of Gifu Eki. ⊠ *5–8 Nagazumi-chō, Gifu-shi, Gifu-ken 500-8175*, ☎ *058/267–0330*, 𝔽𝔸𝕏 *058/264–1330*. 147 rooms. Restaurant. AE, V.

$–$$ 🏨 **Grand Palais Hotel.** This friendly, convenient, and comfortable place is directly across from Gifu Eki. Rooms are simple, but elegant, and on-site restaurants serve Western-style, Chinese, Japanese, and Continental menus. ⊠ *8–20 Kogane-machi, Gifu-shi, Gifu-ken 500-8842*, ☎ *058/265–4111*, 𝔽𝔸𝕏 *058/263–5233*. 180 Western-style rooms, 1 Japanese-style room. 4 restaurants, bar, lobby lounge. No credit cards.

Nightlife

Bier Hall (☎ 058/266–8868) is a nice dive with a ¥1,000 food-and-drink special from 5:30 PM to 7:30 PM. To get here from Gifu Eki, go north on Kinkabashi, turn east on Nagazumicho-dōri, and go north again at the second alley on your right. **That's** (☎ 058/265–7318), a fun bar and restaurant with good beer and an eclectic menu, presents live blues music on Friday night. It's on the north side of Yanagase near Nagarabashi-dōri and is closed Monday.

Inuyama

❿ *20 mins east of Gifu by Meitetsu Komaki Line, 30 mins north of Nagoya by Meitetsu Inuyama Line.*

Like Gifu, Inuyama is a cormorant-fishing town, and as in Gifu, spectator-boat tickets are available from the major hotels. They cost ¥3,300. A pleasant way to see the Kiso-gawa is on a completely tame raft. To travel the hour-long, 13-km (8-mi) river trip (¥3,400), take the train on the Meitetsu Hiromi Line from Inuyama to Nihon-Rhine-Imawatari. Once there, check out several companies before selecting the type of boat you prefer.

★ The origins of Inuyama's most famous sight, **Inuyama-jō,** are debated: guidebooks typically state the castle was built in 1440, but local literature, including brochures you'll pick up at the castle itself, say its construction was in 1537. Controversy aside, the castle, which is also known as Hakutei-jō, is set on beautiful grounds on a bluff overlooking the Kiso-gawa. Climb up the creaky staircases to the top floor for a great view of the river and hills. From Inuyama-Yuen Eki, walk southwest along the river for 15 minutes. ☎ *0568/61–1711.* ✆ *¥400.* ◷ *Daily 9–4:30.*

OFF THE BEATEN PATH

TSUGAO-ZAN – A hike to Tsugao-zan will reveal even more of the pleasant scenery near the Inuyama-jō. Start on the riverside trail at the base of Inuyama-jō. Follow the trail east past the Japan Monkey Park, then north to Jakkō-in (built in 654), where the maples blaze in fall. From here you can climb Tsugao-zan or continue northeast to Ōbora Pond and southeast to Zenjino Eki, where you can catch the Meitetsu Hiromi Line two stops back to Inuyama Eki. The train passes through Zenjino four times an hour. From Inuyama-jō to Zenjino Eki is an 8-km (5-mi) hike. Allow 2½ hours from the castle to the top of Tsugao-zan; add another hour if you continue to Zenjino via Ōbora Pond.

The pretty stretch of the **Kiso-gawa** that flows beneath the cliff-top Inuyama-jō has been dubbed the Japanese Rhine. One well-established boating company that offers trips on the Kiso-gawa is **Nippon Rhine Kankō** (☎ *0574/26–2231*).

In Uraku-en, the garden of the Meitetsu Inuyama Hotel, the lovely **Jo-an Teahouse** is a registered National Treasure. The building was constructed in Kyōto by Grand Master Urakusai Oda in 1618 and moved to its present site in 1971. Tea is served for ¥500, or you can hire the teahouse for your own private ceremony for ¥25,000. It's less than ½ km (¼ mi) from Inuyama-jō. ⊠ *107–1 Kita-Koken,* ☎ *0568/61–4608.* ✆ *Teahouse and gardens ¥1,000.* ◷ *Mar.–Nov., daily 9–5; Dec.–Feb., daily 9–4.*

Lodging

$$$–$$$$ 🏨 **Meitetsu Inuyama Hotel.** This hotel's location on the Kiso-gawa gives it good views and convenience to local sights. Sunny rooms all have nice views; those facing the castle are best. The lobby is bright and lively; the hotel grounds and hot springs are relaxing. ⊠ *107–1 Kita-Koken, Inuyama, Aichi-ken 484-0082,* ☎ *0568/61–2211,* ℻ *0568/62–5750. 99 Western-style rooms, 27 Japanese-style rooms. 2 restaurants, hot springs. AE, V.*

Getting Around

If you are headed to Inuyama from Seki, take the JR Line. From Gifu you can take the JR Line, but the privately operated Meitetsu Line is more convenient. If you want to use your JR Pass, take the JR train as far as Unuma and change to the Meitetsu Line for the three-minute last leg to Inuyama. Tajimi and Inuyama are not connected by rail.

Tajimi

⑪ *26 mins from Nagoya on the JR Chūō Line.*

Tajimi has a nearly 2,000-year-old tradition as a ceramics center. Mino Momoyama ceramics, dating from the 16th-century Momoyama period, are legendary, and four major types—Shino, Oribe, Ki-seto, and Seto-guro—are said to be entirely unique to this region. Shino ceramics have a creamy white glaze spotted with dark crimson. Oribe ceramics are a semitranslucent dark green, reflecting the tastes of the 16th-century warrior and tea master Oribe Furuta. Ki-seto pieces, which were popular for tea ceremony during the Momoyama Period, have a light yellowish brown color. Seto-guro ceramics look as if they were excavated from a meteorite: burned, blistered, black as coal, these often distorted pieces reflect the harsh conditions in which they are fired. They are said to have been a favorite of the famed 16th-century tea master Sen-no-Rikyu. Today, ceramics made in this region are called Mino-yaki and make up about half of the tableware ceramics used in Japan. Industry also uses the ceramics made here—for bricks, tiles, and spark plugs, among other things. There are thousands of kilns in the area, as well as numerous factory outlets where you can choose from an infinite range of types, colors, and prices.

At **Azuchimomoyama** (✉ 1–9–17 Higashi-machi, ☎ 0572/25–2233) you can make your own pottery. **Kokei Dojo** (✉ 2–29 Sumiyoshi-chō, ☎ 0572/22–0129) is a ceramics studio where you can try your hand at this ancient art.

The Tajimi **Tourist Information Center** (☎ 0572/24–6460) can help you sort out which ceramic outlets to visit depending on your tastes and budget. It's on the second floor of the building on the right as you exit the front of the station.

ISE-SHIMA NATIONAL PARK AND THE KII PENINSULA

Hanging like a fin underneath central Honshū, the Ise-Shima and Kii peninsulas provide a scenic and sacred counterweight to Japan's over-built industrial corridor. Ise-Shima National Park—which holds the supremely venerated shrines of Ise Jingū—extends from Ise east to Toba (the center of the pearl industry), and south to the indented coastline and pine-clad islands near Kashikojima. Farther down the coast, the Kii Peninsula has magnificent marine scenery, coastal fishing villages and resorts, and the remarkable temple-mountain, Kōya-san. Nearby Yoshino-Kumano Kokuritsu Kōen (Yoshino-KumanoNational Park) has pristine gorges, holy mountains, and another large, ancient Buddhist community at Yoshino-san, with its gorgeous hillside sakura flowering in early April.

Ise

⑫ *80 mins south of Nagoya by Kintetsu Limited Express (longer by JR local), 2 hrs east of Kyōto by JR Kyūko Express, 1 hr and 40 mins east of Nara by JR, 2 hrs east of Ōsaka by private Kintetsu Line.*

Ise is a small town whose income derives mainly from the pilgrims who visit Ge-kū and Nai-kū, the Outer and Inner shrines, respectively. The most crowded times to visit Ise Jingū are during the Grand Festival, held October 15–17 every year, when thousands come to see the pageantry, and on New Year's Eve and Day, when Shintō believers pray for a good new year.

★ Astounding as it may be, all of the temple-complex buildings that make up **Ise Jingū** (Grand Shrines of Ise) are rebuilt every 20 years, in accordance with Shintō tradition. To begin a new generational cycle, exact replicas of the previous halls are erected with new wood, using the same centuries-old methods, on adjacent sites. Then the old buildings are dismantled. The main halls you can now see—the 61st set—were completed in 1993 at a cost estimated to be more than ¥4.5 billion.

Deep in a park full of ancient Japanese cedars, **Ge-kū**, which dates from AD 477, is dedicated to Toyouke Ō-kami, goddess of agriculture. Its buildings are simple, predating the influx of Chinese and Korean influence that swept through the country in the 6th century. Its plain design makes it seem part of the magnificent grounds. It's made from unpainted *hinoki* (cypress), with a fine, closely cropped thatched roof. Again, you can see very little of the exterior of Ge-kū—only its roof and glimpses of its walls—and none of its interior. Four fences surround the shrine, and only the imperial family and its envoys may enter.

The same is true for the even more venerated **Nai-kū**, southwest of Ge-kū. Nai-kū is where the Yata-no-Kagami (Sacred Mirror) is kept, one of the three sacred treasures of the imperial regalia. The shrine, said to date from 4 BC, also houses the spirit of the sun goddess Amaterasu, who, according to Japanese mythology, was born of the left eye of Izanagi, one of the first two gods to inhabit the earth. According to legend, Amaterasu was the great-great-grandmother of the first mortal emperor of Japan, Jimmu. Thus, she is revered as the ancestral goddess-mother and guardian deity of Japan. The Inner Shrine's architecture is simple. If you did not know its origin, you would almost think it classically modern. The use of unpainted cypress causes Nai-kū to blend into the ancient forest that circles it.

Both Grand Shrines possess a natural harmony that the more contrived buildings in later Japanese architecture do not. You can see very little of either through the wooden fences surrounding the shrines. But even though shrine sightseeing has certain limits, the reward is in the spiritual aura surrounding Nai-kū and Ge-kū. This condition, where the inner experience is assigned more importance than the physical encounter, is very traditionally Japanese. Entry to the grounds of both shrines, which are open sunrise to sunset, is free.

From either the Kintetsu or JR Ise-shi station it's only a 10-minute walk through town to the Outer Shrine. A frequent shuttle bus makes the 6-km (4-mi) trip between Ge-kū and Nai-kū; a bus also goes directly from the Inner Shrine to Ise Eki.

Dining and Lodging

$$$$ ✕ **Restaurant Wadakin.** If you love beef, you may want to make a gustatory pilgrimage to Matsuzaka, a train stop west of Ise. Restaurant Wadakin claims to be the originator of Matsuzaka beef's fame. The cattle are raised with loving care on the restaurant's farm. Sukiyaki or the chef's steak dinner satisfy both your taste buds and any craving for red meat. ✉ *1878 Naka-machi, Matsuzaka,* ☎ *0598/21–3291. No credit cards. Closed 4th Tues. of month.*

$ ▦ **Hoshide Ryokan.** A small Japanese inn in a traditional-style wooden building a short walk from the Ge-kū and the Kintetsu Eki, Hoshide Ryokan is bare and simple, with a shared Japanese bath, but it has clean tatami rooms and congenial hosts—at a bargain price. ✉ *2–15–2 Kawasaki, Ise, Mie-ken 516,* ☎ *0596/28–2377,* 📠 *0596/27–2830. 13 Japanese-style rooms with shared bath. AE, MC, V.*

Getting Around

To travel to the shrines from Nagoya by JR, change at Taki (two hours from Nagoya) and take the local line to Ise. The fastest and most direct route is on the privately owned Kintetsu Line's Limited Express (¥2,320) to Uji-Yamada. (Ise has two stations five minutes apart, Ise-shi and Uji-Yamada, the main station.)

Toba

13 *30 mins east of Ise by JR train or bus.*

Before Kokichi Mikimoto (1858–1954) perfected a method for cultivating pearls here in 1893, the little treasures were rarely found. *Ama* (female divers)—women were believed to have bigger lungs—would dive all day long, bringing up a thousand oysters, but they wouldn't necessarily find a valuable pearl. Thanks to Mikimoto, the odds have changed slightly. For even after the considerable effort of injecting an irritating substance—rounded muscarine, as it happens, from Iowa—into two-year-old oysters, only one in two bears pearls, and no more than 5% are of gem quality. Because the two-year-old oyster takes three more years to secrete layer after layer of nacre and conchiolin over this implant to form the pearl, these gems remain expensive.

Before pearl-oyster farming, women dove for pearls with more frequency than now. Such a hit-or-miss operation can no longer support them in the face of the larger quantities (and cheaper prices) possible through Mikimoto's research and farming. However, on the outlying islands, women do still dive for abalone, octopus, and edible seaweed.

Toba today is a resort town filled with resort hotels and resort activities.

On Pearl Island, 500 yards southeast from Toba Eki, **Mikimoto Shinju no Hakubutsukan** (Mikimoto Pearl Museum) gives tours, conducted in Japanese, but the guides usually speak some English, and the accompanying film has an English voice-over. A demonstration is also given by female pearl divers. The museum is on the bay between Toba Eki and Kintetsu Nakajo Eki. ☎ *0599/25–2028,* ✉ *¥1,500.* ⊙ *Apr.–Oct., daily 8:30–5; Nov.–Mar., daily 9–4.*

Toba Suizokukan (Toba Aquarium) showcases native and exotic marine life, such as rare Alaskan sea otters and Baikal seals. The aquarium is across from the Kintetsu Nakajo Eki. ☎ *0599/25–2028.* ✉ *¥2,400.* ⊙ *Mar. 21–Nov. 30, daily 8:30–5; Dec. 1–Mar. 20, daily 9–5.*

Cruise boats make 50-minute tours of the bay (¥1,460) and ferries go to the outer islands from Ise-wan ferry pier south of the Toba Suizokukan.

Lodging

Because Toba is very popular during peak seasons, you might want to consider staying in Kashikojima, 40 minutes away by rail.

$$$$ 🏨 **Toba International Hotel.** Toba's chief resort hotel sits on a bluff overlooking the town and bay. Take a room facing the sea and be sure to get up for the marvelous sunrises. The combination rooms have a Western-style bed and bathroom and a tatami-floor sitting area. ⊠ *1–23–1 Toba, Mie-ken 517-0011,* ☎ *0599/25–3121,* 🖷 *0599/25–3139. 50 Western-style rooms, 30 Japanese-style rooms, 67 combination rooms. 2 restaurants, bar, pool, boating, fishing. AE, DC, V.*

Getting Around

You can take one of two routes from Ise to Toba: a 45-minute bus ride from near Nai-kū, for ¥980, or the more scenic JR train, for ¥610. Buses

run every hour; the last one leaves at 3:56 PM. The bus route follows the Ise-Shima Skyline Drive, which has fine mountainous and wooded scenery.

Kashikojima

★ ⑭ *50 mins south by bus from Toba, 2 hrs south by train on the Kintetsu Line from Nagoya.*

The jagged coastline at Ago-wan (Ago Bay) presents a dramatic final view of the Ise Peninsula, and the approach to Kashikojima is very scenic if you go out to the tip of the headland to Goza, through the fishing village of Goza itself, then into the bay on a ferry, past hundreds of rafts from which pearl-bearing oysters are suspended.

Be sure to visit **Daio,** the fishing village tucked behind a promontory. Standing above the village is a grand lighthouse, open to visitors daily 9–5 for an entrance fee of ¥80. To reach this towering structure, walk up the narrow street lined with fish stalls at the back of the harbor. From this lighthouse, you can see **Anori,** the oldest (1870) stone lighthouse in Japan, 11 km (7 mi) east. Between the two lighthouses on the curving bay are small fishing villages, coffee shops, and restaurants.

Lodging

$$$$ ⊡ **Ryokan Ishiyama-so.** On tiny Yokoyama-jima in Ago-wan, this
★   small concrete inn is just a two-minute ferry ride from Kashikojima. Phone ahead, and your hosts will meet you at the quay. The inn is nothing fancy, but it does offer warmth and hospitality. The meals, included in the room rate, are good, too. ⊠ *Yokoyama-jima, Kashikojima, Ago-chō, Shima-gun, Mie-ken 517-0500,* ☎ *05995/2–1527,* FAX *05995/ 2–1240. 10 rooms, 4 with bath. AE, MC, V.*

$$$$ ⊡ **Shima Kanko Hotel.** This large and established resort hotel has
★   grand views over Ago-wan, especially at sunset. Staff members are friendly and efficient and speak some English. The hotel's restaurants serve the best Western cuisine on the Shima Peninsula, using the delicious local lobster and abalone. The guest rooms, done in beige and white, are spacious and well furnished, and all have views of the bay. A shuttle will pick you up from Kashikojima Eki if you come by train. ⊠ *731 Shimmei Ago-chō, Shima-gun, Mie-ken 517-0502,* ☎ *05994/ 3–1211,* FAX *05994/3–3538. 150 Western-style rooms, 50 Japanese-style rooms. 5 restaurants, pool, hair salon, shops. AE, DC, MC, V.*

Getting Around

The Kintetsu Line continues from Toba to Kashikojima (about ¥900) on an inland route. There are also two buses a day, at 9:40 and 2:25 (¥1,400). To take a coastal route, get off the train at Ugata and take a bus to Nakiri; then change buses for one to Goza, from which frequent ferries go to Kashikojima. A trip directly to Kashikojima from Nagoya on the Kintetsu rail line costs ¥3,300.

It's possible to follow the coast from Kashikojima to the Kii Peninsula, but there is no train, and in many places the road cuts inland, making the journey long and tedious. From Kashikojima or Toba you are better off taking the Kintetsu Line back to Ise to change to the JR Sangu Line and travel to Taki, where you can change to another JR train to go south to the Kii Peninsula. If you prefer to skip the peninsula, take the Kintetsu Line directly to Nagoya or go to Matsuzaka to connect to Nara and Kyōto.

Kii Peninsula

Owase

🕒 *120 km (72 mi) from Kashikojima, 100 km (60 mi) from Ise.*

🕕 The first major town as you head down the coast from Ise-Shima National Park is Owase. **Ōsugi-kyō** with its untrammeled mountain wilderness and many waterfalls, can be accessed by car from near here or by bus from Misedani Eki, a stop on the JR Kisei Line southwest of Taki.

DINING AND LODGING

$–$$$ ✕ **Brasserie Couscous.** Take a rest and savor some excellent Mediterranean food at Brasserie Couscous. The chef will be happy to show you his fishing trophy photos, the authentic pizza is incredible, and the wine and beer selection is impeccable. Selections start at ¥1,300. ⊠ *2–22 Sakae-chō,* ☎ *05972/3–2586. No credit cards. Closed Mon. No lunch.*

$ ⊡ **Business Hotel Phoenix.** Should you want to stay overnight in Owase, check into the very economical and friendly Hotel Phoenix. A room costs ¥9,800: it's nothing fancy, but suffices for a quick stopover. It's a five-minute walk from the JR station. ⊠ *5–25 Sakae-chō, Owase-shi, Mie-ken 519-3618,* ☎ *05972/2–8111,* ℻ *05972/2–8116. 30 rooms. Restaurant. AE, DC, MC, V.*

Shingū

🕗 *2 hrs south of Taki by JR Limited Express, 2 hrs southwest of Kashikojima by the Kintetsu and JR lines, 3½ hrs south of Nagoya by JR.*

Shingū is useful as a jumping-off point for an inland excursion to Doro-kyō. One of the few north–south roads penetrating the Kii Peninsula begins in town and continues inland to Nara by way of Doro-kyō and Gojo. A drive on this winding, steep, narrow road, especially on a bus, warrants a dose of motion-sickness medicine. The mossy canyon walls outside your window, the rushing water far below, and the surrounding luxuriant greenery inspire a deep sense of calm and wonder, but frequent sharp curves provide plenty of adrenaline surges to counteract it.

DINING AND LODGING

$ ✕ **Dai Kichi.** Typical grilled meats such as chicken, pork, and beef are served in this tiny, friendly place across from the station. À la carte orders begin at about ¥300 each. ⊠ *Eki-mae dōri,* ☎ *0735/22–6577. No credit cards.*

$ ⊡ **Shingū-Yui Hotel.** Friendly staff, convenience, and clean, fair-size rooms make this a viable option if you're staying overnight in Shingū. It's next to the post office, a five-minute walk from the train station. ⊠ *6696–10 Shingū, Shingū-shi, Wakayama-ken 647,* ☎ *0735/22–6611,* ℻ *0735/22–4777. 82 rooms. Restaurant. AE, DC, MC, V.*

Doro-kyō

🕘 *40 mins north of Shingū by JR bus.*

As you travel up the Kumano River from Shingū, the walls of the steep-sided Doro-kyō (Doro Gorge) begin to rise around you. From late May to early June, azaleas line the banks. Farther up, sheer 150-ft cliffs tower above the aquamarine Kumano-gawa, which alternates between rapids and quiet stretches.

The best way to take in this gorge, one of the country's finest, is on a four-hour trip (¥5,100) upriver on a flat-bottomed, fan-driven boat. Outside seats on the boats are the best and usually have odd numbers from 3 to 23 or even numbers from 26 through 48. You can book a trip that includes both bus and boat from the tourist information of-

fice in the JR Shingū Eki plaza, or if you have a JR Pass, save ¥1,120 by taking a 40-minute bus ride from Shingū Eki to Shiko, the departure point for the boats going up river.

The boat trip doesn't venture much farther than Doro-hatchō before returning to Shiko. You can, however, hire different boats (two hours round-trip, ¥3,280) to explore the two other gorges and rapids that extend for several miles upstream.

From Doro-hatchō (or Shiko) you can take a bus back to Shingū. If you do not want to continue around the Kii Peninsula, an alternative is to backtrack by bus as far as Shiko and pick up the Shingū-Nara bus. The bus travels seven hours from Shingū (six from Shiko) through the heart of Yoshino-Kumano National Park to Nara, stopping at Gojo, from which you can make your way to Kōya-san and Yoshino-san.

Nachi
19 *10 mins south of Shingū by JR.*

Nachi-no-taki, said to be the highest waterfall in Japan, has a drop of 430 ft. At the bus stop near the falls, a torii at the top of several stone steps leads down to a paved clearing near the foot of the falls. A 20-minute bus ride (¥600) from the Nachi train station gets you here.

For a view from the top, climb up the path from the bus stop to **Nachi Taisha,** one of the three great shrines of the Kii area. Reputed to be 1,400 years old, it's perched just above the waterfall. Next to the shrine is the 1587 Buddhist temple Seiganto-ji, which is the starting point for a 33-temple Kannon pilgrimage through western Honshū.

20 Thirty large, evenly spaced rocks march out into the sea as if following a line from **Kushimoto** toward Ō-shima, an island 2 km (1 mi) offshore. It was here that the first American set foot on Japanese soil, about 100 years before Perry, although only to replenish his ship's water supply. Kushimoto is a resort town, just 35 minutes from Nachi by JR train, and with direct flights to Nagoya and Ōsaka, it's popular among domestic vacationers.

21 A couple of miles from Kushimoto, **Shio-no-misaki** is Honshū's southernmost point. It's marked by a white lighthouse stationed high above its rocky cliffs. Adjacent to the lighthouse is a good spot for picnics and walks along the cliff paths. The beach looks inviting, but due to sharp rocks and currents, swimming is not a good idea.

Shirahama
22 *75 mins southeast of Nachi, 3 hrs south of Ōsaka by JR train.*

Rounding the peninsula, 54 km (34 mi) northeast of Kushimoto, Shirahama is considered by the Japanese to be one of the best hot-spring resorts in the country. It does have attractive craggy headlands and coves. One of the peninsula's few wide, sandy beaches is here. The climate, which allows beach days in the winter, does give Shirahama appeal as a base to explore the area. A 17-minute bus ride from the train station gets you to the town.

Along the beach, between stretches of development, **Sandan-beki** is a cliff with caves underneath, which used to be the lair of pirates during the Heian era (794–1185). It costs nothing to stand on the cliff, but to enter the caves below—a sort of museum where you can see the types of attack boats the pirates used—and to view the pirates' old, dark, forbidding Buddhist sanctuary, it'll cost you ¥1,000. The sight is open daily 10–5:30.

Soak in the open-air **Sakino-yu Onsen,** a hollow among the wave-beaten rocks facing the Pacific, where it's said that Emperors Saimei (594–661) and Mommu (683–707) once bathed. It's free, and it's 1 km (½ mi) south of the main beach, below Hotel Seymor. ⌂ *Free.* ☉ *Daily, except 4th Wed. of each month, dawn–dusk.*

The outdoor spring, **Sogen-no-yu,** is set in a peaceful garden. Bathers are commonly segregated at this (and other outdoor baths). ⌂ *¥500.* ☉ *Daily 6 AM–7 PM.*

LODGING

$$$ ⊡ **Seamone.** Guest rooms here are large and restful and have magnificent views of the coast. Western-style rooms are slightly smaller and less expensive than the Japanese-style rooms. Meals are prepared with attention to detail and presentation and, unless you have a suite, are served in the main dining hall. ⊠ *1821 Shirahama-chō, Nishimuro-gun, Wakayama-ken 049,* ☎ *0739/43–1100,* 𝔽𝔸𝕏 *0739/43–1110. 140 Western-style and Japanese-style rooms. Restaurant, pool. AE, V.*

Gobō

㉓ *40 mins north of Shirahama by JR.*

Between Shirahama and Wakanoura is the famous **Dōjō-ji** in Gobō. According to legend, Kiyohime, a farmer's daughter, became enamored of a young priest, Anchin, who often passed by her house. One day she blurted out her feelings to him. He, in turn, promised to return that night to see her. However, during the course of the day, the priest had second thoughts and returned to Dōjō-ji. Spurned, Kiyohime became enraged. She turned herself into a dragon and set out in pursuit of Anchin, who, scared out of his wits, hid under the temple bell, which had not yet been suspended. Kiyohime sensed his presence and wrapped her dragon body around the bell. Her fiery breath heated the bell until it became red-hot, and the next morning the charred remains of Anchin were found under the bell.

The most interesting thing about the temple is the legend, but if you want to stop, get off the train at Dōjō-ji Eki, one stop south of Gobō Eki. As at most non-heavily touristed temples, you may wander around outside and onto the porch of this one at any time.

KŌYA-SAN AND YOSHINO-SAN

Kōya-san

★ **㉔** *2 hrs east of Wakayama (via Hashimoto) by JR, 90 mins west of Ōsaka's Namba Station on the Nankai Dentetsu Line.*

This is the headquarters of the Shingon sect of Buddhism, founded by Kūkai, also known as Kōbō Daishi, in AD 816. Every year about a million visitors pass through Kōya-san's **Dai-mon** (Big Gate), to enter the great complex of 120 temples, monasteries, schools, and graves on this mesa in the mountains.

If your time is limited, head for **Okuno-in,** a memorial park, first. Many Japanese make pilgrimages to the mausoleum of Kōbō Daishi or pay their respects to their ancestors buried here. Try to arrive very early in the morning, before the groups take over, or even better, at dusk, when things get wonderfully spooky.

Exploring this cemetery is like peeking into a lost and mysterious realm. You can almost feel the millions of prayers said here clinging to the gnarled branches of 300-year-old cedar trees reaching into the sky. This *is* a special place. Its old-growth forest is a rarity in Japan, and among the trees are buried some of the country's most prominent families, their graves marked by mossy little pagodas and red- and white-robed stone Buddhas.

You may exit Okuno-in by way of the 2½-km (1½-mi) main walkway, which is lined with tombs, monuments, and statues. More than 100,000 historical figures are honored. The lane exits the cemetery at Ichi-no-hashi-guchi; follow the main street straight ahead to return to the center of town (a 20-minute walk) or wait for the bus that is headed for Kongōbu-ji.

The path from Okuno-in-mae ends at the **Tōrō-dō** (Lantern Hall), named after its 11,000 lanterns. Two fires burn in this hall: it's said that one has been alight since 1016, the other since 1088. Behind the hall is the mausoleum of Kōbō Daishi. ☑ *Free.* ☉ *Lantern Hall Apr.–Oct., daily 8–5; Nov.–Mar., daily 8:30–4:30.*

On the southwestern side of Kōya-san, **Kongōbu-ji** is the chief temple of Shingon Buddhism. Kongōbu-ji was built in 1592 as the family temple of Hideyoshi Toyotomi. It was rebuilt in 1861 and is now the main temple of the Kōya-san community. ☑ *¥500.* ☉ *Apr.–Oct., daily 8–5; Nov.–Mar., daily 8:30–4:30.*

The **Danjogaran** (Sacred Precinct) consists of many halls centered on the **Kompon-daitō** (Great Central Pagoda). This red pagoda, with its interior of brightly colored beams, contains five sitting images of Buddha. Last rebuilt in 1937, the two-story structure stands out due to its unusual style and rich vermilion color. It's worth taking a look inside. From Kongōbu-ji walk down the temple's main stairs and take the road to the right of the parking lot in front of you; in less than five minutes you will reach Danjogaran. ☑ *Each building ¥100.* ☉ *Apr.–Oct., daily 8–5; Nov.–Mar., daily 8:30–4:30.*

The exhibits at **Reihōkan** (Treasure Hall), given its 5,000 art treasures, continually change. At any given time, some of the 180 pieces that have been designated National Treasures will be on display. Among these are *Shaka-nehan-zō*—the scroll of Reclining Image of Shakamuni Buddha on His Last Day—and the exotic *Hachi-dai-doji-zō*—images of the Eight Guardian Deities. The hall is south of Danjogaran across a small path. ☑ *¥500.* ☉ *Apr.–Oct., daily 9–5; Nov.–Mar., daily 9–4.*

At the T-junction in the center of town, the **tourist office** (✉ 600 Kōya-san, Kōya-chō, Ito-gun, Wakayama-ken, ☎ 07365/6–2616) can be reached by bus for ¥300.

En route from the station to the tourist office, you will pass the **mausoleums** of the first and second Tokugawa shōguns. You may want to walk back and visit these two gilded structures later; they're free, and open daily 9–5.

Dining and Lodging

Kōya-san has no modern hotels. However, 53 of the temples do offer Japanese-style accommodations—tatami floors, futon mattresses, and traditional Japanese shared baths. Only a few accept foreign guests. The two meals served are *shōjin ryōri,* vegetarian cuisine that uses locally made tofu. You eat the same food as the priests. The price is around ¥10,000 per person, including meals. You can reserve through Kōya-san Kankō Kyokai, the Nankai Railway Company office in Namba Station (Ōsaka), and the Japan Travel Bureau in most Japanese cities.

If possible, make reservations for temple rooms in advance through **Kōya-san Kankō Kyokai** (Kōya-san Tourism Society: ✉ Kōya-san, Kōya-machi, Itsu-gun, Wakayama-ken, ☎ 07365/6–2616).

One especially lovely temple that is open and friendly to foreigners is **Rengejo-in** (☎ 07365/6–2231, FAX 0736/56–4743). Both the head priest and his mother speak English. This is a quiet retreat that offers simple, traditional accommodation, good vegetarian food, and a little bit of Buddhism, all in gorgeously enchanting surroundings. You'll be expected for—and you shouldn't miss—the morning prayer service at 6 AM. From the cable car terminus, take the bus and get off at Ishinguchi stop. The drivers and station attendants will help you—just mention Rengejo-in—it's not hard to find.

Getting Around

Depending on where you are coming from, there are many ways to approach Kōya-san. From Wakayama, if you have a JR Pass, you can take the JR Wakayama Line to Hashimoto (80 minutes; ¥820) and change to the Nankai Line for the final 19 km (11½ mi) (40 minutes; ¥430) to Gokuraku-bashi Eki, from which the cable car runs (¥380) to the top of Kōya-san. (If you cut across the Yoshino-Kumano National Park by bus from Shingū or Hongu on Route 168, instead of circling the Kii Peninsula, get off the bus at Gojo and backtrack one station on the JR Line to Hashimoto; then take the Nankai Line.)

From Ōsaka you can take the private Nankai Line to reach Kōya-san from Nankai Namba Eki, from which a train departs for Kōya-san every 30 minutes. (To reach Namba Eki from Shin-Ōsaka Shinkansen Eki, use the Midō-suji subway line.) The Ōsaka–Kōya-san journey takes 90 minutes, including the five-minute cable-car ride up to Kōya-san Eki, and costs around ¥2,200 (try to reserve a seat if you're traveling on a weekend).

By rail, no matter where you start, the last leg of the trip is a five-minute cable-car ride from Gokuraku-bashi Eki. JR Passes are not valid for the cable car. The lift will deposit you at the top of 3,000-ft Kōya-san, where you can pick up a map and hop on a bus to the main attractions, which are about 2½ km (1½ mi) from the station and about 5½ km (3½ mi) from each other, on opposite sides of town. Two buses leave the station every 20 or 30 minutes, when the cable car arrives. One goes to Okuno-in Cemetery, on the east end of the main road, and the other goes to the Dai-mon, to the west.

Yoshino-san

② *3½ hrs east of Kōya-san by cable car, Nankai, JR, and Kintetsu lines; 1 hr south of Nara by JR and private Kintetsu Rail Line.*

Yoshino-san is one of the most beautiful (and crowded) places in Japan to visit during cherry-blossom season. The Sakura Festival, held April 11–12, attracts thousands of visitors. En-no-Ozunu, a 7th-century Buddhist priest who planted the trees and put a curse on anyone who tampered with them, was a skilled gardener. Since he placed the 100,000 trees in four distinct groves in rows up the mountainside, the zone of flowers in full bloom climbs up the slope as the weather warms the trees from bottom to top. As a result, you're virtually guaranteed to see perfect sakura, sometime within a two-week period in mid-April.

Explore the area to see wonderful mountain views and curious temples. The community of temples at Yoshino-san is less impressive than that of Kōya-san, but it's still interesting. Built into the surrounding mountains, shops in Youshino are on the third floor of buildings, and the first and second floors are below the level of the road.

For pilgrims, Sanjo-san is considered the holiest mountain, with two temples at the summit, one of which is dedicated to En-no-Ozunu, the cherry-tree priest who, as you might expect, is revered as something of a saint in the area. Lodging is available at area temples May 8–September 27 and can be booked at the tourist office.

In the middle of the cherry groves is **Kimpusen-ji,** the main temple of the area. The main hall, Zaō-dō, is said to be the second-largest wooden structure in Japan and also has two superb sculptures of Deva kings at the gate. From the parking lot at Yoshino-san, there's basically only one path: it winds inward, curving along the hill-terrace lined with trees, and is heavily traveled. ☎ *¥350 (includes Nyoirin-ji).* ☉ *Daily 9–5.*

Nyoirin-ji, was founded in the 10th century and is located south of Kimpusen-ji. This is supposedly where the last remaining 143 imperial warriors prayed before going into their final battle for the cause in the 14th century. Behind the temple is the mausoleum of Emperor Go-daigo (1288–1339), who brought down the Kamakura Shogunate. ☎ *¥350 (includes Kimpusen-ji).* ☉ *Daily 9–5.*

In addition to reserving temple stays, the **tourist office** (✉ Yoshinoyama, Yoshino-machi, Yoshino-gun, Nara-ken, ☎ 07463/2–3014) can arrange for accommodations at local *minshuku* (private homes providing lodging and meals for travelers).

Getting Around
From Nara take a JR train to Yoshino-guchi or the Kintetsu Line to Kashihara Jingū-mae Eki and connect with a Kintetsu Line train for Yoshino. From Kōya-san return to JR Hashimoto Eki; take a train one hour southeast to Yoshino-guchi and then change for the Kintetsu Line to Yoshino. From Ōsaka take a two-hour ride on the Kintetsu Line from Abeno-bashi Eki.

NAGOYA, ISE-SHIMA, AND THE KII PENINSULA A TO Z

To research prices, get advice from other travelers, and book travel arrangements, visit www.fodors.com.

AIR TRAVEL
There are direct overseas flights to Nagoya on Japan Airlines (JAL) from Honolulu, Hong Kong, and Seoul. The major airlines that have routes to Japan have offices in downtown Nagoya.

CARRIERS

For domestic travel, Japan Airlines (JAL), All Nippon Airways (ANA), and Japan Air System (JAS) have offices in Nagoya and fly from Nagoya to most major Japanese cities. For other airline phone numbers, *see* Air Travel *in* Smart Travel Tips.
➤ AIRLINES AND CONTACTS: **All Nippon Airways** (☎ 052/962–6211). **Japan Air System** (☎ 052/201–8111). **Japan Airlines** (☎ 052/563–4141).

AIRPORT AND TRANSFER
The Meitetsu Airport Bus makes the 30-minute run between Nagoya's airport and the Meitetsu Bus Center, near Nagoya Eki, for ¥870.
➤ CONTACTS: **Komaki Kokusai Kūkō** (Nagoya International Airport: ☎ 0568/29–0765). **Meitetsu Airport Bus** (✉ Nagoya International Airport, ☎ 0581/22–3796).

BUS TRAVEL
Buses connect Nagoya with Tōkyō and Kyōto. The bus fare, ¥5,100 and ¥2,500 respectively, is half that of the Shinkansen trains, but the journey by bus takes three times longer.

JR buses crisscross Nagoya, running either north–south or east–west. The basic fare is ¥200, and an unlimited-use bus and subway pass costs ¥850. Route maps are posted, and tickets are available in the train station—follow the signs. Further information on bus and subway travel can be collected at the Tourist Information Office in the center of the station.

CAR TRAVEL

The journey on the expressway to Nagoya from Tōkyō takes about five to six hours; from Kyōto allow 2½ hours. If you're used to high-traffic, high-stress, jam-prone highways that can go from high-speed to a snail's pace in a jiffy—like those of Los Angeles or Denver, for example—you'll be all right. The traffic-squeamish should definitely steer clear of this mode of transport, however.

EMERGENCIES

➤ CONTACTS: **Ambulance** (☎ 119). **Kokusai Central Clinic** (⊠ Nagoya International Center Bldg., ☎ 0521/201–5311). **National Nagoya Hospital** (⊠ 4–1–1 Sannomaru-ku, Naka-ku, Nagoya, ☎ 0521/951–1111). **Police** (☎ 110).

ENGLISH-LANGUAGE MEDIA

BOOKS

Maruzen, behind the International Hotel Nagoya downtown, has a broad selection of English-language books.
➤ BOOKSTORE: **Maruzen** (⊠ 3–23–3 Nishiki, Naka-ku, Nagoya, ☎ 0521/261–2251).

SUBWAYS

Several main subway lines run under Nagoya's major avenues. The Higashiyama Line runs from the north down to JR Nagoya Eki and then due east, cutting through the city center at Sakae. The Meijo Line runs north–south, passing through the city center at downtown Sakae. The Tsurumai Line also runs north–south through the city, then turns from the JR station to Sakae to cross the city center. A fourth subway line, the Sakura-dōri, cuts through the city center from the JR station, paralleling the east–west section of the Higashiyama Line. The basic fare, good for three stops, is ¥200. A one-day pass, good for Nagoya's subways (and buses), is ¥850.

TAXIS

Taxis are parked at most major stations, hotels, and wherever there may be pedestrians in need of a lift. You can also wave one over on the street; they are not scarce. The initial fare is ¥610. A ride from Nagoya Eki to Nagoya-jō is ¥1,000.

TOURS

The Nagoya Yuran Bus Company runs five different bus tours of the city. The three-hour Panoramic Course tour (¥2,610) includes Nagoya-jō and Atsuta Jingū and has scheduled morning and afternoon departures. A full-day tour (¥6,270) will take you to sights around Nagoya. Trips also run up to Inuyama to watch u-kai (¥7,680 round-trip). These tours have only a Japanese-speaking guide.

You can arrange a full-day tour to Ise and the Mikimoto Pearl Island at Toba from Kyōto or Ōsaka (¥24,800) through Sunrise Tours.
➤ TOUR CONTACTS: **Nagoya Yuran Bus Company** (☎ 052/561–4036). **Sunrise Tours** (☎ 075/361–7241).

TRAIN TRAVEL

Frequent bullet trains run between Tōkyō and Nagoya. The ride takes 1 hour, 52 minutes on the *Hikari* Shinkansen and 2½ hours on the slower

Kodama Shinkansen. JR Passes are not accepted on the ultrafast *Nozomi*, which links Nagoya with Kyōto (43 minutes) and Ōsaka (1 hour). Another option is the less expensive Limited Express trains, which proceed from Nagoya into and across the Japan Alps—to Takayama, Toyama, Matsumoto, and Nagano.

VISITOR INFORMATION

The Nagoya International Center is quite possibly the best-equipped information center in Japan for assisting gaijin. Not only is there an information desk to answer your questions, but there are also audiovisual presentations and an extensive library of English-language newspapers (both Japanese and foreign), magazines, and books. The center also has an English-language telephone hot line available from 9 to 8:30.

The toll-free Japan Travel Phone will answer travel-related questions daily 9–5. Local tourist offices in Ise-Shima and on the Kii Peninsula are located in most train stations.

➤ TOURIST INFORMATION: **Japan Travel Phone** (☎ 800). **Nagoya International Center** (✉ Nagoya Kokusai Center Bldg., 3rd floor, 1–47–1 Nagono 1-chōme, Nakamura-ku, Nagoya, ☎ 052/581–0100 in English).

4 THE JAPAN ALPS AND THE NORTH CHŪBU COAST

Soaring mountain peaks, rocky coastal cliffs, open-air hot springs, and superb hiking and skiing make this central alpine region a great escape from Japan's bustling cities. From the traditional villages of Kiso Valley to the south, through the Nagano slopes, and northeast to the coast of the Japan Sea, this slow-paced region has it all—without the crowds.

By John
Malloy Quinn

SNOW-TOPPED MOUNTAINS, valleys in full bloom, and coastal islets of Honshū's sleepy alpine corridor stand in for the lures of Japan's cosmopolitan cities. In fact, many traditional villages are virtually untouched by development; while other parts of the country have gone "modern," towns within the North Chūbu region (Fukui, Ishikawa, Toyama, Niigata, Nagano, and Gifu prefectures) have largely maintained their locally distinctive architecture. In Ogi-machi and Hida Minzoku Mura, for example, sturdy structures with thatched roofs and open-hearth fireplaces are still used. Famous temples such as Fukui's Zen Eihei-ji Temple and Kanazawa's Nichiren Myōryū-ji Temple, locally called Ninja-dera (Temple of the Ninja), are architectural markers of the region's religious history.

Traditional arts are represented in yearly events, from those as solemn as Sado-ga-shima's performances of melancholic *okesa* (folk dances) and songs to the area's riotous festivals. Although plenty of folklore museums here display Japanese ceramics, pottery, art, and scrolls made over the centuries, you're also welcome to watch craftspeople dye linens, paint silk for kimonos, carve wood, and hand-lacquer objects in workshops and stores.

Japan Alps and North Chūbu Coast Glossary

Key Japanese words and suffixes for this chapter include *asa-ichi* (morning market), *-bashi* (bridge), *-chō* (street or block), *-chōme* (street), *chūō* (central), *daimyō* (feudal lord), *dōri* (avenue), *eki* (train station), *gaijin* (foreigner), *-gawa* (river), *hama* (beach), *-hantō* (peninsula), *-ji* (temple), *jinja* (Shintō shrine), *-jō* (castle), *-ken* (prefecture), *kōen* ("ko-en," park"), *kōgen* (plateau), *-ku* (section or ward), *kūkō* (airport), *kyōkoku* (gorge), *machi* (town), *matsuri* (festival), *-mon* (gate), *Nihon-kai* (Japan Sea), *ōhashi* (large bridge), *onsen* (hot springs), *ryokan* (traditional inn), *sake* (rice wine), *sakura* (cherry blossoms), *-san* (mountain, as in Asama-san, Mt. Asama), *-shima* or *jima* (island), *torii* ("*to*-ree-ee," gate), and *yama* (mountain).

Pleasures and Pastimes

Architecture

The formidable ranges of mountains and heavy snowfall have for centuries isolated the region, making it less susceptible to social and political whimsy and urban development. The preserved old trading-route Kiso Valley towns of Magome and Tsumago typify the way things were before paved highways and express trains brought hints of Tōkyō to the region. In parts of Noto-hantō and in the hills of Toyama, residents live in grand, centuries-old houses. The *gasshō-zukuri* (praying-hands) farmhouses of Ogi-machi, with open hearths and thatched roofs, have survived the harsh, snowy winters—successfully fulfilling their purpose. In Takayama, the traditional wooden teahouses, dye houses, and sake breweries with latticed windows and doors still stand. Matsumoto has one of the few remaining 16th-century feudal castles. In the cities, modern apartment buildings stand next to 700-year-old temples.

Dining

Every microregion has its own specialties, many of which involve varied preparations of delicious and inexpensive fish and seafood from Nihon-kai. Also, seaweed, like vitamin-rich *wakame* and *kombu*, is frequently used, sometimes with tiny clams called *shijimi*, in miso soup.

In and around Toyama, spring brings tiny baby squid called *hotaruika* (firefly squid), which are boiled in soy sauce or sake and eaten whole.

Also try the seasonal *ama-ebi* (sweet shrimp) and *masu-zushi* (thinly sliced trout sushi that's been pressed flat). In winter look for various types of delicious crabs, including the red, long-legged *beni-zuwaigani.*

Fukui also has huge *echizen-gani* crabs, some 28 inches leg to leg. When boiled with a little salt and dipped in rice vinegar, they're pure heaven. A few exceptional varieties of sole, like *wakasa-karei,* are slightly dried before grilling. In both Fukui and Ishikawa, restaurants serve *echizen-soba* (buckwheat noodles, handmade and served with mountain vegetables) with sesame oil and bean paste for dipping, recalling the Buddhist vegetarian tradition.

In Kanazawa and the Noto-hantō, *Kaga-ryōri* (Kaga cuisine) means that seafood, such as *tai* (sea bream), is served with mountain fern brackens, greens, and mushrooms. At Wajima's early morning fish market (daily except the 10th and 25th), near the tip of Noto-hantō, and at Kanazawa's Omi-chō Market, you can see everything from fresh abalone to seaweed, and it's easy to find some nearby restaurant that will cook it for you.

In Niigata Prefecture, try *noppei-jiru,* a hot or cold soup with *satoimo* (a kind of sweet potato) as its base, and mushrooms, salmon, and other local ingredients. It goes with hot rice and grilled fish. *Wappa-meshi* is a hot dish of steamed rice garnished with local ingredients, especially wild vegetables, chicken, fish, and shellfish. In autumn, try *kiku-no-ohitashi,* a side dish of chrysanthemum petals marinated in vinegar. Like other prefectures on the Nihon-kai coast, Niigata has outstanding fish in winter—*buri* (yellowtail), flatfish, sole, oysters, abalone, and shrimp. A local specialty is *namban ebi,* raw shrimp dipped in soy sauce and wasabi. It's butter-tender and especially sweet on Sado-ga-shima. Also on Sado-ga-shima, take advantage of the excellent *wakame* (seaweed) dishes and *sazae-no-tsuboyaki* (wreath shellfish) broiled in their shells with a soy or miso sauce.

The area around Matsumoto is known for its wasabi and chilled *zaru-soba* (buckwheat noodles), a refreshing meal on a hot day, especially when accompanied by a frosty mug of beer or a cold glass of locally brewed sake.

In the mountainous areas of Takayama and Nagano, you'll find *sansai soba* (buckwheat noodles with mountain vegetables) and *sansai-ryōri* (wild vegetables and mushrooms served in soups, tempura, or as garnishes), as well as local river fish such as *ayu* (smelt) or *iwana* (char) grilled on a spit with *shōyu* (soy sauce) or salt. You'll likely also encounter *hoba miso,* which is a dark, slightly sweet type of miso roasted on a large magnolia leaf.

Nagano is also famous for delicacies such as *ba sashi* (raw horse meat), *sakura nabe* (horse meat stew cooked in an earthenware pot), and boiled baby bees. The former two are still very popular; as for the latter, even locals admit they're something of an acquired taste.

For more details on Japanese cuisine, *see* Chapter 14 *and* Dining *in* Smart Travel Tips A to Z.

CATEGORY	COST*
$$$$	over ¥6,000
$$$	¥4,000–¥6,000
$$	¥2,000–¥4,000
$	under ¥2,000

*per person for a main course at dinner

Festivals

Takayama's biannual festival (April 14–15 and October 9–10) goes back 300 or 400 years, possibly originating from an attempt to appease angry gods in a time of plague. This spectacle transforms the usually quiet, conservative town into a rowdy, colorful party machine, culminating in a musical parade of intricately carved and decorated *yatai* (floats) and puppets. Flags and draperies adorn local houses, and at night the yatai are hung with lanterns. Should you plan to attend, book rooms well ahead and expect to pay inflated prices. April's Sannō Matsuri is slightly bigger than October's Hachi-man Matsuri.

Kanazawa's Hyaku-man-goku Matsuri (June 13–15) includes parades of people dressed in ancient costumes, floating lanterns on the Asano-gawa, Nō (old-style Japanese theater) performances, singing and dancing in parks, and a pervasive atmosphere of all-out merrymaking.

Of the *many* festivals on the Noto-hantō, those impressive ones that attract TV cameras and revelers from far and wide are Nanao's famous Seihakusai Matsuri, a 400-year-old tradition, held May 2–5, and Ishizaki Hoto Matsuri, held the first Saturday of August.

Hiking

The Japan Alps and nearby ranges are a hiker's paradise. Although none of the peaks is more than 11,000 ft, they are capable of making an awesome impression *and* of providing a serious workout. The breathtaking Kamikōchi area of Nagano is laced with trails through and around the snow peaks. Trails and lodges line the wooded banks of the Azusa-gawa. Haku-san, in Ishikawa (accessed from Shiramine), and Tate-yama (from Kurobe-kyōkoku), in Toyama, are two surmountable, sizable peaks offering staggering views for the experienced and prepared hiker. Other gentler trails are appropriate for beginners. Kept under snow in winter, the highland slopes and valleys come alive with wildflowers in summer.

Hot Springs

Onsen near coastal regions tend to be salty and high in calcium, while those in mountain areas are usually higher in iron and sulfur. Each lays claim to various benefits to skin, bones, and mental health, but *no one* will deny that hot springs of any kind are a good thing. Mawaki Onsen, in Noto-hantō, overlooks Toyama Bay, while the open-air onsen of Nagano and Gifu, such as Hirayu or Shirahone, deliver crisp mountain air and pine-scented breezes.

Lodging

Accommodations cross the spectrum, from Japanese-style inns to large, characterless, modern resort hotels that have typical chain facilities. All the large city and resort hotels serve Western and Japanese food. In summer hotel reservations are advised.

For a short course on accommodations in Japan, *see* Lodging *in* Smart Travel Tips A to Z.

CATEGORY	COST*
$$$$	over ¥20,000
$$$	¥15,000–¥20,000
$$	¥10,000–¥15,000
$	under ¥10,000

All prices are for a double room, excluding service and tax.

Skiing

Thanks to the 1998 Nagano Winter Olympics, many resorts were upgraded; every skier (and snowboarder) should find something pleasing from the selection of more than 20 resorts. Although the area is not visited by powdery stuff like you find in the Colorado Rockies or Hokkaidō, the Alps are quite popular, particularly on weekends. Shiga Kōgen, near Yudanaka, and Happa-one, near Hakuba, are among the best.

Exploring the Japan Alps and the Chūbu North Coast

The Japan Alps is not a defined political region; it's a name that has come to be accepted for the mountains in Chūbu, the Middle District. That is, Chūbu encompasses nine prefectures in the center of Honshū, three of which—Gifu-ken, Nagano-ken, and Yamanashi-ken—make up the central highlands. Kanazawa, Fukui, and the Noto-hantō, to the northwest, and Niigata and Sado-ga-shima Island, to the northeast, are neighboring coastal areas. Getting around the Alps is somewhat determined by the valleys and river gorges that run north and south. East–west routes through the mountains are nearly nonexistent, except between Matsumoto and Takayama from May through mid-October. It's easier to get around along the coast and in the foothills of Fukui, Ishikawa, Toyama, and Niigata, with the exception of Fukui, which gets hit with furious blizzards that can shut down train routes and highways. In Noto buses and trains can be relied on for trips to key places, but to really explore the scenery and get a feel for rural life, consider renting a car in Kanazawa or Toyama and making the loop at your own pace.

Numbers in the text correspond to numbers in the margin and on the Japan Alps, Takayama, and Kanazawa maps.

Great Itineraries

To see everything—the Alps, the Noto-hantō, the Chūbu Coast, and Sado-ga-shima—you need about two weeks, and because the mountain climate slows, and sometimes impedes travel (from Matsumoto, Kamikōchi can only be reached between May and October), give some thought to your itinerary in advance. The region can be reached either from the Nihon-kai coast or the Pacific coast. To reach the area from Tōkyō, plan to take a Shinkansen to Nagano. Kanazawa and other Chūbu coastal destinations are on the JR Line, with connections to Kyōto, Nagoya, and the Shinkansen Line at Maibara. For points farther north, such as Sado-ga-shima, the Shinkansen to Niigata from Tōkyō is also an option. (Note that this train is on a different line than Nagano and won't stop there.)

IF YOU HAVE 2 DAYS

Whittle your choices down to one interesting destination, such as ⊞ **Kanazawa** ⑲–㉙, only 2½ hours from Ōsaka, for some fun, shopping, culture, and nightlife. Or for a traditional Japanese mountain town, visit ⊞ **Takayama** ⑧–⑰, about two hours from Nagoya. If you'd like a little of everything—nightlife, mountain scenery, and an example of feudal architecture—go to ⊞ **Matsumoto** ⑤, directly linked by train to Tōkyō and Nagoya.

IF YOU HAVE 4 DAYS

Spend one or two nights in ⊞ **Takayama** ⑧–⑰ and take a day trip to **Kamikōchi** ⑦. Then head for ⊞ **Matsumoto** ⑤ for another night or two. This trip involves train and bus travel and takes a total of about an hour and 45 minutes. If you're heading back to Tōkyō, try to see Zenkō-ji, in Nagano, on your way, or if you're bound for Nagoya, stop in Nagiso or Nakatsugawa to explore Tsumago or Magome in the ⊞ **Kiso Valley** ⑥. The train ride from Matsumoto to Nakatsugawa takes 85 minutes, and it's another 55 minutes to Nagoya from there. Direct buses between Magome and Nagoya take about two hours. You could also explore the remote and scenic **Noto-hantō** ㉛ and take a train through

Kurobe-kyōkoku, in Toyama-ken, in four days, using 🚉 **Kanaza-wa** ⑲–㉙ as a base, with a night on the peninsula at Mawaki Onsen.

IF YOU HAVE 7–9 DAYS
From 🚉 **Nagano** ② head to 🚉 **Matsumoto** ⑤, where your trip really begins. On the second day take a day trip to the old post towns of the 🚉 **Kiso Valley** ⑥. On your third day, travel through the mountains to 🚉 **Kamikōchi** ⑦, spending the night here. Take the fourth and fifth nights in 🚉 **Takayama** ⑧–⑰. On the sixth day leave the mountains for 🚉 **Kanazawa** ⑲–㉙. Or, spend only one night in Takayama, and save the last two days for a trip to Kanazawa and the Noto-hantō. From Kanazawa, express trains run south to Nagoya, Kyōto, and Ōsaka.

If you have time to visit **Sado-ga-shima** ㉞–㊱, begin in 🚉 Takayama, head over the mountains through the old farm town of **Ogi-machi** ⑱ to Kanazawa, and then follow the coast to **Niigata** ㉝ for the crossing to the island.

WHEN TO TOUR
Heavy snow in winter makes getting around the Alps by car difficult or altogether impossible, such as when the road between Takayama and Matsumoto becomes one with the mountain landscape. Unless you've got skiing to do, and a direct route by train to get there, winter is not the best time to explore the area. In summer the Alps are visited by lowland city folks (and tourists) trying to beat the heat. A summer visit to the coastal regions, however, should pose no problem.

THE JAPAN ALPS

Karuizawa

❶ *66 mins by Shinkansen from Tōkyō's Ueno Eki.*

Fashionable Karuizawa's popularity began when Archdeacon A. C. Shaw, an English prelate, built his summer villa here in 1886. Other gaijin living in Tōkyō soon followed his example. Today it's the preferred summer resort destination of affluent Tōkyōites, where branches of more than 500 trendy boutiques sell, well, the same goods as their flagship stores in Tōkyō. So, unless you're a Tōkyō weekender, forego shopping and partake of the natural scenery, which deserves much more respect than it gets up here these days.

Asama-san, an active volcano of more than 8,000 ft, intermittently threatens to put an end to the whole "Highlands Ginza" scene going on below it. You can get a view of Asama-san, of a neighboring mountain, Myogi-san, as well as the whole Yatsugatake, a range of eight volcanic peaks, from the observation platform at **Usui-tōge** (Usui Pass). To get there, walk northeast on boutiques-filled Karuizawa Ginza street to the end, past Nite-bashi, and follow the trail to the pass. The view justifies the 1½-hour walk.

Hiking paths at **Shiraito-no-taki and Ryugaeshi-no-taki** (Shiraito and Ryugaeshi Falls) can get very crowded in tourist season. From the trailhead, you come upon Shiraito after about 1½ km (1 mi). From there, the trail swings southeast, and 3 km (2 mi) farther is Ryugaeshi. To get to the falls, take a bus (25 minutes) from Naka-Karuizawa to Mine-no-Chaya.

Yachō-no-mori (Wild Bird Forest) is home to about 120 species of birds. You can look more closely at the birds' habitat from two observation huts along a 2½-km (1½-mi) forest course. To get to the sanctuary, take a five-minute bus ride from Naka-Karuizawa Eki to

KEY
— JR Trains
═ Shinkansen (Bullet Train)
⊢⊣ Private rail line
🚢 Ferry

NIHON-KAI
(Sea of Japan)

Rokkō-misaki

Sosogi
Wajima   Suzu   Tako-jima
Monzen   Noto Ogi
            Anamizu   Mawaki Onsen

Noto-jima

Nanao

31   Noto-hantō

Hakui

Takaoka   Kurobe
                    32 Toyama
        Tonami   Keyakidaira

Kanazawa
19 29
see detail
map   *Chūbu-Sangaku Nat'l Park*

Ogi-machi **18**

Awara Onsen   *Hotaka-dake* ▲
                              Yake-dake   **7**
Haku-san ▲
        Miboro-ko
Fukui **30**
            Katsuyama   Takayama   *Norikura-san* ▲ Shimo
Eihei-ji   *Haku-san*   **8 17**
        Ono   *Nat'l Park* see detail
                              map
                    Izumi   *On-take* ▲

                    Gero

TO
KYOTO   TO
                    NAGOYA
27   Kiso
                                  Valley **6**

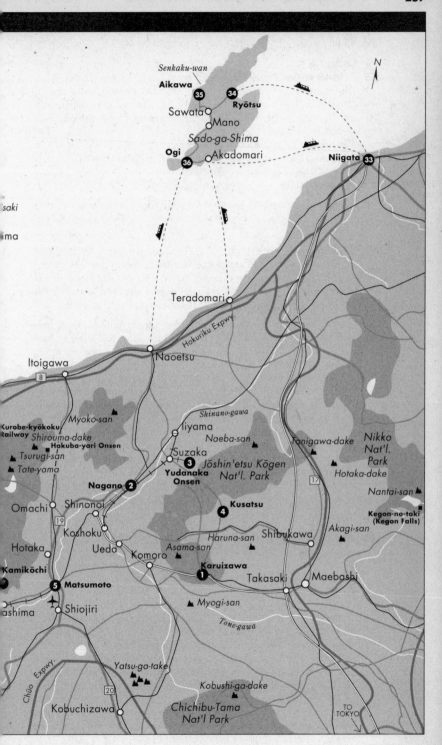

Senkaku-wan

Aikawa

35

34

Sawata○ **Ryōtsu**

○ Mano

Sado-ga-Shima

Ogi

36 ○ Akadomari

Niigata **33**

Teradomari

Hokuriku Expwy

Itoigawa

Naoetsu

8

Shinano-gawa

Kurobe-kyōkoku *Myoko-san*

Railway *Shirouma-dake* Iiyama

Hakuba-yari Onsen *Naeba-san* *Tanigawa-dake*

Tsurugi-san Suzaka

Tate-yama **3** *Jōshin'etsu Kōgen* **Nikko**

Yudanaka *Nat'l. Park* *Hotaka-dake* **Nat'l.**

Onsen **Park**

Nagano 2

Nantai-san

Omachi Shinonoi **4** **Kusatsu** 17

Koshoku *Haruna-san* Shibukawa **Kegon-no-taki**

Hotaka *Akagi-san* **(Kegon Falls)**

Ueda Komoro *Asama-san*

Kamikōchi **1** **Karuizawa**

5 **Matsumoto** Takasaki Maebashi

○ Shiojiri *Myogi-san*

ashima *Tone-gawa*

Chūo Expwy. *Yatsu-ga-take*

20 *Kobushi-ga-dake*

Kobuchizawa *Chichibu-Tama* **TO**

Nat'l Park **TOKYO**

saki

ima

Nishiku-iriguchi, and then walk for 10 minutes up the small road to the entrance. Bikes can be rented at the station for ¥800 an hour or ¥2,000 a day.

Lodging

$$$ ⊞ **Pensione Grasshopper.** This guest house has friendly hospitality, Western beds (great views of Asama-san from Room 208), and a mix of Japanese and Western fare. The owner, Kayo Iwasaki, speaks English. The house is in the suburbs, but the management will transport you to and from the station. There is a standard shared bath. ⊠ *5410 Karyada, Karuizawa, Kitasaku-gun, Nagano-ken 389,* ☎ *0267/46–1333. 10 rooms with shared bath. Dining room. MC, V. EP, MAP.*

Nagano and Environs

97 mins northwest of Tōkyō's Ueno Eki by Shinkansen, 40 mins northwest of Karuizawa by JR, 3 hrs northeast of Nagoya by JR Limited Express.

❷ When **Nagano** (population 300,000) hosted the 1998 XVIII Winter Olympics, a new Shinkansen line was built, connecting Tōkyō and Nagano, and new highways were added to handle the increased car and bus traffic. As a result, the somewhat inaccessible Alps region was opened to visitors and transportation to the region made easier.

★ Nagano's unusual **Zenkō-ji** is the destination for millions of pilgrims each year. Fourteen hundred years old, it has always had an open-door policy, accepting believers of all sects and religions and admitting women when other temples forbade it. As you approach the main hall, do as the pilgrims do and wave the smoke over you to bring good fortune and health. Inside, rub the worn wooden statue of the ancient doctor and his disciple Binzuru for relief of aches and pains. Next, summon your courage and explore the pitch-black tunnel in the basement to see if you can find the handlelike latch on the wall, the seizing of which is said to bring enlightenment. Hop on Bus 33, 40, or 45 for the 10-minute trip (¥100) through the center of Nagano to the temple gate. ⊠ *Motoyoshi 4–9–1,* ☎ *026/234–3591.* ✎ *¥500.* ☾ *Inner sanctuary daily 5:30–4:30.*

You can pick up a free map at the Nagano **City Tourist Office** (☎ 026/226–5626), open daily 9–6, inside the new JR station.

❸ East of Nagano, the **Yudanaka Onsen** area has hot springs made famous by photographs of snow-covered monkeys huddling in open-air thermal pools to keep warm. Between Yudanaka Onsen and Shibu Spa Resort, there are nine open-air hot springs. The specific onsen where the monkeys come to soak is known as Jigoku-dani (Hell Valley) and is just east of Yudanaka and Shibu. A wild monkey park nearby is undoubtedly responsible for their connection to the spas. Yudanaka is the last stop on the Nagano Dentetsu Line (the fare is ¥1230 each way from Nagano), and several spas string out from here. In its natural aspects, the area is not unlike Yellowstone National Park in the United States, with its bubbling, steaming, sulfurous volcanic vents and pools. However, considerable development including more than 100 inns and hotels, several streets, and shops ends the comparison. The spas are the gateway to Shiga Kōgen (Shiga Heights), site of the Olympic alpine skiing and snowboarding slalom events. It's 40 minutes by Nagano Dentetsu Railway from Nagano Eki.

The **Yudanaka Health Center** (☎ 026/933–5888) is a public onsen across the Yomase-gawa from the Yudanaka Eki, and it costs ¥800 for a bath.

The entire spa and Shiga Kōgen ski area falls under the jurisdiction of Yamanouchi Town; the **Tourist Information Center** (☎ 026/933–1107; 026/933–2138 for reservations assistance) is located just south of Yudanaka Eki.

❹ The highly touted hot springs at **Kusatsu** contain sulfur, iron, alum, and even trace amounts of arsenic. Just inside the border of Gunma Prefecture, they can be reached in summer by a bus route across Shiga Kōgen from Yudanaka, or by bus from Karuizawa. More than 130 ryokan cluster around the *yuba* (hot-spring field) that supplies the gushing, boiling, sulfur-laden water. **Netsunoyu** (Fever Bath) is the main and often unbearably hot public bath (open from 7 AM to 10 PM).

For more information on local hot springs and accommodations call the **Kusatsu Information Center** (☎ 027/988–3642).

Lodging

$$$–$$$$ 🏨 **Hotel Fujiya.** The *newest* part of this famous hotel is more than 75
★ years old—the rest has been around for about 340 years. In that time everyone from feudal lords to celebrities has stayed here—and left autographed plaques—en route to Zenkō-ji. Tatami rooms vary from small (¥9,000 per person, including meals) to the royal suite (¥28,000 per person, including meals), which has three rooms with sliding doors that open onto a garden. Among the furnishings are precious antiques and scrolls, and the shared bath is unusually deep. Fujiya is not sophisticated, but it is wonderfully old-fashioned. No English is spoken, but the family who's been running the hotel since its doors first opened are wonderfully friendly and appreciative of respectful foreigners. ✉ *Dai Mon-chō 80, Nagano-shi, Nagano-ken 380-0841,* ☎ *026/232–1241,* ℻ *026/232–1243. 24 rooms, 1 suite. Dining room, Japanese-style bath. AE, DC, MC, V.*

$$ 🏨 **Nagano Sunroute Hotel.** Across from JR Nagano Eki, you enter the marble lobby at street level and take the escalator up to the first-floor reception area and tea lounge. A Japanese restaurant is on the second floor. A coffee table and two easy chairs are squeezed into each compact and clean Western-style room, which is all you need, especially if you're just passing through to other Alps destinations. ✉ *1–28–3 Minami-Chitose, Nagano-shi, Nagano-ken 380,* ☎ *026/228–2222,* ℻ *026/228–2244. 143 rooms. Restaurant, coffee shop, tea shop. AE, DC, MC, V.*

$ 🏨 **Uotoshi Ryokan.** This small inn has a 24-hour, hot springs–fed *hinoki* (cypress) bathtub. The decor is rustic—cozy, but nothing fancy. You can try Japanese archery (*kyūdō*) in the afternoon and look forward to a healthy and delicious dinner of mountain vegetables and Nihon-kai seafood. It's a seven-minute walk from Yudanaka Eki, northeast of Nagano City. ✉ *2563 Sano, Yama-no-uchi-machi, Shimo-Takai-gun, Nagano-ken 381-04,* ☎ *0269/33–1215,* ℻ *0269/33–0074. 8 Japanese-style rooms. Restaurant, mineral bath. AE, MC, V. EP, MAP.*

Matsumoto

❺ *1 hr southwest of Nagano on JR Shinonoi Line, 2 hrs and 40 mins northwest of Tōkyō Shinjuku Eki on JR Chūō Line, 2¼ hrs northeast of Nagoya on JR Chūō Line.*

High snowcapped peaks surround Matsumoto on its alpine plateau, where the air is cool and dry. Here, an interesting variety of restaurants, shops, and nightlife coexist with one of Japan's oldest castles. If you walk to the castle from the JR station, you'll pass through the old section, with its many stone *kura* (warehouses), which are typical of the early Meiji period. They are unusual in their use of irregular stones held in place by mortar.

★ Nicknamed **Karasu-jō** (Crow Castle) for its black walls, Matsumoto's castle began as a small fortress with moats in 1504 and was remodeled into its current three-turreted form at the turn of the 16th century (1592–1614). The 95-ft tall *donjon* (stronghold or inner tower) is the oldest surviving tower in Japan. Inside, the arsenal displays an assortment of weapons from the days of castle-siege warfare. An exhibit on each floor allows you a break from climbing the very steep stairs. You have to wear the slippers offered to you as you enter, but be forewarned: they make the stairs a little tricky. It's worth the maneuvering, because with all those mountains around, the views from the sixth floor are the stuff of postcards.

In the southwest corner of the Karasu-jō grounds, which bloom in spring with cherry trees, azaleas, and wisteria, the **Nihon Minzoku Shiryōkan** (Japan Folklore Museum; ☎ 0263/32–0133) exhibits artifacts of prefeudal days and of the Edo period (1603–1868). In January an ice-sculpture exhibition is held in the museum's park.

The castle is about a 20-minute walk (a few blocks to the east through the old quarter and then north) from the train station. You can make a worthwhile stop for a map at the tourist office, on the right-hand side as you exit the JR station. ✉ *4–1 Maruno-uchi,* ☎ *0263/32–2902.* ✉ *Castle and museum ¥410.* ☉ *Daily 8:30–4:30.*

Matsumoto Mingeikan (Folk Craft Museum) displays more than 600 locally made domestic wood, bamboo, and glass utensils. It's across town from the castle, east of the JR station. To get here, take a taxi or a 15-minute bus ride to the Shimoganai Mingeikan-guchi bus stop. ✉ *1313–1 Satoyamabe,* ☎ *0263/33–1569.* ✉ *¥210.* ☉ *Tues.–Sun. 9–5.*

★ The **Nihon Ukiyo-e Hakubutsukan** (Japan Wood-block Print Museum) is devoted to the lively, colorful, and widely popular *ukiyo-e* wood-block prints of artists from the middle and late Edo period, such as the well-known Hiroshige, Hokusai, and Sharaku. The museum's holdings of 100,000 artworks (displays rotate monthly) contain some of Japan's finest prints and represent the largest collection of its kind in the world. ✉ *2206–1 Koshiba, Shimadachi,* ☎ *026/47–4440.* ✉ *¥1,000.* ☉ *Tues.–Sun. 10–4:30.*

The **Shiho Butsukan** (Japan Judicature Museum), next to the Ukiyo-e Hakubutsukan, is Japan's oldest palatial court building. ✉ *2206–1 Koshiba, Shimadachi,* ☎ *026/47–4515.* ✉ *¥700.* ☉ *Daily 9–4:30.*

These museums are west of the JR station. Unfortunately, it's too far to walk, and there's no bus, so you must invest in a ¥2,000 taxi ride. You can also take the Kamikōchi train (on the private Matsumoto Dentetsu Line) four stops to Oniwa Eki from Matsumoto Eki, from which it's a 10-minute walk to the museum.

Also outside Matsumoto, **Rokuzan Bijutsukan** (Rokuzan Art Museum) displays the work of Rokuzan Ogiwara, a master sculptor, known as the Rodin of Asia. The appeal of Rokuzan's works is complemented by the gallery's setting, against the beautiful backdrop of the northern Japan Alps. The museum is in Hotaka, 10 stops north of Matsumoto Eki on the JR Oito Line (one if you can catch the limited express). From Hotaka Eki it's a 10-minute walk. Ask station attendants to point you in the right direction. ✉ *5095–1 Hotaka-machi,* ☎ *026/82–2094.* ✉ *¥500.* ☉ *Apr.–Oct., Tues.–Sun. 9–5; Nov.–Mar., Tues.–Sun. 9–4.*

Daio Wasabi Nōjo is the largest wasabi farm in Japan. The green horseradish is cultivated in flat gravel beds irrigated with the cold water of melted snow. Surrounded by rows of acacia and poplar trees on the embankments, the fields of fresh, green wasabi leaves bloom with white flowers in late spring. If you're feeling adventurous, try some of the farm's unique products, which range from wasabi cheese and wasabi chocolate to green wasabi ice cream. It's near Hotaka, 10 stops (only one if you take the express) north along the JR Oito Line from Matsumoto. To reach the farm you can rent a bike or take a 40-minute walk along a path from the train station (the station attendant will give you directions).

Dining and Lodging

$-$$ ★ ✕ Kura. For a surprisingly small amount of yen, you can do some serious feasting in this funky 90-year-old Meiji-era warehouse in the center of town. The place serves a full range of sushi and traditional fare: the *aji tataki* (horse-mackerel sashimi) and tempura are particularly good. You can't miss with the traditional, delicious daily lunch courses, either. The owner maintains a stoic face as he expertly prepares your meal, but should his wife spot you relishing the food, you're in for a treat of some downright disarming hospitality—she has an arsenal of potent *ji-zake* (locally brewed sake) and a heart of pure gold. ⊠ *2-2-15 Chūō, northeast of Parco department store,* ☎ *0263/33-6444. AE, MC, V. Closed Wed.*

$-$$ ★ ✕ Tamita Gum Tree. This Japanese-owned bar and restaurant, managed by a friendly Kiwi named Darryl Melville Pearce, is a great place to come if you've been hankering for such diverse Western pleasures as Mexican food, Guinness Stout, fish-and-chips, and heaps of *fair dinkum bush tuck* ("fair dinkum" means "honestly good," and "bush tuck," or "tucker," is "dinner") from Down Under. Try the steak and avocados, sliced in strips and stir-fried in a slightly spicy sauce. Things are always light and lively, and sometimes Darryl rounds up his band for some live rock. ⊠ *1-14-10 Hon-jō, south of Hotel Buena Vista,* ☎ *0263/35-0714. No credit cards. Closed Sun. No lunch.*

$$$-$$$$ ★ 🛏 Hotel Buena Vista. One of Matsumoto's newest and most expensive hotels, the Buena Vista has a bright, spacious marble lobby, a coffeehouse, a café-bar, four restaurants (two Japanese, one Chinese, one French), a disco, *and* a sky lounge on the 14th floor called **Monpage**, with nightly live jazz. The Western-style rooms are decorated in pastels. Single rooms snugly accommodate a small double bed; standard double and twin-bed rooms have enough space for a table and easy chairs. Corner rooms are choice, at ¥21,600. ⊠ *1-2-1 Hon-jō, 4 blocks southeast of Matsumoto Eki, Matsumoto, Nagano-ken 390-0814,* ☎ *0263/37-0111,* FAX *0263/37-0666. 200 rooms. 5 restaurants, bar, coffee shop, dance club. AE, DC, MC, V.*

$$$ ★ 🛏 Enjō Bekkan. This small, friendly ryokan is just outside Matsumoto in Utsukushigahara Onsen. Rooms are neat, clean, and spare, and English is spoken. Unlike many other ryokans, this one doesn't hit you with a curfew, so you can seek out the town's great nightlife. (A transportation tip: bus to and taxi back, as the buses don't run late.) Of course, what makes Enjō exceptional is the access to the thermal waters here 24 hours a day. The Utsukushigahara bus terminal is a 20-minute ride from JR Matsumoto Eki. ⊠ *110 Utsukushigahara-onsen, Matsumoto, Nagano-ken 390-0221,* ☎ *0263/33-7233,* FAX *0263/36-2084. 19 Japanese-style rooms, 11 with bath. Dining room, hot spring. AE, MC, V.*

$$-$$$ 🛏 Hotel New Station. Although other good-value business-class hotels are often rather sterile, this one has character because of the cheerful and attentive staff and touches like a small rock pond just inside the door. The freshwater *iwana* (char) stocked in the pond are unique to the region and can quickly become sashimi (or grilled or boiled in sake) in the hotel restaurant. The hotel's also close to many other restaurants. While rooms are clean and adequate, they are a bit small. To get a "full-size room" by Western standards, you'll have to request a deluxe twin. ⊠ *1–1–11 Chūo, near Matsumoto Eki, Matsumoto, Nagano-ken 390,* ☎ *0263/35–3850,* 𝖥𝖠𝖷 *0263/35–3851. 103 rooms. Restaurant, meeting room. AE, MC, V.*

Nightlife

Off the small park north of the Hotel Buena Vista, **Half Time** (⊠ Takeuchi San-box, 2nd floor, 1–4–10 Shin-en, ☎ 0263/36–4985) is a hip, tiny jazz joint that serves tasty cocktails and snacks from 7 PM into the wee hours. Owner Akira Shiohara, who is quite a trumpet player, will even join in, if you ask him. **Monpage,** a 14th-floor sky lounge, sizzles nightly with live American jazz at the Hotel Buena Vista. The incredible view alone is well worth the cover (up to ¥2,000). **Tamita Gum Tree** has tasty, cheap food and a good choice of beers and cocktails and is an overall lively scene orchestrated by friendly Kiwi bartender Darryl Melville Pearce.

Kiso Valley

★ ❻   *1 hr south of Matsumoto on JR Chūo Line.*

The valley, through which the Kiso-gawa runs, stretches between Matsumoto and Nagoya and has the most scenic landscape in southwestern Nagano Prefecture. The deep, narrow valley is cut by the Kiso-gawa and bounded by the central Alps to the east and the northern Alps to the west. From 1603 to 1867 the river valley called Nakasendo (center highway) was the main route connecting western Japan and Kyōto with eastern Japan and Edo (present-day Tōkyō).

With the pre-Meiji building of the Tōkaidō along the Pacific coast and the later Meiji-era construction of the Chūo train line from Nagoya to Niigata, the 11 **old post villages,** where travelers and traders had stopped to refresh themselves along the difficult journey, were bypassed and left to go the way of ghost towns. Two preserved villages, **Tsumago** and **Magome,** have benefited from recent efforts to retain the integrity and history of these old towns and are within easy reach. Walking through them, you can almost imagine life centuries ago, when the rustic shops were stocked with supplies instead of souvenirs.

The **Magome Tourist Information Office** (☎ 0264/59–2336) is open April to November, daily 9–5, and December to March, Monday through Saturday 9–5. The staff can help you reserve a room. The **Tsumago Tourist Information Office** (☎ 0264/57–3123) is a source of information for the area and can also make reservations for you.

Lodging

Be sure to reserve a room in advance, especially for stays on weekends.

$$$ ▣ **Matsushiro Ryokan.** Tsumago's traditional atmosphere resonates in the operations and accommodations of this small ryokan, operating as a guest house for 140 years. Ten large tatami rooms share a single bath and four immaculately clean old-time pit toilets. Dinner is particularly delicious and is served in your room. No one speaks English here, so a Japanese speaker or the tourist office will need to make your reservation. ⊠ *Tsumago, Nagiso-machi, Kiso-gun, Nagano-ken 399,* ☎ *0264/57–3022. 10 Japanese-style rooms with shared bath. No credit cards. EP, MAP.*

$$$ 🏠 **Onyado Daikichi.** At this particularly good *minshuku* (private residence that offers lodging), all six tatami rooms face the valley. The traditional wooden bath is shared, and the dinners, making good use of the local specialties (horse-meat sashimi, mountain vegetables, fried grasshoppers), are excellent. For the not-so daring, other dinner options are available. With her limited English, owner Nobaka-san makes gaijin feel very welcome. ⊠ *Tsumago, Minami Kiso-machi, Kiso-gun, Nagano-ken 399-54,* ☎ *0264/57–2595,* 🖷 *0274/57–2209. 6 Japanese-style rooms with shared bath. Dining room. No credit cards. MAP.*

Getting Around

The central valley town of Nagiso is one hour south of Matsumoto by JR Chūō Line or two hours north of Nagoya. Tsumago is a 10-minute bus ride (¥240) from JR Nagiso Eki. Magome is closer to JR Nakatsugawa Eki, which is 12 minutes south on the same line. Both towns are served by buses from the Nagiso and Nakatsugawa stations, so you can bus to one village and return from the other. Buses from JR Nagiso Eki leave every hour. There is a direct bus from Nagoya to Magome, but not Tsumago. Local buses between Magome and Tsumago are infrequent.

You can make a hike out of your visit by tracing the old route between Magome and Tsumago, which takes about three hours. Although you find people making this trip in both directions—hilly both ways—it's most commonly taken from Magome to Tsumago. Believe it or not, there is a baggage delivery service between the two towns (generally charging ¥500 per bag): make arrangements at tourist information offices.

To get to Takayama from here, take the 50-minute bus ride from Magome to Gero; then transfer to a JR train for the 45-minute trip to Takayama. Buses leave three times daily (7:21 AM and 12:05 PM with a change at Sakashita for Gero, or a direct bus at 4 PM); the fare is ¥2,300.

Kamikōchi

❼ *2 hrs west of Matsumoto by train (Dentetsu Line) and bus, 2 hrs east of Takayama by bus.*

The incomparably scenic route from Matsumoto to Takayama goes over the mountains and through Chūbu-Sangaku Kokuritsu Kōen (Chūbu-Sangaku National Park) via Kamikōchi, that is, provided it's after the last week of April or first week of May, and the plows have removed the almost 30 ft of snow that accumulates on the road in winter. If you spend the night in Kamikōchi, consider renting a rowboat at Taishō-ike (Taishō Pond)—the view of the snow peaks from the pond is breathtaking.

As you approach Kamikōchi, the valley opens onto a plain with a backdrop of **mountains**: Oku-Hotaka-san is the highest, at 10,466 ft. **Mae-Hotaka-san**, at 10,138 ft, is on the left. To the right is **Nishi-Hotaka-san**, 9,544 ft. The icy waters of the Azusa-gawa flow from the small **Taishō-ike** at the southeast entrance to the basin.

From the many **trails** in and around Kamikōchi, you can reach most of the peaks without too much trouble. One easy three-hour walk follows the river past the rock sculpture of the British explorer Reverend Walter Weston, who first climbed these mountains, and several lodges and ryokan to Kappa-bashi, a small suspension bridge over crystal-clear Azusa-gawa. Continuing on the south side of the river, the trail cuts through pasture to rejoin Myoshin-bashi. On the other side at the edge of the pond, Myoshin-ike, sits the small Hotaka Jinja. From here another bridge leads to the trail on the opposite side of the river back to Kappa-bashi.

From the bus terminal it's a 20-minute walk to Taishō-ike, along the trail that heads southwest from the Kappa-bashi, just a few minutes' walk to northeast from the bus terminal (or you could simply double-back and trudge along the road the bus brought you in on). Here you can rent a boat (¥800 per half hour), or continue for a 45-minute walk east to a bridge, and, 45 minutes farther, to Tokusawa, an area which has camping grounds and great views of other mountains in the area.

Lodging

Hotels and ryokan in Kamikōchi close from mid-November to late April.

$$$$ ☒ **Imperial Hotel.** The most desirable place to stay between Mat-
★   sumoto and Takayama is this alpine lodge. The guest rooms, decorated in brown tones, have sofas and lots of gorgeous woodwork; some even have balconies. Open April–early November, the hotel is owned by Tōkyō's Imperial Hotel, and many of the staff members are borrowed from that establishment for the summer to ensure top service. Although you can see the hotel from the bus terminal, don't just show up—you've got to reserve well in advance. There are Western and Japanese restaurants on the premises. ☒ *Kamikōchi, Azumi-mura, Minami-Azumi-gun, Nagano-ken 390,* ☎ *0263/95–2006; 03/3504–1111 Nov.– Mar.; 212/692–9001 in the U.S.; 0171/355–1775 in the U.K.;* ☒ *0263/ 95–2412. 75 rooms. 3 restaurants, hiking. AE, DC, MC, V.*

Getting Around

To get to Kamikōchi from Matsumoto takes about two hours and costs ¥2,500 in total for the two legs; you pay for them both when you buy the combined ticket to start. Take the Matsumoto Electric Railway from Matsumoto Eki to Shin-Shimashima; at Shin-Shimashima Eki, cross the road for the bus to Naka-no-yu and Kamikōchi.

From Kamikōchi, buses costing ¥1,050 (20 daily, from early May to early November only) take 30 minutes to the mountain resort of **Hirayu Onsen,** 36 km (22 mi) east of Takayama, roughly halfway between Takayama and Matsumoto. Here's where folks coming from the west (as opposed to coming from Matsumoto) have to leave their cars to board a bus to Kamikōchi. Hirayu Onsen may also be reached directly from Matsumoto by bus in 90 minutes for ¥2,300. Year-round hourly buses (12 a day) make the 70-minute trip from Hirayu to Takayama for ¥1,530.

Takayama

2 hrs, 10 mins north of Nagoya by JR Limited Express; 4 hrs north of Matsumoto by JR via Nagoya; 2 hrs, 20 mins by bus from Matsumoto.

In the heart of the Hida Mountains, this tranquil town has held on to its old-fashioned traditions and character, which no doubt is why so many artists have made their homes here. The town is something of a museum piece—it's a perfect place to indulge in fantasies of old Japan. Takayama's hugely popular springtime Sannō Matsuri (April 14–15) and the smaller autumn Hachi-man Matsuri (October 9–10) draw hundreds of thousands of spectators for the parades of floats, which nearly overwhelm Takayama's population of 68,000. During the festivals, hotels are booked solid, so if you plan to visit then, make your reservation months in advance. In addition to the tourist office, throughout Takayama you can get help at businesses that are designated as Travel Information Desks (look for the ? sign in the window).

In the rustic working village of Hida Minzoku Mura (Hida Folk Village), just 3 km (2 mi) west of Takayama, actors in transplanted traditional farmhouses demonstrate how people lived (and some still live) in various parts of the territory.

⑧ Takayama Jinya (Takayama Shrine) will be on your right. This imposing structure, now a museum, was the manor house of the governor, with samurai barracks and a garden. In front of the house, you can buy vegetables, fruits, and local arts and crafts at the **Jinya-mae Asa-ichi** (April–October, 6–noon each day; November–February, 7–noon). From the JR station head east on Hirokoji-dōri for a few blocks, and you come to the old section of town, with its small shops, houses, and tearooms. Before the bridge, which crosses the small Miya-gawa, turn right, pass another bridge, and the Takayama Jinya will be on your right. ⊠ *1–5 Hachiken-machi,* ☎ *0577/32–0643.* ☒ *¥420.* ☉ *Mar.–Oct., daily 8:45–5; Feb.–Mar., daily 8:45–4:30.*

⑨ The main hall of **Shōren-ji** in Shiroyama Kōen (Shiroyama Park) was built in 1504, although it was moved here in 1961 from its original site in Shirakawa-gō before the area was flooded by the Miboro Dam. The temple sits on a hill surrounded by gardens, from where you can see the Takayama skyline and much of the park below. ⊠ *Shiroyama Kōen, across Miya-gawa from Takayama Jinya and up the hill,* ☎ *0577/32–2052.* ☒ *¥200.* ☉ *Apr.–Oct., daily 8–5:30; Nov.–Mar., daily 8–5.*

Takayama-shi Kyōdokan (Takayama City Museum) exhibits antiques, traditional crafts, and folkloric objects of the local Hida people. ⊠ *Sanmachi-dōri and Ichino-machi-dōri,* ☎ *0577/32–1205.* ☒ *¥300.* ☉ *Mar.–Nov., Tues.–Sun. 8:30–5; Dec.–Feb., daily 9–4:30.*

⑩ Today the imposing and magnificent **Tenshō-ji** is both a temple and a youth hostel, although as a hostel, the rooms are drafty and cold in the winter. It's on the east side of the Enako-gawa. ⊠ *San-machi-dōri and Tera-machi-dōri,* ☎ *0577/32–6345 (hostel).* ☉ *Temple daily 9–5.*

⑪ The **Hida Minzoku Kōkokan** (Archaeology Museum) resides in an old house that once belonged to a physician who served the local daimyō. The mansion has mysterious eccentricities—hanging ceilings, secret windows, and hidden passages. Displays include wall hangings, weaving machines, and other Hida regional items. ⊠ *San-machi-dōri, near Sanno-machi-dōri,* ☎ *0577/32–1980.* ☒ *¥400.* ☉ *Mar.–Nov., daily 8:30–6; Dec.–Feb., daily 9–5.*

⑫ The **San-machi-suji** section of town includes Ichino-machi, Ninomachi, and Sanno-machi streets, which all parallel the Miya-gawa. Most of the old teahouses, inns, dye houses, and sake breweries with latticed windows and doors have been preserved, making this neighborhood somewhat of a vestige of pre-Meiji Japan. Along the river is the daily **Miya-gawa Asa-ichi,** where flowers and vegetables are sold until noon. It's generally less interesting than the asa-ichi in front of Takayama Jinya.

★ ⑬ Kusakabe Mingeikan (Folk-Craft Museum), a house from the 1880s, belonged to the Kusakabe family—wealthy merchants in the days of Edo. The handsome interior, with heavy beams of polished wood, acts as an appropriate setting for the Hida folk crafts displayed here. ⊠ *Nino-machi-dōri, north of a small tributary of the Miya-gawa,* ☎ *0577/32–0072.* ☒ *¥500.* ☉ *Mar.–Nov., daily 8:30–5; Dec.–Feb., Sat.–Thurs. 8:30–4:30.*

⑭ The **Yoshijima-ke** is an elegant merchant house museum that was rebuilt in 1908 but retains the distinctive characteristics of the Hida ar-

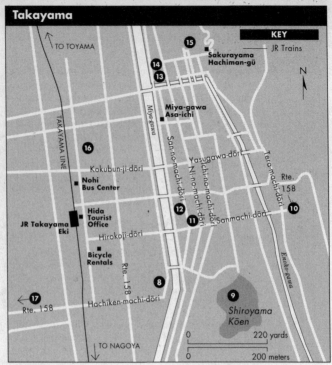

chitectural style. It's next door to Kusakabe Mingeikan. ⌧ *Nino-machi-dōri, north of a small tributary of the Miya-gawa,* ☏ *0577/32–0038.* ⌧ *¥500.* ◷ *Mar.–Nov., daily 9–5; Dec.–Feb., Wed.–Mon. 9–4:30.*

★ ⑮ The **Takayama Yatai Kaikan** (Takayama Float Exhibition Hall) is a community center of sorts that displays four of the 11 Takayama *yatai* (festival floats) used in Takayama's famous Hachi-man Matsuri. More than two centuries ago Japan was ravaged by the plague, and yatai were built and paraded through the streets as a way of appeasing the gods. Because this seemed to work in Takayama, locals built bigger, more elaborate yatai as preventive medicine. Now the yatai are gigantic—the building costs today would exceed ¥1.5 million ($14,000)—and the embellishments of wood-carved panels, carved wooden lion heads for dances, and tapestries are works of art. Technical wizardry is also involved, as each yatai has puppets, controlled by rods and wires that perform amazing feats, which approach Olympic-quality gymnastics. ⌧ *In northeast corner of town, 2 blocks north of the Enako-gawa,* ☏ *0577/32–5100.* ⌧ *¥820.* ◷ *Mar.–Nov., daily 8:30–5; Dec.–Feb., daily 9–4:30.*

⑯ **Kokubun-ji** is the city's oldest temple, dating from 1588, and it houses many objects of art, including a precious sword used by the Heike clan. In the Main Hall (built in 1615) sits a figure of Yakushinyorai (Healing Buddha), and in front of the three-story pagoda is a statue of Kannon. The ginkgo tree standing beside the pagoda is said to be more than 1,200 years old. ⌧ *Off Kokubun-ji-dōri, north of JR station,* ☏ *0577/32–1395.* ⌧ *¥300.* ◷ *Daily 9–4.*

★ ⑰ **Hida Minzoku Mura** (Hida Folk Village), also locally called Hida no Sato (sato is another word for village), is a collection of traditional farmhouses moved to a park from several areas within the Hida region. Because the traditional Hida farmhouse is held together by ropes rather than nails, the dismantling and reassembling of the buildings posed few problems. Many are A-frames with thatched roofs, called *gasshō-zukuri* (praying hands); others are shingle-roofed. Twelve of the buildings are "private houses" displaying folk materials like tableware and weaving tools. In fact, the steeply angled frame of some houses left an atticlike space often used to cultivate silkworms. Another five houses are folk-craft workshops, with demonstrations of *ichii ittobori* (wood carving), *Hida-nuri* (Hida lacquering), and other traditional regional arts. To get to Hida Minzoku Mura, walk 20 minutes south from the JR Takayama station and take a right over the first bridge onto Route 158. Continue west for 20 minutes to the village. You can also take a bus from Platform 6, on the left side of the bus terminal. ☎ *0577/33–4714.* ⊠ *¥700.* ☉ *Daily 8:30–5.*

The **Hida Tourist Information Office** (☎ 0577/32–5328, FAX 0577/33–5565) in front of the JR station is open April–October, daily 8:30–6:30, and November–March, daily 8:30–5. The staff can help you find accommodations, both in town and in the surrounding mountains.

Dining and Lodging

$$$$ ★ ✕ **Kakushō.** Locally famous for Takayama's popular *shōjin-ryōri*, a meal of mountain vegetables, this restaurant uses fresh, regional products. A local miso paste used in the cooking adds extra flavor. If the freshwater ayu is on the menu, be sure to try it. Although there's no dress code per se, you might want to steer toward the semiformal to feel comfortable here. Above all, this is a friendly place, where the owner, Sumitake-san, will happily translate the menu for you. However, there's no English sign out front, so look for a small building with a courtyard patio diagonally across from a parking lot. ⊠ *2 Babachō-dōri, on far side of Miya-gawa, near Tenshō-ji,* ☎ *0577/32–0174. AE, DC, MC, V.*

$$$$ ★ ✕ **Suzaki.** This is Takayama's number one restaurant for *kaiseki*, a carefully prepared and aesthetically arranged 7- to 12-course set meal using the freshest ingredients, served—especially in this case—on beautiful ceramic ware. If making choices among dishes is involved, you'll want to select one prepared with wild plants from the Hida Mountains and salted river fish. ⊠ *4–14 Shinmei, near Naka-bashi,* ☎ *0577/ 32–0023. AE, DC, MC, V.*

$$ ✕ **Susuya.** In a traditional Hida-style house across from the Rickshaw Inn, this delightful, small Japanese restaurant has been owned by the same family for generations. Intimate and wood-beamed, it specializes in superb sansai-ryōri (which you must order a day ahead), mountain plants, and freshly caught river fish, such as ayu, grilled with soy sauce. ⊠ *24 Hanakawa, at Kokobunji-dōri,* ☎ *0577/32–2484. AE, MC, V.*

$$$–$$$$ ★ 🏨 **Hida Plaza Hotel.** With accommodations that are a cut above those of most other lodgings in its price range, this is the best international-style hotel in town. Traditional Hida ambience permeates the older wing. Beautiful wood is used throughout the hotel's tastefully decorated restaurants. Tatami rooms exude elegance and simplicity, and the Western rooms are amazingly large and comfy, with sofas. All rooms have wide-screen TVs, and many have views of the surrounding mountains. Although the newer wing is not nearly as attractive, its rooms are larger. Luxury makes an appearance in the form of mineral baths crafted of fragrant cypress wood. ⊠ *2–60 Hanaoka-chō, north of train station, Takayama, Gifu-ken 506,* ☎ *0577/33–4600,* FAX *0577/ 33–4602. 152 Western-style rooms, 36 Japanese-style rooms. 4 restaurants, coffee shop, indoor pool, mineral baths, sauna, health club, dance club, shops. AE, DC, MC, V.*

$$$ 🏠 **Minshuku Sosuke.** Although this concrete building 15 minutes from town is a private home, it feels more like a traveler's boardinghouse. The owner runs a tight ship and speaks essential English, but don't expect her or her husband to be overly helpful. Rooms are small and basic. The shared rooms, baths, and toilets are kept spotless, which is undoubtedly one of the reasons Sosuke is so popular. Meals are taken at long tables (tatami seating), where you'll meet other guests, although the food's average and the beer expensive. To get here, take a right from the JR Takayama station, then another right at the first bridge, and walk seven minutes; it's opposite the huge, tacky Green Hotel. ✉ *1–64 Okamoto-chō, Takayama, Gifu-ken 506,* 📞 *0577/32–0818,* ℻ *0577/33–5570. 14 rooms. Dining room. No credit cards. EP, MAP.*

$$ 🏠 **Yamakyu.** Cozy, antiques-filled nooks with chairs and coffee tables
★   serve as small lounges in this old Tera-machi minshuku. There's a tiny garden off the central hall. The tatami rooms are not large but are sufficient. In the mineral-water baths, a giant waterwheel turns hypnotically as you're lulled by recorded forest bird songs. Although there's an 11 PM curfew, dinner hours are more flexible than the typical minshuku, and the food, of astonishing local variety, is superb. Yamakyu is east of the Enako-gawa, in the Tera-machi district, a 20-minute walk from Takayama Eki. ✉ *58 Tenshō-ji-machi, near Tenshō-ji, Takayama, Gifu-ken 506,* 📞 *0577/32–3756,* ℻ *0577/35–2350. 30 Japanese-style rooms. Dining room, shop. No credit cards. EP, MAP.*

Nightlife

Nightlife in otherwise sleepy Takayama revolves around locally produced beer and sake. Open for lunch until 3, and then again at 5:30, **Renga-ya** (✉ 58–11 3-chōme Hon-machi, 📞 0577/36–1339) is a brewery, bar, and restaurant. Head left from the station for one block, then turn right on Kokubun-ji-dōri; walk east and cross the Miya-gawa, then turn left. It's one block down, on the left. You'll see the brewery at work through the window. A traditional Hida-style restaurant, **Jizake-ya** sells locally prepared *jizake* (sake) and *jibiru* (beer) to wash down everything from sushi to tempura. It's a lively place where you can meet locals if you're up for it. Look for the amusing English translations on the menu.

Getting Around

Laid out in a grid pattern, compact Takayama is easy to explore on foot or by bicycle—bikes at the rental shop south of the station cost ¥300 per hour. Or, in San-machi-suji, spend ¥3,000 (for two) on a 15-minute old-town ricksha tour (if you just want to pose in one for a photograph, be ready to hand over ¥1,000).

It is easy to get to Takayama by bus from Matsumoto—but only between May and early November, however—and it costs ¥3,100. A highly recommended detour to Kamikōchi will bring the fare to ¥6,260.

Takayama has connections north to Toyama by JR train. There are four train departures daily. The ride takes about 90 minutes and costs ¥1,150 or ¥1,620, depending on whether you reserve a seat and whether the train is running express. There is no direct bus service. From Toyama there are trains east to Niigata or west to Kanazawa and the Noto-hantō via Ogi-machi, which has connections to Nagoya as well.

For Ogi-machi, a Nohi bus makes the 1½-hour trip to Makido (¥1,930); then change to a JR bus for the one-hour trip to Ogi-machi (¥1,430). Six buses depart daily (four from December to March) from Takayama. Connections can be tricky, so inquire at the JR Takayama station tourist office for help before you leave. The Meitetsu express bus from Nagoya to Kanazawa, via the Shōkawa Valley, runs daily in each direction.

Ogi-machi

⑱ *2½ hrs northwest of Takayama by bus.*

It's speculated that Ogi-machi was originally populated by survivors of the powerful Taira family, who were all but killed off in the 12th century by the rival Genji family in western Honshū. The majority of the residents in this quiet Shokawa Valley village strewn with rice fields still live in gasshō-zukuri houses. Both the shape and the materials enable the house to withstand the heavy, wet regional snow, and in summer the straw keeps things cool. Household activities center on the *irori* (open hearth), which sends its smoke up through the timbers and thatched roof. Meats and fish are preserved (usually on a lattice shelf suspended above the hearth) by the ascending smoke, which also does double duty by keeping insects and vermin from taking up residence in the rice-straw thatching. Many of these old houses also function as minshuku. To stay in one, you can make reservations and get maps through the Ogi-machi tourist office.

Opposite Ogi-machi, on the banks of the Shō-gawa, is **Shirakawa Gasshō Mura,** a restored "learning village" that illustrates the rural life of Chūbu farmers through demonstrations and crafts workshops. The 25 gasshō-zukuri–style houses here were actually transplanted from four villages that fell prey to progress—the building of the Miboro Dam upriver in 1972.

Ogi-machi Tourist Office (✉ 57 Ogi-machi, Shirakawa-mura, ☎ 05769/6–1311), open daily 9–5, is next to the Gasshō-shuraku bus stop in the center of Ogi-machi. The staff can help you make accommodation reservations.

Getting Around

Daily service here by Nagoya Meitetsu departs from Nagoya at 8:40 AM from mid-July to mid-November. The fare from Nagoya to Ogi-machi is ¥4,760 (6 hours). A daily bus departing from Ogi-machi at 2:40 PM makes the trip to Kanazawa (¥2,730; 2 hours, 40 minutes). For Kanazawa you can also backtrack and take the JR train from Takayama via Toyama, although you'll see more of the Hida Mountains if you travel by bus.

KANAZAWA AND THE NORTH CHŪBU COAST

Full of culture, fun, and friendliness, Kanazawa ranks among Japan's best-loved cities. To the east rise snowy mountains, including the revered (and hikeable) Haku-san. To the north stretches the mittlike projection of the Noto-hantō, where lush, rolling hills and productive rice fields are bounded by contrasting, highly scenic coastlines. Farther north along the Nihon-kai are the hardworking industrial capitals of Toyama and Niigata and, offshore, the ever-lonely former isle of banishment, Sado-ga-shima.

Kanazawa

2 hrs northeast of Kyōto by JR Limited Express; 3 hrs north of Nagoya by JR Limited Express; 2½ hrs northwest of Takayama by JR Limited Express train, changing trains at Toyama; 3 hrs, 40 mins southwest of Niigata by JR Limited Express.

The bulldozers of modernization have crept slowly into Kanazawa, which today presents a strange mixture of unblemished old Japan and a modern, trendsetting city. Some parts of town have changed surprisingly little in the last 300 years. Yet, as far as modern art, fashion, music, and international dining are concerned, this place is as hip as any in Japan. The Japan Sea gives Kanazawa some of the best seafood in the country but also gives it a climate much like that in Seattle or Vancouver. The cold, gray, and wet winters are more than offset by the welcoming friendliness of its cosmopolitan people.

In the feudal times of the Edo period, the prime rice-growing areas around Kanazawa (known then as the province of Kaga) made the ruling Maeda clan the second wealthiest in the country. Harvests routinely came in at more than *hyaku-man-goku* (1 million *koku,* the Edo-period unit of measurement based on how much rice would feed one person for a year), enough to feed 1 million people for a year. To the Maedas' credit and to the great benefit of the citizens, much of this wealth was used to fund and encourage such cultural pursuits as silk dyeing, ceramics, and the production of gold-leaf and lacquerware—traditions that continue to this day. Education was also fostered, and the town became (and still is) a great center of learning, crafts, and culture.

This prosperity did not pass unnoticed by the power centers to the east. The possibility of attack by the Edo daimyō inspired the Maeda lords to construct one of the country's most massive castles amid a maze-like network of narrow, winding lanes, making the approach difficult and invasion nearly impossible. These tactics paid off, and Kanazawa enjoyed some 300 years of peace and prosperity. However, thanks to seven fires over the centuries, all that remains today of the once-mighty Kanazawa-jō are the castle walls and a single, impressive gate. The former castle grounds are now the site of Kanazawa University.

🔟 The **Kanazawa-jō** area is a good point to start exploring Kanazawa and its history. Only the **Ishikawa-mon** remains intact, although the gate was rebuilt in 1788. It's said that the lead tiles used atop the wall and gate were to act as emergency ammunition in case of a prolonged siege. To reach the castle, take any bus (¥200) from Gate 11 at the bus terminal outside the JR station.

★ 🔟 Across the street from the castle remains is Kanazawa's **Kenrokuen,** (Kenroku Garden) one of the three finest landscaped gardens in the country (the other two are Mito's Kairakuen and Okayama's Kōrakuen). At 25 acres, the largest of the three, Kenrokuen began as the outer garden of Kanazawa-jō in 1676. Many generations of daimyō later, Kenrokuen reached its final form in the early 1880s. Its name means "Garden of Six Qualities" (*ken-roku* means "integrated six"), since it possessed the six superior characteristics judged necessary (since the time of the Chinese Sung Dynasty) for the perfect garden: spaciousness, artistic merit, majesty, abundant water, extensive views, and seclusion. Despite the promise of its last attribute, the gardens attract a mad stampede of visitors—herded by megaphone—in cherry-blossom season (mid-April) and Golden Week (late April and early May). Early morning seems the only sensible option for a visit, when you'll be free from squadrons of people seeking quietude.

While you're strolling through the gardens, note the craftsmanship of the beautifully wrought bridges and fountains. Another Kanazawa-area technique is the elaborate method of bolstering pine boughs in the inevitable event of heavy snowfalls: long ropes tied to a tall pole support individual branches. ⊠ *1 Kenroku-machi, across from Kanazawa-jō,* ☎ *076/221–5850.* 🔁 *¥300, free 3rd Sun. of month.* ☉ *Mar.–mid-Oct., daily 7–6; mid-Oct.–Feb., daily 8–4:30.*

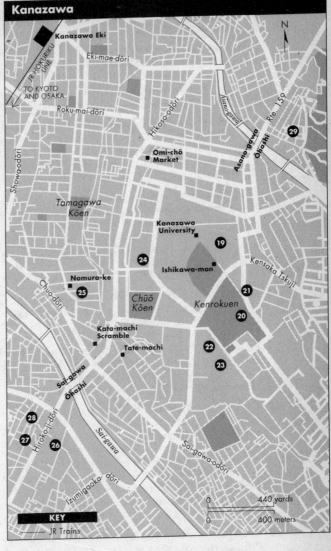

Seisonkaku (Southeast Palace), southeast of Kenrokuen, is a retirement
manor built in 1863 by one of the Maeda lords for his mother. The elegant rooms now house the family heirlooms on display. ☎ 076/221–
0580. ¥600. Thurs.–Tues. 8:30–4.

★ ㉑ **Gyokusenen,** a tiny, intimate garden, is almost as old as its neighbor,
Kenrokuen—dating from the Edo period. Its owner-designer, a wealthy
merchant, sought calm and contemplative peace rather than accolades
for his green thumb. As a result, the garden is spared crowds of visitors, but its intimate repose also seems to come from the imaginative
and subtle arrangement of moss, maple trees, and small stepping-
stones by the pond, which are markedly different from the bold strokes
of Kenrokuen. Efficiently, the garden is landscaped such that silver maples
dangle their leaves over a sunny sunken pond from the perimeter of
another shady pond higher up that is filled with carp and greenery. You
can also have tea here for ¥500. From the Kenrokuen-shita bus stop,
across from the Kankō Bussankan (east of the big gate of the old cas-

tle), go south one block, then turn east onto the small street, and the park entrance is on the right. ☎ 076/221-0181. ➲ ¥700. ☉ Mid-Mar.–mid-Dec., daily 9–4.

At the **Kankō Bussankan** (Prefectural Handicraft Museum), near Gyokusenen, you can see demonstrations of Yuzen dyeing, pottery, and lacquerware production. ☎ 076/224-5511. ➲ ¥700 (includes admission to Gyokusenen). ☉ Apr.–Oct., daily 9–4:30; Nov.–Mar., Fri.–Wed. 9–4:30.

㉒ The **Ishikawa Kenritsu Bijutsukan** (Ishikawa Prefectural Art Museum) displays the country's best permanent collection of Kutani-yaki (colorful overglaze-painted porcelain), dyed fabrics, old Japanese paintings, and various other art objects. ⊠ 2-1 Dewa-machi, southwest of Kenrokuen, ☎ 076/231-7180. ➲ ¥350. ☉ Daily 9–4:30.

㉓ A narrow path behind the Ishikawa Kenritsu Bijutsukan leads to the **Hanrō Honda Zōhinkan** (Honda Museum). The Honda family members were the key political advisers to the Maeda daimyō, and the museum contains 700 art objects used by the Hondas during their term, including armor, uniforms of the family's personal firefighters, and the trousseaus of the Maeda brides who married into the Honda family. ☎ 076/261-0500. ➲ ¥500. ☉ Mar.–Oct., Fri.–Wed. 9–4:30.

Ōmi-chō Ichiba (Ōmi-chō Market), a mazelike warren of fish shops, is sure to delight the visitor with an astonishing variety of the freshest seafood available. You may see delicacies, which were pulled up from the sea that morning, that you've never heard of before. Look for the appallingly ugly but deliciously buttery anko (angler-fish), or the rare and pricey kegani (hairy crab). If you buy something, the merchant can pack it in ice for you, or show you where to have it cooked at a nearby restaurant. ☎ 076/231-1462. ☉ Mon.–Sat. 9–5.

㉔ Built in 1599, **Oyama Jinja** was dedicated to Lord Toshiie Maeda, the founder of the Maeda clan. The shrine's unusual three-story gate, **Shin-mon**, was completed in 1875. A stained-glass window within the squared arch is said to have once functioned like a lighthouse, beaming a light to guide ships in from the Japan Sea to the Kanaiwa port, 6 km (4 mi) northwest. You're free to walk around at any time. To get here from the JR station, you can take Bus 30 or 31 from Gate 8. ⊠ 11-1 Oyama-chō, across from the Kanazawa New Grand Hotel, ☎ 076/231-7210. ➲ Free.

㉕ Behind the modern Kōrinbō 109 shopping center is the **Naga-machi** (Samurai District), where the Maeda clan's samurai lived. Narrow, convoluted streets are lined with beautiful, golden adobe walls 8 ft high, footed with large stones and topped with black tiles.

A few houses have been carefully restored in the Samurai District, including the **Saihitsuan Yuzen Silk Center,** where you can watch demonstrations of Yuzen silk painting, a centuries-old technique in which intricate designs (floral, with exquisite white outlines) are painstakingly painted onto silk used for kimonos. ⊠ 5 blocks southwest of Oyama Jinja, behind the Tōkyū Hotel, ☎ 076/264-2811. ➲ ¥500. ☉ Fri.–Wed. 9–noon and 1–4:30.

Nomura-ke (Nomura House), in Naga-machi, was rebuilt more than 100 years ago by an industrialist named Nomura. Visit the Jōdan-no-ma drawing room made of hinoki (cypress), with elaborate designs in rosewood and ebony. A landscape drawn by Sasaki Senkai of the Kano school is painted on each of the sliding shōji (paper) doors. A small garden with a 400-year-old tree, a winding stream, and a bridge of pink

granite faces the living room. ⊠ *1–3–32 Naga-machi,* ☎ *076/221–3553.*
☎ *¥500.* ⏱ *Apr.–Sept., daily 8:30–5:30; Oct.–Mar., daily 8:30–4:30.*

NEED A BREAK?	While in Naga-machi, you can take green tea and *okashi* (Japanese cookies) at **Nikore** (⊠ 3–1 Naga-machi, 2-chōme, ☎ 076/261–0056), a converted samurai residence where Mrs. Mori and her son serve on a veranda facing a small garden. Nikore is open daily from 10 to 1 (until 2 on weekends and holidays); to find it look for the sign with three yellow *kanji* (Japanese characters).

★ ❷❻ On the south side of the Sai-gawa, a five-minute walk from the Sai-gawa Ōhashi, is the 350-year-old Nichiren-sect temple of **Myōryū-ji.** Its popular name, Ninja-dera (Temple of the Ninja), suggests a secret lure of mysteriously powerful martial-art masters, who protected the daimyō from invaders and assassins. However, if you can understand the Japanese tours, you'll learn that contrary to many of the exciting yet unfounded rumors, there never were "Ninja priests" here, just Nichiren Buddhist ones. The temple *does* have trick doors, hidden chambers, tunnel-like hallways, and an unusual number of extra staircases to its rooms, but this probably reflects the focus on self-preservation among the monks—who were of no small means and lived in dangerous times—rather than any threat of treachery or assassination of the daimyō. Reservations are essential and can be made by phone. ⊠ *1–2–12 No-machi, half a block southeast off Minami Ōdōri,* ☎ *076/241–0888.* ☎ *¥800.* ⏱ *Mar.–Nov., daily 9–4:30; Dec.–Feb., daily 9–4.*

❷❼ At the **Kutani Kōsen Gama** (Kutani Pottery Kiln) you can watch the process of making the local Kutani pottery, which is noted for its vibrant color schemes done in overglaze paints. ⊠ *1 block west and 1 block south of Myōryū-ji.* ☎ *Free.* ⏱ *Mon.–Sat. 8:30–noon and 1–5, Sun. 8:30–noon.*

❷❽ In **Nishi-no-Kuruwa,** the Western Pleasure Quarter, the walls no longer hold back geisha, but the checkpoint that kept them from skipping town has been preserved. Also here are a museum and gallery. From the JR station take Bus 30, 31, or 32 from Gate 8 to Hirokoji.

❷❾ **Higashi-no-Kuruwa,** the Eastern Pleasure Quarter, near the Asano-gawa, was set aside almost 200 years ago as a high-class area of indoor entertainment. Now the pleasures of visiting here are limited to looking at the quaint buildings with wood-slat facades in the narrow, winding streets. Most of the old geisha houses have become tearooms or minshuku, but occasionally you might still see a geisha scuttling to her appointment. Take the JR bus from JR Kanazawa Eki (¥200) to Hachira-chō, just before the Asano-gawa Ōhashi. Cross the bridge and walk northeast into the quarter.

One elegant former geisha house in Higashi-no-Kuruwa, **Shima-ke,** is open to the public for tours. ⊠ *1–13–21 Higashi-yama,* ☎ *076/252–5675.* ☎ *¥400.* ⏱ *Tues.–Sun. 9–5.*

Dining and Lodging

$$$$ ✕ **Goriya.** The specialty here at one of Kanazawa's oldest restaurants, is river fish, including the tiny *gori* (a small river fish usually cooked in soy sauce and sugar syrup). More than 200 years old, Goriya is justly famous for its garden on the banks of the Asano-gawa, although the cooking may not be Kanazawa's finest. Several small rooms compose the dining area. Dress is somewhat formal. You may get the most out of a daytime visit, when a modestly priced lunch (around ¥7,000) is served. ⊠ *60 Tokiwa-chō,* ☎ *076/252–5596. AE, MC, V.*

$$$$ ✕ **Tsubajin.** One of Kanazawa's best restaurants for Kaga-ryōri, Tsub-
★ ajin is actually part of a small, traditional, and expensive ryokan. Try

the crab, as well as the house specialty, a chicken stew called *jibuni*. Be forewarned that dinner for one will exceed ¥20,000, but a less elaborate and less expensive lunch is also served. ⊠ *5–1–8 Tera-machi,* ☎ *076/241–2181. Reservations essential. AE, MC, V.*

$$–$$$ ✕ **Kincharyō.** The menu changes seasonally in the showpiece restaurant
★ of the Kanazawa Tōkyū Hotel. The private dining room's ceiling is an impressive piece of delicate craftsmanship; the lacquered, curved countertop of the sushi bar is uniquely beautiful. And in the kitchen, the chef's culinary skill is superb. In the spring your seven or eight dishes may include *hotaru-ika* (firefly squid) and *idoko* (baby octopus), no larger than a thumbnail. The bargain-priced lunches and seasonal specials come highly recommended. ⊠ *Kanazawa Tōkyū Hotel, 3rd floor, 1–1 Korimbo, 2-chōme,* ☎ *076/231–2411. Reservations essential. AE, DC, MC, V.*

$$–$$$ ✕ **Miyoshian.** Excellent *bentō* (box lunches) and fish and vegetable din-
★ ners have been served here for about 100 years in the renowned Kenrokuen garden. The bentō prices are still pretty reasonable, at about ¥2,000. ⊠ *11 Kenroku-chō,* ☎ *076/221–0127. AE, MC, V. Closed Tues.*

$–$$ ✕ **Hot House.** Chefs from India and Nepal prepare delicious and in-
★ credibly cheap (¥1,000) Thali lunch sets, which include four curries, *nan* (an unleavened, tortilla-like Indian bread), rice, salad, yogurt, and even a beer. Also recommended are the Tandoori chicken and the chicken curry. ⊠ *3–11 Ikeda-machi,* ☎ *076/232–4036,* 𝔽𝔸𝕏 *076/232–9903. No credit cards.*

$ ✕ **Capricciosa.** Stick to the scrumptious pizza and pasta—including gar-
★ lic and chili, carbonara, and the *ika-sumi* (squid-ink) spaghetti (servings big enough for two, ¥1,600). The puffy calzones are just a lot of hot air. Capricciosa is across from the McDonald's at the entrance of Tate-machi between Daiwa and the Kata-machi Scramble. ⊠ *Tōku Tate-machi Bldg., 1–4–18 Kata-machi,* ☎ *076/260–8855. No credit cards.*

$ ✕ **Legian.** You might be surprised to find a funky Balinese eatery
★ alongside the Sai-gawa. But if you try the *gado-gado* (vegetables in a spicy sauce), *nasi goreng* (Indonesian-style fried rice), or chicken *satay* (grilled on a skewer, with peanut sauce), you'll be very glad you did. Indonesian beer and mango ice cream are also available. Since it's open late (Monday–Thursday until 12:30 AM; Friday and Saturday until 4:30 AM), you might want to hang around after dinner for drinks when things get interesting. From Kata-machi Scramble (the central intersection in this area), turn right, before the bridge, over the Sai-gawa and follow the narrow lane along the river. ⊠ *2–31–30 Kata-machi 2-chōme,* ☎ *076/262–6510. No credit cards. Closed Wed.*

$ ✕ **Noda-ya.** Slip into this little tea shop for a scoop of delicious *macha softo creamu* (green tea ice cream), or—oh, yes—a cup of tea. You can sit in the little garden or out front to people-watch. At the far end of the Tate-machi mall, it's a little hard to spot but you can smell the heavenly fragrance of roasting green tea leaves from far off. It's open daily from 9 to 8. ⊠ *3 Tate-machi,* ☎ *076/22–0982. No credit cards.*

$$$$ ⊡ **ANA Kanazawa.** Adjacent to Kanazawa Eki, this member of the ANA chain has a crescent-shape tower, an expansive lobby with a waterfall and pond, and more than its share of marble glitter. Guest rooms are remarkably soothing, with soft beige wallpaper, fabrics, and furnishings, and the L-shape plan is a welcome change from the usual boxiness of most hotel rooms. Staff, most of whom speak English, go out of their way to help foreign guests. Of the several restaurants, the penthouse Teppanyaki offers sumptuous meals with a panoramic view of the city, while Unkai serves kaiseki dinners, with excellent sashimi and a view of a miniature version of Kenrokuen. ⊠ *16–3 Showa-chō, Kanazawa, Ishikawa-ken 920,* ☎ *076/224–6111,* 𝔽𝔸𝕏 *076/224–6100. 255 rooms. 5 restaurants, coffee shop, health club, shops, free parking. AE, DC, MC, V.*

$$$$ ★ 🏨 **Hotel Nikkō Kanazawa.** The gorgeous, bright lobby of this 30-story hotel is more reminiscent of Singapore than Japan, and it has plenty of intimate nooks with luxurious furniture for lounging. Service is attentive, and the staff members are eager to practice their English with you. Western-style rooms beckon with creamy pastels, blond-wood furnishings, and striking views—of sea, city, or mountains. Le Grand Chariot, the top-floor lounge, has a panoramic view, French cuisine, and soft piano music. From here it's 10 minutes by taxi to Kanazawa's center. On the premises is a JAL ticket counter, and the hotel connects via an underground passageway with the JR station. ⊠ *2–15–1 Honmachi, across from Kanazawa Eki, Kanazawa, Ishikawa-ken 920-0853,* ☎ *076/234–1111,* 🆑 *076/234–8802. 256 rooms, 4 suites. 5 restaurants, coffee shop, lobby lounge, pool, gym, shops. AE, DC, MC, V.*

$$$$ ★ 🏨 **Ryokan Asadaya.** A small luxury ryokan designed in a stately style, Asadaya combines modernity with classical simplicity. Antique furnishings and exquisite scrolls and paintings create a pleasing setting—there's no plastic here. Enjoy superb regional cuisine in your room or in the restaurant. ⊠ *23 Jukken-machi, Kanazawa, Ishikawa-ken 920,* ☎ *076/232–2228,* 🆑 *076/252–4444. 5 Japanese-style rooms. Restaurant. AE. EP, MAP.*

$$$ ★ 🏨 **Kanazawa New Grand Hotel.** English is spoken at this established, international hotel in the city center, across from the Oyama Jinja. The hotel is not much to look at on the outside, and since the ANA and Nikkō hotels opened, it's no longer even in the top ranks. Old as the hotel may be, the service is still excellent. From the sky lounge and restaurant, Sky Restaurant Roi, which serves some of the city's best contemporary French cuisine, you can watch the sun set. The spacious rooms, though far from new, are done in white and beige tones, and there's a sofa. Japanese-style rooms are slightly larger but more spartan in furnishings. ⊠ *1–50 Takaoka-machi, Kanazawa, Ishikawa-ken 920,* ☎ *076/233–1311,* 🆑 *076/233–1591. 106 Western-style rooms, 3 Japanese-style rooms. 3 restaurants, coffee shop, shops. AE, DC, MC, V.*

$$$ 🏨 **Kanazawa Tōkyū Hotel.** In the heart of town, this sleek, modern hotel has a spacious lobby on the second floor with lots of red granite and plush carpets. It's brightly lit, with many plants. The elegantly furnished Western-style rooms are comfortable in size (not too large, not too small) and have pale cream walls. Kincharyō is a superb Japanese restaurant on-site; the Schloss Restaurant, on the 16th floor, serves French cuisine and offers a skyline view. ⊠ *1–1 Korimbo 2-chōme, Kanazawa, Ishikawa-ken 920,* ☎ *076/231–2411,* 🆑 *076/263–0154. 120 rooms. 3 restaurants, coffee shop, shops, meeting room. AE, DC, MC, V.*

$$ 🏨 **Kanazawa Station Hotel.** A convenient location and a reasonable price are the Kanazawa Station Hotel's strongest assets. It's nothing fancy, but rooms are larger than at most inexpensive business hotels, and they have refrigerators. The hotel is only a three-minute walk from the train station. ⊠ *18–8 Horikawa-chō, Kanazawa, Ishikawa-ken 920,* ☎ *076/223–2600,* 🆑 *076/223–2607. 62 rooms. Restaurant, coffee shop, refrigerators. AE, DC, MC, V.*

$ 🏨 **Yogetsu.** In a century-old geisha house in the Eastern Pleasure Quarter, Yogetsu is a small, stylish minshuku. Owner Temeko Ishitata is a welcoming hostess, and the price is nice. The guest rooms are small and have ancient-looking exposed beams, and there's a shared Japanese-style bath. ⊠ *1–13–22 Higashiyama, Kanazawa, Ishikawa-ken 920,* ☎ *076/252–0497. 5 Japanese-style rooms with shared bath. Dining room. No credit cards. EP, MAP.*

Nightlife

Some fine all-night fun is right here, and you won't have to burn much money to chase it down, either, since most of it's in the center of town. Be warned: these places don't take credit cards.

Free billiard tables make **Apre** (⊠ 4th floor, Laporto Bldg., ☎ 076/221–0090) a fun place to hang out on weekends (it's closed Monday). When it opens at 8 PM, the tables fill up, and the action is quite competitive. It's tricky to find, though, so don't hesitate to call for directions. **Pole-Pole** ("*po*-ray-*po*-ray"; ⊠ 2–31–31 Kata-machi, ☎ 076/260–1138) is a reggae bar run by the same jolly owner as Legian restaurant. Things get going after midnight, but if you want a place to sit, get here before then, as the two dark and cramped rooms fill quickly. Very often the crowd spills out into the hallway. The place is closed on Sunday but open until 5 AM the rest of the week.

Getting Around

From the JR station to downtown, Oyama Jinja, or the New Grand or Tōkyū hotels, take Bus 30, 31, or 32 from Gate 8 or Bus 20, 21, 22, or 41 from Gate 9. You might want to purchase the intracity Free Pass (¥900) from the Hokutetsu bus ticket office, in front of the JR station. You'll get unlimited travel on the city's buses.

Visitor Information

The **Kanazawa Information Office** (☎ 076/232–6200, FAX 076/238–6210) has two desks at the train station and a extremely helpful volunteer staff that will help you find accommodations. It's open daily 9–7; an English speaker is on duty 10–6.

Fukui

③⓪ *40 mins southwest of Kanazawa by JR Limited Express, 2 hrs north of Nagoya by JR Limited Express.*

One of the two main Buddhist Soto sect temples, **Eihei-ji,** 19 km (12 mi) southeast of the town, is Fukui's main draw. Founded in 1244, the complex of 70 temple buildings sits on a hillside surrounded by hinoki and *sugi* (cedar) trees hundreds of feet tall, some of which are as old as the original structures. The temple is still very active, and there are 200 monks in training at any given time. You can stay at the temple (for ¥7,000 a night, including two meals) with two weeks' advance notice in writing. If you stay, arrive by 4 PM, prepare to rise at 3 AM, and check out at 8 AM. The easiest way to get to Eihei-ji from Fukui is by train. If you do not want to return to Fukui and reboard the train for Kyōto and Ōsaka, take a bus to the JR line, then ride up to Ono and through two beautiful gorges, Kuzuryu and Managawa. ⊠ *Eiheiji-chō; for reservations: Eihei-ji Kokusaibu (International Dept.), Yoshida-gun, Fukui 920,* ☎ *0776/63–3102.* ⌷ *Tours ¥300.* ☯ *Daily 5–5.*

The **Awara Onsen,** northwest of Fukui, shoulders the rocky Nihonkai shore and is a popular resort town for Japanese families. Since it's right on the JR line, it's a good place to take the waters and spend a night or two on the coast. Here you'll find attractive and expensive ryokan as well as less expensive minshuku. From Fukui take the JR local train to the Awara Eki (¥320), and then take a bus from Gate 2 to Awara-chō Onsen (about ¥300).

Lodging

$$$ ⊡ **Hotel Akebono Bekkan.** Think of this small, two-story wooden hotel as a weekend retreat destination: the owners can arrange training sessions in Zen meditation and classes in pottery and papermaking. Both Japanese and Western breakfasts are served, but only Japanese food is available at dinner. All of the small tatami rooms share a communal bath. The inn, a member of the Welcome Inn group, is next to Sakura Bridge, a 10-minute walk from JR Fukui Eki. ⊠ *3–9–26 Chūo, Fukui-shi, Fukui-ken 910,* ☎ *0776/22–0506,* FAX *0776/22–8023.* 10 *Japanese-style rooms with shared bath. Restaurant. AE, V. EP, MAP.*

$$ ⊡ **Minshuku Kimuraya.** A quiet minshuku in the center of the spa town, Kimuraya is a perfect alternative to staying in one of Fukui's plain hotels. Knowing a few words of Japanese helps here, but the family that runs the place will do its best to understand your sign language. Rooms are large—8 or 10 tatami mats—and heated by kerosene stoves. A *kotatsu* (table with an under-blanket electric heater) is the sole furnishing. Home-style Japanese fare is served for breakfast and dinner. From JR Awara Onsen Eki take a bus from Gate 2 to the Awarayu-no-machi stop in town. The minshuku is a three-minute walk west from the stop, which is in front of the park. ⊠ *910–41 Awara-chō Onsen, Fukui-shi, 910,* ☎ *0776/77–2229. 10 Japanese-style rooms with shared bath. No credit cards. EP, MAP.*

Noto-hantō (Noto Peninsula)

③① *Nanao, on the east coast of the peninsula, is 52 mins northeast from Kanazawa by JR Limited Express. Wajima, on the north coast of Noto-hantō, is 2¼ hrs northeast of Kanazawa by JR Limited Express.*

Thought to be named after an indigenous Japanese Ainu word for "nose," the Noto-hantō juts out into the Nihon-kai and shelters the bays of both Nanao and Toyama. A spine of steep, densely forested hills lines the west coast, which is wind- and wave-blasted in winter and ruggedly beautiful in other seasons. The eastern shoreline is lapped by calmer waters and has stunning clear-weather views of Tate-yama, the Hida Mountains, and even of some of Nagano's alpine peaks, more than 105 km (70 mi) away. Rice fields are scattered throughout. This is a good place to explore by car, or even by bicycle. Although the interior routes can be arduous, the coastal roads are relatively flat and good for biking. Or you can explore by combining train and bus trips or guided tours, which can be arranged in Kanazawa.

The Nanao-sen (Nanao Line) runs from Kanazawa through Nanao and all the way to Wajima, via Anamizu, where it's often necessary to change trains. From Anamizu, the private Noto Line goes northeast to Tako-jima. The line to Wajima turns inland after Hakui, however, and misses some of the peninsula's best sights.

A quick sightseeing circuit of the Noto-hantō, from Hakui to Nanao, can be done in six to eight hours, but if your aim is to absorb the peninsula's scenery, stay two or three days, stopping in Wajima and at one of the minshuku along the coast; arrangements can be made through the tourist information offices in Kanazawa, Nanao, or Wajima.

In **Hakui,** a 40-minute train ride away from Kanazawa, ride a bicycle along the coastal path as far as beautiful Gan-mon (Sea Gate), some 26 km (16 mi) away, where you can stop for lunch. Just north of Chirihama, a formerly popular and now unkempt beach, the scenery improves.

You can rent a bike from **Kato Cycle** (☎ 0767/22–0539), across from Joyful Supermarket, west of the JR station in Hakui.

Myōjō-ji, a Nichiren-sect temple complex founded in 1294, is a few miles north by bus from Hakui (buses leave outside the train station). Look for an impressive five-story pagoda. Beside it is a squat wooden building, which appears from the outside too small to be housing the very large, colorful Buddhist statue inside. A recorded announcement on the bus tells where to get off for Myōjō-ji. It's a 10-minute walk to the temple from the bus stop. ⊠ *1 Taki-tani-machi Yo-no,* ☎ *0767/27–1226.* ⊠ *¥350.* ☉ *Daily 8–5.*

Although you can take the inland bus route north from Hakui to Monzen, the longer (70-minute) bus ride that runs along the coast is more scenic. It also allows you to see the 16-km (10-mi) stretch between Fuku-ura and Sekinohana known as **Noto-Kongo** (Noto Seacoast), which is noted for fantastic wind- and wave-eroded rocks. There are many different formations, from craggy towers cut off from the mainland to partly submerged checkerboard platforms, but among the best known is **Gan-mon,** a rocky cave cut through by water. Gan-mon is about 45 minutes north of Hakui and is a stop on tour-bus routes, but in any case you can still see all kinds of wave- and wind-blasted rocks from the road without leaving your car or bus seat.

The Zen temple complex **Sōji-ji** at Monzen once held the headquarters of the Soto sect. A fire destroyed most of the buildings of in 1818, however, and the sect moved its headquarters to Yokohama. Strolling paths still traverse the grounds, past some spectacular red maples, and through an impressive, elaborately carved gate. The Sōji-ji-mae bus stop is directly in front of the temple. It can also can be reached from the Anamizu bus station in 40 minutes. ⊠ *Monzen, Monzen-machi,* ☎ *0768/42–0005.* ☞ *¥400.* ⊘ *Daily 8–5.*

Only 16 km (10 mi) up the road from Monzen, one bus stop away, is **Wajima,** a fishing town at the tip of the peninsula known not only for its fish but for its lacquerware. To see how the laborious manufacturing process is carried out, you can visit the **Wajima Shikki Kaikan** (Lacquerware Hall). To make a single piece involves more than 20 steps and 100 processes, from wood preparation and linen reinforcement to the application of numerous layers of lacquer, with careful drying and polishing between coats, but you can pick some up effortlessly in almost any store in town. Wajima Shikki Kaikan is in the center of town on the north side of Route 249, just before Shin-bashi (New Bridge). To get here from the station, turn left when you exit and walk straight (northwest) about four blocks until you hit Route 249. Turn left again—there's a Hokuriku Bank on the corner—and continue southwest along Route 249 for about four blocks. ☎ *0768/22–2155.* ☞ *¥300.* ⊘ *Daily 8:30–5:30.*

The **asa-ichi** (☎ 0768/22–7653 mornings only) in Wajima is held daily between 8 and 11:30, except the 10th and 25th of each month. You can buy seafood, fruit, vegetables, local crafts, and lacquerware. Local sages advise coming at 11:15, ready to bargain hard. A *yū-ichi* (evening market), a smaller version of the asa-ichi, starts around 3 PM. Ask most anyone for directions, and you'll get pointed there.

NEED A BREAK? Missed the morning market? Various sashimi and sushi (sets) are reasonably priced at **Shin-puku** (⊠ 41 Kawai-chō, Go-bu, Wajima-shi, ☎ 0768/22–8133), a small but beautiful sushi bar just a 10-minute walk from the train station. To get here from the station, turn left when you exit at the front and walk northwest (left) for about four blocks until you hit the main road, Route 249. Then turn right and walk northeast about three blocks along Route 249. One block past the Cosmo gas station (on the left), you'll see Shin-puku on the right.

Wajima's **tourist office** (☎ 0768/22–1503), at the station, offers assistance with accommodations, and maps of the area; it's open daily 10–6.

From Wajima a bus runs hourly for **Sosogi,** a small village 20 minutes to the northeast, passing the terraced rice fields of **Senmaida,** where innumerable rice fields descend from the hills to the edge of the sea.

At Sosogi the road forks inland, and about 8 km (5 mi) beyond the fork are two **traditional farm manor houses.** The Shimo-Tokikunike (Shimo-Tokikuni House; ☎ 0768/32–0075) is more than 300 years old and is furnished with antiques. Rent a tape recorder at the entrance for an English explanation of each room. Close by is **Kami-Tokiku-nike** (Kami-Tokikuni House; ☎ 0768/32–0171), which took 28 years to build in the early 1800s and remains in near-perfect condition. Each room in this house had a special purpose coinciding with the rigid social hierarchy of 19th-century Japan. Both houses charge a small admission fee and are open daily 9–4:30.

You can continue around the peninsula's northern tip by bus—from Sosogi to **Rokkō-misaki** (Cape Rokkō), where there's a small lighthouse, and down to the northern terminus of the Noto Railway Line at Tako-jima. However, unless you have a car, the views and scenery don't quite justify the infrequency of the service on this particular leg of the peninsula, so it's better to take the inland route from Sosogi to Suzu.

The same hourly bus that runs between Wajima and Sosogi continues on to **Suzu** on the *uchi* (inside) coast. Just south of Suzu, near Ukai station, is an interesting offshore rock formation called **Mitsuke-jima**—look for a wedge of rock topped with lush vegetation.

Southeast of Suzu is the superior open-air **Mawaki Onsen.** Artifacts, including pottery perhaps 6,000 years old from the Jōmon (straw-rope pattern) period, were found here. Mawaki is well known for its wonderful hilltop view, which overlooks the rice fields and fishing villages along the edge of Toyama Bay (so feel free to bypass the gaudy new tourist attractions, and head straight for the baths). One bath-and-sauna complex is done in stone, the other in wood; on alternate weeks they open to men and women. A hotel is connected to the bath complex. To get here, it's a bit of a hike up the hill or a short taxi ride from Jōon Mawaki Eki on the Noto Line. Mawaki can also be reached in 2¼ hours by car from Kanazawa—via a scenic toll road as far as Anamizu and then free from there—or 2½ hours by train (with a change in Wakura). ⊠ *19–39 Mawaki,* ☎ *0768/62–4567,* FAX *0768/62–4568.* ☞ *¥450.* ⊙ *Mon. noon–10, Tues.–Sun. 10–10.*

As you make your way south to Mawaki Onsen, there are fine opportunities for hiking, swimming, and camping, as well as a terrific brewery and log-cabin-style restaurant called the **Heart and Beer Nihonkai Club** (⊠ 92 Jitateheki, Uchiura-machi, ☎ 0768/72–8181). It's operated by two beer masters from Eastern Europe and an association that helps the disabled. Specials include delicious fried emu, raised on-site, and tasty local Noto beef, along with some very good microbrewed beer. Open from Thursday through Tuesday, it's about five minutes by taxi from Matsunami Eki (on the Noto Tetsudō).

Nanao is best known for its festivals. **Seihakusai Matsuri,** a 400-year-old tradition held May 2–5, is when huge (26-ft), 10-ton floats resembling ships called *deka-yama* (big mountains) are paraded through the streets for three days and nights of nonstop partying. Since it's celebrated during Golden Week, when everyone enjoys holidays from school and work, it's quite a frenetic scene. At midnight or thereabout the real madness begins: the deka-yama become miniature Kabuki stages upon which costumed children dance while crowds mill and chant below. The men pulling these contraptions at risk of life and limb are given generous and frequent libations of beer and sake for their efforts, and those in the crowd suffer no shortage of such staples either. During the day the floats are parked at community centers, where you can look at them close up. The wheels alone, made of ingeniously joined wooden sections, are 6½-ft tall and weigh enough to shake streets and houses as they pass. On the final day the three deka-yama are gathered together near the wharf amid a carnival-like atmosphere of eating, drinking, and socializing.

During **Ishizaki Hoto Matsuri,** celebrated the first Saturday of August, many beautiful paper lanterns more than 6 ft tall are carried on platforms and poles by participants delirious with excitement. As with the Seihakusai Matsuri, much alcohol is consumed, and the proceedings continue long into the night, rain or shine. The entire town, a fishing village suburb of Nanao, opens its doors and parlors to invite everyone to drink and feast.

Contact the **International Exchange Office in Nanao** (☎ 0767/53–8448, ℻ 0767/54–8117) to get festival details or to arrange for accommodations—or even a home stay.

Takaoka, the southern gateway to the Noto Peninsula, is not especially worth lingering in, though it does have Japan's third-largest **Daibutsu** (Great Buddha), after those at Kamakura and Nara. It's made of bronze and stands 53 ft high. Also in Takaoka, a 10-minute walk from the station, is **Zuiryu-ji,** a delightful Zen temple that doubles as the local youth hostel. A sprawling park, **Kojō-kōen,** not far from the station, is particularly stunning in autumn, with its stands of red and silver maples. Takaoka is mostly known for its traditions of copper-, bronze-, and iron-smithing and remains a major bell-casting center.

Lodging

$$$$ 🏨 **Mawaki Pō-re Pō-re.** This interesting little hotel, which connects to the bath complex at Mawaki, is nestled into the side of a hill and has great views of the sea and surrounding hills. Breakfast is included, and the staff is helpful and friendly. The Western-style rooms are done with blue and purple accents; the Japanese-style rooms are slightly larger, but simpler, bright, and with shōji screens. A restaurant here serves freshly caught local seafood. Best of all, you're just a minute away from the mineral baths. ⌧ *19–110 Mawaki, Noto-machi, Mawaki Onsen, Ishikawa-ken 927,* ☎ *0768/62–4700,* ℻ *0768/62–4702. 5 Western-style rooms, 5 Japanese-style rooms. Restaurant. No credit cards.*

Toyama

③② *30 mins southeast of Takaoka by JR local; 1 hr east of Kanazawa by JR Limited Express; 3 and 4 hrs north of Kyōto and Nagoya, respectively, by JR.*

Busy, industrial Toyama is beautified by Toyama-jōshi (Toyama Castle Park), a spread of greenery with a reconstructed version of the original (1532) castle.

A slow, noisy, open-air train called the **Kurobe-kyōkoku Railway** operates May through November 30 and runs through the mountain valley, past gushing springs and plunging waterfalls along the Kurobe-kyōkoku to Keyakidaira 20 km (12½ mi) away; the fare is ¥1,350. You might catch a glimpse of wild monkeys or *serow,* a native type of mountain goat, from the train. Bring a windbreaker jacket, even in summer, as it's a cold, clammy, long ride (90 minutes each way). Contact the tourist office for times and directions.

From Keyakidaira, you can proceed on foot to two **rotemburo** (open-air spas) nearly 100 years old: Meiken Onsen is a 10- to 15-minute walk; Babadani Onsen, 35–40 minutes.

If you're a serious hiker, **trails** from Keyakidaira can lead you to the peak of **Mt. Shirouma,** more than 9,810 ft high, in several hours. Nearby **Tate-yama** rewards experienced hikers with stunning views. You can also hike to Kurobe Dam, and to the cable car that can take you to the tunnel through Tate-yama to Murodō. If you have several days to spare, camping gear, and a map of mountain trails and shelters, you can go as far as Hakuba in Nagano.

For more information on the Kurobe-kyōkoku Railway, hiking, camping or the town, you can contact the **tourist information office** (☎ 0764/44–3200) in Toyama Eki.

The **National Parks Association of Japan** (✉ Toranomon Denki Bldg., 8–1 Toranomon 2-chōme, Minato-ku, Tōkyō, ☎ 03/502–0488) is a good source of help on hiking and camping near Toyama.

Niigata

By James
Vardaman ③③ *3 hrs from Toyama on the JR Hokuriku line; 1½ hrs northwest of Tōkyō's Ueno Eki by Shinkansen; 2 hrs, 15 mins northwest of Tōkyō on the Toki local line.*

The coast between Kurobe and Niigata is flat and not so interesting. Two towns along the way, Naoetsu and Teradomari, are useful as ferry ports for Ogi and Akadomari, respectively, on Sado-ga-shima. Niigata is likewise most useful as the port from which to board the ferry to Sado. As Japan's major shipping center and industrial city on the Nihon-kai coast, it is a good place for replenishing supplies and changing money. The **tourist information office** (☎ 025/241–7914) to the left of the station can help you find a hotel and supply city maps and ferry schedules for Sado-ga-shima.

Dining and Lodging

$$–$$$ ✕ **Marui.** *The* place in Niigata for fresh fish is Marui. For starters, order the *nami nigiri* (standard sushi set) and a bottle of chilled sake; the local Kitayuki is a good choice. While savoring these, glance at what your neighbors are ordering and ask for what looks good. You can't go wrong with the freshest fish, abalone, sea urchin, and squid in town—at a reasonable price. Marui closes during mid-afternoon. It's one block off the Furu-machi arcade, around the corner from Inaka-ya. ✉ *1411 Hachiban-chō, Higashi-bori-dōri, ☎ 025/228–0101. No credit cards.*

$–$$ ✕ **Inaka-ya.** In the heart of Furu-machi, the local eating and drinking district, this universally recommended restaurant welcomes you warmly. The specialty, *wappa-meshi* (rice steamed in a wooden box with toppings of salmon, chicken, or crab), makes an inexpensive (¥600–¥800) but excellent lunch. The *yanagi karei hitohoshi-yaki* (grilled flounder), *nodo-kuro shioyaki* (grilled local whitefish), and *buri teriyaki* (yellowtail) at ¥1,500–¥2,000 will make you want to become a regular customer. Inaka-ya closes between lunch and dinner. ✉ *1457 Kyūban-chō, Furu-machi-dōri, ☎ 025/223–1266. Reservations not accepted. No credit cards.*

$$$$ ⌂ **Okura Hotel Niigata.** A sophisticated, first-class hotel on the Shinano-gawa, 15 minutes on foot from the station, the Okura is one of Niigata's international accommodations. Rooms overlooking Shinano-gawa have the best views. If you plan to read or work at the hotel, the Okura's rooms have ample lighting. A formal French restaurant in the penthouse looks down on the city and over the Nihon-kai to Sado-ga-shima. Breakfast and lighter meals are served in the Grill Room. ✉ *6-53 Kawabata-chō, Niigata City, Niigata-ken 951-8053, ☎ 025/224–6111, FAX 025/224–7060. 300 Western-style and Japanese-style rooms. 3 restaurants, shops, business services. AE, DC, MC, V.*

$$–$$$ ⌂ **Niigata Toei Hotel.** For an inexpensive business hotel located a block and a half from the station, this ranks the best. The ninth floor has two restaurants and a bar for evening entertainment. ✉ *1–6–2 Benten, Niigata 950-0901, ☎ 025/244–7101, FAX 025/241–8485. 134 rooms. 2 restaurants, bar, meeting room. AE, D, MC, V.*

Sado-ga-shima (Sado Island)

1 hr by hydrofoil from Niigata, 2½ hrs by car ferry.

Sado has always been a melancholy island. Its role in history has been as a place where antigovernment intellectuals, such as the Buddhist monk Nichiren, were banished to endure the harshest exile. Then, when gold was discovered during the Edo period (1603–1868), the homeless, especially those from Edo, were sent to Sado to work as forced laborers in the mines. This heritage of hardship has left behind a tradition of soulful ballads and folk dances. Even the bamboo grown on the island is said to be the best for making *takohachi,* the plaintive flutes that accompany the ballads.

From May through September is the best time to visit Sado. At other times weather can prevent sea and air crossings, and in January and February the weather is bitterly cold. Though the island is Japan's fifth largest, it's comparatively small, at 530 square km (331 square mi). Two parallel mountain chains, running along the north and south coasts, are split by an extensive plain containing small rice farms and the island's principal cities. Despite the million-plus tourists visiting the island each year (more than 10 times the number of island inhabitants), the pace of life is slow, even preindustrial. That is Sado's appeal.

34 Sado's usual port of entry is **Ryōtsu,** the island's largest township. The center of town is the strip of land that runs between Kamo-ko (Kamo Lake) and the Nihon-kai, with most of the hotels and ryokan on the shore of the lake. Kamo-bo is actually connected to the sea by a small inlet running through the middle of town. Ryōtsu's Ebisu quarter has the island's concentration of restaurants and bars.

35 The simplest way to begin exploring Sado is to take the bus from Ryōtsu west to **Aikawa.** This was once a small town of 10,000 people. When, in 1601, gold was discovered, the rush was on. The population swelled to 100,000 until the ore was exhausted. Now it's back to 10,000 inhabitants, and tourists coming to see the old gold mine are a major source of the town's income.

Though some 10,000 tons of silver and gold ore are still mined annually, Aikawa's **Sōdayū-kō** (Sōdayū Mine) is more of a tourist attraction than anything else. There are about 325 km (250 mi) of underground tunnels, some running as deep as 1,969 ft beneath sea level; some of this extensive digging is open to the public. Instead of the slave labor that was used throughout the Edo period, now robots serve in the mine. These robots are, in fact, quite lifelike, and they demonstrate the appalling conditions that were endured by the miners. Sound effects of shovels and pick axes add to the sobering reality. The mine is a tough 40-minute uphill walk or a five-minute taxi ride (about ¥900) from the bus terminal. The walk back is easier. ☎ 0259/74–2389. ✑ ¥700. ☉ Apr.–Oct., daily 8–5:10; Nov.–Mar., daily 8–sunset.

★ North of Aikawa is **Senkaku-wan** (Senkaku Bay), the most dramatic stretch of coastline and a must-see on Sado-ga-shima.

Information on sightseeing boats is available from **Senkaku-wan Kankō** (Senkaku Bay Tourism; ☎ 0259/75–2221). From the water you can look back at the fantastic, sea-eroded rock formations and cliffs that rise 60 ft out of the water. You will get off the boat at Senkaku-wan Yuen (Senkaku Bay Park), where you can picnic, stroll, and gaze upon the varied rock formations offshore. From the park, you return by bus from the pier to Aikawa. To reach the bay, take a 15-minute bus from Aikawa to Tassha for the 40-minute sightseeing cruise. The one-way cruise-boat runs April–November (¥700, glass-bottom boat ¥850).

The most scenic drive on Sado is the **Ōsado Skyline Drive.** No public buses follow this route. You must take either a tour bus from Ryōtsu or a taxi from Aikawa across the skyline drive to Chikuse (¥4,200), where you connect with a public bus either to Ryōtsu or back to Aikawa.

To reach the southwestern tip of Sado, first make your way on a bus to Sawata from Aikawa or Ryōtsu, and then transfer to the bus for Ogi; en route you may want to stop at the town of **Mano,** where the emperor Juntoku (1197–1242) is buried. The **Mano Goryō** (Mano Mausoleum) and the museum that exhibits some of Emperor Juntoku's personal effects are in the park, Toki-no-Sato, a half-hour walk from the center of town. There is a sadness to this mausoleum built for a man who at 24 was exiled on Sado for life by the Kamakura shogunate for his unsuccessful attempt to regain power. Admission to the mausoleum and museum is ¥500; it's open daily April–mid-November.

At Mano, the *tsuburo-sashi* dance is put on nightly at the **Sado New Hotel** (⊠ 278 Shinmachi, Mano-machi, ☎ 0259/55–2511). The unique display is performed by a man holding a *tsuburo* (phallic symbol) dancing with the goddesses Shagri and Zeni Daiko.

㊱ The trip from Sawata to **Ogi** takes 50 minutes, the highlight of it being the beautiful *benten-iwa* (rock formations), just past Tazawaki. Be sure to take a window seat on the right-hand side of the bus. You can use Ogi as a port for returning to Honshū by the ferry (2½ hours to Naoetsu) or on the hydrofoil (1 hour).

Ogi's chief attractions are the **taraibune,** round, tublike boats used for fishing. You can rent them now (¥500 for a 30-minute paddle) and with a single oar wend your way around the harbor. Taraibune can also be found in Shukunegi, a more attractive town on the Sawasaki coast, where the water is dotted with rocky islets and the shore is covered with rock lilies in summer.

Shukunegi has become a sleepy backwater since it stopped building small wood ships to ply the waters between Sado and Honshū, and it has retained its traditional atmosphere and buildings. You can reach Shukunegi from Ogi by a sightseeing boat or by bus. Both take about 20 minutes, so consider using the boat at least one way for the view of the cliffs that were created by an earthquake 250 years ago.

Lodging
You can make hotel reservations at the information counters of Sado Kisen ship company at Niigata Port or Ryōtsu Port.

$$$$ 🏨 **Sado Royal Hotel Mancho.** This is the best hotel on Sado's west coast. It caters mostly to Japanese tourists, but the staff makes the few Westerners who come feel welcome, even if they don't speak English. Breakfast and dinner are included in the rate. ⊠ *58 Shimoto, Aikawa, Sado-ga-shima, Niigata-ken 952-1575,* ☎ *0259/74–3221,* ℻ *0259/74–3738. 87 rooms. Restaurant. DC, V. MAP.*

$$$ 🏨 **Sado Seaside Hotel.** Twenty minutes by foot from Ryōtsu Port, this ★ is more a friendly inn than a hotel. If you telephone before you catch the ferry from Niigata, the owner will meet you at the dock. He'll be carrying a green Seaside Hotel flag. Breakfast and dinner are included in the rate. ⊠ *80 Sumiyoshi, Ryōtsu, Sado-ga-shima, Niigata-ken 952-0015,* ☎ *0259/27–7211,* ℻ *0259/27–7213. 12 Japanese-style rooms, 5 with bath. Dining room, laundry service. AE, V. MAP.*

Getting Around

BY BUS

Frequent bus service is available between major towns on Sado-ga-shima, making travel around the island simple. For example, buses leave Ryōtsu every 30 minutes for Aikawa. The trip takes about 90 minutes and costs ¥740.

May through November, there are also four- and eight-hour tours of the island that depart from both Ryōtsu and Ogi. However, these buses seem to have a magnetic attraction to souvenir shops. The best compromise is to use the tour bus for the mountain skyline drive (¥4,030) or the two-day skyline and historic site combined tour (¥7,690), then rent a bike to explore on your own. You can make bus tour reservations directly with the **Niigata Kōtsū Regular Sightseeing Bus Center** (☎ 0259/52–3200).

BY FERRY

Sado Kisen (☎ 025/245–1234 in Niigata; 0225/43–3791 in Naoetsu) has two main ferry routes, each with both a regular ferry and a hydrofoil service. From Niigata to Ryōtsu the ferry crossing takes 2½ hours, with six or seven crossings a day; the fare is ¥2,060 for ordinary second class, ¥2,920 for a seat reservation, ¥4,140 for first class, and ¥6,210 for special class. The jetfoil (¥5,960 one-way, ¥10,730 round-trip) takes one hour, with 7 to 10 crossings daily in summer, 3 in winter, and between 3 and 8 at other times of the year (depending on the weather). In February, hydrofoils make the crossing only three times per day. The bus from bay No. 6 at the terminal in front of the JR Niigata Eki takes 15 minutes (¥180) to reach the dock for the ferries sailing to Ryōtsu.

Between Ogi and Naoetsu the hydrofoil cost is the same as the Niigata–Ryōtsu crossing, while the regular ferry is ¥2,060 for second class, ¥2,920 for a seat reservation, ¥4,140 for first class, and ¥6,210 for special class. The Naoetsu ferry terminal is a ¥150 bus ride or ¥900 taxi ride from the JR Naoetsu Eki.

Depending on the season, one to three ferries sail between Teradomari (between Niigata and Naoetsu) and Akadomari, taking two hours. The fare is ¥1,410 for second class and ¥2,840 for first class. The port is five minutes on foot from the Teradomari bus station, and 10 minutes by bus from the JR train station (take the Teradomari-ko bus).

JAPAN ALPS A TO Z

To research prices, get advice from other travelers, and book travel arrangements, visit www.fodors.com.

AIR TRAVEL

The flight from Tōkyō's Haneda Kūkō to Komatsu Kūkō in Kanazawa takes one hour on Japan Airlines (JAL) or All Nippon Airlines (ANA); allow 55 minutes for the bus transfer to downtown Kanazawa.

Japan Air System (JAS) offers daily flights to and from Fukuoka, Ōsaka, and Sapporo to Matsumoto.

ANA has five flights daily between Tōkyō and Toyama. For more details on airlines, *see* Carriers *in* Smart Travel Tips A to Z.

Kyokushin Kōkū (Kyokushin Aviation) has small planes that take 25 minutes to fly from Sado-ga-shima from Niigata; there are five round-trip flights a day in summer and three in winter; the one-way fare is ¥7,350.

➤ CONTACT: **Kyokushin Kōkū** (☎ 025/273–0312 in Niigata; 0259/23–5005 in Sado).

CAR RENTAL

Although train and bus travel are better for getting around the region, rental cars are available at all major and some smaller stations, but it's best to reserve the car before you leave Tōkyō, Nagoya, or Kyōto. In Kanazawa, try Nissan Rent-a-Car at the East Exit of the train station. In Wajima your best bet is Eki Rent-a-Car at Wajima Station. An economy-size car will cost about ¥8,000 per day, or about ¥50,000 per week.

During winter certain roads through the central Japan Alps are closed. In particular, the direct route between Matsumoto and Takayama via Kamikōchi is closed November–April.

➤ LOCAL AGENCIES: **Eki Rent-a-Car** (✉ Kanazawa Eki, ☎ 0768/22–0315). **Nissan Rent-a-Car** (✉ 14–27 Shōwa-machi, Wajima, ☎ 0762/32–4123).

EMERGENCIES

➤ CONTACTS: **Ambulance** (☎ 119). **Police** (☎ 110).

TOURS

The Japan Travel Bureau runs a five-day tour from Tōkyō that departs every Tuesday from April through October 26. The tour goes via Shirakaba-ko to Matsumoto (overnight), to Tsumago and Takayama (overnight), to Kanazawa (overnight), to Awara Onsen (overnight), and ends in Kyōto. The fare is ¥150,000, including four breakfasts and two dinners.

The Kanazawa Hokuriku-Tetsudō Co. has a 6½-hour tour that covers much of the Noto-hantō for ¥6,200, with a Japanese-speaking guide. It operates year-round and departs from Kanazawa Eki.

Contact the Niigata Kōtsū Information Center at the Ryōtsu bus terminal for a tour of Sado-ga-shima. It covers Skyline Drive, where public buses don't run. Tours, from May to November, depart from Ryōtsu and cost ¥6,440.

➤ TOUR CONTACTS: **Hokuriku-Tetsudō Co.** (☎ 076/237–8111). **Japan Travel Bureau** (☎ 03/3281–1721). **Niigata Kōtsū Information Center** (☎ 0259/27–3141).

TRAIN TRAVEL

Tōkyō–Nagano Shinkansen service has effectively shortened the distance to the Alps from the east: the trip on the Nagano Shinkansen only takes about 90 minutes. From Kyōto and Nagoya the Alps are three and more hours away on the Hokuriku and Takayama lines. Unless you are coming from Niigata, you will need to approach Takayama and Kanazawa from the south (connections through Maibara are the speediest) on JR.

TRANSPORTATION AROUND THE JAPAN ALPS

Roads and railways through the Japan Alps follow the valleys. This greatly lengthens trips *around* mountains—as in the four-hour Matsumoto–Takayama ride via Nagoya. But traveling in the Alps is about taking in the scenery. Route maps are available for Shinkansen and JR lines at any train station or bookstore. Always scan the train station for a tourist office to provide you with maps and help you find accommodations. Remember that the last train or bus in the evening can be quite early and may leave as early as 8 PM. Most major train stations have an English-speaking information agent to help you.

Getting around by bus in Japan is not as convenient as by train, but it's not unpleasant, and information is easy to come by. Any bus station, which is always adjacent, in front of, or across from the train station, will provide you with maps and schedules, which may be viewed or bought in bookstores as well. Of course, the local tourist-information office—also always in or near the train station—will help you decipher timetables and fares if you're bewildered.

VISITOR INFORMATION

Offices of the JR Travel Information Center and Japan Travel Bureau are at all major train stations. They can help you book local tours, hotel reservations, and travel tickets. Though you should not assume that any English will be spoken, you can usually find someone whose knowledge is sufficient for your basic needs. Travel through the Alps is very straightforward using public transportation. If you get a map and schedule, you'll be able to get around easily. Where public transportation is infrequent, such as the Noto-hantō and Sado-ga-shima, local tours are available; however, the guides speak only Japanese.

The Japan Travel Phone is a nationwide toll-free service for English-language assistance and travel information, available 9–5 daily. When using a yellow, blue, or green public phone (do not use the red phones; they're for local calls only), insert a ¥10 coin, which will be returned.

The Hida Tourist Information Office, in front of the JR station, is open daily April–October 8:30–6:30, November–March 8:30–5, and serves the Takayama region. The Kanazawa Tourist Information Service is inside the JR station; the Nanao International Exchange Office is in Nanao City Hall, a few minutes east of the station; the Niigata City Tourist Information Center, open daily 8:30–7, is to the left of the JR station exit; the Magome Tourist Information Office is open April–November, daily 8:30–5, and December–March, Monday–Saturday 8:30–5; the Matsumoto City Tourist Information Office is to the right as you exit the JR station; the Karuizawa Eki Tourist Office is at the JR station; the Tsumago Tourist Information Office is open daily 9–5; the Wajima Station Tourist Center is in front of the station.

➤ TOURIST INFORMATION: **Hida Tourist Information Office** (☎ 0577/32–5328). **Japan Travel Phone** (☎ 0120/444–800). **Kanazawa Tourist Information Service** (☎ 076/232–6200, FAX 076/238–6210). **Karuizawa Eki Tourist Office** (☎ 0267/42–2491). **Magome Tourist Information Office** (☎ 0264/59–2336). **Matsumoto City Tourist Information Office** (☎ 0263/32–2814). **Nanao International Exchange Office** (☎ 0767/53–8448, FAX 0767/54–8117). **Niigata City Tourist Information Center** (☎ 0252/41–7914). **Tsumago Tourist Information Office** (☎ 0264/57–3123). **Wajima Station Tourist Center** (☎ 0768/22–1503 or 0768/22–4277).

5 KYŌTO

Kyōto is a cross section of a dozen centuries of Japan's history—including the present. Its hundreds of magnificent temples and shrines and its impeccable gardens entice Japanese and foreigners alike. Add to that traditional shopping districts and intriguing local foods, and you come up with some of the best reasons to travel to Japan.

KYŌTO'S HISTORY IS FULL OF CONTRADICTIONS: famine and prosperity, war and peace, calamity and tranquillity. Although the city was Japan's capital for more than 10 centuries, the real center of political power was often elsewhere, be it Kamakura (1192–1333) or Edo (1603–1868). Such was Kyōto's decline in the 17th and 18th centuries that when the power of the government was returned from the shōguns to the emperor, he moved his capital and imperial court to Edo, renaming it Tōkyō. Though that move may have pained Kyōto residents, it actually saved the city from destruction. While most major cities in Japan were bombed flat in World War II, Kyōto survived. And where old quarters of Tōkyō have been replaced with characterless modern buildings—a fate that Kyōto has shared in part—much of the city's wooden architecture of the past still stands.

By Nigel Fisher

Updated
by Lauren
Sheridan

Until 710 Japan's capital was moved to a new location with the succession of each new emperor. When it was decided that the expense of this continuous movement had become overly bloated with the size of the court and the number of administrators, Nara was chosen as the permanent capital. Its life as the capital lasted only 74 years, during which time Buddhists rallied for, and achieved, tremendous political power. In an effort to thwart them, Emperor Kammu moved the capital in 784 to Nagaoka, leaving the Buddhists behind in their elaborate temples. Within 10 years, Kammu decided that Kyōto (then called Uda) was better suited for his capital. Poets were asked to compose verse about Uda, and invariably they included the phrase *Heian-kyō*, meaning "Capital of Peace," reflecting the hope and desire of the time.

For 1,074 years, Kyōto remained the capital, though at times only in name. From 794 to the end of the 12th century, the city flourished under imperial rule. Japan's culture started to grow independent of Chinese influences and to develop its unique characteristics. Unfortunately, the use of wood for construction, coupled with Japan's two primordial enemies, fire and earthquakes, has destroyed all the buildings from this era, except Byōdō-in in Uji. The short life span of a building in the 11th century is exemplified by the Imperial Palace, which burned down 14 times in 122 years. As if natural disasters were not enough, imperial power waned in the 12th century. There followed a period of shogunal rule, but each shōgun's reign was tenuous. By the 15th century civil wars tore the country apart. Many of Kyōto's buildings were destroyed or looted.

The Ōnin Civil War (1467–77) was particularly devastating for Kyōto. Two feudal lords, Yamana and Hosokawa, disputed who should succeed the reigning shōgun. Yamana camped in the western part of the city with 90,000 troops, and Hosokawa settled in the eastern part with 100,000 troops. Central Kyōto was the battlefield.

Not until the end of the 16th century, when Japan was brought together by the might of Nobunaga Oda and Hideyoshi Toyotomi, did Japan settle down. This period was soon followed by the usurpation of power by Ieyasu Tokugawa, founder of the Tokugawa Shogunate, which lasted for the next 264 years. Tokugawa moved the political center of the country to Edo, current-day Tōkyō. Kyōto did remain the imperial capital—the emperor being little more than a figurehead—and the first three Tokugawa shōguns paid homage to it by restoring old temples and building new villas. In the first half of the 17th century, this was yet another show of Tokugawa power. Much of what you see in Kyōto dates from this period.

Steeped in history and tradition, Kyōto has in many ways been the cradle of Japanese culture, especially with its courtly aesthetic pastimes, such as moon-viewing parties and tea ceremonies. A stroll through Kyōto today is a walk through 11 centuries of Japanese history. The city has been swept into the modern industrialized world with the rest of Japan—plate-glass windows, held in place by girders and ferroconcrete, dominate central Kyōto. Elderly women, however, continue to wear kimonos as they make their way slowly along the canal walkways. Geisha still entertain, albeit at prices out of reach for most visitors. Sixteen hundred temples and several hundred shrines surround central Kyōto. There's rather a lot to see, to say the least, so keep this in mind and don't run yourself ragged. Balance a morning at temples and museums with an afternoon in traditional shops and a morning at the market with the rest of the day in Arashiyama or at one of the imperial villas.

Kyōto Glossary

Key Japanese words and suffixes for this chapter include -*bashi* (bridge), *bijutsukan* (art museum), -*chō* (street or block), -*chōme* (street), -*den* (hall), -*dō* (temple or shrine), *dōri* (street), *eki* (train station), *gaijin* (foreigner), -*gawa* or -*kawa* (river), -*gū* (Shintō shrine), *hakubutsukan* (museum), *higashi* (east), -*in* (Buddhist temple), -*ji* (temple), *jingū* or *jinja* (Shintō shrine), -*jō* (castle), *kado* (street corner), *kita* (north), *kōen* (park), -*ku* (section or ward), *machi* (town), *matsuri* (festival), *michi* (street), *minami* (south), -*mon* (gate), *nishi* (west), *ryokan* (traditional inn), *sakura* (cherry blossoms), -*shi* (city or municipality), *Shinkansen* (bullet train, literally "new trunk line"), *taisha* (Shintō shrine), *torii* ("*to*-ree-ee," gate), *yama* (mountain), and -*zan* (mountain, as in Hiei-zan, Mt. Hiei).

Pleasures and Pastimes

Although Tōkyō has been the imperial capital since 1868, Kyōto—which wore the crown for the 10 centuries before—is still the classic Japanese city. The traditional arts, crafts, customs, language, and literature were all born, raised, and refined here. Kyōto has the matchless villas, the incomparable gardens, the magnificent temples and shrines. And Kyōto has the most artful Japanese cuisine.

Architecture

No other city in Japan has such a glorious array of religious architecture. Over its 1,200-year history the city has accumulated more than 1,600 Buddhist temples (30 of which are the headquarters for major sects spread throughout Japan), 200 Shintō shrines, and three imperial palaces. All of these vying for your attention can be a bit daunting, but there are clear standouts, places at which you can get the best of Japan's harmonious, graceful architectural styles without having to dash back and forth with a checklist.

Crafts

Temples, shrines, gardens, and the quintessential elements of Japanese culture are all part of Kyōto's appeal, but you can't take them home with you. You can, however, pack up a few *omiyage* (mementos)—the take-home gifts for which this city is famous. The ancient craftsmen of Kyōto served the imperial court for more than 1,000 years, and the prefix *kyō*- before a craft is synonymous with fine craftsmanship. The wares you will find in Kyōto are, for their superb artistry and refinement, among the world's finest.

Kyō-ningyō, exquisite display dolls, have been made in Kyōto since the 9th century. Constructed of wood coated with white shell paste and clothed in elaborate, miniature patterned-silk brocades, Kyōto dolls

Kyōto *(Boxes Refer to Detail Maps)*

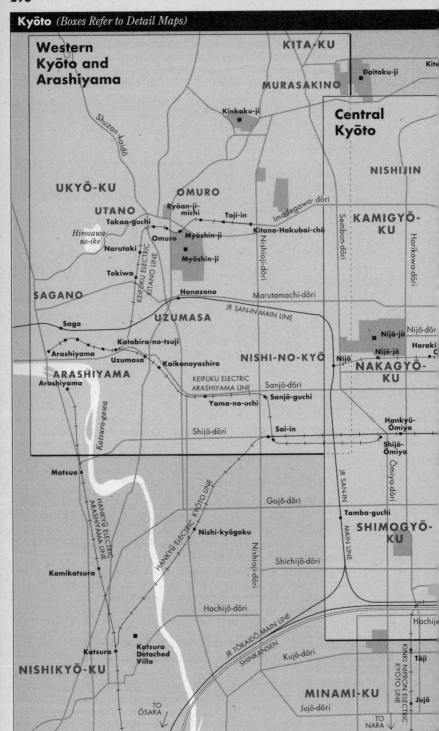

Western Kyōto and Arashiyama

KITA-KU

Kite

Daitoku-ji

MURASAKINO

Kinkaku-ji

Central Kyōto

NISHIJIN

UKYŌ-KU

OMURO

UTANO

Ryōan-ji-michi

Toji-in

Imadegawa-dōri

KAMIGYŌ-KU

Takao-guchi

Kitano-Hakubai-chō

Omuro

Myōshin-ji

Hirosawa-no-ike

Narutaki

Myōshin-ji

Sembon-dōri

Horikawa-dōri

Nishioji-dōri

Tokiwa

SAGANO

Hanazono

Marutamachi-dōri

Saga

JR SAN-IN MAIN LINE

UZUMASA

Katabira-no-tsuji

Nijō-jō

Nijō-dōri

Arashiyama

Uzumasa

NISHI-NO-KYŌ

Nijō-jō

Haraki

Kaikonoyashiro

Nijō

NAKAGYŌ-KU

ARASHIYAMA

KEIFUKU ELECTRIC ARASHIYAMA LINE

Arashiyama

Sanjō-dōri

Yama-no-uchi

Sanjō-guchi

Katsura-gawa

Shijō-dōri

Sai-in

Hankyū-Ōmiya

Matsuo

Shijō-Ōmiya

HANKYŪ ELECTRIC ARASHIYAMA LINE

Gojō-dōri

Ōmiya-dōri

HANKYŪ ELECTRIC KYŌTO LINE

Tamba-guchi

JR SAN-IN MAIN LINE

SHIMOGYŌ-KU

Nishi-kyōgoku

Kamikatsura

Shichijō-dōri

Nishioji-dōri

Hachijō-dōri

Hachijo

Katsura

Katsura Detached Villa

JR TŌKAIDŌ MAIN LINE

Tōji

KINKI NIPPON ELECTRIC KYŌTO LINE

NISHIKYŌ-KU

SHINKANSEN

Kujō-dōri

TO ŌSAKA

MINAMI-KU

Jujō

Jūjō-dōri

TO NARA

KEIFUKU ELECTRIC KITANO LINE

- Botanical Garden
- Kamigamo Jinja
Kita-ōji-dōri

Kita-ōji

Kamo-gawa

SHIMOGAMO

SUBWAY

Kurama-guchi

Takano-gawa

TAKANO

KITA-SHIRAKAWA

Ichijō-ji

Chayama

Mt. Uryu

EIZAN ELECT. KURAMA LINE
EIZAN ELECT. LINE
EIZAN ELECT. LINE

KEY
— JR Trains
— Shinkansen (Bullet Train)
╍ Subway
─┼─ Private rail line

Eastern Kyōto

SAKYO-KU

Mototanaka

Imadegawa

Karasuma-dōri

Kyōto Imperial Palace

Kawara-machi-dōri

Demachi-Yanagi

Imadegawa- dōri

Demachi-Yanagi Keihan

Ginkaku-ji

Shirakawa-dōri

Shishi
gatani-dōri

N

Maruta-machi

Maruta-machi
Maruta-machi-dōri

Karasuma-dōri

Kawara-machi-dōri

Higashiōji-dōri

Heian Jingū

OKAZAKI

Nyoigatake

kima-Oike

ōri

Karasuma-Oike

Oike-dōri

Higashiyama

Sanjō-dōri

Keage

AWATAGUCHI

Sanjō-Keihan

Keishin-Sanjō

TŌZAI LINE

Shijō-dōri

Karasuma
Shijō

Kawara-
machi

Shijō
Keihan

GION

Kujō-yama

Gojō-dōri

Gojō

Gojō

Kiyomizu-dera

Hino-oka

Mt. Kazan

YAMASHINA-KU

TO TŌKYŌ

Misasagi

Yamashina

HIGASHIYAMA-KU

Mt. Kiyomizu

Keihan-Yamashina

Shinomiya

Shichijō

Kyōto Eki

Mt. Rokujō

JR TŌKAIDŌ MAIN LINE

JR NARA LINE

SHINKANSEN

hijō-dōri

Kujō-dōri

Tōfukuji

KEIHAN ELECTRIC MAIN LINE

KANSAI REGION

Kyōto

Lake Biwa

Kōbe

Ōsaka

Osaka Bay

Nara

Jūjō-dōri

Tobakaidō

Yoshino-san

Kōya-san

are considered the finest in Japan. Kyōto is also known for fine ceramic dolls and *Kyō-gangu,* its local varieties of folk toys.

Kyō-sensu are embellished folding fans used as accoutrements in Nō theater, tea ceremonies, and Japanese dance. They also have a practical use—to keep you cool. Unlike other Japanese crafts, which have their origin in Tang dynasty China, the folding fan originated in Kyōto.

Kyō-shikki refers to Kyōto lacquerware, which also has its roots in the 9th century. The making of lacquerware, adopted from the Chinese, is a delicate process requiring patience and skill. Finished lacquerware products range from furniture to spoons and bowls, which are carved from cypress, cedar, or horse-chestnut wood. These pieces have a brilliant luster; some designs are decorated with gold leaf and inlaid mother-of-pearl.

Kyō-yaki is the general term applied to ceramics made in local kilns; the most popular ware is from Kyōto's Kiyomizu district. Often colorfully hand-painted in blue, red, and green on white, these elegantly shaped teacups, bowls, and vases are thrown on potters' wheels located in the Kiyomizu district and in Kiyomizu-danchi in Yamashina. Streets leading up to Kiyomizu-dera—Chawan-zaka, Sannen-zaka, and Ninen-zaka—are sprinkled with kyō-yaki shops.

Kyō-yuzen is a paste-resist silk-dyeing technique developed by 17th-century dyer Yuzen Miyazaki. Fantastic designs are created on plain white silk pieces through the process of either *tegaki yuzen* (hand-painting) or *kata yuzen* (stenciling).

Nishijin-ori is the weaving of silk. *Nishijin* refers to a Kyōto district producing the best silk textiles in all of Japan, which are used to make kimonos. Walk along the narrow backstreets of Nishijin and listen to the persistently rhythmic looms.

Dining

"Paris East" is a difficult epithet for Kyōto to live up to, but in many ways the elegant sister cities do seem to be of the same flesh and blood—not least in that both serve up their nation's haute cuisine. The presence of the imperial court was the original inspiration for Kyōto's exclusive *yusoku ryōri.* Once presented on lacquered pedestals to the emperor himself, it is now offered at but one restaurant in the city, Mankamero.

The experience not to miss in Kyōto is *kaiseki ryōri,* the elegant full-course meal that was originally intended to be served with the tea ceremony. All the senses are engaged in this culinary event: the scent and flavor of the freshest ingredients at the peak of season; the visual delight of a continuous procession of porcelain dishes and lacquered bowls, each a different shape and size, gracefully adorned with an appropriately shaped morsel of fish or vegetable; the textures of foods unknown and exotic, presented in sequence to prevent boredom; the sound of water in a stone basin outside in the garden. Even the atmosphere of the room enhances the experience: a hanging scroll displayed in the alcove and a carefully crafted flower arrangement evoke the season and accent the restrained appointments of the tatami room. Kaiseki ryōri is often costly yet always unforgettable.

For an initiation or a reasonably priced sample, the *kaiseki bentō* (box lunch) served by many *ryōtei* (high-class Japanese restaurants) is a good place to start. Box lunches are so popular in Kyōto that restaurants compete to make their bentō unique, exquisite, and delicious.

Because it is a two-day journey from the sea, Kyōto is historically more famous for ingenious ways of serving preserved fish—dried, salted, or pickled—than for its raw-fish dishes, though with modern transport have come good sushi shops. Compared with the style of cooking elsewhere in Japan, *Kyōto-ryōri* (Kyōto cuisine) is lighter and more delicate, stressing the natural flavor of ingredients over enhancement with heavy sauces and broths. *Tsukemono* (pickled vegetables) and *wagashi* (traditional sweets) are two other local specialties; they make excellent souvenirs. Food shops are often kept just as they were a century ago—well worth the trip if only to browse.

Kyōto is also the home of *shōjin ryōri,* the Zen vegetarian-style cooking, best sampled on the grounds of one of the city's Zen temples, such as Tenryū-ji in Arashiyama. Local delicacies like *fu* (glutinous wheat cakes) and *yuba* (soy-milk skimmings) have found their way into the mainstream of Kyōto ryōri but were originally devised to provide protein in the traditional Buddhist diet.

Famed throughout Japan for the best in traditional Japanese cuisine, Kyōto was slower to pick up the fine French, American, Indian, and Chinese restaurants that it now has. Try them if you need a break from Japanese fare.

For more on Japanese cuisine, *see* Chapter 14 *and* Dining *in* Smart Travel Tips A to Z.

Gardens
Simplicity and symbolism are the perfected goals of Kyōto's temple gardens. The tea garden at Kinkaku-ji, with stepping stones paving the way through manicured grounds, sets the spirit at rest. The timeless arrangement of the *karesansui* (dry-garden) sand and rocks at Ryōan-ji is an eternal quest for completeness. The tree-shrouded gardens at Jakkō-in feed melancholy.

Lodging
Considering the huge numbers of people who visit Kyōto, the city has a surprising dearth of good hotels. Apart from pricey ryokan, the hotels do not compare with their counterparts in Ōsaka or Tōkyō. So don't expect too much, and you won't be disappointed. As for the very expensive ryokans, $500–$600 per night will bring genteel attention, an elegant dinner, and the classical harmony of the tatami rooms. No other Japanese city can compete with Kyōto for style and grace, but it is not always given freely to foreigners. Remember that it helps to have a Japanese person make a reservation for you at a ryokan, unless you can speak Japanese yourself. The idea is to let the ryokan know that you understand the customs of staying at traditional inns.

For a short course on accommodations in Japan, *see* Lodging *in* Smart Travel Tips A to Z.

Matsuri (Festivals)
Kyōto's festival calendar includes five spectacular events: the Aoi (hollyhock), Gion (geisha), Jidai (costume), and the Daimon-ji and Kurama fire matsuri, held between May and October. For more information *see* Festivals and National Holidays *in* Smart Travel Tips A to Z.

Museums
Kyōto and Tōkyō are rivals for the role as the nation's leading repository of culture. Certainly Kyōto wins hands down for its traditional and courtly treasures. You won't get this feeling from walking the busy, congested streets of modern downtown, but a step into any of the nine major museums will sweep you back to the days of refinement and artistic perfection.

Shopping

Perhaps even more than Tōkyō, Kyōto is *the* Japanese city in which to shop for gifts to take home. As Japan's self-proclaimed cultural capital, Kyōto has no shortage of art and antiques shops. Folk crafts from surrounding regions are brought into town for shops to sell. Second-hand kimonos can be a steal at $50, after image-conscious Japanese discard them for new ones priced in the thousands of dollars. Ceramics and woven bamboo make great souvenirs, and if you're looking for odds and ends, there are always the flea markets.

Exploring Kyōto

Most of Kyōto's interesting sights are north of Kyōto Eki. Think of this northern sector as three rectangular areas abutting each other.

The middle rectangle fronts the exit of Kyōto Eki. This is central Kyōto. Here are the hotels, the business district, the Ponto-chō geisha district, and the Kiya-machi entertainment district. Central Kyōto also contains one of the oldest city temples, Tōji; the rebuilt Imperial Palace; and Nijō-jō, the onetime Kyōto abode of the Tokugawa shōguns. Eastern Kyōto, Higashiyama, is chockablock with temples and shrines, among them Ginkaku-ji, Heian Jingū, and Kiyomizu-dera. Gion—a traditional shopping neighborhood by day and a geisha entertainment district by night—is also here. You could easily fill two days visiting eastern Kyōto. Western Kyōto includes the temples Ryōan-ji and Kinkaku-ji, and Katsura Rikyū, a bit south.

You could skim over these three areas, so crowded with historical attractions, in three days. However, two other areas have major sights to lure you. West of the western district is Arashiyama, with its temple, Tenryū-ji. And north of central Kyōto are Hiei-zan and the suburb of Ōhara, where the poignant story of Kenreimonin takes place at Jakkō-in.

Kyōto's sights spread over a wide area, but many of them are clustered together, and you can walk from one to another. Where the sights are not near each other, you can use Kyōto's buses, which run on a grid pattern that is easy to follow. Pick up route maps at the JNTO (Japan National Tourist Organization) office. The following exploring sections keep to the divisions described above so as to allow walking from one sight to another. However, notwithstanding traffic and armed with a bus map, you could cross and recross Kyōto without too much difficulty, stringing together sights of your own choosing.

Unlike other Japanese cities, Kyōto was modeled on the grid pattern of the Chinese city of Xian. Accordingly, addresses in the city are organized differently than in other parts of the country. Residents will assure you that this makes the city easier to navigate; confounded tourists may disagree. Many of the streets are named and east–west streets are numbered—the *san* in San-jō-dōri, for example, means "three." *Nishi-iru* means "to the west," *higashi-iru,* "to the east." *Agaru* is "to the north" and *sagaru* "to the south." These directions are normally given in relation to the closest intersection. Thus the ryokan Daimonjiya's address, Nishi-Iru, Kawara-machi-Sanjō, means "to the west of the junction of Kawara-machi Street and Sanjō (Third Street)."

Admission to Kyōto sights adds up. Over the course of three days, charges of ¥400–¥500 at each sight can easily come to $100 per person.

Great Itineraries

IF YOU HAVE 1 DAY

Heaven forbid if you have such limited time. Should it be so, start in eastern Kyōto with Ginkaku-ji for the simplicity of its exterior shape and its gardens. Walk a little way down the Path of Philosophy (Tetsugaku-no-Michi) before taking a taxi to Kiyomizu-dera, a vast wooden temple built on the side of a hill. Walk through Maruyama Kōen to Chion-in, taking special notice of the awesome San-mon at its entrance. From here take a taxi to the Kyōto Craft Center to browse through the traditional and regional crafts. You may also want to take a break for lunch here. Another taxi ride will take you to central Kyōto and Nijō-jō, a grandiose statement of Tokugawa military might. Now make tracks for western Kyōto, where you should have time for abbreviated visits to Kinkaku-ji, built in 1393, and Ryōan-ji, for its soul-searching garden. You can travel between the two on Bus 12. Or you could go from lunch to Nishiki-kōji, a food market, before heading out to Kinkaku-ji. Because you're here so briefly, don't miss an all-out kaiseki dinner for a magical end to the day.

IF YOU HAVE 3 DAYS

Give your first day to visiting the attractions in eastern Kyōto described above, but after Ginkaku-ji and the Path of Philosophy, slip in Nanzen-ji, the Heian Jingū, and Sanjūsangen-dō before going on to Kiyomizu-dera. On your second day spend the morning in central Kyōto at the Imperial Palace and Nijō-jō. In the afternoon cover western Kyōto and include Kinkaku-ji, Ryōan-ji, Ninna-ji, and Myōshin-ji. The morning of the third day take the Hankyū Railway Line from Kyōto's Hankyū Kawara-machi Eki to Katsura Eki and walk 15 minutes to get to Katsura Rikyū (having obtained your permit to do so the morning before). Then return to Kyōto and head to northern Kyōto and Hiei-zan to spend a calm afternoon wandering through the temple complex to appreciate the views of Kyōto below. Or get in a little shopping so as not to miss local foods and crafts to stuff into your suitcase.

IF YOU HAVE 6 DAYS

Concentrate on eastern Kyōto for your first day. Then take on the Imperial Palace and Nijō-jō in central Kyōto the next morning and western Kyōto in the afternoon. On the third day visit the Katsura Rikyū in the morning and the sights in Arashiyama in the afternoon. When you come back into central Kyōto, try to visit Higashi-Hongan-ji. On the fourth day leave early for northern Kyōto to visit the temples in Ōhara—Sanzen-in, Jikkō-in, and Jakkō-in. By lunchtime, be at Hiei-zan to spend the afternoon on top of the world exploring the temple complexes. On the fifth day head for the Kyōto Craft Center, traditional shops, and Nishiki-kōji for a few treasures to bring home. Finish off your visit with a day trip to nearby Nara.

When to Tour Kyōto

Cherry-blossom time in spring is remarkable. And except for the depths of winter, Kyōto's climate is mild enough to make sightseeing pleasant for 10 months of the year. In the high season (May–October) the large numbers of visitors to the city can make accommodations scarce, and you must apply in advance to visit those attractions that require permits, such as Katsura Rikyū and the Shūgaku-in imperial villas. You can also expect lines for admission tickets to the Imperial Palace.

Religious buildings are generally open seven days a week, but many museums close Monday. If you are lucky enough to be in Kyōto for the Jidai Festival, held on October 22, which celebrates the founding of Kyōto, be sure to head for the Heian Jingū for the procession of about 2,000 people in costumes from every period of Kyōto history.

EASTERN KYŌTO

Start your Kyōto odyssey in Higashiyama (literally, "Eastern Mountain"). If you have time to visit only one district, this is the one. There's more to see here than you could cover comfortably in one day, so pick and choose from the following tour according to your interests.

Numbers in the text correspond to numbers in the margin and on the Eastern Kyōto map.

A Good Walk

Ginkaku-ji ① is one of Kyōto's most famous sights, a wonderful villa turned temple. To get here, take Bus 5 from Kyōto Eki to the Ginkaku-ji-michi bus stop. Walk on the street along the canal, going east. A hundred yards after the street crosses a north–south canal, you'll see **Hakusha Son-sō Garden**, a small villa with an impeccable garden, and then Ginkaku-ji. You'll want to spend a good half hour here soaking up the atmosphere. When you can tear yourself away from Ginkaku-ji, retrace your steps on the entrance road until you reach, on your left, the **Path of Philosophy** ②, which follows alongside the canal. At the first large bridge as you walk south, turn off the path, cross the canal, and take the road east to the modest **Hōnen-in** ③, with its thatched roof and quiet park. After Hōnen-in, return to the Path of Philosophy and continue south. In 15 minutes or so you'll reach, on your left, the temple **Eikan-dō** ④. If you cross the street from Eikan-dō and continue south, you'll see, on the right, the **Nomura Bijutsukan** ⑤, a museum with a private collection of Japanese art.

If the day is close to an end, walk from the Nomura Bijutsukan to Heian Jingū and the Kyōto Handicraft Center, on Maruta-machi-dōri behind it. If not, continue this tour, which returns shortly to Heian Jingū.

Walk south from Nomura Bijutsukan and follow the main path. On your left will be **Nanzen-ji** ⑥, headquarters of the Rinzai sect of Zen Buddhism, with its classic triple gate, San-mon. See also Nanzen-in, a smaller temple within Nanzen-ji. Outside the main gate of Nanzen-ji but still within the complex, take the side street to the left, and you will come to **Konchi-in** ⑦, with its pair of excellent gardens. At the intersection at the foot of the road to Nanzen-ji, you'll see the expansive grounds of the **Kyōto International Community House** ⑧, across the street to the left. Walk back to the main road to Nanzen-ji and turn left. Cross at the traffic light to get to the Meiji-period **Murin-an Garden** ⑨, whose entrance is on a side road half a block east. Walk back north toward the canal and turn left. If you were to cross the canal at the first right, you would be at the **Dōbutsu-en** ⑩, Kyōto's zoo. But there's no pressing reason to visit it, unless you have children in tow. If you skip the zoo, continue to the next right and cross the bridge over the canal. You'll see an immense vermilion torii that acts as a distant entry for Heian Jingū. There are two museums flanking the other side of the torii, the **Kyōto-shi Bijutsukan** ⑪, on your right, and the **Kindai Bijutsukan** ⑫, on your left. Close by is the **Dentō Sangyō Kaikan** ⑬, which exhibits traditional Kyōto crafts. Pass through the torri to get to the **Heian Jingū** ⑭.

If the urge comes on to do some shopping, cross Maruta-machi-dōri and turn left, and you'll come to the **Kyōto Handicraft Center** ⑮. At the crossroads of Maruta-machi-dōri and Higashi-ōji-dōri, west of the handicraft center, is the Kumano Jinja-mae bus stop. If you've had enough sightseeing for one day, take Bus 202 or 206 five stops south on Higashi-ōji-dōri to the Gion bus stop; here, some of the city's best restaurants and bars are at your disposal. If you are going to continue

Eastern Kyōto

sightseeing, stay on Bus 202 for five more stops (to Higashiyama-Shichijō) to explore the southern part of Higashiyama, starting with the temple of **Sanjūsangen-dō** ⑯. If you have taken Bus 206, stay on it for one more stop (it makes a right turn onto Shichijō-dōri and heads for the station) and get off at the Sanjūsangen-dō-mae bus stop. To start exploring here, take Bus 206 or 208 from Kyōto Eki to the Sanjūsangen-dō-mae stop.

From the Sanjūsangen-dō-mae stop, the temple is to the south just beyond the Kyōto Park Hotel. If you get off Bus 202 at the Higashiyama-Shichijō stop, walk west down Shichijō-dōri and take the first major street to the left. If you plan to see Chishaku-in, go there first. It will allow you to avoid doubling back.

From Sanjūsangen-dō retrace your steps back to Shichijō-dōri and take a right. **Chishaku-in** ⑰, famous for its paintings, will be facing you on the other side of Higashi-ōji-dōri. Back across Higashi-ōji-dōri is the prestigious **Kokuritsu Hakubutsukan** ⑱. Just north, less than a five-minute walk along Higashi-ōji-dōri of Kokuritsu, is the **Kawai Kanjirō Kinenkan** ⑲, which houses the works of renowned potter Kanjirō Kawai. The next place to visit is a very special temple, **Kiyomizu-dera** ⑳. To get there from the museum, cross the major avenue Gojō-dōri and walk north along Higashi-ōji-dōri. The street to the right, Gojō-zaka, leads into Kiyomizu-zaka, which you'll take to the temple.

If you take a right halfway down the road (Kiyomizu-zaka) leading from Kiyomizu-dera, you can walk along the Sannen-zaka and Ninen-zaka (slopes). Take a left after Ninen-zaka and then an immediate right, and continue walking north. After another five minutes you will see, on the right, **Kōdai-ji** ㉑, a sedate nunnery founded in the early 17th century. Keep heading north; by doing a right–left zigzag at the Maruyama Music Hall, you'll get to **Maruyama Kōen** ㉒. The road to the right (east) leads up the mountainside to **Chōraku-ji** ㉓, a temple famous today for the stone lanterns that lead to it. Proceed north through Maruyama Kōen, and you'll find **Chion-in** ㉔, headquarters of the Jōdo sect of Buddhism. More paintings by the Kanō school are on view at **Shōren-in** ㉕, a five-minute walk north of Chion-in.

Should you have missed visiting the Heian Jingū, Kindai Bijutsukan, or Kyōto-shi Bijutsukan described in the first part of this tour, note that these are just 10 minutes north of Shōren-in on foot, on the other side of Sanjō-dōri. If you turn right (east) from Shōren-in on Sanjō-dōri, you'll eventually reach the Miyako Hotel; left (west) on Sanjō-dōri leads across Higashi-ōji-dōri to the downtown area and the covered mall. If you turn left on Higashi-ōji-dōri, you will reach Shijō-dōri and the **Gion** district, where geisha live and work.

At the Gion bus stop, Shijō-dōri goes off to the west. Before going down this street, consider taking a short walk east (back into Maruyama Kōen) to **Yasaka Jinja** ㉖, a shrine that is said to bring good health and wealth. Walk back from Yasaka Jinja, cross Higashi-ōji-dōri, and you are in Gion, on Shijō-dōri. On the right-hand corner is the **Kyōto Craft Center** ㉗.

Parallel to Shijō-dōri and to the north is Shinmonzen-dōri, a great place to do a little shopping and browsing. Shijō-dōri itself has interesting, less expensive items.

Off Shijō-dōri, halfway between Higashi-ōji-dōri and the Kamo-gawa, is Hanami-kōji-dōri. The section of this street that runs south of Shijō-dōri (on the right, if you are walking back from the river) will bring you into the heart of the Gion district and the **Gion Kaburenjō Theater** ㉘.

If you continue west on Shijō-dōri, you'll cross over the Kamo-gawa. Pontochō-dōri is on the right. Like Gion, this area is known for its nightlife and geisha entertainment. At the north end of Pontochō-dōri, the **Ponto-chō Kaburenjō Theater** ㉙ puts on geisha performances.

TIMING

This route is extensive, and it would, if you dutifully covered everything along it, require at least two days. You do need to be selective, especially because you might want to spend 40 minutes or more at such places as Ginkaku-ji, Sanjūsangen-dō, the Kokuritsu Hakubutsukan, and Kiyomizu-dera.

Sights to See

★ ㉔ **Chion-in.** The entrance to the temple is through the 79-ft, two-story San-mon. In many people's minds, this is the most daunting temple gate in all of Japan, and it leads to one of Japan's largest temples, the very headquarters of the Jōdo sect of Buddhism, the second-largest Buddhist sect in Japan. The temple has won this distinction because it's the site on which Hōnen, the founder of the Jōdo sect, chose to take his leave of this world by fasting to death in 1212. Chion-in was built in 1234. Because of fires and earthquakes, the oldest standing buildings are the Hon-dō (Main Hall, 1633) and the Daihōjō (Abbots' Quarters, 1639). The temple's belfry houses the largest bell in Japan, which was cast in 1633 and requires 17 monks to ring. The corridor behind the Main Hall, which leads to the Assembly Hall, is an *uguisu-bari* (nightingale floor). This type of floor is constructed to "sing" at every footstep to warn the monks of intruders. Walk underneath the corridor to examine the way the boards and nails are placed to create this inventive burglar alarm. From Kyōto Eki take Bus 206 to the Gion stop. The temple is north of Maruyama Kōen. ✉ *400 Hayashi-shita-chō 3-chōme, Yamato-ōji, Higashi-hairu, Shimbashi-dōri, Higashiyama-ku.* 🎟 *¥400.* 🕐 *Mar.–Oct., daily 9–4:30; Nov.–Feb., daily 9–4; not all buildings open to public.*

★ ⑰ **Chishaku-in.** The major reason for visiting this temple is for its famous paintings, which were executed by Tōhaku Hasegawa and his son Kyūzo—known as the Hasegawa school, rivals of the Kanō school—and are some of the best examples of Momoyama-period art. These paintings were originally created for the sliding screens at Shōun-in, a temple built in 1591 on the same site but no longer in existence. Shōun-in was commissioned by Hideyoshi Toyotomi. When his concubine, Yodogimi, bore him a son in 1589, Hideyoshi named him Tsurumatsu (crane pine), two symbols of longevity. But the child died at age two, and Shōun-in was built for Tsurumatsu's enshrinement. The Hasegawas were commissioned to make the paintings, which were saved from the fires that destroyed Shōun-in and are now on display in the Exhibition Hall of Chishaku-in. Rich in detail and using strong colors on a gold background, they splendidly display the seasons by using the symbols of cherry, maple, pine, and plum trees and autumn grasses.

You may also want to take a few moments in the pond-viewing garden. It has only a vestige of its former glory, but from the temple's veranda you'll have a pleasing view of the pond and garden. From Kyōto Eki take Bus 206 or 208 to the Higashiyama-Shichijō stop. Chishaku-in is on the east side of Higashi-ōji-dōri. 🎟 *¥350.* 🕐 *Daily 9–4:30.*

★ ㉓ **Chōraku-ji.** Mostly it is the procession of stone lanterns along the path that gives this temple a modest fame. Although it's a pleasant temple, it may not be worth the hard climb up the mountainside. Chōraku-ji is east of Maruyama Kōen. 🎟 *¥400.* 🕐 *Daily 9–5.*

⓭ **Dentō Sangyō Kaikan** (Kyōto Museum of Traditional Crafts). This museum displays a wide array of traditional Kyōto crafts, hosts educational crafts-making demonstrations, and even has a shop where you can pick up crafts souvenirs. In the basement is a model interior of a traditional town house. From the Dōbutsu-en-mae bus stop, head down the street that leads to Heian Jingū. The museum is inside the torii on your left after the Kindai Bijutsukan. ⊠ *9–2 Seishōji-chō, Okazaki, Sakyō-ku,* ☏ *075/761–3421.* ☜ *Free.* ☉ *Tues.–Sun. 9–5 (last entry at 4:30).*

☃ ⑩ **Dōbutsu-en** (Kyōto Zoo). The prime reason to stop at the zoo is to entertain your children, if you have any in tow. The zoo has a Children's Corner, where your youngsters can feed the farm animals. It's across from the Dōbutsu-en-mae bus stop. ⊠ *Hoshōji-chō, Okazaki, Sakyō-ku,* ☏ *075/771–0210.* ☜ *¥500.* ☉ *Tues.–Sun. 9–5 (winter 9–4:30); when Mon. is national holiday, zoo stays open Mon. and closes the following day.*

★ ➍ **Eikan-dō.** Officially this temple, founded in 855 by Priest Shinshō, is named Zenrin-ji, but it honors the memory of an 11th-century priest, Priest Eikan, and has popularly come to be known as Eikan-dō. He was a man of the people, and he would lead them in a dance in celebration of Amida Buddha. According to tradition, the Amida statue came to life on one occasion and stepped down from his pedestal to join the dancers. Taken aback, Eikan slowed his dancing feet. Amida looked back over his shoulder to reprimand Eikan for slowing his pace. This legend explains why the unusual statue in the Amida-dō has its face turned to the side, as if glancing backward. A climb to the top of the pagoda affords superb views of the grounds below and Kyōto beyond. With colorful maple trees, the grounds are magnificent in autumn. The buildings here are 16th-century reconstructions made after the originals were destroyed in the Ōnin Civil War (1467–77). Eikan-dō is a 15-minute walk south of Hōnen-in on the Path of Philosophy. ☜ *¥500.* ☉ *Daily 9–5 (last entry at 4:30).*

★ ➊ **Ginkaku-ji.** Ginkaku-ji means "Temple of the Silver Pavilion," but the temple is not silver; it was only intended to be. Shōgun Yoshimasa Ashikaga (1435–90) commissioned this villa for his retirement. He started it as early as the 1460s, but it was not until 1474 that, disillusioned with politics, he gave his full attention to the construction of his villa and to romance, moon gazing, and the tea ceremony, which he helped develop into a high art. Though he never had time to complete the coating of the pavilion with silver foil, he constructed a dozen or so buildings. Many were designed for cultural pursuits, such as incense and tea ceremonies. On his death, the villa was converted into a Buddhist temple, as was often the custom during the feudal era. However, with the decline of the Ashikaga family, Ginkaku-ji fell into decline, and many buildings were destroyed.

All that remain today of the original buildings are **Tōgu-dō** (East Request Hall) and Ginkaku-ji itself. The four other structures on the grounds were built in the 17th and 19th centuries. The front room of Tōgu-dō is where Yoshimasa is thought to have lived, and the statue of the priest is probably of Yoshimasa himself. The back room, called Dojin-sai (Comradely Abstinence), became the prototype for traditional tea-ceremony rooms.

Ginkaku-ji is a simple and unadorned two-story building. Its appeal lies in the serene exterior shape, which combines Chinese elements with the developing Japanese Muro-machi (1333–1568) architecture. The upper floor contains a gilt image of Kannon (goddess of mercy) said to have been carved by Unkei, a famous Kamakura-period sculptor; it's not, however ordinarily open to public view.

★ Ginkaku-ji overlooks the complex **gardens,** attributed to artist and architect Soami (1465–1523), which consist of two contrasting garden sections that together create a balanced, harmonious result. Adjacent to the pavilion is a pond garden, with a composition of rocks and plants designed to afford different perspectives from each viewpoint. The other garden has two sculpted mounds of sand, the higher one symbolizing, perhaps, Mt. Fuji. The garden sparkles in the moonlight and has been aptly named Sea of Silver Sand. The composition of the approach to the garden is also quite remarkable.

To reach Ginkaku-ji, take Bus 5 from Kyōto Eki to the Ginkaku-ji-michi bus stop. Walk on the street along the canal, going east. Cross a north–south canal and Hakusha Son-sō Garden on your right; then continue straight and Ginkaku-ji will be in front of you. ⊠ *Ginkaku-ji-chō, Sakyō-ku.* ▨ *¥500.* ☉ *Mid-Mar.–Nov., daily 8:30–5; Dec.–mid-Mar., daily 9–4:30.*

★ **Gion** (ghee-*own*). Arguably Kyōto's most interesting neighborhood, this is the legendary haunt of geisha. In the evening, amid the glow of teahouse and restaurant lanterns, you can see them scurrying about, white faced, on the way to their appointments. In their wake their *maiko* follow—the young apprentice geisha whom you can identify by the longer sleeves of their kimonos. On a level equal to the world of temples and gardens, Gion is the place for gaijin to fantasize about Japan's fabled floating world.

The heart of the district is on Hanami-kōji-dōri. Heading north, the street intersects with Shinmonzen-dōri, which is famous for its antiques shops and art galleries. Here you'll find collectors' items—at collectors' prices—which make for interesting browsing, if not buying. The shops on Shijō-dōri, which parallels Shinmonzen-dōri to the south, carry slightly more affordable items of the geisha world, from handcrafted hair ornaments to incense to parasols.

★ ㉘ **Gion Kaburenjō Theater.** Because Westerners have little opportunity to enjoy a geisha's performance in a private party setting—which would require a proper recommendation of, and probably the presence of, a geisha's respected client—a popular entertainment during the month of April is the Miyako Odori (Cherry-Blossom Dance), presented at this theater. During the musical presentations, geisha wear their elaborate traditional kimono and makeup. Next door to the theater is **Gion Corner,** where demonstrations of traditional performing arts take place nightly March–November (☞ Nightlife and the Arts, *below*). ⊠ *Gion Hanami-kōji, Higashiyama-ku,* ☎ *075/561–1115.*

Hakusha Son-sō Garden. The modest villa of the late painter Hashimoto Kansetsu has an exquisite stone garden and teahouse open to the public. To get here, take Bus 5 from Kyōto Eki to the Ginkaku-ji-michi stop. Walk east on the street along the canal. Just after the street crosses another canal flowing north–south, Hakusha Son-sō will be on the right. ▨ *¥800; with tea and sweets, an extra ¥800.* ☉ *Daily 10–5 (last entry at 4:30).*

★ ⑭ **Heian Jingū.** One of the city's newest historical sites, Heian Jingū was built in 1894 to mark the 1,100th anniversary of the founding of Kyōto. The shrine honors two emperors: Kammu (737–806), who founded the city in 794, and Kōmei (1831–66), the last emperor to live out his reign in Kyōto. The new buildings are for the most part replicas of the old Imperial Palace, at two-thirds the original size. In fact, because the original palace (rebuilt many times) was finally destroyed in 1227, and only scattered pieces of information exist relating to its construction, Heian Jingū should be taken as a Meiji interpretation of the old palace. Still, the dignity and the relative spacing of the **East Honden** and **West Hon-den** (the Main Halls), and the **Daigoku-den** (Great Hall of State), in which the Heian emperor would issue decrees, conjure up an image of how magnificent the Heian court must have been. During New Year's, kimono-clad and gray-suited Japanese come to pay homage, trampling over the imposing gravel forecourt leading to Daigoku-den.

There are three stroll gardens at Heian Jingū positioned east, west, and north of the shrine itself. They follow the Heian aesthetic of focusing on a large pond, a rare feature at a Shintō shrine. Another notable element is the stepping-stone path that crosses the water—its steps are recycled pillars from a 16th-century bridge that spanned the Kamogawa before an earthquake destroyed it.

Spring, with sakura in full bloom, is a superb time to visit. An even better time to see the shrine is during the Jidai Festival, held on October 22, which celebrates the founding of Kyōto. The pageant, a procession of 2,000 people attired in costumes from every period of Kyōto history, winds its way from the original site of the Imperial Palace and ends at the Heian Jingū.

Another choice time to come to the shrine is on June 1–2 for **Takigi Nō performances,** so named because they are held at night, in open air, lighted by *takigi* (burning firewood). Performances take place on a stage built before the shrine's Daigoku-den.

From the Dōbutsu-en-mae bus stop, follow the street between the Kyōto-shi Bijutsukan and the Kindai Bijutsukan directly to the shrine. ⊠ *Okazakinishi Tennō-chō, Sakyō-ku.* 🖼 *Garden ¥600; Takigi Nō ¥3,300 at the gate, ¥2,500 in advance. Call Tourist Information Center for advance tickets: 075/371–5649.* ☉ *Mid-Mar.–Aug., daily 8:30–5:30; Sept.– Oct. and early Mar., daily 8:30–5; Nov.–Feb., daily 8:30–4:30.*

★ ❸ **Hōnen-in.** The walk through the trees leading to the temple is mercifully quiet and comforting, but not many people come to this humble, thatched-roof structure. The temple was built in 1680, on a site that in the 13th century simply consisted of an open-air Amida Buddha statue. Hōnen-in honors Priest Hōnen (1133–1212), the founder of the Jōdo sect, who brought Buddhism down from its lofty peak to the common folk by making the radical claim that all were equal in the eyes of Buddha. Hōnen focused on faith in the Amida Nyorai; he believed that *nembutsu*—"Namu Amida Butsu," the invocation of Amida Buddha—which he is said to have repeated up to 60,000 times a day, and reliance on Amida, the "all-merciful," were the path to salvation. His ideas threatened other sects, especially the Tendai. The established Buddhist powers pressured then-emperor Gotoba to diminish Hōnen's influence over the masses. At about the same time, two of the emperor's concubines became nuns after hearing some of Hōnen's disciples preaching. The incident provided Gotoba with an excuse to decry the Jōdo sect as immoral, with the charge that its priests were seducing noblewomen. Emperor Gotoba had Anraku and Juren, two of Hōnen's disciples, publicly executed and Hōnen sent into exile. Eventually, in 1211, Hōnen was pardoned and permitted to return to Kyōto, where a year later, at Chion-in, he fasted to death at the age of 79. From the Path of Philosophy, at the first large bridge as you walk south, turn off the path and take the road east. 🖼 *Free.* ☉ *Daily 7–4.*

🔞 **Kawai Kanjirō Kinenkan** (Kawai Kanjirō Memorial House). Taking his inspiration from a traditional rural Japanese cottage, Kanjirō Kawai, one of Japan's most renowned potters, designed and lived in this house, now a museum. He was one of the leaders of the Mingei (folk art) movement, which sought to revive interest in traditional folk arts during the 1920s and '30s, when all things Western were in vogue in Japan. On display are some of the artist's personal memorabilia and, of more interest, some of his exquisite works. An admirer of Western, Chinese, and Korean ceramics techniques, Kawai won many awards, including the Grand Prix at the 1937 Paris World Exposition. From Kyōto Eki take Bus 206 or 208 to the Sanjūsangen-dō-mae stop and then head east to the end of Shichijō-dōri. The house is a five-minute walk north along Higashi-ōji-dōri. ⊠ *Gojō-zaka, Higashiyama-ku,* ☎ *075/561-3585.* 🎫 *¥900.* ⊘ *Tues.–Sun. 10–5; when Mon. is national holiday, museum stays open Mon. and closes the following day. Closed Aug. 10–20 and Dec. 24–Jan. 7.*

⑫ **Kindai Bijutsukan** (National Museum of Modern Art). The museum is known for its collection of 20th-century Japanese paintings and its ceramic treasures by Kanjirō Kawai, Rosanjin Kitaōji, Shōji Hamada, and others. Established in 1903, it reopened in 1986 in a building designed by Fumihiko Maki, one of the top contemporary architects in Japan. From the Dōbutsu-en-mae bus stop, walk down the street that leads to the Heian Jingū. The museum is on the left inside the torii. ⊠ *Enshōji-chō, Okazaki, Sakyō-ku,* ☎ *075/761-4111.* 🎫 *¥420; additional fee for special exhibitions.* ⊘ *Tues.–Sun. 9:30–5.*

★ ⑳ **Kiyomizu-dera.** Unique Kiyomizu-dera, one of the most visited temples in Kyōto and a prominent feature in the city's skyline, stands out because it is built into a steep hillside, with 139 giant pillars supporting part of its main hall. In the past people would come here to escape the open political intrigue of Kyōto and to scheme in secrecy.

The temple's location is marvelous—one reason for coming here is the view. From the wooden veranda, one of the few temple verandas where you can walk around without removing your shoes, there are fine views of the city and a breathtaking look at the valley below. "Have you the courage to jump from the veranda of Kiyomizu?" is a saying asked when someone sets out on a daring new venture.

Interestingly enough, Kiyomizu-dera does not belong to one of the local Kyōto Buddhist sects but rather to the Hossō sect, which developed in Nara. The temple honors the popular 11-faced Kannon (goddess of mercy), who can bring about easy childbirth. Over time Kiyomizu-dera has become "everyone's temple." You'll see evidence of this throughout the grounds, from the little Jizō Bosatsu statues (representing the god of travel and children) stacked in rows to the many *koma-inu* (mythical guard dogs) marking the pathways, which have been donated by the temple's grateful patrons. The original Kiyomizu-dera was built here in 798, four years after Kyōto was founded; the current structure dates to 1633.

Shops selling souvenirs, religious articles, and ceramics line Kiyomizu-zaka, the street leading to the temple. There are also tea shops where you can sample *yatsuhashi*—doughy, triangular sweets filled with cinnamon-flavor bean paste—a Kyōto specialty. Because of the immense popularity of the temple on the hill above it, this narrow slope is often crowded with sightseers and bus tour groups, but the magnificent temple is worth the struggle. From Kyōto Eki take Bus 206 to the Kiyomizu-michi stop. From Kawai Kanjirō Kinenkan cross the major avenue, Gojō-dōri, and walk up Higashi-ōji-dōri. The street to the right,

Gojō-zaka, leads into Kiyomizu-zaka, which you'll take to the temple. ✉ *Kiyomizu 1-chōme, Higashiyama-ku.* ☎ ¥300. ☉ *Daily 6–6.*

NEED A
BREAK?
Kasagi-ya has been serving tea at the foot of Kiyomizu-dera for more than a century. Step inside, and you'll feel as if you've been whisked back in time. Order the *o-hagi*, the sweet bean and rice dumplings; they'll complement the bitterness of your tea and give you a sugar rush for your final assault on the temples. ✉ *349 Masuya-chō, Kōdai-ji, Higashiyama-ku,* ☎ *075/561–9562. Closed Tues. No dinner.*

★ ㉑ **Kōdai-ji.** This quiet nunnery established in the early 17th century provides a tranquil alternative to the crowds of nearby Kiyomizu-dera. The temple was built as a memorial to Hideyoshi Toyotomi by his wife, Kita-no-Mandokoro, who lived out her remaining days in the nunnery there. The famous 17th-century landscaper Kobori Enshū designed the gardens, and artists of the Tosa school decorated the ceilings of the Kaisan-dō (Founder's Hall) with raised lacquer and paintings. The teahouse above on the hill, designed by tea master Sen-no-Rikyū, has a unique umbrella-shape bamboo ceiling and a thatched roof. From Kyōto Eki take Bus 206 to the Higashiyama-yasui bus stop. ☎ ¥500. ☉ *Apr.–Nov., daily 9–4:30; Dec.–Mar., daily 9–4.*

⑱ **Kokuritsu Hakubutsukan** (Kyōto National Museum). Exhibitions at this prestigious museum change regularly, but you can count on an excellent display of paintings, sculpture, textiles, calligraphy, ceramics, lacquerware, metalwork, and archaeological artifacts from its permanent collection of more than 8,000 works of art. From Kyōto Eki take Bus 206 or 208 to the Sanjūsangen-dō-mae stop. The museum is across Higashi-ōji-dōri from Chishaku-in. ✉ *Yamato-ōji-dōri, Higashiyama-ku,* ☎ *075/541–1151.* ☎ ¥420; additional fee for special exhibitions. ☉ *Tues.–Sun. 9–4:30.*

★ ❼ **Konchi-in.** The two gardens of this shrine especially merit a visit: famous tea master and landscape designer Kobori Enshū completed them in 1632, under commission by Zen priest Sūden in accordance with the will of Ieyasu Tokugawa. One has a pond in the shape of the Chinese character *kokoro* (heart). The other is a dry garden with a gravel area in the shape of a boat, a large flat worshiping stone, and a backdrop of *o-karikomi* (tightly pruned shrubbery). The two rock groupings in front of a plant-filled mound are in the crane-and-tortoise style. Since ancient times these creatures have been associated with longevity, beauty, and eternal youth. In the feudal eras the symbolism of the crane and the tortoise became very popular with the samurai class, whose profession often left them with only the hope of immortality. Though not on the same grounds as ☞ **Nanzen-ji,** this temple is in fact part of the Nanzen-ji complex. To get here, leave Nanzen-ji and take the side street to the left. ✉ *86 Fukuchi-chō, Nanzen-ji, Sakyō-ku.* ☎ ¥400. ☉ *Mar.–Nov., daily 8:30–5; Dec.–Feb., daily 8:30–4:30.*

㉗ **Kyōto Craft Center.** Kyōto residents know to come to this collection of stores to shop for fine contemporary and traditional crafts—ceramics, lacquerware, prints, and textiles. You can also purchase moderately priced souvenirs, such as dolls, coasters, bookmarks, and paper products. From Kyōto Eki take Bus 206 to the Gion stop. The center is on the corner of Shijō-dōri and Higashi-ōji-dōri. ✉ *Shijō-dōri, Gionmachi, Higashiyama-ku,* ☎ *075/561–9660.* ☉ *Thurs.–Tues. 11–7.*

⑮ **Kyōto Handicraft Center.** Seven floors of everything Japanese, from dolls to cassette recorders, is on sale. The center caters to tourists with its English-speaking staff. It's a good place to browse, even if you end up deciding that prices are too high. From the Gion bus stop take Bus 202 or 206 five stops north on Higashi-ōji-dōri to the Kumano Jinja-mae bus stop. From Kyōto Eki use Bus 206; the center is across Maruta-machi-dōri from the Heian Jingū. ⊠ *Kumano Jinja Higashi, Sakyō-ku,* ☎ *075/761–5080.* ☉ *Mar.–Nov., daily 9:30–6; Dec.–Feb., daily 9:30–5:30.*

⑧ Kyōto International Community House. On expansive grounds, the center has library and information facilities and rental halls for public performances. The bulletin board by the entryway is full of tips on housing opportunities, study, and events in Kyōto. The KICH also offers weekly lessons in tea ceremony, *koto* (a 13-stringed instrument), calligraphy, and Japanese language at reasonable prices. The book *Easy Living in Kyōto* (available free) gives helpful information for a longer stay. The Community House is just off the intersection at the foot of the road to Nanzen-ji. ⊠ *2–1 Torii-chō, Awata-guchi, Sakyō-ku,* ☎ *075/752–3010.* 🎟 *Free.* ☉ *Tues.–Sun. 9–9; when Mon. is national holiday, Community House stays open Mon. and closes the following day.*

⑪ Kyōto-shi Bijutsukan (Kyōto Municipal Museum of Art). This space serves mostly as a gallery for traveling shows and local art-society exhibits. It owns a collection of Japanese paintings of the Kyōto school, a selection of which goes on display once a year. From the Dōbutsu-en-mae bus stop, walk down the street that leads to the Heian Jingū. The museum is on the right inside the torii. ⊠ *Enshōji-chō, Okazaki, Sakyō-ku,* ☎ *075/771–4107.* 🎟 *Depends on exhibition, but usually around ¥1,000.* ☉ *Tues.–Sun. 9–5 (last entry at 4:30); when Mon. is national holiday, the museum stays open Mon. and closes the following day.*

㉒ Maruyama Kōen. You can rest your weary feet at this small park, home to the Maruyama Music Hall. There are usually a few wandering vendors around to supply refreshment. From Kyōto Eki take Bus 206 to the Higashiyama stop; the park is north of Kōdai-ji.

⑨ Murin-an Garden. The property was once part of Nanzen-ji, but in 1895 it was sold to Prince Yamagata, a former prime minister and advocate of the reforms that followed the Meiji Restoration. Unlike more traditional Japanese gardens, which adopt a more restrained sense of harmony, Murin-an allows more freedom of movement. This is right in step with the Westernizing that the Meiji Restoration brought upon Japan. The garden is south of the Dōbutsu-en-mae bus stop. Enter from the side road on the other side of a canal. 🎟 *¥350.* ☉ *Daily 9–4:30.*

★ ⑥ Nanzen-ji. Like the nearby temple of Ginkaku-ji, this former aristocratic retirement villa was turned into a temple on the death of its owner, Emperor Kameyama (1249–1305). The 15th-century Ōnin Civil War demolished the buildings, but some were resurrected during the 16th century. Nanzen-ji has become one of Kyōto's most important temples, in part because it is the headquarters of the Rinzai sect of Zen Buddhism. You enter the temple through the 1628 **San-mon** (Triple Gate), the classic "gateless" gate of Zen Buddhism that symbolizes entrance into the most sacred part of the temple precincts. From the top floor of the gate you can view Kyōto spread out below. Whether or not you ascend the steep steps, give a moment to the statue of Goemon Ishikawa, a Robin Hood–style outlaw of Japan who hid in this gate until his capture.

On through the gate is **Hōjō** (Abbots' Quarters), a National Treasure. Inside, screens with impressive 16th-century paintings divide the chambers. These wall panels of the *Twenty-Four Paragons of Filial Piety and Hermits* were created by Eitoku Kanō (1543–90) of the Kanō school—

in effect the Kanō family, because the school consists of eight generations, Eitoku being from the fifth, of one bloodline. Kobori Enshū created the Zen-style garden, commonly called the Leaping Tiger Garden
and an excellent example of the karesansui style, attached to the Hōjō.
Unusual here, the large rocks are grouped with clipped azaleas, maples,
pines, and moss, all positioned against a plain white well behind the
raked gravel expanse. The greenery serves to connect the garden quite
effectively with the lush forested hillside beyond.

Within Nanzen-ji's 27 pine-tree-covered acres sit several other temples,
known more for their gardens than for their buildings. One worth visiting if you have time is **Nanzen-in**, once the temporary abode of Emperor Kameyama. Nanzen-in has a mausoleum and a garden that dates
to the 14th century; a small creek passes through it. Nanzen-in is not
as famous as other temples, making it a peaceful place to visit. From
Nomura Bijutsukan, walk south along the main pat to Nanzen-ji; the
temple complex will be on your left. ☒ *Main temple building ¥400,
entrance to San-mon or Nanzen-in ¥200.* ☉ *Mar.–Nov., daily 8:40–5;
Dec.–Feb., daily 8:40–4:30.*

❺ Nomura Bijutsukan. Instead of bequeathing their villas to Buddhist sects,
the modern wealthy Japanese tend to donate their art collections to
museums, as was the case here. Tokushichi Nomura, founder of the
Daiwa Bank and a host of other companies, donated his collection of
scrolls, paintings, tea-ceremony utensils, ceramics, and other art objects to establish his namesake museum. The museum is south of
Eikan-dō on the west side of the street. ☒ *61 Shimogawara-chō,
Nanzen-ji, Sakyō-ku,* ☎ *075/751–0374.* ☒ *¥700.* ☉ *Late Mar.–mid-
June and mid-Sept.–early Dec., Tues.–Sun. 10–4:30 (last entry at 4).*

❷ Path of Philosophy. Cherry trees, which are spectacular in bloom, line
this walkway along the canal, known in Japanese as Tetsugaku-no-michi.
It has traditionally been a place for contemplative strolls since a famous
scholar, Ikutaro Nishida (1870–1945), took his constitutional here.
Now professors and students have to push their way through tourists
who take the same stroll and whose interest lies mainly with the path's
specialty shops. Along the path are several coffee shops and small
restaurants. Omen, one block west of the Path of Philosophy, is an inexpensive, popular restaurant, known for its homemade white noodles.

From Kyōto Eki take Bus 5 to the Ginkaku-ji-michi bus stop. Walk
east on the street that follows the canal. Just after the street crosses a
north–south canal, the path begins on your right.

㉙ Ponto-chō Kaburenjō Theater. Like Gion, Ponto-chō is known for its
nightlife and geisha entertainment. At the north end of Pontochō-dōri,
the Ponto-chō Kaburenjō presents geisha song-and-dance performances
in the spring (May 1–24) and autumn (October 15–November 7). The
theater sits on the west side of the Kamo-gawa between Sanjō and Shijō
streets. ☒ *Ponto-chō, Sanjō-sagaru, Nakagyō-ku,* ☎ *075/221–2025.*

★ ⑯ Sanjūsangen-dō. Everyone knows this temple as Sanjūsangen-dō even
though it's officially called Rengeō-in. *Sanjūsan* means "33," which is
the number of spaces between the 35 pillars that lead down the narrow, 394-ft-long hall of the temple. Enthroned in the middle of the hall
is the 6-ft-tall, 1,000-handed Kannon—a National Treasure—carved
by Tankei, a sculptor of the Kamakura period (1192–1333). One thousand smaller statues of Kannon surround the large statue, and in the
corridor behind are the 28 guardian deities who protect the Buddhist
universe. Notice the frivolous-faced Garuda, a bird that feeds on dragons. Are you wondering about the 33 spaces mentioned earlier? Kannon can assume 33 different shapes on her missions of mercy. Because

there are 1,001 statues of Kannon in the hall, 33,033 shapes are possible. People come to the hall to see if they can find the likeness of a loved one (a deceased relative) among the many statues.

From Kyōto Eki take Bus 206, 208, or 100 to the Sanjūsangen-dō-mae stop. The temple will be to the south, just beyond the Kyōto Park Hotel. ✉ *657 Sanjūsangen-dō Mawari-chō, Higashiyama-ku.* 🎟 *¥600.* ☉ *Apr.–mid-Nov., daily 8–5; mid-Nov.–Mar., daily 9–4.*

Sannen-zaka and Ninen-zaka (Sannen and Ninen slopes). With their cobbled paths and delightful wooden buildings, these two lovely winding streets are fine examples of old Kyōto. This area is one of four historic preservation districts in Kyōto, and the shops along the way sell local crafts and wares such as *Kiyomizu-yaki* (Kiyomizu-style pottery), Kyōto dolls, bamboo basketry, rice crackers, and antiques. From Kiyomizu-dera turn right halfway down the Kiyomizu-zaka.

★ ㉕ **Shōren-in.** Paintings by the Kanō school are on view at this temple, a five-minute walk north of Chion-in. Though the temple's present building dates only from 1895, the sliding screens of the Hon-dō (Main Hall) have the works of Motonobu Kanō, second-generation Kanō, and Mitsunobu Kanō of the sixth generation. In the pleasant gardens an immense camphor tree sits at the entrance gate, and azaleas surround a balanced grouping of rocks and plants. It was no doubt more grandiose when artist and architect Soami designed it in the 16th century, but with the addition of paths through the garden, it's a pleasant place to stroll. Another garden on the east side of the temple is sometimes attributed, probably incorrectly, to Kobori Enshū. Occasionally, koto concerts are held in the evening in the Soami Garden (check with a Japan Travel Bureau office for concert schedules). From Kyōto Eki take Bus 206 to the Higashiyama-Sanjō stop. 🎟 *¥500.* ☉ *Daily 9–5.*

★ ㉖ **Yasaka Jinja.** Your business and health problems might come to a resolution at this Shintō shrine—leave a message for the god of prosperity and good health, to whom Yasaka Jinja is dedicated. Because it's close to the shopping districts, worshipers drop by for quick salvation. Especially at New Year's, Kyōto residents flock here to ask for good fortune in the coming year. From Kyōto Eki take Bus 206 or 100 to the Gion bus stop; the shrine is just off Higashi-ōji-dōri. ✉ *625 Gionmachi, Kitagawa, Higashiyama-ku.* 🎟 *Free.* ☉ *24 hrs.*

WESTERN KYŌTO

This tour of western Kyōto begins with the major northern sights, Kitano Tenman-gū first of all. If you're short on time, start instead at Daitoku-ji. Southwest of this group of shrines and temples, Arashiyama is a delightful hillside area along and above the banks of the Oi-gawa (the local name for the Katsura-gawa as it courses through this area). As in eastern Kyōto, the city's western precincts are filled with remarkable religious architecture, in particular the eye-popping golden Kinkaku-ji and Kitano Tenman-gū, with its monthly flea market.

Numbers in the text correspond to numbers in the margin and on the Western Kyōto and Arashiyama map.

A Good Tour

Start with the Shintō **Kitano Tenman-gū** ㉚, where a flea market is held on the 25th of each month. About a five-minute walk north of Kitano is **Hirano Jinja** ㉛, a shrine with wonderful cherry trees in its garden. After visiting the shrine, head for **Daitoku-ji** ㉜, a large 24-temple complex. To get there from Hirano Jinja head east to the bus stop at the intersection of Sembon-dōri and Imadegawa-dōri. Climb on Bus 206

Western Kyōto and Arashiyama

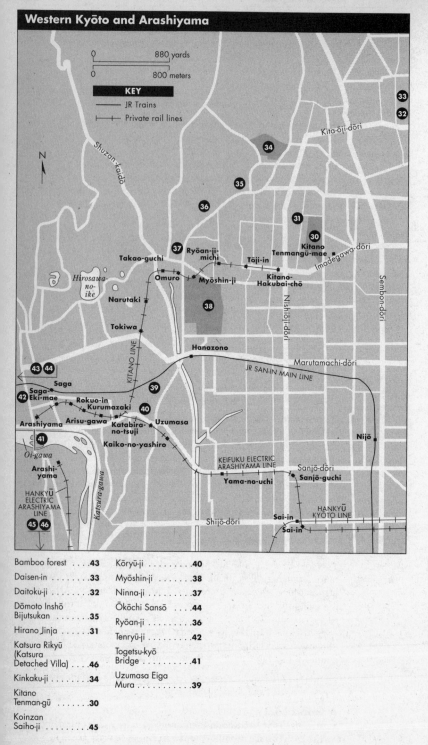

```
0                880 yards
0                800 meters
```

KEY
— JR Trains
⊢—⊢ Private rail lines

Shuzan-kaidō

Kita-ōji-dōri

N

㉝
㉜

㉞

㉟

㊱

㉛

㉚

Kita-ōji-dōri

Imadegawa-dōri

Hirosawa-
no-
ike

Takao-guchi

㊲ Ryōan-ji-
michi

Tōji-in

Kitano
Tenmangū-mae

Omuro

Myōshin-ji

Kitano-
Hakubai-chō

Narutaki

㊳

Tokiwa

Hanazono

Marutamachi-dōri

JR SAN-IN MAIN LINE

KITANO LINE

㊸ ㊹

Saga

㊴

Saga-
㊷ Eki-mae

Rokuo-in

Kurumazaki

㊵

Uzumasa

Arashiyama

Arisu-gawa

Katabira-
no-tsuji

Kaiko-no-yashiro

Nijō

㊶

Oi-gawa

Arashi-
yama

KEIFUKU ELECTRIC
ARASHIYAMA LINE

Sanjō-dōri

Sanjō-guchi

Yama-no-uchi

HANKYŪ
ELECTRIC
ARASHIYAMA
LINE

HANKYŪ
KYOTO LINE

Shijō-dōri

Sai-in

㊺ ㊻

Sai-in

Katsura-gawa

Nishiōji-dōri

Sembon-dōri

and take it north for about 10 minutes. Be sure to see the subtemple, **Daisen-in** ㉝, well known for its landscape paintings and for its kare-sansui garden. Other subtemples to visit if you have time are Kōtō-in and Ryogen-in. To get to the next stop, the impressive **Kinkaku-ji** ㉞, hop on Bus 12 west on Kita-ōji-dōri for a 10-minute ride to the Kinkaku-ji-mae stop.

From Kinkaku-ji walk back to the Kinkaku-ji-mae bus stop and take Bus 12 or 59 south for 10 minutes to the Ritsumeikan-daigaku-mae stop. The nearby **Dōmoto Inshō Bijutsukan** ㉟ exhibits works by the 20th-century abstract artist Inshō Dōmoto. When you leave the museum, either get on Bus 12 or 59 or walk for about 10 minutes south; **Ryōan-ji** ㊱ will be on your right.

From Ryōan-ji it's about 1½ km (1 mi) farther south on Bus 26 to Myōshin-ji. En route you'll pass **Ninna-ji** ㊲ on the right, a temple that was once the palace of Emperor Omuro. From Ninna-ji, take the street veering to the left (southwest); within ¾ km (½ mi) you'll reach **Myōshin-ji** ㊳. Another option from Ryōan-ji is to take Bus 12 or 59 three stops south to Ninna-ji and then change to Bus 8 or 10 to Myōshin-ji. Here you can see Japan's oldest bell. The other (sub-) temple to visit here is Taizō-in, which contains the painting *Four Sages of Mt. Shang,* by San-raku Kanō. Leave the temple complex by the south side, and you can pick up Bus 61 or 62; both go southwest to **Uzumasa Eiga Mura** ㊴, Japan's equivalent of Hollywood's Universal Studios. If you have no interest in stopping here—a visit will take at least two or three hours—continue on the bus to **Kōryū-ji** ㊵, a short walk south of Uzumasa Eiga Mura. Kōryū-ji is one of Kyōto's oldest temples, with many famous works of art, including the Miroku Bosatsu.

You're close to the Arashiyama district now and can take the Keifuku Electric Railway Arashiyama Line west to Tenryū-ji Eki and the bamboo forest just to the north for a pleasant end to the day. You may get the chance to watch some cormorant fishing on the Oi-gawa.

If you'd rather head back into central Kyōto, it's easy to do so from Kōryū-ji. Either take the bus (60–64) back past the Movie Village to JR Hanazono Eki, where the JR San-in Main Line will take you into Kyōto Eki, or take the privately owned Keifuku Electric Railway Arashiyama Line east to its last stop at Shijō-Ōmiya. This stop is on Shijō-dōri, from which Bus 201 or 203 can take you to Gion; or take Bus 26 to Kyōto Eki.

TIMING

If you're quick, you can cover all these sights in a day. If you don't have a lot of time in Kyōto, it would be better, while you're in western Kyōto, to skip a few sights so that you can make your way to Arashiyama in the afternoon.

Sights to See

★ ㉝ **Daisen-in.** Of all the subtemples at ☞ Daitoku-ji, Daisen-in is perhaps the best known—in part for its excellent landscape paintings by the renowned Soami (1465–1523), as well as its karesansui garden, which some attribute to Soami and others to Kogaku Soko (1465–1548). In the garden, the sand and stone represent the eternal aspects of nature, while the streams suggest the course of life. The single rock, once owned by Shōgun Yoshimasa Ashikaga, may be seen as a ship. Be aware that Daisen-in has its share of commercial accretions. *See* Daitoku-ji, *below,* for directions to Daisen-in. ☞ ¥400. ⊘ *Daily 9–5 (9–4:30 in winter).*

★ ㉜ **Daitoku-ji.** The Daitoku-ji complex of the Rinzai sect of Zen Buddhism consists of 24 temples in all, several of which are open to the public.

The original temple was founded in 1319 by Priest Daito Kokushi (1282–1337), but fires during the Ōnin Civil War destroyed it in 1468. Most buildings you see today were built under the patronage of Hideyoshi Toyotomi. However, it is thought that Priest Ikkyū oversaw its development. Ikkyū, known for his rather startling juxtapositions of the sacred and the profane—he was a priest and a poet—is reported to have said, "Brothels are more suitable settings for meditation than temples."

The layout of the temple is straightforward. Running from north to south are the Chokushi-mon (Gate of Imperial Messengers), the San-mon (Triple Gate), the Butsu-den (Buddha Hall), the Hattō (Lecture Hall), and the Hōjō (Abbots' Quarters). The 23 subtemples are on the west side of these main buildings and were donated mainly by the wealthy vassals of Toyotomi.

The **Chokushi-mon** originally served as the south gate of Kyōto's Imperial Palace when it was constructed in 1590. Then, Empress Meisho in the mid-17th century bequeathed it to Daitoku-ji. Note the curved-gable style of the gate, typical of the Momoyama period. The **San-mon** is noteworthy for the addition of its third story, designed by tea master Sen-no-Rikyū (1521–91), who is buried in the temple grounds. Three subtemples in the complex are noteworthy: ☞ **Daisen-in,** Kōtō-in, and Ryogen-in.

The subtemple **Kōtō-in** is famous for its long, maple-tree-lined approach and the single stone lantern that is central to the main garden. The fee is ¥400, and the temple stays open from 9 until 4:30 or 5 (enter 30 minutes before closing).

Ryogen-in is not as popular as some of the other temples of Daitoku-ji, but it is often quiet and peaceful. The subtemple has five small gardens of moss and stone, one of which, on the north side, is the oldest in Daitoku-ji. The fee is ¥350, and the temple stays open 9–4:30 (enter 30 minutes before closing).

There are several ways to get to the temple from downtown Kyōto. Take the subway north from Kyōto Eki to Kita-ōji Eki, from which any bus going west along Kita-ōji-dōri will take you to the Daitoku-ji-mae stop. You can also take Bus 12 north up Horikawa-dōri and disembark soon after the bus makes a left on Kita-ōji-dōri. From western Kyōto Bus 204, which runs up Nishi-ōji-dōri, and Bus 206, which runs up Sembon-dōri, will also take you to the temple. ✉ *Daitoku-ji-chō, Murasakino, Kita-ku.* 🎫 *Admission to different temples varies; the average is ¥500.* 🕐 *Daily; temple hrs vary between 9 and 4.*

㉟ Dōmoto Inshō Bijutsukan (Dōmoto Inshō Art Museum). Twentieth-century abstract artist Inshō Dōmoto created the painting and sculpture exhibited here. From the Kinkaku-ji-mae bus stop, take Bus 12 or 59 south for 10 minutes to Ritsumeikan-Daigaku-mae. ✉ *Kami-Yanagi-chō, Hirano, Kita-ku,* ☎ *075/463–1348.* 🎫 *¥500.* 🕐 *Tues.–Sun. 10–5.*

★ ㉛ Hirano Jinja. This complex of four shrine buildings dates from the 17th century, but its ancestry is ancient. The shrine was brought from Nagaoka—Japan's capital after Nara and before Kyōto—as one of many shrines used to protect the budding new Heian-kyō, as Kyōto was then called, during its formative years. The buildings are less remarkable than the gardens, with their 80 varieties of cherry trees. Take either Bus 50 or 52 from downtown Kyōto or Kyōto Eki. The ride takes a little more than half an hour. The shrine is about a 10-minute walk north of the Kitano Tenman-gū-mae bus stop. ✉ *Miyamoto-chō 1, Hirano, Kita-ku.* 🎫 *Free.* 🕐 *Daily 6–5.*

★ ㉞ **Kinkaku-ji** (Temple of the Golden Pavilion). For a retirement home, Kinkaku-ji is pretty magnificent. Shōgun Yoshimitsu Ashikaga (1358–1409) had it constructed in 1393 for the time when he would quit politics—the following year, in fact—to manage the affairs of state through the new shōgun, his 10-year-old son. On Yoshimitsu's death, his son followed his father's wishes and converted the villa into a temple named Rokuōn-ji. The structure sits, following the Shinden style of the Heian period, at the edge of the lake. Pillars support the three-story pavilion, which extends over the pond and is reflected in the calm waters. It's a beautiful sight, designed to suggest an existence somewhere between heaven and earth. The pavilion was the shōgun's statement of his prestige and power. To underscore that statement, he had the ceiling of the third floor of the pavilion covered in gold leaf. Not only the harmony and balance of the pavilion and its reflection, but also the richness of color shimmering in the light and in the water, make Kinkaku-ji one of Kyōto's most powerful visions.

In 1950 a student monk with metaphysical aspirations torched Kinkaku-ji, burning it to the ground. (Yukio Mishima's book *Temple of the Golden Pavilion* is a fictional attempt to get into the mind of the student.) Kinkaku-ji was rebuilt in 1955 based on the original design, except that all three stories were covered with gold leaf, in accordance with the shōgun's original intention, instead of only the third-floor ceiling.

Marveling at this pavilion, you might find it difficult to imagine the era in which Shōgun Yoshimitsu Ashikaga lived out his golden years. The country was in turmoil, and Kyōto residents suffered severe famines and plagues—local death tolls sometimes reached 1,000 a day. The temple is a short walk from the Kinkaku-ji-mae bus stop. From Daisen-in the ride on Bus 12 takes about 10 minutes. ⊠ *1 Kinkaku-ji-chō, Kitaku.* ☎ *¥400.* ☉ *Daily 9–5.*

★ ㉚ **Kitano Tenman-gū.** This shrine was originally dedicated to Tenjin, the god of thunder. Then, around 942, Michizane Sugawara was enshrined here. In his day, Michizane was a noted poet and politician—until Emperor Go-daigo ascended to the throne. Michizane was accused of treason and sent to exile on Kyūshū, where he died. For decades thereafter Kyōto suffered inexplicable calamities. The answer came in Go-daigo's dream: Michizane's spirit would not rest until he had been pardoned. Because the dream identified Michizane with the god of thunder, Kitano Tenman-gū was dedicated to him. On top of that, Michizane's political rank was posthumously restored. When that was not enough, he was promoted to a higher position and later to prime minister.

Kitano Tenman-gū was also the place where Hideyoshi Toyotomi held an elaborate tea party, inviting the whole of Kyōto to join him—creating a major opportunity for the local aristocracy to show off their finest tea bowls and related paraphernalia. Apart from unifying the warring clans of Japan and attempting to conquer Korea, Toyotomi is remembered in Kyōto as the man responsible for restoring many of the city's temples and shrines during the late 16th century. The shrine's present structure dates from 1607. A large **market** is held on the grounds on the 25th of each month. There are food stalls, and an array of antiques, old kimonos, and other collectibles are sold. Take either Bus 100 or 50 from Kyōto Eki and get off at Kitano Tenman-gū-mae. The ride takes a little more than a half hour. ⊠ *Imakoji-agaru, Onmaedori, Kamigyō-ku.* ☎ *Shrine free, plum garden ¥500 (includes green tea).* ☉ *Shrine Apr.–Oct., daily 5–5; Nov.–Mar., daily 5:30–5:30; plum garden Feb.–Mar., daily 10–4.*

★ ⓴ **Kōryū-ji.** One of Kyōto's oldest temples, Kōryū-ji was founded in 622 by Kawakatsu Hata in memory of Prince Shōtoku (572–621). Shōtoku, known for issuing the Seventeen-Article Constitution, was the first powerful advocate of Buddhism after it was introduced to Japan in 552. In the Hattō (Lecture Hall) of the main temple stand three statues, each a National Treasure. The center of worship is the seated figure of Buddha, flanked by the figures of the Thousand-Handed Kannon and Fukukenjaku-Kannon. In the Taishi-dō (Rear Hall), there is a wooden statue of Prince Shōtoku, which is thought to have been carved by him personally. Another statue of Shōtoku in this hall was probably made when he was 16 years old.

The numerous works of art in Kōryū-ji's Reihō-den (Treasure House) include many National Treasures. The most famous of all is the **Miroku Bosatsu,** Japan's number one National Treasure. This image of Buddha is the epitome of serenity, and of all the Buddhas in Kyōto, this is perhaps the most captivating. No one knows when it was made, but it is thought to be from the 6th or 7th century, carved, perhaps, by Shōtoku himself.

From Kyōto Eki take the JR San-in Main Line to Hanazono Eki and then board Bus 61. From Shijō-Ōmiya Eki, in central Kyōto, take the Keifuku Electric Arashiyama Line to Uzumasa Eki. From central or western Kyōto, take Bus 61, 62, or 63 to the Uzumasa-kōryūji-mae stop. ✉ *Hachigaoka-chō, Uzumasa, Ukyō-ku.* 🎫 *¥600.* ⊙ *Mar.–Nov., daily 9–5; Dec.–Feb., daily 9–4:30.*

★ ⓲ **Myōshin-ji.** Japan's oldest bell—cast in 698—hangs in the belfry near the South Gate of this 14th-century temple. When Emperor Hanazono died, his villa was converted into a temple; the work required so many laborers that a complex of buildings was built to house them. In all, there are some 40 structures here, though only four are open to the public. Beware of the dragon on the ceiling of Myōshin-ji's Hattō (Lecture Hall). Known as the "Dragon Glaring in Eight Directions," it looks at you wherever you stand.

Within the complex, the temple **Taizō-in** has a famous painting by Sanraku Kanō called *Four Sages of Mt. Shang,* recalling the four wise men who lived in isolation on a mountain to avoid the reign of destruction. The garden of Taizō-in is gentle and quiet—a good place to rest. The temple structure, originally built in 1404, suffered like the rest of the Myōshin-ji complex in the Ōnin Civil War (1467–77) and had to be rebuilt.

Buses 61, 62, and 63 all stop at the Myōshin-ji-mae stop. 🎫 *¥400 for Myōshin-ji; additional ¥400 for Taizō-in.* ⊙ *Daily 9:10–11:50 and 1–4.*

★ ⓱ **Ninna-ji.** The original temple here was once the palace of Emperor Omuro, who started the building's construction in 896. Nothing of that structure remains; the complex of buildings that stands today was rebuilt in the 17th century. There's an attractive five-story pagoda (1637), and the Hon-dō (Main Hall), which was moved from the Imperial Palace, is also worth noting as a National Treasure. The temple's focus of worship is the Amida Buddha. Take either Bus 26 or 59 to the Omuro-ninna-ji stop. 🎫 *¥500.* ⊙ *Daily 9–4:30.*

★ ⓰ **Ryōan-ji.** The garden at Ryōan-ji, rather than the temple, attracts people from all over the world. Knowing that the temple belongs to the Rinzai sect of Zen Buddhism may help you appreciate the austere aesthetics of the garden. It's a karesansui, a dry garden: just 15 rocks arranged in three groupings of seven, five, and three in gravel. From the temple's veranda, the proper viewing place, only 14 rocks can be seen at one time. Move slightly and another rock appears and one of the original 14 disappears. In the Buddhist world the number 15 denotes completeness. You must have a total view of the garden to make it a whole and meaningful experience—and yet, in the conditions of this world, that is not possible.

If possible, visit Ryōan-ji in the early morning before the crowds arrive and disturb the garden's contemplative quality. If you need a moment or two to yourself, head to the small restaurant on the temple grounds near an ancient pond, where you can find solace with an expensive beer if need be. From a southbound 12 or 59 bus, the temple will be on your right. ⊠ *13 Goryoshita-machi, Ryōan-ji, Ukyō-ku.* ☎ ¥500. ⊙ *Mar.–Nov., daily 8–5; Dec.–Feb., daily 8:30–4:30.*

☟ ㊴ **Uzumasa Eiga Mura** (Uzumasa Movie Village). This is Japan's answer to Hollywood, and had Kyōto been severely damaged in World War II, this would have been the last place to glimpse old Japan, albeit as a reproduction. Traditional country villages, ancient temples, and old-fashioned houses make up the stage sets, and if you're lucky, you may catch a couple of actors dressed as samurai snarling at each other, ready to draw their swords. You can visit the stage sets where popular traditional Japanese television series are filmed, or take in the *Red Shadow* action show, based on a popular TV series derived from a comic book. Also part of Eiga Mura is **Padios,** a small amusement park. Eiga Mura is a fine place to bring young children. For adults, whether it's worth the time depends on your interest in Japanese movies and your willingness to give Eiga Mura the two or three hours it takes to visit. The village is on the 61, 62, and 63 bus routes. ⊠ *10 Higashi-hachigaoka-chō, Uzumasa,* ☎ *075/881–7716.* ☎ *¥2,200.* ⊙ *Mar.–Nov., daily 9–5; Dec.–Feb., daily 9:30–4.*

Arashiyama and Katsura Rikyū

The pleasure of Arashiyama, the westernmost part of Kyōto, is the same as it has been for centuries. The gentle foothills of the mountains, covered with cherry and maple trees, are splendid, but it is the bamboo forests that really create the atmosphere of untroubled peace. It's no wonder that the aristocracy of feudal Japan came here to escape the famine, riots, and political intrigue that plagued Kyōto with the decline of the Ashikaga Shogunate a millennium ago.

A Good Tour

The easiest ways to get to Arashiyama are by the JR San-in Main Line from Kyōto Eki to Saga Eki, or via the Keifuku Electric Railway to Arashiyama Eki. South of Arashiyama Eki (Saga Eki is just north of Arashiyama Eki), the Oi-gawa flows under the **Togetsu-kyō Bridge** ㊶, where you can watch *ukai* (cormorant fishing) July and August evenings. The first temple to visit is **Tenryū-ji** ㊷—walk north from Arashiyama Eki or west from JR Saga Eki. One of the best ways to enjoy some contemplative peace is to walk the estate grounds of Denjiro Ōkōchi, a silent-movie actor of samurai films. To reach Ōkōchi's villa, either walk through the temple garden or leave Tenryū-ji and walk north on a narrow street through a **bamboo forest** ㊸, one of the best you'll see around Kyōto. The **Ōkōchi Sansō** ㊹ will soon be in front of you. To reach the final two sights on the tour, both south of Arashiyama, you'll need to take the Hankyū Arashiyama Line; the station is south of the Togetsu-kyō-bashi. Head first to Matsuno Eki and the nearby Moss Temple, **Koinzan Saihō-ji** ㊺, popularly known as Kokedera. Note that you'll need to arrange special permission ahead of time to visit the temple and garden here. The final sight is the imperial villa, **Katsura**

Rikyū ④, which reaches the heights of cultivated Shoin architecture and garden design. Continue on the Hankyū Arashiyama Line to Katsura Eki. You'll need to make reservations in advance for one of the scheduled guided tours of Katsura. To return to central Kyōto, take the Hankyū Kyōto Line from Katsura Eki to one of the central Kyōto Hankyū stations: Hankyū-Ōmiya, Karasuma, or Kawara-machi.

TIMING

You can see most of Arashiyama in a relaxed morning or afternoon, with the jaunt south to Saihōji and Katsura—where you should plan to spend at least an hour at each location—at the beginning or end of the tour.

Sights to See

④ **Bamboo forest.** Dense bamboo forests provide a feeling of composure and tranquillity quite different from the wooded tracts of the Western world. Nowadays they are few and far between. This one, on the way to Ōkōchi Sansō from Tenryū-ji, is a delight.

★ ④ **Katsura Rikyū** (Katsura Detached Villa). Built in the 17th century for Prince Toshihito, brother of Emperor Go-yōzei, Katsura is beautifully set in southwestern Kyōto on the banks of the Katsura-gawa, with peaceful views of Arashiyama and the Kameyama Hills. Perhaps more than anywhere else in the area, the setting is the most perfect example of Japanese integration of nature and architecture.

Here you'll find Japan's oldest surviving stroll garden. As is typical of the period, the garden makes use of a wide variety of styles, with elements of the pond and island, karesansui, and tea gardens, among others. The garden is a study in the placement of stones and the progressive unfolding of the views that the Japanese have so artfully mastered in garden design. Look out from the three *shōin* (a style of house that incorporates alcoves and platforms for the display of personal possessions) and the four rustic tea arbors around the central pond, which have been strategically placed for optimal vistas. Bridges constructed from earth, stone, and wood connect five islets in the pond.

An extensive network of varied pathways takes you through a vast repertoire of Katsura's miniaturizations of landscapes: an encyclopedia of famous Japanese natural sites and literary references, such as the 11th-century *Tale of Genji*. These associations might be beyond the average foreigner's Japanese education, but what certainly isn't is the experience of the garden that the designer intended for all visitors. Not satisfied to create simply beautiful pictures, Kobori Enshū focused on the rhythm within the garden: spaces open then close, are bright then dark; views are visible and then concealed.

The villa is fairly remote from other historical sites—allow several hours for a visit. Katsura requires special permission for a visit. Applications must be made, preferably a day in advance, in person to the **Imperial Household Agency** (✉ Kyōto Gyoen-nai, Kamigyō-ku, ☎ 075/211–1215), open weekdays 8:45–4. You will need your passport to pick up a permit, and you must be at least 20 years of age. The time of your tour will be stated, and you must not be late. The tour is in Japanese only, although a videotape introducing various aspects of the garden in English is shown in the waiting room before each tour begins.

To reach the villa, take the Hankyū Railway Line from one of the Hankyū Kyōto Line stations to Katsura Eki; then walk 15 minutes to the villa from the station's east exit or take a taxi for about ¥600. ✉ *Katsura Shimizu-chō, Ukyō-ku,* ☎ *075/211–1215 (inquiries only).* 🎫 *Free.* ♡

Tours weekdays at 10, 11, 2, and 3; Sat. tours 1st and 3rd Sat. of month; every Sat. in Apr.–May and Oct.–Nov.

★ ④⑤ **Koinzan Saihō-ji** (Moss Temple). Entrance into the temple precincts transports you into an extraordinary sea of green: 120 varieties of moss create waves of greens and blues that eddy and swirl gently around Koinzan Saihō-ji's garden and give the temple its popular name, Kokedera—the Moss Temple. Surrounded by the multihued moss, many feel the same sense of inner peace that comes from being near water.

The site was originally the villa of Prince Shōtoku (572–621). During the Tempyō era (729–749) the emperor Shōmu charged the priest Gyogi Bosatsu to create 49 temples in the central province, one of which was this temple. The original garden represented Jōdo, the Pure Land, or western paradise of Buddhism. The temple and garden, destroyed many times by fire, lay in disrepair until 1338, when the chief priest of nearby Matsuno-jinja had a revelation here. He convinced Musō Soseki, a distinguished Zen priest of Rinzenji, the head temple of the Rinzai sect of Zen Buddhism, to preside over the temple and convert it from the Jōdo to Zen sect. Soseki, an avid gardener, designed the temple garden on two levels surrounding a pond in the shape of the Chinese character for heart. Present-day visitors are grateful for his efforts. The garden is entirely covered with moss and provides a unique setting for a contemplative walk. May and June, when colors are brightest due to heavy rains, are the best times to see the garden.

Another interesting aspect to your temple visit is the obligatory *sha-kyō,* writing of sutras. Before viewing the garden, you enter the temple and take a seat at a small, lacquered writing table where you'll be provided with a brush, ink, and a thin sheet of paper with Chinese characters in light gray. After rubbing your ink stick on the ink stone, dip the tip of your brush in the ink and trace over the characters. A priest explains in Japanese the temple history and the sutra you are writing. If time is limited you don't have to write the entire sutra; when the priest has ended his explanation, simply place what you have written on a table before the altar and proceed to the garden.

To gain admission send a stamped, self-addressed postcard to: Saihō-ji Temple, 56 Matsuno Jinjatani-chō, Nishikyō-ku, Kyōto 615-8286. Include the date and time you would like to visit. You can write in English, and the response will also be in English. The postcard must reach the temple at least five days prior to your visit. It's also possible to arrange a visit through the Tourist Information Center. To reach the temple, take the Hankyū Line from Arashiyama to Matsuno Eki. ☒ ¥3,000 *(have exact change).*

④④ **Ōkōchi Sansō.** Walk the estate grounds of Ōkōchi's Mountain Villa to breathe in some contemplative peace—Denjiro Ōkōchi, a renowned silent-movie actor of samurai films, chose this location for his home because of the superb views of Arashiyama and Kyōto. Admission to the villa includes tea and cake to enjoy while you absorb nature's pleasures. ☒ *8 Tabuchiyama-chō, Ogurayama, Saga, Ukyō-ku,* ☎ *075/872-2233.* ☒ *¥900.* ☉ *Daily 9–5.*

★ ④② **Tenryū-ji.** For good reason is this known as the Temple of the Heavenly Dragon: Emperor Go-Daigo, who had successfully brought an end to the Kamakura Shogunate, was unable to hold on to his power and was forced from his throne by Takauji Ashikaga. After Go-Daigo died, Takauji had twinges of conscience. That's when Priest Musō Sōseki had a dream in which a golden dragon rose from the nearby Oi-gawa. He told the shōgun about his dream and interpreted it to mean the spirit of Go-Daigo was not at peace. Worried that this was an ill omen, Takauji built Tenryū-ji in 1339 on the same spot where Go-Daigo had his favorite villa. Apparently that appeased the spirit of the late emperor. In the Hattō (Lecture Hall), where today's monks meditate, a huge "cloud dragon" is painted on the ceiling. The temple was often ravaged by fire, and the current buildings are as recent as 1900; the painting of the dragon was rendered by 20th-century artist Shōnen Suzuki.

The **Sōgenchi garden** of Tenryū-ji, however, dates from the 14th century and is one of the most notable in Kyōto. Musō Soseki, an influential Zen monk and skillful garden designer, created the garden to resemble Mt. Hōrai in China. It is famed for the arrangement of vertical stones in its large pond and for its role as one of the first gardens to use "borrowed scenery," incorporating the mountains in the distance into the design of the garden.

If you visit Tenryū-ji at lunchtime, consider purchasing a ticket for Zen cuisine served at **Shigetsu**, within the temple precinct. The ¥3,500 price includes lunch in the large dining area overlooking a garden, as well as admission to the garden itself. Here you can experience the Zen monk's philosophy of "eating to live" rather than "living to eat." While you won't be partaking of the monk's daily helping of gruel, a salted plum, and pickled radishes, you will get to try Zen cuisine prepared for festival days. The meal includes sesame tofu served over top-quality soy sauce, a variety of fresh boiled vegetables, miso soup, and rice. The *tenzo*, a monk specially trained to prepare Zen cuisine, creates a multicourse meal that achieves the harmony of the six basic flavors—bitter, sour, sweet, salty, light, and hot—required to enable the monks to practice Zen with the least hindrance to their body and mind. It's an experience not to be missed. Though advance reservations are not required for the ¥3,500 course, there are more elaborate courses for ¥5,500 and ¥7,500 that do require reservations (☎ 075/882–9725); ask someone at your hotel or at the Tourist Information Center to make a reservation for you. Take the JR San-in Main Line from Kyōto Eki to Saga Eki or the Keifuku Electric Railway to Arashiyama Eki. From Saga Eki walk west; from Arashiyama Eki walk north. ✉ *68 Susuki-no-bamba-chō, Saga-Tenryū-ji, Ukyō-ku.* ✉ *Garden ¥500; ¥100 additional to enter temple building.* ⊙ *Apr.–Oct., daily 8:30–5:30; Nov.–Mar., daily 8:30–5.*

④ **Togetsu-kyō-bashi.** Spanning the Oi-gawa, the bridge is a popular spot from which you can watch ukai during the evening in July and August. Fisherfolk use cormorants to scoop up small sweet fish, which are attracted to the light of the flaming torches hung over the boats. The cormorants would swallow the fish for themselves, of course, but small rings around their necks prevent this. After about five fish, the cormorant has more than his gullet can hold. Then the fisherman pulls the bird back on a string, makes the bird regurgitate his catch, and sends him back for more. The best way to watch this spectacle is to join one of the charter passenger boats. Make a reservation using the number below, call the **Japan Travel Bureau** (☎ 075/361–7241), or use your hotel information desk. Take the JR San-in Main Line from Kyōto Eki to Saga Eki or the Keifuku Electric Railway to Arashiyama Eki. The bridge is south of both stations. ✉ *Reservations: Arashiyama Tsusen, 14–4 Nakaoshita-chō, Arashiyama, Nishikyō-ku,* ☎ *075/861–0223 or 075/861–0302.* ✉ *¥1,400.*

CENTRAL AND SOUTHERN KYŌTO

Central Kyōto is usually easier to explore after eastern and western Kyōto because the sights here are likely to be convenient to your hotel, and you're likely to see each individually rather than combining them into a single itinerary. Treat sights south of Kyōto Eki the same way, choosing the most interesting for a morning or afternoon venture. The two major sights in central Kyōto are Nijō-jō and the Kyōto Gosho, the castle and the Imperial Palace. The latter requires permission, and you must join a guided tour. The most interesting southern Kyōto sights are Tōfuku-ji and Byōdō-in and the tea-producing Uji-shi.

Numbers in the text correspond to numbers in the margin and on the Central Kyōto map.

A Good Tour

The easiest ways to reach **Kyōto Gosho** ㊼, the Imperial Palace, are to take the subway to Imadegawa or to take a bus to the Karasuma-Imadegawa stop. You can join the tour of the palace at the Seisho-mon entrance on Karasuma-dōri. You can easily combine Kyōto Gosho with **Nijō-jō** ㊽, Kyōto residence of the Tokugawa Shogunate, on the same trip. Take the Karasuma subway line from Imadegawa Eki toward Kyōto Eki to Ōike (two stops) and change to the Tōzai subway line. Board the car heading for Nijō and get off at the next stop, Nijō-jō-mae.

For an excursion into the culture of the tea ceremony, make your way west to the **Raku Bijutsukan** ㊾, a museum that displays the Raku family's tea bowls. For another change of pace, visit the Nishijin silk-weaving district, north of the Raku Bijutsukan on Horikawa-dōri at the corner of Imadegawa-dōri. At the **Nishijin Orimono** ㊿, you can watch demonstrations. The Raku Bijutsukan and the Nishijin Orimono are both roughly halfway between the Gosho and Nijō-jō. Buses 9, 12, 50, and 52 run up and down Horikawa-dōri past these two sights.

From the museum, the textile center, or Nijō-jō, take Bus 9 south on Horikawa-dōri. Disembark at the Nishi-Hongan-ji-mae bus stop. Across from the temple, on the fifth floor of the Izutsu Building at the intersection of Horikawa and Shin-Hanaya-chō, is the **Fūzoku Hakubutsukan** (51), which has clothes that were worn from the pre-Nara era, before 710, to the Meiji period, post-1868. The most famous temples in the area are nearby **Nishi-Hongan-ji** (52) and **Higashi-Hongan-ji** (53). Higashi-Hongan-ji is the second-largest wooden structure in Japan. Nishi-Hongan-ji has interesting art objects, but the temple proper requires special permission to enter.

From Nishi-Hongan-ji it's a 10-minute walk southeast to **Kyōto Eki.** Take some time to look around the station building—it's a sight in its own right. If you still have time, visit **Tō-ji** (54), one of Kyōto's oldest temples, southwest of the station. It holds a flea market on the 21st of each month. The best way here is to leave Nishi-Hongan-ji by the west exit and take Bus 207 south on Ōmiya-dōri. Get off at the Tō-ji-Higashimon-mae bus stop, and Tō-ji will be across the street. From Kyōto Eki, Tō-ji is either a 10-minute walk southwest; or you can take the Kintetsu Kyōto Line to Tō-ji Station and walk west for 5 minutes.

Points of interest south of Kyōto Eki require individual trips, returning each time to Kyōto Eki. **Byōdō-in,** a former 10th-century residence turned temple, is in Uji, a famous tea-producing area where you can taste the finest green tea. **Daigo-ji,** in the Yamashina suburb southeast of Kyōto, is a charming 9th-century temple with a five-story pagoda. To reach Daigo-ji, in the southeast suburb of Yamashina, take the Tōzai subway line to Daigo Eki. **Tōfuku-ji,** a Zen temple of the Rinzai sect,

318

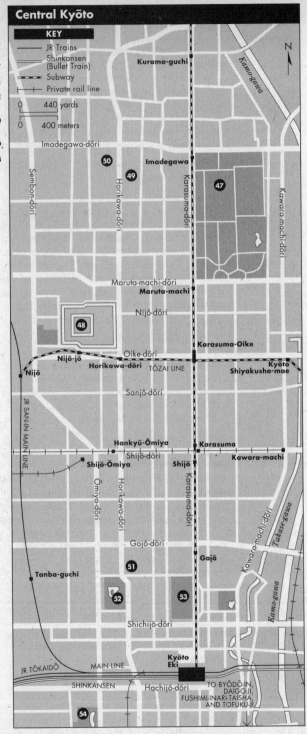

Central Kyōto

KEY

— JR Trains
Shinkansen
(Bullet Train)
Subway
Private rail line

0   440 yards
0   400 meters

Kurama-guchi

Imadegawa-dōri

Imadegawa

Sembon-dōri

Horikawa-dōri

Karasuma-dōri

Kawara-machi-dōri

Kamo-gawa

Maruta-machi-dōri
Maruta-machi

Nijō-dōri

Karasuma-Oike

Oike-dōri
Nijō-jō
Horikawa-dōri   TŌZAI LINE   **Kyōto Shiyakusho-mae**

Nijō

Sanjō-dōri

JR SAN-IN MAIN LINE

Hankyū-Ōmiya   **Karasuma**

Shijō-dōri
Shijō-Ōmiya   **Shijō**   **Kawara-machi**

Ōmiya-dōri

Horikawa-dōri

Karasuma-dōri

Takase-gawa

Gojō-dōri

Tanba-guchi

Gojō

Kawara-machi-dōri

Kamo-gawa

Shichijō-dōri

**Kyōto
Eki**

JR TŌKAIDŌ   MAIN LINE

SHINKANSEN   Hachijō-dōri   TO BYŌDŌ-IN,
DAIGO-JI,
FUSHIMI-INARI-TAISHA,
AND TOFUKU-JI

ranks as one of the most important Zen temples in Kyōto. It's on the Bus 208 route from Kyōto Eki; or it's a 15-minute walk from Tōfuku-ji Eki on the JR Nara Line or the Keihan Main Line. You may want to combine a visit here with a stop at the **Fushimi-Inari Taisha,** farther south. This shrine is one of Kyōto's oldest and most revered. Fushimi-Inari Taisha is a three-minute walk from the JR Nara Line's Fushimi-Inari Eki.

TIMING

The temples and shrines in southern Kyōto are a distance from one another, so traveling time can eat into your day. But central Kyōto's sights are fairly close to each other and quickly accessible by bus or taxi. A morning would be mostly taken up with the Imperial Palace and Nijō-jō. Remember that the Imperial Palace is closed Saturday afternoon and Sunday, and also all day on the second and fourth Saturday of the month in winter and summer.

Sights to See

★ **Byōdō-in.** South of Kyōto in Uji-shi, this temple was originally the villa of a 10th-century member of the influential Fujiwara family. The Amida-dō, also called the Phoenix Hall, was built in the 11th century by the Fujiwaras and is still considered one of Japan's most beautiful religious buildings—something of an architectural folly—where heaven is brought close to earth. Jōchō, one of Japan's most famous 11th-century sculptors, crafted a magnificent statue of a seated Buddha here. Uji itself is a famous tea-producing district, and the slope up to the temple is lined with shops where you can sample the finest green tea and pick up a small package to take home. Take the JR Nara line to Uji Eki; from there the temple is a 12-minute walk. ⊠ *Ujirenge, Uji-shi,* ☎ *0774/21–2861.* ☒ *¥500; additional ¥300 for Phoenix Hall.* ۞ *Temple Mar.–Nov., daily 8:30–5:30; Dec.–Feb., daily 9–4:30; Phoenix Hall Mar.–Nov., daily 9–5; Dec.–Feb., daily 9–4.*

★ **Daigo-ji.** This temple was founded in 874, and over the succeeding centuries, other buildings were added and its gardens expanded. Its five-story pagoda, which dates from 951, is reputed to be the oldest existing structure in Kyōto. By the late 16th century the temple had begun to decline in importance and showed signs of neglect. Then Hideyoshi Toyotomi paid a visit one April, when the temple's famous cherry trees were in blossom. Hideyoshi ordered the temple restored. The smaller **Sambo-in** houses paintings by the Kanō school. To reach Daigo-ji, in the southeast suburb of Yamashina, take the Tōzai subway line to Daigo Eki. ⊠ *22 Higashi Ōji-chō, Fushimi-ku.* ☒ *¥500.* ۞ *Mar.–Oct., daily 9–5; Nov.–Feb., daily 9–4.*

★ **Fushimi-Inari Taisha.** One of Kyōto's oldest and most revered shrines, the Fushimi-Inari honors the goddesses of agriculture (rice and rice wine) and prosperity. It also serves as the headquarters for all the 40,000 shrines representing Inari. The shrine is noted for its bronze foxes and for some 10,000 small torii, donated by the thankful, which stretch up the hill behind the structure. If possible, visit near dusk—you'll be among the only people wandering through the tunnels of torii in the quiet woods, a nearly mystical experience as daylight fades. Take the JR Nara Line to Fushimi-Inari Eki, from which it is a three-minute walk to the shrine. From Tōfuku-ji join the JR train at Tōfuku-ji Eki and go one stop south, toward Nara. ⊠ *68 Fukakusa Yabu-no-uchi-chō, Fushimi-ku.* ☒ *Free.* ۞ *Daily sunrise–sunset.*

★ ⑤ **Fūzoku Hakubutsukan** (Kyōto Costume Museum). It's well worth a stop here to marvel at the range of fashion, which starts in the pre-Nara era and works its way up through various historical eras to the

Meiji period. The museum is one of the best of its kind and, in its own way, gives an account of the history of Japan. Exhibitions, which change twice a year, highlight a specific period in Japanese history. From the Raku Museum, the Nishijin Textile Center, or Nijō-jō, take Bus 9 south on Horikawa-dōri. Disembark at the Nishi-Hongan-ji-mae bus stop. The museum is on the fifth floor of the Izutsu Building, which is at the intersection of Horikawa and Shin-Hanaya-chō, north of the temple on the other side of the street. ⊠ *Izutsu Bldg., Shimogyō-ku,* ☎ *075/342–5345.* 🖾 *¥400.* ☉ *Oct. 9–Sept. 2, Mon.–Sat. 9–5 (closed Apr. 1–8, July 1–8, and Dec. 23–Jan. 6).*

★ ❸ **Higashi-Hongan-ji.** Until the early 17th century Higashi-Hongan-ji and Nishi-Hongan-ji were one temple. Then Ieyasu Tokugawa took advantage of a rift among the Jōdo Shinshu sect of Buddhism and, to diminish its power, split them apart into two different factions. The original faction has the west temple, Nishi-Hongan-ji, and the latter faction the eastern temple, Higashi-Hongan-ji.

The rebuilt (1895) structure of Higashi-Hongan-ji is the second-largest wooden structure in Japan, after Nara's Daibutsu-den. The **Daishi-dō,** a double-roofed structure, is admirable for its curving, swooping lines. Inside are portraits of all the head abbots of the Jōdo Shinshu sect, but, unfortunately, it contains fewer historical objects of interest than does its rival, Nishi-Hongan-ji. From Kyōto Eki walk 500 yards northwest; from the costume museum walk south on Horikawa-dōri. ⊠ *Shichijō-agaru, Karasuma-dōri, Shimogyō-ku.* 🖾 *Free.* ☉ *Mar.–Oct., daily 5:50–5:30; Nov.–Feb., daily 6:20–4:30.*

Kyōto Eki. Kyōto's train station, opened in 1997, is more than just the city's central point of arrival and departure: its impressive marble-and-glass structure makes it as significant a building as any of Kyōto's ancient treasures. Hiroshi Hara's modern design was at first controversial, but his use of space and lighting—and the sheer enormity of the final product—eventually won over most of its opponents. The station houses a hotel, a theater, a department store, and dozens of shops and restaurants.

❹ **Kyōto Gosho** (Imperial Palace). The present palace, a third-generation construction, was completed in 1855, so it has housed only two emperors, one of whom was the young emperor Meiji before he moved his imperial household to Tōkyō. The original, built for Emperor Kammu to the west of the present site, burned down in 1788. A new palace, modeled after the original, then went up on the present site, but it, too, ended in flames. The Gosho itself is a large but simple wooden building that can hardly be described as palatial. On the one-hour tour, you'll only have a chance for a brief glimpse of the Shishin-den—the hall where the inauguration of emperors and other important imperial ceremonies take place—and a visit to the gardens. Though a trip to the Imperial Palace is on most people's agenda and though it fills a fair amount of space in downtown Kyōto, it holds somewhat less interest than do some of the older historic buildings in the city.

Guided tours start at the Seisho-mon entrance. You must arrive at the Imperial Palace before 9:40 AM for the one-hour 10 AM guided tour in English. Present yourself, along with your passport, at the office of the **Kunaichō** (Imperial Household Agency) in the palace grounds. For the 2 PM guided tour in English, arrive by 1:40 PM. The Kunaichō office is closed on weekends, so visit in advance to arrange a Saturday tour. To get to the palace, take the Karasuma Line of the subway in the direction of Kokusaikaikan. Get off at Imadegawa Station, and use the Number 6 Exit. Cross the street and turn right. Enter the palace

When you pack your MCI Calling Card, it's like packing your loved ones along too.

Your MCI Calling Card is the easy way to stay in touch when you travel. Use it to call to and from over 125 countries. Plus, every time you call, you can earn frequent flier miles. So wherever your travels take you, call home with your MCI Calling Card. It's even easy to get one. Just visit **www.mci.com/worldphone.**

EASY TO CALL WORLDWIDE

1. Just enter the WorldPhone® access number of the country you're calling from.

2. Enter or give the operator your MCI Calling Card number.

3. Enter or give the number you're calling.

Australia ◆	1-800-881-100
China	108-12
Hong Kong	800-96-1121
India	000-127
Japan ◆	00539-121▶
Kenya	080011
Morocco	00-211-0012
South Africa	0800-99-0011

◆ Public phones may require deposit of coin or phone card for dial tone.
▶ Regulation does not permit intra-Japan calls.

EARN FREQUENT FLIER MILES

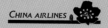

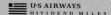

SEE THE WORLD
IN FULL COLOR

Fodor's Exploring Guides bring all the great sights vividly to life with hundreds of photographs, fascinating historical background, and colorful anecdotes. Detailed maps and practical information keep you headed in the right direction.

Pair a **Fodor's** Exploring Guide with your trusted Gold Guide for a complete planning package.

through the Inui Go-mon on your left. ⊠ *Kunaichō, Kyōto Gyoen-nai, Kamigyō-ku,* ☎ *075/211–1215 (information only).* ☒ *Free.* ☉ *Office weekdays 8:45–12 and 1–4; tours weekdays at 10 AM and 2 PM (Sat. tours on 1st and 3rd Sat. of month; every Sat. in Apr.–May and Oct.–Nov.).*

★ ➍ **Nijō-jō.** Nijō-jō was the local Kyōto address for the Tokugawa Shogunate. Dominating central Kyōto, it's an intrusion, both politically and artistically. The man who built the castle in 1603, Ieyasu Tokugawa, did so to emphasize that political power had been completely removed from the emperor and that he alone determined the destiny of Japan. As if to emphasize that statement, Tokugawa built and decorated his castle with such ostentation as to make the populace cower in the face of his wealth and power. This kind of display was antithetical to the refined restraint of Kyōto's aristocracy.

Ieyasu Tokugawa had risen to power through skillful political maneuvers and treachery. His military might was unassailable, and that is probably why his Kyōto castle had relatively modest exterior defenses. However, as he well knew, defense against treachery is never certain. The interior of the castle was built with that in mind. Each building had concealed rooms where bodyguards could maintain a watchful eye for potential assassins, and the corridors had built-in "nightingale" floors, so no one could walk in the building without making noise. Rooms were locked only from the inside, thus no one from the outer rooms could gain access to the inner rooms without someone admitting them. The outer rooms were kept for visitors of low rank and were adorned with garish paintings that would impress them. The inner rooms were for the important lords, whom the shōgun would impress with the refined, tasteful paintings of the Kanō school.

The opulence and grandeur of the castle were, in many ways, a snub to the emperor. They relegated the emperor and his palace to insignificance, and the Tokugawa family even appointed a governor to manage the emperor and the imperial family. The Tokugawa shōguns were rarely in Kyōto. Ieyasu stayed in the castle three times, the second shōgun twice, including the time in 1626 when Emperor Gomizuno-o was granted an audience. After that, for the next 224 years, no Tokugawa shōgun visited Kyōto, and the castle started to fall into disrepair and neglect. Only when the Tokugawa Shogunate was under pressure from a failing economy, and international pressure developed to open Japan to trade, did the 14th shōgun, Iemochi Tokugawa (1846–66), come to Kyōto to confer with the emperor. The emperor told the shōgun to rid Japan of foreigners, but Iemochi did not have the strength. As the shōgun's power continued to wane, the 15th and last shōgun, Keiki Tokugawa (1837–1913), spent most of his time in Nijō-jō. Here he resigned, and the imperial decree was issued that abolished the shogunate after 264 years of rule.

After the Meiji Restoration in 1868, Nijō-jō became the Kyōto prefectural office until 1884; during that time it suffered from acts of vandalism. Since 1939 the castle has belonged to the city of Kyōto, and considerable restoration work has taken place.

You enter the castle through the impressive **Kara-mon** (Chinese Gate). Notice that you must turn right and left at sharp angles to make this entrance—a common attribute of Japanese castles, designed to slow the advance of any attacker. From the Kara-mon, the carriageway leads to the **Ni-no-maru Goten** (Second Inner Palace), whose five buildings are divided into many chambers. The outer buildings were for visits by men of lowly rank, the inner ones for those of higher rank. The most notable room, the **Ōhiroma** (Great Hall), is easy to recognize. In the room, costumed figures reconstruct the occasion when Keiki Tokugawa returned the power of government to the emperor. This spacious hall was where, in the early 17th century, the shōgun would sit on a raised throne to greet important visitors seated below him. The sliding screens of this room have magnificent paintings of forest scenes.

Even more impressive than the palace itself is its garden, created by landscape designer Kobori Enshū shortly before Emperor Gomizuno-o's visit in 1626. Notice the crane-and-tortoise islands flanking the center island (called the Land of Paradise). The symbolic meaning is clear: strength and longevity. The garden was originally designed with no deciduous trees, for the shōgun did not wish to be reminded of the transitory nature of life by autumn's falling leaves.

The other major building on the grounds is the **Hon-maru Palace**, a replacement of the original, which burned down in the 18th century. It's not normally open to the public. To reach the castle, take the bus or subway to Nijō-jō-mae. ✉ *Horikawa Nishi-Iru, Nijō-dōri, Nakagyō-ku,* ☎ *075/841–0096.* 🎫 *¥600.* ☉ *Daily 8:45–5 (last entry at 4).*

....

NEED A BREAK? After your visit to the palace take a break at the traditional Japanese candy store **Mukashi Natsukashi**, on the corner of Ōmiya-dōri, three blocks west of the intersection of Horikawa-dōri and Oike-dōri. Browse through the quaint candy store, grab a cold drink from a cedar bucket filled with cold water, and try the specialty of the house, *dorobo* (a molasses-covered rice-flour crispy snack). You can rest on the bench outside the shop while sampling your wares. ✉ *Oshikoji-dōri, Ōmiya-dōri, Nakagyō-ku.* ☎ *075/841–4464.*

....

★ 🔢 **Nishi-Hongan-ji.** The marvelous artifacts at this temple were confiscated by Ieyasu Tokugawa from Hideyoshi Toyotomi's Jurakudai Palace, in Kyōto, and from Fushimi-jō, in southern Kyōto. He had the buildings dismantled in an attempt to erase the memory of his predecessor.

Hideyoshi Toyotomi was quite a man. Though most of the initial work in unifying Japan was accomplished by the warrior Nobunaga Oda (he was ambushed a year after defeating the monks on Hiei-zan), it was Hideyoshi who completed the job. Not only did he end civil strife, he also restored the arts. For a brief time (1582–98), Japan entered one of the most colorful periods of its history. How Hideyoshi achieved his feats is not exactly known. He was brought up as a farmer's son, and his nickname was Saru-san (Mr. Monkey) because he was small and ugly. According to one legend—probably started by Hideyoshi himself—he was the son of the emperor's concubine. She had been much admired by a man to whom the emperor owed a favor, so the emperor gave the concubine to him. Unknown to either of the men, she was soon pregnant with Hideyoshi. Whatever his origins (he changed his name frequently), he brought peace to Japan after decades of civil war.

Because much of what was dear to Hideyoshi Toyotomi was destroyed by the Tokugawas, it is only at Nishi-Hongan-ji that you can see the artistic works closely associated with his personal life, including the great **Kara-mon** (Chinese Gate) and the **Daisho-in,** both brought from Fushimi-jō, and the **Nō stage** from Jurakudai Palace.

Nishi-Hongan-ji is on Horikawa-dōri, a couple of blocks north of Shichijō-dōri. Visits to some of the buildings are permitted four times a day by permission from the temple office. Phone for an appointment once you arrive in Kyōto; if you don't speak Japanese, you may want to ask your hotel to place the call for you. Tours of Daisho-in (in Japanese) are given occasionally throughout the year. ✉ *Shichijō-agaru, Horikawa-dōri, Shimogyō-ku,* ☎ *075/371–5181.* 🎫 *Free.* ⊗ *Mar.–Apr. and Sept.–Oct., daily 5:30–5:30; May–Aug., daily 5:30 AM–6 PM; Nov.–Feb., daily 6–5.*

50 Nishijin Orimono (Textile Center). The Nishijin district still hangs on to the artistic thread of traditional Japanese silk weaving. Nishijin Orimono hosts demonstrations of age-old weaving techniques and presents fashion shows and special exhibitions. On the mezzanine you can buy kimonos and gift items, such as *happi* (workmen's) coats and silk purses. The center is on the 9 and 12 bus routes, north of the Raku Bijutsukan, at the corner of Horikawa-dōri and Imadegawa-dōri. ✉ *Horikawa-dōri, Imadegawa-Minami-Iru, Kamigyō-ku,* ☎ *075/451–9231.* 🎫 *Free, kimono show ¥600.* ⊗ *Daily 9–5. Closed Aug. 13–15, Dec. 29–Jan. 15.*

49 Raku Bijutsukan. Any serious collector of tea-ceremony artifacts is likely to have a Raku bowl in his or her collection. Here you'll find tea bowls made by members of the Raku family, whose roots can be traced to the 16th century. As a potter's term in the West, *raku* refers to a low-temperature firing technique, but the word originated with this family, who made exquisite tea bowls for use in the shōgun's tea ceremonies. The museum is to the east of Horikawa-dōri, two blocks south of Imadegawa-dōri; take Bus 9 or 12 to Ichi-jō-modōri-bashi. ✉ *Aburakōji, Nakadachuri-agaru, Kamigyō-ku,* ☎ *075/414–0304.* 🎫 *¥700–¥1,000 (depending on exhibition).* ⊗ *Tues.–Sun. 10–4:30.*

★ **Tōfuku-ji.** In all, two dozen subtemples and the main temple compose the complex of this Rinzai-sect Zen temple, established in 1236, which ranks as one of the most important in Kyōto, along with the Myōshin-ji and Daitoku-ji. Autumn is an especially fine time for visiting, when the burnished colors of the maple trees add to the pleasure of the gardens. There are at least three ways to get to Tōfuku-ji, which is southeast of Kyōto Eki: Bus 208 from Kyōto Eki, a JR train on the Nara Line to Tōfuku-ji Eki, or a Keihan Line train to Tōfuku-ji Eki. From the trains, it's a 15-minute walk to the temple. Consider combining a visit here with one to Fushimi-Inari Taisha, farther south. ✉ *Hon-machi 15-chōme, Higashiyama-ku.* 🎫 *¥400.* ⊗ *Daily 9–4.*

54 Tō-ji. Established by imperial edict in 796 and called Kyō-ō-gokoku-ji, Tō-ji was built to guard the city. It was one of the only two temples that Emperor Kammu permitted to be built in the city—he had had enough of the powerful Buddhists during his days in Nara. The temple was later given to Priest Kūkai (Kōbō Daishi), who founded the Shingon sect of Buddhism. Tō-ji became one of Kyōto's most important temples.

Fires and battles during the 16th century destroyed the temple buildings, but many were rebuilt, including the Kon-dō (Main Hall) in 1603. The Kō-dō (Lecture Hall), on the other hand, has managed to survive the ravages of war since it was built in 1491. Inside this hall are 15 original statues of Buddhist gods that were carved in the 8th and 9th centuries. Perhaps Tōji's most eye-catching building is the 180-ft, five-story pagoda, reconstructed in 1695.

An interesting time to visit the temple is on the 21st of each month, when a market, known locally as Kōbō-san, is held. Antique kimonos, fans, and other memorabilia can sometimes be found at bargain prices if you know your way around the savvy dealers. Many elderly people flock to the temple on this day to pray to Kōbō Daishi and to shop. A smaller antiques market is held on the first Sunday of the month. From Kyōto Eki take the Kintetsu Kyōto Line one stop to Tō-ji Eki or walk

10 minutes west from the central exit of JR Kyōto Eki. Bus 207 also runs past Tō-ji: either south from Gion, then west; or west from Kara-suma-dōri along Shijō-dōri, then south. Get off at the Tō-ji-Higashimon-mae stop. ⊠ *1 Kujō-chō, Minami-ku.* ⊡ *Main buildings ¥500, grounds free.* ⊙ *Mar. 20–Sept. 19, daily 9–5; Sept. 20–Mar. 19, daily 9–4:30.*

NORTHERN KYŌTO

Hiei-zan and Ōhara are the focal points in the northern suburbs of Kyōto. Ōhara was for several centuries a sleepy Kyōto backwater surrounded by mountains. Although it is now catching up with the times, it still has a feeling of old Japan, with several temples that deserve visits. Hiei-zan is a fount of Kyōto history. On its flanks Saichō founded Enryaku-ji and with it the vital Tendai sect of Buddhism. It's an essential Kyōto site, and walking on forested slopes among its 70-odd temples is one reason to make the trek to Hiei-zan.

A Good Tour

To get to Ōhara, take private Kyōto Line Bus 17 or 18 from Kyōto Eki and get out at the Ōhara bus stop. The trip takes 90 minutes and costs ¥480. From the bus station, walk northeast for about seven minutes along the signposted road to **Sanzen-in,** a small Tendai-sect temple on delightful grounds with a remarkable carved Amida Buddha. Two hundred yards from Sanzen-in sits the quiet **Jikkō-in,** where you can drink traditional *matcha* (powdered tea-ceremony tea). On the other side of Ōhara and the Takano-gawa is **Jakkō-in,** a romantic temple full of pathos and a sanctuary for nuns. To get here, return to the Ōhara bus stop and walk 20 minutes north up the road.

The next stop is **Hiei-zan.** Take Kyōto Line Bus 16, 17, or 18 down the main highway, Route 367, to the Yase Yuenchi bus stop, next to Yase Yuen Eki. You'll see the entrance to the cable car on your left. It departs every 30 minutes, and you can transfer to the ropeway at Hiei for the remaining distance to the top. At the summit is an observatory with panoramic views of the mountains and of Biwa-ko (Lake Biwa). From the observatory, a mountain path leads to **Enryaku-ji,** an important center of Buddhism. Before day's end, return from Hiei-zan by taking the Eizan Railway from Yase Yuen Eki to Shūgaku-in Eki and making a 15-minute walk to the **Shūgaku-in Imperial Villa,** which consists of a complex of three palaces. The return to downtown Kyōto takes an hour on Bus 5 to Kyōto Eki or 20 minutes by Keifuku Eizan train to Demachi-Yanagi Eki, just north of Imadegawa-dōri.

One final sight, closer to central Kyōto, is **Kamigamo Jinja,** built by the legendary warrior Kamo. It's near the end of the Bus 9 route north from Kyōto Eki by the Kamigamo-Misonobashi stop.

TIMING

It's best to make this a day trip to allow for unhurried exploration of Ōhara and on Hiei-zan. If you're short on time, you could cover the sights in about four hours.

Sights to See

Hiei-zan and Enryaku-ji. From the observatory at the top of Hiei-zan, a serpentine mountain path leads to Enryaku-ji, which remains a vital center of Buddhism. At one time it consisted of 3,000 buildings and had its own standing army. That was its downfall. Enryaku-ji really began in 788. Emperor Kammu, the founding father of Kyōto, requested Priest Saichō (767–822) to establish a temple on Hiei-zan to protect the area (including Nagaoka, then the capital) from the evil spirits. Demons and evil spirits were thought to come from the northeast, and

Hiei-zan was a natural barrier between the fledgling city and the northeastern Kin-mon (Devil's Gate), where devils were said to pass. The temple's monks were to serve as lookouts and, through their faith, keep evil at bay.

The temple grew, and because police were not allowed on its mountaintop sanctuary, criminals flocked here, ostensibly to seek salvation. By the 11th century the temple had formed its own army to secure order on its estate. In time, this army grew and became stronger than that of most other feudal lords, and the power of Enryaku-ji came to threaten Kyōto. No imperial army could manage a war without the support of Enryaku-ji, and when there was no war, Enryaku-ji's armies would burn and slaughter monks of rival Buddhist sects. Not until the 16th century was there a force strong enough to sustain an assault on the temple. With accusations that the monks had concubines and never read the sutras, Nobunaga Oda (1534–82), the general who unified Japan by ending more than a century of civil strife, attacked the monastery in 1571 to rid it of its evil. In the battle, monks were killed, and most of the buildings were destroyed. Structures standing today were built in the 17th century.

Enryaku-ji has three main precincts: the Eastern Precinct, where the main building in the complex, the **Kompon Chū-dō**, stands; the Western Precinct, with the oldest building, the **Shaka-dō**; and the Yokawa district, a few miles north. The Kompon Chū-dō dates from 1642, and its dark, cavernous interior quickly conveys the sense of mysticism for which the esoteric Tendai sect is known. Giant pillars and a coffered ceiling shelter the central altar, which is surrounded by religious images and sacred objects. The ornate lanterns that hang before the altar are said to have been lighted by Saichō himself centuries ago.

The Western precinct is where Saichō founded his temple and where he is buried. An incense burner wafts smoke before his tomb, which lies in a small hollow. The peaceful atmosphere of the cedar trees surrounding the main structures—Jōdo-in, Ninai-dō, and Shaka-dō—suggests an imitation of the essence of the life of a Tendai Buddhist monk, who devotes his life to the esoteric. Enryaku-ji is still an important training ground for Buddhism, on a par with the temples at Kōya-san. The value of coming here is in experiencing Enryaku-ji's overall aura of spiritual profundity rather than its particular buildings. Though the temple complex is only a 20th of its original size, the magnitude of the place and the commitment to esoterica pursued here are awesome.

Take Kyōto Line Bus 16, 17, or 18 up the main highway, Route 367, to the Yase Yuenchi bus stop, next to Yase Yuen Eki. You'll see the entrance to the cable car on your left. It departs every 30 minutes, and you can transfer to the ropeway at Hiei for the remaining ride to the summit, where an observatory affords panoramic views of the mountains and of Biwa-ko. *Enryaku-ji:* ✉ *4220 Sakamoto-hon-machi, Ōtsushi.* 🎫 *Enryaku-ji ¥800; Hiei-zan cable car ¥530, ropeway ¥310.* ☯ *Enryaku-ji Mar.–Nov., daily 8:30–4:30; Dec.–Feb., daily 9–4. Hiei-zan ropeway Apr.–Sept., daily 9–6; Oct.–Mar., daily 9–5 (mid-July–late Aug., observatory stays open until 9).*

★ **Jakkō-in.** In April 1185 the Taira clan met its end in a naval battle against the Minamoto clan. For two years Yoshitsune Minamoto had been gaining the upper hand in the battles. In this one, the Minamotos slaughtered the Tairas, turning the Seto Nai-kai (Inland Sea) red with Taira blood. Recognizing that all was lost, the Taira women drowned themselves, taking with them the young infant Emperor Antoku. His mother,

Kenreimonin, too, leaped into the sea, but Minamoto soldiers snagged her hair with a grappling hook and hauled her back on board their ship. She was the sole surviving member of the Taira clan and, at 29, she was a beautiful woman.

Taken back to Kyōto, Kenreimonin shaved her head and became a nun. First, she had a small hut at Chōraku-ji in eastern Kyōto, and when that collapsed in an earthquake, she was accepted at Jakkō-in. She lived in solitude in a 10-ft-square cell made of brushwood and thatch for 27 years, until death erased her memories and with her the Taira. Her mausoleum is in the temple grounds.

When Kenreimonin came to Jakkō-in, it was far removed from Kyōto. Now Kyōto's sprawl reaches this far and beyond, but the temple, hidden in trees, is still a place of solitude and a sanctuary for nuns. From Kyōto Eki take Kyōto Line Bus 17 or 18 for a 90-minute ride and get out at the Ōhara bus stop; the fare is ¥480. Walk 20 minutes or so along the road leading to the northwest. ⊠ ¥500. ☉ Mar.–Jan., daily 9–5; Dec.–Feb., daily 9–4:30.

★ **Jikkō-in.** At this small, little-frequented temple you can sit, relax, and have a taste of the powdered matcha of the tea ceremony. To enter, ring the gong on the outside of the gate and then wander through the carefully cultivated garden. Take Kyōto Line Bus 17 or 18 for 90 minutes from Kyōto Eki; the fare is ¥580. From the Ōhara bus stop, walk northeast for about seven minutes along the signposted road. Jikkō-in is 200 yards from Sanzen-in. ⊠ ¥500. ☉ Daily 9–5.

Kamigamo Jinja. The warrior Kamo built Kamigamo and its sister shrine, Shimogamo Jinja (farther south on the Kamo-gawa), in the 8th century. Such is Kamo's fame that even the river that flows by the shrine and through the center of Kyōto bears his name. Kamigamo has always been associated with Wakeikazuchi, a god of thunder, rain, and fertility. Now the shrine is famous for its Aoi (Hollyhock) Festival, which started in the 6th century when people thought that the Kamigamo deities were angry at being neglected. Held every May 15, the festival consists of 500 people wearing Heian-period costumes riding on horseback or in ox-drawn carriages from the Imperial Palace to Shimogamo and then to Kamigamo. To get to the shrine, take Bus 9 north from Kyōto Eki or from a stop on Horikawa-dōri. Or take the subway north to Kitayama Eki, from which the shrine is 20 minutes on foot northwest. ⊠ Motoyama, Kamigamo, Kita-ku. ⊠ Free. ☉ Daily 9–4:30.

Miho Bijutsukan (Miho Museum). Built in and around a mountaintop and thoughtfully landscaped—its wooded setting in the hills of Shigariki north of Kyōto is part of the experience of a visit here—the I. M. Pei–designed Miho Museum houses the remarkable Shumei family collection of traditional Japanese art and Asian and Western antiquities. An Egyptian falcon-headed deity, a Roman fresco, a Chinese tea bowl, and a Japanese Bosatsu (Buddha) are among the superb pieces here. A restaurant on-site sells bentō with organic ingredients, and a tearoom serves Japanese and Western beverages and desserts. From Kyōto Eki take the JR Tōkaidō Line (¥230 to Ishiyama Eki, 15 minutes); from there the bus to the museum will take 50 minutes. There are only two buses a day, at 9:10 AM and 11:55 AM during the week; bus service is extended on weekends and public holidays. ⊠ 300 Momodani, Shigariki, ☎ 0748/82–3411. ⊠ ¥1,000. ☉ Mid-Mar.–mid-June and Sept.–mid-Dec., Tues.–Sun. 10–5 (last entry at 4).

Sanzen-in. This small temple of the Tendai sect was founded by a renowned priest, Dengyo-Daishi (767–822). The Hon-dō (Main Hall) was built by Priest Eshin (942–1017), who probably carved the temple's Amida Buddha—though some say it was carved 100 years after Eshin's death. Flanked by two disciples, Daiseishi and Kannon, the statue is a remarkable piece of work, because rather than representing the bountiful Amida, it displays much more the omnipotence of Amida. Although Eshin was not a master sculptor, this statue possibly reflects his belief that, contrary to the prevailing belief of the Heian aristocracy that salvation could be achieved through one's own actions, salvation could be achieved only through Amida's limitless mercy. The statue is in the Main Hall. Unusual for a Buddhist temple, Sanzen-in faces east, not south. Note its ceiling, on which a painting depicts the descent of Amida, accompanied by 25 bodhisattvas, to welcome the believer.

The grounds are also delightful. Full of maple trees, the gardens are serene in any season. During autumn the colors are magnificent, and the approach to the temple up a gentle slope enhances the anticipation for the burned gold trees guarding the old, weathered temple. Snow cover in winter is also magical. Take Kyōto Line Bus 17 or 18 north for 90 minutes from Kyōto Eki; the fare is ¥580. From the Ōhara bus station walk northeast for about seven minutes along the signposted road. ⊠ *Raigōin-chō, Ōhara, Sakyō-ku.* 🔄 *¥600.* ☉ *Mar.–Nov., daily 8:30–4:30; Dec.–Feb., daily 8:30–4.*

Shūgaku-in Rikyū (Shūgaku-in Imperial Villa). Three palaces make up this villa complex with pleasant grounds. The Upper and Lower villas were built in the 17th century by the Tokugawa family to entertain the emperor; the Upper Villa provides nice views. The Middle Villa was added later as a palace home for Princess Ake, daughter of Emperor Gosai. When she decided that a nun's life was her calling, the villa was transformed into a temple.

Special permission is required to visit the villa from the Imperial Household Agency, preferably a day in advance (☞ Kyōto Gosho *in* Central and Southern Kyōto, *above*). From Hiei-zan take the Eizan Railway from Yase Yuen Eki to Shūgaku-in Eki. The villa is a 15-minute walk from there. From downtown Kyōto the trip takes an hour on Bus 5 from Kyōto Eki. Or take the 20-minute ride north on a Keifuku Eizan Line train from the Demachi-Yanagi terminus, which is just northeast of the intersection of Imadegawa-dōri and the Kamo-gawa. ⊠ *Yabusoe Shūgaku-in, Sakyō-ku.* 🔄 *Free.* ☉ *Tours (in Japanese only) weekdays at 9, 10, 11, 1:30, and 3 (Sat. tours on 1st and 3rd Sat. of month; every Sat. Apr.–May and Oct.–Nov.).*

DINING

Most of Kyōto's restaurants accept credit cards; however, some of the finest traditional restaurants do not, so it's wise to check ahead, especially since traditional kaiseki ryōri can be quite expensive. People generally dine early in Kyōto, between 7 PM and 8 PM, so most restaurants apart from hotel restaurants and bars close relatively early. In some cases this means 7, though most are open until 9. The average Japanese businessman wears a suit and tie to dinner—anywhere. Young people tend to dress more informally. If you think that you'll feel uncomfortable without a jacket, take one along. Many Kyōto restaurants do have someone who speaks English if it turns out that you need assistance making reservations.

Apart from the restaurants listed below, Kyōto has its share of the sort of budget quasi-Western–style chain restaurants found all over Japan, serving sandwiches and salads, gratins, curried rice, and spaghetti. These are easy to locate along Kawara-machi-dōri downtown, and they usually come complete with plastic models in the window to which you can point if spoken language fails you.

For more on Japanese cuisine, *see* Chapter 14 *and* Dining *in* Smart Travel Tips A to Z.

CATEGORY	COST*
$$$$	over ¥12,000
$$$	¥6,500–¥12,000
$$	¥2,500–¥6,500
$	under ¥2,500

per person for a main course at dinner

Eastern Kyōto

Japanese

$$$–$$$$ ✕ **Ashiya Steak House.** A short walk from the Gion district, famous for its teahouses and geisha, Ashiya Steak House is the best place in Kyōto to enjoy "a good steak . . . a real martini . . . and the essence of traditional Japan," in the words of owner Bob Strickland and his wife, Tokiko. While you're seated at a *kotatsu* (recessed hearth), your *teppanyaki* dinner of the finest Ōmi beefsteak, grilled and sliced in style, will be prepared as you watch. Cocktails, domestic and imported wines, and beer are available, as well as the best sake. You can take cocktails in the art gallery upstairs, which has a display of traditional and contemporary arts and crafts. ✉ *172–13 4-chōme, Kiyomizu, Higashiyama-ku,* ☎ *075/541–7961. Reservations essential. AE, DC, V. Closed Mon.*

$$$$ ✕ **Kikusui.** Near Nanzen-ji temple, Kikusui serves up traditional kaiseki ryōri and a view of an elegant Japanese stroll garden. The colors of Nanzen-ji-michi are particularly beautiful in the spring, when a large, umbrella-like cherry tree spreads its pink and white blossoms overhead like a canopy. Autumn, when maples explode in a firework display of reds and oranges, is also lovely. You can sample the subtle flavors and beautiful colors of Kyōto's traditional cuisine by ordering the *kyō-no-aji* (mini kaiseki) at lunchtime for a reasonable ¥5,000. ✉ *31 Fukui-cho, Nazenji, Sakyō-ku,* ☎ *075/771–4101. Reservations essential. AE, DC, V.*

$$$–$$$$ ✕ **Matsuno.** Eel may not sound very appetizing at first, but the appeal of *unagi* is slightly more obvious. Once most visitors taste the succulent broiled fish served in its own special sweet sauce, they don't feel so squeamish. Two doors down from the Kabuki theater Minami-za, Matsuno serves unagi to an after-theater crowd in simple but elegant surroundings. Its prices match its century-old reputation; try the *unagidomburi* (grilled eel on rice) for a simple (and cheaper) version of this delicacy. ✉ *Minamiza-higashi 4-ken-me, Shijō-dōri, Higashiyama-ku,* ☎ *075/561–2786. MC, V. Closed Thurs.*

$$–$$$$ ✕ **Nontaro.** If you're looking for a great sushi experience in the heart of the geisha district, try popular Nontaro, which has been serving sushi to visitors to Gion for more than 40 years. You can order sushi à la carte or choose one of the *omakase* (chef's choice) selections. If you're in the mood for something different, try the *kokesushi*—a giant sushi roll. ✉ *Hanamikō-ji Shijō-agaru, Higashiyama-ku,* ☎ *075/561–3189. Reservations essential. AE, DC, MC, V. Closed Sun.*

$$–$$$$ ✕ **Rokusei Nishimise.** Few restaurants in Kyōto have matched Rokusei Nishimise's magical combination of traditional cuisine and contemporary setting. Polished marble floors and manicured interior-garden niches complement the popular ¥3,000 *te-oke bentō* lunch, a collage of flavors and colors presented on a serving tray that's a handmade cypress-wood bucket. With a history as a caterer of formal kaiseki cuisine that began in 1899, Rokusei also serves a different exquisite full-course meal each month for ¥10,000—expensive, you may say, but in the world of Kyōto's haute cuisine, this is reasonable. A three-minute walk west of the turn-of-the-20th-century gardens of the Heian Jingū, the restaurant itself overlooks a tree-lined canal and is famous for its colorful azaleas in May. ✉ *71 Nishitennō-chō, Okazaki, Sakyō-ku,* ☎ *075/751–6171. AE, DC, V. Closed Mon.*

$$–$$$ ✕ **Yagembori.** North of Shijō-dōri in the heart of Kyōto's still-thriving geisha district, this restaurant is in a teahouse just a few steps down a cobbled path from the romantic Shira-kawa, a small tributary of the Kamo-gawa, in Gion. The *o-makase* full-course meal is an elegant sampler of Kyōto's finest kaiseki cuisine, with local delicacies presented on handmade ceramics. The *shabu-shabu* (thinly sliced beef, dipped briefly into hot stock) and *suppon* (turtle dishes) are excellent. Don't miss the *hoba miso*—bean paste with *kinoko* mushrooms and green onions, which are wrapped in a giant oak leaf and grilled at your table—on the à la carte menu. ✉ *Sueyoshi-chō, Kiridoshi-kado, Gion, Higashiyama-ku,* ☎ *075/551–3331. AE, DC, V.*

$$ ✕ **Omen.** Just south of Ginkaku-ji, this is one of the best places to stop for an inexpensive home-style lunch before proceeding down the old canal—the walkway beneath the cherry trees known as the Path of Philosophy—on the way to Nanzen-ji. Omen is not only the name of the shop but also the name of the house specialty: thick white noodles brought to your table in a basket with a bowl of hot broth and a platter of seven vegetables. The noodles—along with vegetables such as spinach, cabbage, green onions, mushrooms, burdock root, eggplant, radishes, and others, depending on the season—are added to the broth a little at a time. Sprinkle the top with roasted sesame seeds, and you have a dish so popular that you can expect a few minutes' wait before you're seated. Like the food, the restaurant is country style, with a choice of counter stools, tables and chairs, or tatami mats. The waiters dress in *happi* coats and headbands; the atmosphere is lively and comfortable. Reservations are only accepted on weekdays. ✉ *74 Ishi-bashi-chō, Jōdo-ji, Sakyō-ku,* ☎ *075/771–8994. No credit cards. Closed Thurs.*

$–$$ ✕ **Grill Kodakara.** Although you may recognize the names on the menu, you probably won't recognize the dishes themselves. Locals consider the food served at this clean, quiet restaurant on Okazaki-michi near Heian Jingū to be Western, but it has a Japanese flair that comes from its subtle yet rich demi-glace sauce. The sauce, which is stewed for five days to bring out its full flavor, is used in the beef stew, hashed-beef rice, and rice omelet. For a small fee, you can take home a Grill Kodakara Print Club sticker with your photo as a souvenir. ✉ *46 Kitagosho-chō, Okazaki, Sakyō-ku,* ☎ *075/771–5893. MC, V. Closed Wed.*

$ ✕ **Rakushō.** Flowering plum trees, azaleas, irises, camellias, and maple trees take turns coloring the four seasons while countless visitors slip in and out, sipping bowls of frothy matcha or freshly brewed coffee and taking in the scenery. Along the path between Maruyama Kōen and Kiyomizu-dera, this tea shop in a former villa is a pleasant place to stop for morning coffee or afternoon tea. You can also order *warabi mochi,* a dessert that resembles Jell-O in a sweet, sticky sauce. A table beside the sliding glass doors looks out on an elaborately landscaped garden; in the pond in the garden, the owner's colorful prize-winning koi (carp) lurk just beneath the surface. The tea shop is minutes on foot from Sannen-zaka, one of Kyōto's historic preservation districts—a cobblestone path lined with shops on the way to Kiyomizu-dera. Rakushō closes at 6 PM. ✉ *Kōdai-ji Kitamon-mae-dōri, Washio-chō, Higashiyama-ku,* ☎ *075/561–6892. Reservations not accepted. No credit cards. Closed 4 times a month (call ahead).*

330

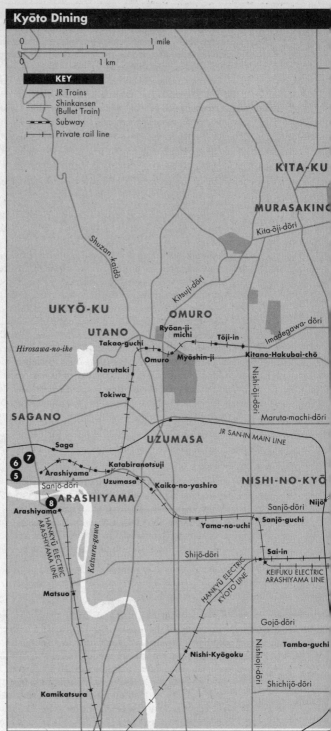

Kyōto Dining

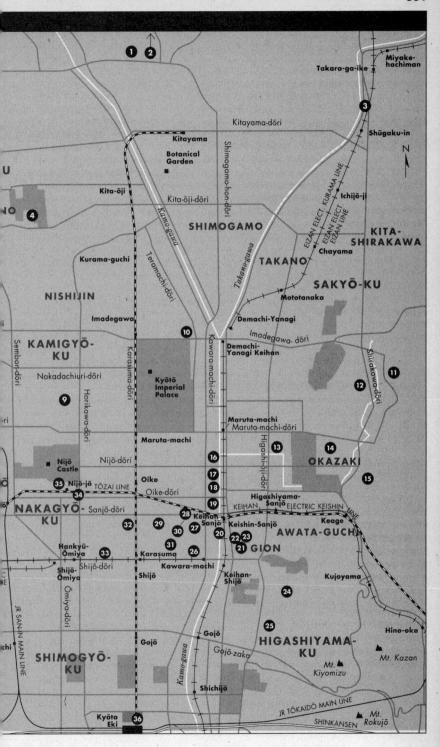

Takara-ga-ike
Miyake-hachiman

① **②**

③
Shūgaku-in

Kitayama-dōri

Kitayama

Botanical
Garden

Kita-ōji
Kita-ōji-dōri

④

SHIMOGAMO

KITA-
SHIRAKAWA

Ichijō-ji

Chayama

Kurama-guchi

TAKANO

SAKYŌ-KU

NISHIJIN

Mototanaka

Imadegawa

⑩

Demachi-Yanagi

Imadegawa- dōri

KAMIGYŌ-
KU

Demachi-
Yanagi Keihan

⑪

Nakadachiuri-dōri

Kyōto
Imperial
Palace

⑫

⑨

OKAZAKI

Maruta-machi
Maruta-machi-dōri

Maruta-machi

⑬

⑭

Nijō-dōri

⑯

Nijō
Castle
Nijō-jō

⑰

⑮

㉟

TŌZAI LINE

Oike

⑱

㉞

Oike-dōri

⑲

Higashiyama-
Sanjō

NAKAGYŌ-
KU

Sanjō-dōri

㉘ Keihan-
Sanjō

KEIHAN

ELECTRIC KEISHIN

LINE

Keage

AWATA-GUCHI

㉜

㉙

㉗

Keishin-Sanjō

㉚

⑳

Hankyū-
Ōmiya

㉝

㉛

㉖

㉒㉓
㉑

GION

Karasuma

Shijō-dōri

Kawara-machi

Kujoyama

Shijō-
Ōmiya

Shijō

Keihan-
Shijō

㉔

Gojō

Gojō

㉕

Hino-oka

Gojō-zaka

HIGASHIYAMA-
KU

Mt. Kazan

SHIMOGYŌ-
KU

Mt.
Kiyomizu

Shichijō

JR TŌKAIDŌ MAIN LINE

Kyōto
Eki

㊱

SHINKANSEN

Mt.
Rokujō

Western Kyōto

Japanese

$$$$ ✕ **Kitcho.** What Maxim's is to Paris, Kitcho is to Kyōto—classic cuisine, an unparalleled traditional atmosphere, exclusive elegance. Lunch
here starts at ¥45,000, dinner at ¥50,000, making this perhaps the
world's most expensive restaurant. Although the original restaurant
is in Ōsaka, the Kyōto branch has the advantage of a stunning location beside the Oi-gawa, nestled at the foothills of Arashiyama. Here
you can experience the full sensory delight of formal kaiseki cuisine.
Only the finest ingredients are used, prepared by master chefs and served
in exquisite antique porcelain ware on priceless lacquered trays—all
in an elegant private room sparsely decorated with a hanging scroll
painted by a famous master, whose message sets the seasonal theme
for the evening. The ability to identify the vessels used, an appreciation of the literary allusions made in the combination of objects and
foods served, and knowledge of the arts of Japan all add depth to the
experience. Expect to spend a minimum of two hours here. Kitcho closes
for dinner at 7. ⊠ *58 Susuki-no-bamba-chō, Tenryū-ji, Saga, Ukyō-
ku,* ☎ *075/881–1101. Reservations essential. Jacket and tie. AE, DC,
MC, V. Closed Wed.*

$$–$$$ ✕ **Nishiki.** Tucked behind a rustic bamboo fence, Nishiki sits on an is-
   ★   land in the middle of the Oi-gawa, surrounded by the densely forested
Arashiyama mountains. The *oshukuzen-bentō* lunch is the best sampler of formal, Kyōto-style kaiseki cuisine, for the reasonable price of
¥3,800. Unlike most other bentō lunches, it is served in seven courses
and is so beautifully presented in a tiered lacquer box, with meticu-
lous attention to the finest seasonal ingredients, that it rivals other meals
at three times the price. A summer lunch might include a course of *kamo-
nasu*, the prized Kyōto eggplant, served *dengaku*-style—smothered in
sweet miso sauce in a silver serving dish the shape of an eggplant. The
top layer of the lacquer box might be covered with a miniature bamboo trellis in which are nestled tiny porcelain cups the shape of morning glories, a favorite summer flower in Kyōto, each one filled with a
different appetizer—a touch of sea urchin or a few sprigs of spinach
in sesame sauce. Nishiki is close to Togetsu-kyō Bridge. Call for reservations or expect a 30-minute wait. The last dinner order is taken at
7:30. ⊠ *Nakanoshima Kōen-guchi, Arashiyama, Ukyō-ku,* ☎ *075/871–
8888. DC, MC, V. Closed Tues.*

$$ ✕ **Sagano.** Amid Arashiyama's lush, green bamboo forests, this quiet
   ★   retreat serves one of the finest *yudōfu* meals—cubes of bean curd sim-
mered in a broth at your table—in Kyōto. The full course includes such
local delicacies as tempura and *aburage* (deep-fried tofu) with black sesame
seeds and a gingko-nut center garnished with a sprig of *kinome* leaves
from the Japanese pepper tree. Take a seat at the sunken counter, and
waitresses in kimonos will prepare the meal in front of you—with a back-
drop of antique wood-block prints on folding screens, surrounded by
walls lined with delicately hand-painted antique porcelain bowls—or
walk out through the garden to private, Japanese-style rooms in the back.
If weather permits, you can dine on low tables in the courtyard garden
beneath towering bamboo. Reservations are a good idea year-round,
and particularly during fall foliage season, when the maple trees of
Arashiyama are stunning. Arrive before 5:30 for dinner in the tatami
rooms, before 6:30 for counter service. ⊠ *45 Susuki-no-bamba-chō, Saga,
Tenryū-ji, Ukyū-ji, Ukyō-ku,* ☎ *075/861–0277. No credit cards.*

Spanish

$$–$$$ ✕ **Bodegon.** A white-walled, tile-floored, wrought-iron, and blown-
glass Spanish restaurant in Arashiyama is about as rare (and welcome)

as decent paella in a neighborhood famous for its tofu. Bodegon sits unobtrusively along the main street that runs through the center of this scenic district, combining Spanish fare and wine with Kyōto hospitality. A wildly popular tourist area in daylight, Arashiyama rolls up its sidewalks after dark, so Bodegon is a good place to escape the crowds downtown in the evening after other places close. ⊠ *1 Susuki-no-bamba-chō, Saga, Tenryū-ji,* ☎ *075/872–9652. MC, V. Closed Thurs.*

Central Kyōto

Coffee Shops

$ ✕ **Honyaradō.** This log cabin–like coffee shop, east of Doshisha University, is a "home away from dormitory" for students. Here you'll find
★ what's left of the peace movement—environmentalists, poets, and musicians—eating their lunches. The notices on the bulletin board are of a less incendiary nature these days, but the sandwiches are still on homemade wheat bread, and the stew is still good. Take along a good book (this guide, perhaps?), order some food, and relax. ⊠ *Imadegawa-dōri, Tera-machi Nishi-Iru, Kamigyō-ku,* ☎ *075/222–1574. Reservations not accepted. No credit cards.*

$ ✕ **Inoda.** Hidden down a side street in the center of town, this century-old establishment is one of Kyōto's oldest and best-loved *kissaten* (coffee shops). The turn-of-the-20th-century, Western-style brick buildings along Sanjō-dōri nearby are part of a historic preservation district, and Inoda's original old shop blends well with its surroundings. Floor-to-ceiling glass windows overlook an interior garden, and the place even has some stained-glass windows and a pair of witty parrots. The coffee is excellent, to boot: for breakfast, lunch, or a break from sightseeing. Inoda closes at 6 PM. ⊠ *Sakai-machi-dōri, Sanjō-sagaru, Nakagyō-ku,* ☎ *075/221–0507. Reservations not accepted. No credit cards.*

$ ✕ **Starbucks.** Yes, the rumor is true. Kyōto welcomed its first branch of "McCoffee" in June 1999. If you're pining for a cup of stronger-than-it-should-be brew, just head to Shijō-dōri near the Karasuma subway station, east of the Daimaru department store. ⊠ *Yasaka Shijō Bldg., Tachi-uri Nakano-machi 106, Shijō-dōri, Yanaginobaba Nishi-Iru,* ☎ *075/231–5008. MC, V.*

French

$$$ ✕ **Natsuka.** This fine French restaurant with a reasonably priced lunch
★ menu overlooks the Kamo-gawa. The Japanese couple who manage the place lived and learned their trade in Paris for several years. The dessert tray here is sumptuous, with a choice of two freshly baked delights from about eight possibilities. The last order must go in by 8. ⊠ *Ponto-chō, Shijō-agaru, Higashi-gawa, Nakagyō-ku,* ☎ *075/255–2105. MC. Closed Wed.*

$$$ ✕ **Ogawa.** Down a narrow passageway across from the Takase-gawa
★ is the place to taste the best in Kyōto-style nouvelle cuisine. Finding a seat at the counter of this intimate French restaurant is like getting tickets for opening night at the opera—one you've never seen. With particularly Japanese sensitivity to the best ingredients only in the peak of the season, proprietor Ogawa promises never to bore by serving the same meal twice. *Ayu,* a popular local river fish, is served in summer, salmon in fall, crab in winter, shrimp in spring. Ogawa prepares marvelous sauces and puddings—even fresh papaya sherbet and mango mousse with mint sauce. The full-course meal at lunch and dinner is spectacular, but some prefer to order hors d'oeuvres with wine. Counter seating is available for only 16. ⊠ *Kiya-machi Oike-agaru Higashi-Iru, Nakagyō-ku,* ☎ *075/256–2203. Reservations essential. Jacket and tie. AE, DC, MC, V. Closed Tues.*

Indian

$–$$ ✕ **Ashoka.** Kyōto, although more famous for its fine Japanese restaurants, has begun to look to the rest of the world for dining options. One of the first such international restaurants to open its doors in the capital of culinary daintiness was Ashoka. The dazzling *Thali* course dinner (about 10 small plates) consists of half a dozen curries in small bowls on a brass tray with rice and tandoori dishes—order this only if you're very hungry. Red carpets, carved screens, brass lanterns, and tuxedoed waiters set the mood, and diners wear everything from denim to silk. The last food order is at 9 PM, 8:30 PM on Sunday. ✉ *Kikusui Bldg., 3rd floor, Tera-machi-dōri, Shijō-agaru, Nakagyō-ku,* ☎ *075/ 241–1318. AE, DC, MC, V. Closed 2nd Tues. of month.*

Italian

$$$ ✕ **divo-diva.** As Japan enjoys an Italian food boom, divo-diva continues
★ to set the standard in Kyōto. Its 31 seats are usually all occupied, often with weary Daimaru shoppers. The chefs here have all trained in Italy, and the fare is authentic Italian but with a Japanese flair for color and design. The wine list is interesting and the pasta and breads homemade. Lunch sets are an especially good value. Tasteful lighting sets off the contemporary decor. ✉ *Nishiki-kōji, Takakura-Nishi-Iru, Nakagyō-ku,* ☎ *075/256–1326. AE, DC, MC, V. Closed Wed. and 2nd and 3rd Tues. of month.*

$$ ✕ **Cucina Il Viale.** The house speciality is not green eggs and ham, but
★ Dr. Seuss would be thrilled nonetheless by the electric-pink tomato sauce served over handmade pasta at Cucina Il Viale. This Italian restaurant a few blocks from Nijō-jō dishes up pasta and fresh seasonal vegetables at a comfortable wooden counter or tables. The two chef-owners are usually quite busy behind the counter preparing the day's menu, but if they have time they may show you how the pasta is made. Courses A and B include antipasti; pasta topped with the house specialty, a pink sauce made from pureed sweet tomatoes; dessert; and espresso. Course B also comes with a fish or meat dish, which changes periodically and is always an authentic Italian creation with a twist. Enjoy a glass of extremely spicy ginger ale while you watch the chef weigh out your pasta and prepare the meal. The light mousse and litchi dessert alone is worth the visit. ✉ *Horikawa, Oike Nishi-iru, Nakagyō-ku,* ☎ *075/812–2366. AE, V. Closed Mon. No lunch Tues.*

$ ✕ **Capricciosa.** Simple decor in striking colors and huge bowls of
★ steaming spaghetti make this unpretentious Italian restaurant, part of a nationwide chain, a popular venue. The pasta dishes are large enough to share, and the pizzas are a good value. Lovers of Italian food may take issue with what is essentially a poor imitation of the real thing, but those looking for a cheap feed before boarding the Shinkansen (the restaurant is conveniently located under Kyōto Eki) won't be disappointed. Capricciosa has two more branches, on Kawara-machi-dōri in the Opa department store and in the Vox building. ✉ *Kyōto Eki basement, Porta Restaurant Zone,* ☎ *075/343–3499,* 🖳 *www. capricciosa.com. No credit cards. Closed 3rd Tues. of month.*

Japanese

$$$$ ✕ **Mankamero.** Established in 1716, Mankamero is the only restaurant in Kyōto that offers formal *yusoku ryōri*, the type of cuisine once served to members of the imperial court. A specially appointed imperial chef prepares the food, using utensils made only for this type of cuisine. Dressed in ceremonial robes, the chef "dismembers" the fish and elaborately arranges its sections to have them brought to you on pedestal trays. Prices are also quite elaborate—up to ¥30,000 per person for the full yusoku ryōri repertoire—though in recent years an incomparable *take-kago bentō* lunch (served in a bamboo basket) has been within reach of wealthy commoners at ¥6,000. Mankamero is on the west side of Inokuma-dōri north of Demizu-dōri. It closes at 8 PM. ⊠ *Inokuma-dōri, Demizu-agaru, Kamigyō-ku,* ☎ *075/441–5020. Reservations essential. Jacket and tie. AE, DC, MC, V. Closed once a month.*

$$$–$$$$ ✕ **Ebisugawa-tei.** Housed in a Meiji-era villa of former industrialist Baron Fujita are two excellent steak restaurants, both serving the celebrated beer-fed and massaged Ōmi beef. The more expensive and more formal Ōmi serves slightly higher-quality beef (men should wear jacket and tie). The **Chidori** is a bit less formal but also serves superb beef and has a better view of the garden. You can stop in at the bar in the basement of the Fujita Hotel for a drink beside the beautiful duck pond and waterfall. ⊠ *Fujita Hotel, Nijō-dōri, Kiya-machi Kado, Nakagyō-ku,* ☎ *075/222–1511. AE, DC, MC, V.*

$$–$$$$ ✕ **Yoshikawa.** This quiet, traditional inn with landscaped gardens is within walking distance of the downtown shopping area. The specialty of the house is tempura, either a full-course dinner served in a tatami room or a lunch at the counter in its cozy "tempura corner," where the chef fries each vegetable and shrimp in front of you while you wait. Tempura should be light and crisp—best right from the pot—and for this Yoshikawa is famous. English is spoken. Yoshikawa closes at 8:30. ⊠ *Tomino-kōji, Oike-sagaru, Nakagyō-ku,* ☎ *075/221–5544 or 075/221–0052. Jacket and tie at dinner. AE, DC, MC, V. Closed Sun.*

$$$ ✕ **Mishima-tei.** This is really the one choice for sukiyaki in Kyōto. In the heart of the downtown shopping district, it is also one of the best restaurants in the area. Kyōto housewives line up out front to pay premium prices for Mishima-tei's high-quality beef, sold by the 100-gram over the counter at the meat shop downstairs. Mishima-tei was established in 1904, and climbing the staircase of this traditional wood-frame restaurant with its turn-of-the-20th-century atmosphere is like journeying into the past. Down the long, dark corridors, with polished wood floors, kimono-clad servers bustle about with trays of beef and refills of sake to dozens of private tatami-mat rooms. Ask for a room that faces the central courtyard garden for the best view. Plan on dining by 7, as the service—and the preparation of your food—can be rushed toward the end of the evening. ⊠ *Tera-machi, Sanjō-sagaru, Higashi-Iru, Nakagyō-ku,* ☎ *075/221–0003. AE, DC, MC, V. Closed Wed.*

$$ ✕ **Ōiwa.** Ōiwa, which is at the head of the Takase-gawa (canal), south of the Fujita Hotel, serves *kushikatsu,* skewered meats and vegetables battered, deep-fried, and then dipped in a variety of sauces. The building itself is actually a *kura* (treasure house) that belonged to a kimono merchant family, and it's one of the first to have been turned into a restaurant in Kyōto, where restorations of this type are still a relatively new idea. The Japanese chef trained in one of the finest French restaurants in Tōkyō, and his version of kushikatsu (usually considered a working man's snack with beer) has an unpretentious elegance. Order by the skewer or ask for the *o-makase* set course. Ōiwa is a fine place to spend a relaxing evening. ⊠ *Kiya-machi-dōri, Nijō-sagaru, Nakagyō-ku,* ☎ *075/231–7667. No credit cards. Closed Wed.*

$$ ✕ **Shinsen-en Heihachi.** Imagine munching on a foot-long hot dog while gazing upon the Rose Garden at the White House. You'll be doing the Japanese equivalent of this when you order a pot-for-two of Japan's fattest *udon* noodles and view all that remains of the once extensive garden of Kyōto's first imperial palace. When Emperor Kammu established Heian-kyō in 794, he built a pleasure garden within the main enclosure of the new capital's first Imperial Palace. The 33-acre Sacred Spring Garden contained pleasure pavilions for moon-viewing, fish-

ing, and waterfall-viewing as well as pavilions for dance, sumō wrestling, and poetry contests. Today, all that remains of the garden's original Chinese design is a garden pond with a brilliant red bridge. Occupying the land, now owned by Tōji temple, is a restaurant famous in southwestern Japan for its extremely fat udon noodles. You can also sample the kaiseki ryōri here while viewing an elegant reminder of Heian-kyō's glorious past. The northern entrance of the restaurant faces the southern wall of Nijō-jō. ⊠ *Nijō-jō Minami-gawa, Nakagyō-ku,* ☎ *075/ 841–0811. AE, MC, V.*

$–$$ ✕ **Agatha.** This restaurant offers a "mystery" twist on the *robatayaki* (charcoal grill). The decor is period Agatha Christie—'40s book covers and movie posters, polished marble walls, potted palms, decent jazz, black-and-white-checkerboard floors. Watch the chef grill interesting variations on traditional delicacies, such as white, long-stem *enoki* mushrooms wrapped in strips of thinly sliced beef, scallops in bacon, or pork in *shiso* (a mintlike leaf). Both the A course and the B course combine these treats with unadorned standards such as *tebasaki* (grilled chicken wings). Salad and appetizers are included, and a wide selection of drinks are available—everything from sake to a gin fizz. Popular with the *juppie* (Japanese yuppie) crowd, this restaurant has two other branches in Kyōto, and one each in Ōsaka and Tōkyō. ⊠ *Yurika Bldg., 2nd floor, Kiya-machi-dōri, Sanjō-agaru, Nakagyō-ku,* ☎ *075/ 223–2379. AE, DC, MC, V. No lunch.*

$–$$ ✕ **Tagoto.** One of the best noodle shops in the downtown area has been serving soup with homemade *soba* (buckwheat noodles) for more than a hundred years in the same location on a shopping street that is now almost completely modernized. Tagoto, too, has remodeled, and the result is a pleasant surprise—modern yet in traditional Japanese style, with natural woods, *shōji* (rice-paper) windows, tatami mats, and an interior garden integrated with slate floors and the comfort of air-conditioning. Tagoto serves both thin soba and thick white udon noodle dishes with a variety of ingredients, such as shrimp tempura, hot or cold to suit the season. It's on the north side of the covered Sanjō Arcade, half a block west of Kawara-machi-dōri ⊠ *Sanjō-dōri, Tera-machi Higashi-Iru, Nakagyō-ku,* ☎ *075/221–3030. Reservations not accepted. AE, DC, MC, V.*

$ ✕ **Daikokuya.** If you're shopping downtown and want a quick meal, stop in at Daikokuya for a soba dish or *domburi,* a bowl of rice with your choice of toppings. The *oyako domburi,* rice with egg and chicken, is the best choice (*oyako* means "parent and child"). The buckwheat for the soba is ground in-house on an antique stone mill powered by a wooden waterwheel. Fresh noodles are also served with exceedingly delicate tempura. Both tatami and table-and-chair seating are available. You can recognize Daikokuya by its red lantern and water mill. ⊠ *281 Minami-kurumaya-chō, Takoyakushi, Kiya-machi Nishi-Iru, Nakagyō-ku,* ☎ *075/221–2818. Reservations not accepted. AE, D, MC, V. Closed Tues.*

Thai

$$–$$$ ✕ **E-san.** Sitting at tables decorated with elephant carvings in a restaurant where spicy food and Thai karaoke are the order of the day, you might be convinced you're a million miles from Kyōto's Imperial Palace; in fact, you're only a stone's throw away. E-san's popular lunch buffet is filling and a good value at ¥1,200; dinner prices start at ¥6,000. If the food is too hot for your taste, order a bowl of delicious sweet-potato ice cream to cool down. ⊠ *Imadegawa-dōri, Kamigyō-ku,* ☎ *075/441–6199. MC, V.*

Northern Kyōto

To get to restaurants in northern Kyōto, take the Eizan Electric R way on the Kurama Line to Shūgaku-in Eki; then proceed by taxi.

Japanese

$$$–$$$$ ✕ **Heihachi-Jaya.** A bit off the beaten path in the northeastern corner
★ of Kyōto, along the old road to the Sea of Japan, this roadside inn has provided comfort to many a weary traveler during its 400-year history. Heihachi-Jaya hugs the levee of the Takano-gawa and is surrounded by maple trees in a quiet garden with a stream. Apart from the excellent *mugitoro* bentō lunch—which includes, among other dishes, grated mountain-potato salad served with barley rice—and the full-course kaiseki dinner, what makes this restaurant special is its clay sauna, the *kamaburo*, a mound-shape clay steam bath heated from beneath the floor by a pinewood fire. Have a bath and sauna, change into a cotton kimono if you wish, and retire to the dining room (or to a private room) for a *very* relaxing meal—an experience not to be missed. Heihachi-Jaya closes at 9 PM. ✉ *8–1 Kawagishi-chō, Yamabana, Sakyō-ku,* ☎ *075/781–5008. AE, DC, MC, V.*

$$$–$$$$ ✕ **Sagenta.** Discovering the town of Kibune is one of the best parts of
★ summer in Kyōto. A short bump-and-rumble train ride into the mountains north of Kyōto on the nostalgic little Keifuku train leaves you on a mountain path that leads farther up into the forest beside a cool stream. The path is lined with restaurants that place tables near the stream in summer, when you can dine beneath a canopy of trees, with the water flowing at your feet. Sagenta is the last of these restaurants, at the very top of the slope, and it serves kaiseki lunches year-round, as well as one-pot *nabe* (stew) dishes in fall and winter. It's reasonably priced, particularly for its popular summertime specialty, *nagashi-somen,* chilled noodles that flow down a bamboo spout from the kitchen to a boat-shape trough; you catch the noodles from the trough as they float past, dip them in a sauce, and eat them with mushrooms, seasonal green vegetables, and shrimp. Reservations are advised in summer. To get here take the Eizan Electric Railway on the Kurama Line to Kibuneguchi Eki and then transfer to the Keifuku train to Kibune. Allow a good 45 minutes from central Kyōto. ✉ *76 Kibune-chō, Kurama, Sakyō-ku,* ☎ *075/741–2244. AE, DC, MC, V. Closed periodically in winter.*

$–$$$ ✕ **Azekura.** On the northern outskirts of Kyōto, not far from Kamig-
★ amo Jinja, Azekura serves home-style buckwheat noodles under the giant wooden beams of a 300-year-old sake warehouse. Originally built in Nara, the warehouse was moved here more than 25 years ago by kimono merchant Mikio Ichida, who also maintains a textile exhibition hall, a small museum, and a weavers' workshop within the walls of this former samurai estate. Have lunch on low stools around a small charcoal brazier or on tatami next to a window overlooking the garden and waterwheel outside. The soba noodles at Azekura have a heartier country flavor than you'll find in most of the other noodle shops in town. This is a perfect place to stop while exploring the Shake-machi district around the shrine, an area in which priests and farmers have lived for more than 10 centuries. Azekura closes at 5 PM. ✉ *30 Okamoto-chō, Kamigamo, Kita-ku,* ☎ *075/701–0161. Reservations not accepted. No credit cards. Closed Mon.*

$$ ✕ **Izusen.** In the garden of Daiji-in, a subtemple of Daitoku-ji, this restaurant specializes in shōjin ryōri, vegetarian Zen cuisine. Lunches are presented in sets of red-lacquer bowls of diminishing sizes, each one fitting inside the next when the meal is completed. Two Kyōto specialties, *fu* (glutinous wheat cake) and *yuba* (curd from steamed soy milk), are served in a multitude of inventive forms—in soups and sauces that prove veg-

arian cuisine to be as exciting as any meat dish. You can dine in tatami-
at rooms, and in warm weather on low tables outside in the temple
rden. Reservations are recommended in spring and fall. Izusen closes
4 PM. ⊠ 4 *Daitoku-ji-chō, Murasakino, Kita-ku,* ☎ *075/491–6665.*
credit cards. Closed Thurs.

LODGING

Kyōto is a tourist city, and its hotel rooms are often designed merely
as places to rest at night. Most rooms are small by international standards, but they are adequate for relaxing after a busy day of sightseeing. As it is throughout Japan, service in this city is impeccable; the
information desks are well stocked with maps and pamphlets about
the sights. Assistant managers, concierges, and guest-relations managers
are always available in the lobby to respond to your needs, although
English may or may not be spoken.

Each room in expensively ($$$–$$$$) and moderately ($$) priced
lodgings comes with a hot-water thermos and tea bags or instant coffee. Stocked refrigerators, television with English-language CNN, and
radio are standard, as are *yukata* (cotton kimonos).

Kyōto has Western- and Japanese-style accommodations, including traditional ryokan. Some ryokan have shared toilets and baths, so ask about
these if you don't like to share facilities.

Most accommodations in the $$, $$$, and $$$$ categories have rep-
resentation abroad, and the nearest Japan National Tourist Organi-
zation (JNTO) office will have information on booking. Do check out
the listed Web sites. Many of the hotels offer heavily discounted rates
in summer. You can often check room availability and reserve rooms
on-line. Book at least a month in advance, or as early as three months
ahead if you're traveling during peak spring and autumn seasons or
around important Japanese holidays and festivals. Keep in mind the
following festival dates when making reservations: May 15, July 16–
17, August 16, and October 22. Rooms will be scarce at these times.

For a short course on accommodations in Japan, *see* Lodging *in* Smart
Travel Tips A to Z.

CATEGORY	COST*
$$$$	over ¥30,000
$$$	¥20,000–¥30,000
$$	¥8,000–¥20,000
$	under ¥8,000

All prices are for a double room, excluding service and tax.

Central Kyōto

$$$$ 🏠 **Hiiragiya.** For more than 150 years the Nishimura family has been
  ★   welcoming dignitaries and celebrities to this elegant inn. Founded in 1818
to accommodate provincial lords visiting the capital, the inn has welcomed Charlie Chaplin, Elizabeth Taylor, and Yukio Mishima in addition to its 19th-century samurai visitors. The inn is representative of
Kyōto itself in the way it skillfully combines ancient and modern. Where
else could you find cedar baths with chrome taps? And look out for the
lacquered gourd designed by the present owner's great-grandfather.
Not only does it turn on the lights, but it allows you to open and close
the curtains by remote control. Those on a budget might consider a room
in the newer annex. Breakfast and dinner are included in the rate. ⊠
Nakahakusan-chō, Fuyachō-Anekōji-agaru, Nakagyō-ku, Kyōto-shi

Kyōto Lodging

604-8094, ☎ 075/221–1136, 🆀 075/221–1139, 🆆 *www.hiiragiya.co.jp.*
33 Japanese-style rooms, 28 with bath. AE, DC, MC, V. MAP.

$$$$ 🏠 **Tawaraya.** The most famous of Kyōto's inns, this is the abode of
kings and queens, princes and princesses, and presidents and dictators
when they visit Kyōto. Tawaraya was founded more than 300 years ago
and is currently run by the 11th generation of the Okazaki family. For
all its subdued beauty and sense of tradition, the inn does have modern comforts such as heat and air-conditioning, but they hardly detract
from the atmosphere of yesteryear. The rooms' superb antiques come
from the Okazaki family collection. The service and food here might
be disappointing, however, if you have not been recommended to the
ryokan by a respected Japanese. You are given the option of staying on
a European Plan basis and, if you wish, of ordering a selection of dinners from ¥12,000 to ¥60,000, the former option being rather meager.
✉ *Fuyachō-Aneyakōji-agaru, Nakagyō-ku, Kyōto-shi 604-8094, ☎ 075/
211–5566, 🆀 075/211–2204. 18 Japanese-style rooms. AE, DC, V.*

$$$–$$$$ 🏠 **Kyōto Brighton Hotel.** The Brighton is unquestionably the city's best
★   hotel in this price range. Its simple, clean design gives it an airy and
spacious quality lacking in most other Kyōto hotels. Hallways circle
a central atrium, and plants hang from the banisters of every floor. Glass
elevators carry you up into the atrium to your room. Large by Japa-
nese standards, rooms have separate seating areas with a couch and
TV. No need to worry about city noise: the Brighton is on a quiet side
street close to the Imperial Palace, although not within walking dis-
tance of most of Kyōto's main attractions. ✉ *Nakadachiuri, Shin-machi-
dōri, Kamigyō-ku, Kyōto-shi 602-8071, ☎ 075/441–4411; 800/223–
6800 in the U.S.; 0800/181–123 in the U.K.; 🆀 075/431–2360, 🆆
www.brightonhotels.co.jp. 181 rooms, 2 suites. 5 restaurants, 2 bars,
pool, hair salon, shops. AE, DC, MC, V.*

$$–$$$$ 🏠 **Hotel Granvia Kyōto.** Combining the traditional design elements of
★   Kyōto in its interior with the ultramodern exterior of the Kyōto Eki
building in which it is located, this hotel provides both comfort and
convenience. Rooms are spacious; a standard double room has two double beds, a desk, a little sitting area, and the best combination of West-
ern- and Japanese-style bathrooms. Sliding glass doors separate a bidet
toilet and sink from the shower and bath. The showerhead is mounted
on the wall next to the bathtub, allowing guests to shower outside the
tub and then relax in the tub as the Japanese do. Rooms have wallpaper and decorative headboards of *washi* in various colors. Take
some time to walk between the north and south towers along the
glassed walkway, taking in the view of the city. ✉ *Karasuma, Oshikoji-
dori-sagaru, Kyōto-shi 600-8216, ☎ 075/344–8888, 🆀 075/344–
4400, 🆆 www.granvia-kyoto.co.jp. 539 rooms. 15 restaurants, pool,
hair salon, health club, shops. AE, DC, MC, V.*

$$$ 🏠 **Daimonjiya.** This tiny inn just off the busy shopping area of Sanjō-
dōri is as famous for its guest rooms as for the food served (in the guest
rooms). Each room, with fine wood interiors, overlooks a small gar-
den. Kaiseki is the specialty of the house; the chef was trained at the
best Kyōto culinary establishment. You do not need to be a guest to
use one of the rooms for a meal, but then you would be missing out
on the quintessential ryokan experience. ✉ *Nishi-Iru, Kawara-machi-
Sanjō, Nakagyō-ku, Kyōto-shi 604-8031, ☎ 075/221–0603. 7 Japa-
nese-style rooms. AE, DC. MAP.*

$$–$$$ 🏠 **ANA Hotel Kyōto.** The best thing about this hotel is its location, di-
rectly across from Nijō-jō. If your room faces the castle rather than
another high-rise, you can be assured that you are indeed in Kyōto.
Now for the less-good news: off the long, narrow, rather depressing
corridors are long, narrow guest rooms that could use refurbishing—
especially considering the rates. There are French, Chinese, and Japa-

nese restaurants. ✉ *Nijō-jō-mae, Horikawa-dōri, Nakagyō-ku, Kyōto-shi 604-8301,* ☎ *075/231–1155,* FAX *075/231–5333,* WEB *www.anahotels.com. 303 rooms. 7 restaurants, 3 bars, indoor pool, health club, shops. AE, DC, MC, V.*

$$–$$$ ⊞ **Hotel Fujita Kyōto.** In the light of a full moon, the waterfall in this
★ pleasant hotel's garden sparkles while waterfowl play. The lobby is narrow and long, with comfortable gray armchairs playing nicely against deep red carpeting. The Fujita has Japanese and Scandinavian decor throughout, and 18 rooms have Japanese-style furnishings. The two main restaurants are a kaiseki dining room and a steak house with counter and table service. Not far from the nightlife center of Gion, this pleasant hotel is situated along the Kamo-gawa. ✉ *Nishizume, Nijō-Ōhashi, Kamo-gawa, Nakagyō-ku, Kyōto-shi 604-0902,* ☎ *075/222–1511,* FAX *075/256–4561,* WEB *www.fujita-kanko.co.jp. 177 Western-style rooms, 18 Japanese-style rooms. 4 restaurants, 2 bars, hair salon, shops. AE, DC, MC, V.*

$$–$$$ ⊞ **Kyōto Kokusai Hotel.** Across the street from Nijō-jō, Kokusai provides excellent views from the rooftop lounge and rooms on the west side of the castle and is only a few yards from the entrance to the Nijō-jō-mae stop on the Tōzai subway line. Perhaps the best reason to choose this hotel, aside from its convenient location, is the Lounge Miyabi, where you can look out through large glass windows into a beautiful courtyard garden. A stage with a thatched roof and lacquered flooring floats on the garden's pond. In the daytime, you can relax with matcha and a sweet while watching a single swan swim gracefully on the pond. At night, have your picture taken with a maiko. Then, take your seat either inside or outside to watch her perform two dances. Pictures are taken every night from 7 to 7:20, and the performance lasts from 7:20 to 7:40. Beds swathed in golden, silken duvets grace the large double rooms. Japanese-style paper screens shade the windows. ✉ *Nijō-eki-mae, Horikawa-dori, Nakagyō-ku, Kyōto-shi 604-8502,* ☎ *075/222–1111,* FAX *075/231–9381,* WEB *www.kyoto-kokusai.com. 277 rooms. 5 restaurants, bar, 2 lounges, shops. AE, DC, MC, V.*

$$–$$$ ⊞ **Kyōto Tōkyū Hotel.** The pillared main entrance, entrance hall, and lobby are expansive, and the courtyard, with its reflecting pool and waterfall, creates a dramatic atmosphere. The well-appointed rooms of this large chain hotel, predominantly in off-white tones, are comfortable and spacious. ✉ *580 Kakimoto-chō, Gojō-sagaru, Horikawa-dōri, Shimogyō-ku, Kyōto-shi 600-8357,* ☎ *075/341–2411,* FAX *075/341–2488,* WEB *www.tokyuhotel.com. 437 rooms. 3 restaurants, 2 bars, pool, hair salon, shops, travel services. AE, DC, MC, V.*

$$–$$$ ⊞ **New Miyako Hotel.** The 10-story white edifice has two protruding wings with landscaping and street lamps reminiscent of a hotel in the United States. Its location in front of Kyōto Eki makes it attractive if you're planning train trips from the city. ✉ *17 Nishi-Kujōin-chō, Minami-ku, Kyōto-shi 601-8412,* ☎ *075/661–7111,* FAX *075/661–7135,* WEB *www.mykhtls.co.jp. 71 Western-style rooms, 4 Japanese-style rooms. 3 restaurants, bar, tea shop, barbershop, shops. AE, DC, MC, V.*

$$–$$$ ⊞ **Rihga Royal Hotel Kyōto.** The rooms at this well-established chain hotel vary in price according to size, but even the smallest rooms don't seem claustrophobic thanks to the added Japanese touch of doors made from shōji. On the 14th floor is Kyōto's only revolving restaurant, which offers splendid views of the city. There's also a branch of the Kitcho on the premises. You'll find their famous parent restaurant in western Kyōto. The hotel is only a five-minute walk from Kyōto Eki, but a shuttle bus leaves the Hachijō Guchi Exit every 15 minutes. ✉ *Horikawa-Shiokōji, Shimogyō-ku, Kyōto-shi 600-8327,* ☎ *075/341–1121; 800/877–7107 in the U.S.;* FAX *075/341–3073,* WEB *www.*

rhiga.com. 498 rooms. 6 restaurants, 3 bars, coffee shop, deli, no-smoking rooms, indoor pool, barbershop, hair salon, sauna, shops, travel services. AE, DC, MC, V.

$ 🏠 **Hiraiwa.** Imagine the ambience of a friendly, Western-style youth hostel with tatami-mat rooms, and you have the Hiraiwa ryokan, a member of the hospitable and economical Japanese Inn Group. To be a member, inns must have English-speaking staff and provide clean, comfortable accommodations. Hiraiwa is the most popular of these inns in Kyōto; it's a great place to meet fellow travelers from around the world. Rules and regulations during your stay are posted on the walls. Guests are welcome to eat with the owners in the small kitchen. The inn has shared toilets and showers. ✉ *314 Hayao-chō, Kaminoguchi-agaru, Ninomiya-chō-dōri, Shimogyō-ku, Kyōto-shi 600-8114,* ☎ *075/351–6748. 21 Japanese-style rooms. AE, MC, V.*

Eastern Kyōto

$$$–$$$$ 🏠 **Miyako Hotel.** The Miyako, the grande dame of Kyōto's Western-style hotels, has been around for more than a century. The hotel spreads across the hills of Kyōto, near the temples and shrines of the eastern district. Be sure to request a room with a view of the surrounding hills. Twenty Japanese-style rooms in two annexes have the feel of a traditional ryokan. ✉ *Sanjō-Keage, Higashiyama-ku, Kyōto-shi 605-0052,* ☎ *075/771–7111; 800/223–6800 in the U.S.; 0800/181–123 in the U.K.;* FAX *075/751–2490,* WEB *www.miyakohotel.co.jp. 300 Western-style rooms, 20 Japanese-style rooms. 5 restaurants, 2 bars, coffee shop, pool, shops, meeting rooms. AE, DC, MC, V.*

$$$–$$$$ 🏠 **Seikōrō.** This lovely inn, established in 1831, is a short walk from
★   busy Gojō Eki, a convenience that makes it popular among both gaijin and Japanese. A local resident who speaks English fluently manages the ryokan. Among the interesting decor are Western antiques that mysteriously blend in quite well with the otherwise traditional setting. When you return to Seikōrō after a day of sightseeing, you may get the distinct feeling that you're returning to your Japanese home. ✉ *Toiya-machi-dōri, Gojō-sagaru, Higashiyama-ku, Kyōto-shi 605-0907,* ☎ *075/561–0771,* FAX *075/541–5481. 23 Japanese-style rooms. AE, DC, MC, V. MAP.*

$$$–$$$$ 🏠 **Yachiyo.** Carefully shaped bushes, pine trees, and rocks surround
★   the woodwork and low-hanging tiled eaves of the special entrance to this ryokan, and the sidewalk from the gate curves into the doorway. Yachiyo is less expensive than its brethren in the deluxe category but nevertheless provides fine, attentive care. Perhaps the biggest draw of the inn is its proximity to Nanzen-ji, one of the most appealing temples in Kyōto. You can reduce the cost of staying at this ryokan by choosing not to dine here. ✉ *34 Nanzen-ji-fukuchi-chō, Sakyō-ku, Kyōto-shi 606-8435,* ☎ *075/771–4148,* FAX *075/771–4140. 25 rooms, 20 with bath. AE, DC, MC, V.*

$$ 🏠 **Holiday Inn Kyōto.** With a bowling alley and an ice-skating rink, this member of the American chain has the best sports facilities of any hotel in Kyōto. The hotel is in a residential area with small, modern houses, occasionally interrupted by large, traditional estates. To compensate for its location away from most of the action, the hotel provides a shuttle bus to make the 30-minute run to and from Kyōto Eki every 90 minutes. The hotel is a 15-minute taxi ride from Kyōto's downtown area. ✉ *36 Nishihiraki-chō, Takano, Sakyō-ku, Kyōto-shi 606-8103,* ☎ *075/721–3131,* FAX *075/781–6178,* WEB *www.holiday-inn.com. 270 rooms. 3 restaurants, 2 bars, coffee shop, indoor pool, sauna, driving range, tennis court, bowling, gym, ice-skating, shops. AE, DC, MC, V.*

$$ 🏠 **Kyōto Traveler's Inn.** This no-frills modern inn is in the perfect spot for sightseeing, with Heian Jingū, Nanzen-ji, and the museums in

Okazaki Park just minutes away on foot. Its Western-style and Japanese-style rooms are plain and small but clean and practical; all have a private bath and toilet. Ask for a room with a view (most don't have one). Because of its location, size, and price, the hotel often hosts large travel groups. Head for the coffee shop on the first floor to look out over the river and plot your course for the day. In contrast to some of Kyōto's other budget inns, this one imposes no curfew. ⊠ *Heian Jingū Torii-mae, Okazaki, Sakyō-ku, Kyōto-shi 606-8344,* ☎ *075/771–0225. 40 Western-style rooms, 38 Japanese-style rooms. Coffee shop, meeting room. AE, MC, V.*

$$ 🏠 **Pension Higashiyama.** A 10-minute walk from downtown and the major temples along the eastern foothills, this small pension overlooks the lovely Shira-kawa Canal, south of Sanjō-dōri. The pension has created a friendly atmosphere for families on a budget and is accustomed to gaijin. Several rooms have tatami, and all share bath. ⊠ *474-23 Umemiya-chō, Shirakawa-suji, Sanjō-sagaru, Higashiyama-ku, Kyōto-shi 605-0061,* ☎ *075/882–1181. 15 rooms, 3 with toilet. Dining room. AE.*

$$ 🏠 **Three Sisters Inn Annex** (Rakutō-sōso Bekkan). A traditional inn popular with gaijin for decades, the annex—which is nicer than the main branch—sits on the northeast edge of Heian Jingū, down a trellised path that hides it from the street. This is a quiet and friendly place, and a good introduction to inn customs because the management is accustomed to foreign guests. On the down side, the rooms could use refurbishment, and the doors close at 11:30 PM sharp. ⊠ *Heian Jingū, Higashi-kita-kado, Sakyō-ku, Kyōto-shi 606-8322,* ☎ *075/761–6333,* FAX *075/761–6335. 12 rooms. AE, DC.*

$–$$ 🏠 **Ryokan Yuhara.** Yuhara draws repeat visitors wishing to save a few yen while exploring Kyōto. The friendliness of the staff more than compensates for the spartan amenities. Especially rewarding is a springtime stay, when the cherry trees are in full bloom along the Takase-gawa, which the inn overlooks. This is a 15-minute walk from Gion and Pontochō. ⊠ *188 Kagiya-chō, Shomen-agaru, Kiya-machi-dōri, Higashiyama-ku, Kyōto-shi 605-0909,* ☎ *075/371–9583. 8 Japanese-style rooms. No credit cards.*

Northern Kyōto

$$$$ 🏠 **Takaraga-ike Prince Hotel.** Although some distance north of the center, Kyōto's only deluxe hotel is close to the Kokusaikaikan subway station and is especially convenient for the nearby International Conference Hall. Its unusual doughnut-shape design provides each room with a view of the surrounding mountains and forests. Inside corridors overlook an inner garden. The tasteful, spacious guest rooms are decorated with colors that complement the greenery of the outside views, and all have beds that are probably the largest you'll find in Japan. Details include impressive chandeliers all around the building, Miró prints hanging in every suite, and an authentic teahouse beside a pond. Demonstrations of the tea ceremony can be arranged upon request. The hotel offers tremendous discounts in summer; check out the Web site for special packages. ⊠ *Takaraga-ike, Sakyō-ku, Kyōto-shi 606-8505,* ☎ *075/712–1111; 800/542–8686 in the U.S.;* FAX *075/712–7677,* WEB *www2.princehotels.co.jp. 322 rooms. 3 restaurants, 2 bars, tea shops. AE, DC, MC, V.*

Western Kyōto

$$$ 🏠 **Syōensō-Hosogawa-tei.** In the *onsen* (hot springs) village of Yunohana, set in the mountains of Tamba northwest of Kyōto, this hotel allows you to soak in your own *rotemburo* (outdoor bath) overlooking a private garden. If you're feeling adventurous you can get into the full swing of an onsen visit by joining other guests in one of the communal baths (separated by gender). The building itself looks like something out of *The Twilight Zone,* but the *machiya* (layers of sliding paper screens) facade of the lobby and the steps bordered on one side by a gently sloping waterfall suggest Old Kyōto. A kaiseki dinner is prepared with seasonal favorites, including Tamba boar in winter. An overnight stay at the hotel complements a trip to Arashiyama. For ¥600, you can take the scenic Sagano Torokko train, which leaves Saga Torokko station in Arashiyamas six minutes before the hour, for the 20-minute ride to Kameoka, where Yunohana is located. Call ahead to ask the hotel shuttle bus to meet you at the station. To return to Arashiyama, take the Hosogawa-kudari boat the next day. Alternatively, you can take the JR line between Kameoka and Kyōto stations. ⊠ *Kameoka City, Yunohana-onsen, 621-0034,* ☎ *0771/22–0903,* FAX *0771/23–6572,* WEB *www.syoenso.com. 56 Japanese-style rooms, 7 with bath. Restaurant, 2 lounges, hot springs, sauna, shops. AE, MC, V. MAP.*

$ 🛏 **Utano Youth Hostel.** If you like the onsen feel, without the onsen price, try the Utano, which provides a communal, indoor hot spring bath. Located near Kinkaku-ji and Ryōan-ji, the hostel is convenient for sightseeing in Arashiyama and western Kyōto. Rooms, which have bunk beds, accommodate up to eight people. Sip tea or coffee with the other guests every night from 10 to 10:30. The friendly staff speaks English. Dinner and breakfast are served for a small additional fee, and you can even rent a bicycle here for ¥600 a day. Internet access is available. ⊠ *29 Nakayama-cho, Uzumasa, Ukyō-ku Kyōto-shi 6160-8191,* ☎ *075/462–2288,* FAX *075/462–2289,* WEB *web.kyoyo-inet.or.jp/org/ utano-yh/. 25 rooms. Cafeteria, hot springs, tennis court, bicycles, coin laundry. AE, MC, V.*

NIGHTLIFE AND THE ARTS

The Arts

Kyōto is quickly following Tōkyō and Ōsaka on domestic and international performing artists' circuits. The city has hosted the likes of Bruce Springsteen, but it's better known for its traditional performances—dance and Kabuki and Nō theater. All dialogue at theaters is in Japanese, of course. *See also* Chapter 14 for descriptions of Japanese performing arts.

Information on performances is available from a number of sources; the most convenient is your hotel concierge or guest-relations manager, who may even have a few tickets on hand, so don't hesitate to ask. For further information on Kyōto's arts scene check the music and theater sections of the monthly magazine **Kansai Time Out,** available at bookshops for ¥300; you can also find information on the Web site (www.kto.co.jp). Another source is the **Kyōto Visitor's Guide,** which devotes a few pages to "This Month's Theater." It's available free from JNTO's Tourist Information Center (TIC), directly across from Kyōto Eki. It's strongly suggested that you stop by the TIC if you're interested in the performing arts in Kyōto, but if you don't have time to visit in person, you can call and speak with an English-speaking information officer.

Gion Corner

Some call it a tourist trap, but for others it's a comprehensive introduction to Japanese performing arts. The one-hour show combines court music and dance, ancient comic plays, Kyōto-style dance performed by *maiko* (apprentice geisha), and puppet drama. Segments are also offered on tea ceremony, flower arrangement, and koto music.

Before attending a show, walk around Gion and Ponto-chō. You're likely to see beautifully dressed geisha and maiko making their way to work. It's permissible to take their picture—"*Shashin o totte mō ii desu ka?*" is the polite way to ask—but as they have strict appointments, don't delay them.

For tickets to Gion Corner, contact your hotel concierge or call the theater directly (✉ Yasaka Hall, 1st floor, Gion, ☎ 075/561–1119). The show costs ¥2,800—a bargain considering that it would usually cost 10 times as much to watch maiko and geisha perform. Two performances are held nightly at 7:40 and 8:40 March–November. No performances are offered August 16.

An even less expensive introduction to geisha arts can be had at the **International Hotel Kyōto** (✉ Horikawa, Nijō-jō-mae, ☎ 075/222–1111), which has free maiko dance performances in its first-floor lounge every evening 7:20–7:40. The hotel is opposite Nijō-jō.

Seasonal Dances
In the **Miyako Odori,** in April, and the **Kamo-gawa Odori,** in May and October, geisha and maiko dances and songs pay tribute to the seasonal splendor of spring and fall. The stage settings are spectacular.

Tickets to performances at the **Gion Kaburenjō Theater** (✉ Gion Hanami-kōji, Higashiyama-ku, ☎ 075/561–1115) cost ¥1,900, ¥3,800, and ¥4,300. Tickets at the **Ponto-chō Kaburenjō Theater** (✉ Ponto-chō, Sanjō-sagaru, Nakagyō-ku, ☎ 075/221–2025) range from ¥1,650 to ¥3,800.

Kabuki
Kabuki has found quite a following in the United States due to tours by Japanese Kabuki troupes in Washington, D.C., New York, and a few other cities. Kabuki is faster paced than Nō, but a single performance can easily take half a day. Devoted followers pack bentō and sit patiently through the entire performance, mesmerized by each movement of the performers.

For a first-timer, however, the music and unique intonations of Kabuki might be a bit of an overload. Unless you're captured by the Kabuki spirit, don't spend more than an hour or two at Kyōto's famed **Minami-za** (✉ Shijō Kamo-gawa, Higashiyama-ku, ☎ 075/561–1155), the oldest theater in Japan. Beautifully renovated, it hosts a variety of performances year-round. Top Kabuki stars from around the country make guest appearances during the annual, monthlong **Kaomise** (Face Showing) Kabuki Festival, in December. Ask at the Tourist Information Center for information. Tickets range from ¥2,000 to ¥9,000.

Nō
A form of traditional theater, Nō is more ritualistic and sophisticated than Kabuki. Some understanding of the plot of each play is necessary to enjoy a performance, which is generally slow moving and solemnly chanted. Major Nō theaters often provide synopses of the plays in English. The carved masks used by the main actors express a whole range of emotions, though the mask itself may appear expressionless until the actor "brings it to life." Particularly memorable are outdoor performances of Nō, especially **Takigi Nō,** held outdoors by firelight on the nights of June 1–2 in the precincts of the Heian Jingū. For more information about the performances, contact the Tourist Information Center.

Nō performances are held year-round and range from ¥4,000 to ¥6,000. **Kanze Kaikan Nō Theater** (⊠ 44 Enshōji-chō, Okazaki, Sakyō-ku, ☎ 075/771–6114). **Kongo Nō Theater** (⊠ Muro-machi, Shijō-agaru, Nakagyō-ku, ☎ 075/221–3049).

Nightlife

Though Kyōto's nightlife is more sedate than Ōsaka's, the areas around the old geisha quarters downtown still thrive with nightclubs and bars. The Kiya-machi area along the small canal near Ponto-chō is as close to a consolidated nightlife area as you'll get in Kyōto. It's full of small watering holes with red lanterns (indicating inexpensive places) or small neon signs in front. It is also fun to walk around the Gion and Ponto-chō areas to try to catch a glimpse of a geisha or maiko stealing down an alleyway on her way to or from an appointment.

Kyōto's only venue for acoustic, folk, and bluegrass is **Cup of Sun** (⊠ west of junction of Shirakawa-dōri and Higashi-kurumaguchi-dōri, ☎ 075/791–1001). Though only open on Saturday night from 8:30 to 11:00, **Kenny's** (⊠ northwest corner of Shimei-dōri and Karasuma-dōri, ☎ 075/415–1171) is a well-known country-and-western bar with live performances by one of Japan's C&W legends. Kenny has even played the Grand Ol' Opry in Nashville. **Le Club Jazz** (⊠ Sanjō Arimoto Bldg., 2nd floor, Sanjō-Gokōmachi Nishi-Iru, ☎ 075/211–5800) has jazz, blues, and soul gigs on Tuesday and sessions every night from Thursday to Monday. There's a ¥2,000 cover charge (including two drinks) on weekends. **Live Spot Rag** (⊠ Kyōto Empire Bldg., 5th floor, Kiya-machi, ☎ 075/241–0446), a jazz place north of Sanjō-dōri, has a reasonable cover charge of about ¥1,200 for its live sessions between 7 and 11. **Mamma Zappa** (⊠ Takoyakushi-dōri, off Kawara-machi-dōri, south of Maruzen, ☎ 075/255–4437) was David Bowie's choice of watering hole when he was in town. An arty crowd munches on Indonesian food while sipping cocktails. One of three Kansai-area **Pig & Whistle** pubs (⊠ across from Keihan Sanjō Eki, Shobi Bldg., 2nd floor, ☎ 075/761–6022) is a popular hangout, and every weekend the Kyōto branch bulges at the seams.

One of the best clubs in Kansai is Kyōto's **Metro** (⊠ Ebisu Bldg., 2nd floor, Shimotsutsumi-chō 82, Maruta-machi Sagaru, Kawabata-dōri, Sakyō-ku, ☎ 075/752–4765), which has an extremely wide range of regular events, from salsa to reggae, as well as frequent guest appearances by famous DJs from Tōkyō and abroad.

OUTDOOR ACTIVITIES AND SPORTS

Participant Sports

Biking

If you'd like to cycle around Kyōto's main sights, try renting a bike from **Rental Cycle Yasumoto Kawabata** (⊠ Kawabata-dori, just north of Sanjō-dori, ☎ 075/751–0595), open Monday–Saturday 9–5, for ¥1,000 per day.

Boating

You can rent a rowboat in Arashiyama and row on the Oi-gawa while enjoying a view of the mountains. **Arashiyama Tsūsen** (☎ 075/861–0223), near Togetsu-kyō Bridge, rents rowboats for ¥1,400 an hour.

Jogging and Walking

Broad pathways alongside the banks of the **Kamo-gawa,** from Kita-ōji-dōri in the north to Shijō-dōri in the south, accommodate joggers, walkers, and occasionally groups practicing tai chi.

Swimming

Pool admissions are pricey in Kyōto. The Kyōto Tourist Information Center can provide a list of pools open to the public. In late July and August, try the **Tokyu Inn Hotel** (✉ 35-1 Hananooka-cho, Kamikazan, Yamashina-ku, ☎ 075/593–0109), which provides a shuttle bus from JR Kyōto Eki and charges ¥2,000.

Spectator Sports

Martial Arts

At the **Budō Center** (✉ Shōgoin Entomichō, Sakyō, ☎ 075/751–1255) you can watch masters of the martial arts, such as *kyūdō* (Japanese archery) and *kendō* (Japanese fencing), demonstrate their finely honed techniques A schedule is available at the Kyōto Tourist Information Center.

SHOPPING

Most shops slide open their doors at 10, and many shopkeepers partake of the morning ritual of sweeping and watering the entrance to welcome the morning's first customers. Shops lock up at 6 or 7 in the evening. Stores often close sporadically once or twice a month, so it's a good idea to call in advance if you're making a special trip. As Sunday is a big shopping day for the Japanese, most stores remain open.

The traditional greeting of a shopkeeper to a customer is *o-ideyasu* (Kyōto-ben, the Kyōto dialect for "honored to have you here"), voiced in a lilting Kyōto dialect with the required bowing of the head. When a customer makes a purchase, the shopkeeper will respond with *o-okini* ("thank you" in Kyōto-ben), a smile, and a bow. Take notice of the careful effort and adroitness with which purchases are wrapped; it's an art in itself. Also, you'll still hear the clicking of an abacus, rather than the crunching of a cash register, in many Kyōto shops. American Express, MasterCard, Visa, and traveler's checks are widely accepted.

If you plan to make shopping one of your prime pursuits in Kyōto, look for a copy of Diane Durston's thorough *Old Kyōto: A Guide to Traditional Shops, Restaurants, and Inns.*

Shopping Districts

Compared with sprawling Tōkyō, Kyōto is compact and relatively easy to navigate. Major shops line both sides of **Shijō-dōri,** which runs east–west, and **Kawara-machi-dōri,** which runs north–south. Concentrate on Shijō-dōri between Yasaka Jinja and Karasuma Eki as well as Kawara-machi-dōri between Sanjō-dōri and Shijō-dōri. Nearby **Kiya-machi-dōri,** famous for its watering holes, has expensive fashion outlets, like that of Paul Smith and other European designers.

Some of modern Kyōto's shopping districts are to be found underground. **Porta,** under Kyōto Eki, hosts more than 200 shops and restaurants in a sprawling, subterranean arcade. **Zest Oike,** which is newer than Porta, is accessible from the Kyōto Shiyakusho-Mae subway station.

Roads leading to Kiyomizu-dera are steep inclines, yet you may hardly notice the steepness for all of the alluring shops that line the way to the temple. Be sure to peek in for unique gifts. Food shops offer sample morsels, and tea shops serve complimentary cups of tea.

Shin-Kyōgoku, a covered arcade running parallel to Kawara-machi-dōri, is another general-purpose shopping area with many souvenir shops.

Crafts Centers

For a description of Kyōto crafts, *see* Pleasures and Pastimes, *above.*

The **Kyōto Craft Center,** on Shijō-dōri in Gion, has two floors of contemporary and traditional crafts for sale in a modern setting. More than 100 crafts studios are represented, giving a diversity to the products for sale. ⊠ *Shijō-dōri, Gion-machi, Higashiyama-ku,* ☎ *075/561–9660.* ⊗ *Thurs.–Tues. 11–7.*

The **Kyōto Handicraft Center,** a seven-story shopping emporium, sells everything from tape decks and pearl necklaces to porcelain and lacquerware designed to appeal to tourists. It's a good place to compare prices and grab last-minute souvenirs. ⊠ *Kumano Jinja Higashi, Sakyō-ku,* ☎ *075/761–5080.* ⊗ *Feb.–Dec., daily 9:30–6; Jan., daily 9:30–5:30.*

Depāto

Kyōto *depāto* (department stores) are small in comparison to their mammoth counterparts in Tōkyō and Ōsaka. They still, however, carry a wide range of goods and are great places for one-stop souvenir shopping. Wandering around the food halls (in all but Hankyū) is also a good way to build up an appetite. Note that all the stores close irregularly for a few days each month. You can call at the beginning of the month to find out about scheduled closures.

Daimaru is conveniently located on the main Shijō-dōri shopping avenue. Its basement food hall is the best in town. ⊠ *Shijō-Karasuma, Shimogyō-ku,* ☎ *075/211–8111.* ⊗ *Daily 10–7:30.*

Hankyū, directly across from Takashimaya on Kawara-machi-dōri, has two restaurant floors. Window displays show the type of food served, and prices are clearly marked. ⊠ *Shijō-kawara-machi, Shimogyō-ku,* ☎ *075/223–2288.* ⊗ *Daily 10–7:30.*

Isetan, in the Kyōto Eki building, has 13 floors, including a restaurant floor, an amusement arcade, and an art gallery. It closes periodically on Tuesday. ⊠ *Karasuma-dōri, Shimogyō-ku,* ☎ *075/352–1111.* ⊗ *Daily 10–7:30.*

Kintetsu is on Karasuma-dōri, the avenue leading north from Kyōto Eki. ⊠ *Karasuma-dōri, Shimogyō-ku,* ☎ *075/361–1111.* ⊗ *Daily 10–7:30.*

Takashimaya, on Kawara-machi-dōri, has a well-trained English-speaking staff at its information desk, as well as a convenient money-exchange counter on its premises. ⊠ *Shijō-kawara-machi, Shimogyō-ku,* ☎ *075/221–8811.* ⊗ *Daily 10–7:30.*

Food and Temple Markets

Kyōto has a wonderful food market, **Nishiki-kōji,** which branches off from the Shin-Kyōgoku covered arcade across from the Daimaru department store in central Kyōto. Look for delicious grilled fish dipped in soy for a tasty snack. Try to avoid the market in late afternoon, when housewives come to do their daily shopping. The market is long and narrow; in a sizable crowd there's always the possibility of being pushed into the display of fresh fish.

Several **temple markets** take place in Kyōto each month. These are great places to pick up bargain kimonos or unusual souvenirs. They're also some of the best spots for people-watching. The largest and most famous is the market at Tō-ji (☞ Central and Southern Kyōto, *above*), which takes place on the 21st of each month. The temple also hosts a smaller market devoted to antiques on the first Sunday of the month.

The market at **Kitano Tenman-gū** (☞ Western Kyōto, *above*) is held on the 25th of each month. A market specializing in homemade goods is held at **Chion-ji** on the 15th. To get to the Chion-ji market, take Bus 206 from Kyōto Eki to Hyakumanben.

Traditional Items and Gift Ideas

Art and Antiques

Nawate-dōri between Shijō-dōri and Sanjō-dōri is noted for fine antique textiles, ceramics, and paintings.

Shinmonzen-dōri holds the key to shopping for art and antiques in Kyōto. It's an unpretentious little street of two-story wooden buildings that is lined with telephone and electricity poles between Higashi-ōji-dōri and Hanami-kōji-dōri, just north of Gion. What gives the street away as a treasure trove are the large credit-card signs jutting out from the shops. There are no fewer than 17 shops specializing in scrolls, *netsuke* (small carved figures to attach to Japanese clothing), lacquerware, bronze, wood-block prints, paintings, and antiques. Shop with confidence, because shopkeepers are trustworthy and goods are authentic. Pick up a copy of the pamphlet *Shinmonzen Street Shopping Guide* from your hotel or from the Tourist Information Center.

Tera-machi-dōri between Oike-dōri and Maruta-machi is known for antiques of all kinds and tea-ceremony utensils.

Bamboo

The Japanese wish their sons and daughters to be as strong and flexible as bamboo. Around many Japanese houses are small bamboo groves, for the deep-rooted plant withstands earthquakes. On the other hand, bamboo is so flexible it bends into innumerable shapes. Bamboo groves surround the entire city of Kyōto. The wood is carefully cut and dried for several months before being stripped and woven into baskets and vases.

Kagoshin has been making bamboo baskets since 1862. Only the best varieties of bamboo are used in this fiercely proud little shop. ☒ *Ōhashi-higashi, Sanjō-dōri, Higashiyama-ku,* ☏ 075/771–0209. ☉ *Mon.–Sat. 9–6.*

Ceramics

Asahi-do, in the heart of the pottery district near Kiyomizu-dera, specializes in Kyōto-style hand-painted porcelain. ☒ *1–280 Kiyomizu, Higashiyama-ku,* ☏ 075/531–2181. ☉ *Daily 9–6.*

Tachikichi, on Shijō-dōri west of Kawara-machi, has contemporary and traditional wares and the best reputation in town. ☒ *Shijō-Tominokōji, Nakagyō-ku,* ☏ 075/211–3143. ☉ *Thurs.–Tues. 10–7.*

Dolls

Ningyō were first used in Japan in the purification rites associated with the Doll Festival, an annual family-oriented event on March 3. Kyōto ningyō are made with fine detail and embellishment.

Nakanishi Toku Shōten has old museum-quality dolls. The owner, Mr. Nakanishi, turned his extensive doll collection into the shop two decades ago and has since been educating customers with his vast knowledge of the doll trade. ☒ *359 Moto-chō, Yamato-ōji Higashi-Iru, Furumonzen-dōri, Higashiyama-ku,* ☏ 075/561–7309. ☉ *Daily 10–5.*

Folk Crafts

For many the prize souvenir of a visit to Kyōto is the **shuinshu,** a booklet usually no larger than 4 by 6 inches. It's most often covered with brocade, and the blank sheets of heavyweight paper inside continuously fold out. You can find them at stationery stores or at temples for as little as ¥1,000 and use them as "passports" to collect ink stamps from places you visit while in Japan. Stamps and stamp pads are ubiquitous in Japan—at sights, train stations, and some restaurants. Most ink stamping will be done for free; at temples monk will write calligraphy over the stamp for a small fee.

Kuraya Hashimoto has one of the best collections of antique and newly forged swords. ⊠ *Nishihorikawa-dōri, Oike-agaru (southeast corner of Nijō-jō), Nakagyō-ku,* ☎ 075/821–2791. ⊙ *Daily 10–6.*

At **Ryushido** you can stock up on calligraphy and *sumi* supplies, including writing brushes, ink sticks, ink stones, paper, paperweights, and water stoppers. ⊠ *Nijō-agaru, Tera-machi-dōri (north of Nijō), Kamigyō-ku,* ☎ 075/252–4120. ⊙ *Daily 10–6.*

Yamato Mingei-ten, next to the Maruzen Bookstore downtown, has the best selection of folk crafts, including ceramics, metalwork, paper, lacquerware, and textiles. ⊠ *Kawara-machi, Takoyakushi-agaru, Nakagyō-ku,* ☎ 075/221–2641. ⊙ *Wed.–Mon. 10–8:30.*

Kimono and Accessories

Shimmering new silk kimonos can cost more than ¥1,000,000—they are art objects, as well as couture—while equally stunning old silk kimonos can cost less than ¥3,000. You can find used kimonos at some local end-of-the-month temple markets.

Aizen Kobo, two blocks east of the textile center on Imadegawa-dōri and a block south, specializes in the finest handwoven indigo-dyed textiles. The shop is in a traditional weaving family's home, and the friendly owners will show you a wide variety of dyed and woven goods, including garments designed by Hisako Utsuki, the owner's wife. ⊠ *Ōmiya Nishi-Iru, Nakasuji-dōri, Kamigyō-ku,* ☎ 075/441–0355. ⊙ *Mon.–Sat. 9–5:30.*

Jūsan-ya has been selling *tsugekushi* (boxwood combs) for more than 60 years. *Kanzashi,* the hair ornaments worn with kimonos, are also available. ⊠ *Shinkyōgoku Higashi-Iru, Shijō-dōri, Shimogyō-ku,* ☎ 075/221–2008. ⊙ *Daily 10–6.*

Umbrellas protect kimonos from the scorching sun or pelting rain. Head for **Kasagen** to purchase authentic oiled-paper umbrellas. The shop has been around since 1861, and its umbrellas are guaranteed to last years. ⊠ *284 Gion-machi, Kita-gawa, Higashiyama-ku,* ☎ 075/561–2832. ⊙ *Daily 10–9.*

The most famous fan shop in all of Kyōto is **Miyawaki Baisen-an,** in business since 1823. It delights customers not only with its fine collection of lacquered, scented, painted, and paper fans but also with the old-world atmosphere that emanates from the building that houses the shop. ⊠ *Tominokōji Nishi-Iru, Rokkaku-dōri, Nakagyō-ku,* ☎ 075/221–0181. ⊙ *Daily 9–6.*

The **Nishijin Orimono** (Textile Center; ☞ Central and Southern Kyōto, *above*) provides an orientation on silk-weaving techniques. ⊠ *Horikawadōri, Imadegawa-Minami-Iru, Kamigyō-ku,* ☎ 075/451–9231. ▨ Free. ⊙ *Daily 9–5.*

Visit **Takumi** for kimono accessories like obis, handbags, and *furoshiki* (gift-wrapping cloth). ⊠ *Sanjō-sagaru, Kawara-machi-dōri, Nakagyō-ku,* ☎ 075/221–2278. ⊙ *Daily 10:30–9.*

KYŌTO A TO Z

*To research prices, get advice from other travelers, and book travel ar-
rangements, visit www.fodors.com.*

AIRPORTS AND TRANSFERS

The closest international airport to Kyōto is Kansai International Airport (KIX), near Ōsaka. KIX does have domestic flights, particularly
to major cities, but the majority of internal air traffic uses Ōsaka's Itami
Airport. Flight time between Tōkyō and Ōsaka is about 70 minutes.
➤ AIRPORT INFORMATION: **Itami Airport** (☎ 06/6856–6781). **Kansai International Airport** (☎ 0724/55–2500).

AIRPORT TRANSFERS

From KIX to Kyōto Eki, take the JR Haruka Limited Express, which
departs every 30 minutes to make the 75-minute run and costs ¥3,490
including charges for a reserved seat; or use a JR Pass. From Itami, buses
depart for Kyōto approximately every 20 minutes from 8:10 AM to 9:20
PM. Some stop at major hotels, but most go straight to Kyōto Eki. The
trip takes from 55 to 90 minutes and costs ¥1,280 or ¥1,370, depending
on the Kyōto destination.

Taxis cost more than ¥10,000 from KIX and Itami to Kyōto.

BIKE TRAVEL

For the most part Kyōto is flat, making getting around by bicycle easy
and very convenient. Rental Cycle Yasumoto Kawabata has bikes at
¥200 per hour or ¥1,000 per day.
➤ BIKE RENTALS: **Rental Cycle Yasumoto Kawabata** (✉ 243 Sanjūsangen-dō, Higashiyama-ku, ☎ 075/751–0595).

BUS TRAVEL

A network of bus routes covers the entire city. Most city buses run 7
AM–9 PM daily, but a few start as early as 5:30 AM and run until 11 PM.
The main bus terminals are Kyōto Eki, Keihan Sanjō Eki, Karasuma-
Kitao-ji, and at the Shijō-dōri–Karasuma-dōri intersection. Many city
buses do not have signs in English, so you'll need to know the bus num-
ber. Because you will probably ride the bus at least once in Kyōto, try
to pick up a bus map early in your stay from the Tourist Information
Center at the Kyōto Tower Building, across from JR Kyōto Eki.

At each bus stop a guidepost indicates the stop name, the bus route,
and the bus-route number. Because the information at most guideposts
is only in Japanese (except for the route number, which is given as an
Arabic numeral), you are advised to ask your hotel clerk beforehand
to write down your destination in Japanese, along with the route number, to show to the bus driver and fellow passengers; this will allow
the driver and others to help you if you get lost. You might also ask
your hotel clerk beforehand how many stops your ride will take.

Within the city the standard fare is ¥220, which you pay before leaving the bus; outside the city limits the fare varies according to distance.
Several special transportation passes are available, including the following: a one-day city bus pass for ¥500; a multiday discount bus pass
that provides ¥2,250 worth of riding for ¥2,000; and the *torafikka kyō*
pass, which provides ¥3,300 worth of transport via city bus or subway for ¥3,000. Additionally, you can purchase combination one-day
(¥1,200) or two-day (¥2,000) passes that cover travel on city buses,
the subway, and private Kyōto Line buses, with restrictions on some
routes. The ¥3,000 *surutto Kansai,* a versatile multiday pass, covers
transportation on city buses, the subway, and all the major Kansai rail-

ways except the JR line. All of these passes are sold at travel agencies, main bus terminals, and information centers in Kyōto Eki.

You can use a JR Pass on the local bus that travels between Kyōto Eki and Takao (in northwestern Kyōto), passing close to Nijō Eki.

CONSULATES

The nearest American, Canadian, and British consulates are in Ōsaka.

EMERGENCIES

The Sakabe Clinic has 24-hour emergency facilities.

➤ DOCTORS: **Daiichi Sekijuji** (Red Cross Hospital; ⊠ Higashiyama Hon-machi, Higashiyama-ku, ☎ 075/561–1121). **Daini Sekijuji Byoin** (Second Red Cross Hospital; ⊠ Kamanza-dōri, Maruta-machi-agaru, Kamigyō-ku, ☎ 075/231–5171). **Japan Baptist Hospital** (⊠ Kita-Shi-rakawa, Yamanomoto-chō, Sakyō-ku, ☎ 075/781–5191). **Sakabe Clinic** (⊠ 435 Yamamoto-chō, Gokō-machi, Nijō Sagaru, Nakagyō-ku, ☎ 075/231–1624).

➤ EMERGENCY SERVICES: **Ambulance** (☎ 119). **Police** (☎ 110).

ENGLISH-LANGUAGE MEDIA

BOOKS

Izumiya Book Center, across from Kyōto Eki on the Shinkansen side, devotes a large corner to English-language books. Maruzen Kyōto has the city's broadest selection of books. Nearby, Media Shop carries a wide range of coffee-table books and titles on art and architecture in English and Japanese.

➤ BOOKSTORES: **Izumiya Book Center** (⊠ Avanti Bldg., 6th floor, Mi-nami-ku, ☎ 075/671–8987). **Maruzen Kyōto** (⊠ 296 Kawara-machi-dōri, Nakagyō-ku, ☎ 075/241–2169). **Media Shop** (⊠ Vox Bldg., 1st floor, Kawara-machi, San-jō, Nakagyō-ku, ☎ 075/255–0783).

NEWSPAPERS AND MAGAZINES

Established in 1977, the monthly *Kansai Time Out* publishes comprehensive events listings for Kōbe, Kyōto, Nara, and Ōsaka. It costs ¥300 and is available in major hotels and bookshops throughout the region.

INTERNET CAFÉS

➤ CONTACTS: **Meix** (⊠ Crista Plaza M Bldg., Karasuma-dōri Takeya-machi-agaru, Nagakyō-ku, ☎ 075/212–7511), open Monday–Saturday noon–7. **Net Surf** (⊠ Kawabata Bldg., Shijō Takakura Nishi-Iru, Shimogyō-ku, ☎ 075/221–2707), open Monday–Saturday 10–6.

SIGHTSEEING GUIDES

Contact Joe Okada at Kyōto Specialist Guide Group or consider hiring an English-speaking taxi driver to be your guide from MK Taxi. Volunteer guides are available free of charge through the Tourist Information Center, but arrangements must be made one day in advance.

➤ CONTACTS: **Kyōto Specialist Guide Group** (☎ 0773/64–0033). **MK Taxi** (☎ 075/721–2237).

SUBWAY TRAVEL

Kyōto has a 26-station subway system. The Karasuma Line runs north to south from Kokusai Kaikan to Takeda. The Tōzai Line runs between Nijō in the west and Daigo in the east. Purchase tickets at the vending machines in stations before boarding. Fares increase with distance traveled and begin at ¥200. Service runs 5:30 AM–11:30 PM. Discounted passes are available for tourists (☞ Bus Travel, *above*).

TAXIS

Taxis are readily available in Kyōto. Fares for smaller-size cabs start at ¥650 for the first 2 km (1 mi), with a cost of ¥90 for each additional

⅔ km (⅓ mi). Many taxi companies provide guided tours of the city, priced per hour or per route. Keihan Taxi has four-hour tours from ¥14,600 per car; MK Taxi runs similar tours for ¥16,600. There are fixed fares for some sightseeing services that start and end at Kyōto Eki. A 7½-hour tour of the city's major sights will cost ¥26,000 with any of 17 taxi companies, including Keihan Taxi and MK Taxi.

➤ LOCAL COMPANIES: **Keihan Taxi** (☎ 0120/113–103). **MK Taxi** (☎ 075/721–2237).

TOURS

EXCURSIONS

Hozugawa Yūsen organizes excursions down a 15-km (9-mi) stretch (about 90 minutes) of the Hozu Rapids in flat-bottom boats, from Kameoka to Arashiyama, which cost ¥3,900. Sunrise Tours, a subsidiary of Japan Travel Bureau, conducts full- and half-day tours to Nara and Ōsaka. An afternoon tour to Nara costs ¥6,300. Morning and afternoon trips to Ōsaka, for ¥8,900 and ¥6,200, respectively, are not worth the cost, especially if you have a JR Pass.

➤ TOUR INFORMATION: **Hozugawa Yūsen** (☎ 0771/225–846). **Sunrise Tours** (☎ 075/341–1413).

ORIENTATION TOURS

Sunrise Tours organizes half-day morning and afternoon deluxe coach tours highlighting different city attractions. Pickup service is provided from major hotels. A ¥5,300 morning tour commonly covers Nijō-jō, Kinkaku-ji, Kyōto Imperial Palace, Higashi-Hongan-ji, and the Kyōto Handicraft Center. A ¥5,300 afternoon tour includes the Heian Jingū, Sanjūsangen-dō, and Kiyomizu-dera. A ¥11,200 full-day tour covers all the above sights and includes lunch.

➤ TOUR INFORMATION: **Sunrise Tours** (☎ 075/341–1413).

SPECIAL-INTEREST TOURS

Kyōto Specialist Guide Group conducts special tours of Kyōto and arranges home visits for individuals and groups. Contact Joe Okada, who will tailor your tour to fit your interests and budget. Private tours are more expensive, so it's best to assemble a group if possible. The Tourist Section of the Department of Cultural Affairs and Tourism can arrange home visits.

➤ TOUR INFORMATION: **Kyōto Specialist Guide Group** (✉ 1137 Amarube-shimo, Maizaru-shi, ☎ 0773/64–0033). **Tourist Section, Department of Cultural Affairs and Tourism** (✉ Kyōto City Government, Kyōto Kaikan, Okazaki, Sakyō-ku, ☎ 075/752–0215).

WALKING TOURS

The Japan National Tourist Office (JNTO) publishes suggested walking routes, which offer maps and brief descriptions for five tours, ranging in length from about 40 minutes to 80 minutes. The walking-tour brochures are available from the JNTO's Tourist Information Center (☞ Visitor Information, *below*) at the Kyōto Tower Building in front of Kyōto Eki. Personable Kyōto-ite Johnnie Hajime Hirooka conducts walking tours of Kyōto, in English, that leave from Kyōto Eki at 10:15 AM Monday–Thursday, early March–late November, rain or shine. Itineraries vary—he often takes people to sights they might not otherwise see. Walks last four hours and cost ¥2,000 per person, ¥3,000 per couple.

➤ TOUR INFORMATION: **Johnnie Hajime Hirooka** (☎ FAX 075/622–6803).

TRAIN TRAVEL

Frequent daily Shinkansen run between Tōkyō and Kyōto (2 hours, 40 minutes). The one-way fare, including charges for a reserved seat, is ¥13,220. Train service between Ōsaka and Kyōto (30 minutes) costs ¥540 one-way. From Shin-Ōsaka Eki, you can take the Shinkansen and be in Kyōto in 15 minutes; tickets cost ¥1,380. You may use a Japan Rail Pass on the Hikari and Kodama Shinkansen.

The Keihan and the Hankyū limited express trains (40 minutes each) are less expensive than the JR, unless you have a JR Pass. The one-way Ōsaka–Kyōto fare is ¥400 or ¥460 on the Keihan Line and ¥390 on the Hankyū Line. They depart every 15 minutes from Ōsaka's Yo-doyabashi and Umeda stations respectively.

In Kyōto, the Keihan Line from Ōsaka is partly underground (from Shichijō Eki to Demachi-Yanagi Eki) and extends all the way up the east bank of the Kamo-gawa to Imadegawa-dōri. At Imadegawa-dōri a passage connects the Keihan Line with the Eizan Railway's Demachi-Yanagi Eki. The Eizan has two lines, the Kurama Line, running north to Kurama, and the Eizan Line, running northeast to Yase. The Hankyū Line, which runs to the Katsura Rikyū, connects with the subway at Karasuma Eki. From Shijō-Ōmiya Eki the Keifuku Arashiyama Line runs to western Kyōto. JR also runs to western Kyōto on the San-in Main Line.

VISITOR INFORMATION

The Japan National Tourist Organization's (JNTO) Tourist Information Center (TIC) is in the Kyōto Tower Building, in front of JR Kyōto Eki. (Take the Karasuma exit, on the side opposite the Shinkansen tracks.) Japan Travel Phone, a nationwide English-language information line for visitors, is available 9–5 daily, year-round. It's run out of the same office as the TIC.

The Japan Travel Bureau (JTB) and Keihan Travel Agency provide information on tours, such as the Sunrise Tours JTB offers; conferences and symposiums; and obtaining Japan Rail Passes. The JTB Web site lists contact numbers outside of Japan.

The Kyōto city government operates a tourist-information office in the Kyōto Eki Building; it's open daily 8:30–7.

➤ TOURIST INFORMATION: **Japan Travel Bureau** (✉ Kyōto Eki-mae, Shiokōji Karasuma Higashi-Iru, Shimogyo-ku, ☎ 075/361–7241, WEB www.jtb.co.jp/eng/). **Japan Travel Phone** (☎ 075/371–5649). **Keihan Travel Agency** (✉ 12 Mori-chō, Fushimi-ku, ☎ 075/602–8162). **Kyōto City Government** (✉ Kyōto Eki Bldg., Higashi-Shiokōji-chō, Shimogyō-ku, ☎ 075/343–6655). **Tourist Information Center** (✉ Karasuma-dōri, Higashi-Shiokōji-chō, Shimogyō-ku, ☎ 075/371–5649).

6 NARA

Nara, with its ancient temples and quaint shopping streets, dates from the 8th century, when the city served as Japan's capital. It might not have the volume of sacred sights that Kyōto has—or all of its concrete and steel—but Nara's historical shrines, sprawling parks, and elaborate kaiseki restaurants are among the country's finest. That this quiet, quintessential old city exists in the midst of Japan's overbuilt industrial corridor makes Nara's understated tranquility all the more precious.

Updated
by Aidan
O'Connor

T HE ANCIENT CITY OF NARA was founded in 710 by Emperor Kammu—thus predating Kyōto—and it was the first Japanese capital to remain in one place over a long period of time. Until then capitals had been established in new locations with each successive ruler. The founding of Nara, then known as Heijō-Kyō, occurred during a period when Japan's politics, arts, architecture, and religion were being heavily influenced by China. Also at this time, the Japanese began using and incorporating *kanji,* Chinese characters, in their writing system.

Introduced from China in the 6th century, Buddhism flourished in Nara and enjoyed the official favor of the rulers and aristocracy, even as it coexisted with well-established Shintō beliefs. Many of Nara's Buddhist temples and monasteries were built by emperors and noble families, while other temples were transferred to Nara from former capitals. At its peak during the 8th century, Nara was said to have had as many as 50 pagodas. The grandest of the Buddhist temples built in this era was Tōdai-ji, which Emperor Shōmu intended to serve as a central monastery for all other provincial monasteries. The emperor, who saw much to emulate in Chinese culture, also hoped that religion could help to consolidate Japan and established Tōdai-ji not only for spiritual purposes but as a symbol of a united Japan.

In 784 Kyōto became Japan's capital, and Nara lost its status as a city of political consequence. The move proved beneficial for Nara's many venerable buildings and temples, however, which remained essentially untouched by the ravages of civil wars that later damaged Kyōto. Of the surviving temples, Kōfuku-ji recalls the power of the Fujiwara clan in the 7th century. Its close connection with Kasuga Taisha, the Fujiwara family shrine, exemplifies the peaceful coexistence of Buddhism and Shintoism. And, both Tōdai-ji and Tōshōdai-ji demonstrate how pervasively and consistently Buddhism has influenced Japanese life.

Nara Glossary

Key Japanese words and suffixes in this chapter include -*chō* (street or block), -*den* (temple hall), -*dō* (temple), *dōri* (avenue), *eki* (train station), -*gū* (shrine), *ike* ("*ee*-keh," pond), -*in* ("*een,*" temple), *izakaya* (pub), -*ji* (temple), -*kan* (museum hall), -*ken* (prefecture), *kōen* ("*ko*-en," park), *machi* (town), -*mon* (gate), *sakura* (cherry blossoms), -*san* (mountain), and *torii* ("*to*-ree-ee," gate).

Pleasures and Pastimes

Architecture

Nara's temples and shrines are among the oldest wooden structures in the world—unlike the replicas found elsewhere in Japan. Paradoxically, the large concentration of old buildings here is somewhat due to their neglect as the city's sociopolitical importance diminished. Crafted in the Chinese style when Buddhism was first imported to Japan, they're a snapshot of old Japan that represents the spirit of newly born imperial and religious institutions.

Dining

Like Kyōto, Nara's specialty is *kaiseki,* a carefully prepared and aesthetically arranged 7- to 12-course set meal using the freshest ingredients. Simpler set meals might include tempura and *soba* (buckwheat noodles). One popular local dish, *cha-gayu,* rice porridge flavored with green tea and served with seasonal vegetables, is known for its healthfulness. Both local wisdom—which attributes Nara's low rate of stomach cancer to cha-gayu—and Western doctors have acknowledged its benefits. Often with traditional meals you'll be served *nara-zuke*, tangy vegetables pickled in sake, as a side dish.

It's a mistake to visit Nara without experiencing an elegant Japanese meal in a traditional kaiseki restaurant—even if you're just here for the day. The thoughtfully prepared food here is remarkably good. If you don't have time for dinner, at least have a leisurely lunch.

Traditional restaurants are often small and tend to have limited menus with set courses only (though this does make ordering simple—choose the meal you want and allow yourself to be regaled), so it's a good idea to make reservations. Also, restaurants tend to close early; plan accordingly. Because some places don't have English-speaking staff or English menus, ask someone from your hotel to help make your arrangements. Alternatively, and much simpler, consider staying in a *ryokan* (traditional inn), where a kaiseki dinner is included in the room rate.

Small restaurants and izakaya are dispersed throughout the maze of streets that make up Nara-machi. Unless you know a few words of Japanese, you may need to point to an appetizing dish that another diner is enjoying. Remember that each time you point it may be interpreted as placing an order and add ¥500–¥800 to your bill. Expect to pay about ¥750 for a large bottle of beer.

For more on Japanese cuisine, *see* Chapter 14 *and* Dining *in* Smart Travel Tips A to Z.

CATEGORY	COST*
$$$$	over ¥7,000
$$$	¥5,000–¥7,000
$$	¥3,500–¥5,000
$	under ¥3,500

*per person for a main course at dinner

Lodging

Nara has accommodations in every style and price range, and because most people treat the city as a day-trip destination, at night the quiet streets are the domain of Nara's residents. If you stay over, you'll have a chance to stroll undisturbed beside the ponds and on temple grounds. Baths are communal unless noted otherwise.

For a short course on accommodations in Japan, *see* Lodging *in* Smart Travel Tips A to Z.

CATEGORY	COST*
$$$$	over ¥30,000
$$$	¥20,000–¥30,000
$$	¥10,000–¥20,000
$	under ¥10,000

*All prices are for a double room, excluding tax and service.

Shopping

Alongside the merchants' houses and traditional restaurants of Nara-machi's narrow backstreets, just south of Sarusawa-ike, old wooden shops sell the crafts for which Nara is famous: *fude* (*foo*-deh, hand-made brushes) and *sumi* (ink sticks) for calligraphy and ink painting, Nara dolls carved in wood, and Nara *sarashi-jofu*—fine handwoven, sun-bleached linen.

EXPLORING NARA

In the 8th century Nara was planned as a rectangular city with checkerboard streets, modeled after the Chinese city of Ch'ang-an. Its well-organized layout has endured, and today Nara is still extremely easy to navigate. Central sights are within walking distance of picturesque Nara Kōen. Other major temples in western Nara, such as Hōryū-ji, Yakushi-ji, and Tōshōdai-ji, are all on one bus route.

Great Itineraries

Many visitors try to see Nara in one day, but you simply cannot do justice to all of its temples and shrines this way. It's best to allow yourself two days here—one for central Nara and another for western Nara. If you have just a day, start with the sights around Nara Kōen, such as Tōdai-ji and its Daibutsu-den, Kōfuku-ji with its five-story pagoda, and Kasuga Taisha. Leave the afternoon to see western Nara's Hōryū-ji, the oldest remaining temple complex in all of Japan, and possibly Yakushi-ji or Tōshōdai-ji.

When to Tour Nara

As in most of Japan, spring is ideal, especially during sakura time. Springtime also draws hordes of Japanese tourists, so accommodations should be reserved in advance, especially on weekends. Winter can be chilly, but you may be blessed with a crisp, clear sky. Summer is invariably hot and humid. Autumn, like spring, has the best temperature for walking from sight to sight while gazing at the colors of the fall foliage.

Numbers in the text correspond to numbers in the margin and on the Central Nara and Western Nara Temples maps.

Central Nara

Much of what you'll come to Nara to see will be in the central part of the city, such as the temples and Great Buddha in Nara Kōen and the historical backstreets of Nara-machi.

A Good Walk

Begin exploring at the resplendent **Tōdai-ji** ①, in Nara Kōen. To get here, board Bus 2 from the front of either JR or Kintetsu Nara Eki; get off at Daibutsu-den. Cross the street to reach the path that leads to the Tōdai-ji complex. You can also walk from Kintetsu Nara Eki to Tōdai-ji in about 15 minutes. To do this, walk east from the station on Noboriōji-dōri, the avenue that runs parallel to the station. In Nara Kōen turn left onto the pedestrians-only street, lined with souvenir stalls and small restaurants, that leads to Tōdai-ji. You can also walk from JR Eki along Sanjo-dōri and turn left up Yasuragi-no-michi to Noboriōji-dōri. From here you can walk east as from Kintetsu Nara Eki, but the route is longer and passes through the less attractive modern sections of town.

As you walk along the path leading to the temple complex, you'll pass through the impressive dark wooden front gate known as **Nandai-mon** ②, which is supported by 18 large wooden pillars.

Continue straight to the main buildings of the Tōdai-ji temple complex. The Daibutsu-den entrance is in front of you, but first you may wish to visit the small temple on the left, **Kaidan-in** ③, guarded by four ferocious-looking statues. From Kaidan-in, return to the **Daibutsu-den** ④, purportedly the largest wooden structure in the world. The Daibutsu, Nara's famous statue of Buddha, is inside.

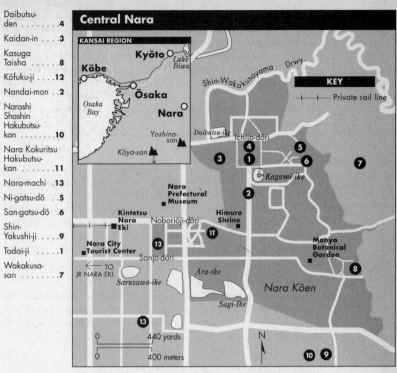

As you exit the Daibutsu-den, turn left and walk up the winding path to the left of the torii. Turn right, ascend the stone staircase, and then veer left on the slope lined with stone lanterns. On your left, on top of the slope, you will come to the **Ni-gatsu-dō** ⑤, which has expansive views of Nara Kōen. Return along the same incline that led to Ni-gatsu-dō and turn left. The wooden structure on your left is **San-gatsu-dō** ⑥, the oldest Tōdai-ji building. The entrance is on the right side as you face the building.

From the entrance of San-gatsu-dō, walk straight ahead, toward **Wakakusa-san** ⑦. On the left is the base of the mountain. Because there are so few areas in which to eat in Nara Kōen, this street is a good place to take a break.

If you continue south past all the restaurants and shops, at the end of the street you'll see stone steps. Descend these and cross a small bridge over a stream; then walk for about 10 minutes along the path that leads into shady and peaceful woods. At its end, turn left up the staircase, to **Kasuga Taisha** ⑧, at the top.

Leaving Kasuga Taisha, walk south down the path lined with stone lanterns past the Kasuga-Wakamiya Shrine. Continue on this wooded path until you reach a paved road. Cross the road and take the first right onto a residential street with many traditional Japanese houses. Take the first left and follow it south about 300 ft, until it curves to the right and leads you directly to **Shin-Yakushi-ji** ⑨, founded in 747. Of the many original buildings that once stood here, only the Main Hall remains. For a glimpse of seldom-visited rural Japan through photographs, head for the **Narashi Shashin Bijutsukan** ⑩, a modern structure discreetly hidden under a traditional tiled roof. As you leave the temple, the museum is to your immediate right.

From the museum retrace your steps past Shin-Yakushi-ji to the residential street you walked down earlier. Turn left onto this street and walk to the major intersection at the end of it. Across the street you will see a bus stop, where you can board Bus 1 back to the Daibutsu-den stop. Or if you've got a second wind, visit **Nara Kokuritsu Hakubutsukan** ⑪ via Bus 1 and the Kokuritsu Hakubutsukan stop, in front of the museum. Leaving the west exit of the east wing of the museum, walk west along the path for about five minutes to the **Kōfuku-ji** ⑫ complex, which once contained 175 buildings; fewer than a dozen remain. The most eye-catching structure is the Five-Story Pagoda. There are good restaurants within minutes of the Kōfuku-ji Pagoda complex.

Before continuing to western Nara and Hōryū-ji, take some time out from temple viewing to walk through the old neighborhood of **Nara-machi** ⑬, just south of Sarusawa-ike. This section of Nara has retained many of its traditional houses and shops, some of which have been selling the same arts and crafts for centuries. Maps to the area are available from the city's tourist information centers and the Shiryōkan. A signboard map on the southwest edge of Sarusawa-ike shows the way to all the important shops, museums, and galleries.

TIMING

To appreciate Nara's relaxed atmosphere and unhurried pace don't try to see everything. Instead, choose six or seven religious sights to visit over the course of a morning, have lunch around Wakakusa-san or in Nara-machi, and visit Nara-machi in the afternoon.

Sights to See

TŌDAI-JI TEMPLE COMPLEX

The temple complex of Tōdai-ji was conceived by Emperor Shōmu in the 8th century as the seat of authority for Buddhist Japan. The impact of Tōdai-ji is in its many structures, among which the ☞ Daibutsu-den is the most grand, with its huge beams that seem to converge somewhere in infinity just beyond the mind's eye.

★ ❹ **Daibutsu-den** (Hall of the Great Buddha). This white, elegant, austere building, its wooden beams darkened with age, is an impressive sight. A pair of gilt ornaments decorate the roof ridge. These are called *kutsu-gata* (shoe-shape) because they resemble footwear and were once believed to ward off fire. Unfortunately, they didn't prevent the original building from burning. The current Daibutsu-den was restored in 1709 at two-thirds its original scale. At 157 ft tall and 187 ft long, it's still considered the largest wooden structure in the world.

Inside Daibutsu-den is the **Daibutsu**, a 53-ft bronze statue of Buddha that is perhaps the most famous sight in Nara. The Daibutsu was originally commissioned by Emperor Shōmu in 743. After numerous unsuccessful castings, this figure was finally made in 749. A statue of this scale had never before been cast in Japan, and it was hoped that it would serve as a symbol to unite the country. The Daibutsu was dedicated in 752 in a grand ceremony attended by then-retired Emperor Shōmu, the imperial court members, and 10,000 priests and nuns.

Behind the Daibutsu to the right, look for a large wooden pillar with a hole at its base. You'll see many Japanese visitors attempting to crawl through the opening, which is barely large enough for a child. Local tradition has it that those who pass through the opening will find their way to an afterlife paradise. Children in particular love darting in and out and watching adults suffer the indignity of barely squeezing through. Behind the Daibutsu, to the left, is a model of the original Tōdai-ji. 🎟 *¥400.* ☉ *Jan.–Feb. and Nov.–Dec., daily 8–4:30; Mar., daily 8–5; Apr.–Sept., daily 7:30–5:30; Oct., daily 7:30–5.*

❸ **Kaidan-in.** Inside this small temple are clay statues of the Four Heavenly Guardians, depicted in full armor, wielding weapons and displaying fierce expressions. *Kaidan* is a Buddhist word for the terrace on which priests are ordained; the Chinese Buddhist Ganjin (688–763) administered many induction ceremonies of Japanese Buddhists here. The original temple was destroyed repeatedly by fire; the current structure dates to 1731. Kaidan-in is in northwestern Nara Kōen, west of Daibutsuden. ▦ ¥400. ☉ *Apr.–Oct., daily 8–5; Nov.–Mar., daily 8–4:30.*

❷ **Nandai-mon** (Great Southern Gate). The impressive Tōdai-ji Gate is supported by 18 large wooden pillars, each 62 ft high and nearly 3⅓ ft in diameter. The original gate was destroyed in a typhoon in 962 and rebuilt in 1199. Two outer niches on either side of the gate contain wooden figures of Deva kings, who guard the great Buddha within. They are the work of master sculptor Unkei, of the Kamakura period (1185–1335). In the inner niches are a pair of stone *koma-inu* (Korean dogs), mythical guardians that ward off evil. Nandai-mon stands over the path to the Tōdai-ji complex.

❺ **Ni-gatsu-dō** (Second Month Temple). Named for the religious ritual that used to be performed here each February, Ni-gatsu-dō was founded in 752. It houses some important images of the Buddha that are, alas, not on display to the public. Still, its hilltop location and veranda afford a breathtaking view of Nara Kōen. ▦ *Free.* ☉ *Daily 8–5:30.*

❻ **San-gatsu-dō** (Third Month Temple). Founded in 733, this temple, which takes its name from a March ritual, is the oldest original building in the Tōdai-ji complex. As you enter, to your left are some benches covered with tatami mats, where you can sit and contemplate the 1,200-year-old National Treasures that crowd the small room. The principal image is the lacquer statue of Fukūkenjaku Kannon, the goddess of mercy, whose diadem is encrusted with thousands of pearls and gemstones. The two clay *bosatsu* (bodhisattvas) statues on either side of her, the Gakkō (Moonlight) and the Nikkō (Sunlight), are considered fine examples of the Nara (or Tenpyo) period, the height of classic Japanese sculpture. ▦ ¥400. ☉ *Jan.–Feb. and Nov.–Dec., daily 8–4:30; Mar., daily 8–5; Apr.–Sept., daily 7:30–5:30; Oct., daily 7:30–5.*

★ ❶ **Tōdai-ji.** It's hard to say which is the most magnificent Buddhist temple in Nara, but resplendent Tōdai-ji in Nara Kōen is certainly a contender. It was completed in 752, and even though the imperial household later left Nara, Tōdai-ji remained the symbol of Buddhist authority. An earthquake damaged it in 855, and in 1180 the temple was burned to the ground. Its reconstruction met a similar fate during the 16th-century civil wars. A century later only the central buildings were rebuilt; these are what remain today.

To reach the Tōdai-ji complex, board Bus 2, which departs from in front of the JR and Kintetsu stations, and get off at the Daibutsu-den. Across the street is the path that leads to the complex. You can also walk from Kintetsu Nara Eki to Tōdai-ji in about 15 minutes. Exit the station and walk east along Noborioji-dōri into Nara Kōen. At the next large intersection turn left onto the pedestrians-only street, lined with souvenir stalls and small restaurants, that leads to Tōdai-ji. The walk from the JR station takes about 20 minutes on Sanjo-dōri. Once in Nara Kōen, take the same pedestrian-only street to Tōdai-ji.

ELSEWHERE IN NARA KŌEN

★ ❽ **Kasuga Taisha.** Kasuga is famous for the more than 2,000 stone lanterns that line the major pathways that lead to it, all of which are lighted three times a year on special festival days (February 2 and August 14–15). Kasuga was founded in 768 as a tutelary shrine for the

Fujiwaras, a prominent feudal family. For centuries, according to Shintō custom, the shrine was reconstructed every 20 years on its original design. Many Shintō shrines, like the famous Ise Jingū in Mie Prefecture, are rebuilt in this way, not merely to renew the materials but also to purify the site. It's said that Kasuga Taisha has been rebuilt more than 50 times; its current incarnation dates to 1893. After you pass through the torii, the first wooden structure you'll see is the **Hai-den** (Offering Hall); to its left is the **Naorai-den** (Entertainment Hall). To the left of Naorai-den are the four **Hon-den** (Main Shrines). They are designated as National Treasures, all built in the same Kasuga style and painted vermilion and green—a striking contrast to the dark wooden exterior of most other Nara temples.

To get to Kasuga Taisha, walk east on Sanjo-dōri, Nara's main street. You'll find the shrine just past the Manyo Botanical Garden, at the western end of Nara Kōen. *Kasuga Shrine Museum ¥420, shrine's outer courtyard free, inner precincts with 4 Hon-den structures and gardens ¥500. ☉ Museum daily 9–4; inner precincts Apr.–Oct., daily 9–5; Nov.–Mar., daily 9–4:30.*

⑫ Kōfuku-ji (Happiness-Producing Temple). This Buddhist temple was originally founded in 669 in Kyōto by the Fujiwara family. After Nara became the capital, Kōfuku-ji was moved to its current location in 710. It was an important temple encompassing 175 buildings, of which fewer than a dozen remain. The history of Kōfuku-ji reflects the intense relationship between Buddhism and Shintoism in Japan. In 937 a Kōfuku-ji monk had a dream in which the Shintō deity Kasuga appeared in the form of a Buddha, asking to become a protector of the temple. In 947 a number of Kōfuku-ji monks held a Buddhist ceremony at the Shinto Kasuga Taisha to mark the merging of the Buddhist temple with the Shinto shrine.

Of the many buildings in this temple complex, perhaps the most interesting is the **Kokuhōkan** (National Treasure House). Ironically, the unattractive, modern concrete building has a fabulous collection of National Treasure sculpture and other works of art from the Nara period.

Kōfuku-ji also has two magnificent pagodas. The **Five-Story Pagoda,** at 164 ft, is the second tallest in Japan. The original pagoda here was built in 730 by Empress Kōmyō. It and several succeeding pagodas were destroyed by fire, but the current 1426 pagoda is an exact replica of the original. The **Three-Story Pagoda** was built in 1114 and is renowned for its graceful lines and fine proportions.

Kōfuku-ji is a five-minute walk west of Nara Kokuritsu Hakubutsukan in the central part of Nara Kōen, and it is an easy 15-minute walk from the JR or Kintetsu station. *Great Eastern Hall ¥300, National Treasure House ¥500. ☉ Daily 9–5.*

★ Nara Kōen. It's a singular pleasure to wander around this lush green park and its ponds as you stroll from temple to temple. Nara Kōen is inhabited by some 1,000 tame, if at times aggressive, deer, which roam freely around the various temples and shrines. They are considered to be divine messengers and are particularly friendly when you feed them deer crackers, which you can buy at stalls in the park.

⑪ Nara Kokuritsu Hakubutsukan (Nara National Museum). The East Wing, built in 1973, has many examples of calligraphy, paintings, and sculpture. The West Wing, built in 1895, displays objects of archaeological interest. During the driest days of November, the Shōsō-in Repository (closed to the public), behind the Tōdai-ji, displays some of its magnificent collection here. ✉ *10–6 Noborioji-chō,* ☎ *0742/22–*

7771. 🖾 ¥420. ⊘ *Apr.–Nov., Tues.–Thurs. and weekends 9–4:30, Fri. 9–8; Dec.–Mar., Tues.–Sun. 9–4:30 (enter by 4).*

OTHER CENTRAL NARA SIGHTS

⑬ Nara-machi. This neighborhood is a maze of narrow residential streets lined with traditional houses and old shops, many of which deal in Nara's renowned arts and crafts. Whether you go on foot or by bicycle, Nara-machi can offer a change of pace from ordinary sightseeing, and local residents are willing to point you in the right direction.

For the best of local goods, you'll want to visit **"Yu" Nakagawa** (☎ 0742/22–1322), which specializes in handwoven, sun-bleached linen textiles, a Nara specialty known as *sarashi-jofu.* For 400 years **Kobaien** (☎ 0742/23–2965) has made fine ink sticks for calligraphy and ink painting. From October to April make an appointment here to watch the actual production of the ink sticks. Visit the Silk Road folk-craft shop **Kikuoka** (☎ 0742/26–3889), near Nara-machi Shiryōkan. Gango-ji temple is Nara-machi's focal point, and near it is the little museum known as **Nara-machi Shiryōkan** (Historical Library) with Buddhist statuary and other artwork.

Nara-machi is just south of Sarusawa-ike. Maps to the area are available at the city's tourist information centers and at the Shiryōkan: a signboard map on the southwest edge of Sarusawa-ike shows the way to all the important shops, museums, and galleries. Coming from the JR station, walk up to the top of the main street and turn right.

⑩ Narashi Shashin Bijutsukan (Nara City Museum of Photography). Through the evocative postwar photography of Irie Taikichi, who documented the people and ways of the rural, pre-industrial Yamato area around Nara, you'll experience a way of life that has all but vanished from contemporary Japan. Other exhibits, usually related to Nara's history and culture, are regularly on display in the underground exhibition space. The museum is just west of Shin-Yakushi-ji. ⊠ 600–1 Takabatake-chō, ☎ 0742/22–9811. 🖾 ¥500. ⊘ *Daily 9:30–5 (last entry at 4:30).*

⑨ Shin-Yakushi-ji. This temple was founded in 747 by Empress Kōmyō (701–760) as a prayer requesting the recovery of her sick husband, Emperor Shōmu. Most of the temple buildings were destroyed over the years; only the Main Hall, which houses many fine objects of the Nara period, still exists. In the center of the hall is a wood statue of Yakushi Nyorai, the Physician of the Soul. Surrounding this statue are 12 clay images of the Twelve Divine Generals who protected Yakushi. Eleven of these figures are originals. The generals stand in threatening poses, bearing spears, swords, and other weapons, and display terrifying expressions. ⊠ 1289 Takabatake-chō. 🖾 ¥500. ⊘ *Daily 9–5.*

❼ Wakakusa-san. Each January 15, 15 priests set Wakakusa-san's dry grass afire, and the blazes that engulf the hill create a grand spectacle. The rest of the year, the street at the base of Wakakusa-san is a good place to have a cup of coffee, a snack, or even lunch when you are visiting the sights of Nara Kōen. The restaurants facing the hill serve standard lunch sets and noodle dishes.

From San-gatsu-dō in the Tōdai-ji complex, walk south, passing Tamukeyama-hachimangu Shrine, to get to Wakakusa-san.

Western Nara

Of the four major temples on the western outskirts of Nara, Hōryū-ji is the most famous. It should be one of the places you visit if you have just one day in Nara. If you're in Nara for two days, you may want to spend the second day in western Nara.

A Good Tour

It's easy to get to the four major temples on the outskirts of Nara from JR Nara Eki or Kintetsu Nara Eki. Bus 52 stops at Tōshōdai-ji, Yakushi-ji, Hōryū-ji, and Chūgū-ji, returning along the same route. It takes 50 minutes and costs ¥760. If you're only going to Hōryū-ji, it's quicker and more pleasant to take the JR train on the Kansai Main Line to Hōryū-ji Eki (¥210); from here the temple is a short shuttle-bus ride or a 15-minute walk. **Hōryū-ji** ⑭ is the most remarkable temple in western Nara, and its complex contains buildings that are among the oldest wooden structures in the world.

A path of carefully raked pebbles behind Hōryū-ji's eastern precinct leads to the quiet nunnery of **Chūgū-ji** ⑮, home to a graceful statue of Buddha that dates from the Asuka period (552–645). If you are pressed for time, you might want to skip this temple.

Get back on Bus 52 in the direction from which you came and get off at Yakushi-ji-mae. **Yakushi-ji** ⑯ was founded in 680 and moved to its current location in 718. As you enter the temple grounds, on your right you'll see the East Pagoda, which dates to 1285. The West Tower, to your left, was built in 1981. The new vermilion building in the center is Yakushi-ji's Kon-dō.

From the back gate of Yakushi-ji it's a 10-minute walk to the 8th-century temple **Tōshōdai-ji** ⑰ down the "Path of History," lined with clay-wall houses, gardens, restaurants, and small shops selling antiques, crafts, and nara-zuke. You'll pass through the Nandai-mon to enter the temple complex. The first building, an excellent example of Nara architecture, is the Kon-dō. Outside, and behind the Kon-dō, is Tōshōdai-ji's Daikō-dō, once the Nara Imperial Court's assembly hall. When you leave Tōshōdai-ji, you can take Bus 63 back to Kintetsu Nara Eki or JR Nara Eki; the bus stop is in front of the temple.

TIMING

At a leisurely pace, you can visit one or two temples in an afternoon—Hōryū-ji should be one of them—but a day's exploration of western Nara's sights is warranted to see some of Japan's finest religious architecture.

Sights to See

⑮ **Chūgū-ji.** Chūgū-ji was originally the home of Prince Shōtoku's mother in the 6th century. When she died, it became a temple dedicated to her memory. Today this quiet nunnery houses a graceful wooden image of the Miroku Bodhisattva, the Buddha of the Future. The statue dates from the Asuka period (552–645), and its gentle countenance has made it famous as an ageless view of hope. Also of interest here is the oldest example of embroidery in Japan, which also dates from the Asuka period. The framed cloth depicts Tenjukoku (Land of Heavenly Longevity). In front of the temple is a small, carefully tended pond with a rock garden emerging from just below the surface.

From the JR or Kintetsu station, take Bus 52, which stops at all the Western temples. From Hōryū-ji, the path at the rear of the temple's eastern precinct takes you to Chūgū-ji. ✉ ¥400. ☉ Daily 9–4:30 (9–4 Oct.–Mar.).

★ ⑭ **Hōryū-ji.** This is the most captivating of the temples in western Nara. Hōryū-ji was founded in 607 by Prince Shōtoku (573–621), and its original wooden buildings are among the world's most ancient. The first gate you pass through at Hōryū-ji is **Nandai-mon**, which was rebuilt

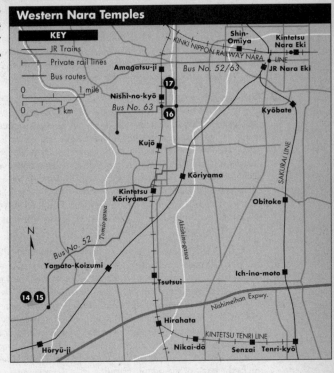

Western Nara Temples

KEY
— JR Trains
— Private rail lines
— Bus routes

0   1 mile
0   1 km

in 1438 and is therefore a young 500 years old. Remarkably, the second gate, **Chū-mon** (Middle Gate), is the 607 original—almost 1,400 years old. Unlike most other Japanese gates, which are supported by two pillars at the ends, this gate is supported by central pillars. Note their unusual entastic (curved outward in the center) shape, which is an architectural technique used in ancient Greece that traveled as far as Japan. Entastic pillars in Japan exist only in the 7th-century structures of Nara.

After passing through the gates, you enter the temple's western precincts. The first building on the right is the **Kon-dō** (Main Hall), a two-story reproduction of the original 7th-century hall, which displays Buddhist images and objects dating from as far back as the Asuka period (552–645). The five-story pagoda to its left was disassembled in World War II to protect it from air raids, after which it was reconstructed in its original form, with the same materials used in 607. Behind the pagoda is the **Daikō-dō** (Lecture Hall), destroyed by fire and rebuilt in 990. Inside is a statue of Yakushi Nyorai (Physician of the Soul) carved from a camphor tree.

From the Daikō-dō, walk back past the Kon-dō and Chū-mon; then turn left and walk past the pond on your right. You'll come to two concrete buildings known as the **Daihōzō-den** (Great Treasure Hall), which display statues, sculptures, ancient Buddhist religious articles, and brocades. Of particular interest is a miniature shrine that belonged to Lady Tachibana, mother of Empress Kōmyō. The shrine is about 2½ ft tall; the Buddha inside is about 20 inches tall.

Tōdai-mon (Great East Gate) opens onto Hōryū-ji's eastern grounds. The octagonal **Yumedono** (Hall of Dreams) was so named because Prince Shōtoku used to meditate in it.

To get here, take a JR Kansai Main Line train to Hōryū-ji Eki (¥210). The temple is a short shuttle ride or a 15-minute walk. Alternatively, Bus 52 to Hōryū-ji is a 50-minute ride from the JR Nara Eki and Kintetsu Nara Eki (¥760). The Hōryūji-mae bus stop is in front of the temple. 🔳 ¥1,000. ⊙ Feb. 23–Nov. 3, daily 8–5; Nov. 4–Feb. 22, daily 8–4:30 (last entry 1 hr before closing).

⑰ Tōshōdai-ji. The main entrance to this temple is brazenly called the "Path of History," since in Nara's imperial days dignitaries and priests trod this route; today it's lined with clay-wall houses, gardens, and small shops selling antiques, crafts, and nara-zuke, a popular local specialty. There are also several good restaurants here, such as Van Kio. Tōshōdai-ji was built in 751 for Ganjin, a Chinese priest who traveled to Japan at the invitation of Emperor Shōmu. At this time, Japanese priests had never received formal instruction from a Buddhist priest. The invitation was extended by two Japanese priests who had traveled to China in search of a Buddhist willing to undertake the arduous and perilous journey to Japan.

On Ganjin's first journey, some of his disciples betrayed him. His second journey resulted in a shipwreck. During the third trip his ship was blown off course, and on his fourth trip he was refused permission to leave China by government officials. Before his next attempt, he contracted an eye disease that left him blind. He persevered, nevertheless, and finally reached Japan in 750. Ganjin shared his knowledge of Buddhism with his adopted country and served as a teacher to many Japanese priests as well as Emperor Shōmu. He is also remembered for bringing the first sampling of sugar to Japan. Every June 6, the **Miei-dō**, in the back of the temple grounds, displays a lacquer statue of Ganjin that dates from 763 to commemorate his birthday.

The temple's entrance, the **Nandai-mon** (Great South Gate), is supported by entastic pillars like those in the Chū-mon of Hōryū-ji. Beyond Nandai-mon, the **Kon-dō** (Main Hall) is a superb example of classic Nara architecture. Inside the hall is a lacquer statue of Vairocana Buddha, the same incarnation of Buddha that's enshrined at Tōdai-ji. The halo surrounding him was originally covered with 1,000 Buddhas—only 864 remain. In back of the Kon-dō sits the **Daikō-dō** (Lecture Hall), formerly an assembly hall of the Nara Imperial Court. It's the only remaining example of Nara palace architecture.

Tōshōdai-ji is a 10-minute walk from the rear gate of Yakushi-ji along the Path of History. From central Nara or Hōryū-ji take Bus 52 to the stop in front of Tōshōdai-ji. 🔳 ¥600. ⊙ Daily 8:30–5.

★ ⑯ Yakushi-ji. Officially named one of the Seven Great Temples of Nara, Yakushi-ji was founded in 680 and moved to its current location in 718. Yakushi-ji's **East Pagoda** dates from 1285 and has such an interesting asymmetrical shape that it inspired Boston Museum of Fine Arts curator Ernest Fenollosa (1853–1908), an early Western specialist in Japanese art, to remark that it was as beautiful as "frozen music." Although it appears to have six stories, in fact it has only three—three roofs with smaller ones attached underneath. The **West Tower** was built in 1981, and the central **Kon-dō** (Main Hall) was rebuilt in 1976 and painted a garish vermilion. These newer buildings are not nearly as attractive as the older structures, and they look out of place in the otherwise appealing temple complex. However, they do house important works of Buddhist art dating as far back as the 8th century.

From central Nara take either the Kintetsu Line train, changing at Saidaiji to Nishinokyo, or Bus 52 to Yakushi-ji; from Hōryū-ji or Chūgū-ji, take Bus 52 back to Yakushi-ji-mae. 🔳 ¥500. ⊙ Daily 8:30–5.

DINING

$$$$
★
✕ **Onjaku.** Hidden down a quiet street just south of Ara-ike in Nara Kōen is this intimate restaurant serving exquisitely presented traditional kaiseki meals. Inside the faded wooden exterior walls, a common architectural motif in Nara, you can sit at a rustic counter or in one of two serene tatami rooms. Choose from one of the two set meals on offer. This is definitely a place to linger and be spoiled. ⊠ *1043 Kita-temma-chō,* ☎ *0742/26–4762. Reservations essential. No credit cards. Closed Sun.*

$$$$
★
✕ **Tsukihitei.** Deep in the forest behind Kasuga Taisha, Tsukihitei is the perfect setting for kaiseki. From the walk up a wooded path to the tranquility of your own tatami room, everything is conducive to experiencing the beautiful presentation and delicate flavors. When reserving a table, enlist the help of a good Japanese-speaker to select a set meal for you as well, and then allow yourself to be regaled. The lunch sets run from ¥10,000 to ¥15,000. ⊠ *158 Kasugano-chō,* ☎ *0742/26–2021. Reservations essential. DC, V.*

$$$$
★
✕ **Uma no Me.** In a little 1920s farmhouse just south of Nara Kōen, this delightful restaurant with dark beams and pottery-lined walls serves delicious home-style cooking. Everything is prepared from scratch in the time-honored way. Highly recommended is the ¥3,500 lunch course with seasonal vegetables, melt-in-your-mouth tofu, and succulent fried fish. As there is only one set meal, ordering is no problem. ⊠ *1158 Takabatake-chō,* ☎ *0742/23–7784. No credit cards. Closed Thurs.*

$$$–$$$$
✕ **Bek-kan Kikusuiro.** Bek-kan Kikusuiro serves what it calls "mini kaiseki," an abridged version with fewer courses, as well as full kaiseki courses all day. The reasonably priced lunch courses start at ¥3,500. Intricately prepared dishes are brought to you in the large, graceful dining room overlooking a garden or in a private room with tatami mats. The sister restaurant next door, **Kikusuiro** (☎ 0742/23–2001), serves French cuisine. ⊠ *1130 Takabatake-chō,* ☎ *0742/23–2001. DC, MC, V.*

$$–$$$$
✕ **To-no-chaya.** One of Nara's most distinctive meals is cha-gayu, green tea–flavored rice porridge. During the day To-no-chaya serves a light meal of this special dish, with sashimi and vegetables, plus a few sweetened rice cakes for dessert. The restaurant was named To-no-chaya, which means "tearoom of the pagoda," because you can see the Five-Story Pagoda of Kōfuku-ji from here. Bento-box meals are served 11:30–4. You must reserve ahead for cha-gayu. ⊠ *47 Noboriōji-chō,* ☎ *0742/22–4348. No credit cards. Closed Wed. No dinner.*

$$–$$$$
✕ **Van Kio.** This large, well-established restaurant, just south of Yakushi-ji's south gate, is famous for its *suien mushi* (hot-stone steam cuisine). Other specialties from the extensive menu (in English) include the *ta-matebako* set meal, in which chicken and vegetables are sealed in earthenware, baked, and then opened before you with some fanfare. From the sumptuous dining room you look out onto a garden where concerts occasionally take place. The restaurant stays open all day. ⊠ *410 Rokujo-chō,* ☎ *0742/33–8942. AE, MC, V. Closed Mon.*

$$$
★
✕ **Yanagi-cha-ya.** Though the building is unassuming from the outside, once you enter the revered old Yanagi-cha-ya you're transported to a bygone age. In a secluded tatami room overlooking a garden, you'll be served elegantly simple bento meals of sashimi, stewed vegetables, and tofu in black-lacquer boxes. Lunch runs ¥4,000–¥6,000. There are two branches: the original shop on the north bank of Sarusawa-ike and another just east of Kōfuku-ji. *Original:* ⊠ *49 Noboriōji-chō,* ☎ *0742/22–7460. Closed Wed. Newer branch:* ⊠ *48 Teraoji-chō,* ☎ *0742/22–7560. Closed Mon. Reservations essential. No credit cards.*

$–$$$ ✗ **Harishin.** Because this Nara-machi restaurant is traditional and quite rustic, you sit in either a large tatami room overlooking a garden or around a large *irori* (hearth). The Kamitsumichi bento, with a selection of sashimi, tofu, fried shrimp, vegetables, and homemade strawberry liqueur, is a bargain at ¥2,500. From the southwest corner of Sarusawa-ike, head south into Nara-machi. Harishin is on your right, shortly after crossing the main road. ✉ *15 Chushinya-chō,* ☎ *0742/22–2669. Reservations not accepted. DC, MC, V. Closed Mon.*

$–$$ ✗ **Tempura Asuka.** If you choose from the selection of set meals, make sure you pick one with tempura—the house specialty, of course. Other fare ranges from a light tempura-soba lunch to an elaborate kaiseki dinner. Lunch options start at only ¥1,000. As with other less formal Nara-machi restaurants, you can sit at the counter, at a table overlooking the garden, or in a tatami room. ✉ *11 Chonanin-chō,* ☎ *0742/26–4308. AE, DC, MC, V. Closed Mon.*

$ ✗ **Muku.** Housed in a former artisan's home full of antiques and pottery, this lunch-only restaurant is a delight. The daily lunch course (there is only one) consists of healthful home-style dishes with *genmai* (brown rice), tofu, and seasonal vegetables. At ¥1,000, it's an excellent value. Seating is at cozy tables on tatami mats. Walk south from the southwest corner of Sarusawa-ike into Nara-machi. Muku is the last building on your left before the first major road. It's open 1–6. ✉ *22-3 Chūin-chō,* ☎ *0742/25–5140. Reservations not accepted. No credit cards. No dinner.*

LODGING

$$$$ ⌂ **Edo-San.** Individual cottages, some thatched, make up this ryokan in the greenery of Nara Kōen. Deer may wander to your door from the park. A kaiseki dinner, served in your cottage, is included in the price. There is a communal bath. The one drawback is its proximity to a rather noisy, major road. ✉ *1167 Takabatake-chō, Nara-shi, Nara-ken 630-8103,* ☎ *0742/26–2662,* ℻ *0742/26–2663. 11 Japanese-style cottages. AE, DC, V.*

$$$$ ⌂ **Kankaso.** At once exquisitely refined and delightfully friendly, ★ Kankaso exemplifies the best of Japanese hospitality. Beautiful gardens surround this intimate ryokan near Tōdai-ji, and inside, carefully arranged flowers adorn the alcove. Each room is tastefully decorated with scrolls and pottery. Although the building has been renovated extensively over the centuries, a testament to its longevity is its 1,200-year-old central beam. The communal baths look out onto the gardens. A delicious kaiseki dinner is included, as is breakfast. ✉ *10 Kasuganochō, Nara-shi, Nara-ken 630-8212,* ☎ *0742/26–1128,* ℻ *0742/26–1301. 10 Japanese-style rooms. V.*

$$$$ ⌂ **Nara Kikusuiro.** It's understandable that this historic, grand old ryokan, just south of Kōfuku-ji, is often the choice of visiting royalty and dignitaries. Built in the Meiji era, the inn has rooms lavishly furnished with antiques; the gardens are immaculately kept with a stunning variety of plants and flowers. Service is thorough and attentive. Room rates, which start at ¥70,000, include a superb kaiseki dinner. In the morning you can choose either a Western or Japanese breakfast, also included in the price. ✉ *1130 Takabatake-chō, Nara-shi, Nara-ken 630-8301,* ☎ *0742/23–2001,* ℻ *0742/26–0025. 20 Japanese-style rooms. DC, MC, V.*

$$$ ⌂ **Hotel Fujita Nara.** Centrally situated between JR Nara Eki and Nara Kōen, this modern hotel has attractive rooms in light shades. Rates run ¥20,000–¥23,000 in peak season (April, October, and November) but drop considerably to ¥12,000–¥15,000 the rest of the year. The restaurant, Hanakagami, serves Japanese cuisine. ⊠ *47–1 Shimo Sanjo-chō, Nara-shi, Nara-ken 630-8236,* ☎ *0742/23–8111,* ⅎ *0742/22–0255. 115 rooms. Restaurant, bar, coffee shop. AE, DC, MC, V.*

$$$ ⊞ **Nara Hotel.** Overlooking several temples, this establishment is it-
★ self a site of historical and architectural interest. Built in 1909, it has a graceful tiled roof and a magnificent lobby with high wooden ceilings. It's no wonder the emperor and his family stay here when visiting Nara. Although most rooms have a good view of the temples, those in the new wing are not as interesting as the turn-of-the-20th-century-style rooms in the old wing. Dining is a special event in the superb, old-fashioned Edwardian-style room—mostly Japanese fare is served, and there are a few Western choices as well. ⊠ *1096 Takabatake-chō, Nara-shi, Nara-ken 630-8301,* ☎ *0742/26–3300,* ⅎ *0742/23–5252. 132 rooms. Restaurant, tea shop. AE, DC, MC, V.*

$$–$$$ ⊞ **Nara Garden Hotel.** As the name suggests, this inviting little hotel on a hillside above Tōdai-ji sits amid attractive gardens. Rooms are comfortable and simply decorated and look out onto the gardens. A French and Japanese restaurant here has a delightful terrace opening onto cherry trees. ⊠ *Wakakusa, Sanroku-chō, Nara-shi, Nara-ken 630-8212,* ☎ *0742/27–0555,* ⅎ *0742/27–0203. 21 rooms. Restaurant, coffee shop. AE, DC, MC, V.*

$$ ⊞ **Kotton Hyaku-pasento.** The name of this popular little family-run hotel is a play on words that means "100% old capital" rather than "100% cotton." It's in a good location just south of Nara Kōen, near Sarusawa-ike, and a short stroll from restaurants. A Western breakfast is included. ⊠ *1122–21 Bodaiji-chō, Nara-shi, Nara-ken 630-8301,* ☎ *0742/22–7117,* ⅎ *0742/22–0607. 14 rooms. MC, V.*

$$ ⊞ **Mitsui Garden Hotel.** Nara's largest hotel sets out to provide comfort at reasonable rates. Rooms are bright and cheerful, with large windows. Sitting atop a shopping arcade next to Nara JR Eki, it's convenient for sights and restaurants. The hotel has both private and public baths. ⊠ *8–1 Sanjohommachi, Nara-shi, Nara-ken 630-8122,* ☎ *0742/35–8831,* ⅎ *0742/35–6868. 330 rooms. AE, DC, MC, V.*

$$ ⊞ **Nara Washington Hotel Plaza.** The snug rooms in this central hotel, part of a nationwide chain, are simply decorated in pale shades. The beds are on the small side. ⊠ *31–1 Shimo Sanjo-chō, Nara-shi, Nara-ken 630-8236,* ☎ *0742/27–0410,* ⅎ *0742/27–0484. 204 rooms. Restaurant. AE, DC, MC, V.*

$$ ⊞ **Pension (Nara Club).** On a quiet street behind Tōdai-ji, this small family-run establishment is reminiscent of a European hotel. The plainly decorated rooms have simple, dark-wood furniture and private bathrooms. A meal plan is available. ⊠ *21 Kita Gomon-chō, Nara-shi, Nara-ken 630-8204,* ☎ *0742/22–3450,* ⅎ *0742/22–3490. 8 rooms. Restaurant. AE, V.*

$ ⊞ **Nara-machi Seikanso.** Of the many inexpensive, small ryokans in Nara-machi, this friendly, family-run establishment is the pick of the bunch for its spotlessness and attentive service at a good price. The quiet neighborhood contributes to the inn's relaxed atmosphere. Simple rooms overlook a large, central garden. It's very popular with international and domestic travelers, so it's best to book a room far in advance. ⊠ *29 Higashikitsuji-chō, Nara-shi, Nara-ken 630-8327,* ☎ *0742/22–2670,* ⅎ *0742/22–2670. 13 Japanese-style rooms. AE, MC, V.*

NARA A TO Z

To research prices, get advice from other travelers, and book travel arrangements, visit www.fodors.com.

AIRPORTS AND TRANSFERS

The nearest airports are in Ōsaka. All international and a few domestic flights use Kansai International Airport (KIX). Most domestic flights use Itami Airport. The hourly airport limousine bus from KIX takes 90 minutes and costs ¥1,800. From Itami, buses leave hourly, take 55 minutes, and cost ¥1,440.

BIKE TRAVEL

Because Nara is a small city with relatively flat roads, biking is a good way to get around. You can rent a bicycle from Kintetsu Sunflower. The cost is ¥900 for the day (until 5); on weekends it's ¥1,000. Ask the Nara City Tourist Information Office, in Kintetsu Nara Eki, for further information or directions. Some hotels also rent bicycles.
➤ BIKE RENTALS: **Kintetsu Sunflower** (⊠ on Konishi-dōri, near Kintetsu Nara Eki, ☎ 0742/24–3528).

BUS TRAVEL

The most economical way to explore Nara is by bus. Two local routes circle the main sites (Tōdai-ji, Kasuga Taisha, and Shin-Yakushi-ji) in the central and eastern parts of the city: Bus 1 runs counterclockwise, and Bus 2 runs clockwise. This urban loop line costs ¥180. Both stop at JR Nara Eki and Kintetsu Nara Eki. Bus 52 west to Hōryū-ji (with stops at Tōshōdai-ji and Yakushi-ji) takes about 50 minutes and costs ¥760; you can catch it in front of either station. Pick up a bus map at the Nara City Tourist Center.

EMBASSIES AND CONSULATES

The nearest U.S., U.K., and Canadian consulates are in Ōsaka; the nearest Australian and New Zealand embassies are in Tōkyō (☞ Embassies *in* Smart Travel Tips A to Z).

EMERGENCIES

➤ CONTACTS: **Ambulance** (☎ 119). **Nara National Hospital** (☎ 0742/24–1251). **Nara police station** (☎ 0742/35–1110). **Police** (☎ 110).

SIGHTSEEING GUIDES

The Student Guide Service and the YMCA Guide Service are free and depart from the JR Nara Eki information center and Kintetsu Nara Eki. Guides are friendly and helpful, though not always fluent in English. And because they're volunteers, it's best to call in advance to determine availability.
➤ CONTACTS: **Student Guide Service** (⊠ Sarusawa Tourist Information Center, 4 Nobori Oji-chō, north side of Sarusawa-ike, ☎ 0742/26–4753). **YMCA Guide Service** (⊠ Kasuga Taisha, ☎ 0742/44–2207).

TAXIS

The rate is ¥610 for the first 1½ km (1 mi) and ¥90 for each additional 1,300 ft. From Kintetsu Nara Eki to Kasuga Taisha it's about ¥900; to Hōryū-ji, about ¥5,000.

TOURS

The Japan Travel Bureau conducts daily tours of Nara in English. The five-hour (¥6,300) tour departs from Kyōto at 1:40. Reservations must be made one day in advance.

The Japan National Tourist Office (JNTO) publishes the leaflet "Walking Tour Courses in Nara," for a self-guided two-hour tour of Nara Kōen and several nearby temples and shrines; other tours start with a bus ride from the city center. There's no JNTO office in Nara; *see* Visitor Information *in* Smart Travel Tips A to Z for addresses elsewhere in Japan.

➤ CONTACT: **Japan Travel Bureau** (☎ 075/341–1413).

TRAIN TRAVEL

From Kyōto, the private Kintetsu Railway's Limited Express trains (¥1,110) leave every half hour for the 33-minute trip to Nara. Three JR trains from Kyōto run every hour. The express takes 45 minutes; the two locals take 70 minutes. All JR trains cost ¥740 without a JR Pass (☞ Train Travel in Smart Travel Tips A to Z).

From Ōsaka's Kintetsu Namba Eki, Nara is a 31-minute ride on a Limited Express (¥1,040). Trains leave every hour. Ordinary Express trains (¥540) leave every 20 minutes, and the trip takes 35 minutes. The JR Line from Tennō-ji Eki takes 50 minutes and costs ¥450; from JR Namba it costs ¥540 and takes 40 minutes; from Ōsaka Eki it takes one hour and costs ¥780.

From Kōbe, take the JR Tōkaidō Line rapid train from San-no-miya Eki to Ōsaka and transfer to one of the trains listed above.

Both JR Nara Eki and Kintetsu Nara Eki are close to major sights. Because these sights are concentrated in the western part of the city, you'll do much of your sightseeing on foot. One exception is Hōryū-ji, which is best accessed by a JR train from JR Nara Eki. The ride to Hōryū-ji Eki takes 11 minutes and costs ¥210.

VISITOR INFORMATION

The Nara City Tourist Information Office is on the first floor of Kintetsu Nara Eki and is open daily 9–5.

A city information window, open daily 9–5, can be found at JR Nara Eki—and its staff is always helpful.

Nara City Tourist Center is open daily 9–9, but the English-speaking staff is only on duty until 7 PM. The center is a 10-minute walk from both Kintetsu Nara Eki and JR Nara Eki and has free maps, sightseeing information in English, a souvenir corner, and a lounge where you can rest and plan your day.

Japan Travel Phone, a nationwide service for English-language assistance or travel information, is available seven days a week, 9–5. When using a yellow, blue, or green public phone (do not use red phones), insert a ¥10 coin, which will be returned.

➤ TOURIST INFORMATION: **City Information Window** (☎ 0742/22–9821). **Nara City Tourist Center** (✉ 23–4 Kami-sanjo-chō, Nara-shi, ☎ 0742/22–3900). **Nara City Tourist Information Office** (✉ Kintetsu Nara Eki, ☎ 0742/24–4858). **Japan Travel Phone** (☎ 0120/444–800).

7 ŌSAKA

Japan's second city in terms of industry, commerce, and technology—after Tōkyō, naturally—Ōsaka is known for its dynamic spirit, superb restaurants, and Bunraku puppet theater. It is not a window to Japan's past—go to Kyōto and Nara for that—but a storefront display of what moves the country today.

By Nigel Fisher

Updated
by Dominic
Al-Badri

OSAKA BEGAN EXPANDING as a trading center at the end of the 16th century. But until the Meiji Restoration, in 1868, the merchant class was at the bottom of the social hierarchy, even though plenty of merchants were among the richest people in Japan. Denied the usual aristocratic cultural pursuits, merchants sought and developed their pleasures in the theater and in dining. Indeed, it is often said that many a successful Ōsaka businessman has eventually gone bankrupt by spending too much on eating.

In the 4th and 5th centuries, the Ōsaka-Nara region was the center of the developing Japanese (Yamato) nation. It was through Ōsaka that knowledge and culture from mainland Asia filtered into the fledgling Japanese society. During the 5th and 6th centuries, several emperors maintained an imperial court in Ōsaka, but the city lost its political importance after a permanent capital was set up in Nara in 694.

For the next several hundred years, Ōsaka, then known as Naniwa, was just another backwater port on the Seto Nai-kai (Seto Inland Sea). At the end of the 16th century, Hideyoshi Toyotomi (1536–98), the great warrior and statesman, had one of Japan's most majestic castles built in Ōsaka following his successful unification of Japan. The castle took three years to complete. Hideyoshi encouraged merchants from around the country to set up their businesses in the city, which soon prospered.

After Hideyoshi died, Ieyasu Tokugawa usurped power from the Toyotomi clan in 1603. But the clan maintained Ōsaka as its base. In 1614 Ieyasu sent his troops from Kyōto to Ōsaka to oppose rebellious movements supporting the Toyotomis. Ieyasu's army defeated the Toyotomi clan and its followers and destroyed the castle in 1615. Even though the Tokugawa Shogunate eventually rebuilt the castle, Ōsaka once again found itself at a distance from Japan's political scene. Ōsaka's merchants, left to themselves far from the shōgun's administrative center in Edo—now Tōkyō—continued to prosper, and they channeled products from the hinterland to Kyōto and Edo.

During this time of economic growth, some of Japan's business dynasties were founded, whose names still reign today—Sumitomo, Marubeni, Sanwa, and Daiwa. Their growing wealth gave them the means to pursue culture, and by the end of the Genroku era (17th century), Ōsaka's residents were giving patronage to such literary giants as the dramatist Chikamatsu (1653–1724) and the novelist Saikaku Ihara (1642–93). Chikamatsu's genius as a playwright elevated Bunraku, traditional Japanese puppet drama, to a dignified dramatic art. Also at this time, Ōsaka merchants' patronage of comic Kabuki theater helped the form grow to maturity.

With the opening of Japan to Western commerce in 1853 and the end of the Tokugawa Shogunate in 1868, Ōsaka stepped into the forefront of Japan's commerce. At first Yokohama was the major port for Japan's foreign trade, but the Great Kantō Earthquake leveled it in 1923, and foreigners looked to Kōbe and Ōsaka as alternative gateways for their import and export businesses. Ōsaka's merchant heritage positioned it well for industrial growth—iron, steel, fabrics, ships, heavy and light machinery, and chemicals all became part of its output. As a result, the region accounts for 25% of Japan's industrial product and 40% of the nation's exports. Since the building of its harbor facilities, Ōsaka has become a major port in its own right, and it relies less on the facilities in Kōbe.

Anyone older than 65 in Japan remembers Ōsaka as an exotic maze of crisscrossing waterways that provided transportation for the booming merchant trade. All but a few of the canals and nearly all traditional wooden buildings were destroyed by the bombings of World War II. Architecturally, the city is leaping into the future with buildings like the Imperial Hotel on the banks of the Yodo-gawa and the dazzling Twin 21 Towers. At the moment, the city is working hard to restore some of the beauty that was lost, with a movement for the greening of Ōsaka running strong.

Ōsaka is still a merchant city, with many streets devoted to wholesale commerce. For example, medical and pharmaceutical companies congregate in Dosho-machi, and fireworks and toys are found in Matcha-machi-suji, which is also famous for shopping. Head to Umeda, Shin-Sai-bashi, or Namba for the greatest concentration of department stores, movie theaters, and restaurants. The city's nightlife is also legendary. Be sure to stroll through Dōtombori-dōri area, beside Dōtombori-gawa, which has more nightclubs and bars per square foot than any other part of town. Although Ōsaka may not have many sites of historical interest, it's a good starting point for trips to Nara, Kyōto, Kōya-san (Mt. Koya), and Kōbe.

Ōsaka Glossary

Key Japanese words for this chapter include -*bashi* (bridge), *bijut-sukan* (art museum), -*chō* (street or block), -*chōme* (street), *Chūō-ku* (Central District), *depāto* (department store), *dōri* (avenue), *eki* ("eh-kee," station), -*gawa* (river), *higashi* (east), -*jō* (castle), *Kita-ku* (North District), *kōen* ("ko-en," park), -*ku* (district or ward), *matsuri* (festival), *Minami-ku* (South District), *nishi* (west), *ōhashi* (large bridge), *onsen* (hot springs), *ryokan* (traditional Japanese inn, -*shi* (city or municipality), -*shima* (island), *Shinkansen* (bullet train, literally "new trunk line"), *shōgun* (general or commander-in-chief), -*suji* (street), *taisha* (grand shrine), and *torii* ("*to*-ree-ee," gate).

Pleasures and Pastimes

Dining

Osakans are passionate about food. As the old saying goes, *Ōsaka wa kuida-ore*—Ōsaka people squander their money on food. They expect the restaurants they frequent to use the freshest ingredients available—a reasonable conceit that developed over centuries of reliance on the nearby Seto Inland Sea, which allowed all classes easy access to fresh seafood. Osakans continue to have discriminating palates and demand their money's worth. Prices in Ōsaka, both for food and lodging, are generally a better value for the money than in Kyōto.

Ōsaka cuisine is flavored with a soy sauce that is lighter in color, milder in flavor, and saltier in content than the soy used in Tōkyō. One local delicacy is *okonomiyaki*, pancakes filled with cabbage, mountain yams, pork, shrimp, and other ingredients, then grilled.

Ōsaka-zushi (Ōsaka-style sushi), made in wooden molds, has a distinctive square shape. Another type is wrapped around an omelet and filled with pickles and other delights. *Unagi* (eel) prepared in several styles remains a popular local dish; grilled unagi is often eaten in summer for quick energy. *Fugu* (blowfish) served boiled or raw is a delicacy that is less expensive in Ōsaka than in other Japanese cities.

Another Ōsaka invention is *takoyaki*, griddle-cooked dumplings with bits of octopus, green onions, and ginger smothered in a delicious sauce. Sold by street vendors in Dōtombori, these tasty snacks also appear at every festival and street market in Kansai.

For more on Japanese cuisine, *see* Chapter 14 *and* Dining *in* Smart Travel Tips A to Z.

CATEGORY	COST*
$$$$	over ¥6,000
$$$	¥4,000–¥6,000
$$	¥2,000–¥4,000
$	under ¥2,000

per person for a main course at dinner

Lodging

Ōsaka is known more as a business than as a tourist destination. The city has modern accommodations for almost every taste, from first-class hotels to more modest business hotels, which unfortunately aren't very distinctive. Guest quarters aren't exactly stylish: Japanese hotel designers are often concerned with efficiency rather than elegance. However, you should appreciate the individual attention of solicitous staff at most hotels. Because Ōsaka hotels offer much the same both in decor and room size within a given price range, choose accommodations in terms of location rather than amenities.

A hotel room in Ōsaka does cost less than one of comparable size in Tōkyō. And Ōsaka has more hotels to choose from than Kyōto, which is important to keep in mind during peak tourist seasons.

For a short course on accommodations in Japan, *see* Lodging *in* Smart Travel Tips A to Z.

CATEGORY	COST*
$$$$	over ¥20,000
$$$	¥15,000–¥20,000
$$	¥10,000–¥15,000
$	under ¥10,000

All prices are for a double room, excluding service and tax.

Performing Arts

Ōsaka is the home of Bunraku (puppet drama), which originated during the Heian period (794–1192), and in the late 17th and early 18th centuries the genius of local playwright Chikamatsu distilled Bunraku as an art form. Bunraku puppets are about two-thirds human size. Three puppeteers move the puppets, and they are completely visible to the audience. These master puppeteers not only skillfully manipulate the puppets' arms and legs but also roll the eyes and move the lips so that the puppets express fear, joy, and sadness. A typical play deals with themes of tragic love or stories based on historical events. At the National Bunraku Theater, the story is chanted in song by a *joruri,* who is accompanied by ballad music played on a three-stringed instrument, the *shamisen.* Although you may not understand the words, the tone of the music will set an appropriate mood of pathos.

Also, perhaps out of rivalry with Tōkyō, the city has renovated an old theater and incorporated technological innovations that are better than those found in the capital. The Sho-chiku-za Kabuki Theater puts on Kabuki in addition to modern plays and variety shows.

Shopping

Ōsaka's 1,500-year mercantile history means a significant stock of the latest fashions and electronics for today's shoppers.

Sumō

Ōsaka is one of Japan's centers for sumō wrestling, in which athletes weighing from 90 to 160 kilograms (198 to 352 pounds) battle to throw an opponent to the floor or out of the ring. Bouts in Ōsaka are held from the second through the fourth Sunday in March.

EXPLORING ŌSAKA

Ōsaka is divided into 26 wards, and though the official city population is only 2.6 million, if you were to include the suburbs, this number would jump to around 6 million. Central Ōsaka is predominantly a business district, with some shopping and entertainment. The JR Kanjō-sen (Loop Line) circles the city center. The primary Ōsaka Eki is at the north end of this loop. In front of Ōsaka Eki is the center of Kita-ku. Although ultramodern skyscrapers soar above the streets, Umeda Chika Center is an underground maze of malls, crowded with dozens of restaurants, shops that sell the latest fashions, and *depātos* (department stores) that offer every modern gadget. Kita-ku is one of Ōsaka's two major shopping areas.

If you continue south, you come to two rivers, Dojima-gawa and Tosa-bori-gawa, with the Naka-no-shima (Inner Island) separating them. Here is Ōsaka's oldest park, which is home to many of the city's cultural and administrative institutions, including the Bank of Japan and the Shiritsu Tōyō Jiki Bijutsukan.

South of these rivers and Naka-no-shima are the Minami and Shin-Sai-bashi districts. They are close together and are surrounded by the Loop Line. Shin-Sai-bashi is Ōsaka's expensive shopping street. Nearby Amerika Mura, with American-style boutiques, and Yoroppa Mura, with Continental shops, appeal to young Ōsaka trendsetters. Minami-ku has a wonderful assortment of bars and restaurants, especially on Dōtombori-dōri. The National Bunraku Theater is also close by, a few blocks southeast, near the Nippon-bashi subway station.

You are likely to arrive in town at Shin-Ōsaka Eki, the Shinkansen terminal. Three kilometers (2 miles) north of Ōsaka Eki, the main railway station, amid some of the city's most modern architecture, Shin-Ōsaka is close to Senri Expo Park. From Shin-Ōsaka Eki, take either the Midō-suji subway line to Umeda or, if you have a Japan Rail Pass, the JR Kōbe Line to Ōsaka Eki. The Umeda subway station and Ōsaka Eki are next to each other, on the edge of central Ōsaka.

Numbers in the text correspond to numbers in the margin and on the Ōsaka map.

Great Itineraries

Ōsaka is known for its dynamism, and you can enjoy the fruits of this energy in a couple of days. If you stay longer, use Ōsaka as a base to explore the surrounding Kansai region—Kyōto, Nara, and Kōbe are each but 30 minutes away by train. Ōsaka is also the most convenient jumping-off point for a trip to the mountainside monasteries of Kōya-san, two hours away on the Nankai private rail line.

IF YOU HAVE 1 DAY

Twenty-four hours in Ōsaka will give you a chance to catch many of the city's major sights. Ōsaka-jō should be first on your list. Then head south to Tennō-ji Kōen, a park that contains the Shiritsu Bijutsukan and its collection of classical Japanese art. Shitennō-ji, or Tennō-ji, is the oldest Buddhist temple in Japan. In the afternoon head to Den Den Town to browse through the gadget stores or to Yoroppa Mura and Amerika Mura for fashion. At the end of the day, Dōtombori-dōri is the place to go for dinner and nightlife.

With two full days in Ōsaka, you can cover all the city's major sights. To the above day-in-town suggestions, add Sumiyoshi Taisha, one of the three most famous shrines in Japan, Senri Expo Park and its museums, Shiritsu Tōyō Jiki Bijutsukan in Naka-no-shima Kōen, and the shops on Midō-suji. Instead of heading to Dōtombori-dōri after dark, go to central Ōsaka and, if you plan ahead and buy tickets, attend a performance at the National Bunraku Theater.

When to Tour Ōsaka

The crisp air of spring and fall are the best seasons to visit—Ōsaka can become quite hot and humid in the summer, and winter can get a bit chilly. Most museums are closed Monday. One notable exception is Senri Expo Park, which closes Wednesday instead. Museums stay open on Monday national holidays, closing the following day instead. Likewise, Senri Expo Park stays open on Wednesday holidays, closing Thursday instead.

A Good Tour

Start your exploration of Ōsaka with the city's major landmark, **Ōsaka-jō** ①, the castle that Hideyoshi Toyotomi built in the late 16th century. It is easily reached by taking the Loop Line from JR Ōsaka Eki to Ōsaka-jō Kōen Eki, from which it is a 10-minute walk uphill through the park.

Leave the castle and, facing north, walk down the hill past Ōsaka-jō Hōru (Ōsaka-jō Hall), which is used for sports competitions and concerts, and cross the overpass near the Aqua Liner water-bus pier. On Sunday afternoons this area hosts to amateur bands, each with its own gaggle of adoring fans. Enthusiasm and fashionable outfits make up for the often rudimentary music skills. On the other side of Hirano-gawa is the Hotel New Otani and Ōsaka Business Park, full of modern, high-rise office blocks. The two mighty skyscrapers you see within the business park are the Twin 21 Towers, a symbol of Japan's rush into the 21st century.

Next, stop in to see the ceramic exhibits of **Shiritsu Tōyō Jiki Bijutsukan** ②, on Naka-no-shima. The art museum sits on the eastern end of the island in Naka-no-shima Kōen, the city's oldest park, which opened in 1891. To get to it from Ōsaka Business Park, take the JR train from Katamichi Eki to the Kyō-bashi stop and transfer to the Keihan Line, which you take to the Yodoya-bashi stop. The museum is a five-minute walk away. Ōsaka University and Ōsaka Festival Hall, which is considered the city's best concert hall, are also on the island.

From here it is a 15-minute walk up to the city's Umeda district, home to JR Ōsaka Eki, three of the city's department stores and the **HEP Five** ③ shopping plaza, complete with a giant Ferris wheel on its roof.

Take the Midō-suji subway line from Yodoya-bashi to Shin-Sai-bashi Eki. When you emerge, you're on **Midō-suji** ④. Shin-Sai-bashi and Ebisu-bashi, which run parallel to Midō-suji, are two of Ōsaka's best shopping and entertainment streets. West of Midō-suji, **Amerika Mura** ⑤ is a group of streets with trendy American clothing stores. East of Midō-suji, **Yoroppa Mura** ⑥ is chockablock with fashionable European boutiques.

Walk south on Midō-suji and cross Dōtombori-gawa to **Dōtombori-dōri** ⑦, a broad cross street that runs alongside the canal. The street and the area around it are filled with bars, restaurants, and nightclubs.

Ōsaka

N

TO SHIN-ŌSAKA, MINŌ KŌEN, HATTORI RYOKUCHI KŌEN

Hankyū Umeda Station

Naka-Zaki-chō

Tenma

Ogi-machi
Umeda

14 Sakura-no-miya

JR KANJO (LOOP LINE)

Tourist Information **3**

Higashi-Umeda

JR Ōsaka Eki

Yodogawa

KITA

Nishi-Umeda

Kita-Shinchi

JR TŌZAI LINE

Minami-Mori-machi

Tenma-gū

Osakajo Kitazume

Kyōbashi

Yodoya-bashi

Naka-no-shima

Tenman-gū

Kata-machi

Dōjima-gawa

2

Naka-no-shima Kōen

KEIHAN MAIN LINE

Tosabori-gawa

Kitahama

Tenma-bashi

Ōsaka Business Park

Higo-bashi

Tenma-bashi

Ōsaka-jō Kōen

1

Hon-machi

Tani-machi 4-Chōme

Mori-no-miya

Chūō-ōdōri

Hanshin Expwy.
Higashi-Ōsaka Line

Sakai-suji-hon-machi

4

Shin-Sai-bashi

Nagahori-bashi

Tani-machi 6-Chōme

Nagahori-dōri

Yatsu-bashi

5 **6**

Sakai-suji

Tamatsukuri

Dotonbori-gawa

7

MINAMI

Namba

Sennichi-mae-dōri

Tsuruhashi

Minato-machi

Nippon-bashi

Ue-hon-machi

15

Ashihara-bashi

Nankai Namba Eki

8

Tanimachi 9-Chōme

Ima-miya

Daikoku-chō

Momodani

Ebisu-chō

Tennō-ji Kōen

0   1 mile

0   1 km

Shin-Imamiya

9 **10**

11

12

Shitennō-ji-mae

Tennō-ji

Terada-chō

Dobutsuen-mae

JR KANSAI MAIN LINE

Hanazono-chō

Abeno

TO NARA

Tobushijo-mae

Kishinosato

TO KANSAI INTERNATIONAL AIRPORT

Showacho

Fuminosato

Kishinosato

NANKAI MAIN LINE

NANKAI KŌYA LINE

NANKAI HANKAI LINE

Tamade

KEY

JR Trains
Subway
Private rail line

TO NINTOKU MAUSOLEUM

KANSAI REGION

Kyōto

Kōbe

Biwa-ko

Ōsaka

Osaka Bay

Nara

Sumiyoshi-Higashi

13

Sumiyoshi Torii-mae

Nagai

JR HANWA LINE

Yoshino-gawa

Kōya-san

At the far southern end of Midō-suji are the Kabuki-za and the Takashimaya depātos. East of the southern terminus of Nankai Namba Eki is **Den Den Town** ⑧, *the* place to go for discounted electronics.

From Namba Eki (the subway station, not Nankai Namba Eki, the train station), take the Sennichi-mae subway line one stop east to Nippon-bashi Eki; try to attend an afternoon performance at the **National Bunraku Theater,** which begin at 4 PM. Take Exit 7, and you will be right outside the theater.

Now head for **Tennō-ji Kōen** ⑨ and its peaceful ponds and gardens. In the park, consider visiting the **Shiritsu Bijutsukan** ⑩, with its ancient and modern art and ancient pottery and artifacts. Rest awhile in the adjacent **Keitakuen** ⑪, a calming garden with cherry trees and azaleas around a pond. Your next stop is **Shitennō-ji** ⑫, usually referred to as Tennō-ji. Founded in 593, though resurrected many a time, it's said to be the oldest Buddhist temple in Japan. To get here straight from Ōsaka-jō, take the Loop Line from Ōsaka-jō Kōen Eki or Kyo-bashi Eki going south. If you exit at Tennō-ji Eki, you'll see the street going north up to Shitennō-ji; Tennō-ji Kōen will be on the left.

To supplement or substitute sights on the tour above, keep in mind the following. At the southern reaches of Ōsaka is one of the three most famous shrines in Japan, **Sumiyoshi Taisha** ⑬. In the city's northern quarters you'll find **Senri Expo Park** ⑭ and its four museums. Two are particularly worth your time: **Nihon Mingei-kan,** for its outstanding traditional regional handicrafts, and **Kokuritsu Minzokugaku Hakubutsukan,** for its exhibits on comparative cultures of the world.

Finally, film buffs and amusement park fans will want to add a day to enjoy the attractions of **Universal Studios Japan** ⑮.

Sights to See

North of Chūō-dōri

❸ **HEP Five.** HEP Five (the acronym *HEP* is short for Hankyū Entertainment Plaza) was completed at the end of 1998, adding yet another enormous shopping palace to Ōsaka's already world-class collection. Inside are 11 floors of restaurants, shops, and entertainment facilities. What makes HEP Five special, though, is the enormous Ferris wheel on its roof, which at its apex is a good 40 ft taller than the Statue of Liberty. It's a very popular place for young couples and in 2000 was rated as the number one spot to go on a date by the city's youth, so expect a wait to ride the wheel on weekends. ⊠ *3 mins north of Hankyū Umeda terminus.* ☉ *Hrs vary.*

Minō Kōen. Osakans come here in autumn to admire the dazzling fall foliage, especially the maple trees, whose leaves turn brilliant crimson. The path along the river leads to the Minō-no-taki (Minō Waterfall). Monkeys reside here in a protected habitat, which is always open with no fee. ⊠ *30 mins from Hankyū Umeda Eki on Minō subway line, north of Minō Eki.*

★ ❶ **Ōsaka-jō.** Ōsaka's castle, one of Hideyoshi Toyotomi's finest buildings, is without doubt the city's most famous sight. The first stones were laid in 1583, and for the next three years as many as 100,000 workmen labored to build a majestic and impregnable castle. Note the thickness and the height of the walls. In order to demonstrate their loyalty to Hideyoshi, the feudal lords from the provinces were requested to contribute immense granite rocks. The largest piece of stone is said to have been donated by Hideyoshi's general, Kiyomasa Katō (1562–

1611), who had it brought from Shodo-shima off Shikoku. Known as Higo-Ishi, the rock measured a gigantic 19 ft high and 47 ft wide.

Hideyoshi was showing off with this castle. He had united Japan after a period of devastating civil wars, and he wanted to secure his western flanks. He also wanted to establish Ōsaka as a merchant town that could distribute the produce from the surrounding wealthy territories. The castle was intended to demonstrate Hideyoshi's power and commitment to Ōsaka in order to attract merchants from all over Japan.

Hideyoshi's plan succeeded, but within two years of his death in 1598, Ieyasu Tokugawa, an executor of Hideyoshi's will, took power and got rid of Hideyoshi's son's guardians. However, it was not until 1614 that Ieyasu sent his armies to defeat the Toyotomi family and their allies. In 1615 the castle was destroyed.

During a 10-year period the Tokugawa Shogunate rebuilt the castle according to original plans, and this version stood from 1629 until 1868, when the Tokugawa Shogunate's power came to an end. Rather than let the castle fall into the hands of the forces of the Meiji Restoration, Tokugawa troops burned it. In 1931 the present five-story (eight stories inside) *donjon* (stronghold) was built in ferroconcrete for the prestige of the city. An exact replica of the original, though marginally smaller in scale, it stands 189 ft high and has 46-ft-high stone walls. At night, when illuminated, it becomes a brilliant backdrop to the city.

Inside the castle, there is a museum with artifacts of the Toyotomi family and historical objects relating to Ōsaka prior to the Tokugawa Shogunate. Unless you are a Hideyoshi fan, these exhibits are of marginal interest. The castle's magnificent exterior and the impressive view from the eighth floor of the donjon are the reasons to see Ōsaka-jō. If you plan ahead, and get lucky, you might catch the cherry blossoms and **Nishi-no-maru Teien** (Nishi-no-maru Garden) at its best.

From Ōsaka-jō Kōen-mae Eki it's about a 10-minute walk up the hill to the castle. You can also take the Tani-machi subway line from Higashi-Umeda Eki (just southeast of Ōsaka Eki) to Tani-machi 4-chōme Eki. From there it is a 15-minute walk. ✉ *1–1 Ōsaka-jō, Chūō-ku,* ☎ *06/6941–3044.* 🎫 *Castle ¥600, garden additional ¥210.* ☉ *Sept.– mid-July, daily 9–5 (last entry at 4:30); mid-July–Aug., daily 9–8:30 (last entry at 8).*

② Shiritsu Tōyō Jiki Bijutsukan (City Art Museum of Asian Ceramics). Set in Naka-no-shima Kōen, the island's park, this world-class museum houses about 1,000 pieces of Chinese, Korean, and Japanese ceramics. The work comes mostly from the priceless Ataka collection, which belonged to a wealthy industrialist and was donated to the museum by the giant Sumitomo Group conglomerate. The collection, rated as one of the finest in the world, includes 14 works that have been designated National Treasures or Important Cultural Properties. In 1999 the museum was enlarged to contain pieces from the Rhee collection and varying special exhibits (which cost extra).

Take the Sakai-suji subway line to Kita-hama or the Midō-suji subway line to Yodoya-bashi and walk north across the Tosabori-gawa to the museum. ✉ *1–1 Naka-no-shima, Kita-ku,* ☎ *06/6223–0055.* 🎫 *¥500.* ☉ *Tues.–Sun. 9:30–5 (last entry at 4:30).*

Tenman-gū. This 10th-century shrine is the main site of the annual **Tenjin Matsuri,** held July 24–25, one of the three largest and most enthusiastically celebrated festivals in Japan. During Tenjin Matsuri, dozens of floats are paraded through the streets, and more than 100 vessels, lighted by lanterns, sail along the canals amid a dazzling display of fireworks. A renowned scholar of the 9th century, Michizane Sugawara, is enshrined at Tenman-gū; he is now considered the god of academics. Tenman-gū is a short walk from Minami-Mori-machi Eki on the Tani-machi-suji subway line. ⊠ *2–1–8 Tenjin-bashi, Kita-ku,* ☎ *06/ 6353–0025.* 🎫 *Free.* ☉ *Apr.–Sept., daily 5:30 AM–sunset; Oct.–Mar., daily 6 AM–sunset.*

🖐 ⑮ **Universal Studios Japan.** Combining the most popular rides and shows from Universal's Hollywood and Florida movie-studio theme parks, along with special, all-new attractions designed specifically for Japan, the 140-acre Universal Studios Japan (USJ) opened with much fanfare at the end of March 2001. Though critics have worried about the vast sums of money pumped into the project by the Ōsaka municipal government, as well as the park's long-term viability, USJ has proved itself to be a star attraction with visitors pouring in from not only all over the country but from as far away as South Korea, Taiwan, and Hong Kong.

Popular rides include those based on Hollywood films such as *Jurassic Park* (which ends with an 82-ft plunge), *Jaws,* and *ET,* and the Japan-only Snoopy attraction appeals to the local infatuation with all things cute. Numerous restaurants and food outlets abound throughout the park, and the road from the JR Universal City Eki is lined with well-known names such as the Hard Rock Cafe and Starbucks, along with local fast-food chain Mos Burger.

USJ is easily reached by direct train from JR Ōsaka Eki or by changing to a shuttle train at JR Nishi-kujo Eki on the Loop Line. Journey time from JR Ōsaka Eki is approximately 20 minutes. Tickets can be bought at numerous locations throughout the city, including branches of Lawson convenience stores and at larger JR stations, as well as at USJ itself. However, due to high demand on weekends and during holiday periods, tickets need to be bought in advance and are not available at the gate. ⊠ *2–1–33 Sakurajima, Konohana-ku,* ☎ *06/4790– 7000,* WEB *www.usj.co.jp.* 🎫 *¥5,500.* ☉ *Daily 10–10.*

Zōhei (Mint Museum). Part of the Ministry of Finance, this money museum exhibits some 16,000 examples of Japanese and foreign currencies. Also on display are Olympic medals, prehistoric currency, and ancient Japanese gold coins. Part of the Mint Bureau's grounds are open to the public for a short period during the cherry-blossom season (usually April). At that time you can stroll on a path shaded by blossoms along the Yodo-gawa. The Zohei is a 15-minute walk east of Minami-Mori-machi station on the Tani-machi subway line. ⊠ *1–1–79 Tenma, Kita-ku,* ☎ *06/6351–8509,* WEB *www.mint.go.jp.* 🎫 *Free.* ☉ *Weekdays 9–4:30 (last entry at 4).*

SENRI EXPO PARK

To get to the park, take the Midō-suji subway line to Senri-Chūō Eki (20 minutes from Umeda); then take the Expo Land bus to Nihon Teienmae Eki (30 minutes) or monorail to Bampaku Kōen-mae (10 minutes). ⊠ *Senri, Suitashi,* ☎ *06/6877–0560 for Expo Land.* 🎫 *Natural garden ¥150, garden ¥310, Expo Land ¥1,100; other facilities vary.* ☉ *Mar.–late Dec., Thurs.–Tues. 9–5.*

Kokuritsu Minzokugaku Hakubutsukan (National Museum of Ethnology). Established in 1974, this modern black-and-silver building has a variety of regional exhibits on world cultures that include good displays on the Ainu, the original inhabitants of Japan, and other aspects of Japanese culture. Automatic audiovisual equipment, called Videotheque, provides close-up views of customs of the peoples of the world. An English pamphlet that comes with your admission ticket explains these fascinating displays. Comprehensive information sheets explaining all the sections of the museum are also available on request. The museum is on the east side of the main road that runs north–south through Senri Park. ✉ *Senri Expo Park, Senri, Suitashi,* ☎ *06/6876–2151.* 🖭 *¥420.* ☉ *Thurs.–Tues. 10–5 (last entry at 4:30).*

Nihon Mingei-kan. Containing many outstanding examples of traditional regional handicrafts, the Japan Folk Art Museum is one of the best places in all Japan to see ceramics, textiles, wooden crafts, and bamboo ware and to familiarize yourself with Japanese handicrafts. ✉ *10–5 Bampaku Kōen, Senri, Suitashi,* ☎ *06/6877–1971.* 🖭 *¥550.* ☉ *Thurs.–Tues. 10–5 (last entry at 4:30).*

⓮ **Senri Expo Park.** On the former site of Expo '70—one of the defining events in Ōsaka's postwar history—this 647-acre park contains sports facilities, a garden with two teahouses, other gardens, a vast amusement park called Expo Land that's popular with families and young couples, the ☞ **Kokuritsu Minzokugaku Hakubutsukan,** ☞ **Nihon Mingei-kan,** and two other smaller museums.

South of Chūō-dōri

❺ **Amerika Mura** (America Village). Though it takes its name from the original shops that opened up here selling cheap American fashions and accessories, Ame-Mura (*ah*-meh *moo*-ra), as it's called, is now a bustling district full of trendy clothing shops, record stores, bars, cafés, and clubs that cater to teenagers and young adults. Shops are jammed on top of each other, and it is virtually impossible to walk on the streets weekends. For a glimpse of the variety of styles and fashions prevalent among urban youth, Ame-Mura is *the* place to go in Ōsaka. ✉ *On west side of Midō-suji, 6 blocks south of Midō-suji subway line's Shin-Sai-bashi Eki.*

❽ **Den Den Town.** Ōsaka's equivalent of Tōkyō's Akihabara district may not be quite as large as its cousin, but it still offers several hundred specialty shops for gadget fans to dive into. All the latest electronic wonders—video games, calculators, and computers to cameras and CD players—are discounted here. ✉ *2 blocks east of southern terminus of Namba Eki.*

★ ❼ **Dōtombori-dōri.** The good life of Dōtombori's restaurants and bars lures flocks of Osakans here to forget their daily toils. The street—a virtual feast for neonophiles—runs alongside Dōtombori-gawa, and it's the best place to stroll in the evening for a glimpse of Ōsaka nightlife. Look for the giant, undulating Kani Dōraku crab sign, a local landmark. Movie fans may be interested to know that parts of *Black Rain,* starring Michael Douglas and Andy Garcia, were filmed in the immediate area. ✉ *From Umeda, take Midō-suji subway line to Namba and walk north 2 blocks up Midō-suji; or walk south from Yoroppa Mura 5 blocks on Midō-suji and cross Dōtombori-gawa.*

Fujii-dera. An 8th-century, 1,000-handed, seated statue of Kannon, the goddess of mercy, is the main object of worship at this temple. The statue is a National Treasure, the oldest Buddhist sculpture of its kind. Take the Midō-suji subway line to Tennō-ji Eki; then transfer to the Kintetsu Minami–Ōsaka Line and take it to Fujii-dera Eki. The temple is a few minutes' walk away. ✉ *1–16–21 Fujii-dera, Fujii-dera-shi,* ☎ *0729/38–0005.* ☉ *Statue on view 18th of month.*

In **Hattori Ryokuchi Kōen,** the main appeal is the open-air **Nihon Minka Shūraku Hakubutsukan** (Museum of Old Japanese Farmhouses), which has full-size replicas of traditional rural buildings from all over the country. Also in this recreational park are facilities for horseback riding, a youth hostel, a swimming pool, and an open-air stage, which hosts concerts and other events in the summer. No reservation is necessary for tennis (¥610–¥710) during the week; for weekend play you need to reserve in advance. Take the Midō-suji subway line from Umeda to Ryokuchi Kōen Eki. The park is a 10-minute walk away. ☎ 06/6862–4946 *park office; 06/6862–3137 museum.* ✉ *Museum* ¥410. ☉ *Apr.–Oct., daily 9:30–5 (last entry at 4:30); Nov.–Mar., daily 9:30–4 (last entry at 3:30).*

⑪ Keitakuen. This garden, originally constructed in 1908 as a circular garden, was given to the city by the late Baron Sumitomo. Its cherry trees and azaleas surrounding a pond are lovely when in bloom. The garden offers a welcome respite from the city. Keitakuen is adjacent to Shiritsu Bijutsukan in Tennō-ji Kōen. ✉ *Free once inside Tennō-ji Kōen.* ☉ *Tues.–Sun. 9:30–4:30 (last entry at 4).*

④ Midō-suji. This is one of Ōsaka's major boulevards, with the Midō-suji subway running underneath it. If you're in town on the second Sunday in October, try to catch the annual Midō-suji Parade, with its colorful procession of floats and musicians. Shin-Sai-bashi and Ebisu-bashi parallel Midō-suji and are two of Ōsaka's best shopping and entertainment streets. The Shin-Sai-bashi stop on the Midō-suji subway line is in the heart of the city's shopping districts.

Nintoku Mausoleum. The 4th-century mausoleum of Emperor Nintoku is in Sakai City, southeast of Ōsaka. The mausoleum was built on an even larger scale than that of the pyramids of Egypt—archaeologists calculate that the central mound of this site is 1.3 million square ft. Construction took more than 20 years and required a total workforce of about 800,000 laborers. Surrounding the emperor's burial place are three moats and pine, cedar, and cypress trees. You can walk around the outer moat to get an idea of the size of the mausoleum and the grounds. However, entry into the mausoleum is not allowed. From Tennō-ji Eki, take the JR Hanwa Line to Mozu Eki (a half-hour ride). From there the mausoleum is a five-minute walk. ✉ *7 Daisen-chō, Sakai-shi,* ☎ *0722/41–0002.*

⑩ Shiritsu Bijutsukan (Municipal Museum of Fine Art). Having been taken over by the Japanese Army during WW II, then used as a center for the occupation forces after the war, the museum has suffered significant wear and tear over the years. Although the building might not be terribly impressive, its exceptional collection of 12th- to 14th-century classical Japanese art is. Other collections include the works of Edo-period artist Ogata Korin, some modern art, more than 3,000 examples of modern lacquerware, and a collection of Chinese paintings and artifacts, including several Important Cultural Properties.

Take the Loop Line or the Midō-suji subway line to Tennō-ji Eki, or the Tani-machi subway to Shitennō-ji-mae. The museum is in Tennō-ji Kōen, southwest of Shitennō-ji. ✉ *1–82 Chausuyama-chō, Tennō-ji-ku,* ☎ *06/6771–4874.* ✉ *¥300.* ☉ *Tues.–Sun. 9:30–5 (last entry at 4:30).*

⑫ Shitennō-ji. Tennō-ji, as it is popularly known, is one of the most important historical sights in Ōsaka. Architecturally, it's gone through the wringer, having been destroyed by fire many times. And the last reconstruction of the Kon-dō (Main Hall), Kodo Taishi-den, and the five-story pagoda in 1965 has maintained the original design and adhered to the traditional mathematical alignment. What has managed to survive from earlier times is the 1294 stone torii that stands at the main entrance. (Torii are rarely used at Buddhist temples.)

Shitennō-ji claims to be the oldest temple in Japan. Outdating Hōryū-ji in Nara (607), it was founded by Prince Shōtoku in 593. Umayado no Mikoto (573–621), posthumously known as Prince Shōtoku, or Shōtoku Taishi, is considered one of early Japan's most enlightened rulers for his furthering of Buddhism and his political acumen. He was made regent over his aunt, Suiko, and set about instituting reforms and establishing Buddhism as the state religion. Buddhism had been introduced to Japan from China and Korea in the early 500s, but it was seen as a threat to the aristocracy, which claimed prestige and power based upon its godlike ancestry. Prince Shōtoku recognized both the power of Buddhism and its potential as a tool for the state. His swords and a copy of his *Hokkekyo Lotus Sutra*, written during the Heian period (897–1192), used to be stored at Shitennō-ji. Now they are kept in the National Museum of Tōkyō. On the 21st of every month, the temple has a flea market that sells antiques and baubles; go in the morning for a feeling of old, pre-prosperity Japan.

Three train lines will take you near Shitennō-ji. The Tani-machi-suji subway line's Shitennō-ji-mae Eki is closest both to the temple and the temple park. The Loop Line's Tennō-ji Eki is several blocks south of the temple. The Midō-suji subway line also has a Tennō-ji stop, which is next to the JR station. Or, you can transfer from the Sakai-suji subway line to the Midō-suji line at the Dobutsu-en-mae stop, then continue to the Tennō-ji stop. ✉ *1–11–18 Shitennō-ji-ku, Tennō-ji,* ☎ *06/6771–0066.* 💴 *¥200.* 🕙 *Apr.–Sept., daily 8:30–4:30; Oct.–Mar., daily 8:30–4.*

⑬ Sumiyoshi Taisha. Most Shintō shrines in Japan today were built after the 8th century and were heavily influenced by Buddhist architecture. Sumiyoshi Taisha is one of three shrines built prior to the arrival of Buddhism in Japan (the other two are the great Ise Jingū and Izumo Taisha near Matsue).

Sumiyoshi Taisha honors the goddess of sea voyages, Sumiyoshi, and, according to legend, was founded by Empress Jingū in 211 to express her gratitude for her safe return from a voyage to Korea. In those days the shrine faced the sea rather than the urban sprawl that now surrounds it. On the shrine's grounds are many stone lanterns donated by sailors and shipowners as dedications to Sumiyoshi and other Shintō deities that guard the voyages of seafarers. Note the arched bridge, said to have been given by Yodogimi, the consort of Hideyoshi Toyotomi, who bore him a son. Of the three ancient shrines, only Sumiyoshi has a Japanese cypress structure that is painted vermilion; the other two have a natural wood finish. According to Shintō custom, shrines were torn down and rebuilt at set intervals to the exact specifications of the original. Sumiyoshi, which, incidentally, is also the name given to the style of architecture of this shrine, was last replaced in 1810.

Every June 14, starting at 1 PM, a very colorful rice-planting festival takes place at the taisha with various traditional folk performances and processions. Sumiyoshi Matsuri, one of the city's largest and liveliest festivals, is held from July 30 to August 1. A crowd of rowdy young men carries a 2-ton portable shrine from Sumiyoshi Taisha to Yamato-gawa and back; this event is followed by an all-night street bazaar. To reach the shrine, take the 20-minute ride south on the Nankai Main Line from Nankai Namba Eki to Sumiyoshi Kōen Eki. ✉ *2–9–89 Sumiyoshi, Sumiyoshi-ku,* ☎ *06/6672–0753.* 💴 *Free.* 🕙 *Apr.–Oct., daily 6–5; Nov.–Mar., daily 6:30–5.*

⑨ Tennō-ji Kōen. This park not only contains the ☞ **Shiritsu Bijutsukan** and the garden of ☞ **Keitakuen**, it's also the site of the **Tennō-ji Shokubutsuen** (Botanical Gardens). In Tennō-ji Kōen you might notice a prehistoric burial mound, **Chausuyama Kofun,** that was the site of Ieyasu Tokugawa's camp during the siege of Ōsaka-jō in 1614–15. Take the Loop Line from Ōsaka Eki to Tennō-ji Eki. The park is on the left side of the road going north to Shitennō-ji. ⊠ *6–74 Chausuyama-chō, Tennō-ji-ku,* ☎ *06/6771–8401.* ☞ *¥150 (park only).* ⊘ *Tues.–Sun. 9:30–4:30 (last entry at 4).*

❻ **Yoroppa Mura** (Europe Village). Not as well defined as Amerika Mura, Yoroppa Mura is a more refined and cosmopolitan area, with cobbled sidewalks and European-style cafés that re-create the atmosphere of a Continental city. Many of Japan's top department stores, like Parco, Sogo, and Daimaru, have branches here. At the north end, Sony Tower has imported goodies for sale and the latest technological wonders on display. ⊠ *East side of Midō-suji, 6 blocks south of Midō-suji subway line's Shin-Sai-bashi Eki.*

DINING

Surrounding Ōsaka Eki are a number of self-proclaimed "gourmet palaces," each with several floors of restaurants. Exploring them can be fun. Head for restaurants in the Hankyū Grand Building, the Hankyū Samban-gai (in the basement below Hankyū Eki), and Acty Ōsaka (in front of JR Ōsaka Eki). Most large department stores also house scores of good restaurants, notably the Daimaru in front of JR Ōsaka Eki.

Ōsaka's shopping arcades and underground shopping areas abound in affordable restaurants and coffee shops, but when in doubt, head to Dōtombori and Soemon-chō ("*so*-eh-mon cho-oh"), two areas along Dōtombori-gawa that spill over with restaurants and bars. Kita-shinchi is the city's most exclusive dining quarter—the local equivalent of Tōkyō's Ginza. Food of all kinds is available in Ōsaka, with the notable exception of good Middle Eastern and Mediterranean cooking. If you feel like you're in a Japanese food rut, this is the place to get out of it. Or if you're into the local culinary groove, Ōsaka cuisine won't disappoint.

$$$$ ✕ **Benkay.** If you appreciate *tai* (Japanese-style red snapper), which is served with *ume* (stewed plums), Benkay is the place to go. Sea urchin, squid, and prawns are staples on the menu here; tempura and sushi are popular as well. The restaurant uses traditional blond-wood paneling, and there's a sushi bar to one side. ⊠ *Hotel Nikkō Ōsaka, 1–3–3 Nishi-Shin-Sai-bashi, Chūō-ku,* ☎ *06/6244–1111. Reservations essential. Jacket and tie. AE, DC, MC, V.*

$$$$ ✕ **La Baie.** The city's premier hotel restaurant serves innovative and
★ extremely good Franco-Japanese fusion food. The wood-paneled La Baie is more akin to a British country-house dining room than a formal hotel restaurant—smart but relaxed. Service is impeccable, and wines are specially chosen to complement each of the four full-course menus available. ⊠ *The Ritz-Carlton Ōsaka, 2–5–25 Umeda, Kita-ku,* ☎ *06/6343–7020. Reservations essential. Jacket and tie. AE, DC, MC, V.*

$$–$$$$ ✕ **Ume no Hana.** A high-class chain restaurant, Ume no Hana offers healthful, multicourse menus of tofu-based cuisine—particularly refreshing on hot summer days. Or try one of the cheaper lunch sets as a break from shopping in Shin-Sai-Bashi. Private dining rooms are all in a traditional Japanese style with pottery and *ikebana* (flower arrangement) artfully displayed. Reserve ahead on weekends. ⊠ *Shin-sai-bashi OPA Bldg., 11th floor, 1–4–3 Nishi-Shin-sai-bashi, Chūō-ku,* ☎ *06/6258–3766. AE, DC, MC, V.*

$$–$$$ ✕ **Kani Dōraku.** The enormous mechanical crab above the door to Kani Dōraku is more than just a sign for the restaurant—it's become a local landmark and often features in promotional literature extolling Ōsaka's well-founded reputation for being a food lover's paradise. The most famous restaurant on Dōtombori-dōri, Kani Dōraku is noted for fine crab dishes at reasonable prices. As you sit at tables or on tatami mats overlooking Dōtombori Canal, the ultramodern Kirin Plaza Building glitters across the water. For lunch, a crab dish will run around ¥4,000, while dinner will be more than ¥6,000. Other, less expensive dishes include delicious *nabe* (one-pot stews). There is another branch in Umeda, and both have English-language menus. Reserve ahead on weekends. ⊠ *1–6–18 Dōtombori, Chūō-ku,* ☎ *06/6211–8975;* ⊠ *Sonezaki Shinchi 1–6–7, Kita-ku,* ☎ *06/6344–5091. AE, DC, MC, V.*

$$–$$$ ✕ **Kanki.** *Akachō-chin,* or red lanterns, are the symbol of inexpensive eating in Japan, but the wonderful combination of Western and Japanese dishes offered at this friendly place makes it different from most other *nomi-ya,* as these inexpensive drinking places are called. Ordering is simple at Kanki, since there are only three options—set dinners at ¥4,000, ¥5,000, and ¥6,000, the contents of which are seasonal in theme and are left to the whims of the master chef behind the first-floor counter. You might end up with Florentine-style scallops or some raw squid. Table seating is available on the second and third floors. ⊠ *1–3–11 Shibata-chō, Kita-ku (at northwest end of Hankyū Umeda Eki),* ☎ *06/6374–0057. No credit cards. Closed Sun.*

$$–$$$ ✕ **Osteria Gaudente.** Relatively authentic decor, attentive waiters, and its popularity with the younger set—especially at lunchtime—make Gaudente an agreeable Italian option. The fish dishes are particularly good, and set dinner menus change daily, depending on what delicacies the chef unearths at the Ōsaka central fish market each morning. Lunch courses are a great value. ⊠ *Dai-yon Bldg., B1 floor, Ōsaka Eki-mae-dōri, 1–11–4 Umeda, Kita-ku,* ☎ *06/6344–8685. Reservations essential weekends. AE, DC, MC, V.*

$$–$$$ ✕ **Tako-ume.** Take a rest from the glitter of Dōtombori nightlife at this
★ 200-year-old dining spot, which specializes in *oden*—a mixture of vegetables, fish cakes, hard-boiled eggs, and fried tofu, cooked in a broth they say has been simmering here in the same pot for the past 30 years (just add liquid. . .). Sake is poured from pewter jugs that were handmade in Ōsaka. A hot Chinese mustard dip is mixed with sweet miso—a house recipe. This is one of Ōsaka's most famous establishments. Reserve ahead on weekends. ⊠ *1–1–8 Dōtombori, Chūō-ku,* ☎ *06/6211–0321. No credit cards. Closed Wed.*

$$ ✕ **Checkers.** You'll find one of Ōsaka's best deals in the comfortable,
★ casual setting of the Hilton's ever-popular buffet-style restaurant. There is a wide range of hot and cold dishes, as well as a fine array of desserts. The menu's theme, ranging from Asian to Californian, depends on the day of the week. The wine list has a fairly wide and reasonable selection. ⊠ *Ōsaka Hilton International, 8–8 Umeda 1-chōme, Kita-ku,* ☎ *06/6347–7111. AE, DC, MC, V.*

$$ ✕ **Fuguhisa.** Expect a warm and hearty welcome at this no-nonsense little restaurant, which specializes in *fugu ryōri,* the blowfish delicacies for which Ōsaka is famous. Extremely expensive almost everywhere else, chef Kato's *tessa* (raw blowfish) and *techiri* (one-pot blowfish stew) are extremely reasonable and very tasty to boot. What the place lacks in glamour it makes up for in good, down-to-earth Ōsaka-style food. It's across from the central exit of Tsuru-hashi Eki on the Loop Line. ⊠ *3–14–24 Higashi Ōhashi, Higashi-Nari-ku,* ☎ *06/6972–5029. No credit cards. Closed Mon.*

$$ ✕ **Kirin Plaza Ōsaka.** Designed by Shin Takamatsu, one of Japan's most controversial architects, this branch of the Kirin City beer-hall chain makes four of its own brews inside the Kirin Plaza Building (a complex that also plays host to contemporary art exhibitions and installations). The restaurant, on the third floor, serves mixed Japanese and Western dishes such as avocado tempura and hot salads. ⊠ *Kirin Plaza Bldg., 3rd floor, 7–2 Soemon-chō, Chūō-ku,* ☎ *06/6212–6572. V.*

$$ ✕ **Kohinoor.** Offering quality Indian cuisine, Kohinoor is upmarket without being intimidatingly expensive. Fish *tikka* (curried and grilled) and chicken kebabs are particularly tasty, and there's a full range of vegetarian options. Six set menus are also available, but be warned—the portions are more filling than they may appear. ⊠ *Herbis Plaza, B2 floor, 2–5–25 Umeda, Kita-ku,* ☎ *06/6343–7112. AE, DC, MC, V.*

$$ ✕ **La Bamba.** The owner-chef here learned his craft in Mexico, and
★ the sombreros and posters at his small restaurant can—for a time—release you from the land of raw fish and chopsticks. Good tacos, guacamole, burritos, quesadillas, and magnificent pitchers of margaritas are all on the menu, along with Caribbean cuisine. ⊠ *2–3–23 Dōtombori, Chūō-ku,* ☎ *06/6213–9612. AE, MC, V. Closed Mon.*

$$ ✕ **Yasubei.** This small *izakaya* (pub) has a fun atmosphere and good food. Sit at the counter, where you can watch the chefs at work, or at a table, and select from an extensive menu that includes grilled fish, hibachi-grilled chicken, and scallops wrapped in bacon. ⊠ *Ōsaka Ekimae Dai-ichi Bldg., B1 floor, 1–3 Umeda, Kita-ku,* ☎ *06/6344–4545. No credit cards.*

$–$$ ✕ **Kitano Brewery.** The vast majority of beer in Japan may still be produced by one of the big four breweries—Kirin, Asahi, Sapporo, or Suntory—but due to recent changes in brewing laws, microbreweries are springing up throughout the country. The Kitano Brewery is one that brews its beer on the premises, and there are three tasty ales. A wide-ranging menu includes German beer-hall fare, as well as pasta, pizza, and salads. The atmosphere is definitely European—with lots of dark-wood furnishings—and for the no-malt-and-hops crowd, there's a decent selection of wines. ⊠ *DD House, 1st floor, 1–8–1 Shibata, Kita-ku (near Hankyū Umeda Eki),* ☎ *06/6292–0343. V. Closed 3rd Mon. of month.*

$–$$ ✕ **Kushitaru.** Specializing in dinners served piping hot on skewers, Kushi-
★ taru is an Ōsaka favorite (note that there's no English menu). Possible selections include *tsukune* (chicken meatballs), celery with sea eel, quail egg with half beak, and oysters with bacon. Of the two dining rooms, the one upstairs is a throwback to the 1970s, with period furniture and music. Kushitaru is behind the Hotel Nikkō—and well worth a visit. ⊠ *Sander Bldg., 13–5 Nishi-Shin-Sai-bashi 1-chōme, Unagidani, Chūō-ku,* ☎ *06/6281–0365. AE, DC, MC, V. Closed Sun.*

$–$$ ✕ **Mimiu.** *Udon-suki*—the thick, white noodle stew with Chinese cabbage, clams, eel, yams, shiitake mushrooms, *mitsuba* (greens), and other seasonal ingredients simmered in a pot over a burner at your table—was born here. Indeed, so successful has the recipe become that there are now branches of Mimiu throughout the city—another convenient location is on the 10th floor of the Hanshin department store, opposite JR Ōsaka Eki. ⊠ *6–18 Hirano-machi, 4-chōme (near Hon-machi subway station), Chūō-ku,* ☎ *06/6231–5770. Reservations not accepted. V. Closed Sun.* ⊠ *1–13–13 Umeda, Kita-ku,* ☎ *06/6345–6648. V.*

$ ✕ **Madonna.** Restaurants that prepare the local dish okonomiyaki can be found throughout the city, but those served here are outstanding. Often mistakenly called "Japanese pizza," okonomiyaki are really pancakes made of cabbage and mountain yams and filled with ingredients like bacon or shrimp. Try the *yakitsubo*, a sample of five mini okonomiyaki, to experience different flavors. ⊠ *Hilton Plaza, B2 floor, 1–8–16 Umeda, Kita-ku,* ☎ *06/6347–7371. No credit cards.*

LODGING

$$$$ 🏨 **ANA Hotel Ōsaka.** One of Ōsaka's oldest deluxe hotels, the ANA overlooks the city's picturesque Naka-no-shima Kōen. Though showing its age a little, the building remains a handsome 24-story white-tile structure, with some unusual architectural features—including great fluted columns in the lobby. There's also an enclosed courtyard with trees. Guest rooms are done in pastel shades and have travertine marble baths. Each room is furnished with twin or double beds; some come with pull-out sofas. ✉ *1–3–1 Dojimahama, Kita-ku, Ōsaka 530-0004,* ☎ *06/6347–1112; 800/262–4683 for U.S reservations; 0171/995–8211 for U.K. reservations;* FAX *06/6347–9208. 500 rooms. 5 restaurants, coffee shop, indoor pool, sauna, health club, business services, parking (fee). AE, DC, MC, V.*

$$$$ 🏨 **Hilton Ōsaka.** Glitz and glitter draw both tourists and expense ac-
★   counters to the Hilton Ōsaka, the city's most convenient hotel, across from Ōsaka Eki in the heart of the business district. It's a typical Western-style hotel, replete with marble and brass. The high-ceiling lobby is dramatic, and the hotel's arcade contains designer boutiques. Standard rooms come with almost all the extras, and three executive floors provide a lounge for complimentary Continental breakfasts and evening cocktails. Checkers, which serves various buffet dinners, is among its 11 restaurants. ✉ *8–8 Umeda 1-chōme, Kita-ku, Ōsaka 530-0001,* ☎ *06/6347–7111,* FAX *06/6347–7001,* WEB *www.hilton.co.jp/osaka. 525 rooms. 11 restaurants, café, coffee shop, indoor pool, massage, sauna, 2 tennis courts, health club, shops, business services. AE, DC, MC, V.*

$$$$ 🏨 **Hotel New Otani Ōsaka.** Popular with Japanese and Westerners, the
★   New Otani has such amenities as indoor and outdoor pools, tennis courts, superior rooms, and a sparkling marble atrium lobby. The rooms, large by Japanese standards, afford handsome views of Ōsaka-jō and the Neya-gawa. Room decor is modern, with twin or double beds, light color schemes, dining tables, and excellent bathrooms. A large number of bars and restaurants provides enough diversity to suit almost any taste. Indeed, the New Otani is like a mini-city within the Ōsaka Business Park. The hotel's one drawback is the result: whenever you need to go to midtown Ōsaka, you have to take the Aqua Liner water bus, which stops in front of the hotel. The hotel is next to Ōsaka-jō Kōen on the Loop Line. ✉ *4–1 Shiromi 1-chōme, Chūō-ku, Ōsaka 540-0001,* ☎ *06/ 6941–1111,* FAX *06/6941–9769,* WEB *www.osaka.newotani.co.jp/e/. 559 rooms. 12 restaurants, 3 bars, 1 indoor and 1 outdoor pool, hair salon, health club. AE, DC, MC, V.*

$$$$ 🏨 **Hotel Nikkō Ōsaka.** An impressive and rather striking white tower in the colorful Shin-Sai-bashi Eki area, this Nikkō is within easy reach of Ōsaka's nightlife. The hotel's atmosphere is lively, even exciting: as you enter, you may be greeted by a doorman in top hat and tails. Some rooms have contemporary furnishings with Japanese touches and traditional light decor. Higher-priced rooms have expensive furniture, thick carpets, and bedside controls. Tiled baths on executive floors are particularly well appointed. The bars and restaurants, including Benkay, are varied, and service here is an art. ✉ *1–3–3 Nishi-Shin-Sai-bashi, Chūō-ku, Ōsaka 542-0086,* ☎ *06/6244–1111,* FAX *06/6245–2432,* WEB *www.hno.co.jp/. 640 rooms. 3 restaurants, 3 bars, coffee shop, shops. AE, DC, MC, V.*

$$$$ 🏨 **Hyatt Regency Ōsaka.** If you're going to the Universal Studios Japan theme park, the Hyatt, in the Nanko development area, is quite convenient, and Kansai International Airport is a 45-minute bus ride away. Otherwise the 20-minute subway trip into the city center may be a bit long for the usual sightseeing. Modern comforts abound: guest rooms are spacious, especially deluxe doubles and junior suites. Choose

a room on an upper floor for grand views of Ōsaka Bay. Marble bathrooms have separate shower stalls. For entertainment and dining, choose from 15 restaurants and bars. Across the street, the Asia and Pacific Trade Center has a host of other restaurants, as well as the enormous Intex convention center. ⊠ *1–13 Nanko-Kita, Suminoe-ku, Ōsaka 559-0034,* ☎ *06/6612–1234; 800/233–1234 in the U.S.; 0171/580–8197 in the U.K.;* FAX *06/6614–7800,* WEB *www.hyatt.com. 500 rooms. 12 restaurants, 3 bars, 1 indoor and 1 outdoor pool, health club, free parking. AE, DC, MC, V.*

$$$$ ⛨ **Imperial Hotel.** Inspired by the old Frank Lloyd Wright–designed Imperial Hotel in Tōkyō, Ōsaka's riverfront Imperial is one of only two hotels in Ōsaka allowed to receive official state guests (the other is the Rihga Royal Hotel). So it's understandable that service is of the highest benchmark. The hotel's fitness center is superb, with three tennis courts, an indoor pool, a squash court, and a sauna, among myriad other facilities. All guest rooms come equipped with fax machines and separate phone lines for computer use. Elegant and understated furnishings fill the rooms, and high ceilings meet the sky through great picture windows showcasing city views. Imperial Tower rooms include separate concierge service, as well as special floor keys for added privacy and security. Adjacent to the hotel, the Imperial Plaza has more than 30 brand-name boutiques and eateries, and river tours depart hourly from a pier close by. A shuttle runs regularly to JR Ōsaka Eki. ⊠ *8–50 Temmabashi 1-chōme, Kita-ku, Ōsaka 530-0042,* ☎ *06/6881–1111; 800/223–6800 in the U.S; 0800/181–123 in the U.K.;* FAX *06/6881–4111. 390 rooms. 7 restaurants, 2 bars, 2 coffee shops, in-room data ports, sauna, 3 tennis courts, health club, squash, shops, concierge, business services, free parking. AE, DC, MC, V.*

$$$$ ⛨ **Miyako Hotel Ōsaka.** A practical, well-appointed hotel, the Miyako is very popular with Western travelers. Guest rooms are modern and inviting, and some have extras such as dining tables. Public rooms are impressive too, none more so than the two-story lobby decorated with marble columns and attractive pastel color schemes. Executive rooms occupy two floors and have plusher appointments. The Miyako is near the Tani-machi-9-chōme subway station, and trains for Nara and Kyōto on the private Kintetsu Line leave from the next-door Ue-hon-machi station. The National Bunraku Theater and Shitennō-ji are also fairly close. A regular limousine bus runs to Kansai International Airport from the hotel. ⊠ *6–1–55 Ue-hon-machi, Tennō-ji-ku, Ōsaka 543-0001,* ☎ *06/6773–1111; 800/333–3333 in the U.S.; 0800/37–4411 in the U.K.;* FAX *06/6773–3322,* WEB *www.miyako-o.co.jp. 586 rooms. 11 restaurants, 2 bars, 2 coffee shops, grill, lounge, indoor pool, health club, racquetball, shops, concierge floor, airport shuttle. AE, DC, MC, V.*

$$$$ ⛨ **Nankai South Tower Hotel.** Rooms in this convenient and modern hotel are decorated in three color schemes—light shades of blue, brown, or purple—with low-pile rugs, electronically controlled curtains, and brass fixtures. Bathrobes are supplied on executive floors, where a special lounge is set with complimentary breakfast and beverages. Expect first-rate comfort but little character. Be sure to have a drink in the Sky Lounge. On-site are both a Christian and a Shintō chapel. ⊠ *1–60 Namba 5-chōme, Chūō-ku, Ōsaka 542-0076,* ☎ *06/6646–1111,* FAX *06/6648–0331,* WEB *www.southtower.co.jp. 535 rooms, 11 Western-style suites, 2 Japanese-style suites. 11 restaurants, indoor pool, hot tub, massage, sauna, health club, shops, chapel, concierge floor. AE, DC, MC, V.*

$$$$ ⛨ **Rihga Grand Hotel.** A sister to the Rihga Royal, the Grand is a lively first-class commercial hotel with free shuttle service every few minutes to the Royal and to the Yodoya-bashi subway station. Everything is neat and clean. The staff is large and hardworking, housekeeping is very good, and the rooms are bigger than average for Japanese accommodations. The decor is somewhat dated but in good repair. ✉ *2–3–18 Naka-no-shima, Kita-ku, Ōsaka 530-0005,* ☎ *06/6202–1212,* FAX *06/6227–5054,* WEB *www.rihga.com/osgrand/. 346 rooms. 3 restaurants, shops, business services, meeting rooms. AE, DC, MC, V.*

$$$$ 🏨 **Ritz-Carlton Ōsaka.** Smaller than Ōsaka's other top-class hotels, the
★ Ritz-Carlton manages to combine a homey feel and old-world European elegance into the city's most luxurious hotel. The reception area and lounge are small even by Japanese standards, while the hotel's non-standard layout makes you feel as if you are wandering around a sprawling country home. This gives the hotel its character, which explains the consistently high occupancy rates. Guest rooms have very well appointed bathrooms, king-size beds with goose-down pillows, plenty of dark-wood furnishings—including large desks and chairs—and plush bathrobes and towels. Stay on a Club floor to have the use of a special lounge with complimentary drinks and food throughout the day, as well as free use of the hotel's fitness center (other guests pay ¥3,000). All this comes, of course, at a price—the Ritz-Carlton is also Ōsaka's most expensive hotel. ✉ *2–5–25 Umeda, Kita-ku, Ōsaka 530-0001,* ☎ *06/6343–7000; 800/241–3333 in the U.S.;* FAX *06/6343–7001,* WEB *www.ritzcarlton.com. 292 rooms. 5 restaurants, bar, coffee shop, pool, health club, concierge floor, business services, free parking. AE, DC, MC, V.*

$$$$ 🏨 **The Westin Ōsaka.** Though its location is slightly inconvenient, the Westin has a good reputation and provides standard rooms that are larger than those at the Ritz-Carlton. Rooms are decorated in a European style, with wooden desks and comfortable chairs accompanying the large beds. Guests staying in Executive rooms have the use of a lounge with free drinks and breakfast. The hotel abuts the Umeda Sky Building, so make sure you get a room on the opposite side if you want a good view of the city. The Amadeus restaurant has a reputation for serving up innovative dishes, and a shuttle bus runs to and from JR Ōsaka Eki. ✉ *1–1–20 Oyodo Naka, Kita-ku, Ōsaka 531-0076,* ☎ *06/6440–1111,* FAX *06/6440–1100. 304 rooms. 4 restaurants, café, coffee shop, indoor pool, massage, sauna, health club, shops, business services. AE, DC, MC, V.*

$$$–$$$$ 🏨 **Hotel New Hankyū and Hotel New Hankyū Annex.** The single rooms here are not enormous but are cozy in Japanese fashion. All rooms have modem jacks. This very convenient hotel complex is in Umeda, close to many restaurants and shopping outlets. The 17-story Annex, a block from the main hotel, offers a buffet breakfast and a fitness club with an indoor pool (you have access if you stay in either building). Japanese, French, Chinese, and steak restaurants are located in the main building. ✉ *1–1–35 Shibata, Kita-ku, Ōsaka 530-8310,* ☎ *06/6372–5101,* FAX *06/6374–6885,* WEB *hotel.newhankyu.co.jp. 1,224 rooms. 5 restaurants, bar, breakfast room, lounge, tea shop, in-room data ports, indoor pool, mineral baths, sauna, health club. AE, DC, MC, V.*

$$$–$$$$ 🏨 **Rihga Royal Hotel.** A veritable city within a city built in the 1930s, the Royal encompasses more than 20 restaurants, bars, and karaoke rooms and no fewer than 60 shops—in addition to nearly 1,000 rooms. Standard rooms are spacious and well equipped, with, among other things, in-room data ports, comfortable armchairs, and plenty of closet space. A stay in the VIP tower allows you free access to the swimming club's two sun-roof pools (other guests pay ¥2,000). The Royal Suite—the city's most expensive hotel room at ¥1 million per night—has been the room of choice for such VIPs as Al Gore and opera singer Placido Domingo. The hotel also provides shuttle service to the nearby Rihga Grand Hotel, JR Ōsaka Eki, and the Yodoya-bashi subway station. You can easily walk to the Shiritsu Tōyō Jiki Bijutsukan. ✉ *5–3–68 Naka-no-shima, Kita-ku, Ōsaka 530-0005,* ☎ *06/6448–1121,* FAX *06/6448–*

4414, WEB *www.rihga.com. 980 rooms. 20 restaurants, 2 bars, in-room data ports, 1 indoor pool, 2 outdoor pools, barbershop, hair salon, massage, sauna, steam room, health club, shops, baby-sitting, concierge, business services. AE, DC, MC, V.*

$$$–$$$$ ⊡ **Umeshin East Hotel.** In the antiques-shop and art-gallery neighborhood near the U.S. consulate, this small brick hotel has an attractive modern design, with a café in the lush green interior garden, a restaurant, and a bar in its tiled lobby. Rooms are small but comfortably furnished. ⊠ *4–11–5 Nishi-Tenma, Kita-ku, Ōsaka, 530-0047 (10-min walk from Midō-suji subway line and Ōsaka Eki),* ☎ *06/6364–1151,* FAX *06/6364–1150. 144 rooms. Restaurant, bar, café. AE, DC, MC, V.*

$$–$$$$ ⊡ **Hotel Do Sports Plaza.** In the heart of Ōsaka's colorful nightlife district, the Do Sports Plaza earned its reputation by catering to sports enthusiasts and athletic teams. Most rooms are small but fairly bright singles; doubles are not much larger. Fitness activities are the main attraction here: The hotel adjoins a members-only sports club that is open to hotel guests for an additional ¥2,000 per person. ⊠ *3–3–17 Minami-Semba, Chūō-ku, Ōsaka 542-0081,* ☎ *06/6245–3311,* FAX *06/6245–5803,* WEB *www.hotwire.co.jp/do/. 208 rooms. Restaurant, coffee shop, pub, indoor pool, sauna, health club. AE, DC, MC, V.*

$$$ ⊡ **Ōsaka Airport Hotel.** This is *the* place if you have an early flight out of Ōsaka's Itami Airport: it's right inside the terminal building. These are hardly the most luxurious rooms for the price, but the location is a lifesaver if you're short on time. ⊠ *Ōsaka Airport Bldg., 3rd floor, Tōyō-naka, Ōsaka 560-0036,* ☎ *06/6855–4621,* FAX *06/6855–4620,* WEB *www.j-hotel.or.jp. 105 rooms. 2 restaurants, 2 bars, shops. AE, DC, MC, V.*

$$$ ⊡ **Ōsaka Dai Ichi Hotel.** As Japan's first cylindrical skyscraper—known as the Maru-Biru (Round Building)—the Dai Ichi is easily picked out of the Ōsaka cityscape. The rooms are wedge shape, and half are small singles that are usually occupied on weekdays by businessmen. The hotel has a coffee shop, open around-the-clock, and an underground shopping arcade. The Dai Ichi is conveniently located next to the Hilton Ōsaka, across from Ōsaka Eki. ⊠ *1–9–20 Umeda, Kita-ku, Ōsaka 530-0001,* ☎ *06/6341–4411,* FAX *06/6341–4930,* WEB *www.daiichihotels.com. 478 rooms. 6 restaurants, bar, shops. AE, DC, MC, V.*

$$–$$$ ⊡ **Hotel Echo Ōsaka.** Recommended for those seeking good, moderately priced accommodations, the Echo Ōsaka is near the JR Tennō-ji Eki, though far from other major parts of the city. Eighty-three plain rooms have air-conditioning and basic furnishings, including double or twin beds, uncoordinated carpeting, and small baths. The hotel is neat and clean, if nothing more, and has an accommodating young staff. ⊠ *1–4–7 Abeno-suji, Abeno-ku, Ōsaka 545-0052,* ☎ *06/6633–1141,* FAX *06/6633–3849. 84 rooms. 2 restaurants, bar, coffee shop. AE, DC, MC, V.*

$$ ⊡ **Ōsaka International Community Center Hotel.** The city community center has a hotel with pleasant, well-furnished rooms at reasonable rates. The center hosts lectures and cultural events and offers simultaneous interpreting services. ⊠ *8–2–6 Kamimoto-chō, Tennō-ji-ku, Ōsaka 543-0001,* ☎ *06/6773–8181,* FAX *06/6772–7600. 50 rooms. Restaurant, bar, café, library, meeting room. AE, DC, MC, V.*

$ ⊡ **Ebisu-so Ryokan.** This, Ōsaka's only member of the inexpensive Japanese Inn Group, is a partly wooden structure with 15 Japanese-style rooms. It's a very basic, no-frills operation, with traditional shared baths and no restaurant, though there are plenty nearby. Close to the electrical appliance and computer center of Den Den Town and the National Theater, Ebisu-so Ryokan is a five-minute walk from Ebisu-chō Eki on the Sakai-suji subway line. ⊠ *1–7–33 Nippon-bashi-nishi, Naniwa-ku, Ōsaka 556-0004,* ☎ *06/6643–4861. 15 Japanese-style rooms with shared bath. AE, MC, V.*

NIGHTLIFE AND THE ARTS

The Arts

National Bunraku Theater. Osakans have helped make Bunraku a sophisticated art form—so a performance here is not to be missed. The theater is active in January, March, April, June, July, August, and November, and each run starts on the third of the month and lasts about three weeks. The Ōsaka tourist offices will have the current schedule, which is also printed in *Kansai Time Out* and the quarterly tourist booklet, *Meet Ōsaka*. Tickets are ¥4,400 and ¥5,600; performances usually begin at 11 AM and 4 PM.

From the Namba subway station, take the Sennichi-mae subway line one stop east to Nippon-bashi Eki. Take Exit 7, and you will be right outside the theater. ✉ *12–10 Nippon-bashi 1-chōme, Chūo-ku,* ☎ *06/ 6212–2531,* WEB *www.osaka.isp.ntt-west.co.jp.*

Sho-chiku-za Kabuki Theater. Since 1997 Ōsaka's Kabuki theater has rivaled Tōkyō's Kabuki-za. Technology has been cleverly incorporated into Sho-chiku-za (originally built in 1923 as Japan's first Western-style theater) alongside traditional theater design. The house hosts Kabuki for about half the year, with major performances most months. The rest of the year it hosts musicals and other concerts. Tickets range in price from ¥4,000 to ¥20,000. ✉ *1–9–19 Dōtombori, Chūo-ku,* ☎ *06/6214–2211; 06/6214–2200 for reservations.*

Nightlife

Ōsaka has as diverse a nighttime scene as Japan's capital, Tōkyō. The Kita (North) area surrounds JR Umeda Eki; and the Minami (South) area is between the Shin-Sai-bashi and Namba districts. Part of Chūo-ku (Central Ward) is in Minami. Many Japanese refer to Minami as being "for kids," but there are still a great number of good restaurants and drinking spots for more seasoned bon vivants. Ōsaka's hip young things hang out in Amerika Mura, in the southern part of Chūo-ku, where there are innumerable bars and clubs.

The mainstay of foreign bars is the **Pig & Whistle** (Kita: ✉ Ohatsutenjin Bldg., basement, 2–5 Sonezaki, Kita-ku, ☎ 06/6361–3198; Minami: ✉ ACROSS Bldg., 2nd floor, 6–14 Shin-Sai-bashi-suji 2-chōme, Chūo-ku, ☎ 06/6213–6911) minichain of English pub–style places. Established in the early 1980s, the chain now has three locations—two of which are in Ōsaka. Fish-and-chips (what else?) is served with Guinness, as well as with bottled beers and a good selection of spirits. These places get very busy on weekends.

Canopy (✉ IM Excellence Bldg., 1st floor, 1–11–20 Sonezaki-shinchi, Kita-ku, ☎ 06/6341–0339) stays open until 5 AM. Portions are healthy, the happy hour is generous, and a terrace allows for open-air dining in summer. **Club Karma** (✉ Kasai Bldg., 1st floor, 1–5–18 Sonezaki-shinchi, Kita-ku, ☎ 06/6344–6181) has become a trendy place where style gurus and businesspeople coexist in harmony. It's expensive, but the people-watching is great. Club Karma hosts all-night techno rave dance parties on weekends and sometimes during the week as well (cover from ¥2,500). **Club Quattro** (✉ Shin-Sai-bashi Parco Bldg., 8th floor, Shin-sai-bashi-suji 1–9–1, Chūo-ku, ☎ 06/6281–8181) features up-and-coming Japanese rock bands as well as popular British and (more expensive) American bands almost every night. The sound system is excellent.

The popular **Club Joule** (✉ Brutus Bldg., 2nd and 3rd floors, 2–11–30 Nishi-Shin-sai-bashi, Chūo-ku, ☎ 06/6214–1223) caters to R&B

and hip-hop fans during the week and house and techno clubbers on weekends. A café-style seating area upstairs is a good place to recuperate between dances—or an ideal location for those who'd rather just watch the action. **Underlounge** (✉ 634 Bldg., B1 floor, 2–7–11 Nishi-Shin-sai-bashi, Chūō-ku, ☎ 06/6214–3322) is perhaps the city's slickest and most modern dance club, with a state-of-the-art sound system and regular appearances by big-name international DJs.

For those who'd rather relax with a beer than spend the night on the dance floor, **Balabushka** (✉ Nippo Mittera Kaikan, 4th floor, 9–5 2-chōme Nishi-Shin-Sai-bashi, Chūō-ku, ☎ 06/6211–5369) has happy hour, pool tables, dartboards, and plenty of places to sit even when it's busy. The **Cellar** (✉ Dai-3-Hirata Bldg., basement, 2–17–13 Nishi-Shin-Sai-bashi, Chūō-ku, ☎ 06/6212–6437) is a smaller bar than Balabushka but has live music three times a week.

OUTDOOR ACTIVITIES AND SPORTS

Participant Sports

Jogging

With its extensive grounds, **Ōsaka-jō Kōen** (Ōsaka Castle Park) is the best place to jog in the city. ✉ *Next to JR Ōsaka-jō Kōen-mae Eki.*

Skating

Ōsaka Pool Skating Rink (✉ 3–1–20 Tanaka, Minato-ku, ☎ 06/6571–2010) is open November to March, daily from 9 to 9. It's easily accessible, near JR Ashiobashi Eki on the Loop Line and costs ¥1,400 to enter this world-class facility.

Swimming

If you're not staying in one of the high-end hotels with a swimming pool, you have a few other options. **Ogimachi Pool** (✉ Ogimachi Kōen, Kita-ku, ☎ 06/6383–8911), completed in 2001, is a modern affair close to JR Tenma Eki, one stop from JR Ōsaka. It's closed Wednesday. **Ōsaka Pool** (✉ 3–1–20 Tanaka, Minato-ku, ☎ 06/6571–2010), closed Monday, is near JR Ashiobashi Eki on the Loop Line. The 50-meter swimming pool (10 lanes) was designed with an eye toward the city's (unsuccessful) Olympic bid.

Spectator Sports

Baseball

Ōsaka Dōmu (Ōsaka Dome). For a taste of Japanese *besuboru* (baseball), this futuristic stadium is where the local Kintetsu Buffaloes square off against national rivals. Tickets can be had for as little as ¥1,600. Buy them at the gate, at branches of Lawsons convenience store in the city, or by telephone from Ticket Pia. ✉ *Next to Ōsaka Dōmu-mae Chiyozaki subway station on Nagahori Tsurumi-ryokuchi line.* ☎ *06/6363–9999 Ticket Pia.*

Soccer

Ōsaka is home to two J. League soccer teams, Cerezo Ōsaka and Gamba Ōsaka. The announcement that Japan and South Korea would be joint hosts of the Soccer World Cup 2002 (Nagai stadium will host a game) brought about a resurgence of popularity in the nation's professional J. League. Tickets are reasonably priced, starting at ¥1,500 for adults, ¥800 for children, from March to November. J. League games rarely sell out, as the stadiums are very big.

The Cerezo Ōsaka play at the **Nagai Stadium** (☎ 06/6692–9011) in south Ōsaka, close to Nagai Eki on the JR Hanwa Line or Midō-suji subway line. The Gamba Ōsaka play at **Bampaku EXPO Memorial Stadium** (☎ 06/6202–5201) in the north of the city. Access is via the Ōsaka Monorail to Kōen Higashi-guchi Eki.

Sumō

From the second Sunday through the fourth Sunday in March, one of Japan's six sumō tournaments takes place in the **Ōsaka Furitsu Taiikukaikan** (Ōsaka Prefectural Gymnasium: ⊠ 3–4–36 Namba-naka, Naniwa-ku, ☎ 06/6631–0120). Most seats, known as *masu-seki*, are prebooked before the tournament begins, but standing room is usually available for ¥1,000. The ticket office opens at 9 AM. The stadium is a 10-minute walk from Namba Eki.

SHOPPING

Ōsaka is known for its vast underground shopping malls, which, even to the long-term resident, are notoriously difficult to navigate, especially the ones underneath JR Ōsaka Eki. Seemingly the human equivalent of rabbit warrens, the various shopping malls merge with one another along ill-defined boundaries, but the wealth of shops makes strolling a pleasure, especially if it is raining, or in the summer as a respite from the heat. Everything from cafés and Italian restaurants to second-hand CD shops, fashionable clothing boutiques, and discount ticket outlets can be found underground. A good place to start exploring these malls is from JR Ōsaka Eki in the northern part of the city or from Namba subway station in the south. Signposting is in both English and Japanese in many places, and if you're ever not quite sure of your bearings, all you have to do is pop up to ground level, like some sort of urban submariner.

In addition to numerous shopping arcades and underground malls, there are specialized wholesale areas throughout the city, many of which have a few retail shops and are worth a visit.

Depātos

All major Japanese department stores are represented in Ōsaka. Some of them, like Hankyū and Kintetsu, are headquartered here. All are open 10–7 and but close on Wednesday or Thursday. The following are some of Ōsaka's leading depātos. **Daimaru** (⊠ 1–7–1 Shin-Sai-bashi-suji, Chūō-ku, ☎ 06/6343–1231). **Hankyū** (⊠ 8–7 Kakuta-chō, Kita-ku, ☎ 06/6361–1381). **Hanshin** (⊠ 1–13–13 Umeda, Kita-ku, ☎ 06/6345–1201). **Kintetsu** (⊠ 1–1–43 Abeno-suji, Abeno-ku, ☎ 06/6624–1111; ⊠ 6–1–55 Ue-hon-machi, Tennō-ji-ku, ☎ 06/6775–1111). **Matsuzakaya** (⊠ 1–1 Tenma-bashi Kyo-machi, Chūō-ku, ☎ 06/6943–1111). **Mitsukoshi** (⊠ 7–5 Korai-bashi 1-chōme, Chūō-ku, ☎ 06/6203–1331). **Takashimaya** (⊠ 5–1–5 Namba, Chūō-ku, ☎ 06/6631–1101).

Gifts

At one time famous for its traditional crafts—particularly its *karaki-sashimono* (ornately carved furniture), its fine Naniwa Suzuki pewterware, and its *uchihamono* (Sakai cutlery)—Ōsaka lost much of its traditional industry during World War II. The simplest way to find a wide selection of Ōsaka crafts is to visit one of the major department stores, many of which carry a selection of locally made wares.

For folk crafts from all over the country, including ceramics, basketry, paper goods, folk toys, and textiles, visit the **Nihon Kogeikan Mingei Fukyubu** (Japan Folkcraft Collection: ⊠ 4–7–15 Nishi-Tenma, Kita-ku, ☎ 06/6362–9501), near the Umeshin East Hotel in the popular gallery district, within walking distance of the U.S. consulate. It's open Monday–Saturday 10–5:30.

Electronics

Though some Japanese electronic goods may be cheaper in the United States than in Japan due to discounting policies, bear in mind that many of the latest electronics products are released on the Japanese market from 6 to 12 months before they reach shops in the West.

Den Den Town has about 300 retail shops that specialize in electronics products (Den Den is a takeoff on the word *denki,* which means electricity) as well as stores for cameras and watches. The area is near Ebisu-chō Eki on the Sakai-suji subway line (Exit 1 or 2), and Nippon-bashi Eki on the Sakai-suji and Sennichi-mae subway lines (Exit 5 or 10). Shops are open 10–7 daily. Take your passport, and make your purchases in stores with signs that say TAX FREE in order to qualify for a 5% discount.

ŌSAKA A TO Z

To research prices, get advice from other travelers, and book travel arrangements, visit www.fodors.com.

AIR TRAVEL

CARRIERS

International carriers include Air Canada and Northwest Airlines to North America, and Japan Airlines to the United Kingdom. Flights from Tōkyō, which operate frequently throughout the day, take 70 minutes. Japan Airlines (JAL), All Nippon Airways (ANA), and Japan Air System (JAS) have domestic flights to major cities. For airline toll-free phone numbers in the United States, *see* Air Travel *in* Smart Travel Tips A to Z.
➤ AIRLINES AND CONTACTS: **Air Canada** (☎ 06/6252–4227). **All Nippon Airways** (☎ 0120/02–9222). **Japan Air System** (☎ 0120/51–1283). **Japan Airlines** (☎ 0120/255–931 international; 0120/255–971 domestic). **Northwest Airlines** (☎ 0120/120–747).

AIRPORTS AND TRANSFERS

AIRPORTS

All international flights arrive at Kansai International Airport (KIX). There are also connecting domestic flights to major Japanese cities. The airport, constructed on reclaimed land in Ōsaka Bay, is laid out vertically—the buildings, not the runways. The first floor is for international arrivals, the second floor is for domestic departures and arrivals, the third floor has shops and restaurants, and the fourth floor is for international departures.

About 60% of domestic flights still use Ōsaka's old airport, Itami Airport, half an hour or so northwest of Ōsaka. Flights from Tōkyō, which operate frequently throughout the day, take 70 minutes.

TRANSFERS

KIX was designed to serve the entire Kansai region (Kōbe, Kyōto, and Nara) not just Ōsaka. There are four main access routes to Ōsaka: to Shin-Ōsaka take the JR Kansai Airport Express Haruka for the 45-minute run (¥2,930); to Tennō-ji Eki, the same JR train will take about 29 minutes (¥2,250); to JR Kyo-bashi Eki take the Kansai Airport Rapid train for a 70-minute run (¥1,140); finally, to Nankai Namba Eki take the Nankai Rapid Limited Express (private line) for a 29-minute trip (¥1,370). No English-language hot line for JR schedules exists, but tourist information offices and hotel staff should be able to help.

The airport is not that large: as soon as you come out through customs you are in the arrivals lobby, where you'll find English-language tourist information and direct access to limousine buses. Airport bus limousine service runs between KIX and many of Ōsaka's downtown hotels. The very comfortable bus takes about 60 minutes (¥1,300–¥1,800).

Buses from Itami Airport operate at intervals of 15 minutes to one hour, 6 AM–9 PM, and take passengers to seven locations in Ōsaka: Shin-Ōsaka Eki, Umeda, Namba (near the Nikkō and Holiday Inn hotels), Ue-hon-machi, Abeno, Sakai-higashi, and Ōsaka Business Park (near the New Otani Hotel). Buses take 25–50 minutes, depending on destination, and cost ¥340–¥680. Schedules, with exact times and fares, are available at the information counter at the airport.

Taxis to the city from Kansai International Airport are prohibitively expensive; between Itami Airport and hotels in central Ōsaka, taxis cost approximately ¥7,500 and take about 40 minutes.

BUS TRAVEL
Economical one-day transportation passes for Ōsaka are valid on bus lines as well as subway routes, and the service operates throughout the day and evening, but bus travel is a challenge best left to local residents or those fluent in Japanese.

BUSINESS ASSISTANCE
Contact Information Service System Co., Ltd. for business-related assistance, including quick-print business cards and interpreting.
➤ CONTACT: **Information Service System Co., Ltd.** (✉ Hotel Nikkō Ōsaka, 1–3–5 Nishi-Shin-Sai-bashi, Chūō-ku, ☎ 06/6245–4015).

CONSULATES
Canada (✉ 2–2–3 Nishi-Shin-Sai-bashi, Chūō-ku, ☎ 06/6212–4910). **U.K.** (✉ Seiko Ōsaka Bldg., 19th floor, 35–1 Bakuro-machi, Chūō-ku, ☎ 06/6281–1616). **U.S.** (✉ 2–11–5 Nishi-Tenma, Kita-ku, ☎ 06/6315–5900).

EMERGENCIES
For medical advice, call the International Medical Information Center or the International Medical Center Kansai.
➤ DOCTORS AND HOSPITALS: **International Medical Information Center** (☎ 06/6213–2393). **International Medical Center Kansai** (☎ 06/6636–2333). **Sumitomo Hospital** (✉ 2–2 Naka-no-shima 5-chōme, Kita-ku, ☎ 06/6443–1261). **Tane General Hospital** (✉ 1–2–31 Sakai-gawa, Nishi-ku, ☎ 06/6581–1071). **Yodo-gawa Christian Hospital** (✉ 9–26 Awaji 2-chōme, Higashi Yodo-gawa-ku, ☎ 06/6322–2250).
➤ EMERGENCY SERVICES: **Ambulance** (☎ 119). **Metropolitan Police Office Service** (☎ 06/6943–1234). **Police** (☎ 110).

ENGLISH-LANGUAGE MEDIA
BOOKS
Kinokuniya Book Store Co., Ltd. is open daily 10–9, except for the third Wednesday of the month. It is across the street from the Midō-suji entrance of Ōsaka Eki in the Hankyū Eki complex. Maruzen sells English-language books and is open daily 10–8 on Shin-sai-bashi-suji, north of Shin-sai-bashi subway station.
➤ MEDIA CONTACTS: **Kinokuniya Book Store Co., Ltd.** (✉ Hankyū Samban-gai 1–1–3, Shibata, Kita-ku, ☎ 06/6372–5821). **Maruzen** (✉ 3–3–2 Bakuromachi, Chūō-ku, ☎ 06/6251–2700).

NEWSPAPERS AND MAGAZINES
Established in 1977, *Kansai Time Out* is a monthly publication listing all sorts of events in Kōbe, Kyōto, Nara, and Ōsaka. There are also

topical articles written for travelers and residents. It costs ¥300 and is available at all major hotels and bookshops throughout the region.

SUBWAYS

Ōsaka's fast, efficient subway system offers the most convenient means of exploring the city—complicated bus routes display no signs in English, and taxis, while plentiful, are costly. There are seven lines, of which Midō-suji is the main one; it runs between Shin-Ōsaka and Umeda in 6 minutes, Shin-Ōsaka and Shin-Sai-bashi in 12 minutes, Shin-Ōsaka and Namba in 14 minutes, and Shin-Ōsaka and Tennō-ji in 20 minutes.

Subways run from early morning until nearly midnight at intervals of three to five minutes. Fares begin at ¥200 and are determined by the distance traveled. You can purchase a one-day pass (¥850)—which provides unlimited municipal transportation on subways, the New Tram (a tram line that runs to the port area), and city buses—at the commuter ticket windows in major subway stations and at the Japan Travel Bureau office in Ōsaka Eki. A very useful subway network map of Ōsaka is available in city tourist offices, most hotels, and from the Japan National Tourist Organization in the United States or in Tōkyō (☞ Visitor Information *in* Smart Travel Tips A to Z).

Adding to the efficiency of the subway system is the Loop Line, which circles the city aboveground and intersects all subway lines. Fares range from ¥180 to ¥420, or you can use your JR Pass.

TAXIS

You'll have no problem hailing taxis on the street or at specified taxi stands. (A red light in the lower left corner of the windshield indicates availability.) The problem is moving in Ōsaka's heavy traffic. Fares are metered at ¥640 for the first 2 km (1 mi), plus ¥80 for each additional 500 yards. Few taxi drivers speak English, so it is advisable to have your address written in Japanese characters to show to the driver. It's not customary to tip, and an increasing number of taxis now accept credit cards.

TELEPHONES

➤ DIRECTORY AND OPERATOR ASSISTANCE: **Directory assistance in English** (☎ 0120/364–463).

TOURS

The Aqua Liner runs a 60-minute tour (¥1,800) through Ōsaka's waterways, departing daily every hour from 10 to 4 from April to September. There are also evening tours from 6 to 7 on Friday, Saturday, Sunday, and national holidays departing from three piers, at Ōsaka-jō, Tenma-bashi, and Yodoya-bashi. This is the only tour of Ōsaka conducted in both Japanese and English.

Japan Amenity Travel has two full-day tours: one to Kyōto only (¥12,000) and one to Kyōto and Nara (¥13,500). Tours depart from the Ōsaka Hilton International and include train fare to Kyōto. Staff at the hotel can help you with bookings. Japan Travel Bureau runs afternoon tours daily to Kyōto and Nara. Pickup is available at several hotels.

Japan's Home Visit System, which enables foreign visitors to meet local people in their homes for a few hours and learn more about the Japanese lifestyle, is available in Ōsaka. Apply in advance through the Ōsaka Tourist Information Center at JR Shin-Ōsaka Eki or at the Ōsaka City Tourist Information Office at the JR Ōsaka Eki.

➤ CONTACTS: **Aqua Liner** (☎ 06/6942–5511). **Japan Amenity Travel** (☎ 075/222–0121 in Kyōto). **Japan Travel Bureau** (☎ 06/6343–0617).

TRAIN TRAVEL

Hikari Shinkansen trains from Tōkyō to Shin-Ōsaka Eki take just under three hours and cost ¥13,750 for reserved seats, ¥12,980 for non-reserved. You can use a JR Pass for the *Hikari* but not for the faster *Nozomi* Shinkansen, which cost ¥14,720. Shin-Ōsaka Eki, on the north side of Shin-Yodo-gawa, is linked to the city center by the JR Kōbe Line and the Midō-suji subway line. The ride, which takes 6–20 minutes, depending on your mid-city destination, costs ¥180–¥230. Train schedule and fare information can be obtained at the Travel Service Center in the Shin-Ōsaka Eki. A taxi from Shin-Ōsaka Eki to central Ōsaka costs ¥1,500–¥2,700.

VISITOR INFORMATION

The main Ōsaka Tourist Information Center, open daily 8–8 and closed December 31–January 3, is on the east side of the main exit of JR Shin-Ōsaka Eki. There is another location at the Midō-suji gate of JR Ōsaka Eki, open daily from 8 to 8 and closed December 31–January 4. A small branch on the first floor of the passenger terminal building in Kansai International Airport is open daily 9–5. The Ōsaka-jō center is open daily 9–5.

Japan Travel Phone, available daily 9–5, provides free information in English.

Academy Travel, No. 1 Travel, and STA Travel sell cheap air tickets, and staff are well versed in English.

➤ TOURIST INFORMATION: **Academy Travel** (✉ Takada II, 4th floor, 2–6–8 Juso Higashi, Yodo-gawa-ku, ☏ 06/6303–3538). **Japan Travel Phone** (☏ 0088/22–4800). **No. 1 Travel** (✉ Nisshin Bldg., 11th floor, 8–8 Taiyuji-chō, Kita-ku, ☏ 06/6363–4489). **Ōsaka City Tourist Information Center** (✉ JR Shin-Ōsaka Eki, ☏ 06/6305–3311; ✉ JR Ōsaka Eki, ☏ 06/6345–2189; ✉ Kansai International Airport, ☏ 0724/56–6025; ✉ Ōsaka-jō, ☏ 06/6941–0546). **STA Travel** (✉ Hon-machi Meida Bldg., 4th floor, 2–5–5 Azuchi-machi, Chūō-ku, ☏ 06/6262–7066).

8 KŌBE

Kōbe is unique in Japan for its blending of European and Japanese influences, both in its architecture and in the attitudes of its inhabitants. For these reasons, Kōbe is often the choice of residence for many Westerners, who would rather avoid the bustle and crowds of more expensive Ōsaka.

By Nigel Fisher

Updated
by Dominic
Al-Badri

KŌBE HAS BEEN A PROMINENT HARBOR CITY throughout Japanese history. In the 12th century the Taira family moved the capital from Kyōto to Fukuhara, the western part of modern Kōbe, with the hope of increasing Japan's international trade. Fukuhara remained the capital for a mere six months, but its port, known as Hyōgo, continued to flourish. Japan didn't officially open its ports to Western trade until 1868, after a long period of isolationism. At the time, in order to prevent foreigners from using the profitable port of Hyōgo, the more remote port of Kōbe was opened to international trade. Within a few years, Kōbe, slightly northeast of Hyōgo, eclipsed it in importance as a port. Now a major industrial city, Kōbe has an active port that serves as many as 10,000 ships a year.

A century of exposure to international cultures has left its mark on Kōbe, a sophisticated and cosmopolitan city. Of its population of 2 million, some 70,000 residents are *gaijin* (foreigners). Most are Chinese or Korean, but a noticeable European contingent also lives and works in Kōbe. Over the years foreign merchants and traders have settled in the hills above the port area. Western-style houses built in the late 19th century are still inhabited by Kōbe's large foreign population, although others have been opened to the public as buildings of historical interest. Many sailors who passed through Kōbe were attracted by the charm of this city and have settled here. So don't come to Kōbe looking for traditional Japan. Instead, visit to relax in a cosmopolitan setting with excellent shopping and international cuisines.

Though the damage wreaked by the Great Hanshin Earthquake in January 1995 was indeed tremendous—more than 5,000 people were killed and some 100,000 buildings destroyed—the process of recovery has been speedy, especially in the city proper. The only cultural attractions completely wiped out were the wonderful 19th-century sake breweries that had been converted into museums. Among Kōbe's suburban shoreline sprawl, a few buildings remain in ruins.

Plans for a domestic airport, to be built on a man-made island, continue apace, even though some 300,000 signatures were collected protesting that it was an unnecessary waste of taxpayers' money. Kōbe Kūkō (Kōbe Airport) is due for completion in 2005 and remains a controversial talking point among the city's residents.

Kōbe Glossary

Key Japanese words and suffixes in this chapter include *-chō* (street or block), *-chōme* (street), *chūō* (central), *depāto* (department store), *-dōri* (street or avenue), *eki* (station), *ijinkan* (Western-style house), *jinja* (Shintō shrine), *kōen* ("*ko*-en," park), *-san* (mountain), *-ku* (section or ward), *onsen* (hot springs), Seto Nai-kai (Seto Inland Sea), *-shi* (city or municipality), Shinkansen (bullet train, literally "new trunk line"), and *torii* ("*to*-ree-ee," gate).

Pleasures and Pastimes

Dining

Think Kōbe, think beef. Kōbe beef is considered a delicacy all over Japan—and the world. Tender, tasty, and extremely expensive, it's a must for beef lovers. Raised in the nearby Tajima area of Hyōgo Prefecture, Kōbe cows are fed beer and are massaged to improve the quality of their meat and give it its marbled (with fat) texture.

There are many international cuisines available in Kōbe. Some sailors stay on in the city and open restaurants that become popular with the large foreign community and with resident and visiting Japanese. The quality and authenticity of these places are unsurpassed.

CATEGORY	COST*
$$$$	over ¥6,000
$$$	¥4,000–¥6,000
$$	¥2,000–¥4,000
$	under ¥2,000

*per person for a main course at dinner

Lodging

Kōbe has a wide range of hotels varying in price and quality. Because it's a heavily industrialized city, Kōbe caters to a lot of business travelers. As a result, the business hotels are conveniently located. Most are quite comfortable.

CATEGORY	COST*
$$$$	over ¥20,000
$$$	¥15,000–¥20,000
$$	¥10,000–¥15,000
$	under ¥10,000

*All prices are for a double room, excluding service and tax.

EXPLORING KŌBE

Downtown Kōbe, the site of most businesses, is near the harbor area. The rest of Kōbe is built on slopes that extend as far as the base of Rokko-san—this hill-and-harbor combination brings San Francisco to some people's minds. In the middle of the harbor is the man-made Pōto Airando (Port Island), which has conference centers, an amusement park, and the Portopia Hotel. The island is linked with downtown by a fully computerized monorail—with no human conductor. The major nightlife area, Ikuta (a part of the Kitano area), is just north of San-no-miya Eki.

Numbers in the text correspond to numbers in the margin and on the Kōbe map.

Great Itineraries

If you are interested in seeing local Japanese culture—as opposed to the expatriate culture of Kōbe—this city needn't be high on your list. It does make for a good break from a standard Japan itinerary, though, and a stroll around its hillside precinct punctuated by a café stop and a great dinner is time well spent. A short day is usually enough as an excursion from Ōsaka or Kyōto. You could even stop off for a few hours on your way down the San-yō Coast. You could spend a second day here if you plan to make a couple of side trips to Rokko-san and Arima Onsen.

When to Tour Kōbe

Except for during the cold days of winter, Kōbe enjoys a mild climate tempered by the Seto Nai-kai. Spring, especially at cherry-blossom time, and autumn are the optimal seasons to visit Kōbe, as well as most of Japan. Midsummer can be quite humid; winter is wet, chilly, and damp, though the sea keeps it from getting very cold.

A Good Tour

A good place to start your visit to Kōbe is the **Phoenix Plaza** ①, close to JR San-no-miya Eki, an information centerdedicated to the devastating 1995 earthquake. A few minutes' walk away is the **Kōbe Shiritsu Hakubutsukan** ②, a museum where you can take in the history of this international port town, including memorabilia from the heyday of the old foreign settlement. To get to the museum, walk south down

Flower Road from San-no-miya Eki, past the Flower Clock and City Hall, to Higashi-Yuenchi Kōen. Walk through the park to the Kōbe Minato post office, across the street on the west side. Walk east on the road in front of the post office toward the Oriental Hotel. Turn left at the corner in front of the hotel; the museum is in the old Bank of Tōkyō building, at the end of the block.

Return to San-no-miya Eki, browsing through **Nankin-machi** (China-town) ③ and the Moto-machi and San-no-miya shopping arcades if time permits. Then, down by the water, stop into Meriken Kōen and the **Kōbe Kaiyō Hakubutsukan** ④, with its exhibits of ships and all things nautical. Once back at San-no-miya Eki, begin your tour of the northern district by crossing the street that runs along the tracks and turning left at the first main intersection to see the classic outline of the orange torii at **Ikuta Jinja** ⑤. The road that runs up the right side of the shrine leads up the slope to Nakayamate-dōri. Cross the avenue and continue up the slope. Turn right at the corner of Yamamoto-dōri, a road lined with high-fashion boutiques and restaurants. Turn left at Kitano-zaka, which leads to **Kitano-chō,** an area where Western traders and businessmen have lived since the late 19th century. Many of the older ijinkan have been turned into museums. Continue up the slope from Nakayamate-dōri. At the first intersection after Yamamoto-dōri (nicknamed Ijinkan-dōri), just past Rin's Gallery, which is filled with boutiques of Japan's top designers, turn right and walk east to visit the 1907 **Eikoku-kan** ⑥.

Three ijinkan in the Kitano-ku area are publicly owned. **Rhein-no-Yakata** ⑦, opposite Eikoku-kan, has a German-style coffee shop inside. Near Kitano Tenman Jinja at the top of the hill is the **Kazami-dōri-no-Yakata** ⑧, made famous on a national TV series some years ago. Continue back down the slope via Kitano-zaka toward San-no-miya Eki and turn right on Yamamoto-dōri. One ijinkan house not to miss is the 1869 **Choueke Yashiki** ⑨, full of interesting turn-of-the-20th-century items. Return to San-no-miya Eki and walk to the **Port-liner** ⑩ platform, and take the automated train to the consumeristic diversions on **Pōto Airando** (Port Island) ⑪.

Sights to See

Downtown Kōbe and Port Island

⑤ **Ikuta Jinja.** Entrance to this Shintō shrine is through an impressive orange torii, which was rebuilt after the 1995 earthquake. According to legend, the shrine was founded by Empress Jingū in the 3rd century and therefore is one of the oldest in Japan. The shrine is about 450 yards west of San-no-miya Eki.

④ **Kōbe Kaiyō Hakubutsukan** (Kōbe Maritime Museum). To the right of Meriken Kōen, on Port Island, stands the Port Tower, Kōbe's Eiffel Tower. From the revolving restaurant at its top, you can look out on a magnificent view of the harbor and the prowlike roof of the museum, which is well worth a visit. Models of all kinds of vessels, from ancient designs to modern hydrofoils, are on display. Look for the Oshoro Maru model—it was one of Japan's earliest sailing ships and is adorned with pearls, rubies, gold, and silver. On the first floor is a model of the HMS *Rodney,* the British flagship that led a 12-ship flotilla into Kōbe Harbor on January 1, 1868—the date that marked the official opening of Japan after 250 years of isolationism. In contrast to all of this backward looking, the *Submarine Travel 2090* puts you in the center of a biosphere on the sea floor. ✉ *Meriken Kōen,* ☎ *078/391–6751.* 🖃 ¥500. ☉ *Tues.–Sun. 10–5.*

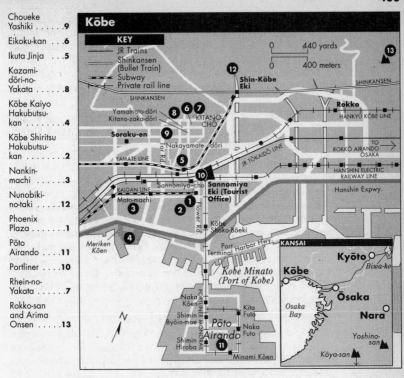

★ **②** **Kōbe Shiritsu Hakubutsukan** (Kōbe City Museum). Look into the past life of this international port town: Alongside earlier artifacts, the museum has an interesting collection of memorabilia from the heyday of the old foreign settlement, including a scale model of the foreign concession. Three entire rooms from a turn-of-the-20th-century Western house are on display. You'll also discover selections from the museum's famous *namban* collection of prints, screens, and paintings by Japanese artists of the late 16th to 17th centuries that depict foreigners in Japanese settings from that period. (Namban refers to anything or any person that came from outside Japan when the first contact occurred between Japan and the West in the 16th and 17th centuries.)

From San-no-miya Eki, walk south on Flower Road to Higashi-Yuenchi Kōen. Walk through the park to the Kōbe Minato post office, across the street on the west side. Walk east on the road in front of the post office toward the Oriental Hotel. Turn left at the corner in front of the hotel, and the City Museum is in the old Bank of Tōkyō building, at the end of the block. ⊠ *24 Kyō-machi, Chūō-ku,* ☎ *078/391–0035.* ⊠ *¥200 (more for special exhibitions).* ⊙ *Tues.–Sun. 10–5.*

③ **Nankin-machi** (Chinatown). Centered at Daimaru Depāto, Nankin-machi is a hot-spot destination for Japanese who come to buy souvenirs and try the many Chinese restaurants. To find Chinatown from Moto-machi Eki, walk on the port side and enter the neighborhood through the large, fake marble gate.

① **Phoenix Plaza.** Completed in 1996, this center details the ongoing reconstruction work following the devastating 1995 earthquake, in addition to acting as a memorial to those who lost their lives in the disaster. There are plenty of photographs and multimedia displays, a number of which are in English. An English pamphlet is also available. ⊠ *1–7 Sannomiya-chō, Chūō-ku,* ☎ *078/325–8558.* ⊠ *Free.* ⊙ *Daily 10–7.*

⓫ **Pōto Airando** (Port Island). The degree to which Kōbe has been internationalized is reflected in the Japanese name for this piece of landfill: Pōto Airando is a wholesale borrowing from English pronounced Japanese-style to sound like Port Island. The Portliner monorail's Shimin Hiroba Eki is right in the heart of the island's futuristic complex, with parks, hotels, restaurants, and fashion boutiques to explore.

⓾ **Portliner.** This digitally driven monorail departs San-no-miya Eki every six minutes from 6:05 AM until 11:44 PM on its loop to and around Port Island, with eight stops along the way. The ride affords a close-up view of Kōbe Harbor. ☞ ¥520 *round-trip.*

Kitano-chō

★ In the area known as **Kitano,** wealthy foreigners in the late 19th century set up residences, bringing to Japan Western-style domestic architecture, referred to in Kōbe as ijinkan. The district is extremely popular with young Japanese tourists, who enjoy the opportunity of seeing old-fashioned Western houses, which are rare in Japan. The curious mélange of Japanese and Western Victorian and Gothic architecture makes for an interesting walk in the hills of this neighborhood. Many residences are still inhabited by Westerners, but more than a dozen 19th-century ijinkan in Kitano-chō are open to the public. Seeing all of them can get repetitious.

To get to Kitano-chō to see the ijinkan, take a 15-minute walk north along Kitano-zaka-dōri from San-no-miya Eki or a 10-minute walk west along Kitano-dōri from Shin-Kōbe Eki. Yamamoto-dōri (nicknamed Ijinkan-dōri) is Kitano's main street, and the ijinkan are on the small side streets ascending the hill.

★ ❾ **Choueke Yashiki** (Choueke ["choo-eh-keh"] Mansion). Built in 1889, this is the only house open to the public that is still inhabited. It's filled to the rafters with memorabilia from East and West. Mrs. Choueke is on hand to show you her treasures, which include many namban wood-block prints, and to share her vast knowledge of Kōbe. Her ijinkan is not to be missed. ☒ *Yamamoto-dōri (street also known as Ijinkan-dōri), Chūō-ku,* ☎ *078/221–3209.* ☞ *¥500.* ⊗ *Wed.–Mon. 9–5.*

❻ **Eikoku-kan** (*"eh*-ee-ko *koo*-kan," English House). This typical old-fashioned Western house—with Union Jacks draped outside—was constructed in 1907 by an Englishman named Baker and served as a makeshift hospital during World War II when the city's main hospital was damaged in an air attack. It's currently a house museum, furnished in period style and complete with an authentic black taxi from London in the driveway. ☒ *2–3–16 Kitano-dōri, Chūō-ku,* ☎ *078/241–2338.* ☞ *¥700.* ⊗ *Daily 9–5.*

❽ **Kazami-dōri-no-Yakata** (Weathercock House). More elaborate than any other Kōbe ijinkan, this one, built in 1909, is listed as an Important Cultural Property. Kazami-dōri-no-Yakata is near Kitano Tenman Jinja at the top of the hill. The interior of this building reflects various traditional German architectural themes, including that of a medieval castle. ☒ *Kazami-dōri, Chūō-ku,* ☎ *078/243–3223.* ☞ *Free.* ⊗ *Wed.–Mon. 10–5.*

❼ **Rhein-no-Yakata** (Rhein House). Opposite Eikoku-kan, Rhein-no-Yakata has a pleasant German-style coffee shop inside, and you can tour the house. ☒ *Kitano-dōri, Chūō-ku,* ☎ *078/222–3403.* ☞ *Free.* ⊗ *Fri.–Wed. 10–5.*

Around Kōbe

⓬ **Nunobiki-no-taki** (Nunobiki Falls). A quiet side trip from the city is the 20-minute walk up the hill behind Shin-Kōbe Eki to Nunobiki Falls, whose beauty has been referred to in Japanese literature since the 10th century. The four cascades of varying heights are collectively known as one of the three greatest falls in Japan.

⑬ Rokko-san and Arima Onsen. A cable car climbs this, the highest peak in the Rokko Mountains, which form a backdrop to Kōbe. Some of the most exciting views are en route, so have your camera ready. Once at the top in the cool mountain air—a delight in summer—you get a staggering view of the city and the Seto Nai-kai. On the mountain are various recreational areas, including the oldest golf course in Japan, designed in 1903 by resident English merchant Arthur H. Gloom, and the summer houses of some of Kōbe's wealthier residents.

To get to Rokko-san, take the Hankyū Kōbe Line from JR San-no-miya Eki to Rokko Eki (¥180). From there take either a taxi or a bus to Rokko Cable-shita Eki. A funicular railway travels up the mountain to Rokko-sanjo Eki (¥570). You can either return to Kōbe by the cable car or go directly back on the Kōbe Dentetsu (electric railway; ¥650), which uses Shin-kaichi Eki, two stops west of Kōbe's Moto-machi Eki. Or take the Kōbe Dentetsu to Tanigami Eki and change for the subway back to San-no-miya (¥900).

Even before Nara became the capital in the 7th century, **Arima Onsen** had established itself as a place to take the thermal waters. The hot spring's fame reached a high point when Hideyoshi Toyotomi took the waters here in the late 16th century. Arima is on the north slope of Rokko-san and is a maze of tiny streets still lined with traditional houses. Some 30 ryokan have established themselves, using the thermal waters' reputed curative powers to attract guests. As the water gushes up freely from springs, some ryokan charge as much as ¥10,000, for use of their baths. Go instead to the public bath, **Arima Onsen Kaikan,** in the center of the village near the bus terminal. Here ¥550 gets you entrance and a soak in the steaming waters. Arima Onsen Kaikan is open daily 8 AM–10 PM (closed the first and third Tuesday of the month). A cable car continues after Rokko-sanjo Eki over the mountain's crest at Country Station before traversing a beautiful valley to Arima Onsen (¥1,460 one-way, ¥2,640 round-trip).

DINING

North of San-no-miya Eki in the Kitano area—from the corner of Hanta-dōri and Yamamoto-dōri, also known as Ijinkan-dōri—there are at least a dozen good Italian, German, French, Swiss, Middle Eastern, Thai, American, and, of course, Japanese restaurants. Port Island also has taken on a reputation for its variety—look near the Portopia Hotel.

$$$$ ✕ Aragawa. Japan's first steak house is famed for its superb hand-fed
★ Kōbe beef. The wood-panel dining room with chandelier has an old-country atmosphere. Aragawa serves melt-in-your-mouth *sumiyaki* (charcoal-broiled) steak that is worth its weight in yen. An evening here is the ultimate splurge, but this is considered *the* place for Kōbe beef—as well it should be, at ¥20,000. ✉ 2–15–18 Nakayamate-dōri, Chūō-ku, ☎ 078/221–8547. Jacket and tie. AE, DC, MC, V.

$$$$ ✕ Totenkaku. This restaurant has been famous among Kōbe residents since 1945 for its Peking duck, flown in fresh from China, but the building itself is worth the proverbial cost of admission. Built at the turn of the 20th century, Totenkaku is located in one of Kōbe's ijinkan, the F. Bishop House. You can keep the price down by ordering one of the Chinese noodle specialties to fill you up. ✉ 3–14–18 Yamamoto-dōri, Chūō-ku, ☎ 078/231–1351. AE, DC, MC, V.

$$$$ ✕ **Wakkoku.** If you want to try Kōbe beef without spending a bundle, come at lunchtime to this smart but plain restaurant on the third floor of the shopping plaza underneath the Oriental Hotel, across from Shin-Kōbe Eki. Don't be distracted by the other restaurants on this floor—Wakkoku is the best choice. Prices at lunchtime—count on ¥3,000 for Kōbe beef—are lower than they are at dinner. ✉ *Kitano-chō 1-chōme, Chūō-ku,* ☎ *078/262–2838. AE, DC, V.*

$$$–$$$$ ✕ **A-1.** For affordable Kōbe beef in the neighborhood north of Hankyū San-no-miya Eki, come to A-1. The *teppan* (broiled on a hot plate) steak is served on a hot grill with a special spice-and-wine marinade that is as memorable as the garlicky crisp-fried potatoes. Right across from the Washington Hotel, A-1 has a relaxed and friendly atmosphere. ✉ *Lighthouse Bldg., ground floor, 2–2–9 Shimoyamate-dōri, Chūō-ku,* ☎ *078/331–8676. No credit cards. Closed Tues.*

$$–$$$$ ✕ **Gaylord.** A few minutes' walk north of San-no-miya Station, this Indian restaurant with flashy decor is a favorite with Kōbe's resident gaijin. Curries are on the mild side but are very tasty, and if you can get a window table, the restaurant also has a good view of the city. Portions can be very filling, so be careful not to order too much unless you're ravenous. ✉ *Bacchus Bldg., 7th floor, 1–26–1 Nakayamate-dōri, Chūō-ku,* ☎ *078/251–4359. AE, DC, MC, V.*

$$–$$$$ ✕ **Highway.** This small, exclusive restaurant has a reputation for serving fine Kōbe beef. The quality of the meat *is* extraordinary. ✉ *13–7 Shimoyamate-dōri 2-chōme, Chūō-ku,* ☎ *078/331–7622. No credit cards. Closed Mon., 3rd Tues. of month.*

$$–$$$$ ✕ **Rote Rose.** A block east of the Kōbe Club on the west end of Kitano, this basement restaurant is owned by a wine importer and is most famous for its wine list, with more than 180 fine German vintages. To sample them, order the six-glass flight. Rote Rose serves a range of European dishes, including French sausage and *tournedos aux champignons* (filet mignon with mushrooms). The ground floor is a *weinstube* (wine bar). ✉ *9–14 4-chōme, Kitano-chō, Chūō-ku,* ☎ *078/222–3200. AE, V. Closed Tues.–Wed.*

$–$$ ✕ **Angel's Share.** A tastefully decorated English-style basement pub, the Angel's Share has a number of imported beers on tap, Guinness among them. The menu is reasonably extensive, with specials including beef and mushrooms cooked in Guinness and oxtail stew alongside the usual fish-and-chips. ✉ *1–4–9 Sannomiya-chō, Chūō-ku,* ☎ *078/333–0190. V.*

$–$$ ✕ **Attic.** Back in the '80s, former U.S. baseball player and newspaper columnist Marty Kuehnert opened this little haven for ballpark refugees and beer lovers of all sorts. Along with the Budweiser, Marty brought to Kōbe his American take on eating—complete with pizza, fried chicken, roast beef, jukeboxes, and peanut shells. ✉ *Ijinkan Club Bldg., 3rd floor, 4–1–12 Kitano-chō, Chūō-ku,* ☎ *078/222–1586 or 078/222–5368. AE, DC, MC, V. Closed Tues.*

$–$$ ✕ **Raja.** This small, unassuming place near Moto-machi Eki was
★ opened by a former chef at Gaylord restaurant. Raja serves home-style Indian food, with spicy curries and excellent saffron rice. ✉ *Sanonatsu Bldg., basement, Sakae-machi 2-chōme, Chūō-ku,* ☎ *078/332–5253. AE, DC, V.*

LODGING

$$$$ 🏨 **Hotel Okura Kōbe.** A 35-story hotel on the wharf in Meriken Kōen,
★ this is Kōbe's finest. Beautifully furnished, the property lives up to the Okura chain's worldwide reputation for excellence. Rooms were done by David Hicks, who has designed interiors for the royal family. The hotel has a well-equipped health club and stunning views of the bay

from the Emerald Restaurant. ⊠ *Meriken Kōen, 2–1 Hatoba-chō, Chūō-ku, Kōbe-shi, Hyōgo-ken 650-8560,* ☎ *078/333–0111,* FAX *078/333–6673,* WEB *www.kobe.hotelokura.co.jp. 489 rooms. 5 restaurants, 2 bars, coffee shop, indoor pool, health club. AE, DC, MC, V.*

$$$$ 🏨 **Kōbe Bay Sheraton.** The city's most international hotel is ideally located for business travelers—on the man-made Rokko Airando (Rokko Island), Kōbe's commercial center. Rooms are comfortable and have interesting views of the surrounding commercial and industrial areas, and service is of the highest order. However, unless you're on business, there's little to see or do on Rokko Island, which makes this less than convenient as a base for sightseeing. ⊠ *2–13 Koyo-chō-naka, Higashi-nada-ku, Kōbe-shi, Hyōgo-ken 658-0032,* ☎ *078/857–7000,* FAX *078/857–7041. 276 rooms. 4 restaurants, coffee shop, sports bar, pool, health club, shops. AE, DC, MC, V.*

$$$$ 🏨 **Shin-Kōbe Oriental Hotel.** The tallest building in Kōbe, this archi-
★ tecturally stunning luxury hotel viewed from downtown at night appears as a brightly lit needle-thin tower jutting into the sky. Guest rooms, with marble-tiled bathrooms, are neatly decorated in pastel fabrics and furnished with a desk, a coffee table, and two reading chairs. Corner rooms on higher floors have superb views over Kōbe. Beneath the hotel there are five floors of shops and restaurants. The hotel faces JR Shin-Kōbe Eki, where the Shinkansen arrives, and is three minutes from downtown by subway. ⊠ *Kitano-chō 1-chōme, Chūō-ku, Kōbe-shi, Hyōgo-ken 650-0002,* ☎ *078/291–1121,* FAX *078/291–1154,* WEB *www.orientalhotel.co.jp. 600 rooms. 5 restaurants, indoor pool, hair salon, sauna, gym, shops. AE, DC, MC, V.*

$$$–$$$$ 🏨 **Hotel Monterey.** With its marvelous Mediterranean-style courtyard fountains and European furnishings, the Hotel Monterey takes you off Kōbe's busy streets and into old Italy. Modeled after a monastery in Florence, the hotel has modern features that many hotels in Japan lack, such as a fitness room, Jacuzzi, and pool (for a small fee). Twin rooms are standard size; duplex (maisonette) rooms come with a carpeted bedroom upstairs and a small lounge area with a tiled floor. Both the Italian and Japanese restaurants on the premises are charming. ⊠ *2–11–13 Shimoyamate-dōri, Chūō-ku, Kōbe-shi, Hyōgo-ken 650-0011,* ☎ *078/392–7111,* FAX *078/322–2899. 164 rooms. Restaurant, bar, pool, gym. AE, DC, MC, V.*

$$$–$$$$ 🏨 **Kōbe Portopia Hotel.** A dazzling modern hotel with every facility imaginable, the Portopia suffers from its location on the otherwise bland, man-made Port Island. Spacious rooms overlook the port, and the restaurants and lounges on the top floors have panoramic views of Rokko-san and Ōsaka Bay. Because of its location, the hotel can only be reached by the Portliner monorail or by taxi. This inconvenience is countered by the fact that everything from food—Chinese, Japanese, and French—to clothing is available inside the hotel. ⊠ *6–10–1 Minato-jima Naka-machi, Chūō-ku, Kōbe-shi, Hyōgo-ken 650-0046,* ☎ *078/302–0111,* FAX *078/302–6877,* WEB *www.portopia.co.jp. 761 rooms. 3 restaurants, coffee shop, 1 indoor and 1 outdoor pool, hair salon, sauna, tennis court, health club, shops. AE, DC, MC, V.*

$$$ 🏨 **San-no-miya Terminal Hotel.** In the terminal building above JR San-no-miya Eki, this hotel is extremely convenient, particularly if you need to catch an early train. The rooms are large for the price and are clean and pleasant. ⊠ *8 Kumoi-dōri, Chūō-ku, Kōbe-shi, Hyōgo-ken 651-0096,* ☎ *078/291–0001,* FAX *078/291–0020. 190 rooms. 8 restaurants. AE, DC, MC, V.*

$$–$$$ 🏨 **Union Hotel.** The most attractive feature of this business hotel is its location, a few minutes' walk from San-no-miya Eki. Rooms are comfortable, if somewhat bland. A 24-hour convenience store is next door. ⊠ *2–1–10 Goko-dōri, Chūō-ku, Kōbe-shi, Hyōgo-ken 651-0087,* ☎

078/242–3000, ℻ *078/242–0220. 167 rooms. Restaurant. AE, DC, MC, V.*

$$ 🏨 **Arcons.** Many of the immaculate rooms at this little white hotel up on the hill in Kitano-chō have a view out over the city to the sea. There's patio dining in the first-floor café when the weather is good. Take a taxi from San-no-miya Eki, as it's in the heart of the ijinkan district. ✉ *3–7–1 Kitano-chō, Chūō-ku, Kōbe-shi, Hyōgo-ken 650-0002,* ☎ *078/231–1538. 22 rooms. Café. AE, DC, V.*

$$ 🏨 **Kōbe Gajoen Hotel.** This delightful hotel is a change from the modern, impersonal hotels that flourish in Japan. Although it's distinctly Japanese, with delicate Japanese cuisine served in a dining room paneled with decorated screens and a staff that bows to guests, the hotel has European furnishings, reminders of the time when Kōbe was a major port for Western traders. Close to downtown, it's a couple of minutes' walk from the west exit of Hanakuma Eki on the Hankyū Line. ✉ *8-4-23 Shimoyamate-dōri, Chūō-ku, Kōbe-shi, Hyōgo-ken 650-0011,* ☎ *078/ 341–0301,* ℻ *078/341–0353. 52 rooms. Restaurant. AE, DC, MC, V.*

NIGHTLIFE

Though Kōbe doesn't have as diverse a nighttime scene as Ōsaka does, its compactness is an advantage—virtually all of the choice places have live music and are within walking distance of each other. One of the best Western bars in Kansai is **Dubliners' Irish Pub** (✉ 47 Akashi-chō, Chūō-ku, ☎ 078/334–3614)—a gathering place for many gaijin residents without being a foreigners-only hangout. It has good food and drink, a friendly staff, and a relaxed atmosphere. Another popular watering hole is **Ryan's** (✉ Rondo Bldg., 7th floor, north side of San-no-miya Eki, ☎ 078/391–6902), named after owner Alan Ryan. It's a lively place, with a younger crowd than Dubliners'. The **Polo Dog** bar (✉ K Bldg., 2nd floor, 1–3–21 Sannomiya-chō, Chūō-ku, ☎ 078/ 331–3944) serves reasonable meals and is tastefully arrayed with '50s and '60s Americana.

SHOPPING

Kōbe is a shopper's paradise. Unlike in Tōkyō, Ōsaka, and other places in Japan where individual shops are scattered all over the city, most of the shopping districts in Kōbe are in clusters, so you can cover a lot of ground with ease.

Kōbe's historic shopping area is known as **Moto-machi,** which extends for 2 km (1 mi) between JR Moto-machi Eki and the department store Daimaru. Much of the district is under a covered arcade, which allows for inclement weather forays. You can find most everything in Moto-machi—from antiques to cameras and electronics. Try **Harishin** (✉ 3–10–3 Moto-machi-dōri, Chūō-ku, ☎ 078/331–2516), on the west end of the arcade, for antiques. **Maruzen** (✉ 1–4–12 Moto-machi-dōri, Chūō-ku, ☎ 078/391–6003), at the entrance on the Moto-machi Eki side of the arcade, has an excellent selection of books in English. **Naniwa-ya** (✉ 3–8 Moto-machi-dōri 4-chōme, Chūō-ku, ☎ 078/341–6367) sells excellent Japanese lacquerware at reasonable prices. **Sakae-ya** (✉ 8–5 Moto-machi-dōri 5-chōme, Chūō-ku, ☎ 078/341–1307) specializes in traditional dolls.

Nearly connected to the Moto-machi arcade, extending from the department store Sogo to the Moto-machi area for 1 km (½ mi), is the **San-no-miya Center Gai** arcade. Because it's right next to San-no-miya Eki, this is a good place for a quick bite to eat.

The famous pearl company **Tasaki Shinju** (✉ Tasaki Bldg., 6–3–2 Minatojima Naka-machi, Chūō-ku, ☎ 078/302–3321), on Port Island, has a museum and demonstration hall along with its retail pearl shop.

The **Santica Town** underground shopping mall, which runs for several blocks beneath Flower Road south from San-no-miya Eki, has 120 shops and 30 restaurants. It's closed the third Wednesday of the month.

Kōbe's trendy crowd tends to shop in the exclusive shops lining **Tor Road,** which stretches north–south on a slope lined with trees. Fashionable boutiques featuring Japanese designers and imported goods alternate with chic cafés and restaurants.

KŌBE A TO Z

To research prices, get advice from other travelers, and book travel arrangements, visit www.fodors.com.

AIRPORTS AND TRANSFERS

Kansai International Airport (KIX) in Ōsaka handles the region's international flights as well as some domestic flights to and from Japan's larger cities. Most domestic flights still fly out of Ōsaka's Itami Airport, approximately 40 minutes away from Kōbe.

AIRPORT TRANSFERS

From KIX take the JR Kansai Airport Express Haruka to Shin-Ōsaka and change to the JR Tōkaidō Line for Kōbe's JR San-no-miya Eki, a 70-minute (¥1,800) trip. You can also ride a boat from the airport ferry terminal to Kōbe City Air Terminal (K-CAT), which takes 30 minutes (¥2,200). Or take the comfortable limousine bus (70 minutes; ¥1,800), which drops you off in front of San-no-miya Eki.

From Itami Airport, buses to San-no-miya Eki leave from the domestic terminal's main entrance and from a stop between the domestic and international terminals approximately every 20 minutes, 7 AM–10 PM. The trip takes about 40 minutes (¥940).

Excellent public transport from the airports makes using taxis impractical.

BUS TRAVEL

City bus service is frequent and efficient, though it might be somewhat confusing to first-timers. At each stop a pole displays a route chart of official stops; the names of stops are spelled out in Roman letters. Enter at the rear or center of the bus; pay your fare with exact change as you leave at the front. The fare is ¥200, regardless of the distance. A special city loop bus that looks like a trolley and has a wood interior with brass fittings stops at 15 major sights on its 12½-km (7½-mi), 80-minute run between Nakatottei Tsutsumi (Nakatottei Pier) and Shin-Kōbe. The buses operate at 16- to 20-minute intervals and cost ¥250 per ride or ¥650 for a day pass, which you can purchase on the bus or at the Kōbe Information Center. (LOOP BUS signs in English indicate stops along the route.) Service runs 9:30–4:25 weekdays, 9:30–5:25 weekends and holidays.

EMERGENCIES

Daimaru Depāto has a pharmacy that's a three-minute walk from JR Moto-machi Eki.

➤ DOCTORS: **Kōbe Adventist Hospital** (✉ 4–1 Arinodai 8-chōme, Kitaku, ☎ 078/981–0161). **Kōbe Kaisei Hospital** (✉ 3–11–15 Shinohara-Kita-machi, Nada-ku, ☎ 078/871–5201).

➤ EMERGENCY SERVICES: **Ambulance** (☎ 119). **Police** (☎ 110).

➤ PHARMACY: **Daimaru Depāto** (✉ 40 Akashi-chō, Chūō-ku, ☏ 078/331–8121).

ENGLISH-LANGUAGE MEDIA

BOOKS

Maruzen Books stocks a small selection of new English-language novels as well as guidebooks, books on Japan, and Japanese study guides. Those looking for a wider selection of English reading material should head to Wantage Books, the only second-hand English-language bookshop in the Kansai region.

➤ BOOKSTORES: **Maruzen Books** (✉ 1–4–12 Moto-machi-dōri, Chūō-ku, ☏ 078/391–6003). **Wantage Books** (✉ 1–1–13 Ikuta-chō, Chūō-ku, ☏ 078/232–4517).

NEWSPAPERS AND MAGAZINES

Kansai Time Out is a monthly publication listing all sorts of events in Kōbe, Kyōto, Nara, and Ōsaka. There are also topical articles written for travelers and residents. It costs ¥300 and is available at all major hotels and bookshops throughout the region.

TAXIS

Taxis are plentiful; hail them on the street or at taxi stands. Fares start around ¥600 for the first 2 km (1 mi) and go up ¥90 for each additional ½ km (¼ mi).

TOURS

Between March 21 and November 30, the City Transport Bureau has several half-day and full-day tours of major attractions in and around the city. The tours are conducted in Japanese, but they do provide an overview of Kōbe. Buses depart from the south side of the Kōbe Kotsu Center Building, near San-no-miya Eki. Information and tickets, which start at ¥3,300, can be obtained at the Shi-nai Teiki Kankō Annaisho (Sightseeing Bus Tour Information Office), on the second floor of the Kōbe Kotsu Center Building.

Authorized taxi services also run tours (¥4,200 per hour) that cover 11 different routes and last from two to five hours. Reserve at the Kōbe Tourist Information Center, on the south side of JR San-no-miya Eki.

➤ CONTACT: **Kōbe Tourist Information Center** (☏ 078/271–2401). **Shi-nai Teiki Kankō Annaisho** (☏ 078/391–4755).

TRAIN TRAVEL

The Hikari Shinkansen runs between Tōkyō and Shin-Kōbe Eki in about 3½ hours. If you don't have a JR Pass, the fare is ¥14,000. The trip between Ōsaka Eki and Kōbe's San-no-miya Eki takes 20 minutes on the JR Tōkaidō Line rapid train, which leaves at 15-minute intervals throughout the day; without a JR Pass the fare is ¥390. The Hankyū and Hanshin private lines run between Ōsaka and Kōbe for ¥310.

The Portliner is a computerized monorail that serves Port Island. Its central station is connected to JR San-no-miya Eki; the ride from the station to Port Island takes about 10 minutes (¥520 round-trip).

Within Kōbe, Japan Railways and the Hankyū and Hanshin lines run parallel from east to west and are easy to negotiate. San-no-miya and Moto-machi are the principal downtown stations. Purchase tickets from a vending machine; you surrender them upon passing through the turnstile at your destination station. Fares depend on your destination.

The city's subway system main line runs from Shin-Kōbe Eki west to the outskirts of town. Another line—opened in July 2001—running along the coast from San-no-miya links up with the main line at Shin-

Nagata Eki. Fares start at ¥180 and are determined by destination. The San-no-miya–Shin-Kōbe trip costs ¥200.

VISITOR INFORMATION

The Kōbe Information Center, on the south side of JR San-no-miya Eki, is open daily 9–7. You can pick up a free detailed map of the city in English. The tourist information center has branches at JR Kōbe Eki and Shin-Kōbe Eki, both open daily 10–6.

The Japan Travel Bureau can arrange for hotel reservations, train tickets, package tours, and more throughout the country and abroad. The Japan Travel Phone, available daily 9–5, provides free information in English on all of Japan.

➤ TOURIST INFORMATION: **Japan Travel Bureau** (✉ JR San-no-miya Eki, ☎ 078/231–4118). **Japan Travel Phone** (☎ 0088/22–4800). **Kōbe Information Center** (✉ JR San-no-miya Eki, ☎ 078/322–0220; ✉ JR Kōbe Eki, ☎ 078/341–5277; ✉ Shin-Kōbe Eki, ☎ 078/241–9550). **Kōbe Tourist Information Center** (☎ 078/271–2401).

9 WESTERN HONSHŪ

The two coasts of western Honshū reveal two very different experiences of Japan. Along the industrial San-yō strip are some attractive cities, most notably Kurashiki and Hiroshima. Nearby, at Miyajima, the vermilion torii rises famously out of the water. The more remote northern San-in region has a slower pace. Here the ceramics city of Hagi, the mountain town of Tsuwano, and the coastal village of Matsue make great escapes from the overdevelopment of the modern world.

By John
Malloy Quinn

Western Honshū is bisected by an east–west range of mountains called the Chugoku San-chi. Two distinct regions lie on either side of this division. The north side, which faces the Nihon-kai (Japan Sea), is called San-in. The south side faces the Seto Nai-kai (Inland Sea) and is referred to as San-yō.

Of the two, San-yō has most of the population, industry, and transportation. This does not mean it is without scenic merit, however. Consider Miyajima, the small island off Hiroshima world famous for its vermilion floating torii, and Kurashiki, with its willow-lined canals and quaint old warehouses. Kōrakuen, in Okayama, is one of Japan's Top Three gardens (a centuries-old distinction). And no one should miss Himeji's graceful castle.

The San-in coast provides a more quintessentially Japanese experience, due in part to the isolation of the region. Traditional customs remain at the core of many people's lives here. Charming fishing villages, hot-spring hideaways, and rocky, unpolluted bays speckle the entire coastline. Inland, tiny towns tucked into mountain-ringed valleys are blessed with some of the freshest air and sweetest water you'll find anywhere.

Western Honshū Glossary

Key Japanese words and suffixes for this chapter include the following: *-bashi* (bridge), *-chō* (street or block), *chūō* (central, as in Central Street), *daimyō* (feudal lord), *donjon* (castle stronghold), *-dōri* (street or avenue), *eki* (train station), *gaijin* (foreigner), *-gama* or *-kama* (kiln), *-gawa* (river), *-gū* (Shintō temple), *hantō* (peninsula), *-in* (Buddhist temple), *jima* (island), *-jinja* (Shintō shrine), *-jō* (castle), *kawa* (river), *-ken* (prefecture), *-ko* (lake), *kōen* ("ko-en," park), *-ku* (section or ward), *kūkō* (airport), *-machi* (town), *Nihon-kai* (Japan Sea), *onsen* (hot springs), *rōmaji* (Japanese words rendered in roman letters), *ryokan* (traditional Japanese inn), *Seto Nai-kai* (Inland Sea), *-shima* (island), *Shinkansen* (bullet train, literally "new trunk line"), *taisha* (Shintō shrine), *torii* ("to-ree-ee," gate), *-yaki* (pottery), and *yama* (mountain).

Pleasures and Pastimes

Culture

As much as or more than in any other region, cultural events are part of daily life in Western Honshū. The pottery centers of Bizen and Hagi host numerous annual ceramics festivals, which are not only educational but make great shopping opportunities as well. Arts and music are of prime importance in Kurashiki, and exhibits and concerts take place regularly. Hiroshima has an international element that leavens all that happens there. Second only to Ise Jingū in importance, the shrine at Izumo provides many Japanese with a firm foundation in their culture.

Dining

Western Honshū is definitely one of the best regions in which to sample local Japanese seafood, thanks to regional specialties from the Nihon-kai and Seto Nai-kai. Oysters in Hiroshima and sashimi and sushi on the San-in coast are superb. Matsue's proximity to the water makes a variety of both freshwater and saltwater fish available and provides for truly delicious eating experiences.

Most reasonably priced restaurants will have a visual display of the menu in the window. On this basis, you can decide what you want before you enter. If you cannot order in Japanese and no English is spoken, after you secure a table, lead the waiter to the window display and point.

For more details on Japanese cuisine, *see* Chapter 14 *and* Dining *in* Smart Travel Tips A to Z.

CATEGORY	COST*
$$$$	over ¥4,500
$$$	¥2,500–¥4,500
$$	¥1,500–¥2,500
$	under ¥1,500

*per person for a main course at dinner

Lodging

Accommodations cover a broad spectrum, from pensions and *minshuku* (private residences that rent rooms) to large, modern resort hotels that have little character but all the facilities of an international hotel. Large city and resort hotels have Western as well as Japanese restaurants. In summer hotel reservations are highly advised.

For a short course on accommodations in Japan, *see* Lodging *in* Smart Travel Tips A to Z.

CATEGORY	COST*
$$$$	over ¥20,000
$$$	¥15,000–¥20,000
$$	¥10,000–¥15,000
$	under ¥10,000

*All prices are for a double room, excluding service and tax.

Outdoor Activities and Sports

The Seto Nai-kai and the San-in seascapes are impressive. The San-in coast is perfect for bicycling—the scenery changes frequently enough to sustain interest, and the air is clear and cool. Tottori with its dunes and beaches is a magnet for surfers and parachute jumpers. Matsue is known as a haven for water-sports enthusiasts. Daisen-san offers good climbing, and many ski areas in the region open for the winter. The Oki Retto (Oki Islands) are a good destination for hiking and camping.

Exploring Western Honshū

This chapter sketches an itinerary from Ōsaka down the San-yō coast, stopping at Himeji, Okayama, Kurashiki, Hiroshima, and Miyajima before reaching Honshū's western point, Shimonoseki. Next is a return to Kyōto by way of the San-in coast. The scenic and cultural highlights of the San-in are in and around Hagi, Tsuwano, Matsue, and Tottori. Farther east on the way to Ama-no-hashidate, in spots like Kundani, Kinosaki, and Misasa Onsen, you can enjoy an even slower pace.

Numbers in the text correspond to numbers in the margin and on the Western Honshū, Hiroshima, and Hagi maps.

Great Itineraries

The Shinkansen makes getting around the San-yō easy, but since the San-in's attractions are not well connected by trains, it might be a good idea to look at train timetables beforehand and plan accordingly. If you don't like traveling between places as much as staying in them, it might be better to stick to one coast or the other, or to focus on smaller, more manageable zones.

IF YOU HAVE 2 DAYS

You have three options, all of which will give you a glimpse of old and new Japan. You can cover 🔲 **Hiroshima** ⑤–⑬ the first day and take a scenic excursion to either **Hagi** ⑮–㉕ or **Tsuwano** ㉖ the second. Another possibility is to spend a day and night in 🔲 **Kurashiki** ④ and continue

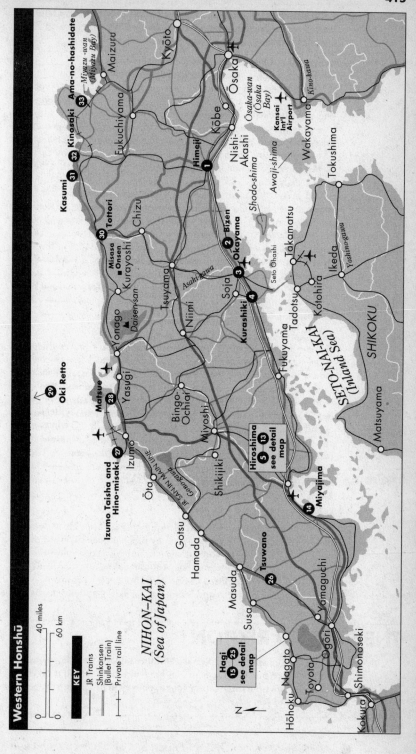

Western Honshū

KEY
JR Trains
Shinkansen (Bullet Train)
Private rail line

0 — 40 miles
0 — 60 km

NIHON-KAI (Sea of Japan)

Ama-no-hashidate
Miyazu-wan (Miyazu Bay)
Maizuru
Kyōto
33 Kinosaki
32 Kasumi
31 Kasumi
Fukuchiyama
Ōsaka
Kōbe
Kino-kawa
Kansai Int'l Airport
Osaka-wan (Osaka Bay)
Wakayama
1 Himeji
Nishi-Akashi
Shodo-shima
Awaji-shima
Tokushima
30 Tottori
Chizu
Misasa Onsen
Kurayoshi
Daisensan
2 Okayama
Bizen
Takamatsu
Ikeda
Kotohira
Yoshino-gawa
SHIKOKU
Yonago
Tsuyama
Niimi
Soja
3 Kurashiki
4
Seto Ōhashi
Tadotsu
Asahi-gawa
29 Oki Retto
28 Matsue
Yasugi
Izumo
27 Izumo Taisha and Hino-misaki
Bingo-Ochiai
Miyoshi
Fukuyama
SETO-NAI-KAI (Inland Sea)
Matsuyama
Hiroshima
5 – 13 see detail map
Ōta
Shikijiki
JR SAN-IN MAIN LINE
Gotsu
Gōno-sen
Hamada
14 Miyajima
Masuda
Tsuwano
26
Yamaguchi
Susa
Ogōri
Shimonoseki
Hagi
15 – 25 see detail map
Hōhoku
Nagato
Toyota
Kokura

N

to Hiroshima. Finally, a more focused (and therefore more leisurely) itinerary could comprise a two-day visit to ☷ **Matsue** ㉘, with an excursion to nearby **Izumo Taisha** ㉗.

IF YOU HAVE 4 DAYS

Four days is plenty to cover either the San-yō or San-in coast. In fact, the Shinkansen will enable you to cover most of the San-yō coast in four days. Make your first stop on your way down the coast **Himeji** ① and visit the castle. Then head west to ☷ **Okayama** ③, possibly hitting the pottery town of **Bizen** ② as a side trip. Spend one night in Okayama and the next in traditional ☷ **Kurashiki** ④. ☷ **Hiroshima** ⑤–⑬ will require at least a full day. On the fourth day you can visit ☷ **Miyajima** ⑭, spending the fourth night either on the rather touristy island or heading back to Hiroshima. A four-day San-in itinerary would need to focus on either the east or west end of the coast. On the east end you could begin with a visit to ☷ **Kinosaki** ㉜, ☷ **Kundani**, or ☷ **Kasumi** ㉛, with a night spent in one of those towns, and then a trip to ☷ **Tottori** ㉚ and Daisen-san on day two. Continuing west, you could finish up with **Izumo Taisha** ㉗ and ☷ **Matsue** ㉘. On the western end of the coast, spread your four days among ☷ **Hagi** ⑮–㉕, ☷ **Tsuwano** ㉖, **Izumo Taisha** ㉗, and ☷ **Matsue** ㉘. It wouldn't be too hard to divide four days among Matsue, Kurashiki, Okayama, and Bizen, either, since there are good connections between Yonago (east of Matsue) and these locations.

IF YOU HAVE 7–10 DAYS

You can cover most of Western Honshū in seven days. Start with a two-night stay in ☷ **Hiroshima** ⑤–⑬ and ☷ **Miyajima** ⑭ before continuing on to ☷ **Hagi** ⑮–㉕, one of the most beautiful coastal towns in all Japan. If you have time, the mountain town of ☷ **Tsuwano** ㉖ is a worthwhile side trip—a night here makes for a charming adventure. Then head back east through the San-in to **Izumo Taisha** ㉗ and ☷ **Matsue** ㉘. Spend at least a night here. You can then go out to the ☷ **Oki Retto** ㉙, see some sights of interest between Yonago and ☷ **Kinosaki** ㉜, or head south from Yonago to ☷ **Kurashiki** ④ or **Okayama** ③. Each of these options is worth a day or two, so choose according to your interests. Finally, on your way back to Kyōto or Ōsaka you can stop in **Bizen** ② and/or **Himeji** ①.

When to Tour

The San-in coast has a beautiful, long spring. Though it does get muggy like most of the rest of Japan by mid-summer, the wind off the Nihon-kai manages to cool the coast, and it makes Shinji-ko near Matsue an ideal windsurfing spot. Autumn colors are spectacular, especially in the mountains. The northern shore gets a stronger dose of winter than the southern and is popular for skiing and onsen-soaking in colder months.

THE SAN-YŌ REGION

Although the stretch from Ōsaka to Hiroshima is well developed, so you can't see much of the Seto Nai-kai from the train, all it takes are small detours from the main corridor to put you in touch with the beauty you came to see.

Himeji

❶ *42 mins west of Shin-Ōsaka; 1 hr west of Kyōto; 3 hrs, 52 mins west of Tōkyō by Shinkansen.*

★ You can see **Himeji-jō,** also known as Shirasagi-jō (White Egret Castle), as soon as you exit the station. Universally loved, it stands on a hill and dazzles the city. A visit to Himeji-jō could well be one of the high points of your trip to Japan, especially if you can manage to see the brilliantly lighted white castle soaring above cherry blossoms or pine branches at night. Thanks to frequent rail service, it should be easy to hop off, visit the castle, and jump on another train two hours later.

Himeji-jō could be regarded as medieval Japan's crowning achievement of castle design and construction. It arrived at its present state of perfection after many transformations, however. It was first a fortress in the year 1333. Notable enlargements took place in 1581, 1608, and between 1615 and 1624.

The five-story, six-floor main *donjon* (stronghold) stands more than 100 ft high and is built into a 50-ft-high stone foundation. Surrounding this main donjon are three smaller ones; all four are connected by covered passageways. Enemies would have had to cross three moats, penetrate the outer walls, and then withstand withering attack from the four towers and the more than 30 other buildings within. It was an impregnable fortress then, and its grace and grand proportions still inspire a great deal of awe. Filmmaker Akira Kurosawa used Himeji-jō's exterior and the castle's grounds in his 1985 movie *Ran.*

From the central north exit of JR Himeji Eki, the castle is a 15- to 20-minute walk or a 5-minute bus ride (¥160). The bus departs from the station plaza, on your left as you exit. ☎ 0792/85–1146. ⧉ ¥500. ☽ *Daily 9–5 (grounds until 6).*

Easy to visit in the vicinity of the castle (walk five minutes north) is the **Hyōgo Ken Shiryōkan** (Hyōgo Prefectural Museum of History), which not only details the history of Himeji-jō but of other castles in Japan and all over the world. There are exhibits of prehistoric bones found in the area, and a room where from one to three times a day a volunteer is allowed to try on some samurai armor or a traditional kimono, which with its 12 layers is a sort of armor itself. Architect Kenzo Tange designed the plain-fronted, postmodern building. ⊠ *68 Hon-machi,* ☎ *0792/88–9011.* ⧉ *¥200.* ☽ *Tues.–Sun. 10–4:30.*

The small **Himeji Bungaku Kan** (Himeji Museum of Literature), which is dedicated to the work of Himeji's men and women of letters (including philosopher Tetsuro Watsuji), is more celebrated for its unique exterior than for the memorabilia that lies within. Designed by renowned architect Tadao Andō, the museum makes use of Andō's trademark reinforced concrete and is a minimalist masterpiece in the shadow of the mighty Himeji-jō. ⊠ *84 Yamanoi-chō,* ☎ *0792/93–8228.* ⧉ *¥300.* ☽ *June–Aug., Tues.–Sun. 10–6; Sept.–May, Tues.–Sun. 10–5.*

If you are interested in getting out onto the Seto Nai-kai, you can take one of five ferries a day leaving Himeji Port for **Shōdo-shima,** near Shikoku. The 1-hour, 40-minute trip costs ¥1,170. However, there are even shorter sea crossings to Shodo-shima from Okayama if you are headed there next.

Getting Around

Himeji is served by Shinkansen, with trains arriving and departing every 15 minutes during the day. The Shinkansen to Okayama, farther west, arrives and departs every hour during the day.

Visitor Information

There is a **Tourist Information Office** (☎ 0792/85–3792) to the right of the station's north exit.

Bizen

② *35 mins from JR Higashi-Okayama Eki on the Akō Line.*

Bizen pottery looks deceptively simple. It is unglazed. It is unpainted. It is often plain, even rough, in texture and appearance. Yet it is expensive. There are several reasons for this. Many stages of mixing, settling, aging, and drying are involved before the special clay is ready to be worked into Bizen-yaki. Bizen pottery is also fired much longer than usual—for anywhere from one to two weeks, which require more than 1,000 bundles of split red pine. If the firing is successful, the result is a unique, very directly expressionistic work of art, highly sought after by connoisseurs of tea ceremony and flower arrangement.

In the 4th through the 7th centuries, pots used for the functions of daily life were only being made and used in areas somewhat far from here. Later, the makers of these pots migrated into the Bizen area and struck—literally—pay dirt. The stuff of their trade existed everywhere here. The clay from the mountains was high in iron and crushed-stone content, firing rough and reddish. The clay from the rice field bottoms was lighter in color, softer, and easier to work with on potter's wheels, when those came along. Sometime during the 1700s Bizen-yaki began to show up all over Japan. Though other types are arguably more popular today, Bizen-yaki remains a favorite of many.

Many variations of colors and textures exist in Bizen pottery. Red pine is the fuel for firing, which scatters a lot of ash, producing color when it lands on the pots and melts onto the clay. Pieces that are buried in ash on the kiln floor do not get much oxygen and are likely to be marked by matte gray and blue spots. Artists also produce this effect by inserting charcoal into the kiln at certain temperatures to rob the fire of oxygen. Shiny blues and grays are produced by nature when dense, random clouds of gases form around pieces. This also happens when salt is tossed into the fire, which not only causes intense coloration and texturing but also severely damages the inside of the kiln, requiring frequent rebuilding. Another process involves wrapping lighter-color pieces in rice straw before firing. Where the straw, called *wara,* touches the pot, there will be permanent firebrands of vivid oranges and reds.

Bishu-gama is a kiln and studio that welcomes visitors, offering you a chance to see master potters in action and to participate in workshops and classes for trying your own hand at the craft. For workshops reservations are officially required, but walk-ins are sometimes accepted (¥1,300 to make a teacup, 30 minutes; ¥2,500 to make a larger piece, 60–90 minutes). If you're interested primarily in shopping, a large selection is for sale in the shop that fronts the kiln and studios, and there's many a bargain to be found.

The kiln complex can be reached via a pleasant 15-minute stroll through streets lined with studios and shops selling Bizen-yaki. Cross the highway and take the street going slightly right (directly away from the station) and go up two blocks; then turn right and follow the sweeping curve back down to where it meets the main road. Then turn left and enter the first big parking lot. Or you can simply follow the main road (Route 2) in front of Bizen/Inbe Eki (turn right as you come out) down the hill and then turn left on Route 374 and then left again into the lot. The first route is highly recommended and could also include a detour and visit to the charming café-gallery affiliated with the kiln called Riho. ⊠ *302-2 Inbe,* ☏ *0869/64-1160.* ⊙ *Daily 9-5.*

The **Bizen Pottery Traditional and Contemporary Art Museum,** with a diverse collection of pottery new and old, is a useful stop for anyone interested in Bizen-yaki. The little office on the right as you enter the hall is also a tourist information center of sorts, and the helpful crew will answer questions, provide maps of the area, and direct you to the scores of other artists' studios and shops that line the streets of Bizen. Some English is spoken. The museum is next to Inbe Eki on the right side as you exit. ⊠ *1659–6 Inbe,* ☎ *0869/64–1400.* ⌦ *¥500.* ☉ *Apr.– May and Oct.–Nov., Mon.–Thurs. 9:30–4:30; June–Sept. and Dec.– Mar., Tues.–Thurs. 9:30–4:30.*

Dining

$ ✕ **Riho.** This is the perfect place to enjoy tea, coffee, or lunch served in, on, and surrounded by works of ceramic art created by the world-famous Yuichi Yamamoto—all for sale, too. His daughter, Ruriko, is one of the friendly staff. The family also owns several other galleries, shops, and the kiln Bishu-gama. Recommended are the sandwich set (¥700) and the *matcha* (¥650), powdered green tea with a kick, served with a bite-size sweet to counteract the slight bitterness between sips from the priceless bowl. Riho is only five minutes from Inbe Eki. Walk two blocks straight up the street leading away from the station, turn left, and Riho is the second establishment on your left. ⊠ *1530 Inbe,* ☎ *0869/64–1187. MC, V. Closed Thurs.*

Okayama

★ ❸ *30 mins west of Himeji and 1 hr west of Ōsaka by Shinkansen.*

Okayama is a pleasant, cosmopolitan town famous for its black castle and spacious garden. The thickly forested, wonderfully sculpted mountains in the interior of the prefecture are among the country's most beautiful as well. The Shinkansen station makes this an attractive base for visiting the quaint charms of Kurashiki—only a nine-minute local-JR-train hop to the west. The city is the best departure point for Shōdo-shima (near Shikoku) if you're coming from Ōsaka or Hiroshima and is also a fine gateway to the remote and beautiful realm of Matsue, 2 hours, 40 minutes by JR train to the northwest. Twenty-three ferries a day make the 40-minute run from Okayama Port to the island. From JR Okayama Eki, it takes 45 minutes on Bus 12 to reach the port. Also keep in mind that if you're headed for Kurashiki, it's fairly convenient to visit the attractions of Okayama while you're here, since you'll need to change to a local train anyway, and the castle, museums, and park are all only a short distance from the station.

Kōrakuen is a fine garden for strolling, with charming tea arbors, green lawns, ponds, and hills that were laid out three centuries ago on the banks of the Asahi-gawa. The maple, apricot, and cherry trees give the 28-acre park plenty of flowers and shade. Kōrakuen's riverside setting, with Okayama-jō in the background, is delightful. The garden's popularity increases in peak season (April, May, and August), but this is perhaps the most spacious park in Japan, so don't be put off from seeing it. Bus 20 (¥160) from Platform 2 in front of the JR station goes directly to Kōrakuen. Okayama claims to have the most sunshine in the country, and if the weather's nice you may want to hop on one of the frequent streetcars plying Momotaro-dōri, the main boulevard heading east from the station (¥100); ride three stops east; and walk southeast to the castle, park, and museums from there. For ¥530, you can buy a combined park-castle ticket. ⊠ *1–5 Korakuen,* ☎ *086/272– 1148.* ⌦ *¥350.* ☉ *Apr.–Sept., daily 7:30–6; Oct.–Mar., daily 8–5.*

Painted black, **Okayama-jō** is known as U-jō (Crow Castle). Though the castle was built in the 16th century, only the "moon-viewing" outlying tower survived World War II. A ferroconcrete replica was painstakingly constructed in 1966. The middle floors now house objects that represent the region's history, including a nice collection of armor and swords. Unlike many other castles with great views from the top, here there's an elevator to take you the six floors up. Less than a five-minute walk across the bridge brings you from the south exit of Kōrakuen to the castle, and there are also various boats for rent on the attractive river below. ⊠ *2–3–1 Marunouchi,* ☎ *086/225–2096.* ⌨ *¥300.* ☉ *Daily 9–5.*

The **Orient Bijutsukan** (Museum of Oriental Art) has a Parthenon-like temple front and 2,000 items on display inside. Its special exhibits show how Middle Eastern art reached Japan via the Silk Road and range from displays of Persian glass goblets and mirrors to stringed instruments. To reach the museum from the JR station, take the streetcar (¥140) bound for Higashiyama directly north for 10 minutes. The museum is across Asahi-gawa from Kōrakuen (about a 10-minute walk). ☎ *086/232–3636.* ⌨ *¥300.* ☉ *Daily 9–5.*

Lodging

$$$–$$$$
★
🏨 **Hotel Granvia Okayama.** This large, luxurious hotel makes a superb, comfortable base for exploring the area. The lobby is done in white marble and wood paneling, and, like the friendly bilingual staff, exudes a bright, cheery confidence. The rooms are amazingly spacious and have a fair share of opulence. It's conveniently connected to the JR Okayama Eki—stay on the second (Shinkansen) level and follow the signs toward the south end. ⊠ *1–5 Ekimoto-chō, Okayama-shi, Okayama-ken 700-8515,* ☎ *086/234–7000,* ℻ *086/234–7099. 323 Western-style rooms, 3 Western-style suites, 2 Japanese-style suites. 7 restaurants, bar, coffee shop, shops. AE, DC, MC, V.*

Visitor Information

Should you need a map or city information, head to the **Tourist Information Office** (☎ 086/222–2912), open daily 9–6, in the JR station.

Kurashiki

★ ➍ *1½ hrs west of Ōsaka by Shinkansen to Okayama, then 8 mins by local train.*

You could hardly find a better place to make you feel as if you're in old Japan than Kurashiki. In centuries past, this vital shipping port supplied the metropolis of Ōsaka with cotton, textiles, and rice. Those days are long past, but Kurashiki lives on, thriving on the income from more than 4 million visitors a year.

You can see most of Kurashiki's sights in a half day or so, but it's worth staying longer, perhaps in a rustic ryokan, to fully appreciate the place. The stucco walls with their slate gray, burnt brown, and black tiles, which line the willow-shaded canals and cobblestone streets, can transport you to an entirely different frame of time and mind.

Virtually the entire town shuts down on Monday. Some lodgings actually boot out their guests for that day and night, so inquire ahead and plan accordingly.

Ōhara Bijutsukan (Ōhara Art Museum), in the old town, is the main museum. Magosaburo Ōhara built this Parthenon-style building to house a collection of art that includes works by El Greco, Corot, Manet, Monet, Rodin, Gauguin, Picasso, Toulouse-Lautrec, and many other Western artists. A newer (1961) wing exhibits modern Japanese paintings, tapestries, wood-block prints, pottery, and antiques. ⊠ *1–15–Chūō,* ☎ *086/422–0005.* ⌨ *¥1,000.* ⏰ *Tues.–Sun. 9–4:30.*

In four converted granaries, which still have their Edo-period white walls and black-tile roofs, the **Kurashiki Mingeikan** (Kurashiki Folk Craft Museum) houses some 4,000 folk-craft objects, including ceramics, rugs, wood carvings, and bamboo wares from all over the world. The Mingeikan is near the tourist office. ⊠ *1–4–11 Chūo,* ☎ *086/422–1637.* ⊡ *¥700.* ◷ *Mar.–Nov., Tues.–Sun. 9–5; Dec.–Feb., Tues.–Sun. 9–4:15.*

The **Nihon Kyōdo Gangukan** (Japan Rural Toy Museum) is one of the two top toy museums in Japan and is more worthwhile if you can find a Japanese person to show you around and explain the stories behind the toys. It displays some 5,000 toys from all regions of the country and has one room devoted to foreign toys. The toy museum is near the Mingeikan on the north bank of the Kurashiki-gawa. ⊠ *1–4–11 Chūo,* ☎ *086/422–8050.* ⊡ *¥500.* ◷ *Daily 8:30–5.*

Ivy Square is an ivy-covered complex that used to be a weaving mill. Artfully renovated, it contains the Ivy Hotel, several boutiques, three museums, a restaurant, and, in the central courtyard, a summer beer garden. The most interesting of the museums in the complex, **Kurabo Kinen Butsukan** (Kurabo Memorial Hall) shows the history of spinning and textiles, an industry that helped build Kurashiki. The other two are the **Torajiro Kajima Kinen Butsukan** (Torajiro Kajima Memorial Hall), which has Western and Asian art, and the **Ivy Gakkan** (Ivy Academic Hall), an educational museum that uses reproductions to explain Western art to the Japanese. Ivy Square is across the bridge from Chūo (the short street of museums) and up the alleyway. ⊡ *Kurabo ¥350, all 3 museums ¥600.* ◷ *Tues.–Sun. 9–5.*

Kanryu-ji and Achi Jinja stand atop the only real hill in Old Kurashiki and provide an excellent view of the town as well as a short, easy walk. You can see the hill straight ahead when you exit the Ōhara Bijutsukan. ⊡ *Free.* ◷ *Daily 9–5.*

Kurashiki Tourist Information Office (☎ 086/422–0542), located inside the station across from the turnstiles, is staffed with friendly locals who can give you useful maps and information.

Dining and Lodging

$$$–$$$$ ✕ **Hamayoshi.** Only three tables and a counter bar make up this personable restaurant specializing in fish from the Seto Nai-kai. Sushi is just one option; another is *mamakari,* a kind of sashimi that's sliced from a fish caught in the Seto Nai-kai. Other delicacies are *shako-ebi,* a type of spiny prawn, and lightly grilled fillet of fish. No English is spoken, but the owner will help you order and instruct you on how to enjoy the chef's delicacies. Hamayoshi is on the main street leading from the station just before the Kurashiki Kokusai Hotel. ⊠ *Achi 2–19–30,* ☎ *086/421–3430. No credit cards.*

$$–$$$$ ✕ **Kiyutei.** For the best grilled steak in town, come to this attractive restaurant, where chefs work over the fires cooking your steak to order. The entrance to the restaurant is through a courtyard just across from the entrance to the Ōhara Museum. ⊠ *1–2–25 Chūo,* ☎ *086/ 422–5140. DC, MC, V. Closed Mon.*

$ ✕ **KuShuKuShu (9494).** Cool music and loud laughter can be heard coming from this place when all else on the streets is locked up tight. An eclectic mix of traditional white stucco, black wooden beams, bright lights, and Western jazz makes this a great place to unwind with hip locals. Scores of tasty à la carte snacks, such as grilled meats or cheese and salami plates, and low-price beer add to the fun. It's tucked along the east side of the covered Ebisu-dōri shopping arcade halfway between the station and Kanryu-ji. ⊠ *Achi 2–16–41,* ☎ *086/421–0949. No credit cards. No lunch.*

$$$$ ✕⊞ **Ryokan Kurashiki.** With the Kurashiki-gawa flowing gently before
★ it, the elegant Ryokan Kurashiki maintains its serenity—no matter how
many visitors are walking the streets in town. The kitchen is famous
for regional dishes, making the most of the oysters in the winter, fish
straight from the Seto Nai-kai in spring and autumn, and freshwater
fish in summer. There is a wonderful inner garden on which to gaze while
sipping green tea in the afternoon. Here is Japanese hospitality at its
best. If you are not staying here, experience the ryokan by having lunch
(¥10,000 per person) or dinner (¥14,000 per person). ⊠ *4–1 Hon-machi,
Kurashiki, Okayama-ken 710,* ☎ *086/422–0730,* ℻ *086/422–0990.
19 rooms, 5 with bath. Restaurant. AE, DC, MC, V. EP, MAP.*

$$$ ✕⊞ **Kurashiki Kokusai Hotel.** Owned by Japan Airlines, this is the best
Western-style hotel in town. The lobby has a black-tile floor and dra-
matic Japanese wood-block prints. Ask for a room in the newer annex
at the back of the building overlooking a garden. The location of the
Kokusai is ideal—a 10-minute walk on the main road leading from the
station and just around the corner from the old town and the Ōhara
Museum. The Alicante Western and Japanese restaurant serves fresh
seafood from the Seto Nai-kai with an interesting mélange of Mediter-
ranean and Japanese ingredients; the wine list is international and rea-
sonable. ⊠ *1–1–44 Chūō, Kurashiki, Okayama-ken 710,* ☎ *086/422–
5141,* ℻ *086/422–5192. 106 Western-style rooms, 4 Japanese-style
rooms. Restaurant, bar, hair salon, free parking. AE, DC, MC, V.*

$$$$ ⊞ **Tsurugata Ryokan.** A merchant's mansion and a converted rice and
★ sugar storehouse make up this delightful ryokan with an Edo-era atmo-
sphere. The window bars, the roof ends and outer wall tiles, and the brass
plates at the intersections of the beams prove the authenticity of this nearly
300-year-old structure. Rooms are on the cozy side, but the pine bath-
tubs and the hotel's location—directly across the bridge from the art mu-
seum—create a feeling that you are experiencing life in another era. The
suite overlooking the garden is especially fine. Since the ryokan is man-
aged by the Kurashiki Kokusai Hotel, staff members tend to speak some
English. ⊠ *1–3–15 Chūō, Kurashiki, Okayama-ken 710,* ☎ *086/424–
1635,* ℻ *086/424–1650. 10 Japanese-style rooms. AE, DC, MC, V.*

$$$ ⊞ **Hotel Kurashiki.** If you have an early train to catch, this efficient
business hotel just above the station is especially convenient. Rooms,
which are done in pink and green pastels, are fairly large, and the bathrooms are custom-made—not the usual plastic cubicles. Eight very large
"family rooms" are available, and north-facing rooms have views of
the expensive and missable Tivoli Theme Park. ⊠ *1–1–1 Achi, Kurashiki,
Okayama-ken 710,* ☎ *086/426–6111,* ℻ *068/426–6163. 133 rooms.
Restaurant. AE, DC, MC, V.*

$$ ⊞ **Kamoi.** This delightfully antique hostelry is the best bargain in
Kurashiki. An eight-minute walk from the Ōhara Bijutsukan, this min-
shuku is next to Achi Jinja. The rooms are simple, and the food is good—
a multicourse breakfast (Western-style or Japanese-style) and dinner
are available. The 10 PM curfew sounds troubling, but wait until you
see how early the sidewalks are rolled up in this part of town. Note
that in true Kurashiki fashion, the entire place is shut down (after check-
out time) on Monday; guests must leave the premises for that day and
night. ⊠ *6–21 Hon-machi, Kurashiki, Okayama-ken 710,* ☎ *086/422–
4898,* ℻ *086/427–7615. 17 Japanese-style rooms with shared bath.
No credit cards. Closed Mon.*

Hiroshima

2 hrs west of Ōsaka by Shinkansen.

At 8:15 in the morning on August 6, 1945, the next hottest thing to a
star glowed 1,900 ft above the center of Hiroshima for only an instant.

That's all it took. Half the city was leveled, the rest in flames. A half-hour later rain fell, but it only wrought more misery: the black precipitation carried deadly radioactive fallout and other by-products of the fission reaction. All told, some 200,000 people died, including 10,000 hapless Korean prisoners of the Japanese.

One site that still bears witness to that mind-boggling release of atomic energy remains in modern Hiroshima: the Gembaku Dōmu, or A-Bomb Dome, which, despite its location almost directly below the blast, did not completely collapse. Its twisted, charred concrete-and-iron structure stands largely untouched since that ill-fated morning, darkly brooding next to the river and surrounded at a respectful distance by a vibrant, entirely rebuilt city.

Heiwa Kinen Kōen Area

The **Heiwa Kinen Kōen** (Peace Memorial Park) contains the key sights in Hiroshima. The monuments and the museum in the park are dedicated to "No More Hiroshimas." The park sits in the top of the triangle formed by two of Hiroshima's rivers, the Ota-gawa (also called Hon-kawa) and Motoyasu-gawa. Take Streetcar 2 or 6 to the Gembaku-Dōmu-mae stop and cross Aioi-bashi. In the middle of the bridge is the entrance to Peace Memorial Park, which is at the far end. En route are statues and monuments, but if you'll be returning through the park, head straight for the museum, about a 10-minute walk from the bridge. A less dramatic approach from Hiroshima Eki is to take the Hiroshima Bus Company's red-and-white Bus 24 to Heiwa Kōen, which is only a two-minute walk from the museum, or to take Streetcar 1 to Chūden-mae for a five-minute walk to the museum.

★ ❺ The **Gembaku Dōmu** (A-Bomb Dome) is a poignant symbol of man's apparently unlimited capacity for destruction. The twisted, half-shattered structure of the city's old Industrial Promotion Hall stands in stark contrast to the new Hiroshima. If you go there at dusk, its foreboding appearance and derelict pose can be absolutely overwhelming. But be prepared—a grizzled old Japanese war veteran might just shuffle over and ask you to take his photo in front of it. The Gembaku Dōmu in Peace Memorial Park, a World Heritage Site, is the sole structural ruin of the war left erect in Hiroshima and because of this its impact is even more powerful.

❻ A visit to the disturbing and educational **Heiwa Kinen Shiryōkan** (Peace Memorial Museum) may be too intense an experience for some to stomach. Through exhibits of models, charred fragments of clothing, melted ceramic tiles, lunch boxes, and watches—and hideously surreal photographs—Hiroshima's story of death and destruction is told. Nothing can quite recapture the reality of witnessing an atomic chain reaction, but the ineffably sad heat-ray-photographed human shadow permanently imprinted on granite steps and the Dalí-esque watch forever stopped at 8:15 do leave a lasting impression. Most exhibits have brief explanations in English. However, more detailed information is available on audiocassettes, which you can rent for ¥150. The museum is in Peace Memorial Park. ☎ *082/241–4004.* 🖅 *¥50.* ☉ *May–July, daily 9–5:30; Aug. 1–15, daily 9–6:30; Aug. 16–Nov., daily 9–5:30; Dec.–Apr., daily 9–4:30.*

❼ The **Gembaku Shibotsusha Irei-hi** (Memorial Cenotaph), designed by Japanese architect Kenzō Tange, resembles the primitive A-frame houses of Japan's earliest inhabitants. Buried inside is a chest containing the names of those who died in the destruction. On the exterior is the inscription (translated), REST IN PEACE, FOR THE ERROR SHALL NOT BE REPEATED. The cenotaph is in front of the Heiwa Kinen Shiryōkan on its north side.

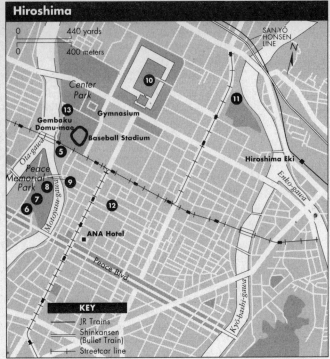

Hiroshima

★ **8** The **Flame of Peace** burns behind the Memorial Cenotaph. The flame will be extinguished only when all atomic weapons are banished. In the meantime, every August 6 there is a solemn commemoration in which the citizens of Hiroshima float paper lanterns on the city's rivers for the repose of the souls of the atomic-bomb victims.

9 Pause before the **Children's Peace Monument** before you leave the park. Many visitors consider this the most profound memorial in Peace Memorial Park. The figure is of a Sadako, a young girl who at age 10 developed leukemia as a result of exposure to atomic radiation. Her will to live was strong, and she believed that if she could fold 1,000 paper *senbazuru* (cranes)—a Japanese symbol of good fortune and longevity—her illness would be cured. She died before finishing the thousand, and her schoolmates finished the job for her. But her story, which has become a folktale of sorts, inspired a nationwide paper-crane folding effort among schoolchildren that continues to this day. The colorful chains of paper cranes—delivered daily from schools all over the world—are visually striking.

Elsewhere in Hiroshima

Hatchobori, Yagenbori, and Nagarekawa are entertainment districts east of the Hon-dōri shopping district. This side of Hiroshima offers some of Japan's hottest nightlife.

10 **Hiroshima-jō** was originally built by Terumoto Mōri on the Ota-gawa delta in 1589. He gave the surrounding flatlands the name *Hiro-Shima,* meaning wide island, and it stuck. By using the castle as headquarters in World War II, the Japanese army made it one of the legitimate targets of the bomb, and it was destroyed in 1945. In 1958 the five-story donjon was rebuilt to its original specifications. Inside, a historical museum of Hiroshima has exhibits from Japan's feudal period. It's a 15-

minute walk north from the Gembaku Dōmu. 🔲 *Castle and museum ¥340.* ☉ *Apr.–Sept., daily 9–5:30; Oct.–Mar., daily 9–4:30.*

⑪ The garden laid out in 1630 by Lord Naga-akira Asano, **Shukkeien,** resembles the design of a famed scenic lake in Hangzhou, China. Streams and islets wind their way between the sculpted pine trees. Small bridges cross the waters, which are filled with colorful carp, a fish praised for long life. Shukkeien is east of the castle on the banks of the Kyō-bashi-gawa. Return to the JR station on Streetcar 9; at the end of the line transfer to Streetcar 1, 2, or 6. 🔲 *¥250.* ☉ *Apr.–Sept., daily 9–5:30; Oct.–Mar., daily 9–4:30.*

⑫ Around **Hon-dōri,** Hiroshima's central district, hundreds of shop-keepers sell their wares. The big department stores are at the east end of the arcade, near the Hatchobori streetcar stop: Sogo (closed Tues-day) is open from 10 to 8; Fukuya (closed Wednesday) and Tenmaya (closed Thursday) are open from 10 to 7:30; and Mitsukoshi (closed Monday) is open from 10 to 7. Many restaurants, and a range of mod-ern hotels from which to choose, are here in the city center to the east of the Peace Memorial Park near the JR station.

☝ ⑬ The **Kodomo Bunka Kagakukan** (Hiroshima Science and Cultural Museum for Children) is a hands-on museum. The happiness of the youngsters here can dispel some of the depression that the Peace Memorial Park is bound to cause. To get here, cross the Aioi-bashi at the park's northern entrance and walk north and east, keeping the river on your left and the baseball stadium on your right. There is a plane-tarium next door. ☎ *082/222–5346.* 🔲 *Center free, planetarium ¥440.* ☉ *Tues.–Sun. 9–5.*

Dining and Lodging

$$$$ ✕ **Kanawa Restaurant.** Hiroshima is known for its oysters. Kanawa, ★ on a barge moored on the Motoyasu-gawa, near the Peace Memorial Park, is Hiroshima's most famous oyster restaurant. *Kaiseki ryōri* (Japanese haute cuisine) is also a top draw. Dining is on tatami mats, with river views. ✉ *Moored on river at Heiwa-bashi, Naka-ku,* ☎ *082/ 241–7416. AE, DC, MC, V. Closed Sun. Apr.–Sept.*

$$$$ ✕ **Mitakiso Ryokan.** For a kaiseki lunch or an elaborate kaiseki din-★ ner in a private tatami room, Mitakiso Ryokan is superb. You need-n't stay at the ryokan in order to enjoy its cuisine; it's an excellent place to entertain Japanese guests. If you do stay, it's worth going all out and choosing a room with sliding doors onto the private garden. ✉ *1–7 Mitaki-machi, Nishi-ku,* ☎ *082/237–1402. Reservations essential. AE, MC, V.*

$–$$$ ✕ **Suishin Restaurant.** Famous for its sashimi and sushi, this restau-rant serves the freshest fish from the Seto Nai-kai—globefish, oysters, and eel, to name but a few. If you don't like raw fish, try the rockfish grilled with soy sauce. Suishin has an English-language menu. It's a plain and simple place with a counter bar and four tables. ✉ *6–7 Tate-machi, Naka-ku,* ☎ *082/247–4411. AE, DC, MC, V. Closed Wed.*

$–$$ ✕ **Sawadee.** A tiny but wonderful Thai restaurant, Sawadee serves up ★ some of the finest green curry and *tom yum kung* (a delicious soup of coconut milk, chilies, lemongrass, and seafood) this side of the Chao Praya. Be forewarned that if you tell the Thai cook you like it hot, she will make you sweat. ✉ *4–6 Fukuru-machi, 3rd floor, Naka-ku,* ☎ *082/243–0084. AE, DC, MC, V. Closed Mon.*

$ ✕ **Okonomi Mura** (Village of Okonomiyaki). In this enclave there are 20 shops serving *okonomi-yaki,* literally, "as you like it." Okonomi-yaki is best described as an everything omelet—a crepe of sorts topped with noodles, bits of shrimp, pork, squid, or chicken, cabbage, and bean sprouts. Different areas of Japan make different kinds of okonomi-yaki;

in Hiroshima the ingredients are layered rather than mixed. Seating in these shops, many of which are open late, is either at a wide counter in front of a grill or at a table with its own grill. The complex is near the Hon-dōri shopping area, just west of Chūō-dōri. ☒ *Shintenchi Plaza, 5–13 Shintenchi, 2nd–4th floors, Naka-ku. No credit cards.*

$$$–$$$$ 🏨 **ANA Hotel Hiroshima.** With glittering chandeliers, beige marble, and Chinese-style carpets, the bright lobby and tea lounge look onto a small garden with a waterfall. Rooms are pink and gray, with small baths. The Unkai restaurant, on the fifth floor, has good Japanese food and a view onto a garden of dwarf trees, rocks, and a pond with colorful carp. The hotel is within walking distance of the Peace Museum. Unfortunately, this makes it very popular with tour groups. ☒ *7–20 Naka-machi, Naka-ku, Hiroshima, Hiroshima-ken 730,* ☎ *082/241–1111,* 𝙁𝘼𝙓 *082/241–9123. 427 Western-style rooms, 4 Japanese-style rooms. 4 restaurants, beer garden (May–Aug.), indoor pool, sauna, health club, shops. AE, DC, MC, V.*

$$$ 🏨 **Hiroshima Prince.** The location beside Motoujina Park on the tip of a peninsula jutting into Hiroshima Bay assures peace and quiet. But although a nap will come easily to a weary traveler, the views of boats plying between the islands that dot the spectacular bay will be hard to resist. All the large rooms overlook the Seto Nai-kai and are done up in relaxing hues of blues and violets. The friendly staff speaks English. The sushi bar in the Hagoromo restaurant, on the 20th floor, serves some of the freshest, tastiest sushi in the country. For a beer with a view, take the elevator to the 23rd-floor (top) lounge. The hotel is 15–20 minutes by taxi from Hiroshima JR Eki, and from the pier behind the hotel you can hop a fast ferry to Miyajima (32 minutes; ¥2,800 round-trip). Tickets are sold in the travel-agency office off the lobby. You can also get here via Bus 21 from the train station. ☒ *23–1 Motoujina-machi, Minami-ku, Hiroshima, Hiroshima-ken 734,* ☎ *082/256–1111,* 𝙁𝘼𝙓 *082/256–1134. 550 rooms. 4 restaurants, bar, breakfast room, pool, bowling, shops, travel services. AE, DC, MC, V.*

$$$ 🏨 **Sera Bekkan.** Experience a great bargain at this basic, no-frills ryokan. The building is rather nondescript, but the rooms are traditional enough, with tatami floors. The location is central; it's only 10 minutes by taxi from Hiroshima Eki. ☒ *4–24 Mikawa-chō, Naka-ku, Hiroshima, Hiroshima-ken 730,* ☎ *082/248–2251,* 𝙁𝘼𝙓 *082/263–2768. 25 Japanese-style rooms. AE, V. EP, MAP.*

$$ 🏨 **Kenmin Bunka Center.** Strictly a business hotel, with small rooms and tiny bathrooms, the Kenmin Bunka Center has cheerful, refreshing decor, and the bathtubs are deep enough for a good soak. For a no-nonsense place to stay close to the Peace Memorial Park, this accommodation is the best value in Hiroshima. Check-in is at 4 PM and advance reservations are recommended. ☒ *1–5–3 Ote-machi-ku, Hiroshima, Hiroshima-ken 730,* ☎ *082/245–2322,* 𝙁𝘼𝙓 *082/245–2315. 50 rooms. Coffee shop. No credit cards.*

Nightlife

Every night in Nagarekawa, the incredibly hip rooftop **Jazznese** (☒ Carp Bldg., 5th floor, 2–16 Nagarekawa, Naka-ku, ☎ 082/246–2949) features live jazz, funk, fusion, or a mix thereof Monday through Saturday—all easily heard from down in the street. Pop in here for a drink, and you may find it hard to leave.

Rock rules at **MAC** (☎ 082/243–0343), where Mac himself—the closest thing you'll see to a Japanese Keith Richards—likes to grab a guitar and get in front of the crowd to jam with the boys at least once a night. The bands here cover everything from Joe Walsh to Van Morrison, often all on one night. Wear your dancing shoes, and be ready to rock till sunup. The place is on a side street halfway between the Ritz movie theater (on Nagarekawa Street) and Chūō Street. Don't be shy about calling for directions; Mac and his fantastic crew speak English.

Getting Around

The streetcar (tram) is the easiest form of transport in Hiroshima. Enter the tram from its middle door and take a ticket. Pay the driver at the front door when you leave. All fares within the city limits are ¥130. A one-day pass is ¥600, available for purchase at the platform outside JR Hiroshima Eki. There are seven streetcar lines; four of them either depart from the JR station or make it their terminus. Stops are announced by a tape recording, and each stop has a sign in rōmaji posted on the platform. Buses also ply Hiroshima's streets; the basic fare is ¥180. Information in English can be gathered at the Hiroshima Station Tourist Info Center.

Taxis can be hailed throughout the city. The initial fare for small taxis is ¥570 (¥620 for larger taxis) for the first 1½ km (1 mi), then ¥70 for every 335 yards.

Hiroshima is Western Honshū's major city, and it is a major terminal for the JR Shinkansen trains; several Shinkansen end their runs at Hiroshima rather than continuing to Hakata on Kyūshū. During the day Shinkansen arrive and depart for Okayama, Ōsaka, Kyōto, and Tōkyō approximately every 30 minutes and about every hour for Hakata. From Tōkyō travel time is 4 hours, 37 minutes, and unless you have a Japan Rail pass, the fare is ¥18,050. Hiroshima Eki also serves as the hub for JR express and local trains traveling along the San-yo Line. There are also two trains a day that link Hiroshima to Matsue, on the northern shore (the Nihon-kai coast) of Western Honshū.

Tours

A number of sightseeing tours are available, including tours of Hiroshima and cruises on the Seto Nai-kai, in particular to Miyajima, the island with the famous sea-bound torii.

To arrange for a sightseeing taxi ahead of time, telephone the **Hiroshima Station Tourist Information Center** (☎ 082/261–1877). A two-hour tour is approximately ¥8,400. Because these taxi drivers are not guides, you should rent a taped recording describing key sights in English. These special taxis can be picked up from a special depot in front of Hiroshima Eki at the Shinkansen entrance.

A 4-hour, 40-minute tour operated by **Hiroshima Bus Company** (☎ 082/243–7207, FAX 082/243–0272) to the city's major sights costs ¥3,510. An eight-hour tour of both the city and Miyajima costs ¥9,470. You depart from in front of Hiroshima Eki's Shinkansen entrance. All tours are in Japanese, but the sights visited are gaijin friendly.

Hiroshima International Relations (☎ 082/247–8007, FAX 082/247–2464) has a home-visit program. To make arrangements, go the day before you wish to visit a Japanese home to the International Center on the ground floor of the International Conference Center in Peace Memorial Park. An inexpensive gift such as flowers or treats from home is not required but will ensure a successful beginning for your visit.

The **Seto Nai-kai Kisen Company** (☎ 082/255–1212, FAX 082/505–0134) operates several cruises on the Seto Nai-kai. Its cruise boat, the *Southern Cross,* operates a 7¼-hour trip (9:30–4:45) daily, March–November, which takes in Etajima, Ondo-no-Seto, Kure-wan (Kure [*koo*-reh] Bay), and Ōmishima (¥4,500–¥6,500 includes lunch and soft drinks). There are also a variety of river cruises, one of which includes dinner (¥6,000–¥10,000). Tours are in Japanese only.

Visitor Information

There are two **Tourist Information Offices** (✉ Hiroshima Eki, ☎ 082/261–1877 south exit; 082/263–6822 north exit) at JR Hiroshima Eki: one at the south exit, the exit for downtown, and one at the north exit, the exit for the Shinkansen. Both provide free maps and brochures as well as help in securing accommodations.

The main tourist office, **Hiroshima City Tourist Information** (☎ 082/247–6738) is in Peace Memorial Park.

Miyajima

★ ⑭ *30 mins southwest of Hiroshima by ferry.*

Miyajima is a small, picturesque island just off the coast in the Seto Nai-kai, and the site of Itsukushima Jinja, a shrine built on stilts above a tidal flat. The majestic vermilion torii in front of the shrine is one of the most widely known symbols of Japan and is one of what the Japanese call the country's Top Three scenic attractions.

The most exciting—and the most congested—time to visit Miyajima is in June, for the annual Kangen-sai Matsuri (Kangen-sai Festival), when three stately barges bearing a portable shrine, priests, and musicians cross the bay, followed by a fleet of decorated boats.

When you arrive in Miyajima, follow the coast to the right (west) from the pier. This leads to the village, which is crowded with restaurants, hotels, and souvenir shops. This part of the island is very touristy. At the far end of the village is a trail that passes by the torii and continues to Itsukushima Jinja. Expect to be greeted—or bothered—by completely fearless deer as you walk through the park.

★ **O-torii,** 500 ft from the shore at an entrance to the cove where the shrine stands, rises 53 ft out of the water, making it one of the tallest torii in Japan. Built with trunks of camphor trees in 1875, it has become a national symbol. As the sun sets over the Seto Nai-kai, the gate and its reflection are an unforgettable sight. At low tide, neither the torii nor the shrine appears to "float" on the water but, instead, stands looking rather forlorn above the mud and sand flats. Most hotels and ferry operators have tide charts you can check to maximize your photo opportunities.

Itsukushima Jinja was founded in 593 and dedicated to the three daughters of Susano-o-no-Mikoto, the Shintō god of the moon and the oceans. The shrine has been continually repaired and rebuilt, and the present structure is thought to be a 16th-century copy of 12th-century buildings. Most of the shrine is closed to the public, but you can walk around its deck, which gives gorgeous views of the torii. ✆ *¥300, combined ticket with Hōmotsukan ¥500.* ⊙ *Mar.–Oct., daily 6:30–6; Nov.–Feb., daily 6:30–5:30.*

The **Hōmotsukan** (Treasure House) at Itsukushima Jinja is a must-see. Because the victor of every battle that took place on the Seto Nai-kai saw fit to offer his gratitude to the gods by giving gifts to Itsukushima Jinja, the Hōmotsukan is rich with art objects, 246 of which have been designated as either National Treasures or Important Cultural Properties. It's across from Itsukushima Jinja's exit. ✆ *¥300, combined ticket with Itsukushima Jinja ¥500.* ⊙ *Daily 8:30–5.*

Atop a small hill overlooking Itsukushima Jinja, **Gojū-no-to** (Five-Story Pagoda) dates to 1407. If you climb up the steps to this buildings for a closer look, a small street on the other side (away from the shrine) serves as a shortcut back to the village.

Senjōkaku (Hall of One Thousand Mats), dedicated by Hideyoshi Toyotomi in 1587, has rice scoops attached to the walls, symbols of the soldiers who died fighting for Japan's expansionism. It's next to the Five-Story Pagoda. Go to look at the outside, and if you're lucky a door may be open.

Though many people spend only a half day on Miyajima, if you have more time to enjoy its beauty, take a stroll through **Momijidani Kōen** (Red Maple Valley Park), inland from Itsukushima Jinja. Here in the park is the start of the mile-long gondola that takes you virtually to the summit of **Misen-dake** (Mt. Misen). It's just a short hike past the top of the cable car, and the views of the Seto Nai-kai and Hiroshima beyond. ✆ *Cable car ¥900 one-way, ¥1,500 round-trip; park free.*

Dining and Lodging

$$$$
★
✕ ▣ **Iwaso Ryokan.** For tradition and elegance, this is the best Japanese inn on the island. Older rooms are full of character, those in the newer wing less so. Two cottages on the grounds have suites superbly decorated with antiques. Prices vary according to the size of your room, its view, and the kaiseki dinner you select, so be sure to specify what you want when you reserve. Breakfast (Western style if you ask) and dinner are usually included. Nonguests are welcome to dine here. ✉ *345 Miyajima-chō, Hiroshima, Hiroshima-ken 739,* ☎ *0829/44–2233,* FAX *0829/44–2230. 45 Japanese-style rooms, 33 with bath. Restaurant. AE, DC, V. EP, MAP.*

$$$–$$$$
▣ **Jyukeiso Ryokan.** This modest family ryokan makes a pleasant home away from home. It is to the east of the ferry pier, away from the town and shrine, which might be a bit inconvenient. Check to be sure that breakfast (Western-style available) and dinner are included. The owner speaks English. ✉ *50 Miyajima-chō, Hiroshima, Hiroshima-ken 739-0533,* ☎ *0829/44–0300,* FAX *0829/44–0388. 13 Japanese-style rooms. Restaurant. AE, DC, MC, V.*

Getting Around

The easiest, least expensive way to Miyajima is to take the commuter train on the JR San-yō Line from Hiroshima Eki to Miyajima-guchi Eki. From Miyajima-guchi Eki, a three-minute walk takes you to the pier from which ferries depart for Miyajima. The train takes about 25 minutes and departs from Hiroshima every 15–20 minutes. The first train leaves Hiroshima at 5:55 AM; the last ferry returns from Miyajima at 10:05 PM. There are two boats, one of which belongs to Japan Rail: your JR pass is valid on this boat only. The one-way cost for the train and ferry, without a JR pass, is ¥560. There are also eight direct ferries (¥1,440 one-way, ¥2,800 round-trip) daily from Hiroshima Ujina Port, next to the Prince Hotel, that make the 32-minute trip. Allow a minimum of three hours for the major sights of Miyajima, one hour or so to have a stroll and get some photos of O-torii and the shrine.

THE SAN-IN REGION

The mountains make transport between the north and south coasts of Western Honshū expensive and slow and keep the modern urbanization that has encroached upon so much of the San-yō coast at bay. You will find a special type of scenery here—one without power lines, skyscrapers, ugly blocks of corporate housing, or traffic jams. Another bonus is the relative dearth of tourists, both foreign and domestic, in San-in, except during national holidays—a decidedly good thing.

The JR San-in Main Line from Shimonoseki to Kyōto is the second longest in Japan, at 680 km (422 mi). It has the most stations of any line, which means plenty of stops and longer traveling times. Only two

Limited Express trains a day cover the Shimonoseki–Kyōto route in either direction. Local trains and buses run frequently between major towns on the San-in coast but still nowhere near as often nor as quickly as in San-yō. Keep this in mind when you make your plans so you can actually enjoy the deliciously slower pace of the region.

Hagi

3½ hrs north of Ogōri by JR train, 1½ hrs by JR bus; 2½ hrs north of Ogōri by JR Yamaguchi Line only; 2 hrs northeast of Shimonoseki by JR Limited Express.

Hagi fits almost entirely within the bounds of an area surrounded by a moat of two forks of the Abu-gawa—the south fork, Abu-gawa, and the north fork, Matsumoto-gawa—which in turn are backed by wave after wave of evocative, shadowy, symmetrical mountains, all looking toward a clean, jewel-blue sea full of potentially delicious fish.

Although the castle was razed in 1874 as a feudal relic, Hagi retains the atmosphere of a traditional castle town. The city is rich with history and, from 1865 to 1867, was of critical importance in the movement to restore power to the emperor. Hagi can also claim credit for supplying much of the intellectual framework for the new Japan: Japan's first prime minister, Hirobumi Ito (1841–1909), was born and educated in Hagi.

Hagi claims distinction beyond the realm of politics, too. The city is famous for Hagi-yaki, a pottery with soft colors and milky, translucent glazes ranging from beige to pink. In feudal times commoners were not permitted to own fine teacups and other such accoutrements of culture. Some clever artist started the tradition of deliberately defacing his work—with a chink in the base, for example—making it unfit for nobles but okay for his own use. Most Hagi-yaki still bears these marks.

Hagi-yaki got its start in a rather shameful way. Japan's attempt to invade Korea in the 16th century was a failure but not a total one. A Mōri general brought home with him two captive Korean potters, who created it (to save their lives, no doubt) for their new masters. Hagi-yaki has since become second to Raku-yaki as the most esteemed pottery in Japan. The Hagi-yaki Festival takes place yearly May 1–5.

Central Hagi

⑮ The second-floor **Ishii Chawan Bijutsukan** (Ishii Tea-Bowl Museum) displays a small collection of rare antique tea bowls produced in Hagi. Also in this prized collection are Korean celadon tea bowls made during the Koryo dynasty (916–1392). For connoisseurs this museum is a pleasure, but if you are short on time, you may want to skip it. From Higashi-Hagi Eki, cross the bridge over the Matsumoto-gawa and, keeping right, continue on the street until you reach the Hagi Grand Hotel. Turn left here, walk seven blocks, and then turn right. Walk straight for at least 10 minutes until you reach a curve. Take the first right after the curve; the museum is on the left. 🔲 ¥1,000. 🕑 Jan.–May and July–Nov., Tues.–Sun. 9–noon and 1–5.

⑯ **Tamachi Mall** is the busiest street in Hagi, with some 130 shops selling local products from Yamaguchi Prefecture. Two stores worth noting are **Harada Chojuan** and **Miwa Seigado**. The latter is at the top end of Tamachi, past the San Marco restaurant. Another gallery and store is **Saito-an,** in which both the masters and "unknown" potters display their works for sale. Prices range from ¥500 for a small sake cup to ¥250,000 for a tea bowl by such "living National Treasure" potters as Miwa

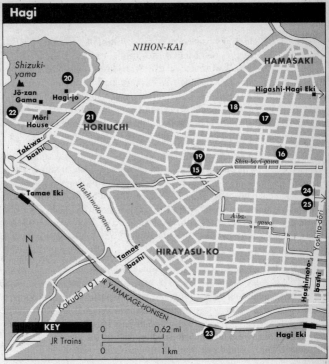

Hagi

NIHON-KAI

HAMASAKI

Shizuki-yama

Jō-zan Gama

Hagi-jo

Higashi-Hagi Eki

Mōri House

HORIUCHI

Shin-bori-gawa

Hashimoto-gawa

Tokiwa-bashi

Tamae Eki

Aiba-gawa

Yoshita-dōri

N

Tamae-bashi

HIRAYASU-KO

Hashimoto-bashi

Kokudō 191 JR YAMAKAGE-HONSEN

KEY
JR Trains

0   0.62 mi

0   1 km

Hagi Eki

Kyusetsu. Tamachi Mall is six blocks southwest from the Hagi Grand Hotel, across the Matsumoto-gawa from Higashi-Hagi Eki.

⑰ The **Tera-machi** section of town has about 10 temples to explore, and each has something of interest, from the old wooden temple of **Hōfukuji**, with its bibbed statues of Jizo, guardian deity of children, to **Kaicho-ji**, with its two-story gate and veranda around the Main Hall's second floor. From the top of Tamachi Mall, a right turn toward Hagi Bay will take you to Tera-machi.

⑱ The **Kumaya Bijutsukan** (Kumaya Art Museum) was once the home of a wealthy merchant, and the warehouse has been made into a museum of art objects and antiques. Of special note are the scrolls, paintings, a screen from the Kano school, and a collection of ceramics, which include some of the first Hagi-yaki produced. Instead of walking all the way to Hagi-wan (Hagi Bay), take a left after Kaicho-ji, and the museum will be on the left at the large metal gate. ☎ 0838/22–7547. ☒ ¥700. ☺ *Daily 9–5.*

⑲ The **Kikuya-ke Jūtaku** (Kikuya House) was once the home of the chief merchant family to the Mōri clan. Though the Kikuya were only traders, their connections allowed them to live ostentatiously. To get here from the Kumaya Art Museum, take the next left (south and away from the sea); it's not far after the turn. ☎ 0838/25–8282. ☒ ¥500. ☺ *Daily 9–5.*

Elsewhere in Hagi

⑳ **Shizuki Kōen**, bounded on three sides by the sea, surrounds 475-ft Shizuki-yama, at the western end of Hagi. The park contains the ruins of Hagi-jō and Hana-no-e Teahouse. ☒ *Shizuki-kōen, Horiuchi,* ☎ *0838/ 25–1826.* ☒ ¥210 *(includes admission to Hagi-jō grounds and the Mōri*

House). ⊗ *Apr.–Oct., daily 8–6:30; Nov.–Feb., daily 8:30–4:30; Mar. daily 8:30–6.*

Hagi-jō was destroyed as a symbol of backward ways by the hell-bent-for-progress Meiji Restoration. Yes, they pulled it down, during peace-time, and intentionally. Walls and moats are the only remains of the old castle; all of this is contained in Shizuki Kōen. Inside the castle grounds you'll find **Shizuki-yama Jinja**, a shrine with a nice, rustic feel, built in 1879. From the top of the castle walls, there is a panoramic view of Hagi, the bay, and the surrounding mountains.

Mōri House is a long, narrow building that was once home to samurai foot soldiers. Rooms in the house are sparely decorated and lie in a straight line, one next to the other. This peculiar arrangement allowed the sol-diers to be in rank at a moment's notice. The house is near the Jō-zan Kiln complex, and the ticket from Shizuki Kōen, just to the south, al-lows entry here as well. ⊠ *Ō-aza Horiuchi,* ☎ *0838/25–1826.* ⌑ *¥210 (includes admission to Shizuki Kōen and Hagi-jō grounds).* ⊗ *Apr.–Oct., daily 8–6:30; Nov.–Feb., daily 8:30–4:30; Mar., daily 8:30–6.*

★ The **Hana-no-e Teahouse** is set amid peaceful gardens and greenery and is one of many attractions contained in Shizuki Kōen (and included in its admission fee). The attendants will make the classic, slightly bitter-tasting *matcha* for you while you meditate. ⌑ *Tea ¥500.*

At **Jō-zan Gama** (Jō-zan Kiln), near Shizuki Kōen, stop in and browse through its Hagi-yaki and, if finances allow, purchase some of the mag-nificent work. Most of the time you will be welcome to enter the stu-dios and see the kilns (across the street from the shop) where the pieces are made and fired. Classes or chances to make your own may also be available. Bicycles can be rented through this outfit as well. ⊠ *Hagi-jo-ato, Horiuchi,* ☎ *0838/25–1666.* ⊗ *Daily 8–4.*

㉑ **Horiuchi,** the samurai section of town, has several interesting architectural features. The tomb of **Tenjuin** is a memorial to Terumoto Mōri, who founded the clan that ruled in the area for 13 generations. From Shizuki Kōen, head back toward downtown and recross the canal (on the mid-dle bridge) to the east side to get here. Next you come to the **Outer Gate of Mōri;** the **Toida Masuda House Walls** are on your right as you head south. These are the longest mud walls in the area, and for a mo-ment they can thrust you back in time. At the next chance, turn right and head west to check out the ancient, wooden **Fukuhara Gate.**

㉒ **Hagi Kirishitan Junkyosha Kinen Kōen** (Hagi Catholic Martyrs' Memo-rial Park), south of Shizuki Kōen and Jō-zan Kiln, is a graveyard where some Christians exiled to Hagi around 1868 for brainwashing and tor-ture are buried. The government officials, perfectly content to worship the sun and long accustomed to feudal loyalty, were confounded by devotion to an unseen lord and resorted to unspeakable cruelty in their efforts to weaken and disperse the Christians. Before the international community forced an end to the killing, many Japanese Christians died for their unfashionable faith.

Outer Precincts

㉓ The first two Mōri generations are buried at **Daishō-in.** Thereafter, even-numbered generations are buried at Daishō-in, odd-numbered gener-ations at Tōkō-ji. When Hidehari Mōri died, seven of his principal retainers—and one of their retainers—followed him in death, dutifully committing ritual suicide. Aghast, the Tokugawa Shogunate promptly declared such demonstrations of loyalty illegal. Future generations of retainers donated lanterns instead, and the path leading to the main hall of Daishō-in is lined with more than 600 of them. In May the wisteria blossoms are an eyeful. Another special time to visit is from August 13 to 15, when all the lanterns are lighted for Obon, the Buddhist festival of the dead.

Daishō-in is on the southern outskirts of Hagi, 650 yards west of JR Hagi Eki. You can take a train from Higashi-Hagi Eki to Hagi Eki or take a bus south to the Hagi-eki-mae bus stop. From Shizuki Kōen, Daishō-in is about 20 minutes by bicycle: ride across the canal that marks the boundary of Shizuki Kōen and follow it south to the Tokiwa-bashi. Once over the Hashimoto-gawa, take the main road that follows the river upstream. Daishō-in is on the right, on the other side of the JR San-in Main Line tracks. ☎ *0838/22–2134.* 🗏 *¥200.* ⊙ *Daily 8:30–5.*

㉔ **Tōkō-ji** contains the other cemetery of the Mōri family. Directly east of Matsumoto-bashi, the temple was founded by the Zen priest Domio in 1691. It's here that he (and every succeeding odd-numbered generation of the Mōri family) is buried. On August 15, during the Obon festival, all 500 stone lanterns lining the mossy lanes are lighted.

If you are coming from Daishō-in on foot, take the train from Hagi Eki to Higashi-Hagi Eki, and then walk south to Matsumoto-bashi and turn left to cross the river. If you have a bicycle, return to Hashimoto-gawa, follow it upstream to Hashimoto-bashi, and then head into central Hagi. At the Bōchō Bus Center, turn right and cross Matsumoto-bashi over the river. ✉ *Ō-aza Higashi,* ☎ *0838/26–1052.* 🗏 *¥200.* ⊙ *Daily 8:30–5.*

㉕ The **Monument to Shōin Yoshida** (1830–59) commemorates a young teacher and important revolutionary who, with the coming of Commodore Matthew Perry's Black Ships in 1853, recognized the need for Japan to tear down the walls of feudalism and embrace at least a few Western ideas. He was caught by the shogunate and kept under house arrest. When he went so far as to suggest introducing democratic elements into the government, he was executed, an act that inflamed and united the antishogunate elements of Hagi and the Namoto Province (now Yamaguchi Prefecture). The monument is a short walk southwest of Tōkō-ji on the loop road.

Dining and Lodging

$$–$$$$ ✕ **Chiyo.** Local sea delicacies are served here, such as sashimi and sushi, in classically elegant surroundings. Dining here, you have views of a small garden. ✉ *20–4 Kinko,* ☎ *0838/22–1128. No credit cards. Closed Sun.*

$$–$$$$ ✕ **Hyakumangoku.** The San-in coast has some of the best seafood in ★ the world, and there's no finer or friendlier place in Hagi to try it. Most of the fish is served as sashimi, but a few items are lightly grilled, and the crabs are boiled. Absolutely the best *uni* (sea urchin) in the world is served here—don't even think of dunking it in soy sauce! The *maguro* (tuna) melts in your mouth. These and more local wonders are part of the very reasonably priced *sashimi-teishoku* (raw fish set). The 100-year-old building itself is a visual treat. Ask the master to open the upper-level wooden shutters from behind the cash register, using an interesting and complicated series of pulleys and ropes. ✉ *Shimo Goken-machi,* ☎ *0838/22–2136. No credit cards.*

$$$ ✕ **Nakamura.** Set-menu courses here might include sashimi, baked fish, fish grilled in soy sauce, mountain vegetables, miso soup, and steamed rice. Nakamura has tatami and Western seating but no English-language menu. You can select your food from the window display. ✉ *Furu-Hagi-chō,* ☎ *0838/22–6619. Reservations not accepted. No credit cards.*

$ ✕ **Fujita-ya.** This is a casual restaurant, full of color, where locals come for handmade *soba* (thin wheat noodles) and hot tempura served on handmade cypress trays. ⊠ *Kumagai-chō,* ☎ *0838/22–1086. No credit cards. Closed 2nd and 4th Wed. of month.*

$$$$ 🏯 **Hagi Royal Hotel.** In the Rainbow Building above JR Higashi-Hagi Eki, this former business hotel has become a ryokan. Guest rooms are on the small side for the money, but they are clean and comfortable. ⊠ *3000–5 Chinto, Hagi, Yamaguchi-ken 758,* ☎ *0838/25–9595,* FAX *0838/25–8434. 51 Japanese-style rooms, 4 Western-style rooms. AE, DC, MC, V.*

$$$$ 🏯 **Hokumon Yashiki.** An elegant ryokan with luxurious rooms, the Hokumon Yashiki has gracious, refined service that makes you feel pampered in a style to which the ruling Mōri clan were surely accustomed. Meals are served in your room. The inn overlooks a garden in the samurai section of town, near the castle grounds. ⊠ *210 Horiuchi, Hagi, Yamaguchi-ken 758,* ☎ *0838/22–7521,* FAX *0838/22–7521. 42 Japanese-style rooms, 5 Western-style rooms. Japanese-style bath. No credit cards. MAP.*

$$$ 🏯 **Fujita Ryokan.** This two-story concrete building has tatami rooms that are standard but better kept than at the nearby Higashi-Hagi Minshuku, and the common bath is clean. There is a small lounge for relaxing. Ask for a room facing the river so you can watch the fishermen at work. The owners prefer that their guests take two meals (breakfast and dinner) here, but if you'd rather dine elsewhere, you might be able to arrange to do so. Fujita is across the river from downtown Hagi, a five-minute walk from JR Higashi-Hagi Eki. ⊠ *Shinkawa Nishi-ku, Hagi, Yamaguchi-ken 758,* ☎ *0838/22–0603,* FAX *0838/26–1240. 13 Japanese-style rooms. V. MAP.*

$$$ 🏯 **Hagi Grand Hotel.** Convenience to JR Higashi-Hagi Eki makes this the most desirable international-style hotel in Hagi. The staff members are helpful, and guest rooms, half of which are Western style, are relatively spacious. There are Japanese- and Western-style restaurants on-site. ⊠ *25 Furu-Hagi-chō, Hagi, Yamaguchi-ken 758,* ☎ *0838/25–1211,* FAX *0838/25–4422. 190 rooms. 2 restaurants, shops, travel services. AE, DC, MC, V.*

$$ 🏯 **Minshuku Susa.** If you have the means or time to get to the small fishing village of Susa, instead of staying in Hagi consider taking one of this minshuku's huge rooms—at least 10 tatami mats in size, with an alcove for a coffee table and two chairs. The best rooms look onto the harbor of this picturesque fishing village between Hagi and Masuda on the Nihon-kai. The shared bathroom is splendid, with an iron Goemon tub (Goemon Ishikawa, a Japanese version of Robin Hood, was boiled alive, giving his name to this tub). Traditional service includes such niceties as an orange in the bath to scent the water. No English is spoken, but the staff's friendliness overcomes any language barrier. Dinner served in a tatami-floor dining room is an occasion to try the region's seafood delicacies. Trains running to Susa are infrequent at best, but it's well worth staying here if you have a car. ⊠ *Irie, Susa-chō, Abu-gun, Yamaguchi-ken 690,* ☎ *08387/6–2408. 6 Japanese-style rooms. Dining room. No credit cards. EP, MAP.*

Getting Around

The most convenient way to get to Hagi is by crossing the mountains from the San-yō town of Ogōri, at which the Hiroshima–Hakata Shinkansen stops. From Ogōri you can take a train to Tsuwano, then continue to Hagi by bus. You can also travel directly to Hagi from Ogōri by JR bus, which is the quicker way. Without a JR pass, the one-way bus fare is about ¥2,000. Remember, the bus is covered by the JR pass, even if some JR-seat reservation clerks seem to think otherwise.

The ideal way to explore Hagi is by bicycle, and there are many out-lets where you can rent a bike for approximately ¥1,000 per day. Try the shop across from the Rainbow Building, left of the station plaza. As an alternative, you can hire a "sightseeing taxi" (¥4,300 per hour); it takes about three hours to complete a hurried city tour.

The **Bōchō Bus Company**'s (☎ 0838/25–3131 sightseeing bus tour; Jap-anese-speaking guides only) departs from the Bōchō bus station on the eastern edge of the central city. The ¥2,810 fare, plus ¥1,200 for lunch, varies with the departure time; the 8:35 AM tour from Higashi-Hagi is the best deal.

Visitor Information

The **City Tourist Office** (☎ 0838/25–3131) is downtown in city hall, virtually in the center of the island that is Hagi. There's a lot more to do in and around this beautiful town than you might think, and the staff here can help you find it. City information is also available at the very friendly **Hagi City Tourist Bureau** (☎ 0838/25–1750) office next to Hagi Eki. For local information at Higashi-Hagi Eki try **Hagi Ryokan Kyōdō-kumiai** (☎ 0838/22–7599, FAX 0838/24–2202). Its main busi-ness is booking accommodations, but its English-speaking owner serves as a helpful adviser to tourists and dispenses official guide maps. The agency is in the Rainbow Building to the left of the station, in the first office on the left side of the shopping arcade.

Tsuwano

★ ㉖ *1 hr, 20 mins northeast of Hagi; 1 hr northeast of Ogōri by JR Yam-aguchi Line. (Ogōri is 1 hr west of Hiroshima by Shinkansen.)*

This hauntingly beautiful mountain town may well be the most pic-turesque hamlet in all Japan. If you catch it on a clear day, the view from the old castle ruins can simply take your breath away. Even if skies are not blue, the mist often seen hanging among the trees and ridges here only adds to its romantic appeal. Many of the stucco-and-tile walls are reminiscent of those in Hagi and Kurashiki, and the clear carp- and iris-filled streams running beside the streets make for pleas-ant strolls or bike rides.

The **Catoriku Kyokai** (Catholic church: ☎ 08567/2–0251), built in 1931, is unusual for its tatami floors. It's a replica of a church in Oura, Na-gasaki, and set among trees next to the road and a stream. Masses are Monday–Wednesday and Friday–Saturday at 6:30 AM and Sunday at 9 AM. Doors are left open till 5.

The **Shiryōkan** was originally a feudal school where the sons of samu-rai would train in the arts of manhood. Today, in its fencing hall, there's a folk-craft museum. It's a few steps past the Catholic church on the left side of Tono-machi-dōri. ☎ *08567/2–1000.* 🎫 *¥200.* 🕓 *Daily 8:30–5.*

The **Kyōdōkan** is a museum with a collection of exhibits that recount regional history. At the top of Tono-machi-dōri, the road crosses the Tsuwano-gawa. Kyōdōkan is on the other side of the bridge. 🎫 *¥350.* 🕓 *Daily 8:30–5.*

The **Taikodani Inari Jinja** (Taiko Valley Inari Shrine) is one of the five most important Inari shrines in Japan. Inari shrines, of which there are thousands scattered around the country, are connected with the fox, a Shintō symbol of luck and cleverness. The approach to this shrine resembles a tunnel because you pass under numerous red torii—1,174 of them—to reach the shrine high on the cliff side. Or you can opt out of the ascent on a bus that takes another road. **Yasaka Jinja** is another shrine on the site where, every July 20, 24, and 27, the Heron Dance Festival is held.

From the ruins of **Tsuwano-jō,** the panoramic view of the sleeping volcano, Aono-yama, the surrounding ridges, and the valley below is positively awe-inspiring. To get here, you can hike from the Inari shrine, or take the chairlift for ¥450, round-trip. The chairlift takes 5 minutes, and from there it's about a 10-minute hike to the castle foundations. Like Hagi-jō, Tsuwano Castle was a casualty of the Meiji "Restoration."

The **Old House of Ōgai Mōri** is worth a visit. Ōgai Mōri (1862–1922) was one of the prominent literary figures in the Meiji Restoration. The museum is spartan; he lived the simplest of lives (and a lot of his belonging are in the Tsuwano Historical Museum). To get to the house from the bottom of the Tsuwano-jō chairlift, turn left and then right to cross over the Tsuwano-gawa. Immediately after crossing the river, take the right-hand street and follow it around to the left. From the center of town, take a bus west to Kyūkyo-mae stop, from which the house is a short walk.

The tomb of Ōgai Mōri is at **Yōmei-ji,** east of JR Tsuwano Eki. ✉ ¥500. ☯ *Daily 8:30–5.*

Sekishūkan (Mori Ogai Museum) displays *washi,* Japanese handmade paper. There are demonstrations of papermaking, as well as a display of Iwami-style paper. On the second floor there are displays of washi from other regions of Japan. If you have not seen the process of creating handmade paper, this is a good museum to visit. It's next door to the Old House of Ōgai Mōri. ✉ *Free.* ☯ *Daily 8:30–5.*

A surprising local find is Tsuwano's **Katsushika Hokusai Bijutsukan** (Katsushika Hokusai Art Museum), just a block from the train station. Katsushika Hokusai (1760–1849) was the famous *ukiyo-e* (floating world) painter from the end of the Tokugawa era who influenced future generations of painters in Japan and overseas. This museum exhibits his wood-block prints, books, and paintings. ☎ 08567/2–1850. ✉ ¥500. ☯ *Daily 9:30–5.*

Tsuwano has put its geothermal gifts to good use at the spa at **Nagomi-no-Sato.** Inside and out, the tubs give you great views of the surrounding gumdrop-shape volcanic peaks marching into the distance. Scent fills the air due to liberal use of delightfully fragrant *hinoki* (Japanese cypress, a type of redwood). The wood's color contrasts with earth-tone tiles, and the waters are of a temperature just right for the interminable soaking of your travelers' aches. It's a bit west of everything else in town, across the river from the Washibara Hachiman-gū, but still not too far to get to by rented bike (and well worth getting to in any case). There's also a decent restaurant and a gift shop full of local specialties, from crafts and green tea to strong, excellent Tsuwano sake. ✉ 257–Ō-aza Washibara, ☎ 0856/72–4122, ✉ ¥500. ☯ *Hot springs daily 10–8, except the 2nd and 4th Thurs. month; restaurant daily 10–8, except 1st and 3rd Thurs.*

OFF THE BEATEN PATH

Otometōge Maria Seido – Between 1868 and 1870, in an effort to disperse Christian strongholds and cause them extreme hardship—and in the hope that they would recant their faith—the Tokugawa Shogunate sent 153 Christians from Nagasaki to Tsuwano. Many gave in to the torture, but in the end 36 held firm and died for it. Otometōge Maria Seido (St. Maria's Chapel at the Pass of the Virgin) was built in 1951 to commemorate them. Near Tsuwano, the 36 martyrs were imprisoned and tortured. Their plight is portrayed in the stained-glass windows. The chapel is a pleasant 1-km (½-mi) walk from Tsuwano Eki. Go right out of the station, make another right at the first street (which leads to Yōmei-ji), and just after crossing the tracks, turn right again and walk up the hill. Every May 3 a procession begins at the church in town and ends in the courtyard of the chapel, where a large outdoor mass is held.

Dining and Lodging

$$–$$$ ✕ **Yūki.** Carp dishes (such as carp sashimi and carp miso soup) and mountain vegetables are what made Yūki's reputation. The decor includes traditional beams and a stream running through the center of the dining room. There are sunken pits for your feet under the tables. ✉ Hon-chō-dōri, ☎ 08567/2–0162. No credit cards. Closed Thurs.

$–$$ ✕ **Aoki.** A great, friendly, reasonably priced sushi restaurant, Aoki is
★ not far from Tsuwano Eki. Try the jyo-nigiri (deluxe sushi set) for ¥1,300. That and a frosty mug of beer only sets you back ¥1,900. ✉ Takaoka-dōri, ☎ 08567/2–0444. No credit cards.

$$$ 🏨 **Tsuwano Lodge.** Kick back and relax in style at this jewel of a spot
★ tucked in along the way to the Washibara Hachiman-gū. The owners are friendly, the rooms are nice, and the food is outstanding. Perhaps best of all, there's a rotemburo (outside bath) full of sulfur-laden water—good for the skin, hair, and nails—to die for. As with the rest of this region, little English is spoken here. ✉ Rte. 345, Washibara, Tsuwano-chō, Kanoashi-gun, Shimane-ken 699-5613, ☎ 08567/2–1683. 8 Japanese-style rooms with shared baths. Dining room, mineral baths. No credit cards. EP, MAP.

$$ 🏨 **Sunroute Tsuwano.** The only place in town with Western-style accommodations, Sunroute Tsuwano has compact rooms with tiny bathrooms. Still, all is clean, and the staff, though unable to speak much if any English, is friendly. The place is a 10-minute walk from town and the station. ✉ Terada, Tsuwano-chō, Kanoashi-gun, Yamaguchi-ken 699, ☎ 0856/72–3232, FAX 08567/2–2805. 50 rooms. Restaurant, bar. AE, MC, V.

$$ 🏨 **Wakasagi-no-Yado.** Despite the limited English of the family that
★ runs this small minshuku, the staff is eager to help overseas tourists and will meet you at Tsuwano Eki, an eight-minute walk away. Typical of minshuku, there is a common bath. A Japanese and Western breakfast is served. ✉ Mōri, Tsuwano-chō, Kanoashi-gun, Shimane-ken 699-0056, ☎ 08567/2–1146. 8 Japanese-style with shared baths. No credit cards. BP.

Getting Around

JR train routes from Hagi to Tsuwano involve layovers in Masuda. To use a JR pass without going through Masuda, you could take a JR bus from Iwakuni (west of Hiroshima and site of a famous five-arch bridge); this takes two hours. An attractive option is to get to Ogōri (which is not far from Hiroshima on the Shinkansen line); from there, it's just an hour to Tsuwano by JR train.

You can also take a bus from Hagi's **Bōchō Bus Center** (☎ 08567/2–0272) directly to Tsuwano, a trip that takes 1 hour, 20 minutes (¥2,080). **Iwami Kotsu** (☎ 0856/24–0085) has a Hiroshima–Tsuwano bus route (you change at Nichihara). The ride takes a total of three hours and costs ¥3,550.

In Tsuwano all sights are within easy walking distance, or rent a bicycle from one of the four shops near the station plaza (two hours; ¥500; for each additional hour add ¥100).

Visitor Information

A **Tourist Information Office** (☎ 0856/72–1144) is inside the Photograph Gallery, to the right of the railway station. It's open daily 9–5, has free brochures, and staff members will help you reserve accommodations. As with most places in town, little or no English is spoken here.

Izumo Taisha and Hino-misaki

㉗ *2 hrs, 45 mins northeast of Tsuwano on the JR San-in Line Oki Limited Express; 1 hr west of Matsue by Ichibata Dentetsu (electric railway); 40 mins west of Matsue by JR Kunibiki Ltd. Exp.*

Although **Izumo Taisha** is Japan's oldest Shintō shrine, the *honden* (main building) you'll see dates from 1744, and most of the others from 1874. The architectural style, with its projecting, saddled crests, and ornamental roof fixtures resembling crossed swords, is said to be unique to the Izumo region, but some similarities with Ise Jingū on the Kii Peninsula can be noted. The taisha is dedicated to a male god, Ōkuninushi, known in mythology as the creator of the land and god of marriage and fortune.

On either side of the compound there are two rectangular buildings that are believed to house the Shintō gods during the 10th lunar month of each year. Accordingly, in the rest of Japan, the lunar October is referred to as Kaminazuki, "month without gods," while in Izumo, October is called Kamiarizuki, "month with gods." The shrine is a five-minute walk from Izumo Taisha-mae Eki. ⊠ *Izumo Taisha, Izumo-shi,* ☎ *0853/53–2298.* ⊡ *Free.* ☉ *Daily 8:30–5:30.*

From its perch 208 ft above the sea, **Hino-misaki Tō-dai** (Cape Hino Lighthouse) towers another 145 ft. Its height makes for stunning views of the San-in coast and, in fine weather, the Oki Islands. The lighthouse is open to the public for a fee of ¥150, daily 8:30–4 from April to September (from 9 AM the rest of year). To get to Hino-misaki, go west from Izumo Taisha and take a bus (hourly) from the Ichibata bus terminal for the 25-minute ride (¥1,150).

Just southwest of Hino-misaki Tō-dai are **Hino-misaki Jinja,** a pair of shrines dedicated to the goddesses Amaterasu and Susonō. Brightly painted on the outside, they have colorful murals inside. ⊡ *Free.* ☉ *Daily 9–5.*

Getting Around

From Tsuwano, the ride to Izumo Taisha is 2 hours, 45 minutes on the JR San-in Line Oki Limited Express.

To go from Matsue Onsen to Taisha, the location of Izumo Taisha, takes only one hour on the Ichibata Dentetsu (electric railway, ¥790), leaving from Matsue Onsen Eki. You will need to change trains at Kawato Eki for the final leg to Izumo Taisha-mae Eki. You can also get there by taking the JR train from Matsue Eki to Izumo, then transferring to the JR Taisha Line and taking that to Taisha Eki, where you can either take a 5-minute bus ride to Taisha-mae Eki or walk to the shrine in about 20 minutes.

Matsue

★ ㉘ *1 hr from Izumo Taisha by Ichibata Dentetsu; 3½ hrs northeast of Tsuwano by JR Limited Express; 5 hrs northeast of Hiroshima by JR Geibi and Kisuki lines (1 train daily departs Hiroshima at 8:45 AM); 2 hrs, 20 mins northwest of Okayama by JR Yakumo Limited Express (13 daily).*

One could easily argue that Matsue has it all. Few cities are blessed with as much beauty, elegance, history, and delicious food as this one.

Working hard to keep it that way, its friendly people help make this
relatively isolated realm a refreshing favorite.

Matsue lies at the point where Shinji-ko empties into Nakaumi-ko, which
connects with the sea. This makes Matsue a seafood-lover's paradise,
with fish from the Nihon-kai and delicacies such as eel, shrimp, shellfish, carp, sea bass, smelt, and whitebait from Shinji-ko as well. The
water has also created a lovely network of canals.

★ Start a tour of Matsue at **Matsue-jō** and its spacious, meditative
grounds. Constructed entirely of pine, Matsue-jō was completed in 1611
and partially reconstructed in 1642, and it was neither ransacked nor
burned during the Tokugawa Shogunate.

Built by the daimyō of Izumo, Yoshiharu Horio, for protection, Matsue-jō is a beautiful structure as well. Its donjon, at 98 ft, is said to be
the second tallest among originals still standing in Japan. Camou-
flaged among the surrounding trees, Matsue-jō seems almost spooky
at times. Note the overhanging eaves above the top floor, designed to
cut down glare that might have prevented the spotting of an attack-
ing force. The castle is fabulously preserved, with six interior levels be-
lied by a facade that suggests only five. The lower floors exhibit a
collection of samurai swords and armor. The long climb to the castle's
uppermost floor is worth it—the view encompasses the city, Shinji-ko,
the Shimane Peninsula, and the distant mountains.

The castle and park are a nice stroll to the northwest from the station,
but if you're not up for it, there's an amazing choice of buses—none
of which are run by JR, however. The cheapest and best option is to
take the Lakeline Bus from Terminal 7 in front of the station and get
off at Ote-mae. The fare is only ¥100. ☎ 0852/21–4030. ✉ ¥550. ☉
Daily 8:30–6.

The **Matsue Kyōdōkan** (Matsue Cultural Museum) displays art, folk
craft, and implements used during the first three imperial eras after the
fall of the Tokugawa Shogunate. The Kyōdōkan is in the two-story,
white Western-style building just south of the castle. ☎ 0852/22–
3958. ✉ *Free.* ☉ *Daily 8:30–5.*

Meimei-an Teahouse was built in 1779 and is one of the best-preserved
teahouses of the period. For ¥300 you can take in a fine view of Matsue-jō, and for ¥360 more, you get tea and a sweet. To get here, leave
Jōzen Kōen, the castle park, at its east exit and follow the moat going
north; at the top of the park a road leads to the right, northwest of the
castle. The teahouse is a short climb up this road. ☎ 0852/21–9863.
☉ *Daily 9–5.*

Buke Yashiki (Samurai Mansion), built in 1730, belonged to the well-
to-do Shiomi family, chief retainers to the daimyō. Note the separate
servant quarters, a shed for the palanquin, and slats in the walls to allow
cooling breezes to flow through the rooms. Buke Yashiki is on the main
road at the base of the side street on which Meimei-an Teahouse is located (keep the castle moat on your left). ☎ 0852/22–2243. ✉ ¥300.
☉ *Apr.–Sept., daily 8:30–6:30; Oct.–Mar., daily 8:30–5.*

Tanabe Bijutsukan (Tanabe Art Museum), dedicated mainly to objects
of the tea ceremony, exhibits beautiful ceramics and tea sets from the
region. The museum is next to Buke Yashiki. ☎ 0852/26–2211. ✉ ¥500
(varies with exhibit). ☉ *Tues.–Sun. 9–4:30.*

The **Koizumi Yakumo Kyūkyo** (Lafcadio Hearn Residence), next to the
Tanabe Bijutsukan, has remained unchanged since the famous writer
left Matsue for Tōkyō in 1891. Born of an Irish father and a Greek

mother, Lafcadio Hearn (1850–1904) spent his early years in Europe, then moved to the United States to become a journalist. In 1890 he traveled to Japan and began teaching in Matsue, where he met and married a samurai's daughter. Later, he even became a Japanese citizen, taking the name Koizumi Yakumo. He spent only 15 months in Matsue, but it was here that he became fascinated with Japan. ☎ 0852/ 23–0714. ☞ ¥250. ☉ Daily 9–4:30.

The **Koizumi Yakumo Kinenkan** (Lafcadio Hearn Memorial Hall) contains a good collection of the author's manuscripts and other items that reflect his life in Japan. It is adjacent to Koizumi Yakumo Kyūkyo. Two minutes from the Memorial Hall is the Hearn Kyūkyo bus stop, where you can catch a bus back to the center of town and the station. ☎ 0852/ 21–2147. ☞ ¥300. ☉ Daily 8:30–5.

When dusk rolls around, position yourself for a good view of the sunset over **Shinji-ko.** You can watch it from Shinjiko Ōhashi, the town's westernmost bridge, but the best spot is south of the bridge along the road, at water level in **Shiragata Kōen,** the narrow lakeside park just west of the NHK Building and the hospital. This is a fabulous place to kick back and enjoy some carry-out sushi.

En Route   A couple of stops on the way from Matsue to Tottori are worth considering. In the town of Yasugi is the **Adachi Bijutsukan** (Adachi Museum of Art), which exhibits the works of both past and contemporary Japanese artists and has an inspiring series of gardens. ✉ 320 Furukawa-chō, Yasugi, Shimane-ken, ☎ 0854/28–7111. ☞ ¥2,200, half price if you show your passport. ☉ Daily 9–4:30.

Daisen-dake (Mt. Daisen), popular with hikers, is a volcanic cone that locals liken to Mt. Fuji. On the slopes above the town of Daisen there is an 8th-century Tendai sect temple, **Daisen-ji.** The peak can be climbed in about seven hours (round-trip) from here. If it's clear, you can even see Shikoku from the top. **Dōmyō-in** (☎ 0859/52–2038) is a subtemple that offers lodging. Subtemple **Renjō-in** (☎ 0859/52–2506) has accommodations you can rent. Buses leave Yonago, in Tottori-ken, every hour for the 50-minute ride to Daisen (¥730).

Near Yonago is the largest flower park in the country, the 124-acre **Hana-Kairo** (Flower Gallery). Here 750,000 flowers bloom each year. It's a half-hour bus ride from Yonago JR Eki, or you can take the Hakubi Line train to Hōkimizuguchi Eki and a five-minute taxi ride from there. ✉ Kaiken-machi, Tsuru 110, Nishi-haku-gun, Tottori-ken, ☎ 0859/48–3030. ☞ Apr.–Nov. ¥1,000, Dec.–Mar. ¥700. ☉ Apr.–Nov., daily 9–5; Dec.–Mar., daily 9–4:30.

Up the coast from Mt. Daisen, toward Tottori, **Misasa Onsen** is a famous 1,000-year-old hot-spring resort claiming the highest radium-content waters (reputed to have strong curative powers) in the country. It's a 20-minute bus ride from Kurayoshi Eki.

Dining and Lodging

$$–$$$ ✕ **Kawakyō.** This is the best place in town to try the seven famous
  ★   delicacies from Shinji-ko: *suzuki* (or *hosho-yaki*), sea bass wrapped in *washi* (paper) and steam-baked over hot coals; *unagi* (freshwater eel) split, broiled, and basted in sweet soy sauce; *shirao,* a small whitefish often served as sashimi or cooked in vinegar-miso; *amasagi* (smelt), teriyaki-grilled or cooked in tempura; *shijimi,* small black-shelled clams served in miso or other soup; *koi,* string-bound, washi-wrapped, steam-baked carp; and *moroge-ebi,* steamed shrimp. And here, prices are low enough that some diners can consume the whole list in a single evening. Especially good is the hosho-yaki. The folks who run the

place are amazingly friendly, as is the regular crowd. Among them all there will be enough English for those who don't speak Japanese to fill up and have a wonderful time doing so. For those who *do* speak Japanese, now's a great time to practice—master-san and his wife are lots of fun. Don't forget to ask for one of the delicious *ji-zake* (locally made sake) samplers. The few seats here are often occupied, so reservations are a good idea. Kawakyō is less than a block west of the Washington Hotel (north of the river). ⊠ *65 Suetsugu Honmachi,* ☎ *0852/ 22–1312. No credit cards. Closed Sun. No lunch.*

$ ✕ **Daikichi.** For having fun and socializing with locals, this *yakitori* (grill) bar with counter service offers an evening's entertainment, good grilled chicken, and flowing sake. The owner, Toshiyuki Hidaka, speaks English and welcomes foreigners. The place is easily recognized by its red lanterns outside. ⊠ *Asahi-machi,* ☎ *0852/31–8308. No credit cards. No lunch.*

$ ✕ **Yakumo-an.** This traditional house is a lovely setting in which to
★ enjoy the best soba in town. A colorful garden surrounds the dining area. Recommended dishes include the *sanshurui soba* (three kinds of soba) for ¥750. Take the top dish and, leaving the garnishes in, pour the broth into it; then dunk the three different dishes of noodles. Drink the leftover broth, too; it's full of B vitamins and good for you. ⊠ *Just west of Tanabe Bijutsukan (north of the castle),* ☎ *0852/22–2400. No credit cards.*

$$$$ ✕🏠 **Minami-kan.** An elegant and prestigious ryokan, Minami-kan is known for its refined service and tasteful furnishings. It also has the best restaurant in Matsue for kaiseki, cooked on hot stones, and *tai-meshi* (sea bream with rice). Even if you do not stay here, you can make dinner reservations. ⊠ *Ōhashi, Matsue, Shimane-ken 690,* ☎ *0852/ 21–5131,* ℻ *0852/26–0351. 9 Japanese-style rooms. Restaurant. DC, MC, V. EP, MAP.*

$$$$ 🏠 **Hotel Ichibata.** In the Matsue Onsen section of town, fronting Shinji-ko, the Ichibata has well-known thermal waters and some great views. All rooms are large, but only Japanese-style rooms face the lake. The view of the sunsets from the top-floor Vermilion Lounge is stunning, but beware: drink prices can be outrageous. The hotel is a 20-minute bus ride from the station or a 10-minute, ¥1,000 taxi ride. ⊠ *30 Chidōri-chō, Matsue, Shimane-ken 690,* ☎ *0852/22–0188,* ℻ *0852/22–0230. 74 Japanese-style rooms, 74 Western-style rooms. 2 restaurants, beer garden, hot springs. AE, DC, MC, V.*

$$ 🏠 **Matsue Washington Hotel.** The best thing about the Washington is its location in the part of town that has lots to do, see, and eat. A short walk away are a pedestrian mall lined with shops, Shinji-ko, and Matsue-jō. The rooms are modern, nice, and generally a good value, if not particularly large. The coffee shop on the ground floor serves a decent breakfast buffet and light meals. There is also a more formal restaurant serving Western and Chinese fare. ⊠ *2–22 Higashi Hon-machi, Matsue, Shimane-ken 690-0842,* ☎ *0852/22–4111,* ℻ *0852/22–4120. 158 rooms. 2 restaurants, coffee shop. AE, DC, MC, V.*

$$ 🏠 **Ryokan Terazuya.** Treat yourself to a stay here. The friendly fam-
★ ily that runs this riverside ryokan has kept up the tradition since 1893, and they really know how to make guests feel at home. The rooms are all air-conditioned, and the location is perfect for those incomparable Shinji-ko sunsets. The food is superb and is of an astounding variety. English is spoken, and if guests are interested, the gregarious owner will teach sushi making, and his charming wife will teach tea ceremony. ⊠ *60–3 Tenjin-machi, Matsue, Shimane-ken 690-0064,* ☎ *0852/21– 3480,* ℻ *0852/21–3422. 10 Japanese-style rooms. No credit cards. EP, MAP.*

Nightlife

For a town of its size, Matsue is unusually flush with the expensive, shady bars called "snacks," where women pour drinks and provide company. Unless you've just won the lottery, you'll want to avoid such places.

Filaments (⊠ 5 Hakkenya-chō, ☎ 0852/24–8984), an upstairs place, hops all night long—every night. Osamu-san, the hip, friendly proprietor, speaks English, and his collection of music will amaze anyone. You name it, he's probably got it—and will play it for you within moments of your request. The drinks are good and cheap (from ¥500), and tasty food is served, too, at prices from ¥650 to ¥1,000. It's located just south of the river near the second of the four main bridges.

Getting Around

Most sights in Matsue are within walking distance of each other. Where they are not, the buses fill in. The bus station faces the train station.

To arrange for a Goodwill Guide, contact the **Matsue Tourist Information Office** (⊠ Asahi-machi, ☎ 0852/27–2598) a day in advance. English-speaking volunteers show you around the city or escort you to Izumo Taisha. There's no charge for the service, though you should pay your guide's expenses, including lunch. The office is in JR Matsue Eki and open daily 9:30–6. You can also collect free maps and brochures here.

Oki Retto (Oki Islands)

㉙ *1 hr northeast of Matsue by bus to Shichirui, then 2½ hrs by ferry.*

The stark Oki Islands were a place of exile for fallen nobility since before the 7th century. Today it's mostly fishing and farming that sustain island residents. Few tourists find their way here; those who do see an untamed landscape with some cliffs more than 800 ft high and a few odd attractions. One peculiar local activity is a type of bullfighting in which two bulls pair off—against each other—in a ring. You can also watch this sport on Shikoku and in Okinawa (and in Indonesia), but it's said to have originated here out of the exiles' boredom. There are four main islands: Dōgo is the largest, and the other three are in a group called Dōzen. The most spectacular cliffs are part of the Oki Kuniga coast on Nishino-shima. Chibu-jima also has great natural beauty. Bullfighting can be observed on Dōgo in the summer.

Sightseeing boats (☎ 08514/6–0016) leave from Urago and Beppu harbors (from ¥2,040).

Dining and Lodging

The only city with Honshū-style hotels is Saigo, on Dōgo Island. There are also ryokan and minshuku; camping is an option, too.

The restaurant at the 38-room **Island Hotel Shimaji** (⊠ Minato-machi, Saigo-chō, Oki-gun, Shimane-ken 685, ☎ 08512/2–1569) serves beautiful meals of freshly caught fish.

The **Oki Viewport Hotel** (⊠ Naka-machi, Saigo-chō, Oki-gun, Shimane-ken 685, ☎ 08512/2–7007, FAX 08512/2–7020) is directly across from the ferry pier. It has 160 rooms and two restaurants.

Getting Around

If you want to travel by air to the Oki Islands, **JAC** (Japan Air Commuter; ☎ 0853/72–0001) flights leave from Izumo Airport. The flight to Saigo takes 30 minutes and costs ¥9,100.

Oki Line (☎ 08512/2–1122) boats leave from Shichirui or Sakaiminato, both near Yonago. Prices for ferries to Saigo range from ¥2,530 to ¥7,110, depending on your class of ticket; the ride is 2½ hours.

Visitor Information

Call the **Tourist Association** (☎ 08512/2–1577, FAX 08512/2–1406) for information on the September bull tournament details, which change annually.

Tottori

30 *2 hrs east of Matsue by JR San-in Main Line, 4½ hrs north of Ōsaka by Bantan and San-in Main lines.*

If you're passing through Tottori, you should by all means visit the *sakyū* (dunes) on the coast north of the city. Other attractions, all within about 1 km (½ mi) of Tottori Eki, include the ruins of a former castle, a French Renaissance building called Jinpukaku, and a few small museums: the Watanabe Bijutsukan (Watanabe Art Museum), the Kenritsu Hakubutsukan (Tottori Prefectural Museum), and the Mingei Bijutsukan (Folk Craft Museum). There's a hot spring only five minutes from the station.

The **sakyū** stretch along the shore for more than 10 km (6 mi); some of the crests rise 300 ft or more. Climb to the top of one and watch the sea in the foreground with the green, mist-covered hills behind. If you can, get here in time to watch the first rays of light start to dance on the still-dewy sand. *Woman in the Dunes,* Kobo Abe's haunting story about a bug collector who himself becomes trapped in a sandpit, like a bug, is set here.

Tourists and surfers come for the miles of fine beaches and waves in summertime, and parachute jumpers like to leap from the top of the highest dune, riding the breeze and landing just in front of the ocean far below. First thing in the morning or late in the day, you don't have to walk far to escape the crowds if you're seeking solitude. Better yet, you can rent a bicycle from the Cycling Terminal at Kodomo-no-kuni, near the entrance to the dunes, and work your way east to the Uradome ("oo-ra-*do*-meh") Seashore. You can follow the roads next to the sand.

To get to the dunes, take Bus 20, 24, 25, or 26 from Gate 3 at the bus terminal in front of the JR station for the 20-minute ride (¥330) north.

At the pier near Iwamoto-bashi, you can board the **San-in Matsushima Yuran** (☎ 0857/73–1212) sightseeing boat for a 50-minute trip (¥1,000) along the coast to see the twisted pines and eroded rocks of the many islands that stand offshore.

The **City Tourist Information Office** (☎ 0857/22–3318) in Tottori is at the station.

Lodging

$$$–$$$$ 🏨 **New Otani.** This tall red-concrete building across from the JR station and next to the Daimaru department store is the most modern hotel in town. The bright lobby, with white and pink marble, green-and-white-striped chairs, and light-wood paneling, is gorgeous. The guest rooms on higher floors have views over Tottori; be sure to request one on the west side. ⊠ *2–153 Ima-machi, Tottori-shi, Tottori-ken 680-0822,* ☎ *0857/23–1111,* FAX *0857/23–0979. 136 rooms. 5 restaurants. AE, DC, MC, V.*

$$–$$$ 🏨 **Tottori Washington Hotel Plaza.** On your right as you exit the station, this tall white hotel offers good value. All of the pastel-color rooms are spacious and look out on the Chugoku Sanchi-chi (Chugoku Mountains) and/or the Nihon-kai. ⊠ *102 Higashi Honji-chō, Tottori-shi, Tottori-ken 680-0835,* ☎ *0857/27–8111,* FAX *0857/27–8125. 156 rooms. 2 restaurants. AE, DC, MC, V.*

Kasumi to Kinosaki

70 mins east of Tottori by JR.

③① The scenery along the coast east of Tottori, part of San-in Kaigan National Park, is remarkable. **Kasumi** is a pleasant, if sleepy, fishing village in which to stay overnight.

Worth visiting in Kasumi is **Daijō-ji,** 1½ km (about 1 mi) south of JR Kasumi Eki. This temple's history began in 746, but it didn't become well known until the 18th century, when Maruyama Okyo, a leading artist of the time, came from Kyōto on a field trip with his students. Inspired, he assigned his students to paint various themes in several rooms of the temple. His fervor caught on—the field trip lasted eight years. Admission to the temple is ¥500; it's open to visitors daily from 8:30 to 4:30.

Kundani, a tiny fishing village where there's nothing to do but relax, is an option for an overnight—the Minshuku Genroku Bekkan is a real find. To get here, take the train to the Satsu Eki, two stops past Kasumi.

③② Near **Kinosaki,** a village set among hills, are a notable temple, Onsen-ji, and a cable car up Daishi-san, but the real draw is the onsen. Every inn and hotel has its own springs, and there are seven traditional public baths. Each charges about ¥300 and closes at around 10:30 PM.

Dining and Lodging

$–$$$ ✕ **Hyōtan.** Convivial and small, Hyōtan in Kasumi has counter seating for about 10 people and tatami space for only a small group. The Nishimoto family work behind the counter, fulfilling requests for beer, sake, sashimi, and grilled fish. Recommended is the *hata-hata,* a small fish dusted with salt and grilled—an order is usually three, and they taste like they were caught moments ago. ⊠ *340–1 Nonokaichi, Kasumi-chō,* ☎ *0796/36–4047. Reservations not accepted. No credit cards. No lunch.*

$$$$ ⊡ **Mikiya Ryokan.** In Kinosaki, this three-story wooden inn is perfectly old-fashioned, with creaking timbers and spacious tatami rooms. It has its own thermal baths, which look out onto the nicely kept garden. ⊠ *Kinosaki-gun, Hyōgo-ken 669,* ☎ *0796/32–2031. 20 rooms. Hot springs. AE, DC, V.*

$$ ⊡ **Marusei Ryokan.** A small, quiet place, Marusei Ryokan is in a two-story concrete building between JR Kasumi Eki and the harbor. The tatami rooms are quite spacious, with minimal furnishings. Bathrooms are cramped, but the narrow tubs are deep. Meals are served in your room on request, but unless the *kani-suki* (crab casserole) is being offered, you may want to venture out to a restaurant instead. ⊠ *Kasumi-chō, Kinosaki-gun, Hyōgo-ken 669,* ☎ *0796/36–0028,* ℻ *0796/36–2018. 11 rooms, 4 with bath. AE, V. EP, MAP.*

$–$$ ⊡ **Minshuku Genroku Bekkan.** This minshuku is in the center of the quiet Kundani, two streets from the sea. The eight tatami-mat guest rooms are spacious and freshly decorated, though none has a private bath. Breakfast and an excellent dinner are served. The owner speaks English and may invite you to join him at the local bar after dinner. The closest JR station is Satsu; if you call on arrival, the owners will meet you at the station. ⊠ *Kundani Kasumi, Kinosaki-gun, Hyōgo-ken 669,* ☎ *0796/38–0018. 8 Japanese-style rooms with shared bath. No credit cards. MAP.*

Ama-no-hashidate

③③ *45 mins east of Kinosaki by JR; 1 hr, 55 mins north of Kyōto by the Tokkyu Line.*

Ama-no-hashidate, along with Miyajima and Matsushima, is one of the Big Three Japanese scenic wonders. The Big Three list dates from centuries ago, when the beauty of these sights so captivated artists and poets that it earned them this distinction. These days, however, many visitors find that tourism and development have taken over the once inspiring beauty.

Ama-no-hashidate, the "Bridge of Heaven," is really just a very narrow 3-km-long (2-mi-long) sandbar that stretches almost completely across Miyazu-wan (Miyazy Bay). Most likely the bay itself was once pristine enough to do the trick, but nowadays people stand with their heads between their legs to make Ama-no-hashidate look like a bridge in the sky.

To get here, take the 15-minute bus ride from JR Ama-no-hashidate Eki to Ichinomiya, or take the ferry boat from Ama-no-hashidate Pier. There are also bicycles for rent at stores in front of the JR station. A leisurely ride along the coastal plain might take 30–40 minutes.

WESTERN HONSHŪ A TO Z

To research prices, get advice from other travelers, and book travel arrangements, visit www.fodors.com.

AIRPORTS

Hiroshima Kūkō is the major airport for this region, with many daily flights to Haneda Kūkō in Tōkyō and direct daily flights to Kagoshima, Okinawa, Sendai, and Sapporo. There are connections with many major Asian cities as well. Other airports in Western Honshū—at Izumo, Tottori, and Yonago—have daily flights to Tōkyō. JAS and ANA fly out of Iwami Airport, which serves Hagi, Tsuwano, and Masuda, to Tōkyō and Ōsaka. For airline phone numbers, *see* Air Travel *in* Smart Travel Tips A to Z.

Seven daily flights travel between Hiroshima and Tōkyō's Haneda Kūkō, and there are flights to Kagoshima, on Kyūshū, and to Sapporo, on Hokkaidō. There are also many flights to Singapore, Hong Kong, Seoul, and other regional hubs.

BOAT AND FERRY TRAVEL

Hiroshima is a ferry hub. Seto Nai-kai Kisen Company runs eight boats daily to Miyajima (¥1,460 round-trip). Two important connections are to and from Matsuyama on Shikoku—14 hydrofoil ferries a day take one hour (¥5,800), and 12 regular ferries a day take three hours (¥4,340 first class, ¥2,170 second class); and to and from Beppu on Kyūshū—one departs Hiroshima at 9:30 PM to arrive at Beppu at 6 AM, and another departs Beppu at 2 PM to arrive at Hiroshima at 7 PM (¥4,000–¥16,000).

➤ BOAT AND FERRY INFORMATION: **Seto Nai-kai Kisen Company** (✉ 12–23 Ujinakaigan 1-chōme, Minami-ku, Hiroshima, ☎ 082/253–1212, FAX 082/505–0134).

EMERGENCIES
➤ CONTACTS: **Ambulance** (☎ 119). **Police** (☎ 110).

TRAIN TRAVEL

By far the easiest way to travel to Western Honshū and along its southern shore is by Shinkansen from Tōkyō, Kyōto, and Ōsaka. Major Shinkansen stops are Himeji, Okayama, and Hiroshima. It takes approximately 5 hours on the Shinkansen to travel to Hiroshima from Tōkyō; 1 hour, 40 minutes from Ōsaka (times vary depending on which stops trains make). To cover the length of the San-yō coast from Ōsaka to Shimonoseki takes 3 hours, 10 minutes.

JR express trains run along the San-yō and San-in coasts, making a loop beginning and ending in Kyōto. Crossing from one coast to the other in Western Honshū requires traveling fairly slowly through the mountains. Several train lines link the cities on the northern Nihon-kai coast to Okayama, Hiroshima, and Ogōri on the southern.

TRANSPORTATION AROUND WESTERN HONSHŪ

Except for the short crossing to Miyajima from Hiroshima, traveling through San-yō means hopping on and off JR's Shinkansen and local trains on the main railway line that follows the southern shore of Western Honshū between Ōsaka and Shimonoseki. Local buses or street-cars are the best way to get around major cities. If you know a little Japanese, can handle both middle-of-nowhere navigation and hectic urban traffic situations, and are traveling with one or more other peo-ple (the highway tolls and gas equal the train fare for one), you might consider renting a car and exploring Western Honshū at your own pace.

Routes cross the mountains to cities on the Seto Nai-kai at several points along the San-in coast. The major connecting train routes are Himeji–Kasumi, Okayama–Tottori, Hiroshima–Izumo, Ogōri–Tsuwano, and Ogōri–Hagi.

JR and Bōchō bus lines also run over the mountains. It's important to call ahead and reserve seats for these buses. Local tourist information offices will help reserve tickets for non-Japanese speakers.

VISITOR INFORMATION

Most major towns or sightseeing destinations have tourist information centers that offer free maps and brochures. They will also help you se-cure accommodations.

The Japan Travel Bureau (JTB) has offices at every JR station in each of the major cities and can assist in local tours, hotel reservations, and ticketing. Except for JTB's Hiroshima office, you should not assume that any English will be spoken beyond the essentials.

The Japan Travel Phone, a nationwide service for English-language as-sistance and travel information, is available seven days a week from 9 to 5. Dial toll-free from outside Tōkyō or Kyōto. When using a gray, blue, or green public phone, insert a ¥10 coin or telephone card be-fore dialing, which will be returned when you hang up.

➤ Tourist Information: **Hagi City Information Office** (☎ 0838/25–3131). **Hagi City Tourist Association** (☎ 0838/25–1750). **Hiroshima City Tourist Office** (☎ 082/247–6738). **Hiroshima Prefectural Tourist Office** (☎ 082/228–9907). **Hiroshima Tourist Information Office** (☎ 082/249–9329). **Japan Travel Bureau Hiroshima** (☎ 082/261–4131). **Japan Travel Phone** (☎ 0120/444–800 or 0088/22–4800). **Matsue Tourism Association** (☎ 0852/27–5843). **Matsue Tourist Informa-tion Office** (☎ 0852/21–4034). **Miyajima Tourist Association** (☎ 08294/4–2011). **Okayama Prefectural Tourist Office** (☎ 086/224–2111). **Okayama Tourist Association** (☎ 086/256–2000). **Okayama Tourist Information Office** (☎ 086/222–2912).

10 SHIKOKU

The smallest of Japan's four main islands,
Shikoku rests neatly beneath western Honshū,
a comfortable distance across the famed
Seto Nai-kai. Rugged east–west mountain
ranges halve Shikoku, where you will be
treated more as a welcome foreign emissary
than as an income-bearing tourist. Perhaps
that reflects on the Japanese who still make
pilgrimages to the island's 88 sacred
temples, as they have done for centuries.

By Nigel Fisher
and Simon
Richmond

Updated
by Suzanne
Kamata

FOR QUITE SOME TIME, Japanese and international vacationers left Shikoku off their itineraries, perhaps because the ferry ride across the Seto Nai-kai (Inland Sea) discouraged most people. But with the recent spate of bridge building, the island has become more popular. An ambitious set of 10 bridges completed in 1999, Shimanami Kaidō, leapfrogs across seven islands and carries the Nishi-seto Expressway from Onomichi, in Hiroshima Prefecture, to Imabari, on Shikoku's northwest coast. The Akashi Kaikyō Ōhashi—the longest single-span suspension bridge in the world—joins Shikoku to Honshū via Awaji-shima, an island to the west of Tokushima. At night, the lights of the bridge, which change color according to the season, resemble a necklace strung across the water, thus the nickname, "Pearl Bridge." Shikoku is also linked to Honshū via the Seto Ōhashi, a 12-km-long (7½-mi-long) series of six bridge spans that connect the islands in great arching leaps. Driving across it you can get off on the various small islands with lookout areas and souvenir shops.

Otherwise, the train from Okayama will whisk you across the Seto Nai-kai in 15 minutes, before turning east to Takamatsu and Tokushima, west to Matsuyama, or south to Kōchi. These four cities are the capitals of the four prefectures—Kagawa, Tokushima, Kōchi, and Ehime—which explains the island's name: *shi* (four) *koku* (countries).

The rugged heart of Shikoku consists of mountain ranges that run from east to west, dividing the island in two. The northern half, which faces the Seto Nai-kai, has a dry climate, with only modest autumn rains during typhoon season. The southern half, which faces the Pacific, is more likely to have ocean storms sweep in, bringing rain throughout the year. With its shores washed by the warm waters of the Kuroshio (Black Current), it has a warmer climate and especially mild winters. The mountain ranges of the interior are formidable, achieving heights up to 6,400 ft, and are cut by wondrous gorges and valleys. Nestled in these valleys are small farming villages that have remained almost unchanged since the Edo period (1603–1868).

Although Shikoku has been part of Japan's political and cultural development since the Heian period (794–1192), the island maintains a certain independence from mainstream Japan. Some factories litter the northern coast, but to a great extent, Shikoku has been spared the ugliness of Japan's industrialization. The island is still considered by many Japanese as a rural backwater where pilgrims follow the route of the 88 sacred temples.

The Buddhist saint Kōbō Daishi was born on Shikoku in 774, and it was he who founded the Shingon sect of Buddhism that became popular in the shōgun eras. (During the Tokugawa Shogunate, travel was restricted, except for pilgrimages.) Pilgrims visit the 88 temples to honor the priest, and by doing so, they can be released from having to go through the cycle of rebirth. Many Japanese wait until they retire to make this pilgrimage, in part because the time is right and in part because it takes two months on foot—the traditional way to visit all the temples. Most pilgrims now scoot around by bus in 13 days and have become more numerous.

Towns large and small all over Shikoku have constructed tourist attractions, such as Uzu-no-michi in Naruto, and American-style outlet malls in order to attract busloads from other parts of Japan. In spite of increased development, however, the island continues to be known as a place of abundant natural beauty and traditional ways.

Shikoku Glossary

Key Japanese words and suffixes in this chapter include -*bashi* (bridge), *bijutsukan* (art museum), -*chō* (street or block), *chūō* (central), *daimyō* (feudal lord), *donjon* (castle stronghold), *dōri* (avenue), *eki* (train station), *gaijin* (foreigner), *gū* (Shintō shrine), *hama* (beach), *hōmotsukan* (treasure house), -*jō* (castle), -*ken* (prefecture), *kōen* ("*ko*-en," park), -*kyōkoku* (gorge), -*misaki* (cape), *ōhashi* (large bridge), *onsen* (hot springs), *Seto Nai-kai* (Inland Sea), -*shima* (island), *Shinkansen* (bullet train, literally "new trunk line"), *ryokan* (traditional Japanese inn), and *torii* ("*to*-ree-ee," gate), -*yama* (mountain).

Pleasures and Pastimes

Dining

The delight of Shikoku is the number of small Japanese restaurants that serve the freshest fish, either caught in the Seto Nai-kai or in the Pacific. You will know that the seafood is fresh because it's often killed in front of you—or because it arrives still wriggling on the plate. Takamatsu and Kōchi are the best places to eat seafood, especially Kōchi, which specializes in *Tosa ryōri* (Tosa is the old name for Kōchi, and *ryōri* means cooking), which are bonito dishes *tataki* style: tender fresh fish steaks seared lightly over a fire of pine needles and served with garlic-flavored soy sauce. In Matsuyama the local specialty is *ikezukuri*, a live fish with its meat cut into strips. In Tokushima try *kaizoku ryōri* (pirate's cuisine), in which you grill seafood on your own earthenware brazier. Also consider ordering what the chef recommends—that dish is always the best. Just mention if you wish to keep the price within certain limits.

Noodle restaurants abound, too: in Takamatsu you should try *sanuki udon* (a thick noodle slightly firmer in texture and more elastic than udon served elsewhere in Japan), while in Matsuyama go for *somen* (thin wheat noodles usually served cold), which traditionally come in five colors. Each of the main cities has lively entertainment districts where you will have no problem finding a range of other cuisines, if Japanese food does not appeal. Outside the main cities, make sure you eat earlier in the evening: few places remain open after 8:30.

For more on Japanese cuisine, *see* Chapter 14 *and* Dining *in* Smart Travel Tips A to Z.

CATEGORY	COST*
$$$$	over ¥4,500
$$$	¥2,500–¥4,500
$$	¥1,500–¥2,500
$	under ¥1,500

*per person for a main course at dinner

Local Traditions

Geographical isolation has allowed Shikoku to preserve more of its traditional arts and culture than other parts of Japan have. You can learn about pottery and indigo dyeing near Matsuyama and Tokushima and even try your hand at *washi* (papermaking) close to Kōchi and Tokushima. The performing arts are represented by *ningyō joruri* puppet shows in Tokushima, and Kabuki at Uchiko and Kotohira, which has the oldest Kabuki stage in Japan. In country towns like Kotohira, Uwajima, and Uchiko, narrow streets and well-preserved old wooden houses are a delight. And there are late-summer dance festivals in Kōchi, Naruto, Takamatsu, and the most famous of all—perhaps in all of Japan—Tokushima's Awa Odori.

Lodging

Accommodations on Shikoku range from pensions and *minshuku* (rooms for rent in private homes) to large, modern resort hotels that have little character but all the facilities of an international hotel. Large city and resort hotels serve Western and Japanese food. During summer and major Japanese holiday periods, such as Golden Week in late spring, reservations are essential.

For a short course on accommodations in Japan, *see* Lodging *in* Smart Travel Tips A to Z.

CATEGORY	COST*
$$$$	over ¥20,000
$$$	¥15,000–¥20,000
$$	¥10,000–¥15,000
$	under ¥10,000

All prices are for a double room, excluding service and tax.

Outdoor Activities

The dramatic interior of Shikoku, especially around Ōboke-kyōkoku and Iya-dani (Iya Valley), is great for hiking and cycling. On the southern coast of the island, the rocky capes, Ashizuri and Muroto, lapped by the unimpeded Pacific Ocean, are favored by Japan's surfing fraternity. Takamatsu, with its excellent Ritsurin Kōen, one of the best traditional gardens in Japan, and Matsuyama, with Dogo Onsen—a 2,000-year-old hot-spring resort—are particularly worth visiting.

Exploring Shikoku

With more than just a couple of days, you can take in the island's mountainous interior, the sun-kissed city of Kōchi with its castle and rugged coastline, and Uwajima, another castle town with interesting shrines. Two weeks would easily allow you to add Shikoku's other major sights, including Tokushima as a base from which you can practice traditional handicrafts, and a trip out to Shōdo-shima, the second-largest island in the Seto Nai-kai.

Numbers in the text correspond to numbers in the margin and on the Shikoku map.

Great Itineraries

IF YOU HAVE 2 DAYS

Spend a day in ⓣ **Takamatsu** ① strolling around Ritsurin Kōen and then go on to **Kotohira** ④ and its much-revered Kotohira-gū (Kotohira Shrine). From here the obvious choice is to travel west along the northern coast to ⓣ **Matsuyama** ⑫ for its castle and justly famous Dogo Onsen. From Matsuyama you can take a hydrofoil to Hiroshima. Alternatives include a visit to **Yashima** ② for Shikoku Mura, a collection of traditional Edo-period houses, and the highland plateau, which provides a stunning view of the Seto Nai-kai; a trip out to Naruto Kaikyō to see the whirlpools; or a trip to ⓣ **Tokushima** ⑤ to take part in making traditional crafts.

IF YOU HAVE 4 DAYS

In addition, or as an alternative, to the sights around ⓣ **Takamatsu** ①, take a day trip to **Shōdo-shima** ③, a rural island in the Seto Nai-kai. A more adventurous option is to head for the mountainous interior after checking out **Kotohira** ④ and stop off at **Ōboke-kyōkoku** ⑥, where you can inspect the gorge from a boat. If you start off early enough, you should be able to make ⓣ **Kōchi** ⑦ for the night. Spend the third day at Kōchi's castle and nearby Katsura-hama (Katsura Beach) before heading across to ⓣ **Matsuyama** ⑫.

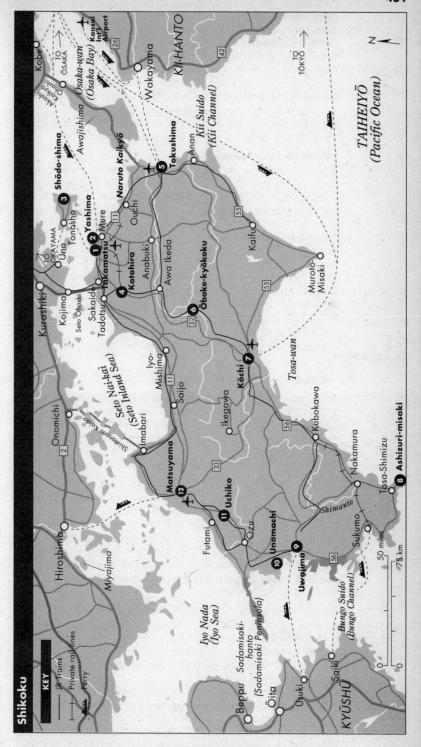

Shikoku

KEY
— JR Trains
— Private rail lines
— Ferry

N

Kobe

Akashi Kaikyō Ōhashi

Osaka-wan (Osaka Bay)
Kansai Intl Airport
TO OSAKA
26

Wakayama
42
KII-HANTŌ

TO TŌKYŌ

TAIHEIYŌ (Pacific Ocean)

Shōdo-shima
3

Tonoshō
Yashima
Mure
Naruto Kaikyō
Tokushima
5
Anan

Awajishima

Uno
1 2
Takamatsu
Ouchi
11
55

TO OKAYAMA
Kojima
Sakaide
Tadotsu
Seto Ōhashi
Kotohira
4
Anabuki
Awa Ikeda
Oboke-kyōkoku
Kaifu

Kurashiki
55

Seto Ohashi
32
6

Seto Nai-kai (Seto Inland Sea)
Iyo-Mishima
7
Kōchi
Muroto-Misaki

Onomichi
2

Saijo
11
Tosa-wan

Shimanami Kaidō

Imabari

Ikegawa
Kubokawa
56

Hiroshima
Matsuyama
33

12
Uchiko
11
Ōzu
Nakamura
Tosa-Shimizu
Ashizuri-misaki
8

Miyajima
Futami
Unomachi
Shimanto
Sukumo

56

10
Uwajima
9
56

Iyo Nada (Iyo Sea)
Sadamisaki-hantō (Sadamisaki Peninsula)

50 miles
75 km

Bungo Suidō (Bungo Channel)

Beppu
Ōita
Usuki
Saiki
KYŪSHŪ

Kii Suidō (Kii Channel)

Ōnaruto Ōhashi

You can see all of Shikoku's major sights in a week by spending two nights in ☷ **Takamatsu** ①; a night each in ☷ **Kōchi** ⑦ and ☷ **Uwajima** ⑨, for its castle and fertility shrine; and the final two nights in ☷ **Matsuyama** ⑫. As an alternative, you could use Matsuyama as a base for forays out to Uwajima and the well-preserved country towns of **Unomachi** ⑩ and **Uchiko** ⑪. Or you could strike out from Kōchi for either of the rugged capes, **Ashizuri-misaki** ⑧ or Muroto. Completing the 1,000-plus-km (620-plus-mi), 88-temple pilgrimage on foot is the biggest challenge. It would take at least six weeks.

When to Tour Shikoku

In winter only the snowbound valleys and hills of the interior are difficult to pass. In February crimson camellias bloom along the south coast of the island, particularly at Ashizuri-misaki. April is the only month in which Kabuki plays are performed in Kotohira, at Kompira O-Shibai, the oldest such theater in Japan. June is the time to head for Ritsurin Kōen to see its ponds filled with purple and white irises, although at any time of the year there are flashes of color in the garden. In summer head for the cool of the mountains or stay by the coast and its sea breezes. Dance festivals run in late summer, the Awa Odori from August 12 to 15. The bullfights in Uwajima are held on January 2, the third Sunday in March, the second Sunday in April, July 24, August 14, and the third Sunday in November. Plan to be in Kōchi on a Sunday for antiques and farm produce.

Takamatsu

❶ *1 hr from Okayama by JR.*

Sprawling, prosperous Takamatsu is most people's first stop on Shikoku. Come here to stroll in the gardens of Ritsurin Kōen—the city's major landmark after wholesale destruction of Takamatsu during World War II—and to admire the Seto Nai-kai panorama from Yashima plateau. Many ferries still call at Takamatsu from Honshū—and the central port area has been redeveloped—but because of the Seto Ōhashi, you are most likely to come by train, bus, or car.

★ Once the summer retreat of the Matsudaira clan, **Ritsurin Kōen** is the number one attraction in Takamatsu. The gardens—for there are actually two: the northern Hokutei and the southern Nantei—were completed in the late 17th century after 100 years of careful planning, landscaping, and cultivation. The Hokutei is more modern and has wide expanses of lawns, in addition to an exhibition hall that displays and sells local products from Kagawa Prefecture, including wood carvings, masks, kites, and umbrellas

Ritsurin's real gem is the Nantei section of the park, which follows a classical Japanese design. The southern garden's six ponds and 13 scenic mounds are arranged to frame a new view or angle to hold your attention at virtually every step on the intersecting paths. You cannot hurry through: each rock, each tree shape, each pond rippling with multicolored carp—and in turn the reflections of the water and the shadows of the trees—beckons. The teahouse, Kikugetsutei, looks as if it is floating on water. Here you can sip *sencha* (green tea; ¥510) and muse on the serene harmony of the occasion, or experience *matcha* (powdered tea-ceremony green tea; ¥710) just as the lords of Matsudaira did in previous centuries. Combination tickets for the gardens and tea are ¥880 (sencha) and ¥1,080 (matcha).

Sanuki Mingeikan (Sanuki Folk Art Museum), next to the park office, is also worth a visit for its interesting displays of local handicrafts and folk crafts. It is open Thursday–Tuesday 8:45–4:30 and Wednesday until 4; admission is free.

To get to Ritsurin Kōen, which is at the far end of Chūō-dōri, take a 10-minute ride (¥220) on any bus that leaves from in front of the Grand Hotel, stop No. 2. (The bus makes a short detour from the main avenue to include a bus depot on its route. Don't disembark from the bus until it rejoins the main avenue—Chūō-dōri—and travels two more stops.) Or take the JR train toward Tokushima and disembark five minutes later at the second stop, Ritsurin Kōen Kita Guchi. ☎ 087/833–7411. ⌨ ¥400. ⊙ Daily 7–5.

Tamamo-jō, built in 1588, was once the home of the Matsudaira clan, who ruled Takamatsu during the Edo period. All that is left of the castle in Tamano Kōen are a few turrets and the inner section of its three-ring moat, but the surrounding park, with the Seto Nai-kai in the background, makes it a pleasant place to relax while waiting for a train or ferry. The park's entrance is beside the Chikko terminus for the Kotoden tram network at the top of Chūō-dōri, where the JR station and main ferry pier are located. ⌨ ¥150. ⊙ Daily 9–5.

The department stores, shops, and restaurants of the city's **covered shopping arcades** are 300 yards down Chūō-dōri from the JR station on the left-hand side. The east–west Hyōgo-machi arcade is intersected by the Marugama-machi arcade running north–south (parallel to Chūō-dōri). The small streets off the arcades are crowded with bars, cabarets, and smaller restaurants.

Takamatsu-shi Bijutsukan (City Museum of Art) has a small permanent collection of local Sanuki lacquerware and contemporary Japanese art. Visiting exhibitions are also likely to be interesting. It's in the shopping area on Bijutsukan-dōri. ☎ 0878/23–171. ⌨ ¥200. ⊙ Tues.–Sun. 9–5.

The studio of the late Japanese-American sculptor Isamu Noguchi (1904–88) has been converted into **Isamu Noguchi Teien Hakubutsukan** (Isamu Noguchi Garden Museum), which is in Mure, a 20-minute drive from Takamatsu. The museum includes about 150 complete and incomplete works of the 20th-century master, revealing his creative process (another studio-museum exists in Long Island City, New York). Noguchi was originally attracted to the area by the local high-quality granite and other stone materials he found there. His stone, terra-cotta, cement, and wood pieces often reflect a Japanese influence. Reservations are required for viewing the collection. Take a JR train to Yashima Eki (15 minutes). From there, it's a seven-minute taxi ride to the museum. ⌨ 3–5–19 Mure, Mure-chō, ☎ 087/870–1500. ⌨ ¥2,000. ⊙ Tues., Thurs., and Sat. at 10, 1, and 3 by appointment.

Dining and Lodging

$$–$$$ ✕ **Tenkatsu.** This classy restaurant serves all manner of fish dishes, from succulent sushi to steaming *nabe* (one-pot) stews, at the far west end of the Hyōgo-machi shopping arcade. Elegant, kimono-clad waitresses pad silently between tatami rooms and a jet-black counter bar that surrounds a central sunken pool where the fish swim until their number is up. ⌨ Nishizumi Hiroba, Hyōgo-machi, ☎ 0878/21–5380. AE, DC, MC, V.

$–$$ ✕ **Kamaizumi.** The sound of plucked koto strings sets the tone for this intimate sanuki udon restaurant. The set meals (you can choose from a picture menu) come with a wooden brazier to keep the udon and *dashi* (fish stock) warm while you decide how much of the spring onions, freshly ground ginger, seaweed flakes, tiny bird's eggs, and sesame seeds to add to the noodle broth. Top it off with a flask of sake. To get here, look for the huge, red paper lantern hanging outside the entrance. In the afternoon one of the chefs makes noodles inside the front window. ✉ *Ferry-dōri,* ☎ *0878/21–6688. AE, MC, V.*

$ ✕ **Ikkaku.** Unfinished concrete on this ultramodern single-story restaurant close to Kotoden Yashima Eki might make it look like a nightclub, but once you sit down in its stylish, brightly lighted interior, the reason for the lines of people waiting for a table becomes clear. The food—spicy barbecued chicken, served on silver platters with an accompaniment of raw cabbage leaves—is delicious. Side dishes are available, and it would be an oversight not to have a glass of the restaurant's own brewed beer. ✉ *Yashima Naka-machi,* ☎ *0878/44–3711. No credit cards.*

$ ✕ **Macou's Bagel Café.** Authentic bagels—made on the premises—and a fantastic range of freshly ground coffees are the order of the day at this sleek venture, worth considering for breakfast or lunch. You can either sip a Seattle-style cappuccino and munch on a bagel with cream cheese and lox in the bright interior, or take out for a picnic lunch. Add a salad and dessert to make it a full meal. Macou's is a two-minute walk west of Chūō-dōri, along Route 11. ✉ *9–11–5 Ban-chō,* ☎ *0878/22–3558. No credit cards. No dinner.*

$$–$$$$ ▥ **Takamatsu Grand Hotel.** Tamamo Kōen and the remains of Tamamo-jō are behind the hotel, so the views on that side of the building are quite splendid. The lobby here is on the third floor (there are nine independently owned restaurants on the second floor), and the main Yashima restaurant is on the seventh floor. Some of the guest rooms could use refurbishing, but they are all clean. Right on the city's main avenue, Chūō-dōri, the Grand is within a five-minute walk of the JR station. ✉ *1–5–10 Kotobuki-chō, Takamatsu, Kagawa-ken 760,* ☎ *0878/51–5757,* ℻ *0878/21–9422. 136 rooms. 2 restaurants. AE, DC, MC, V.*

$$–$$$ ▥ **Kawaroku Ryokan.** The original Kawaroku was destroyed in World ★ War II. This replacement—the best hotel in the center of town—is unappealing from the outside but pleasantly furnished on the inside. The rooms are in light colors, and all have private bath. The restaurant serves French food, but Japanese food can be eaten in your room. ✉ *1–2 Hyakken-chō, Takamatsu, Kagawa-ken 760,* ☎ *0878/21–5666,* ℻ *0878/21–7301,* ⓦ *www.kawaroku.co.jp. 21 Western-style rooms, 49 Japanese-style rooms. Restaurant. AE, V.*

Visitor Information

The **Takamatsu Information Office** (☎ 0878/51–2009) is just outside the JR station. The maps and brochures are limited to Kagawa Prefecture, of which Takamatsu is the capital. If you need information on the entire island, make sure that you visit the Tourist Information Center in Tōkyō or Kyōto before you set out for Shikoku. A bus tour (Japanese-speaking guide only) departs at 8:45 AM from the Takamatsu-Chikko Bus Station (near the JR station) and covers Ritsurin Kōen, Kotohira, and other sights. The tour takes about 8 hours, 45 minutes.

Yashima

② *20 mins by JR or Kotoden tram from Takamatsu.*

Once an island, Yashima is now connected to Shikoku by a narrow strip of land. Its tabletop plateau, standing nearly 1,000 ft above Seto Nai-kai, is an easy half-day trip from Takamatsu. This was the battle site where the Minamoto clan defeated the Taira family in 1185, allowing Yoritomo Minamoto to establish Japan's first shogunate in Kamakura, southwest of what is now Tōkyō.

★ Easily the most interesting sight in the area, **Shikoku Mura** is an open-air village museum. Similar to Hida Village, near Takayama in the Japan Alps, Shikoku Mura has 21 houses that have been relocated from around Shikoku to represent what rural life was like during the Edo period and earlier, 200–300 years ago. The village may be artificial, but in this age, in which ferroconcrete has replaced so much of old Japan, Shikoku Mura provides an opportunity to see traditional thatched-roof farmhouses, a papermaking workshop, a ceremonial teahouse, a rural Kabuki stage, and other buildings used in earlier times. ☎ 087/843–3111. *☒ ¥800. ◷ Apr.–Oct., daily 8:30–5; Nov.–Mar., daily 8:30–4:30.*

Ascend to the top of **Yashima** for the expansive vista from the plateau over the Seto Nai-kai and Shōdo-shima. A five-minute walk west of Shikoku Mura's entrance is a cable car that takes five minutes to climb to the top of the plateau; it costs ¥700 one-way, ¥1,300 round-trip.

Near the upper terminus for the cable car on Yashima Plateau, **Yashima-ji,** originally constructed in 754, is 84th of the 88 temples in the sacred pilgrimage. The temple's museum contains some interesting screens and pottery and a mixed bag of relics of the battle between the Minamoto and Taira clans. The shrine is free and can be seen at any time. ☎ 087/841–9418. *☒ Museum ¥500. ◷ Museum daily 9–5.*

Getting Around

Local JR trains from Takamatsu Eki run at least every hour to Yashima Eki, from which it is a 10-minute walk north to Shikoku Mura. You can also take the Kotoden tram from the Chikko terminal (across from the JR station). These run 10 times a day; the tourist office can supply a schedule. Kotoden Yashima Eki is only a couple minutes' walk from both Shikoku Mura (to the east) and the Yashima cable car station (directly north).

Shōdo-shima

★ ❸ *35 mins north of Takamatsu by hydrofoil, 1 hr by ferry.*

For something of a rural escape, take a ferry out to the principle town of Tonosho on Shōdo-shima, the second-largest island in the Seto Nai-kai. Shōdo's craggy mountains are spectacular, and its seacoasts equally so for the contrast of ruggedness with sandy beaches. The island is also the site of quarries from which the stone used to build the original Ōsaka-jō was cut.

Inland, the 6-km by 4-km (3½-mi by 2½-mi) **Kankakei-kyōkoku** is hemmed in by a wall of mountainous peaks with weather-eroded rocks. The thick maple and pine forest lining the gorge is splashed with color in autumn; in spring the profusion of azaleas makes for an equally colorful spectacle. Walks among the rocks and stream are excellent. If you'd rather not hike, you can gain the summit on an aerial tramway that travels frighteningly close to the cliffs' walls. Kankakei is an hour by bus from Tonosho, including a change at Choshikei O-saru no Kuni (¥610.)

At **Kujakuen** (Peacock Garden), 15 minutes by bus from Tonosho, 3,000 peacocks roam the grounds of a garden.

The water-carved walls of **Choshikei-kyōkoku** (Choshikei Gorge), 25 minutes by bus from Tonosho, extend along the upper stream of the Dempo-gawa (Dempo River).

Seven hundred wild monkeys cavort freely at **Choshikei O-saru no Kuni** (Choshikei Monkey Land). Weather permitting, there's a monkey show twice daily and visitors can feed the animals peanuts. The park

is a 40-minute bus ride from Tonosho Port. ☎ 0879/62–0768. *🎫 ¥370.*
🕐 Daily 8:10–4:50.

You can rent motorized bicycles for ¥3,000 a day, including insurance,
from **Ryobi Rent-a-Bike** (☎ 0879/62–6578) near Tonosho's pier, open
daily 8:30–5.

Dining and Lodging

$–$$ ✕ **Shimamusume.** At mealtime try this restaurant, which serves thin
somen noodles with hot or cold dipping sauce, depending on the season, along with sashimi and other Japanese delicacies. This place caters
to group tours, but individuals are welcome, of course. It's close to
Tonosho Port. ✉ *Tonosho-cho, Tonosho ko mae,* ☎ 0879/62–1666.
No credit cards.

Minshuku in Tonosho are a reasonable way to stay on the island and
will allow you to get closer to Shōdo-shimans. **Chushichi** (☎ 0879/62–
3679) is a minshuku with 10 rooms. **Maruse** (☎ 0879/62–2385) is a
minshuku with 6 rooms.

Getting Around

To get to Tonosho, the island's largest port and town, from Takamatsu
Pier, there are two options: a ferry (¥510) and a hydrofoil (¥1,000).
There's also a hydrofoil to Shōdo-shima (40 minutes; ¥1,600) from
Okayama Port (take Bus 12 from JR Okayama Eki to Okayama Port)
and a regular ferry from Himeji Port (1 hour, 40 minutes; ¥1,300).

Sightseeing buses depart from Tonosho to all island sights; public
buses cover the island efficiently and thoroughly.

Visitor Information

Tonosho Ko no Kanko Center (☎ 0879/62–1205), located near the ferry
terminal, can provide bus and sightseeing information.

Kotohira

★ **❹**   *55 mins by JR or Kotoden tram from Takamatsu.*

Visit Kotohira to climb the 785 steps to its shrine, **Kotohira-gū.** Fondly
known as Kompira-san, the shrine may not be quite as important as
the Grand Shrines at Ise or Izumo Taisha near Matsue, but it's one of
Japan's oldest and most stately. It's also one of the most popular: 4
million pay their respects each year.

Founded in the 11th century and built on the slopes of Zozu-zan, Kotohira-gū is dedicated to Omono-nushi-no-Mikoto (also called Kompira), the guardian god of the sea and patron of seafarers. Traditionally,
fishermen and sailors would visit the shrine and solicit divine assur-
ance for a safe sea passage. However, their monopoly on seeking the
aid of Kompira has ended, as his role has expanded to include all travelers, including tourists—though it's uncertain whether messages written in English will be understood.

To reach the main gate of the shrine, you have to mount 365 granite steps.
On either side of the steps are souvenir and refreshment stands, but don't
dawdle. Beyond the main gate, the souvenir stands are replaced by stone
lanterns, and the climb becomes a solemn, spiritual exercise. Just before
the second torii is the shrine's **hōmotsu-kan,** with a rather dry display
of sculpture, scrolls, and, despite their potentially interesting Buddhist
origins, Nō masks. It's open daily 9–4; the entrance fee is ¥200.

The next important building, on your right, is the 1659 **Shoin** (formerly
a reception hall), its interior covered in delicate screen paintings by the
famous 18th-century landscape artist Okyo Maruyama (1733–95).

Maruyama came from a family of farmers and, not surprisingly, looked to the beauty of nature for his paintings. Such was his talent that a new style of painting—the Maruyama school—a sort of return to nature, developed. Entrance to the Shoin is ¥200; it's open daily 9–4.

Onward and forever upward, the intricate carvings of animals grace the facade of **Asahi-no-Yashiro** (formerly the main shrine; the name means that it is the first building to receive light when the sun comes up in the morning). At the next landing, you'll finally be at the main shrine, a complex of buildings that were rebuilt 100 years ago. Aside from the sense of accomplishment in making the climb, the views over Takamatsu and the Seto Nai-kai to the north and the mountain ranges of Shikoku to the south justify the effort, even more, perhaps, than a visit to the shrine itself—that is, unless you ask Kompira for good fortune. And after climbing 785 steps, you might just want to.

Allow a total of an hour and a half from the time you start your ascent up the granite stairs until you return. Just as the feudal lords once did, you may hire a palanquin to porter you up and down; the fee is ¥5,000 one-way, ¥6,500 round-trip. Riding in a palanquin certainly saves the calf muscles, but the motion and narrow confines are not exactly comfortable.

Kanamaru-za—the oldest Kabuki theater in Japan—hosts performances only in April, but throughout the year the theater is open for viewing. Because it was built in 1835, one of the interesting aspects is how the theater managed its special effects without electricity. Eight men in harness, for example, rotate the stage. Within the revolving stage are two trap lifts. The larger one is used for quick changes in stage props, the smaller one for lifting actors up to floor level. Equally fascinating are the sets of sliding *shōji* (screens) used to adjust the amount of daylight filtering onto the stage. The theater is exceptionally large and was moved, from the overcrowded center of Kotohira to Kotohira Kōen, and restored in 1975. It's a 10-minute walk from Kotohira Eki, near the first flight of steps leading to Kotohira-gū. ☎ 0877/73–3846 ✉ ¥500. ☉ Wed.–Mon. 9–4.

Getting Around

From JR Kotohira Eki it's an eight-minute walk to the steps of Kotohira-gū. There's a cloakroom to the left of the JR station (¥200), which is open daily 6:30 AM–9 PM. Even if you're only visiting for the day, travel lightly—small packs become very heavy while you are mounting the 785 stairs to the shrine. The Kotoden tram runs every half hour between Kawara-machi Eki in Takamatsu and Kotoden Eki in Kotohira.

From Kotohira Eki, trains continue south to Kōchi, the principal city of Shikoku's south coast. If you aren't heading south to the coast, you can return to the north coast of Shikoku and travel west to Matsuyama, or change at Awa Ikeda for the branch line east to Tokushima.

Tokushima

⑤ *1 hr, 10 mins by JR from Takamatsu and from Awa Ikeda.*

If you decide to visit Tokushima, count yourself among few gaijin who do. Between August 12 and 15, you can witness one of the liveliest, most humor-filled festivals in Japan, Awa Odori. At other times of the year, come to Tokushima for the opportunity to watch and participate in local traditional Japanese crafts, such as papermaking, indigo dyeing, and pot making. Although the city is quite modern, its small-scale and well-designed riverside walkways make it a pleasant place to spend a day.

★ The **Awa Odori** dance festival is an occasion for the Japanese to relax. Prizes are even given to the "Biggest Fool" in the parades, and gaijin are welcome to compete for these awards. Make sure you reserve accommodations well in advance, since more than a million people pack the city during the four-day event.

At **ASTY Tokushima,** a state-of-the-art tourist facility, **Tokushima Taikenkan** (Tokushima Tourist and Special Product Hall) has a 360-degree cinema in which you will find yourself at the center of the Awa Odori festival. After the film, you can practice the dance routines and play the instruments—all with the assistance of immaculately dressed women. Simulated bus, bike, and windsurfing rides take you on a virtual tour through the prefecture. The *ningyō joruri* ("*neen*-gyo jo-*roo*-ee," puppet) section has displays and daily shows. Also inside ASTY, there's a large shopping area where you can make *washi* (handmade Japanese paper), practice indigo dyeing, and watch many other local crafts being made, including ningyō joruri. A conference hall and restaurants are on-site. ASTY Tokushima is a 15-minute bus ride from Tokushima Eki. ☒ ¥900. ☉ *Daily 9–5.*

Tokushima Chūō Kōen is a pretty park on the site where the first lord of Tokushima, Hachisuka Iemasa, built his fortress in 1586 (his family lived in it for the next 280 years). In 1896 the castle was destroyed; all that remains are a few stone walls, moats, and a beautiful formal garden that has been designated a National Scenic Spot. The **Tokushima-jō Hakubutsukan** (Tokushima Castle Museum), built in 1992, is not out of place amid these refined surroundings. Displays relate to the Hachisuka clan and give a good idea of what the castle looked like. The park is five minutes east of the JR station on foot. ☎ 088/656–2525. ☒ *Museum ¥300.* ☉ *Museum Tues.–Sun. 9:30–5.*

At each ebb and flow of the tide in the **Naruto Kaikyō** (Naruto Straits), the currents rush through this narrow passage to form hundreds of foaming whirlpools of various sizes—some giant. One hour on either side of the tidal change, the Awa-no-Naruto whirlpools are at their fiercest, below the beginning of the long Naruto Ōhashi (Naruto Suspension Bridge), which crosses the straits to Awaji-shima. To get here, take yellow Bus 1 from JR Tokushima Eki Plaza to Seto Nai-kai Kokuritsu Kōen (Seto Inland Sea National Park), of which the Naruto whirlpools are a part.

You can see the Awa-no-Naruto whirlpools from **Uzu-no-michi,** a walkway recently constructed along the girders of Naruto Ōhashi. Panes of glass in the floor of the Observation Room yield a pulse-quickening view of the whirlpools 149 ft below. Internet terminals in the waiting room provide visitor information. From the station it's a 15-minute walk to the bridge; the bus fare is ¥690. ☎ 088/683–6262. ☒ ¥500. ☉ *Tues.–Sun. 9:30–5.*

For a close encounter with the swirling waters of Naruto Kaikyō, hop aboard a sightseeing boat operated by **Naruto Kankō-Kisen** (P 088/687–0101). The 40-minute cruise costs g̀1,300 and the dock is a 5-minute walk downhill from the Seto Inland Sea National Park.

A few minutes' walk up the hill from the whirlpools, the unique **Ot-suka Bijutsukan** opened in 1998 to commemorate the 75th anniversary of the Otsuka Group (makers of Pocari Sweat, the soft drink that's ubiquitous in Japan). This three-story art museum houses the largest permanent exhibit in Japan. The works on display are not paintings but ceramic-board reproductions of Western masterpieces such as da Vinci's *Mona Lisa,* Rembrandt's *Nightwatch,* and Picasso's *Guernica,* exactly the same dimensions as the originals. Although the price of admission is a bit steep, the museum is worth a visit for its kitsch value alone. ✉ *65–1 Fukuike, Aza, Ura, Tosadomari, Naruto-chō, Naruto-shi,* ☎ *088/687–3737.* ⊡ *¥3,150.* ◷ *Fri.–Wed. 9:30–5.*

During World War II, Naruto was the site of the Bando POW camp, and in the spirit of international friendship the **Naruto Doitsu-kan** (Naruto German House) was constructed in its place. Colonel Matsue, camp director, operated under a highly humane administration policy that allowed soldiers to interact with townspeople and to engage in athletic, creative, and intellectual pursuits. Here you can see photos and other memorabilia, as well as dioramas depicting the soldiers' daily lives. The museum is a 30-minute bus ride from Naruto JR station. You can also take a JR train on the Takamatsu-Tokushima line and get off at Bando station. ✉ *55–2 Higashi-yamada, Aza, Hinoki, Ōasa-chō, Naruto-shi,* ☎ *088/689–0099.* ⊡ *¥400.* ◷ *Tues.–Sun. 9:30–4:30.*

En Route On the way back to Tokushima from Naruto on the JR Naruto branch line, the town of **Otani** is the home of Otani-yaki, a distinctive local pottery that has a heavy texture and is traditionally crafted into enormous standing pots. There are several places in town where you can make your own cups or plates, if you make an appointment first. To make a simple cup costs around ¥3,000, and after firing, the finished result is mailed to your home. **Yano Toen** (✉ 71 Kuhara, Aza, Otani, Oasa-chō, ☎ 088/689–0023). **Harumoto Togyo Kai-kan** (✉ 0-1 Michino-ue, Otani, Oasa-chō, ☎ 088/689–0048).

Natural indigo dyeing in Tokushima dates back at least 400 years: learn about the local craft at the informative **Ai-no-Yakata** (House of Indigo), where mini-dioramas show the coloring process and examples of blue-patterned cloth. You can wander around the old buildings of the complex and try your hand at dyeing. A handkerchief costs ¥500, a T-shirt ¥2,800. The museum is 20 minutes by bus from JR Tokushima Eki (get off at Higashi Nakatomi). ☎ *088/692–6317.* ⊡ *¥300.* ◷ *Daily 9–5.*

At the **Awa Washi Dentō Sangyō Kai-kan** (Hall of Awa Handmade Paper), you might be able to meet "Prefectural Intangible Cultural Asset" Fujimori Minoru—a genial, gray-haired expert in the art of papermaking. The hall holds exhibitions, a shop where its multicolored products are sold, and a huge work space in which you can try your hand at making washi postcards. Take the JR Tokushima main line west to Yamakawa Eki; the hall is then a 15-minute walk south. ☎ *0883/42–6120.* ⊡ *¥300.* ◷ *Tues.–Sun. 9–5.*

Dining and Lodging

A variety of reasonably priced restaurants serve Indian, Chinese, French, and Japanese cuisine on the fifth floor of **Clement Plaza,** above Tokushima Eki.

$ ✗ **Big Brothers.** Located two blocks east of Tokushima Eki, this cozy eatery run by a pair of ex-pats bills itself as a cross between Starbucks and Subway. The menu features foot-long sandwiches with all-American fillings such as turkey, roast beef, and pastrami. Coffees, salads, homemade pumpkin pie, and cheesecakes are also served by a friendly, English-speaking staff members in a bright, clean setting. ✉ *Fuku Building, Terashima Honchō, Higashi 1-chōme,* ☎ *088/624–0340. No credit cards.*

$$$$ ✗▥ **Kappo Hotel Isaku.** At the foot of Mt. Bizan, just to the left of the atmospheric Zuigan-ji (temple), this is one of the most traditional ryokans in Tokushima. The tatami rooms are of a good standard, and some open onto a delightful ornamental garden. Breakfast and dinner are included in the room rate. You can also eat in Isaku's restaurant if you are not a ryokan guest. Meals start at ¥3,000 for a beautifully presented bentō box and ¥5,000 for full course, which includes seafood,

tempura, and other delights. ✉ *1 Iga-chō, Tokushima, Tokushima-ken 770-0831,* ☎ *0886/22–1392,* ℻ *0886/23–8764. 24 Japanese-style rooms. Restaurant. AE, DC, MC, V. MAP.*

$ ⌂ **Four Season.** The dagger-sharp triangular window design of this small business hotel, just west of the JR station, first catches your eye. Inside, rooms are functional and comfortable, and the management is friendly. It's owned by the same family that runs the larger, Grand Palace Hotel nearby. The son, who is the chef in the adjoining café, speaks fluent English and serves his own special variation on curry rice. ✉ *1–54 Terashima Honchō-Nishi, Tokushima, Tokushima-ken 770-0831,* ☎ *088/ 622–2203,* ℻ *088/656–6083. 23 rooms. Restaurant. AE, MC, V.*

Getting Around

Trains arrive at Tokushima Eki from Takamatsu and Kōchi via the Dosan and Tokushima lines. City and prefectural buses depart from outside Clement Plaza. For the airport, take the bus from platform 2. Tokushima is also connected by bus to Kansai International Airport, Kyōto, Ōsaka, and Tōkyō.

Visitor Information

For brochures and other information in English, **Tokushima Prefecture International Exchange Association** (✉ TOPIA: Clement Plaza, 6th floor, ☎ 088/656–3303) is just outside the Tokushima Eki and is open daily 10–6.

Obōke-kyōkoku

❻ *50 mins by JR from Kotohira.*

On the way south to Kōchi, explore the area around **Obōke-kyōkoku,** where the road and rail lines south from Awa Ikeda follow the valleys, cut deep by swift-flowing rivers. The earth is red and rich, the foliage lush and verdant. It's an area of scenic beauty that lends itself to exploration by car, though once you are off the main roads, a little knowledge of Japanese will help your navigation. You can also take a boat trip down the river from near Obōke Eki; check with the tourist section of the town hall in Awa Ikeda.

OFF THE BEATEN PATH | **KAZURA-BASHI –** In the heart of the mountains, this 50-yard-long bridge made of vines and bamboo spans the Iyadanikei-kyōkoku (Iyadanikei Gorge). For ¥500 you can walk across; it's safe enough, since the bridge is remade every three years and is strung through with steel cables. The bridge is a 20-minute bus ride from Obōke Eki and is open during daylight hours.

Getting Around

To get here, take the branch rail line that runs from Tokushima to Kōchi or the main line that runs from Okayama on Honshū to Kōchi via Kotohira. The jumping-off point is Awa Ikeda, an unremarkable town at the head of the gorge. Very infrequent buses run from Awa Ikeda and Obōke to Kazura-bashi.

Visitor Information

The **tourist section** of Awa Ikeda's town hall (✉ 2415 Machi, Aza, ☎ 0883/72–1111) has bus and other information.

Kōchi

❼ *50 mins by JR from Obōke-kyōkoku, 2 hrs by JR from Kotohira.*

On the balmy southern coast of Shikoku, Kōchi is a relaxed city with a cosmopolitan atmosphere, enhanced by its trundling trams and the swaying palms that line the streets. The prefecture is reputed to be one of the poorest in Japan, with residents relying on fishing and agriculture for their living. However, perhaps because of its warm climate, the people of Kōchi are full of humor. Even their local folk songs poke fun at life, for example, "On Harimaya-bashi, people saw a Buddhist priest buy a hairpin. . . ." Priests in those days were forbidden to love women, and they shaved their heads—so it's implied in the lyrics that some naughty business must have been afoot.

Except for Kōchi-jō and Kenritsu Bijutsukan, Kōchi is not architecturally inspired, but it is friendly and fun-loving. People congregate every evening in the compact downtown area. Several downtown streets closed to traffic form shopping arcades.

★ **Kōchi-jō** dominates the town and is the only castle in Japan still to have both its donjon and its daimyō's residence intact. The donjon—its stone foundation seemingly merging into the cliff face—admittedly was rebuilt in 1753, but it faithfully reflects the original (1601–03). The donjon has the old style of watchtower design, and, by climbing up to its top floor, you can appreciate its purpose—the view is encompassing, and splendid. The daimyō's residence, **Kaitoku-kan,** is southwest of the donjon. The formal main room is laid out in Shoin style, which is known for its decorative alcove, staggered shelves, decorative doors, tatami-covered floors, and shōji screens reinforced with wooden lattices. The easiest way to get here is to hop on a green Yosakoe Gurarin Bus in front of Kōchi Eki. The fare is ¥100. ☎ *088/824–5701.* ✎ *¥350.* ☽ *Daily 9–5 (last entry at 4:30).*

The main collection of **Kenritsu Bijutsukan,** a spacious two-story facility set in landscaped grounds, includes modern Japanese and Western art. One room is dedicated to works by Marc Chagall. Take any tram from Harimaya-bashi bound for Kenritsu Bijutsukan-dōri, a 15-minute ride, to get here. ☎ *0888/66–8000.* ✎ *¥350.* ☽ *Tues.–Sun. 9–4:30.*

Should you be in town on a Sunday morning, go to the approximately 650 stalls at the **Nichiyō-ichi** (Sunday open-air market). Farmers have been bringing their produce to sell here for 300 years. You might see the incredibly long-tailed (more than 20 ft) *Onagadori* roosters, for which Kōchi is known. The market runs from the main gate of Kōchi-jō for 1 km (½ mi) along Otetsuji-dōri.

In summer Kōchi-ites flock to **Katsura-hama,** 13 km (8 mi) southeast of town. The beach consists of gravelly white sand, but the swimming is good, and there are scenic rock formations offshore.

On the headland above Katsura-hama is the architecturally dazzling **Sakamoto Ryoma Kinen-kan** (Sakamoto Ryoma Memorial Museum), built in memory of local hero Ryoma, a progressive samurai who helped bring about the Meiji Restoration of the 19th century. It is open daily 9–5; entry costs ¥350.

If you prefer to spend an afternoon amid lawns and greenery, take a bus to Godai-san and **Godai-san Kōen,** designed to have something in bloom all year. Inside the park, visit **Chikurin-ji,** a temple with an impressive five-story pagoda, which is in fact a fairly uncommon sight in Japan. This structure compares to those of Kyōto, and the people from Kōchi say it's more magnificent. Belonging to the Shingon sect of Buddhism, the temple was founded in 724 and is the 31st temple in Shikoku's sequence of 88 sacred temples. The bus to Godai-san Kōen departs from the Toden stop, next to Seibu department store on Harimaya-bashi. The ride costs ¥300 and takes 20 minutes.

Near Chikurin-ji in Godai-san Kōen, **Makino Shokubutsuen** (Makino Botanical Garden: ☎ 0888/82–2601) was built to honor the botanist Dr. Tomitaro Makino (1862–1957). The greenhouse has a collection of more than 1,000 plants. ☞ ¥500. ◷ Daily 9–5.

Half-day and full-day sightseeing tours of Kōchi and environs are offered by **Kochi-ken Kotsu** (✉ 70 Banchi, Iku, ☎ 088/845–1607) and leave from the JR bus terminal at Kōchi Eki at 8:30 AM and 1:50 PM.

Full-day sightseeing tours by **Senan Kotsu** (✉ 434-1 Saoka, Nakamura-shi, ☎ 0888/34–1266) leave from Nakamura Eki; these are not available throughout the whole year, so be sure to call ahead.

OFF THE
BEATEN PATH
MUROTO-MISAKI – The road east (there's no train line) follows a rugged shoreline cut by frequent inlets and indentations. Most of the coast consists of a series of 100- to 300-ft terraces. Continuous wave action, generated by the Kuroshio (Black Current), has shaped these terraces. The result is a surreal coastline of rocks, surf, and steep precipices. It's about a 2½-hour drive along the coast road out to the cape, a popular sightseeing and surfing spot, where the sea crashes against the cliffs and there are black-sand beaches.

Dining and Lodging

$–$$ ✕ **Tosahan.** This outlet of a famous local chain serving Tosa ryōri is decorated in farmhouse style, with dark wooden beams and red paper lanterns. A picture menu and plastic food displays in the window help you select a meal. Seafood *nabe* (stews), cooked at the table, and tataki are particularly good bets. It's easy to find at the start of the Obiya-machi shopping arcade, close by Harimaya-bashi. ✉ 1–2–2 Obiya-machi Arcade, ☎ 0888/21–0002. AE, DC, MC, V.

$$$$ 🏨 **Joseikan.** A rather monumental exterior masks a more restrained, airy lobby and a small central garden in this elegant Japanese-style hotel, which has hosted the emperor on his visits to Kōchi. Tatami suites are immaculate, and a communal sauna and bath on the eighth floor have a spectacular night view of Kōchi-jō. The ryokan is close to the castle, two stops west of Harimaya-bashi by tram. ✉ 2–5–34 Kami-machi, Kōchi-shi, Kōchi-ken 780-0901, ☎ 0888/75–0111, FAX 0888/24–0557, WEB www.jyoseikan.co.jp. 72 Japanese-style rooms. Restaurant, coffee shop. AE, DC, MC, V.

$$$–$$$$ 🏨 **Hotel Shin-Hankyu.** Within sight of Kōchi-jō, the Shin-Hankyu is indisputably the best hotel in Kōchi. The ground floor has a modern, open-plan lobby, with a lounge away from the reception area and a small cake-and-tea shop to the side. On the second floor are several excellent restaurants that serve Japanese, Chinese, and French fare. Spacious guest rooms, most of which are Western style, are pleasantly decorated with light pastel furnishings, and the staff is extremely helpful to foreign guests. ✉ 4–2–50 Hon-machi, Kōchi-shi, Kōchi-ken 780-0870, ☎ 0888/73–1111, FAX 0888/73–1145, WEB hotel.newhankyu.co.jp. 201 Western-style and Japanese-style rooms. 4 restaurants, health club. AE, DC, MC, V.

$$$ 🏨 **Washington Hotel.** Part of a nationwide chain of business hotels, this establishment has a prime position on the street leading to Kōchi-jō, on which the Sunday market is held. There is a small restaurant, and rooms are a good size for this kind of lodging. It's a 15-minute walk to JR station. ✉ 1–8–25 Otetsuji, Kōchi-shi, Kōchi-ken 780-0842, ☎ 0888/23–6111, FAX 0888/25–2737. 172 rooms. Restaurant. AE, V.

Getting Around

Kōchi Eki is a 10-minute walk from the city center at Harimaya-bashi. The tram system, which starts directly opposite the station, costs a flat ¥180. A taxi ride from Kōchi Eki to downtown is about ¥550.

If you want direct Matsuyama–Kōchi transportation, take the three-hour JR bus from Kōchi Eki (there is no direct train). The fare is covered by the JR Pass. For the Kōchi–Uwajima train trip, you will need to change at Kubokawa, where you must pick up a branch line.

Visitor Information

Kōchi's helpful **Tourist Information Office** (☎ 0888/82–1634), with an English-speaking assistant, is to the left of Kōchi Eki's exit.

Ashizuri-misaki

❽   *2½ hrs by JR from Kōchi to Nakamura, 1 hr by bus from Nakamura.*

Part of Ashizuri Kokuritsu Kōen (Ashizuri National Park), at the southwestern tip of Shikoku, this is wonderfully wild country—with a skyline-drive road running down the cape's middle. Keep in mind that the Kubokawa–Nakamura leg of the journey is on the private Kuroshio Tetsudō Line (¥210, not covered by the JR Pass). At Nakamura Eki, continue by bus to Ashizuri-misaki—you might have to change buses at Tosa Shimizu.

At the tip of Ashizuri-misaki is a lighthouse and **Kongōfuku-ji**, 38th of Shikoku's 88 sacred temples. Its origins go back 1,100 years, although what you see was rebuilt 300 years ago.

Kochi-ken Kotsu (☎ 088/824–5535) buses travel from JR Kōchi Eki to Ashizuri-misaki, but don't accept JR Passes.

Exhibits in **John Mung House** tell the story of Nakahama Manjiro's extraordinary life. In 1841 the 14-year-old Manjiro, who hailed from Ashizuri, was shipwrecked on a remote Pacific island. He was eventually rescued by an American whaling ship. The ship's captain, John Whitfield, took a shine to Manjiro and nicknamed him John Mung. The boy stayed with the whaling crew for years and eventually settled in Bedford, Massachusetts, where Whitfield educated him. Mung's fluency in English lead him to play a pivotal role in negotiating the opening of Japan to the world after Commodore Perry's Black Ships arrived in 1853. ⊠ *Ashizuri-misaki, Tosa Shimizu-shi,* ☎ *0880/88–1136.* ▭ *¥200.* ☉ *Sept.–July, daily 8–5:30; Aug., daily 8–6.*

En Route   Returning from Ashizuri-misaki, you can follow the coastline west to Sukumo, or return to Nakamura for a bus there (1 hour; ¥1,100). Change buses to continue north to Uwajima, the terminal for JR rail lines running between Matsuyama and Kōchi. Four ferries a day (2½ hours; ¥1,650) sail from Sukumo for Saiki, on Kyūshū.

Uwajima

❾   *4½ hrs by bus from Ashizuri-misaki, 3½ hrs by JR from Kōchi.*

Like Kōchi, Uwajima contains one of Japan's 12 extant feudal castles. This agreeable, peaceful town is famous for its bullfights sans matador and its fertility shrine.

Uwajima's **Warei-Taisai Matsuri** is celebrated every July 23–24 with a parade of *mikoshi* (portable shrines), decorated fishing boats, and two giant *uni-oshi* (demon bulls). The climax is a mock battle in the local river between the teams carrying the bulls.

Uwajima-jō, a compact, friendly castle, is free of the usual defensive structures, such as a stone drop. The first castle on-site was torn down and replaced with this updated version in 1665—suggesting that by the end of the 17th century, war (at least the kind fought around castles) was a thing of the past. It's a 10-minute walk south of Uwajima Eki. 🚉 ¥200. ⊙ *Daily 9–4.*

For a shrine dedicated to fertility, the small, shady **Taga-jinja** strikes, at first glance, a modest pose. It's only on closer inspection that you notice the distinctly phallic nature of the statues and stones, and of course the giant, penis-shape tree trunk beside the main shrine. There are many, many more similar artifacts in the three-story museum, where every available inch of space is used to display some kind of sexual object. You can marvel suspiciously at the dedication of the priest who spent a lifetime collecting this stuff, but the overall effect is more clinical than titillating. The shrine is 10 minutes on foot northwest of Uwajima Eki, beside the Suka-gawa. ☎ *0895/22–3444.* 🚉 *¥800.* ⊙ *Daily 8–5.*

Most people come to Uwajima for the **tōgyū,** a sport in which two bulls lock horns and, like sumō wrestlers, try to push each other out of the ring. Though there are very similar bouts in the Oki Islands, Uwajima claims that these bullfights are a unique tradition dating back 400 years—an obvious tourism ploy. There are six tournaments a year: January 2, the third Sunday in March, the first Sunday in April, July 24, August 14, and the second Sunday in November. The stadium is at the foot of Maru-yama, a 30-minute walk from Uwajima Eki.

The **Tourist Information Centre** (☎ 0895/22–3934), opposite Uwajima Eki, is open daily 9–5.

Dining

$–$$$$ ✕ **Kadoya.** This bustling two-story restaurant specializes in crab and *tai-meshi* (flaked sea bream on top of rice). Set menus, which include tempura and noodle dishes, are a good value. For quieter dining you can choose a private tatami room. The restaurant is near Uwajima Eki. ✉ *8–1 Nishiki-machi,* ☎ *0895/22–1543. DC, MC, V.*

Getting Around

JR trains connect Uwajima with Kōchi and Matsuyama. Ferries depart from Uwajima for Usuki, two JR train stops from Beppu on Kyūshū, and cost about ¥2,200.

Unomachi and Uchiko

Unomachi is 17 mins and Uchiko is 1 hr north of Uwajima by JR. Uchiko is 30 mins south of Matsuyama by JR.

⑩   **Unomachi** is a charming town with a well-preserved strip of old Japanese houses.

★   The **Ehime-ken Rekishi Bunka Hakubutsukan** (Museum of Ehime History and Culture), a huge new facility perched on a hill overlooking Unomachi, provides a wonderful overview of Ehime Prefecture's history from prehistoric times to today. Whole buildings, including a shrine and thatched-roof house, have been reconstructed inside the museum, which is made up of four linked exhibition areas that use state-of-the-art technology. The highlight is being able to see close-up the fabulous portable shrines and decorations used in local festivals, such as Uwajima's Warei-Taisai Matsuri. ✉ *Uno-chō* ☎ *0894/62–6222.* 🚉 *¥500.* ⊙ *Tues.–Sun. 9–5.*

⑪   **Uchiko** prospered during the Edo era from the development of its *Moku-ro* (wax industry), and it has preserved some of its architectural heritage.

Yokaichi, a 650-yard stretch of old wooden and white-and-cream plaster buildings, is a highlight of Uchiko. Some of the houses are now gift shops and teahouses; others have been preserved as they once were. Yokaichi is a 1½-km (¾-mi) walk from Uchiko Eki.

The impressive Kami-Haga Residence, built in 1894 by a family of rich wax merchants, houses the **Mokurō Shiryokan** (Japan Wax Museum), which is the best place to learn about the industry. ☎ 0893/44–2771, 🎫 ¥400. ⊘ *Daily 9–4:30.*

Uchiko-za, an attractive, restored Kabuki theater, was originally built in 1916. ☎ 0893/44–2840. 🎫 ¥300. ⊘ *Tues.–Sun. 9–4:30.*

Matsuyama

⑫ *30 mins by JR from Uchiko; 3 hrs west of Takamatsu by JR; 1 hr south of Hiroshima by fast boat, 3 hrs by ferry.*

Shikoku's largest city, Matsuyama bristles with industry: from chemicals to wood pulp and textiles to porcelain. Most of its appeal is in its famous literary associations, its castle, and the spas of Dogo Onsen. Matsuyama was the home of Masaoka Shiki, one of Japan's most famous haiku poets, and city officials encourage its residents to continue the haiku tradition.

Matsuyama-jō—the third such feudal castle in Shikoku to have survived intact, though barely—is on top of Katsu-yama, right in the center of the city. Construction began in 1602; then the original five-story donjon burned down in 1784, to be rebuilt in 1820 with a complex of a major three-story donjon and three lesser donjons. The lesser ones succumbed to fire in this century, but all have been reconstructed. Unlike other postwar reconstructions, these smaller donjons were rebuilt with original materials, not ferroconcrete. The main donjon now serves as a museum for feudal armor and swords owned by the Matsudaira clan, the daimyō family that lorded over Matsuyama and Takamatsu throughout the Edo period.

Ninomaru Shiseki Teien, an agreeable park on the west side of the hill, includes the grounds of the former outworks of the castle. The park and grounds are open Tuesday–Sunday 9–4:30, with a fee of ¥100. Walk through Ninomaru Shiseki Teien and up the hill to get to the castle. If you're not feeling so plucky, you can take a cable car or chairlift to the castle from Okaido, the shopping street on the east side of the hill; the fare is ¥210 one-way, ¥400 round-trip. ☎ 089/921–2000. 🎫 ¥350. ⊘ *Daily 9–5.*

Matsuyama has eight of Shikoku's 88 sacred temples. The best known is **Ishite-ji,** 20 minutes on foot east of Dogo Onsen Hon-kan. The Kamakura-style temple has its origins early in the 14th century, and its simple three-story pagoda is a pleasant contrast to the public bathhouse. Note the two Deva king statues at the gate. One has an open mouth, representing life; the other's closed mouth represents death. Praying at Ishite-ji is said to cure one's aching legs and crippled feet—the elderly hang up their sandals here as a hope offering.

Downtown Matsuyama revolves around the **Okaido covered shopping arcade,** at the foot of the castle grounds, and is best reached by taking Tram 5 (fare ¥170) from the plaza in front of Matsuyama Eki.

★ Rather than staying downtown in Matsuyama, consider spending the night at **Dogo Onsen.** With a history that is said to stretch back for more than 2 millennia, Dogo Onsen is one of Japan's oldest hot-spring resort areas. It hasn't outlived its popularity, either. More than 60 ryokan and hotels, old and new, operate here, and most now have their own thermal waters. Dogo Onsen is 18 minutes away from Matsuyama on

Tram 5, which you can take from Matsuyama Eki or catch downtown at the stop in front of the ANA Hotel (Trams 3, 5, and 6).

At the turn of the last century, bathing was done at public bathhouses, and the grandest of them all was—and still is—**Dogo Onsen Hon-kan** (⊠ Dogo Yu-no-machi, ☎ 089/921–5141) the municipal bathhouse. Bathing is a social pastime in Japan, and to stay in the area and not socialize at the municipal bathhouse is to miss the delight of this spa town. The grand, three-story, castlelike wooden building was built in 1894, and with its sliding panels, tatami floors, and shōji screens, it looks like an old-fashioned pleasure palace. In many ways, it is. More than 2,000 bathers come each day for a healthy scrub and soak. Many pay extra to lounge around after their bath, drinking tea in the communal lounge or private rooms. Even if you decide not to pay for a private room, make sure you visit the third floor to see the Botchan Room, named after the comic novel by local writer Natsume Sōseki.

There are different price levels of enjoyment: a basic bath is ¥300; a bath, rented *yukata* (cotton robe), tea and snack, and access to the communal tatami lounge are ¥620; access to a smaller lounge and bath area away from the hoi polloi is ¥980; and a private tatami room is ¥1,240. A separate wing was built in 1899 for imperial soaking. It is no longer used, but for ¥210 you can follow a guide through this royal bathhouse daily from 6:30 AM to 9 PM. The baths are open 6:30 AM–11 PM.

Dining and Lodging

$$–$$$$ ✕ **Kaiseki Club Kawasemi.** At this modern interpreter of traditional *kaiseki ryōri* (a style of food and service that is a traditional art) you can sit at tables or on tatami in private booths and savor delicate morsels of marinated seafood, or slivers of poached fish and vegetables artfully arranged in a mound, surrounded by a savory coulis. A slightly gloomy interior, decorated in minimalist black and grays, has seasonal flower arrangements, which add splashes of color. The restaurant is on the second floor, two streets east of Okaido—look for a purple sign with CLUB on it in English. ⊠ 2–5–18 Niban-chō, ☎ 089/933–9697. AE, MC, V.

$$–$$$ ✕ **à table.** If you're in the mood for delicious French country cooking by a French chef, set out for the heart of town to this slightly offbeat place. Dark-wood beams line the ceiling, some tinsel and risqué photographs serve as decorations, and you sit either at long wooden bench tables or around the kitchen, watching the burly chef hard at work with his assistant. Lunchtime set menus from only ¥850 are a bargain, and they can tempt you to return for more expensive dinner courses. There is a good selection of wines and teas. ⊠ 5–2–6 Chifune-machi, ☎ 089/947–8001. No credit cards.

$$ ✕ **Nikitatsu-an.** A traditionally designed Japanese restaurant, this innovative place is attached to a beer and sake brewery. Dishes include grilled fish, marinated beef strips, and specially prepared rice. Delicate Japanese presentation of the food and a more Western use of pungent spices come together in interesting combinations of crunchy, soft, and silky textures. Try the brewery's light Botchan ale and heavier brown Madonna ale. ⊠ 3–18 Dogo Shita-machi, ☎ 089/924–6617. No credit cards.

$ ✕ **Dan Dan Jaya.** A large *izakaya* (pub) with counter seating encircles the cooking area, and there are small, semi-enclosed areas with tatami seating to the sides. The menu has helpful pictures, and there are dozens of hearty country dishes that range in price from ¥500 to ¥1,000. Dan Dan Jaya is handily located near the Okaido shopping arcade. ⊠ 3–7–1 Niban-chō, ☎ 089/945–7101. AE, DC, MC, V.

$$$–$$$$ 🏨 **ANA Hotel Matsuyama.** The best international hotel downtown, the ANA is five minutes on foot from the cable car to Matsuyama-jō, and Tram 5 out to Dogo Onsen stops out front. Guest rooms are well maintained, reasonably spacious, and fully equipped, with everything from bathrobes to hair dryers. Ask for a room on the 11th or 12th floor that overlooks the Bansuiso Mansion, an imitation French château (housing the missable Prefectural Museum Annex), which is floodlighted at night. The hotel has shopping arcades, several restaurants, and a rooftop beer garden. ⊠ *3–2–1 Ichiban-chō, Matsuyama, Ehime-ken 790-8520,* ☎ *089/933–5511,* FAX *089/921–6053,* WEB *www.anahotels. com. 330 rooms. 4 restaurants, beer garden, hair salon. AE, DC, V.*

$$$–$$$$ 🏨 **Funaya Ryokan.** The best Japanese inn in Dogo Onsen, this is where the imperial family stays when it comes to take the waters. The ryokan has a long history, but the present building was constructed in 1963 and has some Western-style rooms. The finest rooms look out on the garden. Breakfast and dinner are included in the rate. ⊠ *1–33 Dogo Yu-no-machi, Matsuyama, Ehime-ken 790-9842,* ☎ *089/947–0278,* FAX *089/943–2139. 54 Japanese-style and Western-style rooms. Japanese-style baths. AE, DC, MC, V. MAP*

$$–$$$$ 🏨 **Hotel Patio Dogo.** Many of the spacious, well-furnished rooms in this Western-style hotel overlook the Dogo Onsen Hon-kan, which is right outside the lobby door. The hotel has business facilities and is small enough for the friendly staff to take an interest in you—something that doesn't always happen at the larger hotels in Dogo, geared up for the package-tour trade. There's also a good-value sushi restaurant on the ground floor. ⊠ *20–12 Dogo Yu-no-machi, Matsuyama, Ehime-ken 790-9842,* ☎ *089/941–4128,* FAX *089/941–4129,* WEB *www.patio-dogo.co.jp. 101 rooms. Restaurant, business services. AE, DC, MC, V.*

$$–$$$ 🏨 **Hotel Sunroute.** This business hotel has no particular charm, but its rooms are not too small, and it's just a five-minute walk from Matsuyama Eki. The best part of the hotel is its rooftop beer garden (open in the summer), from which you can catch a glimpse of the castle. ⊠ *391–8 Miyata-chō, Matsuyama, Ehime-ken 790-0066,* ☎ *089/933–2811,* FAX *089/933–2763. 109 rooms. Beer garden. AE, DC, MC, V.*

Getting Around

Frequent JR train service runs between Matsuyama and Takamatsu, and high-speed boat service and ferry service can shuttle you between Matsuyama and Hiroshima.

Visitor Information

The **City Tourist Information Office** (☎ 089/931–3914) in Matsuyama Eki provides maps and brochures Monday–Saturday 8:30–5. **Ehimeken Kokusai Senta** (Ehime Prefectural International Centre; ☎ 089/943–6688), on the south side of Katsu-yama below the castle, has information in English on the rest of the prefecture and on the city's efforts to encourage haiku poetry.

SHIKOKU A TO Z

To research prices, get advice from other travelers, and book travel arrangements, visit www.fodors.com.

AIR TRAVEL

Japan Air System, All Nippon Airways, and Japan Airlines provide domestic flights to and from Shikoku's four airports. Takamatsu is served by 7 daily flights from Tōkyō and by 10 daily flights from Ōsaka; Tokushima by 5 daily from Tōkyō and 10 from Ōsaka; Kōchi by 5 daily from Tōkyō and 23 from Ōsaka; and Matsuyama by 6 daily from Tōkyō and 6 from Ōsaka.

➤ CARRIERS: **All Nippon Airways** (☎ 0120/02–9222). **Japan Air System** (☎ 0120/51–1283). **Japan Airlines** (☎ 0120/25–5971).

BOAT AND FERRY TRAVEL

The Kansai Kisen (Kansai Steamship) to Takamatsu takes 5½ hours from Ōsaka's Bentenfuto Pier and 4½ hours from Kōbe's Naka-Tottei Pier. The boat leaves Ōsaka at 8:30 AM and 2:20 PM and Kōbe at 9:50 AM and 3:40 PM. It arrives at Takamatsu at 2 PM and 8:10 PM. From Ōsaka, the cost is ¥2,500 and up; it's slightly less from Kōbe.

Nankai Tokushima Shuttle Line provides ferry connections between Tokushima and Kansai International Airport via Wakayama. The journey takes about two hours and costs ¥3,390 one-way, ¥5,400 round-trip.

To Kōchi from Tōkyō a ship operated by Blue Highway Line departs at 7:40 PM, stops in Katsura, Wakayama Prefecture, at 8:50 AM, and arrives in Kōchi at 5 AM.

Hourly high-speed boat service by Ishizaki Kisen takes one hour to travel between Matsuyama and Hiroshima (¥5,700). Ferry service by Seto Nai-kai Kisen (three hours) costs ¥4,260 for first class, ¥2,130 for second class.

➤ CONTACTS: **Blue Highway Line** (☎ 0888/31–0520; Japanese only). **Ishizaki Kisen** (☎ 089/953–1003). **Kansai Kisen** (☎ 06/573–0530; Japanese only). **Nankai Tokushima Shuttle Line** (☎ 088/664–3330; Japanese only). **Seto Nai-kai Kisen** (☎ 082/253–1212).

CAR TRAVEL

Because traffic is light, the scenery marvelous, and the distances relatively short, Shikoku is one region in Japan where renting a car makes sense. (Remember that an international driver's license is required.) Budget Rent-a-Car has rental offices in Matsuyama, Takamatsu, and Kōchi, as do other car-rental agencies.

➤ CONTACTS: **Budget Rent-a-Car** (⊠ Kūko-dori 1–13–6, Matsuyama, ☎ 089/973–0543; ⊠ Nishinomaru-chō 2–20, Takamatsu, ☎ 087/851–6543; ⊠ Kitahon-machi 4-chōme 6–48, Kōchi, ☎ 088/884–0543).

EMERGENCIES

➤ CONTACTS: **Ambulance** (☎ 119). **Police** (☎ 110).

TOURS

No guided tours covering the island of Shikoku are conducted in English, though the Japan Travel Bureau (JTB) will make individual travel arrangements. JTB has branches in each of the prefectural capitals and can assist in local tours, hotel reservations, and ticketing onward travel. Local city tours, conducted in Japanese, cover the surrounding areas of each of the four major cities in Shikoku. You can arrange these through your hotel.

TRAIN TRAVEL

To get to Shikoku, take the JR Hikari Shinkansen to Okayama (4 hours from Tōkyō; 1 hour from Ōsaka), then transfer to the JR Limited Express for either Takamatsu (1 hour) or Matsuyama or Kōchi (3 hours).

You can also get to Matsuyama by taking the JR Shinkansen to Hiroshima (5 hours, 10 minutes from Tōkyō; 2 hours, 20 minutes from Kyōto). From Hiroshima's Ujina Port, the ferry takes 3 hours to cross the Seto Nai-kai to Matsuyama; the high-speed boat takes 1 hour.

All major towns on Shikoku are connected either by JR express and local trains or by bus. Because of the lower population density on Shikoku, transportation is not so frequent as on the southern coast of Honshū. So before you step off a train or bus, find out how long it will be before the next one departs for your next destination.

The main routes are from Takamatsu to Matsuyama by train (2 hours, 45 minutes); from Takamatsu to Kōchi by train (3 hours), from Takamatsu to Tokushima (90 minutes); from Matsuyama to Kōchi by JR bus (approximately 3 hours, 15 minutes); from Matsuyama to Uwajima by train (3 hours); and from Kōchi to Nakamura by train (2 hours).

VISITOR INFORMATION

Major tourist information centers are located at each of Shikoku's main cities: Takamatsu, Kōchi, Matsuyama, and Tokushima.

A nationwide service for English-language assistance or travel information is available daily 9–5. Throughout Shikoku, dial the hot line toll-free for information on western Japan. When using a yellow, blue, or green public phone (do not use red phones), insert a ¥10 coin, which will be returned.

➤ TOURIST INFORMATION: **English-language hot line** (☎ 0120/444–800 or 0088/224–800). **Kōchi** (☎ 0888/82–1634). **Matsuyama** (☎ 089/931–3914). **Takamatsu** (☎ 0878/51–2009). **Tokushima** (☎ 088/656–3303).

11 KYŪSHŪ

The relatively quiet island of Kyūshū, which hangs like a tail off the south end of Honshū, has a mild climate, lush green countryside, hot springs, and awesome volcanic formations. Its cities are mostly free of skyscrapers and filled with sights of historical and cultural significance.

By Kiko Itasaka

Updated by
Julie Nootbaar

JAPANESE CIVILIZATION as we know it was born in Kyūshū. Because of its geographic proximity to Korea and China, from the 4th century Kyūshū was the first area of Japan to be culturally influenced by its more sophisticated neighbors. Through the gateway of Kyūshū, Japan was first introduced to Buddhism, the Chinese writing system, pottery techniques, and other aspects of Chinese and Korean culture. Legend has it that the grandson of Amaterasu Ōmikami, the sun goddess, first ruled Japan from Kyūshū. Another tale relates that Jimmu Tenno, Japan's first emperor, traveled from Kyūshū to Honshū, consolidated Japan, and established the imperial line that exists to this day.

Not all outside influence was welcome, however. In 1274 Kublai Khan led a fleet of Mongol warriors in an unsuccessful attempt to invade Japan. The Japanese, in preparation for further attacks, built a stone wall along the coast of Kyūshū. Remnants of it still stand outside Fukuoka. When the Mongols returned in 1281 with a force 100,000 strong, they were repelled by the stone wall and by the fierce fighting of the Kyūshū natives. The fighters were aided by a huge storm, known as *kamikaze* (divine wind), which blew the Mongol fleet out to sea. (This term is likely more familiar in its World War II context, when it was used to describe suicide pilots.)

In the mid-16th century, Kyūshū was once again the point of contact with the outside world, when Portuguese ships landed on the shores of Japan. The arrival of these ships signaled Japan's initial introduction to the West and its medicine, firearms, and Christianity. The Portuguese were followed by the Dutch and the Spanish. The Tokugawa Shogunate was not entirely pleased with the intrusion of the Westerners and feared political interference: in 1635 the shogunate established a closed-door policy that permitted *gaijin* (foreigners) to land only on a small island, Dejima, in the harbor of Nagasaki. As a result, until 1859, when Japan opened its doors to the West, the small port town of Nagasaki became the most important center for both trade and Western learning for Kyūshū and the entire nation. The historical influence of Europe is still apparent in Nagasaki, with its 19th-century Western-style buildings and the lasting presence of Christianity.

Kyūshū Glossary

Key Japanese words and suffixes for this chapter include *bijutsukan* (art museum), *-chō* (street or block), *-chōme* (street), *chūō* (central), *daimyō* (feudal lord), *dake* (mountain), *dōri* (avenue), *eki* (train station), *gaijin* (foreigner), *-gawa* (river), *-gun* (county or district), *izakaya* (pub), *-ji* (Buddhist temple), *jinja* (Shintō shrine), *-jō* (castle), *-ken* (prefecture), *kōen* ("*ko*-en," park), *-ku* (section or ward), *kūkō* (airport), *onsen* (hot springs), *rotemburo* (open-air thermal bath), *sake* (rice wine), *sakura* (cherry blossoms), *-san* (mountain, as in Aso-san, Mt. Aso), *-shi* (city or municipality), *-shima* (island), *Shinkansen* (bullet train, literally "new trunk line"), and *-yama* (mountain).

Pleasures and Pastimes

Arts and Culture

Because Kyūshū was the threshold of artistic influences arriving from the wider world, the history of Japanese porcelain—craftsmanship "borrowed" from Korea—begins here. And the pottery towns of Arita and Ōkawachi-yama, in Imari, are interesting windows on the arts, trade, and foreign relations in Edo-era Japan. In 1616, after waging war on Korea, the Japanese brought the artisan Ri Sampei to Kyūshū in order to produce ceramic objects for the shōgun. The kilns that sprung up to support him continue to produce exquisite pieces of art for the emperor and other dignitaries.

Fukuoka is known for its *kyōgen*—traditional Japanese drama unique for its singsong dialogue—and its position as a center of contemporary pan-Asian commerce. Nagasaki's internationalism is based on the port's history of Buddhism, Christianity, and *Ran-gaku* (Dutch studies).

Dining

Until the 20th century Kyūshū was the most international part of Japan. So certain Kyūshū dishes, not surprisingly, show the influence of China and Europe. Tempura, for example, is often thought of as a standard Japanese dish. In fact, it was introduced by Europeans to Kyūshū in the 17th century. Particularly in Nagasaki, the influence of foreign cuisines is still apparent.

Beppu is famous for its seafood. Because it is primarily a resort town, most people tend to remain in their hotels for meals, and thus many hotels have fresh, locally caught fish. One particularly popular local dish is *fugu*, the potentially poisonous blowfish, which restaurants must be licensed to serve.

Fukuoka, Kyūshū's largest city, has excellent Japanese and Western restaurants. Many of the best Western restaurants are in hotels. One well-known dish is *Hakata ramen*, noodles with a strongly flavored pork-based soup with *negi* (scallions) and strips of roast pork. It is also known for its *ikesu* restaurants, places that have a fish tank from which you can select your entrée, guaranteed to be fresh.

The regional specialty of Kumamoto is *basashi* (horse meat), which is served roasted, fried, or raw. An easier-to-take delicacy is *dengaku*, tofu or fish covered with a strong bean paste and grilled. In contrast to the delicate taste of Kyōto cuisine, dengaku is a good example of Kyūshū's stronger flavors.

Shippoku, available only in Nagasaki, is a variety of dishes that, when combined, make a full meal. Dinner centers on a fish-soup base with European flavorings, to which many foods are added, including rice cakes, a variety of vegetables, and stewed pork cubes marinated in ginger and soy sauce. Shippoku is usually served in one large communal dish, very unlike the individual portions typically served in Japan. Another distinctive Nagasaki favorite, *champon*, consists of heavy Chinese-style noodles in a soup. Not surprisingly, Nagasaki also has some of the best Western restaurants in Kyūshū.

For more details on Japanese cuisine, *see* Chapter 14 *and* Dining *in* Smart Travel Tips A to Z.

CATEGORY	COST*
$$$$	over ¥4,500
$$$	¥2,500–¥4,500
$$	¥1,500–¥2,500
$	under ¥1,500

per person for a main course at dinner

Lodging

Accommodations in Kyūshū are plentiful, and it's almost always possible to get reservations. Fukuoka has major hotels with excellent facilities. Nagasaki has grand old hotels and ryokan that, like the city itself, seem to be frozen in the 19th century. If you are looking for a more active vacation, spend a few days in the Aso-san region at a pension, which is something like a bed-and-breakfast where supper is served as well. Pensions near Aso are set in the mountains and are near trails for hiking.

For a short course on accommodations in Japan, *see* Lodging *in* Smart Travel Tips A to Z.

CATEGORY	COST*
$$$$	over ¥20,000
$$$	¥15,000–¥20,000
$$	¥10,000–¥15,000
$	under ¥10,000

All prices are for a double room, excluding service and tax.

Onsen (Hot Springs)

Kyūshū is a center of one of the greatest Japanese pastimes: bathing in onsen, or natural hot springs. No doubt the Japanese love of bathing has something to do with the hundreds of onsen that bubble out of their volcanic island. Many are surrounded by resorts, ranging from overlarge Western-style hotels to small, humble inns; all are extremely popular among Japanese tourists. And some onsen have rotemburo where you can soak outdoors even in the midst of a snowy winter landscape. *See* Chapter 14 for more about the art of bathing in Japan.

Outdoor Activities

Kyūshū is one of the best Japanese islands on which to enjoy the outdoors. Outside Nagasaki and Fukuoka there is plenty of natural drama—from mountains and volcanoes to islands and seascapes that all afford great hiking and cycling. You can climb an active volcano at Aso-san National Park and enjoy views of the surrealistically green hills surrounding the mountain. The islands west of Fukuoka and Nagasaki are good for a bit of adventure, likewise those south of Kagoshima. Hot springs in Kagoshima make it ever so easy to relax after a long trip, as does Aso-san, and the landscapes between Aso and Beppu are particularly beautiful.

Exploring Kyūshū

One approach to touring Kyūshū is to circle the island, which will bring you past rich green rice fields, mountains, and the ocean. The starting point of most visits is Fukuoka, where there is a major airport and JR Shinkansen connections to Tōkyō and other points north. Of course, you can take in the island's sights in any order; here we circle through Fukuoka to Nagasaki on the west coast, then go east to Kumamoto, south to Kagoshima, and north to Mt. Aso, concluding at the hot-springs resorts of Beppu and Yufuin, from which you can easily return to Fukuoka.

Numbers in the text correspond to numbers in the margin and on the Kyūshū and Nagasaki maps.

Great Itineraries

Kyūshū is most noted for its history, food, and natural beauty. And you can cover the island's must-sees in a brief tour from Nagasaki to Beppu via Mt. Aso, with pauses for local wonders and delicacies. Ferries run frequently between peninsulas, but express trains and buses will be your principle mode of transport if you're planning a rapid tour of Kyūshū.

IF YOU HAVE 2 DAYS

In two days you can easily get a sense of Kyūshū's relaxed, international atmosphere and still have a chance to see some gorgeous countryside. Spend one day en route from ☗ **Fukuoka** ① to ☗ **Nagasaki** ④–⑫. It's a beautiful (and easy) ride by train, but if you're traveling by

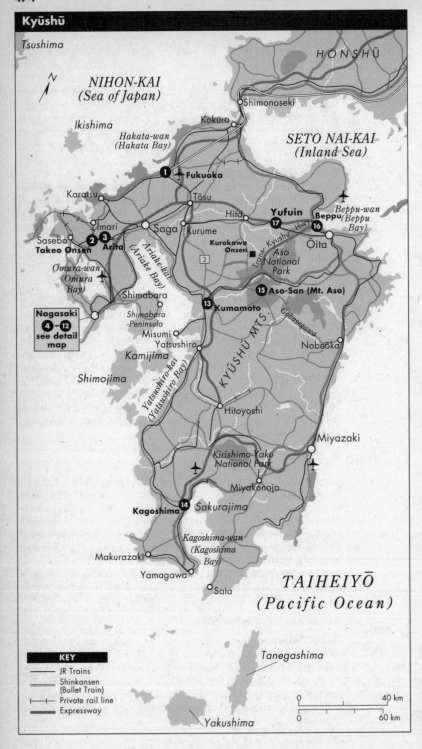

car, adopt a leisurely pace and enjoy the pottery town of **Arita** ③, set among misty valleys and rich green mountains, en route to the culinary treats of Nagasaki. The **Gembaku Shiryōkan** (Atomic Bomb Museum) ⑪ in Nagasaki is the one must-see if time is limited.

IF YOU HAVE 4 DAYS

Leave ⛩ **Fukuoka** ① right away for the cultural and athletic opportunities that are in easy reach of the city or en route to Nagasaki. Spend the first day in **Arita** ③, ending up in ⛩ **Takeo Onsen** ② for the night. ⛩ **Nagasaki** ④–⑫, the hilly, cosmopolitan setting for *Madame Butterfly* and an atomic bomb site, is a lesson in the history of Japan's relations with the West, for better and worse, from the 16th century to World War II. From Nagasaki go straight to ⛩ **Aso-san** ⑮ for a day amid its geological wonders or a two-day stint of intense hiking. Recover at a hot-springs resort in ⛩ **Beppu** ⑯ or ⛩ **Yufuin** ⑰. Travel distances are not terribly far (except for the Nagasaki–Mt. Aso leg), but changing trains and getting between places always takes more time than expected.

IF YOU HAVE 7 DAYS

You can cover all of Kyūshū's major points in seven days without running yourself ragged. Start in ⛩ **Fukuoka** ① to get a taste of the island's main metropolis; then head to ⛩ **Nagasaki** ④–⑫ for a day and a half of easygoing exploring. From here it's a three-hour train ride to ⛩ **Kumamoto** ⑬. As you drop south on Kyūshū, mellow ⛩ **Kagoshima** ⑭ scores points for its unique twist on "Japanese-ness," particularly since Sakurajima, the local active volcano, is often spewing smoke. Nearby Ibusuki city is worth the hour-long train ride from Kagoshima solely for a soak in the therapeutic hot-sand baths. Next stop from Kagoshima is the Japanese hot-springs resort experience. You can choose what some call an over-the-top (if authentically Japanese) hot-springs experience in ⛩ **Beppu** ⑯, or for something more elegant and sedate, head to ⛩ **Yufuin** ⑰. On your way back to Fukuoka, stop at ⛩ **Aso-san** ⑮ for a dramatic Kyūshū finale.

When to Tour Kyūshū

Kyūshū is at its most beautiful in early spring when the greenery is richest—and because much of the island is nearly tropical, temperatures will be plenty warm. April can be magical; late May to June tends to be wet. Summer is usually hot and sticky, more so than elsewhere in Japan. Autumn colors are rich and luxurious, particularly in the north, and they arrive in mid- to late October. Winter sees little snow, except in mountainous central Kyūshū, and the island's weather is milder than in most of Honshū. Look for the migration of cranes from Siberia, which adds drama to Kyūshū's winter landscape.

FUKUOKA AND NORTHERN KYŪSHŪ

Fukuoka

❶ *1½ hrs west of Tōkyō by plane, 5–7½ hrs west of Tōkyō by Shinkansen, 2½–4⅓ hrs west of Ōsaka by Shinkansen (both depending on which train you take).*

Fukuoka is the most logical starting point for travel around Kyūshū. The commercial, political, and cultural center of the island—and its largest city—has 1.2 million inhabitants, making it the eighth largest in Japan. World War II bombing virtually flattened the town, which was rebuilt on a grid plan. Small and provincial in comparison to Tōkyō, there's still a dynamic quality about Fukuoka, whose city council is determined to position it as Japan's gateway to Asia.

You'll find most activities and entertainment around the two city centers, Hakata Eki and the downtown Tenjin district; use the subway to travel between them. The city is divided in two by the Naka-gawa. All areas west of the river are known as Fukuoka; everything east of it is known as Hakata. Fukuoka was originally a castle town founded at the end of the 16th century, and Hakata was the place for commerce. In 1889 the two districts were officially merged as Fukuoka, but the historical names are still used. Nakasu—the largest nightlife district in western Japan, with 3,000 bars, restaurants, and street vendors—is along the Naka-gawa and Hakata-gawa.

Eisai (1141–1215) founded **Shōfuku-ji** in 1195 upon his return to Kyūshū after years of study in China. He was one of the first Japanese priests to introduce Zen Buddhism to Japan—the claim is often made that this is the site of Japan's first Zen temple. Eisai is also said to have brought the first tea seeds from China to Japan. Note the Korean-style bronze bell in the belfry, designated an Important Cultural Property by the Japanese government. The temple is a 15-minute walk from Hakata Eki, or a 5-minute Nishitetsu bus ride from the adjacent Hakata Kōtsū Bus Center to the Okunodo stop. ▨ *Free.* ☉ *Daily 9–5.*

The grounds of **Sumiyoshi Jinja,** dotted with camphor and cedar trees, make it a peaceful retreat from the bustling city. The shrine, founded in 1623, can be reached from Hakata Eki by taking a bus from the adjacent Hakata Kōtsū Bus Center to the Sumiyoshi stop. ▨ *Free.* ☉ *Daily 9–4.*

Believed to have been founded in AD 757, **Kushida Jinja** is the oldest shrine in Fukuoka City and the home of the annual Yamakasa Festival. Destroyed by fires during battles in the 16th century, the shrine was rebuilt and has been renovated and repaired every 25 years—most recently in 2000. A five-minute walk will get you here from Shōfuku-ji, or it's just three minutes from the Canal City-mae bus stop. ▨ *1 Kamikawabata-chō.* ▨ *Free.* ☉ *Daily 9–5.*

Three renovated merchant residences house the **Hakata Machiya Furusato-kan** (Hakata Machiya Folk Museum), with displays on early 20th-century Hakata and demonstrations on the making of traditional dolls and kimono sashes. The gift shop sells a range of traditional crafts and old-fashioned toys. It is across the street from Kushida Jinja. ▨ *6-10 Reisen-machi,* ☎ *092/281–7761.* ▨ *¥200.* ☉ *Daily 10–6.*

The lake at **Ōhori Kōen** was once part of a moat surrounding **Fukuoka-jō,** of which little remains. The spacious park has bridges that connect to three small islands in the center of the lake. In early April the northern part of the park is graced with the blossoms of 2,600 sakura. Many Fukuoka residents take advantage of this oasis in the middle of an otherwise industrial city on weekends. Bring a picnic, enjoy a leisurely walk, or boat and fish on the lake. To get here from town, take the subway from Hakata Eki to Ōhori Kōen Station; it's about a 20-minute ride.

Dining and Lodging

$$$–$$$$ ✕ **Ikesu Kawataro.** A tank full of fish—your dinner—sits in the middle of this large establishment, which has counter seating, Japanese-style rooms with tatami mats, and regular tables. If you don't mind sitting on the floor for the duration of the meal, the tatami section is the most pleasant; other areas of the restaurant tend to be noisy. Try any of the remarkably fresh sashimi dishes; some are so fresh, in fact, that they're still wriggling when served. ▨ *1–6–6 Nakasu, Hakata-ku,* ☎ *092/271–2133. AE, DC, MC, V.*

$ ✕ **Deko.** A cheerful izakaya three minutes on foot from the Hotel New
★ Otani Hakata, here you can while away an evening over good food.

The best seating is Japanese-style at the counter and at shared tables (there are wells for your legs). Western-style seating toward the back of the restaurant lies outside the fraternity of communal dining. Deko has no English menu, but the staff will do its best to make suggestions. The daily special is usually a good bet, and mackerel lightly grilled in soy sauce and salt is superb. ⊠ *1–24–22 Takasago, Chūō-ku,* ☎ *092/ 526–7070. AE, DC, MC, V.*

$ ✕ **Ichiki.** If you're interested in checking out area nightlife, try this bar-restaurant and see how locals spend a free evening. In this relaxed and friendly atmosphere, as the evening wears on, it's more likely than not that one of your Japanese neighbors will attempt to make your acquaintance. Try *kushiyaki,* a sort of shish kebab with fish, meat, and vegetables, fried on a hot, flat grill and served on a wooden skewer. Plan to settle in for a while, have a few beers, and order a few small dishes at a time. ⊠ *1–2–10 Maizuru, Chūō-ku,* ☎ *092/751–5591. No credit cards.*

$$$$ 🏨 **Hotel Il Palazzo.** A showpiece of contemporary design, this boutique hotel created by art director Shigeru Uchida and architect Aldo Rossi is Fukuoka's most chic lodging. The interior is classically simple yet dramatic. Muted lights in the Italian restaurant reflect off the walls, and the ceiling lights sparkle like stars. The Western-style guest rooms have simple furnishings; rich, deep-pile carpets; and soft colors. The nine Japanese-style rooms are traditional except for half partitions that create a feeling of increased space. ⊠ *3–13–1 Haruyoshi, Chūō-ku, Fukuoka, Fukuoka-ken 810-0003,* ☎ *092/716–3333,* 𝖥𝖠𝖷 *092/724–3330. 53 Western-style rooms, 9 Japanese-style rooms. Restaurant, 2 bars, café. AE, DC, MC, V.*

$$$$ 🏨 **Hotel New Otani Hakata.** Like other New Otani properties, this hotel provides modern Japanese comforts—it's smart, characterless, and efficient. It's a top Fukuoka hotel and a quick taxi ride from the station. The rooms, decorated in quiet tones, are spacious and have a writing table and easy chair. This is one of the few hotels in all of Kyūshū where you can expect most of the staff to speak English. The large lobby reception area has a coffee lounge and adjoins a complex of high-fashion, high-price boutiques. ⊠ *1–1–2 Watanabe-dōri, Chūō-ku, Fukuoka, Fukuoka-ken 810-0004,* ☎ *092/714–1111,* 𝖥𝖠𝖷 *092/715–5658,* 𝖶𝖤𝖡 *www.kys-newotani.co.jp/en. 396 rooms. 4 restaurants, bar, barbershop, hair salon, massage, shops, travel services. AE, DC, MC, V.*

$$$$ 🏨 **Hyatt.** There are two Hyatts in Fukuoka, the Hyatt Regency, near the station, and the Grand Hyatt in Canal City, an American-style shopping mall between Tenjin and Hakata stations. The Hyatt Regency, eight minutes from Hakata Eki (on the Shinkansen side), focuses on business travelers looking for polite, efficient service with comfortable guest rooms filled with plastic-veneer furniture. The Grand Hyatt is a bit more flashy, with sleek black marble accents to its modern interior and a bustling open floor of restaurants below the lobby. *Hyatt Regency:* ⊠ *2–14–1 Hakata Eki-higashi, Hakata-ku, Fukuoka, Fukuoka-ken 812-0013,* ☎ *092/412–1234,* 𝖥𝖠𝖷 *092/414–2490. 248 rooms. 2 restaurants, bar, café, shops, concierge floor, meeting room. AE, DC, MC, V. Grand Hyatt:* ⊠ *1–2–82 Sumiyoshi, Fukuoka, Fukuoka-ken 812-0018,* ☎ *092/282–1234,* 𝖥𝖠𝖷 *092/282–2817,* 𝖶𝖤𝖡 *www.hyatt.com/ japan/fukuoka/hotels,* 𝖶𝖤𝖡 *www.hyatt.com/japan/fukuoka/hotels. 3 restaurants, 2 bars, pool, health club. AE, DC, MC, V.*

$$$ 🏨 **Fukuoka Yama-no-ue Hotel.** The name of this hotel means "on a mountain," and it is on a hill above Fukuoka with excellent views of the ocean on one side and the city on the other. The service is quietly polite and extremely helpful. Rooms are on the small side but not uncomfortably so, and there's a public bath. The hotel is a little out of the way—20 minutes from Hakata Eki by taxi or bus (Nishitetsu Bus

58)—but the views make the travel time worthwhile. ⊠ *1–1–33 Terukuni, Chūō-ku, Fukuoka, Fukuoka-ken 810-0032,* ☎ *092/771–2131,* ℻ *092/771–8888. 50 rooms. 2 restaurants. AE, DC, MC, V.*

$$
★   ▦ **Clio Court Hotel.** The best value in Fukuoka has remarkably attractive rooms furnished with great care in a variety of styles, such as art deco and early American (you can request your preferred decor when you make your reservation). Rooms in the front—1202 and 1203—are particularly good choices for the city view. One whole floor contains tea-ceremony rooms modeled on designs by Kamiya Sotan and Hosokawa-Sansai, both disciples of the founder of the tea ceremony, Sen-no-Rikyū. Another tea-ceremony room is furnished with benches and tables for gai-jin. One floor higher is the hotel's revolving restaurant: in 60 minutes you take one full turn around Fukuoka. Clio Court Hotel is just outside Hakata Eki on the Shinkansen side. ⊠ *5–3 Hakata Eki, Chūō-gai, Hakata-ku, Fukuoka, Fukuoka-ken 812-0012,* ☎ *092/472–1111,* ℻ *092/474–3222. 192 rooms. 4 restaurants, bar, café. AE, DC, MC, V.*

Shopping

Fukuoka is famous for two local products—*Hakata ningyō* (dolls) and *Hakata obi* (kimono sashes). Hakata ningyō are popular throughout Japan. They are made with fired clay and are hand-painted with bright colors and distinctive expressions. The dolls are mostly ornamental, representing children, women, samurai, and geisha. Hakata obi are made of a local silk that has a rougher texture than most Japanese silk, which is usually perfectly even and smooth. For local girls, the purchase of their first Hakata obi is an initiation into adulthood. Other products, such as bags and purses, are also made of this silk.

The **Kawabata-dōri Shōtengai** (Kawabata Shopping Arcade), stretching from Nakasu Kawabata Station on the subway line parallel to the Hakata-gawa, is lined with a multitude of shops and restaurants.

Downtown **Tenjin,** which you can reach by taking a 10-minute subway ride on the Kūkō Line from Hakata Eki, is a fashionable area for shopping, with boutiques, department stores, and restaurants both above and below ground.

Masuya (⊠ 6–138 Kami-Kawabata, Hakata-ku, ☎ 092/281–0083) is a specialty shop for Hakata ningyō located in the Kawabata arcade (there's also a branch in Hakata Eki).

Iwataya (⊠ 2–11–1 Tenjin, Chūō-ku, ☎ 092/721–1111), a department store in Tenjin, carries the most complete selection of local merchandise, including Hakata ningyō, Hakata silk, and Kyūshū's distinctive pottery.

Takeo Onsen and Arita

1 hr southwest of Fukuoka by JR; 1 hr, 35 mins north of Nagasaki by JR.

②   **Takeo Onsen,** a small town in Saga Prefecture known for its hot springs, is an easy stop en route from Fukuoka to Nagasaki. Surrounded by mountains, the spa became famous when, approximately 1,700 years ago according to legend, Empress Jingū stopped in Takeo Onsen to recover from childbirth on her way home from invading Korea. Since that time the Japanese have been coming here to take its waters.

The town's other claim to fame is pottery, crafted after the traditions of Korean potters whom Hideyoshi Toyotomi's armies imported to Kyūshū 400 years ago. The pottery is noted for its simple designs and subdued natural colors. Takeo Onsen is also home to three lofty camphor trees, all more than 3,000 years old and designated National Natural Monuments. Takeo Onsen may not be postcard perfect, but it does have an intimate atmosphere not found in big-city Japan. This makes it an intriguing and convenient overnight alternative to Fukuoka or Nagasaki. All the ryokan and izakaya are within walking distance of the station.

❸ The small village of **Arita** has one main street, which is entirely lined with family-owned pottery shops—each has its own kiln and tradition that has been passed on from generation to generation. Prices increase with quality, but you can get a beautiful handmade teacup for around ¥2,000 or a set of five cups and a teapot for ¥10,000. Once a year, from April 29 to May 5, there is a large pottery fair, when everything in all the shops goes on sale. At these times many of the ceramic pieces are priced as low as ¥500. Arita is about 20 minutes by local train from Takeo Onsen, and Imari is 20 minutes beyond Arita.

OFF THE
BEATEN PATH

ŌKAWACHI-YAMA – "The village of the secret kilns," Ōkawachi-yama is a picturesque town on a mountain surrounded by high cliffs where pottery was reportedly first made in the area. It's a short taxi ride from Imari, which is 20 minutes by local train from Arita.

For more information on local pottery, contact the **Arita town office** (✉ 2–8–1 Iwatanigawauchi, ☎ 0955/43–5068).

Dining and Lodging

$ ✗ **Muraichi-ban.** This cheerful izakaya is for the young or young at heart. The centerpiece of the restaurant is a large, square kitchen where cooks energetically fillet fish and stir-fry noodles, performing for whomever is at the counter. If you don't want distractions, sit in one of the booths around the edge of the dining room. Bric-a-brac hangs from the wood-beamed ceilings, and posters on the walls give a light ambience to this local pub. The menu includes foods from sashimi to grilled fish, *yakitori* (soy-roasted skewer chicken) to omelets. ✉ 7283 *Ōaza Takeo, Takeo-chō,* ☎ *0954/23–4995. No credit cards.*

$$$ ⌷ **Kyōto-ya.** A comfortable choice, Kyōto-ya genuinely welcomes gaijin guests. Tatami rooms are reasonably spacious and include a separate alcove with a table and two chairs by a window. The open-air thermal baths here are not as hot as other onsen, and those with tender skin will find them wonderfully soothing and relaxing. Meals are brought to your room, though you can opt to pay for just the room and eat at a local restaurant. ✉ *Onsen-dōri, Takeo-shi, Saga-ken 843-0022,* ☎ *0954/23–2171,* ℻ *0954/23–2176. 35 rooms, 30 with bath. Hot springs, shop. AE, DC, MC, V. EP, MAP*

$$$ ⌷ **Takeo Century Hotel.** A convenient location from which to explore the pottery towns of Arita and Imari, the Takeo Century has Western amenities and a traditional public bath. Rooms in the back of the hotel overlook a garden and the swimming pool. The staff is extremely helpful. It is 10 minutes by taxi from Takeo Onsen. ✉ *4075–13 Takeo-chō, Takeo-shi, Saga-ken 843-0022,* ☎ *0954/22–2200,* ℻ *0954/22–2888. 50 rooms with bath. 3 restaurants, bar, café, pool, 2 tennis courts. AE, DC, MC, V.*

Fukuoka and Northern Kyūshū A to Z

To research prices, get advice from other travelers, and book travel arrangements, visit www.fodors.com.

AIRPORTS

Fukuoka Kūkō is Kyūshū's primary international airport. Skymark Airlines (SKY), Japan Airlines (JAL), All Nippon Airways (ANA), and Japan Air System (JAS) fly the 1½-hour route here from Haneda Kūkō, in Tōkyō. JAL also flies once daily (1 hour, 45 minutes) between Tōkyō's Narita International Airport and Fukuoka Kūkō. JAS, JAL, and ANA also offer a total of nine direct flights between Ōsaka's Kansai International Airport and Fukuoka (1 hour, 45 minutes).

For airline phone numbers, *see* Air Travel *in* Smart Travel Tips A to Z.

Fukuoka Airport is very near the center of the city. Kūkō subway line links the airport with JR Hakata Eki in three minutes.

BUS TRAVEL

An easy way to get around Fukuoka is by bus. Buses leave from Kōtsū Bus Center, just across the street from Hakata Eki, and from Fukuoka Bus Center, at Tenjin.

Sightseeing buses leave from Tenjin Bus Center and from Hakata Kōtsū Bus Center. Very few tours are given in English, so it is better to have your hotel call in advance or to ask at the tourist information office. A four-hour tour costs approximately ¥2,400.

➤ BUS INFORMATION: **Hakata Kōtsū Bus Center** (☎ 092/431–1171). **Tenjin Bus Center** (☎ 092/771–2961).

CONSULATES

➤ UNITED STATES: **U.S. Consulate** (✉ 5–26 Ōhori 2-chōme, Chūō-ku, Fukuoka, ☎ 092/751–9331).

EMERGENCIES

➤ CONTACTS: **Ambulance** (☎ 119). **Nakagawa Hospital** (✉ 17–17 Mukaishin-machi 2-chōme, Minami-ku, Fukuoka-shi, Fukuoka-ken 811-1345, ☎ 092/565–3531). **Police** (☎ 110).

SUBWAYS

The city's two major transportation centers are around Hakata Eki and Tenjin, the terminal station for both subway lines. The Kūkō Line runs downtown through Tenjin to Hakata Eki and Fukuoka Airport, and the Hakozaki Line runs from downtown toward the bay. Fares are from ¥ 200.

TRAIN TRAVEL

JR *Hikari* Shinkansen trains travel between Tōkyō and Hakata Eki in Fukuoka (6½–7½ hours) through Ōsaka and Hiroshima. The superfast *Nozomi* Shinkansen takes only five hours, but it is not included in the JR Pass. There are 15 daily runs. Regular JR express trains travel these routes but take twice as long.

VISITOR INFORMATION

The Fukuoka International Association in Rainbow Plaza is a good source of information for both travelers and residents of Fukuoka. The English-speaking staff is very helpful, and English-language newspapers and periodicals are available for visitors to read. Japan Travel Bureau offers domestic and international travel services.

➤ TOURIST INFORMATION: **Fukuoka International Association** (✉ Rainbow Plaza, IMS, 8th floor, 1–7–11 Tenjin, Chūō-ku, ☎ 092/733–2220, FAX 092/733–2215). **Japan Travel Bureau** (✉ Yamato Seimei Kaikan Bldg., 1–14–4 Tenjin, Chūō-ku, ☎ 092/731–5221).

NAGASAKI

2 hrs southwest of Fukuoka by JR; 1 hr, 35 mins south of Takeo Onsen by JR.

A quiet city of hills with a peaceful harbor, Nagasaki is often called the San Francisco of Japan. Its harbor, now serenely dotted with a few fishing boats, was once the most important trading port in the country.

In 1639 Japan closed its ports to all gaijin and designated the small island of Dejima, in Nagasaki Harbor, as the one place where foreign boats were allowed to land. The Tokugawa Shogunate established this isolationist policy to prevent Western powers from having political influence in Japan, and the only Japanese allowed to have contact with the gaijin were Nagasaki's merchants and prostitutes. So from this sole international port, knowledge of the West, particularly in fields such as medicine and firearms, spread throughout Japan. Such was Nagasaki's role until Japan reopened its doors to the West in 1859. Western-style buildings and churches from the 19th century still stand as testaments to the city's unique history.

After more than two centuries of mercantile importance, Nagasaki had become a relatively obscure city until an atomic bomb was dropped on it in 1945. Although the bomb destroyed one-third of the city, enough remained standing so that, to this day, Nagasaki retains an atmosphere that mixes both Eastern and Western traditions from the last century.

Exploring Nagasaki

Nagasaki is a beautiful harbor city, small enough to cover on foot if you have the energy to attack some of the steep inclines, which veer and meander. Most of the interesting sights, restaurants, and shopping areas are south of Nagasaki Eki. When you consider all of Nagasaki's picturesque sights, the city might seem like a quaint port town that time and progress have somehow passed by. But it's important to remember that Nagasaki suffered the devastation of an atomic bomb. The Gembaku Shiryōkan (Atomic Bomb Museum) and Heiwa Kōen (Peace Park)—the memorial and ruins left in memory of the victims of the second atomic bomb in 1945—and Nishi-zaka are to the north.

❹ **Heiwa Kōen** (Peace Park) was built at the epicenter of the August 9, 1945, atomic blast. In a blinding flash, 6.7 square km (2.59 square mi) were obliterated and 74,884 people were killed, with another 74,909 injured out of an estimated population of 204,000. At one end of the park, a black pillar grimly marks the exact center of the blast. At the other end is a graceless 32-ft statue of a male figure with one arm pointing horizontally (symbolizing world peace), the other pointing toward the sky (indicating the harm of nuclear power). Despite the park's small size—only a fraction of Hiroshima's Heiwa Kōen—an appropriately somber gloom pervades this memorial. Every year on August 9 there is an anti-nuclear-war demonstration here. From the JR station, take either Streetcar 1 or 3 to the Matsuya-machi stop, about a 10-minute ride. ⊠ *Free.* ⊙ *Daily 9–6.*

❺ **Gembaku Shiryōkan** (Atomic Bomb Museum) challenges and informs with interactive TV displays, video testimonies, and hands-on exhibits. The architecture literally steers you spiraling downward into the displays of photos and objects demonstrating the devastation. A section dedicated to the foreign victims of the bomb dropped by the American B-29 *Bockscar* tells of the 500 Allied POWs interned in the middle of a factory site that was decimated (although 200 of them had died as a result of disease, malnutrition, and torture before the bomb was dropped). You can also hear the testimonies of Korean bomb survivors, victims of neglect. The museum is far more grim than Peace Park. To get to the museum, take Streetcar 1 to the Hamaguchi stop; then follow the road in front of you up the slope to the modern building built into the hill next to the tall red Nagasaki Municipal Museum, which you can see from the streetcar stop. ⊠ *7–8 Hirano-machi,* ☎ *0958/44–1231.* ⊠ *¥200, audio tour ¥150.* ⊙ *Daily 8:30–5:30.*

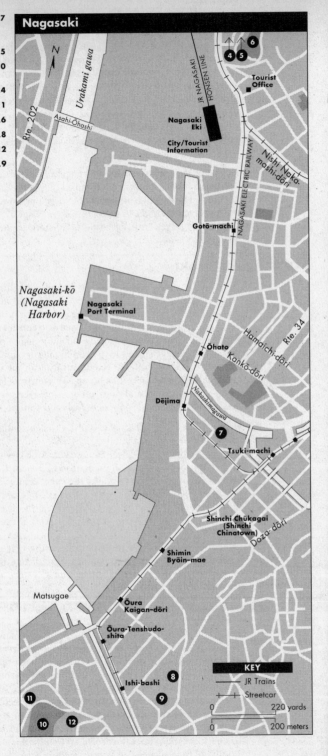

Nagasaki

N

Urakami gawa

JR NAGASAKI HONSEN LINE

Tourist
Office

4 5 6

Asahi-Ōhashi

Rte. 202

Nagasaki
Eki

City/Tourist
Information

Nishi Naka-
mashi-dōri

NAGASAKI ELECTRIC RAILWAY

Gotō-machi

Nagasaki-kō
(Nagasaki
Harbor)

Nagasaki
Port Terminal

Hamaichi-dōri

Rte. 34

Ōhato

Kankō-dōri

Dējima

Nakashimagawa

7

Tsuki-machi

Shinchi Chūkagai
(Shinchi
Chinatown)

Doza-dōri

Shimin
Byōin-mae

Matsugae

Ōura
Kaigan-dōri

Ōura-Tenshudo-
shita

KEY

JR Trains

Ishi-bashi

8

9

Streetcar

11

0   220 yards

10   12

0   200 meters

❻ **Nishi-zaka** (West Slope), a short walk from Nagasaki Eki, is the site of 16th-century Christian martyrdom. At the time missionaries had successfully converted many Japanese to Christianity. Because Japanese leaders feared the potential influence of Christianity, they banned its practice in 1587. Ten years later, 20 Japanese and 6 Europeans were crucified on this hill for refusing to renounce their religious beliefs. A monument was built in 1962 dedicated to the memory of the 26 martyrs, and a small museum documents the history of Christianity in Japan. To get there, exit at the front of the JR station, turn left, and walk along the road next to the train tracks for a few minutes. Turn right on the first major road, and you will be at Nishi-zaka. ☎ 0958/22–6000. ☒ ¥250. ⊙ Daily 9–5.

❼ Five buildings are now open at **Dejima,** the former Dutch East India Company Factory, as the complete restoration of the entire man-made island (now surrounded by land) continues until 2050. This island was built in 1636 to prevent missionary work by the Portuguese and was subsequently used for 220 years by Dutch merchants during the period when foreigners were prohibited from crossing onto Japanese soil by the isolationist government. The limited interaction between the Japanese and the Dutch at this trading post provided the only contact with the outside world until the government abandoned its seclusionist policy in the late 19th century. Visitors may now view exhibitions and films in the restored buildings that give fascinating insight into the lifestyles and trading practices of the Dutchmen here during that time. Dejima is visible from the Dejima and Tsuki-machi streetcar stops. ☒ 6–3 Dejima-machi, ☎ 095/821–7200. ☒ ¥300. ⊙ Daily 9–5.

❽ **Oranda-zaka** (Holland Slope) is a cobblestone incline with 19th-century wooden houses built by Dutch residents. Several of these buildings are open with tea shops or exhibits, including an interesting collection of 19th-century Nagasaki photographs. To get there, follow the street on the southeast side of the Kōshibyō; after about 100 yards, the pleasant walk begins on your left.

❾ The **Kōshibyō** (Chinese Mansion), a Confucian shrine, was built in 1893 by the Chinese residents of Nagasaki. The hall now houses treasures on loan from the Palace Museum, Beijing, which are rotated every two years. Many descriptions are in English, and though the collection is small, it is a worthwhile introduction to the Chinese influence on Nagasaki. Walk southeast from the Ishi-bashi streetcar stop, take the first left turn toward Oranda-zaka, then take the first right, and walk straight ahead to the Chinese wall in front of you. ☎ 0958/24–4022. ☒ ¥525. ⊙ Daily 8:30–5.

★ **❿** **Gloveren** (Glover Gardens) affords panoramic views of Nagasaki and the harbor. The gardens contain Western-style houses built in the late 19th century. The main house is Glover Mansion (1863), former home of Thomas Glover, a British merchant who married a Japanese woman and settled in Nagasaki. Glover introduced the first steam locomotive and established the first mint in Japan. The house remains as it was in Glover's time, and his furniture and possessions are on display. The story for Puccini's opera *Madame Butterfly* is said to have been set here. Escalators going up the slopes toward the Glover Mansion seem out of place, but after a day of walking, they can be a welcome way to ascend the hill. The gardens are distinctly Western in design, providing a sense of what Glover's little colonial sanctuary was like when Japan opened up to the West.

To get to Glover Gardens, board Streetcar 1 from the JR station to the downtown stop Tsuki-machi and transfer (don't forget to collect a transfer ticket) to Streetcar 5. Get off at the Ōura-Tenshudo-shita stop (the second-to-last stop on the line). Take the side street to the right, cross the bridge over the small canal, and then take the second street on your left up the hill. ANA Glover Hill Hotel, a place to keep in mind for an afternoon refreshment, is on the left, and there is an array of souvenir shops to the right. The Ōura Catholic Church faces you as you turn one corner on the hill. ☎ 0958/22–8223. ☞ ¥600. ⊙ Oct.–July, daily 8–6; Aug.–Sept., daily 8–6.

⓫ **Jurokuban-kan** (Building 16) was built in 1860 as accommodations for the American consular staff. The mansion is now a museum that displays Dutch and Portuguese objects related to the history of trade between these countries and Japan. It's outside the exit of Glover Gardens and was built before the street filled with shops. ☎ 0958/27–6111. ☞ ¥400. ⊙ Daily 8:30–6.

⓬ **Ōura Tenshu-dō** (Ōura Catholic Church) is the oldest Gothic-style building in Japan. The church was constructed in 1865 by a French missionary and was dedicated to the memory of the 26 Christians who were crucified in 1597 after Christianity was outlawed. The church has beautiful stained-glass windows. It's a few minutes past Glover Gardens on foot. Look for the stairs to the church on your right. ☎ 0958/23–2628. ☞ ¥250. ⊙ Dec.–Feb., daily 8:30–5; Mar.–Nov., daily 8–6.

Dining and Lodging

$$$$ ✕ **Fūkirō.** Some of the best shippoku in Nagasaki is served in this roomy restaurant with tatami mats and *shōji* (decorative screens). Shippoku combines a series of tasty morsels from Chinese and Japanese cuisine, including sashimi, seasonal vegetable and meat dishes, and fish soup— all presented in an aesthetically pleasing way. The restaurant is housed in an old building with a tiled roof and long wooden beams. To get to Fūkirō, you must first walk up a steep set of stone steps. Lunch courses are ¥5,000 and ¥6,000; dinner courses run from ¥9,000 to ¥17,000. ✉ 5–4 Kaminishi-yama-machi, ☎ 095/822–0253. DC.

$$$$ ✕ **Kagetsu.** This quiet hilltop restaurant is Nagasaki's most prestigious. Dishes are served as *kaiseki* (Kyōto-style set meals), but the menu combines Japanese and Chinese cuisine. The building that houses Kagetsu was visited long ago by the Meiji Restoration leader, Ryōma Sakamoto. According to local legend, Sakamoto, while involved in a fight, slashed his sword into a wooden pillar and left a gash that is still visible in the restaurant today. Lunch runs from ¥5,200 to ¥11,000; dinners are from ¥11,000 to ¥18,000. ✉ 2–1 Maruyama-chō, ☎ 095/822–0191. DC, MC, V.

$$$–$$$$ ✕ **Harbin.** It isn't difficult to imagine residents of the 19th-century Western-style houses of Nagasaki eating at this dark, romantic Continental enclave. Sauces are a bit heavy, and the food on the prix-fixe menu can be slightly overcooked—perhaps the chef is trying to re-create authentically the dishes as they are served in Europe. ✉ 2–27 Kōzen-machi, ☎ 095/822–7443. AE, DC, MC, V.

$ ✕ **Hamakatsu.** Fans of *tonkatsu* (fried pork cutlets) will enjoy the Nagasaki version, which uses ground pork mixed with scallions. Hamakatsu specializes in this local treat. Other dishes are available, but most people stick to tonkatsu, especially because it is one of the lower-priced dishes on the menu. ✉ 1–14 Kajiya-machi, ☎ 095/827–5783. AE, DC, MC, V.

$ ✕ **Kōzanrō.** Within Nagasaki's compact Chinatown district are a dozen or so Chinese restaurants, and the most famous among them is Kōzanrō. Dining is on the second floor, though you'll probably have to wait in the ground-floor lobby for a table. Dishes run the gamut from champon to egg rolls and sweet-and-sour pork. Even though its reputation is grander than its cooking, Kōzanrō is a fun, lively restaurant, especially for groups. ⊠ *12–2 Shinchi-machi,* ☎ *095/821–3735. MC, V.*

$$$$ ⚏ **Hotel New Nagasaki.** Sharing the local spotlight with the Nagasaki
★ Prince Hotel, this hotel has the advantage of being just a two-minute walk from Nagasaki Eki. Standard twin guest rooms, the largest in the city, have enough space for a couple of easy chairs and a table. The lobby lounge is sparklingly fresh, and the French restaurant, Hydrangea, has the airy ambience of a conservatory. On the 13th floor are a Chinese restaurant and the Moonlight Lounge for cocktails; the Steak House serves beef from Gotō Island. Many staff members speak fluent English. ⊠ *14–5 Daikoku-machi, Nagasaki-shi, Nagasaki-ken 850-0057,* ☎ *095/826–8000,* ℻ *095/823–2000. 145 rooms. 8 restaurants, indoor pool, sauna, gym, shops. AE, DC, MC, V.*

$$$$ ⚏ **Nagasaki Prince Hotel.** The interior of the city's grandest—and most expensive—accommodation is the closest imitation of a fine European hotel in Kyūshū. The long, rectangular lobby shimmers with glass, marble, and ponds, but the warm red carpet softens the glare. Sharply dressed staff in suits or uniforms hurry to cater to your every need; concierges are particularly attentive. Guest rooms, decorated in pastels, have natural-color processed-wood furniture. Each room has bedside panels and is equipped with the amenities of a first-class hotel. Restaurants run the gamut from the New York Steak and Seafood dining room to a sushi bar. The Prince is a 10-minute walk from Nagasaki Eki in the opposite direction from downtown, though the streetcar passes by the front entrance and taxis are plentiful. ⊠ *2–26 Takara-machi, Nagasaki-shi, Nagasaki-ken 850-0045,* ☎ *095/821–1111,* ℻ *095/ 823–4309. 183 rooms. 5 restaurants, room service, hair salon, concierge, parking (fee). AE, DC, MC, V.*

$$$$ ⚏ **Sakamoto-ya.** This ryokan, opened in 1895, seems to have changed
★ very little from its founding days. Cedar baths are offered, and the wooden building reflects the simple beauty of Japanese architecture. The inn is very small and has extremely personalized service. The cost of the rooms varies depending on size and location but always includes breakfast and dinner. The restaurant specializes in shippoku. ⊠ *2–13 Kanaya-machi, Nagasaki-shi, Nagasaki-ken 850-0037,* ☎ *095/826–8211,* ℻ *095/ 825–5944. 14 Japanese-style rooms. Restaurant. AE, DC, MC, V. MAP.*

$$$$ ⚏ **Yataro.** On top of a mountain, about 20 minutes by taxi from the center of Nagasaki, this ryokan and its hotel annex have excellent views of Nagasaki. The vista from the shared bath is particularly good. The two meals included are plentiful and presented with great care. In the ryokan, meals are served in your room, and in the hotel annex there's a restaurant. Request a room with a view when you make your reservation. ⊠ *2–1 Kazagashira-machi, Nagasaki-shi, Nagasaki-ken 850-0803,* ☎ *095/822–8166,* ℻ *095/828–1122. 133 Western-style rooms, 56 Japanese-style rooms. Restaurant. AE, DC, MC, V. MAP.*

$$$ ⚏ **Nagasaki Grand Hotel.** This hotel is small and quiet, with a dignified atmosphere. Rooms are compact but pleasantly decorated. Best of all is the outdoor beer garden; there are Japanese and Western restaurants as well. ⊠ *5–3 Manzai-machi, Nagasaki-shi, Nagasaki-ken 850-0033,* ☎ *095/823–1234,* ℻ *095/822–1793. 97 Western-style rooms, 8 Japanese-style rooms. 2 restaurants, bar. AE, DC, MC, V.*

$ ⚏ **Hotel WingPort.** PC rentals and in-room Internet access make the WingPort especially popular with business travelers. Guest quarters are small but pleasant at this hotel two minutes' walk from the station (across the pedestrian bridge on the narrow road past the convenience store). ⊠ *9–2 Daikoku-machi, Nagasaki-shi, Nagasaki-ken 850-0057,* ☎ *095/833– 2800,* ℻ *095/833–2801. 200 rooms. Restaurant. AE, DC, MC, V.*

Shopping

Castella cake has long been the most commonly known Nagasaki product and was popular here when baked goods were still unknown in the rest of Japan. Based on a Dutch cake, the dessert resembles a pound cake with a moist top.

Not far from Dejima, **Hamano-machi** is the major shopping district in downtown Nagasaki. Here you can find traditional crafts, antiques, and restaurants.

Fukusaya (✉ 3–1 Funadaiku-machi, ☎ 0958/21–2938) bakery has been in business since the beginning of the Meiji period (1868). When you say "castella," most people think of this famous shop and its distinctive yellow packaging of the cake. There are two satellite shops in the shopping complex at Nagasaki Eki.

Glass Road 1571 (✉ 2–11 Minami-yamate-machi, ☎ 0958/22–1571) is noted for its Nagasaki glassware, the product of an art that was introduced by the Dutch during the Tokugawa period. The shop is near the Ōura Catholic Church, and items here range from ¥250 to ¥100,000.

Nagasaki A to Z

To research prices, get advice from other travelers, and book travel arrangements, visit www.fodors.com.

AIRPORTS
Nagasaki Kūkō is approximately one hour by bus or car from Nagasaki. JAL, ANA, and JAS fly daily from Haneda Kūkō in Tōkyō to Nagasaki Kūkō (1¾ hours). From Ōsaka the flights are 1 hour, 10 minutes. For airline phone numbers, *see* Air Travel *in* Smart Travel Tips A to Z.

A regular shuttle bus travels between Nagasaki Kūkō and Nagasaki Eki in 55 minutes and costs ¥1,200.

BUS TRAVEL
The Kyūshū Kyūkō Bus Company runs between Fukuoka and Nagasaki (two hours); the bus leaves from Tenjin Bus Center in Fukuoka. Bus service is also available between Nagasaki and Kumamoto.
➤ BUS INFORMATION: **Kyūshū Kyūkō Bus Company** (☎ 092/734–2500). **Nagasaki Ken-ei Bus Terminal** (✉ 3–1 Daikoku-machi, Nagasaki-shi, ☎ 095/826–6221).

EMERGENCIES
➤ CONTACTS: **Ambulance** (☎ 119). **Nagasaki University Hospital** (✉ 7–1 Sakamoto-machi 1-chōme, ☎ 095/847–2111). **Police** (☎ 110).

TOURS
A 60-minute port cruise of Nagasaki Harbor departs at 11:25, 1:45, and 3:15 and costs ¥1,980. Take a streetcar to Ōhato Eki, and then go to the Port Terminal.

Rickshas, once ubiquitous, are now a rare sight in Japan. Prices vary according to the course you take, but the minimum is ¥1,000 per person. A couple of privately run rickshaws hang out on the streets of Chinatown waiting to pick you up. Or you can call in advance to order one.
➤ CONTACTS: **Port Cruise** (☎ 095/824–0088). **Rickshaws** (☎ 095/824–4367).

TRAIN TRAVEL
Take the JR Nagasaki Line Limited Express train from Fukuoka (two hours). To get to Kumamoto from Nagasaki by train, take the Kamome

Line from Nagasaki to Tosu Eki (two hours). From Tosu board the Kagoshima Main Line and get off at Kumamoto (one hour).

➤ Train Information: **Nagasaki Eki** (✉ 1–1 Onoue-machi, Nagasaki-shi, ☎ 095/826–4336).

TRANSPORTATION AROUND NAGASAKI

If you don't care to walk Nagasaki, streetcars are the most convenient way of getting around this hilly city. They can be slow, but they do stop at most major sights, and many stops have signs in English. You can purchase a one-day pass (¥500) for unlimited streetcar travel at tourist offices or at major hotels. Otherwise, you pay ¥100 as you get off the streetcar. If you wish to transfer from one streetcar to another, take a *norikae kippu* (transfer ticket) from the driver of the first streetcar.

VISITOR INFORMATION

The City Tourist Information Center, open daily 9–6 inside the JR station complex, provides English maps and brochures. The city's Web site has detailed information on the Atomic Bomb Museum and Peace Park.

The Nagasaki Prefecture Tourist Office is across the street from the JR station one floor above street level in the bus terminal. To reach it from the station, use the pedestrian bridge. Maps and bus schedules to various areas within the prefecture are available daily from 9 to 5:30. English-speaking staff are happy to help.

➤ Tourist Information: **City Tourist Information Center** (✉ 8–7 Onoue-machi, ☎ 095/823–3631, WEB www.city.nagasaki.nagasaki.jp). **Nagasaki Prefecture Tourist Office** (✉ Nagasaki Kōtsū Sangyō Bldg., 2nd floor, 3–1 Daikoku-machi, ☎ 095/826–9407).

KUMAMOTO

❸ *1½ hrs east of Nagasaki by ferry, 1½ hrs south of Fukuoka by JR Limited Express.*

Kumamoto was one of Japan's major centers of power in the years of the Tokugawa Shogunate (1603–1868). The city's primary historical sights—the castle and the gardens of Suizen-ji Kōen—date from this period and are among the most famous in Japan. Kumamoto may no longer be a major city, but with its broad tree-lined avenues, it *is* attractive.

Exploring Kumamoto

Unlike in many other Japanese cities, there's very little activity around the JR station in Kumamoto. Instead shops, restaurants, and hotels are clustered downtown under the shadow of the castle. The center of town is a broad shopping arcade; small streets branch off it. The area comes alive at night, with neon lights advertising restaurants and bars.

Kumamoto-jō, in the heart of Kumamoto, was first built in 1607 under the auspices of Kiyomasa Katō, the area's daimyō. It's especially famous for unique, massive concave defensive walls, *mushagaeshi,* which are exceedingly difficult for attackers to scale. The castle is also referred to as Ginko-jō, after a giant ginkgo tree that was supposedly planted by Lord Katō. Much of the original castle was destroyed in 1877—after it lay under siege for 57 continuous days by an army from Kagoshima led by Takamori Saigō—and was rebuilt in 1960.

Reconstructed buildings can be bland and boring, but this concrete replica manages to evoke the magnificence of the original. By walking around the expansive grounds, you can get a sense of the grandeur of feudal Japan. Few castles in Japan today—reconstructed or not—have as many as Kumamoto-jō's 49 turrets, 18 turret gates, and 29 castle gates. Further reconstruction work is still in progress. Inside exhibits include samurai armor and palanquins. As you look at the displays, you cannot help but imagine samurai in full regalia, fiercely protecting their lord. From the top floor there is an excellent view of Kumamoto. If time permits, conclude your visit in the lovely **Higo Gardens.** To get to the castle, board Streetcar 2, get off at the Kumamoto-jō-mae stop, and walk up a tree-lined slope. Volunteer guides offer tours in English, or you can take a self-guided, audiocassette tour for ¥300. ☎ *096/352–5900.* ✉ *¥500.* ⊙ *Apr.–Oct., daily 8:30–5:30; Nov.–Mar., daily 8:30–4:30.*

The **Kyū-Hosokawa Gyōbutei** (Hosokawa Mansion) residence was built by Okitaka, who founded the Hosokawa-Gyōbu clan in 1646, and was remodeled repeatedly through the beginning of the 18th century. Now it stands as an excellent, and quite rare, example of a high-ranking samurai residence. English-speaking guides lead a detailed tour, pointing out architectural features such as hallways subtly laid out to thwart attacks on the lord. You can purchase a combined admission ticket (¥640) at the castle and follow the signs out from the main castle entrance through the park to Gyōbutei. ✉ *3–1 Furukyō-machi,* ☎ *096/352–6522.* ✉ *¥300.* ⊙ *Apr.–Oct., daily 8:30–5:30; Nov.–Mar., daily 8:30–4:30.*

Daimyō Kiyomasa Katō built **Honmyō-ji,** a Nichiren temple (Nichiren is a type of Buddhism with its own architectural style). And Katō is buried here, in the tomb at the top of a flight of stairs, so that his spirit may look across at eye level to the *donjon* (stronghold) of his castle, Kumamoto-jō. The temple's small museum contains Katō's personal effects but is of marginal interest. On the hill to the west of town, take a streetcar from JR Kumamoto Eki and change at Kumamoto-jō-mae or take the bus to get here from the Kōtsū Center. ✉ *¥300.* ⊙ *Tues.–Sun. 9–4:30.*

Spring and fall are really the only times worth visiting the **Kumamoto Kenritsu Bijutsukan** (Kumamoto Prefectural Art Museum). During those seasons the famous Hosokawa collection of antiques from the Tokugawa era is on exhibit. Be sure to see the full-scale models of the burial chambers, with Kumamoto's design of painted geometrical shapes. The bijutsukan is west of Kumamoto-jō in a modern redbrick building. ☎ *096/352–2111.* ✉ *¥260.* ⊙ *Tues.–Sun. 9:30–5.*

Suizen-ji Kōen, a 300-year-old garden that is an example of classic Japanese landscape design, was originally created in 1632 by the Hosokawa clan as part of the grounds of their villa. Part of the garden re-creates the 53 stations of the Tōkaidō—the old post road between Edo (Tōkyō) and Kyōto—and its prominent features, Biwa-ko (Lake Biwa) and Fuji-san, with ponds and small artificial mounds. To get to Suizen-ji Kōen, take Streetcar 2 or 3 east from the castle to the Suizen-ji Kōen-mae stop. ✉ *¥400. Mar.–Nov., daily 7:30–6; Dec.–Feb., daily 8:30–5.*

NEED A BREAK?	In Suizen-ji Kōen, stop at the small, **old-fashioned teahouse** by the garden's pond. Here, for ¥600, you can enjoy green tea and a small sweet as you sit on tatami mats and appreciate the exquisite view. It's open daily from 9 to 5.

Dining and Lodging

$$$$ ✕ **Loire.** On the 11th floor of the Kumamoto Castle Hotel, Loire has an excellent view of Kumamoto-jō, which is beautifully lighted at night. The prix-fixe French dinners at the elegant, spacious restaurant typically feature meat or fish entrées and can provide welcome respite from Japanese cuisine. ✉ *4–2 Jōtō-machi,* ☎ *096/326–3311. AE, DC, MC, V.*

$$$$ ✕ **Tagosaku Honten.** This is formal Japanese cuisine at its best. The
★ set-menu meals are not only delicious but are also presented with
exquisite beauty. Seated at low tables, you'll be served several small
courses of fish, meat, tofu, and vegetables. Prices are high, but your
yen are well spent. Tagosaku Honten overlooks a peaceful garden, and
the staff is formal and polite without being stiff. Ask for a table with
a view when you make reservations. ⊠ *1–15–3 Hanazono,* ☎ *096/
353–4171. Reservations essential. AE, DC, MC, V.*

$–$$$ ✕ **Mutsugorō.** Adventurous eaters, take note: this casual dining spot,
on the lower level of the Green Hotel, serves horse meat 40 different
ways, including raw horse-meat sashimi and fried horse meat. You can
also choose from a variety of seafood dishes. For a full meal you will
probably want four or five small plates. ⊠ *12–11 Hanabata-chō,* ☎
096/356–6256. No credit cards. No lunch.

$$$–$$$$ 🏨 **Hotel New Otani Kumamoto.** Weary travelers welcome the sight of
this sleek chain hotel just outside Kumamoto Eki. With just 130 rooms,
this is a small New Otani, which still offers many of the fine services
and amenities as its big-city counterparts. ⊠ *1–13–1 Kasuga, Ku-
mamoto-shi, Kumamoto-ken 860-0047,* ☎ *096/326–1111,* ℻ *096/326–
0800. 130 rooms. 4 restaurants, bar, sauna. AE, DC, MC, V.*

$$–$$$ 🏨 **Ark Hotel Kumamoto.** The modern lobby of this newly built hotel
has wooden floors and a small inner bamboo courtyard flooded with
sunlight. Be sure to request a room with a view, well worth the extra
¥1,000–¥1,500. It's conveniently located across the moat from the cas-
tle and near the shopping and nightlife districts. ⊠ *5–16 Jōtō-machi,
Kumamoto-shi, Kumamoto-ken 862-0846,* ☎ *096/351–2222,* ℻ *096/
326–0909. 300 rooms. 2 restaurants. AE, DC, MC, V.*

$$ 🏨 **Fujie.** On the main street leading directly away from the station is
this serviceable business hotel with Western-style single rooms and Jap-
anese-style doubles. The lobby lounge faces a garden, and the restaurant serves decent Japanese food. Service is personable and friendly.
⊠ *2–2–35 Kasuga, Kumamoto-shi, Kumamoto-ken 860-0047,* ☎
096/353–1101, ℻ *096/322–2671. 44 Western-style and Japanese-
style rooms. Restaurant. AE, DC, MC, V.*

$ 🏨 **Minshuku-ryokan Kajita.** This two-story wooden house has been
made into a friendly inn (part of the Japanese Inn Group). The small
public room has some Western trappings, but the tatami rooms, also
small, are typically Japanese and share a bath. Breakfast (¥700) and
dinner (¥2,000) are optional. To reach the inn, take a city bus from
JR Kumamoto Eki to the Shin-machi bus stop, and then cross the street
and walk two minutes up the side street. ⊠ *1–2–7 Shin-machi, Kumamoto-shi, Kumamoto-ken 860-0004,* ☎ *096/353–1546. 10 Japanese-style rooms with shared bath. AE, V. EP, MAP.*

Shopping

One of Kumamoto's most famous products is *higo zōgan,* a form of
metalwork consisting of black steel inlaid with silver and gold that creates a delicate yet striking pattern. Originally an ornamentation technique used to make the samurai swords, scabbards, and gun stocks of
the Hosokawa clan, it's now used mostly in jewelry and other accessories. The more higo zōgan is worn, the glossier it becomes.

Another popular local product is the *Yamaga dōro,* lanterns of gold
paper. On August 16, as part of the annual Bon Festival, young women
carry these gold lanterns through the streets of Kumamoto.

One of the best places for local handiwork is **Dentō Kōgei-kan** (Kumamoto Traditional Crafts Center; ⊠ *3–35 Chiba-jō,* ☎ *096/324–4930),*
a combination gallery and shop that displays crafts from all over Ku-

mamoto Prefecture. Located in a redbrick building across from the
Akazumon entrance to the castle, it's open Tuesday to Sunday from 9
to 5. At **Shimatōri-Kamitōri Shōtengai** (Shimatōri-Kamitōri Shopping
Arcade), you can find everything from toothpaste to local crafts. It's
near Kumamoto-jō; the Tōrichō-Suji bus and streetcar stops are located
at the midpoint of the arcade. The **Tsuruya** department store (✉ Tetori-
hon-chō-dōri, ☎ 096/356–2111) is a good source for *Yamaga dōro*
(gold paper lanterns) and other local souvenirs.

Kumamoto A to Z

*To research prices, get advice from other travelers, and book travel ar-
rangements, visit www.fodors.com.*

AIRPORTS
Flights on JAL, ANA, and JAS connect Tōkyō's Haneda Kūkō with
Kumamoto Kūkō (1¾ hours). JAL and ANA fly the hour-long route
from Ōsaka Kūkō several times a day. For airline phone numbers, *see*
Air Travel *in* Smart Travel Tips A to Z.

The Kyūshū Sankō bus makes the 55-minute run from the airport to
JR Kumamoto Eki for ¥670.

BUS TRAVEL
The bus from Nagasaki Ken-ei Bus Terminal takes three hours to get
to Kumamoto Kōtsū Center via expressway on the Nagasaki Ken-ei
Bus (¥3,600). A sightseeing bus, Kyūshū Sankō, makes the trip through
Mt. Fugen to Shimabara, then ferries across Ariake Bay to Kumamoto-
kō, then goes directly to Kumamoto Kōtsū Center. This trip takes
about four hours through some of Kyūshū's most beautiful scenery and
costs ¥3,790.
➤ Bus Information: **Kumamoto Kōtsū Center** (✉ 3–10 Sakura-machi,
☎ 096/354–6411). **Kyūshū Sankō Bus** (☎ 096/355–2525). **Nagasaki
Ken-ei Bus** (☎ 095/823–6155).

EMERGENCIES
➤ Contacts: **Ambulance** (☎ 119). **Kumamoto Chūō Hospital** (✉ 96
Tamukae, ☎ 096/370–3111). **Police** (☎ 110).

TRAIN TRAVEL
JR's Limited Express from Hakata stops in Kumamoto (1½ hours) en
route to Kagoshima. From Nagasaki, take JR to Tosu and change to
the train to Kumamoto (three hours total).
➤ Train Information: **Kumamoto Eki** (✉ 3–15–1 Kasuga, ☎ 096/
211–2406).

TRANSPORTATION AROUND KUMAMOTO
The easiest way to get around Kumamoto is by the two streetcar lines
(No. 2 and No. 3) that connect the major areas of the city. When you
board the streetcar, take a ticket. When you get off, you will pay a fare
based on the distance you traveled. A fare chart is posted at the front,
to the left of the driver. Your ticket will bear the number of the zone
in which you boarded the bus; on the chart the fare will flash for each
numbered zone. From the Kumamoto Eki-mae streetcar stop, it's a 10-
minute ride downtown (¥150). One-day travel passes, good for use on
streetcars and municipal *shiei* (buses), are available for ¥500 from the
City Tourist Information Office.

VISITOR INFORMATION
The City Tourist Information Office, open daily 9–5, is inside the JR
Kumamoto Eki complex, to the left as you exit the platform. The

city's Web site offers good descriptions of major sights, as well as maps and transportation information in English.

➤ TOURIST INFORMATION: **City Tourist Information Office** (✉ 3–15–1 Kasuga, ☎ 096/352–3743, 𝚆𝙴𝙱 www.city.kumamoto.kumamoto.jp).

KAGOSHIMA

⑭ *3 hrs south of Kumamoto, 4 hrs south of Fukuoka by JR.*

The scenic train ride south from Kumamoto or Fukuoka to Kagoshima passes mountains to the west and sea to the east. Kagoshima's climate gives it a tropical, relaxed feeling. This southernmost city is not so much a destination in itself as it is a jumping-off point to the surrounding countryside, Okinawa, and neighboring islands. Looking out across the Kinkō Bay, Kagoshima faces the active volcano Sakurajima, which has spewed smoke and ash almost continuously since a large explosion in 1955. A visit to the hot-sand spas of Ibusuki or a hike to see giant camphor trees on Yakushima, to the south, will take you through gorgeous landscapes on roads less traveled.

Tenmonkan-dōri, the downtown shopping-arcade area, is five minutes on foot from JR Nishi-Kagoshima Eki.

Across Kinkō Bay from Kagoshima is the smoking volcanic cone of **Sakurajima.** You must take a boat to the island (which is actually a peninsula since lava from an eruption in 1914 connected it with the mainland).

A **24-hour ferry** operates between Kagoshima Port and Sakurajima Port. Ferries leave every 10–15 minutes, with fewer connections after 10 PM. The ride costs ¥150 each way and lasts 15 minutes. ✉ *Kagoshima Port: 4–1 Shinmachi, Honkō,* ☎ *099/223–7271;* ✉ *Sakurajima Port: 61–4 Yokoyama, Sakurajima-chō,* ☎ *099/293–2525.*

Yunohira Tozan Kankō Bus offers tours to the major sights at Sakurajima: Yunohira Tenbōjō (Yunohira Observatory), where you can see the volcano; the lava outcrops; the Sakurajima Visitor Center; and Sakurajima Pottery. When you arrive at Sakurajima Port, go to the first floor of the ferry terminal and follow signs (in English) for Yunohira Tozan Kankō Bus. Tours (¥1,000) depart twice daily and last 90 minutes. ✉ *Sakurajima Port,* ☎ *0992/93–2525.*

Dining and Lodging

$–$$$ ✕ **Edokko.** Settle in at the counter or at a table with tatami seating at this moderately priced but excellent sushi bar. The hospitable owner will put you at ease in no time. To get to Edokko, on downtown Tenmonkan-dōri, take the first right off Yubudo (the wide shopping-arcade street); it's the last restaurant on your left. ✉ *4–1 Sennichi-chō,* ☎ *099/225–1890. No credit cards.*

$$$ 𝕋 **Furusato Kankō Hotel.** The rotemburo of this hotel on Sakurajima
★ affords a superb view of the Pacific Ocean. Bathers at the open-air thermal pool wear *yukata* (cotton kimono) to show respect to the dragon god living inside the large, old tree at the back of the bath. If you prefer a swim, head to the small pool on the beach. A stay here can completely relax you with a large indoor onsen, a meditation room, and two meals included in the room rate. All rooms have a view of the water; five have miniature gardens. A free shuttle runs every half hour between the hotel and the Sakurajima ferry port. ✉ *1076–1 Furusato-chō, Kagoshima-shi, Kagoshima-ken 891-1592,* ☎ *099/221–3111,* 𝙵𝙰𝚇 *099/221–2345. 40 Japanese-style rooms. Restaurant, bar, pool, hot springs. AE, DC, MC, V. MAP.*

$$ ☑ **Urban Port Hotel.** Though rooms are small and functional, the modern Urban Port is still a step up from the typical Japanese business hotel. Bathrooms are equipped with telephones and hair dryers. It's a 10-minute walk from both Kagoshima-kō and the streetcar to Tenmonkan-dōri. ☒ *15–1 Ogawa-chō, Kagoshima-shi, Kagoshima-ken 892-0817,* ☎ *099/239–4111,* FAX *099/239–4112. 102 rooms. Restaurant, pool, massage, health club. AE, MC, V.*

Kagoshima A to Z

To research prices, get advice from other travelers, and book travel arrangements, visit www.fodors.com.

AIRPORTS
JAL, JAS, and ANA fly daily connections between Tōkyō's Haneda Kūkō and Kagoshima Kūkō (1¼ hours). From Ōsaka the flight takes 1 hour and 10 minutes. For airline phone numbers, *see* Air Travel *in* Smart Travel Tips A to Z.

The Airport Limousine picks up passengers every 10 minutes (until 9 PM) at bus stop No. 2 outside the airport. The 55-minute trip to Nishi-Kagoshima Eki costs ¥1,150.
➤ AIRPORT INFORMATION: **Airport Limousine** (☎ 099/256–2151).

BUS TRAVEL
Frequent buses make the four-hour trip from Fukuoka (departing Hakata Kōtsū Bus Center and Tenjin Bus Center) to Nishi-Kagoshima Eki. Sankō buses leave from Kumamoto Kōtsū Center and take three hours to get to Kagoshima.
➤ BUS INFORMATION: **Kōsoku Bus Center** (☒ 11–5 Chūo-chō, ☎ 092/734–2727). **Sankō buses** (☎ 096/355–2525).

EMERGENCIES
➤ CONTACTS: **Ambulance** (☎ 119). **Kagoshima City Hospital** (☒ 20–17 Kajiya-chō, ☎ 099/224–2101). **Police** (☎ 110).

TRAIN TRAVEL
The JR Kagoshima Line Limited Express arrives at Nishi-Kagoshima Eki from Hakata Station in Fukuoka to Nishi-Kagoshima Eki (3¼ hours) and from Kumamoto (2½ hours).
➤ TRAIN INFORMATION: **Nishi-Kagoshima Eki** (☒ 1–1 Chūo-chō, ☎ 099/256–1585).

TRANSPORTATION AROUND KAGOSHIMA
The easiest way to get around Kagoshima is by streetcar. Two streetcar lines cover the city, and ¥160 takes you any distance. A one-day travel pass for ¥600 is good for unlimited rides on streetcars and municipal buses. You can buy the pass at the Nishi-Kagoshima Eki Tourist Office or on the bus.

VISITOR INFORMATION
The Nishi-Kagoshima Eki Tourist Office, open daily 8:30–6, is a short walk north of the station's east exit. There's always at least one English-speaking person on hand to help you make hotel reservations. The office's excellent map (in English) will help you find your way to historic sites and tourist facilities and provide information about public transportation. Here you can buy a pass (¥600) good for admission to 330-year-old Iso Garden and the adjacent Satsuma Glass Factory.
➤ TOURIST INFORMATION: **Nishi-Kagoshima Eki Tourist Office** (☒ 1–1 Chūo-machi, ☎ 099/253–2500).

ASO-SAN

★ ⑮ *3½ hrs northeast of Kagoshima by JR; 1 hr east of Kumamoto by JR, then 40 mins by bus.*

The road to Aso-san (Mt. Aso) passes through the splendor of rural Kyūshū. As you look upon farmers bent over rice fields and at bamboo groves, you will get a sense of the relationship that people of this region have with the land. That serene image quickly fades when you arrive at the Mt. Aso volcano, where the bare force of Pacific Rim geology smokes and rumbles.

Mt. Aso is in fact a series of five volcanic peaks, one of which, Nakadake, is still active. The five peaks, along with lakes and fields at its base, form a beautiful national park. You can take in Mt. Aso either on a day trip from Kumamoto or as a stop on the way from Kumamoto to Beppu or Yufuin. If you want to spend more time in the park, you can stay in one of the many mountain pensions or ryokan on the south side of Mt. Aso.

Exploring Aso-san

The one active volcano, **Nakadake,** is a fine reason to come to Aso-san National Park. From the inside of the crater, which is 1,968 ft across and 525 ft deep, you hear the rumbling of the volcano and see billowing smoke. Nakadake can be reached from Asosanjō Eki. The cable car leads you to the top of the crater in four minutes and costs ¥410 one-way, weather and volcano conditions permitting. You can either descend the same way or walk down along a path that leads you back to the cable car station in about 20 minutes. Sometimes the volcano is too dangerous to view up close—so be sure to check in Kumamoto or Beppu before you make this excursion.

From the Kusasenri parking and rest area you can take one of several hiking trails that start and finish here. The easiest loop, 5½ km (3½ mi) around the base of Kijimadake crater, takes only one hour, and the views of the surrounding peaks and fields are breathtaking. More ambitious hikers can choose from several trails of various lengths and intensities in the area. Be sure to pick up the *Aso Trekking Route Map* and inquire about current hiking conditions at the information center in JR Aso Eki or at Kusasenri.

If you do reach Aso-san on a day when the Nakadake crater is too active to ascend, stop by the **Aso Kazan Hakubutsukan** (Aso Volcano Museum) at the Kusasenri parking and rest area, where you can view live footage of the volcanic activity on a monitor along with exhibits about Mt. Aso. ⊠ *Kusasenri-ga-hama,* ☎ *0967/34–2111.* 🎫 *¥840.* ☻ *Daily 9–5.*

OFF THE BEATEN PATH
KUROKAWA ONSEN – Nestled in the mountains between Mt. Aso and Yufuin in the Aso-Kujū National Park is this unspoiled village that attracts those seeking a quiet, natural onsen retreat. It's not easy to get to Kurokawa, but those who make the effort are rewarded by the sound of the rushing stream and the view of the surrounding mountains as you relax outdoors in a rotemburo. Book well in advance to stay the night, or buy a pass (¥1,200) for entrance to three baths of your choice in any of the rustic inns.

Lodging

$$$$ 🏨 **Aso Prince Hotel.** Tucked away at the base of Nakadake, this hotel in the Prince chain is stunning. Half of its 180 rooms overlook two uncrowded golf courses designed by Arnold Palmer, and the long drive-

way running through the golf course from the road to the hotel is quite impressive. The public bath is tapped from a mineral source, and a stay here will take you to heights of luxury. ⊠ *Akamizu, Komezuka Onsen, Aso-chō, Aso-gun, Kumamoto-ken 869-2232,* ☎ *0967/35–2111,* FAX *0967/35–1124. 180 rooms. Restaurant, bar, massage, mineral baths, 2 golf courses, 6 tennis courts; shops. AE, DC, MC, V.*

$$$–$$$$ 🏯 **Yamaguchi Ryokan.** Deep in the forest of Mt. Aso, at Tarutama, this rustic 113-year-old ryokan is a 15-minute taxi ride from Shimoda Eki. Soak in any of the three indoor spas, or cross the narrow red bridge to the rotemburo situated under a waterfall cascading from the cliffs. Two meals are included, and dinner is served in your Japanese-style room. To get here, take the Minami Aso Tetsudō Line (change from the Hōhi Line at Tateno). ⊠ *Kawayō, Chōyō-son, Aso-gun, Kumamoto-ken 860-1404,* ☎ *0967/67–0006,* FAX *0967/67–1694. 33 Japanese-style rooms, 5 with bath. Mineral bath, spa. AE, DC, MC, V. MAP.*

$$ 🏯 **Pension Okanoie.** This small retreat is one of six in the Pension Nombiri Village. The rooms are simple but comfortable, and the owner is friendly and happy to pick guests up at the station or drive them to the cable car. The Western-style rooms come with small bath-showers, and there are two larger (family-size) mineral baths which can be shared (when you go in, put out an occupied sign so no one else will enter). Rates are for bed and breakfast, but arrange to have the nice Western-style dinner and spend a quiet evening working on the locally crafted wooden puzzles while chatting with the owner. It's located 10 minutes from Tateno Eki (on the JR Hōhi Line). ⊠ *4732–10 Kawayō, Chōyō-son, Aso-gun, Kumamoto-ken 869-1404,* ☎ *0967/67–1818,* FAX *0967/67–2156,* WEB *www.asopension.com/okanoie. 10 rooms. Japanese baths. No credit cards. CP.*

Aso-san A to Z

To research prices, get advice from other travelers, and book travel arrangements, visit www.fodors.com.

BUS TRAVEL

Sankō Buses leaving from the Kumamoto Kōtsū bus terminal go directly to the Aso Nishi cable car station (1½ hours).
➤ BUS INFORMATION: **Aso-san cable car** (⊠ Furubōchū, Aso-chō, ☎ 0967/34–0411). **Sankō Buses** (☎ 096/355–25259).

TRAIN TRAVEL

The JR Hōhi Line runs between Kumamoto Eki and Aso Eki (56 minutes). From Aso Eki to Beppu there are three JR express trains daily. From JR Aso Eki, you must board a bus (40 minutes; ¥620) to get to the Aso Nishi cable car station at Asosanjō. It's better to begin your trip well before noon, because the last buses for the cable car station leave mid-afternoon.
➤ TRAIN INFORMATION: **JR Aso Eki** (⊠ Kurokawa, Aso-chō, ☎ 0967/34–0101).

VISITOR INFORMATION

➤ CONTACT: **Aso Information Center** (⊠ JR Aso Eki, ☎ 0967/34–0751).

BEPPU AND YUFUIN

Threading your way through the Aso and Kujū mountain ranges on the Yamanami Highway, you pass lush and gentle mountain scenery on the route from Aso to Yufuin and Beppu. For centuries Beppu's onsen have been used as health curatives by the Japanese. Ancient stories tell of residents of the island of Shikoku crossing the ocean for the medicinal effects. In the early 1900s the variety of hot mineral springs, especially in the Kannawa area, drew those who came for extended periods of time seeking health in the mineral springs. With the sea in the foreground and the mountains to the rear, Beppu is still a favorite vacation spot for Japanese today. Unfortunately, garish popular culture thrives; Beppu's neon signs, amusement centers, *pachinko* (gambling done on upright, pinball-like machines) halls, and souvenir shops make the town unappealing at first glance.

Yufuin, developed more recently, has suffered less than Beppu from the pitfalls of modern tourism. It has succeeded in creating a quieter, more tasteful getaway. An hour's bus or train ride inland from Beppu, Yufuin sits on a plateau at 1,400 ft above sea level. The air is intoxicatingly fresh as you browse through antiques shops and art galleries. You will find onsen here, as well as traditional and modern arts and crafts.

Beppu

⑯ *2 hrs northeast of Aso-san by JR; 1 hr, 50 mins southeast of Fukuoka; 5 hrs, 50 mins northeast of Kagoshima.*

Beppu is of little interest, and sometimes even offensive, to many visitors from the West. Over-the-top hot-springs resorts and entertainment complexes have made the town a crowded, overdeveloped tour-group destination for the Japanese and their neighbors. Nonetheless, Beppu can be a multilayered experience for the tourist willing either to embrace—or to venture beyond—the neon palaces. Foray into old Beppu by relaxing in a hot-sand bath in Takegawara Onsen, a 100-year-old public bath near the city center; by dining at a local izakaya; and by spending the night at a friendly *minshuku* (a private home that takes in guests) with its own spa. In such a welcoming atmosphere you may not even notice the garish pachinko halls as you walk to the station the next morning.

To be a part of traditional Japanese tourism, stay at a minshuku or ryokan in **Kannawa,** a neighborhood in northern Beppu, 30 minutes by bus from Beppu Eki. Buses for Kannawa leave five to six times per hour from the JR station (¥330).

In Kannawa visit **Jigoku Meguri** (Eight Hells; ☎ 0977/66–1577) for eight types of natural springs. The most distinctive are Bōzu Jigoku (Monk's Hell), with bubbling mud springs; Umi Jigoku (Sea Hell), with water the color of the ocean; Chi-no-ike Jigoku (Blood Pond Hell), a boiling spring with gurgling red water; and the Tatsumaki Jigoku (Cyclone Hell), a geyser that erupts every 25 minutes. Each spring charges ¥400 for admission; a combined ticket (¥2,000) will admit you to all except Bōzu Jigoku. After your tour of the springs, take a bath, and then join fellow tourists in their yukata and *geta* (wooden sandals) for an evening stroll. Pick up a map of the Hells at Beppu Station before you board the bus for Kannawa so you know where to head when you get off. Six of the eight Hells are located within easy walking distance of each other, but you might want to take another bus to the Blood Pond Hell and the Cyclone Hell.

☾ A day at **Suginoi Palace** is an immersion course in commercial Japanese tourism. Its two large hot springs are named Dream Bath and Flower Bath, enormous multibath rooms full of plants, trees, and garish decorations. Outside the baths are food stalls, arcade games, and souvenir shops. For separate admission you can entertain yourself in "zones" containing water slides and wave pools, a batting cage, virtual golf, arcades, and a synthetic ice rink. The amusement complex is next to the Suginoi Hotel. ⊠ *1 Kankai-ji,* ☎ *0977/24–1160.* ⊡ *¥2,000.* ☉ *Daily 9 AM–11 PM.*

Approximately 1,700 monkeys roam free at **Takasaki-yama Shizen Dōbutsuen** (Mt. Takasaki Monkey Park) in three distinct packs. Once a menace to local farmers, the monkeys are now fed several times daily in the park area where they run around among the throngs of tourists. Buses headed for Ōita and stopping at Takasaki-yama leave frequently from Beppu Station or Kitahama, and it takes about 15 minutes. ⊠ *3098– 1 Kanzaki, Oita-shi,* ☎ *097/532–5010.* ⊡ *¥500.* ☉ *Daily 8:30–5.*

Baths

Hyōtan Onsen has indoor and outdoor baths with waterfalls, stone pools, and sand. It's across the road from Kamenoi Bus Station in Kannawa. ⊠ *159–2 Kannawa,* ☎ *0977/66–0527.* ⊡ *¥700.* ☉ *Daily 8 AM–9 PM.*

Takegawara Onsen, an impressive wooden structure, was built in 1880. It has mineral springs and a hot-sand bath. Bring a towel to cover yourself as you are buried up to your neck in the therapeutic sand. ⊠ *16–23 Moto-machi,* ☎ *0977/23–1585.* ⊡ *Sand bath ¥710, mineral springs ¥100.* ☉ *Daily 8 AM–9:30 PM.*

Dining and Lodging

$–$$$ ✕ **Fugumatsu.** A small, popular restaurant, with a simple, Japanese-style interior, Fugumatsu has counters, tables, and private rooms. Its specialty is a local favorite, fugu. In summer the restaurant also serves a type of *karei* (flatfish) that can be caught only in Beppu Bay. Multi-course meals start at ¥7,000. Upon request you can have less or more expensive food; the restaurant will adjust to your budget. It's one block north of the Tokiwa department store and one block from the bay. ⊠ *3–6–14 Kitahama,* ☎ *0977/21–1717. No credit cards.*

$ ✕ **Jin.** For an inexpensive evening of beer, sake, and izakaya cuisine that includes yakitori and grilled local seafood, Jin is popular with both Japanese and foreign visitors. You sit either at wooden tables or at the bar looking over displays of fish on crushed ice. The mood is jovial, and the people are friendly. Jin is easy to find: walk from the JR station on the right side of Eki-mae-dōri and toward the bay; it's just before the T-junction and across from the Tokiwa department store. ⊠ *1–15–7 Eki-mae-dōri,* ☎ *0977/21–1768. No credit cards.*

$$$$ 🏨 **Suginoi Hotel.** This is more than a hotel: it's a miniresort, and the most famous place in Beppu. Once you check in, you may not feel any need to leave the grounds. Suginoi sits on a hill with a panoramic view of the city and the ocean, connected to the Suginoi Palace. Guests tend to wander the grounds and attend meals in their yukata. Rooms range from simple, Western-style twins to large, combination Japanese-style/Western-style rooms. Palace entrance is free for hotel guests. ⊠ *1 Kankai-ji, Beppu-shi, Ōita-ken 874–0822,* ☎ *0977/24–1141,* FAX *0977/ 21–0010. 111 Western-style rooms, 34 Japanese-style rooms, 403 combination rooms. 4 restaurants, 3 bars, 2 cafés, hair salon, hot springs, shops. AE, DC, MC, V.*

$ 🏨 **Nogamihonkan Ryokan.** You know this Japanese-style inn is mod-ern since it offers free, 24-hour Internet access for guests to check e-mail or browse the Web. Located in the downtown shopping area in front of Beppu Station near Takegawara Onsen, it's a convenient stop-ping place for all transport connections. Rooms are Japanese-style, with dinner served in your room and breakfast served in the communal din-ing room. Full-course dinner (¥4,000), tempura dinner (¥2,500), and Japanese or Western-style breakfast (¥1,000) are available. ⊠ *1–12– 1 Kitahama, Beppu-shi, Ōita-ken 874-0920,* ☎ *0977/22–1334,* FAX *0977/ 22–1336. 26 rooms, 19 with bath. Mineral baths. MC, V. EP, MAP.*

$ ⊞ **Sakaeya.** This minshuku, a rare gem in a beautiful old wooden build-
★ ing, has surprisingly low rates. Arrange to have your meals included
and watch as food is prepared in the backyard oven, which is heated
by the hot springs. The only hot-spring bath is public, but as you relax
with your fellow guests, you have a sense that this is how the Japanese
have been enjoying the wonders of hot springs for centuries. Reserve
ahead, and be sure to ask for the minshuku accommodations, since there
is a pricey ryokan as well. To reach the inn, take any bus for Kannawa
from Beppu Station (a 30-minute ride), and get off at Kamenoi Bus Center. ⊠ *Ido 2 kumi, Ida, Kannawa, Beppu-shi, Ōita-ken 874-0046,* ☎
0977/66–6234, ℻ *0977/66–6235. 10 Japanese-style rooms with shared
bath. Hot springs. No credit cards. EP, MAP.*

Yufuin

★ ⑰ *70 mins by bus or 1 hr by JR west of Beppu, 1 hr west of Ōita by JR,
2 hrs southeast of Fukuoka by JR.*

Yufuin, a hot springs village in the shadow of majestic Yufudake, has
become the resort of choice for those seeking an unspoiled alternative
to Beppu. Quiet clusters of museums and galleries in wooded settings
are interspersed with shops selling local crafts and foods and small,
Japanese country-style inns. Book lodgings early during peak seasons,
as people throng to Yufuin in the fall and during the music and film
festivals held in late July and August.

To enjoy the best of Yufuin in a day, start by picking up an English map
at the information counter in Yufuin Eki and take a five-minute taxi
ride to the Kūsō-no-Mori cluster of art galleries tucked into the mountainside; then go down the hill to Kinrinko, stopping in at Sendō for a
dip in its rotemburo. From here you can take the secluded path behind
Tamanoyu Ryokan into the woods dotted with galleries and museums,
then walk toward the station along the river beside meadows and rice
fields. Or follow the tourists and return to the station as you browse
through country-style crafts and gift shops on the main street.

Watakushi Bijutsukan, a small gallery in the Kūsō-no-Mori area, exhibits
whimsical pieces ranging from wood-block prints to pottery. On the left
as you enter are innovatively designed and brightly colored objects made
by mentally handicapped artists. Most objects on display are for sale.
⊠ *1860–8 Kawakami,* ☎ *0977/84–2961.* ☞ *¥300.* ☉ *Daily 9–6.*

On most days an artist is painting at the large wooden table in the center of the **Yutaka Isozaki Gallery.** Small cards with illustrations such
as persimmons and wildflowers and inspirational messages (¥300–
¥2,000) are popular souvenirs. In the rear of the gallery are crafts including clothing made from antique kimonos. Sift through the piles of
antique cotton and silk textiles and kimonos in **Itoguruma,** the little
shop to the right of the entrance, for a unique memento of old Japan.
⊠ *1266–21 Kawakami,* ☎ *0977/85–4750.* ☞ *Free.* ☉ *Daily 9–6.*

Among the galleries and museums near Kinrinko, **Sueda Bijutsukan**
(Sueda Art Museum) exhibits modern sculpture. ⊠ *Aza Tsue, Kawakami,
Yufuin-machi,* ☎ *0977/85–3572.* ☞ *¥700.* ☉ *Daily 9–6.*

At the **Yufuin Mingei Mura** (Yufuin Folk Crafts Museum) local artisans turn out traditional crafts such as blown glass, toys, and steel blades.
⊠ *1542–1 Kawakami, Yufuin-machi,* ☎ *0977/85–2288.* ☞ *¥650.* ☉
Daily 8:30–5:30.

NEED A **Tenjōsajiki Coffeeshop** (⊠ 2633-1 Kawakami, ☎ 0977/85–2866),
BREAK? open 9 AM to 7 PM in the Kamenoi Bessō Ryokan complex, makes a
sumptuous wild strawberry ice cream. At night, the establishment be-

comes a bar. **Tearoom Nicol** (⊠ Kawakami Yufuin-chō, ☎ 0977/84–2158), at Tamanoyu Ryokan, serves a delicious, homemade apple pie in the daytime and alcohol at night.

Dining and Lodging

$$$–$$$$ ✕ **Budōya.** The restaurant inside Tamanoyu Ryokan, Budōya has an interior of tatami, wooden beams, and bamboo-mat ceiling and serves regional dishes. For lunch, try the *Amiyaki* course, with charcoal-grilled beef, seasonal vegetables, and homemade *kabosu* (citrus sherbet). Another good choice is *Ki*, a course with fresh tofu and vegetable dishes, soup, and sherbet. Chopstick rests made of seasonal flowers and leaves add an innovative touch to an already delightful experience. ⊠ *Kawakami Yufuin-chō,* ☎ *0977/84–4918. AE, DC, MC, V.*

$$$–$$$$ ✕ **Kitayama.** This restored, 120-year-old former *minka* (village house)
★   serves traditional Japanese kaiseki ryōri on dinnerware dating from the late Edo period. One of the dining rooms has a painted paper ceiling. To accompany regional delicacies in summer, try the locally produced *Daiginjyōshu* (high-grade sake), chilled on a bed of crushed ice in an antique ceramic dish. Coffee and dessert are served in the late-19th-century, Western-style room upstairs, among paintings (note the original Chagall) and antiques. To get here, turn left onto Hananoki-dōri, the first tiled street from the station. ⊠ *Hananoki-dōri Yufuin-chō,* ☎ *0977/84–5576. Reservations essential. No credit cards.*

$$$$ 🛏 **Yufu Ryōchiku.** In the winter, warm yourself by the fire of the *irori* (sunken hearth) in the lobby of this inn built in 1925. The small hot-spring baths (the only baths) here are "family-style," meaning you may reserve one for private use with the members of your party. Breakfast and dinner are included and are served in your room. It's located among the shops and galleries near Kinrinko. ⊠ *1097–1 Kawakami, Yufuin-chō Ōita-gun, Ōita-ken 879-5102,* ☎ *0977/85–2526,* 𝖥𝖠𝖷 *0977/ 85–4466. 8 Japanese-style rooms without bath. Hot springs (2 outdoor, 2 indoor). MC, V. MAP.*

$$ 🛏 **Pension Momotaro.** The owners of this modern pension go out of their way to make you feel at home—they'll even take you to the station when you depart. Momotaro has three thermal baths, one of which is a rotemburo where you can view the mountains while you soak. Both Western-style and Japanese-style rooms are available in the main building, and Japanese-style rooms occupy four A-frame chalets. Rates include breakfast; add ¥2,000 per person for dinner. ⊠ *1839– 1 Kawakami, Yufuin-chō, Ōita-gun, Ōita-ken 879-5102,* ☎ *0977/ 85–2187,* 𝖥𝖠𝖷 *0977/85–4002. 6 Western-style rooms, 3 Japanese-style rooms, 4 chalets. Dining room, hot springs. No credit cards. BP, MAP.*

$$ 🛏 **Sendō.** Walk through the trees along a path laid with straw matting and over a small pond to reach the entrance to this rustic inn, hidden away behind Kamenoi Bessō. The exterior is quaintly Japanese, but simple Western-style bedrooms inside can be a welcome sight for travelers. Arrange to eat breakfast and dinner in the cozy dining room (¥2,000). ⊠ *2634–1 Kawakami, Yufuin-chō, Ōita-gun, Ōita-ken 879-5102,* ☎ *0977/84–4294,* 𝖥𝖠𝖷 *0977/84–4143. 9 Western-style rooms, 4 Japanese-style rooms with shared bath, 2 cottages. Dining room, hot springs. AE, MC, V. EP, MAP.*

Beppu and Yufuin A to Z

To research prices, get advice from other travelers, and book travel arrangements, visit www.fodors.com.

AIRPORTS

The closest airport to Beppu and Yufuin is Ōita Kūkō, which is served by JAL, ANA, and JAS domestic flights from Tōkyō's Haneda Kūkō

(1½ hours) and from Ōsaka Kūkō (1 hour). For airline phone numbers, *see* Air Travel *in* Smart Travel Tips A to Z.

Ōita Kōtsu Bus Company runs the hourly airport shuttle to the Kitahama bus stop in Beppu. The trip takes about 45 minutes and costs ¥1,450. Reservations are not required. From Beppu, take a local bus or JR to Yufuin.

➤ AIRPORT INFORMATION: **Ōita Kōtsu Bus Company** (☎ 097/534–7455). **Ōita Kūkō** (✉ 3600 Itohara, Musashi-machi, Higashi Kunisaki-gun, ☎ 0978/67–1174).

BOAT AND FERRY TRAVEL

Three ferries connect Beppu with Ōsaka on the Kansai Kisen Line. These overnight ferries leave in the early evening. The direct ferry for Ōsaka departs Beppu at 7 PM and arrives at 6:20 AM (second class ¥7,400). Reservations are necessary for first class (from ¥14,600 to ¥22,900 for a deluxe room).

➤ BOAT AND FERRY INFORMATION: **Kansai Kisen Line** (☎ 0977/22–1311 in Beppu; 06/6572–5181 in Ōsaka).

BUS TRAVEL

The Kyūshū Ōdan Teiki Kankō Bus, *Kujūgō,* travels between Kumamoto and Beppu on the Trans-Kyūshū Highway, stopping in Yufuin in minutes. A one-way fare from Kumamoto to Yufuin is ¥3,450; to Beppu, ¥3,850. Regular bus service between Yufuin and Beppu costs ¥980.

City buses can take you to most places of interest in Beppu—destinations are written in English. The main terminal, Kitahama Bus Station, is down the road from JR Beppu Eki. Ask at the Foreign Tourist Information Service for a one-day pass, a good buy at ¥900. It's best to walk or take a taxi from the bus station in Yufuin to the sights, as local bus service does not travel through the village.

➤ BUS INFORMATION: **Kitahama Bus Station** (✉ 2–10–4 Kitahama, ☎ 0977/23–0141). **Kyūshū Ōdan Teiki Kankō Bus** (☎ 096/355–2525). **Yufuin Bus Terminal** (✉ 3–1 Kawakita, ☎ 0977/85–3048).

EMERGENCIES

➤ CONTACTS: **Ambulance** (☎ 119). **Nakamura Hospital** (✉ 8–24 Akiba-chō, Beppu-shi, ☎ 0977/23–3121). **Police** (☎ 110).

TAXIS

Because most sights in Beppu are relatively close to one another—but too far to walk—this is one of the few places in Japan where it may be worthwhile simply to hop in a taxi. Fares range from ¥1,000 to ¥3,000. Hiring a taxi for two hours to visit the major thermal pools would run approximately ¥8,000. Note, however, that most taxi drivers in the area don't speak English.

TOURS

Kamenoi Bus runs several sightseeing tours that leave from Beppu Eki and Kitahama Bus Station. There are eight tours of the Eight Hells daily, which take about 2½ hours each and cost ¥3,850 including entrance fees. No English-speaking guides are available, but the sights are self-explanatory.

➤ CONTACT: **Kamenoi Bus** (☎ 0977/23–5170).

TRAIN TRAVEL

The JR Hōhi Main Line travels between Kumamoto and Beppu (three hours), stopping at Aso-san. The JR Nichirin Limited Express runs more than 10 times daily (two hours) between Beppu and Hakata Eki in

Fukuoka. JR Yufugō and Yufuin-no-Mori express trains run six times daily between Hakata and Yufuin, but only Yufugō trains are included in the JR rail pass.

➤ Train Information: **Beppu Eki** (✉ 12–13 Ekimae, ☎ 0977/22–0585). **Yufuin Eki** (✉ 8–2 Kawakita, ☎ 0977/84–2021).

VISITOR INFORMATION

The Beppu Foreign Tourist Information Service is in Beppu Eki. Open Monday to Saturday 9 to 5, it has many useful maps and brochures in English. A well-staffed office of enthusiastic volunteers can help with sightseeing information, local and long-distance transportation information, and reservations for hotels and restaurants. A list of accommodations that welcome non-Japanese speaking tourists is available.

The Yufuin Tourist Information Office at Yufuin Eki is open daily 9–5 and can make hotel reservations for you. More detailed information can be obtained at the main office about five minutes from the station. Bicycles can be rented from either office.

➤ Tourist Information: **Beppu Foreign Tourist Information Service** (✉ Beppu Eki, ☎ 0977/23–1119, FAX 0977/21–6220, WEB www.oitaweb.ne.jp/hp/ftis). **Yufuin Tourist Information Office** (main office: ✉ 2863 Kawakami, ☎ 0977/85–4464; ✉ Yufuin Eki, ☎ 0977/84–4464).

12 TŌHOKU

Tōhoku is, undeservedly, one of Japan's least-visited areas. Almost a world apart from the Japan of the Tōkyō–Ōsaka corridor, Tōhoku is one of the best places to take in rural Japan, high-country plateaus and volcanic lakes, and mountainside temples. Summer here is refreshingly cool, and the sensational August festivals held in the cities of Akita, Aomori, Hirosaki, and Sendai provide a convenient excuse for a trip to the north.

By James M.
Vardaman Jr.

T IS A SHAME that so few foreign travelers venture farther above Tōkyō than the monument town of Nikkō, because Tōhoku, the name given to the six prefectures of northern Honshū, has an appealing combination of country charm, coastal and mountain scenery, old villages, and revered temples. For a long time the area was known as Michinoku—the "end of the road" or "backcountry"—and it retains the spirit of Bashō's poetic travel journal, *Narrow Road to the North*. Many Japanese still hold that image of remote rusticity, with the result that Tōhoku is one of the least-visited areas in modern Japan.

In a nation where politeness is paramount, the people in Tōhoku are friendlier than their more urbanized fellow Nihon-jin. With the exception of Sendai, Tōhoku's cities are small, and the fast pace of city life is foreign to their residents. Bullet train lines extend only halfway into the region, and most of the people of Tōhoku live their lives with less of the postmodern intensity than is the norm in the southern two-thirds of Honshū.

Tōhoku's six largest cities are prefectural capitals, and they have the amenities of any international community. With the exception of Sendai, these cities don't have many sights to explore. In hopes of attracting tourists, they have built modern complexes that serve as giant souvenir shops, museums, and information centers in one, but these aren't what you would come halfway around the world to see.

Instead, come to see the traditional ways and folk arts that are still alive in the north, along with the independence of spirit that locals share with people in Hokkaidō, even farther north. In the Tōno Valley people still live in the traditional northern Japan *magariya* (houses), and the old people still know the stories of mystical creatures and how placenames came into being. The architecture of the *bushi* (warrior class) residences is preserved in Kakunodate, and its people continue to make traditional folk crafts from cherrywood and bark.

Ruggedness is a feature of the people and of the landscape, be it the windblown slopes of Tappi-zaki (Cape Tappi) or Zaō-san's huddled "ice monster" trees, which get covered with airborne crystals. In the midst of the mountains is the verdant calm of Lake Towada and the gurgling Oirase-kyōkoku (Oirase ["oh-*ee*-ra-seh"] Gorge), where the gentle passage of water replaces the violence of volcanic eruptions.

Tōhoku Glossary

Key Japanese words and suffixes for this chapter include the following: *-bashi* (bridge), *bijutsukan* (art museum), *-chō* (street or block), *-chōme* (street), *chūō* (central), *-den* (hall), *-dera* (Buddhist temple), *dōri* (avenue), *eki* (train station), *gaijin* (foreigner), *-gawa* (river), *hakubutsukan* (museum), *hama* (beach), *-hashi* (bridge), *-in* (Buddhist temple), *izakaya* (pub), *-ji* (Buddhist temple), *jinja* (Shintō shrine), *-jō* (castle), *kawa* (river), *-ken* (prefecture), *kita* (north), *-ko* (lake, as in Tazawa-ko, Lake Tazawa), *kōen* ("*ko*-en," park), *kōgen* (plateau), *-ku* (section or ward), *kyōkoku* (gorge), *minami* (south), *-mon* (gate), *Nihon-kai* (Japan Sea), *ōhashi* (large bridge), *onsen* (hot springs), *-san* (mountain, as in Haguro-san, Mt. Haguro), *-shi* (city or municipality), *-shima* (island), *Shinkansen* (bullet train, literally "new trunk line"), and *yama* (mountain).

Pleasures and Pastimes

Dining

Tōhoku is famous for its clean water and its rice, and these two ingredients are made into delicious sake throughout the region. *Sansai* (wild vegetables) and mushrooms appear in an amazing variety of dishes, as do river fish (mostly carp and sweetfish). Along the coast you can find squid so fresh it's translucent, along with *uni* (sea urchin) so delectable it will convert even the squeamish.

In Sendai look for Sendai miso—the heartier red northern version of the staple fermented soybean paste—in soups, and grilled *gyūtan* (beef tongue) for which locals stand in line. Akita's *kiritampo* is boiled rice that's pounded into cakes, molded on sticks, and simmered in broth with chicken and vegetables. Aomori and Iwate's apples often appear in the form of desserts and juice.

For more details on Japanese cuisine, *see* Chapter 14 *and* Dining *in* Smart Travel Tips A to Z.

CATEGORY	COST*
$$$$	over ¥4,000
$$$	¥2,500–¥4,000
$$	¥1,500–¥2,500
$	under ¥1,500

per person for a main course at dinner

Lodging

Tōhoku has a broad spectrum of accommodations, from inns and *minshuku* (private homes that accept lodging guests) to large, modern resort hotels. Because the region has only recently opened up to tourists, many accommodations are modern and have little local character. That means that hotels are often utilitarian and functional. Higher prices tend to mean larger lobby areas and guest rooms.

Price categories below reflect the cost of a double room with private bath. As in other regions of the country, cities and town have Western-style rooms, while in smaller towns and villages, most lodging is Japanese-style. All large city and resort hotels serve Western and Japanese food. In summer hotel reservations are advised. For more on accommodations in Japan, *see* Lodging *in* Smart Travel Tips A to Z.

CATEGORY	COST*
$$$$	over ¥20,000
$$$	¥15,000–¥20,000
$$	¥10,000–¥15,000
$	under ¥10,000

All prices are for a double room, excluding service and tax.

Mountains, Lakes, and Hot Springs

In a country that is split by mountains top to bottom, Tōhoku, because of its relative emptiness, is one of the best places in Japan to take in its rugged landscapes. Deep, volcanic lakes and a slew of onsen resorts are classic Japanese escapes.

Rural Japan

The Japanese, like the rest of the modernized world, have turned their backs on their rural areas. If seeing traditional farmhouses and agricultural areas has some appeal, visit the Tōno Basin near Morioka for, among other things, traditional L-shape magariya.

Exploring Tōhoku

The mountains that rise on the spine of Honshū run north all the way through Tōhoku. Most of the island's trains and highways travel north–south on either side of the mountains. Hence, when taking the major roads or railway trunk lines, you tend to miss some of the grandest mountain scenery. This chapter, laid out as an itinerary up the Pacific side of Tōhoku's spine and down the Nihon-kai side, takes in the best of Tōhoku, using the JR trains as much as possible, but it covers more remote areas as well. If you plan to cross north into Hokkaidō from Aomori, consider heading down the quieter west coast of Tōhoku on the way back.

Keep in mind that Shinkansen lines don't go any farther north than the central cities of Yamagata and Morioka, and the west-coast city of Akita (via Morioka). Travel slows beyond these points—which is part of what Tōhoku is all about.

Numbers in the text correspond to numbers in the margin and on the Tōhoku map.

Great Itineraries

IF YOU HAVE 3 DAYS

In ⊡ **Sendai** ④, start at Aoba-jō, and then walk down to the Sendai-shi Hakubutsukan for a visual and historical overview of the city. From there stroll along the Hirose-gawa to Zuihō-den, the extravagant mausoleums of the Date ("da-teh") leaders. Then spend the afternoon at **Yamadera** ⑥, climbing to the top of the mountainside temple for spectacular views of the town and the Yamagata Basin, returning to Sendai or spending the night at ⊡ **Sakunami Onsen.** The next day travel to ⊡ **Matsu-shima** ⑤, relaxing on the ferry that travels through the islets of the bay to Matsu-shima itself. Spend the night in Matsu-shima or return to Sendai. On the third day take the train north for a day outdoors in one of two areas. See **Gembikei-kyōkoku** ⑩ and then continue to **Mōtsu-ji** in **Hiraizumi** ⑪. From there wander along the fields to **Chūson-ji** and **Konjiki-dō.** Or, if you pick ⊡ **Tōno** ⑫ instead, get an early start in order to have a full afternoon to cover the distances around town. See Kappa-buchi, a small riverside pool of local lore, and then, for a look at farm life, the Denshō-en folk museum. On foot or bicycle, this will take the afternoon. If you go by taxi, also go up the mountainside to see the images of Buddha, Go-hyaku Rakan, carved on moss-covered boulders.

IF YOU HAVE 5 DAYS

One five-day approach to Tōhoku would include two days for ⊡ **Sendai** ④, another day for an excursion to the temple of **Yamadera** ⑥ or the temples and gorges in and around **Hiraizumi** ⑪, then the final two days for the rural splendor of ⊡ **Tōno** ⑫. You would also have the option of heading farther north: two days in ⊡ **Sendai** ④ and either **Yamadera** ⑥ or ⊡ **Matsu-shima** ⑤; a third day in **Hiraizumi** ⑪, ending for the night in ⊡ **Morioka** ⑬; then the last two days taking in the scenery at ⊡ **Towada-ko** ⑳ from sightseeing boats or on a hike along the **Oirase-kyōkoku,** on the east side of the lake, and see the stream cascading gently downward. Spend the night at the resort of ⊡ **Yasumi-ya,** taking a morning hike before moving on.

IF YOU HAVE 7 DAYS

With a week to take in Tōhoku's natural beauty, start in ⊡ **Sendai** ④; then take a second day jaunt west for a climb up **Yamadera** ⑥ and a relaxing bath in the open-air hot springs at ⊡ **Sakunami Onsen.** From there return to Sendai Eki and transfer to the train out to see the **Shiogama Jinja** in Hon-Shiogama and take the ferry to ⊡ **Matsu-shima** ⑤; spend the night there or return to Sendai. On the third day head north, either to **Hiraizumi** ⑪ or **Tōno** ⑫ for a day of strolling between sights. On day four take it easy in ⊡ **Morioka** ⑬ and enjoy some of the best Tōhoku cooking at dinner. On the fifth day head by bus to ⊡ **Towada-ko** ⑳ and take on the 9-km (5½-mi) trail that parallels the Oirase-kyōkoku before spending the night at ⊡ **Yasumi-ya.** From there take

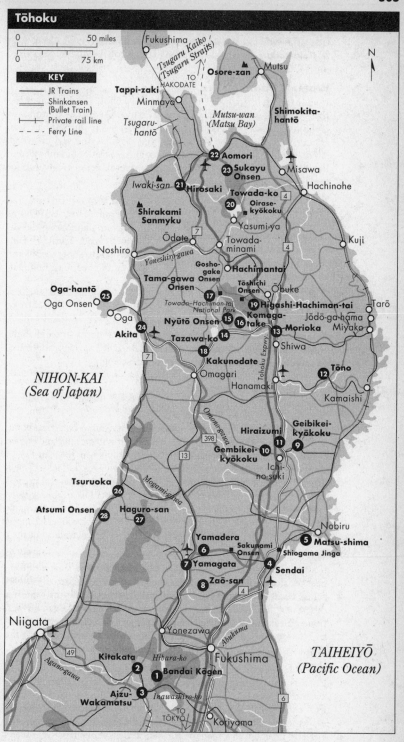

Tōhoku

KEY

— JR Trains
═ Shinkansen (Bullet Train)
+—+ Private rail line
- - - Ferry Line

0   50 miles
0   75 km

Tsugaru Kaikō (Tsugaru Straits)

Fukushima

TO HAKODATE

Tappi-zaki

Minmaya

Tsugaru-hantō

Osore-zan

Mutsu

Mutsu-wan (Matsu Bay)

Shimokita-hantō

㉒ **Aomori**

㉓ **Sukayu Onsen**

Misawa

Iwaki-san ㉑ **Hirosaki**

Shirakami Sanmyku

⑳ **Towada-ko**

Oirase-kyōkoku

Hachinohe

④

Ōdate

Yasumi-ya

Towada-minami

Kuji

Noshiro

Yoneshiro-gawa

⑦

④

Gosho-gake Onsen

Tama-gawa Onsen

⑰

Hachimantai

Tōshichi Onsen

Ōbuke

Towada–Hachiman-tai National Park

⑲ **Higashi-Hachiman-tai**

Tarō

Oga-hantō ㉕

Oga Onsen

Nyūtō Onsen

⑮ ⑯ **Komaga-take**

⑬

Morioka

Jōdō-ga-hama

Miyako

Oga

㉔

Akita

⑭

Tazawa-ko

Shiwa

Tōhoku Expwy

⑫ **Tōno**

⑱

Kakunodate

Omagari

Hanamaki

Kamaishi

⑦

Omonogawa

Hiraizumi

Geibikei-kyōkoku

398

⑪ ⑨

Gembikei-kyōkoku ⑩

Ichi-no-seki

13

Tsuruoka

Mogami-gawa

Atsumi Onsen ㉘

Haguro-san ㉗

Nobiru

Yamadera

⑤ **Matsu-shima**

Sakunami Onsen

⑥

Shiogama Jinga

㉖

Yamagata ⑦

④

Sendai

⑧ **Zaō-san**

④

NIHON-KAI (Sea of Japan)

Niigata

49

Agano-gawa

Yonezawa

Abukuma

TAIHEIYŌ (Pacific Ocean)

Kitakata

Hibara-ko

② ① **Bandai Kōgen**

③

Aizu-Wakamatsu

Inawashiro-ko

Fukushima

TO TŌKYŌ

Kōriyama

⑥

the bus to ⊞ **Hirosaki** ㉑ for a look at the castle town and the Neputa museum on day six. On the seventh day begin heading south, with seaside stops either at the **Oga-hantō** (Oga Peninsula) ㉕, ⊞ **Akita** ㉔, or ⊞ **Kakunodate** ⑱ for a look at a small castle town with buildings from the Tokugawa era.

When to Tour Tōhoku

If your timing is perfect, you can see all of Tōhoku's big summer festivals, starting with Hirosaki's Neputa Festival (August 1–7), Aomori's Nebuta (August 3–7), Akita's Kantō (August 5–7), and Sendai's Tanabata (August 6–8). The festivals are very popular and very crowded. All of Tōhoku's energy is released in colorful parades of lanterns and floats and wild dancing. Reserve at least several weeks in advance for hotels and trains.

Tōhoku's climate is similar to New England's. Winters are cold, and in the mountains snow blocks some of the minor roads. At the same time, snow rarely falls in Sendai and Matsu-shima and along the Pacific coast, and temperatures rarely dip below freezing. Spring and autumn are the most colorful seasons. Summer is refreshingly cool and as a result attracts Japanese tourists escaping the heat and humidity of Tōkyō and points south.

SOUTH TŌHOKU

Fukushima Prefecture is tamer both in scenery and in attitude than the rest of Tōhoku. Nonetheless, there are lakes, hot springs, and traces of traditional Japanese life that are worth seeing.

Bandai Kōgen (Bandai Plateau)

❶ *30 mins northwest of JR Inawashiro Eki by bus.*

Fukushima was the first region in northern Honshū to become a popular resort area for Japanese families, especially around the tableland known as Bandai Kōgen. The volcano Bandai-san erupted in 1888 and in 15 short minutes wiped out more than 40 small villages, killing 477 people and resculpting the landscape. The eruption dammed several streams to form hundreds of lakes, the largest of which is Hibara-ko, with its crooked shoreline and numerous islets. Bandai Kōgen is also the name for the tourist center at Hibara-ko, where Japanese vacationers disperse to their campgrounds, bungalows, or modern *ryokan* (a traditional inn).

Though the Bandai Kōgen area is somewhat spoiled by hordes of tourists, a particularly pleasant walk, the Go-shiki-numa Trail, meanders past the dozen or more tiny lakes (ponds, really) that are collectively ★ called **Go-shiki-numa** (Five-Color Lakes), because each throws off a different color. The trail begins across from the Bandai Kōgen bus station and runs in the opposite direction from Lake Hibara; the round-trip takes two hours. There are other lake and mountain trails in the area as well.

Inawashiro-ko is Japan's third-largest lake, and the town of Inawashiro is on its northern shore. Unlike Tōhoku's other large lakes, Towada-ko and Tazawa-ko, Inawashiro-ko is not a caldera lake but instead is formed by streams. So its flat surrounding shore isn't exactly spectacular, though the scenery is pretty enough as far as Japanese beaches go. The Japanese like the lake for the gaudy, swan-shape sightseeing cruise boats that circle on the water.

Of cultural interest is **Noguchi Hideo Kinen-kan** (Hideo Noguchi's Birthplace and Memorial Museum) in honor of his life and his research of yellow fever, which eventually killed him in Africa in 1928. It's 10 minutes by bus from the Inawashiro station and the bus between Bandai Kōgen and Aizu-Wakamatsu stops at Inawashiro. ☎ 0242/65–2319. 🎟 ¥400. ⏰ Apr.–Oct., daily 8:30–4:15; Nov.–1st wk Dec., daily 9–4; 3rd wk Dec.–Mar., daily 9–4.

Lodging

$$$$ 🏨 **Ura-Bandai Royal Hotel.** A comfortable resort hotel with a magnificent setting, the Royal also has seven restaurants, including traditional Japanese, robatayaki (grill), sushi, and French. Rooms come with two meals, served in the main dining room, or you can pay for a room alone and choose where you eat. In the back garden behind the hotel there is a path leading around a small lake, and the west entrance of the Go-shiki-numa Trail is nearby. If you are just visiting the hotel for the day, try its rare blueberry cheesecake in the coffee shop. ✉ 1093 Hibara Kengamine, Kita-Shiobara Mura, Yama-gun, Fukushima-ken 969-2701, ☎ 0241/32–3111, FAX 0241/32–3130. 227 Western-style and Japanese-style rooms. 4 restaurants, coffee shop. AE, DC, MC, V. MAP.

$$$ 🏨 **Pension Heidi.** The ever-accommodating manager of this pension deserves an award. Rooms are simple but comfortable, and the location (within walking distance of the Kengamine intersection at Ura-Bandai) is certainly convenient, but what wins return visits and two-night stays is the food—very few pensions in Japan offer this level of cuisine in an area so delightful for hiking. And, so guests won't get bored, the chef alternates nightly between French and Chinese cooking. Breakfast and dinner are included in the price. ✉ 1093 Ura-Bandai Kengamine, Kita-Shiobara Mura, Yama-gun, Fukushima-ken 969-2701, ☎ 0241/32–2008, FAX 0241/32–3456. 10 rooms, 2 with bath. AE, DC, MC, V.

Kitakata

★ ❷ 45 mins west of Bandai Kōgen by bus (summer only); 1 hr, 50 mins northwest of Kōriyama by JR.

Mud-wall kura can be seen all over Japan, but for some reason Kitakata has more than 2,600 of them. A kura is a thick-walled, tile-roofed storehouse that is usually two stories high and has small windows with thick shutters at the top—which can be quickly shoved shut and sealed with mud when there's danger of fire. Kura are not only simple places to store rice, miso, soy sauce, sake, fertilizer, and charcoal, they're also status symbols of the local merchants. In the past the kura fascination spread so much that shops, homes, and inns were built in this architectural style as people tried to outdo their neighbors. You can quickly use up a couple of rolls of film taking photographs of the many different kura—some are of black-and-white plaster, some simply of mud, some with bricks, and some with thatched roofs; still others have tiles. If you are short on time, head to the area northeast of the station, which has a selection of storehouses, including Kai Shōten, a black kura storefront of an old miso and soy-sauce factory.

A renowned variety of delicious ramen noodles are made in Kitakata; several tourism-conscious entrepreneurs have combined the two attractions by converting storehouses into ramen shops. The town also has a kura-shape carriage, towed by a brawny cart horse, in which you can ride if the spirit of Japanese kitsch moves you.

Kai Honke Kura Zashiki, an elaborate mansion that took seven years to build, provides an example of how efficient and beautiful the kura were in times past. ✉ 1-4611 Aza, Kitakata-shi, Fukushima-ken, ☎ 0241/22–0011. 🎟 ¥200. ⏰ Mid-Mar.–early Dec., daily 9–5.

Aizu Urushi Bijutsu Hakubutsukan (Aizu Lacquer Museum) displays elegant local lacquer products from trays and bowls to tables. ⊠ *4095 Higashi-machi, Kitakata-shi, Fukushima-ken,* ☎ *0241/24–4151.* ☞ *¥300.* ⊙ *Daily 9–5.*

Yamatogawa Sake Brewery consists of seven kura, one of which serves as a small museum to display old methods of sake production. The other buildings are still used for making sake. After a dutiful tour, you are offered the pleasurable reward of tasting different types of sake. The brewery is across the center of town from the Lacquer Museum. ⊠ *4761 Aza Teramachi, Kitakata-shi, Fukushima-ken.* ☞ *Free.* ⊙ *Daily 9–4:30.*

The **tourist office** (☎ 0241/24–2633) at the local JR station has a kura walking-tour map for the city. It's open Monday–Saturday 9:30–5:30, Sunday 10–5. There is JR service to Kitakata from Kōriyama.

Aizu-Wakamatsu

❸ *20 mins by JR south of Kitakata, 70 mins west of Kōriyama.*

As the locus of a tragic, if partly misconceived, event in the course of the Meiji overthrow of Japan's feudal shogunate in the mid-1800s, Aizu-Wakamatsu has a couple of relevant sights. That said, the compelling story of the Byakkotai far outshines the town itself.

Byakkotai Monument. Every Japanese knows this story, so it bears telling: Twenty young warriors, known as Byakkotai (White Tigers), had been fighting pro-Restoration forces outside the city when they were sent back to Tsuruga-jō to aid in its defense. The boys arrived on a nearby hillside, Iimoriyama. To their horror, they saw smoke rise from the castle and mistakenly believed the castle to be overrun by the enemy. As good samurai, all 20 boys began a mass suicide ritual. One boy was saved before he bled to death. For a samurai this was a curse. He spent the rest of his life with a livid scar and the shame of having failed to live up to the samurai code. Ironically, the castle had not at that point fallen into enemy hands, and the fighting continued for another month—indeed, had they lived, the Byakkotai might have helped to turn the battle in their side's favor. On the hill next to their graves there is now a monument to the 19 who died. The small memorial museum and a strange hexagonal Buddhist temple, Sazaedō, are reached by a 10-minute bus ride from the station. You may want to visit Iimoriyama September 22–24, when a special festival is held in memory of the Boshin civil war and the Byakkotai. ☞ *¥400.* ⊙ *Apr.–end of June and 2nd wk of July–end of Nov., daily 8–5; 2nd wk of Dec.–Mar., daily 8:30–4.*

Tsuruga-jō was the most powerful stronghold of the northeast during the shōgun period. The Aizu clan was closely linked to the ruling family in Edo and remained classically loyal until the end. When the imperial forces of the Meiji Restoration pressed home their successful attack in 1868, that loyalty caused the castle, which had stood for five centuries, to be partly burned down, along with most of the city's buildings. The new government destroyed the castle completely in 1874. The five-story castle was rebuilt in 1965 as a museum and is said to look like its original, but without the presence it must have had in 1868, when 19 Byakkotai committed ritual suicide. From the JR station plaza, take a bus from Gate 14 or 15, but check with the information booth first. The bus loops around the city past the castle and the Byakkotai monument. ☞ *¥400.* ⊙ *Daily 8:30–5 (last entry at 4:30).*

★ Aizu Buke Yashiki (Aizu Samurai Residence). To the east of the castle is an excellent reproduction of a wealthy samurai's manor house. The 38-room house gives an idea of how well one could have lived during the shōgun period. A museum on the grounds displays Aizu craft, culture, and history, and there are several other old or reconstructed buildings in addition to the manor house. To get here take the Higashiyama bus from the JR station. ☞ ¥850. ☉ *Apr.–Nov., daily 8:30–5; Dec.–Mar., daily 9–4:30.*

The city **tourist office** is in the center of town (☎ 0242/32–0688). The **JR information and reservation office** at the station distributes a free English-language map and leaflets about the area.

Higashiyama Onsen

30 mins from Aizu-Wakamatsu by bus.

Higashiyama Onsen, a spa town with several modern ryokan, is an alternative overnight spot to Aizu-Wakamatsu, especially if you enjoy hot mineral baths. The village is in a gorge, and the bus route terminates at the bottom end of the village. Most ryokan will send a car for you so you don't have to hike up the narrow village street. The village's scenic location and its shambles of older houses deserve better than the new and monstrous-looking ryokan that have supplanted most of the old. Nevertheless, Higashiyama is a spa town and a pleasant place to stay.

The **tourist information booth** at the Higashiyama bus stop will telephone a ryokan for you if you give the attendant the ¥10 for the pay phone.

Lodging

$$$–$$$$ 🏨 **Hotel Kōyō.** Although the Kōyō is in the upper part of Higashiyama Onsen, the buildings across the street block its view of the gorge. This is a modest hotel with large, 10-tatami-mat rooms at a reasonable price. The owner also has a fish market, so the meals, served in your room and included in the price, are prepared with good, fresh seafood. Meat can be provided if requested in advance. Two staff members speak some English. A driver will pick you up at the bus stop. ⊠ *241 Hara, Yumoto, Higashiyama-machi, Aizu-Wakamatsu, Fukushima-ken 965-0814,* ☎ *0242/26–9000; 0120/26–4504 toll-free,* ℻ *0242/26–9166. 18 Japanese-style rooms. Snack bar, mineral bath. AE, V.*

$$$–$$$$ 🏨 **Mukaitaki Ryokan.** This is the one ryokan in Higashiyama Onsen that retains a traditional ambience, thanks to its plank floors, shōji screens, and screen prints. English is spoken, and rooms can be reserved until 9:30 PM, though the place is open 24 hours a day. The inn serves Japanese food only. ⊠ *200 Kawamukai, Yumoto-aza, Higashiyama-machi, Oaza, Aizu-Wakamatsu, Fukushima-ken 965-0814,* ☎ *0242/ 27–7501. 25 Japanese-style rooms. Mineral bath. AE, DC, MC, V.*

Getting Around South Tōhoku

The easiest way in and out of Tōhoku is on the Tōhoku Shinkansen. A detour west will take you to Kōriyama and Ura-Bandai and farther to Kitakata and Aizu-Wakamatsu. What you will lose in backtracking to Kōriyama you will make up in reduced travel time and more interesting sights.

From Kōriyama, Inawashiro-ko is reached by local train on the Banetsusai Line (30 minutes). Buses connect from JR Inawashiro Eki and the Noguchi Hideo Kinen-kan to the lake area's main Bandai-Kōgen stop in 30 minutes. From the city of Fukushima buses depart from near Shinkansen Eki daily between April 22 and November 5 and travel the Bandai-Azuma Skyline Drive, offering splendid views of mountains by climbing up through Jōdōdaira Pass at 5,214 ft. The whole mountain resort is, in fact, crisscrossed by five scenic toll roads. All sightseeing buses and local Inawashiro buses arrive at the Bandai Kōgen bus stop.

Train and bus routes run south from Aizu-Wakamatsu to Nikkō. Traveling east by train to Kōriyama puts you back on the Tōhoku Shinkansen for Sendai to the north and Tōkyō to the south. The train going west leads you to Niigata and the Nihon-kai.

To get to Higashiyama, take the bus from Platform 4 at JR Aizu-Wakamatsu Eki for the 20-minute ride, which costs ¥310.

SENDAI

④ *By Shinkansen, 40 mins north of Kōriyama, 2 hrs north of Tōkyō.*

With a population of nearly 900,000, Sendai is the largest city between Tōkyō and Sapporo, the northern island of Hokkaidō's major city. Because American firebombs left virtually nothing unscorched by the end of World War II, it's a very modern city. The buildings that replaced the old ones are not particularly attractive, but Sendai is an open city with a generous planting of trees that justifies its nickname *mori-no-miyako*, "the city of trees." With eight colleges and universities, including the prestigious Tōhoku University, the city has intentionally developed an international outlook and appeal. This has attracted many foreigners to take up residency. Sendai's old customs and modern attitudes make it a comfortable base from which to explore Tōhoku.

Sendai is easy to navigate, and even the major streets have signs in *romaji* (Japanese words rendered in roman letters). The downtown is compact, with modern hotels, department stores with fashionable international clothing, numerous Japanese and Western restaurants, and hundreds of small specialty shops. Three broad avenues, Aoba-dōri, Hirose-dōri, and Jōzen-ji-dōri, and the Chūō-dōri shopping arcade head out from the station area toward Sendai Castle and cut through the heart of downtown, where they are bisected by the wide shopping arcade of Ichiban-chō. Between these two malls and extending farther east are narrow streets, packing in the 3,000 to 4,000 bars, tea shops, and restaurants that make up Sendai's entertainment area.

Unlike other urban centers in Tōhoku, Sendai has a larger number of sights worth visiting, and you can easily spend a day looking around. Sendai's history focuses almost entirely on a fantastic historic figure, Date Masamune (1567–1636). Affectionately called the "one-eyed dragon" for his valor in battle and the loss of an eye from smallpox when he was a child, Date Masamune established a dynasty that maintained its position as one of the three most powerful *daimyō* (feudal lord) families during the shōgun period. In addition to his military skills and progressive administration—he constructed a canal linking two rivers, thus improving the transport of rice—he was also an artist and a scholar open to new ideas.

Sendai's big festival, Tanabata, is held August 6–8, and, although similar festivals are held throughout Japan (usually on July 7), Sendai's is the largest, swelling the city to three times its normal size with Japanese tourists. The celebration stems from a poignant Chinese legend of a weaver girl and her boyfriend, a herdsman, represented by the stars Vega and Altair. Their excessive love for each other caused them to become idle, and the irate king of heaven exiled the two lovers to opposite sides of heaven. However, he permitted them to meet one day a year—and that day is now celebrated as Tanabata, highlighted with a theatrical stage performance of the young lovers' anguish. For the festival, locals decorate houses and streets with colorful paper and bamboo streamers fluttering from poles.

To get an overview of the city and save yourself an uphill hike, take a bus up Aobayama to **Aoba-jō.** There never was a traditional military stronghold, but the grand building that once stood here was the Date clan's residence for 266 years. Because it sat 433 ft above the city on Aobayama and was protected by the Tatsunokuchi-kyōkoku to the south, even without a traditional castle the site was considered impregnable when the first structure went up in 1602. The later castle was destroyed during the Meiji Restoration. The outer gates managed to survive another 70 years, until firebombs destroyed them in 1945. The rather grandiose, heavy, and cumbersome **Gokoku Jinja** is the main feature of the area where the castle stood. Near the observation terrace is a mounted statue of the city's founder, Date Masamune, who looks out over the city with his one good eye. On a clear day you can see the Pacific Ocean on the horizon to the right. Take a bus from stop number 9 in front of Sendai Eki, or ride the Loople tourist bus to get here. 🖂 *Free.* ☉ *Daily dawn–dusk.*

At the foot of the hill beneath Aoba-jō, **Sendai-shi Hakubutsukan** (Sendai Municipal Museum) has a nicely presented history of the Date family and the history of the city. The café on the second floor is a good place to get refreshments before the walk to Zuihō-den. The museum is closed the last day of each month, the day following special exhibits, and national holidays. 🖂 *¥400.* ☉ *Tues.–Sun. 9–4:30 (last entry at 4:15).*

★ **Zuihō-den** burned during the firebombing in 1945 but was reconstructed in a five-year period beginning in 1974. During the excavation, Date Masamune's well-preserved remains were found and have been reinterred in what appears to be a perfect replica of the original hall. Two other mausoleums for the remains of the second (Date Tadamune) and third (Date Tsunamune) lords of Sendai were also reconstructed. These mausoleums, which cost in excess of ¥800 million to rebuild, are astounding in their craftsmanship and authenticity in the architectural style of the Momoyama period (16th century). Each mausoleum is the size of a small temple, and the exterior is inlaid with figures of people, birds, and flowers in natural colors, all sheltered by elaborate curving roofs. Gold leaf is used extravagantly on the pillars and in the eaves of the roofs, creating a golden aura. To get here take Bus 11 from JR Sendai Eki to the Otamaya-bashi Zuihō-den stop. The mausoleum is a short walk up the hill. Or it's a 30-minute walk down the Aobayama and across the Hirose-gawa from the Aoba-jō. 🖂 *¥550.* ☉ *Daily 9–4:30.*

Ōsaki Hachiman Jinja survived the war and is the main historic building in Sendai that did. Built in Yonezawa, in 1527, the shrine was later moved to Toda-gun. Date Masamune liked it and, in 1607, had it moved from its second site to be rebuilt in Sendai. Its free-flowing architectural form has a naturalness similar to that of buildings in Nikkō, and its rich, black-lacquered main building more than justifies its designation as a National Treasure. In the northwest section of the city, it's about 10 minutes from downtown or Aobayama by taxi and 15 minutes from the Zuihō-den area. You can also take Bus 15 from JR Sendai Eki for ¥220. 🖂 *Free.* ☉ *Daily dawn–dusk.*

★ Peace fills the Zen temple garden at **Rinnō-ji.** A small stream leads the eye to the lotus-filled pond, the garden's focal point. Waving, undulating hummocks covered with clusters of bamboo flow around the pool, with each of the two elements in balance. In June the garden is a blaze of color, with irises everywhere, but there are so many visitors that you might feel like you're missing out on the tranquillity you thought you came for. The temple is a 20-minute walk from Ōsaki Hachiman Jinja, northwest of the city center. Use Bus 24 if you are going directly there from JR Sendai Eki. 🚏 *¥300.* ⊙ *Daily 8–5.*

The top three floors of the 30-story **SS 30 Building** (⊠ 4-6-1 Chūō) are reserved for restaurants and viewing galleries. If you want a bird's-eye view of the city, you can't get any higher. At night, riding up in the outside elevator, with the city lights descending below, is quite a thrill.

Dining

The main cluster of restaurants is on the parallel streets Ichiban-chō, Inari-kōji, and Kokubun-chō. Most places display their menus in their windows, along with the prices for each dish. Also, in the JR station, there are tempting arrays of prepared foods and numerous restaurants in the underground mall called Restaurant Avenue.

$$$–$$$$ ✕ **Gintanabe Bekkan.** This is the place for fish in any form—sashimi, fried, boiled, baked, or grilled—and it's a favorite with local people. You can sit at the counter and order one item at a time or ask for a room in the back where complete courses are available, with the catch of the day brought in from Pacific fishing ports. The sashimi *moriawase,* assorted sashimi, at ¥5,000 is an excellent selection for two people. From the Ichiban-chō exit of Mitsukoshi department store, turn left, take a right at the first narrow street, walk two short blocks, turn left, and walk 50 yards. It's the restaurant with the tub-shape fish tank. ⊠ 2-9-34 Kokubun-chō, 🕾 022/227-3478. *AE, DC, MC, V. Closed 2nd Sun. of month. No lunch.*

$$$–$$$$ ✕ **Santarō.** Known especially for delicious tempura, Santarō also serves
★ *shabu-shabu*—thin slices of Sendai beef briefly simmered in broth—as well as sukiyaki, *fugu* (blowfish), and *kaiseki* (Kyōto-style set meals). Tempura courses start at ¥4,000, sukiyaki start at ¥5,000, and shabu-shabu start at ¥5,000. To enjoy the refined atmosphere at a lower price, try weekday lunch specials for ¥1,000–¥3,000. The restaurant is just off Bansui-dōri several blocks south of Jōzen-ji-dōri. ⊠ 1–20 Tachi-machi, 🕾 022/224-1671. *AE, DC, MC, V. Closed mid-Aug.*

$$–$$$$ ✕ **Jirai-ya.** A curtain next to a big red paper lantern leads to a real Sendai gem. Chef Itaru Watanabe keeps a sharp eye on the grill, where *kinki* (deepwater white fish) are prepared to go with *sansai*—tempura in spring and mushrooms in autumn. Try *kinoko-jiru* (mushroom soup), a local dish popular at picnics in autumn. The ingredients are all fresh, and the warm atmosphere makes this a local favorite. It's just off Ichiban-chō, near Hirose-dōri. ⊠ 2-1-15 Kokubun-chō, 🕾 022/261-2164. *MC, V. Closed Sun.*

$–$$$$ ✕ **Kaki-toku.** Matsu-shima Bay is famous for its *kaki* (oysters), and even when they are unavailable locally, this shop brings in the best available. In business for more than 70 years, the place specializes in raw oysters, vinegar oysters, and fried oysters. If you're not crazy about oysters, you can order steak or other entrées while your friends revel in their shellfish. ⊠ 4-9-1 Ichiban-chō, 🕾 022/222-0785. *AE, DC, MC, V. Closed Mon.*

$–$$ ✕ **Aji Tasuke.** This small shop, with a counter and several tables that
★ seat 30 max, is a local institution that serves delicious meals at inexpensive prices, beating similar shops hands down. Order *shokuji* (a meal), and ¥1,350 will get you the full set of grilled beef tongue and pickled cabbage, oxtail soup, and a bowl of barley mixed with rice. From the Ichiban-chō exit of Mitsukoshi department store turn left, walk to the first narrow street, turn right, turn left at the next corner, and Aji Tasuke is 50 yards down on the left next to a small shrine. ⊠ 4-4-13 Ichiban-chō, 🕾 022/225-4641. *No credit cards. Closed Tues.*

Lodging

$$$-$$$$ 🏨 **Hotel Metropolitan Sendai.** Adjacent to the railway station, this up-scale business traveler's hotel has reasonably large guest rooms decorated in light colors. The 21st-floor Sky Lounge restaurant offers the best city view—and French food to go with it. Simpler fare at more reasonable prices is found in the coffee shop. ⊠ *1–1–1 Chūō, Aoba-ku, Sendai, Miyagi-ken 980-8477,* ☎ *022/268–2525,* FAX *022/268–2521. 300 rooms. 5 restaurants, coffee shop, indoor pool, gym. AE, DC, MC, V.*

$$$-$$$$ 🏨 **Sendai Kokusai Hotel.** This newest of Sendai's hotels (next to the
★ SS 30 complex) immediately won attention as the town's leading hotel. The lobby glistens with marble and stainless steel, guest rooms are furnished in light pastels, and larger rooms have stucco arches to exaggerate their size. Fresh flowers add a touch of color. Hotel restaurants serve French, Chinese, and Japanese fare. The Kokusai is a short walk from downtown. ⊠ *4–6–1 Chūō, Aoba-ku, Sendai, Miyagi-ken 980-0021,* ☎ *022/268–1112,* FAX *022/268–1113. 234 rooms. 10 restaurants, bar, coffee shop, sushi bar, shop. AE, DC, MC, V.*

$$ 🏨 **Hotel Shōwa.** A five-minute walk from JR Sendai Eki, this business hotel is convenient for sightseeing and getting to the best downtown restaurants. The simple, clean rooms come at a reasonable price. From the station walk to the Chūō-dōri arcade and turn left. In the second block on the right, take one flight up to the hotel entrance. ⊠ *2–6–8 Chūō, Aoba-ku, Sendai, Miyagi-ken 980-0021,* ☎ *022/224–1211,* FAX *022/224–1214. 117 rooms. Breakfast room. AE, DC, MC, V.*

Shopping

Bustling downtown Sendai is a shopper's paradise. The area is compact, and many of the stores and small shops are in or connected to the two main shopping arcades, Ichiban-chō and Chūō-dōri. Sendai is the unofficial capital of the Tōhoku region, and you can find many of the regional crafts here—cherry-bark letter boxes and *washi* (handmade paper) most notably, which are made outside Miyagi Prefecture.

Shimanuki (⊠ 3–1–17 Ichiban-chō, ☎ 022/223–2370), is tops for folk crafts from around Tōhoku. It's open daily 10:30–9:30.

Getting Around

Although it's easy to get your bearings in Sendai, public transport is not so convenient. The subway awkwardly runs north–south only, and its stations are far from the most interesting sights. A new east–west subway line is planned, which may improve the situation. Fortunately, the center of the city is an easy walk from the train station, and all hotels are between the center and the station. City buses will work for sightseeing, but it's advisable to consult the bus and subway information office, near the subway station in front of the JR station, beforehand. Here you can pick up English-language brochures that tell you about bus departure points, stops, and fares for each of the major sights. Otherwise, taxis are a convenient way of covering the (generally) short distances.

Visitor Information

The **tourist information office** on the second floor of Sendai JR Eki has essential maps with bus routes to help you get to the main places in and around Sendai. **Sendai International Center** (☎ 022/224–1919 hot line) is across the street from the Sendai-shi Hakubutsukan; this has more English information than the downtown office, which makes it a good stop before you cross Hirose-gawa on your way to Zuihō-den.

The office also operates an English-language hot line to answer questions about the city and prefecture.

En Route On your way to Matsu-shima, you can stop in Hon-Shiogama to see its shrine, **Shiogama Jinja** and views of the bay. Shiogama itself has little appeal—except for Shiogama Jinja, supposedly the home of guardian deities who look after mariners and expectant mothers. Its buildings, with bright orange-red exteriors and simple, natural wood interiors, are worth seeing. To reach the shrine, turn left from the station and walk for about 10 minutes. Be warned that after passing through the main entrance, you have to clamber up 202 stone steps. Shiogama Jinja is the main building of the complex, and the second one you come to. **Shiwahiko Jinja** is the first; admission is free. On the grounds is a 500-year-old Japanese holly tree, easily identified by the crowds taking photographs of themselves standing before it. A modern building in the complex houses swords, armor, and religious articles on its first floor and exhibits about fishing and salt manufacturing on its second. ☞ ¥200. ⊙ *Apr.–Nov., daily 8–5; Dec.–Mar., daily 9–4.*

SIDE TRIPS FROM SENDAI

Matsu-shima

❺ *25 mins northeast of Sendai by JR.*

The Japanese have named three places as their Three Big Scenic Wonders—Ama-no-hashidate, on the Sea of Japan in Western Honshū; Miyajima, in Hiroshima Bay; and Matsu-shima Bay. Hands down, Matsu-shima and its bay are the most popular coastal resort destinations in Tōhoku. Matsu-shima owes its distinction to the Japanese infatuation with oddly shaped rocks, which the bay has in abundance. Counts vary, but there are about 250 small, pine-clad islands scattered in the bay. Some are mere rocks with barely enough room for a couple of trees; others are large enough to shelter a few families. Each of the islets has a unique shape. Several have tunnels large enough to pass through in a rowboat. Its mass appeal aside, the bay is beautiful indeed, and it makes for a pleasant day's excursion from Sendai. You can either go directly to Matsu-shima by train or opt for the scenic route by sea. The key sights are within easy walking distance of each other. For maps and brochures, visit the tourist office at the end of the Matsushite Kaigan Pier.

Once you are in Matsu-shima, the small temple of **Godai-dō** is just to the right as you step off the boat on the pier. Constructed at the behest of Date Masamune in 1609, this temple is on a tiny islet connected to the shore by two small arched bridges. Weathered by the sea and salt air, the small building's paint has peeled off, giving it an intimacy often lacking in other temples. Animals are carved in the timbers beneath the temple roof and among the complex supporting beams. If you hope to inspect the temple's interior, you'll have a long wait: it's open to the public only during special ceremonies held once every 33 years, and the next opening is scheduled for 2006.

★ **Zuigan-ji,** Matsu-shima's main temple, dates from 828, but the present structure was built on Masamune's orders in 1609. Designated a National Treasure, Zuigan-ji is the most representative Zen temple in the Tōhoku region. The main hall is a large wood structure with ornately carved wood panels and paintings (faded with age) from the 17th century. Surrounding the temple are natural caves filled with Buddhist statues and memorial tablets that novices carved from the rock face as part of their training. The grounds surrounding the temple are full of trees, two of which are plum trees brought back from Korea in 1592 by Date Masamune after an unsuccessful military foray. Zuigan-ji is down the street from Godai-dō, across Route 45 and the central park. ☒ ¥500. ⊙ *Apr.–Sept., daily 8:30–5; Oct.–Mar., daily 9–4.*

For a glimpse at how people looked and dressed during Date Masamune's time, visit the wax museum, **Michinoku Date Masamune Rekishi-kan** (Date Masamune Historical Museum). With life-size figures, the museum displays scenes from the feudal period—battles, tea ceremonies, and processions. ☒ *Rte. 45 (from Zuigan-ji, turn left and walk back toward the bay).* ☒ ¥1,000. ⊙ *Daily 8:30–5.*

★ **Kanrantei,** translated as "Water Viewing Pavilion," was originally part of Fushimi-Momoyama-jō in Kyōto, but when that castle was demolished, it was moved to Edo (Tōkyō), before being shifted again by Date Tadamune—the great Masamune's eldest son—to its present location in Matsu-shima. Here, the Date family held their tea parties for the next 270 years. **Matsu-shima Hakubutsukan** next to Kanrantei, is a museum with a full collection of the Date family's armor, swords, pikes, and more genteel items, including an array of lacquerware. Kanrantei is on the south side of the harbor opposite Godai-dō. ☒ ¥200. ⊙ *Apr.– Oct., daily 8–5; Nov.–Mar., daily 9–4:30.*

From Godai-dō it's a short walk across the 250-yard pedestrian bridge near the Matsu-shima Century Hotel to **Fukurajima.** For the ¥150 toll, you can walk away from the crowds to enjoy a picnic in the park or a brief nap while looking out across the bay from one of the islands.

From April to November, between 9 AM and 3 PM, **sightseeing ferries** leave from Shiogama every 30 minutes for Matsu-shima (they run every hour from December to March). Whether you catch the gaudy Chinese dragon ferry or one that is less ostentatious, the route through the bay will be the same. So will the incessant and distracting loud-speaker naming (in Japanese) the islands. The first 10 minutes of the hour-long trip are dismal. Don't fret! Shiogama's ugly port and the oil refinery on the promontory soon give way to the beauty of Matsu-shima Bay and its islands. The dock is to the right (seaward side) of Hon-Shiogama Eki. ☒ ¥1,420 *one-way, 2nd class;* ¥2,600 *for upper deck in 1st class.*

Lodging

$$$$ ⊞ **Hotel Ichinobo.** An elegant if somewhat pricey hotel, this resort has a large garden consisting of a small man-made island, which is connected by bridges and is lighted up at night. All rooms overlook the bay and are spacious; the hotel's facilities are attractively designed. ☒ *1–4 Takagi Aza Hama, Matsu-shima-chō, Miyagi-ken 981-0215,* ☎ *022/353–3331,* ℻ *022/353–3339. 20 Western-style rooms, 104 Japanese-style rooms. Restaurant, coffee shop, pool. AE, DC, MC, V.*

$$$$ ⊞ **Matsu-shima Century Hotel.** In the heart of Matsu-shima, with an ★ excellent view of the bay, this luxury hotel has all the amenities of an international resort hotel. Many rooms are lavish, and the meals include the best ingredients from the coastline and the deep Pacific. ☒ *8 Sensui Aza Matsu-shima, Matsu-shima-chō, Miyagi-ken 981-0213,* ☎ *022/354–4111,* ℻ *022/354–4191. 192 Western-style and Japanese-style rooms. 2 restaurants, coffee shop, pool. AE, DC, MC, V.*

Getting Around

For the 30-minute trip to Hon-Shiogama Eki, take the JR Senseki Line. Its platforms are reached from the Sendai Eki basement. The same train goes on to Matsu-shima Kaigan Eki, so this itinerary may be done in reverse if you want to ferry straight to the island. Fares from Sendai are ¥320 to Hon-Shiogama and ¥400 to Matsu-shima Kaigan.

Yamadera and Yamagata

Yamadera

6 *By JR, 50 mins west of Sendai.*

A delightful day trip from Sendai is Yamadera, more formally known as Risshaku-ji.

Built 1,100 years ago, Yamadera's complex of temples with steeply pitched slate roofs on the slopes of **Hōju-san** is the largest one of the Tendai sect in northern Japan. It attracts some 700,000 pilgrims a year. Walk through the village, cross the bridge, and turn right: just inside the entrance is **Kompon Chū-dō**, the temple where the sacred Flame of Belief has been burning constantly for 1,000 years—with, admittedly, one interruption: in 1521 a local lord called Tendo Yorinaga ransacked the complex and extinguished the flame, so that a replacement had to be brought from the original sacred fire at Mt. Hiei in Kyōto.

Near Kompon Chū-dō there is a statue of the Japanese poet **Matsuo Bashō** (1644–94), who wrote extensively of his wanderings throughout Japan in 17-syllable haiku. The path continues up 1,015, well-tended steps; the best views are from the **Niō-mon**. The ascent is relatively easy, but the path can be crowded in summer and treacherous with snow in winter.

Finally, after a steep ascent, you reach **Oku-no-in**, a hall at the summit dedicated to the temple founder, Jikaku Daishi. After your descent, on the way back to the station, grab a snack at the shop to the right of the bridge, where you can sit and look out over the river. You should allow two hours for the climb up and back down. 🎫 *¥300.* ⊙ *Daily dawn–dusk.*

OFF THE BEATEN PATH

SAKUNAMI ONSEN – The train from Sendai to Yamadera passes through Sakunami. Within the Sendai city limits (40 minutes by train from the main station), the town and its hot springs are close enough to make it an alternative spot to overnight.

LODGING

$$$$ 🏨 **Iwamatsu Ryokan.** Though called an inn, Iwamatsu is more of a hotel with full amenities. Built along a cascade, the rooms look out on trees and the stream. The original open-air bath is covered with a wooden roof, but it's at river level, allowing views of spring leaves, autumn foliage, or winter snow. Dinner is Japanese, with several local specialties. Breakfast is a buffet with a variety of Japanese and Western foods that will fill anyone's plate. The inn has a shuttle bus service from JR Sakunami Eki, and regular bus service from Sendai Eki stops in front of the inn. ✉ *16 Sakunami Motoki, Aoba-ku, Sendai-shi, Miyagi-ken 989-3431,* ☎ *022/395–2211,* 📠 *022/395–2020. 102 Japanese-style rooms. Restaurant, tea shop, hot springs, dance club. AE, MC, V.*

GETTING AROUND

To get to Yamadera, take the Senzan Line from Yamagata (20 minutes) or from Sendai (50 minutes). Sakunami Onsen is 40 minutes from Yamagata or Sendai on the JR Senzan Line.

Yamagata

7 *20 minutes west of Yamadera, 1 hr west of Sendai by JR.*

Yamagata, with a population of 240,000, is the capital of the prefecture of the same name. It's a friendly town that's working to improve its appeal to travelers. Yamagata Prefecture, incidentally, has at least one onsen in each of its 44 municipalities—the only 100% thermal Japanese prefecture.

At the **Hana-gasa Festival** (August 5–7), some 10,000 dancers from the entire area dance their way through the streets in traditional costume and *hana-gasa*, hats so named for the safflowers used to decorate them. Floats are interspersed among the dancers, and stalls provide food and refreshments.

❽ Most people come to Yamagata for **Zaō-san,** where nearly 1.4 million alpine enthusiasts ski its 14 slopes between December and April. In summer hikers come, though in smaller numbers, to walk among the colored rocks and take in **Zaō Okama,** a caldera lake with a diameter of nearly 1,200 ft. Cable cars leave from **Zaō Onsen,** the mountain's resort town, one to climb 1,562 ft from the base lodge, which is 2,805 ft above sea level, another to make the final ascent, an additional 1,083 ft. Even nonskiers make the wintertime trip to see the *juhyō*: layer after layer of snow covers the fir trees, creating weird, cylindrical figures that look like fairy-tale monsters—a phenomenon caused by heavy snow on the conifers. Zaō Onsen is 19 km (12 mi) from Yamagata Eki—45 minutes by bus. In winter there are direct buses between Tōkyō and Zaō Onsen.

If you have an interest in pottery, take a trip to **Hirashimizu** on the outskirts of the city. This small enclave of traditional buildings and farmhouses is a step back in time and a sharp contrast to the modern urban sprawl of Yamagata. About six pottery families live here, each with its own kiln, each specializing in a particular style. Two of them, the Shichiemon and Heikichi, offer pottery lessons, and participants can have the results fired and then, two to four weeks later, mailed back home. The pottery of the Sei-ryu-gama (kiln) is the best known, and with exhibitions of their wares in America and Europe, their prices are high. Places are generally open daily 9–3, but keep irregular holidays, so it's best to check with the tourist information office at the station. From Bus Stop 5, in front of JR Yamagata Eki, take a bus for Geijutsu Kōka Daigaku, a 15-minute ride (¥210), or take a taxi (¥2,000).

Pick up free maps and brochures from the **tourist information office** opposite the ticket turnstiles inside the JR station. ☎ *023/631–7865.* ◷ *Weekdays 10–6, weekends 10–5.*

DINING AND LODGING

$$$–$$$$ ✕ **Sagorō.** Sukiyaki, shabu-shabu, or a good steak: this stylish restaurant serves excellent Yonezawa beef. Although the set courses of the above are pricey, a plate of *shōga-yaki* (beef grilled in ginger sauce; ¥1,700), *oshinko moriawase* (pickled vegetables; ¥700), rice, and soup make a delicious, fairly reasonable meal. Look for the black bull on the sign above the street and take the stairs up one flight. ⊠ *1–6–10 Kasumi-chō,* ☎ *023/631–3560. No credit cards. Closed Sun.*

$$–$$$ ✕ **Mimasu.** In Nanoka-machi, a short walk from the Washington Hotel, this restaurant serves good sushi, tempura, and *donburi*—bowls with cutlets, tempura, and chicken placed on top of rice. Lunch specials include *danjurō bentō*, a filling assortment of seasonal vegetables and fish. ⊠ *2–3–7 Nanoka-machi,* ☎ *023/632–1252. Closed 2nd Wed. of month.*

$–$$ ✕ **Shōjiya.** Yamagata is famous for *soba* (thin, brown, buckwheat noodles that are often served in a lightly seasoned broth), and this fine shop is one of the best. For lunch or a light dinner, try the simple *kake-soba* (buckwheat noodles served in a hot broth; ¥650), *tempura soba* (with tempura; ¥1,300), or *nameko soba* (with mushrooms; ¥900). For a full meal, consider *aimori itaten*, a course consisting of two different types of noodles and sauces (¥2,000). The staff speaks no English, but the menu has the complete selection in photographs. It's a 10-minute walk from the JR station. ⊠ *14–28 Saiwai-chō,* ☎ *023/622–1380. Closed Mon.*

$$–$$$ 🏨 **Hotel Metropolitan Yamagata.** Leave through the train station door, walk to the right a few paces, and you have arrived. This recent addition to the JR station area has a modern lobby and spacious rooms; it's the best hotel in this small town. It's also a convenient walking distance to downtown restaurants, should you decide to go out for meals. ✉ *1–1–1 Kasumi-chō, Yamagata, Yamagata-ken 990-0039,* ☎ *023/ 628–1111,* 𝔽𝔸𝕏 *012/628–1166. 116 rooms. 3 restaurants. AE, DC, V.*

$$ 🏨 **Yamagata Washington Hotel.** This downtown Yamagata business hotel, a short taxi ride from the station, is smart and efficient and has a friendly staff. The coffee shop is on the ground floor, the reception area and a Japanese restaurant are on the next floor, and guest rooms are above, from the third to the eighth floor. Rooms are compact, and bathrooms are typical prefabricated plastic units. ✉ *1–4–31 Nanoka-machi, Yamagata, Yamagata-ken 990-0042,* ☎ *023/625–1111,* 𝔽𝔸𝕏 *023/624–1512. 223 rooms. Restaurant, coffee shop. AE, DC, MC, V.*

GETTING AROUND

The Yamagata Shinkansen takes just under three hours to get to Yamagata from Tōkyō. There is also direct train service on the JR Senzan Line from Sendai (about an hour). From west-coast towns, travel times to Yamagata by JR are as follows: 3½ hours from Niigata (Yonesaka Line); 2 hours, 20 minutes from Tsuruoka (Uetsu and Riku-u Sai lines); 3 hours from Akita (Ōu Line). The Tazawa-ko and Ōu lines (connecting in Ōmagari) provide access from Morioka in central Tōhoku.

The Gorges and Hiraizumi

35 mins north of Sendai by Shinkansen, 95 mins by JR local.

East of Ichi-no-seki, the Iwai River flows through the naturally carved Geibikei-kyōkoku, and you can either walk along the banks or travel upstream and take a boat through the gorge. Gembikei-kyōkoku is west of Ichi-no-seki, and its proximity to the temples of Hiraizumi makes these two places a good combination for a full-day outing.

❾ Flat-bottom boats, poled by two boatmen, ply the river for a 90-minute round-trip through **Geibikei-kyōkoku.** The waters are peaceful and slow moving, relentlessly washing their way through silver-streaked cliffs. The high point of the trip is reaching the depths of the gorge, faced with 300-ft cliffs. Coming back downstream would be an anticlimax if it were not for the boatmen, who, with little to do but steer the boat, sing traditional songs. The boat trip costs ¥1,500. From Sendai you can head east to Geibikei by changing to the Ōfunato Line for a 30-minute ride to Higashiyama. But the direct route is only about 21 km (13 mi), so a taxi (about ¥2,000) is much more convenient. There is little other than Geibikei to see along this route.

★ ❿ **Gembikei-kyōkoku,** at 1,000 yards long and less than 20 ft deep, is no less than a miniature gorge, but with all the features of the world's best gorges. Once, rushing water carved its path into solid rock; now it's quiet. Because of its small scale, you can walk its entire length and appreciate every detail of its web of sculpted patterns; the circular holes (called Jacob wells) scoured into the rock side will become personal discoveries. To get to Gembikei, take a taxi west (10 minutes) from Ichi-no-seki, or take a bus (22 minutes) from Iwate-ken Kōtsū to the end of the line. From Gembikei you are best off taking a taxi the 1½ km (1 mi) to Mōtsu-ji and Hiraizumi.

⓫ In the 12th century **Hiraizumi** came close to mirroring Kyōto as a cultural center. Hiraizumi was the family seat of the Fujiwara clan, who for three generations dedicated itself to promoting peace and the arts. The fourth-generation lord became power hungry, and his ambition wiped out the dynasty. Little remains of the efflorescence of the first three generations of the Fujiwara clan, but what does—in particular Chūson-ji and the golden Konjiki-dō—is a tribute to Japan's past. From Hiraizumi Eki you can walk to the two major temples. If time is short and you plan to limit your sightseeing to Mōtsu-ji and Chūson-ji, just take the local train from Sendai for the 100-minute run to Hiraizumi.

During the time of the Fujiwara clan, **Mōtsu-ji** was the most venerated temple in northern Honshū. The complex consisted of 40 temples and some 500 lodgings. Eight centuries later, only the foundations remain. The current buildings are of more recent vintage, including the local youth hostel. The Heian period Jōdo-style (paradise-style) gardens, however, which were laid out according to the Buddhist principle in fashion some 700 years ago, have survived in good condition. The gardens are especially beautiful during the **Ayame (Iris) Festival,** from June 20 through July 10. **The Hiraizumi Museum,** with artifacts of the Fujiwara family, is beside the garden. To get to Mōtsu-ji, walk 1,000 yards up the street that leads directly away from JR Hiraizumi Eki. ⌷ *Gardens and museum ¥500.* ◷ *Daily 8–5.*

★ The temple of **Chūson-ji,** set amid thick woods, was founded by the Fujiwara family in 1105. At that time there were more than 40 buildings. In Chūson-ji's heyday the number reached 300. Unfortunately for the northern Fujiwara dream, war and a tremendous fire in 1337 destroyed all but two halls, Kyōzō and Konjiki-dō. The other buildings in the complex are reconstructions from the Edo period.

The small but magnificent **Konjiki-dō** (Golden Hall) is considered one of Japan's most historic temples. Indeed, it was the first of Japan's National Treasures to be so designated. Konjiki-dō's exterior is black lacquer, and the interior is paneled with mother-of-pearl and gold leaf. In the Naijin (Inner Chamber) are three altars, each with 11 statues of Buddhist deities. The remains of the three rulers of the Fujiwara family—Kiyohira, Motohira, and Hidehira—are beneath the central altar.

Of the two original buildings, **Kyōzō** is the less interesting. It once housed the greatest collection of Buddhist sutras (precepts), but fire destroyed many of them, and the remainder have been removed to the **Sankōzō Museum,** next door.

To commemorate the grandeur that once was, two festivals are held every year—the spring and autumn **Fujiwara festivals** (May 1–5 and November 1–3). Costumed warriors line the temple slope on horseback. To get to Chūson-ji, you can walk along a narrow road from Mōtsu-ji (30 minutes), take a taxi, or walk or take a short bus ride from the JR station. ⌷ *Chūson-ji and Sankōzō Museum ¥800.* ◷ *Apr.–Oct., daily 8–5; Nov.–Mar., daily 8:30–4:30; enter 30 mins before closing time.*

Maps are available at the **tourist office** on your right as you leave JR Hiraizumi Eki. ☎ *0191/46–2110.* ◷ *Apr.–Oct., daily 8:30–5; Nov.–Mar., daily 8:30–4:30.*

NORTHERN TŌHOKU

The northern reaches of Tōhoku are distinguished by rugged people and rugged geography—from rocky cliffs along the ocean to volcanic peaks inland—which make for spectacular natural beauty. The Tōno Basin's farmland and the Pacific coastline to the east are easy to reach by train. At the seaside, a sightseeing boat will afford the best look at the work of waves on stone. The national parks of the central highlands are among the best places to view autumn foliage in late September. Oddly enough, Morioka is still considered a castle town, even though its castle was destroyed in the mid-1800s. However, the town still does make its revered *Nambu-tetsu* (Nambu ironware).

Tōno

⑫ *1 hr east of Shin-Hanamaki by local train, and 1 hr by Shikansen from Shin-Hanamaki to Sendai.*

The people of Tōno like their old ways. The town itself is not particularly remarkable, but the Tōno Basin has old buildings and historical remains that take us back to old Japan. Allow a day or two for a turn through this traditional pastoral corner of Japan. Tōno is rich in traditional ways and folklore, and the coast is an ever-changing landscape of cliffs, rock formations, and small coves.

In a peaceful, wooded area above the Atago Jinja southwest of downtown are the **Go-hyaku Rakan** (500 Disciples of Buddha) images carved by a priest on boulders in a shallow ravine. He wanted to appease the spirits of the quarter of Tōno's inhabitants who starved to death in the two-year famine of 1754–55.

Along the valley on either side of Tōno, there are several *magariya* (L-shape, thatched-roofed Nambu-style farmhouses). A good representative is **Chiba-ke Magariya,** 13 km (8 mi) west of the JR station. Families live in the long side of the L, and horses are kept in the short side.

North of Tōno, **Fukusen-ji** contains Japan's tallest wooden Kannon (Goddess of Mercy), which was built by priest Yūzen Suriishi to boost morale after World War II. There are few sign markers, so ask for directions once you get to this small, small village.

A long taxi ride northeast of town will take you to a **suisha** (water mill), one of the few working mills left in Japan—this is not a museum piece.

Kappa-buchi is a reasonable bike or taxi ride northeast of town. It's a pool in a stream where *kappa*, supernatural amphibious creatures, live. They are said to drag people, horses, and cows into the water and to impregnate young girls, who then give birth to demi-kappas. The site is along the edge of the grounds of Jōken-ji, 6 km (4 mi) from the station, which is about as far as you need to go to see interesting countryside.

At **Denshō-en,** a Japanese folk-village museum, you can see a good Nambu magariya, complete with barn, storehouse, mill, and bathhouse. Be sure to go in the room at the back to see the **oshirasama,** 1,000 small carved sticks upon which are placed votive clothes. These small god figures are said to represent the god of silkworm cultivation—who is able to predict the future. The museum is about 6½ km (4 mi) northeast of Tōno Eki and is closed the last day of each month. ✉ *¥300.* ⊙ *Daily 9–4:30.*

Lodging

$$$ 🏠 **Fukuzansō Inn.** Highly polished creaky floors characterize this friendly, old-fashioned ryokan, a five-minute walk from JR Tōno Eki. Rooms, which share a Japanese-style bath, have a dressing room–closet area and a small enclosed balcony with table and chairs. Breakfast is served downstairs for ¥1,000 per person. No English is spoken, but the hospitable staff is all smiles and will lend you a bike for sightseeing. Fukuzansō is open 24 hours a day, 365 days a year. ✉ *5–30 Chūō-dōri, Tōno-shi, Iwate-ken 028-0523,* ☎ *0198/62–4120; 0120/ 48–8588 toll-free. 18 rooms with shared bath. V.*

$$ ⊡ **Forukurōro Tōno.** If you decide to walk or bike around the sights
★ of this small town, this B&B above JR Tōno Eki is a fine choice. With
comfortable beds, simple but clean rooms, and very friendly staff, it's
reliable and convenient for the price—and easily accessible even if you
don't speak Japanese. Reservations are advised, but if you arrive in town
without a place to stay, check here first. Because the last train comes
through around 9:30 PM and the first around 6:30 AM, there's time to
sleep and rates include a light breakfast. ⊠ *5–7 Shinkoku-chō, Tōno-
shi, Iwate-ken 028-0522,* ☎ *0198/62–0700,* FAX *0198/62–0800. 18
rooms. No credit cards. CP.*

$$ ⊡ **Minshuku Magariya.** A highlight if you're planning to overnight in
Tōno, this L-shape farmhouse has been made into a family-run hotel—
without the animals. Two meals including fish, chicken, and wild vegetable dishes are served, and after dinner one of the local elder ladies
tells folktales (in Japanese). Surrounded by fields 7 km (4 mi) west of
town, Magariya is best reached by a taxi from the station in Tōno, unless you prefer the 20-minute walk from the nearest bus stop. ⊠ *30–
58–3 Niisato, Ayaori-chō, Tōno-shi, Iwate-ken 028-0531,* ☎ *0198/62–
4564. 16 rooms. No credit cards.*

Getting Around

To get to the Tōno Basin from Sendai (or Hiraizumi, if you stop there),
take the Shinkansen to Shin-Hanamaki Eki and then board a JR train
eastbound to Tōno.

Distances between Tōno's sights are too far to walk. Unless you have
a car, plan to rent a bicycle from a hotel, bicycle shop, or even the Tōno
tourist office. A sightseeing taxi is a convenient way to see the faraway
places, and even if the driver waits for you here and there, you can see
a lot in one hour, which will cost about ¥6,000. To make the most of
the Tōno experience, you should read Kunio Yanagita's *Tōno Mono-
gatari,* translated into English by Robert Morse as *The Legends of Tōno.*

Morioka

⓭ *By Shinkansen, 45 mins north of Ichinoseki, 50–100 mins north of
Sendai.*

Morioka is a busy commercial and industrial city ringed by mountains.
Westerners will be pleased by the generous amount of information written in English—on street signs and on the destination boards in the
bus terminal, for example. Because the city is at the northernmost end
of the Shinkansen Line, it gets a lot of traffic as a transfer point for
cities in northern Honshū and Hokkaidō. Aside from horses, the major
attraction of Morioka is Nambu-tetsu. The range of ironware articles,
from small wind bells to elaborate statues, is vast, but the most popular items are *Nambu-tetsu-bin* (heavy iron kettles), which come in all
shapes, weights, and sizes. Dozens of shops throughout the city sell
Nambu-tetsu, but the main shopping streets are Saien-dōri and Ō-dōri,
which pass Iwate Kōen.

If you get to town on June 15, stay around the front of the station around
12:15. That is when the parade of grandly decorated, bell-clad horses
passes by during the festival called **Chagu-chagu Umakko.** The horses
parade through the streets between 9:30 and 1:30, so just look for people gathering.

Morioka had a fine castle built by the 26th Lord of Nambu in 1597,
but it was destroyed in the Meiji Restoration, and all that remains of
it are ruins. The site is now **Iwate Kōen,** the focus of town and the place
to escape the congestion of traffic and people in downtown Morioka.
To reach the park from JR Morioka Eki, cross Kai-un-bashi and walk

straight down the middle of the three roads when the road forks. Gozaku is across the river.

Gozaku is the most interesting place to browse for Nambu-tetsu. Across the river from Iwate Kōen, this area of small shops looks much as it did a century ago. To get to Gozaku from Iwate Kōen, cross the Naka-no-hashi and take the first main street on the left. A short way down, just past Hotel Saitō, is the large Nambu Iron Shop and the narrow streets of the Gozaku section on your left. Beyond Gozaku is another bridge, Yonoji-hashi. On the street corner is a very Western-looking fire station, built in the 1920s and still in operation.

Not far from Gozaku is **Kami-no-hashi,** one of the few decorated bridges in Japan. Eight specially crafted bronze railings were commissioned in 1609 and 10 bronze posts added two years later.

Whether you just want to wander around town between train connections or are in Morioka overnight, don't miss a visit to **Kōgensha,** a shop specializing in quality folk crafts like lacquerware, kites, dyed fabrics, and pottery. The main shop is composed of several small buildings along a courtyard. Walk through the courtyard to a relaxing *kissaten* (coffee shop) and farther to the river. Along the wall to the left are poems by Miyazawa Kenji. To get to Kōgensha from Morioka Eki, walk left to the stoplight in front of the Metropolitan Hotel, turn right, and cross the river on Asahi-bashi. Take the first left into an artistically designed street that leads to the main shop 50 yards down on the left and a branch shop across the street that sells basketry and wooden bowls. ✉ *2–18 Zaimoku-chō,* ☎ *019/622–2894.* ☾ *Daily 10–6. Closed the 15th of each month and several days in mid-Aug.*

The **tourist office,** Kankō Center, in the Train Square lounge on the south end of the second floor of JR Morioka Eki, has useful maps and other information on Morioka and Iwate Prefecture. The office can also help arrange accommodations. ☎ *019/625–2090.* ☾ *Daily 9–7.*

Iwate Kankō Bus Company runs a full-day city tour (¥5,400), with a Japanese-speaking guide, which departs daily at 10 AM and returns at 4:30. Half-day (¥3,900) tours depart from Morioka Eki at 9:30 and 1:30 and return three hours later. ✉ *Morioka Eki,* ☎ *019/651–3355.* ☾ *Tours Apr. 20–Nov. 23.*

Dining and Lodging

$$–$$$ ★ ✕ **Banya Nagasawa.** Everyone in town recommends this shop for yellowtail, grilled shellfish—scallops and abalone—mushrooms in the fall, local wild vegetables in spring, and its own original sake. Banya is across the street from the Mister Donut on Ō-dōri, in the building next to the Kita Nippon Bank; take the elevator to the second floor. ✉ *Kirihara Bldg., 2nd floor, 1–10–13 Ō-dōri,* ☎ *019/622–2646. No credit cards. Closed Sun. and mid-Aug.*

$$–$$$ ★ ✕ **Nambu Doburoku-ya.** The milky-looking sake served in huge bowls here is *doburoku,* at one time the moonshine of Tōhoku farmers. To go with a bowl of doburoku (¥600), try the *hyakusho* (farmer) course (¥3,000), which includes stewed meat, fresh squid, grilled fish, tofu, and soup. For local Tōhoku food and atmosphere, this is a place not to forget. ✉ *2–6–21 Ō-dōri,* ☎ *019/622–9212. No credit cards. Closed Mon. and mid-Aug.*

$–$$$ ★ ✕ **Azumaya.** Hearty soba comes from northern Japanese grain, and Azumaya is Morioka's place to eat soba. *Wanko soba* courses, all the soba you can eat, start at ¥2,500, and a delicious tempura soba is only ¥1,200. The *maneki-neko* (decorative beckoning cats) are mascots to ensure that customers will come again and again, and they seem to be doing their job. Azumaya is in Gozaku, 10 minutes from the station by taxi. ⊠ *1–8–3 Naka-no-hashi-dōri,* ☎ *019/622–2252. No credit cards. Closed 1st and 3rd Tues. of month.*

$$$ 🏨 **Hotel Metropolitan Morioka.** Morioka now has two hotels with the
★ same name where the staff is able to speak English. Just to the left of
the station plaza, the older wing continues to provide clean, utilitarian rooms and good service. From the old wing, cross the street facing the hotel and walk one block to the new wing, where the rooms
are larger and average ¥2,000 more. The Giovanni Café, on the second floor of the new wing, serves a reasonable breakfast and lunch for
¥1,200. Both wings have restaurants and a bar. As a guest you can use
the Central Fitness Club facilities for ¥500, including a 25-meter pool,
a machine gym, a sauna, and a Jacuzzi. ⊠ *1–44 Morioka Eki-mae-
dōri (new wing: 2–27 Morioka Eki-mae Kita-dōri), Morioka, Iwate-
ken 020-0034,* ☎ *019/625–1211,* 𝔽𝔸𝕏 *019/625–1210. 134 rooms (old
wing), 121 rooms (new wing). 5 restaurants, 2 bars. AE, DC, MC, V.*

$$$ 🏨 **Morioka Grand Hotel.** The friendliest and smartest modern hotel in
★ town, the Grand is situated on a small hill on the edge of the city, 10
minutes by taxi from the station. Its views are broader, the air is
cleaner, and its rooms are slightly larger than those in most other local
hotels; this is reflected in the price of the rooms, the most expensive
in Morioka. There are both Japanese and Continental restaurants on-
site. Do not confuse this hotel with the cheaper Morioka Grand Hotel
Annex. ⊠ *1–10 Atagoshita, Morioka, Iwate-ken 020-8501,* ☎ *019/
625–2111,* 𝔽𝔸𝕏 *019/622–4804. 21 Western-style rooms, 10 Japanese-
style rooms. 2 restaurants. AE, DC, MC, V.*

$ 🏨 **Ryokan Kumagai.** In a two-story wooden building, this simple
hostelry with basic tatami rooms is a member of the affordable Japa-
nese Inn Group. There's a small dining area where Japanese and West-
ern breakfasts and Japanese dinners are optional. In traditional style,
no rooms have private baths. Located between the station and center
city, it's a 10-minute walk from JR Morioka Eki—cross the river and
walk along Kaiun-bashi-dōri two blocks and turn right (a gas station
is on the left and a bank on the right). Cross over one block, and the
ryokan is on the left. ⊠ *3–2–5 Ōsakawara, Morioka, Iwate-ken 020-
0025,* ☎ *019/651–3020,* 𝔽𝔸𝕏 *019/626–0096. 11 Japanese-style rooms
with shared bath. Dining room. AE, MC, V.*

Getting Around

Morioka is the last stop on the Tōhoku Shinkansen Line: all trains con-
tinuing north, east, or west are "regular" JR trains. So while it can take
less than an hour to get from Sendai and Morioka, the same distance up
to Aomori takes 2 hours and 20 minutes. To get downtown from the JR
station, take Bus 5 or 6 from the terminal in front of the station. There's
also a convenient loop bus for tourists called Denden-mushi, which goes
to Gozaku, departing every 20 minutes 9–6 from Bus Stop 15 or 16 in
front of Morioka Eki (¥100 for one ride, ¥300 for the day pass).

Tazawa-ko and Kakunodate

The lake area of Tazawa-ko and the traditional town of Kakunodate
make for good side trips into Tōhoku's rugged interior from either
Morioka or the west-coast city of Akita. For a little thermal relaxation,
the old spa towns of Tama-gawa Onsen and Nyūtō Onsen lie just north
of Tazawa-ko.

Tazawa-ko

★ ⑭ *40 mins west of Morioka, 70 mins east of Akita by JR Express.*

At 1,390 ft, Tazawa-ko is Japan's deepest lake. Its blue waters in fact
are too alkaline to support any fish. Like most of Japan's other lakes,
Tazawa-ko sits in a volcanic cone, its shape a classic caldera. With clear

waters and forested slopes, it captures a mystical quality that appeals so much to the Japanese. In winter the Tazawa-ko area is a popular and picturesque skiing destination, with the lake visible from the ski slopes. According to legend, the great beauty from Akita, Takko Hime, sleeps in the water's deep as a dragon. The lake never freezes over in winter because Takko Hime and her dragon husband churn the water with their passionate lovemaking. Or, perhaps, as scientists say, the water doesn't freeze because of a freshwater source that enters the bottom of the lake.

A 15-minute bus ride (¥350) from the JR station gets you to the Tazawa-ko-han center on the lakeshore. A 30-minute bus ride from JR Tazawa-ko Eki via Tazawa-ko-han takes you up to Tazawa-ko Kōgen northeast of Tazawa-ko for ¥580. The journey affords spectacular views of the lake, showing off the full dimensions of its caldera shape. A boat takes 40-minute cruises on the lake from late April to November (¥1,150). There is also regular bus service around the lake (halfway around in winter), and bicycles are available for rent at the Tazawa-ko-han bus terminal. If you go by bike, you can take more time to appreciate the beauty of Takko Hime, whose bronze statue is on the western shore.

The **tourist information office** to the left of the JR station for maps and bus schedules. ☎ *0187/43–2111.* ☺ *Daily 8:30–5:15.*

⓯ The bus from Tazawa-ko continues for another 15 minutes to **Nyūtō Onsen,** a collection of small, unspoiled, mountain hot-spring spas in some of the few traditional spa villages left in Tōhoku. Most of these villages have only one inn, so it's advisable to arrange accommodations before you arrive if you plan to stay the night.

⓰ **Komaga-take** (Mt. Komaga) stands a few miles east of Tazawa-ko. At 5,370 ft, it's the highest mountain in the area—and it's one of the easiest to climb. Between June and October a bus from Tazawa-ko Eki runs up to the eighth station, from which it takes an hour to hike to the summit. You can walk through clusters of alpine flowers if you hike in June or July.

★ ⓱ Another traditional spa town, **Tama-gawa Onsen,** is north of Tazawa-ko on Route 341. The spa is quaint and delightfully old-fashioned, with mainly wood buildings surrounding the thermal springs. The elderly who come to take the waters are very serious about the curative qualities of the mineral waters. However, think twice before staying overnight; the inn is a little ramshackle. There is frequent bus service between Tazawa-ko and Tama-gawa Onsen; the ride takes 90 minutes and costs ¥1,340.

LODGING

Nyūtō Onsen consists of six small spa villages, each with an inn, all generally within the same price range (¥16,000–¥30,000). Only Japanese-style rooms are available, and you must take your meals on-site. No Western credit cards are accepted.

Kaniba Onsen (☎ 0187/46–2021). **Kuro-yu Onsen** (☎ 0187/46–2214). **Magoroku Onsen** (☎ 0187/46–2224). **Ogama Onsen** (☎ 0187/46–2438). **Taeno-yu Onsen** (☎ 0187/46–2740). **Tsuro-no-yu Onsen** (☎ 0187/46–2139).

$$$–$$$$ 📷 **Tazawa-ko Prince.** A modern white hotel on the edge of the lake, the Tazawa-ko Prince has views of Komaga-take. Choose from rooms that are large with a lake view, small with a lake view, or small with a mountain view. Aside from the main dining room, there is a garden room down near the lake. ✉ *Nishiki-mura, Semboku-gun, Akita-ken*

014-0511, ☎ 0187/47–2211, ℻ 0187/47–2211. *Dining room, boating, recreation room, shops. 128 rooms. AE, DC, MC, V.*

Kakunodate

★ ⑱ *16 mins southwest of Tazawa-ko by JR.*

The small and delightful town of Kakunodate was founded in 1620 by the local lord, and it has remained an outpost of traditional Japan that, with cause, claims to be Tōhoku's little Kyōto. The whole town is full of weeping cherry trees, more than 400 of them, and they are direct descendants of those imported from Kyōto three centuries ago. A number of them form a 2-km-long (1¼-mi-long) "tunnel" along the banks of Hinokinai-gawa.

Within a 15-minute walk northwest from the station are several well-preserved samurai houses that date back to the founding of the town, the most renowned of which is **Aoyagi,** with its sod-turf roof. The cherry tree in Aoyagi's garden is nearly three centuries old. ☞ ¥500. ☉ *Apr.–Nov., daily 8:30–5; Dec.–Mar., daily 9–4.*

If you have time, visit **Denshō-kan** (Denshō House), a hall in front of a cluster of samurai houses that serves as a museum and a workshop for cherry-bark handicrafts. ☞ ¥300. ☉ *Apr.–Nov., daily 9–5; Dec.–Mar., Fri.–Wed. 9–4:30.*

LODGING

$$ ⊡ **Forukurōro Kakunodate.** The JR people have converted part of Kakunodate Eki into an inexpensive B&B with clean rooms, each having a private bath and toilet. A simple buffet breakfast and unbeatable convenience are included in a low price. It's only 6 ft from the station exit. ⊠ *14 Nakasugasawa, Iwaze-aza, Kakunodate-machi, Akita-ken 014-0314,* ☎ *0187/53–2070,* ℻ *0187/53–2118. 26 rooms. No credit cards.*

Towada–Hachiman-tai National Park

★ *2 hrs northwest of Morioka by JR and bus.*

From Morioka the main railway line runs north to Aomori via Hachinohe, circumventing Tōhoku's rugged interior, Hachiman-tai Kōgen. The mountains of Towada–Hachiman-tai National Park afford sweeping panoramas over the park's gorges and valleys—which form wrinkles in which natives seek shelter during the region's harsh winters—crystal-clear lakes like Towada-ko, gnarled and windswept trees, volcanic mountain cones, and the ubiquitous hot springs. Needless to say, winter weather conditions are not conducive to extensive traveling. If you plan to travel in winter, be sure to check beforehand which bus services are running and which roads are open.

Hachiman-tai Kōgen

⑲ **Higashi-Hachiman-tai** is the resort town where hikers and skiers begin their ascent into the upper reaches of the mountains. The village of **Pūtaro Mura** consists of log cabins with private thermal pools. In this part of the park, you can either bring in your own food and cook in your cabin or eat in the attached restaurant. A few miles from Pūtaro Mura is **Gozaisho Onsen,** a popular spa resort that can be a useful overnight stop.

The left-hand fork of the road from Higashi-Hachiman-tai leads to **Matsu-kawa Onsen,** which is noted for its pure waters. This spa town is on the backside of Mt. Iwate, amid the eerie barrenness left by the volcano's eruption in 1719.

The entrance to the **Aspite Line** is past Gozaisho Onsen. This 27-km-long (17-mi-long) scenic toll road skirts the flanks of Chausu-san

(5,177 ft) and Hachiman-tai-san (5,295 ft). With every turn there is another view of evergreen-clad slopes and alpine flowers. The Aspite Line is closed November–April.

From the Hachiman-tai-chōjō bus stop off the Aspite Line it's a 20-minute walk up a path to **Hachiman-numa** (Hachiman Marsh), originally a crater lake of a volcano. There is a paved esplanade around the crater, and in July and August alpine wildflowers are in peak bloom.

The road turns left (south) after Hachiman-tai-chōjō to **Tōshichi Onsen.** The year-round spa town—elevation 4,593 ft at the foot of Mokko-san—is a popular spring skiing resort.

On the north side of Tōshichi is **Horaikyo,** a natural garden with dwarf pine trees and alpine plants scattered among strange rock formations. In early October the autumn colors are fantastic.

Goshogake Onsen, noted for its abundance of hot water, is just before the western end of the Aspite Line. This spa and Tōshichi are the best spas for overnight stays, especially Goshogake if you want to try *ondoru* (Korean-style) steam baths and box-type steam baths where only your head protrudes. Just outside Goshogake is a mile-long nature trail highlighting the volcanic phenomena of the area, including *doro-kazan* (muddy volcanoes) and *oyu-numa* (hot-water swamps). After Goshogake Onsen, the toll road joins Route 341; a left turn leads south to Lake Tazawa. A right turn at the junction heads north for an hour's bus journey to the town of Hachiman-tai, where you can rejoin the JR Hanawa Line either to return to Ōbuke and Morioka or to travel north toward Towada-ko and Aomori.

LODGING

$$$$ 🏠 **Kyōun-sō Inn.** It's just the essentials at this little two-story wooden inn: small tatami rooms and traditional shared bathroom facilities. Meals are served in a communal room. Open-air hot springs are nearby, and the owners are always delighted to have a Westerner stay. ✉ *Matsukawa Onsen, Matsuo-Mura, Iwate-gun, Iwate-ken 028-7302,* ☎ *0195/78–2256,* 𝖥𝖠𝖷 *0195/78–2818. 18 Japanese-style rooms. Dining room. AE, MC, V.*

$$$$ 🏠 **Matsu-kawa-sō.** This ryokan is popular for rustic flair and rejuvenating spa waters. It's simple, clean, and traditional, with highly polished wooden floors. Two meals are included, and all rooms are Japanese style. ✉ *Matsu-kawa Onsen, Matsuo-mura, Iwate-gun, Iwate-ken 028-7302,* ☎ *0195/78–2255. 62 rooms. Dining room, hot springs. No credit cards.*

$$$ 🏠 **Pūtaro.** Cabins sleep anywhere from 2 to 12 in connecting rooms. The theme is do-it-yourself: basic cooking utensils are provided, and there is a food store; and if you are looking for a place to relax and hike, this is a good base. There's also an athletic course with ropes and bridges. Reservations are strongly advised. ✉ *Hachiman-tai Onsen, Matsuo-Mura Iwate-gun, Iwate-ken 028-7302,* ☎ *0195/78–2277,* 𝖥𝖠𝖷 *0195/78–3283. 66 cabins. Grocery, kitchenettes, miniature golf, 6 tennis courts. MC, V.*

Towada-ko

⑳ The area around **Towada-ko** is one of the most popular resorts in northern Tōhoku—almost crushingly so in autumn. If you choose one lake to visit, this should be it. The caldera lake fills a volcanic cone to depths of 1,096 ft, making it the third deepest in Japan. Towada-ko had no fish in it until Sadayuki Wainai stocked it with trout in 1903. The town of Towada-minami (Towada South) is 20 minutes north of Hachiman-tai on the JR Hanawa Line. From here buses leave on the hour to Towada-ko; the bus fare is ¥1,110.

The road to Towada-ko snakes over **Hakka-tōge** (Hakka Pass), which has some of the best views over the lake. Following a series of switchbacks, the road descends to circle the lakeshore, though the bus from Towada-Minami goes only part of the way around it.

At the village resort of **Yasumi-ya**—the word *yasumi* means "holiday"—pleasure boats run across the lake to **Nenokuchi.** The one-hour trip on the boat (¥1,320) covers the most scenic parts of the lake. Boats run every 30 minutes from mid-April to early November, less frequently until January 31, then not at all until mid-April.

You can rent a bike at Yasumi-ya and Nenokuchi, but you're better off on foot. First, walk along the lakeside at Yasumi-ya, especially to the right from the sightseeing boat pier. Go at least as far as the statue of two women, and if you are a rock-hopper continue on up the trail to the end of the peninsula. A short walk inland from the statue will take you to the impressively carved, weather-beaten **Towada Jinja.** Regular bus service from Yasumi-ya to Nenokuchi and beyond takes about 25 minutes.

An excellent choice for a walk is to the **Oirase-kyōkoku,** northeast of the lake at Nenokuchi. The carefully tended trail along the gorge follows the stream for a total of 8.9 km (5.5 mi; 2 hours and 40 minutes). A two-lane road parallels the river; from it you can catch a bus at intervals of about 2 km (1 mi). The first stop is a 20-minute walk from the lake, and the second is another 50 minutes. Don't miss this easy trail, for it passes through one of the most pristine areas of Tōhoku. Be prepared for rain, take a map of the river and bus stops, and find out the bus schedule before you start out—and don't be daunted by the crowds of tourists, especially in autumn. Buses along the trail go north to Aomori and south to Nenokuchi and Yasumi-ya.

DINING AND LODGING

$$$-$$$$
★ ✕🏠 **Towada Kankō Hotel.** Yasumi-ya is dominated by rather old hotels that cater to busloads of older people and high school excursions, but this hotel is a sophisticated place to make your base for enjoying the lake, which is steps away. Western-style rooms have comfortable beds and a separate tatami area. Kaiseki-style Japanese dinner is served in your room and includes *kiritampo-nabe* (stew made of grilled rice, fish, vegetables, mushrooms, and wild vegetables); Japanese breakfast is served in the dining room. ✉ *Towada-ko Yasumiya, Aomori-ken 018-5501,* ☎ *0176/75–2111,* 🖷 *0176/75–2327. 72 rooms. Restaurant, bar, café, hot springs. AE, DC, MC, V. MAP.*

GETTING AROUND

There are two ways to get from Morioka to Hachiman-tai Kōgen: Take the JR Hanawa Line for a 43-minute ride to Ōbuke, 19 km (12 mi) from the plateau. From there continue by bus 50 minutes to Higashi-Hachiman-tai. The faster way of reaching Higashi-Hachiman-tai is to take one of the seven daily buses directly from Morioka (1 hour, 50 minutes; from the Number 4 bus stop in front of the JR station); the fare is ¥1,090. The bus's last stop is Hachiman-tai Kankō Hotel. Change buses in town for Matsu-kawa.

After exploring that area, you can catch one of the 10 daily buses at Towada-minami, north of the plateau. From here you can take a bus to Towada-ko or connect in Ōdate to Hirosaki and Aomori. The total travel time is less than a day, but you should plan on spending at least one night en route to take in the remarkable scenery.

Hirosaki

★ ㉑   *1 hr, 40 mins north of Towada-minami by JR; 2 hrs, 20 mins northwest of Morioka by express bus, 4 hrs by JR.*

Hirosaki is one of northern Tōhoku's friendliest and most attractive cities. Its major, and really only, sight is Hirosaki-jō, but the town has an intimacy that makes it appealing. Though the city is compact and walkable, finding your bearings in the ancient castle town might be difficult. Hirosaki's streets were designed to disorient invaders before they could get to the battlements. So pick up a map at the tourist information office.

If you want to get into Hirosaki's nightlife, look for the small entertainment area just beyond the river as you head toward the castle, south of the two main streets, Chūō-dōri and Dote-machi; or if you're still baffled by the town's geography, simply mention the name of the area, Kaji-machi, to any citizen, and you'll be directed to its clutter of narrow streets. There are plenty of places to dine, from izakaya to restaurants with picture menus in their windows. And there are coffeehouses, *nomi-ya* (bars), and more expensive clubs.

The first week of August, the city outdoes itself with its famous **Neputa Festival** (August 1–7). Each night floats follow different routes through town, displaying scenes from Japanese and Chinese mythology represented by huge fanlike paintings that have faces on both sides. With lights inside the faces, the streets become an illuminated dreamscape: just follow the throb of the 12-ft-diameter drums.

Hirosaki-jō, still the original, 400-year-old building, is a pleasant change from admirable replicas. Completed in 1611, the castle is perfectly proportioned in its compactness and is guarded by moats. The gates in the outlying grounds are also original, and when the more than 5,000 *someiyoshino* (cherry trees) blossom (a festival takes place around April 25–May 5) or the maples turn red in autumn (festival late October–mid-November), the setting is marvelous. Winter snows mirror the castle's whiteness and give the grounds a sense of stillness and peace. A snow-lantern festival with illuminated ice sculpture is held in early February. The castle is on the northwest side of town, across the river. The grounds, open year-round, daily 7 AM to 9 PM, are free. ✉ *Castle ¥300.* ☾ *Apr.–Oct., daily 9–5.*

On the northeast corner of the castle grounds, **Tsugaru-han Neputa Mura** is an exhibit of the giant drums and floats used in the summer festival. If you miss the real thing, come here to see the 39-ft fan-shape floats lighted from within. In the workshop you can paint your own traditional kite, paper-and-frame goldfish, and *kokeshi* (traditional wooden doll) and take them home as souvenirs. ☎ *0172/39–1511.* ✉ *¥500.* ☾ *Apr.–Nov., daily 9–5; Dec.–Mar., daily 9–4.*

Dining and Lodging

$$$–$$$$ ✕ **Cartie.** This relaxed, attractive restaurant, which serves French cuisine at reasonable prices, is a real find. The pasta lunch or daily special ranges from ¥1,200 to ¥1,500 and dinner from ¥2,500 to ¥3,500. Light meals, as well as cake and desserts, are served on the terrace throughout the day, and the neighboring bakery provides the French bread and desserts for the restaurant. Cartie is a short taxi ride from JR Hirosaki Eki. ✉ *3–17–1 Miyakawa,* ☎ *0172/37–5010. DC, MC, V.*

$$$ ✕ **Yamauta.** Hirosaki's most interesting eatery is a five-minute walk past City Hirosaki Hotel from the station. Yamauta serves sashimi, grilled fish, *yakitori* (grilled, skewered chicken and vegetables), and grilled meat for ¥380–¥2,700 and has live *shamisen* (a three-string banjolike in-

strument) music every hour. The restaurant gets its musical character from its owner, who was once national shamisen champion and now uses the premises as a school for aspiring shamisen artists. Yamauta is closed one day a month; the day varies. ⊠ *1–2–7 Ō-machi,* ☎ *0172/ 36–1835,* ℻ *0172/36–6115. No credit cards.*

$$ ✕ **Anzu.** Performances of live shamisen music take place at 7 PM, 9 PM, and 10:30 PM. Go an hour early to sit on cushions on the floor, in typical local style, and enjoy a menu of seasonal vegetables, sashimi, grilled scallops, grilled fish and rice, and soup for a reasonable ¥3,000. ⊠ *44–1 Oyakata,* ☎ *0172/32–6684. No credit cards.*

$$–$$$$ ⊡ **Hotel New Castle.** Near Hirosaki Castle, this smart business hotel is notable for the friendly staff rather than for its amenities. The restaurants here serve formal and elegant Japanese meals. ⊠ *24–1 Kamisayashi-machi, Hirosaki, Aomori-ken 036-8354,* ☎ *0172/36–1211,* ℻ *0172/ 36–1210. 59 Western-style and Japanese-style rooms. 2 restaurants. AE, DC, MC, V.*

$$$ ⊡ **City Hirosaki Hotel.** This modern, efficient hotel, just to the left as
★ you exit JR Hirosaki Eki, is very well situated and the atmosphere is excellent. Off the second-floor lobby is the Japanese restaurant Kazahana, which serves attractive lunches for ¥1,800. The top-floor La Contre-haut, a French restaurant, is slightly overpriced, but the food is good. The Repos Lounge is a pleasant place to contemplate sightseeing plans. ⊠ *1–1–2 Ō-machi, Hirosaki, Aomori-ken 036-8004,* ☎ *0172/37–0109,* ℻ *0172/37–1229. 141 rooms. 2 restaurants, bar, tea shop. AE, DC, MC, V.*

Visitor Information

The **Hirosaki Sightseeing Information Center** (☎ 0172/37–5501), south of the castle grounds, displays local industry, crafts, and regional art and provides tourist information; it's open daily and is free. There is also a **tourist information office** (☎ 0172/32–0524) on the right side of the station as you exit; it's open January 4–March, daily 8–5; April–December 28, daily 8:45–6.

Aomori

㉒ *40 mins by JR local from Hirosaki; 2 hrs, 10 mins by JR express from Morioka.*

Aomori is another of Tōhoku's prefectural capitals that have more appeal to their residents than to travelers. Foreign visitors used to stop here while waiting for the ferry to cross to Hokkaidō. Now you can transfer to an express train and ride through the Seikan Undersea Tunnel—about 54 km (34 mi) long, with approximately 24 km (14½ mi) of it deep under the Tsugaru Kaikyo (Tsugaru Straits)—to Hokkaidō. The Seikan Tunnel was the world's longest undersea tunnel until the Channel Tunnel linking Britain and France opened in 1994.

Aomori has an excellent way for gaijin staying in Japan one year or less to see the sights of the prefecture: the Aomori Welcome Card, which gets you discounts on public buses (50%), hotels (10%), and museums (discount varies). The card is available upon presentation of your passport, after filling out a short application form. Inquire at JNTO in Tōkyō, the information office at JR Aomori Eki, or at Aomori Airport.

Aomori's main event is its **Nebuta Festival** (August 3–7), which should not be confused with Hirosaki's Neputa Festival (residents of both places get greatly irritated when they are). Though both are held in early August—and both have large, illuminated floats paraded through the streets at night because of an ancient mythology to do with a battle fought by the Tsugaru clan—there are important differences. Hirosaki's festival is rooted in the period before the battle and has a somber atmosphere, with slowly beating drums. Aomori's celebrates the post-battle victory and is thus noisier and livelier. Although spectators in Hirosaki can only watch, at Aomori you can participate if you are willing to jump, yell, and generally shed your inhibitions.

If you are in Aomori when the festival is not on, you might take the JR bus toward Lake Towada from Bus Stop 8 or 9 (30 minutes; ¥450) to **Nebuta-no-Sato** (Nebuta Museum), in the southeast part of town, where 10 of the figures used in Aomori's festival are stored and displayed. The JR bus that runs to Sukayu Onsen and Hachiman-tai Kōgen stops at Nebuta-no-Sato, so if you are coming from that spa, you can get off the bus and poke around the museum before continuing into downtown Aomori. ☎ 017/738–1230. 🖃 ¥420. ☉ July–Sept., daily 9–8 (except during Nebuta Festival in early Aug.); mid-Apr.–June and Oct.–Nov., daily 9–5:30.

Sannai Maruyama Historical Site dates back 5,000-plus years to Japan's Jōmon period. Discovered in the early 1990s while land was being cleared for a proposed sports complex (since relocated), this was quickly recognized as a large, immensely important archaeological site for Japan's early history. Reconstructions of large, raised buildings stand as a testimony to history, and an exhibition hall displays clay figurines, lacquerware, and other items unearthed here. Admission is free, and volunteer guides offer tours in Japanese every two hours. The site is accessible from Bus Stop 2 at JR Aomori Eki (35 minutes; ¥330). ☎ 017/766–8282 (Japanese only). 🖃 Free. ☉ May–Aug., daily 9–6; Sept.–Apr., daily 9–4:30.

Munakata Shikō Kinen-kan, a museum dedicated to native son Munakata Shikō (1903–75), displays the wood-block prints, paintings, and calligraphy of this internationally known artist. The building itself is constructed in the attractive, rough-hewn wooden azekura style. Take a bus from Bus Stop 2 at the JR station in the direction of Tsutsumi and get off at Shimin Bunka Kaikan-mae (15 minutes). Then walk back to the crossing and take a left. The museum is on the left. ☎ 017/777–4567. 🖃 ¥300. ☉ Apr.–Oct., Tues.–Sun. 9:30–4:30; Nov.–Mar., Tues.–Sun. 9:30–4.

Aomori Kenritsu Kyōdo-kan (Prefectural Museum) displays folk crafts and archaeological material. It's a 10-minute bus ride (¥160) from Bus Stop 4 at JR Aomori Eki or a 20-minute walk. 🖃 ¥310. ☉ Apr.–Sept., Tues.–Sun. 9:30–4:30; Oct.–Mar., Tues.–Sun. 9:30–4.

Keiko-kan (Museum of Folk Art) has a large display of local crafts, including fine examples of tsugaru-nuri (lacquerware), which achieves its hardness from 48 coats of lacquer. Dolls representing the Haneto dancing girls of the Nebuta Festival are also on display. The Keiko-kan is 25 minutes away from the JR station by bus (¥290; board at Bus Stop 3) on a busy highway of malls, arcades, and giant pachinko (a kind of gambling played on upright pinball-like machines) parlors, which makes it easy to miss: watch for the Sanwa complex on your right, get off the bus three sets of traffic lights later, and the museum is tucked away on the right side. 🖃 Free. ☉ Daily 9–4:30 (last entry at 4).

For a quick overview of Aomori, you can head up the **Asupamu Biru** (ASPAM Building), 10 minutes' walk from the JR station down by the waterfront, where the Hokkaidō ferryboats used to dock. The 15-story ultramodern facility is easy to recognize by its pyramid shape. An outside elevator whisks you 13 floors up to an enclosed observation deck, which stays open after the lower floors are closed. There are a number of restaurants and exhibits on Aomori's tourist attractions and crafts inside the building. Though the staff speaks little English, a tourist information desk in the entrance lobby is very helpful in supplying details of the prefecture's attractions. Asupamu Biru is closed every fourth Monday and the last Monday to Wednesday in January. ☞ *¥800; deck only, ¥400.* ⊙ *Daily 9 AM–10 PM.*

Auga, one block east of JR Aomori Eki, across from the Aomori Grand Hotel, is a modern building complex with distinctive crimson pillars. For local flavor, go downstairs to the market where fish, shellfish, preserved seaweed, smoked fish eggs, and other marine products are hawked by hundreds of shopkeepers. ⊙ *Daily 5 AM–6:30 PM.*

OFF THE BEATEN PATH	**TAPPI-ZAKI (CAPE TAPPI)** – Northwest of Aomori is the cape on the Tsugaru Kaikyo under which the JR Seikan Tunnel connects Honshū with Hokkaidō. Tappi is the perfect place to enjoy sea urchin fresh from the sea, stroll along steep Nihon-kai cliffs, climb the stairs off National Highway 339 to a windswept lighthouse, observe the power-generating Wind Park turbo fans, and generally get away from it all. Several JR trains per day on the Tsugaru Line pass through Kanita to Mimmaya (1 hour, 40 minutes; ¥1,100), where you change to a bus that goes on to Tappi (30 minutes; ¥200). There are minshuku with minimal facilities for an overnight, but you may prefer to return to the Aomori area by late bus.

OSORE-ZAN – As much as Aomori City might have its shortcomings, Aomori Prefecture possesses a great deal of natural beauty. If you have a day to spare, consider heading to this mountaintop in the center of the Shimokita-hantō (Shimokita Peninsula), the ax-shape piece of land that juts from Aomori's northeastern corner. Osore-zan's temple, Entsū-ji, is dedicated to the spirits of dead children. The atmosphere of otherworldliness is heightened by its setting: the surrounding peaks, the neighboring dead lake, the steam from the hot springs, the desolate grounds that have been whitened by sulfuric rock, and the distinct sulfur smell that hangs in the air. Even eerier are some of the visitors: Crows often come to feed on the crackers and candles left at the shrines by mourning parents, and blind women gather at the site in late July to offer their services as mediums for contacting the dead. The trip to Osore-zan takes a little more than three hours. From JR Aomori Eki take the train to Shimokita Eki (¥1890), transfer by bus to Mutsu Terminal (¥140), then take another bus to Osore-zan (¥750).

Dining and Lodging

$–$$$$ ✕ **Hide-zushi.** You are in a major seafood city, and if you want the very best available, this is the place to eat. Excellent service, bright decor, and sea urchin, salmon roe, scallops, squid, tuna, and crab will make you glad you visited Hide-zushi. ⊠ *1–5 Tsutsumi-machi,* ☎ *017/722-8888. Closed Sun.*

$–$$$$ ✕ **Nishimura.** It'd be hard to walk out of Nishimura hungry: the *Danna* course (¥3,000), for example, includes abalone and sea urchin soup, seaweed and fish, an all-marine hot pot, and fried eggplant. From JR Aomori Eki walk one block east on Shinmachi-dōri, and take the first left. Go two blocks and it's across on your right. ⊠ *1–5–19 Yasukata,* ☎ *017/773-2880. AE, MC, V. Closed Sun.*

$$–$$$ ⊞ **Aomori Grand Hotel.** Close to the station, this is the best place in town for an overnight stay. The lounge for morning coffee has superbly comfortable armchairs, and the Continental Bellevue Restaurant (on the 12th floor) is an enjoyable place to spend an evening. Guest rooms tend to be small. ⊠ *1–1–23 Shin-machi, Aomori-shi, Aomori-ken 030-0801,* ☎ *017/723–1011,* FAX *017/734–0505. 140 Western-style and Japanese-style rooms. Restaurant. AE, DC, MC, V.*

$ ⊞ **Daini Ryokan.** The proprietor keeps this spacious inn neat and warmly welcomes foreign visitors. Guests take turns using the communal bath and private shower facilities. Long-term rates are also available, making this a good base for exploring. Prices are minutely higher in winter due to heating costs. From the JR station, turn right and walk one block to Nikoniko-dōri. Turn left and take the third narrow right. The inn is on the right. ⊠ *1–7–8 Furu-machi, Aomori-shi, Aomori-ken 030–0862,* ☎ *017/722–3037. 19 rooms. No credit cards.*

Visitor Information

There is a **tourist information center** at the station (☎ 017/723–4670), where you can apply for the Welcome Aomori Card; it's open daily 8:30–5:30, with English maps and brochures for the city and prefecture.

Sukayu Onsen

★ ㉓ *1 hr, 10 mins from JR Aomori Eki by bus.*

Instead of staying in Aomori, you might prefer to spend the night at Sukayu Onsen, near the Hakkōda Ropeway. One snag is that the last bus departs Aomori at 3:30 PM.

More than 300 years ago a hunter shot and wounded a deer near here. Three days later he saw the deer again, miraculously healed. He realized that the deer had cured itself in the sulfur springs. Since then, people have been coming to Sukayu for the water's curative powers. The inn—and there is nothing here but the inn—is a sprawling wooden building with highly polished creaking floors. The main bath, known as Sen-nin Buro (Thousand-Person Bath), is made of *hiba* (Japanese cypress), a very strong wood. It's not segregated—men and women bathe together—but there are smaller baths that are segregated. Sen-nin Buro's two big tubs fill the bathhouse: one pool, called Netsu-no-yu, is 42°C (105°F), while the other, Shibu Rokubu, is one degree hotter. The other two bathtubs, called Hie-no-yu, are for cooling off by pouring water on your head only, so as not to wash the minerals off your body.

Lodging

$$$$ ⊞ **Sukayu Onsen.** In a vast wood building in the mountains, this traditional Japanese inn is one of the few left in the country where men and women are not separated in the main baths—except for the few hours it's set aside for women only. Guest rooms are small and only thinly partitioned from each other, which light sleepers might find difficult. A fixed, multidish dinner is served in your room. Japanese breakfasts are served in a large dining room. A taxi to the Onsen from Aomori takes 45 minutes, the bus 80 minutes. The staff does not speak English. ⊠ *Sukayu Onsen, Hakkōda-Sunchu, Aomori-ken 030-0111,* ☎ *0177/38–6400,* FAX *0177/38–6677. 134 rooms. Hot springs. AE, DC, MC, V. BP.*

TŌHOKU WEST COAST

The "backside" of Tōhoku bears the brunt of Siberian cold fronts, and the rugged mountains provide the base of the esoteric religious practices of Shugendō, a sect founded about 1,400 years ago that combines Buddhism and Shintō.

South from Aomori to Akita

Between Aomori and Akita, the train goes back through Hirosaki and past **Iwaki-san** (5,331 ft high), which dominates the countryside. A bus from Hirosaki travels to the foot of this mountain (40 minutes), from which you can take a sightseeing bus up the Iwaki Skyline toll road (open late April–late October) to the eighth station. The final ascent, with the reward of a 360-degree view, is by a five-minute cable car, followed by a 30-minute walk to the summit.

South of Mt. Iwaki, straddling Aomori Prefecture's border with Akita, are the **Shirakami Sanmyaku** (Shirakami Mountains), home of the world's largest virgin beechwood forest. This is one of Japan's entries on UNESCO's list of World Heritage Sites. Access to the mountains is provided by just a few minor roads on their Aomori and Akita flanks, and the area is great for adventurous hiking. Once you're back on the train, soon after Hirosaki and Mt. Iwaki, the mountains give way to the rice fields and flat plains that surround Akita.

Akita

 2½ hrs from Aomori by JR express; 4 hrs, 15 mins from Tōkyō by JR Shinkansen.

Akita, another prefectural capital (population 300,000), is a relaxing city, though not one loaded with sights to see. The surrounding countryside is said to grow the best rice and have the purest water in Japan—the combination produces excellent dry sake.

The major draw here is the famous **Kantō Festival** (August 3–6), during which young men balance a 36-ft-long bamboo pole that supports as many as 46 lighted paper lanterns on its eight crossbars and weighs up to 110 pounds.

If you have time between trains, walk west from the station for 10 minutes on Hiroko-ji-dōri to **Senshū Kōen,** once the site of the now-ruined Kubota-jo. These days it's a pleasant green haven, with cherry blossoms and azaleas adding color in season.

Hirano Masakichi Bijutsukan has a noted collection of paintings by Tsuguji Fujita (1886–1968), as well as works by van Gogh and Cézanne. The most eye-catching work is Fujita's *Events in Akita,* in which three of the local festivals are merged to form a single scene: rendered on a monstrous piece of canvas measuring 11 ft by 66 ft. It took Fujita just 15 days to complete. The artist then bragged that the feat would never be bettered—now there's a way to make good art. The building itself is architecturally interesting for its Japanese palace-style roof covered with copper, which slopes down and rolls outside at the edge. ⊠ ¥610. ☉ *Early Jan.–Apr., Tues.–Sun. 10–5; May–Sept., Tues.–Sun. 10–5:30; Oct.–late Dec., Tues.–Sun. 10–5 (last entry 30 mins before closing).*

For regional arts and crafts, and more information about the prefecture, visit the 12-story **Atorion Building,** a two-minute walk south from the park on the other side of Hirokō-ji. A large shop in the basement (open daily 10–7) sells local crafts and souvenirs. The **Akita Marugoto Plaza** (☎ 0188/36–7835) on the first floor is the prefectural information center, open daily 9–7. The same floor houses a concert hall and the **Akita Senshu Museum of Art** (¥600), which features the work of local artists as well as oil paintings by Okada Kenzō, who achieved some fame in New York after World War II. The museum is open daily 10–6.

Six blocks west of the Atorion, across the Asahi-gawa and slightly to the south, is **Kawabata-dōri.** This avenue is where everyone comes in the evening to sample the regional hot-pot dishes *shottsuru-nabe* (made with salted sand fish) and *kiritampo-nabe* (grilled rice stick stew), drink *ji-zake* (locally brewed sake), and find entertainment at one of the many bars.

㉕ The **Oga-hantō** (Oga Peninsula) coastline is indented by strange rock formations and reefs, its mountains are clad with Akita cedar, and its hills are carpeted with grasses. At the neck of the peninsula, Kampusan's summit affords a panoramic view extending as far as Akita city. Nearby, the town of Oga hosts a strange custom each December 31: men dressed in ferocious demon masks and coats of straw, carrying buckets and huge knives, go from home to home issuing dire warnings against any loafers and good-for-nothings in the households. This ritual is reenacted for the public at the **Namahage Sedo Matsuri** (Namahage Sedo Festival) on February 13–15 on the grounds of the local Shinzan Jinja.

Roads trace Oga's coastline, but public transport is infrequent. The easiest way to tour the peninsula, which is 45 km (28 mi) north and west of Akita, is by using **Akita Chūō Kōtsū bus lines** (☎ 018/823–4411). Full-day tours costing ¥5,150 (not including meals) depart from Akita Eki from late April to early November and are conducted in Japanese.

The **tourist information office** next to the entrance to the Shinkansen tracks at the station has English-language pamphlets.

Dining and Lodging

$$–$$$ ✕ **Dai-ichi Kaikan.** The third-floor restaurant of this complex specializes in Akita cuisine such as kiritampo-nabe: ¥2,000 for just the hot pot alone or ¥3,500 for the full-course. The *Inaniwa Gozen* is a tray with chicken, dried ray, seaweed, wild vegetables, noodles, and *tsukemono* (pickled vegetables). Try it even if you have never seen many of the ingredients before. ⊠ *5–1–17 Kawabata,* ☎ *018/823–4141. MC, V.*

$–$$$ ✕ **Hinaiya.** The restaurant is named for the local breed of chicken that goes into *Hinai-jidōri kiritampo-nabe,* a hot pot made with kiritampo, rice that is cooked, pasted onto skewers, then grilled over a charcoal fire. This rice is then simmered in a pot with chicken broth, seasonal vegetables, burdock, leeks, and mushrooms (¥1,800). In the heart of the Kawabata entertainment district, walk one block from the river on Suzuran-dōri; Hinaiya is on the second floor. ⊠ *4–2–2 Ō-machi,* ☎ *018/823–1718. DC, MC, V.*

$$$–$$$$ 🏨 **Akita Castle Hotel.** With the best location—opposite the moat, a 15-
★ minute walk from the train station—and the most professional service in Akita, the Castle Hotel has well-maintained rooms. The Western-style doubles are spacious, and the three Japanese-style rooms are even more commodious. The bar and the French restaurant have a park view, and there are Japanese and Chinese restaurants on site as well. ⊠ *1–3–5 Naka-dōri, Akita-shi, Akita-ken 010-0001,* ☎ *018/834–1141,* 🖷 *018/834–5588. 179 Western-style rooms, 3 Japanese-style rooms. 3 restaurants, bar. AE, DC, MC, V.*

$$$ 🏨 **Akita View Hotel.** This establishment has clean, fresh rooms and is the largest of the hotels in Akita. On the right side of a Seibu department store, 3 minutes on foot from the JR station, it's convenient to shopping and a 10-minute walk from the entertainment district. The staff will give you advice on what to see and do in the city and prefecture. An indoor pool adds to the hotel's appeal. ⊠ *2–6 Naka-dōri, Akita-shi, Akita-ken 010-0001,* ☎ *018/832–1111,* 🖷 *018/832–0037. 192 rooms. 2 restaurants, bar, coffee shop, indoor pool, gym, shops. AE, DC, MC, V.*

$$ 🏨 **Kohama Ryokan.** This small inn is friendly, homey, and priced right. It's only a five-minute walk to the left of the square in front of JR Akita Eki. The Japanese-style dinner using fresh local seafood is a bargain at ¥2,000, and breakfast goes for ¥1,000. The ryokan has traditional shared baths. ⊠ *6–19–6 Naka-dōri, Akita-shi, Akita-ken 010-0001,* ☎ *018/832–5739,* 🖷 *018/832–5845. 13 rooms with shared bath. AE, MC, V.*

Getting Around

Akita is now connected to Tōkyō by the Akita Shinkansen Ko-machi trains, making a 3-hour, 48-minute trip to Tōkyō and a 2-hour, 11-minute run to Sendai.

Tsuruoka and Haguro-san (Mt. Haguro)

2½ hrs south of Akita by JR.

South of Akita along the Nihon-kai coast, there are small fishing villages, notable only because few gaijin, not to mention Nihon-jin, stop en route.
㉖ The one exception is **Tsuruoka,** the town that serves as the gateway to Haguro-san, the most accessible of the three sacred mountains of the Dewa-san range. All three mountains have this status for the *yama-bushi,* the popular name given to members of the Shugendō sect.

㉗ The climb up **Haguro-san** begins in Haguro Center at **Zaishin-mon** (Zaishin Gate), then up the 2,446 stone steps to the summit. The rigorous climb follows avenues of 300-year-old cedar trees with shafts of sunlight filtering through, the occasional waterfall, tiny shrines, and a tea shop halfway up—which are the reason for reaching the summit. Running alongside the steps is a trail of rock carvings, depicting sake cups, gourds, lotus cups, and so on. According to legend, the lucky pilgrim who locates all 33 of the carvings will have a wish granted. This climb is the main draw to Haguro-san, and you should allow several hours to complete it. At the summit, the thatch-roofed shrine **Dewa Sanzan Jinja** serves as the focus of the mountain-worship of Shugendō, and you may happen upon one of the many festivals and ceremonies held throughout the year.

It's easiest to get to Haguro Center by bus (55 minutes), either from Bus Stop 2, in front of JR Tsuruoka Eki, or from Stop 5, at Shōkō Mall, with four departures in winter and at least hourly departures in summer. A fare of ¥680 will take you from the station to lodgings run by yama-bushi in the village at the entrance to the peak itself. Most buses from Tsuruoka to Haguro Center continue to the summit, **Haguro-san-chō,** which is not much farther, but the fare jumps to ¥990 (because it covers a toll charge for use of a private road). Still, if you decide to skip the climb or have climbed up the mountain from Haguro Center and don't want to hike back down, the bus is an alternative to consider.

㉘ **Atsumi Onsen** is a spa town where the curative waters are good for your skin as well as your digestive system. To reach the village, use the bus from JR Atsumi Onsen Eki; it's a 10-minute journey to town and costs ¥190.

Dining and Lodging

There are several options for spending the night around Tsuruoka. You can stay in town; you can stay on the mountain summit at the Saikan, which is attached by a long stairway to the Dewa Sanzan Jinja; or you can take the JR express train 20 minutes south to Atsumi Onsen. One particularly hospitable ryokan is Tachibana-ya.

$–$$$ ✕ **Kanazawa-ya.** Ten minutes on foot from the JR station, there's an excellent place to eat soba—the *tenzaru* (tempura served with cold soba noodles) and *kamo nanba soba* (duck meat with soba in hot broth) are superb. From the station walk straight to the corner at Marica and Mister Donut, turn left, and walk past the highway. Kanazawa-ya is on the left. ✉ *3–48 Daihōji-machi,* ☎ *0235/24–7208. No credit cards. Closed Wed.*

$$$$ ⌂ **Tachibana-ya.** This resort ryokan in the center of Atsumi Onsen welcomes gaijin, and its accommodations are excellent. Guest rooms are spacious, and there's a *hinoki* (Japanese cypress wood) bathtub with faucets tapped into the thermal springs. Sliding glass doors overlook a landscaped garden that surrounds a large pond filled with carp. Service is efficient and friendly. Breakfast and dinner, served in your room, delight the eye and palate. The common baths are lined with stone and are filled with steaming water from the thermal springs. ⊠ *Atsumi-machi-tei 3, Atsumi Onsen, Yamagata-ken 999-7204,* ☏ *0235/43–3681,* FAX *0235/43–3681. 78 Japanese-style rooms. Bar, coffee shop, mineral bath. AE, DC, MC, V. MAP.*

$$ ⊞ **Dewa Sanzan Jinja Sai-kan.** This facility, connected to the Gosai-den Jinja by a long stairway, provides an excellent alternative to the city accommodations because you can enjoy the atmosphere of the shrine and scenery at the summit when the tourists have gone. This place is unique in that it consists of large tatami-mat rooms that can be separated by *fusuma* (sliding paper doors on wood frames) to make smaller rooms. Or you and a group of 30 could all sleep in the same enclosed area if you wished. Meals are also served in these rooms after the bedding (futon) is put away. The place is jam-packed at festival times, so don't stay here if you need privacy. On the other hand, because Sai-kan is capable of handling 300 guests, one more person can almost always squeeze in. Meals consist of wild vegetables, tofu, fish, and other dishes made from local products. ⊠ *Tōge, Haguro-machi, Higashi Tagawa-gun, Yamagata-ken 997-0211,* ☏ *0235/62–2357,* FAX *0235/62–2352. No credit cards. MAP.*

$$ ⊞ **Tōkyō Dai-ichi Hotel Tsuruoka.** This standard business hotel is a few minutes' walk from JR Tsuruoka Eki and next to the Shōnai Kōtsū Mall bus terminal, from which buses depart for Haguro-san. The facilities are utilitarian but pleasant enough. ⊠ *2–10 Nishiki-machi, Tsuruoka-shi, Yamagata-ken 997-0031,* ☏ *0235/24–7611,* FAX *0235/24–7621. 75 rooms in main building, 49 in annex. AE, MC, V.*

Getting Around

Heading south from Akita, you have two options: to turn inland toward Tazawa-ko or drop down the Nihon-kai coast to Tsuruoka and the sacred mountain Haguro-san. There are five trains a day between Akita and Niigata; that trip takes about 3¾ hours.

TŌHOKU A TO Z

To research prices, get advice from other travelers, and book travel arrangements, visit www.fodors.com.

AIR TRAVEL

CARRIERS

Sendai has fives daily flights from Ōsaka International Airport by ANA. There are also flights to Fukuoka, Nagoya, Hiroshima, and to Sapporo's Chitose Airport.

Yamagata has four daily flights from Tōkyō's Haneda Airport by ANA and three flights from Ōsaka International Airport by JAS. There are also two flights to Fukuoka and one flight to Sapporo.

Morioka (whose Hanamaki Airport is 50 minutes by bus from downtown) has three flights from Ōsaka International Airport by JAS. There are also flights to Nagoya, Fukuoka, and Sapporo's Chitose Airport.

Akita has four daily flights from Tōkyō's Haneda Airport by ANA (All Nippon Airways), which also operates flights from Nagoya. Two flights from Ōsaka International Airport and three flights from Sapporo are provided by JAS (Japan Air System).

Aomori has four daily flights from Tōkyō's Haneda Airport by JAS and one by ANA. Aomori also has two flights from Nagoya, three from Ōsaka, and two from Sapporo's Chitose Airport.

Daily flights connect Shōnai Airport in Sakata, near Tsuruoka and Haguro-san, to Tōkyō, Ōsaka, Sapporo, and other cities in Japan.

For airline phone number, *see* Air Travel *in* Smart Travel Tips A to Z.

BOAT AND FERRY TRAVEL
Three sightseeing boats are especially recommended: at Matsu-shima Bay, near Sendai, and at Towada-ko. Keep in mind that these boats offer constant commentary in Japanese over the loudspeaker. The best way to find out the schedule is to call the national tourist information bureau in Tōkyō (☞ Visitor Information, *below*).

BUS TRAVEL
Although the Tōhoku Kyūkō Express night bus from Tōkyō to Sendai is inexpensive (¥6,210), it takes 7 hours and 10 minutes. It leaves Tōkyō Eki (Yaesu-guchi side, on the left as you walk along Yaesu-dōri, just before you get to the Matsuoka menswear shop) at 11 PM and arrives in Sendai at 6:10 AM. The bus from Sendai departs at 11 PM and arrives in Tōkyō at 6:10 AM. Reservations are required for all buses. You can buy a ticket right at the bus stop.

Buses take over where trains do not run, and in most instances, they depart from JR train stations. You should be able to find someone at the train station to direct you to the appropriate bus.
➤ CONTACTS: **Bus reservations** (☎ 03/3529–0321 in Tōkyō; 022/262–7031 in Sendai).

CAR RENTAL
Once you're in the locale you wish to explore, a car is ideal for getting around. All major towns have car-rental agencies. The Nippon-Hertz agency is the one most frequently represented. Bear in mind, though, that except on the Tōhoku Expressway, few road signs are in romaji. However, major roads have route numbers. With a road map in which the towns are spelled in romaji and *kanji* (the Chinese characters used in Japanese writing), it becomes relatively easy to decipher the directional signs. Note: Maps are not provided by car-rental agencies; be sure to obtain bilingual maps in Tōkyō or Sendai.
➤ MAJOR AGENCY: **Hertz Domestic Reservation Center** (☎ 0120/38–8002 toll-free).

CAR TRAVEL
The Tōhoku Expressway links Tōkyō with Aomori, but the cost of gas, tolls, and car rental makes driving expensive. It's also considerably slower to drive than to ride on the Shinkansen. Assuming you can clear metropolitan Tōkyō in 2 hours, the approximate driving time is 5 hours to Fukushima, 6 hours to Sendai, 8–10 hours to Morioka, and 10–11 hours to Aomori.

EMERGENCIES
➤ CONTACTS: **Ambulance** (☎ 119). **Police** (☎ 110).

TOURS
In summer's tourist season, scenic bus tours run from major tourist areas. The local Japan Travel Bureau at the train station in each area, or at major hotels, can make arrangements. The offices in Tōkyō, Kyōto, and Sendai arrange tours in English.
➤ TOUR CONTACTS: **Japan Travel Bureau** (☎ 03/5620–9500 in Tōkyō; 075/371–7891 in Kyōto; 022/221–4422 in Sendai).

TRAIN TRAVEL

The most efficient way to get to Tōhoku from Tōkyō is on the Tōhoku Shinkansen trains, all of which the JR Pass covers. The *Yamabiko*, which makes the fewest stops, and the slower *Aoba* Shinkansen run to Sendai and Morioka; the *Tsubasa* runs to Yamagata; and the *Komachi* to Akita. There are 63 total Shinkansen runs a day from Tōkyō to Fukushima (1½ to slightly more than 2 hours long), Sendai (2–2⅓ hours), Yamagata (2½ hours), Morioka (2¾–3½ hours), and Akita (3 hours, 50 minutes–4½ hours). North of Morioka, conventional trains continue on Aomori (an additional 2 hours, 10 minutes).

On Tōhoku's west coast, the train from Niigata takes almost 4 hours to travel along the Nihon-kai to Akita, and an additional 3 hours to reach Aomori. From Niigata inland to Yamagata, the train takes 3½ hours. Niigata is connected to Tōkyō's Ueno Eki by the Jōetsu Shinkansen, which at its fastest makes the run in 2 hours.

Elsewhere in Tōhoku, JR local trains are slower and less frequent (every two hours rather than every hour during the day) when they cross the region's mountainous spine. Most railways are owned by Japan Railways, so your JR Pass will work. Be aware that most trains stop running before midnight.

TRANSPORTATION AROUND TŌHOKU

Transportation in rural Tōhoku was, until recently, limited, which is why Tōhoku still has been undiscovered by modern progress and tourists. However, that is changing rapidly. Now, using a combination of trains and buses, most of Tōhoku's hinterland is easily accessible, except in heavy winter snows.

VISITOR INFORMATION

Japan Travel Bureau, a worldwide tourist agency, has offices at every JR station in each of the prefectural capitals and can assist in many areas, including hotel reservations, and ticketing for onward travel. Individual towns and prefectural governments have their own offices which provide local information. The largest and most helpful tourist center that gives information on all of Tōhoku and not just the local area is at Morioka Eki. In Sendai, it might be a better idea to consult the International Center in Aobayama Kōen.

In Tōkyō each prefecture also has an information center near Tōkyō Eki with a few English brochures and maps. The centers for Akita, Iwate, Miyagi, and Yamagata are on the ninth floor of Tetsudō Kaikan (above Daimaru department store at the station's Yaesu exit). The Aomori center is on the second floor of the nearby Kokusai Kankō Kaikan, and Fukushima's center is one floor higher in the same building.

The nationwide Japan Travel Phone service for English-language assistance or travel information is available seven days a week, 9–5. Dial toll-free for information on eastern Japan. When using a yellow, blue, or green public phone (do not use the red phones which are for local calls only), insert a ¥10 coin, which will be returned. There are different numbers for callers in Tōkyō and Kyōto, and in those cities the service costs ¥10 per three minutes.

➤ Tourist Information: **Japan Travel Phone** (☎ 03/3503–4400 in Tōkyō; 075/371–5649 in Kyōto). **JNTO Tourist Information Centers in Tōkyō** (☎ 03/3211–1775 in Akita; 03/3216–6010 in Aomori; 03/ 3214–2789 in Fukushima; 03/3231–2613 in Iwate; 03/3231–0944 in Miyagi; 03/3215–2222 in Yamagata). **Prefectural Government Tourist Information Centers** (☎ 0188/60–2266 in Akita; 017/734–9386 in Aomori; 0245/21–3811 in Fukushima; 019/651–3111 in Iwate; 022/211– 2743 in Miyagi; 0236/30–2373 in Yamagata).

13 HOKKAIDŌ

Hokkaidō is Japan untamed. Its cities
and towns are outposts of modern urban
humanity that wild mountains, virgin forests,
sapphire lakes, and surf-beaten shores keep
at bay. Hokkaidō is Japan's last frontier,
and the attitudes of the inhabitants are akin
to those of the pioneers of the American
West—or any other last places.

By Nigel Fisher

Updated
by Amanda
Harlow

T IS NO SMALL MARK OF ITS REMOTENESS that Hokkaidō was not even mentioned in books until the 7th century. Then for the next millennium it was written off as the place of the "hairy Ainu." The word *Sapporo* is derived from a combination of Ainu words meaning "a river running along a reed-filled plain." The Ainu, indigenous inhabitants of Japan—possibly related to ethnic groups that originally populated Siberia—were always thought of as the inferior race by the Yamato, who arrived in Japan from the south via Kyūshū and founded Japan's imperial house. As the Yamato spread and expanded their empire from Kyūshū through Honshū, the peace-loving Ainu retreated north to Hokkaidō. There they lived, supporting themselves with their traditional pursuits of hunting and fishing. By the 16th century the Yamato had established themselves in the southern tip of Hokkaidō, and they soon began to make incursions into the island's interior.

With the Meiji Restoration in 1868, Japan changed its policy toward Hokkaidō and opened it up as the new frontier to be colonized by the Yamato Japanese. The Tōkyō government encouraged immigration from the rest of Japan but made no provision for the Ainu people. Indeed, the Ainu were given no choice but to assimilate themselves into the life and culture of the colonizers. Consequently, Ainu culture went into a sudden and terminal decline—so much so that it has been fashionable for academics to write them off as a "doomed" or even "extinct" race.

But in recent years there has been something of a revival in Ainu culture and activism. The number of full-blooded Ainu might be very small, but 24,000 people believe themselves to possess enough of the bloodline to have officially declared themselves "Ainu." Similarly, though the Ainu language has virtually disappeared as a native tongue, many people have begun to study it in a burgeoning number of college and evening courses. Ainu activism, meanwhile, received a boost when the United Nations made 1993 the Year of Indigenous Peoples, and the Ainu scored a propaganda victory in 1994 when their leading activist, Shigeru Kayano, was elected to Japan's House of Councillors—the first Ainu to reach such a prominent position. In May 1997 the national government passed belated legislation recognizing Ainu culture. Sadly, little of this may be obvious to tourists who head for Hokkaidō's (reconstructed) Ainu villages, many of which are tourist traps making money for Japanese entrepreneurs rather than for the Ainu themselves. These can be depressing places indeed.

The Ainu are not the only indigenous Japanese peoples. Another nationality, the Moyoro, lived before the Ainu, but little is known about this mysterious people. Anthropological evidence found in the Moyoro Shell Mound, on Hokkaidō's east coast, and now displayed in Abashiri Museum, supports the belief that Moyoro civilization came to an end in the 9th century.

One of the delights of traveling through Hokkaidō is meeting the people, who are known as Dosanko, after the sturdy draft horse introduced from this area to the north. Since virtually all the Japanese on this island are "immigrants to a new frontier," there is less emphasis placed on honoring tradition than on accomplishing the matter at hand. Dosanko are still very Japanese, sharing the same culture as the rest of Japan, but they are also open to new customs and other cultures. They have a great attachment to their island. Hokkaidō consistently ranks at the top of surveys on where Japanese would most like to live.

Hokkaidō as we know it was born during the Meiji Restoration (1868–1912), a time when the Japanese government turned to the West for new ideas. This island looked to America and Europe as models of modern development. In the 1870s some 63 foreign experts came here, including an American architect who designed the prefecture's principal city, Sapporo. Around the same time, agricultural experts from abroad were brought in to introduce dry farming as a substitute for rice, which would not grow in the severe winter climate until hardy varieties were developed, which didn't happen until much later. This history of cooperation has left Dosanko with a peculiar fondness for Europeans. In Sapporo, Westerners are warmly received. In the countryside, Dosanko are shy—but hardly timid—in coming to the aid of Westerners.

Because Hokkaidō consists more of countryside than of cities—which implies language barriers that are more often than not bridged by the friendliness of locals—the number of gaijin who come here has traditionally been small, compared to the many Japanese from elsewhere in the country who come for winter skiing and summer hiking. At the same time ongoing refurbishments at Sapporo's Chitose Airport have opened up the island to more international flights (from such places as Amsterdam and Honolulu), which in turn have brought more people. Because Hokkaidō is Japan's northernmost and least developed island, it is easy to romanticize it as a largely uncharted territory. That is mostly untrue, as road and rail networks crisscross the island. Of course, wild beauty and open space still abound—from volcanic mountains and lakes to the marshlands of the red-crested *tanchō-zuru* (red-crested crane) to the ice floes of the Ohotsuku-kai (Sea of Okhotsk) to the northerly isolation of the Rishiri and Rebun islands.

Hokkaidō Glossary
Key Japanese words and suffixes in this chapter include the following: *-banchi* (street number), *bijutsukan* (art museum), *-chō* (street or block), *-chōme* (street), *chūō* (central), *-dake* ("*da*-keh," peak), *-dōri* (avenue), *eki* (train station), *gaijin* (foreigner), *-gawa* (river), *-hantō* (peninsula), *higashi* (east), *izakaya* (pub), *-jima*, (island), *-kan* (museum), *-kawa* (river), *-ken* (prefecture), *kita* (north), *-ko* (lake, as in Tōya-ko, Lake Tōya), *kōen* ("*ko*-en," park), *-ku* (section or ward), *kūkō* (airport), *minami* (south), *misaki* (cape), *Nihon-kai* (Sea of Japan), *nishi* (west), *Ohotsuku-kai* (Sea of Okhotsk), *onsen* (hot spring), *rotemburo* (outdoor hot spring), *ryūhyō* (ice floes), *sakura* (cherry blossoms), *-san* (mountain), *-shi* (city or municipality), *-shima* (island), *soba* (buckwheat noodles), *-take* ("*ta*-keh," peak), *-tō* (island), *tōge* (pass), *-yama* (mountain), and *-zan* (mountain).

Pleasures and Pastimes

Dining
Eat at local Japanese restaurants as often as possible to experience one of the true joys of Hokkaidō, the regional food. Many reasonably priced restaurants have a visual display of their menu in the window, which allows you to decide what you want before you enter. If you cannot order in Japanese and no English is spoken, lead the waiter to the window display and point, or try sketching for your server the Japanese character for the dish you want.

Hokkaidō is known for its seafood—the prefecture's name means "the Road to the Northern Sea." *Shake* (salmon), *ika* (squid), *uni* (sea urchin), *nishin* (herring), and *kai* (shellfish) are abundant, but the real treat is the fat, sweet scallop, *kaibashira,* collected from northernmost Wakkanai. The other great favorite is crab, which comes in three varieties: *ke-gani* (hairy crab), *taraba-gani* (king crab), and Nemuro's celebrated *hanasaki-gani* (spiny king crab).

Jingisukan is thinly sliced mutton cooked on a dome-shape griddle. The name comes from the griddle's resemblance to helmets worn by Mongolian cavalry under Genghis Khan. Vegetables—usually onions, green peppers, and cabbage—are added to the sizzling mutton, and the whole mix is dipped in a tangy brown sauce. *Ramen* (Chinese noodles served in soup) is extremely popular and inexpensive. Local residents favor miso ramen, which uses a less delicate variety of fermented soybean paste than does miso soup. Ramen with *shio* (salt) or *shoyu* (soy sauce) soup base also is widely available.

Eki-ben—the classic box lunch—is a must in Hokkaidō. Pick one up in JR Hakodate Eki: the local *nishin-migaki-bentō* consists of nishin (herring) boiled in a sweet, spicy sauce until the bones are soft enough to eat. Your appetite will probably return by the time you reach Mori Eki, about an hour north of Hakodate, so you can try another well-known eki-ben, *ika-meshi*, a box lunch made by stuffing a whole *ika* (squid) with rice and cooking it in a sweet, spicy sauce. Each meal includes two or three ika.

For more details on Japanese cuisine, *see* Chapter 14 *and* Dining *in* Smart Travel Tips A to Z.

CATEGORY	COST*
$$$$	over ¥4,000
$$$	¥2,500–¥4,000
$$	¥1,500–¥2,500
$	under ¥1,500

per person for a main course at dinner

Lodging

Accommodations in Hokkaidō tend to consist of modern, characterless hotels built for Japanese tour groups. Large, unattractively furnished sitting areas and spacious lobbies are the norm, with the scenery as the only distinguishing element. Invariably, prices depend on views and the size of public areas and guest rooms. As tourism in Hokkaidō grows, more attractive and comfortable hotels are appearing.

Outside Sapporo and Hokkaidō's industrial and commercial cities, hot-spring hotels charge on a per-person basis including two meals and excluding service and tax. In those cases, the rates listed below are for two people with two meals each, and the Modified American Plan is noted in the service information. If you don't want dinner, it's usually possible to renegotiate the price. Isolated resort areas may offer the limited choice of dining at your hotel or risking the local equivalent of fast food: ramen or Japanese-style curry.

For a short course on accommodations in Japan, *see* Lodging *in* Smart Travel Tips A to Z.

CATEGORY	COST*
$$$$	over ¥20,000
$$$	¥15,000–¥20,000
$$	¥10,000–¥15,000
$	under ¥10,000

All prices are for a double room, excluding service and tax.

Outdoor Activities and Sports

Keeping in step with the seasons is the way to enjoy Hokkaidō, whether by savoring a summer festival, taking in the explosion of autumn colors, schussing down an Olympic ski slope, or soaking in an open-air hot spring. There are endless trails to hike and rivers, lakes, and oceans to fish.

Exploring Hokkaidō

With little visible past and cities that are relatively new, Hokkaidō will provide a respite from the temples, shrines, and castles that dominate itineraries in the rest of Japan. The island is a geological wonderland: lava-seared mountains hide deeply carved ravines; hot springs, gushers, and steaming mud pools boil out of the ground; and crystal-clear caldera lakes fill the seemingly bottomless cones of volcanoes. Half of Hokkaidō is covered in forest. Wild, rugged coastlines hold back the sea, and all around the prefecture, islands surface offshore. Some are volcanic peaks poking out of the ocean, and others were formed eons ago by the crunching of the earth's crust. The remnants of Hokkaidō's bear population, believed to number about 2,000, still roam the forests, snagging rabbits and scooping up fish from mountain streams, and deer wander the pastures, stealing food from cows. Hokkaidō's native crane, the tanchō-zuru, is especially magnificent, with a red-cap head and a white body trimmed with black feathers. Look for it on the ¥1,000 note and in the marshes of Kushiro, east of Sapporo on the Pacific coast.

Numbers in the text correspond to numbers in the margin and on the Hokkaidō map.

Great Itineraries

Hokkaidō's expansiveness is daunting. Fortunately, the main sights—calderas, remote onsen, craggy coasts, dramatic climate—are everywhere. Rather than rushing to see everything, consider balancing the natural with the urban, the inland with the coastal, and figure in the seasonality of sights and activities more heavily than you would elsewhere in Japan. The historically minded should focus on the major cities of southern Hokkaidō. Wilderness lovers should venture east and center.

IF YOU HAVE 3 DAYS

Three days is just enough to take in a slice of southern Hokkaidō. Fly into Chitose Kūkō, outside ⊞ **Sapporo** ②–⑬, and spend a day touring the city, finishing with the neon thrill of the Susukino nightlife district. The next day, head south and east by JR to Tomikawa and then take the Dōnan Bus service up to the Ainu village of **Nibutani** ㉑, backtracking to ⊞ **Shikotsu-ko** ㉒ for the night. That will position you for a final day around the caldera lake, either soaking in the scenery or going for a morning hike up the volcanic cones of Eniwa-dake or Tarumae-zan. Or, instead of two days between Nibutani and Shikotsu-ko, you could head west and south for ⊞ **Niseko** ⑯ and a day's hiking or skiing. Overnight there and return to Sapporo on the third day on a coastal circuit around rocky **Shakotan-hantō** ⑮, stopping in **Otaru** ⑭ for its rustic charm and peerless sushi.

IF YOU HAVE 5 DAYS

Five days will allow a more in-depth tour of southern Hokkaidō or, if you skip Sapporo entirely, a dash around the central, eastern, or northern parts of the island. For the southern option, spend your first day in ⊞ **Hakodate** ① or ⊞ **Sapporo** ②–⑬; then make a thorough loop through **Shikotsu-Tōya National Park,** detouring east to **Nibutani** ㉑ for its Ainu village. You could otherwise spend the last four days passing through ⊞ **Otaru** ⑭, then around the **Shakotan-hantō** ⑮, on the way down to **Niseko** ⑯ for hiking or skiing. If you're hankering to leave civilization behind you, press north for the islands off the tip of Hokkaidō, **Rebun-tō** ㉛ and ⊞ **Rishiri-tō** ㉜. It takes two days of travel round-trip unless you fly, but the tiny fishing villages and their fresh seafood, great hiking, and volcanic scenery will make for a singular experience of Japan.

TO SAKHALIN ISLAND

33 **Sōya Misaki**

Rebun-tō 31

Kafuka

30 **Wakkanai**

Oshidomari

Hama Tonbetsu

32 Kutsugata

Rishiri-tō

Kutcharo-ko

Esashi

Horonobe

238

KITAMI MTNS.

Mombets

Tomamae

Nayoro

Taki

NIHON-KAI
(Sea of Japan)

Teshio-dake

Rumoi

Kamikaw

Mashike

Asahikawa

28

Asahi-dake

Sōun-ky

Daisets

Asahi-dake Onsen

Shirogane Onsen

Daisets Nation

Furano

Tokachi-dake

29

Shakotan-misaki

Shakotan-hantō

Ishikara-wan

Yobetsu

Furubira

Sapporo

2 — 13

Shikaribetsu-ko

Kamui-misaki

15

Yoichi

14 **Otaru**

see detail map

Yūbari-dake

Tomaru Tōge

Kamoenai

Sapporo

Tengu-yama

17

Iwamizawa

5

Kutchan

Jōzankei Onsen

Niseko

16

Yotei-zan

18 **Nakayama Tōge**

Chitose

Shikotsu-Tōya National Park

22 **Shikotsu-ko**

Tōya-ko Onsen

19

21 **Nibutani**

Noboribetsu Onsen

20

Tomakomai

HIDAKA RANGE

Oshamambe

Shiraoi

Tomikawa

Uchiura-wan

Noboribetsu

Muroran

Hiro-

O-shima-hantō

Komaga-dake

Apoi-dake

5

Esashi

1

Hakodate

Fukushima

Tsugaru Kaikyo (Tsugaru Straits)

N

TO AOMORI

Seikan Tunnel

H O N S H Ū

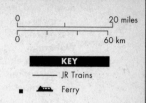

0   20 miles

0   60 km

KEY
— JR Trains
■   ⛴ Ferry

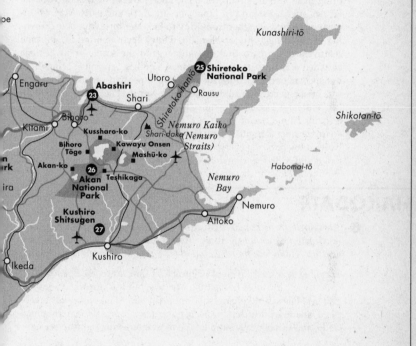

OHOTSUKU-KAI
(Sea of Okhotsk)

Kunashiri-tō

Engaru

Abashiri

Utoro

㉕ **Shiretoko**
National Park

Shari

Rausu

㉓

Bihoro

Kitami

Kussharo-ko

Shiretoko-hantō

Shikotan-tō

Bihoro
Tōge

Kawayu Onsen

Shari-dake

Nemuro Kaiko
(Nemuro
Straits)

Akan-ko

Mashū-ko

Habomai-tō

rk

㉖
Akan
National
Park

Teshikaga

Nemuro
Bay

Nemuro

ira

Kushiro
Shitsugen

Attoko

㉗

Ikeda

Kushiro

TAIHEIYŌ
(Pacific Ocean)

With a week, you can give yourself time in ☷ **Sapporo** ②–⑬ or ☷ **Hako-date** ① and one or two of the farther-flung parks. Skip the areas south of Sapporo and make your way through ☷ **Asahikawa** ㉘ to the gorges and onsen of ☷ **Daisetsu-zan National Park** ㉙ or the Northern Cape's **Wakkanai** ㉚ and the islands in the Nihon-kai. Or continue through Asahikawa and Daisetsu-zan National Park to ☷ **Abashiri** ㉓ to see the wonders of the Ohotsuku-kai and ☷ **Akan National Park** ㉖. Take five days or more to see all of eastern Hokkaidō, including a venture into the end-of-the-world wilds of **Shiretoko National Park** ㉕ and a stop at **Kushiro Shitsugen** ㉗ to see the rare and beautiful tanchō-zuru.

When to Tour Hokkaidō

Hokkaidō has Japan's most dramatic seasons. Festivals predominate in the extreme seasons, summer and winter. May and early summer bring lilacs and alpine flowers. The cherry trees in Hokkaidō are the last to offer up sakura in Japan, in late April and early May. Gloriously refreshing weather from May to October lures Japanese drowning in the muggy air of Honshū. Hotel accommodations become relatively difficult to find in summer, and the scenic areas become crowded with tour groups and Japanese families. September brings brief but spectacular golden foliage, reaching a peak in early October. Fall is as brief as it is crisp and striking, giving way to chilly drizzle in November and early December—times to avoid. Winter makes travel more difficult (some minor roads are closed), and especially on the east coast, weather is frigid. It is no less beautiful a time, however, with crisp white snow covering everything and ice floes crowding the Ohotsuku-kai. If you're here during the second week in February, make your way to Sapporo for the dazzling Snow Festival.

HAKODATE

❶ *3 hrs north from Tōkyō to Morioka by JR Shinkansen, then 2 or 3 hrs north from Morioka to Aomori by JR Limited Express, then 2½ hrs north to Hakodate by JR Rapid via the Seikan Tunnel.*

Traveling by train from Honshū into Hokkaidō, you come first to Hakodate. It isn't the most fascinating of cities, but it is historically important and has several picturesque spots. In 1859 Hakodate was one of three Japanese ports that the Meiji government opened to international trade, and this heritage supplies the most interesting sights to see now.

The **Seikan Tunnel** connects Honshū and Hokkaidō under the Tsugaru Kaikyō (Tsugaru Straits). This civil engineering marvel, completed in 1988, was the longest undersea tunnel in the world until Europe's Channel Tunnel usurped its place. The first stop in Hokkaidō proper is Hakodate. An express ferry makes the crossing in a half hour less (two hours) at half the price (¥1,420).

Hakodate Russian Orthodox Church (✉ 3–13 Moto-machi, ☎ 0138/23–7387) dates from 1859, when it served as the first Russian consulate in the city. After a 1907 fire, it was rebuilt in Byzantine style in 1916. A large-scale restoration project was completed in 1989. The church has become something of an exotic attraction for the city. To get here from the JR station, take Streetcar 5 to the Suehiro-chō stop and walk 10 minutes toward Hakodate-yama.

The **Moto-machi museums,** housed in old buildings with definite European- and American-style architecture, stand clustered in the neighborhood at the foot of Hakodate-yama. **Hakodate-shi Bungaku-kan** (Hakodate City Museum of Literature; ✉ 22–5 Suehiro-chō, ☎ 0138/

22–9014) provides information, some of it in English, about the city's most noted writers. None are household names in the West, but the museum is pleasant and also has a photographic display of the "eight most beautiful scenes in Hakodate"—evidence yet again of the Japanese mania for cataloging and ranking everything. (How it was determined that there were eight such scenes is anyone's guess.) The Bungaku-kan is downhill from the Russian Orthodox church. **Hoppo Minzoku Shiryo-kan** (Museum of Northern Peoples; ✉ 21–7 Suehiro-chō, ☎ 0138/22–4128) gives a straightforward introduction to Hokkaidō's Ainu culture, though it's not nearly as detailed as other museums farther north, and the decor is rather spartan. The **Kyū Igirisu Ryōji-kan** (British Consulate Building; ✉ 33–14 Moto-machi, ☎ 0138/27–8159) is now a museum devoted to the opening of the port in the 19th century. Architecturally, the consulate is picturesque, but the exhibits, alas, have no information in English. **Kyū Hakodate-ku Kokaido** (Old Hakodate Public Hall; ✉ 11–13 Moto-machi, ☎ 0138/22–1001), with its classical columns and antebellum architecture, looks like a manor house in America's Deep South. ✎ ¥840 gains admission to all 4 museums. ☉ Apr.–Oct., daily 9–7; Nov.–Mar., daily 9–5.

★ Jutting out from the city like a spur, the volcanic **Hakodate-yama** rises to a height of 1,100 ft. Views of the city from its summit are especially good at night, with the darkness of the Tsugaru Kaikyō on one side and the brilliant city lights accenting the small isthmus that connects the peak to the downtown. You can take a 30-minute bus ride to the top of Hakodate-yama from the JR station from late April through October, or for a more interesting trip, hop on Streetcar 2 or 5 to the Jūji-gai stop and then walk about seven minutes to the cable car for the three-minute ride up the mountain. The city claims that this cable car, with its capacity of 125 passengers, is the largest in Asia. A restaurant at the top is particularly appealing for its nighttime view. ✎ Cable car ¥640 one-way, ¥1,160 round-trip. ☉ Cable car late Apr.–early May and late July–late Aug., daily 9 AM–10 PM; early May–late July and late Aug–Oct., daily 10–10; Nov.–late Apr., daily 10–9.

In daytime, **Tachi-machi-misaki** (Standing and Waiting Cape) is more dramatic than Hakodate-yama, since you can look down from this cliff to where the ocean batters the coast. The name comes from the promontory's past life as a lookout for the ferry from Honshū, not from its more recent reputation as a place from which people commit suicide. Take Streetcar 2 from Hakodate-eki-mae to Yachigashira, then continue on foot to the cape.

In the center of the city is **Goryōkaku**, a Western-style fort completed in 1864. Its design is unusual for Japan, especially the five-pointed-star shape, which enabled its defenders to rake any attackers with murderous cross fire. In spite of all that protection, the Tokugawa Shogunate was unable to hold out against the forces of the Meiji Restoration, and its walls were breached. Nothing of the interior castle remains, but there is a small museum with relics from the battle. Now the fort area is a park with some 4,000 cherry trees, which, when they bloom in late April, make the stopover in Hakodate worthwhile. An observation tower in the park, at ¥630 admission, is not worth the climb. Take Bus 12, 20, 30, or 27–1 from JR Hakodate Eki's Gate B, or Streetcar 2 or 5 to the Goryōkaku Kōen-mae stop. From either stop, it is a 10-minute walk to the fort. ✎ Free. ☉ Late Apr.–late Oct., daily 8–7; late Oct.–late Apr., daily 9–6.

A number of historic harbor-front warehouses have been restored 250 yards north by northwest of the Jūji-gai streetcar stop, including **Hako-**

date History Plaza (☎ 0138/23–0350), which contains markets, restaurants, and bars (open until 10:30 PM).

Dining and Lodging

$–$$ ✕ **Hakodate Beer Hall.** This seaside hall in Hakodate History Plaza serves seafood specialties, such as squid, octopus, and tofu *shabu shabu* (cooked at the table by dipping in boiling water and then into a sauce) for ¥1,300 and three local brews (wheat beer, ale, and the slightly more bitter "alt" beer). Its spaciousness and conviviality are typical of Hokkaidō and favored by domestic travelers. ✉ *5–22 Ote-machi,* ☎ *0138/23–8000. AE, V.*

$–$$ ✕ **Uoisshin.** Specializing in the best of the morning's catch, served grilled or as sashimi, this two-floor restaurant has both counter and traditional low-table seating. ✉ *3–11 Matsukaze-chō,* ☎ *0138/26–0457. No credit cards. Closed Mon.*

$ ✕ **Lucky Pierrot.** Hakodate's most famous burger shop serves up 14 kinds—including a squid burger—and a range of curries, too. There are only a few seats inside; most customers take out. The shop made news recently when it was chosen to supply hamburgers to a local high school. It's next to Hakodate History Plaza. ✉ *23–18 Suehiro-cho,* ☎ *0138/26–2099. No credit cards.*

$$–$$$$ 🏨 **Harborview Hotel.** This place maintains a fresh, cheerful ambience and has a friendly staff. A pleasant coffee lounge and a sociable bar are in the lobby. Standard Western-style rooms are furnished in light blue or peach—not particularly attractive, but comfortable enough for a night. This hotel is very conveniently located next to JR Hakodate Eki and near buses to in-town destinations. ✉ *14–10 Wakamatsu-chō, Hakodate, Hokkaidō 040–0063,* ☎ *0138/22–0111,* FAX *0138/23–0154. 200 rooms. 3 restaurants, bar, coffee shop. AE, DC, MC, V.*

$$$ 🏨 **Pension Kokian.** A central waterfront location, close to the historic sights, is the reason to select Pension Kokian. On the next street are several cafés and bars. The small tatami rooms are nothing special, with smudged walls and cracked plaster. The shared toilet facilities are basic, and for your bath you have the choice of the communal bath or a 15-minute tram ride to the public baths at Yachigashira Onsen. Better than the accommodations is the restaurant (two meals are included in the room rate). ✉ *13–2 Suehiro-chō, Hakodate, Hokkaidō 040–0053,* ☎ *0138/26–5753,* FAX *0138/22–271. 17 Japanese-style rooms with shared bath. Restaurant. AE, DC, V. MAP.*

$$ 🏨 **Ryokan Hakodate.** This small house with tatami rooms is 10 minutes by foot from the JR station. The price includes breakfast and dinner for two, Japanese style. ✉ *28–7 Omori-chō, Hakodate, Hokkaidō 040–0034,* ☎ *0138/26–1255,* FAX *0138/26–1256. 4 Japanese-style rooms, 14 Japanese-style rooms with shared bath. No credit cards. MAP.*

Getting Around

The cost of travel on streetcars ranges from ¥200 to ¥250 and on the municipal buses from ¥200 to ¥260. You can pick up a one-day bus-and-streetcar pass, available from the tourist information center, for ¥1,000.

Hokuto Kōtsū (☎ 0138/57–7555), a bus company, runs 4½-hour sightseeing tours of the city (in Japanese), leaving from JR Hakodate Eki and covering most of the city sights for ¥4,000.

Visitor Information

For maps and a hotel list in English, stop at the **Hakodate City Tourist Information Center** (☎ 0138/23–5440) just to the right as you exit JR Hakodate Eki. It's open April–October, daily 9–7, and November–March, daily 9–5.

SAPPORO

3½ hrs north of Hakodate by JR.

Sapporo is both Hokkaidō's capital and the island's premier city. With 1.8 million inhabitants, it's four times larger than Asahikawa, the prefecture's next-largest city. And as Hokkaidō's unemployed from the economically depressed farms in the central plains and industrial and fishing towns on the coast migrate to Sapporo for work, it continues to expand. Though it's a large city, it's not confusing or congested. In 1870 the governor of Hokkaidō visited President Grant in the United States and requested that American advisers come to Hokkaidō to help design the capital on the site of an Ainu village. As a result, Sapporo was built on a 330-ft grid system with wide avenues and parks. It's not the exotic and cultural city you expect to find in Japan and is distinctly lacking in pre-Meiji historic sights. On the other hand, you can walk the sidewalks without being swept away in a surge of humanity.

By hosting the 1972 Winter Olympic Games, Sapporo relaunched itself as an international city and took on a cosmopolitan attitude. Developers built plenty of hotels and restaurants that are still up and running. Banks here are used to traveler's checks, and there is always someone on hand to help you out in English. Ultimately, though, Sapporo is best to use as a base from which to make excursions into the wild, dramatic countryside. If you want to explore the city, a day, perhaps two at most, will do.

Sapporo's best-known annual event, held for a week beginning February 5 or 6, the **Sapporo Snow Festival** is the greatest of its kind. More than 300 lifelike sculptures, as large as 130 ft tall by 50 ft deep by 80 ft wide, are created each year. The festival began in 1950 with six statues that were carved to entertain local citizens, depressed by the aftermath of the war and the long winter nights. Now the event is so large that sculpture is displayed in three sections of the city: Ō-dōri Kōen (large sculpture and spectator events), Makomanai (mammoth creations and ice slides for children), and Susukino (magnificent ice sculptures lining Eki-mae-dōri). The festival attracts more than 2 million visitors each year, so book accommodations well in advance.

Numbers in the text correspond to numbers in the margin and on the Sapporo map.

A Good Walk

Most comforting about Sapporo is the simplicity of the city's layout. East–west streets are called *jō*, and those running north–south are *chōme*. They are numbered consecutively, and each block is approximately 100 yards square. The cardinal points are used more often than elsewhere in Japan. North, south, east, and west are *kita, minami, higashi,* and *nishi,* respectively. Ō-dōri Kōen divides the city in half north–south, and the Sosei-gawa separates east from west. Thus, the address Kita 1-jō Nishi 2 means one block north of Ō-dōri Park and two blocks west of the Sosei River, putting you at the Clock Tower.

A good place to start out on foot is **Nakajima Kōen** ②, with its lake, gardens, and two national cultural treasures: the 17th-century Japanese Hasso-an Teahouse and the Western-style Hoheikan. To get to the park, take the Namboku subway line to the Nakajima Kōen stop. You'll exit on the north edge of the park between the blue Park Hotel and the white Hotel Arthur Sapporo.

After touring the park, return to the Nakajima Kōen subway station and walk north on Eki-mae-dōri, leaving the park at your back. This

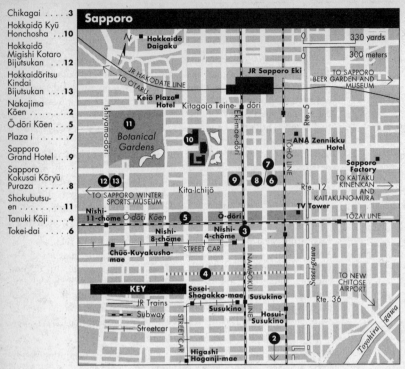

avenue runs through the Susukino entertainment district before slicing Ō-dōri Kōen perpendicularly and being blocked by the JR station. Pass through Susukino for now, and revisit it in the evening. Take time instead to explore the heart of Sapporo's downtown retail center, **Chikagai** ③. Running perpendicular to the north–south access of Chikagai, one block north of Susukino crossing is a covered shopping arcade called **Tanuki Kōji** ④, which provides welcome shelter from the snow during the long winter.

Ō-dōri Kōen ⑤, above the center of Chikagai, is a park in the median of a broad east–west avenue. It's the site of a number of city events, including the Snow Festival. The unappealing TV Tower is at the east end of Ō-dōri Kōen. Sapporo Tourist Association promotes it for the view from its observation platform, but views of the city are better, and free, from any of the high-rise hotels. On Kita-ichi-jō, one block north and one block west of the tower, Sapporo's landmark Russian-style **Tokei-dai** ⑥ is where Japanese tourists photograph each other to prove that they were in Sapporo.

On the first floor of the office building across the street from the Clock Tower is **Plaza i** ⑦, the best place in town for local information in English. **Sapporo Kokusai Kōryū Puraza** ⑧, on the third floor, has a lounge for conversational exchange between foreigners and locals. Back on the streets of Sapporo, head west on the north side of the Kita-ichi-jō block. Past the corner of Eki-mae-dōri, you come upon the classical facade of the **Sapporo Grand Hotel** ⑨.

Just northwest of the Grand Hotel is a complex of municipal buildings, among them a large, redbrick building that houses the **Hokkaidō Kyū Honchōsha** ⑩, the Old Hokkaidō Government Building. West again from here, the **Shokubutsu-en** ⑪ is a good place to stroll amid a profusion of plants. The garden's greenhouse is on the south end of a pond.

Walk four blocks west of the gardens to see the paintings of artist Migishi Kotaro in the **Hokkaidō Migishi Kotaro Bijutsukan** ⑫. On the next block is the attractive **Hokkaidōritsu Kindai Bijutsukan** ⑬, which displays a more general collection of Japanese art. Turn back toward the Botanical Gardens and head back downtown. The other sights listed below are best reached by subway or taxi. Return to Susukino after 7 PM, when the street scene starts to pick up.

TIMING

You can see the sights downtown on foot in about 2½ hours, not including time spent meandering, looking into museums, shopping, and dining. Plan to spend an hour at each art museum, no more than a half hour for the other sites, and at least a half hour at each park. In winter you can use the underground malls to cover large areas of downtown.

Sights to See

❸ **Chikagai.** The Downtown Underground is the heart of Sapporo's retail center. Here, subterranean promenades form a T of shops and restaurants, intersecting at the Ō-dōri subway station, where the Namboku and Tōzai subway lines cross. Pole Town is the T's vertical leg, extending north all the way from beneath the clock in the middle of the Susukino crossing. Aurora Town, the east–west cap to the T, runs from below the TV Tower to Nishi 5-chōe.

Hokkaidō Daigaku (Hokkaidō University). Hokudai, as it's affectionately called, is the most prestigious university in Hokkaidō and one of the best in Japan. A bust on campus honors Dr. William S. Clark, the school's first president and a central figure in Hokkaidō's development. The school was founded in 1878, in the building that is now the Tokeidai. You are more likely to be impressed by the beautifully designed grounds of the spacious campus. It is bordered on the west by Ishiyamadōri, on the east by Hokudai-dōri.

❿ **Hokkaidō Kyū Honchōsha** (Old Hokkaidō Government Building). The grandest structure in Hokkaidō, this Western-style building was erected in 1888 and now contains exhibits about the early development of Hokkaidō. Its nickname, *Aka Renga,* means "Ol' Redbrick." It is just northwest of the Grand Hotel in a complex of municipal buildings and is closed the third Thursday of every month. ☎ *011/231–4111.* ☞ *Free.* ☉ *Apr.–Sept., weekdays 9–5; Oct.–Mar., weekdays 9–5.*

⑫ **Hokkaidō Migishi Kotaro Bijutsukan** (Hokkaidō Kotaro Migishi Art Museum). This gallery was opened in 1983 for the sole purpose of hanging 235 oil and watercolor paintings, drawings, and prints by native son Migishi, who died in 1934 at the age of 31. The museum was designed to reflect the many changes of style that characterize the artist's short career. It is a four-minute walk north of the Nishi-jū-hat-chōme (West 18-chōme) Tōzai Line subway station. ✉ *Kita 1-jō Nishi 16,* ☎ *011/644–8901.* ☞ *¥250.* ☉ *Tues.–Sun. 10–5.*

⑬ **Hokkaidōritsu Kindai Bijutsukan** (Hokkaidō Museum of Modern Art). This museum features local and foreign exhibits. Though it doesn't hold priceless works of art, the museum enables visitors to see what is appreciated by the Japanese. A four-minute walk north of the Nishi-jū-hat-chōme (West 18-chōme) Tōzai Line subway station brings you to the museum. ✉ *Kita 1-jō Nishi 17,* ☎ *011/644–6881.* ☞ *¥250.* ☉ *Tues.–Sun. 10–5.*

Kaitaku Kinenkan (Historical Museum of Hokkaidō). Exhibits range from ancient bones to cultural artifacts, from the propaganda materials created to persuade mainland settlers to head north to bulky early home appliances. The drawback is the location, about 10 km (6 mi) outside Sapporo. Best access is a 15-minute bus or taxi ride from Shin-Sapporo Eki. ✉ *Konopporo, Atsubetsu-chō,* ☎ *011/898–0456.* ◻ *¥300.* ◷ *Tues.–Sat. 9:30–4:30.*

Kaitaku-no-mura (Historical Village of Hokkaidō). More than 60 old buildings from all over Hokkaidō have been brought together in a park, and an excellent English guidebook helps visitors step back into farm and village life of 100 years ago. The centerpiece is the former Sapporo Railway Station, a glorious red-and-white edifice that shames the modern architects who erected the current glass-and-concrete gateway to the city. In winter, horse-drawn sleighs tour the village. Take a JR bus to the village from Sapporo Eki (in the early morning), or Shin-Sapporo Eki (about every hour); if you're traveling in a group, the 15-minute taxi ride from Shin-Sapporo is more convenient and economical. ✉ *1–50–1 Konopporo, Atsubetsu-cho,* ☎ *011/898–2692.* ◻ *¥610.* ◷ *Tues.–Sun. 9:30–4:30.*

❷ Nakajima Kōen. This city park has a couple of historic sites, which, along with its small lake for boating (¥600 for 40 minutes) and Japanese and Western gardens, make it worth a visit.

One of Nakajima Kōen's National Cultural Treasures is the 17th-century **Hasso-an Teahouse,** harmoniously surrounded by a Japanese garden on the west side of the park. Virtually the only traditional Japanese structure in Hokkaidō, it stands in stark contrast to the new frontier style of architecture on the rest of the island. The name means "eight windows." ◻ *Free.* ◷ *May–Oct., daily 9–4.*

The other National Cultural Treasure in Nakajima Kōen is **Hoheikan,** a stately Western-style building originally constructed as an imperial guest house. It's symbolic of the time when Hokkaidō was colonized by the Yamato Japanese and the Meiji government looked to the West as it built a modern nation state. The empty interior, which is hired out for lunch parties, does not offer much to visit, but the blue-and-white exterior makes a grand sight—especially when the cherry blossoms are out. ◻ *Free.* ◷ *Daily 9–5.*

On the west side of the park, one of Japan's finest concert halls stands in modern counterpoint to Hoheikan. **Sapporo Concert Hall,** opened in 1997, has a 500-pipe organ and serves as a central facility to the city's Pacific Music Festival, held the last three weeks of July.

The **Aruku Sukii Muryō Kashidashi-jō** (Free Cross-Country Ski Lending Office; ☎ 011/530–5911) offers three-day loans of cross-country skis. Just leave a piece of identification, and off you go. It's in the Nakajima Sports Center, on the east side of the park. The easiest way to get to the park is by taking the Namboku Line subway to the Nakajima Kōen stop. Exit on the north edge of the park between the blue Park Hotel and Hotel Arthur Sapporo's white tower. The alternative is to walk here from the JR station, heading due south along Eki-mae-dōri for 1½ km (1 mi).

❺ Ō-dōri Kōen. This 345-ft-wide, east–west avenue park bisects the city center. It's a good place to people-watch in summer, when office workers buy lunch from various food vendors and take in the sun, so long absent during the winter months. Skip the park-vendor food. Instead, picnic on box lunches from the basement food floors of the Marui Imai department store, south across the street from the park's West 2 block.

Various events are held here in succession from June through August; in February the park displays large, lifelike snow sculptures that the Japanese Self-Defense Forces create for the Sapporo Snow Festival, which has made the city famous.

❼ **Plaza i.** English-speaking staff members here are extremely helpful in distributing free brochures, maps, and flyers on current happenings in town and will send and receive faxes. They can assist with accommodations throughout the area. You may want to browse through their English-language books on Hokkaidō and other islands of Japan and take a look at the display of local crafts. ✉ *1st floor, Kita 1-jō Nishi 3, Chūō-ku,* ☎ *011/211–3678,* FAX *011/219–0020,* WEB *www.plaza-sapporo.or.jp.* ⏰ *Daily 9–5:30.*

★ **Sapporo Beer Garden and Museum.** During the day, free tours through the redbrick museum will acquaint you with the history and the modern brewing technology of Hokkaidō's most famous product. Museum reservations are required; request a guide who speaks some English. But the real fun of coming here is the huge beer garden and the cavernous, three-tier beer hall. Most of the action occurs during the evening in the hall, which is similar in atmosphere to a German beer hall. It was a German, after all, who, upon finding wild hops growing on Hokkaidō, taught locals how to make beer. Instead of bratwurst, however, the beer garden's griddle-cooked lamb Jingisukan is the highlight.

In summer the beer garden is a gathering place day and evening, good for seeing and meeting the Japanese at play. The *tabe-nomi-hodai* (all you can eat and drink) menu means mugs of lager downed with gusto amid exclamations of "*Kampai!*"—"Bottoms up!" Around February, snow sculptures and igloos festoon the site. The beer garden is about a 15-minute walk east from JR Sapporo Eki, or a ¥1,000 taxi ride from downtown. ✉ *Kita 7-jō Higashi 9,* ☎ *011/731–4368 museum; 011/742–1531 restaurant.* ⬚ *Free.* ⏰ *Museum Sept.–May, daily 9–5; June–Aug., daily 8:40–6 (last entry 80 mins before closing); beer garden May–Sept., daily 11–9:30; Oct.–Apr., daily 11–8:45.*

★ **Sapporo Factory.** If you are more interested in shopping, eating, and drinking than in trekking around to see the sights, Sapporo Factory has enough boutiques, restaurants (the only good Mexican one in Hokkaidō), and entertainment to fill an entire day. Small wonder its promoters call it a "town within a city." The complex occupies several buildings—including an old Sapporo Beer brewery, which retains its distinctive redbrick and chimney—all but one linked by a second-floor passageway. Among the venues are a 1,500-seat beer restaurant, a wine cellar containing some 2,000 varieties of wine, an IMAX theater, and 11 movie theaters. Most striking of all, however, is the 275-ft-high atrium, with an arching glass roof that shields an indoor garden and terrace from the worst that Hokkaidō's climate can offer. It's the largest structure of its type in Japan. **Sapporo Springs** (☎ 011/242–1111), part of the factory, is a hot-spring pool and sauna. For ¥1,800 (three hours) or ¥2,700 (all day), you can be pampered and invigorated in this steaming resort complex. It's open in the summer only. ✉ *Kita 2-jō Higashi 4.* ⏰ *Stores daily 10–8; restaurants daily 11–10 (except Nutberry Club, 11 AM–3 AM).*

❾ **Sapporo Grand Hotel.** Classical European architecture appears so out of place in Japan, especially in modern Sapporo, that the columns and majestic lobby of the Sapporo Grand begin to make it even more of a landmark than the Clock Tower. The hotel has a bustling café looking out on the street, and a lobby display of its famous guests and the food they ate, such as the Tiffin Menu for the New York Yankees in '55. ✉ *Kita 1-jō Nishi 4, Chūō-ku,* ☎ *011/261–3311.*

8 **Sapporo Kokusai Kōryū Puraza** (Sapporo International Communication Plaza). Established to facilitate commercial and cultural relations with the world beyond Japan, this center is the best place for getting suggestions on travel in Hokkaidō and for meeting other people who speak English. It's also a useful place to have something translated from Japanese into English. The center has a salon with books, newspapers, and brochures in English and is meant for informal socializing. Ask foreign residents and Japanese about their favorite restaurants and nightspots. For up-to-date information on local cultural events, pick up a free copy of *What's On in Sapporo* and *Xene* at the salon information counter. The Clock Tower faces the building. ✉ *3rd floor, Kita 1-jō Nishi 3, Chūō-ku,* ☎ *011/221–2105.* ☺ *Mon.–Sat. 9–5:30.*

Sapporo Winter Sports Museum. Leap off a ski jump on a simulator or try your muscles at ice hockey or curling at Sapporo's newest museum near the Olympic Okura Jump. The enormous slope is visible from downtown, and the views from the competitors' chairlift are chilling. Take a 15-minute bus ride from Maruyama Bus Terminal, City Bus Nishi 14 (¥200). ✉ *Miyanomori 1274,* ☎ *641–1972.* 🎟 *¥600.* ☺ *May–Oct., daily 9–6; Nov.–Apr., daily 9:30–5.*

11 **Shokubutsu-en** (Botanical Gardens). With more than 5,000 plant varieties, the Shokubutsu-en makes for a cool retreat in the summer, both for its green space and its shade. 🎟 *May–Oct. gardens and greenhouse ¥400; Nov.–Apr. gardens free, greenhouse ¥110.* ☺ *Apr.–Sept., daily 9–4; Oct.–Nov., daily 9–3:30; Dec.–Mar., weekdays 9–5.*

4 **Tanuki Kōji.** A *tanuki* is a raccoon dog, which in Japanese mythology is known for its cunning and libidinous nature. The Tanuki Kōji covered arcade got its name because the place used to be frequented by prostitutes, who displayed similar characteristics when it came to relieving their clients of cash. Now it's the arcade's merchants who are so eager to lighten the wallets of passersby. Perpendicular to Pole Town, one block north of Susukino Crossing, its sides crowded with small shops selling clothing, footwear, electronics, records, and, inevitably, Ainu-inspired souvenirs of Hokkaidō, Tanuki Kōji has considerably lower prices than the area's department stores. It's also the place to find Hokkaidō specialties—from melon confections to dried salmon and seaweed—which are good presents for Japanese friends on Honshū.

6 **Tokei-dai** (Clock Tower). This is Sapporo's most identifiable landmark. It was built in 1878 in Russian style, and a clock from Boston was added three years later. Other than being on every Sapporo travel brochure, it is rather ordinary. Inside the building a museum recounts the local history of Sapporo and includes displays on the tower and photos from Sapporo's early history. 🎟 *¥200.* ☺ *Tues.–Sat. daily 9–5.*

Dining

Most of Sapporo's restaurants, whatever the culinary origin, use visual displays for their menus. The greatest concentration of restaurants is in the entertainment district of Susukino, although other key locations are the downtown department stores and underneath the JR station. Formal dining rooms and/or coffee shops in all the major hotels serve Continental food. Invariably, the food will be French-inspired and expensive. Most larger hotels also have at least one Japanese restaurant and a Chinese restaurant.

Hokkaidō is known for its ramen, Chinese noodle served in broth, and Sapporo for its miso ramen, with miso broth. To eat cheaply, and without the pressure of the next ramen-shop customer looking over your shoulder, you might try one of the large izakaya in Susukino, which have gaijin-friendly menus with pictures.

The city has more than 1,000 ramen shops, but do try to make it to the **Ramen Yoko-chō** area, a small alley with as many as three dozen tiny shops with counter service. It runs perpendicular to the southern side of Susukino-dōri (Minami 4-jō).

$$$–$$$$ ✕ **Chanko Kita-no-Fuji.** Ever wonder how sumō wrestlers bulk into fighting form? Find the answer here: *chanko nabe*, a hot pot of meat or seafood and vegetables. The restaurant's colorful replica of a sumō ring contributes to the lively atmosphere. The downside is rushed service and dingy tableside ambience. Reservations are strongly recommended, especially in winter—chanko season. ⊠ *Susukino Plaza Bldg., Minami 7-jō Nishi 4, 1st floor, Chūō-ku,* ☎ *011/512–5484. Reservations essential. AE, DC, V.*

$$–$$$$ ✕ **Ambrosia Room.** At this restaurant on the penthouse floor of the Keio Plaza Hotel, the extremely attentive and personable staff serves ambitious French fare. You might find the view over the Shokubutsu-en more memorable than the cooking. ⊠ *Keio Plaza Hotel, Kita 5-jō Nishi 7, Chūō-ku,* ☎ *011/271–0111. AE, DC, MC, V.*

$$$ ✕ **Sapporo Beer Garden.** Jingisukan is popular here and the course price includes as much beer as you can drink in 100 minutes. Other Japanese dishes are also available. The atmosphere is festive in both the garden and in the cavernous halls of the old brewery, where there's a museum, too. ⊠ *Kita 7-jō Higashi 9, Higashi-ku,* ☎ *011/742–1531. AE, DC, MC, V.*

$$–$$$ ✕ **Daruma.** Below the sign with a roly-poly red doll, this 40-year-old establishment serves the freshest Jingisukan mutton barbecue (¥700 a plate). At the end of the meal, you're given hot tea to mix with the dipping sauce remaining from your meat. You drink the tea and sauce together: Delicious! Be sure to wear your oldest clothes, store your coat in one of the lockers, and don a paper bib. ⊠ *Crystal Bldg., Minami 5 Nishi 4,* ☎ *011/552–6013. Reservations not accepted. No credit cards. Closed Mon.* ⊠ *Noguchi Bldg., Minami 6 Nishi 4,* ☎ *011/533–8929. Reservations not accepted. No credit cards. Closed Tues.*

$$–$$$ ✕ **Sushi-zen.** The fresh fish here is so good that even sushi novices may fall in love with it. Sushi-zen is an empire with three restaurants and a delivery service. To taste the best at bargain prices, time your visit to the Maruyama branch for the third Wednesday of every month—when the trainee chefs' sushi is available for ¥200 a piece. ⊠ *Kita 1 Nishi 27, Maruyama,* ☎ *011/644–0071;* ⊠ *109 Building, Minami 4 Nishi 5,* ☎ *011/521–0070;* ⊠ *Minami 7 Nishi 4,* ☎ *011/531–0069. AE, DC MC, V. Closed Wed.*

$–$$ ✕ **Potato Circus.** A popular student and family izakaya, Potato Circus is on the fourth floor of the Urban Sapporo Building. ⊠ *Minami 3-jō Nishi 4,* ☎ *011/221–6060. No credit cards.*

$–$$ ✕ **Tori.** On the first floor of the Sumire Hotel, just northeast of the Clock Tower, this Japanese restaurant is the best lunch value in Sapporo. Try the *chirashi tekka* ladies' set: sliced raw tuna over seasoned rice, with two *yakitori* (skewers of marinated, grilled meat and vegetables), fruit, salad, pickled vegetables, and miso soup. (A "ladies' set" is a set meal with less rice and an additional side dish.) Ask the helpful staff for English explanations of the lunch sets (¥850), all of which are excellent. ⊠ *Sumire Hotel, 1st floor, Kita 1-jō Nishi 2,* ☎ *011/261–5151. AE, DC, MC, V.*

$ ✕ **Aji-no-tokei-dai.** You enter Aji-no-tokei-dai, a well-regarded ramen shop, from street level and go downstairs into the restaurant. (The bushy-eyebrowed elderly gentleman slurping away in the photo is former prime minister Tomiichi Murayama, who ate here.) Choose either the counter or a table, which you might share with other diners if the restaurant is crowded. ⊠ *Sanwa Ginkō Bldg., Kita 1-jō Nishi 3,* ☎ *011/232–8171. Reservations not accepted. No credit cards.*

Lodging

$$$$ 🏨 **ANA Zennikku Hotel.** A 26-floor high-rise, ANA Zennikku is among Sapporo's tallest hotels. Shops and a coffee-and-pastry restaurant are on the ground floor, with an open lobby area with lounges and bars up an escalator. Rooms are spacious and brightly decorated. The Sky Restaurant and Sky Lounge have fine views. The hotel runs buses to and from Chitose Airport, making it particularly convenient if you're flying. It's also close to the JR station. ⊠ *Kita 3-jō Nishi 1, Chūō-ku, Sapporo, Hokkaidō 060–0003,* ☎ *011/221–4411,* FAX *011/222–7624. 412 Western-style and Japanese-style rooms. 6 restaurants, bar, airport shuttle. AE, DC, MC, V.*

$$$$ 🏨 **Keio Plaza Hotel Sapporo.** Because the large, modern Keio stands between the Shokubutsu-en and the Hokkaidō University campus, views from rooms on the upper floors are the best in town—and are very spacious for a Japanese hotel. If you are not staying here, you can see the views from the Ambrosia Room and Miyama (Japanese) restaurants on the 22nd floor. The Jurin coffee shop stays open until 2 AM and is a haven for jet-lagged travelers. There are also an izakaya and sushi bar, a tea lounge, and a delicatessen. The enthusiastic, helpful staff can always find someone to help out in English, if required. It's a five-minute walk west of the JR station. ⊠ *Kita 5-jō Nishi 7, Chūō-ku, Sapporo, Hokkaidō 060–0005,* ☎ *011/271–0111,* FAX *011/221–5450. 525 rooms. 9 restaurants, 2 bars, coffee shop, tea shop, health club, car rental, travel services. AE, DC, MC, V.*

$$$$ 🏨 **Sapporo Grand Hotel.** Built in 1934, and renovated in 1984, Sapporo's oldest Western-style accommodation retains the traditions of a
★ great European hotel. Service is first rate. Rooms in the newer annex have a fresher, more modern air than those in the older wing. The hotel's restaurants—Japanese, Chinese, French, and a pub—are more lively than you might expect from Sapporo's oldest hotel, although locals hint that the food isn't what it once was. ⊠ *Kita 1-jō Nishi 4, Chūō-ku, Sapporo, Hokkaidō 060–0001,* ☎ *011/261–3311,* FAX *011/231–0388,* WEB *www.mitsuikanko.co.jp/sgh/. 560 rooms. 9 restaurants, coffee shop, shops. AE, DC, MC, V.*

$$$–$$$$ 🏨 **Hotel Alpha Sapporo.** You can't beat the location if you want to walk to the downtown shopping area of the city and be close to Susukino's nightlife. Service is excellent, and the decor of warm rust-browns and reds makes it an inviting place to return to after a day of sightseeing. Though the copious facilities include a tea-ceremony room and movie theater, this is smaller than most of the other top hotels, which means that the hotel's staff will soon know you by name. Guest rooms tend to be ordinary, but they are larger than most other standard hotel rooms in Japan. The French restaurant Alsienne, in an elegant wood-paneled dining room, imports many of its ingredients from France. The Chinese restaurant, Tōri, is highly regarded, and the Sunday lunch buffet (¥1,800) is a popular meeting place. ⊠ *Minami 1-jō Nishi 5, Chūō-ku, Sapporo, Hokkaidō 060–0061,* ☎ *011/221–2333,* FAX *011/221–0819. 146 rooms. 4 restaurants, bar, tea shop, hair salon, cinema. AE, DC, MC, V.*

$$–$$$$ ⊞ **Hotel Nikkō Chitose.** Owner Japan Airlines puts up its flight crews to be near Sapporo's closest international airport, about 3 km (2 mi) away. This is the best hotel in the Chitose area, south of the city. ⊠ *4–4–4 Honchō, Chitose-shi, Hokkaidō 066–0047,* ☎ *0123/22–1121,* FAX *0123/22–1153. 258 rooms. 2 restaurants. AE, DC, MC, V.*

$$$ ⊞ **Hotel Arthur Sapporo.** This pleasing white tower rises from north-west corner of Nakajima Kōen. Rooms are reasonably large for Japan, and the dark-stained furniture imparts a European feel. The spacious lobby area has an open lounge where you can dine with views of the park. The 25th floor has a bar and a club called (oddly enough) Bar 21. A restaurant specializing in crab cuisine occupies the two floors below it. Not all staff members speak English, but they are eager to help gaijin guests. ⊠ *Minami 10-jō Nishi 6, Chūō-ku, Sapporo, Hokkaidō 064–0810,* ☎ *011/561–1000,* FAX *011/521–552. 229 rooms. 4 restaurants, bar, lobby lounge, hair salon, nightclub, shop. AE, DC, MC, V.*

$$ ⊞ **Nakamuraya Ryokan.** This inn near the Shokubutsu-en dates from 1898—ancient for Sapporo—though the current building is more recent. The six-tatami-mat rooms seem larger because of their spacious cupboards, built-in minibar, and wide window shelf. Rooms have tiny private bathrooms. The staff are welcoming to foreign guests, particularly if you are carrying this guidebook. The large communal bath is a welcome comfort in winter. The Japanese dinner (included along with breakfast in the rate) is expansive, with a selection of fresh seafood from local waters. ⊠ *Kita 3-jō Nishi 7, Chūō-ku, Sapporo, Hokkaidō 060–0003,* ☎ *011/ 241–2111,* FAX *011/241–2118,* WEB *www.nakamura-ryokan.co.jp/ nakamura-english.htm. 29 Japanese-style rooms. Restaurant, Japanese-style bath. AE, MC, V. MAP.*

$ ⊞ **Hotel Maki.** A family hotel, Maki offers a change of style from the sterility of big city hotels, and the Inada family speaks a little English. Half the rooms have baths; all have toilets and washbasins. There is also a general bath. The hotel is a favorite with out-of-town sports teams, who wolf down the extensive Japanese-style breakfast available for ¥900. It's located in a quiet area just five streetcar stops from Susukino or 10 minutes from Horohirabashi subway station. ⊠ *1–20 Minami 13 Nishi 7, Sapporo 064–0913,* ☎ *011/521–1930,* FAX *011/531–6747. 15 Japanese-style rooms. Breakfast room, Japanese bath. No credit cards. MAP.*

Nightlife

★ **Susukino,** Sapporo's entertainment district, is a night owl's paradise, with more than 5,000 bars, nightclubs, and restaurants providing bacchanalian delights, Japanese style. The compact area, illuminated with lanterns and flashing signs, is mind-boggling and in itself justifies an overnight stay in Sapporo. Most bars remain open until the wee hours, some as late as 5 AM, though restaurants often close before midnight. From Sapporo Factory, walk west to Ō-dōri before heading south down Eki-mae-dōri. Susukino is bounded by Minami 3-jō, Minami 7-jō, Nishi 2-chōme, and Nishi 6-chōme. The seedier alleys are mostly west of Eki-mae-dōri, but all of Susukino is safe.

Make sure that you know what kind of bar you're going into before you enter. There are several kinds: clubs stocked with hostesses who make small talk (¥5,000 and up per hour, proving that talk is *not* cheap); *sunakku* bars (the word sounds like "snack," which translates into fewer hostesses and expensive *ōdoburu*—hors d'oeuvres); izakaya, for different kinds of food and drink; bars with entertainment, either karaoke or live music; and "soapland" and *herusu* (health) massage parlors, which are generally off-limits to non-Japanese lacking an introduction.

If at all possible, go to the clubs and *sunakku* with a Japanese-speaking acquaintance. Signs that say NO CHARGE only mean that there is no charge to be seated; you should beware of hidden extras. Many bars add on all sorts of strange charges for: peanuts, female companionship, song, cold water, hand towel, etc. The term "free drink" refers to an all-you-can-drink special that does cost money.

A Susukino bar that reflects the eclectic Japanese taste for foreign music and styles is the tiny but cozy **Anyway** (✉ Mimatsu Muraoka Bldg., 6th floor, Minami 5-jō Nishi 2, ☎ 011/512–1578), whose affable, Stetson-wearing owner is besotted with country-and-western and speaks English. There is a ¥1,500 cover charge. **Bazoku** (✉ Minami 2-jō Nishi 5, ☎ 011/241–196) is a Japanese take on the American dive. Cheap beer and conviviality complement the occasional weekend live rock show in this basement bar. Look for the English sign reading AMERICAN BAR-BE-QUE. There's never a door charge.

Izakaya are well represented in Susukino, and one that has a menu with a distinctly Hokkaidō flavor is **Irohanihoheto** (✉ Minami 5-jō Nishi 4, ☎ 011/521–1682), on the second floor of the Bacchus Building. Oenophiles might prefer the **Wine Bar** (✉ New Hokusei Bldg., 9th floor, Minami 4-jō Nishi 3, ☎ 011/241–3405), reputed to be Sapporo's number one spot for young courting couples. Be warned, though, that both a seating charge and a 10% service fee are added.

The district's strangest bar, **Susukino Rei-en** (✉ Number Two Green Bldg., 8th floor, Minami 4-jō Nishi 3, ☎ 011/518–2229), whose name means Susukino Cemetery, resembles an Asian graveyard. Despite the awful-sounding concept, it is surprisingly comfortable. The bar is open until 2 AM weekdays (3 AM weekends). Some menu items may put you off if you're not into racy humor. There's a ¥1,000 door charge.

Sapporo A to Z

AIR TRAVEL
BOOKING

Coziness with Japan Airlines tends to make the local Japan Travel Bureau push this carrier. For cheaper fares or additional flight times, inquire about other airlines. For good deals on domestic travel, contact Ticket Super/No. 1 Travel.

CARRIERS

Direct service to Amsterdam debuted in 1998. All Nippon Airways (ANA), Japan Air System (JAS), Japan Airlines (JAL), and KLM Royal Dutch Airlines all serve Chitose. In an attempt to stir competition in Japan's complacent airline industry, Air Do (rhymes with "who") began flying between Tōkyō and Sapporo in 1998. Although other carriers have cut their fares somewhat in response, this Hokkaidō upstart is still cheaper and deserves support for taking on the big guys.
➤ AIRLINES AND CONTACTS: **Air Do** (☎ 011/200–7333). **Japan Air System** (☎ 0120/71–1283 international; 0120/5–11283 domestic). **Japan Airlines** (☎ 0120/255–931 international; 0120/255–971 or 011/232–3690 domestic). **Japan Travel Bureau** (☎ 011/241–6201). **KLM Royal Dutch Airlines** (☎ 0120/86–8862 or 011/232–0775). **Ticket Super/No. 1 Travel** (☎ 011/251–3314, FAX 011/251–4607).

AIRPORTS AND TRANSFERS
Sapporo's Shin-Chitose Kūkō (New Chitose Airport), 40 km (25 mi) south of the city, is Hokkaidō's main airport. More than 30 domestic routes link Chitose to the rest of Japan, and flights from Chitose to other parts of Asia are increasing.

➤ Airport Information: **Shin Chitose Kūkō** (☎ 0123/23–0111).

Japan Railways (JR) runs every 20 minutes or so between the airport terminal and downtown Sapporo. (Shin Chitose Kūkō Eki is the final eastbound stop from Sapporo; do not get off at the Chitose or Minami Chitose stations if you want the airport.) The trip is usually made by rapid transit trains (¥1,040, 40 minutes). Hokuto Bus runs a shuttle bus (¥820) that connects with ANA flights at Chitose and its hotel, the ANA Zennikku, in Sapporo, first stopping at the Renaissance and Sunroute hotels. Chūō Bus (¥820) runs a shuttle between the airport and Sapporo's Grand Hotel, also stopping at Ō-dori Kōen, JR Sapporo Eki, and the Korakuen, Royton, and Keio Plaza hotels. These buses reach the airport in under an hour, though you should allow more time in winter. Taxis are available, but ridiculously expensive.

➤ Contact: **Bus information** (☎ 011/377–3855).

BUS TRAVEL

Local bus fares begin at ¥200. Buses follow the grid system and run until shortly after 11 PM. There is no English schedules for buses in Sapporo, and bus-stand information is all in Japanese. However, two circular route services connect many of the main sites. Factory Line connects downtown shops, the train station, the fish market, Sapporo Factory and Beer Garden for ¥200 a journey. Its bus stops are confusingly marked as Sapporo Walk. Sapporo Lincle Bus runs May to October, and for ¥1,200, the day pass allows passengers to get on and off. From downtown the bus line reaches the Moiwa cable car, Maruyama Zoo, the Okura Ski Jump, and Sapporo Beer Garden.

➤ Bus Information: **Factory Line** (☎ 011/896–2734). **Sapporo Lincle Bus** (☎ 011/231–0500).

CAR TRAVEL

Sapporo has two expressways. The Dō Expressway heads southeast to Chitose, then veers southwest to hug Hokkaidō's underside as far as Oshamanbe. The Sasson Expressway links Otaru to the west with Asahikawa in the northeast.

Information on road conditions is available during the winter. It's only in Japanese, however, so if you're not conversant, ask the staff at your hotel or Plaza i to place the call for you.

➤ Contacts: **Plaza i** (☎ 011/211–3678). **Road Conditions** (☎ 011/281–6511).

CONSULATE

Non-U.S. citizens applying for U.S. visas must do so in Tōkyō.

➤ Contact: **U.S. Consulate** (✉ Kita 1-jō Nishi 28, Chūō-ku, ☎ 011/641–1115).

EMERGENCIES

➤ Contacts: **Ambulance** (☎ 119). **Hokkaidō University Hospital** (✉ Kita 14-jō Nishi 5, ☎ 011/716–1161). **Nighttime Emergency Hospital** (✉ Ōdori Nishi 16, ☎ 011/641–4316). **Police** (☎ 110). **Sapporo City General Hospital** (✉ Kita 11-jō Nishi 13, ☎ 011/726–2211).

ENGLISH-LANGUAGE MEDIA

Outside Sapporo, finding English-language books is difficult, so you may want to browse in Sapporo's two largest bookstores with limited stocks of books in English: Kinokuniya and Maruzen.

Mariya offers an excellent selection of English books. Reasonable book prices can be found at New Day Books. A sprawling Tower Records sells magazines in Japanese and English to trend-hungry young locals. ➤ CONTACTS: **Kinokuniya** (⊠ Dai-ni Yuraku Bldg., 2nd floor, Minami 1-jō Nishi 1, ☎ 011/231–2131). **Mariya** (⊠ Kita 1-jō Nishi 3, ☎ 011/221–3307). **Maruzen** (⊠ Minami 1-jō Nishi 3, 4th floor, ☎ 011/241–7251). **New Day Books** (⊠ Arche Bldg., 5th floor, Minami 3-jō Nishi 4). **Tower Records** (⊠ Pivot Bldg., 7th floor, Minami 2-jō Nishi 4, ☎ 011/241–3851).

STREETCARS

Sapporo has a streetcar service with a flat fare of ¥170. However, it's confined to a single line connecting Susukino with Moiwa-yama in the city's southwest corner—well away from the sights mentioned in this section—and has remained in business more because of public affection than profitability. In an effort to scrape a little more money out of the service, the city has made its streetcars available to be rented out for parties, and you may see the vehicles trundling across town with a crowd of revelers on board.

SUBWAYS

Sapporo's subway is a pleasure. Trains have rubber wheels that run quietly, and most signs include English. There are three lines: the Namboku Line runs south from JR Sapporo Eki past Susukino to Nakajima Kōen; the Tōzai Line bisects the city from east to west. These two cross at Ō-dōri Eki. The third, the Tōhō Line, enters central Sapporo from the southeast of the city, then parallels the Namboku Line from Ō-dōri Eki to the JR station before branching off into the northeastern suburbs.

The basic fare, covering a distance of about three stations, is ¥200. A one-day open ticket (*ichi-nichi-ken*) for ¥1,000 provides unlimited access to the subway, bus, and streetcar (¥800 for the subway alone); a ¥700 Eco-ticket (*ekokippu* in Japanese), intended to encourage residents to leave their cars at home for the day, covers the same three types of public transport on the 5th and 20th of every month. These tickets are available at any subway station and at the Ō-dōri Eki Underground Commuters' Ticket Office, open weekdays 8:30–7, weekends 10–5:30. Prepaid cards (available for ¥1,000, ¥3,000, ¥5,000, and ¥10,000 at vending machines) automatically debit the appropriate amount when you've reached your destination and give you a 10% discount. Trains stop running at midnight.

TAXIS

Taxi meters start at ¥550 or ¥600, depending on the company. Check the basic fare, which is posted on the door, before you get in. An average fare, such as from the JR station to Susukino, runs about ¥800.

TRAIN TRAVEL

All JR trains arrive at the central station, on the north side of downtown Sapporo. Trains depart for Honshū about every two hours. The route sometimes involves a change of trains in Hakodate. As many as six trains per hour run to and from Otaru and east. Every half hour from 7 AM to 10 PM there are trains north to Asahikawa.

TRANSPORTATION AROUND SAPPORO

Sapporo is a walking city with wide sidewalks; it's easy to find your way around. The International Information Corner (☞ Visitor Information) at the Sapporo Eki has a city map, and most hotels have a smaller map marking their hotels and major points of interest. The finest map is in *Travelers' Sapporo,* a free brochure available at all of the tourist offices and at the Ōdori subway station.

VISITOR INFORMATION

The most helpful places for information on Sapporo and Hokkaidō in general are the International Information Corner, open daily 9–5 except the second and fourth Wednesday of the month (second Wednesday only January–February and July–September), in the western portion of Lilac Paseo in the JR station; and the Sapporo International Communication Plaza's tourist office, Plaza i, which is open daily 9–5:30.

Other offices that supply information include Hokkaidō Tourist Association, open weekdays 9–5; Sapporo City Tourism Department Office, open weekdays 8:45–5:15; and Sapporo Tourist Information Center, open daily 10–6.

Look for copies of the magazine *Xene* in hotels and bookstores for its listings of local and Hokkaidō-wide events and festivals, as well as coupons and articles. *What's On in Sapporo* informs readers of local events. You'll find it at Plaza i.

➤ TOURIST INFORMATION: **Hokkaidō Tourist Association** (⊠ Keizai Center Bldg., Kita 2-jō Nishi 1, Chūō-ku, ☎ 011/231–0941). **Kokusai Jōhō** (International Information Corner; ⊠ Sapporo Eki, ☎ 011/213–5062). **Plaza i** (⊠ MN Bldg., Kita 1-jō Nishi 3, Chūō-ku, ☎ 011/211–3678). **Sapporo City Tourism Department Office** (⊠ Kita 1-jō Nishi 2, Chūō-ku, ☎ 011/211–2376). **Sapporo Tourist Information Center** (⊠ Ō-dōri Eki, Ō-dōri Nishi 3, ☎ 011/232–7712).

OTARU AND THE SHAKOTAN-HANTŌ

West of Sapporo, the Shakotan-hantō and its mysteriously shaped rocks jut fanglike into the yawning, bold blueness of the Nihon-kai. The peninsula is ideal for cliff-side drives and, along less precipitous stretches, walks down to the ocean. On the way you might want to stop in the port city of Otaru. Inland, the Niseko resort area is dotted with cozy cottages and rustic open-air hot springs in which outdoors enthusiasts unwind and refuel between days of skiing, snowboarding, hiking, and rafting. A quick circuit of the area takes one or two days by car, two days by public transport.

Otaru

⑭ *50 mins west of Sapporo by JR, 40 km (25 mi) west of Sapporo by car.*

Otaru is known for its canals and old Western-style buildings. Its image as a charming port city and romantic weekend retreat from Sapporo has made Otaru a popular spot for domestic tourists; gaijin are usually less impressed with what is essentially a commercial city in the shadow of Hokkaidō's capital. Otaru has also become infamous as the home of Yunohana Onsen in Temiya, which tried to ban foreign bathers and subsequently got hit by a lawsuit brought by local foreign residents. Nevertheless, Otaru's historical importance and peerless sushi make it worth a stop.

A number of 19th-century wood-frame houses still stand, sandwiched between modern concrete structures, and a busy port area sees ferries departing for Niigata to the south and Russians arriving from the north. They come for the black-market trade of seafood for consumer goods. Otaru once served as a more legitimate financial center, dubbed the Wall Street of the North. Its fortunes plunged with the decline of the fishery industry. Resourceful craftsmen turned from making glass buoys and lamps for squid fishing to fashioning the glass objets d'art now seen in boutiques on a lively strip 10 minutes by foot from JR Otaru Eki in the Otaru Canal area.

Otaru Hakubutsukan (Otaru City Museum), in a former warehouse, combines natural history exhibits with displays about the town's development since the 19th century. It is eight minutes on foot south of the JR station in the direction of the sea. ☎ *0134/33–2439.* ☒ *¥100.* ☉ *Daily 9:30–5.*

Otaru Suizokukan (Otaru Aquarium), Hokkaidō's only worthwhile aquarium, has a marine-mammal show that thrills youngsters. To get here, ride the Suizokukan Yuki bus from the JR station (Chūō bus platform 3) for 20 minutes to the last stop. ☎ *0134/33–1400.* ☒ *¥1,300.* ☉ *Apr.–Oct., daily 9–5; Nov., daily 9–4.*

At **Tengu-yakata** (Goblin Hall) you can come nose to nose with a *tengu* (long-nose goblin). This small museum containing hundreds of goblin masks is incongruously situated alongside a room detailing Japanese success in various Winter Olympics. To get to Tengu-yakata, take a 15-minute Chuo Bus ride from Otaru Eki to the Tengu-yama Ropeway and then ride the cable car (¥1,000) to the top of the mountain. ☒ *Tengu-yama, Otaru,* ☎ *0134/33–7381.* ☒ *Free.* ☉ *Daily 10–5.*

Dining and Lodging

$$$–$$$$ ✕ **Uoisshin.** Hokkaidō's seasonal fishy fare is served fresh from the ocean to sashimi connoisseurs who travel from Sapporo for this restaurant's expertise. ☒ *1–11–10 Hanazono,* ☎ *0134/32–5202. Reservations essential. No credit cards.*

$ ✕ **Kita-no Ice Cream.** Beer ice cream anyone? Maybe you'd prefer sake ice cream—or squid, cherry blossom, or pumpkin flavor? This Otaru institution serves up 20 varieties from a shop in an 1892 warehouse. ☒ *Ironai 1–chōe,* ☎ *0134/23–8983. No credit cards.*

$ ✕ **Shodai.** Steaming bowls of ramen are served here, in an old warehouse, by the team that came second in a nationwide televised competition. ☒ *14–8 Sumiyoshi-cho,* ☎ *0134/33–2626. No credit cards. Closed Tues. No dinner.*

$$$$ ▥ **Otaru Hilton.** The 18 floors of hotel perch atop shops, seven movie theaters, a hot spring, restaurants galore—and there's even a Ferris wheel outside. Western-style rooms, in calming golds, blues, and browns, have large twin or double beds. Other amenities include CNN and English-language programming, a TV remote control, Internet access, and a Sony game system—which are rarer than bear sightings in Hokkaidō. This quality accommodation is connected to one of the largest shopping malls in Japan, the redbrick MYCAL complex, overlooking Otaru Marina. ☒ *Otaru Chikko, Otaru, Hokkaidō 047–0008,* ☎ *0134/21–3111 or 0120/489852 toll free,* 🖷 *0134/21–3322. 289 rooms. 2 restaurants, 2 bars, patisserie. AE, DC, MC, V.*

$$ ▥ **Cottage Sakanouekan Hirao.** With its net curtains, big beds, and stained glass, this aims to be a vaguely Russian experience in the heart of Otaru. The Hirao family have built an extension in their garden, and the large room, which can sleep up to five, comes equipped with a refrigerator and microwave for basic cooking. The bay windows overlook the harbor. No meals are included; it's a short walk up the hill behind the Steam Clock. ☒ *3–10 Sumiyoshi-cho, Otaru, Hokkaidō 047–0015,* ☎ *0134/33–9151. 1 room. Kitchenette. No credit cards.*

$$ ▥ **Otaru Kokusai Hotel.** Above a shopping arcade, this modern hotel is reached by an escalator from the main street. The lobby area is rather bare and uncomfortable, but guest rooms are cheerful if small. The staff speaks little English. ☒ *3–9–1 Inaho, Otaru, Hokkaidō 047–0032,*

☎ 0134/33–2161, FAX 0134/33–7744. *76 Western-style rooms, 4 Japanese-style rooms. 3 restaurants. AE, DC, MC, V.*

Visitor Information

The **Otaru tourist office** (☎ 0134/22–6584) is to the left of the ticket gates inside the station. It's open daily 9–6, but as it shares office space with the JR travel office, staff are somewhat harried. The staff of **Unga Plaza Tourist Office** (☎ 0134/33–1661), by the canal, shows patient attention to questions. From the station Unga Plaza is eight minutes straight down the main street, housed in the stone buildings last on the left.

Shakotan-hantō

★ ⑮ *Yoichi is 30 mins west of Otaru by JR local; Iwanai is 3 hrs, 40 mins southwest of Yoichi by bus on the coastal road.*

Shakotan typifies natural Hokkaidō. Cliffs stave off the endlessly surging sea both on the two capes, Shakotan-misaki and Kamui-misaki, and on the northern and western tips of the peninsula. Sentimental Japanese go to Kamui-misaki to see the sun set over the Sea of Japan. Volcanic mountain peaks, Yobetsu-dake (4,019 ft) and Shakotan-dake (4,258 ft), dominate the peninsula's interior. Thick forests blanket the slopes with dark, rich greens, and ravines crease the mountainsides. Shakotan-hantō has coastal scenery at its most dramatic.

Some of Hokkaidō's best sandy beaches lie west of Otaru along the coastal road leading to **Yoichi** (*Yo-ee-chee*). After you pass the town, beaches soon give way to cliffs rising out of the sea. Yoichi marks the beginning of the Shakotan-hantō.

The road from Yoichi, **Route 229,** circles the peninsula, keeping to the coast as much as the cliffs allow. At Yobetsu, near Kamui-misaki, it gets even more spectacular as it heads south to Iwanai. If you are driving, at Kamoenai you can decide to continue south or to cross the peninsula via a thrilling hairpin road (closed in winter) over Tomaru Tōge that skirts Yobetsu-dake and returns to Furubira.

Shakotan-dake has a gentle round-trip climb of 3¾ hours. Buses run from the JR stations in Otaru and Yoichi to the trailhead.

Getting Around

To tour the peninsula in summer take the **Chuo Bus** (☎ 011/231–0500) on the Grand Blue Shiribeshi-go bus line. With a Free Passport Ticket (¥2,000 for two days), you can get on and off anywhere around the coast. The bus departs from the Otaru bus terminal and no reservations are necessary.

Niseko

⑯ *2 hrs, 10 mins southwest of Otaru by JR.*

For the best skiing in Hokkaidō, and perhaps Japan, head for Niseko. The entire resort area is known by that name, although its sights and activities are spread between two towns: Niseko proper and Kutchan, an adjoining hamlet. Niseko has become an outdoor adventure mecca in Japan, and several outfits, run by ex-pats, offer thrills such as rafting, backcountry ski tours, dog sledding, and bungee jumping. The fastest way to get to Kutchan from Sapporo is by road or rail via Otaru. If you take the inland route through Jōzankei Onsen, Kimobetsu, Rusutsu, and Makkari, smaller roads weave through more spectacular terrain.

Kutchan has a sleepy charm, but the real action is in the collection of peaks that have five ski areas and the stately **Yotei-zan.** Climbing this

Fuji look-alike takes four hours. Two trails lead up the mountain: the more challenging Hirafu Course and the easier but still arduous Makkari Course. Regardless of your approach, you're bound to be taken by the wildflowers in summer, as well as the elderly Japanese chomping on bamboo shoots that grow wild on the hills. A hut at the top provides crude lodging if you decide to hike up to see the next day's sunrise. To get to the trails, take the bus from JR Kutchan Eki 20 minutes to Yotei To-zan-guchi (hiking trail entrance) for the Hirafu Course or 40 minutes to the Yotei Shinzan Kōen stop for the Makkari Course.

Niseko Adventure Centre (☎ 0136/23–2093, WEB www.nac-web.com) is the oldest adventure company in the area. In addition river trips, it also offers indoor rock climbing, winter sports, and mountain biking from the stylish center building. After all that exertion, kick back and relax at the on-site JoJo's bar and café. **Niseko Outdoor Adventure Sports Club** (☎ 0136/23–1688, WEB www.noasc.com) sponsors river activities, and for height lovers: bungy jumping, bridge swinging, mountain boarding, and ice climbing, too. **Scott Adventures** (☎ 0136/21–3333, WEB www.sas-net.com), popular with domestic school groups for their rafting trips, can also arrange hot air ballooning, fishing, snowshoeing, and dogsled riding with a team of huskies.

To the right of the ticket gate at the JR Kutchan station is the excellent **Kutchan Kankō Kyōkai no Kankō Annai-sho** (Kutchan Tourism Association Tourist Office; ✉ Minami 1-jō Nishi 4-chōme, Kutchanchō, ☎ 0136/22–5151).

Dining and Lodging

If you are driving into the area, you might ask at the Kutchan tourist office about staying at pension cottages with hot springs.

$ ✗ **Kurowassan.** This noodle shop is known for *imo udon*, a thick noodle made of potato flour instead of the usual wheat. ✉ *Minami 3-jō Nishi 2*, ☎ *0136/22–0537. No credit cards.*

$ ✗ **Yabutomi.** For superb soba go three blocks from the JR station in Kutchan, and then turn left under the rusty archway to the entertainment area. The shop is the first on the right in a weathered wooden building. ✉ *Kita 1-jō Nishi 1, Kutchan-chō*, ☎ *0136/22–0537. No credit cards.*

$$$ ⊞ **Hotel Yotei.** In the center of town behind the station, this conventional modern accommodation includes a hot spring. Room price includes two meals. ✉ *Asahi 69-banchi, Kutchan-chō, Abuta-cho, Hokkaidō 044–0083,* ☎ *0136/22–1164,* FAX *0136/22–1165. 20 rooms. Hot spring. No credit cards. MAP.*

$$ ⊞ **Minshuku Yamagoya.** If you're relying on public transport, try this modest inn in the center of town. Room price includes two meals. ✉ *Minami 6 Higashi 1, Kutchan, Abuta-cho, Hokkaidō 044–0083,* ☎ *0136/22–0823. 10 rooms. No credit cards. MAP.*

En Route If you have time and a car, take the picturesque detour inland via Jōzankei Onsen when you leave Shakotan-hantō instead of heading straight back to Sapporo along the coast. You'll pass three mountains whose peaks suggest the long-nose goblin known as a *tengu*, which is a folk character in Japanese lore.

From Otaru the road climbs past Asarigawa Onsen to **Tengu-dake** (there are three Mt. Tengus on Hokkaidō), on the Otaru side of the border with Sapporo, and continues through some of Hokkaidō's most scenic mountains. This road is marked Route 1 on better maps, but everyone knows it as the road to Sapporo Kokusai Ski Grounds; it's now open in winter until 7 PM. Follow the ravine that winds its way past the ski resort and Sapporo-ko, traverses Jōzankei Dam, and wraps around

Kotengu-yama (Little Mt. Tengu) before descending to Jōzankei. The forests and rock outcroppings make this trip especially beautiful in late spring, when patches of white snow are melting into crystal streams.

A hiking trail leads from the parking lot at **Jōzankei Dam** to the top of Kotengu-yama, an easy 45-minute climb. The peak overlooks yet another tengu: Tengu-yama, the more massive mountain northwest of Kotengu-yama.

Jōzankei Onsen

⑰ *40 mins southeast of Tengu-dake by car, 1 hr west of Sapporo by bus.*

Because Jōzankei is actually within Sapporo city, weekend day-trippers do crowd in. The resort town itself is wedged in a small valley in the foothills beneath the mountains of Shikotsu-Tōya National Park. Were it not for the modern, square-block hotels, the village would be beautiful. Unfortunately, although it has all the creature comforts of a hotspring resort, developers have managed to spoil the area with architectural monstrosities. Skiers from all over Japan come here in winter, and Hokkaidō residents visit on summer weekends for hiking and camping.

The ski season is in full swing by the beginning of December and lasts through May at **Sapporo Kokusai Ski Resort** (☎ 001/598–4511). The ski area is 25 minutes north by bus from the spa. A one-day lift ticket that includes night skiing costs ¥4,600.

One of the most unusual museums in Hokkaidō attests to Japan's legacy of peasant frankness about things sexual. The coyly named **Hihō-kan** (House of Secret Treasures) is a museum devoted to Japan's tradition of erotica and sexual folk culture, including phallic and yonic objects formerly related to fertility rites. You can locate it by the huge statue of a crying Kannon, the Buddhist goddess of mercy, out front. A restaurant at the top of the building serves Japanese food. ⊠ *Rte. 230, Higashi 2-chōme,* ☎ *011/598–4141.* ☜ *¥1,500.* ☉ *Daily 10–8.*

A more rustic hot-spring experience awaits bathers at **Hoheikyo Onsen,** 1 km (½ mi) southwest of Jōzankei. There are no resort hotels to spoil the view from the rotemburo, which is studded with rock islands and a working waterwheel. This is an onsen as it should be. Leave Jōzankei on Route 230 west, and take the first left at the sign that shows a turbaned man (the hot spring also has a very good Indian restaurant; ask about the onsen-dinner package). The onsen is on the left in a ramshackle building. ⊠ *680-banchi, Minami-ku, Jōzankei,* ☎ *011/598–2410.* ☜ *¥1,000.* ☉ *Onsen daily 10 AM–midnight, restaurant daily 11 AM–10 PM.*

SHIKOTSU-TŌYA NATIONAL PARK

Mountains, forests, refreshing caldera lakes, hot-spring resorts, and volcanoes—all are virtually in Sapporo's backyard in this national park. For a quick tour of the area, plan two days by car and three by public transport.

Nakayama Tōge

★ **⑱** *25 mins southwest of Jōzankei Onsen by car, 1 hr south of Sapporo by bus.*

Once through Jōzankei Onsen, the twisting, winding road, Route 230, presages the high drama of the mountain pass ahead. The final ascent

to 2,742 ft ends after a tunnel that opens on Nakayama Tōge's sweeping panoramas of lonely mountains and peopled plains. In the distance,
beyond the surrounding mountain peaks, the nearly perfect conical shape
of **Yotei-zan** begs comparison to Fuji-san, but any native worth his or
her salt would say that Yotei has no competition.

There are souvenir shops on both sides of the road at Nakayama Pass.
Outward-bound from Sapporo is the larger, newer complex, with a convenience store and fast-food counters. On the second floor is a soba
restaurant and, for nondrivers, a vending machine with 4.5% alcohol-
content Potato Brew or Corn Brew. For those who like to go in style,
this is also the site of Hokkaidō's priciest public toilet, a construction
boondoggle that caused a stink when the million-dollar price tag was
made public.

Tōya-ko

★ *2½ hrs southwest of Sapporo by bus.*

The road descends from Nakayama Tōge to Kimobetsu—where farmers sell fruit and vegetables at roadside stalls—and on to the unsightly
amusement park at Rusutsu. Soon after this it climbs to the vast, active, volcanic cone cradling Tōya-ko in its depths. For the best approach
to the lake, turn left off Route 230 about 11 km (7 mi) from Rusutsu
and follow signs for Toya Mura.

At lunchtime on March 28, 2000, **Usu-zan** erupted for the first time
in 23 years. A 10,500-ft-high cloud of ash and smoke exploded over
the resort. Approximately 16,000 people were evacuated and for three
months life in the town came to a stop while vulcanologists and government members debated the unpredictably of volcanoes. By July 2000,
the resort was back in business, encompassing the still-smoking craters
in its midst. Pleasure boats take day-trippers out to the new islands
that appear to have been dropped into the center of the lake. On the
west-coast-facing side of Usu-zan, 3,960 ft of walkways cross the so-
lidified mudflows where the land has risen by 264 ft, enabling photo
opportunities near the steaming craters. Access is free, and depending
on weather and the volcano conditions, the paths are open from April
to November.

Another view of the action is available from the small road behind the
convenience store as you enter Tōya-ko Onsen from Rusutsu, and from
behind the bus terminal building. Wire and sandbags keep visitors at
a safe distance, and the remains of homes, a school, and a gas station
stand marooned in ash flow. Route 230 between the lake and the
coast is closed due to the volcanic activity.

⑲ The spa town of **Tōya-ko Onsen,** on the southwestern edge of Tōya-
ko, is the chief holiday center for this part of Shikotsu-Tōya Park. Consequently, it's loaded with hotels, inns, and souvenir shops. The hotels
are open all year, but the busiest time is from June through August.
Japanese families come in droves for trout fishing, hiking, boating, visiting Nakajima (Inner Island is the largest of the cluster of islands in
the center of the lake), taking in nightly fireworks in summer, and enjoying the curative waters of the hot springs.

Abuta Kazan Kagaku-kan (Volcanic Science Museum) chronicles the
development of Usu-zan and Shōwa Shin-zan, and the volcanic activity of the entire area—including the 2000 eruption. It's on the second
floor of the Dōnan Bus Terminal in the center of Tōya-ko Onsen, although you must exit the terminal to enter the museum. ☎ *0142/75–
4400.* ☒ *¥600.* ☽ *Daily 9–5.*

Shōwa Shin-zan, a few minutes' drive east from Tōya-ko Onsen, means "new mountain of the Shōwa era." Japan's newest volcano, it made its appearance in 1943, surprising everyone, but no one more than the farmer who watched it emerge from his wheat field. In the course of two years, it grew steadily until it reached its present height of 1,312 ft. A cable-car ride up the eastern flank of the mountain costs ¥600 and is open daily from 9 to 5.

Dining and Lodging

$$ ✕ **Biyotei.** Set back from the main road, in a garden with gnomes, is a relaxing European-style restaurant. A stone floor, low beams, and table legs made from logs provide the atmosphere. The menu is in English and the sizzling hamburger platters are the best choices. ⊠ *Tōya-ko Onsen,* ☎ *0142/75–2311. No credit cards.*

$$$ ⊡ **Hotel Grand Toya.** Faded, rather than grand, but it's as close as you can stay to the volcanic craters. No English is spoken here, but the staff are welcoming and you cannot beat the location between the bus terminal and the lakeside. Room rates include breakfast and dinner for two served in your room. ⊠ *Tōya-ko Onsen, Abuta-cho, Hokkaidō 049–5721,* ☎ *0142/75–2288,* ⅋⅋ *0142/75–3434. 35 Western-style rooms, 4 Japanese-style rooms. No credit cards. MAP.*

$–$$$ ⊡ **Tōya Park Hotel.** This hotel is at the head of the town and on a slight bluff. All the rooms in the newer wing are Japanese style and face the lake. In the original wing, only the Japanese-style rooms face the lake. The room rate includes breakfast and a buffet diner. ⊠ *38 Tōya-ko Onsen, Abuta-cho, Hokkaidō 049–5721,* ☎ *0142/75–2445,* ⅋⅋ *0142/ 75–391. 24 Western-style rooms, 256 Japanese-style rooms. 2 restaurants, pool, hot springs, bowling, recreation room. AE, DC, MC, V.*

Getting Around

The drive from Sapporo to Tōya-ko via Jōzankei is easy. Take the road that runs along the west side of the Botanical Gardens; it is a straight run to Jōzankei, less than an hour south of the city. There are sufficient signs in *romaji* (Japanese written in Roman script) throughout this area to give you directional confidence, and the route number— 230—is frequently displayed.

Direct buses from Sapporo to Tōya-ko Onsen via Nakayama Tōge take 2½ hours (¥2,700). **Jōtetsu Bus** (☎ 011/572–3131) runs between Sapporo and Tōya-ko Onsen; reservations are necessary. **Dōnan Bus** (☎ 011/261–3601) makes the Sapporo to Tōya-ko Onsen trip daily.

Tōya-ko Onsen is on the JR Sapporo-Hakodate Line. Disembark from the train at JR Tōya Eki for a 15-minute bus ride to the lake.

Noboribetsu Onsen

★ **20** *1 hr, 20 mins east of Tōya-ko by bus; 1 hr, 40 mins south of Sapporo by bus.*

Noboribetsu Onsen is the most famous spa in Hokkaidō, perhaps even in all of Japan. It's said that some 34,300 gallons of geothermally heated water are pumped out every hour, making it the most prodigious hot spring in Asia. Its 11 types of water are said to cure ailments ranging from rheumatism to diabetes to menopause. Noboribetsu Onsen *is* a tourist town, so expect masses of hotels and souvenir shops. However, though the modern hotel architecture is decidedly unattractive and out of tune with the mountain and forest surroundings, the village is not without charm. A stream runs through it, the main thoroughfare is cobblestone, and infernal gases billow from every street grate in winter. More important, the buildings do not obscure the mountains. Most hotels in Noboribetsu Onsen have their own baths, and the grandest of all are those at the Dai-ichi Takimoto-kan. The onsen has undergone something of a gentrification in recent years, the cozier ryokan yielding to blockbuster hotels that cater to busloads of visitors. For this reason you might find yourself getting more for your yen if you arrange a tour from Sapporo.

Whatever you do, don't confuse Noboribetsu Onsen with Noboribetsu, a city on the coast that is 13 minutes by bus from its namesake spa town. Noboribetsu is an ugly industrial city on the JR Muroran Line. In fact, the whole coastal area from Date to Tomakomai is an industrial eyesore, worsened by a sagging regional economy. Noboribetsu city is one hour south of Sapporo by JR Limited Express. From the JR station in Noboribetsu, a shuttle bus serves Noboribetsu Onsen.

★ **Jigokudani** (Valley of Hell) is a volcanic crater that looks like a bow-shape valley. Boiling water spurts out of thousands of holes, sounding like the heartbeat of the earth itself—although, because of its strong sulfur smell, others have described it differently. Whereas hot springs elsewhere in Japan were used to dispose of zealous foreign missionaries during the equally zealous periods of xenophobia—Unzen on Kyūshū is a notable example—Jigokudani's natural cauldrons were once favored by suicidal natives. The place is a couple of hundred yards from Noboribetsu Onsen. Set out northeast on Gokuraku Shopping Mall, the town's main drag. Signs will direct you to the crater, a 15-minute walk from the town center. Admission is free.

Dai-ichi Takimoto-kan (✉ 55 Noboribetsu Onsen, ☎ 0143/84–2111) hotel is a monstrosity, but its 12 pools—men's and women's—have seven different waters of varying temperatures and are well worth the ¥2,000 nonoccupant dipping fee (¥3,000 on weekends). Even hot-springs skeptics should consider paying the entrance fee if only for the view beyond the bathhouse's plate-glass window: it looks upon the steaming, volcanic gases of Jigokudani. One floor beneath the baths, there is a swimming pool with a slide. The baths are open to nonoccupants from 9 to 3; once inside you can stay until 5.

Lodging

$$–$$$$
★ **Noboribetsu Manseikaku Hotel.** An outdoor hot spring and Japanese haute cuisine—*kaiseki ryōri*—are the attractions at this Japanese-style inn. Except between 2 PM and 4 PM, use of the baths is restricted to guests. The charge for nonguests is ¥1,000. ✉ *21 Noboribetsu Onsen, Noboribetsu, Hokkaidō 059–0551,* ☎ *0143/84–3500. 19 Western-style rooms, 175 Japanese-style rooms. Dining room, hot springs. AE, DC, MC, V. MAP.*

$$ **Dai-ichi Takimoto-kan.** This monolithic spa hotel can host as many as 1,200 guests at one time. They come to enjoy its thermal pools, the best and most well known in Japan. The hotel is expensive, yet it has zero ambience. It's like a giant youth hostel and always fully booked. Service is efficiently impersonal, and it's a hike from your bedroom to the lobby and to the thermal baths. One indication of the place's size is the English-language map available at reception to help you negotiate the labyrinth of buildings and passageways. A vast dining room, the Attaka-tei, serves average Japanese and Western food, including a suitably sprawling dinner buffet of 75 dishes. ✉ *55 Noboribetsu Onsen, Noboribetsu, Hokkaidō 059–0551,* ☎ *0143/84–2111,* FAX *0143/84–2202,* WEB *takimotokan.co.jp. 393 Western-style rooms, 8 Japanese-style rooms. 2 restaurants, hot springs, shops, recreation room. AE, DC, MC, V, MAP.*

$$ **Noboribetsu Grand Hotel.** This is another huge hotel with large, barren public rooms. Be warned—your luxurious room may overlook the bus station. ✉ *154 Noboribetsu Onsen, Noboribetsu, Hokkaidō 059–*

0551, ☎ 0143/84–2101, ℻ 0143/84–2543. 174 Japanese-style rooms, 87 Western-style rooms. Restaurant, hot springs, shops. AE, DC, MC, V. MAP.

$ ⚑ **Akashiya-sō Youth Hostel.** The older female manager of this rather
★ run-down hostel provides a warm welcome. The place does have a hot-spring bath—and plenty of informative notices in English. Avoid the original wing, which opens on peak days for travelers not averse to roughing it in damp and dingy surroundings. Microwave ovens and refrigerators are available for basic self-catering. Membership in the Youth Hostel Association is not required to stay here. Located at the bottom of the village, it's below the post office. ✉ *6-4 Noboribetsu Onsen, Noboribetsu, Hokkaidō 059–0551, ☎ 0143/84–2616. 13 Japanese-style rooms (8 in new wing). No credit cards. MAP.*

Getting Around

From June to late October three buses per day make the 1¼-hour run between Tōya-ko Onsen and Noboribetsu Onsen; only one bus runs per day the rest of the year (¥1,530; reservations necessary). Heavy snow keeps the road closed until spring. **Dōnan Bus** (☎ 011/261–3601) travels from Sapporo to Noboribetsu Onsen; the trip takes 100 minutes by expressway (¥1,900; reservations advised).

To get to Noboribetsu Onsen by train, take the JR Sapporo-Hakodate Line, disembark at Noboribetsu, and then get on the Donan Bus (a 20-minute ride) to the spa town.

Nibutani

★ ㉑ *45 mins east of Tomakomai by JR, then 30 mins east of Noboribetsu Onsen by bus.*

Nibutani is one of the very last places in Hokkaidō with a sizable Ainu population—or at least part-Ainu, as the number of pure-blooded Ainu is very small now. Consequently, though the usual souvenir shops are much in evidence, there's some comfort in knowing your money has a better chance of finding its way into the pockets of proper Ainu, instead of someone trying to make a fistful of yen off someone else's native heritage.

The surrounding rolling hills and spacious horse ranches make Nibutani a beguiling place to visit in summer, though it has been spoiled somewhat by the building of a dam that put part of the area under water. Unfortunately, much of the lost land was of spiritual or economic value to the local Ainu. Keep in mind that only in 1997, with the passage of a law recognizing Ainu culture, did Japanese authorities begin to treat the group with anything approaching respect.

Nibutani has the excellent **Nibutani Ainu Bunka Hakubutsukan** (Nibutani Ainu Culture Museum). There is a brief bilingual pamphlet, and a selection of videos lets you listen to eerie-sounding traditional Ainu chants and songs. ✉ *Off Rte. 237, Biratori-chō, Saru-gun, ☎ 0145/72–2892. ⚏ ¥400, ¥700 joint ticket with Kayano Shigeru Nibutani Ainu Shiryō-kan. ☉ Mid-Jan.–mid-Dec., Tues.–Sun. 9:30–4;30.*

Five minutes on foot from the Nibutani Ainu Bunka Hakubutsukan is a smaller museum, the **Kayano Shigeru Nibutani Ainu Shiryō-kan** (Shigeru Kayano Nibutani Ainu Archive), which displays artifacts collected by a prominent Ainu activist, Shigeru Kayano, who was a member of Japan's House of Councillors from 1994 to 1998. In 2001 he set up the only Ainu-language radio station, which broadcasts once a month. ☎ *01457/2–3215. ⚏ ¥400, ¥700 joint ticket with Nibutani Ainu Bunka Hakubutsukan. ☉ Mid-Jan.–mid-Dec., Tues.–Sun. 9:30–4:30.*

Getting Around

The simplest way to get to Nibutani is from Sapporo: two buses a day (¥2,000) run from JR Sapporo Eki to the Nibutani Ainu Bunka Shiryō-kan. Buses also run from Nibutani to the JR station in Tomakomai, with bus connections to Shikotsu-ko and Noboribetsu Onsen. Finally, a small railway line provides transport between Tomakomai and Tomikawa, and to the right of the JR station in Tomikawa you can catch a bus to Nibutani. Don't make the mistake of getting off the bus too early, at Biratori.

Shikotsu-ko

★ ㉒   *50 mins south of Sapporo by bus, 2¼ hrs west of Nibutani by bus via Tomakomai.*

Shikotsu-ko is the deepest lake in Hokkaidō—outfathomed only by Honshū's Tazawa-ko as the deepest in all of Japan. Swimmers should remember that although the beach shelves gently for 35 ft, it drops suddenly to an eventual depth of 1,191 ft. The lake's shape is that of a classic caldera, except that the rise of two volcanoes crumbled its peripheral walls on both north and south shores. Both the southern volcano, **Tarumae-zan,** and its northern counterpart, **Eniwa-dake,** remain active. They have fine hikes and summits with superb views of the lake, Eniwa-dake being the more challenging climb.

At the base of Eniwa-dake on Route 435 is **Marukoma Onsen Ryokan** (☎ 0123/25–2341), which has rotemburo along the northwest lakeshore. Few experiences compare to steaming in the waters to the sight of falling snow and the sound of the lake roiling just beyond the rotemburo wall. Non-hotel guests are welcome in the baths from 10 AM to 3 PM (¥1,000). Guests can enjoy the outdoor baths 24 hours a day. The friendly ryokan is used to accommodating foreign visitors, who have included Swedish royalty.

Lodging

$$$–$$$$ 🏨 **Marukoma Onsen Ryokan.** The lobby, lounges, and restaurant of this ryokan—all facing the northwest shore of Shikotsu-ko—compensate for neither the building nor its interior furnishings having great aesthetic value. The tatami-style guest rooms have plain, modern light-wood furnishings, and if you can get a room facing the lake and mountain, the view will be splendid. Service is attentive and tolerant of foreigners; dinner, served in your room, is above average. However, besides the indoor thermal pool facing the water, the real benefit of this ryokan is its public rotemburo on the shore of Shikotsu-ko, as well as its private beach within yards of the hotel. The ryokan is on Route 435. ⊠ *Poropinai, Banga-ichi Chitose-shi, Hokkaidō 066–0287,* ☎ *0123/25–2341. 1 Western-style room, 60 Japanese-style rooms. Restaurant, bar, coffee shop, hot springs, recreation room. AE, DC, MC, V. MAP.*

Getting Around

To reach Shikotsu-ko from Nibutani, take the expressway to Tomakomai and follow Route 276 to Shikotsu Onsen, or follow Route 512 south from Sapporo. You can also take a train to JR Tomakomai Eki, from which Shikotsu-ko is a 40-minute bus ride.

From Shikotsu-ko the quickest route back to Sapporo (by car or bus) is via Chitose and up the expressway. You could also return to Tomakomai by bus and take the JR train back westward in the direction of Hakodate, or take a bus to Chitose Kūkō, then the JR back to Sapporo.

EASTERN HOKKAIDŌ AND THE OHOTSUKU-KAI

Abashiri, on the Ohotsuku-kai, makes a good base from which to head south to explore the mysterious lakes of Akan National Park; east out to the mountains and coastal scenery of Shiretoko National Park; or west to Hokkaidō's ice flow capital, Mombetsu. To see the great wetland breeding grounds for the striking and endangered tanchō-zuru, continue south from Akan National Park to Kushiro.

Abashiri

㉓ *5½ hrs east of Sapporo via Asahikawa by JR Limited Express.*

In the shadow of Tento-zan, Abashiri is the principle Ohotsuku-kai town, but it is quite small. In winter, ryūhyō jam up on its shores and stretch out to sea as far as the eye can see.

Two pleasure boats leave from the **Aurora Terminal** (☎ 0152/43–6000) at the east end of the port. The *Aurora 1* and the *Aurora 2* give you a chance to inspect the ryūhyō at close range from mid-January to mid-April, for ¥3,000.

The **Abashiri Kyōdo Hakubutsukan** (Abashiri Municipal Museum) houses a good collection of Ainu artifacts and anthropological findings taken from the nearby Moyoro Shell Mound that are believed to be relics from aboriginal people who predate the Ainu. The museum's across the railroad tracks to the south of downtown, in Katsuragaokaen (Katsura-gaoka Park), two minutes on foot from Abashiri Shogakko (elementary school). ⊠ *1–3 Katsura-machi 1-chōme, Abashiri-shi*, ☎ *0152/43–3090.* 🎟 *¥100.* ☉ *May–Oct., daily 9–5; Nov.–Apr., Tues.–Sat. 9–4.*

On the southeastern slope of Tento-zan, the **Hoppo Minzoku Hakubutsukan** (Hokkaidō Museum of Northern Peoples) contains artifacts belonging not only to the Ainu but also to indigenous cultures on the neighboring island of Sakhalin and in northern parts of America and Eurasia, such as the Inuit and the Lapps. If the museum's layout seems a little bizarre, it's because the building was designed to resemble the outline of a flying swan. The nodule housing the entrance lobby is fashioned like a conical tent. It is 5 km (3 mi)—a 10-minute drive—from JR Abashiri Eki on the Dōdo Taikan Yama Kōen-sen, a local road. ☎ *0152/45–3888.* 🎟 *¥250.* ☉ *Tues.–Sun. 9:30–4:30.*

★ Down the hill from Tento-zan toward Abashiri-ko, the **Abashiri Kangoku Hakubutsukan** (Prison Museum) recalls the days when convict labor was used to develop the region. Only the most heinous criminals were banished to this forbidding northern outpost, the Alcatraz of Japan. The museum is 10 minutes southwest of downtown on Route 395. ⊠ *Yobito 1–1*, ☎ *0152/45–2411.* 🎟 *¥1,050.* ☉ *Apr.–Oct., daily 8–6; Nov.–Mar., daily 9–5.*

In winter swans migrate from Siberia to **Tofutsu-ko,** just south of Abashiri, to hole up here. To get to the lake, take the train to Kitahama Eki and walk south for 10 minutes. From late June to late July, between Tofutsu-ko and the Ohotsuku-kai, the main attractions are

★ the **Gensai Ka-en** (Wildflower Fields). Spread over 11 km (7 mi) of sand dunes and containing 50 species of flowers, this is where locals take their afternoon promenades.

Dining and Lodging

$–$$ ✕ **Nakazushi.** Sushi combinations here pulled fresh from the nearby sea include salmon roe over rice, sea urchin, and the famous Abashiri scallop. Note that Nakazushi closes irregularly. ⊠ *Minami 2-jō Nishi 2,* ☎ *0152/44–4763. No credit cards.*

$$$$ 🏨 **Hotel Kanihonjin Yuaiso.** This hotel is perched on Tento-zan and overlooks Abashiri-ko. As you might expect at a hotel that calls itself the "Official Inn of Crab Lovers," the restaurant menu includes dishes that give the crustacean a range of Western and Japanese treatments—10 different ones for the *kani-gozen* (crab table d'hôte). The service is haughty to the point of curtness. Guest rooms are well maintained and are done in the muddy green favored by traditional Japanese hotels. Room charges include breakfast and dinner, and there's a karaoke room on-site. The hotel is eight minutes by taxi from the JR station. ⊠ *Omagari 34, Abashiri-shi, Hokkaidō 093–0045,* ☎ *0152/43–0033,* FAX *0152/44–2468. 111 Japanese-style rooms. Restaurant, bar. AE, MC, V.*

$ 🏨 **Hotel Shimbashi.** This basic business hotel has the advantage of a convenient location just across from the train station. Though it is admittedly formal, the proprietors are welcoming. The restaurant serves Japanese food—from soba to sushi to crab—priced from ¥400 to ¥2,000. ⊠ *1 Shin-machi, Abashiri-shi, Hokkaidō 093–0046,* ☎ *0152/ 43–4307,* FAX *0152/45–2091. 45 rooms. Restaurant. AE, DC, MC, V. MAP.*

Getting Around

The significant distance from Sapporo to Abashiri makes it advisable to take a train out, then rent a car or take a bus to get to the surrounding parks and towns. Coastal Highway 238 skirts Saroma-ko between Mombetsu and Abashiri.

A single bus runs to all of the worthwhile sights in Abashiri. It departs hourly from **JR Abashiri Eki** (⊠ Shin-machi 2-chōme 2-banchi); departure times are available at the tourist office.

The **tourist office** (☎ 0152/43–4261) adjoining the JR station can provide information about transportation in the area. Some staff members speak English.

Mombetsu

㉔ *1½ hrs northwest of Abashiri by car.*

Mombetsu feels like the end of the world. The icy waters of the Ohotsuku-kai wash the northeasternmost coast between this small port town and Wakkanai, and when the sea freezes in winter, Mombetsu is bitterly cold and besieged by ice floes. The people here make their living fishing the Ohotsuku-kai in summer. The town has museums; a small, friendly entertainment district; shops on the main street; and a few hotels.

The frigid Ohotsuku-kai waters produce *hokkai shima-ebi* (striped shrimp), the sweetest you'll ever taste, and ke-gani (best in June and July), which may look ugly, but the crab meat is so delicate you'll have no trouble forgiving the creature's appearance. The coastline is relatively flat, and the drama is in its isolation rather than its scenery.

To view the ice floes, you can ride the **Garinko Go,** which in season acts as an icebreaker, pushing out through the floes. The boat runs from late January to mid-October, but there are no departures in April. The dock, Kaiyō Kōryukan, is 10 minutes south by car from the main bus station in Mombetsu. ☎ *01582/4–8000.* ✉ *¥1,500 summer, ¥3,000 winter.*

Mombetsu's municipal museum, **Mombetsu Kyōdo Hakubutsukan,** has examples of Hokkaidō's flora and fauna, some stone arrowheads, and ancient pottery. ✉ *1–33 Hanazono-chō 8-chōme,* ☎ *01582/3–4236.* ✉ *Free.* ◷ *Tues.–Sun. 10:30–5:30.*

Ohotsuku Ryūhyō Kagaku Senta Giza (Okhotsk Giza Sea Ice Science Center) is a museum that aims to promote understanding of ice floes. Its main feature is the Astrovision Hall, where spectacular views of sea ice are projected on a 360-degree dome, re-creating the experience of flying over the Okhotsk Sea when the ice floes are most impressive. There is also a low-temperature simulation room, where, clad in Eskimo-type clothing, you can wander around blocks of sea ice. ✉ *11–6 Moto-mombetsu,* ☎ *01582/3–5400.* ✉ *¥300 (additional fees for Exhibition and Astrovision halls).* ◷ *Tues.–Sun. 9:30–4:30.*

Okhotsk Tower, a unique facility for the observation of ice floes, bills itself as the only place in the world from which ice floes can be viewed from underwater. It outlines the unusual conditions that conspire to bring such ice to this latitude, the southernmost reaches of ice floes in the northern hemisphere. The tower stands at the end of a 1-km-long (½-mi-long) pier, on which there is also a seal pen. ✉ *Motomombetsu 25-banchi 2-saki,* ☎ *01582/3–1100.* ✉ *¥1,200.* ◷ *Apr.–Oct., daily 9–9; Nov.–Mar., daily 10–7.*

Mombetsu Tourist Office (✉ *24–1 Saiwai-cho 5-chōme,* ☎ *01582–4–3900*) is open 9–5:30 year-round and staff members are happy to make local hotel bookings.

<table>
<tr><td>OFF THE
BEATEN PATH</td><td>**TAKINOUE** – Thirty minutes southwest of Mombetsu (via Route 273), this town is famous for its Shiba-zakura Festival (May 1–June 1), when the surrounding hills bloom with *shiba-zakura* (phlox), flowers that form a delicate pink carpet. Japanese drums boom, a photo contest draws shutterbugs hoping to capture the fantasy of the season, and a sideshow contest picks a Miss Phlox, a.k.a. Phlox Cinderella. Many villages on the coast between Mombetsu and Wakkanai host smaller versions of the same festival.</td></tr>
</table>

Dining and Lodging

Mombetsu's entertainment area, three streets up from the Harbor View Hotel, is small, but there are plenty of bars that serve food and one or two modest discotheques. There are fewer restaurants than bars. Although many eateries have visual displays in their windows to indicate prices and the type of food served, the bars do not. Count on about ¥5,000 per person in one of the bars that have hostesses with whom customers are expected to talk—in Japanese, not English. Prices can climb steeply, so establish the costs before you gulp too much whiskey.

$ ⌂ **Harbor View Hotel.** Even though the Harbor View is modest, it *is*
★ clean and comfortable. Request a room overlooking the harbor. Japanese and Western breakfasts are provided, and lunch or dinner might include grilled fish or shellfish. No English is spoken. The hotel is 25 minutes from Ohotsuku-Mombetsu Airport by car or bus; the trip from Memambetsu Airport takes one hour and 45 minutes. ✉ *6 Minato-machi, Mombetsu, Hokkaidō 094–0011,* ☎ *01582/4–6171. 35 Western-style rooms, 1 Japanese-style room. Restaurant. AE, MC, V. BP.*

$ 🏨 **Mombetsu Prince Hotel.** This business hotel's central location makes up for its small rooms. The Prince is a six-minute walk from the JR station and adjoins restaurants in the port. The hotel does not serve lunch, but the room charge includes a Western breakfast buffet and Japanese and Western dinners. For ¥2,500 there is an all-you-can-eat feast that includes crab. Some English is spoken. ✉ *3–26 Honcho 7-chōme, Mombetsu, Hokkaidō 094–0004,* ☎ *01582/3–5411. 135 Western-style rooms, 13 Japanese-style rooms. AE, DC, MC, V. BP.*

Shiretoko National Park

★ ㉕   *45 mins by train to JR Shari Eki, then 45 mins east of Abashiri by bus.*

A combination of somewhat difficult roads, changeable weather, and a local bear population—the last two of which aren't entirely agreeable to hikers—had kept Shiretoko off the Japanese tourist trail. Recently, however, TV shows and guidebooks have trumpeted it as "the last wilderness in Japan." During summer's school holidays it can feel like every rental car in Hokkaidō is here. The last stretch of the peninsular road is now closed to all but tour buses in the high season. Still, visiting outside of the summer crush, Shiretoko is remarkable, an untouched pocket of wilderness in an industrialized and technologically advanced nation.

You enter Shiretoko National Park at Utoro, where there's a **sightseeing boat** (☎ 0152/43–6000 late Oct.–late Apr.; 01522/4–2147 late Apr.–late Oct.) that runs out to the cape from late April to late October. Catch the boat from the *fune noriba* (boat pier), about a 10-minute walk from the Utoro Onsen bus terminal. It departs five times daily (less in winter) and costs ¥2,700 for a 90-minute tour, ¥6,000 for a 3¾-hour excursion. As the boat skirts the shore and rounds the cape's tip, the views are impressive, with 600-ft cliffs breaking straight out of the sea and rugged mountains inland.

Kamui means spirits/god in the Ainu language, and there is certainly something wondrous about **Kamuiwakka Onsen** on the north shore under Io-zan. Steaming hot water rushes down the mountain through a series of falls and pools creating a rotemburo with an ocean view. The pools are free—just strip and hop in. But between July 28 and August 29 visitors must park at the Nature Center and take a tour bus to the onsen.

The **Shari Bus** (☎ 01522/3–3145) runs every 20 minutes from the Shiretoko Nature Center to the rotemburo at Kamuiwakka Onsen. The tour bus takes one hour to travel along the single-track road.

Twenty minutes east of Utoro by car is the **Shiretoko Go-ko** (Five Lakes) area, where a collection of small lakes cling like dewdrops perched above a precipitous northward drop into the ocean.

Getting Around

Frequent train service runs from Sapporo to Abashiri and on to Shari. To get to Shiretoko National Park, continue traveling southeast of Abashiri on the Kanno Line beyond Hama-Koshimizu. Shari is the end of the line and the jumping-off point for Utoro, the gateway to the peninsula and park. Most proper roads end about halfway along the peninsula. The final one terminates at Aidomari, with 30 km (19 mi) remaining before Shiretoko's tip. Bus service is erratic, and winter closes most of the area off to wheeled vehicles. To get to the park by public transport (available in summer only), take the 55-minute bus ride from Shari to Utoro.

Highway 244 heads east to Shari, from which 334 heads onto the Shire-toko-hantō until it dead-ends in the wilds of the national park.

Akan National Park

㉖ *2 hrs southeast of Mombetsu by car.*

Like Shikotsu-Tōya National Park, this national park has some of Hokkaidō's most scenic lakes and mountains. And although the mountains are not as high as those in Daisetsu-zan National Park, they are no less imposing. In addition, Akan has three major lakes, each of which has a distinctive character. And, crucial to the success of any resort in Japan, the park has an abundance of thermal springs.

★ **Akan-ko** is watched over by the smoking volcanoes Me-Akan and O-Akan (Mr. and Mrs. Akan). The lake itself is famous for *marimo*—spherical colonies of green algae that may be as small as a Ping-Pong ball or as large as a soccer ball (the latter taking up to 500 years to form). Marimo are rare, and the only other areas they can be found are in Yamanaka-ko near Fuji-san and in a few lakes in North America, Siberia, and Switzerland. These strange plants act much like submarines, photosynthesizing by absorbing carbon dioxide from the water and then rising to the surface, where they exhale oxygen and sink. They also serve as weather indicators, rising closer to the surface when bright sunshine increases their photosynthesis but less so in inclement weather, when light levels drop. Akan-ko is especially beautiful in winter, when it freezes over and the surrounding mountains are covered with snow. A popular sport from January to March is skating between the *wakasagi* (pond smelt) fishermen. The wakasagi are hooked from ice holes and laid on the ice in order to freeze immediately. Their freshness makes them popular minced and eaten raw, though some people prefer to fry them. Grilled wakasagi often appears on the winter menus of Hokkaidō izakayas.

The town of **Akan-kohan** is the resort area. This small village has expanded around the lake as new hotels go up. As in so much of Hokkaidō, these hotels are not very attractive. The key is to obtain a room over the lake so you are looking at nature and not architectural calamities. The village center is kitschily dressed up for tourists and cluttered with souvenir shops with endless rows of carved bears, which are numerous here because a small Ainu population lives in the village, and the bear features heavily in traditional Ainu spiritual life.

Teshikaga is a small resort town with a few inns. Its JR station goes by the name of Mashū. Mashū Onsen is nearby, and Mashū-ko itself is a 20-minute drive—35 minutes by bus to the nearest observation point—from Teshikaga.

★ **Mashū-ko** is ringed by 656-ft-high rock walls. Curiously, no water has been found either to enter or leave the lake, so what goes on in its 695-ft depths is anybody's guess. Perhaps that mystery and the dark blue water combine to exert a strange hypnotic effect and are what cause tourists to stare endlessly down from the cliffs into the lake. These cliff sides are incredibly steep and have few or no footholds. You may live longer if you forgo the pleasure of inspecting the pristine water, said to be clear to a depth of 115 ft. Instead of climbing, consider taking in the lake from its two observation spots on the west rim. You can recognize them by the parking lots and the buildings housing souvenir and food stands.

Kawayu Onsen, lined with relatively expensive hotels (most of them Japanese style), is for those who believe in the curative value of hot springs. Kawayu is not particularly attractive. However, just before the spa is **Iō-zan** (ee-*oh*-zan), an active volcano that emits sulfurous steam from vents in two ravines. There are a parking lot and souvenir and grocery store just off the road. Buy a couple of fresh eggs from the store and then walk up to one of the saucepan-size pools and boil them. Kawayu is 14 km (9 mi) northwest of Mashū-ko.

Kussharo-ko (sometimes spelled Kutcharo and not to be confused with similarly named lakes in northern and southern Hokkaidō) is Akan National Park's largest lake. Once it had a nearly perfect caldera shape, but other volcanoes have since sprung up and caused its shores to become flat and less dramatic. It is, however, an ideal area for camping and is popular with families who come for boating and paddling in the water. There are also a couple of natural hot springs that can be used free of charge. One other tourist attraction has been enthusiastically promoted in recent years—perhaps with an eye on the profits being made on the shores of Scotland's Loch Ness: "Kusshie," a creature said to inhabit the lake's depths. The lake is at its finest in the autumn, when the different shades of gold and green on the trees extend from the lakeshore into the higher mountain altitudes. From Kawayu the road hugs the eastern side of the lake and connects with Route 243 to the south.

At the northwest end of the Kussharo-ko, the road climbs up the mountains through **Bihoro Tōge,** affording the last great view of Akan National Park's mountains and the green waters of Kussharo-ko below. At Bihoro the road swings west back toward Kitami and Asahikawa, or northeast to Abashiri.

Lodging

$$$ 🏨 **New Akan Hotel.** The prestigious New Akan tends toward sterility
★ and vastness, but it does have an ideal location on Akan-ko. Its newer annex is called Shangri-La; the original hotel is the Crystal Wing. The Western-style rooms are simply furnished in crisp white; Japanese-style rooms can accommodate up to five people. Despite the hotel's size, there are only a few English speakers on staff. There are Western- and Japanese-style restaurants. ✉ *Akan-ko Onsen, Akan-chō, Akan-gun, Hokkaidō 085–0467,* ☎ *0154/67–2121,* 🖷 *0154/67–3339. 75 Western-style rooms, 295 Japanese-style rooms. 2 restaurants, hot springs, shops. AE, DC, MC, V.*

$$–$$$ 🏨 **Hotel Yamaura.** Fronting Akan-ko at the south end of the village, the Yamaura has its own onsen. Half of the rooms are Japanese style, the others a hybrid of Western and Japanese styles. All have private bathrooms. Prices include two meals. Some staff members speak English. ✉ *Akan-kohan Onsen, Akan-chō, Akan-gun, Hokkaidō 085–0467,* ☎ *0154/67–2311,* 🖷 *0154/67–2330. 89 rooms. Restaurant, hot springs, hot tub, sauna. AE, DC, MC, V. MAP.*

$$ 🏨 **Akan Kankō Hotel.** This midsize hotel has its own onsen and a restau-
★ rant that serves local specialties. Rooms are small, well kept, and in subdued tones. The restaurant is open only to guests, and breakfast and dinner are included in the room rate. ✉ *Akan-ko Onsen, Akan-chō, Akan-gun, Hokkaidō 085–0467,* ☎ *0154/67–2611,* 🖷 *0154/67–2520. 3 Western-style rooms, 65 Japanese-style rooms. Bar, café. AE, MC, V. MAP.*

Getting Around

There are buses to Akan-ko from Kushiro. You can also catch a bus from Akan-ko to Abashiri if you change buses in Bihoro. By car from

Kitami, west of Abashiri, a road heads south to the small town of Tsubetsu, where it joins Route 240, entering Akan National Park near Akan-ko. From the southern part of Daisetsu-zan National Park at Nukabira, a road to Kamishihoro continues to Ashoro, which connects with Route 241; this runs directly to Akan.

Kushiro

70 mins south of Teshikaga by JR.

Despite its romantic moniker, the City of Fog, Kushiro is a port town of no great appeal that used to be known for its rather seedy entertainment area aimed at sailors and tourists coming in off the Tōkyō ferry. The city has been trying to reinvent itself as a base for nature conservation and tourism. Downtown, part of the old waterfront, has been restored and now has a complex called, mysteriously, MOO-EGG, which contains souvenir shops and food stalls, cafés, a small botanical garden, and a popular ice cream stand. Even the entertainment district has some revamped bars with traditional fireplaces where fish is cooked to order. Kushiro's fog keeps the city several degrees cooler than other coastal towns in Hokkaidō.

★ ㉗ North and west of Kushiro (35 minutes by bus) is **Kushiro Shitsugen** (Kushiro Marsh), which constitutes 60% of Japan's marshland and was the world's first wetland designated for protection under the 1995 Ramsar Convention. It is the home of the red-crested tanchō-zuru. These cranes were ruthlessly hunted at the beginning of the 20th century and were even believed to be extinct, until a handful of survivors were discovered in 1924. They have slowly regenerated and now number about 650. The crane—long-legged, long-billed, with a white body trimmed in black and a scarlet cap on its head—is a symbol of long life and happiness. Although said to live 1,000 years, the birds nonetheless have made it to a rather impressive 80 in zoos. They pair for life, which has also made them the symbol of an ideal couple—they are frequently cited in Japanese wedding speeches. In March or April females lay two eggs. The male and female play an equal role in looking after the eggs and, later, the chicks.

It is difficult to recommend a trip to see the cranes in summer: the birds are busy rearing their chicks and go deep into the swamps, where you can see them only through binoculars. Only a few are on view at an artificial breeding park, and these are kept behind a fence. In winter, when they come for food handouts (especially near Tsurui), they are easier to spot and no less beautiful in the snowy landscape.

Dining and Lodging

$–$$ ✕ **Uroko.** This riverside *robatayaki* (a restaurant specializing in charcoal grilling) welcomes foreign patrons. There is no English menu, but diners can point to the seafood of their choice—the speciality of the house is *menme* (rockfish). The restaurant is four minutes on foot from the Kushiro Pacific Hotel along the Kushiro-gawa. ✉ *2–24 Suehiro-chō,* ☎ *0154/24–6940. No credit cards. No lunch.*

$$ ▥ **Kushiro Pacific Hotel.** Recommended mainly for its central location, the Kushiro Pacific is five minutes by taxi from the train station. An efficient staff keeps the rather small rooms clean. Chinese and Western breakfast (¥1,100) and lunch (¥880) are served buffet style in the restaurant. For dinner explore the restaurants spread along the river, or ask the concierge for a recommendation. ✉ *2–6 Sakae-machi, Kushiro, Hokkaidō 085–0013,* ☎ *0154/24–8811,* ℻ *0154/23–9191. 132 rooms. Restaurant. AE, DC, MC, V.*

CENTRAL HOKKAIDŌ AND THE NORTHERN CAPE

Taking in Japan's largest national park, its northernmost points, and the island's highest mountain, this area is one of superlatives. After ascending the breathtaking Daisetsu-zan range in central Hokkaidō, get ready for the trek to Sōya-misaki, the northern cape in Japan, and the stark beauty of the Rishiri and Rebun islands.

Asahikawa

28 *1½ hrs northwest of Sapporo by tollway; 1 hr, 20 mins by train.*

Asahikawa, Hokkaidō's second-largest city, is the principal entrance to Daisetsu-zan National Park. The city is vast and sprawling—361,000 people reside in an area of 750 square km (465 square mi)—even though the first pioneers didn't establish a base here until 1885. Cosmopolitan it is not. The endless suburbs can be depressing, but the downtown center contains several international accommodations, including the sparkling Palace Hotel; a pedestrian shopping mall, the first such car-free mall in Japan; and the nightly scene of restaurants, izakaya, and bars. Asahikawa's major attractions are the Ainu Kinen-kan and the Ice Festival—held in February, this is Asahikawa's smaller version of Sapporo's Snow Festival (200 sculptures, compared with the 300 at Sapporo). Here, the celebration has the feeling of a country fair.

The **Kawamura Kaneto Ainu Kinen-kan** (Kawamura Kaneto Ainu Memorial Hall) is a reasonably good Ainu museum, if slightly ramshackle. However, like the Kayano Shigeru Ainu Shiryō-kan in Nibutani, it does have the moral advantage of being run by a genuine Ainu, a man named Kaneto Kawamura, whose family has lived in the Asahikawa area for seven generations. There's a feeling that the museum really does exist to educate people about Ainu culture. To get here, take Bus 24 (¥170) from bus Platform 14, which is two blocks north of the JR station, and get off at Ainu Kinenkan-mae. ☎ 0166/51–2461. ☞ ¥500. ⊙ July–Aug., daily 9–6; Sept.–June, daily 9–5.

The **Kokusai Senshoku Bijutsukan** (International Dying and Weaving Art Museum) displays dye work and textiles from China, Egypt, and elsewhere. ⊠ Minamigaoka 3-chōme, ☎ 0166/61–6161. ☞ ¥550. ⊙ Apr.–Nov., daily 9–5:30.

Yūkara Ori Kōgei-kan (Yūkara Ori Folkcraft Museum) exhibits crafts from around the world, mostly textiles. The wood used for the building comes exclusively from trees native to Hokkaidō. ⊠ Minamigaoka 3-chōme, ☎ 0166/62–8811. ☞ ¥450. ⊙ Apr.–Nov., daily 9–5:30; Dec.–Mar., Tues.–Sun. 9–5.

Dining and Lodging

Far from the sea and from Hokkaidō's breadbaskets, Asahikawa is not known for its cuisine, with two notable exceptions: ramen and *tonkatsu* (breaded, deep-fried pork cutlet). Asahikawa ramen features a distinctively salty pork broth prized by ramen connoisseurs. Several noodle shops pepper the area around the station.

$–$$ ✕ **Jenkatsu Isen.** This chain is famous for tonkatsu; a full-course meal will set you back about ¥1,200. Its many branches include a gaijin-friendly one three minutes from the station on foot. ⊠ 2-jō 7-chōme, ☎ 0166/26–7363. AE, V.

$$–$$$$ 🏨 **Palace Hotel.** Public spaces here are brightly lighted and airy, with
★ plants separating the registration area from the lounge. The Palace is downtown, 10 minutes east of the station on foot. The friendly staff

speaks some English. One of its restaurants, Lila, serves Continental fare. ✉ 7-jō 6-chōme, Asahikawa, Hokkaidō 070–0037, ☎ 0166/25–8811, ✉ 0116/25–8200. 259 rooms. 3 restaurants. AE, DC, MC, V.

$$–$$$ ⊞ **Asahikawa Terminal Hotel.** Although the rooms in this tower are
★ not big, they are bright and tastefully furnished, and the location can't be beat: the hotel is connected to the railway station, which figures, since both are operated by JR Hokkaidō. Fukutsuru-teii, a restaurant on the sixth floor, offers standard Japanese fare with set courses from ¥1,500. The Orion Cafe serves light meals and drinks. ✉ Miyashita-dōri 7-chōme, Asahikawa, Hokkaidō 070–0030, ☎ 0166/24–0111, ✉ 0166/21–2133. 159 rooms. 2 restaurants, bar, tea shop. AE, DC, MC, V.

$$ ⊞ **Toyo Hotel.** The understated lobby here makes for a hotel more appealing inside than out. This small hotel has rooms with white-and-gray decor. No English is spoken; the Toyo is used to serving Japanese guests but is friendly and helpful to Westerners. A Japanese restaurant on the ground floor offers meals from ¥2,500 to ¥3,500. Anjou restaurant serves French fare with courses from ¥4,000 to ¥9,000. ✉ 7-jō 7-chōme, Asahikawa, Hokkaidō 070–0037, ☎ 0166/22–7575, ✉ 0116/23–1733. 104 rooms. 2 restaurants. AE, DC, MC, V.

Daisetsu-zan National Park

29 *50 mins east of Asahikawa by car.*

The geographical center of Hokkaidō and the largest of Japan's national parks, Daisetsu-zan contains the very essence of rugged Hokkaidō: vast plains, soaring mountain peaks, hidden gorges, cascading waterfalls, wildflowers, forests, hiking trails, wilderness, and, of course, onsen. Daisetsu-zan, which means great snow mountains, refers to the park's five major peaks, whose combined altitudes approach 6,560 ft. Their presence dominates the area and channels human access into the park: only a few roads pass through. The rest dead-end in formidable terrain.

As you follow the main route through the park, the first place to go is
★ **Sōun-kyō.** The 24-km (15-mi) ravine extends into the park from its northeast entrance and is doubtless the most scenic wonder therein. For an 8-km (5-mi) stretch, sheer cliff walls rise on both sides of the canyon as the road winds into the mountains. In winter and early spring, foreboding stone spires loom as if in judgment; in other seasons they thrust through glorious foliage. Sōun-kyō Onsen is at the halfway point of the ravine.

Ugly resort hotels do diminish the gorge's impact. Sōun-kyō Onsen is another unfortunate example of how natural splendor can be abused. Resting precariously on the walls of the gorge are grocery stores, houses, inns, and the inevitable souvenir shops that make up the village of Sōun-kyō. Activities take place in resort hotels, not in the village, and during the day most people are out on trails hiking through the park. One popular, if easy, trip combines a seven-minute gondola ride (¥1,600 round-trip) with a 15-minute chairlift ride (¥600 round-trip) up Kuro-dake for great views of Daisetsu-zan. For even finer views, including one of Sōun-kyō, take the hour's walk to the very top. In July and August alpine wildflowers cover the mountain.

The picturesque twin **Ryusei-no-taki** (Shooting-Star Falls) and **Ginga-no-taki** (Milky Way Falls) are 3 km (2 mi) up the road from Sōun-kyō Onsen. Neither is especially dramatic, but because they are a pair, separated by a buttresslike node called Buddhist Rock, they fit well into the Japanese natural aesthetic.

Follow the Ishikari-gawa through perpendicular cliffs and fluted rock columns until it reaches the dammed-up **Daisetsu-ko.** Unfortunately, the path has been closed two-thirds of the way to the dam out of concern for falling rocks. If you have rented a bicycle at the Sōun-kyō bus terminal (¥1,500/day) and hope to reach the dam, the only option is to backtrack to the main road and take the tunnel. The dam is a feat of engineering, its walls constructed only of earth and rubble. In itself, it has no visual merit, but islands appear to float in the lake behind it, surrounded by a backdrop of conifer-clad mountains.

At Daisetsu-ko the road divides. The right fork, Route 273, turns south and traverses the rough wilderness and least-visited part of the park. The road has been upgraded to avoid closure in winter, but there are no public buses. If you do not have a car, you must hitchhike as far as Nukabira, where you can catch buses and trains. This dramatic route climbs up and over **Mikuni Tōge** before it drops into lush valleys and through small ghost towns.

Nukabira is a quiet spa town close to **Shikaribetsu-ko,** the park's only natural lake. Toward the end of December, the lake freezes over, and an igloo village is built on the 3-ft-thick ice in preparation for the Shikaribetsu Kotan Matsuri, the village festival that runs from mid-January to the end of February. The festival celebrates the dramatic Okhotsk winter, with an open-air bath erected on the ice and hot-air balloons taking people up and dotting the shimmering icy landscape with color.

On the west side of the park, two **spa towns** serve as hiking centers in summer and ski resorts in winter. **Shirogane Onsen,** at 2,461 ft, has had especially good skiing since its mountain, Tokachi-dake, erupted in 1962, creating a superb ski bowl. It erupted again in 1988. At **Asahi-dake Onsen,** you can take a cable car up Asahi-dake, Hokkaidō's highest mountain, to an altitude of 5,250 ft, and hike for two hours to the 7,513-ft summit. In late spring and early summer the slopes are carpeted with alpine flowers. Serious skiers come here for Japan's longest ski season.

Lodging

For good or ill, you have no option but to stay in Sōun-kyō Onsen if you want to stay in the northern part of the park. Rates tend to be 20% lower in winter. Because Sōun-kyō's hotels are almost exclusively ryokan, where meals are included, other dining opportunities in town are limited. You can also try the small **youth hostel** (☎ 01658/5–3418).

$–$$$$ ☷ **Choyotei.** Perched on a bluff halfway up the side of the gorge, this hotel has the best views—and, because of this, spoils some of Sōun-kyō's beauty. Its corner window in the huge foyer lounge looks straight down the gorge; however, the hotel itself is an eyesore, cold and sterile in the modern Japanese style. Its sumptuous baths and rooms that face the gorge may merit the price, although rooms at the back overlook a parking lot. ⊠ *Sōun-kyō Onsen, Kamikawa, Hokkaidō 078–1701,* ☎ *01658/5–3241. 5 Western-style rooms, 257 Japanese-style rooms. Bar, hot springs, shops, recreation room. AE, DC, MC, V. MAP.*

$–$$ ☷ **Mount View Hotel.** This hotel was built as a modern interpretation
★ of an alpine inn, a design concept marred by cheap execution. The decor is cheerful, in warm pastels, but the hotel is down by the road and has limited views. Its restaurant, Maple, has a Western-style buffet and offers an unexpectedly large wine list for a hot-spring hotel. There is also a Japanese restaurant. ⊠ *Sōun-kyō Onsen, Kamikawa, Hokkaidō 078–1701,* ☎ *01658/5–3011,* FAX *01658/5–3010. 69 Western-style rooms, 28 Japanese-style rooms. 2 restaurants, hot springs. AE, DC, MC, V.*

$ ⊡ **Pension Yukara.** Small rooms and small furniture make for a cuteness that borders on kitsch. Still, the atmosphere at this cozy Western-style inn is relaxed, and the prices are better than at most others in Sōun-kyō Onsen. Though little English is spoken, the owners are welcoming to overseas visitors. Passable Western-style meals with Hokkaidō ingredients are included in the price, although you would do better to stay without meals (not an option in the peak months of July and August). The management is happy to present picnic *onigiri* (rice balls) if you're planning to hit the hiking trails early. ⊠ *Sōun-kyō Onsen, Kamikawa, Hokkaidō 078–1701,* ☎ ℻ *01658/5–3216. 4 Western-style rooms, 3 Japanese-style rooms with shared bath. Dining room, hot springs. AE, DC, MC, V. MAP.*

Getting Around

Sōun-kyō is two hours southeast of Asahikawa by car. You can catch a bus directly to Sōun-kyō Onsen (¥1,900) from in front of Asahikawa's JR station. If you are using a Japan Rail pass, you can save money by taking the train to Kamikawa Eki and transferring to the Dohoku Bus for the 30-minute run to Sōun-kyō.

Visitor Information

The **Sōun-kyō tourist office** (☎ 01658/5–3350), under the bicycle rental office in the bus terminal, provides hiking maps and information on sightseeing and lodging. English is spoken here.

The Northern Cape

Wakkanai is 5¾ hrs north of Sapporo by JR Limited Express, 1 hr north of Okadama Airport, or ¾ hr north from New Chitose Airport.

30 **Wakkanai** is a working-class town that subsists on farming the scrubland and fishing the cold waters for Alaska pollack and Atka mackerel when the sea is not packed with ice floes. It's an isolated outpost of humanity: winter nights are long, and in summer there is a feeling of poetic solitude that comes from the eerie quality of the northern lights. From Wakkanai Park, on a ridge west of the city, there's a commanding view of Sakhalin, an island taken over by the Russians at the end of World War II. Several monuments in this park are dedicated to the days when Sakhalin was part of Japan. One commemorates nine female telephone operators who committed suicide at their post office in Maoka (on Sakhalin) when the island was taken by the Russians.

Few travelers come as far as Wakkanai for the town itself. You're likely to do the same and stick around only long enough to catch one of the ferries that make the daily crossing to Rebun-tō and to Rishiri-tō.

★ **31** **Rebun-tō** is the older of two Nihon-kai islands created by an upward thrust of the earth's crust. The long, narrow island is oriented on a north–south axis. Along the east coast there are numerous fishing villages where men bring their catch, some of which is made into *nukabokke* (pollack covered in rice-bran paste), while women rake in edible yellow-green kelp, which is often used for soup broth, from the shore. Fleets of uni boats fish just offshore; the prickly sea urchin are spotted through bottomless boxes held over the side of the boat and then raked in.

On the west coast, cliffs stave off the surging waters of the Nihon-kai. Inland, during the short summer months, wild alpine flowers, 300 species in all, blanket the mountain meadows. Momo-iwa, or Peach Rock, is an 820-ft-high mound 2 km (1 mi) west of the ferry landing. Here the wildflowers are in such profusion in mid-June that you almost fear to walk, for each step seems to crush a dozen of the delicate blossoms, including the white-pointed *usuyo-kiso*, which is found only on Rebun. Its name roughly translates as "dusting of snow."

Buses stop at the trailhead to the **Kitosu Course** (midway down the eastern side of the island) and the **Nairo Course** (10 km [6 mi] north). Bamboo and low-lying pines predominate. Leave 1¼ hours to cover the 4½-km (3-mi) loop to the top of 1,600-ft Rebun-dake, which overlooks rolling hills and the ocean beyond. Another hike, the **Eight-Hour Course,** covers the island from top to bottom on the west coast, passing along the way cliffs, waterfalls, and tiny seasonal villages. Buses also go to Sukotan-misaki, a lovely cape on the west side of the island with a cove that is popular with anglers. Be warned that, apart from Kafuka, there are no restaurants on the island and village shops tend to be in the front room of a home and hard to spot.

★ ㉜ **Rishiri-tō** is the result of a submarine volcano whose cone now towers 5,640 ft out of the water. The scenery is wilder than on Rebun-tō, and, though it is a larger island, Rishiri-tō has fewer inhabitants. The ruggedness of the terrain makes it harder to support life and figures for hardier climbing—sometimes too hardy: the Oniwaki Course was closed after a climber suffered a fatal misstep. The intermediate **Kutsugata Course** (four hours to the top), on the west side of the island, will take you past patches of wildflowers, including the buttercup-like *botan kimbai,* vibrant purple *hakusan chidori,* and numerous bird species.

To get the lay of the island, it's a good idea to take one of the regularly scheduled buses, which make a complete circle in two hours. From May through November, there are six a day between 6:30 AM and 4:40 PM, which go both clockwise and counterclockwise. Fewer make the circuit the rest of the year. Get off at any of the several tourist stops along the way, and take the hiking routes laid out to the major scenic spots. Once you break above Rishiri-zan's tree line, at about 3,000 ft, the alpine panoramas of wildflowers, cone-shape mountain, and wide expanses of sea are astonishing.

㉝ Halfway between Wakkanai and **Sōya-misaki,** the mountains push out toward the sea. Russia's Sakhalin Island stands out across the frigid waters. Sōya-misaki is at the northernmost limits of Japan. This lonely but significant spot is the site of several monuments marking the end of Japan's territory, as well as a memorial to the Korean airliner downed by the Soviet military north of here in 1982. If you happen to be rounding Sōya-misaki on the way to Wakkanai after a trip up Hokkaidō's east coast, your first glimpse of Rishiri-to and its volcano on the horizon will come soon after you round the cape. A public bus makes the hour-long run between Wakkanai and Cape Sōya six times a day.

Dining and Lodging

$$–$$$ ✕ **Sakatsubo.** Famous for sea urchin, this restaurant serves a variety called *bafun* (literally, "horse turd"). Despite its inauspicious name, it is prized and is served as *domburi* (over steamed rice). The *unigiri* (sea urchin–filled rice balls) go for ¥400. ✉ *Kafuka, Rebun-chō,* ☎ *01638/ 6–1894. No credit cards.*

$$$ 🏠 **Hera-san no Uchi.** Hera's House, as the name translates, typifies the warm, casual atmosphere that makes Hokkaidō so loved by Japanese hippies. Mr. Hera refuses to use artificial or frozen foods for the two meals that come with the Japanese-style rooms, and he welcomes travelers from every nation. Bicycles are available for rent. The house is at the entrance to the Peshi-misaki hiking trail. ✉ *Rishiri-Fuji-machi, Oshidomari, Rish iri-chō, Hokkaidō 097–0400,* ☎ *01638/2–2361. 9*

Western-style rooms, 3 Japanese-style rooms with shared bath. No credit cards. MAP.

$$$ ☎ **Pension Uni.** This sky-blue building is at the top of the cliffs above the village, and although no English is spoken, the family are welcoming to foreigners. Rooms come with bathrooms, and the two meals included in the rate feature ingredients that were swimming only hours earlier. Gargantuan dinners alternate from Western to Japanese for guests who stay more than one night, although maybe only the cutlery-chopsticks switch will give a clue as to which is which. ✉ Tonnai, Kafuka, Rebun-chō Hokkaidō 097–1201, ☎ 01638/6–1541. 9 Western-style rooms, 1 Japanese-style room. No credit cards. MAP.

Getting Around

From June through August, Air Nippon flies from New Chitose Airport directly to Rishiri Airport on Rishiri-tō. Check the departure board for local weather conditions, and if the flights to the island are delayed try to reimburse your ticket and go by ferry instead. Buses meet the planes and take passengers into town; otherwise a taxi for the 25-minute journey will cost about ¥2,000.

Higashi-Nihon Ferry (☎ 0162/23–3780) has boats that make the daily two-hour crossing to Rebun-tō and the one-hour, 40-minute crossing to Rishiri-tō. In summer there are four or five daily ferries, in winter two. Fares to Rebun are ¥3,780 for first class and ¥2,100 second class. Fares to Rishiri are ¥3,360 and ¥1,880. A ferry between the two islands costs ¥730.

HOKKAIDŌ A TO Z

To research prices, get advice from other travelers, and book travel arrangements, visit www.fodors.com.

AIR TRAVEL

Japan Airlines (JAL), Japan Air System (JAS), and All Nippon Airways (ANA) link Hokkaidō to Honshū by direct flights from Tōkyō's Haneda Kūkō to Hakodate, Sapporo (New Chitose Airport), Asahikawa Airport, Abashiri (Memambetsu Airport), Nemuro (Nakashibetsu Airport), and Kushiro Airport. There are also two flights a day from Tōkyō's Narita International Airport. Many other major cities on Honshū have flights to Sapporo, as do several places in the Asian and Pacific region.

The cost by air from Tōkyō to Sapporo is as low as ¥16,500, compared with ¥22,430 by train. Some air travelers arriving in Japan on European flights can, with a change of planes at Tōkyō, fly at no extra charge to Sapporo. If you are flying from overseas to Sapporo via Tōkyō, book the domestic portion when you buy your international ticket; otherwise you will have to fork out for what is, per mile, the most expensive domestic ticket in the world. Two fledgling airlines are starting to rectify this situation. Air Dō (rhymes with "who") debuted in 1998 to slash fares between Tōkyō and Sapporo (¥16,000). Skymark Airlines, another welcome fare slasher, flies between Chitose and Ōsaka's Itami Airport.

The two domestic airlines—Japan Air System (JAS) and All Nippon Airways (ANA)—have local companies connecting Sapporo with Hakodate, Kushiro, Wakkanai, and the smaller Memambetsu, Naka-Shibetsu, and Ohotsuku-Mombetsu airports in eastern Hokkaidō. Hokkaidō Air System is part of JAS. Air Hokkaidō and Air Nippon are part of ANA. There is also daily service between Wakkanai and both Rebun and Rishiri islands. Because of the potential for weather and other delays in Hokkaidō, always check flights before you get to Sapporo.

➤ CONTACTS: **Air Hokkaidō and Air Nippon** (☎ 0120/029–222). **Hokkaidō Air System** (☎ 0120/5–11283).

BOAT AND FERRY TRAVEL

This is the least expensive form of travel to Hokkaidō. First-class fares are typically somewhat more than double the second-class rate. From Tōkyō the luxury ferryboat *Sabrina Blue Zephyr* sails three or four times weekly to Kushiro (32 hours) and is operated by the Kinkai Yusen Company, with rates of ¥9,400.

Higashi Nihon Ferry's express *Unicorn* makes two round-trips daily from Aomori to Hakodate. The express ferry takes 2 hours (to the train's 2½) but costs only ¥1,420 second class. Higashi-nihon boats also make the journey from Hachinohe to Tomakomai in 9 hours (¥3,970); from Hachinohe to Muroran in 8 hours (¥3,970); from Sendai to Tomakomai in 16½ hours (¥9,020); and from Aomori to Muroran in 7 hours (¥3,460).

Shin Nihon Ferry travels from Niigata to Otaru in 18 hours (¥5,250). Taiheiyo Ferry routes include Sendai to Tomakomai (18 hours, ¥7,600) and Nagoya to Tomakomai (36 hours, ¥10,200).

➤ BOAT AND FERRY INFORMATION: **Higashi Nihon Ferry** (☎ 0177/82–3631 in Aomori; 0138/42–6251 in Hakodate; 0178/28–3985 in Hachinohe; 0144/34–5261 in Tomakomai; 0143/34–5261 in Muroran; 022/25–7221 in Sendai). **Kinkai Yusen Company** (☎ 0154/52–4890). **Shin Nihon Ferry** (☎ 025/273–2171 in Niigata; 0134/22–6191 in Otaru). **Taiheiyo Ferry** (☎ 022/25–7221 in Sendai; 052/203–0227 in Nagoya).

BUS TRAVEL

Buses cover most of the major routes through the scenic areas, and all the excursions in this chapter may be accomplished by bus. There's no English-language telephone service for buses in Hokkaidō, although Chuo Bus has an English brochure for Japanese-speaking tours out of Sapporo. Plaza in Sapporo will supply bus route and schedule information and make telephone bookings if required.

CAR RENTAL

Cars are easy to rent. Orix Rent-a-Car has offices in central Sapporo, at Chitose Airport, and at major JR stations in Hakodate and Asahikawa. For the most part, the Japanese are cautious drivers, though a combination of wide straight roads, light traffic, treacherous weather conditions, and Honshū visitors' unfamiliarity with all of the above gives Hokkaidō the worst traffic fatality figures in Japan. However, Dosanko, the area residents, are extremely helpful in giving instructions and directions to Western travelers. The limitation to renting a car is the expense. A day's rental is about ¥11,000 (not including tax), including 220 free km (132 mi), after which you are charged ¥20 per km (½ mi).

➤ LOCAL AGENCY: **Orix Rent-a-Car** (✉ Minami 4 Nishi 1, Chūō-ku, Sapporo, ☎ 011/241–0543).

EMERGENCIES

➤ CONTACTS: **Ambulance** (☎ 119). **Police** (☎ 110).

LODGING

Plaza i in Sapporo can help with telephone reservations for lodgings throughout Hokkaidō and also publishes an excellent camping guide.

➤ CONTACT: **Plaza i** (☎ 011/211–3678).

TOURS

The Japan Travel Bureau runs tours of Hokkaidō from Tōkyō, lasting from a few to several days. These include airfare, hotel, and meals and stop at major cities and scenic areas. Bookings should be made at least 10 days in advance. Although your guide may speak some English, the tours are geared to domestic travelers and are conducted in Japanese.

➤ CONTACT: **Japan Travel Bureau** (☎ 03/5620–9500 in Tōkyō).

TRAIN TRAVEL

With the 55-km (34-mi) Seikan Tunnel permitting train travel between Hokkaidō and Honshū, the train journey from Tōkyō to Sapporo can take as little as 10 hours. This trip involves a combination of the Shinkansen train to Morioka (2½ hours), the northernmost point on the Tōhoku Shinkansen Line, and a change to an express train for the remaining journey to Hakodate (4 hours, 20 minutes) and then on to Sapporo (3¼ hours). The JR pass covers this route (the cost is ¥22,430 without the pass). The Hokutosei sleeper train provides greater comfort if not speed. It makes the voyage in 17 hours and eliminates the need to change trains. The fare is ¥23,520 (¥9,450 for JR pass holders). Forget about local trains from Tōkyō (¥14,070); the combined travel time to Sapporo is 30 hours, not including the required overnight stop in Aomori. Travelers with more time than cash would do better on the ferry.

Japan Railways (JR) has routes connecting most of the major cities. For the most part, trains travel on less scenic routes and are simply efficient means to reach the areas that you want to explore. Bus routes pass through the more scenic areas.

Japan Rail's English-language information line provides price and schedule information for JR lines nationwide.

➤ TRAIN INFORMATION: **Japan Railway Information Line** (☎ 03/3423–0111).

TRANSPORTATION AROUND HOKKAIDŌ

The best way for foreign visitors to explore is by car. Most car rental companies offer the option of having different pick-up and drop-off locations and will meet customers from train, ferries, and local flights. Long-distance buses are a good way to cut some driving miles off a Hokkaidō journey, but check that the service will use the expressways and is not stopping at every village.

VISITOR INFORMATION

The Hokkaidō Tourist Association has an office in Tōkyō, on the second floor of the Kokusai Kankō Kaikan Building, near the Yaesu exit of Tōkyō Eki. The Japan National Tourist Organization's Tourist Information Center (TIC) in Tōkyō has free maps and brochures on Hokkaidō. Within Hokkaidō, the best place for travel information is Sapporo.

Important regional tourist information centers are in Akan-ko, Noboribetsu Onsen, Sōun-kyō Onsen, and Tōya-ko.

There are bus and train travel information centers at all the major train stations.

Japan Travel Phone, the toll-free nationwide service for English-language assistance or travel information, is available from 9 to 5, seven days a week. You may see pamphlets listing other numbers for different areas of Japan; however, these numbers have been consolidated into one toll-free number.

➤ TOURIST INFORMATION: **Hokkaidō Tourist Association** (⊠ Marunōchi 1–8–3, Chiyoda-ku, Tōkyō, ☎ 03/3214–2481). **Japan Travel Phone** (☎ 0088/22–4800). **Regional Tourist Information Centers** (☎ 0154/ 67–2254 in Akan-ko; 0143/84–3311 in Noboribetsu Onsen; 01658/ 5–1811 in Sōun-kyō Onsen; 01427/5–2446 in Tōya-ko). **Tourist Information Center** (TIC: ⊠ Tōkyō International Forum Bldg., floor B-1, 3–5–1 Marunōchi, Chiyoda-ku, Tōkyō, ☎ 03/3201–3331).

14 BASICS AND BACKGROUND

Portraits of Japan

Books and Videos

Chronology

Smart Travel Tips A to Z

Vocabulary

Some aspect of Japnese culture is bound to have led you to pick up this book and contemplate a trip to Japan. Perhaps it was the warm aroma of grilled *unagi sushi* or a steaming bowl of *nabeyaki udon.* It could have been the rustle of a *kimono* or the ancient crackle on a piece of *shino* pottery. Or maybe it was the quiet allure of a haiku by Bashō quoted in something that you read about Japan. Whether or not one of these sparked your interest, no doubt one or more elements of Japanese culture will make your trip unforgettable. In the course of the culture warp you're bound to experience when you set foot on *terra Japonica,* some of the topics below might be useful for getting your bearings.

— Updated by Tamah and
Yoshihiro Nakamura

THE ARTS

Calligraphy

Calligraphy in Japan arrived around AD 500 with Buddhism and its emphasis on writing. By 800 the *kana* of Japanese language—the two alphabets—began to be artistically written as well. The art of calligraphy lies not only in the creative execution of the characters, as in Western calligraphy, but also in the direct expression of the artist's personality and message. Thick, heavy splotches or delicate, watery lines should be viewed first without respect to their meaning, as creative forms displaying emotion. Then the meaning can come to the fore, adding substance to the emotion.

As with all traditional arts in Japan, there are various schools and styles of calligraphy—five in this case—each with more or less emphasis on structure and expression. The Chinese exported the *tenshō* (a primitive style called "seal") and *reishō* (scribe's style, an advanced primitive form) to Japan with written Buddhist scripture. The Japanese developed three other styles: *sōshō* (cursive writing), the looser *gyōshō* (semicursive, or "running" style), and *kaishō* (block, or standard style).

The first two demonstrate the Japanese emphasis on expression to convey an impromptu, flowing image unique to the moment—retouching and erasing is impossible. Kaishō has since developed into carved calligraphy on wood—either engraved or in relief—and the traditional stamp art seen at temples and in print. Avant-garde styles now popular, which are difficult even for Japanese to read, can seem the most interesting to foreigners as an art form. You'll see this style in many traditional restaurants.

Go to visitor centers if you would like to try out a brush, and unless you insist on a famous calligrapher's work, most Japanese can write something interesting for you on a decorative board found at most art stores. Reading: *The Art of Japanese Calligraphy,* by Yujiro Nakata.

Ceramics

With wares that range from clean, flawlessly decorated porcelain to rustic pieces so spirited that they almost breathe, Japanese pottery attracts its share of enthusiasts and ardent collectors for good reason. During the past several decades, it has significantly influenced North American ceramic artists. The popularity of Raku firing techniques, adapted from those of the famous Japanese pottery clan of the same name, is one example.

Japanese ceramic styles are defined regionally. Arita *yaki* (ceramic ware from Arita on Kyūshū), Tobe yaki, Kutani yaki, and Kyōto's Kyō yaki and Kiyomizu yaki are all porcelain ware. True to the nature of porcelain—a delicate fine-particled clay body—these styles are either elaborately decorated or covered with images. Stoneware decoration tends to have an earthier but no less refined appeal, befitting the rougher texture of the clay body. Mashiko yaki's brown, black, and white glazes are often applied in splatters. Celebrated potter Shōji Hamada (1894–1978) worked in Mashiko.

Other regional potters use glazes on stoneware for texture and coloristic effects—mottled, crusty Tokoname yaki; speckled, earth-tone Shigaraki yaki made near Kyōto; and the pasty white or blue-white Hagi yaki come to life with the surface and depth of their rustic glazes. Bizen yaki, another stoneware, has no liquid glaze applied to its surfaces. Pots are buried in ash, wrapped in straw, or colored in the firing process by the potters' manipulations of kiln conditions.

Unless your mind is set on the idea of kiln hopping in pottery towns like Hagi, Bizen, and Arita, you can find these wares in Kyōto and Tōkyō department stores. If you do go on a pilgrimage, call local kilns and tourist organizations to verify that what you want to see will be open and to ask about yearly pottery sales, during which local wares are discounted. Reading: *Inside Japanese Ceramics*, by Richard L. Wilson.

Gardens

What might strike us only second to the sense of beauty and calm that pervades Japanese gardens is how different they are from our own Western gardens. One key to understanding—and more fully enjoying—them is knowing that garden design, like all traditional Japanese arts, emerged out of the country's unique mixture of religious, philosophical, and artistic ideas.

Shintoism, Taoism, and Buddhism all stress the contemplation and re-creation of nature as part of the process of achieving understanding and enlightenment, and from these come many of the principles that most influence Japanese garden design.

From Shintoism, Japan's ancient religion, comes *genus loci* (the spirit of place) and the search for the divine presence in remarkable natural features: special mountains, trees, rocks, and so forth. Prevalent features of Tao influence are islands that act as a symbolic heaven for souls who achieve perfect harmony. Here sea turtles and cranes—creatures commonly represented in gardens—serve these enlightened souls.

Buddhist gardens function as settings for meditation, the goal of which is enlightenment. Shōgun and samurai were strongly drawn to Zen Buddhism and the achievement of enlightenment, and Zen gardens evolved as spaces for individuals to use almost exclusively for meditation and growth. The classic example from this time is the *karesansui*—dry landscape—consisting of meticulously placed rocks and raked gravel. It is a highly challenging style that reflects the skill of the designer.

Historically, the first garden designers in Japan were temple priests. Later, tea masters created gardens in order to refine the tea ceremony experience. A major contribution of the tea masters was the *roji*, the path or dewy ground that emotionally and mentally prepares participants for the ceremony as it leads them through the garden to the teahouse.

Gradually, gardens moved out of the exclusive realm to which only nobles, *daimyō*, wealthy merchants, and poets had access, and the increasingly affluent middle class began to demand professional designers. In the process, aesthetic concerns came to override those of religion.

In addition to genus loci, karesansui style, and the roji mentioned above, here are a few terms that will help you more fully experience Japanese gardens.

Change and movement. Change is highlighted in Japanese gardens with careful attention to the seasonal variations that plants undergo: from cherry blossoms in spring to summer greenery to autumn leaf coloring to winter snow clinging to the garden's bare bones. A water element, either real or abstract, often represents movement, as with the use of raked gravel or a stone "stream."

Mie gakure. The "hide-and-reveal" principle dictates that from no point should all of a garden be visible, that there is always mystery and incompleteness, and that viewers move through a garden to contemplate its changing perspectives.

Miniaturized landscapes. Depicting celebrated natural and literary sites, these references have been one of the most frequently utilized design techniques in Japanese gardens. They hark back to their original inspiration—Fuji-san represented by a truncated cone of stones; Ama-no-Hashidate, the famous spit of land, by a stone bridge; or a mighty forest by a lone tree.

Shakkei. "Borrowed landscape" extends the boundaries of a garden by integrating a nearby attractive mountain, grove of trees, or a sweeping temple roofline, for example, and framing and capturing the view by echoing it with elements of similar shape or color inside the garden itself.

Symbolism. Abstract concepts and mythological legends, readily understood by Japan's homogeneous population, are part of the garden vocabulary. The use of boulders in a streambed can represent life's surmountable difficulties, a pine tree can stand for stability, or islands in a pond for a faraway paradise.

Lacquerware

Japanese lacquerware has its origins in the Jōmon period (10,000–300 BC), when basic utensils were coated with lacquer resin made from tree sap. By the Nara period (AD 710–AD 794) most of the techniques we recognize

today were being used. For example, *maki-e* (literally, "sprinkled picture") refers to several different techniques that use gold or silver powder in areas coated with liquid lacquer. In the Azuchi-Momoyama period (1568–1600), lacquerware exports made their way to Europe. The following period, the Edo (1603–1868), saw the broadening of the uses of lacquer for the newly prosperous merchant class.

The production of lacquerware starts with the draining, evaporation, and filtration of sap from lacquer trees. Successive layers of lacquer are carefully painted on basketry, wood, bamboo, woven textiles, metal, and even paper. The lacquer strengthens the object, making it durable for eating, carrying, or protecting fragile objects, such as fans. Lacquerware can be mirrorlike if polished; often the many layers contain inlays of mother-of-pearl or precious metals inserted between coats, creating a complicated design of exquisite beauty and delicacy. The best places to see lacquerware are Hōryū-ji in Nara—the temple has a beautiful display—and Wajima on Ishikawa. Expensive yet precious lacquerware remains one of the most distinctive and highest-quality crafts of Japan.

Papermaking

Handmade paper and shōji (paper screens) are unique and beautiful Japanese creations that are surprisingly affordable, unlike other traditional crafts. *Washi*, Japanese paper, can have a translucent quality that seems to argue against its amazing durability. Shintō's usage of paper as a decorative symbol in shrines—probably due to its purity when new—gives an added importance to the already high esteem the Japanese hold for paper and the written word. Paper is a symbol of *kami* (god), and the process to make it requires an almost ritualistic sense. Usually, the inner bark of the paper mulberry is used, but leaves, ropelike fibers, even gold flake can be added in the later steps of the process for a dramatic effect. The raw branches are steamed and bleached by exposure to cold or snow. The fibers are boiled with ash lye and subsequently rinsed. After chopping and beating the pulp, it is soaked in a starchy taro solution, and the textures or leaves are added for decoration. A screen is dipped in the floating fibers, and when the screen is pulled up evenly, a sheet of paper is formed. Amazingly, wet sheets when stacked do not stick together.

The best places to view the papermaking process are Kurodani, near Kyōto; Mino, in central Japan; and Yame, near Kurume. Different parts of Japan specialize in different products. Gifu is known for its umbrellas and lanterns, Nagasaki for its distinctive kites, and Nara for its calligraphy paper and utensils. A light, inexpensive, and excellent gift, Japanese paper is a handicraft you can easily carry home as a souvenir.

Textiles

The topic of textiles is invariably linked to the history and nature of kimonos and costumes, which offered the best opportunity for weavers, dyers, and designers to exhibit their skills. Both Buddhism and Confucianism helped to create the four castes in Japan: samurai, Buddhist clerics, farmers, and townspeople (merchants and artisans) in descending order of importance. Courtesans and actors often slipped through the cracks and thus were exempt from the targets of the laws that reinforced these strata by making certain types of dress illegal for lower castes. Outer appearance helped to identify social rank and maintained order. Styles of embroidery and decoration and sumptuous clothing changed legal status in reaction to social upheavals and the eventual rise of the merchant class.

The types of the kimono—Japanese traditional dress attire is unisex in cut—are made from flat woven panels that provide the most surface for decoration. Although Western clothing follows the body line in a sculptural way, the Japanese use of fabric is more painterly and has little concern for body size and shape. No matter the wearer's height or weight, a kimono is made from one bolt of cloth cut and stitched into four panels and fitted with a collar. When creating a kimono, or the Buddhist clerics' *kesa* (a body wrap), no fabric is wasted. Shintō's emphasis is evident in the importance of natural fabrics, as the way of the gods was always concerned with purity and defilement.

Regional designs are the rule in textiles. Kyōto's heavily decorated Nishijin Ori is as sumptuous as Japanese fabric comes. Okinawa produces a variety of stunning fabrics, and both Kyōto and Tōkyō's stencil dyeing techniques yield intricate, elegant patterns. The most affordable kimonos are used kimonos—which can be nearly flawless or in need of minor stitching. Kyōto's flea markets are a good venue for this. Also look for lighter weight *yukata* (robes), *obi* (sashes), or handkerchiefs from Arimatsu, near Nagoya, for example. Good places to see fabrics are Kyōto's Fūzoku Hakubutsukan (Costume Museum), Nishijin Orimono (Textile Center), and the Tōkyō National Museum, which displays garments of the Edo period.

— David Miles and Barbara Blechman

BATHING: AN IMMERSION COURSE

Many Japanese cultural phenomena confound first-time visitors to the country, but few rituals are as opaque to foreigners as those surrounding bathing. Partly because of the importance of purification rites in Shintō, Japan's ancient indigenous religion, the art of bathing has been a crucial element of Japanese culture for centuries. Baths in Japan are as much about pleasure and relaxation as they are about washing and cleansing. Traditionally, communal bathhouses served as centers for social gather-, ings, and even though most modern houses and apartments have bathtubs, many Japanese still prefer the pleasures of communal bathing—either at *onsen* (hot springs) while on vacation or in public bathhouses closer to home.

Japanese bathtubs themselves are different from those in the West—they're deep enough to sit in upright with (very hot) water up to the neck—and the procedures for using them are quite different as well. You wash yourself in a special area outside the tub first. The tubs are for soaking, not washing; soap must not get into the bathwater.

Many hotels in major cities offer only Western-style reclining bathtubs, so to indulge in the pleasure of a Japanese bath you'll need to stay in a Japanese-style inn or find an *o-furo* (public bathhouse). The latter are clean, hygienic, and easy to find. You may at first feel justifiably apprehensive about bathing (and bathing *properly*) in an o-furo, but if you're well versed in bathing etiquette, you should soon feel at ease. And once you've experienced a variety of public baths—from the standard bathhouses found in every neighborhood to the idyllic outdoor hot springs on Kyūshū, for example—

you may find yourself an unlikely advocate of this ancient custom.

The first challenge in bathing is acknowledging that your Japanese bath mates will stare at your body. Take solace, however, in the fact that their apparent voyeurism most likely stems from curiosity.

When you enter the bathing room, help yourself to two towels, soap, and shampoo (often included in the entry fee), and grab a bucket and a stool. At one of the shower stations around the edge of the room, crouch on your bucket (or stand if you prefer) and use the handheld showers, your soap, and one of your towels to wash yourself thoroughly. A head-to-toe twice-over will impress onlookers. Rinse off, and then you may enter the public bath. When you do, you'll still have one dry towel. You can use it to cover yourself, or you can place it on your head (as you'll see many of your bath mates doing) while soaking. All you need to do then is lean back, relax, and experience the pleasures of Shintō-style purification—cleanse your body and enlighten your spirit. It seems, in Japan, cleanliness is next to godliness.

— David Miles

RITUAL AND RELIGION

Buddhism
Buddhism in Japan grew out of a Korean king's symbolic gift of a statue of Shaka—the first Buddha, Prince Gautama—to the Yamato court in AD 538. The Soga clan adopted the foreign faith and used it as a vehicle for changing the political order of the day. After battling for control of the country, the Soga clan established itself as political rulers, and Buddhism took permanent hold of Japan. Shōtoku Taishi, the crown prince and regent during this period, sent the first Japanese ambassadors to China, which inaugurated the importation of Chinese culture, writing, and religion in Japan. Since that time several eras in Japanese history have seen the

equation of consolidating state power with promulgating Buddhist influence and building temples. By the 8th century AD Japanese Buddhism's six schools of thought were well established, and priests from India and Persia came for the ceremonial opening of Tōdai-ji in Nara. Scholars argue that the importation of architectural styles and things Buddhist in this period may have had more to do with the political rather than religious needs of Japanese society. Likewise, the intertwining of religion and state and the importation of foreign ideas had undeniably political motivations during the Meiji Restoration and Japanese colonial expansion early in the 20th century. And the use of foreign ideas continues to be an essential component of understanding the social climate in Japan today.

Three waves in the development of Japanese Buddhism followed the religion's Nara-period (710–84) florescence. In the Heian period (794–894), two priests who studied in China—Saichō and Kūkai—introduced esoteric Buddhism. Near Kyōto, Saichō established a temple on Mt. Hiei—making it the most revered mountain in Japan after Mt. Fuji. Kūkai established the Shingon sect of Esoteric Buddhism on Mt. Kōya, south of Nara. It is said he is still in a state of meditation and will remain so until the arrival of the last bodhisattva (Buddhist messianic saint, *bosatsu* in Japanese). In Japanese temple architecture, Esoteric Buddhism introduced the separation of the temple into an interior for the initiated and an outer laypersons' area. This springs from Esoteric Buddhism's emphasis on *mikkyō* (secret rites) for the initiated.

Amidism was the second wave, and it flourished until the introduction of Zen in 1185. Its adherents saw the world emerging from a period of darkness, during which Buddhism had been in decline, and asserted that salvation was offered only to the believers in Amida, a Nyorai (Buddha), an enlightened being. Amidism's promise of salvation and its subsequent versions of heaven and hell earned it the appellation "Devil's Christianity" from visiting Christian missionaries in the 16th century.

The influences of Nichiren and Zen Buddhist philosophies pushed Japanese Buddhism in the unique direction it heads today. Nichiren (1222–82) was a monk who insisted that repetition of the phrase "Hail the miraculous law of the Lotus Sutra" would bring salvation, the Lotus Sutra being the supposed last and greatest sutra of Shaka. Zen Buddhism was attractive to the samurai class's ideals of discipline and worldly detachment and thus spread throughout Japan in the 12th century.

Japanese Buddhism today, like most religions in Japan, plays a minimal role in the daily life of the average Japanese. Important milestones in life provide the primary occasions for religious observance. Most Japanese have Buddhist burials. Weddings are usually in the Shintō style; recently, ceremonial references to Christian weddings have crept in, added mainly for romantic effect. (This mixing of religions may seem strange in the West, but it is wholly acceptable in Japan.) Outsiders have criticized the Japanese for lacking spirituality, and it is true that many Japanese don't make some kind of religious observance part of their daily or weekly lives. That said, there is a spiritual element in the people's unflinching belief in the group, and Japanese circles around very spiritual issues.

For more information on religious and political history, statuary manifestations of bosatsu and the Buddha, and architectural styles, consult *Buddhism, A History,* by Noble Ross Reat, and *Sources of Japanese Tradition,* by Tsunoda, De Bary, and Keene.

Shintō

Shintō—literally, "the way of the *kami* (god)"—does not preach a moral doctrine or code of ethics to follow. It is a form of animism, nature worship, based on myth and rooted to the geography and holy places of the land. Fog-enshrouded mountains, pairs of rocks, primeval forests, and geothermal activity are all manifestations of the *kami-sama* (honorable gods). For many Japanese the Shintō aspect of their lives is simply the realm of the kami-sama, not attached to a religious framework as it would be in the West. In that sense, the name describes more a philosophy than a religion.

Shintō rites that affect the daily lives of Japanese today are the wedding ceremony, the *matsuri* (festivals), and New Year's Day. The wedding ceremony uses an elaborate, colorful kimono for the bride and a simple, masculine *happi* (short coat) worn over a *furisode*-style (literally, "swinging sleeves") robe for the groom. The number three is significant, and sake, of the fruits of the earth from the gods, is the ritual libation.

The neighborhood shrine's annual matsuri is a time of giving thanks for prosperity and of the blessing of homes and local businesses. *O-mikoshi,* portable shrines for the gods, are enthusiastically carried around the district by young local men. Shouting and much sake drinking are part of the celebration.

New Year's Day entails visiting an important local shrine and praying for health, happiness, success in school or business, or the safe birth of a child in the coming year. A traditional meal of rice cakes and sweet beans is served in stacked boxes at home, as part of a family time not unlike those of traditional Western winter holidays.

Like Buddhism, Shintō was used throughout Japanese history as a tool for affirming the might of a given ruling power. The Meiji Restoration in 1868 used Shintoism to reclaim the emperor's sacred right to rule and to wrest control from the last Tokugawa shōgun. Today shrines are more often visited for their beauty than for their spiritual importance, though there is no denying the ancient spiritual pull of shrines like the Ise Jingū, south of Nagoya.

Tea Ceremony

The tea ceremony was formalized by the 16th century under the patronage of the Ashikaga shōguns, but it was the Zen monks of the 12th century who started the practice of drinking tea for a refresher between meditation sessions. The samurai and tea master Sen-no-Rikyū elucidated "the Way," the meditative and spiritual aspect of the ceremony, and is the most revered figure in the history of tea. For samurai, the ceremony appealed to their ideals and their sense of discipline, and diversions in time of peace were necessary. In essence, tea ceremony is a spiritual and philosophical ritual whose prescribed steps and movements serve as an aid in sharpening the aesthetic sense.

Tea ceremony has a precisely choreographed program. Participants enter the teahouse or room and comment on the specially chosen art in the entryway. The ritual begins as the server prepares a cup of tea for the first patron. This process involves a strictly determined series of movements and actions, common to every ceremony, which include cleansing each of the utensils to be used. One by one the participants slurp up their bowl of tea, then eat the sweet cracker served with it. Finally, comments about the beauty of the bowls used are exchanged. The entire ritual involves contemplating the beauty in the smallest actions, focusing their meaning in the midst of the impermanence of life.

The architecture of a traditional teahouse is also consistent. There are two entrances: a service entrance for the host and server and a low door that requires that guests enter on their knees, in order to be humbled. Tearooms often have a flower arrangement or piece of artwork in the alcove, for contemplation and comment, and tatami (grass mat) flooring. Though much of the process may seem the same wherever you experience the ceremony, there are different schools of thought on the subject. The three best-known schools of tea are the Ura Senke, the Omote Senke, and the Musha Kōji, each with its own styles, emphases, and masters.

Most of your tea experiences will be geared toward the uninitiated: the tea ceremony is a rite that requires methodical initiation by education. If you don't go for instruction before your trip, keep two things in mind if you attend or are invited to a tea ceremony: first, be in the right frame of mind when you enter the room. Though the tea ceremony is a pleasant event, some people take it quite seriously, and boisterous behavior beforehand is frowned upon. Instead, make conversation that enhances a mood of serenity and invites a feeling of meditative quietude. Second, be sure to sit quietly through the serving and drinking—controlled slurping is expected—and openly appreciate the tools and cups afterward, commenting on their elegance and simplicity. This appreciation is an important final step of the ritual. Above all, pay close attention to the practiced movements of the ceremony, from the art at the entryway and the kimono of the server to the quality of the utensils. Reading: *The Book of Tea*, by Kakuzo Okakura; *Cha-no-Yu: The Japanese Tea Ceremony*, by A. L. Sadler.

— David Miles

THEATER AND DRAMATIS PERSONAE

Nō

Nō is a dramatic tradition far older than Kabuki; it reached a point of formal perfection in the 14th century and survives virtually unchanged from that period. Where Kabuki was Everyman's theater, Nō developed for the most part under the patronage of the warrior class. It is dignified, ritualized, and symbolic. Many of the plays in the repertoire are drawn from classical literature or tales of the supernatural, and the texts are richly poetic. Some understanding of the plot of each play is necessary to enjoy a performance, which moves at a nearly glacial pace—the pace of ritual time—as it is solemnly chanted. The major Nō theaters often provide synopses of the plays in English.

Where the Kabuki actor is usually in brightly colored makeup derived from the Chinese opera, the principal character in a Nō play wears a carved wooden mask. Such is the skill of the actor—and the mysterious effect of the play—that the mask itself may appear expressionless until the actor "brings it to life," at which point the mask seems to express a considerable range of emotions. As in Kabuki, the various roles of the Nō repertoire all have specific costumes—robes of silk brocade with intricate patterns that are works of art in themselves. Nō is not a very *accessible* kind of theater: its language is archaic; its conventions are obscure; and its measured, stately pace can put even Japanese audiences to sleep.

In Tōkyō, as a contrast to the rest of the city, Nō will provide an experience of Japan as an ancient, sophisticated culture. In Kyōto the outdoor performances of Nō, especially *Takigi* Nō, held outdoors by firelight on the nights of June 1–2 in the precincts of the Heian Jingū, are particularly memorable.

Somewhat like Kabuki, Nō has a number of schools, the traditions of which developed as the exclusive property of hereditary families. Note that *kyōgen* are shorter, lighter plays that are often interspersed in between Nō performances and are much more accessible than Nō. Consider taking advantage of opportunities to see kyōgen rather than Nō.

Kabuki

Kabuki emerged as a popular form of entertainment by women dancing lewdly in the early 17th century; before long, it had been banned by the authorities as a threat to public order. Eventually it cleaned up its act, and by the latter half of the 18th century it had become Everyman's theater par excellence—especially among the townspeople of bustling, hustling Edo. Kabuki had music, dance, and spectacle; it had acrobatics and sword fights; it had pathos and tragedy and historical romance and social satire. It no longer had bawdy beauties, however—women have been banned from the Kabuki stage since 1629—but in recompense it developed a professional role for female impersonators, who train for years to project a seductive, dazzling femininity. It had—and still has—superstars and quick-change artists and legions of fans, who bring their lunch to the theater, stay all day, and shout out the names of their favorite actors at the stirring moments in their favorite plays.

Edo is now Tōkyō, but Kabuki is still here, just as it has been for centuries. The traditions are passed down from generation to generation in a small group of families; the roles and great stage names are hereditary. The Kabuki repertoire does not really grow or change, but stars like Ennosuke Ichikawa and Tamasaburo Bando have put exciting, personal stamps on their performances that continue to draw audiences young and old. If you don't know Japanese, Tōkyō's Kabuki-za (Kabuki Theater) has superb simultaneous English translation of its plays available on headphones. Reading: *The Kabuki Guide*, by Masakatsu Gunji.

Bunraku

The third major form of traditional Japanese drama is Bunraku puppet theater. Itinerant puppeteers were plying their trade in Japan as early as the 10th century. Sometime in the late 16th century, a form of narrative ballad called *jōruri*, performed to the accompaniment of a three-string banjolike instrument called the *shamisen*, was grafted onto their art, and Bunraku was born. The golden age of Bunraku came some 200 years later, when most of the form's great plays were written and the puppets themselves evolved to their present form— so expressive and intricate in their movements that they require three people at one time to manipulate them. Puppeteers and narrators, who deliver their lines in a kind of high-pitched croak from deep in the throat, train for many years to master this difficult and unusual genre of popular entertainment. Puppets are about two-thirds human size and are large enough to cover the puppeteers underneath them. Elaborately dressed in period costume, each puppet is made up of interchangeable parts—a head, shoulder piece, trunk, legs, and arms. Various puppet heads are used for roles of different sex, age, and character, and a certain hairstyle will indicate a puppet's position in life.

To operate one puppet, three puppeteers must act in complete unison. The *omozukai* controls the expression on the puppet's face and its right arm and hand. The *hidarizukai* controls the puppet's left arm and hand along with any props that it is carrying. The *ashizukai* moves the puppet's legs. This last task is the easiest. The most difficult task belongs to the omozukai. It takes about 30 years to become an expert. A puppeteer must spend 10 years as ashizukai, an additional 10 as hidarizukai, and then 10 more years as omozukai. These master puppeteers not only skillfully manipulate the puppets' arms and legs but also roll the eyes and move the lips so that the puppets express fear, joy, and sadness. The spiritual center of Bunraku today is Ōsaka. Periodically there are performances in Tōkyō in the small hall of the National Theater.

Geisha

Because the character for the *gei* in *geisha* stands for arts and accomplishments (*sha* in this case means person), the public image of geisha in Japan is one of high status. Although it's a common misconception in the West, geisha are not prostitutes. To become a geisha, a woman must perfect many talents. She must have grace and a thorough mastery of etiquette. She should have an accomplished singing voice and dance beautifully. She needs to have a finely tuned aesthetic sense—with flower arranging and tea ceremony—and should excel at the art of conversation. In short, she should be the ultimate companion.

These days geisha are a rare breed. They numbered a mere 10,000 in the late 1980s, as opposed to 80,000 in the 1920s. This is partly due to the increase of bar hostesses—who perform a similar function in nightclubs with virtually none of a geisha's training—not to mention the refinement and expense it takes to hire a geisha. Because she is essentially the most personal form of entertainer, the emphasis is on artistic and conversational skills, not solely on youth or beauty. Thus the typical geisha can work to an advanced age.

Geisha will establish a variety of relations with men. Besides maintaining a dependable amount of favorite customers, one might choose a *danna*, one man for emotional, sexual, and financial gratification. The geisha's exercise of choice in this matter is due partly to the fact that wages and tips alone must provide enough for her to survive. Some geisha marry, most often to an intimate client. When they do, they leave the profession.

A geisha typically starts her career as a servant at a house until 13. She continues as a *maiko* (dancing child) until she masters the requisite accomplishments at about 18. Before World War II full geisha status was achieved after a geisha experienced a *mizuage* (deflowering), with an important client of the house. Maiko must master the shamisen and learn the proper hairstyles and kimono fittings. They are a sight to see on the banks of the Kamo-gawa in the Gion district of Kyōto, or in Shimbashi, Akasaka, and Ginza in Tōkyō. Today geisha unions, restaurant unions, and registry offices regulate the times and fees of geisha. Fees are measured in "sticks"—generally, one hour—which is the time it would take a stick of *senkō* (incense) to burn.

Sumō

If baseball can be called Japan's modern national pastime, surely sumō is its traditional national pastime, and it remains tremendously popular, even at 2,000 years old. This centuries-old national sport of Japan is not to be taken lightly—as anyone who has ever seen a sumō wrestler will testify.

Indeed, sheer weight is almost a prerequisite to success. Contenders in the upper ranks tip the scales at an average of 350 pounds, and there are no upper limits. There are various techniques of pushing, gripping, and throwing in sumō, but the basic rules are exquisitely simple: except for hitting below the belt (which is all a sumō wrestler wears) and striking with a closed fist, almost anything goes. If you get thrown down or forced out of the ring, you lose.

There are no free agents in sumō. To compete, you must belong to a *heya* (stable) run by a retired wrestler who has purchased that right from the Japan Sumō Association. Sumō is very much a closed world, hierarchical and formal. Youngsters recruited into the sport live in the stable dormitory, doing all the community chores and waiting on their seniors while they learn. When they rise high enough in tournament rankings, they acquire servant-apprentices of their own.

Tournaments and exhibitions are held in different parts of the country at different times, but all stables in the Sumō Association—now some 30 in number—are in Tōkyō. Most are clustered on both sides of the Sumida River near the green-roofed Kokugikan (National Sumō Arena), in the areas called Asakusabashi and Ryōgoku. When wrestlers are in town in January, May, and September, you are likely to see some of them on the streets, cleaving the air like leviathans in their wood clogs and kimonos.

— Jared Lubarsky and David Miles

JAPANESE SOCIETY: A FACTORY OF FADS

It is impossible to summarize the life of a people in brief. Still, there are a few fascinating points about the Japanese that are nonetheless important to mention, even if only in passing.

The Japanese communicate among themselves in what Dr. Chie Nakane, in her *Japanese Society* (1972), calls a "vertical society." In other words, the Japanese constantly vary the way they speak with each other according to the gender, family and educational background, occupation and position, and age of the speakers. Japanese grammar reflects this by requiring different verbs for different levels of interaction. Since it is necessary for individuals to vary the way they speak according to the person, they are always considering the levels of the people around them. In a crowded country, this means the Japanese are often wondering what other people are thinking—often in an effort to gauge where they belong themselves. This constant consideration toward other members of their group makes the Japanese keen readers of other people's emotions and reactions.

Where much of the West—the United States in particular—has shed nearly everything but wealth as an indicator of position in society, the Japanese maintain concepts of social order that have feudal echoes, as in the ideas of *uchi* and *soto*. Uchi refers to the home, the inside group, and, ultimately, Japan and Japaneseness. Soto is everything outside. Imagine uchi being a set of concentric rings, where the most central group is the family; the next is the neighborhood or extended family; then the school, company, or association; then the prefecture, the family of companies, or the region in which they live; and, finally, Japan itself. Japanese verb forms are more casual within the various uchi, as opposed to the more polite forms for those "outside." Interestingly enough, the *gai* in the Japanese word for foreigner, *gaijin*, is the same character as *soto*. Soto—not belonging—is an undeniable barrier for non-Japanese. Translated into feelings, being the "other" can be frustrating and alienating. At the same time, it makes instances of crossing the boundary into some level of uchi that much more precious.

Despite the belief that the American presence after World War II was what built Japan, it is more correctly the sense of tribe or group the Japanese have utilized to their advantage since the Meiji Restoration that really created modern Japan. In the West we might have trouble understanding what we perceive as a lack of individuality in Japanese society, but we tend to ignore the sense of togetherness and joy that comes from a feeling of homogeneity. We might also miss any number of subtleties in interpersonal communication because we are wholly unaccustomed to them. It can take a lifetime to master the finer points of Japanese ambiguities, but even a basic appreciation of shades of meaning and the Japanese vigilance in maintaining the tightness of the group helps to see the beauty of this different way of life.

This beauty might be that much more precious in the face of change. With more of the younger generation traveling and living abroad, women especially, the group mentality and its role in supporting the Japanese socioeconomic structure are eroding rapidly.

You're bound to notice that the Japanese are extremely fond of animation, and they use it in communicating ideas and in advertising far more than we do in the West. So you'll see the anthropomorphizing of garbage cans, signage, and even huge, cute-squid telephone booths. The Japanese also seem to lead the world in the production of purposeless gadgets that astound and delight, if only for a minute or two. If this is your thing, don't miss the shops in downtown Ōsaka, or Harajuku and Shibuya in Tōkyō, because you'll never find these items anywhere else. Some of them are expensive—the mooing cow clock that wakes you up with "Don't-o suleepu yo-ah lie-foo eh-way" looks hardly worth more than $10 but is nearly four times that, if you can even find one available; and the "waterfall sounds" player for shy women using the toilet can run up to $300.

There are reams of books and articles on Japanese English—and how they use and abuse it—but the topic might not come to mind until you set foot in Japan. Throughout the country, on billboards and in stores, on clothes, bags, hats, and even on cars, baffling, cryptic, often side-splitting English phrases leap out at you in the midst of your deepest cultural encounters. For example: "Woody goods: We have a woody heart, now listen to my story." What could this possibly mean? Did it make sense in the original Japanese?

Alas, friends and family might not understand why you find funny English so hilarious, without a firsthand encounter with something like CREAM SODA earnestly printed on a body-builder's T-shirt—or a fashion catalog that cryptically asserts "optimistic sunbeam shines beautifully for you." These tortured meanings are no doubt a compliment to the ascendancy of the English language, which on the world popular-culture stage is, in whatever form, chic and cool. You might find that on a heavy day of temple viewing, funny English might be the straightest path toward *satori* (enlightenment).

The latest obsessions in Japan can take a long time to get rolling, but when they do, they can take over the country. And Japanese homogeneity makes for a certain lemming quality that is utterly intriguing when it comes to observing fads. Take the wild popularity of Tamagotchi and Pokèmon. The international success of these techno-obsessions just goes to show how adept the Japanese are at catering to the world's unrecognized needs.

Whatever the fad is, when you're in Japan, make a note of it and try to remember the Japanese name or words associated with it. When you try to pronounce them, Japanese friends and colleagues will be immensely humored and impressed. Such is the intensity of fads that they act as barometers of the atmosphere of Japan at any given time.

— David Miles

THE DISCREET CHARM OF JAPANESE CUISINE

Leave behind the humidity of Japan in summer and part the crisp linen curtain of the neighborhood *sushi-ya* some hot night in mid-July. Enter a world of white cypress and chilled sea urchin, where a welcome *oshibori* (hot towel for cleaning your hands) awaits and a master chef stands at your beck and call. A cup of tea to begin, a tiny mound of ginger to freshen the palate, and you're ready to choose from the colorful array of fresh seafood on ice inside a glass case before you. Bite-size morsels arrive in friendly pairs, along with a glass of ice-cold beer. The young apprentice runs up and down, making sure everyone has tea—and anything else that might be needed. The chef has trained for years in his art, and he's proud, in his stoic way, to demonstrate it. The *o-tsukuri* (a kind of sashimi) you've ordered arrives; today the thinly sliced raw tuna comes in the shape of a rose. The fourth round you order brings with it an unexpected ribbon of cucumber, sliced with a razor-sharp sushi knife into sections that expand like an accordion. The chef's made your day . . .

Red-paper lanterns dangling in the dark above 1,000 tiny food stalls on the backstreets of Tōkyō . . . To the weary Japanese salary man on his way home from the office, these *akachōchin* (red) lanterns are a prescription for the best kind of therapy known for the "Subterranean Homesick Blues," Japanese style: one last belly-warming bottle of sake, a nerve-soothing platter of grilled chicken wings, and perhaps a few words of wisdom for the road. Without these nocturnal way stations, many a fuzzy-eyed urban refugee would never survive that rumbling, fluorescent nightmare known as the last train home.

And where would half of Japan's night-owl college students be if not for the local *shokudō*, as the neighborhood not-so-greasy spoon is known? Separated at last from mother's protective guidance (and therefore without a clue as to how to boil an egg or heat a bowl of soup), the male contingent of young lodging-house boarders put their lives in the hands of the old couple who run the neighborhood café. Bent furtively over a platter of *kare-raisu* (curry and rice) or *tonkatsu teishoku* (pork cutlet set meal), these ravenous young men thumb through their baseball comics each night, still on the road to recovery from a childhood spent memorizing mathematical formulas and English phrases they hope they'll never have to use.

Down a dimly lighted backstreet not two blocks away, a geisha in all her elaborate finery walks her last silk-suited customer out to his chauffeur-driven limousine. He has spent the evening being pampered, feasted, and fan-danced in the rarefied air of one of Tōkyō's finest *ryōtei*. (You must be invited to these exclusive eateries—or be a regular patron, introduced by another regular patron who vouched for your reputation with his own.) There have been the most restrained of traditional dances, some shamisen playing—an oh-so-tastefully suggestive tête-à-tête. The customer has been drinking the very finest sake, accompanied by a succession of exquisitely presented hors d'oeuvres—what amounts to a seven-course meal in the end is the formal Japanese haute cuisine known as *kaiseki*. If it were not for his company's expense account, by now he would have spent the average man's monthly salary. Luckily for him, he's not the average man.

On a stool now, under the flimsy awning of a street stall, shielded from the wind and rain by flapping tarps, heated only by a portable kerosene stove and the steam from a vat of boiling noodles, you'll find neither tourist nor ptomaine. Here sits the everyday workingman, glass of *shōchū* (a strong liquor made from sweet potatoes) in sun-baked hand, arguing over the Tigers' chances of winning the Japan Series as he zealously slurps down a bowl of hot noodle soup sprinkled with red-pepper sauce—

more atmosphere and livelier company than you're likely to find anywhere else in Japan. The *yatai-san,* as these inimitable street vendors are known, are an amiable, if disappearing, breed.

Somewhere between the street stalls and the exclusive ryōtei, a vast culinary world exists in Japan. Tiny, over-the-counter restaurants, each with its own specialty—from familiar favorites, such as tempura, sukiyaki, or sushi to exotic delicacies, like *unagi* (eel) or *fugu* (blowfish)—inhabit every city side street. Comfortable, country-style restaurants abound, serving a variety of different *nabemono,* the one-pot stew dishes cooked right at your table. There are also lively neighborhood *robatayaki* grills, where cooks in happi coats wield skewered bits of meat, seafood, and vegetables over a hot charcoal grill as you watch.

A dozen years ago, sukiyaki and tempura were exotic enough for most Western travelers. Those were the days when raw fish was still something a traveler needed fortitude to try. But with *soba* (buckwheat noodle) shops and sushi bars popping up everywhere from Los Angeles to Paris, it seems that—at long last—the joy of Japanese cooking has found its way westward.

There *is* something special, however, about visiting the tiger in his lair—something no tame circus cat could ever match. Although tours to famous temples and scenic places can provide important historical and cultural background material, there is nothing like a meal in a local restaurant—be it under the tarps of the liveliest street stall or within the quiet recesses of an elegant Japanese inn—for a taste of the real Japan. Approaching a platter of fresh sashimi in Tōkyō is like devouring a hot dog smothered in mustard and onions in Yankee Stadium. There's nothing like it in the world.

The Essentials of a Japanese Meal

The basic formula for a traditional Japanese meal is deceptively simple. It starts with soup, followed by raw fish, then the entrée (grilled, steamed, simmered, or fried fish, chicken, or vegetables), and ends with rice and pickles, with perhaps some fresh fruit for dessert, and a cup of green tea. It's as simple as that—almost.

An exploration of any cuisine should begin at the beginning, with a basic knowledge of what it is you're eating: rice, of course—the traditional staple; and seafood—grilled, steamed, fried, stewed, or raw; chicken, pork, or beef, at times—in that order of frequency; a wide variety of vegetables (wild and cultivated), steamed, sautéed, blanched, or pickled, perhaps—but never overcooked; soybeans in every form imaginable, from tofu to soy sauce; and seaweed, in and around lots of things.

The basics are just that. But there are, admittedly, a few twists to the story. Beyond the raw fish, it's the incredible variety of vegetation used in Japanese cooking that still surprises the Western palate: *take-no-ko* (bamboo shoots), *renkon* (lotus root), and the treasured *matsutake* mushrooms (which grow wild in jealously guarded forest hideaways and sometimes sell for more than $60 apiece), to name a few.

Tangy garnishes, both wild and domestic, such as *kinome* (leaves of the Japanese prickly ash pepper tree), *mitsuba* (trefoil, of the parsley family), and *shiso* (a member of the mint family), are used as a foil for oily foods. The more familiar-sounding ingredients, such as sesame and ginger, appear in abundance, as do the less familiar—*wasabi* (Japanese horseradish), *yuri-ne* (lily bulbs), *gin-nan* (ginko nuts), and *daikon* (gigantic white radishes). Exotic? Perhaps, but delicious, and nothing here bites back. Simple? Yes, if you understand a few of the ground rules.

Absolute freshness is first. According to world-renowned Japanese chef Shizuo Tsuji, soup and raw fish are the two test pieces of Japanese cuisine. Freshness is the criterion for both: "I can tell at a glance by the texture of their skins—like the bloom of youth on a young girl—whether the fish is really fresh," Tsuji says in *The Art of Japanese Cooking*. A comparison as startling, perhaps, as it is revealing. To a Japanese chef, freshness is an unparalleled virtue, and much of a chef's reputation relies on the ability to obtain the finest ingredients at the peak of season: fish brought in from the sea this morning (not yesterday) and vegetables from the earth (not the hothouse), if at all possible.

Simplicity is next. Rather than embellishing foods with heavy spices and rich sauces, the Japanese chef prefers flavors au naturel. Flavors are enhanced, not elaborated, accented rather than concealed. Without a heavy dill sauce, fish is permitted a degree of natural fishiness—a garnish of fresh red ginger will be provided to offset the flavor rather than to disguise it.

The third prerequisite is beauty. Simple, natural foods must appeal to the eye as well as to the palate. Green peppers on a vermilion dish, perhaps, or an egg custard in a blue bowl. Rectangular dishes for a round eggplant. So important is the seasonal element in Japanese cooking that maple leaves and pine needles will be used to accent an autumn dish. Or two small summer delicacies, a pair of freshwater *ayu* fish, will be grilled with a purposeful twist to their tails to make them "swim" across a crystal platter and thereby suggest the coolness of a mountain stream on a hot August night.

Mood can make or break the entire meal, and the Japanese connoisseur will go to great lengths to find the perfect yakitori stand—a smoky, lively place—an environment appropriate to the occasion, offering a night of grilled chicken, cold beer, and camaraderie.

Atmosphere depends as much on the company as it does on the lighting or the color of the drapes. In Japan this seems to hold particularly true. The popularity of a particular *nomiya*, or bar, depends entirely on the affability of the *mama-san,* that long-suffering lady who's been listening to your troubles for years. In fancier places, mood becomes a fancier problem, to the point of quibbling over the proper amount of "water music" trickling in the basin outside your private room.

Culture: The Main Course

Sipping coffee at a sidewalk café on the Left Bank, you begin to feel what it means to be a Parisian. Slurping noodles on tatami in a neighborhood soba shop overlooking a tiny interior garden, you start to understand what it's like to live in Japan. Food, no matter which country you're in, has much to say about the culture as a whole.

Beyond the natural dictates of climate and geography, Japanese food has its roots in the centuries-old cuisine of the imperial court, which was imported from China—a religiously formal style of meal called *yusoku ryōri*. It was prepared only by specially appointed chefs, who had the status of priests in the service of the emperor, in a culinary ritual that is now nearly a lost art. Although it was never popularly served in centuries past (a modified version can still be found in Kyōto), much of the ceremony and careful attention to detail of yusoku ryōri are reflected today in the formal kaiseki meal.

Kaiseki Ryōri: Japanese Haute Cuisine

Kaiseki refers to the most elegant of all styles of Japanese food available today, and *ryōri* means cuisine. Rooted in the banquet feasts of the aristocracy, by the late 16th century it had developed into a meal to accompany ceremonial tea. The word *kaiseki* refers to a heated stone (*seki*) that Buddhist monks placed inside the folds (*kai*) of their kimonos to keep off the biting cold in the unheated temple halls where they slept and meditated.

Cha-kaiseki, as the formal meal served with tea (*cha*) is called, is intended to take the edge off your hunger at the beginning of a formal tea ceremony and to counterbalance the astringent character of the thick green tea. In the tea ceremony balance—and the sense of calmness and well-being it inspires—is the keynote.

The formula for the basic Japanese meal derived originally from the rules governing formal kaiseki—not too large a portion, just enough; not too spicy, but perhaps with a savory sprig of trefoil to offset the bland tofu. A grilled dish is served before a steamed one, a steamed dish before a simmered one; a square plate is used for a round food; a bright green maple leaf is placed to one side to herald the arrival of spring.

Kaiseki ryōri appeals to all the senses at once. An atmosphere is created in which the meal is to be experienced. The poem in calligraphy on a hanging scroll and the flowers in the alcove set the seasonal theme, a motif picked up in the pattern of the dishware chosen for the evening. The colors and shapes of the vessels complement the foods served on them. The visual harmony presented is as vital as the balance and variety of flavors of the foods themselves, for which the ultimate criterion is freshness. The finest ryōtei will never serve a fish or vegetable out of its proper season—no matter how marvelous a winter melon today's modern greenhouses can guarantee. Melons are for rejoicing in the summer's bounty . . . period.

Kaiseki ryōri found its way out of the formal tearooms and into a much earthier realm of the senses when it became the fashionable snack with sake in the teahouses of the geisha quarters during the 17th and 18th centuries. Not only the atmosphere but the Chinese characters used to write the word *kaiseki* are different in this context; they refer to aristocratic "banquet seats." And banquets they are. To partake in the most exclusive of these evenings in a teahouse in Kyōto still requires a personal introduction and a great deal of money, though these days many traditional restaurants serve elegant kaiseki meals (without the geisha) at much more reasonable prices.

One excellent way to experience this incomparable cuisine on a budget is to visit a kaiseki restaurant at lunchtime. Many of them offer *kaiseki bentō* lunches at a fraction of the dinner price, exquisitely presented in lacquered boxes, as a sampler of their full-course evening meal.

Shōjin Ryōri: Zen-Style Vegetarian Cuisine

Shōjin ryōri is the Zen-style vegetarian cuisine. Traditional Japanese cuisine emphasizes the natural flavor of the freshest ingredients in season, without the embellishment of heavy spices and rich sauces. This probably developed out of the Zen belief in the importance of simplicity and austerity as paths to enlightenment. Protein is provided by an almost limitless number of dishes made from soybeans—such as *yu-dōfu,* or boiled bean curd, and *yuba,* sheets of pure protein skimmed from vats of steaming soy milk. The variety and visual beauty of a full-course shōjin ryōri meal offer new dimensions in dining to the vegetarian gourmet. *Goma-dōfu,* or sesame-flavored bean curd, for example, is a delicious taste treat, as is *nasu-dengaku,* grilled eggplant covered with a sweet *miso* sauce.

There are many fine restaurants—particularly in the Kyōto area—that specialize in shōjin ryōri, but it's best to seek out one of the many temples throughout Japan that open their doors to visitors; here you can try these special meals within the actual temple halls, which often overlook a traditional garden.

Sushi, Sukiyaki, Tempura, and Nabemono: A Comfortable Middle Ground

Leaving the rarefied atmosphere of teahouses and temples behind, an entire realm of more down-to-earth gastronomic pleasures waits to be explored. Sushi, sukiyaki, and tempura are probably the three most commonly known Japanese dishes in the Western world. Restaurants serving these dishes are to be found in abundance in every major hotel in Japan. It is best, however, to try each of these in a place that specializes in just one.

An old Japanese proverb says *"Mochi wa mochi-ya e"*—if you want rice cakes, go to a rice-cake shop. The same goes for sushi. Sushi chefs undergo a lengthy apprenticeship, and the trade is considered an art form. Possessing the discipline of a judo player, the *itamae-san* (or, "man before . . . or behind . . . the counter," depending on your point of view) at a sushi-ya is a real master. Every neighborhood has its own sushi shop, and everyone you meet has his or her own secret little place to go for sushi.

The Central Wholesale Market district in Tōkyō is so popular for its sushi shops that you usually have to wait in line for a seat at the counter. Some are quite expensive, while others are relatively cheap. "Know before you go" is the best policy; "Ask before you eat" is next. Among the dozens types of sushi available, some of the most popular are *maguro* (tuna), *ebi* (shrimp), *hamachi* (yellowtail), *uni* (sea urchin), *anago* (conger eel), *tako* (octopus), *awabi* (abalone), and *aka-gai* (red shellfish). The day's selection is usually displayed in a glass case at the counter, which enables you to point at whatever catches your eye.

Tempura, the battered and deep-fried fish and vegetable dish, is almost certain to taste better at a small shop that serves nothing else. The difficulties of preparing this seemingly simple dish lie in achieving the proper consistency of the batter and the right temperature and freshness of the oil in which it is fried.

Sukiyaki is the popular beef dish that is sautéed with vegetables in an iron skillet at the table. The tenderness of the beef is the determining factor here, and many of the best sukiyaki houses also run their own butcher shops so that they can control the quality of the beef they serve. Although beef did not become a part of the Japanese diet until the turn of the 20th century, the Japanese are justifiably proud of their notorious beer-fed and hand-massaged beef (e.g., the famous Matsuzaka beef from Kōbe and the equally delicious Ōmi beef from Shiga Prefecture).

Shabu-shabu is another possibility, though this dish has become more popular with tourists than with the Japanese. It's similar to sukiyaki in that it is prepared at the table with a combination of vegetables, but it differs in that shabu-shabu is swished briefly in boiling water, while sukiyaki is sautéed in oil and, usually, a slightly sweetened soy sauce. The word *shabu-shabu* actually refers to this swishing sound.

Nabemono, or one-pot dishes, are not as familiar to Westerners as the three mentioned above, but the possibilities are endless, and nothing tastes better on a cold winter's night. Simmered in a light, fish-based broth, these stews can be made of almost anything: chicken (*tori-nabe*), oysters (*kaki-nabe*), or the sumō wrestler's favorite, the hearty *chanko-nabe*...with something in it for everyone. Nabemono is a popular family or party dish. The restaurants specializing in nabemono often have a casual, country atmosphere.

Bentō, Soba, Udon, and Robatayaki: Feasting on a Budget

Tales of unsuspecting tourists swallowed up by money-gobbling monsters disguised as quaint little restaurants on the backstreets of Japan's major cities abound. There are, however, many wonderful little places that provide excellent meals and thoughtful service—and have no intention of straining anyone's budget. To find them, you must not be afraid to venture outside your hotel lobby or worry that the dining spot has no menu in English. Many restaurants have menus posted out front that clearly state the full price you can expect to pay (some do add a 10% tax, and possibly a service charge, so ask in advance).

Here are a few suggestions for Japanese meals that do not cost a fortune and are usually a lot more fun than relying on the familiar but unexciting international fast-food chains for quick meals on a budget: *bentō* (box) lunches, *soba* or *udon* (noodle) dishes, and the faithful neighborhood *robatayaki* (grills), ad infinitum.

The Bentō. This is the traditional Japanese box lunch, available for takeout everywhere and usually comparatively inexpensive. It can be purchased in the morning to be taken along and eaten later, either outdoors or on the train as you travel between cities. The bentō consists of rice, pickles, grilled fish or meat, and vegetables, in an almost limitless variety of combinations to suit the season. The basement levels of most major department stores sell beautifully prepared bentō to go. In fact, a department-store basement is a great place to sample and purchase the whole range of foods offered in Japan: among the things available are French bread, imported cheeses, traditional bean cakes, chocolate bonbons, barbecued chicken, grilled eel, roasted peanuts, fresh vegetables, potato salads, pickled bamboo shoots, and smoked salmon.

The *o-bentō* (the *o* is honorific) in its most elaborate incarnation is served in gorgeous, multilayer lacquered boxes as an accompaniment to outdoor tea ceremonies or for flower-viewing parties held in spring. Exquisite *bentō-bako* (lunch boxes) made in the Edo period (1603–1868) can be found in museums and antiques shops. They are inlaid with mother-of-pearl and delicately hand-painted in gold. A wide variety of sizes and shapes of bentō boxes are still handmade in major cities and small villages throughout Japan in both formal and informal styles. They make excellent souvenirs.

A major benefit to the bentō is its portability. Sightseeing can take you down many an unexpected path, and if you bring your own bentō you won't need to worry about finding an appropriate place to stop for a bite to eat. No vacationing Japanese family would ever be without one tucked carefully inside their rucksacks right beside the thermos bottle of tea. If they do somehow run out of time to prepare one in advance—no problem—there are hundreds of wonderful options in the form of the beloved *ekiben* (train-station box lunch).

Each whistle-stop in Japan takes great pride in the uniqueness and flavor of the special box lunches, featuring the local delicacy, sold right at the station or from vendors inside the trains. The pursuit of the eki-ben has become a national pastime in this nation in love with its trains. Entire books have been written in Japanese explaining the features of every different eki-ben available along the 26,000 km (16,120 mi) of railways in the country. This is one of the best ways to sample the different styles of regional cooking in Japan and is highly recommended to any traveler who plans to spend time on the Japan Railway trains.

Soba and Udon. Soba and udon (noodle) dishes are another lifesaving treat for stomachs (and wallets) unaccustomed to exotic flavors (and prices). Small shops serving soba (thin, brown buckwheat noodle) and udon (thick, white-wheat noodle) dishes in a variety of combinations can be found in every neighborhood in the country. Both can be ordered plain (ask for o-soba or o-udon), in a lightly seasoned broth flavored with bonito and soy sauce, or in combination with things like tempura shrimp (*tempura soba* or *udon*) or chicken (*tori-namban soba* or *udon*). For a refreshing change in summer, try *zaru soba,* cold noodles to be dipped in a tangy soy sauce. *Nabeyaki-udon* is a hearty winter dish of udon noodles, assorted vegetables, and egg served in the pot in which it was cooked.

Robatayaki. Perhaps the most exuberant of inexpensive options is the robatayaki (grill). Beer mug in hand, elbow to elbow at the counter of one of these popular neighborhood grills—that is the best way to relax and join in with the local fun. You'll find no pretenses here—just a wide variety of plain, good food (as much or as little as you want) with the proper amount of alcohol to get things rolling.

Robata means fireside, and the style of cooking is reminiscent of old-fashioned Japanese farmhouse meals cooked over a charcoal fire in an open hearth. It's easy to order at a robatayaki shop because the selection of food to be grilled is lined up behind glass at the counter. Fish, meat, vegetables, tofu—take your pick. Some popular choices are *yaki-zakana* (grilled fish), particularly *karei-shio-yaki* (salted and grilled flounder) and *asari saka-mushi* (clams simmered in sake). Try the grilled Japanese shiitake mushrooms, *ao-tō* (green peppers), and the *hiyayakko* (chilled tofu sprinkled with bonito flakes, diced green onions, and soy sauce). Yakitori can be ordered in most robatayaki shops, though many inexpensive drinking places specialize in this popular barbecued chicken dish.

The budget dining possibilities in Japan don't stop there. **Okonomiyaki** is another choice. Somewhat misleadingly called the Japanese pancake, it is actually a mixture of vegetables, meat, and seafood in an egg-and-flour batter grilled at your table, much better with beer than with butter. It's most popular for lunch or as an after-movie snack.

Another is **kushi-age,** skewered bits of meat, seafood, and vegetables battered, dipped in bread crumbs, and deep-fried. There are many small restaurants serving only kushi-age at a counter, and many of the robatayaki serve it as a side dish. It's also a popular drinking snack.

Oden, a winter favorite, is another inexpensive meal. A variety of meats and vegetables slowly simmered in vats, it goes well with beer or sake. This, too, may be ordered piece by piece (*ippin*) from the assortment you see steaming away behind the counter or *moriawase,* in which case the cook will serve you up an assortment.

Sake: The Samurai Beverage

With all this talk about eating and drinking, it would be an unforgivable transgression to overlook Japan's number one alcoholic beverage, *sake* (pronounced sa-kay), the "beverage of the samurai," as one brewery puts it. Ancient myths call this rice wine the "drink of the gods," and there are more than 2,000 different brands produced throughout Japan. A lifetime of serious scene-of-the-crime research would be necessary to explore all the possibilities and complexities of this interesting drink.

Like other kinds of wine, sake comes in sweet (*amakuchi*) and dry (*karakuchi*) varieties; these are graded *tokkyū* (superior class), *ikkyū* (first class), and *nikkyū* (second class) and are priced accordingly. (Connoisseurs say this ranking is for tax purposes and is not necessarily a true indication of quality.)

Best drunk at room temperature (*nurukan*) so as not to alter the flavor, sake is also served heated (*atsukan*) or with ice (*rokku de*). It is poured from *tokkuri* (small ceramic vessels) into tiny cups called *choko*. The diminutive size of these cups shouldn't mislead you into thinking you can't drink too much. The custom of making sure that your companion's cup never runs dry often leads the novice astray.

Junmaishu is the term for pure rice wine, a blend of rice, yeast, and water to which no extra alcohol has been added. Junmaishu has the strongest and most distinctive flavor, compared with various other methods of brewing and is preferred by the sake *tsū*, as connoisseurs are known.

Apart from the *nomiya* (bars) and restaurants, the place to sample sake is the *izakaya*, a drinking establishment that serves only sake, usually dozens of different kinds, including a selection of *jizake*, the kind produced in limited quantities by small regional breweries throughout the country.

Regional Differences

Tōkyō people are known for their candor and vigor, as compared with the refined restraint of people in the older, more provincial Kyōto. This applies as much to food as it does to language, art, and fashion. Foods in the Kansai district (including Kyōto, Nara, Ōsaka, and Kōbe) tend to be lighter, the sauces less spicy, the soups not as hardy as those of the Kantō district, of which Tōkyō is the center. How many Tōkyōites have been heard to grumble about the "weak" soba broth on their visits to Kyōto? You go to Kyōto for the delicate and formal kaiseki, to Tōkyō for sushi.

Nigiri zushi (note that the pronunciation of "sushi" changes to "zushi" when combined with certain words), with pieces of raw fish on bite-size balls of rice (the form with which most Westerners are familiar), originated in the Kantō district, where there is a bounty of fresh fish. *Saba zushi* is the specialty of landlocked Kyōto. Actually the forerunner of nigiri zushi, it is made by pressing salt-preserved mackerel onto a bed of rice in a mold.

Every island in the Japanese archipelago has its specialty, and within each island every province has its own *meibutsu ryōri*, or specialty dish. In Kyūshū try *shippoku-ryōri*, a banquet-style feast of different dishes in which you eat your way up to a large fish mousse topped with shrimp. This dish is the local specialty in Nagasaki, for centuries the only port through which Japan had contact with the West.

On the island of Shikoku, try *sawachi-ryōri*, an extravaganza of elaborately prepared platters of fresh fish dishes, which is the specialty of Kōchi, the main city on the Pacific Ocean side of the island. In Hokkaidō, where salmon dishes are the local specialty, try *ishikari-nabe*, a hearty salmon-and-vegetable stew.

The Bottom Line

A couple of things take some getting used to. Things will be easier for you in Japan if you've had some experience with chopsticks. Some of the tourist-oriented restaurants (and, of course, all those serving Western food) provide silverware, but most traditional restaurants in Japan offer only chopsticks. It's a good idea to practice. The secret is to learn to move only the chopstick on top rather than trying to move both at once.

Sitting on the floor is another obstacle for many, including the younger generation of Japanese, to whom the prospect of sitting on a cushion on tatami mats for an hour or so means nothing but stiff knees and numb feet. Because of this, many restaurants now have rooms with tables and chairs. The most traditional restaurants, however, have kept to the customary style of dining in tatami rooms. Give it a try. Nothing can compare with a full-course kaiseki meal brought to your room at a traditional inn. Fresh from the bath, robed in a cotton kimono, you are free to relax and enjoy it all, including the view. After all, the carefully landscaped garden outside your door was designed specifically to be seen from this position.

The service in Japan is usually superb, particularly at a *ryōri-ryokan*, as restaurant-inns are called. A maid is assigned to anticipate your every need (even a few you didn't know you had). "*O-kyakusan wa kamisama desu*" (the customer is god), as the old Japanese proverb goes. People who prefer to dine in privacy have been known to say the service is too much.

Other problems? "The portions are too small" is a common complaint. The solution is an adjustment in perspective. In the world of Japanese cuisine, there are colors to delight in, and shapes, textures, and flavors are balanced for your pleasure. Naturally, the aroma, flavor, and freshness of the foods have importance, but so do the dishware, the design of the room, the sound of water in a stone basin outside. You are meant to leave the table delighted—not stuffed. An appeal is made to all the senses through the food itself, the atmosphere, and appreciation for a carefully orchestrated feast in every sense of the word—these, and the luxury of time spent in the company of friends.

This is not to say that every Japanese restaurant offers aesthetic perfection. Your basic train-platform, stand-up, gulp-it-down noodle stall ("eat-and-out" in under six minutes) should leave no doubts as to the truth of the old saying that "all feet tread not in one shoe."

In the end you'll discover that the joy of eating in Japan lies in the adventure of exploring the possibilities. Along every city street you'll find countless little eateries specializing in anything you can name—and some you can't. In the major cities, you'll find French restaurants, British pubs, and little places serving Italian, Chinese, Indian, and American food. In country towns you can explore a world of regional delicacies found nowhere else.

There is something for everyone and every budget—from the most exquisitely prepared and presented formal kaiseki meal to a delicately sculpted salmon mousse à la nouvelle cuisine, from skewers of grilled chicken in barbecue sauce to a steaming bowl of noodle soup at an outdoor stall. And much to the chagrin of culinary purists, Japan has no dearth of international fast-food chains—from burgers to spareribs to fried chicken to doughnuts to 31 flavors of American ice cream.

Sometimes the contradictions of this intriguing culture—as seen in the startling contrast between ancient traditions and modern industrial life—seem almost overwhelming. Who would ever have thought you could face eating a salad that included seaweed along with lettuce and tomatoes, or that you could happily dig into green-tea ice cream? As the famous potter Kawai Kanjiro once said, "Sometimes it's better if you don't understand everything . . . It makes life so much more exciting."

Manners

- Don't point or gesture with chopsticks. Licking the ends of your chopsticks is rude, as is taking food from a common serving plate with the end of the chopstick you've had in your mouth. Don't stick your chopsticks upright into your food when you're done using them; instead, allow them to rest on the side of your dish or bowl.

- There is no taboo against slurping your noodle soup, though women are generally less boisterous about it than men.

- Pick up the soup bowl and drink directly from it, rather than leaning over the table to sip it. Take the fish or vegetables from it with your chopsticks. Return the lid to the soup bowl when you are finished.

The rice bowl, too, is to be picked up and held in one hand while you eat from it.

- When drinking with a friend, don't pour your own. Take the bottle and pour for the other person. She will in turn reach for the bottle and pour for you. The Japanese will attempt to top your drink off after every few sips.

- The Japanese don't pour sauces on their rice in a traditional meal. Sauces are intended for dipping foods lightly, not for dunking or soaking.

- Among faux pas that are considered nearly unpardonable, the worst perhaps is blowing your nose. Excuse yourself and leave the room if this becomes necessary.

- Although McDonald's and Häagen-Dazs have made great inroads on the custom of never eating in public, it is still considered gauche to munch on a hamburger (or an ice cream cone) as you walk along a public street.

— Diane Durston

WHAT TO READ AND WATCH BEFORE YOU GO

Books

The incredible refinement of Japanese culture has produced a wealth of literature. Yet in the face of thousands of such books, where should you begin? If you are a newcomer to the subject of Japan, start with Pico Iyer's *The Lady and the Monk,* which will charm you through the first five phases of stereotypical infatuation with Japan and leave you with five times as many insights. Then read Seichō Matsumoto's *Inspector Imanishi Investigates,* a superb detective novel that says volumes about Japanese life (make a list of characters' names as you read to keep them straight). As fearsome a topic as it is, the atomic bombing of Hiroshima, as told by John Hersey in his *Hiroshima,* is essential reading both about Japan and about the 20th century. The book is utterly engrossing both as a human story and for what it tells of the Japanese in particular.

Art and Architecture

A wealth of literature exists on Japanese art. Much of the early writing has not withstood the test of time, but R. Paine and Alexander Soper's *Art and Architecture of Japan* remains a good place to start. A more recent survey, though narrower in scope, is Joan Stanley-Smith's *Japanese Art.* Dore Ashton's *Noguchi East and West* looks at one of the 20th century's finest sculptors.

The multivolume *Japan Arts Library* covers most of the styles and personalities of the Japanese arts. The series has volumes on castles, teahouses, screen painting, and wood-block prints. A more detailed look at the architecture of Tōkyō is Edward Seidensticker's *Low City, High City.* Kazuo Nishi and Kazuo Hozumi's *What Is Japanese Architecture?* treats the history of Japanese architecture and uses examples of buildings you will actually see on your travels.

Fiction and Poetry

The great classic of Japanese fiction is the *Tale of Genji;* Genji, or the Shining Prince, has long been taken as the archetype of ideal male behavior. The story, widely considered the world's first novel, was written by a woman of the court, Murasaki Shikibu, around the year 1000. If the 1,000-plus-page complete edition is too daunting, try the abridged version. From the same period, Japan's golden age, *The Pillow Book of Sei Shōnagon* is the stylish and stylized diary of a woman's courtly life.

The Edo period is well covered by literary translations. Howard Hibbett's *Floating World in Japanese Fiction* gives an excellent selection with commentaries. The racy prose of late-17th-century Saikaku Ihara is translated in various books, including *Some Final Words of Advice* and *Five Women Who Loved Love.*

Modern Japanese fiction is more widely available in translation. One of the best-known writers among Westerners is Yukio Mishima, author of *The Sea of Fertility* trilogy, among many other works. His books often deal with the effects of postwar Westernization on Japanese culture. Two superb prose stylists are Junichirō Tanizaki, author of *The Makioka Sisters, Some Prefer Nettles,* and the racy 1920s *Quicksand;* and Nobel Prize winner Yasunari Kawabata, whose superbly written novels include *Snow Country* and *The Sound of the Mountain.* Kawabata's *Thousand Cranes,* which uses the tea ceremony as a vehicle, is an elegant page-turner. Jirō Osaragi's *The Journey* is a lucid, entertaining rendering of the clash of tradition and modernity in postwar Japan. Also look for

Natsume Sōseki's charming *Botchan* and delightful *I Am a Cat*.

Other novelists and works of note are Kōbō Abe, whose *Woman in the Dunes* is a 1960s landmark, and Shūsaku Endō, who brutally and breathlessly treated the early clash of Japan with Christianity in *The Samurai*.

Novelists at work in Japan today are no less interesting. Fumiko Enchi's *Masks* poignantly explores the fascinating public-private dichotomy. Haruki Murakami's *Wild Sheep Chase* is a wild ride indeed; his short stories are often bizarre and humorous, with a touch of the science fiction thrown in for good measure. Murakami's more recent *The Wind-up Bird Chronicle*, a dense and daring novel, fantastically juxtaposes the banality of modern Japanese suburbia with the harsh realities of 20th-century Japanese history. Along with Murakami's books, Banana Yoshimoto's *Kitchen* and other novels are probably the most fun you'll have with any Japanese fiction. Kōno Taeko's *Toddler-Hunting* and Yūko Tsushima's *The Shooting Gallery* are as engrossing and well crafted as they are frank about the burdens of tradition on Japanese women today. Nobel Prize winner Kenzaburō Ōe's writing similarly explores deeply personal issues, among them his compelling relationship with his disabled son.

Haiku, the 5-7-5 syllable form that the monk Matsuo Bashō honed in the 17th century, is the flagship of Japanese poetry. His *Narrow Road to the Deep North* is a wistful prose-and-poem travelogue that is available in a few translations. But there are many more forms and authors worth exploring. Three volumes of translations by Kenneth Rexroth include numerous authors' work from the last 1,000 years: *One Hundred Poems from the Japanese, 100 More Poems from the Japanese,* and *Women Poets of Japan* (translated with Akiko Atsumi). Each has notes and brief author biographies. *Ink Dark Moon*, translated by Jane Hirshfield with Mariko Aratani, presents the remarkable poems of Ono no Komachi

and Izumi Shikibu, two of Japan's earliest women poets. The Zen poems of Ryokan represent the sacred current in Japanese poetry; look for *Dew Drops on a Lotus Leaf*. Other poets to look for are Issa, Buson, and Bonchō. Two fine small volumes that link their haiku with those of other poets, including Bashō, are *The Monkey's Raincoat* and the beautifully illustrated *A Net of Fireflies*.

Another way into Japanese culture is riding on the heels of Westerners who live in Japan. The emotional realities of such experience are engagingly rendered in *The Broken Bridge: Fiction from Expatriates in Literary Japan*, edited by Suzanne Kamata.

History and Society

Fourteen hundred years of history are rather a lot to take in when going on a vacation, but two good surveys make the task much easier: Richard Storry's *A History of Modern Japan* (by modern, he means everything post-prehistoric) and George Sansom's *Japan: A Short Cultural History*. Sansom's three-volume *History of Japan* is a more exhaustive treatment.

If you're interested in earlier times, Yamamoto Tsunetomo's *Hagakure* (*The Book of the Samurai*) is an 18th-century guide of sorts to the principles and ethics of the "Way of the Samurai," written by a Kyūshū samurai. Dr. Junichi Saga's *Memories of Silk and Straw: A Self-Portrait of Small-Town Japan* is his 1970s collection of interviews with local old-timers in his hometown outside Tōkyō. Saga's father illustrated the accounts. Few books get so close to the realities of everyday life in early modern rural Japan. Elizabeth Bumiller's 1995 *The Secrets of Markio* intimately recounts a very poignant year in the life of a Japanese woman and her family.

The Japanese have a genre they refer to as *nihon-jin-ron*, or studies of Japaneseness. Western-style studies of the Japanese way of life in relation to the West also abound. Perhaps the best is Ezra Vogel's *Japan as Number One: Lessons for America*. A fine study of the Japanese mind is found in Takeo Doi's *The Anatomy of De-*

pendence and Chie Nakane's *Japanese Society*.

Karel van Wolferen's *The Enigma of Japanese Power* is an enlightening book on the Japanese sociopolitical system, especially for diplomats and businesspeople intending to work with the Japanese. Roland Barthes's impressionistic *Empire of Signs*, though dated by some of the events he recalls, contains keenly observant vignettes on topics like costume, theater, and the planning of Tōkyō. And as a sounding of the experience of his years in the country, Alex Kerr's *Lost Japan* examines the directions of Japanese society past and present. This book was the first by a foreigner ever to win Japan's Shinchō Gakugei literature prize.

Language

There is an overwhelming number of books and courses available for studying Japanese. *Japanese for Busy People* uses conversational situations (rather than grammatical principles) as a means of introducing the Japanese language. With it you will also learn the two syllabaries, *hiragana* and *katakana*, and rudimentary *kanji* characters. To augment your study of kanji, look for P. G. O'Neill's *Essential Kanji* and Florence Sakade's *Guide to Reading and Writing Japanese*.

Religion

Anyone wanting to read a Zen Buddhist text should try *The Platform Sutra of the Sixth Patriarch*, one of the Zen classics, written by an ancient Chinese head of the sect and translated by Philip B. Yampolsky. Another Zen text of high importance is the *Lotus Sutra*; it has been translated by Leon Hurvitz as *The Scripture of the Lotus Blossom of the Fine Dharma: The Lotus Sutra*. Stuart D. Picken has written books on both major Japanese religions: *Shintō: Japan's Spiritual Roots* and *Buddhism: Japan's Cultural Identity*. William R. LaFleur's *Karma of Words: Buddhism and the Literary Arts in Medieval Japan* traces how Buddhism affected medieval Japanese mentality and behavior.

Travel Narratives

Two travel narratives stand out as superb introductions to Japanese history, culture, and people. Donald Richie's classic *The Inland Sea* recalls his journey and encounters on the fabled Seto Nai-kai. Leila Philip's year working in a Kyūshū pottery village became the eloquent *Road Through Miyama*.

Videos

The Japanese film industry has been active since the early days of the medium's invention. A limited number of Japanese films, however, have been transferred to video for Western audiences, and even these may be hard to locate at your local video store. Many Japanese movies fall into two genres: the *jidai-geki* period-costume films and the *gendai-geki* films about contemporary life. Period films often deal with romantic entanglements, ghosts, and samurai warriors, as in *chambara* (sword-fight) films. Movies set in more recent times often focus on lower- or middle-class family life and the world of gangsters.

Western viewers have typically encountered Japanese cinema in the works of Japan's most prolific movie directors, Kenji Mizoguchi, Yasujirō Ozu, and Akira Kurosawa. Mizoguchi's career spanned a 34-year period beginning in 1922, and three of his finest films investigate the social role of a female protagonist in feudal Japan: *The Life of Oharu* (1952), *Ugetsu* (1953), and *Sanchō the Bailiff* (1954). Ozu directed 54 films from 1927 to 1962; most of his movies explore traditional Japanese values and concentrate on the everyday life and relationships of middle-class families. Among his best works are *Late Spring* (1949), *Early Summer* (1951), *Tōkyō Story* (1953), and *An Autumn Afternoon* (1962).

Kurosawa, who began directing movies in 1943, is the best-known Japanese filmmaker among Western audiences. His film *Rashōmon* (1950), a 12th-century murder story told by four different narrators, brought him international acclaim and sparked world interest in Japanese cinema.

Among his other classic period films are *Seven Samurai* (1954), *The Hidden Fortress* (1958), *Yōjimbō* (1961), *Red Beard* (1965), *Derzu Uzala* (1975), and *Kagemusha* (1980). The life-affirming *Ikiru* (1952) deals with an office worker dying of cancer. *High and Low* (1963), about a kidnaping, was based on a detective novel by Ed McBain. Two of Kurosawa's most honored films were adapted from Shakespeare plays: *Throne of Blood* (1957), based on *Macbeth,* and *Ran* (1985), based on *King Lear.*

Another director in the same generation as Mizoguchi and Ozu was Teinosuke Kinugasa, whose *Gate of Hell* (1953) vividly re-creates medieval Japan. *The Samurai Trilogy* (1954), directed by Hiroshi Inagaki, follows the adventures of a legendary 16th-century samurai hero, Musashi Miyamoto. A whole new group of filmmakers came to the forefront in postwar Japan, including Kon Ichikawa, who directed two powerful antiwar movies, *The Burmese Harp* (1956) and *Fires on the Plain* (1959); and Masaki Kobayashi, whose samurai period film *Harakiri* (1962) is considered his best work. In the late '60s and '70s several new directors gained prominence, including Hiroshi Teshigahara, Shōhei Imamura, and Nagisa Ōshima. Teshigahara is renowned for the allegorical *Woman in the Dunes* (1964), based on a novel by Kōbō Abe. Among Imamura's honored works are *The Ballad of Narayama* (1983), about the death of the elderly, and *Black Rain* (1989), which deals with the atomic bombing of Hiroshima. Ōshima directed *Merry Christmas, Mr. Lawrence* (1983), about a British officer in a Japanese prisoner-of-war camp in Java during World War II.

Other Japanese filmmakers worth checking out are Yoshimitsu Morita, Jūzō Itami, and Masayuki Suo. Morita's *The Family Game* (1983) satirizes Japanese domestic life and the educational system. Itami won international recognition for *Tampopo* (1986), a highly original comedy about food. His other films include *A Taxing Woman* (1987), which pokes fun at the Japanese tax system, and *Mimbō* (1992), which dissects the world of Japanese gangsters. Suo's *Shall We Dance?* (1997) is a bittersweet comedy about a married businessman who escapes his daily routine by taking ballroom dance lessons. *Fireworks* (1997), by Kitano Takeshi, depicts a cop's struggle with loss in modern, frenetic Japan.

JAPAN AT A GLANCE: A CHRONOLOGY

10,000 BC– AD 300 Neolithic Jōmon hunting and fishing culture leaves richly decorated pottery.

AD 300 Yayoi culture displays knowledge of farming and metallurgy imported from Korea.

after 300 The Yamato tribe consolidates power in the rich Kansai plain and expands westward, forming the kind of military aristocratic society that will dominate Japan's history.

ca. 500 Yamato leaders, claiming to be descended from the sun goddess, Amaterasu, take the title of emperor.

538–552 Buddhism, introduced to the Yamato court from China by way of Korea, complements rather than replaces the indigenous Shintō religion.

593–622 Prince Shōtoku encourages the Japanese to embrace Chinese culture and has Buddhist temple Hōryū-ji built at Nara in 607 (its existing buildings are among the oldest surviving wooden structures in the world).

Nara Period
710–784 Japan has first permanent capital at Nara; great age of Buddhist sculpture, piety, and poetry.

Fujiwara or Heian (Peace) Period
794–1160 The capital is moved from Nara to Heian-kyō (now Kyōto), where the Fujiwara family dominates the imperial court. Lady Murasaki's novel *The Tale of Genji,* written circa 1020, describes the elegance and political maneuvering of court life.

Kamakura Period
1185–1335 Feudalism enters, with military and economic power in the provinces and the emperor a powerless, ceremonial figurehead in Kyōto. Samurai warriors welcome Zen, a new sect of Buddhism from China.

1192 After a war with the Taira family, Yoritomo of the Minamoto family becomes the first shōgun; he places his capital in Kamakura.

1274 and 1281 The fleets sent by Chinese emperor Kublai Khan to invade Japan are destroyed by typhoons, praised in Japanese history as kamikaze, or divine wind.

Ashikaga Period
1336–1568 The Ashikaga family assumes the title of shōgun and settles in Kyōto. The Zen aesthetic flourishes in painting, landscape gardening, and tea ceremony. Nō theater emerges. The Silver Pavilion, or Ginkaku-ji, in Kyōto, built in 1483, is the quintessential example of Zen-inspired architecture. The period is marked by constant warfare but also by

increased trade with the mainland. Ōsaka develops into an important commercial city, and trade guilds appear.

1467–1477 The Ōnin Wars that wrack Kyōto initiate a 100-year period of civil war.

1543 Portuguese sailors, the first Europeans to reach Japan, initiate trade relations with the lords of western Japan and introduce the musket, which changes Japanese warfare.

1549–1551 St. Francis Xavier, the first Jesuit missionary, introduces Christianity.

Momoyama Period of National Unification

1568–1600 Two generals, Nobunaga Oda and Hideyoshi Toyotomi, are the central figures of this period. Nobunaga builds a military base from which Hideyoshi unifies Japan.

1592, 1597 Hideyoshi invades Korea. He brings back Korean potters, who rapidly develop a Japanese ceramics industry.

The Tokugawa Period

1600–1868 Ieyasu Tokugawa becomes shōgun after the battle of Sekigahara. The military capital is established at Edo (now Tōkyō), which shows phenomenal economic and cultural growth. A hierarchical order of four social classes—warriors, farmers, artisans, then merchants—is rigorously enforced. The merchant class, however, is increasingly prosperous and effects a transition from a rice to a money economy. Merchants patronize new, popular forms of art: Kabuki, haiku, and the ukiyo-e school of painting. The life of the latter part of this era is beautifully illustrated in the wood-block prints of the artist Hokusai (1760–1849).

1618 Japanese Christians who refuse to renounce their foreign religion are persecuted.

1637–1638 Japanese Christians are massacred in the Shimabara uprising. Japan is closed to the outside world except for a Dutch trading post in Nagasaki harbor.

1853 U.S. commodore Matthew Perry reopens Japan to foreign trade.

The Meiji Restoration

1868–1912 Opponents of the weakened Tokugawa Shogunate support Emperor Meiji and overthrow the last shōgun. The emperor is "restored" (with little actual power), and the imperial capital is moved to Edo, which is renamed Tōkyō (Eastern Capital). Japan is modernized along Western lines, with a constitution proclaimed in 1889; a system of compulsory education and a surge of industrialization follow.

1902–1905 Japan defeats Russia in the Russo-Japanese War and achieves world-power status.

1910 Japan annexes Korea.

1914–1918 Japan joins the Allies in World War I.

1923 The Great Kantō Earthquake devastates much of Tōkyō and Yokohama.

1931 As a sign of growing militarism in the country, Japan seizes the Chinese province of Manchuria.

1937 Following years of increasing military and diplomatic activity in northern China, open warfare breaks out (and lasts until 1945); Chinese Nationalists and Communists both fight Japan.

1939–1945 Japan, having signed anti-Communist treaties with Nazi Germany and Italy (1936 and 1937), invades and occupies French Indochina.

1941 The Japanese attack on Pearl Harbor on December 7 brings the United States into war against Japan in the Pacific.

1942 Japan's empire extends to Indochina, Burma, Malaya, the Philippines, and Indonesia. Japan bombs Darwin, Australia. U.S. defeat of Japanese forces at Midway turns the tide of the Pacific war.

1945 Tōkyō and 50 other Japanese cities are devastated by U.S. bombing raids. The United States drops atomic bombs on Hiroshima and Nagasaki in August, precipitating Japanese surrender.

1945–1952 The American occupation under General Douglas MacArthur disarms Japan and encourages the establishment of a democratic government. Emperor Hirohito retains his position.

1953 After the Korean War, Japan begins a period of great economic growth.

1964 Tōkyō hosts the Summer Olympic games.

late 1960s Japan develops into one of the major industrial nations in the world.

mid-1970s Production of electronics, cars, cameras, and computers places Japan at the heart of the emerging "Pacific Rim" economic sphere and threatens to spark a trade war with the industrial nations of Europe and the United States.

1989 Emperor Hirohito dies.

1990 Coronation of Emperor Akihito. Prince Fumihito marries Kiko Kawashima.

1992 The Diet approves use of Japanese military forces under United Nations auspices.

1993 Crown Prince Naruhito marries Masako Owada.

1995 A massive earthquake strikes Kōbe and environs. Approximately 5,500 people are killed and 35,000 injured; more than 100,000 buildings are destroyed.

Members of a fringe religious organization, the Aum Shinri Kyō, carry out a series of poison-gas attacks on the transportation networks of Tōkyō and Yokohama, undermining, in a society that is a model of decorum and mutual respect, confidence in personal safety.

1997 The deregulation of rice prices and the appearance of discount gasoline stations mark a turn in the Japanese economy toward genuine privatization. These small indications constitute a break from traditional price control policies that support small merchants and producers.

1998   The Japanese economy is crippled from slumps throughout Asia. Banks merge or go bankrupt, and Japanese consumers spend less and less.

1999   In the international arena Japanese toys, films, and other accoutrements of pop culture find themselves in the spotlight like never before. The economy, however, continues to suffer as politicians debate economic measures that foreign economists have been recommending for years. Small businesses are most affected, and the attitude of the average Japanese is grim.

A nuclear accident 112 km (70 mi) northeast of Tōkyō injures few but raises many questions about Japan's vast nuclear-power industry.

2001   In support of the U.S. war against terrorism in Afghanistan, the Japanese government extends noncombat military activities abroad for the first time since World War II by sending support ships to the Indian Ocean under a reinterpretation of the existing post-1945, pacifist constitution. Asian leaders express some concern for a first step for Japanese military presence abroad since 1945.

ESSENTIAL INFORMATION

ADDRESSES

The simplest way to decipher a Japanese address is to **break the address into parts.** The following is an example of a typical Japanese address: 6-chōme 8–19, Chūō-ku, Fukuoka-shi, Fukuoka-ken. In this address the "chōme" indicates a precise area (a block, for example), and the numbers following "chōme" indicate the building within the area (buildings aren't always numbered sequentially; numbers are often assigned as buildings are erected). Only local police officers and mail carriers in Japan seem to be familiar with the area defined by the chōme. Sometimes, instead of "chōme," "machi" (town) is used.

"Ku" refers to a ward (a district) of a city, "shi" refers to a city name, and "ken" indicates a prefecture, which is roughly equivalent to a state in the United States. It's not unusual for the prefecture and the city to have the same name, as in the above address. There are a few geographic areas in Japan that are not called ken. One is Hokkaidō. The other exceptions are greater Tōkyō, which is called Tōkyō-to, and Kyōto and Ōsaka, which are followed by the suffix "-fu"—Kyōto-fu, Ōsaka-fu. Not all addresses conform exactly to the above format. Rural addresses, for example, might use "gun" (county) where cities have "ku" (ward).

Even Japanese people cannot find a building based on the address alone. If you get in a taxi with a written address, do not assume the driver will be able to find your destination. Usually, people provide very detailed instructions or maps to explain their exact locations. It's always good to **know the location of your destination in relation to a major building** or department store.

AIR TRAVEL

BOOKING

When you book **look for nonstop flights** and **remember that "direct" flights stop at least once.** Try to avoid connecting flights, which require a change of plane. For more booking tips and to check prices and make on-line flight reservations, log on to www.fodors.com.

CARRIERS

Japan Airlines (JAL) and United Airlines are the major carriers between North America and Narita Airport in Tōkyō; Northwest, American Airlines, Delta Airlines, and All Nippon Airways (ANA) also link North American cities with Tōkyō. JAL, Cathay Pacific, Virgin Atlantic Airways, and British Airways fly between Narita and Great Britain; JAL, United, and Qantas fly between Narita and Australia; and JAL and Air New Zealand fly between Narita and New Zealand.

➤ AIRLINES & CONTACTS: **American** (☎ 800/433–7300; 0120/000–860 in Japan). **All Nippon Airways** (☎ 800/235–9262; 020/7355–1155 in the U.K.; 03/5489–8800 in Japan for domestic flights; 0120/5489–8800 in Japan for international flights). **British Airways** (☎ 0345/222–111 in the U.K.; 03/3593–8811 in Japan). **Canadian Airlines** (☎ 888/247–2262; 03/3281–7426 in Japan). **Continental** (☎ 800/525–0280). **Delta** (☎ 800/221–1212). **Japan Air System** (☎ 03/3438–1155 in Japan for domestic flights; 0120/511–283 in Japan for international flights). **Japan Airlines** (☎ 800/525–3663; 0345/747–700 in the U.K.; 0120/25–5931 in Japan). **Korean Air** (☎ 800/438–5000; 0800/413–000 in the U.K.; 03/5443–3311 in Japan). **Lufthansa** (☎ 0345/737–747 in the U.K.). **Northwest** (☎ 800/447–4747). **Swissair** (☎ 800/221–4750; 020/7434–7300 in the U.K.;

03/3533–6000 or 0120/120–747 in Japan). **Thai Airways International** (☎ 800/426–5204; 020/7499–9113 in the U.K.; 03/3503–3311 in Japan). **United** (☎ 800/241–6522; 0120/114–466 in Japan).

CHECK-IN & BOARDING

Always **ask your carrier about its check-in policy.** Plan to arrive at the airport about 2 hours before your scheduled departure time for domestic flights and 2½ to 3 hours before international flights.

Assuming that not everyone with a ticket will show up, airlines routinely overbook planes. When everyone does, airlines ask for volunteers to give up their seats. In return, these volunteers usually get a certificate for a free flight and are rebooked on the next flight out. If there are not enough volunteers, the airline must choose who will be denied boarding. The first to get bumped are passengers who checked in late and those flying on discounted tickets, so **get to the gate and check in as early as possible,** especially during peak periods.

Always **bring a government-issued photo ID to the airport;** even when it's not required, a passport is best.

CUTTING COSTS

The least expensive airfares to Japan must usually be purchased in advance and are nonrefundable. It's smart to **call a number of airlines,** and when you are quoted a good price, **book it on the spot**—the same fare may not be available the next day. Always **check different routings** and look into using different airports. Travel agents, especially low-fare specialists (☞ Discounts & Deals, *below*), are helpful.

Consolidators are another good source. They buy tickets for scheduled international flights at reduced rates from the airlines, then sell them at prices that beat the best fare available directly from the airlines, usually without restrictions. Sometimes you can even get your money back if you need to return the ticket. Carefully read the fine print detailing penalties for changes and cancellations, and **confirm your consolidator reservation with the airline.**

➤ CONSOLIDATORS: **Cheap Tickets** (☎ 800/377–1000). **Discount Airline**

Ticket Service (☎ 800/576–1600). **Unitravel** (☎ 800/325–2222). **Up & Away Travel** (☎ 212/889–2345). **World Travel Network** (☎ 800/409–6753).

ENJOYING THE FLIGHT

For more legroom, **request an emergency-aisle seat.** Don't sit in the row in front of the emergency aisle or in front of a bulkhead, where seats may not recline. If you have dietary concerns, **ask for special meals when booking.** These can be vegetarian, low-cholesterol, or kosher. On long flights, try to maintain a normal routine, to help fight jet lag. At night, **get some sleep.** By day, **eat light meals, drink water** (not alcohol), and **move around the cabin** to stretch your legs. For additional jet-lag tips consult *Fodor's FYI: Travel Fit & Healthy* (available at bookstores everywhere).

FLYING TIMES

Flying time to Japan is 13¾ hours from New York, 12¼ hours from Chicago, 9½ hours from Los Angeles, and 11–12 hours from the United Kingdom. Japan Airlines' GPS systems allow a more direct routing, which reduces its flight times by about 30 minutes. Your trip east, because of tailwinds, will be about 45 minutes shorter.

HOW TO COMPLAIN

If your baggage goes astray or your flight goes awry, complain right away. Most carriers require that you **file a claim immediately.**

➤ AIRLINE COMPLAINTS: U.S. Department of Transportation **Aviation Consumer Protection Division** (✉ C-75, Room 4107, Washington, DC 20590, ☎ 202/366–2220, WEB www.dot.gov/airconsumer). **Federal Aviation Administration Consumer Hotline** (☎ 800/322–7873).

AIRPORTS

The major gateway to Japan is Tōkyō's Narita Airport (NRT). To alleviate the congestion at Narita, Kansai International Airport (KIX) opened in 1994 outside Ōsaka to serve the Kansai region, which includes Kōbe, Kyōto, Nara, and Ōsaka. It's also possible to fly from the United States, the United Kingdom, New Zealand, and Australia into Nagoya Airport. A few international flights use Fukuoka Airport, on the island of Kyūshū; these include Northwest flights from Honolulu and flights from other Asian destinations. Shin-Chitose Airport, outside Sapporo on the northern island of Hokkaidō, handles some international flights, though at present these are mostly nonscheduled flights. Most domestic flights to and from Tōkyō are out of Haneda Airport.

Two new airports were in the works at press time—one in Nagoya (slated to open before the 2005 World Expo) and one in Kōbe.

Tōkyō's Narita Airport is 80 km (50 mi) northeast of the city and serves the majority of Japan's international flights. There is a departure tax of ¥2,040, which is waived for children under two and transit passengers flying out the same day as their arrival.

Narita's Terminal 2 has two adjoining wings, north and south. When you arrive, your first task should be to convert your money into yen; you'll need it for transportation into Tōkyō. In both wings money exchange counters are in the wall between the customs inspection area and the arrival lobby. Both terminals have a Japan National Tourist Organization's Tourist Information Center, where you can get free maps, brochures, and other information. Directly across from the customs-area exits at both terminals are the ticket counters for airport limousine buses to Tōkyō. *See* Tōkyō A to Z *in* Chapter 1 for information on the one- to two-hour trip from the airport to Tōkyō proper.

If you plan to skip Tōkyō and center your trip on Kyōto or central or western Honshū, Kansai International Airport (KIX) is the airport to use. Built on reclaimed land in Ōsaka Bay, it's laid out vertically. The first floor is for international arrivals; the second floor is for domestic departures and arrivals; the third floor has shops and restaurants; and the fourth floor is for international departures. A small tourist information center on the first floor of the passenger terminal building is open daily 9–5. Major carriers are British Airways, Canadian Airlines, Japan Airlines, and Northwest Air-

lines. The trip from KIX to Kyōto takes 75 minutes by JR train; to Ōsaka it takes 45–70 minutes. *See* Chapters 5 and 7 for more information.

➤ AIRPORT INFORMATION: **Fukuoka Airport** (☎ 092/483–7007). **Haneda Airport** (☎ 03/5757–8111). **Kansai International Airport** (☎ 0724/55–2500). **Narita Airport** (☎ 0476/34–5000). **Shin-Chitose Airport** (☎ 0123/23–0111).

BIKE TRAVEL

BIKES IN FLIGHT

Most airlines accommodate bikes as luggage, provided they are dismantled and boxed. Airlines sell bike boxes, which are often free at bike shops, for about $5 (it's at least $100 for bike bags). International travelers can sometimes substitute a bike for a piece of checked luggage at no charge; otherwise, the cost is about $100. Domestic and Canadian airlines charge $25–$50.

BOAT & FERRY TRAVEL

Ferries connect most of the islands of Japan. Some of the more popular routes are from Tōkyō to Tomakomai or Kushiro in Hokkaidō; from Tōkyō to Shikoku; and from Tōkyō or Ōsaka to Kyūshū. You can **purchase ferry tickets in advance** from travel agencies or before boarding. The ferries are inexpensive and are a pleasant, if slow, way of traveling. Private cabins are available, but it's more fun to travel in the economy class, where everyone sleeps in one large room. Passengers eat, drink, and enjoy themselves in a convivial atmosphere. For more information *see* the A to Z sections at the end of Chapters 1, 10, 11, 12, and 13.

BUS TRAVEL

Japan Railways (JR) offers a number of overnight long-distance buses that are not very comfortable but are inexpensive. You can use Japan Rail Passes (☞ Train Travel, *below*) on these buses. City buses outside of Tōkyō are quite convenient, but **be sure of your route and destination,** because the bus driver probably won't speak English. Some buses have a set cost, from ¥170 to ¥180, depending on the route and municipality, in which case you board at the front of the bus and pay as you get on. On other buses cost is determined by the distance you travel. You take a ticket when you board at the rear door of the bus; it bears the number of the stop at which you boarded. Your fare is indicated by a board with rotating numbers at the front of the bus. Under each boarding point, indicated by a number, the fare increases the farther the bus travels.

JR also runs buses in some areas that have limited rail service. Remember, these buses are covered by the JR Pass, even if some JR reservation clerks tell you otherwise.

➤ BUS INFORMATION: **Japan Railways** (☎ 03/3423–0111), open weekdays 10–6.

BUSINESS HOURS

General business hours in Japan are weekdays 9–5. Many offices also open at least half of the day on Saturday but are generally closed on Sunday.

BANKS & OFFICES

Banks are open weekdays 9–3.

MUSEUMS

Museums generally close on Monday and the day following national holidays. They are also closed the day following special exhibits and during the weeklong New Year celebrations.

SHOPS

Department stores are usually open 10–7 but close one day a week, which varies from store to store. Other stores are open from 10 or 11 to 7 or 8.

CAMERAS & PHOTOGRAPHY

Before departing, **register your foreign-made camera or laptop with U.S. Customs** (☞ Customs & Duties, *below*). If your equipment is U.S. made, call the Japanese consulate to find out whether the device should be registered with local customs upon arrival.

Fluorescent lighting, which is common in Japan, gives photographs a greenish tint. You can counteract this discoloration with an FL filter.

The *Kodak Guide to Shooting Great Travel Pictures* (available at bookstores everywhere) is loaded with tips.

➤ PHOTO HELP: **Kodak Information Center** (☎ 800/242–2424).

EQUIPMENT PRECAUTIONS

Don't pack film and equipment in checked luggage, where it is much more susceptible to damage. X-ray machines used to view checked luggage are becoming much more powerful and therefore are much more likely to ruin your film. Always **keep film and tape out of the sun.** Carry an extra supply of batteries, and **be prepared to turn on your camera or camcorder** to prove to security personnel that the device is real. Always **ask for hand inspection of film,** which becomes clouded after repeated exposure to airport X-ray machines, and **keep videotapes away from metal detectors.**

CAR RENTAL

Rates in Tōkyō begin at $87 a day and $437 a week for an economy car with unlimited mileage. This does not include tax, which is 5% on car rentals. Reservations in the United States should be made at least a week in advance.

➤ MAJOR AGENCIES: **Alamo** (☎ 800/522–9696; 020/8759–6200 in the U.K., WEB www.alamo.com). **Avis** (☎ 800/331–1084; 800/879–2847 in Canada; 02/9353–9000 in Australia; 09/525–1982 in New Zealand; 0870/606–0100 in the U.K., WEB www.avis.com). **Budget** (☎ 800/527–0700; 0870/156–5656 in the U.K., WEB www.budget.com). **Dollar** (☎ 800/800–6000; 0124/622–0111 in the U.K., where it's affiliated with Sixt; 02/9223–1444 in Australia, WEB www.dollar.com). **Hertz** (☎ 800/654–3001; 800/263–0600 in Canada; 020/8897–2072 in the U.K.; 02/9669–2444 in Australia; 09/256–8690 in New Zealand, WEB www.hertz.com) **National Car Rental** (☎ 800/227–7368; 020/8680–4800 in the U.K., WEB www.nationalcar.com).

CUTTING COSTS

To get the best deal, **book through a travel agent who will shop around.** Payment must be made before you leave home.

INSURANCE

When driving a rented car you are generally responsible for any damage to or loss of the vehicle as well as for any property damage or personal injury that you may cause. Before you rent, see what coverage your personal auto-insurance policy and credit cards provide.

REQUIREMENTS & RESTRICTIONS

In Japan your own driver's license is not acceptable. You need an international driver's permit; it's available from the American or Canadian Automobile Association, or, in the United Kingdom, from the Automobile Association or Royal Automobile Club (☞ Auto Clubs *under* Car Travel, *below*).

SURCHARGES

Before you pick up a car in one city and leave it in another, **ask about drop-off charges or one-way service fees,** which can be substantial. Note, too, that some rental agencies charge extra if you return the car before the time specified in your contract. To avoid a hefty refueling fee, **fill the tank just before you turn in the car,** but be aware that gas stations near the rental outlet may overcharge.

CAR TRAVEL

It's possible for foreigners to drive in Japan with an international driver's license, and though few select this option, it is becoming more popular (to obtain a license, contact your country's major auto club; ☞ *below*). Major roads are sufficiently marked in the roman alphabet, and on country roads there is usually someone to ask for help. However, it's a good idea to **have a detailed map with town names written in** *kanji* **(Japanese characters) and** *romaji* **(romanized Japanese).**

Car travel along the Tōkyō–Kyōto–Hiroshima corridor and in other built-up areas of Japan is not as convenient as the trains. Within the major cities, the trains and subways will get you to your destinations faster and more comfortably. Roads are congested, gas is expensive (about ¥100 per liter, or $4.80 per gallon), and highway tolls are exorbitant (tolls between Tōkyō and Kyōto amount to ¥9,250). In major cities, with the exception of main arteries, English signs are few and far between, one-way streets often lead you off the track, and parking is often hard to find and usually expensive.

That said, a car can be the best means for exploring cities outside the metropolitan areas and the rural parts of Japan. Consider taking a train to those areas where exploring the countryside will be most interesting and renting a car locally for a day or even half a day.

AUTO CLUBS

➤ IN AUSTRALIA: **Australian Automobile Association** (AAA; ☎ 02/6247–7311, WEB www.aaa.asn.au).

➤ IN CANADA: **Canadian Automobile Association** (CAA; ☎ 613/247–0117, WEB www.caa.ca).

➤ IN NEW ZEALAND: **New Zealand Automobile Association** (☎ 09/377–4660, WEB www.aa.co.nz).

➤ IN THE U.K.: **Automobile Association** (AA; ☎ 0870/550–0600). **Royal Automobile Club** (RAC; ☎ 0870/572–2722, WEB www.rac.co.uk).

➤ IN THE U.S.: **American Automobile Association** (AAA; ☎ 800/564–6222, WEB www.aaa.com).

ROAD CONDITIONS

Roads in Japan are often narrower than those found in the United States, but they're well maintained in general.

RULES OF THE ROAD

In Japan people **drive on the left.** Speed limits vary, but generally the limit is 80 kph (50 mph) on highways, 40 kph (25 mph) in cities.

Many smaller streets lack sidewalks, so cars, bicycles, and pedestrians share the same space. Motorbikes with engines under 50 cc are allowed to travel against automobile traffic on one-way roads. Fortunately, considering the narrowness of the streets and the volume of traffic, most Japanese drivers are technically skilled. They may not allow quite as much distance between cars as you're used to. Be prepared for sudden lane changes by other drivers. When waiting at intersections after dark, many drivers, as a courtesy to other drivers, turn off their main headlights to prevent glare.

Japan has very strict laws concerning the consumption of alcohol prior to getting behind the wheel. Given the almost zero-tolerance for driving under the influence and the occasional evening police checkpoint set up along the roads, it's wisest to avoid alcohol entirely if you plan to drive.

CHILDREN IN JAPAN

If you are renting a car, don't forget to **arrange for a car seat** when you reserve. For general advice about traveling with children, consult *Fodor's FYI: Travel with Your Baby* (available in bookstores everywhere).

BABY-SITTING

Some very expensive Western-style hotels and resorts have supervised playrooms where you can drop off your children. The baby-sitters, however, are unlikely to speak English. Child-care arrangements can also be made through your hotel's concierge, but some properties require up to a week's notice.

FLYING

If your children are two or older, **ask about children's airfares.** As a general rule, infants under two not occupying a seat fly at greatly reduced fares or even for free. When booking, **confirm carry-on allowances** if you're traveling with infants. In general, for babies charged 10% of the adult fare you are allowed one carry-on bag and a collapsible stroller; if the flight is full, the stroller may have to be checked or you may be limited to less.

Experts agree that it's a good idea to use safety seats aloft for children weighing less than 40 pounds. Airlines set their own policies: U.S. carriers usually require that the child be ticketed, even if he or she is young enough to ride free, since the seats must be strapped into regular seats. Do **check your airline's policy about using safety seats during takeoff and landing.** And since safety seats are not allowed everywhere in the plane, get your seat assignments early.

When reserving, **request children's meals or a freestanding bassinet** if you need them. But note that bulkhead seats, where you must sit to use the bassinet, may lack an overhead bin or storage space on the floor.

LODGING

Most hotels in Japan allow children under a certain age to stay in their parents' room at no extra charge, but others charge for them as extra adults; be sure to **find out the cutoff age for children's discounts.**

SIGHTS & ATTRACTIONS

Places that are especially appealing to children are indicated by a rubber-duckie icon ( ) in the margin.

CONSUMER PROTECTION

Whenever shopping or buying travel services in Japan, **pay with a major credit card,** if possible, so you can cancel payment or get reimbursed if there's a problem. If you're doing business with a particular company for the first time, **contact your local Better Business Bureau and the attorney general's offices** in your state and (for U.S. businesses) the company's home state as well. Have any complaints been filed? Finally, if you're buying a package or tour, always **consider travel insurance** that includes default coverage (☞ Insurance, *below*).

➤ BBB: Council of Better Business Bureaus (✉ 4200 Wilson Blvd., Suite 800, Arlington, VA 22203, ☎ 703/276–0100, FAX 703/525–8277, WEB www.bbb.org).

CUSTOMS & DUTIES

When shopping, **keep receipts** for all purchases. Upon reentering the country, **be ready to show customs officials what you've bought.** If you feel a duty is incorrect or object to the way your clearance was handled, note the inspector's badge number and ask to see a supervisor. If the problem isn't resolved, write to the appropriate authorities, beginning with the port director at your point of entry.

IN AUSTRALIA

Australian residents who are 18 or older may bring home $A400 worth of souvenirs and gifts (including jewelry), 250 cigarettes or 250 grams of tobacco, and 1,125 ml of alcohol (including wine, beer, and spirits). Residents under 18 may bring back $A200 worth of goods. Prohibited items include meat products. Seeds, plants, and fruits need to be declared upon arrival.

➤ INFORMATION: **Australian Customs Service** (Regional Director, ✉ Box 8, Sydney, NSW 2001, Australia, ☎ 02/9213–2000, FAX 02/9213–4000, WEB www.customs.gov.au).

IN CANADA

Canadian residents who have been out of Canada for at least seven days may bring home C$750 worth of goods duty-free. If you've been away fewer than seven days but more than 48 hours, the duty-free allowance drops to C$200; if your trip lasts 24–48 hours, the allowance is C$50. You may not pool allowances with family members. Goods claimed under the C$750 exemption may follow you by mail; those claimed under the lesser exemptions must accompany you. Alcohol and tobacco products may be included in the seven-day and 48-hour exemptions but not in the 24-hour exemption. If you meet the age requirements of the province or territory through which you reenter Canada, you may bring in, duty-free, 1.14 liters (40 imperial ounces) of wine or liquor *or* 24 12-ounce cans or bottles of beer or ale. If you are 19 or older you may bring in, duty-free, 200 cigarettes and 50 cigars. Check ahead of time with the Canada Customs Revenue Agency or the Department of Agriculture for policies regarding meat products, seeds, plants, and fruits.

You may send an unlimited number of gifts worth up to C$60 each duty-free to Canada. Label the package UNSOLICITED GIFT—VALUE UNDER $60. Alcohol and tobacco are excluded.

➤ INFORMATION: **Canada Customs Revenue Agency** (✉ 2265 St. Laurent Blvd. S, Ottawa, Ontario K1G 4K3, Canada, ☎ 204/983–3500 or 506/636–5064; 800/461–9999 in Canada, WEB www.ccra-adrc.gc.ca).

IN JAPAN

Japan has strict regulations about bringing firearms, pornography, and narcotics into the country. Anyone caught with drugs is liable to be detained, deported, and refused reentry into Japan. Certain fresh fruits, vegetables, plants, and animals are also illegal. Nonresidents are allowed to bring in duty-free: (1) 400 cigarettes or 100 cigars or 500 grams of tobacco; (2) three bottles of alcohol; (3) 2 ounces of perfume; (4) other goods up to ¥200,000 value.

IN NEW ZEALAND

Homeward-bound residents 17 or older may bring back $700 worth of souvenirs and gifts. Your duty-free allowance also includes 4.5 liters of wine or beer; one 1,125-ml bottle of spirits; and either 200 cigarettes, 250 grams of tobacco, 50 cigars, or a combination of the three up to 250 grams. Prohibited items include meat products, seeds, plants, and fruits.

➤ INFORMATION: **New Zealand Customs** (Custom House, ✉ 50 Anzac Ave., Box 29, Auckland, New Zealand, ☎ 09/300–5399, FAX 09/359–6730), WEB www.customs.govt.nz.

IN THE U.K.

From countries outside the European Union, including Japan, you may bring home, duty-free, 200 cigarettes or 50 cigars; 1 liter of spirits or 2 liters of fortified or sparkling wine or liqueurs; 2 liters of still table wine; 60 ml of perfume; 250 ml of toilet water; plus £145 worth of other goods, including gifts and souvenirs. If returning from outside the EU, prohibited items include meat products, seeds, plants, and fruits.

➤ INFORMATION: **HM Customs and Excise** (✉ St. Christopher House, Southwark, London SE1 OTE, U.K., ☎ 020/7928–3344, WEB www.hmce.gov.uk).

IN THE U.S.

U.S. residents who have been out of the country for at least 48 hours (and who have not used the $400 allowance or any part of it in the past 30 days) may bring home $400 worth of foreign goods duty-free.

U.S. residents 21 and older may bring back 1 liter of alcohol duty-free. In addition, regardless of your age, you are allowed 200 cigarettes and 100 non-Cuban cigars. Antiques, which the U.S. Customs Service defines as objects more than 100 years old, enter duty-free, as do original works of art done entirely by hand, including paintings, drawings, and sculptures.

You may also mail or ship packages home duty-free: up to $200 worth of goods for personal use, with a limit of one parcel per addressee per day (except alcohol or tobacco products or perfume worth more than $5); label the package PERSONAL USE and attach a list of its contents and their retail value. Do not label the package UNSOLICITED GIFT or your duty-free exemption will drop to $100. Mailed items do not affect your duty-free allowance on your return.

➤ INFORMATION: **U.S. Customs Service** (✉ 1300 Pennsylvania Ave. NW, Room 6.3D, Washington, DC 20229, WEB www.customs.gov; inquiries ☎ 202/354–1000; complaints c/o ✉ 1300 Pennsylvania Ave. NW, Room 5.4D, Washington, DC 20229; registration of equipment c/o Office of Passenger Programs, ☎ 202/927–0530).

DINING

The restaurants we list are the cream of the crop in each price category. Food, like many other things in Japan, is expensive. Eating at hotels and famous restaurants is costly; however, you can eat well and reasonably at standard restaurants that may not have signs in English. Many less expensive restaurants have plastic replicas of the dishes they serve displayed in their front windows, so you can always point to what you want to eat if the language barrier is insurmountable. A good place to look for moderately priced dining spots is in the restaurant concourse of department stores, usually on the bottom floor. Properties indicated by an ✕☐ are lodging establishments whose restaurant warrants a special trip.

In general, Japanese restaurants are very clean (standards of hygiene are very high). The water is safe, even when drawn from a tap. Most hotels have Western-style rest rooms, but restaurants may have Japanese-style toilets, with bowls recessed into the floor, over which you must squat.

Local and regional specialties are discussed at the beginning of each chapter in this book; for more general information on dining in Japan, *see* The Discreet Charm of Japanese Cuisine *in* Chapter 14.

MEALTIMES

Unless otherwise noted, the restaurants listed in this guide are open daily for lunch and dinner.

RESERVATIONS & DRESS

Reservations are always a good idea: we mention them only when they're essential or not accepted. Book as far ahead as you can, and reconfirm as soon as you arrive. We mention dress only when men are required to wear a jacket or a jacket and tie.

DISABILITIES & ACCESSIBILITY

Generally speaking, Japan has a long way to go before accessibility throughout the country equals that in the West. Though wheelchair navigation is not an impossibility and elevators are everywhere, the sheer numbers of people in larger cities are likely to frustrate even the most determined traveler with disabilities. Such disadvantages may be countered, of course, by the amazing helpfulness of strangers and by their eagerness to extend even the smallest kindness.

RESERVATIONS

When discussing accessibility with an operator or reservations agent, **ask hard questions.** Are there any stairs, inside *or* out? Are there grab bars next to the toilet *and* in the shower/tub? How wide is the doorway to the room? To the bathroom? For the most extensive facilities meeting the latest legal specifications, **opt for newer accommodations.**

SIGHTS & ATTRACTIONS

Many shrines and temples are set on high ground, with steep steps, so people with mobility problems may have difficulty visiting them.

➤ COMPLAINTS: **Aviation Consumer Protection Division** (☞ Air Travel, *above*) for airline-related problems.

Civil Rights Office (✉ U.S. Department of Transportation, Departmental Office of Civil Rights, S-30, 400 7th St. SW, Room 10215, Washington, DC 20590, ☎ 202/366–4648, FAX 202/366–9371, WEB www.dot.gov/ost/docr/index.htm) for problems with surface transportation. **Disability Rights Section** (✉ U.S. Department of Justice, Civil Rights Division, Box 66738, Washington, DC 20035-6738, ☎ 202/514–0301 or 800/514–0301; 202/514–0383 TTY or 800/514–0383 TTY, FAX 202/307–1198, WEB www.usdoj.gov/crt/ada/adahom1.htm) for general complaints.

TRAVEL AGENCIES

In the United States, the Americans with Disabilities Act requires that travel firms serve the needs of all travelers. Some agencies specialize in working with people with disabilities.

➤ TRAVELERS WITH MOBILITY PROBLEMS: **Access Adventures** (✉ 206 Chestnut Ridge Rd., Scottsville, NY 14624, ☎ 716/889–9096, dltravel@prodigy.net), run by a former physical-rehabilitation counselor. **Flying Wheels Travel** (✉ 143 W. Bridge St., Box 382, Owatonna, MN 55060, ☎ 507/451–5005 or 800/535–6790, FAX 507/451–1685, WEB www.flyingwheelstravel.com).

DISCOUNTS & DEALS

Be a smart shopper and **compare all your options** before making decisions. A plane ticket bought with a promotional coupon from travel clubs, coupon books, and direct-mail offers or on the Internet may not be cheaper than the least expensive fare from a discount ticket agency. And always keep in mind that what you get is just as important as what you save.

DISCOUNT RESERVATIONS

To save money, **look into discount reservations services** with toll-free numbers, which use their buying power to get a better price on hotels, airline tickets, even car rentals. When booking a room, always **call the hotel's local toll-free number** (if one is available) rather than the central reservations number—you'll often get a better price. Always ask about special packages or corporate rates.

When shopping for the best deal on hotels and car rentals, **look for guaranteed exchange rates,** which protect you against a falling dollar. With your rate locked in, you won't pay more, even if the price goes up in the local currency.

➤ AIRLINE TICKETS: ☎ 800/AIR–4LESS.

➤ HOTEL ROOMS: **Hotel Reservations Network** (☎ 800/964–6835, WEB www.hoteldiscount.com). **Players Express Vacations** (☎ 800/458–6161, WEB www.playersexpress.com). **Steigenberger Reservation Service** (☎ 800/223–5652, WEB www.srs-worldhotels.com). **Turbotrip.com** (☎ 800/473–7829, WEB www.turbotrip.com). **VacationLand** (☎ 800/245–0050, WEB www.vacation-land.com).

PACKAGE DEALS

Don't confuse packages and guided tours. When you buy a package, you travel on your own, just as though you had planned the trip yourself.

ELECTRICITY

To use electric-powered equipment purchased in the United States or Canada, **bring a converter and adapter.** The electrical current in Japan is 100 volts, 50 cycles alternating current (AC) in eastern Japan, and 100 volts, 60 cycles in western Japan; the United States runs on 110-volt, 60-cycle AC current. Wall outlets in Japan accept plugs with two flat prongs, like in the United States, but do not accept U.S. three-prong plugs.

If your appliances are dual-voltage, you'll need only an adapter. Don't use 110-volt outlets marked FOR SHAVERS ONLY for high-wattage appliances such as blow-dryers. Most laptops operate equally well on 110 and 220 volts and so require only an adapter.

EMBASSIES

➤ AUSTRALIA: **Australian Embassy and Consulate** (✉ 2–1–14 Mita, Minato-ku, Tōkyō, ☎ 03/5232–4111), open weekdays 9–noon and 1:30–5.

➤ CANADA: **Canadian Embassy and Consulate** (✉ 7–3–38 Akasaka, Minato-ku, Tōkyō, ☎ 03/5412–

6200), open weekdays 9–12:30 and 1:30–5:30.

➤ NEW ZEALAND: **New Zealand Embassy** (✉ 20–40 Kamiyama-chō, Shibuya-ku, Tōkyō, ☎ 03/3467–2270), open weekdays 9–12:30 and 1:30–5:30.

➤ UNITED KINGDOM: **British Embassy and Consulate** (✉ 1 Ichiban-chō, Chiyoda-ku, Tōkyō, ☎ 03/3265–5511), embassy open weekdays 9–12:30 and and 2–5:30, consulate weekdays 9–11 and 2–4.

➤ UNITED STATES: **U.S. Embassy and Consulate** (✉ 1–10–5 Akasaka, Minato-ku, Tōkyō, ☎ 03/3224–5000), embassy open weekdays 8:30–12:30 and 2–5:30, consulate weekdays 8:30–12:30 and 2–4.

EMERGENCIES

Assistance in English is available 24 hours a day on the toll-free Japan Helpline.

➤ CONTACTS: **Ambulance and Fire** (☎ 119). **Japan Helpline** (☎ 0120/461–997). **Police** (☎ 110).

ENGLISH-LANGUAGE MEDIA

NEWSPAPERS & MAGAZINES

The *Daily Yomiuri,* an English-language sibling of the *Yomiuri Shimbun;* the *Japan Times;* a daily English-language newspaper; and the *International Herald Tribune* are reliable for national and international news coverage, as well as for entertainment reviews and listings. They're available at newsstands and in bookstores that carry English-language books, and both Japanese papers have Web sites (☞ *below*)—handy if you want to brush up on current events before your trip.

ETIQUETTE & BEHAVIOR

Propriety is an important part of Japanese society. Many Japanese expect foreigners to behave differently and are tolerant of faux pas, but they are pleasantly surprised when people acknowledge and observe their customs. The easiest way to ingratiate yourself with the Japanese is to **take time to learn and respect Japanese ways.**

It is customary to **bow upon meeting someone.** The art of bowing is not simple; the depth of your bow depends on your social position in respect to that of the other person. Younger people, or those of lesser status, must bow deeper in order to indicate their respect and acknowledge their position. You're not expected to understand the complexity of these rules, and a basic nod of the head will suffice. Many Japanese are familiar with Western customs and will offer a hand for a handshake.

Don't be offended if you're not invited to someone's home. Most entertaining among Japanese is done in restaurants or bars. It's an honor when you are invited to a home; this means your host feels comfortable and close to you. If you do receive an invitation, bring along a small gift—a souvenir from your country makes the best present, but food and liquor or anything that can be consumed (and not take up space in the home) is also appreciated. Upon entering a home, **remove your shoes in the foyer and put on the slippers that are provided**; in Japan shoes are for wearing outdoors only. Be sure your socks or stockings are in good condition.

Japanese restaurants often provide a small hot towel called an *oshibori.* This is to wipe your hands but not your face. You may see some Japanese wiping their faces with their oshibori, but sometimes this is considered to be bad form. If you must use your oshibori to remove forehead perspiration, wipe your face first, then your hands. When you are finished with your oshibori, do not just toss it back onto the table, but fold or roll it up. If you're not accustomed to eating with chopsticks, ask for a fork instead. When taking food from a shared dish, do not use the part of the chopsticks that has entered your mouth to pick up a morsel. Instead, use the end that you have been holding in your hand. Never leave your chopsticks sticking upright in your food; this is how rice offerings at funerals are arranged. Instead, rest chopsticks on the edge of the tray, bowl, or plate between bites and at the end of the meal. For more information on dining etiquette, refer to The Discreet Charm of Japanese Cuisine *in* Chapter 14.

BUSINESS ETIQUETTE

Although many business practices are universal, certain customs remain unique to Japan. It's not necessary to observe these precepts, but the Japanese always appreciate it if you do.

In Japan, *meishi* (business cards) are mandatory. Upon meeting someone for the first time, it is common to bow and to proffer your business card simultaneously. Although English will suffice on your business card, it's best to have one side printed in Japanese (there are outfits in Japan that provide this service in 24 hours). In a sense, the cards are simply a convenience. Japanese sometimes have difficulty with Western names, and referring to the cards is helpful. Also, in a society where hierarchy matters, Japanese like to know job titles and rank, so it's useful if your card indicates your position in your company. Japanese often place the business cards they have received in front of them on a table or desk as they conduct their meetings. Follow suit and do not simply shove the card in your pocket.

The concept of being fashionably late does not exist in Japan; it is extremely important to **be prompt for both social and business occasions.** Japanese addresses tend to be complicated (☞ Addresses, *above*), and traffic is often heavy, so allow for adequate travel time. Most Japanese are not accustomed to using first names in business circumstances. Even coworkers of 20 years' standing use surnames. Unless you are sure that the Japanese person is extremely comfortable with Western customs, it is best to **stick to last names and use the honorific word -san after the name,** as in *Tanaka-san* (Mr. or Mrs. Tanaka). Also, respect the hierarchy, and as much as possible address yourself to the most senior person in the room.

Don't be frustrated if decisions are not made instantly. Rarely empowered to make decisions, individual businesspeople must confer with their colleagues and superiors. Even if you are annoyed, **don't express anger or aggression.** Losing one's temper is equated with losing face in Japan.

A separation of business and private lives remains sacrosanct in Japan, and it is best not to ask about personal matters. Rather than asking about a person's family, it is better to **stick to neutral subjects in conversation.** This does not mean that you can only comment on the weather but rather that you should take care not to be nosy.

Because of cramped housing, again, many Japanese entertain in restaurants or bars. It is not customary for Japanese businessmen to bring wives along. If you are traveling with your spouse, do not assume that an invitation includes both of you. You may ask if it is acceptable to bring your spouse along, but remember that it is awkward for a Japanese person to say no. You should pose the question carefully, such as "Will your [wife or husband] come along, too?" This eliminates the need for a direct, personal refusal.

Usually, entertaining is done over dinner, followed by an evening on the town. Drinking is something of a national pastime in Japan. If you would rather not suffer from a hangover the next day, do not refuse your drink—sip, but keep your glass at least half full. Because the custom is for companions to pour drinks for each other, an empty glass is nearly the equivalent of requesting another drink. Whatever you do, **don't pour your own drink, and if a glass at your table happens to be empty, show your attentiveness by filling it for your companion.**

A special note to women traveling on business in Japan: remember that although the situation is gradually changing, many Japanese women do not have careers. Many Japanese businessmen do not yet know how to interact with Western businesswomen. They may be uncomfortable, aloof, or patronizing. Be patient and, if the need arises, gently remind them that, professionally, you expect to be treated as any man would be.

GAY & LESBIAN TRAVEL

It is no small feat to orient yourself as a gay or lesbian traveler to Japan's gay nightlife. Forget about gay restaurants, cafés, even bookstores that sell more than "adult" books. A few words about the Japanese attitude toward homosexuality will help you in Japan. Because Japan does not have the religious opposition to homosexuality that the West does, the major barrier that continues to suppress gay lifestyle in Japan is the Confucian duty to continue the family line, to bring no shame to the family, and to fit into Japanese society. So gay and lesbian travelers aren't likely to stumble upon many establishments that cater to a gay clientele.

There *are* bars, karaoke lounges, discos, "snacks" (a type of bar), hostess bars, host bars, and drag king/queen bars—the trick is finding them. Even the gay district of Tōkyō, Shinjuku 2-chōme (a 15-minute walk west of Shinjuku Station) leaves you wondering if you've found the place. When you get there, look for people who live in the area, particularly Westerners, and approach them. The Japanese would never broach the subject except, perhaps, at the end of a night of drinking. In fact, it is a bad idea to broach the subject with a Japanese: It will cause much awkwardness, and the response will be nowhere near as sophisticated as it has become in the West. All of this said, homosexuality (as an interest but not a life choice) is more accepted in the realm of human expression than it is in the West. This may sound quite discouraging, but in actuality, Japan can prove to be an outlet of immense freedom for gays if you are successful in making friends in Tōkyō, the Kansai area (Kyōto–Ōsaka–Kōbe), and Hiroshima.

International Gay Friends is a gay meeting group in Tōkyō. Occur Help Line sets aside different days of the month for women and men. *Out in Japan* magazine is available at Tower Records in Tōkyō.

➤ CONTACTS & INFORMATION: International Gay Friends (☎ 03/5693–4569). Occur Help Line (☎ 03/3380–2269).

➤ GAY- & LESBIAN-FRIENDLY TRAVEL AGENCIES: **Different Roads Travel** (✉ 8383 Wilshire Blvd., Suite 902, Beverly Hills, CA 90211, ☎ 323/651–5557 or 800/429–8747, FAX 323/651–3678, lgernert@tzell.com). **Kennedy Travel** (✉ 314 Jericho Turnpike, Floral Park, NY 11001, ☎ 516/352–4888 or 800/237–7433, FAX 516/354–8849, WEB www.kennedytravel.com). **Now Voyager** (✉ 4406 18th St., San Francisco, CA 94114, ☎ 415/626–1169 or 800/255–6951, FAX 415/626–8626, www.nowvoyager.com). **Skylink Travel and Tour** (✉ 1006 Mendocino Ave., Santa Rosa, CA 95401, ☎ 707/546–9888 or 800/225–5759, FAX 707/546–9891, WEB www.skylinktravel.com), serving lesbian travelers.

GUIDEBOOKS

Plan well and you won't be sorry. Guidebooks are excellent tools—and you can take them with you. You may want to check out color-photo-illustrated *Fodor's Exploring Japan*, thorough on culture and history, and pocket-size *Citypack Tokyo,* which includes a foldout map. Both are available at on-line retailers and bookstores everywhere.

HEALTH

Tap water everywhere is safe in Japan. It may be difficult to buy the standard over-the-counter remedies you're used to, so it's best to bring with you any medications (in their proper packaging) you may need. Medical treatment varies from highly skilled and professional treatment at major hospitals to somewhat less advanced procedures in small neighborhood clinics. At larger hospitals you have a good chance of encountering English-speaking doctors who have been partly educated in the West.

HOLIDAYS

As elsewhere, peak times for travel in Japan tend to fall around holiday periods. You'll want to avoid traveling during the few days before and after New Year's; during Golden Week, which follows Greenery Day (April 29); and in mid-July and mid-August, at the time of Obon festivals, when many Japanese return to their hometowns (Obon festivals are celebrated July or August 13–16, depending on the location). Note that when a holiday falls on a Sunday, the following Monday is a holiday. *See* also Festivals and National Holidays, *below.*

January 1 (*Ganjitsu,* New Year's Day); the second Monday in January (*Senjin-no-hi,* Coming of Age Day); February 11 (*Kenkoku Kinen-no-bi,* National Foundation Day); March 20 or 21 (*Shumbun-no-hi,* Vernal Equinox); April 29 (*Midori-no-hi,* Greenery Day); May 3 (*Kempo Kinen-bi,* Constitution Day); May 5 (*Kodomo-no-hi,* Children's Day); September 15 (*Keiro-no-hi,* Respect for the Aged Day); September 23 or 24 (*Shubun-no-hi,* Autumnal Equinox); the second Monday in October (*Taiiku-no-hi,* Sports Day); November 3 (*Bunka-no-hi,* Culture Day); November 23 (*Kinro Kansha-no-hi,* Labor Thanksgiving Day); December 23 (*Tennō Tanjobi,* Emperor's Birthday).

INSURANCE

The most useful travel-insurance plan is a comprehensive policy that includes coverage for trip cancellation and interruption, default, trip delay, and medical expenses (with a waiver for preexisting conditions).

Without insurance you will lose all or most of your money if you cancel your trip, regardless of the reason. Default insurance covers you if your tour operator, airline, or cruise line goes out of business. Trip-delay covers expenses that arise because of bad weather or mechanical delays. Study the fine print when comparing policies.

If you're traveling internationally, a key component of travel insurance is coverage for medical bills incurred if you get sick on the road. Such expenses are not generally covered by Medicare or private policies. U.K. residents can buy a travel-insurance policy valid for most vacations taken during the year in which it's purchased (but check preexisting-condition coverage). British and Australian citizens need extra medical coverage when traveling overseas.

Always **buy travel policies directl** **from the insurance company**; if buy them from a cruise line, airline, or tour operator that goes out of business you probably will not be covered for the agency or operator's default, a major risk. Before making any purchase, **review your existing health and home-owner's policies** to find what they cover away from home.

➤ TRAVEL INSURERS: In the United States: **Access America** (✉ 6600 W. Broad St., Richmond, VA 23230, ☎ 800/284–8300, FAX 804/673–1491, WEB www.etravelprotection.com), **Travel Guard International** (✉ 1145 Clark St., Stevens Point, WI 54481, ☎ 715/345–0505 or 800/826–1300, FAX 800/955–8785, WEB www.travelguard.com).

➤ INSURANCE INFORMATION: In the United Kingdom: **Association of British Insurers** (✉ 51–55 Gresham St., London EC2V 7HQ, U.K., ☎ 020/7600–3333, FAX 020/7696–8999, WEB www.abi.org.uk). In Canada: **RBC Travel Insurance** (✉ 6880 Financial Dr., Mississauga, Ontario L5N 7Y5, Canada, ☎ 905/791–8700, 800/668–4342 in Canada, FAX 905/816–2498, WEB www.royalbank.com). In Australia: **Insurance Council of Australia** (✉ Level 3, 56 Pitt St., Sydney NSW 2000, ☎ 02/9253–5100, FAX 02/9253–5111, WEB www.ica.com.au). In New Zealand: **Insurance Council of New Zealand** (✉ Level 7, 111–115 Customhouse Quay, Box 474, Wellington, New Zealand, ☎ 04/472–5230, FAX 04/473–3011, WEB www.icnz.org.nz).

LANGUAGE

Communicating in Japan can be a challenge. This is not because the Japanese don't speak English but because most of us know little, if any, Japanese. Take some time before you leave home to **learn a few basic words,** such as where (*doko*), what time (*nan-ji*), bathroom (*o-te-arai*), thank you (*arigatō gozaimasu*), excuse me (*sumimasen*), and please (*onegai shimasu*).

English is a required subject in Japanese schools, so most Japanese study English for nearly a decade. This does not mean everyone *speaks* English. Schools emphasize reading, writing, and grammar. As a result, many Japanese can read English but can speak only a few basic phrases. Furthermore, when asked, "Do you speak English?" many Japanese, out of modesty, say no, even if they do understand and speak a fair amount of it. It is usually best to simply ask what you really want to know slowly, clearly, and as simply as possible. If the person you ask understands, he or she will answer or perhaps take you where you need to go.

Although a local may understand your simple question, he or she cannot always give you an answer that requires complicated instructions. For example, you may ask someone on the subway how to get to a particular stop, and he may direct you to the train across the platform and then say something in Japanese that you do not understand. You may discover too late that the train runs express to the suburbs after the third stop; the person who gave you directions was trying to tell you to switch trains at the third stop. To avoid this kind of trouble, **ask more than one person for directions every step of the way.** You can avoid that trip to the suburbs if you ask someone *on* the train how to get to where you want to go. Also, remember that politeness is a matter of course in Japan and that the Japanese won't want to lose face by saying that they don't know how to get somewhere. If the situation gets confusing, **bow, say *arigatō goza-imashita* ("thank you" in the past tense), and ask someone else.** Even though you are communicating on a very basic level, misunderstandings can happen easily.

Traveling in Japan can be problematic if you don't read Japanese. Before you leave home, **buy a phrase book** that shows English, English transliterations of Japanese (*romaji*), and Japanese characters (*kanji* and *kana*). You can read the romaji to pick up a few Japanese words and match the kanji and kana in the phrase book with characters on signs and menus. When all else fails, ask for help by pointing to the Japanese words in your book.

Learning Japanese is a major commitment. Japanese writing alone consists of three character systems: kanji, characters borrowed and adapted from China centuries ago, which represent ideas; and two forms of kana—*hiragana* and *katakana*—which represent sounds. Hiragana is used to write some Japanese words, verb inflections, and adjectives; katakana is used for foreign words, slang expressions, and technical terms. There are two sets of 47 kana and more than 6,000 kanji, although most Japanese use fewer than 1,000 kanji. This is obviously more than a tourist can learn in a short stay, so you'll probably find yourself scanning your surroundings for romaji, which are easier to interpret.

The most common system of writing Japanese words in Roman letters is the modified Hepburn system, which spells out Japanese words phonetically and is followed in this book.

For information on pronouncing Japanese words, notes on how Japanese words are rendered in this guide, and a list of useful words and phrases, *see* An English-Japanese Traveler's Vocabulary *in* Chapter 14.

Note: There is some disagreement over the use of gaijin (literally, "outside person") as opposed to *gai-koku-jin* (literally, "outside country person") because the former has negative echoes of the days of Japanese isolationism. In the 17th and 18th centuries, when the Japanese had contact only with Dutch traders, Westerners were called *buttā-kusai* (literally, "stinking of butter")—obviously a derogatory term. Gaikoku-jin, on the other hand, has a softer, more polite meaning, and many Westerners in Japan prefer it because it has no xenophobic taint.

Gaijin is used to translate the word *foreigner* throughout this guide for two reasons. First, it is commonly used in books written by Westerners who have lived in Japan, and as such it has wider recognition value. Second, as Japan becomes more global—especially its younger generation—gaijin is losing its negative sense. Many Japanese use gaijin as the one word they know to describe non-

Japanese and most often mean no offense by it.

So if children giggle and point at the *gaijin-san*, know that it is meant with only the kindest fascination. And if you feel that extra politeness is appropriate, use gai-koku-jin with colleagues whom you respect—or with whomever might be using gaijin a bit too derogatorily.

CHAPTER GLOSSARIES

At the beginning of each chapter is a glossary of words that appear elsewhere in the chapter untranslated. Getting to know these Japanese words will help you if you need to ask directions from a non-English speaker. Even among Japanese who know English, using Japanese words whenever possible—*eki*, for example, which means train station—makes getting around that much easier.

LODGING

Overnight accommodations in Japan run from luxury hotels to *ryokan* (traditional inns) to youth hostels and even capsules (☞ Hotels, *below*). Western-style rooms with Western-style bathrooms are widely available in large cities, but in smaller, out-of-the-way towns it may be necessary to stay in a Japanese-style room—an experience that can only enhance your stay.

The lodgings we list are the cream of the crop in each price category. We always list the facilities that are available—but we don't specify whether they cost extra: when pricing accommodations, always ask what's included and what costs extra. Properties indicated by an ✕⛉ are lodging establishments whose restaurant warrants a special trip.

LODGING PRICES

Outside cities and major towns, most lodgings quote prices on a per-person basis with two meals, exclusive of service and tax. If you do not want dinner at your hotel, it is usually possible to renegotiate the price. Stipulate, too, whether you wish to have Japanese or Western breakfasts, if any. When you make reservations at a noncity hotel, you are usually expected to take breakfast and dinner at the hotel—this is the rate quoted to you unless you specify otherwise.

Assume that hotels operate on the **European Plan** (EP, with no meals) unless we specify that they use the **Continental Plan** (CP, with a Continental breakfast), **Modified American Plan** (MAP, with breakfast and dinner), or the **Full American Plan** (FAP, with all meals).

APARTMENT & VILLA RENTALS

If you want a home base that's roomy enough for a family and comes with cooking facilities, **consider a furnished rental.** These can save you money, especially if you're traveling with a group. Home-exchange directories sometimes list rentals as well as exchanges.

In addition to the agents listed below, English language-newspapers and magazines, such as the *Hiragana Times, Tokyo Journal,* or *Tokyo Classified,* or the *City-Source English Telephone Directory* may be helpful in locating a rental property.

➤ INTERNATIONAL AGENT: **Property Rentals International** (✉ 1008 Mansfield Crossing Rd., Richmond, VA 23236 USA, ☎ 804/378–6054 or 800/220–3332, FAX 804/379–2073).

➤ LOCAL AGENTS: **Tsukasa Weekly/ Monthly Mansion** (✉ 6–4–14 Koyama, Shinagawa-ku, Tōkyō 142-0062, ☎ 03/3784–0631 or 03/3440–0111, FAX 03/3784–1167; ✉ 1–3–2 Tokui-machi, Chūō-ku, Ōsaka 540-0025, ☎ 06/6949–4471, FAX 06/6942–9373; Japanese guarantor required).

HOME VISITS

Through the home visit system, travelers can get a sense of domestic life in Japan by visiting a local family in their home. The program is voluntary on the home owner's part, and there is no charge for a visit. The system is active in many cities throughout the country, including Tōkyō, Yokohama, Nagoya, Kyōto, Ōsaka, Hiroshima, Nagasaki, and Sapporo. To make a reservation, **apply in writing for a home visit at least a day in advance** to the local tourist information office of the place you are visiting. Contact the Japan

urist Organization (☞
...mation, *below*) before
...apan for more informa-
...program.

No matter what your age, you can **save on lodging costs by staying at hostels.** In some 4,500 locations in more than 70 countries around the world, Hostelling International (HI), the umbrella group for a number of national youth-hostel associations, offers single-sex, dorm-style beds and, at many hostels, rooms for couples and family accommodations. Membership in any HI national hostel association, open to travelers of all ages, allows you to stay in HI-affiliated hostels at member rates; one-year membership is about $25 for adults (C$26.75 in Canada, £9.30 in the United Kingdom, $30 in Australia, and $30 in New Zealand); hostels run about ¥3,000–¥4,000 per night. Members have priority if the hostel is full; they're also eligible for discounts around the world, even on rail and bus travel in some countries.

➤ ORGANIZATIONS: **Hostelling International—American Youth Hostels** (✉ 733 15th St. NW, Suite 840, Washington, DC 20005, ☎ 202/783–6161, FAX 202/783–6171, WEB www.hiayh.org). **Hostelling International—Canada** (✉ 400–205 Catherine St., Ottawa, Ontario K2P 1C3, Canada, ☎ 613/237–7884; 800/663–5777 in Canada, FAX 613/237–7868, WEB www.hostellingintl.ca). **Japan Youth Hostels, Inc.** (✉ Suido-bashi Nishiguchi Kaikan, 2–20–7 Misaki-chō, Chiyoda-ku, Tōkyō 101–0061, ☎ 03/3288–1417). **Youth Hostel Association Australia** (✉ 10 Mallett St., Camperdown, NSW 2050, Australia, ☎ 02/9565–1699, FAX 02/9565–1325, WEB www.yha.com.au). **Youth Hostel Association of England and Wales** (✉ Trevelyan House, 8 St. Stephen's Hill, St. Albans, Hertfordshire AL1 2DY, U.K., ☎ 0870/8708808, FAX 01727/844126, WEB www.yha.org.uk). **Youth Hostels Association of New Zealand** (✉ Level 3, 193 Cashel St., Box 436, Christchurch, New Zealand, ☎ 03/379–9970, FAX 03/365–4476, WEB www.yha.org.nz).

HOTELS

Full-service, first-class hotels in Japan resemble their counterparts all over the world, and because many of the staff members speak English, these are the easiest places for foreigners to stay. They are also among the most expensive.

Business hotels are a reasonable alternative. These are clean, impersonal, and functional. All have Western-style rooms that vary from small to minuscule; service is minimal. However, every room has a private bathroom, albeit cramped, with tub and handheld shower, television (with Japanese-language channels), telephone, and a hot-water thermos. Business hotels are often conveniently located near the railway station. The staff may not speak English, and there is usually no room service.

Designed to accommodate the modern Japanese urbanite, the capsule hotel is a novel idea. The rooms are a mere 3½ ft wide, 3½ ft high, and 7¼ ft long. They have an alarm clock, television, and phone, and little else. Capsules are often used by commuters who have had an evening of excess and cannot make the long journey home. Although you may want to try sleeping in a capsule, you probably won't want to spend a week in one.

All hotels listed have private bath unless otherwise noted.

➤ TOLL-FREE NUMBERS: **Best Western** (☎ 800/528–1234, WEB www.bestwestern.com). **Choice** (☎ 800/221–2222, WEB www.choicehotels.com). **Clarion** (☎ 800/252–7466, WEB www.clarionhotel.com). **Comfort** (☎ 800/228–5150, WEB www.comfortinn.com). **Hilton** (☎ 800/445–8667, WEB www.hilton.com). **Holiday Inn** (☎ 800/465–4329, WEB www.basshotels.com). **Hyatt Hotels & Resorts** (☎ 800/233–1234, WEB www.hyatt.com). **Inter-Continental** (☎ 800/327–0200, WEB www.interconti.com). **Marriott** (☎ 800/228–9290, WEB www.marriott.com). **Nikko Hotels International** (☎ 800/645–5687, WEB www.nikkohotels.com). **Radisson** (☎ 800/333–3333, WEB www.radisson.com). **Renaissance Hotels & Resorts** (☎ 800/468–3571,

WEB www.renaissancehotels.com/).
Ritz-Carlton (☎ 800/241–3333,
WEB www.ritzcarlton.com). **Sheraton**
(☎ 800/325–3535, WEB www.
starwoodhotels.com). **Westin Hotels
& Resorts** (☎ 800/228–3000,
WEB www.westin.com).

INEXPENSIVE ACCOMMODATIONS

JNTO publishes a listing of some 200
accommodations that are reasonably
priced. To be listed, properties must
meet Japanese fire codes and charge
less than ¥8,000 per person without
meals. For the most part, the properties charge ¥5,000–¥6,000. These
properties welcome foreigners (many
Japanese hotels and ryokan do not
like to have foreign guests because
they might not be familiar with tradi-
tional-inn etiquette). Properties include business hotels, *ryokan* (☞
below) of a very rudimentary nature,
minshuku (☞ *below*), and pensions.
It's the luck of the draw whether you
choose a good or less-than-good
property. In most cases rooms are
clean but very small. Except in business hotels, shared baths are the
norm, and you are expected to have
your room lights out by 10 PM.

Many establishments on the list of
reasonably priced accommodations—
and many that are not on the list—can
be reserved through the nonprofit
organization **Welcome Inn Reservation
Center.** Reservation forms are available from your nearest JNTO office
(☞ Visitor Information, *below*). The
Japanese Inn Group, which provides
reasonable accommodations for
foreign visitors, can be reserved
through this same service. The center
must receive reservation requests at
least one week before your departure
to allow processing time. If you are
already in Japan, JNTO's Tourist
Information Centers (TICs) at Narita
Airport, downtown Tōkyō, and Kyōto
can make immediate reservations for
you at these Welcome Inns.

➤ RESERVATIONS: **Welcome Inn
Reservation Center** (✉ Tōkyō
International Forum B1, 3–5–1
Marunouchi, Chiyoda-ku, Tōkyō
100–0005, ☎ 03/3211–4201,
FAX 03/3211–9009).

MINSHUKU

Minshuku are private homes that
accept guests. Usually they cost about
¥6,000 per person, including two
meals. Although in a ryokan you need
not lift a finger, don't be surprised if
you are expected to lay out and put
away your own bedding in a minshuku. Meals are often served in
communal dining rooms. Minshuku
vary in size and atmosphere; some are
private homes that take in only a few
guests, while others are more like no-
frill inns. Some of your most memorable stays could be at a minshuku, as
they offer a chance to become ac-
quainted with a Japanese family and
their hospitality.

➤ INFORMATION: **Japan Minshuku
Center** (✉ Tōkyō Kōtsū, Kaikan
Building, B1, 2–10–1 Yūrakuchō,
Chiyoda-ku, Tōkyō, ☎ 03/3216–
6556, FAX 03/3216–6557,
WEB www.minshuku.co.jp).

RYOKAN

If you want to sample the Japanese
way, **spend at least one night in a
ryokan (inn).** Usually small, one- or
two-story wooden structures with a
garden or scenic view, they provide
traditional Japanese accommodations:
simple rooms in which the bedding is
rolled out onto the floor at night.

Ryokan vary in price and quality.
Some older, long-established inns
cost as much as ¥80,000 per person,
whereas humbler places that are more
like bed-and-breakfasts are as low as
¥6,000. Prices are per person and
include the cost of breakfast, dinner,
and tax. Some inns allow you to stay
without having dinner and lower the
cost accordingly. However, this is not
recommended, because the service
and meals are part of the ryokan
experience.

It is important to **follow Japanese
customs in all ryokan.** Upon entering,
take off your shoes, as you would do
in a Japanese household, and put on
the slippers that are provided in the
entryway. A maid, after bowing to
welcome you, will escort you to your
room, which will have *tatami* (straw
mats) on the floor and will probably
be partitioned off with *shōji* (sliding
paper-paneled walls). Remove your
slippers before entering your room;

you should not step on the tatami with either shoes or slippers. The room will have little furniture or decoration—perhaps one small low table and cushions on the tatami, with a long, simple scroll on the wall. Often the rooms overlook a garden.

Plan to arrive in the late afternoon, as is the custom. After relaxing with a cup of green tea, have a long, hot bath. In ryokan with thermal pools, you can take to the waters anytime, although the doors to the pool are usually locked from 11 PM to 6 AM. In ryokan without thermal baths or private baths in guest rooms, guests must stagger visits to the one or two public baths. Typically the maid will ask what time you would like your bath and fit you into a schedule. In Japanese baths, washing and soaking are separate functions: wash and rinse off entirely, and then get in the tub. Be sure to keep all soap out of the tub. Because other guests will be using the same bathwater after you, it is important to observe this custom. After your bath, change into a *yukata*, a simple cotton kimono, provided in your room. Don't worry about walking around in what is essentially a robe—all other guests will be doing the same.

Dinner, included in the price, is served in your room at smaller and more personal ryokan; at larger ryokan, especially the newer ones, meals will be in the dining room. After you are finished, a maid will discreetly come in, clear away the dishes, and lay out your futon. In Japan *futon* means bedding, and this consists of a thin cotton mattress and a heavy, thick comforter. In summer the comforter is replaced with a thinner quilt. The small, hard pillow is filled with grain. The less expensive ryokan (under ¥7,000 for one) have become slightly lackadaisical in changing the sheet cover over the quilt with each new guest; feel free to complain (in as inoffensive a way as possible, of course, so as not to shame the proprietor). In the morning a maid will gently wake you, clear away the futon, and bring in your Japanese-style breakfast. If you are not fond of Japanese breakfasts, which often consist of fish, pickled vegetables, and rice, the staff will usually be able to rustle up some coffee and toast.

Because most ryokan staffs are small and dedicated, it is important to be considerate and understanding of their somewhat rigid schedules. Guests are expected to arrive in the late afternoon and eat around 6. Usually the doors to the inn are locked at 10, so plan for early evenings. Breakfast is served around 8, and checkout is at 10.

A genuine traditional ryokan with exemplary service is exorbitantly expensive—more than ¥30,000 per person per night with two meals. Many modern hotels with Japanese-style rooms are now referring to themselves as ryokan, and though meals may be served in the guests' rooms, they are a far cry from the traditional ryokan. There are also small inns claiming the status of ryokan, but they are really nothing more than bed-and-breakfast establishments where meals are taken in a communal dining room—for an additional fee—and service is minimal. In lesser-priced inns, which run from ¥5,000 for a single room to ¥7,000 for a double, tubs are likely to be plastic rather than cedarwood, and small rooms might overlook a street rather than a garden. Rooms have tatami straw mat floors, futon bedding, and a scroll and/or flower arrangement in its rightful place. JNTO offers a publication listing some of these.

Bear in mind that not all inns are willing to accept foreign guests because of language and cultural barriers. This makes calling ahead for a room important so you can be sure to get one. Also, top-level ryokan expect even new Japanese guests to have introductions and references from a respected client of the inn, which means that you, too, might need an introduction from a Japanese for very top-level ryokan. On the other side of this issue, inns that do accept foreigners without introduction sometimes treat them as cash cows, which means giving you cursory service and a lesser room. When you reserve a room, try to have a Japanese make the call for you, or you can do it yourself if you know Japanese; this will convey the idea that you understand the customs of staying in a traditional inn.

➤ INFORMATION: **Japan Ryokan Association** (✉ 1–8–3 Maru-no-uchi, Chiyoda-ku, Tōkyō, ☎ 03/3231–5310). **JNTO** (☞ Visitor Information, *below*).

TEMPLES

You can also arrange accommodations in Buddhist temples. JNTO has lists of temples that accept guests. A stay at a temple generally costs ¥3,000–¥9,000 per night, including two meals. Some temples offer instruction in meditation or allow you to observe their religious practices, while others simply offer a room. The Japanese-style rooms are very simple and range from beautiful, quiet havens to not-so-comfortable, basic cubicles. Either way, temples provide a taste of traditional Japan.

MAIL & SHIPPING

The Japanese postal service is very efficient. Air mail between Japan and the United States takes between five and eight days. Surface mail can take anywhere from four to eight weeks. Express service is also available through post offices.

Although numerous post offices exist in every city, it is probably best to **use the central post office near the main train station** because the workers speak English and can handle foreign mail. Some of the smaller post offices are not equipped to send packages. Post offices are open weekdays 9–5 and Saturday 9–noon. Some of the central post offices have longer hours, such as the one in Tōkyō, located near Tōkyō Eki (train station), which is open 24 hours year-round. Most hotels supply stamps and mail your letters and postcards, usually with no service fee.

The Japanese postal service has implemented use of three-numeral-plus-four postal codes, but its policy is similar to that in the United States regarding ZIP-plus-fours; that is, addresses with the three-numeral code will still arrive at its destination, albeit perhaps one or two days later. Mail to rural towns may take longer.

POSTAL RATES

It costs ¥110 to send a letter by air to North America and Europe. An airmail postcard costs ¥70. Aerograms cost ¥90.

RECEIVING MAIL

To get mail, **have parcels and letters sent "poste restante" at the central post office in major cities**; unclaimed mail is returned after 30 days.

MONEY MATTERS

Japan is expensive, but there are ways to cut costs. This requires, to some extent, an adventurous spirit and the courage to stray from the standard tourist paths. One good way to hold down expenses is to **avoid taxis** (they tend to get stuck in traffic anyway) and **try the inexpensive, efficient subway and bus systems**; instead of going to a restaurant with menus in English and Western-style food, go to places where you can rely on your good old index finger to point to the dish you want, and **try food that the Japanese eat** (☞ The Discreet Charm of Japanese Cuisine *in* Chapter 14).

A cup of coffee costs ¥350–¥600; a bottle of beer, ¥350–¥1,000; a 2-km (1-mi) taxi ride, ¥660; a McDonald's hamburger, ¥340; a bowl of noodles, ¥700; an average dinner, ¥2,500; a double room in Tōkyō, ¥11,000–¥45,000.

Prices throughout this guide are given for adults. Substantially reduced fees are almost always available for children, students, and senior citizens. For information on taxes, *see* Taxes, *below.*

ATMS

Some major branches of the post office in large cities like Tōkyō have ATMs that accept Visa, MasterCard, American Express, Diners Club, and Cirrus cards. Elsewhere, especially in more rural areas, it's difficult to find suitable ATMs.

CREDIT CARDS

MasterCard and Visa are the most widely accepted credit cards in Japan. Throughout this guide, the following abbreviations are used: **AE,** American Express; **DC,** Diners Club; **MC,** MasterCard; and **V,** Visa.

➤ REPORTING LOST CARDS: **American Express** (☎ 03/3220–6100). **Diners Club** (☎ 03/3499–1181). **Master-Card** (☎ 0031/113–886). **Visa** (☎ 0120/133–173).

CURRENCY

The unit of currency in Japan is the yen (¥). There are bills of ¥10,000, ¥5,000, ¥2,000, and ¥1,000. Coins are ¥500, ¥100, ¥50, ¥10, ¥5, and ¥1. Japanese currency floats on the international monetary exchange, so changes can be dramatic. Some vending machines will not accept the newly introduced ¥2,000 bill or the new version of the ¥500 coin, but these older machines are gradually being replaced. At press time the exchange rate was about ¥123 to the U.S. dollar, ¥77 to the Canadian dollar, and ¥175 to the pound sterling.

CURRENCY EXCHANGE

For the most favorable rates, **change money through banks.** Although ATM transaction fees may be higher abroad than at home, ATM rates are excellent because they are based on wholesale rates offered only by major banks. You won't do as well at exchange booths in airports or rail and bus stations, in hotels, in restaurants, or in stores. To avoid lines at airport exchange booths, **get a bit of local currency before you leave home.**

➤ EXCHANGE SERVICES: **International Currency Express** (☎ 888/278–6628 for orders, WEB www.foreignmoney. com). **Thomas Cook Currency Services** (☎ 800/287–7362 for telephone orders and retail locations, WEB www.us.thomascook.com).

TRAVELER'S CHECKS

Do you need traveler's checks? It depends on where you're headed. If you're going to rural areas and small towns, go with cash; traveler's checks are best used in cities. Even hotels in smaller cities will often cash them for guests, so long as the checks are in major currencies. Lost or stolen checks can usually be replaced within 24 hours. To ensure a speedy refund, buy your own traveler's checks—don't let someone else pay for them: irregularities like this can cause delays. The person who bought the checks should make the call to request a refund.

PACKING

Because porters can be hard to find and baggage restrictions on international flights are tight, **pack light.** What you pack depends more on the time of year than on any dress code. For travel in the cities, pack as you would for any American or European city. At more expensive restaurants and nightclubs, men usually need to wear a jacket and tie, and women need a dress or skirt. Wear conservative-color clothing at business meetings. Casual clothes are fine for sightseeing. Jeans are as popular in Japan as they are in the United States and are perfectly acceptable for informal dining and sightseeing.

Although there are no strict dress codes for visiting temples and shrines, you will be out of place in shorts or immodest outfits. For sightseeing leave sandals and open-toe shoes behind; you'll need sturdy walking shoes for the gravel pathways that surround temples and fill parks. Make sure to bring comfortable clothing that isn't too tight to wear in traditional Japanese restaurants, where you may need to sit on tatami-matted floors. For beach and mountain resorts pack informal clothes for both day and evening wear.

Japanese do not wear shoes in private homes or in any temples or traditional inns. Having shoes you can quickly slip in and out of is a decided advantage. Take some wool socks along to help you through those shoeless occasions during the winter.

If you're a morning coffee addict, **take along packets of instant coffee.** All lodgings provide a thermos of hot water and bags of green tea in every room, but for coffee you'll either have to call room service (which can be expensive) or buy very sweet coffee in a can from a vending machine. If you're staying in a Japanese inn, they probably won't have coffee, and it may be hard to find in rural areas.

Although sunglasses, sunscreen lotions, and hats are readily available, you're better off buying them at home, because they're much more expensive in Japan. It's a good idea to carry a couple of plastic bags to protect your camera and clothes during sudden cloudbursts.

Take along small gift items, such as scarves or perfume sachets, to thank hosts (on both business and pleasure trips), whether you've been invited to their home or out to a restaurant.

In your carry-on luggage, **pack an extra pair of eyeglasses or contact lenses and enough of any medication** you take to last the entire trip. You may also ask your doctor to write a spare prescription using the drug's generic name, since brand names may vary from country to country. In luggage to be checked, **never pack prescription drugs or valuables.** To avoid customs delays, carry medications in their original packaging. And don't forget to carry with you the addresses of offices that handle refunds of lost traveler's checks. Check *Fodor's How to Pack* (available in bookstores everywhere) for more tips.

CHECKING LUGGAGE

You are allowed one carry-on bag and one personal article, such as a purse or a laptop computer. Make sure that everything you carry on-board will fit under your seat or in the overhead bin. Get to the gate early, so you can board as soon as possible, before the overhead bins fill up.

If you are flying internationally, note that baggage allowances may be determined not by piece but by weight—generally 88 pounds (40 kilograms) in first class, 66 pounds (30 kilograms) in business class, and 44 pounds (20 kilograms) in economy.

Airline liability for baggage is limited to $1,250 per person on flights within the United States. On international flights it amounts to $9.07 per pound or $20 per kilogram for checked baggage (roughly $640 per 70-pound bag) and $400 per passenger for unchecked baggage. You can buy additional coverage at check-in for about $10 per $1,000 of coverage, but it excludes a rather extensive list of items, shown on your airline ticket.

Before departure, **itemize your bags' contents** and their worth, and label the bags with your name, address, and phone number. (If you use your home address, cover it so potential thieves can't see it readily.) Inside each bag, **pack a copy of your itinerary.** At check-in, **make sure that each bag is correctly tagged** with the destination airport's three-letter code. If your bags arrive damaged or fail to arrive at all, file a written report with the airline before leaving the airport.

PASSPORTS & VISAS

When traveling internationally, **carry your passport** even if you don't need one (it's always the best form of I.D.) and **make two photocopies of the data page** (one for someone at home and another for you, carried separately from your passport). If you lose your passport, promptly call the nearest embassy or consulate and the local police.

ENTERING JAPAN

Visitors from the United States, Canada, Great Britain, Australia, and New Zealand can enter Japan for up to 90 days with a valid passport; no visa is required.

PASSPORT OFFICES

The best time to apply for a passport or to renew is in fall and winter. Before any trip, check your passport's expiration date, and, if necessary, renew it as soon as possible.

➤ AUSTRALIAN CITIZENS: **Australian Passport Office** (☎ 131–232, WEB www.dfat.gov.au/passports).

➤ CANADIAN CITIZENS: **Passport Office** (☎ 819/994–3500; 800/567–6868 in Canada, WEB www.dfait-maeci.gc.ca/passport).

➤ NEW ZEALAND CITIZENS: **New Zealand Passport Office** (☎ 04/494–0700, WEB www.passports.govt.nz).

➤ U.K. CITIZENS: **London Passport Office** (☎ 0870/521–0410, WEB www.ukpa.gov.uk) for fees and documentation requirements and to request an emergency passport.

➤ U.S. CITIZENS: **National Passport Information Center** (☎ 900/225–5674; calls are 35¢ per minute for automated service, $1.05 per minute for operator service; WEB www.travel.state.gov/npicinfo.html).

REST ROOMS

The most hygienic rest rooms are found in hotels and department stores and are usually clearly marked with international symbols. You may encounter Japanese-style toilets, with bowls recessed into the floor, over which you squat facing the hood. This may take some getting used to, but it's completely sanitary as you don't come into direct contact with the facility.

In many homes and Japanese-style public places, there will be a pair of slippers at the entrance to the rest rooms. Change into these before entering the room, and change back when you exit.

SAFETY

Even in its major cities, Japan is a very safe country with one of the lowest crime rates in the world. You should **avoid Ura-Kabuki-chō in Tōkyō's Shinjuku district and some of the large public parks at nighttime.**

SENIOR-CITIZEN TRAVEL

Senior citizens often qualify for discounts at museums. To qualify for age-related discounts, **mention your senior-citizen status up front** when booking hotel reservations (not when checking out) and before you're seated in restaurants (not when paying the bill). When renting a car, ask about promotional car-rental discounts, which can be cheaper than senior-citizen rates.

➤ EDUCATIONAL PROGRAMS: **Elderhostel** (✉ 11 Ave. de Lafayette, Boston, MA 02111-1746, ☎ 877/426–8056, FAX 877/426–2166, WEB www.elderhostel.org). **Interhostel** (✉ University of New Hampshire, 6 Garrison Ave., Durham, NH 03824, ☎ 603/862–1147 or 800/733–9753, FAX 603/862–1113, WEB www.learn.unh.edu).

SHOPPING

Despite the high price of many goods, shopping is one of the great pleasures of a trip to Japan. You may not find terrific bargains here, but if you know where to go and what to look for, you can purchase unusual gifts and souvenirs at reasonable prices. In particular, **don't shop for items that are cheaper at home;** Japan is not the place to buy a Gucci bag. Electronics, too, are generally cheaper in the United States. Instead, **look for things that are Japanese made** for Japanese people and sold in stores that do not cater primarily to tourists.

Don't pass up the chance to purchase Japanese crafts. Color, balance of form, and absolutely superb craftsmanship make these items exquisite and well worth the price you'll pay. Some items can be quite expensive; for example, Japanese lacquerware carries a hefty price. But if you like the shiny boxes, bowls, cups, and trays and consider that quality lacquerware is made to last a lifetime, the cost is justified. Be careful, though: some lacquer items are made from a pressed-wood product rather than solid wood, and only experts can tell the difference. If the price seems low, it probably means the quality is low, too.

For more information on Japanese crafts, *see* Chapter 14.

SIGHTSEEING GUIDES

The Japan National Tourist Organization (JNTO) sponsors a Good-Will Guide program in which local citizens volunteer to show visitors around; this is a great way to meet Japanese people. These are not professional guides; they usually volunteer both because they enjoy welcoming foreigners to their town and because they want to practice their English. The services of Good-Will Guides are free, but you should pay for their travel costs, their admission fees, and any meals you eat with them while you are together. To participate in this program, **make arrangements for a Good-Will Guide in advance through JNTO** in the United States or through the tourist office in the area where you want the guide to meet you. The program operates in 75 towns and cities, including Tōkyō, Kyōto, Nara, Nagoya, Ōsaka, and Hiroshima.

STUDENTS IN JAPAN

➤ IDs & SERVICES: **Council Travel** (CIEE; ✉ 205 E. 42nd St., 15th floor,

New York, NY 10017, ☎ 212/822–2700 or 888/268–6245, ℻ 212/822–2699, WEB www.councilexchanges.org) for mail orders only, in the United States. **Travel Cuts** (✉ 187 College St., Toronto, Ontario M5T 1P7, Canada, ☎ 416/979–2406 or 800/667–2887 in Canada, ℻ 416/979–8167, WEB www.travelcuts.com).

TAXES

HOTEL

A 5% national consumption tax is added to all hotel bills. Another 3% local tax is added to the bill if it exceeds ¥15,000. You may **save money by paying for your hotel meals separately** rather than charging them to your bill.

At first-class, full-service, and luxury hotels, a 10% service charge is added to the bill in place of individual tipping. At the more expensive ryokan, where individualized maid service is offered, the service charge is usually 15%. At business hotels, minshuku, youth hostels, and economy inns, no service charge is added to the bill.

SALES

There is an across-the-board, nonrefundable 5% consumer tax levied on all sales. Since the tax was introduced in 1989, vendors have either been absorbing the tax in their quoted retail prices or adding it on to the sale. Before you make a major purchase, inquire if tax is extra. A 5% federal consumer tax is added to all restaurant bills. Another 3% local tax is added to the bill if it exceeds ¥7,500. At the more expensive restaurants, a 10%–15% service charge is added to the bill. Tipping is not customary.

TAXIS

Taxis are an expensive way of getting around cities in Japan. The first 2 km (1 mi) cost about ¥660, and it's ¥80 for every additional 280 meters (400 yards). If possible, avoid using taxis during rush hours (7:30 AM–9:30 AM and 5 PM–7 PM).

In general, it's easy to hail a cab: do not shout or wave wildly—simply **raise your hand if you need a taxi.** Japanese taxis have automatic door-opening systems, so **do not try to open the taxi door.** Stand back when the cab comes to a stop—if you are too close, the door may slam into you. When you leave the cab, do not try to close the door; the driver will do it automatically. Only the curbside rear door opens. A red light on the dashboard indicates an available taxi, and a green light indicates an occupied taxi.

Drivers are for the most part courteous, although sometimes they balk at the idea of a foreign passenger because they do not speak English. Unless you are going to a well-known destination such as a major hotel, it is advisable to **have a Japanese person write out your destination in Japanese.** Remember, there is no need to tip.

TELEPHONES

AREA & COUNTRY CODES

The country code for Japan is 81. When dialing a Japanese number from outside of Japan, drop the initial 0 from the local area code. The country code is 1 for the United States and Canada, 61 for Australia, 64 for New Zealand, and 44 for the United Kingdom.

DIRECTORY & OPERATOR ASSISTANCE

Operator assistance at 104 is in Japanese only. Weekdays 9–5 (except national holidays), English-speaking operators can help you at the toll-free NTT Information Customer Service Centre.

➤ CONTACTS: **Directory Assistance** (☎ 104). **NTT Information Customer Service Centre** (☎ 0120/364–463).

INTERNATIONAL CALLS

Many gray, multicolor, and green phones have gold plates indicating, in English, that they can be used for international calls. Three Japanese companies provide international service: KDDI (001), Japan Telecom (0041), and IDC (0061). Dial the company code + country code + city/area code and number of your party. KDD offers the clearest connection but is also the most expensive. Telephone credit cards are especially convenient for international calls. For operator assistance in English on long-distance calls, dial 0051.

LONG-DISTANCE SERVICES

AT&T, MCI, and Sprint access codes make calling long distance relatively convenient, but you may find the local access number blocked in many hotel rooms. First ask the hotel operator to connect you. If the hotel operator balks, ask for an international operator, or dial the international operator yourself. One way to improve your odds of getting connected to your long-distance carrier is to travel with more than one company's calling card (a hotel may block Sprint, for example, but not MCI). If all else fails, call from a pay phone.

➤ ACCESS CODES: For local access numbers abroad, contact one of the following: **AT&T Direct** (☎ 800/222–0300). **MCI WorldPhone** (☎ 800/444–4444). **Sprint International Access** (☎ 800/877–4646).

PUBLIC PHONES

Pay phones are one of the great delights of Japan. Not only are they conveniently located in hotels, restaurants, and on street corners, but at ¥10 for three minutes, they have to be one of the few remaining bargains in Japan.

Telephones come in various colors, including pink, red, and green. Most pink and red phones, for local calls, accept only ¥10 coins. Green and gray phones accept ¥10 and ¥100 coins as well as prepaid telephone cards. Domestic long-distance rates are reduced as much as 50% after 9 PM (40% after 7 PM). Green phones take coins and accept telephone cards—disposable cards of fixed value that you use up in increments of ¥10. Telephone cards, sold in vending machines, hotels, and a variety of stores, are tremendously convenient because you will not have to search for the correct change.

TIME

All of Japan is in the same time zone, 9 hours ahead of Greenwich Mean Time and 14 hours ahead of U.S. Eastern Standard Time. Daylight saving time is not observed.

TIPPING

Tipping is not common in Japan. It's not necessary to tip taxi drivers, or at hair salons, barbershops, bars, or nightclubs. A chauffeur for a hired car usually receives a tip of ¥500 for a half-day excursion and ¥1,000 for a full-day trip. Porters charge fees of ¥250–¥300 per bag at railroad stations and ¥200 per piece at airports. It's not customary to tip employees of hotels, even porters, unless a special service has been rendered. In such cases, a gratuity of ¥2,000 or ¥3,000 should be placed in an envelope and handed to the staff member discreetly.

TOURS & PACKAGES

Because everything is prearranged on a prepackaged tour or independent vacation, you spend less time planning—and often get it all at a good price.

BOOKING WITH AN AGENT

Travel agents are excellent resources. But it's a good idea to collect brochures from several agencies as some agents' suggestions may be influenced by relationships with tour and package firms that reward them for volume sales. If you have a special interest, **find an agent with expertise in that area**; the American Society of Travel Agents (ASTA; ☞ Travel Agencies, *below*) has a database of specialists worldwide.

Make sure your travel agent knows the accommodations and other services of the place being recommended. Ask about the hotel's location, room size, beds, and whether it has a pool, room service, or programs for children, if you care about these. Has your agent been there in person or sent others whom you can contact?

Do some homework on your own, too: local tourism boards can provide information about lesser-known and small-niche operators, some of which may sell only direct.

BUYER BEWARE

Each year consumers are stranded or lose their money when tour operators—even large ones with excellent reputations—go out of business. So **check out the operator.** Ask several travel agents about its reputation, and try to **book with a company that has a consumer-protection program.** (Look for information in the company's brochure.) In the United States, members of the National Tour Association and the United States Tour Operators Association are required to set aside funds to cover your payments and travel arrangements in the event that the company defaults. It's also a good idea to choose a company that participates in the American Society of Travel Agents' Tour Operator Program (TOP); ASTA will act as mediator in any disputes between you and your tour operator.

Remember that the more your package or tour includes the better you can predict the ultimate cost of your vacation. Make sure you know exactly what is covered, and **beware of hidden costs.** Are taxes, tips, and transfers included? Entertainment and excursions? These can add up.

➤ TOUR-OPERATOR RECOMMENDA-TIONS: **American Society of Travel Agents** (☞ Travel Agencies, *below*). **National Tour Association** (NTA; ✉ 546 E. Main St., Lexington, KY 40508, ☎ 859/226–4444 or 800/682–8886, WEB www.ntaonline.com). **United States Tour Operators Association** (USTOA; ✉ 342 Madison Ave., Suite 1522, New York, NY 10173, ☎ 212/599–6599 or 800/468–7862, FAX 212/599–6744, WEB www.ustoa.com).

TRAIN TRAVEL

Riding Japanese trains is one of the pleasures of travel in the country. Efficient and convenient, trains run frequently and on schedule. The Shinkansen (bullet train), one of the fastest trains in the world, connects major cities north and south of Tōkyō. It is only slightly less expensive than flying but is in many ways more convenient because train stations are more centrally located than airports (and, if you have a Japan Rail Pass [☞ Cutting Costs, *below*], it's extremely affordable). On the main line that runs west from Tōkyō, there are three types of Shinkansen. The *Nozomi* makes the fewest stops, which can cut as much as an hour from long, cross-country trips; it is the only Shinkansen on which you cannot use a JR Pass. The *Hikari* makes just a few more stops than the

Nozomi. The *Kodama* is the equivalent of a Shinkansen local, making all stops along the Shinkansen lines. The same principal of faster and slower Shinkansen also applies on the line that runs north from Tōkyō to Morioka, in the Tōkyō region.

Other trains, though not as fast as the Shinkansen, are just as convenient and substantially cheaper. There are three types of train services: *futsū* (local service), *tokkyū* (limited express service), and *kyūkō* (express service). Both the tokkyū and the kyūkō offer a first-class compartment known as the Green Car.

Because there are no porters or carts at train stations, and the flights of stairs connecting train platforms can turn even the lightest bag into a heavy burden, it's a good idea to **travel light when getting around by train.** Savvy travelers often have their main luggage sent ahead to a hotel that they plan to reach later in their wanderings. It's also good to know that every train station, however small, has luggage lockers, which cost about ¥300 for 24 hours.

CUTTING COSTS

If you plan to travel by rail, **get a Japan Rail Pass,** which offers unlimited travel on Japan Railways (JR) trains. You can purchase one-, two-, or three-week passes. A one-week pass is less expensive than a regular round-trip ticket from Tōkyō to Kyōto on the Shinkansen. You must **obtain a rail pass voucher prior to departure for Japan** (you cannot buy them in Japan), and the pass must be used within three months of purchase. The pass is available only to people with tourist visas, as opposed to business, student, and diplomatic visas.

When you arrive in Japan, you must exchange your voucher for the Japan Rail Pass. You can do this at the Japan Railways desk in the arrivals hall at Narita Airport or at the JR stations of major cities. When you make this exchange, you determine the day that you want the rail pass to begin, and, accordingly, when it ends. You do not have to begin travel on the day you make the exchange; instead, **pick the starting date to maximize use.** The Japan Rail Pass allows you to travel on all JR-operated trains (which cover most destinations in Japan) but not lines owned by other companies.

The JR Pass is also valid on buses operated by Japan Railways (☞ Bus Travel, *above*). You can make seat reservations without paying a fee on all trains that have reserved-seat coaches, usually the long-distance trains. The Japan Rail Pass does not cover the cost of sleeping compartments on overnight trains (called blue trains), nor does it cover the newest and fastest of the Shinkansen trains, the *Nozomi*, which make only one or two stops on longer runs. The pass covers only the *Hikari* Shinkansen, which make a couple more stops than the *Nozomi*, and the *Kodama* Shinkansen, which stop at every station along the Shinkansen routes.

Japan Rail Passes are available in coach class and first class (Green Car), but most people find that coach class is more than adequate. A one-week pass costs ¥28,300 coach class, ¥37,800 first class; a two-week pass costs ¥45,100 coach class, ¥61,200 first class; and a three-week pass costs ¥57,700 coach class, ¥79,600 first class. Travelers under 18 pay lower rates. The pass pays for itself after one Tōkyō–Kyōto round-trip Shinkansen ride. Contact a travel agent or Japan Airlines to purchase the pass.

➤ INFORMATION: **Japan Railways Group** (✉ 1 Rockefeller Plaza, Suite 1622, New York, NY 10020, ☎ 212/332–8686, FAX 212/332–8690).

➤ BUYING A PASS: **Japan Airlines** (JAL; ✉ 655 5th Ave., New York, NY 10022 USA, ☎ 212/838–4400). **Japan Travel Bureau** (JTB; ✉ 810 7th Ave., 34th floor, New York, NY 10019, ☎ 212/698–4900 or 800/223–6104). **Nippon Travel Agency** (NTA; ✉ 111 Pavonia Ave., Suite 317, Jersey City, NJ 07310, ☎ 201/420–6000 or 800/682–7872).

FARES & SCHEDULES

➤ TRAIN INFORMATION: **JR Hotline** English-language information service (☎ 03/3423–0111), open weekdays 10–6.

RESERVATIONS

Many travelers assume that rail passes guarantee them seats on the trains they wish to ride. Not so. If you're using a rail pass, there's no need to buy individual tickets, but you should **book seats ahead.** This guarantees you a seat and is also a useful reference for the times of train departures and arrivals. You can reserve up to two weeks in advance or just minutes before the train departs. If you fail to make a train, there is no penalty, and you can reserve again.

Seat reservations for any JR route may be made at any JR station except those in the tiniest villages. The reservation windows or offices, *midori-no-madoguchi*, have green signs in English and green-stripe windows. If you're traveling without a Japan Rail Pass, there's a surcharge of approximately ¥500 (depending upon distance traveled) for seat reservations, and if you miss the train, you'll have to pay for another reservation. When making your seat reservation, you may request a no-smoking or smoking car. Your reservation ticket shows the date and departure time of your train as well as your car and seat number. On the platform you can figure out where to wait for a particular train car. Notice the markings painted on the platform or on little signs above the platform; ask someone which markings correspond to car numbers. If you don't have a reservation, ask which cars are unreserved. Sleeping berths, even with a rail pass, are additional. Unreserved tickets can be purchased at regular ticket windows. There are no reservations made on local service trains. For traveling short distances, tickets are usually sold at vending machines. A platform ticket is required if you go through the wicket gate onto the platform to meet someone coming off a train. The charge is ¥140 (in Tōkyō and Ōsaka, the tickets are ¥130).

Most clerks at train stations know a few basic words of English and can read roman script. Moreover, they are invariably helpful in plotting your route. The complete railway timetable is a mammoth book written only in Japanese; however, you can **get an English-language train schedule from** the **Japan National Tourist Organiza-tion** (JNTO; ☞ Visitor Information, *below*) that covers the Shinkansen and a few of the major JR Limited Express trains. JNTO's booklet *The Tourist's Handbook* provides helpful information about purchasing tickets in Japan.

TRAVEL AGENCIES

A good travel agent puts your needs first. Look for an agency that has been in business at least five years, empha-sizes customer service, and has some-one on staff who specializes in your destination. In addition, **make sure the agency belongs to a professional trade organization.** The American Society of Travel Agents (ASTA)—the largest and most influential in the field with more than 26,000 members in some 170 countries—maintains and enforces a strict code of ethics and will step in to help mediate any agent-client disputes if necessary. ASTA (whose motto is "Without a travel agent, you're on your own") also maintains a Web site that includes a directory of agents. (If a travel agency is also acting as your tour operator, *see* Buyer Beware *in* Tours & Pack-ages, *above*.)

➤ LOCAL AGENT REFERRALS: **Ameri-can Society of Travel Agents** (ASTA; ⊠ 1101 King St., Suite 200, Alexan-dria, VA 22314, ☎ 800/965–2782 24-hr hot line, ℻ 703/739–7642, ᗯ웹 www.astanet.com). **Association of British Travel Agents** (⊠ 68–71 Newman St., London W1T 3AH, ☎ 020/7637–2444, ℻ 020/7637–0713, ᗯ웹 www.abtanet.com). **Association of Canadian Travel Agents** (⊠ 130 Albert St., Suite 1705, Ottawa, On-tario K1P 5G4, ☎ 613/237–3657, ℻ 613/237–7052, ᗯ웹 www.acta.net). **Australian Federation of Travel Agents** (⊠ Level 3, 309 Pitt St., Sydney NSW 2000, ☎ 02/9264–3299, ℻ 02/9264–1085, ᗯ웹 www.afta.com.au). **Travel Agents' Associa-tion of New Zealand** (⊠ Level 5, Paxus House, 79 Boulcott St., Box 1888, Wellington 10033, ☎ 04/499–0104, ℻ 04/499–0827, ᗯ웹 www.taanz.org.nz).

VISITOR INFORMATION

For information before you go, contact the Japan National Tourist Organiza-tion (JNTO). You may also want to check out their Web site at www.jnto.go.jp. When you get there, call or stop by one of the Tourist Informa-tion Centers (TIC) for information on western or eastern Japan and use the Japan Travel Phone (daily 9–5); for recorded information 24 hours a day, call the Teletourist service.

➤ JAPAN NATIONAL TOURIST ORGANI-ZATION (JNTO): **Canada:** (⊠ 165 University Ave., Toronto, Ontario M5H 3B8, ☎ 416/366–7140). **Japan:** (⊠ 2–10–1 Yūrakuchō 1-chōme, Chiyoda-ku, Tōkyō, ☎ 03/3502–1461; ⊠ Kyōto Tower Bldg., Higashi-Shiokoji-chō, Shimogyo-ku, Kyōto, ☎ 075/371–5649). **United Kingdom:** (⊠ Heathcoat House, 20 Savile Row, London W1X 1AE, ☎ 020/7734–9638). **United States:** (⊠ 1 Rocke-feller Plaza, Suite 1250, New York, NY 10020, ☎ 212/757–5640; ⊠ 401 N. Michigan Ave., Suite 770, Chicago, IL 60611, ☎ 312/222–0874; ⊠ 1 Daniel Burnham Court, San Francisco, CA 94109, ☎ 415/292–5686; ⊠ 515 S. Figueroa St., Suite 1470, Los Angeles, CA 90071, ☎ 213/623–1952).

➤ JAPAN TRAVEL PHONE: **Throughout Japan** (☎ 0088/22–4800 throughout Japan outside of Tōkyō and Kyōto; 03/3201–3331 in Tōkyō; 075/371–5649 in Kyōto).

➤ TELETOURIST SERVICE: **Tōkyō** (☎ 03/3201–2911).

➤ TOURIST INFORMATION CENTERS (TIC): ⊠ Tōkyō International Forum B1, 3–5–1 Marunouchi, Chiyoda-ku, Tōkyō, ☎ 03/3201–3331; ⊠ Main Terminal Bldg., Narita Airport, Chiba Prefecture, ☎ 0476/34–6251; ⊠ Kyōto Tower Bldg., Shichijo-Karamasu Sagaru, Shimogyo-ku, Kyōto, ☎ 075/371–5649; ⊠ Kansai International Airport, Ōsaka, ☎ 0724/56–6025.

➤ U.S. GOVERNMENT ADVISORIES: **U.S. Department of State** (⊠ Over-seas Citizens Services Office, Room 4811 N.S., 2201 C St. NW, Washing-ton, DC 20520, ☎ 202/647–5225 for interactive hot line, ᗯ웹 http://travel.state.gov/travel/html); enclose a self-addressed, stamped, business-size envelope.

WEB SITES

Do check out the World Wide Web when planning your trip. You'll find everything from weather forecasts to virtual tours of famous cities. Be sure to **visit Fodors.com** (www.fodors. com), a complete travel-planning site. You can research prices and book plane tickets, hotel rooms, rental cars, vacation packages, and more. In addition, you can post your pressing questions in the Travel Talk section. Other planning tools include a currency converter and weather reports, and there are loads of links to travel resources.

Cultural resources and travel-planning tools abound for the cybertraveler to Japan. Good first stops include the Web sites of Japan's two major English-language daily newspapers, the *Daily Yomiuri* and the *Japan Times*. For travel updates, visit the Web site of the Japan National Tourist Office (JNTO). You'll also find a links page, which connects you to an amusing if random assortment of sites that somehow relate to Japan.

Tokyo Classified and *Tokyo Journal,* slick on-line magazines for the English expat community in Tōkyō, will catch you up on the latest goings-on in the capital city. Both have up-to-date arts, events, and dining listings.

On-line resources abound for information on traveling by public transportation. Visit Business Insight Japan's invaluable "Expert on Travel Planner." You enter the town from which you're departing and your destination, and the planner presents you with the travel time, fare, and distance for all possible routes. Japan Rail's sites are handy planning tools as well, and provide fare and ticket information. Both the JR East and the JR West sites will direct you to detailed information about the Japan Rail Pass (☞ Train Travel, *above*). For local info, RATP, the French rail-transit authority, maintains a useful subway navigator, which includes the subway systems in Tōkyō and Sapporo.

On the Web site of the Japan City Hotel Association, you can search member hotels by location and price and make reservations on-line. Japan Economy Hotels Reservation Service, Inc., is another on-line lodging resource.

Japanese-Online is a series of on-line language lessons that will help you pick up a bit of Japanese before your trip. (The site also, inexplicably, includes a sampling of typical Japanese junior high school math problems.) Kabuki for Everyone provides a comprehensive and accessible introduction to the dramatic form; on the site you'll find video clips of Kabuki performances, summaries of major plays, an audio archive of Kabuki sounds, and a bibliography for further reading. Finally, for fun, stop by the Web site of Tōkyō's Tsukiji Central Wholesale Market—where else can you see tunas as big as cars on-line?

➤ URLs: **Business Insight Japan** (WEB www.businessinsightjapan.com). *Daily Yomiuri* (WEB www.yomiuri. co.jp/index-e.htm). **Japan City Hotel Association** (WEB jcha.yadojozu.ne.jp/ english/index.htm). **Japan Economy Hotels Reservation Service, Inc.** (WEB www.inn-info.co.jp/english/ home.html). **Japan National Tourist Office** (WEB www.jnto.go.jp). **Japan Rail East** (WEB www.jreast.co.jp/e). **Japan Rail West** (WEB www.westjr.co. jp/kou/english/index.html). *Japan Times* (WEB www.japantimes.co.jp). **Japanese-Online** (WEB www.japanese-online.com). **Kabuki for Everyone** (WEB www.fix.co.jp/kabuki/kabuki. html). **RATP Subway Navigator** (WEB www.subwaynavigator.com). *Tokyo Classified* (WEB www.tokyoclassified. com). *Tokyo Journal* (WEB www. tokyo.to/index.html).**Tsukiji Central Wholesale Market** (WEB www. tsukiji-market.or.jp/tukijiže.htm).

WHEN TO GO

The best seasons to travel to Japan are spring and fall, when the weather is at its best. In the spring, the country is warm, with only occasional showers, and flowers grace landscapes in both rural and urban areas. The first harbingers of spring are plum blossoms in early March; *sakura* (cherry blossoms) follow, beginning in Kyūshū and usually arriving in Tōkyō by mid-April. Summer brings on the rainy season, with particularly heavy rains and humidity in July. Fall is a welcome relief, with clear blue skies and glorious foliage. Occasionally a few surprise typhoons occur in early fall, but the storms are usually as quick to leave as they are to arrive. Winter is gray and chilly, with little snow in most areas. Temperatures rarely fall below freezing.

For the most part, the climate of Japan is temperate and resembles that of the east coast of the United States. The exceptions are the subtropical southern islands of Okinawa, south of Kyūshū, and the northern island of Hokkaidō, where it snows for several months in the winter and is pleasantly cool in the summer.

To avoid crowds, **do not plan a trip for times when most Japanese are vacationing.** For the most part, Japanese cannot select when they want to take their vacations; they tend to do so on the same holiday dates. As a result, airports, planes, trains, and hotels are booked far in advance. Many businesses, shops, and restaurants are closed during these holidays. Holiday periods include the few days before and after New Year's; Golden Week, which follows Greenery Day (April 29); and mid-August at the time of the Obon festivals, when many Japanese return to their hometowns.

CLIMATE

The following is a list of average daily maximum and minimum temperatures for major cities in Japan.

➤ FORECASTS: **Weather Channel Connection** (☎ 900/932–8437), 95¢ per minute from a Touch-Tone phone.

TŌKYŌ

Jan.	46F	8C	**May**	72F	22C	**Sept.**	78F	26C
	29	− 2		53	12		66	19
Feb.	48F	9C	**June**	75F	24C	**Oct.**	70F	21C
	30	− 1		62	17		56	13
Mar.	53F	12C	**July**	82F	28C	**Nov.**	60F	16C
	35	2		70	21		42	6
Apr.	62F	17C	**Aug.**	86F	30C	**Dec.**	51F	11C
	46	8		72	22		33	1

KYŌTO

Jan.	48F	9C	**May**	75F	24C	**Sept.**	82F	28C
	35	2		56	13		68	20
Feb.	53F	12C	**June**	82F	28C	**Oct.**	74F	23C
	32	0		66	19		53	12
Mar.	59F	15C	**July**	93F	34C	**Nov.**	62F	17C
	40	4		72	22		46	8
Apr.	65F	18C	**Aug.**	89F	32C	**Dec.**	53F	12C
	44	7		74	23		33	1

FUKUOKA

Jan.	53F	12C	**May**	74F	23C	**Sept.**	80F	27C
	35	2		57	14		68	20
Feb.	58F	14C	**June**	80F	27C	**Oct.**	74F	23C
	37	3		68	20		53	12
Mar.	60F	16C	**July**	89F	32C	**Nov.**	65F	18C
	42	6		75	24		48	9
Apr.	62F	17C	**Aug.**	89F	32C	**Dec.**	53F	12C
	48	9		75	24		37	3

SAPPORO

Jan.	29F	– 2C	May	60F	16C	Sept.	72F	22C
	10	–12		40	4		51	11
Feb.	30F	– 1C	June	70F	21C	Oct.	60F	16C
	13	11		50	10		40	4
Mar.	35F	2C	July	75F	24C	Nov.	46F	8C
	20	– 7		57	14		29	– 2
Apr.	51F	11C	Aug.	78F	26C	Dec.	33F	1C
	32	0		60	16		18	– 8

FESTIVALS AND NATIONAL HOLIDAYS

Matsuri (festivals) are very important to the Japanese, and a large number are held throughout the year. Many of them originated in folk and religious rituals and date back hundreds of years. Gala matsuri take place annually at Buddhist temples and Shintō shrines, and many are associated with the changing of the seasons. Most are free of charge and attract thousands of visitors as well as locals. For the big three festivals of Kyōto (the Gion, Jidai, and Aoi festivals), hotel bookings should be made well in advance. That said, the same applies to almost all holiday times in Japan, whether nationally or locally.

Many of the matsuri below are elaborated upon in the relevant chapters of this guide, especially when local history is involved. To find out specific matsuri dates, contact the Japan National Tourism Organization (☞ Visitor Information, *below*).

When national holidays fall on Sunday, they are celebrated on the following Monday. Museums and sights are often closed the days after these holidays.

➤ JAN. 1: **New Year's Day**, along with the days preceding and following, is the festival of festivals for the Japanese. Some women dress in traditional kimonos, and many people visit shrines and hold family reunions. Although the day is solemn, streets are often decorated with pine twigs, plum branches, and bamboo stalks.

➤ 2ND MON. OF JAN.: **Adults' Day** honors those who have reached the voting age of 20.

➤ FEB.: During the first week more than 300 pieces of ice sculpture, some huge, populate the **Sapporo Snow Festival**, bringing some 2 million people to the city to see them. Asahikawa's **Ice Festival** is a smaller counterpart to Sapporo's, with more of a country-fair atmosphere.

➤ FEB. 11: **National Foundation Day** celebrates accession to the throne by the first emperor.

➤ FEB. 13–15: Akita (in Tōhoku) City's **Namahage Sedo Festival** enacts in public a ritual from nearby Oga of threatening "good-for-nothings": men in demon masks carrying buckets and huge knives issue dire warnings to loafers.

➤ MAR. 21 (OR 20): **Vernal Equinox Day** celebrates the start of spring.

➤ APR. 14–15: Takayama's **Sannō Festival** transforms this sleepy time machine of a town into a rowdy party.

➤ APR. 29: Greenery Day marks the first day of **Golden Week**—when many Japanese take vacations, and hotels, trains, and attractions are booked solid. This is *not* a good time to visit Japan.

➤ MAY 2–5: Nanao's 400-year-old **Seihakusai Festival** enlivens the rustic Noto Peninsula fishing town with three days and nights of pulling huge 10-ton floats called *deka-yama* through the streets amid much all-night revelry.

➤ MAY 3: **Constitution Memorial Day** commemorates the adoption of the Japanese constitution.

➤ MAY 5: On **Children's Day** families with little boys display paper or cloth carp on bamboo poles outside the house or a set of warrior dolls inside the home.

➤ MAY 15: Dating to the 6th century, the **Aoi Festival**, also known as the

Hollyhock Festival, is the first of Kyōto's three most popular celebrations. An "imperial" procession of 300 courtiers starts from the Imperial Palace and makes its way to Shimogamo Jinja to pray for the prosperity of the city. Today's participants are local Kyōtoites.

➤ 3RD WEEKEND OF MAY: The **Sanja Festival,** held at Tōkyō's Asakusa Jinja, is the city's biggest party. Men, often naked to the waist, carry palanquins through the streets amid revelers. Many of these bare bearers bear the tattoos of the Yakuza, Japan's Mafia.

➤ JUNE: On Miyajima near Hiroshima, the lunar calendar determines the timing of three stately barges' crossing of the bay to the island's shrine for the **Kangen-sai Festival.** During the first weekend in June, **Yosakoi Soran Festival** explodes with 41,000 noisy and colorful dancers on the streets of Sapporo. Based on a blending of Koichi's Yosako dance festival and Hokkaido's fishing folk-song Soranbushi, the festival has 30 venues in the city.

➤ JUNE 13–15: **Hyaku-man-goku** means the rice needed to feed one for a year, and Kanazawa's festival of the same name commemorates the city's rich rice-growing history with celebrations with floating lanterns, an amazing variety of parades, and a great deal of merrymaking.

➤ JULY 16–17: The **Gion Festival,** which dates to the 9th century, is perhaps Kyōto's most popular festival. Twenty-nine huge floats sail along downtown streets and make their way to Yasaka Jinja to thank the gods for protection from a pestilence that once ravaged the city.

➤ JULY 20: A recent addition to the calendar, **Umi no hi** (Marine Day) marks the start of school summer holidays.

➤ JULY 24–25: Ōsaka's **Tenjin Festival** is a major event, with parades of floats, nighttime fireworks, and processions of 100-plus lighted vessels on the city's canals.

➤ AUG.: The first week's dreamlike **Neputa Festival,** held in the Tōhoku city of Hirosaki, involves nightly processions of floats, populated with illuminated paintings of faces from mythology, through the streets.

➤ 1ST SAT. IN AUG.: At Noto Peninsula's **Ishizaki Hoto Festival** celebration, paper lanterns more than 6 ft tall are carried on the shoulders of townfolk, who open their houses to all guests for one night of lavish feasting and drinking.

➤ AUG. 3–7: The **Nebuta Festival** in northern Tōhoku's Aomori noisily celebrates an ancient battle victory with a nighttime parade of illuminated floats.

➤ AUG. 5–7: At Yamagata's **Hanagasa Festival,** in southern Tōhoku, celebrants dance through the streets in local costume among floats. Food and drink are on hand for spectators.

➤ AUG. 6–8: Sendai's **Tanabata** celebrates two legendary astrological lovers with a theatrical rendition of their tale, and city residents decorate their streets and houses with colorful paper and bamboo streamers.

➤ AUG. 13–16: During the **Obon Festival,** a time of Buddhist ceremonies in honor of ancestors, many Japanese take off the entire week to travel to their hometowns—try to avoid travel on these days.

➤ AUG. 16: For the **Daimonji Gozan Okuribi,** huge bonfires in the shape of kanji characters illuminate five of the mountains that surround Kyōto. The most famous is the *Dai,* meaning "big," on the side of Mt. Daimonji in Higashiyama (Kyōto's eastern district). Dress in a cool yukata (cotton robe) and walk down to the banks of the Kamo-gawa to view this spectacular summer sight, or catch all five fires from the rooftop of your hotel downtown or a spot in Funaokayama or Yoshida-yama parks. There are Bon dances as well as the floating of lanterns in Arashiyama (the western district).

➤ AUG.: Another loud Tōkyō blowout, the **Kanda Festival,** which takes place in odd-numbered years, is all about taking the Kanda shrine's gods out for some fresh air in their *mikoshi* (portable shrines)—not to mention drinking plenty of beer and having a great time.

➤ SEPT. 15: **Keiro-no-hi** (Respect for the Aged Day).

➤ SEPT. 23 (OR 24): **Shubun-no-hi** (Autumnal Equinox Day).

➤ 2ND MON. OF OCT.: **Health-Sports Day** commemorates the Tōkyō Olympics of 1964.

➤ OCT. 22: Kyōto's **Jidai Festival**, the Festival of Eras, features a colorful costume procession of fashions from the 8th through 19th century. The procession begins at the Imperial Palace and winds up at Heian Jinja. More than 2,000 Kyōtoites voluntarily participate in this festival, which dates to 1895.

➤ OCT. 22: The **Kurama Fire Festival**, at Kurama Shrine, involves a roaring bonfire and a rowdy portable shrine procession that makes its way through the narrow streets of the small village in the northern suburbs of Kyōto. If you catch a spark, it is believed to bring good luck.

➤ NOV. 3: **Culture Day**, a fairly new holiday, encourages the Japanese to cherish peace, freedom, and culture, both old and new.

➤ NOV. 23: **Kinro Kansha-no-hi** (Labor Thanksgiving Day) is recognized by harvest celebrations in some parts of the country.

➤ DEC. 23: **Tennō Tanjobi** (Emperor's Birthday).

➤ DEC. 27: Travel is *not* recommended on the first day of the weeklong **New Year** celebrations.

WORDS AND PHRASES

Japanese sounds and spellings differ in principle from those of the West. We build words letter by letter, and one letter can sound different depending where it appears in a word. For example, we see *ta* as two letters, and *ta* could be pronounced three ways, as in *tat, tall,* and *tale.* For the Japanese, *ta* is one character, and it is pronounced one way: *tah.*

The *hiragana* and *katakana* (tables of sounds) are the rough equivalents of our alphabet. There are four types of syllables within these tables: the single vowels *a, i, u, e,* and *o,* in that order; vowel-consonant pairs like *ka, ni, hu,* or *ro;* the single consonant *n,* which punctuates the upbeats of the word for bullet train, *Shinkansen* (*shee*-n-*ka*-n-*se*-n); and compounds like *kya, chu,* and *ryo.* Remember that these compounds are one syllable. Thus Tōkyō, the capital city, has only two syllables—*tō* and *kyō*—not three. Likewise pronounce Kyōtō *kyō-tō,* not *kee-oh-to.*

Japanese vowels are pronounced as follows: *a*–ah, *i*–ee, *u*–oo, *e*–eh, *o*–oh. The Japanese *r* is rolled so that it sounds like a bounced *d.*

No diphthongs. Paired vowels in Japanese words are not slurred together, as in our words *coin, brain,* or *stein.* The Japanese separate them, as in *mae* (*ma*-eh), whch means in front of; *kōen* (*ko*-en), which means park; *byōin* (*byo*-een), which means hospital; and *tokei* (to-*keh*-ee), which means clock or watch.

Macrons. Many Japanese words, when rendered in *romaji* (roman letters), require macrons over vowels to indicate correct pronunciation, as in Tōkyō. When you see these macrons, double the length of the vowel, as if you're saying it twice: *to-o-kyo-o.* Likewise, when you see double consonants, as in the city name Nikkō, linger on the Ks—as in "bookkeeper"—and on the O.

Emphasis. Some books state that the Japanese emphasize all syllables in their words equally. This is not true. Take the words *sayōnara* and *Hiroshima.* Americans are likely to stress the downbeats: sa-yo-*na*-ra and hi-ro-*shi*-ma. The Japanese actually emphasize the second beat in each case: sa-*yō*-na-ra (note the macron) and hi-*ro*-shi-ma. Metaphorically speaking, the Japanese don't so much stress syllables as pause over them or race past them: Emphasis is more a question of speed than weight. In the vocabulary below, we indicate emphasis by italicizing the syllable that you should stress.

Three interesting pronunciations are in the vocabulary below. The word *desu* roughly means "is." It looks like it has two syllables, but the Japanese race past the final *u* and just say "dess." Likewise, some verbs end in -*masu,* which is pronounced "mahss." Similarly, the character *shi* is often quickly pronounced "sh," as in the phrase meaning "pleased to meet you:" *ha*-ji-me-*mash(i)*-te. Just like *desu* and -*masu,* what look like two syllables, in this case *ma* and *shi,* are pronounced *mahsh.*

Hyphens. Throughout *Fodor's Japan,* we have hyphenated certain words to help you recognize meaningful patterns. This isn't conventional; it is practical. For example, *Eki-mae-dōri,* which literally means "Station Front Avenue," turns into a blur when rendered Ekimaedōri. And in the Kyōto chapter, where you'll run across a number of sight names that end in -*jingū* or -*jinja* or -*taisha,* you'll soon catch on to their meaning: Shintō shrine.

Chapter glossaries. In the same spirit, we have added glossaries to each chapter to signal important words that appear in the city or region in question. From studying the Japanese language, we have found that knowing these few words and suffixes adds meaning to reading about Japan and makes asking directions from Japanese people a whole lot more productive.

Basics 基本的表現

Yes/No	*ha-i/ii*-e	はい／いいえ
Please	o-ne-*gai* shi-masu	お願いします
Thank you (very much)	(*dō*-mo) a-*ri*-ga-to go-*zai*-ma su	(どうも)ありがとう ございます
You're welcome	*dō* i-ta-shi-ma-shi-te	どういたしまして
Excuse me	su-mi-ma-*sen*	すみません
Sorry	*go*-men na-*sai*	ごめんなさい
Good morning	o-*ha*-yō go-zai-ma-su	お早うございます
Good day/afternoon	kon-*ni*-chi-wa	こんにちは
Good evening	kom-*ban*-wa	こんばんは
Good night	o-*ya*-su-mi na-*sai*	おやすみなさい
Goodbye	sa-yō-na-ra	さようなら
Mr./Mrs./Miss	-san	一さん
Pleased to meet you	*ha*-ji-me-*mashi*-te	はじめまして
How do you do?	*dō*-zo yo-*ro*-shi-ku	どうぞよろしく

Numbers 数

The first reading is used for reading numbers, as in telephone numbers, and the second is often used for counting things.

1	*i*-chi / hi-*to*-tsu	一／一つ	17	*jū*-shi-chi	十七
2	ni / fu-*ta*-tsu	二／二つ	18	*jū*-ha-chi	十八
3	san / *mit*-tsu	三／三つ	19	*jū*-kyū	十九
4	shi / *yot*-tsu	四／四つ	20	*ni*-jū	二十
5	go / i-*tsu*-tsu	五／五つ	21	*ni*-jū-i-chi	二十一
6	ro-ku / *mut*-tsu	六／六つ	30	*san*-jū	三十
7	*na*-na / *na*-na-tsu	七／七つ	40	yon-jū	四十
8	*ha*-chi / *yat*-tsu	八／八つ	50	go-jū	五十
9	kyū / *ko*-ko-no-*tsu*	九／九つ	60	*ro*-ku-*jū*	六十
10	jū / tō	十／十	70	na-na-jū	七十
11	*jū*-i-chi	十一	80	*ha*-chi-jū	八十
12	*jū*-ni	十二	90	kyū-jū	九十
13	*jū*-san	十三	100	*hya*-ku	百
14	*jū*-yon	十四	1000	sen	千
15	*jū*-go	十五	10,000	*i*-chi-man	一万
16	*jū*-ro-ku	十六	100,000	*jū*-man	十万

Days of the Week 曜日

Sunday	*ni*-chi yō-bi	日曜日
Monday	*ge*-tsu yō-bi	月曜日
Tuesday	*ka* yō-bi	火曜日
Wednesday	*su*-i yō-bi	水曜日
Thursday	*mo*-ku yō-bi	木曜日
Friday	*kin* yō-bi	金曜日
Saturday	*dō* yō-bi	土曜日
Weekday	hei-ji-tsu	平日
Weekend	Shū-ma-tsu	週末

Months 月

January	*i*-chi *ga*-tsu	一月
February	*ni* ga-tsu	二月
March	*san* ga-tsu	三月
April	*shi* ga-tsu	四月
May	*go* ga-tsu	五月
June	*ro*-ku *ga*-tsu	六月
July	*shi*-chi *ga*-tsu	七月
August	*ha*-chi *ga*-tsu	八月
September	*ku* ga-tsu	九月
October	*jū* ga-tsu	十月
November	*jū*-i-chi *ga*-tsu	十一月
December	*jū*-ni *ga*-tsu	十二月

Useful Expressions, Questions, and Answers   よく使われる表現

Do you speak English?	*ei*-go ga wa-*ka*-ri-ma-su *ka*	英語が。 わかりますか
I don't speak Japanese.	*ni*-hon-go ga wa-*ka*-ri-ma-*sen*	日本語が わかりません。
I don't understand.	wa-*ka*-ri-ma-*sen*	わかりません。
I understand.	wa-*ka*-ri-ma-shi-*ta*	わかりました。
I don't know.	*shi*-ri-ma-*sen*	知りません。
I'm American (British).	wa-*ta*-shi wa a-*me*-ri-ka (i-*gi*-ri-su) jin *desu*	私はアメリカ （イギリス）人です。
What's your name?	o-*na*-ma-e wa *nan* desu *ka*	お名前は何ですか。
My name is . . .	. . . to *mo*-shi-*ma*-su	…..と申します。
What time is it?	*i*-ma *nan*-ji desu *ka*	今何時ですか。
How?	*dō* yat-te	どうやって。
When?	*i*-tsu	いつ。
Yesterday/today/ tomorrow	ki-*nō*/kyō/*ashi*-ta	きのう／きょう／ あした
This morning	*ke*-sa	けさ
This afternoon	*kyō* no *go*-go	きょうの午後
Tonight	*kom*-ban	こんばん
Excuse me, what?	su-*mi*-ma-*sen*, *nan* desu *ka*	すみません、 何ですか。
What is this/that?	*ko*-re/*so*-re wa *nan* desu *ka*	これ／ それは何ですか。
Why?	*na*-ze desu *ka*	なぜですか。
Who?	*da*-re desu *ka*	だれですか。
I am lost.	*mi*-chi ni ma-yo-i-*mash*-ta	道に迷いました。
Where is [place]	[place] wa *do*-ko desu *ka*	…..はどこですか。
Train station?	e-ki	駅
Subway station?	chi-*ka*-te-tsu-no eki	地下鉄の駅
Bus stop?	*ba*-su *no*-ri-*ba*	バス乗り場
Taxi stand?	*ta*-ku-shi-i *no*-ri-*ba*	タクシー乗り場
Airport?	kū-kō	空港

Post office?	yū-bin-kyo-ku	郵便局
Bank?	gin-kō	銀行
the [name] hotel?	[name] ho-te-ru	ホテル
Elevator?	e-re-bē-tā	エレベーター
Where are the restrooms?	to-i-re wa do-ko desu ka	トイレは どこですか。
Here/there/over there	ko-ko/so-ko/a-so-ko	ここ／そこ／あそこ
Left/right	hi-da-ri/mi-gi	左／右
Straight ahead	mas-su-gu	まっすぐ
Is it near (far)?	chi-ka-i (to-i) desu ka	近い (遠い) ですか。
Are there any rooms?	he-ya ga a-ri-masu ka	部屋がありますか。
I'd like [item]	[item] ga ho-shi-i no desu ga	…..がほしいの ですが。
Newspaper	shim-bun	新聞
Stamp	kit-te	切手
Key	ka-gi	鍵
I'd like to buy [item]	[item] o kai-ta-i no desu ke do	…..を買いたいの ですけど。
a ticket to [event]	[event] ma-de no kip-pu	…..までの切符
Map	chi-zu	地図
How much is it?	i-ku-ra desu ka	いくらですか。
It's expensive (cheap).	ta-ka-i (ya-su-i) de su ne	高い (安い) ですね。
A little (a lot)	su-ko-shi (ta-ku-san)	少し (たくさん)
More/less	mot-to o-ku/ su-ku-na-ku	もっと多く／少なく
Enough/too much	jū-bun/o-su-gi-ru	十分／多すぎる
I'd like to exchange ...	... ryō-ga e shi-te i-ta-da-ke-masu ka	…..両替して 頂けますか。
dollars to yen	do-ru o en ni	ドルを円に
pounds to yen	pon-do o en ni	ポンドを円に
How do you say ... in Japanese?	ni-hon-go de ... wa dō i-i-masu ka	日本語で…..は どう言いますか。
I am ill/sick.	wa-ta-shi wa byō-ki desu	私は病気です。
Please call a doctor.	i-sha o yon-de ku-da-sa-i	医者を呼んで 下さい。
Please call the police.	ke-i-sa-tsu o yon-de ku-da-sa-i	警察を 呼んで下さい。
Help!	ta-su-ke-te	助けて！

Restaurants　レストラン

Basics and Useful Expressions　よく使われる表現

A bottle of ...	... ip-pon	…..一本
A glass/cup of ...	... ip-pai	…..一杯
Ashtray	ha-i-za-ra	灰皿
Plate	sa-ra	皿
Bill/check	kan-jō	かんじょう

Bread	pan	パン
Breakfast	*chō*-sho-ku	朝食
Butter	ba-*tā*	バター
Cheers!	kam-*pai*	乾杯！
Chopsticks	*ha*-shi	箸
Cocktail	*ka*-ku-te-ru	カクテル
Dinner Does that include...	yū-sho-ku *ga tsu-ki-ma-su-ka*	夕食が付きますか。
Excuse me!	su-mi-ma-*sen*	すみません
Fork	*fō*-ku	フォーク
I am diabetic.	wa-*ta*-shi wa tō-*nyō*-byō de su	私は糖尿病です。
I am dieting.	*da*-i-et-to *chū* desu	ダイエット中です
I am a vegetarian.	sa-i-*sho*-ku *shū*-gi-sha de-su	菜食主義者です。
I cannot eat [item]	[item] wa *ta*-be-ra-re-ma-*sen*	.....は食べられません。
I'd like to order.	*chū*-mon o shi-*tai* desu	注文をしたいです。
I'd like [item]	[item] o o-ne-*gai*-shi-ma su	.....をお願いします。
I'm hungry.	*o*-na-ka ga *su*-i-te i-*ma su*	お腹が空いています。
I'm thirsty.	*no*-do ga ka-*wa*-i-te i-*ma su*	喉が渇いています。
It's tasty (not good)	*o*-i-shi-i (ma-*zu*-i) desu	おいしい（まずい）です。
Knife	*na*-i-fu	ナイフ
Lunch	*chū*-sho-ku	昼食
Menu	me-nyū	メニュー
Napkin	*na*-pu-*kin*	ナプキン
Pepper	ko-*shō*	こしょう
Please give me [item]	[item] o ku-da-*sa*-i	.....を下さい。
Salt	*shi*-o	塩
Set menu	*te*-i-sho-ku	定食
Spoon	su-*pūn*	スプーン
Sugar	sa-to	砂糖
Wine list	*wa*-i-n *ri*-su-*to*	ワインリスト
What do you recommend?	*o*-su-su-me *ryō*-ri wa *nan* desu ka	お勧め料理は何ですか。

Meat Dishes　肉料理

焼き肉	yaki-niku	Thinly sliced meat is marinated then barbecued over an open fire at the table.
すき焼き	sukiyaki	Thinly sliced beef, green onions, mushrooms, thin noodles, and cubes of tōfu are simmered in a large iron pan in front of you. These ingredients are cooked in a mixture of soy sauce, mirin (cooking wine), and a little sugar. You are given a saucer of raw egg to

		cool the suki-yaki morsels before eating. Using chopsticks, you help yourself to anything on your side of the pan and dip it into the egg and then eat. Best enjoyed in a group.
しゃぶしゃぶ	shabu-shabu	Extremely thin slices of beef are plunged for an instant into boiling water flavored with soup stock and then dipped into a thin sauce and eaten.
肉じゃが	niku-jaga	Beef and potatoes stewed together with soy sauce.
ステーキ	sutēki	steak
ハンバーグ	hambāgu	Hamburger pattie served with sauce.
トンカツ	tonkatsu	Breaded deep-fried pork cutlets.
しょうが焼	shōga-yaki	Pork cooked with ginger.
酢豚	subuta	Sweet and sour pork, originally a Chinese dish.
からあげ	kara-age	deep-fried without batter
焼き鳥	yaki-tori	Pieces of chicken, white meat, liver, skin, etc., threaded on skewers with green onions and marinated in sweet soy sauce and grilled.
親子どんぶり	oyako-domburi	Literally, "mother and child bowl"—chicken and egg in broth over rice.
他人どんぶり	tanin-domburi	Literally, "strangers in a bowl"—similar to oyako domburi, but with beef instead of chicken.
ロール・キャベツ	rōru kyabetsu	Rolled cabbage; beef or pork rolled in cabbage and cooked.
はやしライス	hayashi raisu	Beef flavored with tomato and soy sauce with onions and peas over rice.
カレーライス	karē-raisu	Curried rice. A thick curry gravy typically containing beef is poured over white rice.
カツカレー	katsu-karē	Curried rice with tonkatsu.
お好み焼き	okonomi-yaki	Sometimes called a Japanese pancake, this is made from a batter of flour, egg, cabbage, and meat or seafood, griddle-cooked then covered with green onions and a special sauce.
シュウマイ	shūmai	Shrimp or pork wrapped in a light dough and steamed.
ギョウザ	gyōza	Pork spiced with ginger and garlic in a Chinese wrapper and fried or steamed.

Seafood Dishes 魚貝類料理

焼き魚	yaki-zakana	broiled fish
塩焼	shio-yaki	Fish sprinkled with salt and broiled until crisp.

さんま	samma	saury pike
いわし	iwashi	sardines
しゃけ	shake	salmon
照り焼き	teri-yaki	Fish basted in soy sauce and broiled.
ぶり	buri	yellowtail
煮魚	nizakana	soy-simmered fish
さばのみそ煮	saba no miso ni	Mackerel stewed with soy-bean paste.
揚げ魚	age-zakana	deep-fried fish
かれいフライ	karei furai	deep-fried breaded flounder
刺身	sashimi	Very fresh raw fish. Served sliced thin on a bed of white radish with a saucer of soy sauce and horseradish. Eaten by dipping fish into soy sauce mixed with horseradish.
まぐろ	maguro	tuna
あまえび	ama-ebi	sweet shrimp
いか	ika	squid
たこ	tako	octopus
あじ	aji	horse mackerel
さわら	sawara	Spanish mackerel
しめさば	shimesaba	Mackerel marinated in vinegar.
かつおのたたき	katsuo no tataki	Bonito cooked just slightly on the surface. Eaten with cut green onions and thin soy sauce.
どじょうの柳川なべ	dojo no yanagawa nabe	Loach cooked with burdock root and egg in an earthen dish. Considered a delicacy.
うな重	una-jū	Eel marinated in a slightly sweet soy sauce is charcoal-broiled and served over rice. Considered a delicacy.
天重	ten-jū	Deep-fried prawns served over rice with sauce.
海老フライ	ebi furai	Deep-fried breaded prawns.
あさりの酒蒸し	asari no sakamushi	Clams steamed with rice wine.

Sushi 寿司

| 寿司 | sushi | Basically, sushi is rice, fish, and vegetables. The rice is delicately seasoned with vinegar, salt, and sugar. There are basically three types of sushi: nigiri, chirashi, and maki. |
| にぎり寿司 | nigiri zushi | The rice is formed into a bite-sized cake and topped with various raw or cooked fish. The various types are usually named after the fish, but not all are fish. Nigiri zushi is eaten by picking up the cakes with chopsticks or |

		the fingers, dipping the fish side in soy sauce, and eating.
ちらし寿司	chirashi zushi	In chirashi zushi, a variety of seafood is arranged on the top of the rice and served in a bowl.
巻き寿司	maki zushi	Raw fish and vegetables or other morsels are rolled in sushi rice and wrapped in dried seaweed. Some popular varieties are listed here.
まぐろ	maguro	tuna
とろ	toro	fatty tuna
たい	tai	red snapper
さば	saba	mackerel
こはだ	kohada	gizzard shad
しゃけ	shake	salmon
はまち	hamachi	yellowtail
ひらめ	hirame	flounder
あじ	aji	horse mackerel
たこ	tako	octopus
あなご	anago	conger eel
えび	ebi	shrimp
甘えび	ama-ebi	sweet shrimp
いか	ika	squid
みる貝	miru-gai	giant clam
あおやぎ	aoyagi	round clam
卵	tamago	egg
かずのこ	kazunoko	herring roe
かに	kani	crab
ほたて貝	hotate-gai	scallop
うに	uni	sea urchin
いくら	ikura	salmon roe
鉄火巻	tekka-maki	tuna roll
かっぱ巻	kappa-maki	cucumber roll
新香巻	shinko-maki	shinko roll (shinko is a type of pickle)
カリフォルニア巻	kariforunia-maki	California roll, containing crabmeat and avocado. This was invented in the U.S. but was re-exported to Japan and is gaining popularity there.
うに	uni	Sea urchin on rice wrapped with seaweed.
いくら	ikura	Salmon roe on rice wrapped with seaweed.
太巻	futo-maki	Big roll with egg and pickled vegetables.

Vegetable Dishes　野菜料理

おでん	oden	Often sold by street vendors at festivals and in parks, etc., this is vegetables, octopus, or egg simmered in a soy fish stock.
天ぷら	tempura	Vegetables, shrimp, or fish deep-fried in a light batter. Eaten by dipping into a thin sauce containing grated white radish.
野菜サラダ	yasai sarada	vegetable salad
大学いも	daigaku imo	fried yams in a sweet syrup
野菜いため	yasai itame	stir-fried vegetables
きんぴらごぼう	kimpira gobō	Carrots and burdock root, fried with soy sauce.
煮もの	nimono	vegetables simmered in a soy- and sake-based sauce
かぼちゃ	kabocha	pumpkin
さといも	satoimo	taro root
たけのこ	takenoko	bamboo shoots
ごぼう	gobō	burdock root
れんこん	renkon	lotus root
酢のもの	sumono	Vegetables seasoned with ginger.
きゅうり	kyūri	cucumber
和えもの	aemono	Vegetables dressed with sauces.
ねぎ	tamanegi	onions
おひたし	o-hitashi	Boiled vegetables with soy sauce and dried shaved bonito or sesame seeds.
ほうれん草	hōrenso	spinach
漬物	tsukemono	Japanese pickles. Made from white radish, eggplant or other vegetables. Considered essential to the Japanese meal.

Egg Dishes　卵料理

ベーコン・エッグ	bēkon-eggu	bacon and eggs
ハム・エッグ	hamu-eggu	ham and eggs
スクランブル・エッグ	sukuramburu eggu	scrambled eggs
ゆで卵	yude tamago	boiled eggs
目玉焼	medama-yaki	fried eggs, sunny-side up
オムレツ	omuretsu	omelet
オムライス	omuraisu	Omelet with rice inside, often eaten with ketchup.
茶わんむし	chawan mushi	Vegetables, shrimp, etc., steamed in egg custard.

Tōfu Dishes　豆腐料理

Tōfu, also called bean curd, is a white, high-protein food with the consistency of soft gelatin.

冷やっこ	hiya-yakko	Cold tōfu with soy sauce and grated ginger.
湯どうふ	yu-dōfu	boiled tōfu
あげだしどうふ	agedashi dōfu	Lightly fried plain tōfu dipped in soy sauce and grated ginger.
マーボーどうふ	mābō dōfu	Tōfu and ground pork in a spicy red sauce. Originally a Chinese dish.
とうふの田楽	tōfu no dengaku	Tōfu broiled on skewers and flavored with miso.

Rice Dishes　ごはん料理

ごはん	gohan	steamed white rice
おにぎり	onigiri	Triangular balls of rice with fish or vegetables inside and wrapped in a type of seaweed.
おかゆ	okayu	rice porridge
チャーハン	chāhan	Fried rice; includes vegetables and pork.
ちまき	chimaki	A type of onigiri made with sweet rice.
パン	pan	Bread, but usually rolls with a meal.

Soups　汁もの

みそ汁	miso shiru	Miso soup. A thin broth containing tōfu, mushrooms, or other morsels in a soup flavored with miso or soy-bean paste. The morsels are taken out of the bowl and the soup is drunk straight from the bowl without a spoon.
すいもの	suimono	Soy sauce flavored soup, often including fish and tofu.
とん汁	tonjiru	Pork soup with vegetables.

Noodles　麺類

うどん	udon	Wide flour noodles in broth. Can be lunch in a light broth or a full dinner called *nabe-yaki udon* when meat, chicken, egg, and vegetables are added.
そば	soba	Buckwheat noodles. Served in a broth like udon or, during the summer, cold on a bamboo mesh and called *zaru soba*.
ラーメン	rāmen	Chinese noodles in broth, often with *chashu* or roast pork. Broth is soy sauce, miso or salt flavored.
そう麺	sōmen	Very thin wheat noodles, usually served cold with a tsuyu or thin sauce. Eaten in summer.

ひやむぎ	hiyamugi	Similar to somen, but thicker.
やきそば	yaki-soba	Noodles fried with beef and cabbage, garnished with pickled ginger and vegetables.
スパゲッティ	supagetti	Spaghetti. There are many interesting variations on this dish, notably spaghetti in soup, often with seafood.

Fruit 果実

アーモンド	āmondo	almonds
あんず	anzu	apricot
バナナ	banana	banana
ぶどう	budō	grapes
グレープフルーツ	gurēpufurūtsu	grapefruit
干しぶどう	hoshi-budō	raisins
いちご	ichigo	strawberries
いちじく	ichijiku	figs
かき	kaki	persimmons
キーウィ	kiiui	kiwi
ココナツ	kokonatsu	coconut
くり	kuri	chestnuts
くるみ	kurumi	walnuts
マンゴ	mango	mango
メロン	meron	melon
みかん	mikan	tangerine (mandarin orange)
桃	momo	peach
梨	nashi	pear
オレンジ	orenji	orange
パイナップル	painappuru	pineapple
パパイヤ	papaiya	papaya
ピーナッツ	piinattsu	peanuts
プルーン	purūn	prunes
レモン	remon	lemon
りんご	ringo	apple
さくらんぼ	sakurambo	cherry
西瓜	suika	watermelon

Dessert デザート類

アイスクリーム	aisukuriimu	ice cream
プリン	purin	caramel pudding
グレープ	kurēpu	crepes
ケーキ	kēki	cake
シャーベット	shābetto	sherbet
アップルパイ	appuru pai	apple pie
ようかん	yōkan	sweet bean paste jelly

コーヒーゼリー	kōhii zeri	coffee-flavored gelatin
和菓子	wagashi	Japanese sweets

Drinks　飲物

Alcoholic　酒類

ビール	biiru	beer
生ビール	nama biiru	draft beer
カクテル	kakuteru	cocktail
ウィスキー	uisukii	whisky
スコッチ	sukocchi	scotch
バーボン	bābon	bourbon
日本酒（酒）	nihonshu (sake)	Sake, a wine brewed from rice.
あつかん	atsukan	warmed sake
ひや	hiya	cold sake
焼酎	shōchū	Spirit distilled from potatoes.
チューハイ	chūhai	Shōchū mixed with soda water and flavored with lemon juice or other flavors.
ワイン	wain	wine
赤	aka	red
白	shiro	white
ロゼ	roze	rose
シャンペン	shampen	champagne
ブランデー	burandē	brandy

Non-alcoholic　その他の飲物

コーヒー	kōhii	coffee
アイスコーヒー	aisu kōhii	iced coffee
日本茶	nihon cha	Japanese green tea
紅茶	kō-cha	black tea
レモンティー	remon tii	tea with lemon
ミルクティー	miruku tii	tea with milk
アイスティー	aisu tii	iced tea
ウーロン茶	ūron cha	oolong tea
ジャスミン茶	jasumin cha	jasmine tea
牛乳／ミルク	gyū-nyū/miruku	milk
ココア	kokoa	hot chocolate
レモンスカッシュ	remon sukasshu	carbonated lemon soft drink
ミルクセーキ	miruku sēki	milk shake
ジュース	jūsu	juice, but can also mean any soft drink
レモネード	remonēdo	lemonade

More Useful Phrases よく使われる表現

Temple	otera/odera/-ji/-in/-dō	堂／寺
Shrine	jinja/jingū/-gū/-dō/taisha	神社／神宮／大社
Castle	-jō	城
Park	kōen	公園
River	-kawa/-gawa	川
Bridge	hashi/bashi	橋
Museum	hakubutsukan	博物館
Zoo	dōbutsu-en	動物園
Botanical gardens	shokubutsu-en	植物園
Island	shima/jima/tō	島
Slope	saka/zaka	坂
Hill	oka	丘
Lake	-ko	湖
Marsh	shitsugen	湿原
Pond	-ike	池
Bay	-wan	湾
Plain	hara/bara/taira/daira	平
Peninsula	hantō	半島
Mountain	yama/-san/-take	山
Cape	misaki/saki	岬
Sea	kai/nada	海
Gorge	kyōkoku	峡谷
Plateau	kōgen	高原
Train line	sen	線
Prefecture	-ken/-fu	県／府
Ward	-ku	区
Exit	deguchi/-guchi	出口
Street, avenue	dōri/-dō/michi	道
main road	kaidō/kōdō	街道／公道
In front of	mae	前
North	kita	北
South	minami	南
East	higashi	東
West	nishi	西
Shop, store	mise/-ya	店
Hot-spring spa	onsen	温泉

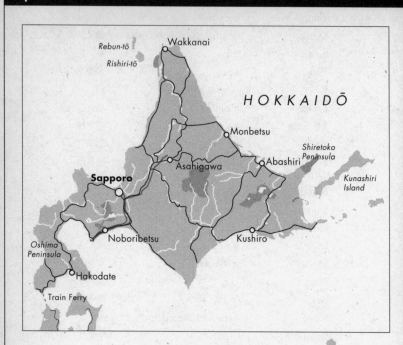

Rebun-tō

Rishiri-tō

Wakkanai

HOKKAIDŌ

Monbetsu

Shiretoko Peninsula

Asahigawa

Abashiri

Kunashiri Island

Sapporo

Noboribetsu

Kushiro

Oshima Peninsula

Hakodate

Train Ferry

N

Oki Islands

Matsue

Tsushima

Tottori

Hagi

Yamaguchi

Hiroshima

Okayama

Iki Island

Fukuoka

Kōbe

Ōs

Takamatsu

Seto Nai-k

Awaji Island

Goto Islands

Matsuyama

Beppu

Tokushima

Wakaya

Nagasaki

Aso

Oita

Uwajima

Kōchi

Kii Peninsula

Amakusa Islands

Kumamoto

SHIKOKU

Sh

Shimo-Koshiki Island

KYŪSHŪ

Kagoshima

Miyazaki

Kuchinoerabu Island

Yaku Island

Tanega Island

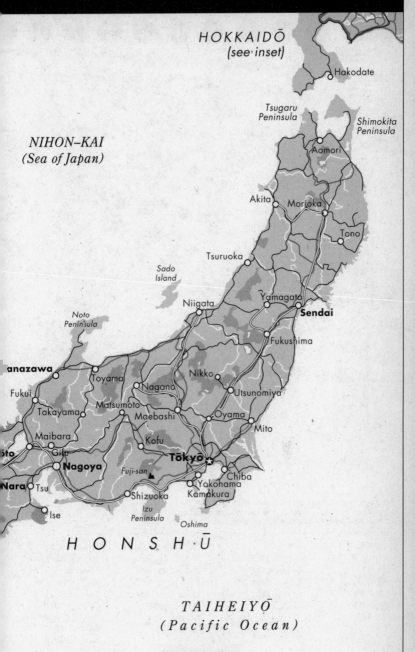

HOKKAIDŌ
(see inset)

Hakodate

Tsugaru
Peninsula

Shimokita
Peninsula

NIHON–KAI
(Sea of Japan)

Aomori

Akita   Morioka

Tono

Tsuruoka

Sado
Island

Yamagata

Niigata   Sendai

Noto
Penin'sula   Fukushima

anazawa   Toyama   Nikko

Fukui   Nagano   Utsunomiya

Takayama   Matsumoto   Oyama

Maibara   Maebashi   Mito

to   Gifu   Kofu

Nagoya   Tōkyō

Nara   Tsu   Fuji-san   Chiba

Shizuoka   Yokohama
Kamakura

Ise   Izu
Peninsula

Oshima

H O N S H Ū

TAIHEIYŌ
(Pacific Ocean)

KEY		
—— JR Trains	0	50 miles
—— Shinkansen (Bullet Train)		
—— Roads	0	75 km

World Time Zones

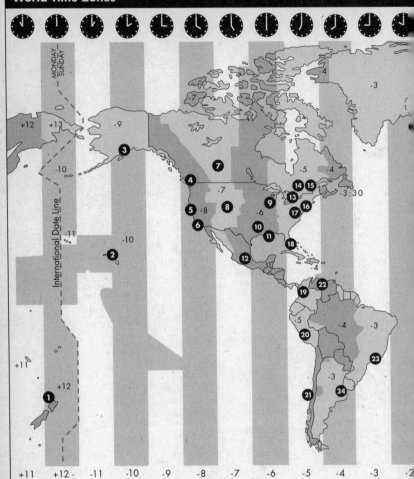

Numbers below vertical bands relate each zone to Greenwich Mean Time (0 hrs.).
Local times frequently differ from these general indications,
as indicated by light-face numbers on map.

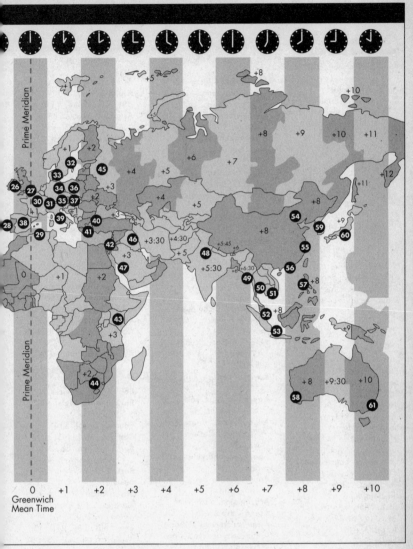

0 +1 +2 +3 +4 +5 +6 +7 +8 +9 +10

0
Greenwich
Mean Time

Mecca, **47**
Mexico City, **12**
Miami, **18**
Montréal, **15**
Moscow, **45**
Nairobi, **43**
New Orleans, **11**
New York City, **16**

Ottawa, **14**
Paris, **30**
Perth, **58**
Reykjavík, **25**
Rio de Janeiro, **23**
Rome, **39**
Saigon (Ho Chi Minh City), **51**

San Francisco, **5**
Santiago, **21**
Seoul, **59**
Shanghai, **55**
Singapore, **52**
Stockholm, **32**
Sydney, **61**
Tokyo, **60**

Toronto, **13**
Vancouver, **4**
Vienna, **35**
Warsaw, **36**
Washington, D.C., **17**
Yangon, **49**
Zürich, **31**

NOTES

NOTES

NOTES

NOTES

NOTES

NOTES

ABOUT OUR WRITERS

The more you know before you go, the better your trip will be. Japan's best sushi bar could be just around the corner from your hotel, but if you don't know it's there, it might as well be on the other side of the globe. That's where this book comes in. It's a great step toward making sure your next trip lives up to your expectations. As you plan, check out the Web as well. Guidebooks have been helping smart travelers find the special places for years; the Web is one more tool. Whatever reference you consult, be savvy about what you read, and always consider the source. Images and language can be massaged to make places appear better than they are. And one traveler's quaint is another's grimy. Here at Fodor's, and at our on-line arm, Fodors.com, our focus is on providing you with information that's not only useful but accurate and on target. Every day Fodor's editors put enormous effort into getting things right, beginning with the search for the right contributors—people who have objective judgment, broad travel experience, and the writing ability to put their insights into words. There's no substitute for advice from a like-minded friend who has just come back from where you're going, but our writers, having seen all corners of Japan, are the next best thing. They're the kind of people you'd poll for tips yourself if you knew them.

About Our Writers

Dominic Al-Badri, who updated the Ōsaka and Kōbe chapters, studied biochemistry at the University of London's Imperial College but after graduating found himself a long way from both home and profession teaching English in rural Japan. Since 1997 he has been the editor of *Kansai Time Out,* Japan's oldest English-language monthly magazine.

After graduating from Cambridge University with a degree in French and Russian, **Matthew Green** made the incongruous decision to come to Japan. He lived in the Kansai region for three years where he wrote articles on Japanese pop culture. He now lives in Tōkyō where he works as a speech writer for an international organization. He updated the Tōkyō nightlife section and wrote the Great Itineraries.

Hokkaidō updater **Amanda Harlow** dropped out of provincial journalism in the south of England to travel the world for a year—and never went back. She settled in Japan in 1993, first in Saitama and finally in Hokkaidō, where she now works proofreading, teaching, and narrating government videos about clearing snow from roads. Her perfect Hokkaidō day is skiing followed by a hot spring, sushi, and a beer.

Most recently from South Carolina, **Suzanne Kamata,** who updated the Shikoku chapter, has lived in Tokushima Prefecture since 1988. Her writing has been published widely and she is the editor of *The Broken Bridge: Fiction from Expatriates in Literary Japan* (Stonebridge Press).

Jared Lubarsky, who worked on the Tōkyō and Side Trips from Tōkyō chapters, has lived in Japan since 1973. He has worked for cultural exchange organizations, taught at public and private universities, and written extensively for travel publications. He still ponders the oddities of Japanese culture, wondering why, for instance, the signs that advise you not to ride in elevators during an earthquake are posted *inside* the elevators.

Tamah Nakamura and **Yoshihiro Nakamura** have explored their interests in food and culture living in Singapore, Korea, and Japan and traveling throughout Asia. Longtime residents of Fukuoka, Kyūshū, they teach, write, and lecture on intercultural issues. Their idea of paradise is a getaway to Kyūshū's lush countryside for a soak in hot springs and a taste of regional specialities. They updated the Background and Essentials chapter.

Originally from California, Kyūshū updater **Julie Nootbaar** came to Japan in 1990 after graduating from Mount Holyoke College with a degree in Asian Studies. Living with her husband and two small children in rural Kyūshū, she teaches English at a local university and is currently working on a master's degree in Advanced Japanese Studies. In addition to teaching, she has also translated tourism material for government offices in Kyūshū and has served as a tour guide for visiting dignitaries.

Nara updater **Aidan O'Connor** first came to Japan under the auspices of the Japanese government–run JET Program. He returned to Europe for graduate studies and a life in academia but soon found himself lured back east. Now living in Ōsaka, Aidan is a contributing writer for *Kansai Time Out* magazine and teaches at a local university.

John Malloy Quinn, who got his master's in English from the University of Colorado at Boulder, lived and taught English for two years among the tea terraces of Shizuoka and seven years in the wilds of Ishikawa. Although he's been everywhere from Mount Everest to the Great Barrier Reef and Bali, he considers Japan to be his favorite friendly planet. He's written for the *Colorado Daily* and *Boulder Magazine* and has exhibited his photos and ceramics in Colorado and Japan. He worked on the Nagoya, Ise-Shima, and the Kii Peninsula; Japan Alps and the North Chūbu Coast; and Western Honshū chapters.

Kyōto updater **Lauren Sheridan** spent more than five years living and studying at various universities in Kyōto. A recipient of the prestigious Japanese Ministry of Education Research scholarship, she studied at Kyōto University for two years.

Her research topic focused on the lives of women working in the entertainment district of Gion. She now enjoys studying about Kyōto's traditional crafts, such as *temari* (balls decorated with brightly colored silk thread in complex geometric shapes) and *kyō-ningyō* (display dolls).

Tennessee-born **James Vardaman** wrote the guidebook *In and Around Sendai* and co-authored *Japanese Etiquette Today* and *Japan from A to Z: Mysteries of Everyday Life Explained*. He has been a professor of English at Surugadai University in Saitama Prefecture and has worked as a translator. James updated the Tōhoku chapter, Smart Travel Tips A to Z, and the Niigata and Sado-ga-shima section of the Japan Alps and the North Chūbu Coast chapter.

Don't Forget to Write

Your experiences—positive and negative—matter to us. If we have missed or misstated something, we want to hear about it. We follow up on all suggestions. Contact the Japan editor at editors@fodors.com or c/o Fodor's, 280 Park Avenue, New York, NY 10017. And have a fabulous trip!

Karen Cure
Editorial Director

FODOR'S JAPAN

EDITORS: Deborah Kaufman, Lisa Dunford

Editorial Contributors: Dominic Al-Badri, Barbara Blechman, Diane Durston, Nigel Fisher, Matthew Green, Amanda Harlow, Kiko Itasaka, Suzanne Kamata, Jared Lubarsky, David Miles, Tamah Nakamura, Yoshihiro Nakamura, Julie Nootbaar, Aidan O'Connor, John Malloy Quinn, Lauren Sheridan, James Vardaman

Editorial Production: Stacey Kulig

Maps: David Lindroth, *cartographer;* Rebecca Baer and Robert Blake, *map editors*

Design: Fabrizio La Rocca, *creative director;* Guido Caroti, *art director;* Jolie Novak, *senior picture editor;* Melanie Marin, *photo editor*

Cover Design: Pentagram

Production/Manufacturing: Robert B. Shields

Cover Photograph: Brian Lovell/Nawrocki Stock Photo

SPECIAL SALES

Fodor's Travel Publications are available at special discounts for bulk purchases for sales promotions or premiums. Special editions, including personalized covers, excerpts of existing guides, and corporate imprints, can be created in large quantities for special needs. For more information, contact your local bookseller or write to Special Markets, Fodor's Travel Publications, 280 Park Avenue, New York, NY 10017. Inquiries from Canada should be directed to your local Canadian bookseller or sent to Random House of Canada, Ltd., Marketing Department, 2775 Matheson Boulevard East, Mississauga, Ontario L4W 4P7. Inquiries from the United Kingdom should be sent to Fodor's Travel Publications, 20 Vauxhall Bridge Road, London, England SW1V 2SA.

PRINTED IN THE UNITED STATES OF AMERICA

10 9 8 7 6 5 4 3 2 1

IMPORTANT TIP

Although all prices, opening times, and other details in this book are based on information supplied to us at press time, changes occur all the time in the travel world, and Fodor's cannot accept responsibility for facts that become outdated or for inadvertent errors or omissions. So always confirm information when it matters, especially if you're making a detour to visit a specific place.

PHOTOGRAPHY

Nawrocki Photo Studio: *Brian Lovell, cover. (Tea Plantation, Mt. Fuji)*

Axiom: *Jim Holmes, 24B. Kutomi, 15D.*

Tibor Bognar, *30F.*

Corbis: *2 bottom left, 2 bottom center, 3 top right, 3 bottom right, 9E, 14C. AFP, 19C, 28D, 29E. Ric Ergenbright, 32. Jack Fields, 19B. Michael Freeman, 10C, 11D, 18B. Peter Guttman, 13E. Bob Krist, 15 bottom right. Chris Lisle, 14B, 30J. Galen Rowell, 13D, 13F. Sakamoto Photo Research Laboratory, 16A. Michael S. Yamashita, 18C, 30B, 30C, 30D.*

The Image Bank: *Luciano Lepre, 7C.*

Japan National Tourist Organization, *2 top right, 3 bottom left, 12C, 24A, 28C.*

Hiroshi Mochizuki, *7E, 30A.*

Network Aspen: *Jeffrey Aaronson, 15E. Paul Chesley, 21B. Nicholas Devore III, 25D.*

Nomadstock: *Tony Martorano, 6B, 7D, 17A, 30G.*

Pacific Press Service: *Masami Goto, 25E. Takashi Ito, 10B. Takao Nishida, 4–5, 22A. Ben Simmons, 8B. Ken Straiton, 11E, 21A, M. Tomioka, 23E. Takashi Yamaguchi, 12B, T. Yoshimura, 22C.*

PhotoDisc, *1, 8A, 12A, 16C, 18A, 19A, 22B, 25C, 26 top, 30H, 30I.*

PictureQuest: *Photosphere, 2 top left, 2 bottom right, 3 top left, 10A, 14A, 17C, 20A, 20B, 20C, 21C, 23D, 23F, 27A, 27B, 30E.*

Stone: *Christopher Arnesen, 8C. Charles Gupton, 6A. Ernst Haas, 16B. Paolo Negri, 17B. Orion Press, 9D.*